PRAISE FOR *ELEANOR AND FRANKLIN*

"The intimate chronicle of a woman and a marriage. The woman was Eleanor Roosevelt, and her marriage to Franklin D. Roosevelt—with its painful secrets and public triumphs—played a vital role not only in the lives of these two extraordinary human beings but in the lives of all humanity. Here is one of the great and moving stories of our time—a masterpiece of vivid evocation and sympathetic understanding. 'Monumental.'"

—*New York Times*

"WHOLLY ABSORBING AND RICHLY DOCUMENTED.... Eleanor Roosevelt's major burdens as a woman were two: the first was Sara Delano Roosevelt, her mother-in-law, oppressor, tyrant, self-appointed possessor of her son Franklin and every thing and person close to him. The other was Eleanor's burden of anguish born through Franklin's love affair with Lucy Mercer, whom Eleanor had employed as a social secretary."

—Marya Mannes, *The Atlantic*

"AN EXCEPTIONALLY CANDID, EXHAUSTIVE...HEART-RENDING BOOK.... The highest praise one can pay Mr. Lash is that he has proved worthy in every particular of an immense and chancy undertaking."

—Brendan Gill, *The New Yorker*

"A STUNNING, MAGNIFICENT ACHIEVEMENT—that combination of scholarship and narrative drive which is so rare. I had thought I understood Eleanor Roosevelt. Now I know how little I knew."

—William Manchester

"EXTRAORDINARY...a unique American drama!"
—William Hogan, *San Francisco Chronicle*

"A MARVELOUS BOOK."
—Donald Meyer, *The New Republic*

ELEANOR AND FRANKLIN

ELEANOR AND FRANKLIN

The Story of Their Relationship,
Based on Eleanor Roosevelt's Private Papers

JOSEPH P. LASH

FOREWORD BY
Arthur M. Schlesinger, Jr.

INTRODUCTION BY
Franklin D. Roosevelt, Jr.

W. W. NORTON & COMPANY

NEW YORK LONDON

To my wife Trude

Contents

III. THE EMERGENCE OF ELEANOR ROOSEVELT

IV. THE WHITE HOUSE YEARS

Foreword

ARTHUR M. SCHLESINGER, JR.

⬦

I BEGAN TO READ THE MANUSCRIPT OF THIS WORK WITH A CERtain apprehension. I knew that no one was better qualified by close and sympathetic acquaintance to write the biography of Eleanor Roosevelt than Joseph P. Lash. But one also knew of Joe Lash's profound, almost filial, devotion to Mrs. Roosevelt and feared that affection might conflict with the austere obligations of the biographer. Moreover, his friendship with Mrs. Roosevelt covered only the last twenty-two years of a long and varied life, and one wondered how someone coming along at the verge, so to speak, of the last act could do justice to the earlier years—above all, to an intense and crucial girlhood lived so many years before in what was not only another century but another world. Nor could one be certain that Mr. Lash, for all his experience as a newspaperman, would not be lost in the staggering mass of Mrs. Roosevelt's personal papers; even a professional historian might well have been daunted by this form of total immersion.

My apprehension was unjustified. Mr. Lash has written, I believe, a beautiful book—beautiful in its scholarship, insight, objectivity, and candor. He portrays Eleanor Roosevelt's anguished childhood with marvelous delicacy and understanding, and he skillfully evokes the social milieu in which she grew up—the old New York of Edith Wharton, where rigid etiquette concealed private hells and neurosis lurked under the crinoline. He perceives and reconstructs the complex reciprocity of the partnership between Eleanor and Franklin Roosevelt with immense subtlety, sensitivity, and honesty. He faithfully records the moving, often painful, process by which a tense and humorless girl overcame personal insecurity and private adversity and emerged as a powerful woman in her own right, spreading her influence not only across her own country but around much of the planet. As he does all this, he gives a story long familiar in its broad outline a fresh and compelling quality.

A word about the author. Mr. Lash, born in New York City in 1909, graduated from the City College of the City University of New York in 1931 in the depth of the Depression. In the next year he became an officer of the Student League for Industrial Democracy, a Socialist youth organization; and in 1935, when the Comintern Congress in Moscow gave the international Communist movement a more moderate party line, he overcame his earlier distrust of the American Communists and led the SLID into one of the first American experiments in a "united front" against fascism—the American Student Union. American students were politically concerned as they would not be for another thirty years, and Joe Lash was one of their more conspicuous leaders. In the Popular Front enthusiasm after 1935, he moved closer to the Communists and was discussing a job with the *Daily Worker* in August, 1939, when the news came through of the Nazi-Soviet Pact.

For the idealistic fellow-travelers of the period, the pact was a stunning blow. It separated the democrats from the Stalinists; and Lash found himself in growing conflict with his Communist associates in the ASU. Then in November, 1939, three months after the pact, Lash, with other youth leaders, received a summons from the House Committee on Un-American Activities, already well embarked on its long career of saving the republic by hit-and-run investigations of the radical left. It was in this connection that he had his first serious encounter with Mrs. Roosevelt.

The president's wife had a conviction, hard to oppose but not widely shared, that the youth constituted the future of a nation; and, in this time before the young had quite become a distinct and impassioned constituency, she sought to find out on behalf of her husband what they believed and needed. She not only advised the student leaders of 1939 how they should conduct themselves before Congressman Dies's committee but attended the hearings herself and took half a dozen of the young firebrands back to the White House for dinner. Joe Lash, after Stalin's deal with Hitler, was both in inner turmoil and somewhat isolated within the ASU; his personal dilemma appealed to Mrs. Roosevelt. Moreover, she soon found she could rely a good deal more on his word and judgment than on that of his pro-Soviet colleagues.

Soon she invited him to Hyde Park. In spite of considerable disparities in age and background, a warm friendship developed. This continued when as a soldier he went to the South Pacific and in the years after the war when he wrote for the *New York Post*. Clearly he filled some need in her own life—in particular, perhaps the compelling emotional need, so perceptively analyzed in the pages that follow, to offer help, attention, tenderness, and to receive unquestioning love in return. Mrs. Roosevelt may have made occasional mistakes in her desire to provide succor, but her trust in Joe Lash was not misplaced. He has now repaid this trust by writing a book which, because it sees Eleanor Roosevelt with love but without illusion or sentimentalism, makes her, in her fortitude and in her triumph, an even more remarkable figure than we had supposed before.

Americans over thirty, whether they admired or detested her, will not forget Mrs. Roosevelt. But for those under thirty—and this was the group she cared about most—she can only in the 1970s, I imagine, strike faint chords of third-hand recollection, probably arousing faint memories of maternal benevolence. As the young read this book, they will discover that while the do-good thing was there all right, while an indestructible faith in human decency and possibility was the center of her life, all this was accompanied by an impressive capacity for salty realism and, on occasion, even for a kind of quasi-gentle mercilessness. She was, in fact, a tough old bird who saw earth as well as stars. People mixed with her at their peril, as even such tough citizens as Harry S. Truman, Cardinal Spellman, Carmine de Sapio, and Andre Vishinsky learned. Her air of artlessness was one of her most deadly weapons; no one could slice off a head with more benign innocence. But her toughness was tempered by tolerance and tied to a belief in humanity.

The young will discover, too, how contemporary the past may, after all, be. They will find students in revolt, marching, picketing, fighting cops, heckling presidents. They will see the first American war against poverty and the greatest American effort to humanize industrial society. And they will see in Eleanor Roosevelt herself, though she would doubtless have smiled over the overwrought ideology and dramatics of Women's Lib, the most liberated American woman of this century.

But what Mr. Lash understands so well and sets forth so lucidly is that her liberation was not an uncovenanted gift. She attained it only through a terrifying exertion of self-discipline. It was terrifying because the conviction of her own inadequacy was so effectively instilled in Eleanor Roosevelt as a child, and because her adult life had so much disappointment and shock, that it required incomparable and incessant self-control to win maturity and serenity. If her mastery of herself was never complete, if to the end of her life she could still succumb to private melancholy while calmly meeting public obligation, this makes her achievement and character all the more formidable. Her life was both ordeal and fulfillment. It combined vulnerability and stoicism, pathos and pride, frustration and accomplishment, sadness and happiness. Mr. Lash catches all this and, in a remarkable American biography, recreates for a new generation a great and gallant—and, above all, a profoundly good—lady.

Introduction

Franklin D. Roosevelt, Jr.

———————————————— ✧ ————————————————

My mother's will named me her literary executor,
responsible for her private papers which she deposited with the Franklin D. Roosevelt Library at Hyde Park, New York. After consulting
with my sister Anna and my brothers, I asked Joseph P. Lash to undertake the very extensive research and the writing of this biography
based on these papers. Joe Lash has been a close friend of mine and of
my entire family for over thirty years, and during this period I have
developed great respect for his integrity and objectivity. In inviting Joe
to go through my mother's papers, I was also mindful of the fact that
in 1947 she had selected him to assist my brother, Elliott, in editing
volumes III and IV of my father's letters. She further attested to her
confidence in Joe in the authorization she gave him to go through her
papers while she was still alive in connection with the book he was
writing on the youth movement of the thirties.

The library at Hyde Park houses the papers of both my father and
my mother and of many who were associated with them during their
public careers. Those careers cover the period in American history
during which time the United States grew from a nation isolated not
only by geography but often by national policy into the most powerful
country in the world, the most advanced industrial society, as well as
a nation of great social conscience. That transformation is reflected in
the papers in the Roosevelt Library, which make it a fascinating and
unique collection of source materials.

Each of us sees a person differently. My brothers and sister in our
family conclaves have often argued vehemently, though lovingly, about
our parents. It was natural that Joe Lash would see some matters differently from us. I read this book carefully while it was in preparation.
I had many sessions with the author, and we discussed his assessments
and reconstructions and occasionally disagreed. But I felt from the
beginning that this had to be the writer's book.

My parents are figures in history. They were also human beings with foibles and frailties as well as great strength and vitality. Their marriage lasted forty years. To us, as children, they were wonderful parents. Inevitably, there were times of tension and unhappiness as well as years of joy and companionship. For this book to be of value to the present generation the whole picture, insofar as it could be ascertained, had to be drawn.

Many people have written about my mother's contribution to my father's work. This book documents her part in that work. They were a team, and the Roosevelt years, I believe, were more fruitful and creative as a consequence of that partnership.

It was my hope that Joe Lash would present a portrait of my mother that would be objective yet sympathetic and recapture something of her reality as she moved through eight of the most significant decades in our country's history. This book fulfills my hope.

Author's Note

✦

WHEN I FINISHED MY LITTLE BOOK, *ELEANOR ROOSEVELT: A Friend's Memoir,* I did not think that I would again be involved in writing about Eleanor Roosevelt, but then Franklin Roosevelt, Jr., invited me to do a biography based on his mother's papers and I accepted happily. Not the least part of my pleasure was the prospect of again working closely with my old friend Franklin.

Many people have aided in the writing of this book, but I particularly want to acknowledge my indebtedness to Eleanor Roosevelt's children for talking with me freely and at length. Anna Roosevelt Halsted's vivid recollections were invaluable, and our many three-hour luncheons were among the most pleasant parts of my research. The footnotes list the names of the many relatives, friends, and co-workers of Mrs. Roosevelt who were kind enough to share their memories with me. My sessions with Eleanor Roosevelt's two remarkable cousins, Alice Longworth and Corinne Cole, and with Mrs. Roosevelt's ninety-six-year-old uncle by marriage, the late David Gray, were especially memorable, as were my many talks with such long-time friends and collaborators of Mrs. Roosevelt's as Esther Everett Lape, Marion Dickerman, Earl R. Miller, Dr. David Gurewitsch, and Maureen Corr.

Dr. Viola W. Bernard read the first half of the manuscript and devoted several evenings to giving me a psychiatrist's view of Eleanor Roosevelt's psychosocial development. She was very helpful; however, she is not responsible for the way I have made use of her observations, nor, for that matter, are the others who talked with me.

The distinguished New Dealer and wise counselor, Benjamin V. Cohen, read the entire manuscript and made helpful comments, as did Nancy and James A. Wechsler, who provided a constant support through their friendship. Mrs. Suzanne P. Roosevelt, who was trained by her father to look at a writer's copy with a grammarian's eye, reviewed part of the manuscript. A promising young writer, Noemi

Emery, helped me with some of the research and made many useful observations.

Living in a lovely old house, Wildercliffe, overlooking the Hudson, I spent three winters going through Mrs. Roosevelt's papers at the Franklin D. Roosevelt Library at Hyde Park, and immersing myself in the Dutchess County countryside and traditions. Research is a lonely task, but the loneliness in this case was offset by the companionship of the Richard Roveres and of the staff of the Roosevelt Library: Dr. Elizabeth B. Drewry, its former director; her successor, Dr. James O'Neill; William J. Stewart, the assistant director; James Whitehead, the curator; Jerry Deyo, the archivist; and Joseph Marshall, in charge of the Search Room.

The typing was done by my sister, A. Elsie Lash, a formidable task to which she gave all of her free time because of her devotion to the memory of Mrs. Roosevelt.

It was my good fortune when I turned the manuscript in to W. W. Norton & Company to have it reviewed by Evan W. Thomas, an exacting but sensitive critic.

The spare words with which I have dedicated this book to my wife do not convey the help she has given me in its writing. There is scarcely a page which does not bear her imprint.

JOSEPH P. LASH

Preface

THE FIRST ROOSEVELT, CLAES MARTENSZEN VAN ROSENVELT, arrived from Holland in the 1640s when New Amsterdam was a tiny settlement of 800 huddled in some eighty houses at the foot of Manhattan. Who Claes Martenszen was, whether solid Dutch burgher in search of larger opportunities or solemn rogue "two leaps ahead of the bailiff," as his witty descendant Alice Roosevelt Longworth has suggested, is not known. In either case, by the eve of the American Revolution when New York had become a bustling port of 25,000, there were fifty Roosevelt families, and Claes's descendants were already showing an "uncanny knack" of associating themselves with the forces of boom and expansion in American economic life.

In the Roosevelt third generation two of the brothers, Johannes and Jacobus, took the family into real estate with the purchase of the Beekman Swamp, a venture that was to have "a lasting effect on the city and their own family fortunes." It was these two brothers, also, who started the branches that led ultimately to Oyster Bay (Johannes) and to Hyde Park (Jacobus). The pre-Revolutionary Roosevelts were prosperous burghers but not of the highest gentry, and in civic affairs they were aligned with the popular faction against the aristocrats.

The first Roosevelt to achieve gentility and distinction was Isaac, the great-great-great-grandfather of Franklin, who for his services to the American cause was called "Isaac the Patriot." Isaac was a trader in sugar and rum but ended his business career as president of New York's first bank. At his death Philip Hone, the diarist, spoke of him as "proud and aristocratical," part of the "only nobility" the country had ever had.

It took the Johannes–Oyster Bay branch of the Roosevelts a little longer to advance from trader to merchant prince. Isaac's cousin James, after service with the Revolutionary army, founded Roosevelt & Son, a hardware business on Maiden Lane that swiftly expanded into building supplies. When James's grandson, Cornelius Van Schaack

Roosevelt, was head of the firm, it imported most of the plate glass that was used in the new homes being built in the prospering nation. Cornelius' chief distinction was his wealth; he was listed among the five richest men in New York. His son, on the other hand, the first Theodore, retired from business early in order to devote himself to civic activity and was one of the most esteemed men in the city.

By the beginning of the twentieth century the Roosevelt family was one of the oldest and most distinguished in the United States. Its men had married well—a Philadelphia Barnhill, one of whose ancestors arrived with William Penn; a Yankee Howland, whose family had arrived on the *Mayflower*; a Hoffman of Swedish-Finnish descent, one of the richest heiresses in Dutchess County; and one of the Bullochs of Georgia. The Hudson River Roosevelts led the leisurely life of country squires and Johannes' clan was building its country houses, stables, and tennis courts along the north shore of Long Island.

Conscious of having played their part in the transformation of New York from a frail Dutch outpost into a cosmopolitan city and of the country from a handful of seaboard colonies into a continent-spanning imperial republic, the Roosevelts had a firm sense of their roots. While most of them had changed their church affiliation from Dutch Reform to Protestant Episcopal, they remained faithful churchgoers and believers in the Protestant ethic, which sanctified a ruthless competitive individualism on the one hand and, on the other, the love and charity that were the basis of the family's strong sense of social obligation. Standards of honor, conduct, and manners—the caste marks of the old-stock upper class—were further bred into the Roosevelt sons at Groton and Harvard. They went on to become bankers, sportsmen, financiers, and, in two cases, president of the United States. The Roosevelt women, however, were essentially private individuals concerned with supervising large households and launching their daughters into fashionable society. With a few notable exceptions, they led lives of genteel conformity and escaped public notice—until the advent of a girl who was to become known as First Lady of the World.

I

CHILDHOOD
AND
YOUTH

1. ELEANOR'S FATHER

ELEANOR ROOSEVELT WAS BORN ON OCTOBER 11, 1884. ANNA Hall Roosevelt, her mother, died when she was eight and her father, Elliott Roosevelt, when she was ten.

"He was the one great love of my life as a child," Eleanor wrote about her father almost forty years after his death, "and in fact like many children I have lived a dream life with him; so his memory is still a vivid, living thing to me."

Seeking to give some shape and meaning to his brief existence, she called him a "sportsman." He was that, but as one contemplates the promise of his early years, it is the pathos of wasted talents, the stark tragedy of an enormously attractive man bent on self-destruction that reaches across the decades to hold us in its grip.

Elliott's brother Theodore became president of the United States, one of its outstandingly "strong" chief executives. What made Theodore resolute and Elliott weak? It was a question the many who loved Elliott sought to answer all their lives, for the pain of Elliott's death remained in their hearts to the end of their days, such was the spell this man cast over those around him.

It was her father who acquainted Eleanor Roosevelt, his gravely gay Little Nell, with grief. But he also gave her the ideals that she tried to live up to all her life by presenting her with the picture of what he wanted her to be—noble, brave, studious, religious, loving, and good.

The story of Eleanor Roosevelt should begin with him.

Elliott Roosevelt was the third of four children born to Theodore Roosevelt, Sr., and Martha Bulloch. They were a remarkable group. Of Anna, the oldest, born in 1855, whom the family called "Bye" or "Bamie," her niece Alice was to say, "If Aunty Bye had been a man, she would have been President." Theodore Jr., born in 1858, was followed two years later by Elliott, who was called "the most lovable of the Roosevelts." Corinne, the youngest, born 1861, called "Conie" or "Pussie" by her brothers, was described by Clarence Day, whose family's Madison Avenue brownstone adjoined Corinne's in the 1880s, as "a dignified but lively young lady who . . . knew how to write poetry, turn cartwheels and stand on her head."

A childhood friend, recalling the family, spoke of their "gusto," "explosions of fun," "great kindliness and generosity of nature," their "eager friendliness." They were all unabashedly demonstrative in their affections. "Oh! my darling Sweetest of Fathers I wish I could kiss you," a thirteen-year-old Elliott wrote. His southern grandmother's outbursts of affection were so embarrassingly effusive, they were called her "melts."

Their mother, Martha "Mittie" Roosevelt, was a flirtatious southern belle whose dark hair glowed and whose complexion seemed to young Corinne like "moonlight." A vivacious hostess, a spirited and daring horsewoman, she made as lively an impression on New York society as she had on the ante-bellum Savannah society of the early fifties. In the years after the Civil War, Martha Roosevelt was among the five or six gentlewomen of such birth, breeding, and tact that people were "always satisfied to be led by them," acknowledged Mrs. Burton Harrison, one of New York's smartest hostesses.

The children adored her. To Elliott she was "his sweet little China Dresden" mother, and Bamie spoke glowingly of "darling little mother's exquisite beauty." She told stories better than anybody, said Corinne, and her way of describing things was inimitable. Many of these stories were about her "little black shadow," a slave she had been given at birth. She was, however, completely helpless when faced with the smallest everyday task. She was habitually, almost compulsively tardy, and household accounts were a mystery to her. Even when they were very young, her children felt protective toward her, and Theodore Sr. insisted that Bamie, when she was fourteen, take over the reins of the household.

Mittie's Savannah friends later said that the younger Theodore "got his splendid dash and energy" from his southern mother, but the children themselves never doubted that it was from their father that they inherited their zest for life and love of people. The male Roosevelts were solid, industrious, worthy Dutch burghers, and—also in the Dutch tradition—they were a humorless, sobersided lot. But Theodore Sr., who belonged to the seventh generation of American Roosevelts, was also blessed with vivacity and tenderness, and in him there began to emerge that special blend of grace, vitality, courage, and responsibility that is called charisma and that his contemporaries found irresistible.

A big, powerful, bearded man, he moved easily and comfortably in the worlds of Knickerbocker society, business, philanthropy, and civic enterprise. Her father, Corinne said, was "unswerving in duty ... yet responsive to the joy of life to such an extent that he would dance all night, and drive his 'four-in-hand' coach so fast ... that his grooms frequently fell out at the corners!" When Bamie came out in the winter of 1873–74, she had a hard time getting her father—he was then forty-two—to go home from a dance, and he was so popular that she felt like a wallflower.

Theodore Sr. was only twenty-nine when the Civil War broke out, but in deference to the feelings of his wife, whose grandfather had been the first post-Revolutionary governor of Georgia and whose brothers served with the Confederacy, he bought a substitute and limited himself to noncombatant work with the Union armies. Even though this was of sufficient importance to earn him the friendship of Lincoln and a lifelong intimacy with John Hay, the fact that his father did not enlist in the Union fighting forces remained a sore point with young Theodore.

The Confederacy was a living presence in the Roosevelt household. Mittie's sister Anna—later Mrs. James King Gracie—the children's beloved Aunt Gracie—lived with them in New York during the war, as did Grandma Bulloch, and the three women did not hide their passionate southern loyalties, on the occasion of one southern victory, a family legend has it, even breaking out the Confederate flag. The two Bulloch brothers were not included in the post–Civil War amnesty and settled in Liverpool as exiles. From then on, the family never went abroad without visiting Uncle Jimmie and Uncle Irvine in Liverpool.

Theodore Sr. was the son of Cornelius Van Schaack Roosevelt, in whose stately house on Union Square Dutch was still spoken on Sundays. It was he who shifted the family firm into banking and investment. When Cornelius died in 1871, he left ten million dollars to his four sons.

Theodore headed the plate glass division of Roosevelt & Son, but after the Civil War he devoted more and more time to philanthropy and civic enterprise and finally withdrew from business altogether. He was one of the founders of the Metropolitan Museum of Art and the Museum of Natural History, helped start the Orthopedic Hospital, contributed substantial amounts to charities, took a continuing interest in the Newsboys' Lodging House, and led a Mission Class for poor young men.

Public concern for poverty, social welfare, and reform were something new in the elder Theodore's days, as indeed unemployment, slums, and the exploitation of children were new. Fashionable New York, then centered on lower Fifth and Madison Avenues, was only a stone's throw from the tenements on the East Side and the squatters' shanties on the West Side, but most of the wealthy were content to keep them out of sight and out of mind. "At a time when most citizens of equal fortune and education" were not willing to accept any responsibility for reforming and philanthropic enterprises, Theodore "was always engaged in them," commented a colleague in many of those undertakings.

He was not content to serve on boards; he needed to be actively involved with those he sought to help. In the Newsboys' Lodging House he knew the boys by name and was familiar with their histories, and whenever he came they would gather round and he would question each one as to what he was doing and would "give him advice and sympathy and direction." He often brought his children with him, and they remained interested even after his death; one of Eleanor Roosevelt's earliest memories was being taken by her father to the Newsboys' Thanksgiving dinner. Theodore Sr. had a special feeling for children, was full of tenderness when speaking to them, and could not bear the thought of their being shut up in institutions. He had what he called a "troublesome conscience," a burden or a blessing of which his granddaughter Eleanor also would complain.

First and foremost, however, Theodore Sr. was a family man fully involved in the upbringing and education of his children. It was a matter of deep concern to him that Theodore Jr., Bamie, and, later, Elliott suffered from ill health and handicaps which, if not corrected, might seriously limit their activities. The most acutely afflicted was Bamie, who suffered from a curvature of the spine, while Theodore Jr. was sickly and asthmatic. It was largely for Theodore Jr. that the upstairs back of the house was transformed into a large play and exercise "piazza" so that he could build himself up on the exercising devices. The equipment was also a source of joy for the other children, especially Elliott, who quickly became the leader in their youthful sports and won all competitions.

The children's education was centered in the home. Aunt Gracie taught them their letters and there was an occasional tutor, but it was their father who really opened up new worlds of learning for them. On picnics and rides, or before the fire in winter, he discussed authors with them and had them recite their favorite poems. He was a firm believer in the educational effect of travel, and when Elliott was nine took his whole brood on a twelve-month Grand Tour of Europe, and three years later on an even more extended and strenuous pilgrimage to Egypt, the Holy Land, southeastern and central Europe. The children were left in Dresden, where they stayed with German families for "purposes of board and instruction," and where they remained for five months while their family's new house on Fifty-seventh Street was being built. They were getting on in German grammar, Elliott wrote his father, adding "We have learned three pieces of German poetry." But on July 4, he rebelled against the glories of German culture being preached day after day by Fräulein. "Don't you think America is the best country in the world?" he asked his father. "Please, when you write tell me if we have not got as good Musick and Arts as the Germans have at the *present* time." When in September, 1873, the Fifty-seventh Street house was nearing completion—though a hand-carved circular staircase had missed its connection on the second floor by three feet—the children set out for home.

Upon their return Theodore Jr. was given a tutor to prepare him for Harvard. Elliott wanted very much to enter St. Paul's, but he now suddenly began to suffer from severe headaches and dizzy spells. His father, feeling that health was more important than formal education, sent him abroad in 1874 and in 1875 south with a friend of the family who was a doctor in the hopes that two months of outdoor life and hunting would build up his constitution. He loved the shooting, but, he confessed to his "dear funny little Bamie," he was also homesick. "Sometimes I long for Home—what a sweet word it is. I wonder what you all are doing this beautiful moonlit night. I can see you now. Conie and Thee home from dancing class and full of it have finished their storeys and are gone upstairs to study. Papa's pet or the belle of New York is entertaining some friends in the parlor and Father is in his study. And Mother?"

He was lonely, as his loving letter to his father written on his fifteenth birthday showed.

Mar 6th 1875
Saturday.

My own dear Father.*

I got your kinde "Father" like letter with Muzes to day oh! it was
so nice to feel you had thought of me on my birthday....

Dear old Govenor—for I *will* call you that not in publick but
in private for it does seem to suit you, you splendid Man just my
ideal, made to govern & doing it so lightly & affectionately that
I can call you by the name as a pet one.—its not such a long time
since you were fifteen & any way as I was saying to Mrs Metcalfe
today you are one of the few men who seem to remember they were
boy's once them selves & therefore can excuse pieces of boyish folly
committed by their boy's.

Do you think it would be a good plan to send *me* to school again
perhaps as I am not going to college I could make more friends
there. I will do just as you think best, mon père.

I gave you my plan of study in my last letter but I would just
as leif study at school as at home for Thee is way behind or rather
before me & perhaps although I don't now I may in future years
see it was best for me.

I feel rich too in the prospect of my allowance, next first of January, it seemes a long way off.

Are we going to Oyster bay next summer dont you think Thee
& I could spunge on all of our uncles & you & have a sail boat. I
know we could manage her & would not I think be likly to drown.
My darling Father you have made me a companion & a very happy
one I don't believe there is any boy that has had as happy & free of
care life as I have had.

Oh. Father will you ever think *me* a "noble boy", you are right
about Tede he is one & no mistake a boy I would give a good deal
to be like in many respects. If you ever see me not stand by Thee
you may know I am entirely changed, no Father I am not likly to
desert a fellow I love as I do my Brother even you dont know what
a good noble boy he is & what a splendid man he is going to be as
I do No, I love him. love him very *very* dearly & will never desert
him & if I know him he will *never* desert me.

---

*Holograph letter in Halsted File at Franklin D. Roosevelt Library with spelling and
punctuation as in the original.

Father my own dear Father God bless you & help me to be a good boy & worthy of you, good by.

Your Son.

[P.S.] This sounds foolish on looking over it but you touched me when you said always to stand by Thee in your letter.   E.R.

When Theodore Sr. finally gave in to Elliott's pleadings and allowed him to enter St. Paul's in September, 1875, the boy's happiness was brief. "I am studying as hard as I can," he wrote his father on October 1, "and I think all my teachers are satisfied with me." But after a letter full of casual gossip, he added an ominous postscript:

Private
Yesterday during my Latin lesson without the slightest warning I had a bad rush of blood to my head, it hurt me so that I can't remember what happened. I believe I screamed out, anyway the Doctor brought me over to his house and I lay down for a couple of hours; it had by that time recovered and after laying down all the afternoon I was able to go on with my afternoon studies. I lost nothing but one Greek lesson by it. It had left me rather nervous and therefore homesick and unhappy. But I am well now so don't worry about me. I took some of my anti-nervous medicine, and I would like the receipt of more. You told me to write you everything or I would not bother you with this, but you want to know all about me don't you?
P.S. II Don't forget me please and write *often*.
    Love from Ellie

"Poor Ellie Roosevelt," Archibald Gracie wrote his mother, "has had to leave on account of his health. He has 'ever been subject to rush of blood to his head' and while up here he exerted himself too much both physically and mentally. He studied hard and late. One day he fainted just after leaving the table and fell down.... His brother came up to take him home...."

The various doctors who were consulted did not agree on the nature of his malady. According to some reports he had a form of epilepsy, but there is no other record of epilepsy in the family and the seizures of which we have accounts were too infrequent to fit such a diagnosis. Some doctors who have read this account have noted that

Elliott's seizures occurred when he was confronted with demands that evidently were too much for him and have suggested that they may have been, without Elliott's realizing it, a form of escape.

It was the elder Roosevelt's view that bodily infirmities were to be conquered by a strenuous outdoor life and Spartan discipline. He had told the frail and asthmatic Theodore in 1870: "You have the mind but not the body.... You must make your body." And that was exactly what Theodore proceeded to do. Outdoor life was now to cure Elliott; he was sent to Fort McKavett, a frontier post in the hill country of Texas, where the Roosevelts knew many of the officers, including the commander, General Clitz. This may seem to have been an inappropriate treatment for a medical ailment, but in wealthy families of that era travel was the standard prescription for illnesses, nervous disorders, and unhappy love affairs, and Elliott did seem to function more effectively away from his family and school. With an unusual ability to fit into any situation and a zest for adventure, the sixteen-year-old quickly and without complaint made the transition from the comfortable, closed, and protected life of New York society to the rough equalitarianism of the frontier.

Graham, Young Co., Texas

Dear Father: Jan. 12th, 1876

I have gone through some regular roughing since I last wrote you at Weatherford. After we left there we came on slowly camping at night and shooting all that we wanted to eat for we have never been on short rations yet thank goodness. The weather up to last night was very warm and pleasant but suddenly one of those frightfully cold north winds sprang up and from being too warm with our coats off, the addition of blankets, ulsters and mufflers of all kinds did not keep us even tolerably warm. Ed and I left them: that is the two wagons; at about half past five and went on for three or four miles and made a camp fire and prepared everything for them, but we waited and watched and no wagons so at last we concluded that they had gone on to Graham not having seen the fork we turned up it being so dark. We were camped by a house so as we had no blankets and it was most fearfully cold we tied our horses to the gate post and left the saddles on to keep them warm and as Ed said I had a "persuasive air with me" I went up to the little log hut and knocked. The door was opened and the master appeared and I talked with him for a while and then a friend of his appearing on the scene he offered to take Ed with him and the first fellow took me in. The hut was crowded and a single fire burning so although there were chinks on all sides and a cold wind blowing still we kept fairly warm. There were three girls two quite good looking so I made the rest of the evening pass quite pleasantly only I was a little worried about the other chaps not having turned up. At about ten o'clock the landlord or rather ranch man came in with "Gentlemen your beds are ready" where at, as I had been riding since seven o'clock and not had a mouthful to eat either I got up and making my good night to the ladies, the elder of which being the mistress sat pipe in mouth in the chimney corner; I rose followed by some six others all pretty rough looking chaps and followed mine host into an adjoining room no roof but logs and the merest frame work of walls. Three rolls of blankets on the floor, three men took one, two another and a cow boy from way out west and I took the third. I used Tar who had stuck to my heels all the evening in mortal terror of two other dogs belonging to the house, for a pillow partly for warmth and partly to drown the smell of my bed fellow. In this manner I shivered through the night up to five when "breakfast gentlemen" brought us all to our feet and without more ado we ran for the fire in the next room and were served by the old lady still pipe in mouth with bacon and bread a frugal meal but if you laugh at it think I had not a mouthful since six a.m. the day before, roughing it! eh? . . .

Your affectionate
Son.

In two visits Elliott spent over a year with the 500 men, women, and children who lived in Fort McKavett. Officers and enlisted men delighted in regaling the attractive young easterner with tales of Mexican War days and Indian fights. There were elaborately organized wild-turkey shoots in which Elliott did his "fair share of the shooting, also of the eating." He became "chums" with the post commander, boxed, sat on the piazza listening to the post band, read every paper he could lay his hands on, and argued politics. "So Hayes is really counted in," Elliott wrote his father, March 4, 1877. "I wish you could hear the dismal forebodings that the Democratic members of our party (I was the only Republican) have for the 'Old Union' we have had some glorious pitched battles, 'you bet'!" There were also whist parties until three in the morning, and although he assured his family that he neither smoked nor drank, "for wine we drink catawba and the General knows what a good bottle of that is like I can tell you."

The old trouble with his head seemed to be gone but all his attempts to follow an organized course of reading and study came to naught. "It strikes me it's just a sell my being down here...altogether I feel like a general fraud, who ought to be studying," he confessed to his father. He was troubled, but not enough to resist the temptations of the "glorious" life at the fort.

Soon after Elliott returned to New York in 1877, his father became ill with what was later diagnosed as intestinal cancer. For weeks Elliott scarcely left his father's room. That winter, wrote Corinne, "Elliott gave unstintingly a devotion which was so tender that it was more like that of a woman and his young strength was poured out to help his father's condition." Elliott wrote in his diary of his father's "cries for ether," the mercy of "a chloroform sleep," and new agonies on awakening until the final release of death on February 10, 1878, at the age of forty-six.

The family was devastated, and the children vowed to lead lives that would reflect credit on their father's name. "We have been very fortunate," Theodore Jr. wrote Bamie after he returned to Harvard, "in having a father whom we can love and respect more than any other man in the world."

Eighty-nine years later, Theodore Sr.'s granddaughter, Alice Roosevelt Longworth, contrasting her own style and outlook with that of her cousin Eleanor, said that Eleanor "was a do-gooder. She got that from my grandfather. It took with Eleanor, but not with me. I never did those things. They bored me."

Legacies of approximately $125,000 came to each of the children at the death of their father, which gave them an annual income of about $8,000. Of the $125,000, half was given outright, half a trust for life. Each of the children would receive another $62,500 at the death of their mother. And thus their annual income would be about $14,000 if they held onto their capital.

For Elliott, the most sensitive of the children, the death of his father was not only a terrible sorrow but a disaster. Without his father's stern, demanding, but loving guidance he was lost. Although intelligent and eager to learn, he was discouraged by the realization that he was hopelessly outdistanced by his contemporaries. Restless, spoiled by admiration and success out West, he was not prepared to start at the bottom of some business and patiently work his way up. And then there was the strong pull of the exciting world of society and sport, where he was a leader by the sheer force of his personality. His inheritance made it possible for him to live in this world.

Theodore, whom Elliott visited frequently at Harvard, admired his younger brother's social skills and his great popularity with the girls. Although his every instinct was combative and competitive, Theodore was so fond of his brother, he wrote an aunt, that he could "never hold in his heart a jealous feeling toward Elliott" and "gloried" in his accomplishments. This did not stop him from keeping a sharp eye on who was the better man. "Nellie stayed up from town," he wrote in his diary in 1879, "and so I spent the day with him: we rowed around Lloyd's—15 miles, and virtually racing the whole way. As athletes we are about equal; he rows best; I run best, he can beat me sailing or swimming; I can beat him wrestling and boxing. I am best with the rifle, he with the shotgun, etc., etc...." Elliott, although he wrote in 1880 that every day he was "more happy in the dear old brother's good company," must have been somewhat overwhelmed by a brother who, a friend noted, "always thought he could do things a little better than anyone else," and, if he couldn't, set out to overcome the infirmity with awesome resolution. The time was past when Elliott had to shield his older brother from bullies.

The year Theodore graduated from Harvard, Elliott decided to undertake an expedition to India to hunt tiger and elephant, and to the Himalayas for the elusive ibex and markhor. He was pulled by the lure of adventure but was also pushed by the realization that Theodore, who had been his father's favorite son, was returning to New York and would become the head of the family. Another consideration contributed to his decision to abandon New York: he had begun to drink heavily, so much so, one family report has it, that a girl whom he wished to marry refused him unless he changed his ways—which he apparently was unable to do.

Elliott and Theodore spent two months hunting out West before Elliott left for the Orient. It was a happy trip, and they enjoyed "the return to the old delight of dog and gun," Elliott wrote his mother, but it was also the occasion for an uneasy report by Theodore on what he called Elliott's "epicurean" appetites. Only half in jest he reported after a week's hunting in Iowa:

> As soon as we got here he took some ale to get the dust out of his throat; then a milk punch because he was thirsty; a mint julep

because it was hot; a brandy mash 'to keep the cold out of his stomach'; and then sherry and bitters to give him an appetite. He took a very simple dinner—soup, fish, salmi de grouse, sweet-bread, mutton, venison, corn, macaroni, various vegetables and some puddings and pies, together with beer, later claret and in the evening, shandigaff.

When Elliott set out on his big expedition to India, aware that his glorious adventure was also a flight, he assured Bamie that the duties of paterfamilias would be attended to,

and by a far better man. Thee is well able and no mistake—shrewd and clever, by no means behind the age. What I have often smiled at in the old Boy are I am now sure some of his best points—a practical carrying out in action of what I, for example, am convinced of in theory but fail to put into practice.

Even as Elliott was journeying through India his brother won election as assemblyman from the "brownstone district" of New York and completed his first literary venture, *The Naval War of 1812*.

"Has not our dear Thee done well at home this winter," Elliott wrote Bamie from Kashmir, "and his plans for occupying the position he should as Father's son and namesake seem [to be] going so splendidly smoothly—all success to him." Elliott diagnosed correctly that he lacked "that foolish grit of Theodore's." And while he, too, was interested in politics and had helped his brother found the City Reform Club to interest "respectable, well-educated men—young men especially" in the political questions of the day, and he, too, loved being with the News-boys, and he, too, had a literary flair, as was evident in his letters, he was incapable of sustained effort except in sports, and followed the easier and ever more tempting path of achieving success and approval through his charm and his accomplishments as sportsman and man-about-town.

He would make frequent "new starts" in his short life, but the question of "paterfamilias" was settled for good.

His trip to India was a series of glittering triumphs. On shipboard to England the James Roosevelts of Hyde Park, just married, asked him to make their rooms in London his headquarters. He had "long talks and walks" with Thomas Hughes, the author of *Tom Brown's School Days*, and agreed to dine with him in London. His partners at whist were "kind enough to wish me to go to Cannes to play whist with them all winter!" And most important to Elliott, Sir John Rae Reid, "the mighty hunter and second Gordon Cummings has taken me under his especial wing—given me a dozen letters to India and I breakfast with him next Sunday at twelve and on Monday we buy my guns, etc."

From the moment of his arrival in Bombay he was treated like a "grand prince." He could hardly account for it, he wrote his mother, "for if ever there was a man of few resources and moderate talents I am he, yet all events and people seem to give me the best of times on my holiday visit.... I am 'up' at the club and have 'dined,' 'Tiffined' and breakfasted 'out' every meal."

The officers of His Majesty's Forces in India, the princes of India, and the Society of the Bombay Club were charmed by this young man from New York and pressed invitations upon him. Nevertheless, he retained a certain critical detachment. He exulted over an intoxicating feast at Sir Sala Jung's, regent of the Nizam of Hyderabad, to which they were driven in a cortege that was itself a princely pageant and were escorted into dinner "through long lines of motionless blacks holding flaming torches." But he also commented, "This is a picture of a native state—under, unwillingly, British protection. England in power—natives high and low discontented."

"Oh! these people," he wrote en route to Kashmir and the Himalayas,

> what a puzzle to me this world becomes when we find out how many of us are in it. And how easy for the smallest portion to sit down in quiet luxury of mind and body—to say to the other far larger part—lo, the poor savages. Is what *we* call right, right all the world over and for all time?

He was appalled by the "ocean of misery and degradation" that he found on the subcontinent, such total degradation that it

> might teach our "lovers of men" to know new horrors and sadness that the mortal frames and still more the Immortal Souls of Beings in God's image made, should be brought so low. The number and existence of these some millions of poor wretches has upset many preconceived notions of mine.

The journey to Tibet along the Astor Road was shadowed by mishap. In Srinagar he was held over for a week by fever. Impatiently, he pushed on and reached Thuldii in the highest Himalayas, but "that beastly fever" clung to him and he was forced to abandon the expedition and return home without having hunted the ibex and markhor that he had sought.

India had made him deeply conscious of his lack of education. "How I do crave after knowledge, book learning…education and a well-balanced mind," he exclaimed in the Himalayas as he tried to catch hold of "finer subtleties" of description, history, and analysis. Few Americans had had his opportunity, and he wanted to write about his experiences, which would have made as colorful a book as Theodore's about the West. He drafted an account of a tiger shoot in Hyderabad and an elephant hunt in Ceylon. The drafts were good, but he did not persist. The manuscripts did not see the light of day until 1933 when they were edited, along with his letters, and published by Eleanor under the title *Hunting Big Game in the Eighties*.

While the youthful Elliott was disturbed by the way the British held India "in a grip of iron," the way of life of the British rulers— hunts, polo, racing—suited him quite well. "I am very fond of this life, Bammie," he wrote at the end of his trip.

> No doubt about it. I thought to rather put a slight stop to my inclinations by a large dose of it, but—for the great drawback that none of you are with me to enjoy it, it would be very nearly perfect in its way. Not, I think, "our way" for that means life for an *end*. But this for the mere pleasure of living is the only life.

He found it necessary to justify his trip—"There seemed little for me to do in New York that any of you my own people could be proud of me for, and naturally I am an awfully lazy fellow"—and he faced his return to New York with some anxiety.

> I know Sister Anna will keep her eyes open and about her for chances for the boy. If some of the wise and strong among you don't make a *good* chance for me on my coming home I'll make but a poor one for myself I fear. . . .

But fate now intervened in the form of a sparkling debutante, Anna Rebecca Hall.

2. HER MOTHER

ELLIOTT WENT INTO REAL ESTATE ON HIS RETURN FROM INDIA, and even though he dutifully reported to his office on lower Broadway his real life was as man-about-town. Because of his Himalayan exploits he seemed more glamorous than ever and had a kind of Guardsman masculinity that captivated young and old alike. He had the ability when talking with you, said Fanny Parsons, a friend of Corinne's, of shutting out the rest of the world and making you feel as if you were the most important thing to him.

> If he noticed me at all I had received an accolade, and if on occasion he turned on all his charm, he seemed to me quite irresistible. But all the time I knew that his real worship was at the shrine of some mature and recognized belle of the day.

The leading debutante the winter Elliott returned was Anna Hall. He described her excitedly as "a tall slender fair-haired little beauty—just out and a great belle."

Anna, then almost nineteen, was the eldest of four Hall sisters. All four—Anna, Elizabeth (Tissie), Edith (Pussie), and Maude—were society belles, and all were considered slightly but attractively mad. Anna was the most competent, and she was also a little cold. Elliott was all spontaneity and tenderness, while beneath her youth and beauty Anna was a creature of rules and form. She belonged to Edith Wharton's "old New York," an ordered and hierarchical society "which could enjoy with discrimination but had lost the power to create."

The Halls were descendants of the landed Livingstons and Ludlows, and their Tivoli home on the Hudson was on property originally deeded to the lords of Livingston Manor through letters patent of Charles II, James II, and George I. The marriage of Anna's father, Valentine G. Hall, Jr., and her mother, Mary Livingston Ludlow, represented a merger of a wealthy mercantile family of New York City with the landed gentry of the Hudson. The first Ludlow had settled in New York in 1640, and as early as 1699 a Ludlow was one of provincial notables, meaning men of property, and had sat as a member of the Assembly of the Province of New York. The Ludlow social standing, patriot or Tory, was of the highest, but along the upper reaches of the Hudson, from Tivoli to Germantown, they were overshadowed by the Livingstons.

Anna Hall's grandmother, Elizabeth Livingston, the granddaughter of Chancellor Livingston, eloped with Edward H. Ludlow, a doctor. Imperious and strong-willed, she made her young husband give up his profession because she did not like a doctor's hours. He went into real estate where values were booming and in the period after the Civil War became the city's most respected realtor. That did not soften his wife's disdain for those who carried on the world's business. Once when some business associates came to see him at their house on fashionable Fourth Avenue, she stormed into the parlor, turned off the gas, and announced, "Gentlemen, my husband's office is on lower Broadway." They retired in confusion.

Eleanor remembered her great-grandmother as a very old lady whom she, her Aunt Maude, and Grandma visited regularly on Sundays. One Sunday Grandma Hall was ill and Eleanor and Maude went alone. The old lady refused to accept their explanation for Mrs. Hall's absence and told them to go right back and summon "Molly," which they did. Mrs. Hall dutifully got out of bed. When one of Eleanor's cousins, who was also the old lady's granddaughter, inherited some blue Canton china, she asked her father why so many pieces were missing. "Well, my mother used to throw the plates at my father and myself and so a good many of them were broken," he explained. When Mrs. Ludlow wanted something or felt irate, she banged the floor with her cane, which Eleanor remembered as a very long one. "I was terrified of her," Eleanor later said, adding half in amusement, half in admiration, "she was *character.*"

A picture of this iron-willed lady shows a plain but strong mouth, and if the upper half of her face is covered, the mouth and chin are those of Eleanor Roosevelt.

She and Edward Ludlow had two children—Edward, "the gentlest of men," and Mary, who was mild, submissive, and beautiful. Both married children of Valentine G. Hall.

The senior Valentine Hall was an Irish immigrant. He settled in Brooklyn and by the time he was twenty-one had become a partner in one of the largest commercial houses in the city and had married his partner's daughter. The firm—Tonnele and Hall—enjoyed "unlimited credit" throughout the world. "He had remarkable business ability," his contemporaries said, and before he was fifty retired from business "with a large fortune" that included considerable real estate from Fourteenth to Eighteenth Streets along Sixth Avenue. He lived another thirty-five years but contributed little to civic welfare except for his support of religious enterprises.

His son, Valentine G. Hall, Jr., was a gentleman of solemn dignity who, after some sowing of wild oats and a period of penitence that included attending a theological school, assumed his place in society and executed its obligations and those of his church with punctilious regard. He did not go into business but lived the life of a leisured gentleman. He fathered six children—four daughters and two sons, Valentine and Edward; the Ludlows said he was good for little else. That was not his opinion of himself. In 1872 instead of building a larger town house, he built Oak Terrace at Tivoli, next to the house of his brother-in-law.* Its finest room was the library, presided over by a bust of Homer. There, together with a resident clergyman whom he supported, he pursued his interests in the classics and in theological doctrine.

Valentine Jr.'s preoccupation with theology gave a puritanical tone to Tivoli life that was unusual for the Hudson River gentry. He was troubled by man's innate depravity. "I awoke this morning about half-past seven," he wrote in his journal when he was twenty-seven. "Instead of getting up immediately as I should have done, I gave way to one of my many weaknesses and lay instead until the clock struck eight building castles in the air. Oh! how much time, precious time, we waste in worldly thoughts." His austere ways reminded a neighbor of "one of the olden Christians," and the family clergyman later wrote

---

* A family story which Eleanor told with amusement had it that when her Grandfather Hall needed more money to complete his Tivoli house he went to his mother who "would go to the wardrobe and rummage around" and emerge "with a few thousand dollars." Eleanor thought that this harked back to her great-grandmother's immigrant origins "because in Ireland it would be perfectly normal to keep your belongings in whatever was the most secret place in your little house. You would not deposit them in a bank, and this was what . . . my great-grandmother evidently had carried into the new world and proceeded to do." Eleanor added that "as neither of her sons ever added to the fortune but both of them seemed well provided for, I think it is safe to say that the original immigrant great grandfather must have made a considerable fortune."

that "no one could ever forget the morning and evening devotions, the Sunday afternoon recitation of favorite hymns."

In the Roosevelt household religion was seen as the affirmation of love, charity, and compassion; in the Hall household at Tivoli it was felt that only a ramrodlike self-denial was acceptable to God. Religion was also used to justify domestic tyranny. Valentine Hall, Jr., was a despot who had little intellectual respect for his wife. He had married her when she was quite young and had always treated her like a child. He alone decided the education, discipline, and religious training of his children. He did not even permit his womenfolk to go into the shops to choose their own clothes. He ordered dresses to be sent home where they were strewn around the parlor, and the women were allowed to make their choices. At Tivoli youthful spirits constantly rubbed against externally imposed standards. While the Roosevelts welcomed "joy of life" as the greatest of heaven's gifts, the Halls considered pleasure of the senses to be sinful and playfulness an affront to God. As the Hall children grew up, their instincts were often at war with their moral precepts, and they had an especially strong sense of duty and responsibility.

Anna Hall's education, except for religion and manners, was sketchy. A great deal of attention was given to correct posture, dancing, and the social graces; one's debut was more important than the cultivation of one's mind except for a smattering of language, literature, and music. A scrapbook that Anna kept on a trip to England and Ireland the summer before she made her debut contained photographs of the accepted shrines of the culturally refined—Sir Walter Scott's study, Abbotsford Abbey, Holyrood Palace, Windsor Castle. The poems that she transcribed into her exercise book were by the approved poets of the period—Longfellow, Browning, Owen Meredith—and she preferred those that pointed to a moral and suggested a rule of conduct.

The same exercise book contained the beginning of a story she had written. Its language was conventional and its emotions stereotyped, its setting in a British castle suggesting the fascination that British titles had for girls in the 1880s—a form of escape both romantic and decorous. Its theme was the redemption of a dissolute London aristocrat by an equally aristocratic girl of nineteen. High-minded and self-controlled, Anna turned naturally to a man of ardor and bravura, even if he was weak.

When Anna was seventeen her father died without leaving a will, which meant that the properties had to be administered by the court.

Valentine Hall had never taught his wife how to budget and to keep accounts. Mary Hall, who knew nothing about disciplining her children since that had been her husband's prerogative, was left with four daughters and two sons between the ages of three and seventeen. Anna, the oldest, was "the strongest character in the family, very religious"; she "took hold and tried to control the family." But since she was also the most beautiful, she was married within three years of her father's death.

In the brief but strenuous New York season of 1881–82 Anna was acclaimed as one of society's most glamorous women. "She was made for an atmosphere of approval," a friend said, "for she was worthy of it. . . . Her sweet soul needed approbation." Elliott's courtship provided just that, for where she was reserved and circumspect, Elliott was demonstrative and ardent.

It was the springtime of the year, the springtide of their love; their hope was high and their dreams radiant. Elliott introduced her to his Newsboys and she began to do volunteer work at the Orthopedic Hospital. Gallant messages arrived accompanied by flowers and proposals that they ride or dance or boat or dine together. On Sundays there were the church parades along tree-shaded Fifth Avenue past the fashionable residences, the young men top-hatted, the girls elegant, stopping to chat, while horses and carriages jogged northward toward Central Park.

For the wealthy, the New York of the eighties was gracious and society a self-contained little island of brownstones that stretched from Washington Square to Central Park along Fifth and Madison Avenues, with a few Knickerbocker hold-outs at Gramercy Park and Stuyvesant Square—the "Second Avenue set," Elliott called them. Almost everyone to whom Elliott doffed his hat was connected in some way to either the Roosevelts or the Halls.

Anna and Elliott's courtship was ritually decorous.

"My dear Mr. Roosevelt," wrote Anna in her strong, precise handwriting,

> Thank you many times for your very pretty philopena present. I think it was wicked of you to send me anything, yet I must tell you how much pleasure it gave me. I would try and thank you for your note, but feel it would be useless. Let me only say that I fully appreciate your kindness.

Hoping soon to see you, Believe me   Yours very sincerely,

ANNA R. HALL

Monday, March 12th.   11 West 37th St.

And a note from Elliott, impatient to shorten the hours away from her, greeted his "dear Miss Hall" at breakfast.

It will be, I hope, so delightful an afternoon that I will be at the hospital at half after four instead of five, it being so much more pleasant an hour for driving than the later.

I trust that you can get through your work there by that time. Accept these few flowers and wear them for the little children to see. They say that the "lovely lady" always has some with her. Even the flowers are happier at being your servants I am sure.

With regard I am   Faithfully Yours

6 West 57 St.   ELLIOTT ROOSEVELT

Friday

According to Fanny Parsons, Anna and Elliott decided to become engaged at a Memorial Day house party given in the hope of encouraging just this event by lovely Laura Delano, the youngest sister of Mrs. James (Sallie) Roosevelt. The party was at Algonac, the stately Delano mansion overlooking the Hudson at Newburgh. The Roosevelt clan immediately welcomed the nineteen-year-old Anna with an outpouring of affection mingled with relief that as a family man with "something to work for in life," Elliott might perhaps settle down.

"He is such a tender, sympathetic, manly man," Bamie wrote to Anna, that she, though older, had "ever turned toward him in many sad moments for help and strength." Corinne, suffering from a "quincy sore throat," scratched out a note in pencil to express her delight that Anna had made Elliott "so grateful and happy a man. He loves you with so tender and respectful a devotion, that I who love my darling brother so dearly, cannot but feel that you as well as he, have much to be thankful for." Theodore wrote his "dearest Old Brother" that "it is no light thing to take the irrevocable step you have just taken, but I feel sure that you have done wisely and well, and we are all more than thankful to have so lovely a member added to our household circle."

Felicitations poured in, as did invitations to call. From Hyde Park, Elliott's cousin James Roosevelt sent his "warmest congratulations," adding, "Your Godson [F.D.R.] thrives and grows. I have just been teaching him now to climb a ladder in a cherry tree. Your Aunt [Sara] says—'she will send you a line to express her congratulations.'"

Elliott spent most of the summer in town, but on week ends he was at Tivoli and the whole "Tivoli crowd" along the Woods Road came to congratulate the couple. There were tennis and "jolly drives," reading out loud and an evening of fireworks at the R. E. Livingstons'. Moving serenely through it all, reported Elliott to his mother, was his willowy Anna, wearing the magnificent "tiger claw necklace" that Elliott had made after his return from India.

Weekdays in town were not all work. There were "all night talks" with Theodore and frequent dashes out to Hempstead to ride, hunt, and play polo. "The 'Meet' at Jamaica yesterday afternoon was a very pretty one and we had a glorious run," Elliott wrote Anna. "Mohawk [his hunter] did grandly and gave me a good place in the first flight from start to kill." Afterward they "dined quietly at the kennels," and then Elliott sat "cosily over the big wood fire gazing into the flames and wishing for and thinking of my Sweet Heart."

"A jolly afternoon's polo yesterday," he reported a few days later. He was one of the best polo men at Meadow Brook, and his brilliance in this "emperor" of sports thrilled Anna, although she must have worried about the game's hazards. "You will have to hurry up and marry me," he warned her,

if you expect to have anything left to marry. It seems to me that I get from one bad scrape into another. That beastly leg gave me so much pain that I went to the Doctor and I'm in for it this time, I'm afraid, not to get on a horse for a week and not to walk about more than is absolutely necessary. Oh! my! *Poultices! Ointment!* and three evenings alone by myself at 57th St. with my leg on a chair.

Was he really in such a hurry to marry Anna? He was often melancholy that summer and had some sort of seizure at Tivoli. "My old Indian trouble has left me subject to turns like I had Monday from change of weather or some such cause," he wrote Anna reassuringly. The trip down on the train had been "pretty bad," he confessed, but "Herm Livingston and Frank Appleton were on board and very kind so I pulled along very well."

Anna was troubled by his sudden depressions. "Please never keep anything from me," she pleaded with him, "for fear of giving me pain or say to yourself 'There can be no possible use of my telling her.'

Believe me, I am quite strong enough to face with you the storms of this life and I shall always be so happy when I know that you have told and will tell me every thought, and I can perhaps sometimes be of some use to you."

She should not worry, he replied. "I know I am blue and disagreeable often, but please darling, bear with me and I will come out all right in the end, and it really is an honest effort to do the right that makes me so often quiet and thoughtful about it all." And in Anna's moments of doubt and despondency, Elliott comforted and cheered her: "Darling if you care to, we will read some of my favorite chapters and verses in the little Testament together." He had carried that little book all around the world and it had been a "comforting and joyous though silent companion."

Mrs. Hall agreed to a December 1 wedding date. Would Anna really like diamonds for a wedding present, Elliott asked her as summer drew to a close, or would she prefer "a little coupe or Victoria?" He thought he could afford to buy one for her if she would find it useful and enjoy the driving.

As the wedding day neared, Mrs. Hall, although happy for her "darling child," could not help but feel anxious about entrusting her to this dashing young man, so different from her sternly pious husband. "I pray you and Elliott to enter your new life with your hearts turned to God," she wrote her daughter on the eve of the wedding. "Go to him tonight before retiring and in His presence read your Bible and kneel together and ask Him to guide you both through this world which has been so bright to you both, but which must have some clouds, and dearest Anna and Elliott for my sake, and for both of your dear fathers' sakes never fail to have daily prayers."

The wedding ceremony was at Calvary Church, two blocks from Elliott's Twentieth Street birthplace. It was described by the *Herald* as "one of the most brilliant social events of the season.... The bride was every bit a queen and her bridesmaids were worthy of her." The *Herald*'s account of the wedding ended, "It is the desire of the bride to be back by the 11th inst. in order to be present at the time of the Vanderbilt ball."

On their way south they stopped in Philadelphia, and Elliott promptly penned a reassuring note to Mrs. Hall.

Your kind letter we received today and both your children, for I feel for Anna's sake you will consider me one now too, are deeply and truly with you in the spirit of what you say. We both knelt before the Giver of every good and perfect gift and thanked him the source of perfect happiness for His tender loving kindness to us. Dear Lady do not fear about trusting your daughter to me. It shall be my great object all my life to comfort and care for her.

3. THE WORLD INTO WHICH ELEANOR WAS BORN

AFTER HIS MARRIAGE ELLIOTT WENT TO WORK FOR THE LUDLOW firm, the city's leading real-estate establishment. His earnings there supplemented the better than $15,000 annual income that he and Anna had between them. Their income did not permit a gold service or servants in livery drawn up in line in the English fashion as were to be seen at the more formal entertainments of such friends as Mrs. Astor and the Cornelius Vanderbilts. But, in an era when there were no taxes and wages were low, the young couple were able to maintain a well-staffed brownstone house in New York's fashionable Thirties. Anna had her coupe in town and ordered her dresses from Palmers in London and Worth in Paris while Elliott stabled four hunters at Meadow Brook.

The Elliott Roosevelts were among the gayest and most lively members of the younger set—the newspapers called them "the swells"—who pursued their pleasure in the great Fifth Avenue houses, at Meadow Brook, Tuxedo, Newport, Lenox, and the fashionable watering places of Europe. They were prominent members of New York society at a time when the merger between the old Knickerbocker families and the post-bellum barons of oil, steel, and railroads had already been accomplished, and, in emulation of Europe's aristocracies, especially England's, New York society had become a well-defined, self-conscious, codified hierarchy. It was, said Mrs. Winthrop Chanler, "a closed circle to which one either did or did not belong."

Anna and Elliott belonged. They and their friends set the fashion in dress and manners, and the anxious ones knocked at their doors. Anna's graceful beauty and charming manners were everywhere acclaimed. "Fair, frail and fragile, and therefore a good illustration of beauty in American women," a society columnist rhapsodized. Her father's discipline had not been in vain. He had insisted that she and her sisters walk regularly in the country with a stick across their backs held in the crook of their elbows, which had produced an unmistakable bearing.

"The proud set of the head on the shoulders was the distinctive look of the Halls," recalled Mrs. Lucius Wilmerding, whose mother was a close friend of Anna. When *Town Topics* took the young ladies of society to task for their stoop and slouch compared to the "superb" carriage of English girls, it excluded Mrs. Elliott Roosevelt from its strictures and recommended her as a model.

Mr. Peter Marié, writer of *vers de société* and a great beau, was noted for the beautiful women at his entertainments. No greater compliment could be bestowed upon a lady than to have Mr. Marié request a photograph from which he would have some well-known artist paint a miniature for his famous collection. Anna's beauty was accorded this gallant tribute: she was one of his "brilliant creatures." Robert Browning was so taken with her beauty that he came to read to her while she was having her portrait painted during a summer she and Elliott spent in the Engadine.[1]

When Anna and her friends launched the Knickerbocker Bowling Club it became the fashionable thing to do. While the well-turned-out coaches of other women promenaded in Central Park, she and her friends jogged an extra three miles up semirustic Riverside Drive to the Claremont Restaurant for afternoon tea. She was among the women who inaugurated the series of dances at Sherry's, when the "swells" decided that the Assemblies and Patriarchs' Balls had ceased to be select. She was, to use the phrase of one of her contemporaries, "tuned to a ballroom pitch."

She loved the cotillions at eleven and supper at midnight, the Tuesday Evening Dancing Class, the evening at the opera, the annual kennel and horse shows, the amateur theatricals, the polo and tennis matches, the meetings of philanthropic boards, and all the other occasions that constituted a New York season. While a few emancipated spirits considered conformity to society's pleasures and disciplines bondage to a "chain of tyrannical trifles," for Anna Hall Roosevelt they were the very substance of a happy, contented life.

Anna was proud of her handsome husband who was one of society's great gallants. His haunts were the Knickerbocker Club and Meadow Brook, his pleasure a fast game of polo, the cross-country steeplechase, the hunt ball, and the horse show. A young lady's cup flowed over, said Daisy Harriman, when she was asked down to Meadow Brook. "All New York aped the English," Mrs. Harriman said of society in the eighties, especially so in the annual Coach Parade, when the swells in green coats and gray top hats, with lovely ladies gracing the boxes of their four-in-hands, would make the circuit of Central Park. Elliott was a mainstay of this ritual, which ended with dinner at the Brunswick, its dining room festooned with whips, whiffletrees, and coach horns. John Sargeant Wise, son of a well-known Whig politician from Virginia, said that Elliott was "the most lovable Roosevelt I ever knew," adding that "perhaps he . . . was nothing like so aggressive or so forceful a man as Theodore, but if personal popularity could have bestowed public honours on any man there was nothing beyond the reach of Elliott Roosevelt."[2]

In New York, Meadow Brook, Bar Harbor, and Newport, Anna and Elliott gave themselves to a strenuous, fun-loving life. "We play our polo matches on Monday, and Saturday next we go out on Mr. E. T. Gerry's yacht the 'Electra' to see the race tomorrow for the Goelet Cups. We dine, dance, play tennis, polo, sail, swim and live in the open air all the time. It will do you lots of good," Nell assured his "dearest Bye," urging her to join them.

And this letter from Anna to Bamie described their summer:

> 34 Catherine Street
> Dearest Bamie,   Newport
> I want to write you just a few lines in answer to your letter. We arrived here on Saturday & spent until Monday with the Wilsons. Of course I was in bed all day Sunday with one of my headaches. Elliott went everywhere though, & they were awfully kind and made things as pleasant as possible for us.
>
> Elliott's match will come off tomorrow. The Harvards beat the Westchesters on Wednesday. Every one seems to think that Meadow Brook will beat them though. Elliott is very much excited over it, & is playing very well. We have been to the Casino every morning watching the tennis matches. . . . I suppose this is the gayest week here, but I do not care much for it. I liked Bar Harbor much better. The air there is bracing & then you always got to bed early. The life here is too much like New York. This afternoon I am going with Mrs. Vanderbilt to some teas. This evening we dine with the Whitneys & then Elliott is coming home.
>
> I may go to the Kernochan ball for half-an-hour, but doubt it. I am not feeling my best and am on my back—which accounts for this being in pencil.
>
> Last night we had a very jolly spree. First we dined on the

Morgan's yacht after a delightful sail to Bristol & then drove home by moonlight on the coaches. There were three coach leads. . . .

On Monday they play in pairs at polo & if Elliott loses on Monday or Wednesday we will go up the Hudson on Thursday, but if not we will stay for the final game on Saturday.

I shall be delighted to reach Tivoli and see them all. I really feel quite homesick here . . . [rest of letter missing].

There were times when Elliott was full of large plans—to get wealth "for his little wife's sake," to become active in Republican politics, to pull together and publish his notes on India. But his will was as weak as his hopes were high, and the attractions of society and sports quickly reasserted themselves.

In the summer of 1884 Anna was pregnant, and, always of frail health, she often felt unwell and had to rest a great deal. The family was anxious, all the more so because in February of that year Theodore's wife, his adored Alice Lee, had died two days after giving birth to baby Alice. It had been a time of double tragedy in the Roosevelt household, for their beloved mother, Mittie, had died only a few hours earlier. "There is a curse on this house," Elliott cried as he opened the door to Theodore, who had rushed down from Albany; "Mother is dying and Alice is dying too."

Anxiety grew as Anna's confinement approached, and there was general relief when, on October 11, a baby girl was delivered—without complications. Though Elliott and Anna had wished ardently for a "precious boy" and the little girl was "a more wrinkled and less attractive baby than the average," to her father she was "a miracle from heaven." Anna and Elliott named their first-born Anna after her mother and Bamie, their favorite sister and sister-in-law, and Eleanor after her father who had been called "Ellie" and "Nell." Between her parents' disappointment that she was not a boy and the death threat that her advent into the world had represented to her mother, Eleanor, in a sense, came into the world guilty and had to reinstate herself.

As usual, Bamie was on the scene being helpful. From the time of the older Theodore's death, the family had turned to her at moments of crisis. Elliott in particular relied on "the busy Bye" to set his "little world to rights." It was Bamie who notified members of the family, including Aunt Gracie, who immediately replied:

Bamie's telegram at 11:30 this morning brought us the joyful news. I am overjoyed to hear of itty girl's (not itty "precious boy jr") safe arrival and just long to have her in my arms. How well I remember when I held you darling Ellie for the first time. My heart beat so I could hardly hold you! And you were so rosy and so beautiful! Kiss Anna for me.

Eleanor—she never called herself Anna Eleanor except in official documents and in signing checks—was born into a secure golden world in which significant or even ominous events around the globe were hardly noticed—or, if they were, they seemed remote and without relevance to the lives of her parents and their friends.

The foreign cables in the newspapers of October 11, 1884, reported the growth of the empires whose dissolution would occupy so much of the agenda of Eleanor's final years at the UN. Egypt, which had been part of the Ottoman Empire when her father had sailed up the Nile in a dehabeah in 1873, was coming under the rule of Great Britain, and, at the request of the khedive, it was reported, British troops were in the field seeking to suppress the "wild and fanatical" forces of El Mahdi. The same column of foreign notices reported that Paris had heard that "Chinese bands" had been driven off from "Western and Southern Tonquin." "My fleet is closely watching the coast," General Brière de l'Isle reported to Paris. "I assume immediate command of the troops and am about to leave Hanoi." In India Elliott had questioned the universality of the western concepts of right and civilization in defense of which the white man was allegedly assuming his burdens. But gradually he had lost interest in the rights and wrongs of imperialism, and his social ties were now aligned with the propertied classes of western Europe, especially of England.[3]

The foreign cables also noted briefly that "the outrages against the Jews in Morocco have been stopped." New York society had little sympathy for an anti-Semitism that expressed itself in physical brutalities and political repression, but it was nevertheless openly anti-Semitic. Attendance at the Patriarchs' balls at Delmonico's was falling off, *Town Topics*, the self-styled "Journal of Society" noted, adding that the chief beneficiaries of these entertainments now were "the Hebrews," who arranged their own festivities for the days following a Patriarchs' ball so that they could take advantage of the lavish decorations the Patriarchs left behind. Even so enlightened a woman as Mrs. Winthrop Chanler could write of a Jewish friend that "she seemed to descend from prophets rather than from money lenders." Elliott and Anna shared New York society's bias against immigrant foreigners generally, and against the eastern European Jews particularly.

Politics, except on the highest levels of government and statesmanship, was not an occupation for gentlemen in 1884. Theodore's willingness to run for assemblyman in the "brownstone" district—in Eleanor's day it would be known as the "Silk Stocking" district—distressed some members of the family. "We felt that his own father would not have liked it, and would have been fearful of the outcome," Cousin Emlen said. "Uncle Jim, Em and Al bitterly opposed to my candidacy of course," Theodore had noted in his diary in 1881, but Elliott stood by him like a "trump." Elliott even joined his brother in going into the Twenty-first A.D. Republican Club.

The chief item in the newspapers that October, and Theodore's major preoccupation, was the close of the Cleveland-Blaine campaign. Theodore was not happy with a presidential candidate whom he regarded as a special-interests jobber. He had opposed Blaine at the Chicago convention and until a few weeks before Election Day had managed to avoid campaigning for him. But in the end, to the distress of the Reformers, he chose regularity and stumped for Blaine. Presumably Elliott, who, like his sisters, followed his brother in political matters, voted for him, but Anna's side of the family found Grover Cleveland's honesty as well as conservatism more than satisfactory. And, indeed, a substantial part of high society voted for Cleveland. A few days before Eleanor was born Grandfather Ludlow was quoted as saying: "I have been a Democrat for years and will probably vote for Cleveland, but I am not a politician. . . ."

The Roosevelts had all been Democrats before the Civil War but became firm Lincoln Republicans during the war. So did Valentine Hall, although a little less staunchly, motivated by economic self-interest as well as patriotism. A friend who came in after dinner just before the 1864 Lincoln-McClellan race ended announced that he had sold all his stocks. Valentine Hall considered that stupid. "He should have held on until after Lincoln's election," he thought. Everything would go up. He scared another friend with the warning that if McClellan were elected, the Democrats would surely repudiate the debt. But Valentine Hall did not wholly approve of Lincoln, either. When the president sent in a general to take charge of riot-ridden New York, he thought the action "despotic." As for Lincoln's political associates, their pockets were "filled too." He prayed, worried about his health, and though in his twenties, bought a substitute in order to escape military service, as many gentlemen did.

The Oyster Bay Roosevelts stayed Republican, but the Dutchess County branch reverted to the Democratic party. One Roosevelt who voted for Cleveland was the gracious squire of Hyde Park.

Cleveland was the first Democrat to occupy the White House since 1860, but his policies differed little from those of his Republican predecessors. Not until Theodore became president did either Republican or Democrat assert the national interest in any way that angered the rich and privileged.

The Cleveland victory saw the final suppression of the Negro vote in the southern states. "Let the South alone," William E. Dodge, New York capitalist, Grant Republican, and close friend of the elder Theodore, had urged in 1875, and that is what Republican administrations did, beginning with President Hayes, for whom the elder Theodore had worked hard. By 1884 the South had nullified the Fourteenth and Fifteenth Amendments insofar as they applied to Negroes, and white supremacy was effectively re-established.

Because of the Bulloch connection in Georgia, the Roosevelts always had a large circle of southern friends. And because of these southern ties, Elliott and Theodore were undoubtedly sympathetic with the restoration of white rule in the South, although as president, Theodore would shatter precedent and rouse the South to a fury by having Booker T. Washington as a White House luncheon guest.

He was to shatter precedent as well by his enlightened approach to the rights of the workingman, and it was in the year of Eleanor's birth that he began to question the interpretation of the laissez-faire doctrine to which he and most of the members of his class had always subscribed. In 1884 Samuel Gompers of the Cigarmakers Union took Theodore on a tour of the slum sweatshops, and the young assemblyman agreed to sponsor a bill to prohibit the manufacture of cigars in tenements even though it violated his laissez-faire principles. And when the courts, quoting Adam Smith, invalidated his bill saying that they could not see "how the cigar-maker is to be improved in his health or his morals by forcing him from his home and its hallowed associations," Theodore began to be aware, as he wrote later, that complete freedom for the individual could turn out in practice "to mean perfect freedom for the strong to wrong the weak." He would be the first president since Jackson to use the power of government against Big Business—in the 1902 coal strike.

The trade-union movement in the eighties was in its infancy. Labor was cheap. The propertied wanted to keep it that way and rationalized their privileged position by arguing that any man worth his salt could improve his status. The day Eleanor was born, an Episcopal congress met in Detroit to answer the question *Is Our Civilization Just to Workingmen?* "Labor's complaint is poverty," said the keynote speaker, the Reverend Dr. R. H. Newton. "Poverty is the fault neither of the laborer nor of nature. The state crosses the path of the workingman and prevents him from making a fair fight. Labor fails to get favorable legislation; capital secures all it asks."

To the respectable and the upstanding, whether wealthy or not, this was "rot" and heresy. Their laissez-faire individualism was not troubled by the fact that at a time when half-a-million-dollar yachts and million-dollar mansions were being built, thousands of unemployed were looking for work, bread, and shelter, that the average income of eleven million out of the twelve million American families was $380 a year. They approved of industrialists like Pullman, who proclaimed that "the workers have nothing to do with the amount of wages they shall receive." In 1893 they were relieved when the Supreme Court declared unconstitutional a 2-per-cent tax on income of $4,000 and over; a good friend and Roosevelt family adviser, Joseph Choate, had argued the case, denouncing the tax as "a communist march on private property."

"Unfair" taxes and the threat of the nascent labor movement may have invaded the after-dinner conversations of the men, but matters involving politics were of no concern to gentlewomen. *Godey's Lady's Book*, the widely read arbiter of feminine taste and interest in the 1880s, made it a matter of policy to avoid references to public controversy and agitating influence. In 1884 the closest it came to discussing a woman in public life was "Queen Victoria as a Writer." Women's suffrage had become an important issue, but it had no supporters in the Roosevelt family among either the men or the women.

FAMILY LETTERS and recollections provide few glimpses of Eleanor's childhood, yet they were obviously critical years. In Eleanor's later portrayal of these years she emerges as a child who was full of fears—of the dark, of dogs, horses, snakes, of other children. She was "afraid of being scolded, afraid that other people would not like me." She spoke of a sense of inferiority that was almost overpowering coupled with an unquenchable craving for praise and affection. She described her mother as the most beautiful woman she ever knew but also as representing cold virtue, severity, and disapproval, while her father embodied everything that was warm and joyous in her childhood.

Her contrasting memories of her mother and father emerged in a brief account of her first visit to Hyde Park that she included among the explanatory footnotes to her father's letters, in *Hunting Big Game in the Eighties*. On January 30, 1882, "a splendid large baby boy" (Sara Roosevelt's description) had been born to the James Roosevelts. They asked Elliott to be one of the godparents of Franklin Delano, as they decided to name him.

To see this godchild, Eleanor wrote, was the reason

> for that visit which I paid at the age of two with my parents to Hyde Park and I am told that Franklin, probably under protest, crawled around the nursery (which has since been our children's), bearing me on his back. Also, I am told, that I was sent down at tea time to the library in a starched white frock and stood bashfully at the door till my Mother saw me and called "Come in, Granny." She often called me that, for I was a solemn child, without beauty and painfully shy and I seemed like a little old woman entirely lacking in the spontaneous joy and mirth of youth.[4]

From her mother Eleanor received the indelible impression that she was plain to the point of ugliness. As a young woman Anna had been captivatingly beautiful, her face and head so classic in outline that artists had begged to paint her. Anna had been, a friend of the family said, "a little gentlewoman." Eleanor, in her anxiety for people to do right, was more the little schoolmistress, saved from primness only by her grave blue eyes and the sweetness with which she admonished the grownups. To paraphrase Carlyle, who was speaking of the founder of one of the world's great religions, she was one of those who "cannot but be in earnest; whom Nature herself has appointed to be sincere." She is so "old-fashioned," her mother said apologetically. Eleanor, who sensed her mother's disappointment in her, considered this a reproach, but behind the reproach was a mother's bafflement over her little girl's precocious sense of right and wrong and the sadness in her appraising eyes. But these same traits amused and charmed her father, who called her his "little golden hair."

My father was always devoted to me, however, and as soon as I could talk, I went into his dressing room every morning and chattered to him often shaking my finger at him as you can see in the portrait of me at the age of five which we still have. I even danced for him, intoxicated by the pure joy of motion, twisting round and round until he would pick me up and throw me into the air and tell me I made him dizzy.[5]

Eleanor's first nurse was French. "My mother had a conviction that it was essential to study languages, so when I was a baby, she had a French nurse for me, and I spoke French before I spoke English." What this nurse was like, Eleanor nowhere said, but in later life she spoke French as fluently as English, which suggests that this first nurse had the baby's confidence.

While Eleanor's own warmest memories of her early childhood years were all associated with her father, that attractive man was, in fact, putting his little family through a grim ordeal. Nervous and moody, he spent much of his time with the Meadow Brook men, often in reckless escapades and drinking sprees that worried his family and mortified Anna. In the spring of 1887, dissatisfied with himself and his business prospects, he gave up his partnership in the Ludlow firm. Anna prevailed upon him not to risk another Long Island summer. An extended stay in Europe, away from his cronies, she hoped, would enable him to get hold of himself and regain his health. So, on May 19, the Elliott Roosevelt family, a nurse for two-and-a-half-year-old Eleanor, and Anna's sister Tissie sailed for Europe on the *Britannic*.

One day out, the *Britannic* was rammed by the incoming *Celtic* in a fog. "The strain for a few minutes," Anna wrote Bamie, "when we all thought we were sinking was fearful though there were no screams and no milling about. Everyone was perfectly quiet. We were among those taken on life boats to the *Celtic*." Eleanor's recollection of "wild confusion" was significantly different, and closer to reality.

As passengers described the collision to newspapermen, the prow of the *Celtic* struck the *Britannic* a slanting blow, glanced off and then struck again, her nose entering the *Britannic*'s side fully ten feet. Several passengers were killed, a child beheaded, and many injured. The sea foamed, iron bars and belts snapped, and above the din could be heard the moans of the dying and injured. Grownups panicked. Stokers and boiler men emerging from the depths of the *Britannic* made a wild rush for the lifeboats until the captain forced them back at the point of his revolver. The air was filled with "cries of terror," Eleanor's among them. She clung frantically to the men who were trying to drop her over the steep side of the ship into the outstretched arms of her father, who stood in a lifeboat below. Although the sea was calm, the lifeboats were pitching, and the distance seemed vast to Eleanor. The transfer was finally completed despite Eleanor's struggles, and they were rowed to the *Celtic*, which took them back to New York.[6]

Anna and Elliott decided to go through with their plans, because Elliott's health depended on it. But Eleanor, in terror, refused to go and remained unmoved even by her father's endearments and pleas. The puzzled young parents turned to the Gracies, and Eleanor was left to spend the summer with them. "We took a cab," Aunt Gracie wrote to Corinne,

> and called for our sweet little Eleanor and brought her out here with us. She was so little and gentle & had made such a narrow escape out of the great ocean that it made her seem doubly helpless & pathetic to us. . . . She asked two or three times in the train coming out here, where her "dear Mamma was, & where her Papa was, & where is Aunt Tissie?" I told her "They have gone to Europe." She said "where is baby's home now?" I said "baby's home is Gracewood with Uncle Bunkle & Aunt Gracie," which seemed to entirely satisfy the sweet little darling. But as we came near the Bay driving by Mrs. Swan's she said to her uncle in an anxious alarmed way "Baby does not want to go into the water. Not in a boat." It is really touching. . . .

Aunt Gracie's hopeful interpretation of Eleanor's acquiescence may have calmed her own anxiety but showed little real understanding of the ordeal the two-and-a-half-year-old child was going through in numb silence. She had not been able to overcome her terror of the sea. She had disgraced her parents, and as a punishment they had deserted her and she had lost her home.

This violent experience made an indelible impression on Eleanor. She never lost her fear of the sea. Throughout her life she felt the need to prove that she could overcome her physical timidity by feats of special courage. Desertion of the young and defenseless remained an ever present theme—in her reading and her compositions for school; the mere suspicion that someone she loved might have turned away from her always caused the same taut, hopeless bewilderment.

Anna remained uneasy about the separation, "I do so long for her," she wrote from Paris, "but know it was wiser to leave her." And even if Anna had understood how seriously the child was being hurt, she could not have acted differently, because her troubled husband needed his wife's reassuring presence and love if he was to get well.

By August he was "a thousand times better," but he did not wish to risk exposure to his family until he was "really strong and fit to work hard." They returned to New York after six months and Elliott, full of good intentions, joined his Uncle Gracie's banking and brokerage firm. But he also rejoined the hard-drinking, hard-riding Meadow Brook crowd. In spite of his family's misgivings he began to build a large, handsome house in Hempstead, L.I. Polo and hunting became more the center of his life than ever, and he became an ever more reckless rider. One day the hunt started from the Mineola Fair Grounds, the hounds streaking across the Jackson and Titus farms. Forty started out but by the time they were taking the fences of the Titus place only Elliott was following the huntsman. He could hear his companions shouting "don't follow that Irishman, you will be killed" when he was thrown at the third fence and broke his collar bone. On another occasion he arranged a hair-raising midnight steeplechase. "Your father was one of the greatest sports I ever knew," Joe Murphy, the Meadow Brook huntsman, later wrote.[7]

Anna and Eleanor shared Elliott's excitement about the new house in Hempstead—Anna because she hoped it might steady him, Eleanor because it meant she would spend more time with her father. The family rented a cottage nearby to be able to supervise the construction. "Anna is wonderfully well, enjoys everything . . . even the moving and looks the beautiful girl she is. Little Eleanor is as happy as the day is long, plays with her kitten, the puppy & the chickens all the time & is very dirty as a general rule. . . . Baby Eleanor goes up to look after it [the house] every day and calls it hers," a delighted Elliott informed Bamie.

The idyll was brief. In June, 1888, Elliott, exhausted by his hectic life, became seriously ill, and though he rallied miraculously, his family was far from reassured. "Elliott is very much better," Theodore wrote. "I lunched with him Wednesday, and he is now able to go out driving. I wonder if it would do any good to talk to him about his imprudence! I suppose not. I wish he would come to me for a little while; but I guess Oyster Bay would prove insufferably dull, not only for Elliott but for Anna." Soon Elliott was back on his feet, playing polo with Theodore in Oyster Bay. "I know we shall be beaten," Anna confided to her sister-in-law, "since Elliott can barely stay on his pony." Elliott's team lost. "We have great fun here at polo," Theodore wrote Cabot

Lodge. Theodore worked and played strenuously, but he found the pace set by Anna and Elliott too frantic and ultimately meaningless. "I do hate his Hempstead life," he confided to Bye. "I don't know whether he [Elliott] could get along without the excitement now, but it is certainly very unhealthy, and it leads to nothing."

For Eleanor, Hempstead was a happy place. She was not too far away from her cousin Alice, with whom she loved to play. "She and Eleanor are too funny together," Anna reported. They both went to Aunt Gracie's for lessons every morning. "Alice is looking so splendidly and plays so beautifully with Eleanor," was the report. But when Elliott left to go cruising on the *Mayflower,* the 100-foot sloop that had won the America's Cup several years before, Anna made a point of letting him know that "Baby is well but very fiendish." Eleanor's anger did not last, however. Soon she was caught up again in the excitement of her full summer life. "Eleanor is on the piazza building a house with blocks and seems very well and happy," Anna wrote in her next report. "She won't hear of going home as she says, she would not have Alice any more. Aunty and Uncle Bunkle took Alice and Eleanor sailing yesterday. They did enjoy it so much. They are coming over from Sagamore Hill to lunch, and tonight we tea there."

The relationship between Alice and Eleanor, both born in 1884, may not have been as serene as their elders assumed. The two cousins were very different. Though a frail child, "Baby Lee" was as proud, self-assured, and competitive as her father. Golden-curled and saucy, her blue eyes flashed an endless challenge, while Eleanor was gentle, docile, shy, and already painfully aware of her ungainliness. For two years Eleanor wore a steel brace to correct a curvature of the spine, "a very uncomfortable brace." Alice, like Eleanor, idolized her father, and also felt rebuffed and neglected by her mother—in her case, her stepmother. Her response was to rebel, to turn tomboy, which she knew annoyed her stepmother, while Eleanor, much as she would have liked to imitate Alice, withdrew into injured melancholy. Alice seemed "older and cleverer," she said much later, "and while I always admired her I was always afraid of her."

The summer of 1888 had been a time of closeness to her parents and happiness for Eleanor, who was going on four. "The funny little tot had a happy little birthday," her father wrote to Bamie, thanking her for Eleanor's birthday present, "and ended by telling me, when saying good night (after Anna had heard her say her prayers) that she 'loved everybody and everybody loved her.' Was it not cunning?"

That fall and winter were to be the last time Anna, Elliott, and Eleanor enjoyed life as a family. By late spring, 1889, they were finally and fully settled in their "country seat," which they called "½-way Nirvana." Anna was pregnant again and expected to spend a quiet summer.

It was only a few weeks later that Elliott, rehearsing with friends for an amateur circus to be staged at the Waterbury place in Pelham, fractured his ankle in turning a double somersault. The break was incorrectly diagnosed as a sprain, and he was in agony for two weeks after the plaster had been broken off. There were days of such pain "that he could eat nothing and at night he would sob for hours." His leg had to be rebroken and reset. He told Eleanor what the doctors were going to do. She gave him courage and comfort, but it was a thoughtless act, considering that she was not quite five. He did not complain, but Eleanor, being a child of amazing sensitivity, did not have to be told; as leaves moved to the wind, she stirred to the thought of others in pain. If a playmate was injured she wept, and her father was the person she most loved in the world. Her eyes brimmed with tears as he pulled himself on crutches out to the waiting doctors. Eleanor never forgot this experience.

Elliott Jr. was born October 1, 1889, and this event evoked the first letter, dictated to Pussie, from Eleanor, who had been sent to Tivoli to stay with her grandmother.

> Dear Father:
> I hope you are very well and Mother too. I hope little brother doesn't cry and if he does tell the nurse to give him a tap tap. How does he look? Some people tell me he looks like an elephant and some say he is like a bunny. I told Aunt Pussie today she would be very unhappy if she were a man because his wife would send her down downtown every day she could only come home on Sunday and then she would have to go to church. Goodby now dear Father, write me soon another letter. I love you very much and Mother and Brother too, if he has blue eyes.
> Your precious little
> Eleanor.

"And," added Pussie, "Totty [the name by which her Hall aunts called her] is flourishing. She has quite a color and tell Anna the French lessons are progressing, although I am afraid the pupil knows more than the teacher."

"Eleanor is so proud of her baby brother and talks of nothing else," was the next report from Tivoli.

Elliott and Anna were equally pleased. The birth of their first son was the fulfillment of "their hearts' desire." Elliott, in spite of his continuing pain, doted on "Baby Joss," as the new arrival was called. But even though Elliott was with his new son, Eleanor sensed no change in her father's attitude toward her. She never doubted that she was first in his heart.

With her mother, however, the birth of little Ellie and a year later of Hall did make a difference. Forty years later, in 1929, Eleanor wrote a story for a magazine whose fictional heroine, Sally, was obviously herself.

> Her forty-fifth birthday.... As she looked [into the fire] pictures formed in the dancing flames, first, there was a blue-eyed rather ugly little girl standing in the door of a cozy library looking in at a very beautiful woman holding, oh so lovingly, in her lap a little fair-haired boy. Through Sally's heart passed the old sensation, the curious dread of the cold glance which would precede the kindly and indifferent "Come in Sally, and bring your book."

In her autobiography, published in 1937, she was more explicit about her feelings of being left out when her mother was with the two little boys, Ellie and Hall. Her mother did not consciously exclude her; she read to Eleanor and had Eleanor read to her and recite her poems, and Eleanor was allowed to stay after the boys had been sent off to bed. But what Eleanor emphasized was standing in the door, "very often with my finger in my mouth," and her mother bidding her "Come in, Granny," with that voice and look of kind indifference. Child psychologists had not yet discovered the connection between the "finger in the mouth" and the hunger for affection. To visitors her mother would explain that she called Eleanor "Granny" because she was "so old-fashioned."

"I wanted to sink through the floor in shame, and I felt I was apart from the boys."[8]

To Eleanor her mother's sigh and exasperated voice were further proof that only her father understood and loved her. And her father was leaving her again. His foot had to be stretched every day to prevent its shortening. He had begun to take laudanum and morphine and to drink ever more heavily to kill the excruciating pain in his foot.

When his behavior became hostile even to those he loved most and he threatened suicide, the doctors prescribed a complete rest, and at the end of December, 1889, he embarked on a trip to the South—without saying good-by to his wife and children. His wife desperately tried to reach him through his love for the children. "Eleanor came rushing down when she heard the postman to know if there was a letter from you and what you said. I told her you would not be here for two weeks and she seemed awfully disappointed, but was quite satisfied when I told her you were getting well."

Eleanor's whole life was spent waiting for her father. "Eleanor lunched with us yesterday," wrote Tissie; "she rushed to the stairs every time the bell rang to see if it was her Papa. I shall be so glad to see my *dear* Father, she kept saying. She certainly adores you."

4. THE CRACK-UP

THE SOUTHERN CURE DID NOT WORK. ELLIOTT'S DRUNKEN SPREES became more violent and dissipated. In 1890, in a final desperate effort to hold the family together, they decided to lease their houses in town and Hempstead, sell their horses, and go abroad for a tour of mountain resorts and watering places. Anna declined the Gracies' offer to leave the children with them, and Eleanor, almost six, and baby Elliott accompanied their parents on a restless, troubled journey that ended in disaster.

They went directly to Berlin, and Anna's first extended report to Bamie was bright and hopeful. Count Bismarck got them "splendid places" for the parade of the garrison. Count Sierstorff took them to see the cavalry drill. And the only moment of danger came when Buffalo Bill, who was also in Berlin, offered Elliott whiskey to drink to his health. Sierstorff was wonderful, Anna reported, took the glass out of Elliott's hand, and told Buffalo Bill it was against doctor's orders.

From Berlin they proceeded to Reichenhall, in Bavaria, where the Germans were "all of a class that no one would think of meeting," Anna wrote. But Elliott took the baths and drank the waters and except for "awful attacks of depression" was sleeping well and his foot had stopped hurting.

"Elliott is really studying German now," she added, "and I hope he will take some interest in it. Eleanor is beginning to speak a little but teaching her to read is hopeless. She is as good as gold."

After a month in Reichenhall they went on to Munich and then to Oberammergau for the Passion play before heading for Vienna and Italy. Their expenses, lamented Anna, seemed enormous. "I don't know how it is, but we don't seem to be able to travel under $1,500 a month," even though they were not buying things. On the way to Vienna they stopped to visit the estate of Count Arco, and that was a disaster. "Elliott was an angel up to Wednesday night. Then I *think* he drank champagne for dinner, though he denies it." Anna was ill and had to stay in bed, but she tried to accompany Elliott everywhere, "excepting when they were shooting." Elliott, however, finally eluded her, and she found him drinking brandy and water. "I was furious and said so. It affected him at once. . . . I am sure it is the first alcohol he has touched in two months."

That fall they moved south to Italy. From Venice, at the end of October. Elliott wrote "Dear Anna's Mother" that though they had "done so much and worked so hard over our amusements . . . the children and Anna are both very well." Lots of sightseeing and visiting but

her great delight of course; as mine; is in Baby "Joss." He gets stronger and fatter and rosier every day. I am afraid he is a son of his father, though, for he is not at all a "good boy." Eleanor is so sweet and good with him and really is learning to read and write for love of it making it possible to tell him stories which he cannot understand.

He told her of

the little things such as Ellie's feeding the pigeons on the Piazza at St. Marks, the lovely music on the Canal in decorative Gondolas by the band of the "32" Regiment, the delight that Eleanor and I have taken in the Lido Shore, wandering up and down looking over the blue Adriatic watching the gray surf and catching funny little crabs!

For Eleanor, the high point in Venice was her father acting as gondolier and singing along with the other boatmen.

They moved on to Florence and then Naples, because, said Anna, "it is warmer." From Sorrento in November, Anna wrote to Bamie that Elliott

goes sailing every day & takes the children in the morning. I went one afternoon but cannot stand it. Elliott generally takes a nap in the boat in the afternoon. Last night I only got four hours sleep owing to a dear sweet letter from Aunt Annie which completely upset Elliott. Don't repeat this, but beg them to write brightly. Elliott is so nervous everything upsets him. First he sobbed, then got furious and went out, said he would never go home, etc. and worked himself into a perfect fever of excitement.

To her mother she wrote more reassuringly.

> This is the most beautiful place, right on the bay with Naples. Vesu-
> vius and Capri opposite and only a little way off Pompeii. Elliott
> takes both children sailing every morning, while I have an Italian
> lesson from the Priest here, and later in the afternoon we drive and
> then go on the water for the sunset.

Pregnant again and unwell, Anna was in bed much of the time,
and when Elliott proposed a trip to Vesuvius she begged off. He took
Eleanor and her nurse, Albertina. The three were late getting back
and Anna had worried herself into a state close to hysterics. For little
Eleanor it was an exciting but exhausting trip. Years later she recalled
the endless journey down the slope and how it took all her self-control
to stand it "without tears so that my father would not be displeased."
Fear of her father's displeasure also seared Eleanor's memory of the
donkey that she was given in Sorrento.

> "You are not afraid are you?" The tone was incredulous, astonished,
> and the man looked down from his horse to the child on her small
> donkey. The eyes were kind, but she sat shivering and hung back,
> looking at the steep descent. A steely look came into the man's eyes
> and in a cold voice he said: "You may go back if you wish, but I did
> not know you were a coward." She went back and the man went on
> sliding down the hill after the grown-ups—the nurse and the little
> donkey boy escorted the five year old girl along the dusty highway
> back to Sorrento, Italy.[1]

In her autobiography Eleanor recalled another episode with the
donkey and the little donkey boy, whose feet were cut and bleeding.
"On one occasion we returned with the boy on the donkey and I was
running along beside him, my explanation being that his feet bled
too much!"

Grasping at externals, Anna thought Elliott was getting better in
Sorrento. Not that she supposed he could as yet stand temptation, but
she hoped for great things from the next two months; perhaps by the
beginning of March they might be able to return home. But she did
not feel she could manage the homeward trip alone. She was expecting
a baby in June and pleaded with Bye to come over. As the winter rains
started and the children took sick "in the nasty wet cold," the doctors

prescribed a cold, dry climate, and the family settled down for the winter in the old university city of Graz in Austria, in "the beautiful mountains of southern Styria." At first they all felt "the benefit" of the "hardy, honest and healthy climate," and Elliott even managed to get off a cheerful report to Theodore, chiefly about his children.

Tell Alice that Eleanor takes French lessons every day and tries hard to learn how to write so she won't be far behind when we return. Eleanor is learning to skate too, quite well. She has some little German friends with whom she coasts and plays snow balling all day. She really talks German *very* well. Little Boy understands both German and English but can only say "Nein" "Mama" and "da-da" as yet. He is so fat and well. Eats all the time. He looks just like little Ted used to those days at Sagamore when I used to laugh so at his back view digging holes in the walk. And playing he was as big as the other children. Do you remember?

Ever lovingly yours,

Nell.

But the Graz interlude was brief, and on the advice of Vienna specialists Elliott entered the Mariengrund sanitarium for treatment. Bamie was sent for, and persuaded the Vienna doctors to allow her to stay at Mariengrund with him.[2]

April brought a precipitate dash to Paris. It is not clear why, but the departure was so hurried that the children were left behind and traveled to Paris with their nurse Albertina and her husband—Elliot's man Stephen. At one stop the train went off before Eleanor and Albertina managed to get back on, causing much fright and telegraphing back and forth. At the suggestion of the doctor whom they engaged to take care of the pregnant Anna, the family rented a house in Neuilly.

Since it was a small house, it was decided that Eleanor would be better off in a convent, where she would be out of the way when the baby arrived and able to improve her French. The six-year-old child saw this as a banishment. She was miserable, made to feel like an outsider by the other little girls, whose religion she did not share and whose language she spoke awkwardly.

Loneliness, the sense of exclusion, the hunger for praise and admiration led to the episode of the penny. When one of the other little girls became the center of excitement and attention because she had swallowed a coin, Eleanor went to the sisters and announced that she, too, had swallowed a penny. It was a pathetic but revealing bid for the limelight. The sisters did not believe her but could not budge her from her story, so they sent for her mother, who took her away in disgrace. Her father "was the only person who did not treat me as a criminal."

In Paris Elliott's behavior became more frightening and erratic. He disappeared for days on end and then turned up depressed, penitent, full of promises to reform; he made violent scenes and then tried to reassure his family. Anna and he were "quietly happy," he wrote his mother-in-law. "Anna and I walk together in the morning...we often sit and read for two hours at a time while the children play; that is Joss does, for Eleanor is at school except in the afternoon when she comes, too, and feeds the fishes and the ducks." But to his Meadow Brook cronies he wrote boastfully about his good times with the Jockey Club set hunting boar with the Duc de Gramont's hounds.

> ...the horns played a little and then we galloped in single file up and down miles of beaten forest roads (without a chance of danger or excitement unless one should be to sleep in the saddle and fall out) guided by clever Piquers until we killed. It was fun and interesting but how I did long for a gentle school (over Hempstead Plains even) with you or one of your kind.

The family's breakup came soon after the birth of Hall in June, 1891. Elliott seemed to lose control of his actions completely. He feared that he was losing his mind, and the terrified family became afraid to have him with them.

The more frenzied Elliott's excesses, the more his unhappy, sorely tried wife, backed by Bamie, took refuge in strength and rectitude. In desperation, during one of his wilder, more prolonged bouts of drunkenness, they finally had him placed in an asylum for medical treatment. He said they "kidnapped" him. Anna, Bamie, and the children sailed for home, Anna agreeing not to get a divorce if Elliott consented to stay under the care of physicians for six months at the Château Suresnes outside of Paris.

Fearful, however, that he would dissipate the remainder of his estate, the family applied to the U.S. courts to have him adjudged insane and incapable of taking care of himself, and to have his property, which Theodore valued at $175,000, placed in trust for his wife and children. In their affidavits, Theodore and Bamie said that as long ago as 1889 they had noticed the deterioration in Elliott's physical and mental condition, his inability to concentrate, loss of memory, irrational behavior. Three times he had threatened to commit suicide.[3]

The months during which the proceedings dragged on were anguished ones for the family, none of it made easier by the sensation the court move had created in the press. A reporter for the *World* tracked Anna down at her mother's house in Tivoli where she was staying with her children. She was afraid that she would be "nasty" but could not risk having her mother talk to him. Was Elliott really insane, the reporter wanted to know. "I said no doctor had ever thought him so excepting from alcohol," she replied, "and that I considered any man irresponsible when under the influence of alcohol."

Elliott alternately cooperated and resisted. In one letter to Anna, he first accused her of the most "abominable" things and sounded like a "madman," she wrote Bamie, and then after picturing himself as the injured party, abruptly changed his tone and said that she was a "noble woman" and that he trusted her entirely. "His letter is so hopelessly sad and I so long to help him, not to make him suffer more."

The family was divided over the recourse to the courts. The doctors disagreed over the cure. Elliott himself wrote to the court, objecting to the proceedings. Finally, Theodore, who was then a member of the Civil Service Commission and living in Washington, made a hurried trip to Paris. He persuaded Elliott to come home and make a new start, promising that the legal proceedings would be discontinued if Elliott would place most of his money in trust for his family. Elliott agreed to take a course of treatment for alcoholism in the United States, resume a business connection, and prove himself worthy of being reunited with his family.

A woman to whom Elliott had turned in Paris, who met him with welcoming love rather than lectures, passed harsh judgment on Anna and Theodore. While she was clearly a biased witness, Eleanor was not wholly unsympathetic when in later years she came into possession of the journal entries in which this woman's feelings were recorded.

"This morning," this woman wrote,

> with his silk hat, his overcoat, gloves and cigar, E. came to my room to say goodbye. It is all over, only my little black dog, who cries at the door of the empty room and howls in the park, he is all that is left to me. So ends the final and great emotion of my life. "The memory of what has been, and never shall be" is all the future holds. Even my loss was swallowed up in pity—for he looks so bruised so

beaten down by the past week with his brother. How could they treat so generous and noble a man as they have. He is more noble a figure in my eyes with all his confessed faults, than either his wife or brother. She is more to be despised, in her virtuous pride, her absolutely selfish position than the most miserable woman I know, but she is the result of our unintelligent, petty, conventional social life. And why is it that the gentle, strong men always marry women who are so weak & selfish. Perhaps the feeling of protection & care given to a feebler nature is part of the charm. If she were only large-souled enough to appreciate him . . .

In later years Eleanor said that it might have been more helpful to her father if her mother had responded to his drinking with love instead of high-minded strength. Her mother was a good woman, she said, and very strong, but if something was right there was no excuse for not doing it. Her father might not have been able to conquer his drinking, she later concluded, but would have been happier if he had felt loved.

How much six-year-old Eleanor knew of her father's crack-up is unclear. She said that it was only after her mother died that she began to have any awareness that there was something seriously wrong with her father. But she was so bound up with his moods and actions that she could not have been wholly shielded from the sad events that were taking place in the tiny household. But, whatever she heard or saw, her sympathies were with her father.

5. HER MOTHER'S DEATH

ELLIOT RETURNED TO THE STATES ANXIOUS TO REDEEM HIMSELF in the eyes of his family, especially his wife. She had stipulated a year of separation during which he would have to regain command of himself, stop drinking, choose an occupation, and stick to it.

He went, in February, 1892, to Dwight, Illinois, the headquarters of Dr. Keeley and the "Keeley cure" for alcoholism, but undertook this new course of treatment and probation rebelliously. He considered it "wicked and foolish" and only agreed to it because "it is Anna's wish." After drying out in Dwight, he felt that he should return to New York and undergo his final probation "*in my family* with the aid and strengthening influence of Home." To start anew in some western or southern city, as his family was insisting, would only separate him further from his wife and children. He had wanted to see Anna before he went to Dwight so that she should "see me as I *am*. Not as she last saw me, flushed with wine, reckless and unworthy but an earnest, repentant self-respecting gentle-man." But Anna had refused to receive him.

As the five-week treatment drew to a close, Elliott was less rebellious and was prepared to "do *anything* required of me by my loved ones to prove the completeness of my cure and the earnestness of my desire to atone." His brother-in-law, Douglas Robinson, proposed that he go to southwest Virginia to take charge of the large Robinson holdings there. Bamie and Theodore sided with Anna but the Robinsons, especially Corinne, joined the Gracies and the Liverpool Bullochs in taking Elliott's part. The Robinson properties covered a vast, almost primeval wilderness of virgin forest, laurel thicket, and high peaks, which the Douglas Land Company had decided to begin to tap. This meant bringing in railroads, improving mountain trails, settling boundary disputes, selling land to homesteaders.

The work was difficult and hazardous but "by meeting the mountaineers upon their own grounds" Elliott was soon considered a "friend," the Washington County paper wrote. "Children loved him; negroes sang for him; the poor, the needy and the unfortunate had reason to bless him; the young girls and the old ladies 'fell for him;' and men became his intimate friends."[1]

He quickly assembled "a stable of choice mounts," gathered "a rare assortment of dogs, including terriers, setters, pointers, 'coon' dogs, hounds," and hunted everything "from snakes to bears.... He dropped into homes and fitted into every family circle, eating apples by the open fire, reading poetry, talking of local things or about his own wife and children." He always functioned best away from his strong-minded wife and very successful brother but does not seem to have recognized this. And although he carved out a place for himself in Abingdon, he felt exiled, and his letters home were full of remorse and pleas that the "homeless and heartsick and lonely" sinner be forgiven and allowed to return to his family. "You who know no sin which compares with mine," he wrote his wife, "can hardly know the *agony* of shame and repentance I endure and the *self* condemnation I have to face. I need indeed be brave to make my fight...."

Anna had an equally anguished time, torn between wanting to try again yet not daring to hope that Elliott would change. She made few moves without consulting Bamie. "This letter from Elliott worries me so that I send it to you," she wrote from Tivoli. "I am so awfully sorry for him. My heart simply aches and I would do anything I could that could really help him.... It seems to be dawning on him for the first time that he is not coming home this Autumn."

It was the summer of 1892, when Anna was nearly thirty. She suffered from backaches, complained that her eyes were giving out, and was to have an operation in the fall. Eleanor was then sleeping in her mother's room and spent hours rubbing her mother's head with her strong, competent fingers, happy, she said, to be of some use to her suffering parent. Only seven, she was already taking care of her mother.

The life of a beautiful young woman separated from her husband was not an easy one in New York society of the 1890s. Anna was aware of how easily a woman alone might be considered to have overstepped the line of correctness and propriety. When she and Eleanor went to Bar Harbor she was continually preoccupied with how much fun and gaiety she could allow herself. A string of queries went off to Bamie. Should she "matronize" dinners? Could she go rowing or driving in the afternoon with a man, although, of course, she would not go more than once or twice with the same man? It was an awful temptation when one feels desperately lonely and wildly furious with the world at large, not to make up one's mind to pay no attention to criticism as long as one does no wrong and to try to get some fun out of the few years of our youth. I hate everything and everyone so and am most of the time so miserable that I feel anything one could do would be a comfort to forget for one moment.

Many members of her family were at Bar Harbor—her sister, Pussie; her brothers, Vallie and Eddie; Cousin Susie and her husband Henry Parish. There were endless discussions about Elliott. "Something was wrong with my father and from my point of view nothing could be wrong with him," Eleanor wrote much later. But no one told her anything, and the anxious talks, which she now strained to catch, left her confused, torn between her adoration for her father and the distress of her mother.

Anna returned to New York in the autumn, determined to start a new life for her children and herself, a life that would be more than a waiting for a transformation in her husband that deep down she knew would never happen and that would provide a buttress against the now pleading, now threatening letters with which Elliott bombarded her. She moved to a new house at Sixty-first Street and Madison Avenue, two blocks away from Bamie. Her gracious hospitality and charm quickly attracted a widening circle of admiring friends who gathered round her while she presided over the silver tea urn. But no matter how busy her day, she explained to friends, the evening hours from six to seven o'clock were resolutely and dutifully devoted to her children. "If anyone comes to see me during that hour, they must understand they are welcome, but the children are of the first importance then, and my attention must be given to them. I play with them any way they may want. I get down on the floor and we play horse or we play tag, or I read for them—anything, that they may remember the hour happily as 'mother's hour,' and feel assured that nothing whatever is to interfere with it."[2]

A friend was present one day when the children were brought in at six o'clock sharp. "She took the baby in her lap, kissed 'Josh' and moved the footstool for Eleanor to sit upon. A bit of biscuit was given to each, and then they were kissed goodnight 'as tonight Mamma is very tired' and waved to bed, only little Eleanor remaining at her mother's feet."

Anna began to plan her children's education. Little Ellie would go to kindergarten next year, so that was easy; but Eleanor presented a problem. Anna was sure that Eleanor should have a good basic education. She felt keenly her own lack of systematic study, and lamented that her knowledge of history and science was so scanty that she was not able to answer Eleanor's questions. She no longer accepted the premise that beauty and breeding were all that a girl of wealth needed—and, besides, Eleanor would not have beauty to help her succeed as a woman.

At seven Eleanor had had a smattering of reading and writing which had been taught to her by various relatives. Great-Aunt Gracie had tried to teach Eleanor and Alice to read, as she had their fathers. Eleanor adored her, was fascinated by her expressive hands as she told them B'rer Rabbit tales and stories of the vanished ante-bellum life on the Rosewell plantation in Georgia, but she did not learn to read. Another great-aunt, Mrs. Edward Ludlow, whose Hudson River estate bordered her grandmother's, was dismayed to find, when Anna and the children returned from Paris, that seven-year-old Eleanor could not read and hadn't the slightest knowledge of the elementary household tasks that little girls usually learn by playing house in the nursery. Great-Aunt Maggie scolded the embarrassed Anna and sent her companion over every day to make sure that the child got her lessons. And to Eleanor's great sorrow, the nurse, an Alsatian woman whom Eleanor feared, was directed to teach Eleanor to cook and sew, which quite possibly is the reason that Eleanor never was interested in cooking or learned much about it. She did not like Madeleine.

Mrs. Ludlow's reprimand confirmed Anna in her decision to begin Eleanor's formal schooling immediately. In the fall of 1892 she turned part of the upper floor in her house into a schoolroom for Eleanor and a few other girls her age, and invited Frederic Roser, whose classes for the daughters of the highest society were then very fashionable, to teach the little group. Mr. Roser did not like to teach the youngest girls and assigned his assistant, Miss Tomes, to the class.

Eleanor remembered her first days in school as a time of agony and mortification. She was asked to spell simple words such as "horse" that her mother knew she knew, but frozen by shyness and the presence of her mother, who sat in on the class, she misspelled every one. Her mother reproached her—she did not know how Eleanor would end up, she said. Forty years later Eleanor still remembered vividly her feeling of utter misery because of her mother's disgust with her. "I was always disgracing my mother." Perhaps her behavior in the classroom was also a rejection and punishment of her mother, whom she blamed for exiling her beloved father.

Anna realized that her already shy and awkward daughter suffered deeply under the discord in the family and tried to comfort her, making a special effort for her. Anna read to her daily, and Eleanor listened silently and politely but without the rapt attention she had always given to her father. Years later Eleanor's strongest childhood reading memories were associated with her father. "I had a special interest in *The Old Curiosity Shop*, becauses my father used to call me 'Little Nell' after the child in that story, and I first really learned to care for Longfellow's poems because my father was devoted to Hiawatha." At the age of eight she learned almost the entire poem because she was eager to surprise her absent father when she saw him again.[3]

Her sons were a comfort to Anna. "Ellie is a saintlike child, simply perfect, never grumbles or complains of anything and is so loving and attractive," while Baby Hall was a "lovely boy with a strong will" who "rules Ellie even now." Only Eleanor was a problem. She was now so afraid of "strange children" that when her mother took her to children's parties on Saturday afternoons she would break into tears and have to be brought home. Anna arranged to have some boys and girls come in on Friday afternoons to play and stay for tea so that Eleanor could begin to make some friends, but the plan was never carried out. Anna had her operation and Eleanor spent her eighth birthday with the Gracies. "Mother wishes she could be with you," Anna wrote her. "I enclose a letter from Father to you."

Abingdon, Va.
Oct. 9/92

My darling little Daughter,

Many happy returns of this birthday little Nell. I am thinking of you always and I wish for my Baby Girl the greatest of Joy and the most perfect happiness in her sweet young life.

Because Father is not with you is not because he doesn't love you. For I love you tenderly and dearly. And maybe soon I'll come back all well and strong and we will have such good times together, like we used to have. I have to tell all the little children here often about you and all that I remember of you when you were a little bit of a girl and you used to call yourself Father's little "Golden Hair"— and how you used to come into my dressing room and dress me in the morning and frighten me by saying I'd be late for breakfast.

I gave a doll to the little girl you sent the Doll's jewelry to, small

Lillian Lloyd and she has called it Eleanor and another little friend of mine the daughter of my good and dear friend Mr. Blair of Chicago has named her most precious doll Eleanor too; after you they are both named. Some day you must meet little Lillian and little Emily and they will be glad to know you in person; they say they know your photograph so well.

Now I must stop writing dearest little Nell, do take care of yourself and little Brothers, Ellie and Brudie, and kiss them for me. Love dear Mother for me and be very gentle and good to her 'specially now while she is not well. Goodbye my own little Daughter. God bless you.

Give my best love to Aunt Gracie and Uncle.

Your devoted Father

Elliott Roosevelt.

From Aunt Gracie's, Eleanor went to Tivoli and from there wrote her father.

Oak Terrace
Tivoli-on-Hudson

My dear Father:—

Your present which you and Mamma sent me was lovely. It is just what I want for washing the doly's clothes which Aunt Pussie and Auntie Maud gave me. I got a ball, walking doll, violin, music boxes, and a bell to draw around the piaza. The candy Auntie Tissie brought up looks lovely, but I have not tasted it as I do not eat between meals, but will have some after dinner. Elsie, Susie and Kittie Hall are coming to dinner and Auntie Maud is going to have Punch and Judy after dinner which I think will be great fun don't you. I was very glad to get your letter and please thank the clerk for the picture. I thank you again for the present you sent me. I hope you are all well and now I must close dear Father from your little daughter

Baby

Eleanor received two other birthday letters from friends in Abingdon. One was from Lillian Lloyd, daughter of the Episcopalian rector.

Dear Eleanor:

I want to write so badly that Mother is holding my hand. Your nice letter came today. I wish I could play with you. Wont you come down and play with my pretty doll and my brother Hubard and spend a week? I named my pretty doll ELEANOR ROOSEVELT LLOYD....I love your papa dearly, better than any man but Father. He has my picture with my Maltese cats in it. They are dead.

Send me your picture, Eleanor, if you can't come soon....

The other was from the daughter of Daniel Trigg, whose farm was just outside Abingdon. She also mentioned how often Eleanor's father spoke of his daughter, how fond she was of Eleanor's father, and how she hoped Eleanor would soon come down to Abingdon. The letters from the Abingdon children were loving and innocent, but for Eleanor they made the pain of separation from her father almost unbearable.

Elliott had wanted to come north for Anna's operation but was asked to stay away. To explain why Anna did not want him to come even though she was seriously ill, Corinne relayed to Elliott what she had heard from Anna's mother. Elliott responded by writing directly to Mrs. Hall.

Did she say she wanted to die, that I had made her so utterly miserable that she did not care to live any more. And did you say that was what your poor child had been suffering in silence all these past killing months?

He was relieved when he heard that Anna was better but insisted that "in danger my place and my right is to be near her." But Anna did not want him. A new illness at the end of November was diagnosed as diphtheria. "I ought to be with her unless my presence is *actually distasteful* to her," Elliott wrote imploringly, but Mrs. Hall telegraphed "Do not come," which Elliott understood to be Anna's command.

Letters crossed in the mail. Mrs. Hall again wrote sharply that he should not come. Her letters hurt him, he wrote on December 6. They had no right to doubt his word, "and I have pledged it to my wife never to force myself upon her.... You need not fear that even if called to my wife's deathbed that if not at her request I would present myself there." The next day he wrote again.

I am only terribly sad that I should be so repugnant to her.... It is most horrible and full of *awe* to me that my *wife* not only does not want me near her in sickness or trouble but *fears* me. And, before God I say it, I am honestly worthy of her trust and Love—for even in my drinking I never did a *dishonorable* thing, nor *one cruel act* towards my wife or children.

Resigned to staying away from New York, he begged Mrs. Hall to telegraph C.O.D. about his wife's condition. She died that day, and the message reached him while he was at Daniel Trigg's, several miles out in the country. Hurriedly driving over the muddy road to town, he packed a bag hastily and flagged the night train to New York.

Eleanor's account of her mother's death, written almost forty-five years later, did not dwell on the loss of her mother but on the return of her father. "Death meant nothing to me, and one fact wiped out everything else—my father was back and I would see him very soon." Her mother died on December 7, 1892. Her father did not come to see her immediately. Later she realized, she wrote, "what a tragedy of utter defeat" her mother's death meant for her father. "No hope now of ever wiping out the sorrowful years he had brought upon my mother—and she had left her mother as guardian for her children. My grandmother did not feel she could trust my father to take care of us. He had no wife, no children, no hope!"[4]

She wept for her father, not for her mother. Yet that engaging man's capacity for love and devotion was fatally flawed: it was totally self-centered, without steadiness or altruism. He made large promises, was full of warmth, charm, and affection, but there was no follow-through, no constancy, little on which his family could build.

Eleanor refused to recognize this, but the rest of the family, especially Bye and Theodore, saw him clearly and approved Anna's decision, stated in her will, to make her mother the children's guardian. "Good as I firmly believe your advice to have been," Elliott informed Mrs. Lloyd, the wife of the Episcopalian rector in Abingdon,

and sorely as I think myself I need my little ones with me, I will return without them. I have not found one person in either my wife's or my connection who encourages me in the slightest degree when I propose that the children join their Father. If I have a comfortable home they might come down and visit me for a while during the summer. But all seem to think the proper place for them now is with their Grandmother and surrounded by everything in the way of luxury and all the advantages, both educational and otherwise to which they have been accustomed.

Elliott sought to comfort his daughter as well as himself with a gleaming vision of their making a home together again.

After we were installed (at Grandma Hall's house) my father came to see me, and I remember going down into the high ceilinged dim library on the first floor of the house on West 37th Street. He sat in a big chair. He was dressed all in black, looking very sad. He held out his arms and gathered me to him. In a little while he began to talk, to explain to me that my mother was gone, that she had been all the world to him, and now he had only my brothers and myself, that my brothers were very young, and that he and I must keep close together. Some day I would make a home for him again; we would travel together and do many things which he painted as interesting and pleasant, to be looked forward to in the future together.

Somehow it was always he and I. I did not understand whether my brothers were to be our children or whether he felt that they would be at school and college and later independent.

There started that day a feeling which never left me—that he and I were very close together, and some day, would have a life of our own together. He told me to write to him often, to be a good girl, not to give any trouble, to study hard, to grow up into a woman he could be proud of, and he would come to see me whenever it was possible.

When he left, I was all alone to keep our secret of mutual understanding and to adjust myself to my new existence.[5]

6. "HE LIVED IN MY DREAMS"

ELLIOTT'S LETTERS TO HIS DAUGHTER WERE TENDER, CHIVAL-
rous, playful, and, above all, full of protestations of love. After his
death she would carry them around with her for the remainder of her
life. People who lived on in the memories of those alive, she said, were
not dead. She read and reread her father's letters, and each time it was
a fresh invocation of the magic of his presence.

"I knew a child once who adored her father," she wrote in 1927.

> She was an ugly little thing, keenly conscious of her deficiencies,
> and her father, the only person who really cared for her, was away
> much of the time; but he never criticized her or blamed her, instead
> he wrote her letters and stories, telling her how he dreamed of her
> growing up and what they would do together in the future, but
> she must be truthful, loyal, brave, well-educated, or the woman he
> dreamed of would not be there when the wonderful day came for
> them to fare forth together. The child was full of fears and because
> of them lying was easy; she had no intellectual stimulus at that time
> *and yet she made herself as the years went on into a fairly good copy of the
> picture he had painted.*[1]

In his letters her father addressed Eleanor as "Father's Own Little
Nell," and that was the way she signed herself in the letters to him. His
first letter after his return to Abingdon reported on his new puppies.
"They are both in the armchair beside me and the old Dog is curled
up at my feet in the rug dreaming, I suppose of all the rabbits he *did
not* catch today!"

What shall he write about, his next letter asked.

> Shall I tell you of the wonderful long rides, of days through the
> grand snowclad forests, over the white hills, under the blue skies

as blue as those in Italy which you and I and little Ellie, though he was so little he cannot remember it, used to sail over Naples Bay to beautiful Capri. I am afraid in those young "Nell days" you were a little seasick and did not enjoy it as much as you will in the day that is coming when you have worked hard at your lessons and gotten that curious thing they call "education."

After Anna's death "Professor Roser," as Elliott dubbed him, had inquired of Grandma Hall about her plans for Eleanor's education, expressing hope that he would not lose such a promising student. Mrs. Hall consulted Elliott. There was no question "as to the wisdom of Eleanor's undoubtedly remaining in his class. Will you write therefore and have the matter attended to? The tone of his note is very nice, did you not think so? Our little girl is a good little girl and conscientious, I believe, as he says."

His January 20 letter sought to impress on Eleanor the importance of education.

The next time you go walking get your maid to take you where they are building a house and watch the workmen bring one stone after another and place it on top of the one gone before or along side, and then think that there are a lot of funny little workmen running about in your small Head called "Ideas" which are carrying a lot of stones like small bodies called "Facts," and these little "Ideas" are being directed by your teachers in various ways, by "Persuasion," "Instruction," "Love," and "Truth" to place all these "Fact Stones" on top of and alongside of each other in your dear Golden Head until they build a beautiful house called "Education"—*Then*! Oh, my pretty companionable Little Daughter, you will come to Father and what jolly games we will have together to be sure—And in your beautiful house "Education," Father wishes you such a happy life—But those little fact stones are a queer lot, and you have to ask your teachers to look well after the Idea workmen that they don't put some in crooked in the walls of your pretty House. Sometimes you'll find a rough hard fact that you must ask your teacher to smooth down and polish and set straight by persuasion, love and truth. Then you'll find a rebellious little factstone that won't fit where it ought to, though it is intended to go just there like the little factstone "music"—maybe you will have to get your teachers to use Instruction, maybe a great deal of it to get that small stone to fit, but it must go there and it *will*, if the little Idea workmen stick at it long enough. Then there are what seem to be stupid, wearisome, trying factstones that you can't see the use of in your dear house, that the Ideas are building! Like—"Going to bed regularly and early fact stones." "*Not eating candy* fact stones," "Not telling *always* exactly the Truth fact stones," "Not being a teasing little girl fact stones" instead of a precious gentle *Self* amusing and satisfied one.

There are lots of others like those I have mentioned and to have them put in order you must *beg* your teachers to use all four powers of Persuasion, Instruction, Love, Truth and another force too, *Discipline!* Of all the forces your Teachers use, Father and you too, Little Witch, probably like Love best, but we must remember the little fact stones as I said at first are such a queer lot, that we have to trust to your Teachers, who know by Experience in building other Education houses in little brains, how much the Idea workmen can do and how also the character of the fact stones, what forces to apply. Think of your brain as an Education House; you surely always wish to live in a beautiful house not an ugly one, and get Auntie Maude darling to explain what Father means by this letter tale. Little Terrier says I must go to bed. Goodnight *my* darling little Daughter, my "*Little Nell.*"

Miss Tomes was a good teacher who knew how to hold the children's interest, and Eleanor was a diligent pupil. Despite her initial humiliation, she gradually gained self-confidence—only long division eluded her. Usually Mr. Roser urged his girls to skip it on the assumption that well-bred women did not go on to college and would not need mathematics, but her father, while sympathetic, urged her not to give up.

I know division, especially long division, seemed to me at your age a very tiresome and uninteresting study. I too longed to be in fractions—or *infractious* but I found afterwards that it had been better,—as it turns out nine times out of ten, that I stood out against my own impatience and lack of desire to become informed, and devoted myself—howbeit against the grain—to the study of the

life and the interests of those of God's creation, whom He calls
not his own.

Arithmetic aside, she did well. "Your letter was undoubtedly without
mistake, so far as the spelling is to be considered, and I congratulate and
praise you upon the same. You should be proud of, my daughter, Mr.
Rosa's [sic] unlooked for compliment as to your book, and commenda-
tion of the good behavior of so young a child." She was also doing well
in French, not surprisingly since she had spoken French before English
and there had always been someone who spoke French in the house as
long as her mother had been alive.[2] She liked her French teacher Mlle.
LeClerq, and even though she thought memorizing passages of the
New Testament in French a waste of time, she dutifully did so. "I have
received your beautifully written French note of the 26th," her father
wrote her. "I see well que vos leçons de français vous fait beaucoup de
bien, même en style et en facilité il faut me corriger toujours quand je
fait des fautes en vous écrivant."

Eleanor's school work was soon so good that she was singled out
for advanced work. Bursting with importance, she reported to her
Uncle Eddie.

Dear Uncle Edie   March 2d, (1894)
I hope you are well and Mr. Wright also. Are you having a lovely
time in Morroco with hunts and pig sticks and oh so many horses, I
should think you were having a beautiful time with so many things
to do. Are the people out there very bad ones?

Now I want to tell you about what I am going to have next May
in schooll, a written examination in History and Geographay and
I am the youngest one who is to have it.

With a great deal of love from all and a great deal from me I am
your little niece.

Eleanor.

At Easter time she sent her father books and he sent her white vio-
lets, "which you can put in your Prayer book at the XXIII Psalm and
you must know they were Grandmother Roosevelt's favorite flower."
Eleanor did not have to be told what the XXIII Psalm was; her mother
had encouraged her to learn by heart many verses from the Bible. "Is
there anything else in life that can so anchor them to the right?" had

been Anna's view. Elliott was no less religious. He sang in the choir of the little Episcopal church in Abingdon and was a favorite of the local clergy. She wore his flowers to church, Eleanor wrote her father, who replied, "I thought of *You all day long* and blessed you and prayed for your happiness and that of your precious small brothers." There were always special "love messages" for the little boys, Ellie and Brudie, in his letters to her.

Tragedy struck the little household again in May, when both boys came down with scarlet fever. Elliott hastened to New York and sadly telegraphed the Ludlows, to whom Eleanor had been sent, to prepare the little girl for the worst. In addition, he wrote his daughter "to let you know that dear little Ellie is very, very ill and may go to join dear Mother in Heaven. There is just a little chance that he may not die but the doctors all fear that he will."

"Dear father," Eleanor replied,

> I write to thank you for your kind note and to tell you how sorry I am to hear Ellie is so sick, but we must remember Ellie is going to be safe in heaven and to be with Mother who is waiting there and our Lord wants Ellie boy with him now, we must be happy and do God's will and we must cheer others who feel it to. You are alright I hope. I play with the [name indistinct] every day.
>
> It is so cold here that Uncle Ned wears a fur overcoat. I met a lady that used to live down at hemmestid and she new me right away.
>
> Goodbye give my love to all and Ellie and Brudie to and for you O so much love.
>
> Nell.

My darling little Nell,   Monday [May 29, 1893]
I am so glad you wrote Father such a sweet note on Saturday. I received it today and it has comforted me a great deal to know my little daughter was well and happy.

Ask Aunt Maggie to tell you what a sad day today was for all of us. I do not want to write it to you though I would tell you if your dear golden head was on my breast; my dear, *loved* little Nell. But do not be sad my Pretty, remember Mother is with Ellie and Aunt Gracie now.

I sent Morris, my groom, on with your pony and cart tomorrow afternoon's boat so that he will deliver him to you on Wednesday morning with Father's tender love to his sweet Daughter. You must get Aunt Maggie's coachman to teach you how to drive him. He is *perfectly gentle* and only needs reasonable handling for you to drive him *alone*. Tell Aunt Maggie this. In fact let Aunt Maggie or Uncle Ned read this letter. I wish I could be with you to teach you how to drive myself but that can not be. Thank Aunt Maggie for asking me to come on after the 22nd and say that I am writing her.

  With a heart full of love,
  Ever fondly, your Father.

Sympathetic and considerate as Grandma Hall and Great-Aunt Maggie were, Eleanor had only one thought, one purpose—to rejoin her father. That alone would be home. But the family dared not entrust the children to him. "I cannot tell you dear little girl," he wrote her two weeks after Ellie's death, "when you are coming home until I have seen Grandma and consulted her." Mrs. Hall informed Elliott that she did not want him to come to Tivoli during the summer, and that in August Eleanor would be going to Newport. Elliott pleaded with her to bring his children to the city or the seashore "where I can see them and enjoy a little love which my heart craves and for lack of which it has broken. Oh, Mrs. Hall, I have tried so hard and it has been so lonely & weary and the break down seems to me natural in my strained condition. Above all believe me it was not drunkenness. Let me see you soon please Mother. . . ."

It was difficult not to yield to these entreaties, and Mrs. Hall turned to Bamie for advice. She would do anything she could, Bamie told her, but Elliott had turned against her, and if she appeared to be intervening he would take the opposite position. She could no longer influence him. She was heartbroken, but he had put it out of her power to do anything for him unless he specifically asked for something. His greatest chance of stability of purpose in regard to his children "lay in the management being purely between you and himself." There was only one exception to her hands-off attitude: if Elliott tried to take the children from Mrs. Hall, she and Theodore felt that "for Anna's sake" they would have a right to stop him.

Her father's visits brought Eleanor rushing down the stairs to fling herself into his arms, but their reunions were not wholly without anxiety for her. In later years she recalled how one time he called to take her driving in what appeared to be a very high dog cart. On the way to Central Park, along Madison Avenue, a streetcar frightened Mohawk, her father's high-spirited hunter. When the horse shied, her father's hat flew off, and when it was retrieved, Elliott looked at his daughter and asked, "You weren't afraid, were you, little Nell?" She was but she did not want to disappoint him by admitting it. When they reached the park and joined the procession of carriages and horses, her father said teasingly, "If I were to say 'hoop-la' to Mohawk he would try to jump them all." Eleanor prayed he would not. Yet despite her "abject terror," she later wrote, "those drives were the high point of my existence."

Worse trials beset the eight-year-old as, for instance, on one occasion when her father came to take her for a walk. "My father had several fox terriers that he seemed to carry everywhere with him," Eleanor recalled. "One day he took me and three of his fox terriers and left us with the doorman at the Knickerbocker Club. When he failed to return after six hours, the doorman took me home." It was a shattering experience for a child who was already obsessed with a fear of being deserted by those whom she loved, and when she spoke of it in later years, she sometimes added the terrible detail that she saw her father carried out. It was no wonder that Grandma Hall disapproved of his visits so strongly.

While the adults in the Roosevelt and Hall families feared that the hapless Elliott might commit some irredeemable folly in a moment of lonely despair, his letters to his daughter continued to be full of tenderness. He wanted her to learn to ride, "for it will please me so and we can have such fun riding together after you come to the city next fall." She was swimming a little in the Hudson, she told him. That was splendid, he commented, and was Brudie "learning new things, too?" She had a bad habit of biting her fingernails. He wanted her to stop: "I am glad you are taking such good care of those cunning wee hands that Father loves so to be petted by, all those *little* things that will make my dear Girl so much more attractive if she attends to them, not forgetting the big ones. Unselfishness, generosity, loving tenderness and cheerfulness."

But his letters were also full of excuses—why he had not written in "so long," why he had not been able to see her, why he would not be able to visit her. Nor did his vivid accounts of what he did with the children at Abingdon give Eleanor unmixed pleasure. "Little Miriam welcomed me with the fox terriers at the station though I came by an entirely unexpected train," Elliott wrote. "The little girl had been down to *every* train for two days." Realizing perhaps that Eleanor might be jealous of the girls who could be with him, he added, "No other little girl can ever take your place in my heart." Another letter must have caused even sharper pangs of envy.

Miriam, Lillian and the four Trigg children all on their ponies and horses and the fox terriers Mr. Belmont gave me (to comfort me in my loneliness) go out about sunrise and gallop over these broad fields for one or two hours; we rarely fail to secure some kind of game, and never return without roses in the cheeks of those I call now, my children.

In the fall of 1893, he moved in and out of New York, and had become evasive with everyone in his family concerning his whereabouts and intentions. He told the faithful Corinne that he was going to Abingdon, but ten days later she discovered he was still in town. Corinne and Douglas went to his hotel almost daily, but could never find him in. He would promise to come to stay with them or Theodore or Uncle Gracie and then would telephone to break the engagement.

He disappeared from his usual haunts, and they learned only later that, although he received mail at the Knickerbocker Club, he was living under an assumed name on West 102nd Street with a woman whose name was unknown to the family. Theodore and Bamie sadly and reluctantly gave up.

To Bye, Theodore wrote in July, 1894.

I do wish Corinne could get a little of my hard heart about Elliott. She can do, and ought to do nothing for him. He can't be helped, and he simply must be let go his own gait.

He is now laid up from a serious fall; while drunk he drove into a lamp post and went out on his head. Poor fellow! if only he could have died instead of Anna!

Eleanor had known for many months, from the talks and whisperings of the grownups, that something was desperately wrong with her father. She also knew it from her own experience. Her father would send her a message that he was coming to take her for a drive and then not appear. Unthinkingly, he would arouse her hopes that she would be coming "home" to him. He disappointed her in almost everything, yet her love never faltered, her trust never weakend.

With the arrival of summer, 1894, Grandma Hall again closed her Thirty-seventh Street house and Eleanor moved to Tivoli and later to Bar Harbor. A handful of Eleanor's letters to her father that final summer have survived.

Dear Father: June 14th, 1894
I hope you are well. I am very well and so is every one else. We moved to the country and that is why I have not written before we were in such a hurry to get off for it was so hot in New York. We have two people staying with us—cousin Susie Hall and Mable Drake—do you know her? tell me in your next letter. I rode my pony to-day for the first time this summer. I did not go very far but tomorrow I am going for a long ride with Uncle Valley won't it be fun. I wish you were up here to ride with me. Give my love to the puppies and every one else that you know. Madlein Brudie and I often drive with my pony.
  With a great deal of love I am your little daughter
  Nell

Dear Father   July 5th, 1894
I would have written before but I went to Cousin Susie. We are starting to-day for Bar Harbor we are in a great flurry and hurry I am in Uncle Eddie's room. The men are just going to take the trunks away. We are to have lunch at 15 minutes before twelve. We are going to Boston in the one o'clock train. Brudie wears pants now.
  Good-bye I hope you are well *dear Father.*
  With a great deal of love to everybody and you especially I am your little daughter   Nell
P.S. Write to me at W. 37th St.

Dear Father: July 10th, 1894
I hope you are well. I am now in Bar Harbor and am having a lovely time yesterday I went to the Indian encampment to see some pretty things I have to find the paths all alone I walked up to the top of Kebo mountain this morning and I walk three hours every afternoon. Brudie walks from 4 to 5 miles every day. Please write to me soon. We eat our meals at the hotel and the names of the things we get to eat are to funny Washington pie and blanket of Veal are mild to some other things we get. I have lessons every day with Grandma.

With a great deal of love, I am your little daughter   Nell

Dear Father: July 30, 1894
I hope you are well. I enjoyed your last letter very much. I went
fishing the other day I had great fun I caught six fish don't you think
I did well for the first time. I am having lessons with Grandma
every day and go to a french class from half past eleven till half past
twelve. Alice Fix died three days ago and was buried yesterday was
it not very sad.

Goodby dear dear Father I send you a great deal of love I am
your little daughter   Nell

With a Knickerbocker Club return address, Elliott wrote his "little
Nell" that her letters from Bar Harbor had been his "great delight."

When you go to the Indian encampment you must say "How" to
them for your old father's sake, who used to fight them in the old
claims in the West, many years before you opened those little blue
eyes and looked at them making birch bark canoes for Brudie and
Madeleine to go paddling in and upset in the shallow water, where
both might be drowned if they had not laughed so much.

Give my love to all the dear home people and all of my good
friends who have not forgotten me.

Would you like a little cat, very much like the one you used
to have at Hempstead and called an "Angostora" kitten instead of
what was his correct name, "Angora?" If so, I have a dear friend
who wants to make you a present of one. Let me know after you
have asked grandma.

Please do not eat all the things with the funny names you tell
me you have,—that is, if they taste like their names—for a Washington pie with a blanket of veal, and Lafayette left out, would be
enough to spoil your French-American history of the latter part of
the last century, for some time to come, possibly for so long that
I might not be able to correct your superstition. The blanket was
what Washington needed and the pie should have been laid out of
veal and the neglected Lafayette should have eaten it.

Again with dear love, I am   Your affectionate father
                                            Elliott Roosevelt.

On August 12 Theodore wrote Bamie from Washington: "Elliott is up and about again: and I hear is drinking heavily; if so he must break down soon. It has been as hideous a tragedy all through as one often sees."

On August 13 Elliott wrote his last letter to his daughter.

Darling Little Nell—
What must you think of your Father who has not written in so long, but we seem to be quits about that. I have after all been very busy, quite ill, at intervals not able to move from my bed for days. You knew that Uncle Gracie was back. He is so happy at "Gracewood." You know he was going to ask you there. Are you going?

Give my love to Grandma and Brudie and all—I was very much amused by hearing my Darkey coachman in his report of Stable News that he had trained all the Dogs to drive together, four and six in hand, and built a wee cart with wooden wheels. It was really funny to see this great big fat "Irish" colored man in this little cart! and six small Fox Terriers driving for all they were worth. I saw Auntie Corinne and the others the other day. They were so funny— They are very well and sent love to you all. How is your pony and the dogs at Tivoli, too? Tell Madeleine and Brudie that Father often thinks of them—With tender affection ever devotedly

　Your Father
　Elliott Roosevelt

The next day Elliott had a fall, was knocked unconscious, and died with none of his family about him, moaning in his delirium for his sister Corinne.

From the *World,* August 16, 1894:

The curtains of No. 313 West 102nd Street are drawn. There is a piece of black crepe on the door-knob. Few are seen to pass in and out of the house, except the undertaker and his assistants. The little boys and girls who romp up and down the sidewalk will tell you in a whisper; "Mr. Elliott is dead," and if you ask, "Who is Mr. Elliott?" "We don't know, nobody knows," they will answer.

At the door a sad-faced man will meet you. "Mr. Roosevelt died at 10 o'clock Tuesday evening," he will say. In a darkened parlor all day yesterday lay a plain black casket. Few mourners sat about it.

Beneath its lid lay the body of Elliott Roosevelt. Few words will tell of his last days. . . .

The physician and a valet were the only watchers at the end. The first of the family notified was James K. Gracie of Oyster Bay, an uncle of Elliott Roosevelt. To him was left the duty of breaking the news to the others. Many of them did not know that Elliott Roosevelt was in New York. Few of them had seen him for a year. At the clubs no one knew his address. Even the landlord from whom he rented his house knew him only as Mr. Elliott. Under that name he has lived there with his valet for over ten months. He sought absolute seclusion.

Many people will be pained by this news. There was a time when there were not many more popular young persons in society than Mr. and Mrs. Elliott Roosevelt. . . .

Elliott was buried at Greenwood, the Roosevelt burial place. Grandma Hall did not take Eleanor to her father's funeral, and even the flowers she sent from herself and the children arrived too late. Grandma Hall was deeply sorry about that: "Elliott loved flowers and always brought them to us, and to think not one from us or his dear ones went to the grave with him grieves us deeply."

There was one comfort in his death—the harsh and bitter memories were washed away, Theodore wrote Corinne.

I only need to have pleasant thoughts of Elliott now. He is just the gallant, generous, manly loyal young man whom everyone loved. I can think of him when you and I and he used to go round "exploring" the hotels, the time we were first in Europe; do you remember how we used to do it? And then in the days of the dancing class, when he was distinctly the polished man-of-the-world from outside, and all the girls from Helen White and Fanny Dana to May Wigham used to be so flattered by any attention from him. Or when we were off on his little sailing boat for a two or three days' trip on the Sound, or when we first hunted; and when he visited me at Harvard. . . .

Elliott had spent a few weeks of that final tormented summer with the woman who had been his mistress in Paris, who had summoned the doctor to her house on the New England shore and tried to make

Elliott rest. He had often spoken to her of his sister, Corinne Robinson, and she now wrote Mrs. Robinson,

> will you not tell me how he died? He seemed so much stronger when he left, that even the physician was astonished at his vitality, and I hoped for his children, he would try to take care of himself. He was so strong, and had such a gay, sweet nature, that I could not realize seeing him with my children, so interested in their work and play, that he was mentally and physically so worn out.
>
> I do beg of you to have his children's memory of him—a beautiful one; his tender courtesy, his big—generous heart and his wonderfully charming sweet nature, ought to be kept before them. If in saying this, I am overstepping the line of discretion or courtesy, I beg you to forgive me.
>
> Believe me, dear Mrs. Robinson, your brother suffered greatly, only as a big tender man like him could suffer—and while he was here, and I watched him sick and half wandering in his mind while he slept, he spoke constantly of you, how you had held to him and alone had given him the love he needed. Of course you do not need for a stranger to tell you this, but I know what a grief your brother's death must be to you, and it may be a little consolation to you to hear this.
>
> I cannot forgive myself for not keeping him here, where he was loved and guarded, and where he might have regained some strength so as to have gone back a little more able to meet his lonely fight there—but it is too late to even regret. One thing you can do for him—see to it that he does not lose the place he deserves in his children's lives. He loved them, and ought to have been with them.

Two years later, when Mrs. Hall asked that his body be moved to the family vault at Tivoli, Corinne was grateful. "I want to write you a few lines to thank you for having let me know that all was safely accomplished and that Elliott now lies by Anna and his boy. I cannot help but feel glad that it is so, and I must tell you once more how deeply I appreciate the feeling which led you to wish him brought to Tivoli, a feeling which I dared not think could be there, or I should never have laid him at Greenwood."

With her father's death, wrote Eleanor Roosevelt in 1933, "went for me all the realities of companionship which he had suggested for the future, but as I said in the beginning he lived in my dreams and does to this day."[3]

Perhaps it was fortunate for Eleanor that her father died when he did. As Theodore Roosevelt said, now he could again think of Elliott as "the gallant, generous, manly, loyal young man whom everyone loved." By his death Elliott made it possible for his daughter to maintain her dream-picture of him. But somewhere, rarely admitted to conscious awareness, Eleanor carried another picture of her father— the father who sent her messages that he was coming and did not appear, who left her in the cloakroom of his club, who aroused her hopes that she would be coming home to him, hopes that were always disappointed, the father who lacked self-control, who could not face responsibility, who expected to be indulged. Repressing this picture exacted a price: her own sense of reality was impaired. She tended to overestimate and misjudge people, especially those who seemed to need her and who satisfied her need for self-sacrifice and affection and gave her the admiration and loyalty she craved. Just as her response to being disappointed by her father had been silence and depression because she did not dare see him as he really was, so in later life she would become closed, withdrawn, and moody when people she cared about disappointed her.

Although idolization of her father exacted a price, it was also a source of remarkable strength. Because of her overwhelming attachment to him, she would strive to be the noble, studious, brave, loyal girl he had wanted her to be. He had chosen her in a secret compact, and this sense of being chosen never left her. When he died she took upon herself the burden of his vindication. By her life she would justify her father's faith in her, and by demonstrating strength of will and steadiness of purpose confute her mother's charges of unworthiness against both of them.

7. THE OUTSIDER

"Poor child," Mrs. Hall wrote Corinne after Elliott's death; she "has had so much sorrow crowded into her short life she now takes everything very quietly. The only remark she made was 'I did want to see father once more.'"

Her father's death deepened Eleanor's feeling that she was an outsider. She was a shy, solemn, insecure child, tall for her age, badly dressed, with blonde hair falling about her shoulders, and did not make friends easily. She would have to regain her trust in the world before she could act upon the lesson her Grandfather Theodore had impressed upon his children—receive people's love and people will love you.

To some extent her separateness was self-imposed. She wanted to be left alone "to live in a dream world in which I was the heroine and my father the hero." At school her first compositions reflect this fantasy life.[1]

The Tempest*

We were all crowded in the cabin, no one had dared to go to bed for it was midnight on the sea, and there was a dreadful storm raging. It is a terrible thing in winter to be tossed about by the wind, and to hear captain calling through the trumpet "Cut away the mast." So we all sat there trembling, and none of us dared to speak, for even the bravest among us held our breath while the sea was foaming and tossing, and the sailors were talking death. And while we sat there in the dark, all of us saying our prayers, suddenly the captain rushed down the stairs. "We are lost!" he shouted. But his little girl took his cold hand and said. "Is not God on the ocean just as well as on the land?" Then we all kissed the little girl, and we spoke more

---

*Several readers have noted that Eleanor's *The Tempest* is a prose version of a widely reprinted poem by James T. Fields, sometimes entitled "The Captain's Daughters."

cheerfully, and the next day we anchored safely in the harbor when the sun was shining brightly.

This little sketch reversed what had actually happened at sea in 1887 during the collision of the *Britannic* and the *Celtic,* when Eleanor had been terrified and her father had acted as the strong and confident captain. In making the girl the heroine, she betrayed what she wished had happened—that she had been calm and brave and had won the approval of her father and all the passengers so that all would have "kissed the little girl." The poignant tale underscored again how greatly she craved admiration and affection, and yet the reversal of roles also reflected what had happened between the time of the collision and her father's death. In those years her father had been the one who needed help and in reality as well as in fantasy, she had been the one to sustain and comfort him.

Eleanor lived with her grandmother in the brownstone on Thirty-seventh Street, a fashionable part of New York. In addition to the Roser class and French lessons with Mlle. LeClerq, she now attended a music class taught by Frank Damrosch and was brought by her governess to the exclusive Dodworth's, where girls in velvet curtsied to boys in blue and learned the waltz, the two-step, and the polka. But despite her busy life, she was a child as bereaved and lonely as Antoine Lemaire, the hero of another of her early compositions who is cast out of his home by his parents and is befriended by a musician who teaches him to play the violin. Antoine is a "born genius" and plays superbly, but, wrote Eleanor, "the thing which the boy yearned for most was love."

Grandma Hall was well disposed and kindly, but her hands were full with her own rather unruly children, Eleanor's aunts and uncles—Pussie, twenty-one; Maude, sixteen; Vallie, twenty-five; and Eddie, twenty-two. Grandma was only fifty-one, but her temperamental family exhausted her and she withdrew—or, as Eleanor later put it, she was "relegated"—to her own bedroom where her children expected her to sit by the window and mend their clothes. She did everything within her comprehension for Eleanor and Hall, yet they were neglected youngsters, starved for the thousand little parental attentions that build up the security and self-esteem of children.

That is the way some of Eleanor's schoolmates in the Roser classes remembered her.[2] She attended them until she was fifteen. Her classmates were Helen Cutting, Margaret Dix, Jessie Sloane, Gwendolyn Burden, Ruth Twombly, Valerie Hadden, and Sophie Langdon.

"It must have been in our early teens," Helen Cutting (Mrs. Lucius Wilmerding) recalled. "She was visiting me in Tuxedo."

"'Let's go out and do something,' I urged."

Eleanor put her off. "I'll finish the letter I'm writing to Hall. Then we can go out."

"But you wrote him yesterday."

"I write him every day. I want him to feel he belongs to somebody."

Her stay with Helen was one of the rare occasions she was allowed to be away from home. The less her grandmother was able to control her own children, the more rigidly she sought to rein in Eleanor and Hall, and guidance usually meant saying "no." When the father of another of Eleanor's Roser classmates, Jessie Sloane, invited Eleanor to spend a summer out West with his daughter, Eleanor begged to be allowed to go. She had never wanted to do anything as much. Jessie was the prettiest girl in class, and Eleanor, who was gawky, her prominent teeth in braces, admired her for her loveliness. Her grandmother said no.

The girls were reaching the age when they were sensitive about their clothes. Margaret Dix (Mrs. Charles Lawrance), the daughter of the rector of Trinity, "the oldest, wealthiest and most fashionable" parish in the country, first made her appearance in the classroom in a DePinna sailor dress. "A titter in the class—my skirt's too short!" she later wrote.

Eleanor's skirts were always too short. She had few dresses and those she did have were shapeless and fell straight from the shoulders. She wore black stockings and high button shoes, and her grandmother insisted on long flannel underwear from November to April.

"A group of us girls would go to Central Park to skate and play," Helen Cutting has said. "In the spring we went without our coats. Eleanor played very hard and like all of us would fall into puddles and get covered with mud and grime.

"'Couldn't you put on a clean dress?' we asked her the next day.

"'My other dress is in the wash,' she answered."

One day she spilled ink on her dress. When she took it off and tried to wash it in a basin, the ink spot spread all over the dress. "But she had to wear it," said Helen. This was not because of a lack of money but because of a lack of attention and care. Although Grandfather Hall had died intestate and thereby created financial problems for his wife, she received more than $7,500 a year for the care of Eleanor and Hall from various trusts left in their name.

The Thirty-seventh Street house was a dark, gloomy place, "grim and ill-kept," as Helen Cutting remembered it. "Nobody cared how it looked. Eleanor did not have her little friends there often. I don't remember having a meal there."

Eleanor's cousin Corinne, the daughter of her Auntie Corinne (Mrs. Douglas Robinson), lived in a brownstone at Forty-ninth Street and Madison Avenue. "My mother would ask me to go to have supper with Eleanor," recalled Corinne, who was two years younger than her cousin. "I never wanted to go. The grim atmosphere of that house. There was no place to play games, unbroken gloom everywhere. We ate our suppers in silence." It was not a house for children, Corinne added. "The general attitude was 'don't do this.'"[3]

It was also a frightening house. Eleanor's uncles had begun to drink heavily and she was afraid of them. She slept in a hall bedroom on the top floor next door to the room that Madeleine, the governess, occupied with Hall. Madeleine was sweet with Brudie, as Hall was called, but tyrannized Eleanor, pulled her hair "unmercifully," and berated her so violently that if Eleanor did something wrong, she preferred punishment at the hands of her grandmother. It was not until she was fourteen that she dared to tell her grandmother how often Madeleine made her shed bitter tears and was at last taken out of her care.

"I remember Madeleine," said Corinne. "She was a terrifying character. It was the grimmest childhood I have ever known. Who did she have? Nobody."

Eleanor's unhappiness made her even more determined to succeed. Some of her classmates considered her a "grind." They thought she worked harder than the other girls because things did not come easily for her, yet she had a very good memory, turned in compositions that were well written and imaginative, and recited poetry quite well. If she was a grind, it was because she set herself high standards. She wanted to learn, to excel, and thereby gain approval and praise.

Margaret Dix, the clergyman's daughter and, therefore, in the eyes of the other girls—except Eleanor—"a thing apart," had to win acceptance. But she was quick, gay, and mischievous. She inked in faces on her fingernails and held them up behind the teacher's back for the other girls to see. "They would giggle," Margaret recalled. "Eleanor would turn away. That would shock her. She only wanted to be a student."[4]

The Twombly mansion, where the Roser class met when the Cutting house was not available, was next door to St. Thomas' Church at

Fifth Avenue and Fifty-third Street. The day the duke of Marlborough married Consuelo Vanderbilt in one of the most fashionable weddings in society's annals, Margaret found the occasion irresistible and slipped out during the recess to watch the wedding. "Eleanor would never have stepped out of a class to watch a wedding," she said.

Margaret recalled her schooling in the Roser class approvingly: "Mr. Roser gave me an excellent education." A more general verdict was that voiced by Eleanor's cousin Corinne, who was enrolled in a younger class:

> I cannot understand why on earth our mothers fell for the Roser classes. They were held at all the big houses. I wish you could have seen Mr. Roser. A Prince Albert coat. Side whiskers, Not one grain of humor. Nobody in the world as pompous as he. And the things he decided to have us learn!

In the single paragraph that Eleanor Roosevelt devoted to the Roser classes in her autobiography she wrote admiringly of his assistant, Miss Tomes, but with reserve about Mr. Roser himself. He envisaged himself as a headmaster in the British public-school tradition, was learned in a literary kind of way, and expressed himself forcefully. The girls were obliged to stand when he came into the classroom, whereupon he would bow formally and indicate to the "young ladies" that they could be seated, addressing them as "Miss Roosevelt," "Miss Cutting," "Miss Sloane." He had a quotation from some great man or writer, most often from Dr. Johnson, for every occasion. The textbooks—the Nelson School Series, most of them written by William Francis Collier, LL.D., D.D.—were imported from England. History was taught from Dr. Collier's *The Great Events from the Beginning of the Christian Era Till the Present Time*, the present time being 1860, when Dr. Collier had produced this particular text, whose aim was "To give in a series of pictures such a connected view of the Christian Era as may be pleasantly readable and easily remembered." Implausible as the Nelson textbooks appear today, they were, nevertheless, not inferior to the McGuffey reader and Webster Speller that were in use in common schools all over the United States at the time. And if the Reverend Dr. Collier presented Victorian England rather than the American Republic as history's crowning triumph, the aberration would be corrected at home, since most of the Roser pupils came from families whose genealogy was in itself American history.

Mr. Roser was a pedant and rhetorician who expressed himself in a manner that he considered aphoristic.

> Self control is necessary at all ages. We cannot begin too soon to acquire this virtue.

> Without order in the classroom there can be no lesson given.

> Whatever breaches the order of the class constitutes an act of disorder.

> There is a distinction between reasonable and unreasonable merriment.

Occasionally Mr. Roser was driven to less pompous utterances. "Some girls talk too much," he once exploded.

He courted the rich and taught precepts that the wealthy found agreeable. "What is more natural to a good person than to help the poor?" one of his homilies began, and proceeded, "and if we yield to our emotions at the sight of a poor man we shall be surprised to hear that we are not diminishing wretchedness but increasing the number of street beggars." The notion that the poor were victims of their own failings, that no man who was sober, industrious, and prudent went hungry, was part of the Protestant ethic of individualism.

What did young, compassionate Eleanor make of such preachments? Charity, not prudence, even when it was disguised as benevolence, ruled her heart. She felt sympathy and solicitude even for what was alien and hostile. In Italy when she saw her donkey boy's bruised feet, she made him mount the animal while she trotted alongside. While she was in a stagecoach on Fifth Avenue, Eleanor saw an impoverished man try to snatch a purse from a woman sitting nearby, terrifying Eleanor so much that she jumped from the moving vehicle. But afterward she remembered, even more vividly than her fright, the face of the "poor, haunted man."

Eleanor found two Roser subjects difficult—grammar and arithmetic—and her mastery of them was due more to her excellent memory than to her ability to reason. The hours devoted to literature, especially poetry, were more satisfactory. The girls had to recite, and medals were given for the best performance. Gwendolyn Burden did Caroline Norton's "Bingen on the Rhine," which began "A soldier of the Legion lay dying in Algiers," and had them all in tears. Helen Cutting recited "The Old Clock on the Stairs" with a perceptible French accent since she had spent so much time abroad. Eleanor declaimed "The Last Leaf on the Tree," and was awarded a medal for her performance. She loved poetry, and memorized Tennyson's "The Revenge" in one day. Impressed, Mr. Roser had her recite the whole poem. They had no work that day, Helen recalled with delight, for Eleanor took up all the time with the ballad of brave Sir Richard Grenville, "who fought such a fight for a day and a night as may never be fought again."

It was the era of the "Delsarte System" of elocution, which assigned an appropriate flourish or pose to every mood and emotion—remorse, the hand to the head; rejection, the right hand flung out and down as if casting off a scrap of paper. Margaret Dix was a mimic and entertained her classmates with take-offs of their poetry recitations. She often portrayed Eleanor, standing stiffly erect, her face turning from left to right in approved elocutionary style, the hand outflung, the tip of her tongue in a circular movement moistening her lips. Eleanor and Margaret were not congenial.

Some of Eleanor's compositions have survived. Mr. Roser's comment was often a prim "your handwriting is not satisfactory." Even then Eleanor's penmanship was strong, angular, and highly individual. Sometimes Mr. Roser was impressed by Eleanor's vivid imagination, and he would append a "recommended for printing" comment to the end of the exercise, meaning that in his view it was worthy of publication, although apparently there was no school magazine or paper.

One of the first of her compositions, "Gilded Butterflies," showed her to be, as always, the moralist, but she also displayed a growing power of observation. The "butterflies" were characters suspiciously like the people around her, especially her young aunts.

GILDED BUTTERFLIES

Lying one hot July day on my back in the long grass lazily watching the daisies nod their heads as the scarcely felt breeze passed over them I was disturbed by a sound of voices and looking around I could see nothing but a few harmless butterflies fluttering here and there. Listening again I discovered that the voices came from the butterflies. Curiosity sharpening my ears I began to understand what they were saying. Listening to the one which was now speaking I heard him say "Pooh! I'm not going to sit on a daisy always. I have higher aspirations in life. I am going to know a great deal and to see everything. I won't stay here to waste my life. I mean to know something before I've finished."

Then he flew away and I saw a big fat portly old butterfly. He looked after him and said "Dear, dear, dear how dreadful it is to be discontented. For my part I'd rather stay where I am. I've seen life. I've met great men and been to large dinners in the crowded cities and now that it is ended it's a rest to be in the country and to see the flowers from which I can sip as much honey as I want, and besides, here I can be comfortable."

Just then a beautiful young butterfly arrived. "Dear me I am so tired. I've been to at least six dinners and about as many dances in the last week but then it is such fun. What would life be worth if there weren't any dinners, teas or dances but there aren't enough. There ought to be more. O my! there's an old gentleman, I must go. I never can stand these old people."

And she lifted her lovely gilded wings and fluttered by making a great noise and almost blowing the old gentleman off his comfortable seat. His old wings flapped as he muttered, "Poor little gilded butterfly what a lot you've got to learn."

Then came one who settled down next to the old man and said, "O dear, dear what a nuisance it is always racing and tearing for your food and then you don't get anything. Every one gets there before you. What bother life is. I wish I was dead. There are nothing but daisies and buttercups never any change. Now if I were only a genius, or rich then I could buy genius! Then he stopped and the old man gave a low chuckle. Then I heard a soft, lovely voice near my ear so low it was like a whisper. The voice said "Child, learn a lesson from the gilded butterflies and be contented in this world and you will find happiness."

An even more charming fable, written when Eleanor was thirteen or fourteen, was "The Flowers Discussion." Its references to a "conservatory" in which orchids, camellias, and even "a huge palm tree" were growing suggest the kind of great houses where young Eleanor was welcome. This composition was rewarded with the Roser imprimatur "recommended for printing."

THE FLOWERS DISCUSSION

"I am by far the most beautiful." These were the words I heard as I awoke from a nap I had been taking in a conservatory.

I was rather surprised to see that the speaker was a tall red rose which grew not far from me. There was evidently a hot discussion going on among the plants as to which excelled the others. I knew that if they saw I was awake the discussion would cease & as I wished to hear how it ended I feigned sleep.

After the red rose had spoken the beautiful lily raised its head. "You, the most beautiful?" I heard it say. "Look how straight you hold your head. You have no grace. Now mine bends over gracefully & then I am white which is by far a prettier color than red. I rest every eye which looks at me while you tire it. Besides you hurt people with your thorns. I never do. I smell far sweeter than you. Most people think so. Now you see that I excell you all" & she looked around with a proud glance.

There had been several interruptions during her long speech from the smaller flowers but now for a moment there was silence. Then the orchid spoke. "Indeed, you the most beautiful of all the flowers. What an idea. Why if any one is beautiful I am. Look at my varied coloring & how gracefully I hang, far more gracefully than you. Besides everyone likes me. No conservatory is complete without me while any can go without you."

Then a little white camelia spoke. "I hear someone coming. Whichever flower they choose as the prettiest shall excell." The flowers had time to murmur "yes" when in came a little boy of not quite two. He gave a cry of delight as [he] entered. He looked around & then made straight for the orchid & stood by it drawing his finger lightly over the flower murmuring as he did so "Pitty flower pitty flower." His nurse picked it for him & he passed out.

As soon as he had disappeared the discussion began again, the rose & the lily averring that it was not right to stand by his decision. He was too small. This time the modest little violet who had not as yet spoken said "someone is coming. Stand by their decision" & the flowers said yes again. This time a young girl & her lover entered. They seated themselves under a huge palm tree & the young man said "which of all these flowers do you love the best?" "I love the white rose best, she is so sweet and pure," the young girl said. Her lover picked one for her and they went out.

They had hardly gone when the discussion began again. This time it was the orchid who said "The white rose is too small a flower to excell us all & besides the one which excells is king & imagine the white rose ruling us." All the plants laughed at the idea of their obeying the white rose & even I had to smile at the thought of the little flower ruling the haughty red rose, lily & orchid.

The discussion continued for several minutes when the pansy said, "Be quiet. Someone is coming." An old man & his wife now appeared. The flowers whispered as they entered "We will abide by their decision." The old couple seated themselves & the old man said "Is it not beautiful here Jennie. Which of all these flowers do you love the best?" The old wife looked around. "I love them all." she said & then as though she were thinking not talking "As a baby I loved the orchid, then the lily & the rose. As a young girl I loved the violet for it is the flower you picked for me when you told me of your love. Yes I loved it best then. I love it best now.

I thought so, the old man said. Then they went out. I wondered what the flowers would say to this, but I was soon to find out for the old couple had hardly gone when the rose broke out with "The violet excell all of us? The violet rule us? Why the white rose could do it better."

"Yes, indeed," cried all the plants. I could plainly see that all the flowers were bent upon excelling & I do not know how long the discussion would have lasted had not the violet said "Why none of us excell. We are all beautiful in our own way. Some are beautifully colored. Others smell sweetly & again others are graceful. We were all made well. From this day we are all equal."

The other flowers listened & to some it seemed strange that the flower which had been chosen to excel should say this but they all agreed and from that day they were equal.

But I always have and always will love the violet best.

As she passed from childhood to adolescence, the beauty of nature spoke to her awakening senses. The changes of the seasons, the play of light on the river, the color and coolness of the woods began to have the profound meaning to her that they would retain throughout her life. When she was a young girl, she wrote a half century later, "there was nothing that gave me greater joy than to get one of my young aunts to agree that she would get up before dawn, that we would walk down through the woods to the river, row ourselves the five miles to the village in Tivoli to get the mail, and row back before the family was at the breakfast table."

The summer months in her grandmother's house on the Hudson were among her happiest, even though none of her friends lived close by except Carola dePeyster, whose parents' house was five miles away and with whom she exchanged visits twice each summer. All the great houses along the Woods Road were on land rising in terraces.[5] Below, the Hudson was wide, slow, and majestic, while westward the Catskills rose in hushed silence.

A stone gatehouse led into the Hall estate, and the road went by large stables and came out onto a lawn that was shaded by towering oaks. The driveway went past a lawn tennis court said to have been one of the first built in the United States. Vallie and Eddie were both outstanding tennis players, each in turn winning the National Championship for singles and together for doubles. There was an old orchard behind the water tank and a sluggish little stream in which Eleanor and Hall caught tadpoles.

The children loved Oak Terrace, as the high-ceilinged drafty house with fourteen bedrooms was called. On the first floor there were reception, dining, and music rooms and the massive library wing. The large crystal chandeliers were not used, and the rooms were lit by kerosene lamps. Two bathrooms served the square bedrooms upstairs. On the third floor there were the servants' quarters, and the kitchen and storerooms were in a deep cellar, with a dumbwaiter to transport meals to the dining room. Staples were stored in barrels, and every morning Eleanor accompanied her grandmother to the storeroom and watched her measure out exactly what the cook would need. There was also a big, old-fashioned laundry in the cellar, presided over by Mrs. Overhalse, a neighboring farm woman. Eleanor was told that she could help the kindly lady, and she turned the wringer and learned to iron. There were enormous washes "because for every dress" her aunts wore "there were at least three petticoats." Eleanor often watched as her aunts dressed for the evening. "The top dress was pinned to the petticoat all the way round the edge so that the flounces would come straight and they would fall correctly." She watched with envy, wondering when her turn would come.

There were always errands to be run for her aunts and uncles, but in return they played games with the children. They had campfires and evening picnics in the hemlock grove. Uncle Vallie taught her to jump her pony, Captain. Aunt Pussie read her poetry, and Pussie and Maude occasionally permitted Eleanor to accompany them on a drive through the countryside, and she would sit with her legs dangling from the rear of the Hall buggy.

Sunday was a special day in the household. The family drove to church in the victoria, with Eleanor sitting in a little seat that faced backward. Sometimes the victoria swayed so much that she would begin to feel seasick. St. Paul's Church, on the Woods Road, had been built by the Livingstons, Ludlows, dePeysters, Halls, and Clarksons, and its tree-shaded churchyard was little more than a family burial place with a row of vaults built into the side of a hill. The front pews in the little church were reserved for the Livingstons, with Eleanor's branch on the right side. There was a special door for John Watts dePeyster by which that eccentric man came into a transept that was reserved for him. Before church Eleanor gave a Sunday school lesson to the coachman's little daughter. She also recited a hymn and collect to her grandmother.

There was a minimum of cooking, most of the Sunday dinner having been prepared the day before. In the afternoon no games, not even croquet, were allowed, only walks. The religious pattern that had been set by Grandfather Hall was even followed on weekdays. "My grandmother always had family prayers in the morning to which everybody including every servant in the house and even the coachman was expected to come and there were always evening prayers though all the outside people were not expected to come." After her aunts and uncles were grown up, Eleanor noted, "they weren't so good about observing all these rules."

She was a scrupulously well-behaved girl in class, but at Tivoli she sometimes broke her grandmother's rules, playing games along the high gutters of the house with Hall or sliding down the roof of the ice house and getting her clothes dirty, for which she would be sternly scolded. She even practiced high-kicking, although she had to do it secretly because when she expressed admiration for ballet dancing, her grandmother told her that no lady did anything like that.[6]

Most of all, Tivoli was a place for reading. There were long summer days when she would lie on the grass or climb a cherry tree with a book, sometimes forgetting to appear at meals. On rainy days the attic was her favorite spot. She often awakened at dawn and just as often violated her grandmother's injunction that she was not to read in bed before breakfast. The library was full of her grandfather's heavy theological works, but there were also Dickens, Scott, and Thackeray, and "sometimes a forbidden modern novel which I would steal from my young aunts, purely because I heard it whispered that the contents were not for young eyes."

Eleanor read everything, disappearing into the fields or woods, often to "cry and cry" over such books as Florence Montgomery's *Misunderstood* and Hector Mallet's *Sans Famille*. The heroes of both these books were orphaned outcasts with whom she obviously identified. *Sans Famille*, which became *No Relations* in English, began with the declaration "I was a foundling," and the adventures of this waif were reminiscent of those of Antoine Lemaire in Eleanor's composition for Mr. Roser. *Misunderstood* was a great favorite of the Victorians; as a young girl Sara Delano also sobbed over its pages. In that book the lad Humphrey welcomed death because it would reunite him with his mother and end an existence that had been rendered "miserable" by his father's partiality for Humphrey's little brother. She still enjoyed them, Eleanor Roosevelt wrote in 1950, but she thought them "very sentimental, foolish books to allow a rather lonely child to read."★ Sometimes she made a play out of the book she was reading, in which she was the principal character and her brother, six years younger, the supporting cast. *Robinson Crusoe* especially lent itself to such dramatization. The desert island was a secret place in the woods a quarter of a mile away from the main house. Hall was "poor Friday," and in that role was "forced to do many strange things."[7]

Another fictional waif who engaged her sympathy was Peter Ibbetson, the main character in the du Maurier novel by that title which swept romantic young America at the end of the century (probably one of the books she purloined from her aunts). Peter Ibbetson, orphaned at twelve like Eleanor, retreated to an "inner world" where he achieved happiness by learning to "dream true"—that is, to evoke at will the people he loved and to carry on a fantasy life with them in his "private oasis." Generally her reading was not censored, but if she asked inconvenient questions the books prompting them disappeared. On Sunday mornings the book she was reading was taken away "no matter where I was in it," and she was given what were called "Sunday books," works of religious edification.†

★She was often asked in later years to list her favorite girlhood books. "I loved Dickens' *Old Curiosity Shop* and *Tale of Two Cities*; Longfellow's Poems; Kipling's *Light That Failed*; Walter Scott's *The Talisman*; *Sarah Carew*; *The Prince and the Pauper*; *The Little Lame Prince*; Ouida's *Dog of Flanders* and *Nuremberg Stove*." On another occasion she added *Oliver Twist* and *Dombey and Son* as among the books she remembered from girlhood and "with great enthusiasm a long book called *Thaddeus of Warsaw*, which was a historical novel, touching on one phase of Poland's efforts to remain a free nation." In an article for *Girl Scout Magazine*, August, 1933, she said that she had read George Eliot's *The Mill on the Floss, Romola*, and *Silas Marner* as she "grew a little older." Also, a "book which could not be found today in any library—*The Gad Fly*—gave me hours of pleasure."

† *The Sunday at Home: Family Magazine for Sabbath Reading* (Religious Tract Society, London).

At fourteen Eleanor had definite opinions, was reflective, and was capable of a crisp expression of her views. An essay on "Ambition" exists only as a draft, and toward the end the corrections she made in it became somewhat illegible, but the main ideas are clear. She was ambitious. She wanted to succeed.

Ambition

Some people consider ambition a sin but it seems to me to be a great good for it leads one to do & to be things which without it one could never have been. Look at Caesar. It was because he was ambitious that they killed him but would he ever have been as great a man had he not had ambition? Would his name ever have come down to us if he had not had enough ambition to conquer the world? Would painters ever paint wonderful portraits or writers ever write books if they did not have ambition?

Of course it is easier to have no ambition & just keep on the same way every day & never try to do grand or great things, for it is only those who have ambition & who try & who meet with difficulties, they alone feel the disappointments that come when one does not succeed in what one has meant to do for the others say "It was meant that we should not succeed. Fate has so decreed it" and do not think of it again. But those who have ambition try again, & try till they at last succeed. It is only those who ever succeed in doing anything great.

Ambition makes us selfish and careless of pushing others back & treading on them to gain our wish it is true, but we will only be able to push back the smaller souls for the great ones we cannot tread on. Those who are ambitious & make a place & a name in the great world for themselves are nearly always despised & laughed at by lesser souls who could not do as well & all they do for the good of men is construed into wrong & yet they do the good & they leave their mark upon the ages & if they had had no ambition would they ever have made a mark?

Is it best never to be known & to leave the world a blank as if one had never come? It must have been meant it seems to me that we should leave some mark upon the world & not just live [&] pass away. For what good can that do to ourselves or others? It is better to be ambitious & do something than to be unambitious & do nothing.

Ambition is essential for any kind of success. Even those best men who condemn ambition, must have it or they would never do anything good. For it is their ambition that makes them wish to do better things than other people.

Therefore it seems to me that after all people have said against it ambition is still a good thing.

While she considered ambition a virtue, wanted to achieve great things and even echoed Roser's social Darwinism with the suggestion that only the fittest survive—and deserve to survive—these were not really the beliefs by which she lived. Highest in her scale of values were loyalty, friendship, service to others. And women, she lamented in another composition, lacked these qualities, which were so much more desirable than mere beauty. Thus did she seek to come to terms with her own lack of good looks. Her distaste for women who kissed one moment and the next tore each other's characters to shreds was also the response of a judgmental young girl to the mercurial crushes of her schoolmates and aunts—some of whom, at least, thought her too high-minded, too serious, too good.

LOYALTY AND FRIENDSHIP

Loyalty is one of the few virtues which most women lack. That is why there are so few real friendships among women for no friendship can exist without loyalty. With a man it is a point of honor to be loyal to his friend but a woman will kiss her best friend one moment & when she is gone will sit down with another best friend & pick the other's character to pieces.

It may seem strange but no matter how plain a woman may be if truth & loyalty are stamped upon her face all will be attracted to her & she will do good to all who come near her & those who know her will always love her for they will feel her loyal spirit & have confidence in her while another woman far more beautiful & attractive will never gain anybody's confidence simply because those around her feel her lack of loyalty & by not having this great virtue she will lose one of the greatest gifts that God has given man, the power of friendship. . . .

She was, of course, talking about herself. She was the "plain" one, who by her truth and constancy would gain the love and confidence of those around her. She would succeed by the strength of her character since she did not have beauty to fall back upon. The first entry in a briefly kept journal is a careful copying out of a long poem, "My Kate," by Mrs. Browning:

She was not as pretty as women I know, yet one
. . . turned from the fairest to gaze in her face.
And when you had once seen her forehead and mouth
You saw as distinctly her soul and her truth. . . .

She never found fault with you, never implied
Your wrong by her right, and yet men at her side,
Grew nobler, girls purer as through the whole town
The children were gladder that pulled at her gown.

"So like Aunt Pussie," Eleanor wrote at the bottom of the poem. "How I wish I was like her. I don't suppose I ever will be though."

Actually, Pussie, who was the most volatile of the Hall sisters, was not very much like Mrs. Browning's Kate. Pussie was constantly involved in tempestuous love affairs whose ups and downs she shared with Maude and Eleanor, much to their delight. She was also frequently depressed, and when she was she locked her door and talked to no one for days. She was an accomplished pianist, briefly tried her hand at painting, shared her literary enthusiasms with Eleanor, and even took her to meet the great Italian actress Eleanora Duse. Eleanor devotedly served her lovely aunt, rubbed her temples when she complained of headaches, and once even groped tremblingly down three flights of stairs in the dark of night to get her some ice from the backyard icebox at Thirty-seventh Street. Because Eleanor adored Pussie, she invested her with Kate's nobility, but because Pussie was irresponsible as well as irrepressible, she was scarcely a woman, as Eleanor herself later realized, at whose side men grew nobler and girls purer.

"I have a headache journal tonight," Eleanor wrote on November 18, 1898.

I am feeling cross. Poor Auntie Pussie she is so worried. I am going to try and see if I can't do something for her tonight. I have studied hard two lessons but I can't think of a composition. I suppose I can think tomorrow. Am not going to tell you—unless something happens. I've tried to be good and sweet and quiet but have not succeeded. Oh my.

She was setting herself very high ideals, an entry for November 13 indicated.

> To be the thing we seem
> To do the thing we deem enjoined by duty
> To walk in faith nor dream
> Of questioning God's scheme of truth and beauty.

"It is very hard to do what this verse says," Eleanor commented, "so hard I never succeed & I am always questioning, questioning because I cannot understand & never succeed in doing what I mean to do, never, never. I suppose I don't really try. I can feel it in me sometimes that I can do much more [than] I am doing & I mean to try till I do succeed."

The final entry in the journal, dated November 18, also reported that

> Alice did not come. I will never see her I am afraid. I wish I could but I don't dare ask if she is coming to lunch. I *do hope* I will see her. Goodnight journal.

In 1898 Alice was in open rebellion against her stepmother and had been sent to New York to stay with Auntie Bye, now married to Commander William Sheffield Cowles. Alice had grown into a defiant, hoydenish girl who coasted down steep hills with her feet on the handlebars of her bike, rode her pony hard and recklessly, and once, to get an evening out with her teen-age gang (of which she was the leader although its only girl member), had one of the boys call for her dressed in his sister's clothes, a ruse that was discovered.[8]

Not surprisingly, she considered Eleanor too mild. "She was full of duty, never very gay, a frightful bore for the more frivolous people like ourselves." Although Eleanor looked forward to Alice's visits, they never turned out to be as happy as she had anticipated. Alice was a tease, and when she and the other girls excitedly discussed the "facts of life," Eleanor was embarrassed. Once they were all chattering away in Alice's room at Auntie Bye's—Eleanor, Alice, Gwen Burden, Jessie Sloane, Margaret Dix, and Helen Cutting. "No one should talk about things like that," Eleanor indignantly protested. When they told her that everything they were saying could be found in the Bible, she lapsed into injured silence. "What is the meaning of whore?" she asked her grandmother when she returned home, adding, "It is in the Bible." "It is not a word that little girls should use," Mrs. Hall said severely.

Later on, her schoolfriends enlightened her.[9]

After her parents' deaths Eleanor saw little of her Oyster Bay relatives. Grandmother Hall had said that she wanted the children to be "influenced by their father's family as well as by their dear Mother's" but frightened by the gay and strenuous life led by the Teddy Roosevelt clan, she kept Eleanor away, and Theodore's wife did not press Eleanor to visit Oyster Bay. Aunt Edith was standoffish and reserved toward all but her immediate family, but when Eleanor did go to Sagamore Edith saw the child's future with remarkable prescience. "Poor little soul, she is very plain," she wrote Bamie. "Her mouth and teeth seem to have no future. But the ugly duckling may turn out to be a swan." Whatever Aunt Edith's attitude toward her, Uncle Ted's affection was huge and vehement. He loved all his nieces, having what Alice called a "tribal affection," but Eleanor was his favorite because she was Elliott's daughter and "he was very devoted to Uncle Ellie."

"Eleanor, my darling Eleanor," he greeted her as he helped her out of the carriage at Sagamore and crushed her to his chest. "He was a bear," Edith reported, and "pounced upon her with such vigor that he tore all the gathers out of Eleanor's frock and both buttonholes out of her petticoat." Eleanor loved the day and a half she was allowed to stay at Sagamore, but keeping up with her uncle and her cousins turned into another series of mortifying proofs that she was inadequate. Alice was much better at sports. Eleanor did not even know how to swim, she had to confess the first time she went to Oyster Bay, whereupon Uncle Ted told her to jump off the dock, which she obediently did, only to come up panicky and spluttering.[10]

Then he organized a race down Cooper's Bluff, a steep sandy cliff, with each cousin holding onto the hand of another, and Uncle Ted in the lead. Rolling, tumbling, sliding down, she was "desperately afraid" the first time, but then realizing that there was little to fear, entered into the fun. Her Uncle Ted did everything with a boyish zest, chasing the children through the haystacks, into which they burrowed like rabbits, and through the barn in the game of hide and go seek. In the evening around a campfire he would pull out whatever book he had in his pocket and read to them; on rainy days he took them to the gun room and read to them there. A week end in Sagamore was a test of self-control and perseverance, of hiding fears and doing things to the best of her ability, but when Eleanor returned to her lonely existence at Tivoli or Thirty-seventh Street she was again the outsider.

The only other occasion on which she saw her father's family was at the Christmas party that Auntie Corinne gave at Orange. That was the only time she was with boys her own age, and the experience gave her "more pain than pleasure." The other young people knew each other so much better, she was poor at winter sports, and she thought that she danced awkwardly and was not dressed properly.

"Mother would have Eleanor stay with us," her cousin Corinne recalled.

We were a gay ebullient family. Eleanor was just sad. For the big party she was dressed by her grandmother in a short, white nainsook with little blue bows on either shoulder, the hem above her knees all hanging like a child's party dress but she was 14. She was in Alice's age group and Alice had on a sophisticated long dress. We begged her to borrow a dress, but she was noble, martyred and refused.

"We all felt the same way about her—Mother, Auntie Bye and I," Corinne added. "We loved her. We admired her and we were sad about her."[11]

But finally, when Eleanor was just turning fifteen, Grandmother Hall decided it was not good for her to remain at home. Her son Vallie was becoming increasingly difficult to handle, and Pussie had turned out to be a sophisticated but wildly romantic woman who had young men to tea and smoked cigarettes.

"Your mother wanted you to go to boarding school in Europe," Mrs. Hall told Eleanor. "And I have decided to send you, child."

Finishing school in Europe meant Allenswood and Mlle. Souvestre, who had done such wonders in 1869 for Auntie Bye and whom Eleanor's parents had met and liked in 1891 when they were living in the suburbs of Paris.

Another stage of her life was beginning. The years of being an outsider were over.

8. THE SPARK IS STRUCK

A YEAR AFTER ELEANOR ARRIVED AT ALLENSWOOD, ON THE outskirts of London near Wimbledon Common, its remarkable headmistress, Mlle. Souvestre, wrote Mrs. Hall:

> All what you said when she came here of the purity her heart, the nobleness of her thought has been verified by her conduct among people who were at first perfect strangers to her. I have not found her easily influenced in anything that was not perfectly straightforward and honest but I often found she influenced others in the right direction. She is full of sympathy for all those who live with her and shows an intelligent interest in everything she comes in contact with.[1]

Eleanor blossomed in the warm, friendly environment of Allenswood—it was as if she had started life anew. Behind her were the people who pitied her because she was an orphan or who taunted her for her virtues, and for the first time in her life all fear left her and her personality began to shine forth. "As a pupil she is very satisfactory," Mlle. Souvestre's evaluation continued, "but even that is of small account when you compare it with the perfect quality of her soul."

Bamie had been sent to Mlle. Souvestre in 1869 when the latter was headmistress of Les Ruches in Fontainebleau, outside of Paris. Because of an internal crisis precipitated by her co-principal, Marie Souvestre had given up Les Ruches, and years of "cruel sadness" had followed. In the mid-eighties she founded her new school in England.*

---

*A fictional account of the crisis at Les Ruches and a vivid portrait of Mlle. Souvestre are to be found in *Olivia* by "Olivia" (1949). *Olivia* was the pseudonym of Dorothy Strachey-Bussy, the sister of Lytton Strachey who was a pupil at Les Ruches and a teacher at Allenswood when Eleanor was there.

"The elite of many countries" sent their daughters to Allenswood—the Chamberlains, the Roosevelts, the Siemenses, the Stracheys. Henry James thought well enough of the school to suggest that his brother William send his daughter there in 1899, and described the sixty-five-year-old Mlle. Souvestre as "a most distinguished and admirable woman" who

> has had for many years a very highly esteemed school for girls at high, breezy Wimbledon, near London (an admirable situation)—where she has formed the daughters of many of the very good English *advanced* Liberal political and professional connection during these latter times. She is a very fine, interesting person, her school holds a very particular place (all Joe Chamberlain's daughters were there and they adore her,) and I must tell you more of her.

"The one shade of objection," he wrote Mrs. William James a few days later, "is that it is definitely 'middle-class'. But *all* schools here are that." By "middle-class" James meant to differentiate between the upper bourgeoisie and the intellectual elite to which he, as a man of genius, belonged.[2]

While the majority of the 35 to 40 girls enrolled in the school when Eleanor arrived were English-speaking, French was obligatory inside the classroom and out. This was no hardship for Eleanor, and, indeed, in the first few bewildering days she was reassured to see the other new girls having difficulty with the language. At her "first meal," a classmate recalled, "when we hardly dared open our mouths, she sat opposite Mlle. Souvestre chatting away in French . . . we admired her courage."[3]

The American newcomer was turned over to Marjorie Bennett, an English girl who was to be Eleanor's roommate. "Bennett" showed her around the school and explained its rules. Allenswood had some of the austerity and strictness of a British public school. "Its strict discipline suited the temperament of the youthful 'Totty.'"[4] The girls wore long skirts, usually black, white ruffled blouses, and boaters out-of-doors. Their day was fully programmed, and punctuality was mandatory. They made their own beds. Bureau drawers and closets had to be arranged as laid down in the rules and ready for inspection at any moment. At meals everything taken onto a plate had to be eaten. After breakfast there was a brisk walk in the commons in good weather and foul, and in London's damp chill Eleanor gladly began wearing her flannels again.

Classes went on throughout the day with special periods set aside for the preparation of lessons. To encourage concentration, the pupils were obliged to lie down on the floor after their midday meal and fix their minds for an hour on a single thought, which they later discussed at tea in French. Although athletics were not worshiped here as in the British public schools, two hours of exercise in the afternoon were obligatory. Eleanor went out for field hockey. She was not good at sports, but, as one of her classmates put it, "full of duty again,"[5] she persevered and made the first team, one of "the proudest moments" in her life, she said. There was an afternoon snack, more classes and study, and then the bell that alerted them to dress for dinner. Leadership in the school was marked in many ways, and the most ceremonial was to be chosen to sit opposite Mlle. Souvestre at dinner. To occupy this place, Dorothy Strachey wrote, "was an education in itself." It was this girl's duty to rise at a nod from Mlle. Souvestre as a signal that dinner was ended. In time, Eleanor was awarded this coveted honor. "Sou," as the girls called their headmistress, had her favorites. As the students filed by to say good night, she embraced some girls, kissed some, and extended a gracious hand to the rest.

Eleanor, who was drawn to girls who had difficulties, soon developed her own circle of friends. Carola von Passavant, the daughter of a wealthy Frankfort family, arrived in Allenswood shortly after Eleanor. It was her first time away from her parents and her first time out of Germany. The English girls were "very cool and stiff," the other German girls not sympathetic. Mlle. Souvestre saw that Carola was having an unhappy time and asked "Totty," as Eleanor was called at the school, to watch out for her. "That she did and I was thankful for it."[6] Eleanor, Carola, and Marjorie Bennett formed a trio. Eleanor also made friends with Hilda Burkenshaw ("Burky"), whose father was an officer with the British forces in India, and with Avice Horn, who had been sent from Australia to get her education "at home." Two rather schoolmistressy girls, the Gifford sisters, Helen and Leonie, who later started the successor school to Allenswood, were also among Eleanor's intimates.

Eleanor took French with Mlles. Souvestre and Maître, German with Fräulein Prebitsch, and Italian with Signorina Samaia, a mouse-like woman with skirts that swept the floor who had come with Mlle.

Souvestre from Fontainebleau and was now the school's energetic administrator. She studied English literature with Dorothy Strachey, who remembered her as "a tall, slim, elegant young girl who was so much more intelligent than all the others!"[7] and English history, Latin, and algebra with a variety of instructors. She had three years of drawing and design, and her schoolgirl notebooks were adorned with baroque lettering. She toiled away at music—three years of piano lessons and one of violin—but with indifferent results. "I struggled over the piano and was always poor," she wrote many years later. "I could not draw much less paint. I envied every good actress but could not act!" She wanted "desperately to have some form of artistic expression," but soon realized that she had no particular gifts.[8] Classes in the dance and three years of "needlework" rounded out her course of study. Allenswood placed little emphasis on science, and there was little concern with American history and government. Beatrice Webb, who was otherwise a good friend and admirer of Marie Souvestre, criticized the school's "purely literary" training.[9]

In contrast to Mr. Roser's decorous homilies, which had almost turned learning into a chore, Eleanor found the teaching at Allenswood lively and stimulating. According to her teachers, she was eager to learn and keenly interested in all her class work. Her workbooks showed a steady development in standards of taste and judgment, and—after the months when Mlle. Souvestre felt she was "a little bit likely to be influenced in her studies"—a sturdy insistence on thinking for herself.

The girls were encouraged to go to the theater in London and Paris during the holidays. Eleanor sat in the topmost gallery at the Comédie Française and stood and shouted, as did everyone around her, for Sully, then going blind, in Oedipus Rex.[10] She and her friends saw L'Aiglon with Sarah Bernhardt and Cyrano de Bergerac with Coquelin in the leading role. Was it because she remembered these occasions through "the rosy glasses of youth" that she felt in later years they represented the greatest days of the theater?[11] "Cyrano," Eleanor, the Allenswood student, wrote,

seems to me to be a very able piece of work in which the workman has made good use of everything which could make his readers laugh or cry. It is not a burlesque but it is very amusing and the duel scene in which Cyrano fights and rhymes at the same time is very clever. I do not wonder that Coquelin has made such a success of the part, for on the whole Cyrano is a very sympathetic character and

Coquelin is a wonderful actor. I notice his voice which M. told me
was so disagreeable but I think it serves admirably in this part and
helps to enhance the comic effect…it is a play essentially written
for the stage and though interesting to read many of the fine points
can only be brought out by perfect acting.…

But she was not sure, she added, that *Cyrano* merited more than one
or two readings: Shakespeare, on the other hand, was "a continent."

What distinguishes men of great genius? It is the power of creation
and generalization. They gather into one character scattered personalities and they bring to the knowledge of the world new creations.
Do we not believe in Don Quixote's existence as in that of Caesar?
Shakespeare is something terrible [she first used word "gigantic" but
crossed it out] in this respect. He was not one man but a continent.
He had in him great men, entire crowds, and landscapes.

Men of genius, she went on,

do not need to pay attention to style, they are good in spite of their
faults and because of them, but we, the lesser ones, only prevail by
perfect style. Hugo will surpass everyone in this century because
of his inspiration, what inspiration! I hazard here an opinion which
I would not dare speak anywhere. It is that the greatest men often
write very badly and all the better for them. It is not in them that
we must look for perfect style but in the secondary writers (Horace,
Labruyere)—One must know the masters by heart, adore them,
try to think as they do and then leave them forever. For technical
instruction there is little of profit to draw from the learned and
polished men of genius.

The nature of the poetic mission and understanding intrigued her, and
she returned to the subject.

To a poet nothing can be useless. He must be conversant with all
that is terribly awful and wonderfully beautiful. He must be able to
admire alike what is splendidly great or elegantly small. The plants
of the garden, the insects and birds of the air are all important, for
he knows most who is best able to vary his scenes and to furnish
his readers with moral and useful instruction.

But the knowledge of nature "is only half the task of a poet," she wrote in the same essay.

> He must be acquainted with all the different modes of life. He is required to estimate the happiness and misery of every condition, to trace the power of the passions, and to observe all the changes through which the mind passes owing to the different customs and climates from infancy to old age. He must free himself from the ideas of his time and regard right and wrong apart from the customs of his age. He must [word indecipherable] nature and consider himself above the criticism of his time trusting to posterity to acknowledge his merit. He must consider himself the arbiter of the thoughts of future generations as a being superior [?] to time and place.

Her notebook on English literature began with *Beowulf*, devoted a considerable amount of space to the Age of Chaucer and ended with the Age of Johnson. A separate notebook was filled with the passages from Shakespeare's plays that she considered worth transcribing. Her readings in French literature were equally extensive, and in Italian she read *The Divine Comedy* and *Orlando Furioso*.

Her report cards showed a steady progression and mastery:

FRENCH LANGUAGE

SEPTEMBER TO DECEMBER, 1899	"has begun too recently to be able to judge but interests herself very much in her lessons"
JANUARY TO APRIL, 1900	"she works admirably in French and history and is the first out of a class of nine."
MAY TO JULY, 1900	"works at French with much intelligence and taste, has made progress but cannot yet work on her own well enough"
SEPTEMBER TO DECEMBER, 1901	"works with application"
MAY TO JULY, 1902	"very advanced"

GERMAN

SEPTEMBER TO DECEMBER, 1899	"works very well, spelling needs improving"

JANUARY TO APRIL, 1900	"very good pupil, is always interested in her work"
MAY TO JULY, 1900	"excellent"
SEPTEMBER TO DECEMBER, 1901	"worked well"
MAY TO JULY, 1902	"very industrious—has made remarkable progress."

LATIN

| SEPTEMBER TO DECEMBER, 1899 | "is going over the elements with good results" |
| JANUARY TO APRIL, 1900 | "has worked splendidly. Excellent" |

ITALIAN

| SEPTEMBER TO DECEMBER, 1901 | "very good student, she works with zeal and much intelligence" |
| MAY TO JULY, 1902 | "excellent student, she speaks and writes Italian easily." |

ENGLISH LITERATURE

SEPTEMBER TO DECEMBER, 1899	"Intelligent, as far as can be seen in the few lessons she has had"
JANUARY TO APRIL, 1900	"Intelligent, but she is not quite up to the level of the class she is in."
MAY TO JULY, 1900	"Good"
SEPTEMBER TO DECEMBER, 1901	"Works very well. Very satisfactory."
MAY TO JULY, 1902	"Very good. Her progress was very marked this term."

The Allenswood years shaped Eleanor's tastes in literature, music, theater, and the arts generally, but what made those years among the most important in her life was its headmistress, the seventy-year-old Mlle. Marie Souvestre. The daughter of Emile Souvestre, a well-known philosopher and novelist and an innovator in the field of adult education, she inherited his interest in ideas and the arts as well as his moral zeal in politics. Strongly anti-Royalist, almost radical in his sympathies, he had been obliged on occasion to take refuge in Geneva.

His daughter was just as staunchly outspoken and nonconformist in her views. She was at home in the world of high politics and high culture and was welcome in all the great Liberal houses in England. Although her body had thickened with age, she was a woman of striking presence. Her forehead was strong and unlined, her face finely featured, her hair silvery white, and her eyes penetrating. She communicated a sense of force and authority and gave a Gallic flavor to any company she was in. Her lectures in history and literature were wide-ranging discourses on social movements. Beatrice Webb spoke of her "brilliancy of speech," which Dorothy Strachey said "darted here and there with the agility and grace of a hummingbird" and which influenced the literary style and taste of Lytton Strachey. "Cette grande femme," he called her.[12] No one read Racine like Marie Souvestre. She gave the French classics, one of her pupils said, "a new vividness and reality and a wider meaning." Her special gift was "the intense enthusiasm she could inspire in the young for things of the mind, for courageous judgment, and for a deep sense of public duty."

Mlle. Souvestre's classes were conducted in her library, a spacious book-lined room that was always full of flowers. The sculpture and paintings seemed quite daring to the girls—the work of such artist-friends as Rodin, Puvis de Chavannes, Barbedienne. The occasions Eleanor treasured most were the evenings when she and a few other girls were invited to Mlle. Souvestre's study, where for a few hours after dinner Mademoiselle read aloud, encouraged them to recite poems, and talked with them.

A passionate advocate, Mlle. Souvestre "often fought seemingly lost causes," but causes, Eleanor noted, that "were often won in the long run." She was a Dreyfusard, and for years before Captain Dreyfus was vindicated, the spellbound girls heard every move in the case over and over again. From that time on, Eleanor later said, she became conscious of the feeling in herself that "the underdog" was always to be championed.

When the Boer War came along, Mlle. Souvestre was Pro-Boer. She had a great many friends in government circles; in fact, one of her old pupils was a daughter of an Englishman high in the government at that time. But that did not deter her from being a pro-Boer running a girls' school in England or from her out-spoken criticism of British policies. On the other hand, she was scrupulously fair and allowed the British girls to celebrate their victories in South Africa, although she would take the rest of us into her library and talk to us at length on the rights of small nations while the British celebration was going on.[13]

Despite the vigor of her convictions, or perhaps because of them, she insisted that her students think for themselves. Intellectual independence and a lively sense of curiosity, she felt, were the most important traits she could develop in her girls. She wanted them to become personalities without losing the grace, the sweetness, the elegance which she felt were "the charm and smile of life." She herself had broken free from the constraining circle of inherited ideas, and she wanted the girls she cared about to do the same, to be openminded, curious, and to reach out. Eleanor, who had been taught by her mother and grandmother that conformity was the way to win society's approval, was a little upset with the demand that she be herself and self-reliantly say what she, not her teacher, thought.

Mlle. Souvestre's class sat on little chairs in her library, the headmistress in "a tall, straight armchair," with Signorina Samaia "on a little stool close and behind." Mlle. Souvestre talked, gave them a reading list, and asked them to do an essay based on their reading. Later, when the girls read their essays, she devastated those who parroted what she had said. A half-century later Eleanor could still see the indignant headmistress, as one of the girls read her paper aloud, take it away and tear it up. "You are giving me back what I gave you and it does not interest me." She insisted that her girls sift things through their own intelligence. "Why was your mind given you but to think things out for yourself?"

Challenged, Eleanor began to seek points Mlle. Souvestre had not made, and felt that it was even more satisfactory to come up with an idea that she had not found in the assigned reading. She glowed when Mlle. Souvestre returned a paper with the comment "well thought out," even if she added, "but you have forgotten this or that point."

Beatrice Webb was less impressed by Mlle. Souvestre as a thinker. She lamented Mademoiselle's reliance on the sparks of intuition rather than the rigors of scientific method in arriving at social judgments. Like her father, Mlle. Souvestre was primarily a moralist in politics, and she was concerned more with social justice than with social analysis. In this regard she strengthened Eleanor's disposition toward a social idealism based on intuitive reason and the promptings of the heart rather than intellectual analysis.

In what did Mlle. Souvestre succeed, a pupil later asked, and answered her own question—"in exciting, in amusing, in passionately interesting the intellect, in putting such a salt and savour into life, that it seemed as if we could never think anything dull again."

Mlle. Souvestre's fervent concern with public affairs and politics was another novelty for Eleanor; at Grandma Hall's there had been fashionable indifference. Uncle Ted's exploits in Cuba, his progress to the governorship, the vice presidency, and presidency were, of course, discussed at Tivoli, but as part of the family chronicle, not because they were national events. Politics, so far as the women were concerned, was still strictly the business of the men, as it had been in Grandfather Hall's day. Mlle. Souvestre, on the other hand, was "a radical free thinker," an intimate of the group that surrounded Frederic Harrison, leader of the English Positivists, who was a staunch supporter of trade unionism and an advocate of the "religion of humanity."

The headmistress was sensationally different from the devout Christians who directed the English public schools in her attitude toward religion: she called herself an atheist. That shocked Eleanor. If Grandma Hall had had the slightest inkling of this, she would surely have summoned Eleanor home immediately, regardless of Auntie Bye's devotion to the Frenchwoman.

As Mlle. Souvestre explained it, she could not comprehend a God who occupied Himself with the insignificant doings of individual men, and she considered pathetic the belief that He passed out rewards for good behavior and punishment for bad. Right should be done for its own sake; only the weak needed religion. These views were held by a large body of anticlerical opinion on the continent, but they were new and startling to Eleanor.

Did Christians do right only because of the rewards that were promised in heaven? Eleanor puzzled over this for many years, and in the end concluded that the charge was meaningless so far as her own feeling about God was concerned. "I was too young then to come back with the obvious retort that making those around you happy makes you happy yourself and, therefore, you are seeking a reward just as much as if you were asking for your reward in your future life."[14]

But she also maintained that listening to Mlle. Souvestre's anti-clericalism did her no harm in that it prompted her to reexamine her own beliefs. She could not accept Mlle. Souvestre's concept of a God indifferent to man and his activities on earth. Eleanor felt that God commanded what her own heart bid her do. Eleanor has "the warmest heart that I have ever encountered," Mlle. Souvestre noted on Eleanor's first report. Religion and prayer touched mystic chords in Eleanor that bound her to her dead father and to all humanity. Mlle. Souvestre's indifference to religion did not interfere with Eleanor's enjoyment of the Passion play which Aunt Tissie took her to see or of the Christmas midnight mass that she and Burky attended with Mlle. Souvestre in Rome. She concluded, with pathetic eagerness, that the headmistress could not be an atheist "at heart for she was as much moved as we were by the music and the lights!" Beatrice Webb questioned Marie Souvestre's ability to appreciate religious feeling. Yet one of Mademoiselle's dearest friends, the French evangelist the Reverend Charles Wagner, did not consider it a violation of his friend's basic convictions to confide her soul to the hands of the Lord at her funeral in the Church "de L'oratoire Saint-Honoré." So Eleanor may have been more discerning than Mrs. Webb in ascribing some religious sentiment to Mlle. Souvestre.

While Marie Souvestre's agnosticism produced no answering echo in Eleanor, the elder woman's "uncompromising sense of truth"— Beatrice Webb called it her "veracity"—and her "intolerance of pettiness and sham" did. In later years Eleanor did not hesitate to disagree with church or bishop when their actions or words seemed to conflict with Christian spirit or when religious institutions lent support to cruelty, prejudice, and human degradation.

Although Allenswood was notably emancipated if measured against other finishing schools, it was totally innocent in regard to preparing young ladies to deal with the world of men. Except for a few elderly gentlemen teachers, the girls were as cloistered as in a nunnery. On one occasion when Eleanor and Audrey Hartcup, then two of the oldest girls at the school, went into the library to say good night to Mlle. Souvestre, they found her in conversation with Mlle. Samaia and the older brother of one of their classmates. "Mlle. Samaia threw up her hands in horror and shooed us out!" The next day Eleanor and Audrey cornered her and tried to make her understand the absurdity of such squeamishness in view of "how freely we mixed with members of the opposite sex—when at home." If Eleanor, one of the most proper of young ladies, felt that Mlle. Samaia was being overly protective, it must have indeed been a cloistered existence.

Mlle. Souvestre was the most influential figure in Eleanor's early years, second only to her father. Headmistress and pupil were strongly drawn to each other. Marie Souvestre, like Eleanor, had been very attached to her father, who had died when she was quite young, and there were other bonds between the two. Mlle. Souvestre admitted to having a special feeling for Americans, and then there was the family tie. "Believe me," Mlle. Souvestre wrote Mrs. Hall, "as long as Eleanor will stay with me I shall bear her an almost maternal feeling, first because I am devoted to her aunt, Mrs. Cowles, and also because I have known both the parents she was unfortunate enough to lose." But according to Corinne, Eleanor's younger cousin whose first year at Allenswood overlapped Eleanor's last and who also gained a preferred place in the affections of the school's headmistress, the crux of the relationship was Mademoiselle's realization that "she could give a great deal to that really remarkable, sad young girl."

The headmistress' motherly solicitude for Eleanor extended to her clothes, her health, her grooming. She was outraged by Eleanor's made-over dresses but hesitated to say so at first because she was afraid of hurting the sensitive girl. During Eleanor's second year at Allenswood, however, when she and Burky were spending the between-year holiday with a French family in order to improve their French, Mlle. Souvestre, who was also in Paris, finally expressed herself on the subject of Eleanor's clothes. Mlle. Samaia was directed to take Eleanor to a dressmaker, and the dark red gown that was made for her gave Eleanor as much pleasure as if it had come from the most fashionable house in Paris. "I can well remember this red dress," a schoolmate recalled more than sixty-five years later.

Mlle. Samaia also undertook to break Eleanor of the habit of biting her fingernails. She had little success until one day when Eleanor was rereading her father's letters and came to the passage that admonished her to take care of her personal appearance. It hit home, and from that day forward, she said, she let her nails grow.

Her grandmother had alerted the school to her delicate health. "You would enjoy seeing her so well, so rested, so ready for all out-of-door exercises," Mlle. Souvestre wrote Mrs. Hall. "She does not any more suffer of the complaints you told me about. She has a good sleep, a good appetite, is very rarely troubled with headaches and is always ready to enjoy her life." A year later Mlle. Souvestre again reported on Eleanor's physical condition.

> She looks always very thin, delicate and often white and just the
> same I have rarely seen such a power of endurance. She is never
> unwell even when she seems so. Her appetite and sleep are excellent
> and she is never tired of walking and taking exercise.

Photographs of Eleanor at this period show a tall, slim, narrow-waisted girl with soft, wavy hair arranged in a pompadour and braided in the back. Her most distinctive feature was her eyes; blue, serene, and soft, in their gaze one forgot the overly prominent teeth and the slightly receding chin. Her soul, said Mlle. Souvestre, was a radiant thing, and it could be glimpsed in her eyes. Like her father, she had the faculty of concentrating all her attention and sympathy on the person she was with. "She is conscientious and affectionate," the headmistress wrote Mrs. Hall in one of many such reports, "full of regard for others, and of a fineness of feeling truly exquisite. She desires only the good."

Eleanor's schoolmates agreed. Burky, who felt "tired" by comparison with Eleanor, later expressed her gratitude to her for her companionship during holidays, even though "my mind and my body could not keep up with all the things you absorbed so readily and so intelligently." Eleanor was so consistently helpful that even the girls her age looked upon her "as one of the older ones." Avice Horn's sister Dorothy characterized Eleanor "as being entirely sophisticated, and full of self-confidence and *savoir faire*," and Eleanor's cousin Corinne gave this picture of the position that Eleanor held at the school:

> When I arrived she was "everything" at the school. She was beloved
> by everybody. Saturdays we were allowed a sortie into Putney
> which had stores where you could buy books, flowers. Young girls
> have crushes and you bought violets or a book and left them in the
> room of the girl you were idolizing. Eleanor's room every Saturday
> would be full of flowers because she was so admired.

Mlle. Souvestre's aim was to make her girls "cultivated women of the world," and because she knew so many men of arts and letters in all countries she was able to give a few fortunate older pupils special advantages when she took them abroad on vacation. Eleanor was one of those chosen for this privilege.

"If you have no objection to this plan," she wrote Mrs. Hall in February, 1901, "I am thinking of taking her with me to Florence during the Easter holiday. It will be short but I think she may nevertheless derive some benefit of a fortnight in Italy and she is very eager to come with me."

All the practical details of the journey were turned over to the sixteen-year-old girl. Eleanor packed for both of them, looked up train schedules, secured the tickets, arranged for the hansoms and porters. She loved every part of her assignment, and traveling with Mlle. Souvestre was a "revelation" to her: eating native dishes, drinking the *vin du pays* (diluted, of course, with water), being with the people of the country, not one's countrymen. She learned the pleasures of a meal of wine, cheese, bread, and coffee, and the virtue of flexibility in travel; of revising plans in order to see a friend or a church or a painting. In France they were entertained by M. Ribot, a former prime minister. In Alassio they called on Mrs. Humphrey Ward, the novelist. In Florence they stayed with a painter who was doing a gigantic church mural of the Last Supper. While in Florence Mlle. Souvestre told Eleanor to take her Baedeker and go through the sublime city street by street, church by church; "Florence is worth it," said Mlle. Souvestre. And "so, 16 years old, keener than I have probably ever been since and more alive to beauty, I sallied forth to see Florence alone."[15] In addition to the excitement and joy of discovery, there was the pleasure of discussing everything she had seen with Mlle. Souvestre afterward. "It is impossible to wish for one self a more delightful companion in traveling," Mlle. Souvestre wrote Mrs. Hall. "She is never tired, never out of sorts, never without a keen interest in all that she sees."[16]

On her way back to England Eleanor stopped in Paris, where she wanted to get gifts. Like her father, she took pleasure in giving, and also like him she tried to find "just the thing" which would make the recipient feel loved and valued. A list of those to receive presents started with her family:

Maude's baby [Maude was Mrs. Larry Waterbury]
Joe's baby [her Uncle Eddie Hall had married the beautiful Josie
   Zabriskie]
Pussie
Cherub [Hall]
Grandma
Vallie

Tissie [Mrs. Stanley Mortimer]
Cousin Susie [Mrs. Henry Parish]

It also included teachers and her closest school friends, and ended with the redoubtable Madeleine, who had caused her so much grief.

In Paris she ran into the Newbold family, whose Hyde Park estate bordered on that of the Roosevelts'. Mlle. Souvestre did not think Eleanor needed to be chaperoned, and the Newbolds promptly reported to Grandma Hall that they had seen Eleanor in Paris alone. Eleanor worried about her grandmother's reaction to this news; she was to go back to the United States in July and she wanted desperately to return to Allenswood in September. "I sincerely hope she may be able to do that," Mlle. Souvestre wrote to Mrs. Hall. "I am sure another year of a regular and studious life will be in every respect mentally and physically beneficial. Her health though excellent is perhaps not yet settled enough to make it desirable for her to face all the irregularities of a society life. . . . She is very desirous of seeing you and is often anxious for you, now that so many of your daughters are married and away." (Tissie spent a good part of the year abroad; Maude had married Larry Waterbury, the famous polo player; and Pussie, although still unmarried, was totally preoccupied with herself.)

It was Pussie who came to London to accompany Eleanor on her return to America. The voyage was emotionally exhausting. Pussie, in the throes of a romantic crisis about a man she had met in London, was full of tears and avowals that she was going to jump overboard. It was a bad beginning of an unhappy summer, whose only bright note was a visit to Farmington, Connecticut, where Auntie Bye had recently moved. Eleanor helped her aunt get settled, and in the guest book next to her name she wrote "the laborer is worthy of his hire." She was thrown together with Pussie again in Northeast Harbor, Maine, where Pussie was staying with Mrs. Ludlow and Eleanor with Mrs. Ludlow's daughter, her cousin Susie.

Something Eleanor said nettled Pussie. Because she had taken Pussie's threats to jump overboard seriously, Eleanor may have expressed surprise at the speed with which Pussie became involved in a new romantic interest in Maine. Whatever the provocation, Pussie retaliated with gibes intended to hurt Eleanor where she was most vulnerable. She ridiculed Eleanor's appearance, reviving her mother's lament that she was the ugly duckling among all the beautiful Hall women; no men would ever be interested in her, Pussie taunted. But

Eleanor, long reconciled to her plain looks, could not be provoked, so Pussie thrust more savagely. Who was she to talk self-righteously in view of her father's behavior? She hysterically told Eleanor about her father's last years and of the grief and shame his behavior had caused her mother and all the family. Distraught and shattered, Eleanor ran to her grandmother for consolation and denial, whereupon she was told that Elliott *had* ruined her mother's life.

Eleanor was thrown into despair, and wanted only to get back to Allenswood and Mlle. Souvestre. Her grandmother hesitated, but Eleanor's determination and entreaties finally prevailed and Mrs. Hall agreed to let her return for a third year if she could find a chaperone for the voyage. Eleanor went to New York and on her own engaged a "deaconess" through an employment agency to accompany her. With the help of her aunts, she bought her first tailor-made suit with an oxford-gray skirt that fashionably trailed the ground. Accompanied by the respectable-looking deaconess and dressed modishly, she turned away from that unhappy summer and returned to the peace of Allenswood.

It is a measure of how much she had grown in self-assurance that her encounter with Pussie did not cause her to withdraw into feeling unloved except by a father who was dead. Instead, her last year at Allenswood strengthened her leadership qualities.

She was happy and contented, yet she also "knew the sadness of things," a sadness that shadowed even her moments of greatest joy and achievement. She could not abandon herself to frivolity and merriment like other young people. Mlle. Souvestre later talked with Corinne about "Totty," and after enumerating her virtues "would throw up her hands and add 'mais elle n'est pas gaie.'" "She took a serious view of life," Helen Gifford recalled, "and once confided to me that all she wished for was to do something useful: that was her main object."[17]

Because her mother had bred in her an ineradicable sense of inferiority and plainness, Eleanor felt that she could never count on beauty in gaining people's affection—only helpfulness. "The feeling that I was useful was perhaps the greatest joy I experienced," she later wrote. Happiness, she reasoned in an essay she wrote for Mlle. Souvestre, lay in what one did for others rather than in what one sought for oneself.

There is no more fleeting notion than that of happiness. Certain people seem to find happiness in a thoroughly egoistic life. Can we believe however that those socialites who look as if they were enjoying happiness in the bustle of worldly pleasures are actually happy? We don't believe so, for the pleasures of the world are precarious, and there must be moments, even in the gayest and most brilliant life, when one feels sad and lonely in the midst of a frivolous crowd where one cannot find a single friend.

On the other hand, it often happens that those whose existence seems saddest and dullest are in fact the happiest. For instance you sometimes meet a woman who sacrifices her own life for the sake of other people's happiness and is happy nevertheless because she finds in her devotion the best remedy against sadness and boredom....

If no life is without sadness, none is without happiness either, for in the saddest life there are moments of happiness, sometimes produced by comparing the present peace of mind with past sufferings.

Most of all, those who are not looking for happiness are the most likely to find it for those who are busy searching forget that the surest way to be happy is to seek happiness for others.

Eleanor wanted to return for a fourth year, but her grandmother insisted that she come home and be introduced into society since she would be eighteen in October.

"The more I know her the more I see what a helpful and devoted grandchild she will be to you," Mlle. Souvestre wrote to Mrs. Hall at the beginning of 1902, adding, "Ah! to me! What a blank her going away must leave in my life!" And in her final report in July she said, "Elinor [*sic*] has had the most admirable influence on the school and gained the affection of many, the respect of all. To me personally I feel I lose a dear friend indeed."

As for Eleanor, she wrote in an exercise that described Allenswood to an interested parent, "I have spent three years here which have certainly been the happiest years of my life."

9. YOUNG IN A YOUNG COUNTRY IN A YOUNG TIME

———————————————————◇

ELEANOR WAS ALMOST EIGHTEEN WHEN SHE RETURNED TO THE United States in the early summer of 1902. There was a lively perception in her eyes, her face was sensitive and intelligent, and although she was tall, her movements were quick and graceful—like those of a colt, someone said. Full of dreams and hopes, her sky-reaching mood matched that of the country. Reform was in the air. The century was young, and the United States, raucous and self-confident, was responsive to the prophecies of Eleanor's uncle, its most youthful president, that this was destined to be an American and, therefore, a better century. The nation was ready to embark on "a new quest for social justice," historian Harold U. Faulkner wrote, and Roosevelt "instinctively . . . responded to the widespread desires for a better civilization and, rushing to the head of the movement, he rose to unprecedented heights of popularity as the reform wave surged onward."[1]

Radiant, full of optimism, Theodore Roosevelt delighted in the presidency, and the nation was infected with his enjoyment of the office. For the first time not only was a president's policy always on stage, but so was his personality—the warming smile, the outsize teeth, the striking phrase sometimes uttered with a screech, the explosive laugh. Never before had the private lives of the president and his family been so fully and continuously reported. The country adored reading about his dash with children and friends down Cooper's Bluff, his wandering off into the meadows to read an afternoon away, or such greetings to Alice's friends as "Children, come with me—I'll teach you how to walk on stilts."[2] Alice, now dubbed "Princess," was on the front page almost as often as her father, and he, even in his Harvard days, had been, one professor complained, "a great lime-lighter." He now used his showman instincts to promote his public purposes. "On the whole," William James wrote in 1902, "I have rejoiced in Roosevelt so far."[3] His use of the word "rejoiced" caught precisely the national mood of sheer pleasure in its young president. The nation was enchanted, and so was Eleanor, who, soon after her return, made the rounds of her Oyster Bay kin—Auntie Bye and Auntie Corinne, Uncle Gracie and Uncle Ted.

The advance of technology and the resultant new domestic comforts bolstered the sense that the new century would be a better one. "How wonderful the telephone is and how I should miss it at Hyde Park," Mrs. James Roosevelt noted in her journal. Eleanor's family was replacing coal stoves with gas, and kerosene lamps and gas jets with electricity. They were using automobiles as a means of transportation, not only as playthings. When Alice and another girl motored alone "all the way from Newport to Boston" that summer, the newspapers hailed the journey as representing progress in travel by motor, while their families lamented the shift in moral standards among the young implied by the absence of a chaperone.

New York, too, was changing from the quiet city Eleanor had known as a child. It was now Greater New York, a teeming metropolis of 3.5 million people, and the population was still surging upward as immigration, almost wholly from eastern and southeastern Europe, approached a million a year. "More money," the city departments cried. The budget would soon pass the hundred million mark, the editorials warned, while Fusion Mayor Seth Low bewailed the unreasonable limitations that Albany placed upon the city's borrowing powers.

It was a divided city. Jacob Riis had called his book on the subject, published in 1890, *How the Other Half Lives*. A decade later the split was deeper. There was the New York of Eleanor's family and friends, whose resplendent homes along Fifth Avenue now stretched from Washington Square to the upper Eighties. Concentration of wealth was "the outstanding feature of American economic life" in the new century, and on Fifth Avenue it was reflected in the French châteaux, Rhine castles, and Italian Renaissance mansions that replaced the old brownstones.

The other face of New York was the huddle of East Side slums, where two thirds of the city lived in 90,000 tenements, most of them of the gloomy "dumbbell" type in which ten out of the fourteen rooms on a floor were windowless. The male head of the household earned $600 a year, for which he worked a ten-hour day, six days a week. Children and women were "sweated."

These were the ugly realities raising portentous thunderheads over the glitter and elegance of Fifth Avenue when Eleanor returned. But the omens, if more menacing, were not new; what was new were the reforming impulses that could be felt everywhere, especially among women, whose position was changing. The women's rights movement had made enormous strides since 1848, when Elizabeth Cady Stanton had launched it. When she died, just as Eleanor returned, she was no longer a figure of mockery, and some even called her "the greatest woman the world has ever produced." Even Theodore Roosevelt, who was not yet a convert to women's suffrage, called her death a loss to the nation.

By the opening of the new century, American women had broken out of their traditional sphere.

> When I read in the papers and heard in the Club that a dozen women of great wealth were standing along Broadway handing bills and encouragement to the girl shirtwaist strikers of last winter, I was not a bit surprised. Nowadays I can hardly go to a reception or a ball without being buttonholed by somebody and led into a corner to be told about some new reform. It is perfectly amazing, this plague of reform, in its variety, in its volume and in the intensity of earnestness with which it is being pushed.[4]

Some well-born women went further. Charlotte Perkins Gilman challenged members of her sex to seek "economic independence" and to use their economic power for social reform, not simply to salve their consciences by charitable donations. When Professor Vida Scudder of Wellesley advocated "a new Franciscanism" and appealed to students to go into the slums and staff the growing settlement-house movement, a few New York debutantes responded. Mary Harriman and Nathalie Henderson enrolled in Barnard to study economics and sociology and then launched the Junior League, one of whose purposes was to assist the settlements.[5]

Eleanor returned to the United States feeling that she was on the threshold of life, ready to be swept up by such an undertaking. After three years under Mlle. Souvestre's influence, she was open to the reforming currents that were in the air, and she wanted to go on with her education.

But society decreed that at eighteen, young girls who "belonged" came out. The debut was a tribal ritual, "the great test," the society columns cruelly proclaimed, of a young girl's social talents.[6] The approaching rites filled Eleanor with dread, but it never occurred to her not to comply—a resolve that worried Mlle. Souvestre. Her letters cautioned Eleanor against permitting society to "take you and drag you into its turmoil. Protect yourself," she urged.

> Give some of your energy, but not all, to worldly pleasures which are going to beckon to you. And even when success comes, as I am sure it will, bear in mind that there are more quiet and enviable joys than to be among the most sought-after-women at a ball or the woman best liked by your neighbor at the table, at luncheons and the various fashionable affairs.[7]

But society, echoed by her Hall relatives, decreed that her first obligation was to be introduced. So Eleanor prepared for the ordeal.

The social season did not begin until November, and Eleanor spent the intervening months at Oak Terrace in Tivoli. It was a sobering experience. After the protected surroundings of Allenswood, she was suddenly brought face to face with "the serious side of life." It was lonely at Tivoli. Aunt Maude, closest to her in age, was now settled in her own house and was leading a very gay life that was the talk of the society columns. Aunt Pussie, Eleanor reported to Mlle. Souvestre, was involved in "worldly excitements." She was as temperamental as an artist, and when she was at Tivoli she was likely as not to be depressed and would refuse to speak to anyone. And then "she would emerge perfectly delightful and bright and happy as a May morning." The whole family, added Eleanor, who had become quite impatient with her aunt, "had been through a wringer wondering what was the matter and then nothing."

Pussie was quite attached to Hall, Eleanor's eleven-year-old brother, and considered him her child. Eleanor wanted Hall with her although she felt bad about it, she wrote Mlle. Souvestre, because it made her aunt so sad. Mlle. Souvestre consoled her. It was hard for Eleanor to be faced with such problems so soon, but Mademoiselle was pleased that Hall had elected to go with Eleanor. Since Pussie was so busy with society and her gentlemen, the headmistress thought she would easily forget these "regrets of a sentimental character."

The loneliness of Tivoli could have been borne, even when Hall was staying with his Oyster Bay cousins, if it had not been for Uncle Vallie, whose alcoholism was a never-ending nightmare to Eleanor. He would stand at a window with a gun and shoot at members of the family as they crossed the lawn so that they had to take shelter behind the trees. Vallie was often joined in his escapades by his younger brother even though Eddie was now married to the beautiful Josie Zabriskie. Her Allenswood classmate, Leonie Gifford, came to stay with Eleanor, but throughout her visit Eleanor was on tenterhooks. The strain was too much, and she decided that she could no longer invite friends to Tivoli. Two young men, Duncan Harris and Charley Draper, dropped in unannounced and were baffled by her desperate maneuvers to keep them from having a drink with Vallie, who they knew was entertaining the current amateur doubles champions that day.[8] Only once did she depart from her "no guests" rule, and that was when she invited young Franklin Roosevelt, who knew the situation at Tivoli well enough not to be frightened off by Vallie's sudden eruption. Of the visit, Franklin noted in his Line-A-Day diary, "Vallie has been exemplary—I seem to have a good effect on him."

The spectacle of her two uncles losing control of themselves instilled in Eleanor, she said, "an almost exaggerated idea of the necessity of keeping all of one's desires under complete subjugation." She warmed to vitality but disliked abandon, especially the maudlin behavior induced by alcohol. When people let themselves go in that way, she turned rigid and cold. The intensity of her reaction to her uncles was undoubtedly fed by the repressed knowledge of her father's behavior, something that she could not acknowledge but which, after Pussie's outburst the summer before, must have been close to the surface of consciousness.

Between Vallie and Pussie, she had a "liberal education" that summer in how people who were emotionally unstable "can make life miserable for the people around them." She began to have an understanding of what her mother had suffered, although it did not alter her feelings toward her father.

After the new school term began at Allenswood, Mlle. Souvestre wrote Eleanor that she was sorely missed at the school. "There are many new girls with us," Mlle. Souvestre wrote. "As is their custom, the English girls pay no attention to them and leave them alone. You would have known how to act so that they would have felt at ease and happy in conditions so different from their usual life." What a "great void" your departure has created, Mlle. Samaia wrote her. "Tell me when the big season starts in New York," Mlle. Souvestre demanded.

For Eleanor, the coming of autumn only increased her dread of her debut and her first winter in society. Would her Roser-class schoolmates still see her as a girl apart? Would there be the whispered "she has no father or mother, she is so pathetic," or would she be able to repeat her Allenswood triumph and establish a place for herself in New York?

For some, the New York season began with the autumn ball at Tuxedo, but it was the sound of the bugle opening the horse show at Madison Square Garden that announced to the city that society was once more "at home." Splendid animals pranced on the tanbark, and elegant folk thronged the boxes. One of the stalls belonged to Franklin D. Roosevelt's older half brother, James "Rosy" Roosevelt, who had married an Astor, looked Edwardian, worldly, and attractive, and was "a real honest snob." The night the horse show opened James's daughter Helen, who was engaged to Theodore Douglas Robinson, was there with him, as was Eleanor. "Two handsome members of the Roosevelt family," reported the *Herald*, which omitted to note that young Franklin Roosevelt, down from Harvard, was also in the box that evening; he was an unimportant Roosevelt. The center of attention was Alice, who made several circuits of the Garden in a lovely white gown and the strikingly large hat that had already become her trademark, this one of white plumes.

Although the newspapers noted Eleanor's presence at the show and Franklin wrote in his diary, "Dinner with James Roosevelt Roosevelt, Helen Roosevelt Roosevelt, Mary Newbold and Eleanor Roosevelt at Sherry's and horse show," in her own account of her coming out Eleanor failed to mention the occasion. For her the pinnacle was still to be scaled.

The big Assembly Ball at the Waldorf-Astoria took place on December 11. To New York society, said the *New York Times,* it is what "the Drawing Room in Buckingham Palace is to the fashionable world in London." A debutante did not feel she had come out until she had curtsied to the patronesses who received the guests in the smilax-decorated foyer, had entered the great ballroom in her white gown and long white gloves, and had danced in the cotillion with a handsome young man.

Almost all the debutantes considered the ball an ordeal—"ninety-nine per cent of us," said Helen Cutting; "no, I would make that ninety-nine point nine per cent."[9] They all worried over what their peers would say about their gowns, their looks—above all, whether they would be asked by young men to dance. For Eleanor the evening was even more trying because of the inevitable comparisons with her mother's splendid debut. The week before the Assembly, *Town Topics* had commented that Eleanor's coming out recalled the brilliant days of New York society in the late eighties when Mrs. Elliott Roosevelt was one of its "leaders." Society would be thinking of her mother and, she was sure, how far the daughter fell short of being a belle.

She stayed in town that autumn with Pussie, who never let her forget that it was unheard of for a Hall girl not to be a belle at every party. Fourteen years after her debut Pussie was still much admired and much wooed, still had more partners than she could possibly accept for both the cotillion and supper. Both Pussie and Maude caused "raised eyebrows" in New York society; they "broke practically every rule that could be broken" but were always forgiven because of their great beauty and charm. Living with Pussie only added to Eleanor's feelings of gloom and foreboding.

There were five Misses Roosevelt making their appearance in society in 1902. Alice, who had come out the previous January with "the most gala White House ball since the days of Dolly Madison," was coming to the Assembly, as were Christine, Elfrida, Dorothy, and Eleanor—all eighteen years of age. The town was talking about "the Magic Five" and twittering away over who was the prettiest, the most attractive, the most sought after. That Alice was the wittiest—not only among the debutantes but in society generally—was already agreed.

The Assembly, according to Eleanor, was "utter agony." She was adequately gowned in a Callot from Paris, but she knew no one and would have been totally ignored by the men, she claimed, were it not for Forbes Morgan, a suitor of Pussie's, and Bob Ferguson, who was fifteen years older and had been devoted to her mother. They danced with her and introduced her to others at the ball, but she was not a popular debutante, she felt, and left as soon as she could, ashamed that she should be the first girl on her mother's side of the family not to be a belle.

Her agony, though real, was self-inflicted, and revealed more about the immense importance she attached to being a success than it did about how others regarded her. So far as looks were concerned, *Town Topics* commented rather cruelly, the Roosevelt girls were "interesting-looking, but they are not pretty."[10] And what constituted a "popular debutante"? Before going to the Assembly Ball, Eleanor had attended the largest of the dinners that preceded it, an elaborate affair thronged by young men and women given by the Reverend Dr. and Mrs. Morgan Dix for their daughter Margaret. Two days before the Assembly she was at Sherry's for the dinner-dance given by the Emlen Roosevelts for their daughter Christine, and the day after the Assembly she attended the reception and small cotillion given by Mrs. Hilborne L. Roosevelt for Dorothy. The following week she went to a dinner and dance at Sherry's for Gertrude Pell and assisted at Elsie Waterbury's afternoon reception and supper. Before departing for Washington for New Year's at the White House, Aunt Tissie took sixty of Eleanor's friends to see Julia Marlowe in *The Cavalier*. After the play the elegantly begowned ladies and top-hatted young men went by omnibus to Sherry's for supper and informal dancing. In Washington Eleanor was invited to all the big parties and went to most of them. In all, it was hardly the life of a "Miss Lonelyheart."

After the exhausting New Year's gaieties, Eleanor returned to New York for more dinners and private dances in the splendid mansions along Fifth Avenue. "Now comes the critical test of the winter as to who shall be left and who shall be chosen," wrote the *Herald*, adding that a few debutantes—but by no means all—would be invited to the Astor ball, "the most important event of the winter season." To be included on Mrs. Astor's list meant distinction for the girl who had just made her debut. Eleanor was included, and she was also invited to all the so-called "small" dances—those presented by Mrs. Ogden Mills, Mrs. John Jacob Astor, the Elbridge T. Gerrys, the Whitelaw Reids. These entertainments usually began at eleven after the opera, and consisted of dancing until midnight, supper, a cotillion, and further dancing until early morning. Eleanor did not enjoy these parties and left as early as possible. That first winter, she said, society was the all-important thing in her life, but it nearly brought her to a "state of nervous collapse."

"She wasn't a belle by any means," recalled Duncan Harris. "She was too tall for most of the young men. But she was an interesting talker. And she was always gracious and pleasant." Her contemporaries remarked upon her exquisite manners, and older men found her sympathetic and were impressed with her grave thoughtfulness. To her surprise, several times she found herself seated next to the host—but what did such victories matter? At eighteen she would have preferred younger, if less exalted, dinner companions. With men her own age, however, she was insecure and quick to consider them "fresh," and she was overly "proper." During her last month at Allenswood, Leonie Gifford's brother had come to visit his sister, and the two Giffords, Eleanor, and Marjorie Bennett went for a walk in the common. She and Marjorie tossed a coin to decide who should walk with whom. "You walked with me," Walter Gifford reminded her two decades later, "and when I congratulated you on winning the toss you very coldly told me you had lost it, which was rather galling for a 17-year-old male in a very high collar."

The winter over, she was glad to get back to Tivoli. "I only arrived at six last night and I've just finished my third book. I never quite realize when I'm away how much time there is for reading here." She laughed over Charles Flandrau's *Harvard Episodes* and *The Diary of a Freshman* but the third book, *La Gioconda*, "is just tremendous. ...I suppose D'Annunzio meant to show that fate is inexorable and that one may sacrifice all and get nothing for it if such is our destiny. Certainly he did not show men in a very favorable light." She made these comments in a diary she began to keep at the end of May, 1902, because, she wrote, she hoped to do "something which I will want to remember later on." But she also had literary aspirations, and in the briefly kept journal she dramatized an encounter between her grandmother and the cook.

"Do you know Totty I simply cannot get rid of the cook!" was the way Eleanor began the episode; "she simply won't go." Then Eleanor recreated the scene between her grandmother and the cook, Mary Ann—"the scene which had led up to this startling announcement."

> G'ma. "Mary Ann, Mrs. K wants you to go back to her on Monday."
>
> Mary Ann. "Sure Mam and I couldn't think of such a thing (feeble attempt at protest from my G'ma) why should I be after leaving you when the young ladies are so nice and I'm quite completely settled for the summer. (Another attempt at speech on my G'ma's part—unsuccessful of course.) Why now Ma'am I've been with Mrs. K's sister, Mrs. B., and with her brother's sister-in-law and with her cousin so it's natural you know she should want me back but I told her when I was going I wouldn't come back and you don't think I'd be after laving you now?"
>
> Here there was a pause for breath and her grandmother managed to say something.
>
> G'ma. "But Mary Ann if we have a great deal of company can you make ice cream and do all the other work?"
>
> Mary Ann. "Why to be sure, Ma'am an' I can do anything, anything you want, of course ye'll give me some help and don't you worry about me I kin do things just perfect. You just send

word to Mrs. K. I can't come back. I'd do it meself but I can't write you know."

"So G'ma retired," Eleanor finished, "to do as she was bid and Mary Ann is still our cook."

The entry (and the diary) ended with a pathetic declaration: "I won't write again until I've been to the Poor's. Wish me good luck please. I'm usually so hopeless on a house party!"

Despite this self-depreciation, she had begun to develop a circle of friends. Her eyes, Laura Delano later asserted, softened the hearts of all the men, young as well as old, and her face did things that were suddenly lovely.[11] Her male friends came from the group that worked for the Astor Trust—Duncan Harris, Nicholas Biddle, and especially Robert Munro Ferguson, who was the center of a "Ferguson cult" among New York society women. He was a member of an ancient Scotch Highland clan, and his brothers were pillars of the British Liberal establishment and members, along with Asquith, Haldane, and Grey, of the closely knit group called the "Limps." Bob Ferguson had come to the United States in the late 1880s and had been a Rough Rider in the Spanish-American War; Teddy Roosevelt considered him one of the bravest men he had ever known. He had been a frequent visitor at Eleanor's house while her mother was alive and was a favorite of Auntie Bye's. A tall man, rather sad looking except when his face broke up in twinkles, he invited confidences. He was not all surface and Eleanor was strongly drawn to the silent, sensitive, attractive Bob.

Bob Ferguson introduced Eleanor to Bay Emmett, the painter, and escorted her to parties at Miss Emmett's studio in Washington Square. "Not a Four Hundred thing, although it was the Four Hundred,"[12] the Emmett parties were extremely informal and supposedly very Bohemian, although some young men did not stay long because no hard liquor was served. That made the parties even nicer, as far as Eleanor was concerned, and thus she was not, as was customary for her, among the first to leave.

By the autumn of 1903 her Tivoli family was beginning to depend on her a great deal, looking upon her as the strong one. She could cope with Pussie's emotional crises, and when a drunken Vallie, eluding Mrs. Hall in Tivoli, would turn up in New York, it was Eleanor who took command. She gladly assumed responsibility for Hall. Anna Roosevelt had entered Hall's name on the Groton list for his year, and after her death, the headmaster, Reverend Endicott Peabody, wrote Eleanor's father that although Hall was twenty-third on the list, he was sure that Groton would be able to take him. It was Eleanor who accompanied Hall to the school, saw him installed, and chatted with Dr. Peabody and the masters, especially William Amory Gardner (WAG), on whose yacht the *America* her father had sailed. It was the first of what would be many trips, for she thought of Hall as being as much her son as her brother.

She went through her second winter in New York calmly. Just as at Allenswood she had taken the younger girls under her wing, she now eased the ordeal for those in the new crop of debutantes who were close friends. Though society had lost its terrors for her, she did not look forward to another round of parties, she was ready for something more. She joined a German and a Bible class.

Mlle. Souvestre had cautioned her against a preoccupation with social success, and the good example that Auntie Bye set proved Mlle. Souvestre's point to Eleanor. At home in the world of society, Mrs. Cowles did not let herself be limited by its conventions. People said of her, as they did of Eleanor, that she was no beauty but that her quick intelligence and cordiality made them forget that fact. In New York she had turned her drawing room "into a rendezvous for civic reformers, artists, writers, journalists, politicians"[13] at a time when society "fled in a body from a poet, a painter, a musician, or a clever Frenchman."[14] Her at-homes in Washington, Eleanor observed, brought "every kind of person into that house." She enjoyed people, drew them out, and made them feel at their best; later she would discuss them with Eleanor, commenting with sympathy, sometimes with spice. When Eleanor stayed with her, Bye was delighted to take her "soft-eyed" niece—so alert, so shyly curious—everywhere and to encourage her interest in public affairs.

The most important visitor to Bye's little house on N Street was Theodore Roosevelt, who came so frequently to talk with his sister that her home was called "the little White House." Eleanor would talk to her about them afterward, enough so that she could say later,

> There was never a serious subject that came up while he was President that he didn't go to her at her home on N. Street and discuss with her, that was well known by all the family. He may have made his own decisions, but talking with her seemed to clarify things for him.[15]

Uncle Ted's disdain for society no doubt fed Eleanor's matur-
ing determination to free herself from its demands. "It was one of
Roosevelt's definite contributions to his time," wrote Mark Sullivan,
"that he, being a Harvard man, and of inherited wealth, showed to
others of his class ways to spend their lives with satisfaction to themselves and advantage to their country."[16] It was a doctrine that he
particularly preached to the young.

He did not have much success with Alice, who, he wrote his sister Corinne in 1903, was "spending most of her time in Newport
and elsewhere, associating with the Four Hundred—individuals with
whom other members of her family have exceedingly few affiliations."
Eleanor, however, found his attitude congenial.

One day Eleanor was on the Hudson River train with an elderly
relative who never hesitated to state his views. Referring to the newspaper he was reading, he demanded, "What is this Junior League?"
Not waiting for her answer, he rasped out his disapproval of girls who
gave plays and made themselves conspicuous. He did not like it even
if it was in the name of charity. "Young girls are getting altogether
too bold nowadays!" Eleanor kept quiet. That was a time, she said,
when young people did not disagree with their elders.[17] But her interest had been stirred, and later when she was asked why she didn't join
the Junior League, she was the readier to do so because it had been
criticized. She was acquainted with Mary Harriman and Nathalie
Henderson, who were rallying the debutantes to give entertainments
to help finance the "college settlements." While all debutantes were
automatically inscribed as associate members on the lists of the Junior
League, only a few were volunteering for active work in the settlement houses.

Eleanor soon joined this group. Along with Jean Reid, the daughter
of Whitelaw Reid, she was assigned to work with the settlement house
on Rivington Street. After a brief introductory lecture in "practical
sociology," they plunged into teaching calisthenics and dancing to a
group of young East Side girls, although they had had no previous
training in how to manage children in groups. Jean played the piano,
Eleanor was the teacher. "I had been in calisthenics classes and in dancing classes," wrote Eleanor, "and all I could do was put to use methods
I had seen used and which I thought were good." The results were
sometimes ludicrous. "The contribution of the college settlements to
the education of the middle class," observed the historians Mary and
Charles Beard, "was perhaps greater than its services to the poor."[18]

Until then Eleanor's contact with poor children had been slight: she had helped her father serve Thanksgiving dinner to the Newsboys; she had assisted Uncle Vallie in decorating the Christmas tree for children in Hell's Kitchen; and she had trailed along with her aunts to sing at the Bowery Mission. But these activities had been charity, a continuation of the kind of work that had been started by her grandfather. Now she saw misery and exploitation on a scale she had not dreamed possible, and the pleas for legislative reform were more compelling to her because she saw the conditions to which they were addressed.

The Rivington Street Settlement, two blocks south of Houston Street in one of the most densely populated parts of the city, was a harsh introduction to social realities. When the settlement was founded in 1889 the neighborhood had been German. Then it had become predominantly Jewish; and now it was changing again as Italian emigrants flooded into the country. Settlement workers urged the residents to welcome the Italians and not to use the derogatory term "dago." The settlement activities were practical—kindergartens for the young children, a gymnasium, classes in cooking, carpentry, art, and dancing, picnics in the woods and at the beach, and a summer camp in the country—and the settlement was also the center of neighborhood effort for civic improvement. The headworker, in her report for the year Eleanor was there, hailed the advances that had been made— cleaner streets, tenements with more light and air, new schools—and then she added: "That further improvements will follow is assured by the fact that the neighborhood is beginning to demand them and to speak for itself, a most encouraging sign."[19]

The settlement's policy of encouraging slum dwellers to stand together and claim their rights was one phase of Eleanor's education in the realities of social change. Another was in the relationship of law and politics to social conditions. The girls and young women in the clubs and classes often failed to appear, and when the settlement workers investigated they found the explanation in the excessively long hours the poor were obliged to work. The College Settlement Association enlisted the help of Miss Mary Van Kleeck of Smith College to make a study of working hours of women in factories. Such a report, it was hoped, would prod state authorities into enforcing the law that limited the hours that women and children could work to sixty per week.

The Van Kleeck report startled the city. Ten hours, it noted quietly, "make a long day spent watching and feeding a needle which sets

4,000 stitches a minute; or treading in standing position the pedals of an ironing machine." Yet Miss Van Kleeck found that it was "not uncommon" for young girls in factories to work twelve, thirteen, and even fourteen hours a day, six days a week, at a weekly wage of $6.

Eleanor took her duties at Rivington Street very seriously—too much so, in the view of her cousin Susie, in whose home on East Seventy-sixth Street Eleanor was staying. When her afternoon at Rivington Street conflicted with a party, Cousin Susie insisted that Eleanor give up the class; Eleanor gave up the party. "She says I am the most obstinate person she knows as she would have preferred my giving out this afternoon and going to-night!" Cousin Susie pitied the man Eleanor might marry. For her part, Eleanor pitied Cousin Susie's husband, Henry Parish, whom the family described as "a dear sweet man" except that he never dared stand up to his wife and at Newport kept his bottle of Scotch hidden in his hatbox. Cousin Susie was a very tall, very proper woman, who in motion reminded the younger people of "a full-rigged ship."[20] She was strait-laced and opinionated and refused to have anything to do with people who were outside Society. Nevertheless, she was very kind to Eleanor, and although Eleanor refused to be frightened by Susie's apprehensions about her safety on Rivington Street, she was devoted to her and her husband.

Eleanor liked the settlement-house children and they liked her.

> Poor Jean [Reid] has grippe and couldn't go to Rivington Street with me today, so I took my first class alone and I've not had such real fun for weeks. The children were dears, a little obstreperous at times but I hope they enjoyed it in the end as much as I did. Two of them walked back to the cars [?] with me and we had such a nice talk, I cannot see how Caroline and Gwendolyn after going once could miss as they do. I don't believe either of them really cares for children or they would love going down there and not treat it as a burden. I stayed very late and only got home at a quarter to six and it was such a relief to know that I didn't have to start out for the Barker's at once.[21]

Jean recovered and returned to the class, and Eleanor was relieved that she too enjoyed the assignment: "I thought she might hate it and refuse to go again!"[22]

When Gwendolyn Burden needed help in Ludlow Street in her sewing class, Eleanor volunteered, "but the children were not as nice as mine and I am glad I do not have to go regularly." Occasionally she had disciplinary problems at Rivington Street and had to send children home, which she "hated" doing, but on the whole the experience, after the agonies of trying to shine in society, was a reassuring one. Her class at Rivington Street, she summed up, was "the nicest part of the day."[23]

She quickly emerged as one of the leaders of the Junior League. Of a meeting at Nathalie Henderson's, she reported that it had been "a little trying... I made myself disagreeable to Mary Harriman by telling her I could not call meetings at a moment's notice and by opposing several of her suggestions successfully!"

The settlement house was part of a network of reform organizations that included the Public Education Association, the Women's Trade Union League, and the Consumers League. Eleanor became a member of the Consumers League, a militant group devoted to combating the abuses disclosed in the Van Kleeck report. The league was headed by the redoubtable Maud Nathan; Eleanor's aunt, Mrs. Douglas Robinson, was a vice president, as was Mrs. Fulton Cutting, Helen's mother. It operated by means of a "white list" that named the retail establishments which dealt "justly" with their employees and which the league's members and friends were urged to patronize. To get on the "white list" a retail firm, among other requirements, had to give equal pay for equal work, observe a ten-hour working day, and pay a minimum wage of $6 per week. Another of the league's major goals was to obtain legislation that would prohibit child labor, and, in particular, the cruel "sweating system" where children of kindergarten age toiled away in their slum homes at such jobs as making artificial flowers.

The league's key committee was the one that determined whether a merchant had complied with the league's standards. The Rivington Street headworker was on that committee, and Eleanor became involved in its activities.

Her first trip to check on conditions in department stores proved to be valueless. Did the women have stools to sit on behind the counters when they were not waiting on customers, she was asked afterward. She had not looked, she confessed; it had not occurred to her that perhaps they could never sit down and rest. "And if I had looked I would not have understood what it meant until someone else pointed out its meaning." But she was a willing pupil, and the league asked her to investigate the sweatshops in which artificial feathers and flowers were being made.

I was appalled. In those days, these people often worked at home, and I felt I had no right to invade their private dwellings, to ask questions, to investigate conditions. I was frightened to death.

But this was what had been required of me and I wanted to be useful. I entered my first sweatshop and walked up the steps of my first tenement.... I saw little children of four or five sitting at tables until they dropped with fatigue.... [24]

She was finding a vocation and a role, and she applied herself with scrupulous diligence to the settlement tasks. Already her debutante friends were classing her with Mary Harriman and Nathalie Henderson, whom they regarded as "superior beings," and even among her more frivolous debutante associates she was not an object of fun. Would-be scoffers were deterred by Eleanor's dignity and universal helpfulness. She did not have "social lightheartedness," but girls liked to tell her their most intimate secrets because she gave everyone the feeling that she was interested in them, as indeed she was.

Among the young men, too, she had many admirers, including some whose interest was serious. But they had missed their chance. A young man who knew his mind had asked her for her hand, and she had become secretly engaged.

10. "FOR LIFE, FOR DEATH"

―――――――――――――――――――◇

FRANKLIN ROOSEVELT'S MOST FATEFUL ACTION AS A GAY, CHARM-ing, princely young man of twenty-one was to pick shy, somewhat plain Eleanor Roosevelt to be his wife. It showed remarkable per-spicacity. We can only guess at his reasons; his courtship letters were burned—by Eleanor Roosevelt, probably in 1937 when she was writ-ing the first volume of her autobiography and his youthful avowals of constancy unto death were perhaps too painful to reread. She said she burned them because they were too private. He preserved hers.

Franklin was a junior at Harvard when he encountered Eleanor after her return from Allenswood and began to see in her an appealing woman rather than interesting cousin. They had run into each other occasionally before she went abroad. At a Christmas party in 1898 at the West Orange country house of Eleanor's aunt, Corinne Robin-son, a sixteen-year-old Franklin, then a Groton student, had asked an unhappy, pathetically dressed fourteen-year-old Eleanor to dance, for which she had been deeply grateful. But it had not been just cousinly chivalry. A few weeks before the Robinson party Franklin had writ-ten his parents, "How about Teddy Robinson and Eleanor Roosevelt? They would go well and help to fill out the chinks at a Hyde Park Christmas party." It was about this time, too, that he was said to have remarked to his mother, "Cousin Eleanor has a very good mind."[1]

Still, his interest in Eleanor was scarcely distinguishable from his lively awareness of a number of other teen-age girls, including Alice Roosevelt, with whom he exchanged a few teasing letters. And they did not correspond while Eleanor was at Allenswood, although both were already conscientious letter writers. But one day during the sum-mer of Eleanor's return from finishing school, Franklin saw her on the train to Tivoli, hastened over, and took her to the car in which his mother was sitting. Eleanor remembered the occasion all her life. Sara, although her husband had died two years before, was still entirely in black, with a heavy veil that fell from her hat to the ground, as was the custom for widows. Eleanor was held spellbound by her beauty, and the son was as handsome as the mother—tall, slender, with sloping shoulders. His nose, pinched at the bridge, gave him a patrician aspect; his eyes were a cool grayish-blue, arch and gay and jauntily self-confident. And Eleanor, however insecure she may have felt, was outwardly self-assured, clothed with the authority of three years abroad. Eleanor at seventeen, said Caroline Drayton, one of her contemporaries, was "dear [and] affectionate . . . simple [and] spontaneous." She had a Gibson-girl figure, a pensive dignity, the charm of tenderness, and the sweetness of youth.

Franklin's interest was revived, and later that autumn when the social season was under way he came down from Harvard for some of the debutante parties. Although Eleanor nowhere mentioned his presence at the social affairs that were such "agony" to her, her name began to appear in his diary with increasing frequency. He noted that she was at the horse show, and two weeks later, when he was again in New York for Christine Roosevelt's dance, his diary read "Lunched with Eleanor." And before he went to Hyde Park for Christmas he shopped with his mother until 3:30 but then slipped away for "tea with Eleanor."

After Christmas week in Hyde Park and New York he, too, was invited to Washington for the New Year's festivities, and stayed with Mrs. Cowles. She was "Cousin Bamie" to him, and he was one of her favorites in the younger generation. He went to afternoon tea with Alice at the White House and noted in his diary that Eleanor was staying with Alice. At the New Year's Day reception, he and Eleanor stood in the "inner circle" and watched with fascination the thousands filing through the White House to shake hands with the president, who afterward went out for his customary canter "as fresh as a daisy," according to the papers. They all dined with the president, and then "to theatre and sit near Eleanor." "Very interesting day," the young man commented in his diary.[2]

A month later, Eleanor was among those his half brother Rosy invited to celebrate Franklin's twenty-first birthday, an affair that Franklin described as "very jolly!" At the end of the school year in June there was a house party at Hyde Park, and Eleanor's name began to appear in Sara Roosevelt's journal as well as in her son's diary. "Muriel [Robbins, Franklin's cousin, also called Moo], Eleanor and her maid, Franklin, Lathrop Brown and Jack Minturn came yesterday. Mary Edmund and young Hollister came to dine. Had singing after dinner."[3] They all walked to the river "in the rain," Franklin recorded, dined with the Rogers, who were next-door neighbors, played tennis and blind man's bluff. It was a long week end. Eleanor arrived on Saturday, and Franklin took her to the train on Tuesday.

He then dashed back to Cambridge to pick up his diploma. He had obtained it in three years but planned to return to Harvard to do graduate work and, what was more important to him, to run the *Crimson*, of which he had been elected president. His degree in his pocket, he boarded the *Half Moon*, the family's sixty-foot schooner, in New Bedford, raced her off Newport and then sailed her back to Hyde Park. Again there was a house party which Eleanor, accompanied by the inevitable maid, attended, along with those whom Sara described as "my six young people." They sailed, dined on board the *Half Moon*, went on a hay ride, took the cliff walk along the river. A week later Sara noted in her journal that everyone had had tea with Eleanor at Tivoli, but if she suspected that Franklin's interest in Eleanor was becoming serious, she said nothing, not even when, before going abroad July 24, he invited Eleanor to come to Campobello after he returned. She arrived on August 28, and on September 3 Sara noted, "Eleanor left at six with her maid. We took her to Eastport, on the *Half Moon*." A more perceptive observation was made by Mrs. Hartman Kuhn of Boston, whose red-shingled, green-shuttered summer home was next to the Roosevelts' at Campobello. When Franklin and Eleanor announced their engagement fifteen months later, Mrs. Kuhn wrote Eleanor that she could not pretend to be surprised: "The first summer at Campo I saw most clearly how Franklin admired you. . . ."

Few saw that that admiration was turning to love. Already Franklin was a man who masked his deepest feelings in debonair banter, preferring to gain his way by diplomacy and charm rather than by frontal assault. Indeed, many of his contemporaries belittled him as being all shining surface and artifice. Young Corinne Robinson taxed him with lacking conviction and laughingly called him "hypocrite" and "feather duster."[4] His Oyster Bay female cousins did not consider him a great prize in the matrimonial sweepstakes. "He was the kind of boy whom you invited to the dance, but not the dinner," said Alice; "a good little mother's boy whose friends were dull, who belonged to the minor clubs and who never was at the really gay parties."[5] But this was said years later when envy and politics had sharply divided the Oyster Bay and Hyde Park clans.

Some of the Delanos had their own theory to explain Alice's spitefulness. "Alice was angry about Franklin's choosing Eleanor," Franklin's cousin Laura Delano maintained. "That's always in the picture. She was angry because she didn't catch him."[6] In the course of researching this book, when the author asked Mrs. Longworth about this, her expressive face registered incredulity, alarm, and horror, not wholly unmixed with interest, as if her very active mind were examining the story for all its possibilities. "I liked him, of course," she finally said, but he was too "prissy," too much of "a good little mother's boy" for her. And since she was not entirely persuaded that the interviewer believed these protestations, Mrs. Longworth told the *Washington Post* that she had "tape recorded her denial, so that future generations can hear in her own voice and words just how absurd she considers such a suggestion to be."[7]

No other contemporary of Eleanor, Alice, or Franklin confirmed Laura Delano's intriguing theory; on the contrary, everyone was skeptical of it, but they also disagreed with the Oyster Bay portrait of Franklin as a mollycoddled lightweight. "They exaggerate" was the dry comment of a contemporary who went to the same balls, attended the same football games, moved in the same social circles, and was Republican in her sympathies.[8] As an undergraduate, Franklin led a strenuous social life in Boston and New York and suffered from no lack of invitations to dinners as well as dances. His diary was sprinkled with the names of young ladies with whom he teased and flirted, and when the news of his engagement to Eleanor was disclosed more than one young female heart must have fluttered with regret. No, he could pick and choose, and his choice of Eleanor showed that beneath his surface gaiety there was seriousness and a life plan. "We used to say 'poor Franklin,'" Alice Longworth acknowledged. "The joke was on us."

While neither his mother nor his friends seemed to perceive the strength of his feeling for Eleanor, she, persuaded of her plainness, refused to believe it. He had stayed on at Campobello after she left, a good part of the time in the company of Evelyn Carter, daughter of the governor of Barbados, who made no secret of her interest in him. From Campo he went to Oyster Bay to stay with the Emlen Roosevelts; Alice Parker, an attractive debutante whom he had seen in London, was also a guest. And Miss Carter turned up again at Lenox while Franklin was visiting Mrs. Kuhn before returning to Hyde Park. But if these dalliances caused Eleanor to wonder about the young man's intentions, she should have been reassured by her overnight stay at Hyde Park on her way back to Tivoli from Groton, where she had left Hall. Franklin took her on a long ride through the woods in the morning and in the afternoon on a drive in the dog cart. Their talk was intimate and relaxed. She told him of her worries about "the Kid," as she called Hall, and he spoke of his plans for the *Crimson* and his indecision about whether to enroll in the law school or the graduate faculty. She must have sensed that he was eager to please her, for he left for Cambridge the next day, ushered at the football game, and then went immediately to Groton so that he could report to her that "the Kid" was getting on "finely" and was "much liked." No matter how devoted he was to Groton, he hardly would have left Cambridge the week end that he was preparing, almost singlehandedly (since most of the staff was not yet back), to get out the first issue of the *Crimson* if the had not wished to impress the young lady in Tivoli with his thoughtfulness.

She, too, was interested, even to the point of being a little jealous, as her first letter to him after his return to Cambridge reveals, but she was also on guard for a rebuff.

[Oct. 3, 1903]
Tivoli

Dear Franklin   Friday
Many thanks for your note & the "token from the sea," which I think I should have sent to someone else however, don't you?

Hall wrote me that he had seen you at Groton last Sunday. It was kind of you to look him up when you must have had so much to do. I hope he is all right. I can't tell much from his letters.

Did you have to work very hard on the "Crimson"? I hoped someone would turn up to help in the end.

I am so anxious to hear what you have decided to do this year & also whether you can come here on the 16th. I am hoping that you will be able to get down & of course I would like you to come back here after the game on the 17th if Cousin Sally does not mind & you are willing to stay in this quiet spot.

Please don't do anything you don't want to do however as I shall quite understand if you decide to go to Hyde Park instead of coming here.

Yours in haste,

Is the address on this right?   Eleanor Roosevelt.

"It is not so much brilliance as effort that is appreciated here," wrote Franklin in his first editorial, addressed to the freshman class—the "determination to accomplish something." He felt that with Eleanor at his side his own great dreams would stand a better chance of realization. "It was nice of you to write me," Eleanor said in her next letter, "and you know quite well you need not apologize for writing about yourself. I should think history and political economy would be most interesting and much the most useful for you in the future and *of course* you are going to get an A.M."

An indignant reproach in the same letter made it clear that this was more than cousinly advice. "What were you thinking of when you wrote not to tell me whether you could get down on the 16th and come to me or not?" she asked. She cared a great deal, even if convention prescribed that she betray no interest in him and even if her grandmother looked askance when she received a letter from a man. Franklin had not replied to Eleanor because he had wanted to find out first what his mother was planning for the week end of the Harvard–West Point game. Who was coming on the sixteenth, he had written her. "Are H. [Helen] Cutting, Eleanor and Moo [Muriel Robbins] coming to us?" Everything was arranged satisfactorily, and although it poured on the day of the game it was a joyful week end for Franklin and Eleanor. "Harvard wins 5 to 0," he recorded in his Line-A-Day, "Eleanor and I catch train, others miss it, drive up from Poughkeepsie." An unexpected participant in some of their gaieties was Alice Roosevelt, who that week end was a guest of the Ogden Millses at their estate a few miles up the Hudson at Staatsburgh; she came down, escorted by a young man, for tea.

"Cousin Sally [Sara Roosevelt] was very sad after you left on Sunday," Eleanor reported to Cambridge, "and the only thing which cheered her at all was the thought of having you on the 3d all to herself." The romance was flourishing. She now signed herself "Your affectionate cousin" and made her plans with his in mind. She had been invited to a party at the Levi Mortons' and was unable to decide whether or not to go; however, "I think I'll chance there being someone there I like and accept."

She worried about his health. "I suppose you are hard at work now, but please be a little careful of your eyes, for it is really foolish to fool with them you know, and besides it worries Cousin Sally so when you are not all right. She spoke of it several times after you had gone." But then, a little conscience-stricken that she might sound too schoolma'amish, she apologized. "I am afraid this letter has a good deal of horrid advice in it. Please remember, however, that you have told me I was 'grandmotherly' and don't blame me too much!"

Grandmotherly! Do Prince Charmings fall in love with "grandmotherly" young ladies? Yes, if under his gay surface the prince harbors large ambitions that require a helpmate rather than a playfellow to bring them to fruition. "Even at that age," recalled Isabella Greenway, who, as a debutante, took New York society by storm in 1904, "life had, through her orphanage, touched her and made its mark in a certain aloofness from the careless ways of youth. The world had come to her as a field of responsibility rather than as a playground."[9]

Neither young Roosevelt was leading a monastic life. Franklin's letters to his mother spoke of a "small dance" at the golf club, a visit to Beverly, a swimming party at the home of Alice Sohier, a Boston belle, week ends at New Bedford. Eleanor moved from one country house to another: one week end she was at Llewellyn Park, Cousin Susie's estate in the fashionable Oranges; she spent another at Ophir Hall, the Westchester establishment of Whitelaw Reid, owner of the *New York Tribune* and the father of Jean Reid, Eleanor's associate at Rivington Street; and she accepted the invitation of Franklin's cousin Muriel Robbins to attend the Tuxedo Ball. The Boston Brahmins had created Brook Farm; New York society had Tuxedo Park, a 600,000-acre country club community thirty miles from New York City whose "cottages" were casemented in the English style, whose clubhouse was staffed with English servants, and whose grounds were enclosed by a high fence to guard against intruders from the lower orders.

"I am glad you think I am going to enjoy the Tuxedo Ball," she wrote Franklin. "I do not feel quite so confident as I haven't seen any of my last winter's friends in so long that I fully expect to be forgotten." Did she go to the ball in order to prove to him that she was not too "grandmotherly"? "Tuxedo was great fun," her next letter insisted, "and I only wish you had been there, though I don't doubt you had a more restful time wherever you were, as we were up till all hours of the night, which nearly finished me." She would be going up to the Mortons' on the 3:30 train and if he did not have to go up earlier "it would be splendid to go up together." There was a mild rebuke in this letter, one that would be repeated often in the future. "By the way do you know you were an 'unconscionable' time answering my last letter and you would not be hearing from me so promptly if I did not want you surely to lunch with me on the 14th." Sara Roosevelt's entry in her journal for November 14 indicated that the Morton week end had worked out as Eleanor had planned.

> Got up at 7 and at 7:30 Franklin and Lyman came from Boston. After they had their baths, we all had breakfast and we all lunched with Eleanor at Sherry's, also her cousin Mrs. Parish. We came up at 3:30 and Eleanor, Franklin and Lyman went up to Ellerslie to the Mortons to spend Sunday.

Ellerslie was another palatial country house, high above the Hudson at Rhinecliff, owned by Levi P. Morton, who had been governor of New York and vice president under Benjamin Harrison. The Morton girls were sophisticated and fun-loving, temperamentally closer to Alice than to Eleanor. "I am glad you enjoyed the Morton's," Eleanor wrote Franklin, "as I thought it very pleasant." Her praise of the party was tepid, but her comments on a poem that Franklin had sent her on his return to Cambridge were much livelier. She thought it was "splendid" poetry, "but what ideals you have to live up to! I like 'Fear nothing and be faithful unto death,' but I must say I wonder how many of 'we poor mortals' could act up to that!"*

In mid-October Franklin invited her to Cambridge for the Harvard-Yale game, after which he hoped to join her at Groton during her visit to Hall. She would accept, she replied, if Muriel Robbins and her mother also were going. Muriel's brother Warren was at Harvard and they could chaperone her. On Saturday, November 21, Franklin wrote in his diary:

> In town at 10:30 and Eleanor and I walk to the Library, see the pictures, and then walk up Beacon Hill. I out to lunch in Cambridge and lead the cheering at the Harvard-Yale game, 16–0, but our team does well. Show Eleanor my room and see them off to Groton.

The next day he followed Eleanor to Groton and spent the day with her, beginning with church in the morning and ending with chapel in

---

*Efforts by the Library of Congress and others to trace the poem from the line quoted by Eleanor were unsuccessful. Perhaps it was written by young Franklin Roosevelt, in which case the loss to history caused by Mrs. Roosevelt's destruction of his courtship letters is even more regrettable, even though the last part of the line, indeed the whole sentence, echoes the Bible, Revelations 2:10.[10]

the evening. During this visit to Groton he proposed to her. How he put it we do not know. Some biographers have written that he said, "I have only a few bright prospects now," to which the nineteen-year-old Eleanor is said to have replied, "I have faith in you. I'm sure you'll really amount to something someday."[11] This account leaves one dissatisfied. Another version seems more in character. According to this account, Franklin said that he was sure he would amount to something some day, "with your help," and the surprised girl replied, "Why me? I am plain. I have little to bring you."[12]

Eleanor returned to New York trembling with excitement even though she was beset by questions. She found Franklin irresistible, but was he sure? Was she? What would happen to her brother Hall? What was her duty to her grandmother? And, as so often in her life, her joy was shadowed by tragedy. Her Great-Uncle James King Gracie had died, and her first letter to Franklin after the Groton week end first dwelt on that. "I am more sorry than I can say for he has always been very kind and dear to us and he and Aunt Gracie both loved my Father very dearly and so it is just another link gone." She was worried, too, about her Aunt Corinne, for whom the death was a terrible blow and who was "almost crazy" with grief.

> In spite of it all I am very happy. I have been thinking of many things which you and I must talk over on Sunday. Only one thing I want to tell you now. Please don't tell your Mother you have to come down to see Mr. Marvin on Sunday, because I never want her to feel that she has been deceived & if you have to tell her I would rather you said you were coming to see me for she need not know why. Don't be angry with me Franklin for saying this, & of course you must do as you think best. Ellen told me they were all coming down Saturday night by boat so you will have plenty of company. Please don't get tired out this week & try to rest a little bit at Fairhaven. I am afraid this letter sounds very doleful, for I really am sorry about dear Uncle Gracie & the whole day has been a bit trying so please forgive me & the next will be cheerier & more coherent I hope! Goodnight,
> Always affectionately
> Eleanor Roosevelt.

Her next letter reveals something of what she and Franklin had said to each other that Sunday in Groton. It represents the first time she felt free to give voice to the strength of her feeling for Franklin.

[Nov. 24, 1903]

Franklin dear,   Tuesday night

I promised that this letter should be cheerier so I don't suppose I
ought to write to-night for the day has been very trying. I wanted
to tell you though that I *did* understand & that I don't know what I
should have done all day if your letter had not come. Uncle Gracie's
funeral is to be on Friday at ten. I have been twice to-day to Auntie
Corinne's & I have promised to spend to-morrow morning there
also. She looks so worn & I wish I could do something more to help
her. She seems to have every thing to arrange & settle. Teddy came
this afternoon I am thankful to say so he will be some help to her &
a great comfort. I am dreading Friday. I know I ought not to feel as
I do or even to think of myself but I have not been to a funeral in
ten years & it makes me shudder to think of it. The others have all
gone to the play so I am all alone to-night as I would of course go
nowhere this week, & I have been thinking & wishing that you were
here. However, I know it is best for you not [to] come until Sunday
& for me also as I should be a very dreary not to say a very weary
companion just at present & there are so many things I know I ought
to think of before I see you again. I am afraid so far I've only thought
of myself & I don't seem to be able to do anything else just now.

   Do you remember the verse I tried to recite to you last Sunday?
I found it to-day & I am going to write it out for you, because it is
in part what it all means to me:

> *Unless you can think when the song is done,*
>   *No other is left in the rhythm;*
> *Unless you can feel, when left by one,*
>   *That all men else go with him;*
> *Unless you can know, when upraised by his breath,*
>   *That your beauty itself wants proving;*
> *Unless you can swear, "For life, for death!"*
>   *Oh, fear to call it loving!*
>
> *Unless you can muse in a crowd all day*
>   *On the absent face that has fixed you;*
> *Unless you can love, as the angels may,*
>   *With the breath of heaven betwixt you;*
> *Unless you can dream that his faith is fast,*
>   *Through behooving & unbehooving;*

Unless you can die when the dream is past—
  Oh, never call it loving![13]

  I wondered if it meant "for life, for death" to you at first but I
know it does now. I do not know what to write. I cannot write
what I want. I can only wait & long for Sunday when I shall tell
you all I feel I cannot write.

  Goodnight. I hope you will all have a very happy Thanksgiving
at Fairhaven & please don't get tired out by working at night.

  Always devotedly
  Eleanor.

She had wondered whether she, too, cared enough to be able to
say that it was "for life, for death," and she discussed her feelings
with Cousin Susie on her return to New York. Whatever her cousin's
response, Eleanor's "great curiosity" about life and her "desire to participate in every experience that might be the lot of woman" pulled
her toward marriage. She was swept up by "the urge to be a part of
the stream of life," and it seemed entirely natural and right to her to
say yes to Franklin.[14]

  Franklin, meanwhile, had gone to Fairhaven, the Delano clan's
gathering place, where he told his mother that he had proposed to
Eleanor. "Franklin gave me quite a startling announcement," she
wrote in her journal. Then he went to New York where there was a
note from Eleanor: "Mrs. Parish wants you to lunch with us tomorrow
if you can and also to take tea with us. I do hope that you will come
to both if you can for I want you every minute of your stay."

  "It is impossible to tell you what these last two days have been to
me," she wrote him afterward, thinking he was on his way to Cambridge, "but I know they have meant the same to you so that you will
understand that I love you dearest and I hope that I shall always prove
worthy of the love which you have given me. I have never known
before what it was to be absolutely happy."

  But Franklin had not left New York. His mother had returned,
and it is not difficult to sense the surprise and disapproval in the terse
entry, "I find Franklin still in New York." The next day he went to
Seventy-sixth Street and accompanied Eleanor to see Sara. "I had a
long talk with the dear child."[15]

  To Sara, Franklin's announcement meant surrendering her exclusive relationship with her son and her plans for their life together after he left Harvard. She did not surrender easily. Could they *really* be sure they cared enough, she asked them. They were young—shouldn't both of them think it over and see what the lapse of time and being away from each other would do to their feelings? Her father, Warren Delano, had married at thirty-three, after he had made a name for himself and had something to offer a woman. Franklin was only twenty-one and Eleanor was just nineteen; they had plenty of time.

These were the reservations that Sara expressed, but Eleanor thought an additional reason was her desire that he should make "a more worldly and social match."[16] There was probably another constraint that was never voiced but that was always in the background—Eleanor's father's alcoholism, not to mention her uncles'. Girls were carefully chaperoned, and Eleanor radiated purity and innocence, but the maid who invariably accompanied her reflected her own or her family's awareness that she was more vulnerable than other girls her age to rumor and gossip if she overstepped the strict line of decorum that society drew for young ladies. As uneasy as Sara may have been about Eleanor's flawed heritage, she kept it to herself. She only pleaded with them to keep their engagement secret for a year, during which time she would take Franklin on a cruise as a test of how they really felt. They agreed to her conditions.

After Franklin returned to Harvard, he wrote his mother a comforting letter.

> I know what pain I must have caused you and you know I wouldn't do it if I really could have helped it—mais tu sais, me voila! That's all that could be said—I know my mind, have known it for a long time, and know that I could never think otherwise: Result: I am the happiest man just now in the world; likewise the luckiest—And for you, dear Mummy, you know that nothing can ever change what we have always been & always will be to each other—only now you have two children to love & to love you—and Eleanor as you know will always be a daughter to you in every true way—

Eleanor sent a sympathetic and understanding letter to Sara, tenderly buttressing Franklin's point that Sara was gaining a daughter, not losing a son.

8 East 76th Street

Dec. 2d, 1903,

Dearest Cousin Sally,   Wednesday.

I must write you & thank you for being so good to me yesterday.
I know just how you feel & how hard it must be, but I do so want
you to learn to love me a little. You must know that I will always
try to do what you wish for I have grown to love you very dearly
during the past summer.

It is impossible for me to tell you how I feel toward Franklin.
I can only say that my one great wish is always to prove worthy
of him.

I am counting the days to the 12th when I hope Franklin & you
will both be here again & if there is anything which I can do for
you you will write me, won't you?

With much love dear Cousin Sally,

Always devotedly   Eleanor.

Eleanor's days were full of activity but they were dominated by
thoughts of her beloved, to whom she wrote now with ever deepening commitment.

Dearest Franklin,

Though I only wrote last night I must write you just a line this
morning to tell you that I miss you every moment & that you are
never out of my thoughts dear for one moment. I was thinking last
night of the difference which, one short week can make in one's life.
Everything is changed for me now. I am so happy. Oh! so happy &
I love you *so* dearly. I cannot begin to write you all I should like to
say, but you know it all I am sure & I hope that you too dearest are
very, very happy. I am counting the days to the 12th & the days in
between seem so very long.

She was generous to Sara in spite of the onerous conditions the older
woman had exacted from them.

I found the sweetest, dearest letter here from your Mother last night.
Boy dear,* I realize more and more how hard it is for her & we
must both try always to make her happy & I do hope some day she

---

*Eleanor's father had been addressed as "Boy dear" and "Boy darling" by his Aunt Ella.

will learn to love me. She is coming to town to-day for a few days & says she will telephone me & try to see me.

She had told Cousin Susie of Sara's reaction to the engagement. Cousin Susie felt, Eleanor wrote Franklin, "as I do that your Mother's feelings ought to be considered first of all." Cousin Susie also thought it would be all right to tell Eleanor's grandmother what they had decided, and Eleanor went to Tivoli to see Mrs. Hall. "I have told her that I shall not be definitely engaged until next year and she has *promised* me to tell no one that I am even thinking of such a thing, so I hope all will go well."[17]

Was she sure that she was really in love, her grandmother asked. "I solemnly answered 'yes,'" she wrote in her autobiography, "and yet I know now that it was years later before I understood what being in love was or what loving really meant."[18]

11. MOTHER AND SON

◇

AT THE OLDER WOMAN'S REQUEST, ELEANOR MET SARA Roosevelt two days after Franklin's return to Cambridge. The session turned out to be quite painful, the first of many duels that in time would cause all of them great agony. The gracious lady, despite her protestations of regard for "the delightful child of nineteen whom I had known and loved since babyhood," was determined to create difficulties for the two young people. And in the contest of wills that Sara foresaw with her equally stubborn son she did not scruple to take advantage of Eleanor's touching eagerness to "always try to do" what the older woman wished. But if Sara had seen the letter that Eleanor wrote at her request to Franklin, she would not have drawn much comfort from it. Although Eleanor had transmitted Sara's views to Franklin, as Sara had asked, in doing so she made it perfectly clear what she herself wanted.

[Dec. 4, 1903]

Boy darling,   Friday evening

I have rather a hard letter to write you tonight & I don't quite know how to say what I must say & I am afraid I am going to give you some trouble, however I don't see how I can help it.

I went to the apartment this morning & saw your Mother there for a few minutes & then we went out together & had a long talk. She is coming down next Friday to meet you & she wants us to lunch & dine with her & then she wants you to go to Hyde Park with her Sunday morning. Helen and Cousin Rosie have been asking when you were coming home. She thinks they are sure to hear you are in New York & say that you are loafing & never coming home & she also says that if we go to church together we are sure to be seen. She also thinks that you ought to go home on account of the place, & your interest in it. She asked me to write you & I

tell you all this dear because I think it only fair. Of course it will
be a terrible disappointment to me not to have you on Sunday as I
have been looking forward to it & every moment with you is very
precious as we have so little of each other but I don't want you to
stay if you feel it is your duty to go up & I shall understand of course.
I realize that we may be seen if we go to church together, but we
will have to choose some small church. However, I suppose your
Mother feels more strongly on the subject than I do & I am afraid
I must leave the whole thing to you to decide. Whatever you do I
shall know to be right but I don't think your Mother quite realizes
what a very hard thing she was asking me to do for I am hungry
for every moment of your time, but you mustn't let what I want
interfere with what you feel to be right dearest.

Now for the second thing. Cousin Sally said she did not think
you would want to go on a trip now & she said she thought of taking a house in Boston for three months. She said she hoped I would
come & stay once or twice during that time but if she took the house
she did not want you to be coming to New York. I can understand
how she feels but I'm afraid I can't promise not to want you more
than twice in all that time. However I think you & she will have to
talk it over next Saturday & decide that also. We also spoke about
the holidays but I think that will wait until I see you as these were
the only two things she asked me to write about.

I haven't had a letter from you this evening & I am wondering
what has happened. I did so want it, but I hope it will come in the
morning. I am going to Tivoli by the early train & coming down
by the 7.19 on Sunday.

Oh! boy dear, I want you so much. I'm worried & tired & cross &
I don't know what I ought to do. Please be very careful of yourself
dearest & don't work yourself to death & when you can write me
what you decide about Sunday.

Always your loving
Eleanor.

The decision was now up to Franklin, who was already aware of
his mother's feeling; she had taken the precaution of writing him herself. As she had anticipated, he was not impressed by her arguments,
although as a devoted son he was prepared to abide by her wishes if
she insisted on them.

Alpha Delta Phi Club
Dec. 6, 1903,
Dearest Mama—   Sunday.
Yours of Friday came yesterday & I have been thinking over what
you say about next Sunday—I am so glad, dear Mummy, that you
are getting over the strangeness of it all—I knew you would and
that you couldn't help feeling that not only I but you also are the
luckiest & will always be the happiest people in the world in gaining
anyone like E. to love & be loved by.

I confess that I think it would be poor policy for me to go to H.P.
next Sunday—although, as you know and don't have to be told, I
always love & try to be there all I can—I have been home twice
already this term & I feel certain that J.R.R. & Helen w'd be sure
to smell a rat if I went back for *part of a day* just a week before the
holidays, for they would know I had been in N.Y. a whole day. *Also*
if I am in N.Y. on Sunday *not a soul* need know I have been there
at all as if we go to Church at all we can go to any old one at about
100th St. & the rest of the day w'd be in the house where none c'd
see us. Of course I suppose you have told no one you w'd see me
Saturday. Now if you really can't see the way clear to my staying
in N.Y. of course I will go to H.P. with you—but you know how I
feel—and also I think that E. will be terribly disappointed, as I will,
if we can't have one of our first Sundays together—It seems a little
hard & unnecessary on us both & I shall see you all day Saturday
which I shouldn't have done had the great event not "happened." . . .

I am going to accept all invites for Xmas but don't you think
we might have a house party for one or two days—Go ahead & ask
whoever you want, we might have two girls & E. and if you name
date & telegraph I will try to get two or three fellows—Indeed I
don't intend to give up things—it w'd not be right to you or E—&
she also will keep on going to things—You can imagine how completely happy I am—it gives a stimulus to everything I do. . . .

Ever your loving son   F.D.R.

All week the battle of wills raged, although it was couched in
terms of endearment and respect; and all week Eleanor was on tenterhooks awaiting the outcome. He should not work too hard, she cautioned Franklin, "for I don't want to receive a wreck next Saturday.
I am growing more and more impatient as the time draws near and
I can hardly bear to think that you may not be able to stay here on

Sunday." That was Tuesday. On Wednesday she still was hopeful that Sara would not insist on Franklin's going to Hyde Park, "for then I shall have you all to myself on Sunday," but she was afraid that his mother was going to want him on Sunday. "You see it is hard for her to realize that any one can want or need you more than she does, so I suppose I ought not to mind, only I do mind terribly, as you only can understand dear, however I mustn't complain, must I?" Sara evidently tried to force their hand by telling Rosy and his daughter Helen that Franklin was coming to Hyde Park. "I cannot tell you how sorry I am about Sunday," Eleanor wrote resignedly the next day, "but I am not in the least surprised as I knew your Mother would insist on your going to Hyde Park and since she has told Cousin Rosie and Helen it is certainly impossible for you to stay here without running the risk of their knowing it."

But young love prevailed over filial affection. However Franklin managed it, he and Eleanor spent Sunday as well as Saturday with each other. "We have had two happy days together," she wrote him after he had returned to Cambridge, "and you do not know how grateful I am for every moment which I have with you."

"She had already lived through so much unhappiness," a cousin commented, "and then to have married a man with a mother like Cousin Sally."[1] James Roosevelt had died in 1900 when Franklin was in his freshman year at college, and from that time on the forty-six-year-old Sara had focused all her thoughts, love, and energy on Franklin. For two winters she had rented a house in Boston to be close to him; they had traveled abroad together; when they were apart he wrote to her with a remarkable faithfulness. There was almost nothing she would not grant him except what was perhaps beyond the power of a lonely woman to grant an only child—independence.

"She was an indulgent mother but would not let her son call his soul his own" was the way a loyal friend of Eleanor's, quoting P. G. Wodehouse, sought to describe the strong-willed dowager's relationship with her son.[2] Except for Eleanor, no one ever exercised so strong a sway over his development, and Eleanor would always insist that not even she had so great an influence. Sara claimed Franklin as her own, even against her husband: "My son Franklin is a Delano, not a Roosevelt at all," she would assert with a proprietary air after he became president, and, strangely, in his final years his face came more and more to resemble his mother's. But the kinship was more than physical. In his will James Roosevelt had written: "I wish him

[Franklin] to be under the influence of his mother." It was an unnecessary stipulation. He already was.

Handsome Sara (Sally) Delano was twenty-six, half as old as James Roosevelt, a widower of quiet dignity, when they were married in 1880. The marriage united two of the great Hudson River families, but the disparity in their ages had caused some astonishment in society, an amused surprise that had been reflected in a letter that Eleanor's father wrote home from London in 1880.

> The sly old chap took great pleasure as indeed "Aunt Sara" (they passed for my Aunt and Uncle) did also, in relating to me the incidents and course of The Love Affair. When he slipped off before breakfast while he used to visit us in the country and say it was for his a.m. walk, the gay young dog went to post billets to his fair mistress. But truly they are a devoted couple and very kind to me.

The Delano family lived at Algonac, a stately brown and buff Victorian mansion with wide lawns overlooking the Hudson at Newburgh. Sara was born in 1854, the seventh child in a brood of eleven—six boys and five girls. Three years later her father, having lost his first China-trade fortune in the panic of 1857, returned to China to make "another million." This time it took him six years, and in 1862 he sent for his family, and Mrs. Delano and her children, including eight-year-old Sara, embarked on the square-rigger *Surprise* for the 128-day voyage. After their return to the United States at the end of the Civil War, Warren Delano invested his new wealth judiciously in coal and other securities; Sara's share of the legacy at his death was over a million dollars.[3]

Warren Delano was a patriarch, and everyone in his large Algonac household gave him unquestioning obedience. That was the custom of the times, said Sara later. But the Delano children went beyond custom: they were sure their father was infallible and knew best about everything. If her father frowned upon a young man, said Sara, that was the end of him, and she even permitted her father to help her with the letter so telling the gentleman. Perhaps James Roosevelt, twice her age, reminded her of her father, and perhaps that was a strong part of his attraction for her.[4]

James was a seventh-generation Roosevelt. His grandfather, born in 1760, also named James, had been the first of the Jacobus line to settle on the Hudson, after an attempt at gentleman-farming in Harlem had to be abandoned because of its rocky soil. The elder James died in 1847—"a highly respectable gentleman of the old school," wrote Philip Hone—and his son Isaac (1790–1863) completed his family's withdrawal from New York—and from public activity. Isaac was an eccentric. He attended Princeton and obtained a medical degree at Columbia, but never practiced because he was unable to stand the sight of blood or human pain. He turned instead to botanical research and led a secluded country existence in Dutchess County.

His son James (1828–1900), Franklin's father, was more enterprising. He went to Union College and then for two years did the Grand Tour, at one point in the turbulent year of 1848 even enlisting in Garibaldi's Red Shirts, who were then besieging Naples. But a siege can be a tedious affair, and James soon returned to the States. After attending Harvard Law School, he devoted himself to his investments and to cultivating a life of dignified rural amenity on the Hudson in the manor style of the British nobility, whom he much admired. He made several bids for great financial power by putting together mergers in coal and railroads, and even though the mergers failed his fortune was large enough to enable him to sustain the leisured life of a Hudson River gentleman at Springwood, his 1,000-acre Hyde Park estate. "English life to perfection," said Ward McAllister, who passed through Hyde Park and was enchanted with the avenue of old trees, the little village church, the gracious estates, and well-appointed houses.

Not the least of Hyde Park's English flavor came from James Roosevelt himself, a tall man with mutton chop whiskers who was rarely without his riding crop. He bred trotters and built a famous herd of Alderneys that he crossed with Jerseys and Guernseys.[5] He took the cure annually at a German spa, hunted in Pau, shot grouse in Scotland, and as a patriarch was among those who decided who belonged in New York society. While declining to take part in politics as not quite gentlemanly, he fulfilled a squire's obligation to the village, where he was a member of the Democratic caucus, belonged to the Volunteer Fire Company, was warden and vestryman of the church, and served as town supervisor. And as president of a small railroad he was entitled to take his private railroad car, the "Monon," to any part of the country. Such was the man and style of life to which Sara Delano happily accommodated herself.

James' first wife, Rebecca Howland, had died in 1876, and their son, James Roosevelt Roosevelt ("Rosy"), was a river grandee much in the mold of his father. Rosy and Sara were the same age but it was the widower who courted her, and in her eyes James Roosevelt was a delightful gentleman—high-minded, courteously persistent, and well descended. They worshiped the same household gods, had the same convictions about education and manners, *noblesse oblige*, and honor. They shared a love for the tranquil, secluded life of Hudson Valley and agreed that its old families, to most of whom they were related, embodied and defended the precious old standards in which they had been bred.

Warren Delano was not at all pleased with his daughter's choice. Although he was fond of the Hudson River squire—"the first person who has made me realize that a Democrat can be a gentleman"—he felt that James was too old for Sara. But this time she would not be swayed by his wishes, and on October 7, 1880, they were married at Algonac in a ceremony that, according to a New York paper, was witnessed "by a small number of the best representatives of New York Society." That afternoon they drove the twenty miles to Hyde Park, and by evening Sara, installed as mistress of Springwood, contentedly set about giving her husband the worshipful devotion and care she had bestowed upon her father—and removing all traces of her dead predecessor, Rebecca Howland.

Her diaries reflected the sedate, patterned existence into which she slipped without, if one is to judge by what she wrote there, pang or travail.

We drove to church in our new Victoria. In the afternoon James rowed me down to Rosedale. We hung our new water colors. The neighbors all have been to see us . . . so we are busy returning a visit or two each day which gives an object for our drives. James keeps busy. He goes to town at least once a week and has school meetings, etc. I always go to the train with him and go for him again so he is not so long away from me. James is too devoted to me.

If their life together was not as bland as these entries suggest, if the realities were different, the code under which she had been reared would have obliged her to pretend otherwise. It would have been an affront against form and manners to have acknowledged the truth if the truth were unpleasant. This same attitude would be bred into her son Franklin. "If something was unpleasant and he didn't want to know about it, he just ignored it and never talked about it. . . . I think he always thought that if you ignored a thing long enough it would settle itself."[6] James adored her and she leaned on him, endowing his every action with an almost cloying significance. Yet she was no Grandma Hall, satisfied to be cherished, protected, and helpless; she was a woman of dominating will and active mind. When James died she assumed management of Hyde Park and, over her son's protests, kept it as a gentleman's estate rather than farming it as a business. She astutely used the money she had inherited to bolster her position as matriarch. It was perhaps an ideal marriage: she was wholly reverential, always deferred to her husband's wishes, and had everything her own way.

In 1882 the circle of her contentment was complete. A son, Franklin, was born. From then on her diaries reported equally on the doings of "dear James" and "darling Franklin." Franklin's was a happy boyhood. His parents doted on him, and as the first grandchild in the vast Delano clan (a cousin having died) he was petted and made much of by aunts and uncles. His father loved "riding and driving, sailing and ice-boating, skating and tennis" and could not wait to have his son join him as a companion in these interests. Whatever the boy wanted, he was given. A pony? As soon as his legs were long enough to straddle its back. A boat? He had the use of his father's yacht the *Half Moon*, a Campobello sea captain to teach him how to handle it, and a twenty-one footer of his own. A gun? His father handed him one at eleven. There were the neighboring Rogers boys and Mary Newbold for him to play with, trees, cliff, and a river in which to test his mettle, and a succession of nurses, governesses, and tutors to serve and instruct him and for whom he could do no wrong. He did not require strict handling, his mother said, because "instinctively" he was "a good little boy."[7] When he developed an interest in birds, he was encouraged to begin a collection, as he was with stamps. And the wishes and interests that his parents did not anticipate or were reluctant to grant, he learned to obtain by charm and persuasion. What is impressive is the steadiness and professionalism that he brought to these occupations. His interest in birds resulted in the most complete collection of Dutchess County birds in existence; his philatelic interest so impressed his Uncle Fred Delano that Fred turned over his albums to his young nephew, and their combined collection became one of the world's most famous.

In later years Franklin said, "All that is in me goes back to the Hudson." His boyhood world was ordered and harmonious, his childhood secure, happy, and protected—so different from Eleanor's storm-tossed early years. "He never saw ugly moods or emotions," Sara's biographer wrote on the basis of what Sara told her. "He was never the inwardly shrinking victim of conflicting interests, envenomed jealousies or ill-tempered words."[8] If anything, he was overprotected. "Much of his time, until he went to Groton, was spent with his father and me," Sara wrote, and though she disagreed with the assessment, there were "many people who pitied him for a lonely little boy, and thought he was missing a great deal of fun."[9] Geraldine Morgan, a Livingston from Staatsburgh who called herself a tomboy, said that Franklin was unable to make the Hyde Park baseball team recruited from the great houses; that, because he spent so much time with his mother and father, he found it difficult to play with the other children; and that the children who knew him felt sorry for him.[10] In the little memoir *My Boy Franklin*, Sara insisted that she had never tried to influence young Franklin against his own tastes and inclinations, and yet she also disclosed that it was only "eventually" that she had allowed his golden curls to be shorn, and that when, at the age of five, he had become melancholy he had "clasped his hands in front of him and said 'Oh, for freedom'" when she asked him why. She had been genuinely shocked.

> That night I talked it over with his father who, I confess, often told me I nagged the boy. We agreed that unconsciously we had probably regulated the child's life too closely, even though we knew he had ample time for exercise and play.

The training and discipline of young Franklin were left to Sara, who had forceful opinions on the kind of man she wanted him to become. "Never, oh never," she confessed later, had it been her ambition for him that he should become president. "That was the last thing I should ever have imagined for him, or that he should be in public life of any sort." She had only one goal in mind for him:

> that he grow to be a fine, upright man like his father and like her own father, a beloved member of his family and a useful and respected citizen of his community just as they were, living quietly and happily along the Hudson as they had.[11]

If the role of a country squire ever appealed to young Franklin, he was opened to larger ideals, different styles of life, and new heroes when he entered Groton in 1896. His cubicle at Groton was austere and cramped compared to his quarters at home, but it was his own and he loved it. The school's headmaster, the Reverend Endicott Peabody, was a stern and exacting disciplinarian, but his influence upon young Franklin was, next to his parents', greater than anyone's. Dr. Peabody's repeated theme, inside chapel and out, was service, particularly public service. "If some Groton boys do not enter political life and do something for our land it won't be because they have not been urged," he would say.

Groton helped shape Franklin's outlook, but it was not as liberating an influence on him as Allenswood was upon Eleanor. Because Franklin's regard for Endicott Peabody equaled Eleanor's for Marie Souvestre, the differences between headmaster and headmistress—not wholly to be explained by Groton's being a school for boys and Allenswood for girls—are not without interest.

Mlle. Souvestre was an agnostic—indeed, she called herself an atheist—who insisted that no area of human belief should be immune from critical inquiry and objective study. The Reverend Peabody "was by nature a believer rather than an inquirer. Theological perplexities and subtleties simply did not affect him."[12] In politics, Souvestre frequented the great Liberal houses, was a friend of Beatrice Potter Webb and a follower of Harrison's religion of humanity. Peabody was a conservative with an abiding faith in the status quo who shaped Groton into a splendid mechanism for instilling into the sons of the old-stock, white Anglo-Saxon Protestant upper class the elements of a "manly Christian character" that would make them worthy and capable of ruling America. Souvestre sided with the oppressed minorities everywhere. Peabody believed in the superiority of the Anglo-Saxon peoples, especially the English, and considered the Spanish-American War "the most righteous war that has been undertaken in this country." Souvestre's closest friends were in the artistic community and her library was adorned with avant-garde works. Peabody distrusted art and artists, and Groton boys with serious artistic interests had to hide them if they did not wish to be labeled outsiders. Souvestre was impatient with pupils who studied by rote and mechanically repeated what they had heard from her or had read in a book. Interest should motivate study, the rector agreed, but if interest was not aroused "the work should be done as a matter of duty." Souvestre, a Dreyfusard was prepared to uphold the truth even if it meant undermining authority. At Groton "obedience came before all else"; rules and good form were upheld at the price of curiosity, sometimes of truth. In short, Peabody's values were those of order, hierarchy, discipline, and power; Souvestre's were those of heart, vision, and spirit.[13]

When Franklin left Groton he was attuned to the rector's admonitions that Groton boys should go into politics and public service. But service to whom, politics for what ends? To uphold the established order, as the rector preached, or to change it in favor of the victim, as Mlle. Souvestre believed? Roosevelt's answer in the great crisis of the thirties would be to conserve the system through the institution of change, a course that reflected the teachings of the rector tempered by those of Mlle. Souvestre as transmitted through Eleanor Roosevelt.

Sara's hopes that her son would lead the quiet life of a country gentleman were undermined from another quarter—Theodore Roosevelt. Franklin's enthusiasm as a boy at Groton and a young man at Harvard for "Cousin Theodore" was undisguised. Indeed, it was in connection with the Theodore Roosevelts that young Franklin showed that, devoted as he genuinely was to his mother, he could be as stubborn and determined as she. At the end of his first year at Groton (1897), while his parents were taking the annual cure at Bad Nauheim, Bamie wrote and asked whether Franklin could spend the Fourth of July week end with her at Oyster Bay. When his mother refused the invitation for him, he wrote back, "Please don't make any more arrangements for my future happiness." A few days later Theodore came to Groton to talk about his adventures as New York police commissioner—a talk that Franklin called "splendid"—and while there he also invited Franklin to Oyster Bay. The young man promptly accepted and wrote his parents: "I hope you will not refuse that too."

Theodore Roosevelt's compelling personality made a large impact upon the younger generation, and his influence was particularly felt at Harvard, which Franklin entered in 1900, where Theodore's example counteracted the Gold Coast cult of "Harvard indifference." He was a "great inspirer," said Eleanor, and Franklin was one of those whose inclination to enter politics definitely matured under his influence. At Harvard, Franklin was a clubman, went out for the crew, and took a heavy schedule of courses, but he spent most of his time on the *Crimson*, which he later said was probably "the most useful preparation I had in college for public service."

An undergraduate paper that he wrote on the Roosevelts in New Amsterdam should also have warned his mother that he would go with her as far as he could but that he was independent, self-reliant, and thought for himself. To Sara, the Roosevelt and Delano family trees—which she knew in every detail and which she would frequently expound (in later years, much to the irritation and impatience of her daughter-in-law)—were the basis for her feeling of caste and exclusiveness. Franklin's genealogical researches, however, had a democratic emphasis. In a sophomore essay, "The Roosevelt Family in New York before the Revolution," he wrote:

> Some of the famous Dutch families in New York have today nothing left but their name—they are few in numbers, they lack progressiveness and a true democratic spirit. One reason,—perhaps the chief—of the virility of the Roosevelts is this very democratic spirit. They have never felt that because they were born in a good position they could put their hands in their pockets and succeed. They have felt, rather, that being born in a good position, there was no excuse for them if they did not do their duty by the community, and it is because this idea was instilled into them from their birth that they have in nearly every case proved good citizens.[14]

It is true that Franklin was as strong a traditionalist as his mother, and later became a founder and pillar of the Dutchess County Historical Society, but he recognized what his mother did not, and the recognition was implicit in his Harvard essay, that in order to survive America's aristocracy had to justify itself by its works and a willingness to accommodate to change. This was Eleanor's feeling, too, although genealogy never had the fascination for her that it did for Franklin.

Franklin knew his own mind, and was determined to shape his own destiny. Although he was a devoted and loving son, if his views differed from his mother's in matters that he considered important to himself, he held his own course. He preferred to achieve his objectives by diplomacy, patience, and charm, but if it came to a direct collision, he, too, could be stubborn. That was the case with his decision to marry Eleanor.

Eleanor signed the letter she wrote Franklin after their week end together in New York "Little Nell," her father's favorite name for her. It was a sign of how completely she had surrendered her heart to her young lover by admitting him into her most precious secrets and endowing him with all the virtues she had ascribed to her father.

"For many years," she later wrote, her father "embodied all the qualities I looked for in a man." But although he was her father's godson, Franklin was not like her father, nor was her father the "parfit, gentil knight" that in her dream world Eleanor imagined him to be. In this inability to see the man she loved as he really was, she set the stage for much disappointment for herself.

Franklin, like Eleanor, was caught up in the tide of young love. He copied and sent to her his favorite poem from the *Sonnets from the Portuguese.* We can only guess which one it was. It "is an old friend of mine," Eleanor wrote back, "and queerly enough I read it over the other evening also and thought how beautiful and expressive it was." Why did he reread her old letters? she went on. "They really are not worth it. However, I don't suppose I ought to talk as I have kept all yours and probably read them far oftener than you read mine, but you write nice letters and I love them and mine are very often dull I fear."

She was wrapping Christmas presents and he was in the midst of class elections. He had been nominated for class marshal, but, as he had warned his family, he was not elected. The biggest prizes seemed to elude him, at Harvard as well as at Groton. He had entered Groton two years after the other boys in his form, was not a success at athletics, was not elected prefect, and was not one of the really popular boys. "He knew things they didn't; they knew things he didn't," Eleanor later said, commenting on the consequences of his entering his form two years late. "He felt left out. It gave him sympathy for people who are left out." At Harvard he not only missed election as class marshal but was not taken into Porcellian, Harvard's most exclusive club, which was by far "the greatest disappointment" in his life, he later confided to Bye's son, Sheffield Cowles.[15] After he became president, his Republican relatives ascribed his attacks on Wall Street and his hostility to bankers like Morgan and Whitney to his resentment about not making Porcellian. "He was getting back at them," they maintained. He had been disappointed, Eleanor agreed, and even developed something of an inferiority complex as a result; but the blow to his self-esteem at Harvard, like his loneliness at Groton, had widened his sympathies. His childhood had been secure and happy, and his cheerfulness contrasted with Eleanor's gravity. But there was a sense in which he, like Eleanor, was an outsider, and this, too, drew them together, especially since she supported and encouraged him in his large dreams.

She was overjoyed, she wrote him when he was chosen permanent chairman of the Class Committee, "for I know how much it meant to you and I always want you to succeed. Dearest, if you only knew how happy it makes me to think that your love for me is making you try all the harder to do well and oh! I hope so much that some day I will be more of a help to you."

12. JOURNEY'S END

⬥

FOR FRANKLIN AND ELEANOR JANUARY, 1904, WAS SHADOWED by Franklin's impending departure for the Caribbean. If Sara had hoped that a five-week winter cruise would dampen the romance, the urgency of their meetings in January should have told her otherwise.

"I am sorry to part with the old year," Eleanor wrote Franklin on New Year's Eve; "it has been so good to me but the new is going to bring us both I hope still more perfect joy and love, if that is possible. Twelve is striking so goodnight darling 'a Happy New Year to you——.'"

They spent the next two days together in New York, and while Franklin jovially reported to his mother, who had returned to Hyde Park, how they had gone to a play and to church and been to Aunt Corinne's for an "uproarious lunch" and all had tea later at Cousin Susie's, there were things he did not tell her, such as how they had slipped away from Aunt Corinne's early and that he was planning on returning to New York the following week end.

Even with the prospect of seeing him again on Saturday, for Eleanor the hours seemed to drag. "What will you do when you have to stand five weeks?" Cousin Susie admonished her. Eleanor was mortified that anyone else should see how out of humor she was; it spoke badly for her self-control, she felt. She told Franklin that he should not laugh at her work in the Rivington Street Settlement. If he were in New York to take up all her time "I would not be going I'm afraid, but one must do something or not having the person who is all the world to me would be unbearable."

Despite all their stratagems for concealing their relationship, some began to suspect. When challenged or teased, Eleanor found the slightest deviation from a truthful, candid reply excruciatingly difficult. Was she ever going to marry Franklin, her Aunt Pussie asked her flatly one day. She had no right to ask that, replied Eleanor, who was easily exasperated with Pussie; when she intended to marry, she would let

Pussie know. But since she was secretly engaged, this was an evasion and it embarrassed her. "I suppose I could have got out of it without telling such a story if I had thought and I am really quite remorseful."

At a luncheon one day Eleanor's friends began to discuss the approaching marriage of one of their friends, Edith Poor, to a British officer. "Can you imagine loving a man well enough to go to South Africa with him?" the girl next to Eleanor asked her. "Luckily," said Eleanor, someone else chimed in and answered for her. To dissemble made her dreadfully uncomfortable.

For the sake of appearances, Eleanor agreed to accept Lyman Delano, Franklin's cousin and also a student at Harvard, as a supper partner at a theater party and dance to be given by his Aunt Kassie. Lyman was interested enough in Eleanor to get angry when she seemed to elude him. He wrote her from Harvard that he was expecting to come to New York for Aunt Kassie's party—would Eleanor go to supper with him? To avoid difficult explanations, Eleanor accepted. But, she consoled Franklin, "I'll dance with you," and besides, they would be together at Groton before the party and would come to New York on the train together. At the party Lyman wanted to know how she had come down from Boston and by what train, "and when I said the twelve," Eleanor reported to Franklin later, "he said 'why had I not let him know, as he would have met me and been delighted to come down with me!' I did not say that I was escorted by someone else."

In Franklin a relaxed attitude toward the truth produced neither guilt nor embarrassment. Although his trip to New York the second week end in January had been planned the week before, after he was back in Cambridge he wrote to his mother:

> Now I must confess—on Saturday I found I had no engagement and went to N.Y. on the 10 o'clock—E. and I had a quiet evening and went to Church together on Sunday—I lunched at the Parishes' & came on here again on the 3 o'clock getting here at 10, just in time to write my editorial. You know I positively couldn't help it—There was nothing to keep me here and I knew I should be in a much better humor for a short trip to N.Y.!

Countless young men in love have resorted to similar omissions and excuses in communications with their parents, and Franklin's dissemblings were not unusual. Eleanor's scrupulousness was. She had, she said, "painfully high ideals and a tremendous sense of duty at that time, entirely unrelieved by any sense of humor or any appreciation of the weaknesses of human nature."[1]

There was a deep strain of puritanism in her. Grandfather Hall had preached a stern gospel of duty and self-control, and both Grandfather Roosevelt and Uncle Theodore, for all their joy of life, had been accused of priggishness in their youth. Grandma Hall and Cousin Susie both dinned it into her that passions should be mastered, not yielded to. "I don't think I seem a great success at conquering 'my natural inclinations' which seems to be our aim in life," she confessed to Franklin in the course of bewailing her inability to get along with Pussie. Her conscience spoke to her with a strong voice, and it was powerfully reinforced by the repressed knowledge of what self-indulgence had done to her father. Paradoxically, her earnest correctness and the tight control she kept over herself were not, on the conscious level at least, her defense against being like her father but were her way of complying with her father's wishes. He had wanted her to be good, loyal, well educated, truthful; he had wanted her to be the virtuous person he wished he could be and which perhaps she could help him to be; he had wanted her to work against the pleasure-seeking side in him. He, too, had lovingly called her "Granny." Perhaps she appealed to Franklin because he needed someone to temper his fun-loving, easy-going, frivolous side.

She could be quite censorious and prim. Alice was in New York, she informed Franklin, "looking well but crazier than ever. I saw her this morning in Bobbie Goelet's auto quite alone with three other men! I wonder how you would like my tearing around like that. I'm seriously thinking of taking it up, it seems to be the fashion nowadays." Bobbie Goelet was one of the gayest and wealthiest young men about town—"None of us had very much money compared to Bertie and Bobby Goelet," said Duncan Harris, who then worked at the Astor Trust; "they were the big party boys." Bobbie Goelet was also one of the reasons Eleanor disapproved of Pussie, who was to marry Forbes Morgan on February 14. Eleanor was to be her maid of honor and the day before the wedding was busy arranging the house for the ceremony. Pussie, on the other hand, spent a good part of the day with Bobbie Goelet, and Eleanor could not understand "spending the last afternoon like that." But then there was little that Pussie did of which Eleanor approved. She could not forget what Pussie had said about her father. After one of Eleanor's flare-ups with Pussie, Cousin Susie told Eleanor that her face looked as if it were made of stone. Eleanor should read the thirteenth chapter of Corinthians, Cousin

Susie had suggested, "and though she said it laughingly I am quite discouraged with myself for I don't think I shall ever learn how to take Pussie charitably." A few days later Cousin Susie lectured her again, this time on the subject of forgiveness. "She says I do not know the higher meaning of the word because I never forget. Of course, it's true and that makes it all the more disagreeable I suppose...." Eleanor vowed to try to be a better person, "and according to Cousin Susie the first step is peace with Pussie so peace it is to be until we fight again!"

Eleanor's mood softened the day of the wedding: "Pussie was married this afternoon at half past four and really looked so lovely." The ceremony affected Eleanor strongly. "It is a pretty solemn thing when it comes to the point of this getting married and I do not see how anyone who has not a great love in their heart can go through with it. Have you ever read the service through Honey? I wish you would sometime for each time I hear it, I think it more beautiful and it means so much, one's whole life in fact."

She was very firm about not yielding to what she considered her baser instincts. She came very near "gambling" at bridge, she confessed to Franklin, at a dinner party at General and Mrs. Bryce's on Washington Square. Afterward their daughter Leila organized the young people for bridge and suggested that Eleanor and Beatrice Mills play at the same table, which terrified Eleanor, who seldom played bridge. It was a favorite diversion at the Mills' house parties,* and Beatrice was a skilled player. "You can imagine my feelings when I had to say that I never played for money and objected distinctly to having my partner carry me!"

Harnessed to a narrow moralism, Eleanor's ability to say "no" might have landed her in the ranks of the battle-ax feminist crusaders had she not married Franklin, Alice Longworth asserted.[2] She was, moreover, by temperament a "yea-sayer." Overflowing with vital energy, she was eager to experience the world in all its aspects and, like her preceptor Mlle. Souvestre, believed it to be woman's particular function to add a grace note to life. However, she was not as forbidding as she depicted herself in the episode at the Bryces'. Although she was not good at games, she was an easy conversationalist, quick to appreciate merit in others; she took pains to draw shy people out and would not spoil

---

*The palatial Mills' house at Staatsburgh, a few miles north of Hyde Park, is described by Edith Wharton in *The House of Mirth*, where it is called Bellomont.

other people's pleasure if she could help it. Outwardly, little ruffled her. One time a group of young men—Bob Ferguson, Nick Biddle, and Otway Byrd of Westover, Virginia—descended upon one of her tea parties and in high spirits proceeded to telephone her friends, talk Indian language to them, and beat on tom toms. "Finally they left to my great relief," Eleanor recalled, "and I'm glad to say Cousin Susie was out during the whole performance or I'm afraid she wouldn't have approved!" At a dinner party given by Charles Barney, she was seated between Mr. Barney and Bronson Winthrop, the bachelor descendant of Governor Winthrop. "Luckily, I can, with some effort, succeed in making Mr. Winthrop talk but I cannot imagine why I was put next to the host when there were a good many older girls there! I suppose I must resign myself to being considered twenty-five however!" It was part of her code that one tried to put other people at ease, and she was critical of Laura and Ellen Delano, Franklin's cousins, because they would not make the effort to talk with people who were newly introduced to them.

At the Whitelaw Reids' annual ball Edmund Rogers took her into supper, and she had such "nice partners" that she stayed until 4:00 A.M. "for the first and last time this winter." She was "burning the candle at both ends," she confessed to Franklin, and she could never do that for very long.

It was an equally strenuous month for Franklin. He would arrive back in Cambridge from a week end in New York and then doze through his morning classes. "It is dreadfully hard," he wrote his mother, "to be a student, a society whirler, a 'prominent and democratic fellow' and a fiance all at the same time—but it [is] worth while, especially the last and next year, tho' hard will be easier."

Two plays greatly impressed Eleanor that winter, one negatively, the other positively. She went with Maude Waterbury to R. C. Carton's *Lord and Lady Algy*, a popular stock comedy that everyone enjoyed—except Eleanor. The intoxication scene in the second act was the most vivid in the play, and it spoiled the entire work for her. But she saw *Candida* by George Bernard Shaw several times, and was fascinated by Candida, whose love for and care of her husband, James Morell, a popular clergyman and Christian Socialist, made him strong and master of the house. The play's most eloquent speech is made by Candida to the wastrel poet Marchbanks, and its account of what she does for Morell foreshadows the role that for many years Eleanor would have in Franklin's life.

Now I want you to look at this other boy here—my boy—spoiled from his cradle. We go once a fortnight to see his parents. You should come with us, Eugene, and see the pictures of the hero of that household. James as a baby! the most wonderful of all babies. James holding his first school prize, won at the ripe age of eight! James as the captain of his eleven! James in his first frock coat! James under all sorts of glorious circumstances! You know how strong he is... —how clever he is—how happy! [*With deepening gravity*] Ask James' mother and his three sisters what it cost to save James the trouble of doing anything but be strong and clever and happy. Ask me what it costs to be James' mother and three sisters and wife and mother to his children all in one.... Ask the tradesmen who want to worry James and spoil his beautiful sermons who it is that puts them off. When there is money to give, he gives it; when there is money to refuse, I refuse it. I build a castle of comfort and indulgence and love for him, and stand sentinel always to keep vulgar little cares out. I make him master here, though he does not know it....

This outpouring is a revelation to Marchbanks, who gives up his suit; he says despairingly of Candida, upon whose hurt feelings he had hopefully played, "it is she who wants somebody to protect, to help, to work for.... Some grown-up man who has become as a little child again." Eleanor must have identified with the character of Candida, since she, also, wanted somebody to protect and to work for. She had already begun to take care of Franklin. She worried about keeping his relationship with his mother on an even keel: "Boy dear, do you realize you've not written your Mother for over a week," she admonished him. Just as Candida had the will and self-discipline to make a happy marriage, so did she.

January sped past, and the week of Franklin's departure for the Caribbean arrived. Then—dreadful disappointment—Henry Parish had to go to Lakewood for his health, and "of course Cousin Susie goes too so I shall be here alone and no one not even you dear can come to the house till they get back." She hated to upset their plans for being together before Franklin left, "but I cannot help it as long as it is not proper for me to have you come to see me when I'm not chaperoned. ...I don't know what to do but perhaps you can think of something and you know that I will do anything which I possibly can rather than miss seeing you for a whole day before you leave."

Franklin was equal to the emergency. He wrote his mother:

I have just heard from E. that Mr. and Mrs. Parish have gone away and I couldn't see her [*i.e.*, no chaperone] if I went to N.Y. on Wednesday. I find I can get off from here Tuesday night and I feel that I must see all I can of E. these last few days—so I am telegraphing you tonight to see if you won't have her up at Hyde Park—coming Wednesday a.m. and staying till Thursday. Nobody need know a thing about it and she wouldn't be any trouble as far as getting off is concerned—for I can pack all my things in half an hour. If you decide not to telegraph her I think I must go down Thursday so as to have all day Friday with her....

On February 6 Franklin, Sara, and Franklin's Harvard roommate, Lathrop Brown, sailed on the *Prinzessen Victoria Luisa*. "F. is tired and blue," his mother noted. And Eleanor, who fled the city to spend the week end with Muriel Robbins at Tuxedo, confessed when she began her first letter: "I could not write last night. I felt as though you had gone so far away and altogether the world was such a dreary place that I was afraid to trust myself on paper.... I wonder if you know how I hated to let you go on Friday night, five weeks seems a long time and judging by the past two days they will be interminable."

The only consolation was that on his return Franklin would join her in Washington, where she would be visiting Auntie Bye. He gave her three mailing addresses in the Caribbean, and she wrote something each day, sending him three fat letters in which she told him about the people she had seen, the things she had done in society, the books she had read, the plays she had attended, what she had been doing at the settlement house, and occasionally even breaking away from the purely personal to comment on the news.

"The papers are nothing but war and fires," Eleanor's first letter reported. The war referred to was the one between Russia and Japan, the fire the one which had gutted Baltimore. The latter affected the Delano family, for Mrs. Warren Delano III of Barrytown was Jennie Walters, the daughter of one of the richest men in Baltimore, whose inheritance had included many properties in Baltimore.

She had seen Nick Biddle, Eleanor wrote in relation to the larger conflagration in the Far East. "He wants to go to the war but I think it would be foolish when he is getting on so well at the office to throw it all up and I do hope he won't go." "Everyone is talking war madly at present," Eleanor added a few days later; "and the Japanese certainly seem to have made a good beginning. I do hope that they will win for I suppose that their defeat might bring about an international war. Besides they are, from a distance at least, such a plucky and attractive little people, don't you think so?"

Did Franklin, like Nick Biddle, itch to get to the battlefront? He had talked excitedly about enlisting in the Navy in the Spanish-American War, but scarlet fever ended that dream; and he wanted to go to Annapolis, "only my parents objected."[3] "Thank heavens," she wrote, "you are not out there dear, even as a correspondent." Both were sufficiently interested in the Far East to read *Chinese Characteristics*, a book by a Christian missionary, A. H. Smith, which combined penetrating observations of Chinese traits with the argument that China's needs will be met "permanently, completely, only by Christian civilization." The book had impressed Eleanor, and she lent it to Franklin.

She liked to share her literary enthusiasms with him, and one of the books she wanted him to read was Balzac's *La Peau de chagrin*. There was a stoic strain in her, and perhaps the appeal of the book was its thesis that every aspiration of the heart, brain, or will that is fulfilled must in the end be paid for. "There are so many things I want to cover and read with you some day when we have time," she wrote Franklin. Another book that she wanted him to read with her was Ruskin's *Sesame and Lilies*. What in this work particularly attracted her? Was it the metaphor of the library as a silent storehouse where the reader is privileged to hold communion with the kings and prophets of all ages? Or was it Ruskin's passionate outcry against the exploitation and injustice rampant in England and his denomination of idleness and cruelty as the two most heinous sins? Or did she want to see what Franklin's reaction would be to Ruskin's appeal to women to exercise their power against injustice and war? How different in this respect was Ruskin's outlook from that of the Reverend Dr. Morgan Dix, Margaret Dix's father, who weekly inveighed not only against women's suffrage but even against college education for girls. But Eleanor was far from a feminist. She did not go to Barnard as some of her friends did, and she was vigorously opposed to women's suffrage. She even declined an invitation to become a founding member of the Colony Club, the most exclusive of women's clubs, as did Franklin's mother, who said, "She could not see any reason for a women's club and would never have any reason to go inside one."[4]

Eleanor attended church faithfully and was very interested in Janet McCook, one of the girls in society who went to Barnard and also taught Bible classes; she later received an M.A. and became something of a Biblical scholar. Eleanor, who attended Janet's classes and often discussed religion with her, went with her to hear a popular preacher, Dr. G. Campbell Morgan, a leader of the Northfield Extension Movement. "It was really very interesting and impressive but quite at the end he called upon all those who felt themselves to be *really* Christians to get up and that flavored too much of a revival meeting to me but it was interesting to see." She went to hear him a second time, but she felt that his sermon was addressed "to the crowd whose emotions must be touched and that kind of thing does not appeal much to me."

So with attendance at church and the opera and a few parties and Bible classes and lessons in German, the weeks passed and at last she could write Franklin that she was leaving for Washington. "My class in Rivington Street bade me a sad farewell today for two weeks and they all promised to be good with Helen and I feel sure they will be as bad as they can be." She was reluctant to leave, for there were many things in New York she hated to miss, "but I love being with Auntie Bye and I hope it won't be too gay, for a perpetual society would kill me."

She arrived in Washington and was "immediately taken out calling!" Friends came to tea, and then "A. Bye and I went to dine with Uncle Theodore. I am sorry to say A. Edith is away but we had a very pleasant dinner during which I just sat still and listened while the men discussed the appointments for the Panama Commission," she wrote in her last letter to Franklin, whose cruise ended in Nassau. There they were the guests of the C. T. Carters, whose daughter, Evelyn, flirtatiously entertained Franklin and Lathrop. On their way back to Washington, Franklin and his mother stopped briefly in Palm Beach, where they found, according to Sara, "much dressing and display, crowds of overdressed, vulgar people."

A note was waiting for Franklin at the Shoreham in Washington. "Just a line to tell you how *more* than glad I am to have you here at last. I will be home as near twelve as possible Honey, and I hope you will be able to get here. Auntie Bye will I think, be in about then also." Shortly after their arrival Mrs. Cowles called. "Went to Bammie's to tea. Eleanor at Bammie's," Sara noted.

Sara was not ready yet to concede defeat, and tried once more to separate the young couple. She forgot the episode, she said, but years later Mabel Choate reminded her of it.[5] Sara took Franklin to see Joseph Choate, whom Theodore had summoned home from his ambassadorial post in London in connection with the Russo-Japanese War, and asked the ambassador to take Franklin with him to London as his secretary. But Mr. Choate had already engaged a secretary, and, in any event, he felt that Franklin was too young for the job.

Sara had lost.

"Darling Franklin," his mother wrote him when she returned to Hyde Park from Washington,

I am feeling pretty blue. You are gone. The journey is over & I feel as if the time were not likely to come again when I shall take a trip with my dear boy, as we are not going abroad, but I must try to be unselfish & of course dear child I *do* rejoice in your happiness, & shall not put any stones or straws even in the way of it. I shall go to town a week from Friday just to be with you when I can. I have put away your albums & loved fussing over them & I placed the new volumes of Punch in their row. Looked over more papers & pamphlets & have written several notes & now at 11 I think I shall leave the rest until tomorrow & go to bed. Oh how still the house is but it is home and full of memories dear to me. *Do* write. I am already longing to hear.

Back in Tivoli, Eleanor was full of compassion for Sara. "I knew your Mother would hate to have you leave her dear," she wrote Franklin in Cambridge, "but don't let her feel that the last trip with you is over. We three must take them together in the future that is all and though I know three will never be the same to her still someday I hope that she really will love me and I would be very glad if I thought she was even the least bit reconciled to me now. I will try to see her whenever she comes in town if she lets me know."

13. EPITHALAMION

SARA STILL RESENTED THE MATCH, BUT PRUDENCE AS WELL AS breeding now required that she yield gracefully. She realized, moreover, that her best hope for preserving a close relationship with her son lay in Eleanor's extraordinary sense of duty and in the girl's eagerness to be accepted by her future mother-in-law.

Sara's letters to Franklin began to report the things she did with "the dear child": they had spent the afternoon together; Eleanor had accompanied her to the dressmaker's for a fitting; they had had tea; Eleanor has been "as sweet as ever." Sara invoked Eleanor to get Franklin to do things he might otherwise refuse. "Much as I want to see you," she wrote him in early May, even more she wanted him to attend the Thayer-Russell wedding; it would please the Russells—with whom the Delanos had been intimately associated in their China ventures—to have one member of the family there. And then she added, almost in desperation, "I am going to have Eleanor here next week, so you will find her, and I think you will be willing to do what I ask."

Eleanor, whose resentment had given way to magnanimity and duty, was sorry for Franklin's mother and tried to ease her anguish. Sometimes she arranged to be elsewhere so that Sara and Franklin could be alone. When Mrs. Warren Delano invited her to Barrytown for the Fourth of July, she was unable to accept and confessed to Franklin that it was "just as well for Cousin Sally's peace of mind that I can't." She assumed the role of mediator between mother and son, urging Franklin to be forbearing; "We will have to learn to accept the little things," she wrote him after a clash between the two, "and not show our annoyance. I know it is harder for you."

Because of Sara's jealousy, Eleanor rejoiced at all signs that Franklin's family liked and accepted her. She spent a day at Algonac, the home of Mr. and Mrs. Frederic Delano Hitch (Mrs. Hitch was Franklin's Aunt Annie). The place was as lovely as Franklin had said, she wrote him. Mr. Hitch "petrified" her, but Mrs. Hitch took her around the house and grounds and for a long afternoon drive and could not have been sweeter. From Tuxedo she reported with delight that another of Cousin Sally's sisters, Mrs. Price Collier, had asked her to call her "Aunt Kassie." And Franklin was meeting with equal acceptance from her own Hall family, she wrote him happily. They liked him so much, she said in mock despair, that she feared they would not think her half good enough when they learned of the engagement. His mother and Mrs. Parish had had a long talk, and Sara had been "sweet" to Cousin Susie. "I don't think Honey, your Mother could be anything else. Everyone has to fall in love with her."

Helen Roosevelt and Eleanor's cousin Theodore Douglas Robinson were to be married in June at Hyde Park. Eleanor and Helen, who was Franklin's niece, were the best of friends and Eleanor carefully followed the preparations and decisions that Helen made since she soon would confront many of them herself. Uncle Ted was coming for the wedding and Eleanor, Alice, and Corinne were to be among the bridesmaids.

Never had spring been so wonderful as that year—to Eleanor's wide-awake senses it seemed that she heard "all the lovely summer noises beginning" as she walked through the woods. She would awaken early and lie in her bed dreamily, wishing she had Peter Ibbetson's capacity to imagine what her lover was doing. She wondered "how life could have seemed worth living before I knew what 'love' and 'happiness' really meant." She could not see enough of Franklin. When they were together, the world and its cares were banished, but at the moment of separation an uncontrollable sadness would well up in her. She hated partings, and sometimes was overwhelmed by melancholy, almost depression. "A woman's moods are sent her," she wrote Franklin apologetically, "just as a man's temptations."

Eleanor spent the Fourth of July week end in Oyster Bay at Sagamore. Young Corinne and Isabella Selmes were staying nearby with Lorraine Roosevelt at Waldeck, the home of the West Roosevelts. There was dancing, "a nice hen party for lunch," and a great deal of tennis, which Eleanor played poorly; Corinne won the tournament despite an injured leg. Eleanor accompanied her cousin to the doctor in New York, and afterward the two girls lunched with Bob Ferguson and Nick Biddle. The latter, a young man of great gaiety, was taken with Eleanor, but Corinne, who was not aware of her cousin's feeling for Franklin, thought that perhaps Eleanor was interested in Bob.[1]

Eleanor was better than Franklin at playing the Victorian charade that she and Franklin were friendly cousins, not plighted lovers. Her lapses of candor caused twinges of conscience, but to have violated the pledge to Sara to keep their engagement secret would have caused her greater inward stress. Franklin was the opposite: he found it difficult to hide his feeling for Eleanor—or probably he did not wish to and took the pledge to his mother less seriously than Eleanor did. The result was a Shakespearian comedy of errors at Islesboro in Dark Harbor, Maine, where Eleanor went to visit her Aunt Corinne and young Corinne. Caroline Drayton was there, too, and the three girls were reading Browning together when Franklin and some Harvard classmates appeared on the *Half Moon*. The two Corinnes were soon persuaded that Franklin was quite in love with Eleanor but that she did not seem interested in him, which, they thought, was a pity. They noted that Franklin took Eleanor canoeing but that Eleanor seemed indifferent.[2] After the *Half Moon* had departed Eleanor wrote Franklin at Campobello saying that aunt and cousin "both undertook to talk to me seriously yesterday about you, because they thought I did not realize how serious you might be, etc. and I led them on very wickedly and made believe I was much worried at the thought that you might really care for me in more than a friendly way! May I be forgiven for all my white lies, but it seems like I can't help doing it!"

She did not lack attentions from other men, and her Dark Harbor letters were filled with chitchat about Boston boys who had gone to Groton and Harvard and who were "attractive" and "interesting." There was Howard Cary, who was much in evidence at Dark Harbor. His intense, searching eyes seemed to be asking for answers she could not give him, and he invited her to go climbing with him, to explore the other side of the island, to come to dinner, to tea. And when she lunched with Caroline Drayton "it brought me a rather terrifying proposal which I was obliged to accept and in consequence Mr. Drayton and I are going walking together tomorrow morning! I haven't yet recovered from the shock and my terror is great!" Was she wholly teasing? She evidently enjoyed the attentions of other men, and with feminine instinct realized that such interest on their part enhanced her appeal to Franklin and also served to bridle any inclination he might have to philander. The name that cropped up most often was Nick Biddle's. She had seen him frequently in town and invited him to Tivoli in June. He amused her: "Never have I known anyone able to talk the steady stream that Mr. Biddle does," she reported to Franklin.

One of her friends thought they were secretly engaged, and even the astute Mrs. Cowles was puzzled. Auntie Bye had written her, Eleanor informed Franklin, that she wanted a long visit to Oldgate in the autumn "and wanted to have you and Nick Biddle while I was there but thought she had better have you at different times! I really think the family must think me either a dreadful flirt or an awfully poor one, I don't quite know which." Franklin was not leading a cloistered life, either. Evelyn Carter was back on Campobello, staying with Mrs. Kuhn, and one of Eleanor's comments in a letter from Dark Harbor was almost too nonchalant: "I did not know you had Edith Weekes with you."

But this was all froth on the waves of their love. Franklin impatiently urged her to abbreviate her stay at Dark Harbor, and she did her best to accommodate him without wounding Aunt Corinne's feelings. The quickest route to Campobello was by way of Millbridge, and Franklin begged her to take it so that he could meet her there. That would not do, she wrote primly; if the train missed connections, they would be stranded, and even with her maid to chaperone them, that would not be proper. "That is one of the drawbacks dear, to not announcing our engagement, and though we did not think of it at the time, it is one of the things we gave up until January 1st." But she, too, was longing to get to Campobello. Although she had greatly enjoyed Islesboro, "I want a quiet life for a while now and above all I want you."

Franklin's fondness for Campobello was second only to his feeling for Hyde Park, and Eleanor soon came under the enchantment of the "beloved isle," as the James Roosevelts had named it when they first discovered its beauty and peace in 1883. It was pine-smelling and spruce-laden, nine miles long and from one and a half to three miles wide. Franklin took Eleanor for walks over mossy paths and showed her his favorite picnic spots. In the morning the fog rolled in and shut out the world, but in the evening spectacular sunsets were arrayed in the western sky. At Franklin's urging Eleanor ventured onto the tennis court, but even though she loved him dearly she did not see why she had to prove her inability over and over again—play with Evelyn, she entreated him. She went sailing on the *Half Moon* and portrayed a willow tree in the end-of-the-season *tableaux* at the club for the benefit of the island library; Franklin impersonated "a very funny 'Douglas' in kilts." They made eighty dollars, Sara recorded, plus twenty-five cents that Eleanor later sent from Tivoli—"I came away and entirely forgot that I owed it... for a ticket the night of the *tableaux* as I took a small boy in."

The happy time they had together in Campobello was over "oh! so quickly," Eleanor lamented, and Franklin's feelings mirrored her own. "I wish you could have seen Franklin's face the night you left Campo," Mrs. Kuhn wrote. "He looked so tired and I felt everybody bored him. He could not stand Evelyn's chatter."

And increasingly Eleanor could not stand the chatter and triviality of the social game. She spent a week end on Long Island with Aunt Tissie, and wrote Franklin that a number of ladies were coming to tea and bridge. "If you ever find me leading this type of life, stop me, for it's not the way to happiness." Her high-mindedness vexed some of her relatives. She had "the queerest time," she reported of her visit to her Aunt Joe (Eddie Hall's wife): "I don't go there very often and in between times I forgot the impression it always makes on me to see Joe and all the other women there smoking and I find myself constantly the only one who does not do one thing or another, which makes me uncomfortable as they always say 'Oh! well, Totty hasn't been here enough to fall into our ways' and I dare not say that I hope I never shall! Somehow I can't bear to see women act as men do!"

In the autumn of 1904 Franklin entered Columbia Law School. He had planned to go to Harvard Law School, but Columbia meant he could be near Eleanor, and that consideration was more compelling than his fondness for the Yard and Gold Coast society. "I am anxious to hear about the first day [at Columbia Law]," Eleanor wrote from Tivoli, "and whether you found any old acquaintances or had only Jew Gentlemen to work with!"★ Most of the youngsters in her Rivington Street class were Jewish and although that did not inhibit her solicitude for them, she did share society's prejudice against Jews.

Occasionally Franklin met her at the settlement, and once, when a child in her class became ill, he accompanied Eleanor to the tenement in which the child lived. After they came out he drew a long breath of air. "My God," he said, aghast. "I didn't know people lived like that!"

Sara was as pleased as Eleanor that her son was in New York. He should move his chair closer to the light "so as to see the print of those charming and comprehensible law books!" she gaily advised him, adding, "I am so sorry I cannot be there to explain any difficulties you

---

★An inspection of the 1907 class roster showed 21 Jewish names in a graduating class of 74.

meet with." But law school commanded little of Franklin's attention that first year, and even the presidential election does not seem to have been much on his mind, or on Eleanor's, although the campaign was reaching its climax and there must have been a great deal of discussion of Uncle Theodore's prospects the first week in October when they were visiting Auntie Bye at Oldgate in Connecticut. But they were absorbed in each other and in the approaching announcement of their engagement. When? Who would write letters to whom? How soon after should their wedding follow? On October 7 Franklin selected a ring at Tiffany's, "after much inspection and deliberation," and gave it to Eleanor on October 11, her twentieth birthday. "I am longing to have my birthday present from you for good," she wrote him from Tivoli that evening, "and yet I love it so I know I shall find it hard to keep from wearing it! You could not have found a ring I would have liked better, if you were not you! This sounds odd but is quite sensible."

They disclosed their engagement at the beginning of December. Franklin had planned to be at Fairhaven, where the Delano clan would be assembled at Thanksgiving, to announce the news himself, but he came down with jaundice and had to remain in New York. Excited letters were promptly sent to Franklin and Eleanor from Fairhaven telling them what the family's response had been. "All those who know you think it is the luckiest thing that ever happened to Franklin," Muriel Robbins reported. Lyman Delano wrote to both of them: "I have more respect and admiration for Eleanor than any girl I have ever met, and have always thought that the man who would have her for a wife would be very lucky." And to Eleanor he wrote that he would have given anything if she could have been in Fairhaven on Thursday morning "when Franklin's letters came. I never saw the family so enthusiastic in my life and I am sure your ears would have burned if you could have heard some of the compliments paid you."* Lyman's father, Warren Delano, the senior member of the clan, wrote Franklin that "Eleanor must have no doubt about being taken in by all her fiance's family—certainly by those who have learned to know and

---

* Grace Tully, Franklin Roosevelt's secretary during the White House years, once asked him why he departed from custom and congratulated the prospective bride as well as groom. "With the mock sense of injury he sometimes affected, he said that when his engagement was announced, all the congratulations were showered on him for securing Eleanor as a wife. He felt, he said, that some people at least should have congratulated her for securing him as a husband." Grace Tully, *F.D.R. My Boss* (New York, 1949), p. 120.

appreciate her." Another note was struck by Mrs. Hitch, who, aware of the wrench in the relationship between her sister and Franklin that the announcement foretold, wrote Eleanor that she was thankful you "already love my dear Sister" and expressed her pleasure to Franklin "that your devoted Mother will have a devoted daughter in Eleanor."

Eleanor's Hall relatives rejoiced that she would at last have a home of her own, but their hearts ached somewhat at the thought of her leaving Tivoli and Cousin Susie's. She would miss "dear Eleanor very much," Grandma Hall wrote Franklin, but was thankful that Eleanor was "going to marry such a fine man as I believe you to be." Maude, a believer in spiritualism, horoscopes, and fortune tellers, drew a circle in wishing "Totty" happiness, "a perfect circle no break anywhere," and then added, "Do be good to Grandma I think she will miss you frightfully." Cousin Henry, who usually was not given to speaking in a personal vein, wrote Eleanor that she filled a place in Susie's life: "Much as I am to Susie, you are more and I pray that you always will be." Pussie was in ecstasy. "I've always loved Franklin & must write him a tiny line tonight just to ask him if he knows and appreciates what he has won," she wrote, but asked how Hall felt. "I know that he had a secret longing that Mr. Biddle would be the one."

He had to throw away three unsatisfactory starts, Mr. Biddle confessed to Franklin in his congratulatory note. Another disappointed suitor, Howard Cary, wrote him from Cambridge, "You are mighty lucky. Your future wife is such as it is the privilege of few men to have." He was mortified that at Islesboro he had "thoughtlessly put her in a position which must at times have been embarrassing." And Howard's mother, only half in jest, lamented to Eleanor, "and so you are not going to be my daughter-in-law after all."

Letters of congratulations also poured in upon them from friends and former classmates at Allenswood, Groton, and Harvard. "I am afraid I shall bear [Franklin] a grudge though," one of Eleanor's co-workers in the Junior League wrote, "if in consequence we are to lose the most efficient member of the League." Many of the letters to Franklin told him how lucky he was, that he could not have made a better match. "It has been a dream of mine for some years that you would be a man widely useful to your country," Groton's second in command, the Reverend Sherrard Billings, wrote him, "and a sympathetic wife will be a great help to you on the road to realizing my dream and I am thankful and glad." The previous spring when Dr. Peabody had officiated at Flossie Twombly's wedding to William A. M.

Burden, Eleanor had said to Franklin, "It seems quite necessary for a Groton boy to have him," and the rector now shifted an engagement to preach in a Cambridge church in order to be able to officiate at their marriage.

The Oyster Bay side of the family was delighted with the news. "Oh, *dearest* Eleanor—it is simply too nice to be true," wrote Alice from the White House; "you old fox not to tell me before." Young Corinne Robinson bubbled over—"Hurrah, hurrah, hurrah," she wrote, and recalled that when Franklin and Eleanor had come to Orange in the fall she had suggested to Franklin that he was in love with Eleanor and had called him a hypocrite and gay deceiver when he had denied it.

"My own darling soft-eyed child," Auntie Bye wrote Eleanor, "your letter has given me great joy. I love Franklin as you know on his own personal account because he is so attractive & also because I believe his character is like his Father's whom Uncle Will & I always feel was the most *absolutely* honorable upright gentleman (the last in its highest sense) that we ever knew." She was thankful, Auntie Bye went on, "to feel you care for someone in a way that gives you the right to make him first over everyone & be everything to him." Aunt Corinne was equally moved by the news. "I can only hope that when the time comes for [young] Corinne to tell me such a piece of news, that I shall feel as completely satisfied."

Uncle Theodore, always in the pulpit, sermonized a little in his letter to Eleanor: "Married life has many cares and trials; but it is only in married life that the highest and finest happiness is to be found; and I know that you and Franklin will face all that comes bravely and lovingly." A happy married life, he advised Franklin, was more important than political success.

White House
Washington
Nov. 29th 1904

Dear Franklin,

We are greatly rejoiced over the good news. I am as fond of Eleanor as if she were my daughter; and I like you, and trust you, and believe in you. No other success in life—not the Presidency, or anything else—begins to compare with the joy and happiness that come in and from the love of the true man and the true woman, the love which never sinks lover and sweetheart in man and wife. You and Eleanor are true and brave, and I believe you love each other unselfishly; and golden years open before you. May all good fortune attend you both, ever.

Give my love to your dear mother.

Your aff. cousin

Theodore Roosevelt

A few days after the announcement of their engagement Eleanor and Franklin saw Auntie Bye and asked her to find out if Uncle Ted would be able to attend the wedding, which, like Pussie's, would take place in the adjoining Seventy-sixth Street houses of Cousin Susie and her mother, Mrs. Ludlow. A few days later Auntie Bye forwarded Theodore's note: "Tell dear Eleanor that I can attend the wedding if it takes place before March 17." Eleanor promptly wrote the president that the ceremony was scheduled for March 17 and expressed her pleasure that he could come. "I want you & Aunt Edith so much & as I am to be married in the house do you think you could give me away?" Not only would he do so but, wrote Aunt Edith, she and Uncle Theodore had been talking about the wedding and "he feels that on that day he stands in your father's place and would like to have your marriage under his roof and make all the arrangements for it." They would understand if she wished to adhere to her original plans, "but we wish you to know how very glad we should be to do for you as we should do for Alice." Despite the warmheartedness of this offer, Eleanor and Franklin decided to keep the wedding at Cousin Susie's and have the invitations sent by Grandma Hall. Eleanor would have "a bevy of pretty bridesmaids," she wrote to Helen Robinson, including Alice Roosevelt, Ellen Delano, Muriel Robbins, Isabella Selmes, Corinne Robinson and Helen Cutting. "You angel," Alice replied to her invitation,

to ask me to be your bridesmaid. I should love to above anything. It will be too much fun. Let me know where I am to hat (&) cloth myself so I can arrange about fittings.... Really you are a sair to ask me....

Before the wedding the engaged couple took time off to attend Uncle Theodore's inauguration. He had defeated conservative Democrat Judge Alton B. Parker by 2.5 million votes, a landslide, and one of the votes came from Franklin. "My father and grandfather were Democrats and I was born and brought up a Democrat," he later explained

(1938), "but in 1904 when I cast my first vote for a President, I voted for the Republican candidate, Theodore Roosevelt, because I felt he was a better Democrat than the Democratic candidates."[3]

They traveled to Washington in Emlen Roosevelt's private car and stayed with Auntie Bye. During the ceremonies on March 4 they sat on the Capitol steps just behind the president and his family and heard his ringing appeal: "All I ask is a square deal for every man." They went to the White House to lunch with the president and again joined him and his immediate family on the reviewing stand for the parade and at the inaugural ball that evening. Then they hurried back to New York, Eleanor, at least, thinking that was the last inauguration of a member of her family that she would attend.[4]

With the wedding less than two weeks off, many parties were given for them, and wedding presents began arriving. There were in all 340 gifts—flatware and china, glass candlesticks, silver candlesticks, several silver tea sets, cut glass and vases of many descriptions, four inkstands, thirteen silver trays, and thirteen clocks. For Franklin there were golden cigarette cases and a dozen bottles of Madeira, and for Eleanor there was a great deal of jewelry, including a handsome pearl dog collar with diamond bars, a gift from Sara. There were water colors from Uncle Ted and Aunt Edith and a sketch of Auntie Bye from Ellen Emmet. They were given enough sets of books to fill a library— two of Jane Austen, three of Robert Browning, two *Golden Treasuries,* and one set each of Campbell, Motley, Emerson, Mrs. Browning, Symonds, Stevenson, Rossetti, Charlotte Brontë, Whittier, Cowper, and Longfellow's *Dante.* Bridesmaids helped Eleanor acknowledge her presents, and Isabella Selmes was so carried away she began to sign her own name instead of Eleanor's.[5]

Cousin Susie helped Eleanor buy her trousseau and linen, and Sara went with her to Pach's for her wedding photo. On March 6 Sara noted in her journal "Tried on my lace dress for my dear Franklin's wedding. Mama's black lace over white."

On March 16 Sara wrote:

Mr. and Mrs. Peabody came at 3.15. I took them up to see Eleanor's presents. Back to tea. Had Bammie, corinne & Douglas, Mr. & Mrs. Jack Morgan to dine. This is Franklin's last night at home as a boy.

Franklin, meanwhile, was busy with his ushers. Since Rosy, his half brother, was ill, Lathrop Brown was to be his best man, and the ushers were Nicholas Biddle, Owen Winston, Lyman Delano, Warren Robbins, Charles B. Bradley, and Thomas Beal, who had sailed on the *Half Moon* with him the previous summer. He had designed a diamond tie pin for his ushers based on the three feathers in the Roosevelt crest, and he gave Eleanor a watch with her initials in diamonds and a pin with the three feathers to hold it.

On Friday, March 17, Pussie sent Eleanor some last-minute advice:

> Try & forget the crowd & only think of Franklin—if you are wise you will drink a cup of strong tea half an hour before you go down stairs. It will give you color & make you feel well. *No* sugar or cream in it.

She sent three kisses, "one for Father & Mother & Ellie."

From Maude came a note with the hope "that she will always try & think of me as her sister, one who loves her very much." A cable signed "Souvestre" was handed her: "Bonheur," it said.

Downstairs all was in readiness. The two large drawing rooms that opened into each other glowed in candlelight and the reflected tints of the heavy furniture. The yellow brocade with which the walls were hung picked up the glow as did the portraits of the Livingstons and Ludlows. White lilacs, lilies, and pink rosebuds relieved the stately dignity of the two rooms, and clematis and palms shaped the brocaded walls into a tabernacle of blossoms. An altar had been set up at the back of Mrs. Ludlow's drawing room, where an enormous shower bouquet of pink roses combined with palms to form a bower in which the ceremony would be performed.

Outside, traces of winter were still on the street, but the day was balmy, and windows everywhere were open, crowded with spectators. Many little boys had come from the St. Patrick's Day parade and were holding American and Irish flags as they awaited the arrival of the president. The carriages and cars of the guests continuously pulled up to the canopy, and finally everyone had arrived and was seated. Grandma Hall in black velvet and Franklin's mother in white silk trimmed with black lace were ushered to the front. Off in a little room on the side Franklin, Lathrop, and the rector were reminiscing, a little distractedly, about Groton; upstairs the bride and her bridesmaids were waiting for the president. A few moments before 3:30 the squeals of the children, a clatter of hooves, and the shouting of commands signaled his arrival, and—top-hatted and buoyant, a shamrock in his buttonhole—he bounded out of the open landau and hastened upstairs.

The Landers Orchestra, discreetly screened, began to play the wedding march. The bridesmaids, in taffeta, with demiveils and three silver-tipped feathers in their hair, moved with measured step down the circular stairway and up the aisle formed by satin ribbons held by the ushers. Behind them came the gravely beautiful bride on the arm of her uncle. A few, remembering her mother, gasped—today she looked like the beautiful Anna, they thought. Past and present were everywhere. Her satin wedding gown was covered with Grandmother Hall's rose-point Brussels lace, which Eleanor's mother had also worn at her marriage. The veil that covered her hair and flowed over her long court train was secured with a diamond crescent that had belonged to her mother. March 17 was her mother's birthday.

At the altar she was met by Franklin. Alice took her bouquet of lilies of the valley and the rector began the Episcopal wedding service. Once he faltered—the light was dim and he could not lay hold of the words, he explained later. Eleanor knew the service so well she could have helped him out, but he recovered quickly. The vows were exchanged. Hand touched hand. It was done.

"Well, Franklin," the president's high-pitched voice could be heard saying, "there's nothing like keeping the name in the family." He kissed the bride and marched off to the double dining room where refreshments were being served. Others pressed forward to congratulate them, but as the dining room began to crackle with the president's sallies and the guests' appreciative laughter, the bridal couple soon found themselves abandoned. Dr. Dix and his daughter Margaret, arriving a little late for the reception, found Franklin and Eleanor standing quite alone. Eleanor was taking it calmly, Margaret observed, but Franklin was a little put out.[6] The Dixes traipsed off after the others, and soon the newlyweds, too, decided they might as well follow. Ushers and bridesmaids gathered round while Franklin guided Eleanor's hand as she cut the cake. Even the president was made to attend and take his piece. At five the president left, to shouts of "Hooray for Teddy" from the little boys still waiting outside; the president beamed and shook his fist smilingly. Eleanor and Franklin went upstairs to dress, and soon they, too, departed in the traditional shower of rice. With Isabella, they stopped to see Bob Ferguson, who was ill in bed, and then left for Hyde Park, which Sara turned over to them for an interim honeymoon.

Sara, at Tuxedo Park, where she had gone with her sister Kassie, finished the day's chronicle:

March 17th. Took Mrs. Peabody out in the electric to do some errands. Had all the ushers to lunch. Left at 2.30 for 76th Street. Franklin is calm & happy. Eleanor the same. All the family at the wedding. Dora, Annie & Fred, Fred & Tilly, Kassie & all & Mlle. Mathieu. About 200 at the ceremony, a large reception afterward. Theodore Roosevelt, President, gave Eleanor away.

Then she wrote her "precious Franklin and Eleanor" that it was "a delight to write you together & to think of you happy at dear Hyde Park just where my first happiness began."

And the president, addressing the Friendly Sons of St. Patrick at Delmonico's after the wedding, spoke in words intended as much for the Vanderbilts, Sloans, Burdens, Chanlers, Winthrops, Belmonts, and van Rensselaers who had applauded his quips in the Ludlow-Parish dining room as for his immediate audience:

American is not a matter of creed, or birthplace, or descent. That man is the best American who looks beyond the accidents of occupation or social condition, and hails each of his fellow citizens as his brother, asking nothing save that each shall treat the other on his worth as a man, and that they shall join together to do all that in them lies for the uplifting of this mighty and vigorous people.[7]

It began with Theodore Roosevelt as the American century but would progress toward a more ecumenical outlook; and in the broadening of loyalties that the United Nations would represent, the marriage that had been celebrated that day was destined to figure significantly.

II

WIFE
AND
MOTHER

14. HONEYMOON

SOME SITUATIONS BROUGHT OUT ELEANOR'S COMPETENCE, AND others touched the secret springs of her insecurity; her marriage did both. The pathos of orphanage was ended, but the poignancy of wishing to please and be fully accepted by her young husband and his mother began.

For five years before her marriage, beginning with the beneficent influence of Mlle. Souvestre, she had begun to assert her individuality, sense her potentialities, and emerge as a tower of strength to those around her. Suddenly the pattern was reversed, and in return for the privilege of loving and being loved she stifled any impulse to assert herself. "I want him to feel he belongs to somebody," she had said of Hall in the 1890s to explain why she wrote him so often, and it reflected her own yearning to belong, to be part of a family whose members came first with her as she came first with them. She had had the self-discipline to do what she thought needed to be done to bring that about, and now that she wanted to be fully accepted by her mother-in-law she was prepared to dismiss her own wishes and values to gain Sara's love.

There was, moreover, that conscience of hers; if there was any conflict between what she might enjoy doing and what she ought to do, the voice of duty prevailed. The result was that she totally subordinated herself to her husband and her mother-in-law. Their wills became hers; not what she wanted, but what they wanted, mattered.

Since Franklin had to finish his year at Columbia Law School and they could not yet leave on an extended honeymoon, they were to have a week to themselves in Hyde Park and then stay at the Hotel Webster in New York. When Franklin finished his exams they would depart for a three-and-a-half-month honeymoon in Europe. Fifty years later, Eleanor's recollection of the week at Springwood focused on "Elespie"—Elspeth McEachern, the highly competent Scotswoman who, under Sara's direction, ran the efficient and spotless household at Hyde Park. She had been at the door to welcome Sara as James' bride in 1881. "She was in the house when we went to Hyde Park the day of our wedding," said Eleanor, "and she looked me over critically and appraisingly, wondering if I could come up to her expectations as the wife of 'her boy.'"[1]

When they returned to New York on March 25, Sara was there to greet them. "Went to F. & E.'s apartment at Hotel Webster," she noted in her diary; "arranged flowers and went to my French lecture. Returned to find my children and brought them home to lunch with me."

Now that Eleanor was faced with the fulfillment of her dream—an intimate normal life of her own with the man she loved—she was frightened. In her grandmother's house she had never had a chance to learn what went into a serene, well-run household. The hotel apartment was a godsend, because Franklin would not discover how little she knew about managing a household right away. All she had to do was "a little mending."

Despite her inner anxieties, on the surface she was busy cheerfulness and left Franklin free to prepare for his examinations. She arranged for Hall to stay with them at the hotel when he came down from Groton; she went with Franklin and Sara to the wedding of Lucius Wilmerding and Helen Cutting; and there was much family visiting—the large Delano clan, the Oyster Bay and Hudson River Roosevelts. Helen and Teddy Robinson returned from their honeymoon trip around the world, and Sara had everyone to dinner—"Rosy, Corinne and Douglas, Bammie, F. & E." Eleanor had many things to take care of for her own forthcoming honeymoon—purchases to be made, trunks to be packed, letters of credit arranged, tickets to be picked up. She organized it all competently—and quickly. On June 6 Sara wrote, "Franklin got all their luggage put on board the *Oceanic* & lots of friends came to say goodbye. We had Rosy, Helen & Teddy to dine." Then, overcome with a sense of her good fortune, she added, "My dear Franklin & Eleanor."

For Eleanor her honeymoon was a bittersweet affair. Its sweetness was recorded in the long, detailed letters she wrote to her mother-in-law at the time; its harsher side emerged only in her reminiscences three or four decades later when she had become a freer, more independent woman.

"There were certain subjects never discussed by ladies of different ages," she wrote thirty-five years later, "and the result was frequently very bewildered young people when they found themselves faced with some of life's normal situations!" She was commenting on the scene in *Life with Father* where Father announces that he will tell his son "all about women" and then informs him promptly that there are certain subjects never discussed between gentlemen.[2]

And to the extent that there was any discussion between generations of what a woman faced, it was in terms of marital duty. That was Grandma Hall's view. It was also Sara's, so one of her grandchildren, Franklin Jr., learned one day when he sat on the edge of "Granny's" bed and she pressed him to tell her about his girls. The young man parried the question. "What was life like with Grandfather?" he wanted to know. "Did you have any fun?" She was not at all unwilling to answer the charming young man. "Well, you know we were Victorians. I knew my obligations as a wife and did my duty."[3]

That was the case with Eleanor. Sex was an ordeal to be borne, she would later confide to her daughter Anna.[4]

She began her honeymoon trip fearful that she would be seasick and become a burden to her nautical husband, who was never more at home with himself than when on the water. But after four days out Franklin reported to his mother, "Eleanor has been a *wonderful* sailor and hasn't missed a single meal or *lost* any either." And she exulted, "Franklin has been a wonderful maid & I've never been so well looked after." With Eleanor there to prod Franklin, for once Sara would not feel she was being neglected. Almost daily they sent her long letters full of information and affection. Eleanor's effusive avowals of love were pathetic evidence of her eagerness to be fully accepted by the older woman. "Thank you so much dear for everything you did for us," she wrote from the *Oceanic*. "You are always just the sweetest, dearest Mama to your children and I shall look forward to our next long evening together, when I shall want to be kissed all the time!"[5]

She shared amused observations about Franklin with the adoring Sara. "The stewardess informed me the other morning that my husband must be English, he was so handsome and had the real English profile!" she wrote archly. "Of course it was a great compliment but you can imagine how Franklin looked when I told him." Eleanor was always observant, always learning, her heart easily stirred. They toured the ship with the captain, and "it was very interesting, but I am more sorry than ever for the Steerage passengers." Some Japanese were on board on their way to supervise two Japanese battleships being built in

England; Franklin spent most of his time "*trying* to talk to the Japs," Eleanor reported, "and they have proved interesting companions."

After a stop in Liverpool to visit Eleanor's Confederate relatives, the Bullochs, and to weep a little with Aunt Ella, whose heart still ached over her "Ellie boy," they went on to London. Wherever they went in Europe there were family connections or friends of the family to introduce them into the highest circles of society, politics, and art. Their greatest joy, however, was to poke around London, Paris, or Venice— just the two of them. For Eleanor it was a new experience to be able to do the things she had always wished to do without worrying about the cost or what "G'ma" or Cousin Susie would think. Some places had special meaning for her because she had first seen them with her father or Mlle. Souvestre, and she delighted in exploring them anew with Franklin; for his part, he could not wait to take his bride to his favorite bookseller, mountainside spot, or café.

They walked themselves weary in London while Franklin searched for rare books and prints, and ordered, he teasingly wrote his mother, "thousands of dollars worth of clothes." They lunched at the Embassy with the Reids, Eleanor reported, and "I sat next to Mr. Reid!" They had supper at the Carlton and, she said, "were much entertained by some of the English women. It is quite out of date here to appear with your own face or hair. In fact it really looks immodest!" She visited Allenswood, "but it was dreadful without Mlle. Souvestre." She had died a few weeks earlier.

Doing Paris with Franklin was an even greater joy. She went shopping for clothes and ordered "thousands of dollars worth of linen," according to Franklin, while he spent "all I owned" in the first bookshop he entered. He accompanied her to the dressmaker's but insisted that he had dozed off while she ordered "a dozen or so new dresses and two more cloaks." Eleanor scribbled a P.S.: "Don't believe *all* this letter please. I may be extravagant but——!!!" Franklin enjoyed introducing his new wife to the world of high fashion. "This A.M. we went out and Franklin got me such lovely furs," Eleanor wrote; "I don't think he ought to give them to me but they are wonderful and of course I am delighted with them." They dined in out-of-the-way places, ordered *spécialitiés de la maison*, and, since Franklin thought he spoke French well, they had a gay time talking with the *patrons*. Although Franklin's French was hardly as good as Eleanor's, it was good enough for some hard bargaining with booksellers. He would not let Eleanor come along on these bargaining sprees, because her sense of fairness interfered with hard trading. Her Italian, however, was fair, while his was only poor, so in Italy he had to rely on Eleanor for such transactions. In Paris they also visited "Cousin Hortense" Howland, the French woman who had married a brother of James Roosevelt's first wife and whose salon was described in Proust as a meeting place of the Jockey Club. "You would have laughed if you could have heard Mrs. Howland flatter Franklin yesterday," Eleanor wrote. "This isn't true," Franklin commented in the margin; "Eleanor got buttered on both sides!"

For Eleanor, Venice was full of memories of her father and Mlle. Souvestre. Of course they hired a gondola and gondolier. Charles Stuart Forbes, an artist and kinsman, lived in Venice and was their guide. They visited the Palace of the Doges and the artistically interesting churches with him, and at the end of tiring days they all went to little Italian restaurants where they learned the pleasures of superbly cooked but simple Italian food.

They had tea at the Lido, and again Eleanor's strait-laced attitudes asserted themselves. "It is a lovely island with a splendid beach but I never saw anything like the bathing clothes the ladies wear.... But Franklin says I must grow accustomed to it as France is worse!" For Eleanor a decorous bathing costume consisted of a skirt, a long-sleeved, high-necked blouse, stockings, slippers, a sun-bonnet, and gloves. They left Venice reluctantly. Franklin, who had expected to be disappointed with Venice, found the reality "far more wonderful than he had imagined." Eleanor felt that "nothing could be quite so lovely," but then the stern voice of conscience welled up "as long as you wished to be idle!"

From Venice they proceeded to the Dolomites and to Cortina. "An old lady's Paradise," Franklin complained, "and I feel like Satan all right." But among the not-so-old female guests was Kitty Gandy, the attractive owner of a fashionable New York hat shop. She joined them at bridge and, according to Franklin, was "quite nice (smoked all my good cigarettes) and promised *me* a new ostrich feather hat for next winter." When Eleanor, a poor mountain climber, declined to accompany him up the 4,000-foot Faloria, Miss Gandy gaily volunteered. To his letter describing the jaunt, a piqued Eleanor appended: "E.R. spent the morning with the Miss VanBibbers climbing up the landslide, to meet a husband who never turned up till after they got home!" Much later, in her autobiography, she confessed that she had been unspeakably jealous of Kitty Gandy and hadn't breathed easily until they left Cortina to drive through the Alps to St. Moritz. The drive over the Stelvio was "wonderful," and Franklin, in an exuberance of good spirits, leaped out of the coach to pick wild flowers for Eleanor—"the wild jasmine smells sweeter than anything I ever had," she wrote. Aunt Tissie, who often stayed at St. Moritz with her family, had reserved rooms for them, and Eleanor had been a little anxious as to what they might find awaiting them, since Tissie's "ideas of the necessities of life and ours differ"; but, she reported, "we are surviving her extravagance." She went to have her hair washed while "Franklin found a paper and devoured it." They had tea and then went down to dinner, "since when I have been writing this and he has been mending his Kodak and occasionally telling me that I have a wonderful husband, so I suppose he is being successful!"

Fashionable St. Moritz did not respond to their young romantic mood. Eleanor always remembered—and recounted with a smile— that they were underdressed for the Palace Hotel and the management relegated them to a table—with a view of the lake, to be sure—well out of sight of the other guests. Fifty years later, when she was world famous, she returned to St. Moritz but stayed at a rival hostelry and explained to her companions why she was amused by the aggrieved message from the management of the Palace Hotel: "But why didn't Madame Roosevelt stay with us!"[6]

Their next destination was Franklin's boyhood haunts in southern Germany, where they journeyed through the Black Forest. From St. Blasien Franklin reported: "We are full of health and bursting with food (at least I am) and the only unkind word Eleanor has ever said to me is that she would like to see me bust!" Her letter, Eleanor insisted at the beginning of a twelve-page report, was bound to be "unbearably dull"; all her letters were dull, she said deprecatingly, compared to Franklin's "amusing ones." "We are having such a nice lazy time," she reported from St. Blasien. She was reading Anatole France in French, but "he occasionally disgusts me so that I have to stop." Sara had sent them a check, and she had decided to spend her share in Paris. "How I would like to kiss you and *tell* you instead of writing my thanks."

On their return to Paris her clothes and furs were awaiting her for fittings. And awaiting Franklin were his law-school grades, which— not surprisingly for the year in which he was married—included two F's. They immediately cabled for his law books so that Franklin could study on board ship on the way home. He wanted to take make-up examinations in the autumn, Eleanor wrote. "I'm not very confident about his passing but it won't hurt him to try and the work will be that much gained next winter."

In Paris Franklin ran into some college friends who took Eleanor and Aunt Dora to a very "French" play, hoping to shock the ladies, Eleanor reported, a little irritated with their sense of humor. The only one shocked was Eleanor; Mrs. Forbes did not lift an eyebrow. Eleanor's primness came out again at Voisin's, where she saw, she wrote, *Mrs.* Jay Burden and *Mrs.* Harry Whitney with Mr. Bertie Goelet and Mr. Meredith Hare, "so you see it is not fashionable to go out with your husband!"

The honeymoon drew to an end with a visit to Novar, the home of the Ferguson clan, and to Mr. and Mrs. Foljambe, friends of Sara's who lived in a part of England that included Sherwood Forest and was known as the "Dukeries." The opulent estates there eclipsed the great houses on the Hudson, and for Eleanor the visit to Osberton-in-Worksop, as the Foljambe estate was called, was "terrifying." There was a punctilious emphasis on correct behavior, and dinner was austerely formal. Guests of such a great house, it was assumed, would all know each other and thus there were no introductions. After dinner, bridge was played for money, which was against Eleanor's principles, and so arrangements were made for her to be carried by her partner. She was the more embarrassed by this to-do because she was convinced she played badly. She described her feelings at Osberton-in-Worksop with a metaphor whose grisliness underscored her insecurity: she felt like "an animal in a trap" who did not know how to get out or how to act where it was.

Franklin took the Foljambes in his stride. They were flattered by his interest and eagerness to learn all about Osberton. After touring the farms and talking with Mr. Foljambe, he breezily informed his mother that his plans for Hyde Park "now include not only a new house, but new farm, cattle, trees, etc."

The visit with the Fergusons, old friends of Eleanor's father and mother, was more relaxed. Bob's older brother Hector remembered her as a golden-haired three-year-old. Bob Ferguson and Isabella Selmes, who had been married in July, were visiting the family. Eleanor drove over in a two-wheeled cart to see them and wrote Sara delightedly: "It is impossible to imagine how sweet [Isabella] and Bob are together for I would not know him for the same man. He has become demonstrative if you can believe it and they play together like two children."

While they were with the Fergusons, they received news that

Theodore Roosevelt had scored a considerable diplomatic triumph when the Japanese and Russian peace plenipotentiaries, meeting at Portsmouth, New Hampshire, reached agreement on terms of a settlement of the Russo-Japanese War. The Fergusons were part of the Foreign Office establishment, and Sir Ronald Ferguson had played a role in bringing the meeting about. "It is nice news, isn't it?" Eleanor wrote. "We had really begun to think it would not be and I think Uncle Ted must be gratified to have done so much towards it." Franklin jauntily waved the flag. "Everyone is talking about Cousin Theodore saying that he is the most prominent figure of present-day history, and adopting towards our country in general a most respectful and almost loving tone. What a change has come over English opinion in the last five years!" Also while Franklin and Eleanor were at the Fergusons', Sidney and Beatrice Webb came to lunch. "They write books on sociology," was Eleanor's meager description of the couple, "and Franklin discussed the methods of learning at Harvard while I discussed the servant problem with the wife!" Did her exclamation point mean that she sensed that talking with Beatrice Webb about servant problems had been an opportunity wasted? The door was open, as at Uncle Ted's, to talk of high politics, culture, and science. Therefore, when Lady Ferguson asked Eleanor to explain the difference between federal and state governments and Eleanor could not get beyond the fact that there *was* a difference, since Uncle Ted had been governor of New York and now was president of the United States, her mortification was extreme. Fortunately, Franklin came to her rescue—as he did again when she was asked to open the flower show. "She opened it very well," Franklin insisted, "and wasn't a bit rattled and spoke very clearly and well—but I had an awful time of it and wasn't even introduced." Eleanor's account was different. "We opened the flower show at Novar last Saturday and Franklin made a very good speech." In this case, Eleanor was the more accurate reporter; Franklin's talk was graceful and humorous—it was, as his wife said, "a very good speech."

He was fortunate "in having a Highland nurse," he said, "so that I passed my early years with kilts on the outside and oatmeal and scones on the interior." If he began on a note of intentional humor, he ended on one that was unintentional. American women instead of cooking vegetables in water "nearly always cooked them in milk, and this of course makes them more nutritious, besides bringing out the flavor."[7] Little as Eleanor knew about cooking, she knew her husband was drawing on his imagination when he spoke of cooking vegetables in milk and it was a relief when he ended. But his audience loved it and she loved him for coming to her rescue.

As they left for home they received a letter from Sara expressing her delight and gratification over the way they had made her feel she was never far from their thoughts. "I never knew such angels about writing and I *am* so glad Eleanor says that although you have had such a perfect time you are now anxious to see 'home and mother' again!"

15. SETTLING DOWN

At the newlyweds' request, Sara had rented for them the Draper house at 125 East Thirty-sixth Street, just three blocks from her own, and furnished it and staffed it with three servants. If she had looked forward to finding and furnishing her own first house, Eleanor gave Sara no hint of this. "You are an angel to take so much trouble with the house," she wrote from St. Moritz, and thanked Sara for having done "wonders" for them in the way of "a bargain," for now they could get settled "so much sooner than if we waited to choose a house on our return. Altogether we feel jubilant over it and I am looking forward so much to getting it in order with you to help us." Eleanor's requests were minimal: she wanted their bedroom painted white, the kitchen and basement whitewashed, the telephone, if there was one, to remain—and was there a house safe?

Only when Sara offered to spend a considerable amount of money to wire the house for electricity did they demur. "You are a dear, sweet Mama, to want to put it in for us," Eleanor wrote from Paris a month before their return, "but we are pulled two ways for we will only have the house two years."

They moved into their "14 foot mansion," as Franklin called it, as soon as they returned, and two days later he took his make-up exams at Columbia Law School. Sara had sent his law books to London with the advice, "You can do a good deal even crossing an ocean, if you set apart two or three hours a day for work." He had a retentive memory and a good mind, and with Eleanor to see that he stuck to his studies, he passed.

Through the remaining two years at law school Eleanor's quiet confidence in Franklin's abilities fortified him against indolence and irresolution. He passed his bar exam in the early spring of 1907, was sworn in in May, and in September wrote from Campobello to his mother in Europe that by the time she returned he would be "a full-fledged office boy" with Carter, Ledyard and Milburn. "I shall think of you on the 23rd beginning work," his mother wrote back. "I know you will in many ways be glad to start. Try to arrange for systematic air and exercise and keep away from brokers' offices, this advice free gratis for nothing."

While Franklin was busy learning his way around the municipal courts, Eleanor devoted herself to her mother-in-law. Every day she drove with Sara in her brougham up Fifth Avenue and through Central Park, and they had at least one meal a day together. Eleanor consulted Sara on servants and menus and on where to shop and what to buy, and she listened dutifully to Sara's daily briefings about Franklin's health. Often she had to beg off when Helen Robinson or Nathalie Swan or Corinne Robinson wanted to "have a little gossip." She had to lunch with Mama, she excused herself. No, she could not go to the lecture or to the theater with them—she was driving or dining with Mama.

Under the firm guidance of her mother-in-law she was becoming a conventional young society matron.[1] Franklin did not mix socially with his fellow students or professors. The young couple's social life was to be restricted to the group in which they had been raised. New York was throbbing with vital movements in art, politics, and welfare, but for Franklin and Eleanor, New York was limited to the interests of a small group of families of impeccable social standing and long-established wealth. Before her marriage, Eleanor had begun to break loose from this narrow framework through her work at the Rivington Street Settlement and with the Consumers League. But now she was told by Sara and Cousin Susie that if she continued with this work she risked bringing the diseases of the slums into her household. Eleanor's impulse to do things for the less fortunate was to be restricted to serving on proper charitable boards and to making modest donations, the appropriate activity for a young matron, just as the older members of Franklin's family approved of his election as a vestryman of St. James' Episcopal Church and his membership, like his father before him, in the Eagle Engine Company of Hyde Park and the Rescue Hook and Ladder Company of Dutchess County.

The Franklin Roosevelts, while not really wealthy, were well off. Franklin had a $5,000 income from a $100,000 trust fund, and Eleanor had an annual income of $7,500. Also, Sara could always be counted on for generous checks on special occasions. So their life was comfortable and without financial worry.

They were not members of the fastest, gayest crowd, although they saw a good deal of the Teddy Robinsons, who were. Franklin rode and hunted, but hunt-breakfasts, polo, and steeplechasing were never as important to him as they were to Teddy. The Robinsons engaged in such madcap pranks as turning up at dinner dressed in baby clothes. Eleanor was totally incapable of "letting go" in that way, but if Franklin had been married to someone else he might have joined the fun. He enjoyed gay escapades that Eleanor had little use for and that often left her feeling inadequate.

If he wanted to go on a "bat" with his male contemporaries, she encouraged him. She packed him off to Cambridge for a "real spree" with his Fly Club brethren, which gave her a chance to fix up the house, she said, "so it will look a little better for you." In June she bundled him off to Cambridge again, for she realized that the true son of Harvard needed the stimulus of a return to the Yard and participation in commencement festivities.

Eleanor got on easily with older people, and joined her mother-in-law and her friends in their discussions of art, literature, and music. Almost everybody in society was organizing classes. Sara Roosevelt had one in history at her home. "Such a funny combination of people," remarked Helen Robinson, since it consisted mostly of Sara's contemporaries, with only Helen and Mary Newbold and Eleanor representing the younger generation. Around the corner, Eleanor attended the class Aunt Jennie (Mrs. Warren Delano) had in her home in "modern" literature—George Eliot, D. G. Rossetti, Browning, Swinburne, Meredith, Matthew Arnold. She still turned up regularly at the Bible class conducted by Janet McCook.

The pattern of Franklin and Eleanor's life during the first year of marriage was set by Sara, at least to the extent that Eleanor's deliberate self-effacement kept her from expressing her own preferences. No wonder Sara was thankful—she understood what she had gained. In 1905, on Eleanor's twenty-first birthday Sara wrote that she prayed that her "precious Franklin may make you very happy, and thank him for giving me such a dear loving daughter. I thank *you* darling for being what you are to me already."

But Eleanor had Franklin's love and a home, and that was what counted for her. In September Franklin went to New York and she stayed in Hyde Park alone, their first day apart. "I feel quite lost and sad without you," she wrote him, "and it was horrid coming home last night so I don't think we will try this experiment again, do you think? Incidentally I hope you miss me dreadfully too!"

Insecure, unsure of her adequacy as a woman, another of her

anxieties when she married Franklin was that she might prove barren.[2] But not long after they returned from their honeymoon she knew
she was pregnant. The pregnancy was a difficult one, and for the last
three months she was quite ill, but with those around her she remained
calm and cheerful. "Eleanor and I walk every morning at ten. She
is wonderful, always bright and well," Sara noted. Eleanor had little
patience with her own physical ailments and did not allow them to
keep her from doing what had to be done. This had always been one
of her nobler attributes, but it had sometimes made her insufferably
righteous toward others who were less self-disciplined. Her pain and
nausea while carrying Anna, however, humbled and softened her, and
although she still refused to yield to her own infirmities, she became
more tolerant of those who did.

In December, 1905, Alice Roosevelt announced her engagement to
Nicholas Longworth. Since the wedding on February 17, 1906, took
place only a few weeks before Eleanor's confinement she was unable to
attend, but Franklin went with his mother. "Alice looked remarkably
pretty and her manner was very charming," Sara reported to Eleanor.
Cousin Theodore was, "as always, cordial and interesting." "So Alice
is really married," the family noted with considerable surprise and
even more relief.

On May 2, Sara wrote, "Eleanor and I had our usual walk and in the
afternoon she and I drove from 2:30 till four, and Eleanor and Franklin lunched here. I went there to dine. We played cards. Eleanor had
some discomfort." The next day, Miss Spring, a trained nurse, called
Sara at nine. "I went over and Dr. Ely soon came. At 1:15 a beautiful
little girl was born, 10 pounds and one ounce."

Eleanor always remembered the first time she held Anna in her
arms, "just a helpless bundle but by its mere helplessness winding itself
inextricably around my heart." The mother's pleasure in the birth of
her first child was only slightly marred by her knowledge that her
mother-in-law had yearned for a boy.

Eleanor had scarcely recovered from childbirth when she began to
worry about what would happen once the trained nurse left. Stubby
Blanche Spring was so competent and sensible that Eleanor became
quite attached to her, and felt rather lost when the nurse was no longer
with them. "Miss Spring left," Sara noted in her diary. "Poor little
Eleanor is upset by it though she is brave."

Miss Spring urged Eleanor to care for the baby herself, but Sara
argued that a nurse must be employed. So Eleanor added a nurse that

Sara engaged to the household staff of cook, housemaid, and butler. Later she bitterly regretted yielding on this point; if she had insisted on caring for her own children, she felt, instead of turning them over to nurses and governesses, as was customary in her group, she as well as the children would have been happier. In retrospect, she also regretted having been insulated from the household's vital activities; she and Franklin, she said later, would have been better off during the first year of their marriage if they had not had a staff of servants. But Sara shaped their style of life, and when Eleanor had misgivings and consulted her Cousin Susie, she found that Susie was as much a traditionalist as Sara.[3]

The baby was christened "Anna Eleanor" at St. James Church on July 1, 1906. The child's godmothers were Isabella Ferguson and Muriel Robbins, and the godfather was Edmund Rogers. A lunch party for thirty-four at Springwood followed the ceremony.

For Sara, the presence of a grandchild was a fascinating experience, and she found it more difficult than ever not to spend all her waking hours with her son and his family. There were times, nevertheless, when Eleanor escaped her mother-in-law, and managed to join her friends at lunch, to call on them at their homes, and sometimes even to entertain them at dinner. Those were the years when most of her bridesmaids and Franklin's ushers were themselves getting married, settling down, and excitedly reporting to each other on their babies. Helen Robinson's son Douglas Jr. was born on November 8, 1905; Helen Wilmerding (née Cutting) gave birth to a son in January, 1906; and Isabella Ferguson had a daughter in September, 1906. "Will you marry me 21 years from today?" the Robinsons telegraphed the Fergusons on behalf of Douglas Jr. "Sorry," the answer came back, "just eloped with Peter Biddle" (Peter was Nick and Elizabeth Biddle's one-month-old son). The Robinsons took Douglas to call on little Anna Eleanor. "Douglas rather terrifying Anna by his amorous advances," Helen recorded, "as they sat on the floor together. He wanted to hold her hand but she was quite rebellious."

Soon after Anna's christening the Franklin Roosevelt household left for the first of many summers on Campobello Island. Resolutely Eleanor set about mastering her fear of water, because life on Campobello would be tedious for her if she didn't sail. If she wanted to keep her children company—not to mention her husband—she had to learn about boats. They went up to St. Andrews in the launch, Franklin informed his mother, "and though slightly rough in Passamaquoddy

Bay for a few minutes E. did not show the least paleness of cheek or tendency to edge towards the rail!" Eleanor even learned to fish: "F. and I fished yesterday afternoon and caught twelve flounders," she announced laconically.

She wanted to participate in other sports with her husband, but her feelings of awkwardness and shyness as well as her husband's self-centeredness deterred her. Franklin loved golf, and Eleanor practiced secretly, but when she went golfing with him she played so badly and Franklin was so impatient with her that she gave it up then and there. During their courtship he had tried to coax her onto the tennis court, but he now accepted her protestations that she would only spoil the game for others—so she was relegated to entertaining the guests on the sidelines. At Hyde Park, too, her efforts to join in outdoor activities were unsuccessful. Her ankles were too weak for ice-skating. She enjoyed riding and tried Franklin's horse Bobby, but he was used to Franklin's handling and she could not control him. When Sara, who could handle Bobby (the horse at one time had been hers), took the view that there were not enough people at Hyde Park to justify two saddle horses, Eleanor meekly said that she preferred not to ride.[4] As a result, the only outdoor pleasures she shared with her husband were long walks and picnics.

It was not customary for wives to go on long cruises with their husbands, but Eleanor was left out of the carefree active summer life on Campobello more than most young women of her time. She did not complain, however, and at the end of each summer she would busy herself provisioning the *Half Moon* for Franklin and Hall for a run to Nova Scotia or westward to Bar Harbor.*

The first few summers at Campobello the Franklin Roosevelts lived with Sara, who managed not only the household but everything else with great firmness. Franklin was an expert sailor and he loved the *Half Moon*, but for many years Sara, not Franklin, gave the captain his orders, and only when her son had guests at Campobello was the boat turned completely over to him. Sara also kept the management

---

*But secretly she resented her exclusion from the active handling of the boats on which her menfolk sailed. In 1935 Emma Bugbee of the *New York Herald Tribune* was with her in Campobello, and they went sailing. "I shall never forget the satisfaction with which she took the helm from Captain Calder, who had handled Roosevelt family boats for years," Emma later wrote. "'I never get a chance to sail the boat myself,' she beamed. 'There are always so many men around.... One always has to let the men do the sailing'" (*New York Herald Tribune*, July 7, 1963).

of Hyde Park firmly in her own hands. She allowed her son to take some responsibility for the woods and the roads but meticulously kept his operations and hers separate.

Back in New York during the winter of 1906–7, Eleanor led an even quieter life than before, because she still had not completely recovered from her difficult pregnancy and tired easily. Occasionally, however, she and Franklin accepted an invitation to one of the big balls. The night of the Sloane dance, they had the Teddy Robinsons and the Biddles to dinner, went to a play, and then stopped at Mama's to "prink a little" before proceeding to the Sloanes', where they stayed through the cotillion and supper. Sometimes Eleanor encouraged Franklin to go alone or to stay on after she left. At Hyde Park it was customary to dine, dance, and see the New Year in at the Rogers' "with a great deal of noise and a punch bowl." There was ice-skating on the Hudson and tobogganing and skating on the Rogers pond. There were even baseball games on the spacious front lawn when the weather permitted. "We all went to a dinner of 50 at the Rogers," Sara noted New Year's Eve. "A dance after it. . . . E. does not seem at all well." Helen and Teddy were also at the party. "We dined at the Rogers tonight," Helen wrote, "a great big dinner as Edmund has a lot of men with him, & F.D.R. & Eleanor, Sylvia & Corinne are all staying at Cousin Sallie's & were all at dinner. It was great fun. . . . Teddy stayed till quite late . . . & I was tired, so we slept till 10.30 this morning."

Corinne also remembered the party. Eleanor had left with Sara after dinner; Franklin had stayed on, at Eleanor's urging, and had had "a lovely time," Corinne recalled. "It was an all-night affair and he could not have left before three or four in the morning." The next day when Corinne finally arose, she went in to see Eleanor and afterward ran into Franklin in the foyer. "He was pale as a sheet and furious. His mother had upbraided him for staying out so late, especially with his wife unwell, and had forced him to come down for breakfast at 8 A.M." Corinne and Franklin went for a walk and stopped in a greenhouse. "Suddenly there was a clatter of pipes and Franklin literally jumped. 'Are you afraid Mama is after you again?' I teased."[5]

If Eleanor was hurt by Franklin's easy acquiescence in her pulling back from most of the gay life of the young-married set she never said so, but much later she confessed that she had sometimes been jealous. She well remembered a young bride, Eleanor wrote in 1931 in a draft of an article, "The Tests of a Successful Wife" (and the reference, although in the third person, appears to be autobiographical), "who wept many tears because after an absence of some weeks, her husband on his return talked to her more about his business than about his love for her with the result that she thought the romance and glamor of marriage were gone forever."

Franklin, self-centered and flirtatious, would gladly have joined in every game or mischievous escapade of the moment. Banter came easily to him, and he was an incorrigible tease. Although Eleanor could laugh robustly, she was usually over-serious, sensitive, and felt insecure in casual relationships. Thus, not wishing to spoil her husband's fun, nor expose herself to embarrassment and humiliation, she increasingly withdrew.

Their different temperaments, values, and upbringing created problems of adjustment for both. She had high and precise standards of how her young husband should behave. If he disappointed her—if he, like her father, was as invariably late as she was prompt; if he forgot an anniversary by which she set much store; if he was sometimes less than frank; if, without suspecting the inner distress it caused her, he agreed to domestic arrangements she did not like—she did not speak to him about it. Instead, she withdrew into heavy silence. The depressions were a form of passive reproach: she did not dare to be defiant, for that meant risking the approval of those whom she wanted to love her. She called them her "Griselda moods," and she was, like Patient Griselda in Chaucer's "The Clerk's Tale," the medieval archetype of "wifely obedience...all meekness, all yielding, all resignation." Eleanor not only nursed her hurts and disappointments in silence, but performed her wifely duties so excellently, was so helpful, self-effacing, competent, and understanding that, also like Griselda, "Ech her lovede that looked in her face."* Franklin loved and admired his wife but was often puzzled by her "Griselda moods" and wished she would speak up. He wanted to live up to her expectations and was aware of his shortcomings, even if he was not unduly weighed down by them. It

---

* The parallels between Chaucer's Griselda and Eleanor go much beyond this point. The prince's subjects at first could not understand why, with all the beautiful girls in the realm to choose from, he settled on Griselda. But then as she took charge of his household, they recognized her "rype and sad corage," and before long all were her liege supporters, for

> So wyse and wordes hadde she
> And jugements of so greet equitee,
> That she from heaven sent was, as men wende,
> Peple to save and every wrong t'amende.

made him unhappy to see his wife sad or depressed, and at those times he left her alone, hoping it would blow over.

There were other differences between the two. Franklin executed his vestryman's duties at St. James Church faithfully, but often skipped Sunday services to play golf. Eleanor went to church regularly; it took time for her to become reconciled to his casual churchgoing habits. Franklin was dilatory about writing, while she was the most dependable of correspondents. "I was horribly disappointed with your hasty little scrap of a note yesterday after not getting anything for two days," she wrote from Campobello. It was a recurrent reproach.

In the excitement of the moment he often neglected his duties and forgot his promises, assuming that eventually, if others were involved, Sara or Eleanor would square things for him. And they did.

Eleanor took care of the amenities. When babies were born she sent notes of congratulations and ordered the gifts. When someone was ill, she called; when friends or relatives died, it was she who wrote. When Sara was not with them, it was Eleanor who said to Franklin, "I think Mama would love a letter from you" or "Don't forget Mama's birthday is the 21st." When Sara returned from Europe it was Eleanor who advised Franklin to have a man at customs "to see Mama through quickly...she expects us to 'smooth' things." She had an obsession about paying bills promptly; Franklin could be quite casual about this and tended to overlook them. She did not want to bother him in the midst of his Cambridge festivities, Eleanor wrote him in June, 1907, but "this has just come and I thought you said you wrote the man a note...."

Whether gladly or not, she accepted the role of prodder and manager in family affairs in her marriage, just as she had for her brother. On the whole, life seemed good. When two of her bridesmaids, Ellen Delano and Muriel Robbins, wrote her in the spring of 1907 about their young men, she commented to Franklin, "God bless them both and may their husbands be as good to them as you have been to me."

Her preparations at the end of 1907 for the birth of her second child were a model of serene efficiency. "It is a very active infant or infants (!)," she wrote her mother-in-law, "and I have never felt so well but it will stick out in front and I have great difficulty keeping my clothes from rising up to my chin! Miss Spring says if it is twins she will run away!!" On December 16, Miss Spring again came to stay.

Eleanor wrote out a list of things for Franklin to do.

F.D.R. List

Tell Sara she can have Mrs. Keenan for the afternoon & evening on her Sunday out & on Thursday evenings. Speak to Mrs. K. yourself. Tell Nurse to put Anna to sleep in her *crib* until I am well enough for her to go in her cage & to bring her down to you in the mornings as soon as you call & then you get the nursemaid when you leave to bring her sewing & stay with her till Nurse can come for her. Telephone G'ma—47 Germantown, Cousin Susie, Isabella 331 Plaza. A. Corinne 6605 - 38th St. Helen 1008 79th St. Telegraph A. Bye 1733 N. St.

    Milk tags for cans to be given Sara about Jan. 3d are in left hand drawer of my desk. Address envelopes for bills next to tags.

She bought and wrapped the Christmas gifts and filled the stockings, "even [for] Baby Anna and Miss Spring," Sara reported in some astonishment. On December 22, 1907, Eleanor, Franklin, and Hall dined with Sara and at 10:30 walked home. An hour later Hall was sent back to Sara's to spend the night there, as Eleanor's pains had begun. Franklin called his mother at 2:45 in the morning.

"I flew over and found Franklin to greet me with 'a son all right Mummy.'" Sara wrote in her diary. "I hope it will be *James*."

Franklin, elated, could not wait to inform the world. He called Helen and Teddy before breakfast, and Helen arrived almost immediately. Franklin showed her the "cunning baby," she reported. "He is lovely & looked like a 3-weeks-old child instead of only 7 hours! Weighs 10 lbs. 5 oz."

On the day that James was christened, Sara noted in royal phrases, "I gave presents on the place and house in honor of the named." As for Eleanor, her "heart sang," and she greeted the birth of a son with "relief and joy."

Despite James' size he was a sickly baby. He came down with pneumonia, and even after he recovered he was not completely well. The winter was difficult, for both baby and mother—"one of the times" in her life, Eleanor wrote, which she "would rather not live over again." To be near their doctor, the Roosevelts rented a cottage at Seabright, New Jersey, for the summer of 1908. Sara preferred not to be in Campobello without her children, and commuted between Hyde Park and Seabright during the hot summer months as did Franklin.

That summer Franklin had one of the first Fords around—it had no windshield, was cranked by hand, and was prone to frequent blowouts.

"Has Franklin done anything rash yet—such as driving across the lawn and through the hedge?" Hall inquired. But it was Eleanor, not Franklin, who banged into the gate post when she was learning to drive. She gave up the attempt after the mishap, appalled at having damaged something that was Franklin's. She preferred the victoria, in which she and the children took drives along the beach.

Franklin and Eleanor enjoyed their children, whose first lispings were chronicled in detail. "She kept her eyes fixed on the door and said 'pa pa pa' all the time," Eleanor reported of Anna, aged eight months. There wasn't a funnier sight, she told her mother-in-law, than Franklin coming up the hill with Anna on his back, her "two short legs sticking straight out of either side of his head." Anna's first steps were duly noted. "She began on Sunday going from him [Franklin] to Cousin Susie and does better all the time but she loves it so that she really runs instead of walking which is the cause of many tumbles and subsequent tears."

In later years Eleanor described herself as having been a model of innocence and ignorance in her methods of child training. A believer in fresh air, she cradled Anna in a wire contraption rigged up outside a window until outraged neighbors, who allegedly threatened to report Eleanor to the Society for the Prevention of Cruelty to Children, compelled her to give up the experiment. But the other young wives thought her a pioneer. "How well I remember the Tuckermans, etc. on 37th Street agitating over the baby outside the window," Lily Polk later recalled, "and how wise the younger ones thought it and when we copied you how daring we felt!"

Though Eleanor knew what habits she wanted to encourage in her children, she was not sufficiently sure of herself to overrule the formidable array of mother-in-law, nurses, and English governess. In these early years she yielded to their authority against her own better judgment. "Anna is upset today so I am told though I haven't seen her long enough to judge for myself. Mama and Nelly think so, however, so she has gone to bed and had a dose of castor oil." On another occasion she thought that Anna wasn't well, but Sara disagreed. The doctor came and said Anna "should have calomel and I expect all would have been well before had I given it but Mama is so against it I didn't dare!" But if Sara and a nurse disagreed, the headstrong Sara laid down the law: "I told Nurse Watson she *must* get up and turn her [Anna] over and soothe her," Sara once noted in her diary.

When Anna was sixteen months old, Nurse Nelly had to be away. "I am to take charge of her and put her to bed tonight," Eleanor wrote, and noted the next day, "I never knew before how easy it was to take care of Anna." When Nurse Nelly returned, the baby was pleased, but, wrote Eleanor, "I am glad to say I think she missed me a little last night!"

In the autumn of 1908 Franklin and Eleanor moved into a house Sara had had built for them at 49 East Sixty-fifth Street. She had announced her intentions at Christmas in 1905, and the following year had acquired the land and hired Charles A. Platt, the designer of the Freer Gallery of Art in Washington, D.C., to draw up plans for adjoining houses—one for herself and one for the young couple—like the Ludlow-Parish houses on Seventy-sixth Street. The two houses' drawing and dining rooms opened onto each other, there was a connecting door on the fourth floor, and they had a common vestibule.

When Franklin came home on their first evening in the new house, he found his wife in tears. This was not her house, she sobbed. She had not helped plan it, and this wasn't the way she wanted to live. Why hadn't she told him this before, her bewildered husband asked. They had gone over the plans together—why hadn't she spoken up? He told her gently that she was not seeing things as they really were, and quickly left the room.[6]

If Sara knew of Eleanor's unhappiness, she did not admit it, even to herself. "Some of [my] friends were surprised," she told her biographer twenty-five years later, that Franklin and Eleanor had not lived with her after their marriage. That had never occurred to her, she blandly averred; she valued her independence too highly.[7] "You were never quite sure when she would appear, day or night," Eleanor later said of the connecting doors.[8]

With all her benevolence and breeding, Sara was an autocrat and rather enjoyed being regarded as the "redoubted madam" by her staff. She would have been surprised and hurt, however, if she had been told she was trying to rule her children's lives. She was a matriarch who belonged completely to a past generation; she sought to dominate her children's lives as she had dominated her husband's—from behind a façade of total generosity, submission, and love.

"Last night we had such a funny time," Eleanor wrote from Seabright to Nova Scotia, where Franklin was on a hunting expedition with Hall.

You would have enjoyed it for Anna gave Mama a little exhibition of her will power! She wished to sit on a certain chair and Grandma thought by talking to her and diverting her mind she could be made to sit on another and the result was shrieks and G'ma rapidly took to the desired chair.

When she ceased to weep I said "Oh! Anna where did you get all your determination from?" and she looked up at Mama and said "Gaga!"

Of course I almost expired for it did hit the nail so beautifully on the head.

Sara's husband had advised her never to be materially dependent upon her children, but it was all right, she told Eleanor, to have her children be dependent on her. "I think she always reverted that my husband had money of his own from his father and that I had a small incomes of my own," Eleanor said many years later. Their son James stated it more bluntly: "Granny's ace in the hole ... was the fact that she held the purse strings in the family. For years she squeezed all of us—Father included—in this golden loop."

Few in the family were aware that Eleanor found total subordination to her mother-in-law increasingly oppressive. She did confide, often tearfully, Laura Delano said, in Laura's mother, Mrs. Warren Delano, who lived around the corner. But if she could tell Aunt Jennie, Laura wondered, why couldn't she have had it out with her husband and her mother-in-law?[9]

A few of her closest friends eventually became aware of the situation and concluded that she kept silent because she did not wish to do anything that might disturb the relationship between mother and son. Moreover, she could not bear being scolded or rebuked herself. She had developed a sixth sense for Sara's velvety "yes" that really meant "no" and was so sensitive even to these indirect reproaches that she preferred to swallow her discontent. That was the period, a friend recalled, when she was saying "Yes, Mama" or "No, Mama" three or four times in a row.[10] She was "very dependent" on her mother-in-law, Eleanor said forty years later; she had needed Sara's help "on almost every subject and never thought of asking for anything which I felt would not meet with her approval."[11] But this self-subordination exacted its toll in self-doubt, bottled-up anger, and withdrawal into those "Griselda moods" that her husband found so puzzling.

Whatever Eleanor's private frustrations, Sara was oblivious of them in her diaries, which were a serene chronicle of the things she did with Franklin and Eleanor and their children: "A little dinner for F. & E." "To town early. Arranged flowers for F. & E.'s lunch of 22 for the T.R. family." "Today E. & I walked to church." In 1908 Eleanor was pregnant for the third time, and a diary she kept briefly before the baby was born revealed only that, like other young wives, she moved in a world that was still limited to family and old friends, to familiar surroundings and activities. She was very precise in noting the time Franklin came in and when he went out alone. She dined alone with Sara, she recorded in January, 1909, while Franklin went to a dinner pary with Teddy Robinson, played poker at the Knickerbocker Club, and "returned home 4 A.M." Two weeks later there was a similar entry: "F. went to Harvard Club dinner & got home 3:30 A.M. Dined with Mama."

On Wednesday, March 17, she wrote, "St. Patrick's Day, Mother's birthday. Our fourth wedding anniversary!" The next day Franklin Jr. was born.

Again Sara recorded the event.

March 18th Eleanor had her beautiful hair washed, etc. and nails done. At 2 she went to drive with me. We got home at 4. At 5.30 Dr. Ely came. At 8.10 her second son was born. Franklin got home at 4.45 so he was there very soon after Eleanor got home from her drive. The baby is really lovely and very big, 11 lbs.

Franklin Jr. was indeed the biggest and most beautiful of all Eleanor and Franklin's babies. Eleanor had regretted letting Miss Spring go too quickly after the birth of James, and this time she insisted on keeping Miss Spring for several months.

In the summer of 1909 they returned to Campobello but stayed in a house of their own. Mrs. Hartman Kuhn, who had owned the cottage next door to Sara's, had become as fond of Eleanor, who frequently read to her, as she had always been of Franklin. She had died in 1908, and her will stipulated that Sara could have her house for $5,000, if she purchased it for Franklin and Eleanor. Sara did so.

This was the first house that Eleanor felt was her own. "I have moved every room in the house around," she gaily reported to her husband, "and I hope you will like the change," and he should bring up his caribou and wolf skins to spread in front of the fireplace. Now Franklin and Eleanor could have whomever they wished as guests.

Although Sara had encouraged them to invite friends when they stayed with her, her opinions of suitable guests had not always coincided with Eleanor's. Furthermore, Sara did not want her children to form close attachments outside the family circle. Eleanor liked Miss Spring, from whom she had learned a great deal, but when she lunched with Miss Spring she did not dare mention it to Sara and cautioned Franklin not to do so, "for Mama always seems to dislike my doing things with her!" Even after her first summer in her own house in Campobello Eleanor was fearful of Sara's reaction to the announcement that she was inviting Miss Spring to come up for part of the next summer.

"I broke it to Mama Miss Spring was coming up and put it all on you," she advised her husband. Unable to stand up for herself and say "this is what I want," she made use of others. It was a conscious tactic that she would employ in the White House years with great subtlety and sophistication in order to get Franklin to do the things which he might otherwise refuse to do if the suggestions came directly from her.

Eleanor was content at Campobello. The pace there was more sedate than at Bar Harbor or Newport. The summer families had a club of sorts and were satisfied with an occasional dance for which a Victor talking machine provided the music. Eleanor even liked the Bay of Fundy's fogs and its prolonged periods of foul weather, for she was an avid reader and enjoyed reading aloud to family and guests in front of the fireplace in the large living room.

She always arrived at Campobello determined on self-improvement. One summer she and Sara read all of Ferrero's volumes on Rome. She began to study Spanish with the help of recordings. "All my Spanish things are here," she wrote Franklin, "but I am waiting for you to put my phonograph together!" Franklin did, but at the end of the summer she confessed she might never learn the language because she still had not mastered the art of making the phonograph work.

Until his marriage, Hall spent part of his summers at Campobello. Franklin enjoyed and admired his brilliant young brother-in-law, who had been chosen senior prefect at Groton. Whenever Hall arrived, a covey of girls would immediately gather around him, and Franklin and Eleanor spoke teasingly about "Hall and his harem." Hall looked up to his sister, whose selflessness and devotion he appreciated. "I despair of hearing from Eleanor about herself," he wrote Franklin from Groton. "I hope you will drop me a postal some time just to let me know how she is getting on."

When Franklin had to be in New York, Eleanor tried to pinch-hit for him with the children in outdoor activities, and during the summer of 1909, when James was a year and a half and Anna a little over three, she took them sailing on the *Half Moon*. "I think they will sail rather seldom together as James goes round and round the cockpit and won't sit still and Anna kicks him whenever she can." James had his defenses against Anna, however: "He is very naughty and poor Anna's arm is all blue where he bit her yesterday."

There were fond letters from Eleanor and the children.

Dearest Honey—
The enclosure was dictated jointly by Anna & James on the *Half Moon* this afternoon. We got off at three but the wind was light & we didn't get up to G. South Bay but the chicks had supper on board & loved it.

This morning I took Anna & James to the beach & as there was no wind & the sun was hot I put on Anna's bathing suit & she waded until just before we came up when she sat down & kicked & splashed & then ran home & slept 2 hours! She is mad about it & James weeps because he can't sit down & when I say he must stop wading he kicks & howls with rage!...

Ever so much love.   E.R.
(Enclosure)

Dear Fadder,
I had my bathing suit on & go in the water & walked & sat down & splashed. (James) took off his shoes & stockings & was angry as he couldn't walk to the boat. In the morning I say "Good morning Half Moon, Captain, Mother, Old Mother Hubbard.
(Anna) I wouldn't like to go away from Campobello.
(James) Poor Fadder go to New York.
(A. & J.) Like Fadder to come back soon.
Anna's kiss...made by herself.
James' kiss   Your loving
                                                   Anne & James

And there were the detailed orders from an efficient wife in cool Campobello to a husband in the sweltering city. "I enclose my list of things to be done," she wrote Franklin, "and I am sorry for you."

Ask Mary if she knows of two good, *honest* cleaners to come on Monday, Sept. 13th & start at the roof & clean down & be through on Sept. 21st. To take great care with the white paint & get it clean also sun the children's mattresses on the roof & beat them well the last day. I think it would be well for you to ask Harriet to do the library & tell her to take all the books out, wipe them & put them back. She ought to do it in three days & as she can't work steadily I would tell her that we will only pay her $1. a day. The other cleaners get $1.50.

Telephone R. H. Morisson 73rd St. & 3d Avenue to clean all the chimneys between the 9th & 11th as it must be over before the cleaning begins. Also find out from Max if the [word indistinct] cap is on the chimney as we don't want more work than necessary done after the house is clean.

Bring me Aug. & Sept. Harper's when you come. Go to Putnam's & order some nice book not more than $5. sent to Miss Ellen Shipman, Windsor, Vermont, with enclosed card.

If Mary knows no cleaners ask Harriet.

I am anxiously waiting for the wash trunk. Was Mary at the house when you got home? Will you ask her when the trunk left? Don't forget to look in both houses for [words indistinct]. Tell me what Dr. Dailey's bill was. Send Hall his check book.

Subsequent letters supplemented these instructions.

Their return to New York that autumn was shadowed by the illness of Franklin Jr. Although he weighed eleven pounds at birth, he seemed delicate, like James, and Miss Spring was with the family at Campobello most of the summer to care for him. They were worried about his rapid breathing, but they were not prepared for the worsening in his condition that set in late in October. Sara reported the course of the crisis in her journal and the reaction of the three of them to the tragedy.

Oct. 29. Baby cried often in the morning, but was sleeping sweetly in the pram at 12.30 when I went in a motor to the Olins for lunch. Mrs. Howard with me. At 2, Annie the housemaid telephoned me to come as Baby was ill. I *flew* home. . . . Dr. Gribbon was here, holding precious Baby. He just got there in time as the little heart had almost stopped. . . . I telephoned E. she and F. came at 8.30 bringing Miss Spring. Dr. Gribbon stayed till 11.

Oct. 30th. . . . they all leave on the 9.30 train. . . . Dr. Winters in N.Y. confirms Dr. Gribbon that it is serious heart trouble. Some hope is held out. Darling Eleanor is brave and Franklin helps and supports her hopeful spirit.

Oct. 31st. Eleanor says Baby had a fair night and is quiet. They are hopeful. At 2.30 Franklin telephoned me not so well. I went to town, though just as I left, F. said "don't come down." I simply had to go. When I got there, E. said, "Oh I am so glad you came.". . .

Nov. 1st. At a little before 5 I went in. Dr. Carr said "He is holding his own." At a little before 7 A.M. F. telephoned me to my room. "Better come, Mama, Baby is sinking." I went in. The little angel ceased breathing at 7:45. Miss Spring was asleep in her room but Dr. Carr and Miss Battin did what they could. F. and E. are most wonderful, but poor E.'s mother heart is well nigh broken. She so hoped and cannot believe her baby is gone from her. He was 7 months and 9 days old, a beautiful flower he always seemed and yet the delicacy certainly was there and he could not overcome it.

Nov. 2nd. I sat often besides my little grandson. It is hard to give him up and my heart aches for Eleanor.

Nov. 5. F. and E came home (i.e., H.P.) and it is such a sad home-coming. E. is perfectly marvelous the way she bears it.

Nov. 7th. All to church. E. brave and lovely.

For many months Eleanor's life was darkened by the baby's death. She felt she was in some way to blame and reproached herself for not caring for him enough. The baby's death reinforced her sense of inadequacy as a woman and as a mother. When Elliott, born ten months later, turned out to be a more agitated and excitable baby than Anna and James had been, she blamed that, too, on her moodiness while carrying him. Only gradually did she conquer her grief for her dead baby, and she often laid flowers on the quiet little grave in the St. James churchyard and recalled the sad burial scene.

Such tragedies, as she well knew from childhood, were part of the human condition. Religion comforted her, as did her love for Franklin. "I miss you dreadfully and feel very lonely," she wrote him from Campobello the next summer, "but please don't think it is because I am alone, having other people wouldn't do any good for I just want you!"

"Success in marriage," she told an interviewer many years later, "depends on being able when you get over being in love, to really love...you never know anyone until you marry them."[12] Five years after her marriage, just before Franklin entered politics, their friends considered them an exemplary couple and thought Eleanor remarkable for the way she fulfilled her role as wife, mother, mistress of her household, and daughter-in-law.

16. THE WIFE OF A PUBLIC OFFICIAL

————————————————————◇

AFTER TAFT'S ELECTION IN 1908 THEODORE ROOSEVELT INVITED various younger members of the family to the White House for a final visit before inauguration day. Eleanor and Franklin went down early in January, and a week later it was the Teddy Robinsons' turn. "It is rather horrid to feel that is the last time that we will be at the White House in that way," Helen wrote.[1] Franklin had other thoughts. Imbued with Theodore's ideals of public service, he already contemplated a career modeled on Uncle Ted's that would bring him to the White House on his own. To his fellow law clerks he outlined a political timetable like his uncle's—the state legislature, assistant secretary of the Navy, the governorship, and then, with "any luck," the presidency. The law office was only a way station on the road to the livelier world of politics, and "he intended to run for office at the first opportunity."[2]

Franklin's mother did not welcome the idea that her son might become involved in the "messy business" of politics, as she later told her biographer. She did not see why she should receive all these people whom she had never called on and whose families she did not know. Eleanor, however, was neither surprised nor upset by his plans.[3] While Franklin was still in law school she had written Auntie Bye, "he will not find himself altogether happy with the law he is studying at Columbia unless he is able to get a broad human contact through it."[4] A career in politics would assure him of a life full of excitement and variety in which his ability to get along with people would be important.

Franklin had always voted from Hyde Park. Like his father, he was active in village and county affairs, but with Eleanor at his side to encourage him he brushed aside his mother's pleas that he follow his father and lead a "peaceful life among the family, the friends and neighbors at Hyde Park." When John Mack, Democratic district attorney in Dutchess County, dropped into the Carter, Ledyard and Milburn offices early in 1910 to talk Dutchess politics and discuss the possibility of Franklin running for the state legislature, he found an attentive listener.

Eleanor had known enough men in public life to realize that if her husband embarked on a political career it would mean that the family would have to move about a lot, be very adaptable, and make many sacrifices. But she wanted her husband to have large plans, and if realizing those dreams meant she would have to make adjustments, she was prepared to do so—to live in Albany if that was required and to see that his household ran smoothly. Politics was neither new nor threatening to her. She followed public affairs, read the *New York Times* regularly, and, like her husband, had been stirred by Uncle Ted's appeals to the younger generation to devote themselves to the public good. And deep within she must have realized that Franklin's entry into politics would mean an expansion of her horizons as well as his.

In June she and Franklin lunched with Uncle Ted on his return from Europe and Africa, and no doubt they discussed Franklin's decision to go into politics. Theodore was planning to return to the political wars himself, to fight the conservative drift in the Republican party under Taft. Would Uncle Ted be campaigning in Dutchess County, Franklin asked Auntie Bye a few weeks later. "Franklin ought to go into politics without the least regard as to where I speak or don't speak," Theodore advised Bye. Franklin was "a fine fellow," he went on, but he wished he had Joe Alsop's views. Joe Alsop, whom Auntie Corinne described as "a very strong man," had married young Corinne and was involved in Republican politics in Connecticut. And in Herkimer, New York, Teddy Robinson was preparing to run for the state assembly as a Republican.

She had heard an amusing account, Aunt Ella wrote Eleanor from Liverpool, of how Franklin, Teddy, and Joe Alsop were "all in the limelight and Uncle Ted in the extraordinary position of being the arbiter of the Republican destinies. He has certainly infected you all with large ambitions as citizens and I am sure will be proud of you all."[5]

It was a measure of Franklin's independence that, admiring Theodore as greatly as he did, he stuck with the Democrats. Eleanor, although she worshiped her uncle and had been raised in a household and milieu where "Republicanism and respectability went hand in hand,"[6] followed her husband's political allegiance. Any suggestion that she should not would have shocked her, and she certainly did not envisage a political role for herself. She was an anti-suffragette, and vigorously so. Pussie was the only advocate of the women's vote in the family. "The most surprising part to me," Hall commented to Eleanor in 1908, "is that she is trying to convert you of all people." Two years later Eleanor was still disagreeing with Pussie over the suffragette issue, and evidently with some violence, to judge by Hall's reproving remark: "I thought you had more self control."

While Eleanor insisted that politics was a man's domain, she wanted to share her husband's interests and accomplishments, a somewhat contradictory position that was also held by other strong-minded women of that transitional era. Beatrice Webb did not recant her public opposition to women's suffrage until 1909, even though she had renounced her romance with Joe Chamberlain rather than yield to his insistence that he should have the final word in their marriage.[7] Eleanor made no such demand, but she did want to be part of her husband's life away from home as well as in it.

She was at Campobello most of the summer of 1910 when Franklin was meeting with the Dutchess County leaders and party workers. Her letters begged him to keep her informed about his political prospects; it was difficult enough being at Campobello without him, she wrote, but if he did not write she would feel quite lost. And if he was unable to come up as he had planned, "I shall weep." Franklin hoped to run for the assembly, but the incumbent, Lewis Stuyvesant Chanler, finally told him he had no intention of bowing out. This left the state senate seat, which had only once been won from the Republicans, in the 1880s by Roosevelt's neighbor, Thomas Jefferson Newbold. Franklin's chances of winning, Mack cautioned him, were one in five. Undaunted, Franklin decided to make the bid.

On September 23, 1910, Eleanor gave birth to Elliott, an eleven-pound fourteen-ounce baby. Two weeks later, on October 6, the Democratic leaders meeting in convention in Poughkeepsie formally nominated Franklin Roosevelt for state senator. Sara now discovered that pride in her son was stronger than anxiety over the hordes of strangers she might have to receive. She sat proudly through the meeting as he made his acceptance speech, she recalled two decades later, her head held high, sure as she heard his statement of principles that *noblesse oblige* would shape his career in politics as it had that of her old friend Theodore and the sons of her highborn friends in England.[8] In her diary at the time, however, she limited herself to the more pragmatic comment, "Franklin will be here now a great deal."

Eleanor did not hear the speech. Immobilized in New York City with her newly born baby, she had to be satisfied with the lilies, at that time her favorite flower, that Franklin had sent her. "Much love and good luck to you in your campaigning," she wrote him as he set out to reverse the 5 to 1 odds by the unorthodoxy of his campaign tactics. "In the coming campaign," he had pledged in his acceptance speech, "I need not tell you that I do not intend to sit still. We are going to have a very strenuous month." He hired a red Maxwell touring car and decked it out with flags, and "at the dangerous pace of about 22 miles an hour" he and the congressional candidate, Richard Connell, a spread-eagle orator, toured the district, stopping at every country store, talking to every farmer, speaking in every village.* Not even a fall from a moving street car slowed him down. Eleanor spent twenty-four hours soaking his elbows and knees in disinfectant and he was off again. The Saturday before the election Eleanor heard him make his final speech outside the Nelson House in Poughkeepsie, later known as his "lucky corner"—the first time she had heard him make a political speech. She agonized over his slow delivery and frequent pauses,[9] but he managed, nonetheless, to convey warmth, friendliness, and self-confidence. The voters responded. On Election Day, Sara recorded, in the proper order of their importance to her, "Anna weighs 42.8; James 35.13. Franklin elected State Senator with about 1,500 majority."

It was a Democratic sweep in which the governorship as well as both houses of the legislature were captured by the party, but Franklin ran far ahead of the state ticket. His unparalleled 1,140 majority in a rock-ribbed Republican district was noted by politicians throughout the state. "Telegrams coming all day for Franklin," Sara recorded. Eleanor returned to New York to be with her baby, but a new period was beginning in her life, for Franklin had said that if elected he wanted his family with him in Albany. "We're thinking of your move to Albany," Isabella Ferguson wrote Eleanor from Cat Cañon in New Mexico. The Fergusons and their two children had cut loose from

---

* In later years he often regaled his wife and children with the song that he and Connell sang as they neared some port of call:

> Are we almost there?—Are we almost there?
> Said the dying girl as she neared her home.
> Be them the tall poplar trees what rears
> Their lofty heights against Heaven's big dome——
> Are we——al——most there——
>
> (agonized diminuendo)

fashionable New York and were literally tenting down in the south-west desert because the dry air and hot sun had been recommended for Bob's lungs. Eleanor's impending move represented almost as drastic a break with her previous style of life as the Fergusons' had.

The change began in November when she and Franklin, without Sara, went to Albany to look for a house. They picked a large brown-stone with an enormous library and a small garden. Although it seemed quite palatial compared to their narrow New York house, "it is a com-fort to have only three stories instead of six," Franklin commented. Three weeks later they returned with Sara, who approved. "A fine house can be made comfortable."

Albany in 1911 was a cluster of low roofs dominated by a few church spires and the architectural pile on a hill that constituted the center of the state government. For most of the legislators the city was little more than a dormitory and their brief stays were confined to the stretch of pavement between the Hotel Ten Eyck, the capitol, and the railroad station. It was also a pleasant city for those who wanted to live there, with broad avenues, narrow tree-shaded streets, and a spacious park full of lovely walks and drives where Eleanor and the nurses could take the children. Among the brownstones and red brick homes were a few gabled roofs to remind newcomers of the city's Dutch antecedents. The small, compact Albany society was dominated by a few old families of Dutch lineage, and it bid the Roosevelts welcome.

Eleanor was the wife of Albany's most talked-about young politi-cian, and her initiation into official life was swift, sudden, and thor-ough. On the Sunday before Governor Dix's inauguration, with the children, their three nurses, and a household staff barely settled, she and Sara were arranging furniture and hanging photographs when politicians who had come to Albany for the inauguration began to drop by to take a look at Franklin.

The next day, wife, mother, and brother-in-law accompanied the new senator to the assembly chamber, where they listened to the governor's speech and then hurried home because Franklin had announced "open house" for his constituents. A block away, they saw a dense, cheering crowd in the front of their house—the delegation from Franklin's senatorial district, "four hundred strong!" as Franklin told the story. There was a band and the Hyde Park Fife and Drum Corps, both "working overtime," and "all finally managed to get into the house, shaking hands as they passed into the Dining Room." To Eleanor the catered luncheon seemed endless, but Sara thought she "managed splendidly," and Franklin recorded proudly that both "E.R. and S.D.R.... made a hit with the whole delegation."

Eleanor's initiation was not yet over. She and Franklin drove to the executive mansion to pay their formal respects to Governor and Mrs. Dix, and when they returned half the Dutchess County delegation was back at the house to await the departure of their train. It was late afternoon before Franklin coaxed them out and led them down to the station. Scarcely had Eleanor and Sara gone back to moving furniture when the governor called and invited Franklin and Eleanor to come up to the mansion for a "family party" and a little informal dancing; so they quickly dressed and hurried over.[10] The next night they were again with the governor, this time as guests of Colonel and Mrs. William Gorham Rice, old friends of the James Roosevelts. Colonel Rice had been President Cleveland's secretary, and he and Governor Dix were Cleveland Democrats, as Franklin's father had been and as his half brother Rosy still was. Mrs. Rice welcomed Eleanor to Albany with a list of places to shop and a ceremonial offering of "ole Keuken," a cake that was still eaten by the families descended from the original Dutch colonists. Another guest at the Rices' was Thomas Mott Osborne, the former mayor of Auburn. A man of wealth, he was the leader of the anti-Tammany liberal wing of the Democratic party, which he had nurtured along with the help of an upstate newspaperman named Louis Howe.

On Wednesday Sara returned to Hyde Park. "It seems like a very strange dream," she wrote Franklin and Eleanor, "to be here and to think of you dear things all settled in that big Albany house and my boy sitting in the State Senate, a really fine and dignified position, if only lived up to as it should be and I know it *will* be by my dear one. ... I was *so* interested today and were I to be with you I should be very often in that gallery."

For the first time since her marriage, Eleanor was out of immediate reach of Sara and Cousin Susie and had to depend upon herself. Although she was shy and uncertain, necessity was a good teacher. In the few days she had been in Albany, she had met hundreds of new people, had had to cope with all kinds of new situations, and had discovered not only that she could manage, but that she liked it.

She had a lively intellectual curiosity, was as interested in people as her husband was, and found the political atmosphere invigorating. When Franklin turned their State Street house into the headquarters of the insurgents a few days after the session began, Eleanor took it in her stride. At that time U.S. senators were still chosen by the state legislature, and Tammany leader Charles F. Murphy wanted Chauncey M. Depew's successor to be "Blue-eyed Billy" Sheehan. Edmund R. Terry, an independent assemblyman from Brooklyn who had been a classmate of President Taft's at Yale, began the rebellion against Boss Murphy's designation of Sheehan. Franklin was the first senator to join the assembly insurgents and was made the spokesman for the group. He quickly became "the shepherd of the flock," Terry wrote, "and his house was during the early days of the insurgency a harbor of refuge nearly every evening."

Eleanor spent many of these evenings with the men, and later estimated that she got to know at least thirty of them "very well." For her it was a seminar in the more practical side of politics. She made the men feel at home in the library; sometimes she sat with them, but more often they slipped into the living room to talk with her. Terry was one of the most faithful. A prolific writer of verse, he read it to her by the hour while she knitted. At the end of the evening, with Terry's help she brought in crackers, cheese, and beer, which became the signal that it was time, gentlemen, to adjourn.

The press came to the house, another new experience for Eleanor. Louis Howe, a poky little man in disheveled clothes, was often there as reporter and adviser, and Eleanor invited his wife and daughter to lunch. Another day Mr. and Mrs. Sheehan were her luncheon guests. The former Buffalo boss hoped he could soften Franklin's opposition in a direct confrontation, and the men withdrew, leaving the ladies to make polite, uncomfortable small talk. It was sticky going. Finally the parley ended and the Sheehans left. "Did you come to any agreement?" Eleanor anxiously asked. "Certainly not," her huband replied. The struggle went on.

Sara came to Albany. "He is working bravely," she wrote. Uncle Ted also approved: "Just a line to say that we are all really proud of the way you have handled yourself." Franklin felt the same way about his distinguished relative. "Are you an admirer of your uncle-in-law?" a reporter asked him. "Why, who can help but admire him? ... My uncle-in-law will come back all right, no matter what some people believe." Sheehan spread the word that Franklin was really Theodore's agent and was trying to split the Democratic party. "Why I haven't seen my distinguished cousin since the first of the year," Franklin said laughingly, and then added, a little inaccurately, "We've had absolutely no communication on this subject." As Franklin's fight made him known throughout the state, the mail began to pour in, and Eleanor received her first fan letter: "I know very well he never could do so well, and be so brave, if he were not upheld and strengthened in every way by his wife." It was one of the few nonfamily letters she saved from that period.

The meetings continued night after night, and when the children, whose nursery was directly above the library, began to complain about the cigar smoke, Eleanor moved the nursery to the third floor. She presided over frequent dinners and larger entertainments that mixed politicians and local society. She met thirty-three-year-old Robert Wagner, whose nomination as president pro tem of the state senate Franklin had seconded on behalf of the upstate senators. Alfred E. Smith, assembly majority leader and another of Murphy's protégés, came to dinner. When British Ambassador James Bryce addressed a joint session of the legislature, Franklin and Eleanor gave a party for about one hundred people at which Ruth Draper did her monologues and Tammanyites, insurgents, and Albany cliff dwellers rubbed shoulders. "Mr. Grady gratefully acknowledges the honor and accepts the gracious compliment of the invitation of Mrs. Roosevelt to her at home," one reply read, from Senator Tom Grady, the courtly, eloquent, but somewhat bibulous Tammanyite. Although Franklin had helped to depose Grady as senate leader, he liked the young man's wife. "Be with the insurgents," he wrote Eleanor on St. Patrick's Day, "and if needs be with your husband every day in the year but this—to-day he 'wid us.'"

When Sheehan finally withdrew from the race, Murphy put forward the candidacy of Justice O'Gorman, a man of integrity though a former Tammany sachem. The insurgents went along, and newspapermen wrote that Roosevelt had been scalped by Tammany. They failed to note that Franklin Roosevelt's name had become nationally known in connection with the movement for direct, popular election of senators and that he had become identified as part of the progressive wing of the Democratic party. As for Eleanor, she asserted that the rights and wrongs of the Sheehan fight meant very little to her, although she was appalled at the reprisals against some of the more vulnerable insurgents. Franklin, however, later said that the struggle was the beginning of his wife's "political sagacity."

When, at a banquet given by the Columbia County Society, a reporter asked Franklin how country women compared with those in the cities, he replied, "I'm afraid I'm a little prejudiced in that direction," and flashed his broad smile. "I haven't been married long enough to compare any woman favorably with my wife—and she came from the country, from Columbia County which is one of the reasons I am at this banquet. If all country girls are like her, then there can be no comparison—and you must pardon me if I make none."

Their close friends knew how helpful she was to him. "She did everything quietly but calmly and most efficiently," Langdon P. Marvin, one of Franklin's law partners, later recalled. "She was a great manager in the family and in the household and everybody loved her." She was also, he added, "the ardent backer" of her husband, even though he was not able to budge her when he began to shift his position on women's suffrage.[11] His conversion was less than wholehearted at first. With an eye on his rural constituents—and perhaps also on his mother and his wife—he hedged his stand, saying that the voters should express their views through a referendum before the legislature acted. That, said the beautiful and relentless suffragette, Inex Milholland, who lobbied Senator Roosevelt on the issue, was "a very stupid and expensive way" of going about it.

Miss Milholland had come to Poughkeepsie in May, 1911, to fire up the feminist troops, of which the Vassar faculty was a powerful contingent. She marshaled the members of the Dutchess County chapter of the Equal Suffrage League in a series of street-corner meetings and house-to-house canvasses.[12] Senator Roosevelt finally took the correct stand, but without help from his wife, who still considered men superior beings. Nor is there any evidence that Eleanor intervened on behalf of another crusader for women's rights, Frances Perkins, just out of college, who had joined the staff of the Consumers League and, as a lobbyist in Albany for the fifty-four-hour bill for working women, was having difficulty with Franklin.

Eleanor was not yet "the evident force" that she subsequently became, observed Marvin. Within the privacy of the family, however, she was a sympathetic and interested listener who through her questions and comments helped Franklin clarify his opinions by talking them out, as she had seen her Auntie Bye do with Uncle Ted.

She went to the senate gallery regularly to listen to the debates and occasionally visited the assembly side to follow the progress of a bill. She read political materials, including such recondite documents as the proceedings of the 1884 Democratic national convention, which Colonel Rice had sent to her. By the beginning of July, when she transported her large household to Campobello, she had the knowledge of

a political insider to whom Franklin could write in the crisp shorthand that political professionals use about such varied items as the
race-track-gambling bill, the ups and downs of his fight for a direct
primary, or his intricate political maneuvers to defeat a Republican
reapportionment bill.

It was a disturbed summer. No sooner had Eleanor arrived in Campobello than Franklin reported he was having trouble with his sinuses
and that he felt "like a rag and have lost nearly ten pounds. . . . I can't
tell you how I miss you and Mama does not in the least make up."
Eleanor promptly returned to Albany to nurse him. "Eleanor came in
all the heat," Sara noted, adding five days later, "Poor Eleanor returns
alone to Campobello." Franklin stayed to push his direct-primary bill.
When the legislature recessed without action, he hastened to Campobello, but he had to leave again early in September. "I feel lonely
and depressed and wish you were here," she wrote him. "Take care
of yourself and write often and tell me everything."

She realized that she would often have to manage without him in the
summer. She was a conscientious manager. Henry Parish, the banker
who was married to Cousin Susie, taught her to keep her household
accounts, and his lessons were supplemented by those Franklin gave
her. She budgeted carefully. "I enclose Edgar's bill which is a dreadful
surprise to me," she wrote her husband from Campobello. "I had no
idea that you had told him to spend so much on the pool or that he
had to work so many days in the winter. This year we must make it
plain that we want no work done!" Sometimes her efforts at frugality and careful planning ran athwart Sara. Eleanor and Franklin had
decided that instead of opening their townhouse in New York for the
few autumn months before they were back in Albany, they would stay
with Sara and board out the servants they wanted to keep. Sara was
upset over the proposed arrangements, Franklin warned; she wanted
the servants to stay. "Do just as you think best dearest," he wrote
Eleanor, "and you know I'll back you up!" his letter ended.

"Really, Honey, it becomes ludicrous!" Eleanor protested in a spurt
of independence:

> She made an offer then withdrew it and now wants to renew it! I
> think she had better decide another time before speaking and as
> I wrote you it would be foolish to get new servants and put them
> in her house as Lydia is going. I expect to let Emily go also as I
> overheard a conversation which made me decide that she talked

too much even though she might seem nice to me!...After Cousin Susie is in town I'm sure she will love having us stay there if we want to anytime and I would rather do it than go to Mama's now! I simply wrote Mama all my plans were already made and no one would be in her house and I did not expect to go there!

Eleanor's view prevailed. It usually did when she considered it worthwhile to make a stand.

When they returned to Albany for the winter 1911–12 they moved into a new house. Their friends were glad to see them both. They were "exceedingly popular...their home...the scene of good fellowship and real family life."[13] People were as interested in Eleanor as they were in Franklin, and she was now an old Albany hand. She called on the wives of the new legislators and helped make them feel at home, and she dropped in on the wives of newspapermen. Her thoughtfulness and kindness made friends for Franklin everywhere. Teddy Robinson had been elected to the assembly from Herkimer in November's Republican comeback, and the two families saw each other often. For Franklin's birthday Eleanor had the Robinsons, Hall and his fiancée, Margaret Richardson, William Church Osborn, the Rices, and some senatorial colleagues with whom Franklin worked closely. Sara was not there. "I planned to go up and surprise you today," she wrote, "and spend one night but as Hall and Margaret get there today I think it would be foolish and also I should have to sleep with you and Eleanor!" As a birthday gift, she "enclose[d] a little motor car for the winter."

Eleanor found marriage to a man at the center of public activity stimulating. Everyone had something interesting to contribute to her education and, in turn, she gave everyone the feeling that she was interested in them. Eleanor's "dinner record" was crowded with the names of Cleveland Democrats, progressives, and regulars. She and Franklin went to play bridge with Mr. and Mrs. Louis Howe, although Eleanor felt that neither bridge nor Mr. Howe contributed to an attractive evening. Franklin wanted her to go, so she went.

Franklin was a key man in the 1912 legislature. "We are safely organized," he informed Eleanor, who was in New York City, at the beginning of the year. "The Committee appointments were handed down. I drew Chairman of Agriculture, ranking member of Conservation (the old Forest, Fish and Game) and also members of Codes, Railroads and *Military Affairs!* This isn't bad and I am particularly glad that the other members of Agriculture give me control of the

Committee as against our New York City friends." Franklin was even being talked about as a possible candidate for governor. On their wedding anniversary Eleanor gave a political luncheon attended by the governor, the lieutenant governor, Senator O'Gorman, and a gentleman whom she described in her dinner book as the "Secretary of Tammany Hall."

By April, however, his political prospects had darkened. The Republican resurgence dimmed his chance of re-election in 1912, and the Tammany bosses detested him. The Democratic boss of Albany, "Packy" McCabe, upbraided Roosevelt as a "political prig" and said it was time the party leaders stopped coddling these "fops and cads... these political prudes," phrases that echoed those used against Theodore when he was an assemblyman. One hope that Franklin and his fellow progressives had of breaking Murphy's stranglehold on the state Democratic organization was to align themselves with the burgeoning Wilson movement. Although initial efforts to drum up Wilson support at the state convention were a fiasco, Franklin and Thomas Mott Osborne decided to convene a Wilson Conference. But before the preparations were complete Franklin and Hall embarked on a winter cruise to Panama, leaving Eleanor to cope not only with the move back to town but with the Wilson movement as well.

Osborne wrote Eleanor to ask whether there was any objection to signing Franklin's name to the call for the conference, saying he was quite sure it was all right "under the approval he [Franklin] gave; but I should prefer to have your advice on the matter." Eleanor's reply was deliberately noncommittal, which did not help him much, Osborne commented dryly, and left him "in something of a quandary." Osborne's letter, she wrote Franklin, "has given me an uncomfortable day but I can only hope I've done as you would wish." More of a pragmatist in politics than the uncompromising Osborne, he wanted to move slowly. Moreover, he had many irons in the fire, as Eleanor's next letter indicated. "Louis Howe told me to tell you," she wrote, "that Evans etc., were grooming you to run for Governor against Mr. Wadsworth! Also he had a long talk with Mr. C. Osborn and felt that you could count on help from him next autumn."

She had arranged to meet Franklin in New Orleans on his way back, since they did not like to be separated any longer than necessary. "I simply hated to have you go on Saturday," she wrote him after he sailed, and he was also upset. "It is hard enough to be away from the chicks, but with you away from me too I feel very much alone and lost. I hereby solemnly declare that I REFUSE to go away the next time without you...."

Her husband's involvement in the Wilson campaign created a dilemma for Eleanor, since she was devoted to her Uncle Ted. Late in March she had lunched with Auntie Bye and Uncle Ted who, with characteristic energy, was preparing his assault on Taft's renomination. When she joined Franklin in New Orleans in April they went to Cat Cañon for a three-day visit with the Fergusons and found Bob and Isabella passionately absorbed in Theodore's forthcoming campaign. The younger "progressive" elements were hitching themselves to Theodore's star, they told the Roosevelts. Franklin's law partners, Langdon Marvin and Harry Hooker, were for Teddy. Even Sara was in conflict.

Whatever Eleanor's private sentiments, her duty was to be at the side of her husband, who had accepted the chairmanship of the New York State Wilson Conference, and she accompanied him to Baltimore for her first national convention. Many people she knew were there, including Alice and Kermit. Theodore was preparing to run as a third-party candidate. "Pop's been praying for Clark," Kermit told Franklin. Alice looked bad, Eleanor thought; in fact, all of Theodore's supporters who came to Baltimore seemed to her "restless and unhappy."

She found the convention sessions tedious. A moralist in politics, she felt that the ritual of noisy demonstrations, parades, and seconding speeches, while colorful, did not contribute to the thoughtful consideration of the party's purposes and policies. After the first roll call Champ Clark, the candidate of the conservatives, was in the lead; but he could not muster the two-thirds majority for the nomination. As the balloting dragged on, Eleanor saw less and less of her husband, and decided to take the children to Campobello and await the results there. But the significance of the battle between Wilson and Clark had not escaped her; what struck her most was "the contempt in which the New York delegation was held and the animosity shown toward the big financiers. If we are not going to find remedies in Progressivism then I feel sure the next step will be Socialism."[14] This was a remarkably sage and sophisticated perception by someone who only a few years earlier had been the shyest of apprentices in politics.

"Wilson nominated this afternoon," Franklin wired her in Campobello, "all my plans vague splendid triumph." Eleanor rejoiced not only for her husband's sake but because she felt that Wilson offered the best chance for the alleviation of social injustice. However, she felt bad for Uncle Ted, who, she suspected, would not have committed himself so irrevocably to running as a third-party candidate, had he foreseen Wilson would be the Democratic nominee. Wilson's nomination and Theodore's third party transformed the political scene. With the prospect of a Bull Moose candidate in his district who would divide the Republican vote, Franklin's doubts about running for re-election evaporated. He began to press hard for renomination, touring his district tirelessly, rousing his workers, flashing the smile that overcame all resistance. "It appears that Tammany and the 'Interests' are really making an effort to prevent my renomination," he wrote Eleanor, but he thought Tammany's ally in Dutchess County was spineless and would yield in the end.

As Franklin predicted, his Tammany opposition did collapse, and on August 24 he wired Eleanor, "Received designation by unanimous vote. Will wire Sunday if I can leave." He also notified his mother, who was in Paris. She replied, "In one way I wanted you all in New York, but to be sensible and unselfish, I am glad...I hope the 'bull moose' party will endorse you." But the Bull Moosers entered a candidate against him. The Democrats on their side closed ranks around Wilson, and Osborne and Roosevelt quietly shelved their independent Wilson organization. This brought Franklin an anguished plea from Louis Howe, who had been on Osborne's payroll: "If you can connect me with a job during this campaign, for heaven's sake help me out." A few weeks later Franklin was flat on his back with typhoid and asked Eleanor to see if Howe would run his campaign. That eccentric-looking little man had early sensed Franklin's possibilities and had cultivated his friendship. Franklin had reciprocated these overtures, somewhat to the dismay of Eleanor and Sara, who were put off by Howe's untidiness, his tobacco-specked vest, and a face that he himself cheerfully called "one of the four ugliest" in the state. Nevertheless, Howe had a sixth sense for the movement of public opinion and was something of a genius at political analysis. He loved power, Eleanor later wrote, but recognized his own limitations. In 1911 he spotted Franklin as the instrument through which he could realize his own ambitions. For his part, Franklin sensed that here was the perfect aide, brilliant politically but no potential rival. But many years were to pass before Eleanor appreciated Howe's remarkable qualities.[15] A man of great sensitivity, he could not have failed to notice how uncooperative Eleanor was after he hurriedly came down from Horseneck Beach in Massachusetts to take over Franklin's campaign. She fussed over his chain smoking, seemed impatient with the length of his visits, and generally made herself a nuisance, she confessed later, to the man who was to carry the district for her husband.

The fact that she herself was feeling ill no doubt accentuated her irritability. It was Sara who discovered that something was radically wrong when she arrived one day to find her daughter-in-law "so hot I was frightened." Characteristically, Eleanor shrugged off her symptoms; she would get to bed early and be well in the morning. But Sara was not to be put off so easily, and insisted on taking Eleanor's temperature, which was over 103. She summoned the doctor at once and his tests showed that Eleanor, too, had typhoid. A trained nurse was brought in and Eleanor went "into the fever." It was a week before her temperature began to come down. "She sees no one but Franklin, not even me!" Sara reported to Eleanor's Aunt Maude.

Thus the crucial election drew to a close with both Franklin and Eleanor flat on their backs. "Poor Franklin," Eleanor wrote Maude, "has had a horrid time just up and down. . . . He hasn't been able to campaign at all so he feels a little uncertain of election." But Howe was doing a first-rate job, and with the Bull Moose candidate expected to draw off Republican votes, Franklin's chances were good.

Theodore's campaign was roaring to a finish. Isabella wrote Eleanor that she had spent the day with Uncle Ted in Albuquerque: "He was more loveable than ever and of you he said so much that warmed my heart." Eleanor's Uncle Eddie Hall came to tell her that he had registered so he could vote for Theodore. Sara went to Theodore's windup rally with the Parishes one night and the next she was at Madison Square Garden to hear Woodrow Wilson. On election night, however, when Eleanor and Franklin were so weak they could barely sit up, Sara chose to go with Harry Hooker to Bull Moose, not Democratic, headquarters. But there was little cheer there. "Governor Wilson has a landslide," Sara noted in her diary. "Franklin is elected with about 1,500 majority."

"Howe did gallant work under very adverse circumstances," Osborne wrote Franklin. "He was about as loyal and wholehearted as a man could be." And Sara noted critically, "Mr. Howe here a good deal." By December, Eleanor could begin to jest about the fact that both she and Franklin had been ill. Her Christmas presents would be small, she informed Maude, "as the campaign was more expensive than it would have been had Franklin been well and of course the doctors' bills are a bit high for our joint autumn entertainment! However, we ought to be thankful as we got off cheaper than if we had had it separately!" They were not taking a house in Albany this time, only a small apartment, and they planned to be there only from Tuesday to Thursday because, wrote Eleanor, Franklin "thinks he won't have much work this year."

Eleanor was twenty-eight as Franklin's term in Albany ended. She presided over a large household that had to be moved several times a year—from Sixty-fifth Street in New York, to Hyde Park, to Albany, and in June to Campobello. And on each occasion it was like a small army on the march: a nurse for each of the three children, three to five other domestics, and a vast number of trunks, valises, hat boxes, and pets. The trip to Campobello meant an early train to Boston with a stopover during the day at the Hotel Touraine, then a sleeper to Eastport, Maine, and finally the *Half Moon* or the motor launch to Campobello—in all, a considerable exercise in logistics. When Franklin could not be with them, Eleanor handled it alone with a minimum of fuss. She had already developed a reputation within the family for crowding an incredibly large number of activities into a morning. "She got hats, ordered dresses, etc.—all very quickly and I dropped her off at Susie Parish's before one," Sara noted in admiration. When she moved her family down from Albany, Eleanor "had to work awfully hard," Sara recorded, "and think very hard before she got away and she seemed to remember everything, even tho' at one day's notice she moved a whole day earlier than planned."

Eleanor dressed smartly—even the style-conscious Pussie was delighted to get her hand-me-downs. She was slim and tall and the sheath gowns of the era did justice to her Gibson Girl figure. She had tapering, expressive fingers and masses of soft brown hair full of golden tints. Her profile, with its overly prominent teeth and receding chin, was not attractive, but, like Auntie Bye, she had an inner radiance that prevailed over physical looks. Her eyes, as Beatrice Webb had said of her own mother, caressed one with sympathy and studied one with intelligence. Even the self-deprecating Eleanor admitted that her eyes were her best feature. She was glad that her children had inherited their father's looks—his fair skin, his smile, his jutting jaw—but their eyes, she thought, came from her side of the family, and they were good eyes, she said.

The Halls still turned to her in every crisis, and the crises were frequent. "Eleanor has been here every day," Grandma Hall wrote. "She is so good." Tivoli was decaying. Presided over by the violent-tempered Vallie who brandished a gun at visitors, and Grandma Hall, now a roly-poly lady in black dress and bonnet, Oak Terrace was no longer a proud Hudson house but the setting for a Gothic tragedy. "I am so sorry about Grandma," Eleanor wrote Maude,

> and one's hands are tied unless Vallie can be removed from Tivoli, which of course she won't agree to now.... I wish you and I could talk it over as I would do anything to make these next years easier and happier for her. Can't I let you have some money?

An equally urgent problem was what should be done with Eddie's three children, whose beautiful mother had died. "I feel after this," Eleanor wrote when Eddie had disappeared on another prolonged bat, "he should not dream of taking the children to his own house this spring and hope no one will make it possible so long as the Zabriskies are willing to keep them." Her stern advice echoed Auntie Bye's admonition fifteen years earlier to her own family that under no circumstances should Eleanor's father be permitted to have his children. But Eleanor had never acknowledged the wisdom of keeping herself and her father apart; the world of reality and the dream life she lived with her father were still separate.

Eleanor was Maude's confidante in matters of the heart as well as her mainstay in disentangling her private affairs, including some large debts. Maude, with her masses of red hair, great warmth, and puckish sense of humor, charmed men and women alike. She had turned down a Whitney to marry Larry Waterbury, and at one time the society pages were full of her doings. "Seated in a big automobile at the Jockey Club races at Newport last summer, Mrs. Waterbury performed the feat of eating half of a large watermelon without removing her white gloves—and without soiling them." Although Larry Waterbury was attractive and an outstanding polo player, he had no money. The two lived beyond their means, and contracted heavy gambling debts, and finally the marriage broke up. When Maude decided to sell her pearl collar, "Totty" was her agent in the negotiations with Tiffany's and Black, Starr and Gorham. To free herself of debts, Maude, like Lily Bart in *The House of Mirth*, tried running a dress shop and even considered, until Eleanor discouraged her, serving as a hostess in a new restaurant whose owner was eager to have society patronage. Eleanor loved having her aunt at Campobello. Would Eleanor mind, Maude inquired, if a Mr. David Gray joined her on the island?

Eleanor could not quite make up her mind about the romance but she welcomed Mr. Gray to Campobello and undertook to chaperone them. "If you think best casually mention to Mama that Mr. Gray is boarding in the village," she wrote Franklin, "but if you think the surprise is better for her, just let it go." The son of a Buffalo editor, David Gray was witty and charming, wrote fashionable stories about the hunting life, and was much in demand in society.

Eleanor kept Franklin informed of her reactions to Mr. Gray. He had "the best anthology I've ever seen called *The Home Book of Verse*, compiled by a man called Stevenson. You can give it to me for my birthday as he has mended the turntable so I don't need a new one!" Mr. Gray read poetry well, and they were having "a grand poetry orgy," her next letter said. He was a delightful companion "but something is lacking and it worried me. I wish you were here and could form an opinion." He read them a story he had just written. "He certainly has the gift of the short story. Whether he has it for the big things is not yet proved and I wonder if it ever will be." How did Eleanor like him, Maude asked after they had been at Campobello several weeks. "I told her I did not feel I knew him yet. . . . I somehow shall never feel quite straight about it all till I've told him all my fears for them and seen how he takes it."

Meanwhile there was Sara to be dealt with. Appearances meant a great deal to her. Once Harry Hooker, one of Franklin's law partners, had come to Campobello while Franklin was away, and "Mama has chaperoned us pretty carefully," Eleanor noted with amusement. When Eleanor first mentioned David's name to Sara she "fairly snorted," and Eleanor foresaw trouble. Publicly Sara was kind, gracious, and devoted to Maude, but she "confided in Laura (who promptly told me)," wrote Eleanor, "all her outraged feelings in regards to Maude, David and me. . . . I know I'm in for a grand scene with Mama and tears one of these days."

David finally allayed Eleanor's misgivings: "I think you will like David Gray," she advised Franklin. If Maude ever made up her mind to marry him, "he will take good care of her. He strikes me as a man who has enjoyed life, had some big disappointments but kept his ideals, though up to now he has wanted a big incentive for work."

Her doubts about her brother Hall's marriage were of a different kind. A handsome young man, Hall had graduated from Harvard Phi Beta Kappa in 1912 and was about to enter engineering school. Eleanor had great faith in his abilities and wanted to be sure the girl he married would bring out the best in him; she thought of Hall as her oldest child, and if he was ever in trouble she was at his side. "Eleanor is a wonder," a friend remarked who saw them together; "it was delightful to see the sweet feeling between that sister and brother." When Hall first brought Margaret Richardson, a lovely Boston debutante, to meet Eleanor, Eleanor had some reservations. Margaret was a sportswoman who rode, played tennis, and enjoyed camping trips and dancing. "Hall is holding you up as an example to me," Eleanor teasingly reported to her. They were different types, and Eleanor could not get on "an intimate footing" with Margaret, she confessed to Franklin, and Margaret had the same problem with her. Eleanor "was perfectly lovely to me," Margaret recalled, "but I never felt at home with her."[16] Eleanor thought a woman should stir a man to large undertakings and be able to keep up with him intellectually, not just be someone to have fun with, and she was not sure Margaret was the right person for her brother. After Hall and Margaret were married, however, she counseled him not to make too many demands on his young wife. Hall had just awakened to poetry and philosophy, which were like wine in their effect on him, Eleanor observed in a letter to Franklin adding, "He expects Margaret to feel as he does and to grasp things just as quickly and it is very hard on her for she has been accustomed to a sleepy atmosphere. He is impatient of her family and wants her to keep out of the atmosphere of Boston which she has always been in! Oh! these periods of readjustment, they are hard all round, aren't they?"

Painful as the process had been, she had made the adjustment from innocent bride to manager of a large household, from sheltered wife of a fun-loving young lawyer-about-town to competent helpmate of a promising public official. Politics was already for her as well as for her husband a way to self-fulfillment. It was an activity she could share with him, a domain where she could be helpful, unlike sports and frivolities where she so often felt inadequate and excluded. Politics pivoted around Franklin and the family pivoted around her, but she was more than the mother of his children, the custodian of the hearth. He respected her judgment and valued her opinions—how much so he attested in a letter he wrote Maude. He wanted Maude to come back to Campobello next year, "as I know what a delight it is to Eleanor to have you and I am afraid I am sometimes a little selfish and have had her too much with me in past years and made life a trifle dull for her really brilliant mind and spirit."

17. THE ROOSEVELTS GO TO WASHINGTON

⸻✦⸻

IN MID-JANUARY, 1913, FRANKLIN HAD BEEN SUMMONED TO Trenton for a talk with President-elect Wilson about New York patronage. Franklin wanted to serve in the new administration himself, but when he, Eleanor, and Sara went to Wilson's inauguration, he still did not know whether he would be able to get the post he most coveted, the assistant secretary of the Navy, the position that Theodore Roosevelt had held before moving on to the governorship of New York and the presidency.

The morning of the inauguration he ran into Wilson's new secretary of the Navy, Josephus Daniels, homespun editor of the *Raleigh News and Observer*, prohibitionist, pacifist, and progressive. They had met at the Baltimore convention, where Josephus had instantly taken to Franklin, "as handsome a figure of an attractive young man as I had ever seen . . . a case of love at first sight."[1]

"How would you like to come to Washington as assistant secretary of the Navy?" Daniels queried.

"How would I like it? I'd like it bully well," Franklin replied. "All my life I have loved ships and have been a student of the Navy, and the assistant secretaryship is the one place, above all others, I would love to hold." He is "our kind of liberal," Daniels told the president two days later when he brought up Roosevelt's name.

After his confirmation on March 17, Franklin elatedly pulled out an assistant-secretary-of-the-Navy letterhead, impressively embossed in the corner with the office's insignia of four stars around an anchor, and wrote his "own dear Babbie," as he called her. She had remained in New York to hear what was to be "our fate."[2]

I didn't know till I sat down at this desk that this is the 17th of happy memory. In fact with all the subdued excitement of getting confirmed & taking the oath of office, the delightful significance of it all is only just beginning to dawn on me. My only regret is that you could not have been here with me, but I am thinking of you a great deal & sending "wireless" messages!

He was already at work, he went on gaily, "signing vast quantities of 'stuff' about which I know nothing," and would she have calling cards made for him, "by next Monday if possible"?

Eleanor meanwhile had written Franklin:

A telegram came to you from Mr. Daniels so we know you are confirmed & finally launched in your work!

P.S.
March 17th.
Many happy returns of to-day dear. I ordered your 17th of March present as we couldn't do anything else together!

Franklin also had written his mother, "I am baptized, confirmed, sworn in, vaccinated—and somewhat at sea!" She was grateful that her son had thought of her in the moment of his success: "You can't imagine the happiness you gave me by writing to me yesterday. I just *knew* it was a *very* big job, and everything so new that it will take time to fit *into* it." Big jobs, in Sara's mind, required appropriate signatures: "Try not to write your signature too small," she added, "as it gets a cramped look and is not distinct. So many public men have such awful signatures, and so unreadable!"

Shortly after Franklin began his new job he was invited to Raleigh, North Carolina, Josephus Daniels' home town, to address the Agricultural and Mechanical College. Daniels was one of its trustees and was proud of this college of farm boys, as he was of his young aide.

Eleanor, wearing a big hat and a dress with a high choke collar, according to the local paper, accompanied Franklin who sported a derby. "I am a hayseed myself," the pince-nez'd patrician northerner said at one point in his speech, "and proud of it."[3]

Eleanor, more fastidious in her choice of words, would never have called herself "a hayseed," and she was suddenly conscious of a kind of upper-class insularity. "There seems to be so much to see and know and to learn to understand in this big country of ours," she wrote Maude afterward, "and so few of us ever try to even realize that we ought to try when we've lived in the environment that you and I grew up in."[4]

The Wilson years in Washington thrust them on—Franklin toward national leadership, Eleanor toward wider sympathies and a radical independence.

Franklin had to learn the ropes of his new position, and so did Eleanor, whose job was to make things easier and pleasanter for him. But what were the duties of the wife of the assistant secretary? "When I see Eleanor," Theodore wrote Franklin in congratulating him, "I shall say to her that I do hope she will be particularly nice to the naval officers' wives. They have a pretty hard time, with very little money to get along on, and yet a position to keep up, and everything that can properly be done to make things pleasant for them should be done." Auntie Bye, the wife of an admiral and as knowledgeable in the ways of the Navy and the Capital as anyone, gave Eleanor similar advice. Mrs. Cowles also briefed her in the Washington ritual of calls.

As long ago as 1823 General Jackson had protested the practice— "There is nothing done here but visiting [*sic*] and carding each other— you know how much I was disgusted with those scenes when you and I were here, it has been increased instead of diminishing"[5]—but in 1913 it was still a "sacred rite." Ladies in white gloves, carrying card-cases, went forth daily on their appointed rounds, and none was more determined or conscientious than Eleanor: Mondays the wives of the justices of the Supreme Court, Tuesdays Congress, Thursdays Cabinet, Fridays diplomats. Wednesday would be the day she received, but she was sure no one would call on her.

A letter to Maude described her first weeks in Washington that spring.

I've paid 60 calls in Washington this week and been to a luncheon at the Marine barracks, the kind, where the curtains are drawn & candles lit & course after course reduces you to a state of coma which makes it almost impossible to struggle to your feet & leave at 4 P.M. I've received one long afternoon next to Mrs. Daniels until my feet ached and my voice was gone & since then I've done nothing but meet people I saw that day & try to make them think I remember them quite well! We've been out to dinner every night, last night a big Navy League affair for Mr. Daniels where there was some really good speaking. Mrs. Daniels is a dear & I'm looking forward to knowing her better. Mrs. Bryan is nice too though not so attractive, but some of the others are not so exciting.

Ten days later she was still at her calls. "I got here yesterday about 2 and started out at 3 to call on the Navy Yard people & the Justices' wives, about 20 calls in all and the same number almost everyday this week!"

As the wife of the assistant secretary she considered it her duty to master Navy protocol and ceremony, to keep her poise when the guns thundered out a seventeen-gun salute when her husband boarded a flag ship, and to shake hands only with the officers, not the enlisted men, as the Marine guard on the quarter deck presented arms. There were sterner tests of her self-command. The secretary invited members of the cabinet and their wives to join him and the assistant secretary in watching the Navy at target practice at Hampton Roads, "the most spectacular sight on sea or land," he called it. The men went to the firing division and the women were brought aboard the *Rhode Island*, the battleship that was towing the target. The executive officer of the *Rhode Island*, Commander Yates Stirling, detailed an officer to each lady to explain anything she might wish to know. Lieutenant Emory Land was assigned to Eleanor.

As Eleanor recalled the day, the sea had been quite rough and she had begun to feel queasy. When the young officer asked her if she would like to climb the skeleton mast, she quickly agreed—anything to distract her from the way she was feeling would be a relief—and up the mast she went. It was a dizzying climb, but she got over her seasickness. The impression she made on the *Rhode Island*'s officers was totally different.

> She wanted to see all there was, and when I went to the wardroom, where all were assembled, she had donned a suit of dungarees, trousers and all, and Land was taking her up the mast to the top, an excellent place from which to witness the firing. None of the other women seemed willing to risk climbing the mast.[6]

Even in New York and Hyde Park there was no escape from her duties as the wife of the Navy Department's second-in-command. When the secretary did not require them, a 124-foot converted yacht, the *Sylph,* and an older but larger dispatch boat, the *Dolphin*, were at Franklin's disposal, and he made frequent use of them for trips down the Potomac and occasionally up the Hudson. He could also thumb rides on other ships. One time Eleanor asked Maude if she were going to Tivoli, because "if so we want you to go up the River 8 A.M. Saturday with us on a destroyer." When they moored off Hyde Park, Sara went on board with Anna and James, and fifty sailors came up to the house for ice cream.

Life at Campobello was also considerably changed as a result of Franklin's new position. Not only did Eleanor see even less of him, but he was as likely as not to bring a large naval vessel along when he was able to get away from Washington. The first time this happened was when Franklin ordered one of the fleet's most powerful ships, the *North Dakota,* to anchor off Eastport on the Fourth of July week end of 1913. The job of entertaining the ship's senior officers fell on Eleanor, who arranged teas, bridge, games, dinners, and other festivities. After the week end, Franklin left but the *North Dakota* lingered on, delayed by a dense fog. Eleanor played bridge with the captain, the commander, and the paymaster until she was sure they must be quite sick of her; but the children loved it. Eleanor dressed three-year-old Elliott in a blue sailor suit, and when he boarded the ship he faced the stern and saluted the flag as his father had instructed him. He even displayed "a real swaggering walk." Finally the fog cleared and the *North Dakota* departed, "thank heavens." But a few days later Eleanor heard alarming rumors that a flotilla would be turning up in August. "Is it so?" she wrote pleadingly to Franklin. "I could hardly bear such excitement again."

"No, no more battleships coming," he reassured her. "I may come up in a destroyer later, but that means only 3 officers!"

"I shall welcome you on a destroyer or with whole fleet," she wrote back, "if you will just come a little sooner on their account but of course the destroyer will be easier to entertain!"

The Navy yards were under Franklin's jurisdiction, and in the autumn Eleanor accompanied him on a tour of Gulf installations. It was her introduction to the exertions, excitements, and crises of an official inspection. Diminutive, handsome, sharp-tongued Laura Delano also went along. She was having a stormy love affair, and the Roosevelts thought the trip would be good for her.

From the moment they arrived in New Orleans, they were "busy every minute." After breakfast they left with a delegation of "prominent political (not social) citizens," Eleanor said, drawing a distinction that still seemed immensely important to her. At the Navy yard Franklin "counted every rivet," she noted impatiently; a time would come when such inspections would not seem tedious, when she would painstakingly do the same. They were due to dine with a "real old bird," a retired admiral, in one of New Orleans' most elegant cafés, but "of course Franklin had to be late so we started off alone." Not usually given to gourmandizing, Eleanor nevertheless noted that their dinner was exceptional, ending, as it did, "with coffee poured into burning brandy, the prettiest thing and also the best thing I ever tasted," one of the few occasions on which she had anything good to say about liquor. She was less keen on the champagne that was served the next morning before breakfast en route to Biloxi on a yacht. While Franklin inspected the harbor, she and Laura were motored around Biloxi, and in the evening they all attended a banquet "where husbands and wives sat side by side and salad came after the soup!" Afterward she and Laura "just sat down and laughed for 15 minutes." At Pensacola, where they arrived at six the next morning, and at Brunswick they followed the same hectic schedule of tours, picnics, and receptions, their tour ending with a twenty-four-hour train trip back to Washington. It was an exhausting, demanding journey with little sleep and less privacy, but one kept silent about headaches and weariness and extended never-failing courtesy to everyone because, Eleanor said, the point of her presence was "to make life pleasanter" for her husband, not to add to his burdens.[7] The trip, moreover, had been stimulating. It confirmed her view that "it is always good to break away from accustomed surroundings."

In Washington they lived in Auntie Bye's house at 1733 N Street, which they had sublet from her. The red-brick residence on a narrow tree-shaded street had a "postage stamp of a lawn" and a little garden in back with a rose arbor where Eleanor liked to breakfast when the weather permitted. Sara, after her first visit, noted: "Dined at 1733 N. Street. Moved chairs and tables and began to feel at home."

Washington is never as vibrantly alive as in the first months of a new administration. New policies, new men—all things seem possible. The 1912 election had boiled down to a race between Theodore Roosevelt and Woodrow Wilson, but whatever the differences between Wilson's New Freedom and Roosevelt's New Nationalism, both philosophies recognized the need for social change and both were energized by the nation's reforming and humanitarian impulses. Bull Moosers and Wilsonian liberals alike felt a quickening of spirits with the end of Wilson's inaugural address: "Here muster, not the forces of party, but the forces of humanity. I summon all honest men, all patriotic, forward-looking men, to my side."

Since they were related to Theodore and were members of Wilson's official family, Eleanor and Franklin Roosevelt seemed to represent what was best and most promising in both camps. The belief that Franklin was a coming man in politics and would some day be the heir of both progressive traditions enhanced Washington's fascination with him. "It is interesting to see that you are in another place which I myself once held," Uncle Ted had written him, and Josephus Daniels had the same thought. "His distinguished cousin T.R. went from that place to the Presidency," he wrote in his diary. "May history repeat itself."[8] Franklin himself was not averse to pointing up the Theodore Roosevelt analogy. Two days after becoming assistant secretary of the Navy, he assured newsmen that there need be no fear of a repetition of what happened "the last time a Roosevelt was on the job"—a reference to Theodore's reversal of department policies in accordance with his own ideas while his chief was away.[9] Eleanor thought it was "a horrid little remark." Now many men in addition to Louis Howe were busy planning Franklin's future. "My head whirls when I think of all the things you might do this coming year," Eleanor teased him, "run for Governor, U.S. Senator, go to California! I wonder what you really will do!"

They were invited to nearly all the big parties, including occasional dinners, musicales, and receptions at the White House, and Eleanor did her own share of entertaining. Her first big dinner was in honor of Mr. and Mrs. Daniels. "Our dinner went off quite well," she reported to Sara, "and I think the cook is good." The only untoward event was that "the Sec. and Mrs. Daniels came early but luckily I was ready." They gave a dinner for Secretary of State and Mrs. William Jennings Bryan, the most pacifistic member of the cabinet, at which the other guests were chiefly admirals and generals. They dined with Justice and Mrs. Charles Evans Hughes. It was very pleasant, noted Eleanor, and after dinner the attorney general and the justice talked to her and she was fascinated by what they had to say but was unhappy when one of the guests began to play the piano, for that made conversation "rather scrappy." Franklin, she said with mock disdain, "indulged entirely in children. Nona McAdoo and Miss Hughes at dinner and Miss Wolcott afterwards." A few days later they were guests of General John Biddle, who lived next door. "I had Justice Holmes [on] one side (you may remember the speech of his which we read last winter). He is brilliant and full of theories and epigrams and Franklin thinks Mrs. Holmes wonderfully clever and quick so we both enjoyed ourselves." On her other side was Vice President Marshall, who had recently warned the Wall Street plutocracy that "if the tendency of certain men to accumulate vast fortunes is not curbed America may face socialism or paternalism." Eleanor questioned him about the speech; he had not been correctly quoted, he told her, but "nevertheless," she wrote Maude, "he is a good deal of a socialist with a desire for the millennium and it seems to me no very well worked out ideas so far of how we are to get there."[10]

While she did not advocate socialism, she did not approve of Henry Adams' pessimism, either. A frail one-man Greek chorus, the aristocratic, cynical Adams was at that period commenting sourly on the passing Washington scene from his study overlooking Lafayette Square. He had ceased going out socially in Theodore Roosevelt's day, but he would stop his victoria in front of the Roosevelt house on N Street and ask to see the children, whereupon all of them, including the dog, would climb into his carriage. Justice Holmes said that Adams turned everything "to dust and ashes" but Adams was nevertheless attracted by this golden couple and invited them to lunch. Sometimes Eleanor stopped in alone for a cup of tea, "rather exhausted after an afternoon of calls," recalled Aileen Tone, "Uncle Henry's" secretary-companion, who had taken charge of him after his stroke. "She had the routine of calls so well organized that she kept to a schedule of six minutes a call. Uncle Henry liked her—it was difficult not to," Aileen continued; Eleanor had "a kind of universal friendliness and kindness that enveloped you."[11]

All the Roosevelts stopped by to see Uncle Henry whenever they were in Washington, and Eleanor had a quiet, old-fashioned kind of charm of which Adams approved, even though her desire to reform the world, rudimentary as it was at the time, "was not much in Uncle Henry's line." Once, when Franklin was impatiently holding forth about the Wilson administration, Adams stopped him and, according to Eleanor, said, "Young man, I have lived in this house many years and seen the occupant of that White House across the square come and go, and nothing that you minor officials or the occupants of that house can do will affect the history of the world for long!" Eleanor did not consider this good doctrine to preach to the young. Adams' pessimism, she concluded later, was "an old man's defense against his own urge to be an active factor in the work of the world, a role which Henry Adams rejected in his youth."[12]

Washington during the Wilson administration was no longer the slow-moving, parochial Capital it had been when Theodore Roosevelt first arrived there in the 1890s, "where an old resident knew by sight everyone who kept a carriage" and its social life had consisted of walking, driving, bicycling, and paying calls.[13]

Society consisted of three groups—old Washington families called "The Aborigines," top-ranking officials who were also social register, and diplomats. Franklin and Eleanor were immediately placed on the lists of all three. There were the "cave dwellers" like the Misses Patten who knew everyone and at whose Sunday afternoons the latest gossip could be heard (official Washington was said to have three means of communication—telephone, telegraph, and tell-a-Patten). "I called on the Misses Patten this p.m.," Eleanor reported in 1916 when the social tide was running strong against Germany, "and heard the latest German tale."

Another early dinner guest at the Franklin Roosevelts was Belle Hagner, who had been a highly popular Washington debutante and had served as Edith Roosevelt's social secretary and had stayed on in that position with Mrs. Taft and the first Mrs. Wilson. The William Corcoran Eustises were also guests of the Roosevelts. They lived in the Corcoran House, a landmark on Lafayette Square. Mrs. Eustis was the former Edith Morton, daughter of Levi P. Morton, a Dutchess County neighbor of the Roosevelts and vice president under Benjamin Harrison; Willie Eustis was a member of one of the First Families of Virginia. Edith Eustis said the Franklin Roosevelts were "the most attractive and nicest young couple I know." Other families (mostly Republican) of distinguished lineage and public eminence who were kind to them were the Longworths, the Lodges, the Henry Whites, and the William Phillipses.

The Metropolitan and Chevy Chase country clubs were the gathering places of the socially acceptable and politically powerful; businessmen were not admitted—neither were Jews nor, of course, Negroes. (One reason Washington high society suspected Woodrow Wilson of social radicalism was his refusal to accept honorary membership in the Chevy Chase Club.)[14] Franklin spent a great deal of time at both. Their acceptance mattered to him. They were the people who counted, and their recognition eased the pain of his exclusion from Porcellian.[15] Eleanor later said that it was Louis Howe, who had come to Washington as Franklin's aide, who saved Franklin from the snobbishness and total dedication to pleasure-seeking represented by the Metropolitan Club. The Howes lived near the Roosevelts, and every day Louis and

Franklin walked to the Navy Department together. Eleanor and Grace Howe shopped together and occasionally the Howes were guests at 1733 N Street, but although Eleanor was unfailingly courteous, she still discouraged intimacy.

In the diplomatic circle the young Roosevelts inherited most of Uncle Ted's and Auntie Bye's friends and made many of their own, especially among the younger embassy people. The British ambassador, Sir Cecil Spring-Rice, had known Eleanor's parents, and he and his wife became good friends of the young Roosevelts. The French ambassador, Jules Jusserand, who had been a member of Theodore's "walking cabinet," also befriended them.

Within this larger Washington society, the Roosevelts had their own circle of friends, sufficiently intimate, said Eleanor, that protocol could be ignored when they dined together, as they often did. This group included the Charles Hamlins, the William Phillipses, the Franklin K. Lanes, and the Adolph Millers.

Charles Hamlin was assistant secretary of the treasury, a post he had also held under Cleveland. His wife "Bertie" was from Albany and had met Franklin when as a young boy he had come to Albany for his Uncle Ted's inauguration as governor. They lived near the Roosevelts, and although Franklin did not find them exciting, he felt they would make real friends, he told Eleanor.

William Phillips was assistant secretary of state. He was a protégé of Colonel House, who had brought him into the Wilson administration and who often used the Phillips home as his base when he was in Washington. Caroline Phillips, a granddaughter of *the* Mrs. Astor and a voluminous diarist, was an old friend of Eleanor's.

Franklin Lane was secretary of the interior, appointed sight unseen by Wilson on Colonel House's strong recommendation. Mrs. Lane, it was said, had set up "a code of calling which exceeded in exclusiveness anything attempted by the White House," but nevertheless the Lanes were not primarily occupied with social affairs. Lane was known for his buoyant temperament and good advice; although he was a Democrat, he had been appointed to the Interstate Commerce Commission by Theodore, who valued his counsel. A western progressive, he argued the need for government to experiment with a distribution of wealth that would be more equitable than the existing economic order while not destroying individual initiative. A young couple could not have had a wiser mentor or a better friend.

Adolph Miller, an economist brought to Washington by Lane as one of his top aides, was subsequently appointed to the newly established Federal Reserve Board. Although Miller was a strict Dutch Calvinist and not an ebullient conversationalist, his wife Mary was pleasant and gay. Eleanor found both the Millers and the Lanes to be a "joy," and noted that "talk with them is real talk."

These were the friends Franklin and Eleanor saw informally, often on Sunday evenings when Eleanor scrambled eggs in a chafing dish and served cold cuts, a cold dessert, and cocoa. They called themselves "the Club." "Franklin Roosevelt was always gay and amusing. The Lanes and Millers were brilliant conversationalists. Those evenings were among the best of that Washington sojourn," Phillips later wrote.

How little did any of us imagine the great role that Franklin was to play in the future! I knew him then as a brilliant, lovable, and somewhat happy-go-lucky friend, an able Assistant Secretary of the Navy, but I doubt if it ever occurred to any of us that he had the making of a great President.... His wife, Eleanor, whom we all admired, was a quiet member of the little group. She seemed to be a little remote, or it may have been that Franklin claimed the attention, leaving her somewhat in the background.[16]

Eleanor was essentially domestic, said Phillips, "and her interest in public affairs was centered in her husband's career rather than in any thought of a career of her own." Franklin overshadowed her. Although she was still basically shy, occasionally there were thunder-claps that heralded the political activist and militant equalitarian she was to become in later years. For example, she had a violent political argument with Fred Adams, who had married Ellen Delano. "He is most pessimistic about the 'common people,' considers us the worst governed people in the world and would prefer a monarchy! He has about the grasp and vision in big things of a child and it is discourag-ing to think that he is only one of many who think and feel like that about their country!" She could not see how Laura, Ellen's sister, could admire Adams: "It would be deadening to see much of him, much less live in the house with him."[17]

Cousin Susie's preoccupation with herself also irked Eleanor. Now living alone with Henry Parish in big houses in New York and Orange, she complained constantly of her ailments. "She thinks she is dying," Eleanor scoffed, "someone else to think about would be her best cure."

Harry Hooker was in love. Eleanor lunched with the young lady and her mother "and came away with the feeling that Hooligan (Hooker) would never win out unless he could make his own life a big thing and not hang around Tuxedo." She told him so that evening. He should really go to *work* for the progressives, she advised him and not always keep the young lady first in his mind. "Harry came up to dine," she reported to Franklin, "and went home about 9.45 after my having all your theories passed on to him as mine and if they have the desired effect he'll go to supper after his progressive meeting tomorrow night with all 'the boys.'"

Another example of Eleanor's independent thinking was displayed in 1914 during the family contretemps resulting from Rosy Roosevelt's announcement that he had finally persuaded Betty Riley, the gentle Englishwoman who had been his companion for many years, to marry him. Betty had tried to discourage him, because she felt that her lower-middle-class origins were not worthy of his social standing. Sara would have agreed. She was shocked by Rosy's decision and deplored his behavior as a threat to "standards," feeling that it showed he lacked principle. She wanted Eleanor's moral support, but did not get it. "She told me yesterday," Eleanor wrote Franklin, "she could talk it all over with Helen [Robinson] and Helen understood her point of view but I made her feel like a stranger by my curious attitude and I assured her I had no attitude and no opinion and she became enraged and said, *that* she couldn't understand!" The marriage took place before Sara was able to get down to Hyde Park, but Rosy later accepted her invitation to come to Campobello. "Somehow it fills me with amusement for Mama is so happy to be 'the one' and yet feels she must not let me think she approves!"

But such stirrings of nonconformism went unnoticed in Washington society, which saw her as an official's wife who was doing her job, "the embodiment of 20th century activity," one friend marveled. Eleanor was doing her job "a little better than anyone else" was the surprising verdict of Alice Longworth, who herself refused to play the game of calling and being called upon.[18] Alice did only what amused her, but such was her wit and temperament that she could establish her own rules. Eleanor envied Alice's ability to disregard convention,[19] little aware that one day she too would go her own way—but in the interest of those who needed help, not for the sake of her own amusement.

18. BRINGING UP HER CHILDREN

In 1927, Eleanor Roosevelt, by then much freer and more self-reliant than she had been in the years when she was giving birth to one child after another, wrote an article entitled "Ethics of Parents" in which she briskly and self-confidently summed up her views in a seven-point code.

1. Furnish an example in living.
2. Stop preaching ethics and morals.
3. Have a knowledge of life's problems and an imagination.
4. Stop shielding your children and clipping their wings.
5. Allow your children to develop along their own lines.
6. Don't prevent self-reliance and initiative.
7. Have vision yourself and bigness of soul.
   The next generation will take care of itself.[1]

It was observed of Pestalozzi, the great educator, that he could not bring up his own children, and it must be noted that this admirable statement of Eleanor Roosevelt's was written after her youngest child had been delivered to boarding school and she could be more objective about parenthood.

While the Roosevelt children were at home and in their most impressionable stage, Eleanor was ambivalent—on the one hand, she was too deferential to the child-rearing views of her mother-in-law and the nurses and governesses who were usually selected by Sara, and on the other, she was too much of a disciplinarian, reflecting her own austere upbringing.

Two children were born during the years that Franklin was assistant secretary of the Navy. In August, 1914, the second Franklin Jr. was born. Again, as with Elliott, her confinement and recovery took place while Franklin was involved in a political campaign, this time an unsuccessful bid for the Democratic senatorial nomination in New

York. August was also the month when war broke out. Eleanor followed these events as best she could from Campobello. She was leading a very quiet life, she assured her husband, and saw no reason for the baby to arrive "before the date, the 26th." She had arranged with Dr. Ely, one of the country's leading gynecologists, to come up for the delivery, but Miss Spring was to arrive on August 12.

It was fortunate that Miss Spring came early and also that Franklin dashed up for a visit, for on the sixteenth Eleanor felt the baby was about to appear. She awakened Franklin, and he sailed over on the *Half Moon* to get old Dr. Bennett from Lubec. The doctor arrived, but the baby did not. For almost a day everyone sat around while Eleanor felt guilty over the trouble she was causing and sought to persuade Dr. Bennett to leave and take care of his other patients. Finally, late on the seventeenth the second Franklin Jr. made his appearance—another better-than-ten-pound baby. Afterward Dr. Bennett expressed surprise to Miss Spring that when it came to having babies summer people were no different from Down-Easters: "She is just like one of us."

As soon as Franklin was sure Eleanor and the baby were all right he hurried back to his primary fight. Her letters mixed reports about bowel movements with political encouragement. They had put up the poster Franklin had sent them; James wanted more campaign buttons; "I have a little more milk." The baby thrived but Franklin's six-week bid for the Democratic nomination did not—Tammany's candidate, James W. Gerard, defeated him. "I wonder if you are disappointed," his mother wrote consolingly. "I hope not. You made a brave fight and now you can return to the good and necessary work of the Navy Department which must have missed you all these last weeks." Eleanor was so involved with the new baby that the campaign made little impression upon her, but like Sara she thought that Franklin was quite content to get back to his desk at the Navy Department.

Eleanor's last baby, John Aspinwall, was born March 13, 1916. In February she was still dining out almost every night and being hostess at large Navy receptions—"as 225 came last time I don't think there is anyone left to come!" Caroline Phillips, who was also pregnant, dined with her the evening of March 13. After dinner Franklin went out, and at ten Caroline left. Shortly afterward Eleanor called Miss Spring, who summoned the doctor, and by the time Franklin returned the baby had almost arrived—"born at 11 p.m. in Washington," Sara recorded in her diary. John's was the only birth Sara was not on hand for. Later, John, like the other boys, was brought to St. James Episcopal

Church in Hyde Park and christened in his father's christening dress. Henceforth Washington matrons who complained that they could not run their households were told it could be done: "Eleanor Roosevelt . . . has five children and moves them all six times a year—and does everything else besides!"

In later years Eleanor blamed herself for the way she brought up her children: she had been too stern with them; she had not done enough things that they wanted to do and too many that she had thought it was good for them to do; she had deferred too much to nurses and to Sara.[2] The results of this training were described by Mrs. Frances Theodora Parsons, a friend of Eleanor's parents and a well-known writer of books on nature. She was at Susie Parish's when Eleanor was there with Anna and James. Eleanor admired Mrs. Parsons' creativity and sweetness with the children, but Mrs. Parsons was less complimentary about Eleanor. She met James and Anna "primly parading on the asphalt drive with their nursery-governess one June morning," she recalled in *Perchance Some Day*. "I invited them to join me in a hunt for wild flowers up the mountain path. But they were too much appalled by steep curves and outcropping rocks to derive any pleasure" from the expedition.[3] That was before Eleanor had become an independent woman, Mrs. Parsons explained. "I can remember at twenty-two expecting my year old baby to sit on the sofa beside me while I poured tea with all kinds of good things on the tray. Her manners had to be so perfect that she would never even reach or ask for these forbidden goodies!" Eleanor later wrote.[4]

Eleanor's nurses and governesses were supplied by agencies that traditionally served New York's upper-class families, and the schools to which she sent Anna, James, and Elliott were the accepted ones in her milieu. Before she moved the children to Washington in 1913, Anna, then seven, briefly attended classes in New York. Maude had suggested the progressive Ethical Culture school, but Anna was sent to Miss Davidge's. In Washington Anna went to the Misses Eastman, and James and Elliott to the Potomac School. These schools were well-staffed and highly exclusive.

Like other young Washington matrons, Eleanor gave much thought to education, a subject that she discussed endlessly with Caroline Phillips and Lily Polk, who had children the same age as her own. She was principally concerned with what she and Franklin could do to reinforce the classroom. She believed that the early years were decisive and that the home was more important than school; if a child was not taught habits of self-control at home and if parents did not encourage curiosity by the way they responded to a child's queries, formal education was likely to be unproductive.

Eleanor tried a number of ways to teach her children to concentrate. She spent time with them on their lessons and reading to them. She also had a French governess to help them learn French. Elliott "goes to Mlle. now for French every morning & I think has learnt a good deal though if you ask him to say anything he promptly refuses." She had borrowed one of her methods of teaching concentration from Mlle. Souvestre. After lunch she had the children lie flat on the floor.[5] "Relax your muscles completely," she softly commanded. When they were physically relaxed and, she hoped, mentally focused, she read to them. It is difficult to say whether these efforts were effective. The Roosevelt children did show an unusual ability, when interested, to concentrate on what was being said and to pick up ideas and information aurally, but their father and mother had the same faculty and it may have been an inherited rather than a learned trait.

The children did not suffer from lack of motherly care and attention. John was "three months old [and] weighs 14 lbs 13 oz.," Eleanor noted, "which is 15 oz. more than F. jr. weighed." She worried if she had to be away from the children. Before Eleanor left with Franklin on his inspection tour of southern naval facilities, Anna had asked anxiously what would happen if they had to buy anything "or got lost or put into prison." Eleanor was also apprehensive about how the household would manage if a crisis developed while she was away, and the longer she was gone, the stronger her fears became. But after she returned she was able to report to Sara, "All was well here."

Sometimes there *were* mishaps while Eleanor was away. One summer when they were at Campobello she went to St. Andrews to do some shopping, and when she returned she discovered Elliott had fallen into the smoldering ashes of a fire the children had made on the beach while the nurse had wandered off and burned his arms and legs. In the four-page letter that went to Franklin describing what had happened, Eleanor was careful not to alarm him unduly—"he only cried a little & Nurse says they are only skin burns" and they applied Unguentine.

She was as composed and cool-headed in dealing with Elliott as she was in writing Franklin, and later concluded that the spirit with which one faced life's little calamities was the important thing, since children cannot be totally shielded from misadventures. But then when Franklin, perhaps because her letter was so reassuring, made only passing reference to Elliott's injuries, she was indignant. "You are casual about Elliott's burns...he is a very brave young man!"

Because she had been full of fears when she was a child, Eleanor wanted her children to be venturesome and to meet adversity with fortitude. She was pleased when Anna and James entered the swimming pool. "One thing their lessons did for them is that they'll put their heads under & go in to their necks & James seems less timid than Anna," she reported. Since Anna was ten and James nine, it might not appear to be much of an achievement, but the point is that she was determined to have them face up to their fears. She admired spunkiness and detested sniveling. Once when Elliott bit James hard she spanked him with a slipper and explained that no matter whose fault it was, boys didn't bite. Elliott's feelings were hurt and "he made such a long upper lip he looked like a rabbit," but she was pleased with his insistence that "it didn't hurt so very much, Mother!" Another show of defiance was also reported half approvingly: "Elliott went for me with both fists." There were times, however, when she was not so enamored of Elliott's temper. She took him to the Spring-Rice dancing class to look on, "but he is so shy with people and you never are sure that he'll do as you tell him without a scene so it isn't an unmixed joy." Then she added firmly, "The new baby is not going to be allowed to grow up like this!"

Sara often deplored and frequently hindered Eleanor's efforts at shaping the children's character. "Anna and James thrive and have a good time," Eleanor wrote Franklin, "though Mama thinks them much abused." When they all went sailing, she reported on another occasion, "the chicks became obstreperous and I most severe and Mama unhappy!" When James fell off his pony while they were visiting Hyde Park he was scratched but Eleanor did not think he was really hurt; "but of course he cried hard and Mama brought him in and had him lying down before I knew anything was wrong or I would have made him get on again if only for a minute."

Sara should not have interfered with her daughter-in-law's decisions, but Eleanor, as she later realized, was too stern a disciplinarian. She had disliked her mother, but it was her mother's and grandmother's tendency to say "no" rather than her father's life-affirming "yes" that took charge when she was confronted by unruliness in her children. She thought the discipline she had undergone as a child had been beneficial, "and so when I found myself responsible for the bringing up of children, I enforced a discipline which in many ways was unwise."[6]

Having seen what self-indulgence had done to her father and uncles, she was puritanical and repressive toward herself and overly severe in curbing what she considered the "wildness" of her children. "They have been the wildest things you ever saw," she complained to Franklin, "and about ready to jump out of their skins." "Let the chicks run wild at Hyde Park," he advised her. "It won't hurt them." His reaction was the same when she appealed to him to end some roughhousing between James and Elliott: "Oh, let them scrap. It's good exercise for them."

Franklin did not like to administer discipline. As public responsibilities more and more cut down the time he was able to spend with his "chicks," he wanted the hours he was with them to be full of fun, excitement, and affection. His mother had always tried to run him, and he shied away from doing the same to his children. He was loath to hurt anyone's feelings, and preferred to be the agent of good tidings. When one of the children had to be punished, the task usually fell to Eleanor, and if she insisted that it was Franklin's responsibility, wrote James Roosevelt in his engaging memoir, *Affectionately, F.D.R.,* "the punishment simply was not administered."[7]

Sara, however, was the real culprit in undermining the children's discipline. Even the Hyde Park servants thought so. Sara overhead talk in the servants' part of the house that she spoiled the children, that she was "chicken-hearted," and the criticism made her cross, she wrote to Eleanor. Then she added:

> But one sh[d] keep as clear of the opinion of that class as possible I am sure, for they blow hot & cold, the best of them, & if any of them speak to me of how *nice* the children are, I shall not even answer. One thing that makes for good behaviour at table is that we all know everything goes upstairs & outside.

"We 'chicks' quickly learned," wrote James, "that the best way to circumvent 'Pa and Mummy' when we wanted something they wouldn't give us was to appeal to Granny."[8] But Franklin was away so often that it was Eleanor who bore the brunt of Sara's interference. The older woman was motivated by darker, more complicated forces than an overindulgent love of her grandchildren: she was Eleanor's rival for the affections both of the children and of Franklin. James wrote that his grandmother was "in constant competition with Mother" over how the children should be raised. In the article that *McCall's* published posthumously, "I Remember Hyde Park," Eleanor at the end of her life spoke more plainly that ever about this arrangement *à trois*.[9] The Big House at Hyde Park was her mother-in-law's and Franklin's home, but not hers: "For over forty years, I was only a visitor there." In the dining room Franklin sat at one end of the table, Sara at the other, and Eleanor on the side. It was the same in the large library-living room, in the new wing that Sara added to the house in 1915 after consulting Franklin but not her—the two large armchairs on either side of the fireplace were occupied by Franklin and his mother, while Eleanor "sat anywhere."

When Sara had realized that the marriage between Franklin and herself could not be prevented, Eleanor went on, explaining why the Big House had been such an unhappy place for her, "she determined to bend the marriage to the way she wanted it to be. What she wanted was to hold onto Franklin and his children; she wanted them to grow up as she wished. As it turned out, Franklin's children were more my mother-in-law's children than they were mine." This was partly her own fault, she admitted, for having permitted Sara to keep her "under her thumb."

Hall understood his sister's problems with "Cousin Sally," as he called Sara, and with the nurses and governesses that Sara selected for Eleanor. "Are the legions of law and order too strong for you or have you managed this summer without too assiduous attentions?" he sympathetically inquired.

Eleanor tried to lead the children in games and sports. She went fishing with them—"James and Anna and I fished off the float yesterday morning and got about 11 flounders in about an hour and a half." She taught them croquet and found it "a good exercise for her temper" to take their disregard of the rules calmly. She accompanied Anna and James to their dancing class at Lady Spring-Rice's. She took James on a tour of Annapolis and could "hardly drag him past the football practice field." All the children had an assortment of dogs and rabbits—"We had a great tragedy yesterday, one of the bunnies died. . . . The chicks were very sad but they buried it with great ceremony and are going to put a mound of stones above him today and that seems to be a great consolation." When she played with her children she tried to forget herself, to enter into the spirit of the occasion and to be like a child herself, but she was not easy-going in such matters. The moralist in her was always in command, standing between herself and her children, whose irrepressible spirits cried out for acceptance, not judgment. "She felt a tremendous sense of duty to us," Anna later said. "It was part of that duty to read to us and to hear our prayers before we went to bed, but she did not understand or satisfy the need of a child for primary closeness to a parent." "I was certainly not an ideal mother," Eleanor wrote later. "It did not come naturally to me to understand little children or to enjoy them. Playing with children was difficult for me because play had not been an important part of my own childhood."[10]

Even without Sara, Eleanor's overly active conscience would have been both a burden and a blessing to her children, but Sara made escape from the demands of that conscience more difficult. Sara spoiled the children, but she was also very conventional and she imposed her essentially Victorian standards of good behavior on the children by "a procession of 'proper' English 'nannies,'" wrote James, that she "foisted on our household."[11] Their really intimate lives, said Anna, "were run by nurses and governesses."[12] One of these nurses, whom James called "Old Battleaxe," tyrannized the children, cuffing them about, locking them in closets, subjecting them to humiliations, all in the name of discipline. Eleanor discovered that she was also "a secret drinker," and that was her end. "From the time I got rid of that person," she said many years later, reminiscing with her children, "and took over the selection of the type of nurses I wanted, I began to have more confidence in my ability to handle the children."

There was a severe polio epidemic in 1916, which frightened Franklin and Eleanor, and Franklin was glad his family was at Campobello. "The infantile paralysis in N.Y. and vicinity is appalling," he wrote back after leaving them on the island. "*Please* kill all the flies I left. I think it really important." Eleanor tried to do as he wished: "The flies are fairly well exterminated," she reported.

Franklin spent little time at Campobello that summer, and Eleanor was restless and when Franklin intimated he might have to cut short his holiday at Campobello, she proposed to bring the family down earlier: she and the children could "easily go down from here by train alone." But Franklin did not like that idea. "No one is thinking of moving children by rail," he told her. And he wanted his family to stay there until he could get the *Dolphin* to bring them back directly to Washington rather than have them go to Hyde Park as they usually did in September, but that would not be until mid-September. Eleanor did not share Franklin's anxieties about having the children stay at Hyde Park.

I think the chicks will be safest at Hyde Park and even Mama does not seem to worry. They are exposed *possibly* anywhere and all we can do is to keep them as well as we can and I think the long season in Washington would be worse for them than the risks at Hyde Park.

But having made clear how she felt, she would not press the point: "*of course* if you decide it best to go to Washington or to stay later here I will do as you think best."

She yielded to him even though she found it "annoying to have to stay here just the one year I really want to get back!" The *Dolphin* finally picked them up at Eastport at the beginning of October. It was commanded by William D. Leahy, who recalled later that the forty-two-hour journey to New York City was considerably enlivened by the children, who took over the ship. They went to Hyde Park after all, Franklin finally agreeing with Eleanor "that H.P. is really no more risk than a long autumn in Washington."

It was Eleanor's "complete unselfishness," William Phillips wrote, that kept the household on an even keel, although Sara's "jealousy made life difficult in many ways" for her.

Caroline was always impressed by Eleanor's willingness to efface herself so that there would be no trouble between mother and son. It was her thoughtfulness of other people rather than of herself which made it possible to preserve a calm and tranquil attitude in such domestic difficulties.

No wonder we all admired her.[13]

But was her attitude so admirable? She did not think so in later years. Neither did her children.

19. THE APPROACH OF WAR

ACCORDING TO BILL PHILLIPS, WHO KNEW HIM AS WELL AS anyone in World War I Washington, Franklin did not seem fully mature. "He was likable and attractive, but not a heavyweight, brilliant but not particularly steady in his views," Phillips later wrote. "He could charm anybody but lacked greatness."[1] What was more, he was inclined to cockiness in his relation with his superiors, especially Daniels; if audacity did not more often lapse into presumption, he probably had Eleanor to thank for it.

She tried to discipline his brashness, because although she appreciated her husband's abilities and loyally supported his ambitions, she also knew that he could be egocentric and impulsive and give the impression that no one could refuse him anything. She took pleasure in passing on any praise of him that came her way, but usually coupled it with a chastening qualification. Harry Hooker "talked of you last night in a wonderful way and so did Maude and David the other day"—that was the garland; then came the bramble: "It is a great responsibility to feel such trust in one's character and brains and I'm glad it doesn't lie on my shoulders. I'd be bowed down!" Adulation bothered Eleanor. It intoxicated her husband.

His exuberant self-esteem usually amused her, but occasionally she dressed him down sharply. She read in the papers that Franklin had launched his campaign for senator with a statement "congratulating" his old political ally William Church Osborn on his resignation as New York Democratic state chairman by using such snide phrases as "had Mr. Osborn been in the thick of every political contest" and "had Mr. Osborn's political experience been deeper...." "Isn't it just a bit patronizing?" Eleanor rebuked her husband. "If I were 'he' I would rise up and smite you for an impertinent youth."

Bill Phillips recorded an exchange between Franklin and Eleanor that he thought characterized Eleanor's steadying influence on her husband in those years. It took place in a hotel suite in San Francisco which the Phillipses shared with the Roosevelts in March, 1915, when they accompanied Vice President Marshall to the opening of the Panama Pacific Exposition. One morning while the four of them were breakfasting together, Eleanor asked Franklin whether he had received a letter from a certain person. "'Yes,' said F.D.R. and drank his coffee. 'Have you answered it, Dear?' she asked. 'No,' said he and swallowed some more coffee. 'Don't you think you should answer it?' 'Yes,' was the reply. 'Don't you think you should answer it now?' 'Yes.'" Phillips added, "He answered it then and there. I gathered that the letter might never have received a reply without the watchful eye of his wife."[2]

When Josephus Daniels had cleared Roosevelt's appointment as assistant secretary with Elihu Root, then senator from New York, Root had cautioned him that "whenever a Roosevelt rides, he wishes to ride in front," and it was not long after his confirmation that Franklin was confiding to Eleanor how much better he could run the department than his chief. He and the secretary had slaved all day

> on all the things he *should* have decided before and as I expected *most* of them were turned over to me! The trouble is that the Secretary has expressed half-baked opinions on these matters and I don't agree. I know that he would decide right if he'd only give the time to learn. However, he has given me *carte blanche* and says he will abide by my decision.

Eleanor thought this showed Mr. Daniels to be a man of magnanimity and strength. "I think it is quite big of him to be willing to let you decide," she cautioned Franklin. "Most people want to put their opinions through at all costs whether they are half-baked or not! It shows great confidence in you."[3]

At an early meeting of his cabinet President Wilson had referred to the Diary of Gideon Welles, Lincoln's secretary of the Navy, which had prompted Eleanor to read it and to point up its moral to her husband. She was struck by the "pettiness" of the men around Lincoln. "It was very wonderful we ever came through the Civil War. There seems to have been poor management at the War Department and so much jealousy and littleness among Cabinet members."

It was easy to underestimate Daniels, and Franklin did. The secretary's porkpie hat, string tie, and country-editor pleasantries gave him a look of rustic innocence, but underneath there was stubborn character and coherent conviction, and his feeling for power and how to hold onto it was just as strong as his ambitious young aide's. If Franklin raged impatiently against Josephus in the privacy of the N Street dining room, Bill Phillips felt equally strongly about his chief, William Jennings Bryan, who was Daniels' closest political associate. Both secretaries were pacifists, and neither was willing to look at his department through the eyes of its career men—the professional diplomats at State, the admirals at Navy.

To Daniels, navalist meant imperialist, while Franklin was an early disciple of Alfred Thayer Mahan, the great theoretician of sea power in relation to world politics. The admirals considered Franklin a sympathetic soul and cultivated him enthusiastically. The outbreak of war seventeen months after he joined the Navy Department brought Franklin's impatience with the secretary to a boiling point. If Eleanor had misgivings about her husband's hawkish views, she suppressed them and sided with him in the controversies he had with Daniels over the size and pace at which the Navy should be built and the aggressiveness with which the United States should assert its maritime rights against Germany.

The coming of the war shook the foundations of the world in which Franklin and Eleanor had grown up. To Caroline Phillips it seemed "like the end of the world."[4] Like Caroline, Eleanor watched gloomily as diplomatic efforts to damp down the blaze that had been kindled at Sarajevo yielded to inflammatory ultimatums and intimidating mobilizations. "It does seem unthinkable that such a struggle should take place," she wrote her husband from Campobello, where she was awaiting the birth of the second Franklin Jr., and comforting her French and English household help, whose relatives were being called to the colors. "I wonder if war can be averted," she wrote on August 2. War in fact had already begun, and a long letter Franklin wrote her that same day described the situation at the department. He had

> found everything asleep and apparently utterly oblivious to the fact that the most terrible drama in history was about to be enacted. . . . These dear good people like W.J.B. and J.D. have as much conception of what a general European war means as Elliott has of higher mathematics. They really believe that because we are neutral we can go about our business as usual. . . .

"I am not surprised at what you say about J.D. or W.J.B. for one could expect little else," she wrote back. "To understand the present gigantic conflict one must have at least a glimmering of understanding of foreign nations and their histories. I hope you will succeed in getting the Navy together and up to the mark for I think we're going to need its moral support."

Franklin thought a long drawn-out struggle could be averted: "I hope England will join in and with France and Russia force peace *at Berlin!*" Eleanor concurred, and wrote, "The only possible *quick* solution to me seems the banding together of France, Russia and England and then only if England can gain the decisive victory at sea." Three days later a harried Franklin wrote again: "I am running the real work, although Josephus is here! He is bewildered by it all, very sweet but very sad!" Eleanor's reply was sympathetic: "I can see you managing everything while J.D. wrings his hands in horror. There must be so much detail to attend to all the time and so many problems which must, of course, be yours and not J.D.'s."[5]

Over at State the Phillipses were equally discontented with Bryan. William was working sixteen hours a day while "Mr. Bryan spends his time talking local politics with Senators and Congressmen," Caroline recorded, "and has not the slightest realization of the importance of this momentous struggle in Europe, consequently the whole initiative falls on William's and Mr. Robert Lansing's, the Counselor, shoulders. Without the latter, William would really be quite alone."[6]

The illusion persisted that the war might be ended quickly. The captain of the *Half Moon* told Eleanor of a rumor about a big naval battle in which thirty-seven German and six English ships had been sunk. "What a horrible loss of life, if true. One can only hope such a disaster will end the war," Eleanor wrote Franklin, who replied that he was disappointed "that England had been unable to force a naval action—of course it is the obvious course for Germany to hold her main fleet back and try to wear out the blockading enemy with torpedo and submarine attacks in foggy and night conditions."

As the hopes of a quick Allied victory faded, the dreadful consequences of a prolonged struggle loomed larger in Eleanor's mind. "I fear whichever side wins it will be a fearful slaughter," she wrote her husband, adding, "the Belgians have certainly done wonders." She was pro-Ally.

Germany's militarism and its intrigues in the Caribbean, especially in Mexico, the refusal of the Central Powers to submit the Serbian question to arbitration, the invasion of Belgium, despite treaty pledges, and Belgium's "glorious and unexpected resistance," as Franklin put it, all served to turn most Americans into Allied sympathizers, even though the country generally supported Wilson in his proclamation of complete neutrality. In the fervidly pro-Ally circles in which the Roosevelts moved, however, there was less sympathy for the president's subsequent plea that Americans should be neutral in thought as well as in action.

When Franklin lunched with Sir Cecil Spring-Rice at the Metropolitan Club, he informed Eleanor, the German ambassador, Count Johann Heinrich von Bernstorff, was at the next table "trying to hear what we were talking about.... I just *know* I shall do some unneutral thing before I get through." Eleanor also disdained Wilson's plea for impartiality of thought. Sara was always passing on the latest anti-German tidbit; she had heard, for example, that "the big gray building of the German Brothers across the river from Hyde Park (North of it) is full of ammunition."

Eleanor was still in touch with a German schoolmate, Carola von Passavant, whose brother had stayed with her and Franklin during a visit to the States just before the war broke out. In January, 1915, Carola wrote Eleanor:

> Although this war is most terrible, it also makes us feel proud and happy, as it shows clearly all the good qualities, mental and physical strength of our nation. I do not know whether the feelings in America are with us, or against us now. I wonder what sort of an opinion you have formed about the Germans in this war?

Usually the promptest of correspondents, Eleanor delayed her reply until May 14, when she wrote:

> ... you asked questions which I did not just know how to answer.... This whole war seems to me too terrible. Of course it brings out in every nation wonderful, fine qualities for it calls for self-sacrifice and unselfishness, two qualities which are not apt to shine in uneventful and prosperous times but every people believes that it is right! War also brings out in all nations certain qualities which are not beautiful and I wish it could be wiped from the face of the earth though I recognize that in our present state of civilization there comes a time when every people must fight or lose its self-respect. I feel that it is

almost too much to expect that we shall be spared when there is so much sorrow and suffering in so many countries abroad.

As to the opinions we have formed of the Germans in the war, I can only speak for myself, for my husband as you know is a member of the government and not allowed to express any opinions, but I think among the people here there is great respect for the people of Germany and also for the wonderful efficiency and preparedness of her army. Sympathy is pretty well divided I think on both sides but I think Count Bernstorff has been unfortunate in talking too much at first and though Dr. Dernburg has made very able speeches he has alienated many who felt he was trying to appeal to the popular sympathy over the heads of the Government. Just now you know the feeling is very tense but I cannot help hoping some understanding may be reached. . . .

The tense feeling to which Eleanor referred was over Germany's U-boat campaign. A week earlier, a German submarine had sunk the *Lusitania* on the high seas, with a loss of twelve hundred noncombatants, including 120 Americans. The United States was shocked and angered. Theodore Roosevelt wanted to go to war, and when Wilson said, "There is such a thing as a man being too proud to fight," Roosevelt accused him of cowardice and weakness. The Wilson cabinet was divided between Bryan, who favored compromise and arbitration, and those who favored strong action to compel Germany to end submarine warfare against unarmed merchantmen. On June 8, Bryan resigned to head a countrywide peace campaign.

"What d'y' think of W. Jay B?" Franklin wrote his wife. "It's all too long to write about, but I can only say I'm disgusted clear through. J.D. will *not* resign!" Their letters crossed. "I'm so glad Bryan is out," Eleanor commented, "but I can't help admiring his sticking to his principles. How about J.D. I wonder, and how would his resignation affect you! It is all most exciting but above all how will this affect the German question?"[7] In her autobiography two decades later Eleanor wrote that Bryan's pacifism had appealed to her and that she was one of the few people in official Washington who had not laughed at the miniature plowshares made out of old melted-down swords that he sent around: "Anti-war germs must have been in me even then."[8] That is clear, too, from her letter to Carola. There were women who went considerably further, who not only actively preserved their detachment but, impressed with war's futility, sought a peace without victory. In 1915 an international women's congress met at The Hague, under the presidency of Jane Addams, and outlined a peace platform that was the forerunner of Wilson's Fourteen Points. There were forty-seven women in the U.S. delegation, including Dr. Alice Hamilton and Professor Emily Balch, but such movements and actions were still outside Eleanor's ken. Her husband was a leader of the preparedness faction within the government, and she was vigorously pro-Ally, as were her friends. Sir Cecil Spring-Rice was contemptuous of Bryan, whom he portrayed as sighing for the Nobel Prize. German policy, moreover, affronted American feelings.

Anger over the *Lusitania* had scarcely begun to subside when the White Star Liner *Arabic* was torpedoed without warning. "An outrage," commented Eleanor, adding the next day, "We are all wondering whether there are to be more words or action of some sort over the *Arabic*. The Germans are certainly not treating us with great consideration!"[9] Franklin thought the president would act, he replied, "as soon as we can get the facts. But it seems very hard to wait until Germany tells us her version and I personally doubt if I should be quite so polite."

"I think we have a little too much patience with Germany, don't you," Eleanor wrote back. Sara, as usual, was more emphatic. "I feel a little as T.R. feels, in fact a good deal," she wrote her son, adding shortly afterward, "there is one thing that he [Wilson] must remember—the time for dealings with the German criminals is over. Diplomatic relations with Germany are henceforth impossible." But the German government retreated. It disavowed the *Arabic* sinking and revealed that its submarine commanders had been ordered not to sink passenger liners without warning or making sure of the safety of noncombatants.

The U-boat crisis converted Wilson into an advocate of preparedness, vindicating a position that Franklin had long held, particularly with regard to the fleet. His strong feelings on the issue had in fact brought him close to insubordination. "He was young then and made some mistakes," Daniels wrote in 1944. "Upon reflection, although I was older, I made mistakes too."[10]

While Eleanor and Franklin had sympathized with Theodore's demands in 1915 for a tough line against Germany, they had serious reservations about Uncle Ted's politics in 1916. At the Republican convention that year, Theodore made his peace with the party. Although the nomination of Charles Evans Hughes on a platform of "straight and honest" neutrality represented a rejection of both his leadership and his policy of interventionism, Theodore supported the Republican ticket. When a relative said that Uncle Ted in 1916 had shown himself to be a bigger and a finer man than ever before, Eleanor could only express her astonishment. At the time Theodore was abandoning the progressives, Wilson was pushing through Congress most of the planks that Roosevelt had advocated in 1912. The mood of the country was fiercely noninterventionist. The Democrats answered Hughes' slogan of neutrality with the cry "He kept us out of war," and ardent progressives as well as Socialists swung over to Wilson. The election was one of the closest in U.S. history, but Eleanor thought Wilson was certain to lose.

Eleanor was at Hyde Park with the children as the election drew to a close. The Lanes and Millers were there, too, at Sara's invitation. (Lane called Sara "the ducal lady" and Franklin "the lord lover.") Sara was at her most gracious, and Lane reported that they all had "an exquisite time" before they left Eleanor and her children to go to New York City to hear the returns at headquarters.

It was a gloomy night for Democrats; Hughes appeared to be elected when Lane and Roosevelt left the dispirited gathering to return to Washington. But the next day it turned out that the western states were ranged in the Wilson column, and the outlook had altered drastically. "What a close and exciting election," Eleanor wrote her husband, "and all weighing now apparently on California. I can't help feeling Hughes will win in the end but it won't be such a walkover as it appeared to be." To Franklin this was "the most extraordinary day" in his life. "After last night, Wilson may be elected after all," and if he was, Franklin intended to wire his conservative Uncle Warren Delano, who was violently "agin the government," that "the Republican Party has proved to its own satisfaction I hope that the American people cannot always be bought." Then in a postscript addressed as much to himself as to Eleanor, he added, "I hope to God I don't grow reactionary with advancing years."

Despite Wilson's victory, 1916 ended, Eleanor said, with a sense everywhere of impending catastrophe.[11] Franklin was more and more outspokenly interventionist. "We've got to get into the war," he would say to Daniels, who invariably answered, "I hope not."[12] When, on January 22, 1917, Wilson called for a negotiated settlement, a "peace without victory," and an organized postwar order based on self-determination, disarmament, and freedom of the seas, Eleanor, in a departure from Franklin's interventionism, was enthusiastic. "I think the Allies are wild but it may be successful," she wrote Sara.[13] Spring-Rice was cynical about Wilson's motives: "Peace under the President's auspices must mean the permanent glory of the Democratic party in the person of its head."[14]

Germany spared the Allies the necessity of formally rejecting Wilson's bid by resuming unrestricted submarine warfare. On February 3, the president, while not completely abandoning his hopes of a peace without victory, announced a break in relations with Germany. Ambassador Bernstorff was handed his passports.

Franklin, meanwhile, had been sent to the Caribbean to inspect the Marine operations in Haiti and Santo Domingo and to determine whether the approaches to the Panama Canal were wholly secure. Haiti was not entirely pacified and evidently there was some danger in going there—or so Eleanor thought. Franklin was tired and needed the change, she wrote Sara; "also it is good for all men, young men especially, I imagine, to occasionally do something with the spice of risk in it otherwise they lose the love of it and Franklin hadn't had a chance for a long time now!"

This was another side of Eleanor. She was the daughter of her father, with a taste for adventure and a desire to feel not only the balm but the tang of life. Soon there would be hardship and danger enough for everyone.

When Wilson broke relations with Germany, Daniels ordered Roosevelt to return to Washington "at once." But throughout February and March Wilson continued to debate whether or not to declare war. He felt that war was inevitable, but the cost would be so great and the responsibility so heavy that he wanted it to be clear to the world that Germany left no other course open to him.

Daniels shared the president's feelings. "If any man in official life ever faced the agony of Gethsemane, I was the man in the first four months of 1917," he later wrote. "From the very beginning of the war in Europe I had resisted every influence that was at work to carry the United States into the war." Roosevelt felt that Wilson had the power to arm merchant vessels without congressional authorization, as did Lane. "We wait and wait," Lane wrote his brother on February 16. "Daniels said we must not convoy—that would be dangerous. (Think of a Secretary of the Navy talking of danger!)"[15] In his diary Roosevelt noted on March 9, "White House statement that Wilson has power to arm and *inference* that he will use it. J.D. says he will by Monday. Why doesn't President say so without equivocation?"

Again, Germany took the decision out of the president's hands with the Zimmerman telegram, which instructed the German representative in Mexico City to propose an alliance with Mexico in the event the United States entered the war, in return for which Mexico would receive "the lost territory in Texas, New Mexico, and Arizona." Fury swept both the country and the administration. On March 18 German submarines torpedoed three American vessels. Two days later the cabinet, including Daniels, advised Wilson to ask Congress for a declaration of war. "The Cabinet is at last a unit," Lane wrote. But the president, he added, "goes unwillingly." So did Daniels.

Congress was summoned to meet on April 2 "to receive a communication concerning grave matters." It rained on April 2, "a soft, fragrant rain of early spring," Wilson's son-in-law, William G. McAdoo, noted. The president's address was equal to the solemnity of the moment. There was no alternative to war, he explained. Autocracy was the foe of liberty, and "the world must be made safe for democracy."

> ...It is a fearful thing to lead this great peaceful people, into the most terrible and disastrous of all wars, civilization itself seeming to be in the balance. But the right is more precious than peace, and we shall fight for the things which we have always carried nearest our hearts....

"I went," Eleanor wrote, "and listened breathlessly and returned home still half-dazed by the sense of impending change."[16]

The period of privacy, of exclusive devotion to her family and preoccupation with purely social duties, was at an end.

20. PRIVATE INTO PUBLIC PERSON

———————————————◆

A YEAR AFTER AMERICA'S ENTRY INTO THE WAR ELEANOR WROTE her mother-in-law that she was taking on still another assignment: "I'm going to have charge of the knitting at the Navy Department work rooms," in addition to the hours spent at the Red Cross canteen. "It is going to mean part of every day now except Sundays taken up at one place or another but that doesn't seem much to do, considering what the soldiers must do."[1] Eleanor had never shunned work, but the war harnessed her considerable executive abilities to her always active sense of responsibility. The war gave her a reason acceptable to her conscience to free herself of the social duties that she hated, to concentrate less on her household, and plunge into work that fitted her aptitudes. Duty now commanded what she could take pleasure in doing.

During the first few weeks Eleanor was so busy helping entertain the high-ranking allied missions that came hurrying to Washington that she didn't have time to think about what the war demanded of her as a person. The young couple's friendship with British Ambassador Spring-Rice and French Ambassador Jusserand, Franklin's duties with the Navy Department, and the social circles in which they moved meant a great deal of partying with members of the British Mission, headed by Arthur Balfour, whom Eleanor found "charming in the way that a good many Englishmen are and very few of our own men," and with the French Mission, with "Papa" Joffre as the center of attraction.

Marshal Joffre brought sobering news that dispelled the lingering illusion in New York and Washington that all that would be required of the United States would be money, foodstuffs, war materials, and the fleet to see to it that they got safely to Europe. At a luncheon at the Phillipses that included the Lanes, the Eustises, the Roosevelts, the Longworths, and Mrs. Borden Harriman, the Marshal made it clear that France wanted American troops, and as quickly as possible: "You should send 25,000 troops at once, and then again 25,000 and again and again, just as fast as possible."[2] Eleanor later accompanied Franklin to a Navy League reception for the head of the British Naval Mission. Franklin in his remarks sought to awaken the public to the true state of affairs. The British and the French Missions had been given "fair words, and again fair words," he said, but they had a right to ask about "the number of men that have left America for the other side.... It is time that they [Congress and the people] insist on action *at once*. Action that will give something definite—definite ships, definite men—on a definite day."

Eleanor applauded; "Franklin listened to all the polite platitudes and false hopes and was called on to speak last," she wrote Sara, at which time he "said all he has pent up for weeks. It was solemn and splendid and I was glad he did it and I think a good many people were but I shouldn't wonder if the Secretary was annoyed. Mr. Belmont was furious and said he took much too dark a view!"[3]

Franklin espoused a plan to lay a mine barrage across the North Sea to bottle up the submarines in their nests as part of an aggressive antisubmarine strategy. And it *was* originally Franklin's idea, Eleanor claimed. There has been dispute about that claim, but none that he became its chief advocate at a time when Daniels questioned its practicality and the British admiralty dragged its heels. "Franklin has asked to see the President to present his plan for closing the North Sea," Eleanor wrote Sara on May 10, 1917, "but 3 days have passed and he hasn't been granted an interview." She thought Franklin "very brave," Sara wrote back, "and long to hear that he could show his plan to the President." Franklin did not get to see Wilson until June 4, when he obtained the president's support for the establishment of an interdepartmental commission to inquire into the project's advisability. "If it hadn't been for him, there would have been no Scotch mine barrage," Admiral Harris later said,[4] and if the barrage came too late to be a decisive factor in winning the war, the delay was not Franklin's fault.

Theodore Roosevelt visited Washington during the hectic first weeks of the war. Blind in one eye, bothered by the fever he had picked up in the Brazilian jungles, the former president nevertheless came charging into the Capital with characteristic bravura to press his proposal that he be sent to France at the head of a division that he personally would raise. He stayed with Alice, and Franklin and Eleanor saw a good deal of him. When Uncle Ted visited them, the two youngest children, Franklin and John, were soon made aware of his presence. Full of electric vitality, Theodore burst into their room at the top of the house. "Oh, ho, ho," the old lion roared; "these two little piggies are going to market," and he hooked a happily protesting child under each arm and charged down the stairs.[5]

But apart from such family interludes there was little to cheer Theodore. "Though he was kind to us, as he always was," Eleanor said, "he was completely preoccupied with the war."

Franklin thought it was good policy to permit Uncle Ted to go to Europe and arranged for him to see the secretary of war. Sara also approved. "I hope he will be allowed to go," she wrote. More substantial support came from France. "Our *poilus* ask, 'Where is Roosevelt?'" Clemenceau wrote Wilson. "Send them Roosevelt—it will gladden their hearts." But the War Department was afraid a Teddy Roosevelt division would drain off the best officer talent. The war would be won by professionalism, discipline, and organization, it felt, not by gallant charges up the French equivalent of San Juan Hill. "The business now in hand," Wilson coldly announced on May 18, "is undramatic, practical, and of scientific definiteness and precision."

"I hated to have him disappointed," Eleanor wrote, "and yet I was loyal to President Wilson."[6]

All four of Theodore's sons went into the service, and he repeatedly urged Franklin to resign and put on a uniform. But General Leonard Wood, the most prestigious soldier in the Army and a Republican, said in July, 1917, that it would be "a public calamity if Franklin, an advocate of fighting the war aggressively, left at this time." Daniels was equally firm. A year later Eleanor became quite angry with her distinguished uncle when he brought up the subject again at Douglas Robinson's funeral, urging her to use her influence to get him to don a uniform. It was her husband's own business, she felt, and she knew, moreover, how anxious he was to get into the Navy. She was quite prepared to have him serve, but there were decisions a man had to make alone.

When her brother Hall, who was just getting established professionally, teamed up with Theodore's youngest son, Quentin, to go into the fledgling air force, she backed him up, even though he had to cheat a little on the eye test to qualify. But Grandma Hall asked why he didn't buy a substitute, as gentlemen had done in the Civil War, which outraged Eleanor. "Gentlemen" owed the same duty to their country as other citizens, and it would be unthinkable, she flung out at her grandmother, to pay someone to risk his life for you.[7]

The episode stood out in Eleanor's mind as another step on her road to independence. Under the impact of the war, her viewpoint was changing. A letter from Cousin Susie full of complaints about minor inconveniences caused by the war evoked an impatient exclamation: "How can one be like that in these days?"[8]

On all sides noncombatants were being urged to do their bit. "It is not an army we must shape and train for war," said Wilson, "it is the nation." Women, on the point of achieving suffrage—to which Eleanor was now a convert—broke loose from the Good Samaritan services to which tradition had assigned them and rallied to the war effort in every capacity except actual fighting in the field. "Is there any law that says a yeoman must be a man?" asked Daniels when the Navy faced a shortage of office workers. "Then enroll women!" Eleanor yearned to serve, but how? Her first ventures were awkward. Food administrator Herbert Hoover appealed to the country to conserve food; society responded by reducing the eight-course dinner to three, decreeing one meatless day a week, and pledging "simplicity in dress and entertainments." There was an end to calls.

Eleanor introduced her own austerity rules in her household, and her food-saving program was selected by the Food Administration "as a model for other large households," the New York Times reported. "Mrs. Roosevelt does the shopping, the cooks see that there is no food wasted, the laundress is sparing in her use of soap, each servant has a watchful eye for evidence of shortcomings on the part of others; and all are encouraged to make helpful suggestions in the use of 'left overs.'" And Mrs. Roosevelt added, according to the reporter, "Making ten servants help me do my saving has not only been possible but highly profitable."[9]

The story produced guffaws all over Washington. Franklin wrote:

All I can say is that your latest newspaper campaign is a corker and I am proud to be the husband of the Originator, Discoverer and Inventor of the New Household Economy for Millionaires! Please have a photo taken showing the family, the ten cooperating servants, the scraps saved from the table and the hand book. I will have it published in the Sunday Times.... Uncle Fred says, "It's fine, but Gee how mad Eleanor will be!"

Uncle Fred was right about Eleanor's reaction. "I do think it was horrid of that woman to use my name in that way and I feel dreadfully about it because so much is not true and yet some of it I did say. I never will be caught again that's sure and I'd like to crawl away for shame."[10]

Although chagrined, she did not give up. She went to a meeting called by Daisy Harriman to muster support for the Red Cross. Mrs. Harriman proposed the formation of a motor corps auxiliary, but since Eleanor did not drive, she joined the Red Cross canteen, helped Mrs. Daniels to organize the Navy Red Cross, and joined the Comforts Committee of the Navy League, which distributed free wool to volunteer knitters and on Saturdays collected the finished articles.

The war kept Franklin in Washington, and Eleanor had to move the household to Campobello alone. She managed very well, as usual, and as soon as the family was settled went to Eastport to talk about the Red Cross. She wrote that she also brought "6 pyjamas to make and am going to learn to use the machine to make them myself!" She had begun on the machine, she reported the next day, "and hope to work more rapidly as I go on!" A week later she rejoiced that the last pyjama top would be finished that night, "and then I take 6 pair back tomorrow!"

During the summer Franklin was hospitalized with a throat infection, and Eleanor hurried to Washington to be with him. She returned the middle of August, bringing word to Sara that Franklin had petitioned the secretary to be allowed to go overseas in order to urge the British admiralty to use more aggressive antisubmarine tactics.

At the end of the summer, for the first time, Eleanor varied the routine of moving her family off Campobello. She shepherded her whole flock as far as Boston, saw the four younger ones, their nurses, and maids settled on the train to New York, and then Huckins, the Roosevelt chauffeur, drove her and eleven-year-old Anna west along the Mohawk Trail to visit Hall and Margaret and their children in Schenectady. "The views are wonderful and Anna is a most enthusiastic companion," she wrote her husband in Washington. She preferred to do such things with Franklin, but if he wasn't available she would do them nonetheless, and she was determined also to learn to drive. It was another small declaration of independence.

There was also the remarkable letter dated October 14, 1917, that Sara sent Franklin and Eleanor. In 1959 Eleanor told her son James that it had followed an argument about the future of Hyde Park, with Sara on one side and herself and Franklin on the other. Sara wanted the estate to stay in the family, the way Algonac and Fairhaven were kept by the Delanos and her English friends held on to their ancestral acres. Franklin dissented vigorously, Eleanor mildly, but dissent she did. He refused to make any such promise, Franklin declared and then, according to Eleanor's later recollection, forcefully voiced his own social and political credo, an exposition that caused Sara to write the following letter a few hours after her children had left for Washington.

Dearest Franklin
& Dearest Eleanor,
...I think of you almost in New York and I am sorry to feel that Franklin *is* tired and that my views are not his, but perhaps dear Franklin you may on second thoughts or *third* thoughts see that I am not so far wrong. The foolish old saying "noblesse oblige" is good and "honneur oblige" possibly expresses it better for most of us. One can be democratic as one likes, but if we love our own, and if we love our neighbor we owe a great example, and my constant feeling is that through neglect and laziness I am not doing my part toward those around me. After I got home, I sat in the library for nearly an hour reading and as I put down my book and left the delightful room and the two fine portraits, I thought: after all, would it not be better just to spend all one has at once in this time of suffering and need, and not to think of the future; for with the *trend* to "shirtsleeves," and the ideas of what men should do in always being all things to all men and striving to give up the old-fashioned traditions of family life, simple home pleasures and refinements, and the traditions some of us love best, of what use is it to *keep up* things, to hold on to dignity and all I stood up for this evening. Do not say that I *misunderstand*, I understand perfectly, but I cannot believe that my precious Franklin really feels as he expressed himself. Well, I hope that while I live I may keep my "old fashioned" theories and that *at least* in my own family I may continue to feel that *home* is the best and happiest place and that *my* son and daughter and their children will live in peace and happiness and keep from the tarnish which seems to affect so many. Mrs. Newbold's theory that children are "always just like their parents," is pretty true, as *example* is what really counts.

When I *talk* I find I usually arouse opposition, which seems odd, but is perhaps my own fault, and tends to lower my opinion of myself, which is doubtless salutary. I doubt if you will have time dear Franklin to read this, and if you do, it may not please you. My love to our fine little James, and to you two dear ones.

Devotedly
Mama

At the time this was written Eleanor was deeply involved in war work, an experience that was propelling her toward a more radical assertion of independence. "Today I go canteening" had become Eleanor's password. Washington was a major railroad junction, with as many as ten troop trains a day sitting on the sidings in the Washington yards. The Red Cross set up canteens manned by volunteers to provide the waiting soldiers with soup, coffee, and sandwiches. When a train came in the Red Cross ladies were there, lugging baskets of sandwiches and buckets of steaming coffee that had been prepared in the tin shacks where the volunteers worked. His mother was "up at five this morning to go to the canteen," James complained to his grandmother; "do not you think that Mother should not go so early?"

Edith Benham Helm described Eleanor at the canteen:

> We also had a small room where we sold, at cost, cigars, cigarettes, chewing tobacco, picture postcards and candy bars. Here Mrs. Roosevelt shone. We had to make change at quick order when the men were lined up buying the supplies and we were supposed to turn over our finances in perfect order to the incoming shift. In all my experience there were only two women whose financial affairs were in perfect condition. One was Miss Mary Patten and the other, Mrs. Roosevelt.[11]

Eleanor, who once had not known how to keep her own household books, worked out the canteen's accounting system, and Mrs. Helm considered her "the dynamo" behind the canteen service.

Before the troop trains pulled out, the canteen workers picked up the postcards they had furnished for the men, censored them, and saw that they were posted. But handling the mail on top of her other canteen duties was too much even for her, as it ran to about five hundred pieces of mail a day, "This post office game isn't going to work," she informed her husband. "It needs two or three people a day." She persuaded the Red Cross to set up a special unit under Mrs. Vanderbilt.

When she was not at the canteen she gave out wool to knitters and collected the finished products. Then she was placed in charge of the knitting at the Navy Department, which meant supervising more than forty units whose captains reported to her. At the same time she learned that if Mrs. Daniels, who was ill, was not well enough to preside at a Navy Department rally the next day to organize for war work, she would have to preside. She did it—"I hated it but it was not as terrifying as I expected." Then she was asked to report to an assemblage of Red Cross workers on how the Red Cross knitting operation was organized. She was "petrified" when it was her turn to speak in the huge DAR auditorium, but she managed to get through her report, she wrote Sara, "and I hope I was heard."

She did everything that was asked of her. "I pour tea this p.m. at the Navy Yard for a Navy Relief party"; "I am collecting for the Red Cross at the Shoreham Hotel Lobby from 9–12 tomorrow a.m. and then canteen from 1–6." "Sometimes," she wrote Franklin, "I'd rather like to have a little while with you when neither of us had anything we ought to do, but I suppose that isn't to be hoped for till after the war!" Once when Franklin came to pick her up at the canteen they "were so busy he just turned in and worked too for an hour and enjoyed it! We had about 3,700 men during the day." The only concession to family life she made was always to be at home at tea time with the children and to keep them with her until they went to bed.

The winter and spring of 1918 were an anxious time. "I don't think there is any doubt that the Germans will put everything they can muster into a spring offensive," Eleanor wrote Sara.[12]

Sir Cecil Spring-Rice, the British ambassador, was acutely conscious of the dangers of the interval before the weight of the fresh American divisions began to be felt on the western front. Wilson did not like the ambassador, whom he called "that highly excitable invalid," and in January, 1918, Spring-Rice was recalled. "I feel very badly about the Spring-Rices," Eleanor wrote. "I shall be very sorry to have them go, it will really make a big difference here." The Spring-Rice children, Betty and Anthony, brought Anna pictures of themselves as parting gifts, and the ambassador gave Franklin and Eleanor a pen-and-ink drawing of the Washington monument which he had done himself; there was a poem on the back addressed to "sons of honour, richly fathered, scions of a sturdy brood.... Tell again your father's story" and ending with a warning: "Woe to them who lounge and linger when the foe is at the gate." Within a month Sir Cecil was dead. Eleanor framed the poem and drawing and hung them on the wall.

The sorrow and tragedy of the war was always with her. Franklin reported that a transport had been sunk and they feared a thousand men were lost. "All through dinner I felt like Nero." When the word came that Theodore's youngest son, an aviator, had been killed, "Think if it were our John," Eleanor wrote Franklin; "he would still seem a baby to us." She grieved for Aunt Edith and Uncle Ted, "but

I suppose we must all expect to bear what France and England have borne so long."

Sir Cecil was not the only friend who passed from the world's stage that spring. At the end of February they dined with Henry Adams for the last time; on March 27 his "nieces" found him dead.

> Franklin and I went to Mr. Adams funeral at two and I felt very sad for he was a very interesting man and the house had so many associations and now all is ended. There are not too many houses or [interiors] of that kind in this country and the end of things is sad. Alice invited us to lunch next Sunday almost before the Service was over and it offended me and made me angry, it seemed to be lacking in feeling, but Franklin said we'd go.

It was not always easy for Eleanor to follow Franklin into new experiences and to entertain new people whom he considered important to his career. When he brought Felix Frankfurter home, she sensed his brilliance but was bothered by what she considered his Jewish mannerisms—"an interesting little man but very jew," she commented.[13] In her anti-Semitism she belonged to the world of Henry Adams and Spring-Rice, whose hostility to materialism and the new power of money was mingled with dislike of Jews. She had to go to a party given by Admiral Harris for Bernard M. Baruch, "which I'd rather be hung than seen at," she complained to her mother-in-law; "mostly Jews."[14] Two days later she wrote, "The Jew party [was] appalling. I never wish to hear money, jewels and . . . sables mentioned again." Brandeis was exempted from this dislike, as were the young Henry Morgenthaus who had recently settled at Fishkill in lower Dutchess County. Even Sara approved of the Morgenthaus. "Young Morgenthau and his wife called this p.m.," she wrote Eleanor from Hyde Park, "and while they were here Mrs. F.W.V. [Vanderbilt] came bringing 5 people, and we had a pleasant tea. Young Morgenthau was easy and yet modest and serious and intelligent. The wife is very Jewish but appeared very well."

In May, 1918, the Red Cross proposed that Eleanor go to England to organize a Red Cross canteen there. "I really won't go abroad," she assured Sara, "but it is a fearful temptation because I feel I have the strength and probably the capacity for some kind of work and one can't help wanting to do the real thing instead of playing at it over here."[15] Why did she refuse? She was not sufficiently independent to manage such an undertaking, she later wrote, adding that in her heart of hearts she felt her primary obligation was to stay with her children. She did not want to admit this, even to herself, but that is what she felt.[16] And she knew the family—Grandma, Cousin Susie, Sara—would not approve.

Some were even critical when Franklin went abroad on naval business in July. "I think the family are funny not to be interested in F's trip," she wrote Sara,

> for if it served no other purpose, it is really the only way of knowing the "real thing," the problems over there and the men whom this war is daily changing. It is too silly to think you can sit here at a desk and realize them and adequately deal with them, even men of the highest imagination can't and they say so. I hear it all the time.

The next day Franklin was received at Buckingham Palace. To bolster Sara, Eleanor sent her newspaper clippings about the event. Franklin "is surely making a hit," she observed. "The enclosed is from the *Washington Post*. I often think that you must wish his father could be here to be proud with you of Franklin."

She was working hard and tirelessly. Sara wanted her to come up to Hyde Park in May, but when Eleanor told the Navy Department workers that she was thinking of leaving, "they groaned. I really have no right to go unless it is a necessity." One day when there was a rush at the canteen she cut her finger to the bone while using the bread-slicing machine. She applied a bandage and kept on working, and although she saw a doctor later, she carried a scar for the remainder of her life.

She saw Alice at a party. Alice, who amused guests by turning back somersaults, expressed an interest in working at the canteen. "I'm taking Alice down to the canteen but I doubt if she does much and they told me they were almost afraid to take her on!" There were no trains the afternoon Alice came down and she decided, said Eleanor, that "she did not like scrubbing and ironing."

Sara's sister, who lived in Washington, reported that "Eleanor is the 'willing horse' and they call upon her at all hours, all the time." Washington was sticky and torrid that July, especially in the tin shacks in which they worked, but Eleanor made light of the discomfort: "I've come to the conclusion that you only feel heat when idle."

They had eight trains on July 17, a "very hectic day" made more so because the president's daughter Margaret came in to work with Eleanor's shift. Eleanor had

> to introduce her to officers, etc. Mrs. Wilson now has a uniform and comes and works fairly regularly and yesterday late the President came down and walked down the tracks and all around and they tell me seemed much interested. I rather wish I'd been on duty there instead of the station.

A week later she had second thoughts about the president's wife.

> We've become the fashionable sight and yesterday Mrs. Woodrow Wilson came to look on and brought Lady Reading [the wife of the British Ambassador] and Mrs. [Newton D.] Baker and Miss Margaret Wilson worked with us! It rather tries my soul but it is good for my bump of deference.

While Franklin was in Europe she finally had the family chauffeur, Huckins, teach her to drive. She was able to drive their Stutz to the canteen with Huckins on the running board, but just when she learned to handle it, the axle broke. She then used their older Buick, but its brakes "don't hold very well so I've just escaped street cars occasionally. However, Huckins says I'm doing finely." When General Headlam, head of a British military mission, came up from Washington to visit West Point and stayed at Hyde Park, Eleanor drove him about in the Ford, "once nearly dumping him but otherwise all serene." By the end of August she was driving her children and assorted relatives up to Tivoli and back. She was also making a new effort to learn to swim, and thought she might at last succeed.

Sara was happy to have her daughter-in-law at Hyde Park, if only because it meant that Franklin's letters to Eleanor from Europe would be promptly read to her. Please, Eleanor implored her husband, "when you don't write Mama, send messages to her otherwise I have to invent and that is painful! . . . I hate not being with you and seeing it all. Isn't that horrid of me!" She envied him his opportunities and she was lonely, but she hoped he could accomplish "a good deal . . . for I know that is what you really want."

Franklin delayed his departure from Europe because he wanted to avoid the Democratic primary at the beginning of September. The previous summer he had made his peace with Tammany, to the distress of Eleanor and Sara. Just before he had left for Europe he had had to squelch a plan to nominate him for governor that Tammany was prepared to sponsor, and in the process had come out for upstater William Church Osborn, an old comrade in the political wars against Tammany. A letter from Eleanor reported that Louis Howe was in an agitated state because Franklin's support of Osborn was interfering with his appeasement policy toward Tammany. Howe told her, Eleanor reported, that

> he alone kept you from being nominated for governor and now he doesn't know what to do as you came out for Osborn and he is staying in the race and Al Smith wants your endorsement and he, Mr. H. could get no answer as to what the White House wanted you to do, etc! My guess is he's making himself one little nuisance. However, I soothed him by suggesting that as you were out for Osborn you'd have to stick till he withdrew which would doubtless be soon.

As Howe had foreseen, however, Osborn declined to withdraw from the primary and came to Howe to solicit Franklin's help. Howe told him that Franklin would be out of the country, and therefore out of politics, for a long time, and asked Eleanor to pass the word to Franklin confidentially that "the President and Mr. Daniels think that the political situation will be considerably eased if he does not reach this country until at least a week after the primaries, which are sometime in the first week of September."

In a speech in Paris Franklin said that he intended to volunteer for the Navy, and a letter to Eleanor from Brest explained that his place was "not at a Washington desk, even a Navy desk." He added that he expected to be back in the States about September 15.

She next heard that he was ill in Paris, "so I expect it has been a little too strenuous but the trip back if devoid of incidents will be restful!" His illness was more serious than she knew. On September 19, the *Leviathan* docked and Eleanor received a call to come to the pier with a doctor. She summoned Dr. Draper, and two hours later an ambulance drew up at Sara's Sixty-fifth Street house and four Navy orderlies carried Franklin inside. His illness was diagnosed as double pneumonia.

As a consequence, she and Franklin did not get back to Washington until October 18, and a few weeks later the war was over. "This has been an exciting day," Eleanor wrote on November 11, 1918.

> The Secretary got me a ticket for the gallery so I heard the President make his speech to Congress and F. went on the floor with Mr. Daniels. The galleries were packed and it was most inspiring. At the mention of Alsace-Lorraine's evacuation the whole place rose and cheered and the French wept. There was not as much enthusiasm for feeding the Central Powers![17]

"The feeling of relief and thankfulness was beyond description," she later wrote.[18]

At the war's end her attention shifted from the canteen to the wounded, who were being returned to military hospitals. There were men who would never be well enough to go home again, and Christmas no longer was exclusively a family party. Her children, Sara noted, "had a Christmas tree and supper with 12 soldiers from Mrs. Lane's Convalescent Home and 12 sailors from the Naval Hospital." Each man was given a cornucopia of candy, a box of cigarettes, and a tie. "Sec. and Mrs. Lane there and Mrs. (Gladys) Saltonstall played violin and everyone sang."

Except for Eleanor, everyone in the household—all the children, Franklin, and most of the servants—was felled by the influenza epidemic that swept through Washington that winter. Eleanor worked round the clock, putting to good use all the lessons she had learned from Miss Spring. When the children were asleep, she hurried off to assist the Red Cross unit set up to provide help for government offices whose employees were absent with the flu.

After everyone recovered, Eleanor and Franklin went to Europe (more will be said about this journey later) and when they returned on February 24, Eleanor thought her work was "practically over." But soon afterward she agreed to take charge of the Red Cross recreation room at the Naval Hospital. She visited the hospital wards daily, handing out cigarettes, bringing flowers, saying a word of cheer. Her new duties also included reviewing appeals from families of sailors and marines who were in need of help.

"I am taking two ladies of Navy Department Red Cross Auxiliary to St. Elizabeth's this p.m.," she wrote Sara at the end of March. "We have 400 men in the insane asylum there and the Chaplain asked that we go to see the Doctor in charge and find out what could be done for them as very few organizations take any interest in them and many of the men are not insane but shell shock patients."[19] The chief doctor took them through the two naval wards, and pity filled Eleanor's heart. St. Elizabeth's, a federal hospital, was starved for funds, short of attendants, lacking equipment. The men were locked in and moved restlessly around their cagelike porches; they were not permitted to go outside for exercise or sports. Eleanor told the doctor that the Navy Red Cross would supply newspapers, games, a phonograph, and records for a Navy recreation room that the Red Cross would build.

St. Elizabeth's was under the jurisdiction of the Interior Department, headed by Eleanor and Franklin's friend, Franklin Lane, who feared that the program Eleanor and her friends had devised for the Navy boys in the hospital would be considered discriminatory. "It is more and more clear to me," he wrote her, "that we could not have the Navy men treated better than the Army men or the civilians without causing a great deal of trouble." There was a time when Eleanor would have let the matter rest there, but now she asked why the government should not improve the whole hospital, military and nonmilitary. She wanted Lane to visit St. Elizabeth's to see conditions for himself, and although he declined, he appointed a departmental investigatory commission, whose report to the House Committee on Appropriations confirmed the inadequacy of the care provided at St. Elizabeth's. A larger appropriation was voted and the doctors were able to transform the hospital into a model institution.

Far from decreasing, her public activity was so great that, Eleanor lamented late in 1919, she hardly had time to breathe. She had a hand in obtaining rest rooms for the girls who worked in the Navy Department; she was responsible for a ball for the benefit of Trinity Parish; she even agreed to sit in a booth at the New Willard Hotel to help the membership drive of the American Women's Legion. Theodore Roosevelt had died in January, 1919, and a Women's Memorial Committee was being organized. She agreed to work hard for it if someone else took the chairmanship, stating, "This is positively the last thing I'm going to do!"

But there were compensations. On New Year's Eve a Staten Island mother wrote her:

> I want to thank you as the mother of one of the boys who was in the Naval Hospital at Washington from the first of April until July 8th for the kind words—the little favors—the interest you took in my son, which was so much appreciated by him and also his mother.
>
> Perhaps you can't recall the boy. He lay in the T.B. ward.... He

always loved to see you come in. You always brought a ray of sunshine with you, always had something to say to him. . . .

Eleanor acknowledged that being able to help gave her a deep sense of satisfaction. "One of the boys in the Naval Hospital died today," she wrote Sara, "and the little wife who is to have a baby in October and the mother had to borrow money to come to him so the Navy Department Auxiliary is going to refund it and I must go to see them this p.m. It is nice to be able to do such things isn't it?"[20]

In 1920, when Franklin accepted the Democratic nomination for vice president and Eleanor resigned from the Navy Relief Society, the board of managers adopted a resolution praising her for her "valuable services, . . . unfailing interest in the work of the society, . . . patience, good judgment, tact, and amiability."

Once during the war when Sara had been deploring the fact that the war caused a decline in moral standards, Eleanor had remarked that she might be right, "yet I think it is waking people to a sense of responsibility and of obligation to work who perhaps never had it before." She was one of the awakened.

She said, when she was asked to go to work for the Theodore Roosevelt Memorial, and she repeated it in one form or another throughout her life: "I begin to feel that only a hermit's life will ever give me joy again." But her commitment to public activity had been made. The sleeping princess, as Archibald MacLeish later wrote, had been awakened.[21] She would never again be content with purely private satisfactions, and for the rest of her life she would look at the injustice of the world, feel pity for the human condition, and ask what she could do about it.

21. TRIAL BY FIRE

THERE WAS ANOTHER REASON WHY THERE WAS NO TURNING BACK to a wholly private life for Eleanor: her discovery of the romance between her husband and her social secretary, Lucy Page Mercer. In the shaping of Eleanor Roosevelt the Lucy Mercer affair, while neither hammer nor anvil, was the flame whose heat hastened and fixed the change from private into public person. Franklin's love of another woman brought her to almost total despair, and she emerged from the ordeal a different woman. Ended was the subordination to her mother-in-law and to the values and the world Sara represented; emergent was the realization that to build a life and interests of her own was not only what she wanted to do but what she had to do. "The bottom dropped out of my own particular world," she wrote twenty-five years later, "and I faced myself, my surroundings, my world, honestly for the first time. I really grew up that year."[1]

She forgave her husband and they continued to live together, but their relationship was different. She no longer allowed herself to be taken for granted, either as a woman or an instrument of his purposes. And because—to paraphrase Santayana—she felt great things greatly and had the power to relate them to the little things she felt keenly and sincerely, her life became an inspiration to women everywhere. Her relationship with her husband not only stands as one of the most remarkable in American history but had considerable effect upon its course.

The depth of Eleanor's feeling about the Lucy Mercer episode can be gauged by the fact that it is one of the few events that she did not mention in her books and about which she found it difficult to speak. Occasionally in later life Eleanor discussed it with a few of her closest friends, including the writer of this book, when she saw they were puzzled by some of her domestic arrangements or when she thought her own experience might help them disentangle their own problems of love and marriage, but even then she was very reluctant to speak of it. If it were not central to an understanding of husband and wife it might be passed over with the same reticence, but it must be dealt with, even though the story is known only in outline.[2]

Eleanor employed Lucy Page Mercer, then twenty-two, in the winter season of 1913–14 to help with social correspondence three mornings a week. Lucy, an efficient social secretary and a charming person, soon became a household familiar. By later 1914 Franklin was writing Eleanor in Hyde Park that he had arrived safely in Washington, gone to the house, "and Albert telephoned Miss Mercer who later came and cleaned up." (Albert was the Roosevelt chauffeur and general handyman.)

Sara approved of Lucy. In the spring of 1915 when she came down to stay with the children during Franklin and Eleanor's trip to the San Francisco Exposition, a letter that reported such news as "Babs [Franklin Jr.] is splendid, had his one big movement," also included an enthusiastic reference to Eleanor's social secretary: "Miss Mercer is here, she is *so* sweet and attractive and adores you Eleanor."[3]

Sara's approval was in character—Lucy, descended as she was from the Carrolls of Maryland, had an irreproachably patrician background. Her mother had been a famous Washington beauty and her father was Major Carroll Mercer, one of the founders of the Chevy Chase Club, where Franklin played golf, and a pillar of the Metropolitan Club, another favorite haunt of Franklin's. But the family had fallen on hard times and the marriage had broken up, so Lucy's mother had brought her up to be able to earn a living as a social secretary—a job, Jonathan Daniels has written, for young ladies of "impeccable social standing and slim purses." Lucy did her job well, said Aileen Tone, who performed similar functions for Henry Adams. Lucy would sit down on the floor of the living room, Aileen recalled, strew bills, letters, and invitations about, and in the twinkling of an eye have everything in order. "She was a charmer," Aileen added. Lucy Mercer's loveliness, good taste, and exquisite manners enabled her to maintain her footing socially. When Eleanor was short a woman for a dinner party or luncheon, she invited Lucy. Men fell in love with Lucy—"every man who ever knew her," some said; she was good-looking enough "to be generally admired," one of the young men at the British Embassy said, and her voice had the quality of dark velvet. She knew how to please a man, to make his life easy and agreeable, to bolster instead of challenge him.

She had qualities of femininity that Eleanor lacked, and Eleanor was aware of her own shortcomings. Because she could not relax, others found it difficult to be wholly relaxed with her. Duty came first, not fun or pleasure. She still felt awkward at parties, and at dances she put in an appearance and then vanished. While Arthur Schlesinger, Jr., may have exaggerated when he described the Eleanor Roosevelt of that era as "a woman sternly devoted to plain living, invincibly 'sensible' in her taste and dress,"[4] she herself often spoke of the "Puritan" in her that held her back from high living, frivolity and indolence.

Franklin, on the other hand, was, as Lane dubbed him, the "gay cavalier," the "lord lover"—debonair, fun-loving, and able to enjoy making a night of it with the British Embassy "boys" or his intimates at the Metropolitan Club. Franklin was one of the handsomest men in Washington, admired by men and women alike. Walter Camp, the famous Yale coach who came to wartime Washington to keep its executives in trim, described Roosevelt as "a beautifully built man, with the long muscles of an athlete."[5] The assistant military attaché at the British Embassy, Arthur Murray, spoke of Roosevelt as "breathing health and virility."[6] Bill Phillips remembered him as "always amusing, always the life of the party."[7] After Auntie Bye had seen Franklin in Washington, Admiral Cowles (her husband) reported to Franklin that Bye had thought him brave and charming, "but," Cowles added, "the girls will spoil you soon enough Franklin, and I leave you to them."[8]

Eleanor also teased him about his popularity with the ladies. He was going back to the department at five o'clock, she reported to Sara, to review "the yeomen F" (female).[9] She thought that was entertaining, but she might have been happier had the secretary assumed that duty. When Franklin went to Europe in 1918 she was amused at all the lovely creatures in the Navy Department and the Red Cross who took an interest in his safe arrival abroad. The wife of a Marine captain, she wrote Franklin, "told me she knew you were on the way and had been so worried! She's one of my best cooks on the canteen, so it hasn't interfered with her work!"[10] Everyone was so nice about Franklin's safe arrival in Europe, she reported to Sara: "I wish I could tell you how many people speak as though they were lying awake nights over him!"[11]

She knew that she did not satisfy the frivolous, flirtatious side of Franklin's nature. She liked the company of older people while he complained that they were always invited to the stodgy parties where he was usually given the "honor" of taking the oldest dowager present in to dinner. Her letters from Campobello and Hyde Park were filled with expressions of pleasure that he was having a gay time,[12] which reflected an awareness that companionship and love that were not freely offered were not worth having. But she was also jealous, and undoubtedly the more firmly she urged him to go to a party alone, the more she wanted him to say no. She disciplined herself to treat his flirtations as summer shadows. She had long ago learned to repress her jealousy, to think tolerantly, even fondly, of possible rivals when her adored father had filled his letters from West Virginia with accounts of all the things he did with the little girls in Abingdon. She could treat Franklin's dalliances lightly so long as she was sure of his love, sure that she came first with him.

She began to feel uneasy about her husband being alone in Washington during the summer of 1916, the year of the polio epidemic when Franklin insisted that she remain at Campobello until the end of September and she did not want to stay. That was the summer he portrayed himself a veritable wallflower in his letters to Eleanor. "Yesterday I had a very busy time as the Secretary went to Annapolis and left me a thousand loose ends to tie up. I stayed here until just in time to dress for dinner and went out to Chevy Chase with the Blues—a nice dinner. Everybody danced afterwards, except self who lost his nerve, and Mrs. Blue and the Miss Somebody [he couldn't catch her name] who had a sore on her leg—so I had a peaceful evening—and really enjoyed watching the antics of the three or four hundred other bipeds on the floor."[13] That was the summer, too, when their chauffeur, Golden, went joy-riding through Washington in the Roosevelt car and cracked up both the car and himself. "Isn't it horrid to be disappointed in someone," she wrote to Franklin commiseratingly, "it makes one so suspicious!"[14] Suspicious only of servants, or was the comment meant to have a broader application?

In 1917 she delayed her departure to Campobello for reasons that may be surmised from a letter Franklin sent her the day after she left.

I really can't stand that house all alone without you, and you were a goosy girl to think or even pretend to think that I don't want you here *all* summer, because you know I do! But honestly *you* ought to have six weeks straight at Campo, just as *I* ought to, only you can and I can't! I *know* what a whole summer here does to people's nerves and at the end of the summer I will be like a bear with a sore head until I get a change or some cold weather—in fact as you know I am unreasonable and touchy now—but I shall try to improve.[15]

Eleanor was nervous about Lucy Mercer that summer; when she reluctantly left Washington she put Lucy and Mary Munn in charge of the Saturdays when she gave out yarn and collected the sweaters, scarves, and socks that had been finished. Eleanor had insisted that Lucy, who had begun to work in the Navy Department as a yeoman (F), third class, in June, be paid and that the relationship be strictly a business one. She had given Franklin notes on how she wanted her "wool Saturdays" to be handled while she was away. "Your letter of Thursday is here and one from Miss Mercer," she wrote him on July 23. "Why did you make her waste all that time answering those fool notes? I tore them and the answers up and please tear any other results of my idiocy up at once. She tells me you are going off for Sunday and I hope you all had a pleasant trip but I'm so glad I'm here and not on the Potomac!"

The trip to which Miss Mercer referred combined duty with pleasure. "The trip on the Sylph was a joy and a real rest, though I got in a most satisfactory visit to the fleet," Franklin wrote her.

Such a funny party, but it worked out *wonderfully*! The Charlie Munns, the Cary Graysons, Lucy Mercer and Nigel Law, and they all got on splendidly. We swam about four times and Sunday afternoon went up the James to Richmond. We stopped at Lower and Upper Brandon, Westover and Shirley and went all over them, getting drenched to the skin by several severe thunderstorms. Those old houses are really wonderful but *not* comfy![16]

Nigel Law, the third secretary of the British Embassy, was a bachelor and a companion of Franklin's in relaxation at the Chevy Chase Club and at the Lock Tavern Club on the Potomac. Before Eleanor left Washington, she had spent a week end on the *Sylph* at which Lucy Mercer and Nigel Law were present. Did the presence of Nigel Law allay her worry about Lucy?

She was glad he had enjoyed his trip, Eleanor commented, "but sorry you found things not quite right in the fleet. The party sounds delightful to me except the Graysons' but I think you were clever to take them."[17] Eleanor's letter went on to talk of household matters such as reminding him to deposit three hundred dollars into the household account on August 1 as she intended to draw on it that day to pay bills, but she did not manage to conceal her disquiet completely. She was writing for train accommodations early, she announced, but he would see very little of her in Washington in the early autumn because she would have lots of things to do in New York. "I think in spite of all their troubles Mrs. Munn and Miss M. like to run my Sats. so I shall have no scruples there and I don't think I shall have to take over the packing room." Then, in a reference to his protestations of how lonely it was in Washington in the summertime, she remarked "I'm glad you are so gay but you know I predicted it! I hope you'll have this Sunday at H.P."

Then Franklin informed her, "I do miss you so very much, but I am getting busier and busier and fear my hoped-for dash to Campo next week for two days will not materialize. Nor can I get to H.P. for Sunday, as I found my absence last Sunday has put me too far back."[18] "I am sorry," she wrote back, "you can't get to H.P. this Sunday before Mama leaves. I know she will feel badly about it. I hope you won't try to come here. It is too far away and you ought not to do it. It will be better to take 2 weeks at H.P. in September and October."[19] But it was a reproach, because only four days earlier she had written, "I am praying no one will come to stay this summer, I am having such a delightful, unbothered time.... I wish you could come but I want no one else!" And there was another reproach: "I don't think you read my letters for you never answer a question and nothing I ask for appears!"

Although she was having a "delightful, unbothered time" at Campobello, when Franklin came down with his old throat infection at the end of July Eleanor rushed to Washington and did not return to Campobello until the middle of August. En route back she wrote, "I hated to leave yesterday. Please go to the doctor twice a week, eat well and sleep well and remember I *count* on seeing you the 26th. My threat was no idle one."[20]

She did not say what her threat had been, but whatever her suspicion of an attachment between her husband and Lucy, it is obvious that she hadn't mentioned it while in Washington, for on August 20 Franklin wrote her, "I had a very occupied Sunday, starting off for golf at 9 with McIlhenny, Legare, and McCawley, quick lunch at Chevy Chase, then in to town and off in car at 2:30 to the Horsey's place near Harper's Ferry. Lucy Mercer went and the Graysons and we got there at 5:30, walked over the farm—a very rich one and run by the two sisters—had supper with them and several neighbors, left at nine and got home at midnight! The day was magnificent, but the road more dusty and even more crowded than when we went to Gettysburg."

This time Franklin did get to Campobello as he had promised. "It is horrid to be without you," Eleanor wrote him on September 2, the day after he left, "and the chicks and I bemoaned our sad fate all through breakfast." But she continued to be reserved and wary toward Lucy, as indicated by a genteel dispute between the two over Eleanor's insistence on paying Lucy for handling her "wool Saturdays." Eleanor sent a check, which Lucy declined to accept. Eleanor was immovable and Lucy finally said she would abide by her wishes since Eleanor was mistress of the situation. She apologized for having been unbusiness-like, but then she returned the check as the last two collections were not made, on the assistant secretary's instruction; furthermore, on Saturday, July 21, she had not been present, and she had participated the previous Saturday only to the extent of answering questions and listing what came in. Eleanor sent this letter on to Franklin with the comment, "I've written Miss Mercer and returned the check saying I knew she had done far more work than I could pay for. She is evidently quite cross with me!"[21]

"*You* are entirely disconnected and Lucy Mercer and Mrs. Munn are closing up the loose ends," Franklin replied.[22]

That autumn the Roosevelts moved into a larger house at 2131 R Street, and wool distribution and collection were shifted to rooms at the Navy Department. Lucy Mercer, who had been promoted to yeoman, second class, was released from her Navy duty on October 5, 1917, "by special order of Secretary of the Navy"—perhaps for hard-ship, since her father had died a few days earlier—but she still helped Eleanor as social secretary and Eleanor still asked her to fill in when she needed an extra woman for a lunch or dinner party.

On the surface all went on as usual, but Eleanor must have had a sense of impending catastrophe. That winter she wrote almost daily to her mother-in-law, whose standards in regard to the obligations that a husband owed his wife and family were precise and unbudgeable. Her letters to Sara at this time were as warmly affectionate as they had been the year of her honeymoon. It was as if she were seeking to protect herself against the disaster she saw coming by shielding herself in the older woman's lee.

"Much love always dearest Mummy," Eleanor wrote on January 22, 1918. "I miss you and so do the children, as the years go on I realize how lucky we are to have you and I wish we could always be together. Very few mothers I know mean as much to their daughters as you do to me." "I wish you were always here!" she wrote a month later, "There are always so many things I want to talk over and ask

you about and letters are not very satisfactory are they?" She rejoiced
when the time came for Sara's spring visit. "We are all thrilled at the
thought of having you, I am particularly hungry for a sight of you,
only a stern sense of duty has kept me from running away to see you
a number of times."

Sara sent Franklin and Eleanor a letter and telegram on their wedding anniversary and Eleanor replied,

> Thirteen years seems to sound a long time and yet it does not seem
> long. I often think of what an interesting, happy life Franklin has
> given me and how much you have done to make our life what it is.
> As I have grown older I have realized better all you do for us and
> all you mean to me and the children especially and you will never
> know how grateful I am nor how much I love you dear.[23]

Sara reciprocated Eleanor's regard.

When Aunt Kassie's daughter, "Little Kassie," married George B.
St. George, the latter's mother was delighted with her daughter-in-
law. "Well, Kassie, you are running a close second to my Eleanor as
a daughter-in-law," Sara commented. Kassie demurred: "Oh, Aunt
Sallie, I never could be as good and lovely as Eleanor is."

For some her very goodness was a goad. The romance between
Franklin and Lucy did not escape Alice's keen eyes. She saw Franklin
out motoring with Lucy, and called him afterward. "I saw you 20
miles out in the country," she teased. "You didn't see me. Your hands
were on the wheel but your eyes were on that perfectly lovely lady."[24]

"Isn't she perfectly lovely?" he replied.

Alice encouraged the romance. Franklin dined at Alice's when
Eleanor was out of town, and she also invited Lucy. It was good for
Franklin, Alice maintained. "He deserved a good time. He was married to Eleanor."[25] Moreover, since she considered Eleanor "overly
noble," Alice was not beyond enjoying a little one-upmanship at
Eleanor's expense. Alice and Eleanor had run into each other at the
Capitol, but Eleanor had left Alice at the door, she reported to Franklin, "not having allowed her to tell me any secrets. She inquired if you
had told me and I said no and that I did not believe in knowing things
which your husband did not wish you to know so I think I will be
spared any further mysterious secrets!"

When Franklin returned from his 1918 trip to Europe in September
stricken with double pneumonia, Eleanor took care of his mail, and in

the course of doing so she came upon Lucy's letters.[26] Her worst fears were confirmed. Her world seemed to break into pieces. After her wedding there had been a period of total dependency and insecurity from which she had slowly begun to emancipate herself. But Franklin's love was the anchor to which her self-confidence and self-respect were secured, and now the anchor was cut. The thought tortured Eleanor that, having borne him six children, she was now being discarded for a younger, prettier, gayer woman—that her husband's love belonged to someone else. The bottom, she wrote, dropped out of her world. She confronted her husband with Lucy's letters. She was prepared to give her husband his freedom, she told him, if after thinking over what the consequences might be for the children he still wanted to end their marriage.

He soon discovered that divorce might have disagreeable consequences in addition to the effect upon the children. Sara was said to have applied pressure with the threat to cut him off if he did not give up Lucy. If Franklin was in any doubt about what a divorce might do to his political career, Howe was there to enlighten him. Lucy, a devout Catholic, drew back at the prospect of marriage to a divorced man with five children. Eleanor gave him a choice—if he did not break off with Lucy, she would insist on a divorce. Franklin and Lucy agreed never to see each other again.

"I know that marriage would have taken place," Mrs. Lyman Cotten, a North Carolina cousin of Lucy, told Jonathan Daniels, "but as Lucy said to us, 'Eleanor was not willing to step aside.'"[27] Mrs. Cotten is incorrect, not in her impression of what Lucy may have told her, but as to the facts. Franklin may have told Lucy that Eleanor would not give him a divorce, but this was not the story as Eleanor's friends heard it or as Auntie Corinne heard it from Cousin Susie or as Alice Longworth heard it from Auntie Corinne.[28] "I remember one day I was having fun with Auntie Corinne," Alice said; "I was doing imitations of Eleanor, and Auntie Corinne looked at me and said, 'Never forget, Alice, Eleanor offered Franklin his freedom.' And I said, 'But, darling, that's what I've wanted to know about all these years. Tell.' And so she said, 'Yes, there was a family conference and they talked it over and finally decided it affected the children and there was Lucy Mercer, a Catholic, and so it was called off.'"

With Eleanor the paramount, perhaps the only consideration in preserving the marriage was the children, and no doubt Franklin's affection for his children was the major reason for his hesitation. Lucy's guilt feelings as a Catholic and Sara's threat were undoubtedly also influential, but for years Eleanor believed that the decisive factor with Franklin had been his realization that a divorce would end his political career.

A long letter dated February 14, 1920, from Eleanor to Sara full of chitchat about the children and political news ended with the sentence, "Did you know Lucy Mercer married Mr. Wintie Rutherfurd two days ago?"

In later years Eleanor confided to her most intimate friends, "I have the memory of an elephant. I can forgive, but I cannot forget."

22. RECONCILIATION AND A TRIP ABROAD

———————————————◇———————————————

"NO WOMAN MARRIES THE MAN SHE REALLY MARRIES," JOSEPHUS Daniels declared[1] at a party the Roosevelts gave in December, 1918, to celebrate the approaching marriage of Sallie Collier, Aunt Kassie's gayest daughter. The secretary addressed himself to Sallie but it was Eleanor who paid attention. She and Franklin were now each trying to be the partner the other had hoped for when they married. He knew how deeply he had wounded her and sought to do the things that pleased her; she was making an effort to be gay, even frivolous. There was a kind of wistful camaraderie to their relationship. "Last night's party was really wonderful and I enjoyed it," she informed Sara, and Franklin reported the same reaction. Eleanor talked to "heaps and heaps of people" he wrote, "and I actually danced once."[2]

Sunday was still sacred to Chevy Chase and golf, but in the afternoon instead of the morning. Franklin "went to church last Sunday and goes again today, which I know is a great sacrifice to please me," Eleanor noted. Once his casual habits of attendance at church had upset Eleanor, but now she could jest about it. When Franklin was informed that he had been made a vestryman at St. Thomas where they worshiped in Washington, Eleanor described the news as a "fearful shock" to him and expressed the hope that he would decline.[3]

He spent more time with the children. He took James with him to Chevy Chase and let the youngster caddy, and helped Anna with her algebra until Miss Eastman suggested it might be better to drop algebra altogether and concentrate on arithmetic. He read Eleanor his official report to the secretary on his European trip. She thought it very good and undertook to edit the diary he had kept during the trip with a view to publication. "We had a good deal of dictating in the evening for the first time," she wrote Sara.[4] She merged into a single account diary notes, letters, and new material dictated by him, and then dictated the combined account to a stenographer in Franklin's office. A month later they were still working on it—"luckily I'm not as sleepy as last night so I hope we can have some dictating"[5]—but in the end the account was only half completed and was not published until Elliott edited his father's *Personal Letters.*

With the war over, Washington was no longer the focus of excitement and action, and Franklin was restless. *Town Topics,* the society gossip sheet, even said he had resigned and might be slated for a diplomatic post. "Mrs. Franklin Roosevelt," the item added, "has always been retiring and not overwhelmingly in love with Washington." Eleanor thought that was "a funny notice, however, I'm glad I'm retiring enough not to merit any further comments." Yet Franklin was "very discontented with his work. . . . Don't be surprised if we are back with you next winter, if we are not in France," she wrote Sara.[6] It was to Europe that they went.

Franklin proposed to the secretary that a civilian should go to Europe to direct the liquidation of the naval establishments there, and if he were sent, Eleanor should accompany him. "Today the Secretary told Franklin he could sail about the 19th but I still feel it is uncertain," wrote Eleanor, but she nevertheless quietly finished her Christmas shopping "as I felt if we were going I wanted to have everything ready."[7] Daniels, who was not enthusiastic about the idea, signed his orders reluctantly, perhaps as much in the interests of the marital truce as in those of the Navy. "Franklin says we may sail on the 28th and I can probably go."[8] She thought the children, who were recovering from the flu, would be well enough by then. "I never hated to do anything so much and yet I think I'd worry more about Franklin if he went alone. It is rather a horrid world I think."[9]

One of the few things they did in New York before they boarded the U.S.S. *George Washington* was to review the triumphant U.S. fleet in a blinding blizzard. A photograph of Eleanor on the bridge of the reviewing ship, one of the most extraordinary of the thousands taken of her, showed a face ravaged and severe, purged of all softness as if she, not Franklin, was the one who had survived a wasting illness. The night before they sailed Franklin, Eleanor, and Sara dined at the Colony Club with Captain Edward McCauley, the *George Washington*'s skipper. Franklin was "full of enthusiastic anticipation of the adventure before us," he recalled, and in spite of her qualms Eleanor also looked forward to the journey. On New Year's Day they embarked. "Very comfy and well settled in our suite," she noted in the diary that she began to keep.

It was an eventful moment to be going to Europe. Four years

of slaughter had ended, leaving 9 million soldiers dead, 22 million wounded, and immeasurable civilian devastation. Mankind's eyes were now on the Paris Peace Conference, where almost all the great and mighty on the Allied side were in attendance. Wilson, the most powerful of them all, had become the inspired spokesman for a new order of things. Eleanor had seen the president a week before he sailed, at "a really historic party at the French Embassy. The President and Mrs. Wilson came and the Ambassador spoke and then the President and everyone drank to Strassbourg and the President. The National Anthems were played and with all the uniforms and pretty dresses it was a brilliant scene and as Caroline said it will be nice to tell our grandchildren about."[10]

Both Eleanor and Caroline had been critical of Wilson, but both were becoming true believers. Caroline left an account of her change of heart, which became complete when she heard Wilson's address to a joint session of Congress just before he sailed for the Peace Conference:

It began the night that I heard him speak at the French Embassy. ...On Monday last, this experience was more than ever vivid. I was poignantly moved by the ordeal he was facing. I prayed with all my strength for his support, and I felt as though some spiritual aid was really reaching him through my prayers. My conclusion is that in the ordinary things of life he makes continual blunders, has poor judgment of men and affairs, is self-conscious, uncertain, but in the really big things he has a real vision and inspiration which make him a great leader, in fact the *only* man who can lead the way in the upbuilding of a new and better world out of the chaos of the old one....[11]

Eleanor thought Wilson had a remarkable understanding of man in the mass but little of men as individuals. She considered him an inept politician and had criticized his appeal to the country in the November elections to return a Democratic Congress, an appeal which had boomeranged. She thought self-righteousness made him too partisan.[12] But like Caroline she was unhappy over Wilson's blunders because she cared deeply for his ideals.

Eleanor was thirty-five when she sailed for Europe, her first trip abroad since her honeymoon fourteen years earlier.[13] The ocean, like much else, had lost most of its terrors: "Quite a blow and some roll," she noted in her diary; "I feel proud to be so good a sailor so far." It was indeed a "blow"; Livingston Davis, Franklin's partner in Chevy Chase convivialities as well as his assistant for operations and personnel, also kept a diary on that trip. "A heavy sea," he noted that same day; "whole dining room wrecked by heavy roll, also my breakfast landing on top of waiter's head."

Eleanor's sure-footedness compared with 1905 was more than nautical. She entered into all shipboard activities, went to the movies, joined in the singing led by a YMCA man, turned out daily for the "abandon ship drill," and was present for every meal. If a man interested her, she sought him out. She talked with Walter Camp, who exercised the men daily. "I like him," she wrote, and it was for her benefit as well as Franklin's that he came to their suite to show them his back exercises. Charles M. Schwab, the steelman, was another passenger. When Wilson had named him head of the Emergency Fleet Corporation in the spring of 1918 Eleanor considered the appointment "the first sign that the President [was] waking up" to the need for stronger leadership in war production. He and Franklin spoke to the crew, and Eleanor noted that she had "a little walk and talk with him." Bernard Baruch, who had once been a Roosevelt dinner guest, was another illustrious shipmate. Since he was seasick most of the voyage he stayed below, and Eleanor's diary did not refer to him until they reached Paris, when he sent her "a lot of roses." There were Chinese and Mexican delegations aboard on their way to the Peace Conference. "At four Eleanor gave a tea to the Chinese mission," Livy (Davis) noted. "Most of the conversation was in French."

Theodore Roosevelt had died while they were en route. "I feel it must have been sudden and I am so sorry for Aunt Edith and the boys in Europe," Eleanor wrote. She was sorry, too, that the last few years had been so full of disappointments for Uncle Ted. In Europe, when Wilson was informed of the passing of his old antagonist he dictated a cool message of condolence to Mrs. Theodore Roosevelt and remarked to his intimates that Roosevelt had no constructive policy to his record. Eleanor's evaluation of her uncle's role was more just: "Another great figure off the stage," she wrote sadly in her diary.

The news about Uncle Ted's death came while she was reading *The Education of Henry Adams,* which she had given Franklin for Christmas. Theodore was for her a symbol of "active participation in the life of his people," while Adams symbolized withdrawal from life. "Very interesting," she commented on the Adams book, "but sad to have had so much and yet find it so little."

"A wonderfully comfortable and entertaining trip," Eleanor summed up the voyage as the *George Washington* approached the port of Brest. After the landing ceremonies, demobilization business claimed the men of the party, while Admiral Henry B. Wilson took Eleanor and Mrs. Thomas J. Spellacy, the wife of the U.S. attorney from Connecticut who was Franklin's legal adviser on the mission, on a drive through the town and its environs. "Every other woman wears a crepe veil to her knees," Eleanor noted. An exhausted Mrs. Spellacy begged to be allowed to sit in the car during the last part of their tour of the city and naval base and stayed behind when Eleanor walked with the admiral to a shop that sold the work of war widows.

The next day they were in Paris. Eleanor had never seen anything like it, she reported. "It is full beyond belief and one sees many celebrities and all one's friends." In one respect her outlook had changed little since her honeymoon visit; the women still scandalized her. "The women here all look exaggerated, you wonder if any are ladies though all look smart and some pretty." Now, however, puritan ethic was fortified by social outrage. "In contrast to this element are the women in plain black and deep mourning that one sees in all the streets."

She and Franklin went to tea with Mrs. Wilson at the Palais Murat, and it seemed to Eleanor that all of Washington was congregated there. She attended a luncheon given by Admiral Benson's wife, at which Mrs. House and Mrs. Lansing were also present, and noted, "Much talk of the President's not having been to the front yet and Mrs. Wilson only having seen two hospitals." Eleanor helped remedy the latter complaint, according to Miss Benham, Mrs. Wilson's social secretary, who wrote that Eleanor "swept Mrs. Wilson up into her project of visiting the war wounded in the hospitals."[14] Although the president had not yet visited the front, Eleanor did so on the way to Boulogne with Franklin. It was a journey through recently fought-over battlefields that, said Franklin, "we shall never forget." Eleanor, he added, had a "very achy side and shoulder" but insisted "on doing everything and getting out of the car at all points of interest." The land was gashed by trench systems and scarred by barbed-wire entanglements. "Ghastly," Franklin exclaimed at the Somme battlefield. "In the bigger places the Cathedral is *always* destroyed, and the town more or less, mostly more," Eleanor noted. "The streets are all clear, all is neat and clean but you feel as though ghosts were beside you." Their army guides, who had been through the fighting at St. Quentin, described the attack the previous September in the face of massed machine guns and the breakthrough in the Hindenburg line at the St. Quentin Canal. "An almost incredible feat," said Franklin. "How men ever did it I cannot imagine," wrote Eleanor. When they finally arrived at Amiens for the night, they were informed that express orders forbade ladies to go to the front, "but as I'd been," wrote Eleanor, "there was nothing to do about it!"

"Eleanor laid out with pleurisy," Livy recorded when they reached London. Admiral William S. Sims met them at the station and took them to the Ritz, and when Muriel Martineau, one of Eleanor's brides-maids and Franklin's cousin, came to see them, she immediately called a doctor, who ordered a protesting Eleanor to bed. Franklin and his staff had a great deal to do in London, but he came back to the hotel for lunch and later for tea, and at the end of the day dined at the hotel, "bringing me my dinner. He has been too sweet in looking after me," Eleanor recorded. In the next few days she ran a temperature, admitted to feeling tired and even conceded she might have a touch of influenza, but when Franklin insisted on taking her temperature and, finding that it was over 100, would not let her go out, she was furious. "He made me back out to my rage."

After she recovered she had reunions with those of her Allenswood schoolmates who were in London. They recalled the years that were among the happiest in her life, and although she was deeply fond of them she had progressed beyond them in the breadth of her interests and sympathies. Lady Gertrude of Osberton came to call. Eleanor's honeymoon stay at Osberton had been a nightmare; now she was at ease and self-assured. Lady Gertrude was "a dear old Lady" but Eleanor had scant sympathy for her lament that Osberton was ruined because the woods had to be cut down to pay the death duties. And she was amused by Lady Gertrude's distress that her grandson, who had been a prisoner of war, had married his nurse, a Polish woman; "of course one would prefer an Englishwoman even though she was nice and had twice saved his life," Lady Osberton said.

Yet interlaced with judgments and reactions that showed how much Eleanor had grown since her honeymoon days were avowals of allegiance to Sara that were as affectionate as those of 1905. "I do hope we never have to separate again. As I grow older I miss you and the children more and more. I think instead of becoming more independent I am growing into a really clinging vine!" Her old puritan conscience was as outraged in London as it had been in Paris. She and Franklin dined with a British admiral, and she was shocked: "Just wait till I get home and tell you what these respectable people now let their daughters do, your hair will curl as mine did!" Franklin, however, was intrigued. One lady so fascinated him, Eleanor wrote, that it was with difficulty she "dragged" him home at eleven o'clock. "We have nothing like some of their women or some of their men!"

She learned anew how cold London could be in the winter. "I don't wonder they consume much wine here, they have to in order to rise above the cold houses or the cheer would indeed be cold cheer!" She wore spats, a flannel petticoat, and her heavy purple dress "all the time" and never felt even "mildly warm." She was disappointed in herself for minding: "Decidedly we are growing effete at home from too much comfort and I always thought myself something of a Spartan!"

Franklin left on the thirty-first of January for Brussels and the Rhineland without Eleanor; it would be easier for everyone, he told her, not to have women along in the occupied areas. "I hate to miss the trip to Brussels and Coblentz," she wrote in her diary, "and to have him going off without me."

She stayed on in London with Muriel Martineau and then returned to Paris, but it was depressing without Franklin. "I hope he arrives. Somehow I feel lost and lonely in a strange town alone and I do get so blue. I suppose it must be the result of pleurisy!" She decided that activity was the best cure for melancholy.

She and Aunt Dora, who all through the war had refused to abandon her beloved Paris, visited the Val de Grâce Hospital. "It is here that Morestin operates and he has been so successful with the horrible face wounds," she wrote. The sight of shattered faces devastated her, and much as she tried she could not help but feel revolted "even though one does not show it." Aunt Dora seemed to love hearing about the various operations, but it made Eleanor feel ill. She even found the plaster casts oppressive, and "could hardly bear to look at the men with the horrible face wounds." But she did.

The next day was waiting-for-Franklin day, and from 6:00 P.M. on she began her waiting in earnest. Lieutenant Commander John M. Hancock, one of Franklin's aides, came to dine at 8:00; they waited until 8:15 but "still no sign, so we dined." Livy joined them after dinner and stayed until 10:30, when he pleaded sleepiness and went to bed. At 11:30 Hancock felt "it wouldn't do for him to wait longer so he left." Finally, at about 12:30 Franklin and his party turned up. Eleanor had a cold supper waiting for them and Admiral Long, who met them in the hall, "came up with some liquid refreshment."

They were laden with "loot" from the battlefields and were "full of a delightful and interesting trip," she reported. The party broke up at 1:30, probably due to her.

A few days later they prepared to sail for home, again on the *George Washington*. Eleanor was relieved that young Sheffield Cowles and David Gray were going back with them; Paris was "no place for the boys, especially the younger ones, and the scandals going on would make many a woman at home unhappy." Sara sounded a similar theme. "One hears a great deal here from returning officers and privates," she wrote. "One tale is that the common soldier behaves better than the officers, asking 'where is Napoleon's Tomb' 'where is the Louvre gallery' etc. The officers say: 'Where is Maxim's?'"

The president and Mrs. Wilson were also to be on board the *George Washington*. The Covenant of the new League of Nations had been finished on February 12, and Wilson was returning, House said, "to confront his enemies in the Senate." Sara had kept her children apprised of the way sentiment had turned against Wilson, at least in the circles in which she moved. She had stayed away from Mrs. Whitelaw Reid's, she informed them, because everyone had told her that Mrs. Reid did nothing but criticize the president and the administration "and I am rather tired of it." At a luncheon, another report went, she had sat next to Mrs. Berwind, who said that her husband looked upon Wilson as the "head of the Bolsheviki in this country." People generally were "so nasty about the Peace Conference and League of Nations that when anyone is full of admiration of our President and his ideals it is a pleasant surprise."

The boat train on which the Roosevelts were passengers preceded the president's by twenty minutes, and as they flashed by between lines of troops and roofs crowded with Bretons their train was mistaken for the president's. "The troops present arms and gaze in the hope of seeing the President," Eleanor noted in her diary. "It rains gently as usual." A newspaperman gave them a copy of the Covenant. "The High Contracting Parties," they read, "in order to promote international cooperation and to achieve international peace and security...." They read the twenty-six Articles eagerly and had high hopes that the new machinery could effectively safeguard the peace. In Brest they joined the French dignitaries who were there to bid the president good-by. "Great consternation and great upsetting of plans" when Mrs. Wilson and Miss Benham—on the president's insistence, but contrary to Navy custom—went on board ahead of the president. Eleanor and

Franklin went in to talk with the president and Mrs. Wilson. "The President is not very flattering about the French government and people," she recorded. Franklin left to go to the bridge as the vessel got under way, and stayed for nearly an hour's chat with the president, who was also there.

Auntie Bye's son Sheffield, a tall, lantern-jawed, kindly young man, saw a great deal of Eleanor on that trip. "She used always to be telling Franklin, 'I met so-and-so. He's an interesting fellow. You should talk with him. He's interested in more than sailing,'" he recalled.[15] Eleanor did the same kind of reading as his mother, he noted; "I was surprised how much she referred to Mother and was influenced by Mother."

On the fourth day out the president and Franklin made an official inspection of the ship, but "I can't say the President looked as though he saw much!" Eleanor noted. She herself visited the sick bay, and her inspection was thorough. "The arrangements for sick and wounded are ideal in every way. Splendid operating room, cleanliness, good food and good nurses." It was a far cry from the young woman who had complained that Franklin had inspected "every rivet."

One evening the crew put on an entertainment in which a boy dressed up as a chorus girl chucked the president under the chin. "Consternation and later reprimand but the President took it calmly," noted Eleanor. On Washington's Birthday they were invited to lunch with the president and Mrs. Wilson along with Dr. Grayson, Captain McCauley, Miss Benham, and the U.S. ambassador to Russia. The talk, Eleanor said, was, as usual in such cases, "chiefly stories," but two things the president said made a deep impression on her. He had read no papers since the beginning of the war, Wilson told them; Joseph P. Tumulty, his secretary, "read all and cut out important news or editorials," for him. "This is too much to leave to any man," she exclaimed in her diary. She also noted that the president spoke of the League, saying, "The United States must go in or it will break the heart of the world for she is the only nation that all feel is disinterested and all trust."

Eleanor accepted that. Her visits to the hospitals and battlefields of Europe had imbued her with an implacable hatred of war, a sentiment that would be a ruling passion with her for the remainder of her life. Two days later when they landed in Boston and rode in the fifth carriage in the president's procession, she noted approvingly that the streets "were all packed with people wildly shrieking. I never saw a better crowd or more enthusiasm." At the luncheon following the parade she was seated next to Governor Calvin Coolidge. It was, despite her best efforts, a wordless encounter. She thought Mayor Peters of Boston made "a courageous speech," coming out for the League despite the hostility of his Irish constituents. Governor Coolidge meant to speak guardedly but committed himself to "feeling sure the people would back the President." It was the president's speech, however, that set his listeners on fire, a "fighting" pronouncement, the *New York Times* reporter said, in which the president threw down "the glove of defiance to all Senators and others who oppose the League of Nations." "A very wonderful speech," was Eleanor's comment.

On the train to Washington, Miss Benham had tea in their compartment, and when they went to say good-by to the president and Mrs. Wilson, Eleanor had "a nice talk with him" and Mrs. Wilson gave her and Mrs. Spellacy a "bunch of flowers." They were home the next morning: "Greeted by chicks and Mama. All very well and very happy to be together again."

Back in Washington they soon discovered that the opposition was not at all daunted by Wilson's thunderbolts. When they dined with Alice Longworth, Eleanor found the atmosphere "very partisan"—so much so that it was too much for Franklin's customary good nature and he became "rather annoyed."[16] Nevertheless, Alice and her husband were invited to dinner at the Roosevelts', along with the leader of the Senate Democrats, to meet Sir Edward Grey, who had come to Washington as special ambassador to try to persuade Wilson to compromise with Senator Lodge and accept his reservations to the Covenant. "All seemed to enjoy it," Eleanor wrote of her dinner. "Lord G. said to Alice 'I would like to have a list of the books which you have read and I've never even heard of'! She really is extraordinary and kept us all entertained."[17]

Grey's mission was a failure, both with Alice and with Wilson. In a cold rebuff, Wilson, immured behind White House walls after his stroke, declined to receive Grey, and Alice remained a principal crusader against the League. When the Senate rejected the Covenant, the leading irreconcilables adjourned to the Longworth house for a celebratory snack, where, Alice wrote, "Mrs. Harding cooked the eggs."[18]

Eleanor took no part in the League fight, as political activity was still Franklin's domain. Nor did she take part in the final battle for women's suffrage. Although she declined Alice Wadsworth's invitation to join the National Association of Anti-Suffragists and counseled Sara to do likewise, when Franklin went to Hyde Park to vote in November, 1918, he went alone, even though New York women had acquired the vote by state referendum in 1917.

But she was venturing into new fields and was privately expressing views on politics and public affairs that were crisply unequivocal and quite sophisticated. When Wilson dismissed Secretary of State Lansing because he had convened cabinet meetings during the president's disablement without authorization, she was indignant: "I think it will be awkward for whoever is next Secretary of State for he will be branded as a rubber stamp. The President's letter can only be considered that of a sick, peevish man and I think everyone is more seriously worried than at any time."[19] And when New York lawyer Bainbridge Colby was named to succeed Lansing, she was harsh: "Mr. B. Colby is a good speaker and an agreeable person to meet. His 'mind will go along' excellently. He's a non-entity and has never shown in any job much capacity and of course he has no qualifications for this one, except that I feel sure he will never hold an opinion at variance with the President as long as it pays him not to!"[20] Official Washington's unhappy experience with an incapacitated president who was protectively isolated from his cabinet and political associates by his wife and physician made an indelible impression on Eleanor and would influence her own conduct in the final months of Franklin's administration when his strength began to fail.

In the fall of 1919 when Franklin went to New Brunswick for some hunting, Eleanor undertook to keep track of the Industrial Conference for him. Organized under the chairmanship of Secretary Lane, the conference was trying, amid the wave of postwar strikes, to formulate a modus vivendi between employer groups and unions. This activity brought Eleanor in touch with a new range of problems and people. "Heard Mr. Fish of the Employer group speak against a compromise resolution which was brought in on the collective bargaining issue, responded to with much heat by Mr. Wheeler of the public group. Nothing done so far!" The next day she reported, "The industrial conference came to a smash and the labor delegates walked out. Now the public groups are trying to pick up the pieces having asked the employers to withdraw. The President's letter was fine but did no good, even the *Tribune* gave it high praise this morning. The coal situation looks a little better today but the A.F. of L. has called a general conference for November and is preparing for a big struggle."[21]

The labor movement was beginning to engage Eleanor's sympathies.

An International Congress of Working Women took place in Washington at the end of October, 1919, and she went to a tea for the delegates. It was "of course a very advanced and radical gathering presided over by Mrs. Raymond Robins," but evidently its radicalism did not frighten her for she found it "interesting and amusing."[22]

She then invited some of the women to lunch with her. The U.S. delegation, in addition to Mrs. Robins, included Rose Schneiderman of the Cap Makers, Maud Swartz of the Printers, Leonora O'Reilly of the New York Women's Trade Union League, Mary Anderson of the Boot and Shoe Workers Union, Fannia Cohn of the Ladies Garment Workers, Julia O'Connor of the Telephone Operators, and Lois Rantoul of the Federal Employees Union. The time was coming when she would call many of these women her friends.

23. THE REBELLION BEGINS

THE YEARS IN WASHINGTON WERE DRAWING TO A CLOSE. Outwardly they were a time of triumph; they were also a time of deep inner travail.

"I do not think I have ever felt so strangely as in the past year," Eleanor wrote in her diary at the end of 1919, "perhaps it is that I have never noticed little things before but all my self-confidence is gone and I am on edge though I never was better physically I feel sure."[1]

At Christmas time she sent close friends photographs of her family. The handsome group included the five children, Franklin, and, on Eleanor's insistence, Sara. "It looks alarmingly like the ones of families that end up in the White House," a close friend wrote. What "a grand success you've made."

Success! When the rock upon which she had built her life and sought to lay to rest the sense of failure and inferiority had been shattered? Tightly, desperately, Eleanor clung to the old familiar ties and attachments—family, friends, and duties—yet she could not shut off the moods of black despair that seized her when she felt that no one belonged to her and she was of no use to anyone. There were moments when her belief that life had meaning slipped away from her. "There are times," she later said, "in everyone's life when the wish to be done with the burdens and even the decisions of this life seems overwhelming."[2] This was such a time for her. She often took refuge in Rock Creek Cemetery, sitting in front of the haunting memorial that Henry Adams had commissioned Augustus Saint-Gaudens to erect to his wife. The cowled bronze figure had inspired Spring-Rice to write a sonnet, a copy of which was found among Eleanor's bedside papers at her death:

> O steadfast, deep, inexorable eyes
> Set look inscrutable, nor smile nor frown!

O tranquil eyes that look so calmly down
Upon a world of passion and of lies!...

Mrs. Adams, a victim of prolonged depressions, had committed suicide, but the seated figure did not evoke thoughts of despair in Eleanor. The lips were full. The hand was strong. The beautiful face was that of a woman who had achieved absolute self-mastery. Henry Adams had sometimes called the figure the "Peace of God," a peace, Saint-Gaudens said, that was "beyond pain and beyond joy," and for Eleanor these were the years when sometimes she envied the peace that Mrs. Adams had achieved, and sometimes wondered whether such peace could be achieved in life through self-mastery.[3] "There was a time," she would write a friend in 1941, "when I thought happiness didn't matter but I think differently today."[4]

As civilized as she and Franklin were, they had some very bad times, although inner strain flared only rarely into open conflict. "Found F.D. and E. very cool as he had been to the Fly Club dinner night before," Livy Davis had noted in Paris.[5] "Dined alone," Eleanor recorded on April 10, 1919. "Franklin nervous and overwrought and I very stupid and trying, result a dreadful fracas."

It was a time for her of harsh self-reproach and depreciation, of desolating conviction that she had failed as a woman and was in some way responsible for Franklin's involvement with Lucy. But bitter as the experience was, it also matured her. Slowly she won through to the realization that she could not achieve fulfillment through someone else. "Somewhere along the line of development we discover what we really are," she wrote in 1941, "and then we make our real decision for which we are responsible. Make that decision primarily for yourself because you can never really live anyone else's life not even your child's. The influence you exert is through your own life and what you become yourself."[6]

She buried herself in work, especially in her work for St. Elizabeth's where she could find her way back to a firm feeling that she was of some use, where she could feel herself needed. "My experience has been," she wrote in later years, "that work is almost the best way to pull oneself out of the depths."[7] To wean her from self-pity and private woe there were, in addition to her duties with the Red Cross, her children, her household, as well as her obligations as the wife of one of the most promising public men in Washington.

In her final months in Washington she made considerable changes in her household. Servants had ceased to intimidate her. When Blanche, her personal maid, did not do her job, she cheerfully informed Sara, "I blew her up the other day,"[8] and while she did not think it had "much effect" the expression bespoke her growth in self-assurance.

In the choice of governesses she also struck a new note. "I feel when we do *burden* ourselves with one," she told Sara, "it should be to acquire a language not just to be kept up in English to which they devote most of their winter."[9] Their last year in Washington she gave Anna and James the choice of having a governess who would supervise them or making a pledge to perform their chores and duties without supervision. Both chose freedom.

In 1913 Daniels had reproached her for having white household help. Housework should be done by Negro servants, he had said, and the statement had shocked her. But now in 1919 difficulties with her white help persuaded her to restaff her household, except for an English nurse, with Negro servants—cook, kitchen maid, butler, and housemaid. Paradoxically, this was not a compromise with the southern view that such jobs were menial and for Negroes alone but a rejection of New York society's conviction that only whites were qualified and trustworthy enough to serve inside the house. It was Eleanor's first intimate contact with Negroes. "Well, all my servants are gone and all the darkies are here and heaven knows how it will all turn out!" she informed Sara.[10]

Her first big dinner under the new arrangements was to take place on March 13, and she was curious to see how "my darkies manage," but she had already found them "pleasanter to deal with and there is never any question about it not being their work to do this or that."[11] The dinner went off without mishap but sometimes there were problems. On the eve of a buffet luncheon for Marine officers the butler developed pleurisy, which she thought an odd disease for midsummer. "With darkies," she generalized, "one is always suspicious even of a death in the family."[12] But her new cook, Nora, more than made up for the butler's absence and proved to be "a host in herself. . . . She cooked the hams (4) made a wonderful grapefruit punch and vegetable salad in enormous quantities and black coffee in the same quantities." Eleanor never regretted having made the change, although there was a long journey ahead before she freed herself of racial stereotypes and bias.

When in the summer of 1919 racial violence swept Washington, triggered by returned servicemen, her thoughts were of Franklin's safety, not of the causes of the racial outbreak. She and the children were in Fairhaven rather than Campobello, because, she had explained to Sara, it was "a long and expensive commuting trip" to Campobello and that is what it would be for Franklin "and for me."[13] Her anxiety when she did not hear from Franklin seemed excessive, its intensity a reflection of her own edginess. "You seem to have had pretty bad race riots in Washington," she wrote him on arrival at Fairhaven. "Have you seen anything of them?"[14] She was more agitated the next day. "No word from you and I am getting very anxious on account of the riots. Do be careful not to be hit by stray bullets." The riots had not spread to R Street, he assured her, and he had taken pains "to keep out of harm's way."[15] But the mail was slow in reaching Fairhaven. "Still no letter or telegram from you and I am worried to death," she wrote him. "Even if something is wrong why don't you let me know. I'd always rather know than worry. I couldn't sleep at all last night thinking of all the things which might be the matter."[16] She seemed unduly disquieted. Evidently Franklin thought so too. "Your telegram came last night at ten," he informed her; "as I was in my pyjamas and couldn't get Western Union I did not answer it till this a.m. as soon as I got to the office."[17]

If she was strained and jittery in matters involving Franklin, when it came to a crisis involving the children Eleanor was remarkably poised, as she had demonstrated a few weeks earlier at the time of the A. Mitchell Palmer assassination attempt. "Mother's" self-control on that occasion became a legend in the family. Shortly before midnight on June 2, 1919, a bomb went off in front of the house of Attorney General Palmer, shattering its front, killing a man, and blowing out the front windows of the Roosevelt house across the street. Franklin and Eleanor, who arrived shortly after the blast, raced into their house to see what had happened to James, who was the only child at home.

"James did not hear the explosion but heard the ensuing confusion," she wrote Sara.

> However, I stated nothing was the matter "just an explosion" in the most matter-of-fact tone as though it was a daily occurence and he returned to bed and sleep at once. We went over at once and offered to take the Palmers in but they preferred to get out of the street.
>
> Now we are roped off and the police haven't yet allowed the gore to be wiped up on our steps and James glories in every new bone found! I only hope the victim was not a poor passer by instead of the anarchist![18]

She was now asserting a more direct supervision over her children's upbringing. She was discontented with Anna's school—she thought it "stuffy," an expression that indicated her changing standards. Frequent conferences with the Misses Eastman on ways to improve Anna's grades produced middling results. She took Anna to the theater to encourage an interest in the drama, and sent her to music and dancing classes, and when the young men from the British Embassy came to luncheon Anna was sometimes invited to join them in the hope that the combination of handsome young men and good conversation would widen her interests. She was tall, with yellow hair that tumbled over her shoulders, and looked older than her thirteen years. Her parents took her with them to Annapolis, and she was invited to next year's plebe hop. "I declined," her mother wrote Sara.[19]

James also failed to make good grades at the Cathedral School, which he and Elliott now attended. That distressed Eleanor because he needed good grades to qualify for Groton, and it was taken for granted that when they reached their twelfth birthdays all the boys would be handed over to Dr. Peabody. Eleanor tried a winter of getting up early to hear James' lessons before he went off to school, and there were tutors and stern lectures, but all with indifferent results. James continued to do better as left end on the football team than on his exam papers. Elliott's marks were "very good," she informed Sara, but "James is worse than last month, 12th in a class of 26, average way below the class, the only decent mark is 93 in History. I just told him I did not care to discuss it as unfortunately no one else could study for him and he evidently did not care to make use of any of his advantages. He wept as usual and it will have as much effect as usual. I think this summer I shall have him work an hour longer than Anna daily."[20]

Of all her children the two youngest, Franklin Jr. and John, were the ones Eleanor seemed to enjoy most. She was overprotective of Elliott, perhaps because he carried her beloved father's name and seemed to have his proneness for physical mishaps, but with "the babies" she was more relaxed than she had been with the older children, could take their outbursts of wildness more calmly, and on the whole seemed to have more fun with them. Franklin Jr. was the "sunshine" boy, as James later dubbed him. "I went out for a walk with little Franklin this morning," he wrote his grandmother, "and everytime he saw a child he would say hallow as if he knew them." Franklin at five was a flatterer. "I love you very much. I want to kiss you," he wrote his grandmother, adding, "Please give me a light like Anna's and a firecracker." He amused his mother. "I asked Franklin Jr. last night what I was to ask Santa Claus to bring him and without prompting he reeled off more things than you ever heard of. I gasped and he added, 'and John just the same!'"[21] John was already showing the instincts of a businessman; "I feel sure he owns everything by now," Eleanor wrote Sara after the children had been with their grandmother for a week in 1918.[22] She read them a children's life of their Uncle Ted. "Granny, I intend to run for the Presidency, and am beginning my campaign at your tea," Franklin Jr. announced to Sara while he was still in short pants. John had no such interest. Aunt Tissie at Fairhaven was so taken with John's pleasing ways that she told him he would be president some day. "I am *not* going to be President," he replied firmly.[23]

Franklin Jr. and John made a team. Together they went to a party at the Bill Phillipses and had a "fine time," according to their mother, "except for the fact that they did not get enough cereal to eat." On John's fourth birthday she arranged a "Mother Goose" party for "the babies." This was Franklin Jr.'s time to be little Jack Horner as the others had been before him, and she had a large pie filled with little toys which he handed out after supper with much excitement. As the youngest were a pair, so were Anna and James. Elliott was left out, the others sometimes allying themselves against him, spurred on by the feeling that their mother spoiled him. "The other boys ate up his dessert at dinner, because he ate so slowly he wasn't ready for it, and they wouldn't tell him where the w.c. was so just before leaving he had an accident in his pants which upset him a good deal but I think all will go well from now on!"[24]

Gladys Saltonstall, who spent a Sunday evening with the Roosevelts in 1919, found Eleanor's warm, maternal relationship to her children especially attractive. "I secretly envied her."[25] But others who knew the household better doubted that Eleanor gave her children what they needed. Margaret Cutter, who then was her sister-in-law, felt that while Eleanor loved the children she "did not make them her friends."[26] "She did her duty," cousin Corinne remarked. "Nobody in the world did her duty more than Eleanor Roosevelt. But with the children I don't think you can have an understanding of them unless you enjoy them."[27] It was their father who taught them to ride, to love sailing, who during the winter was "the moving spirit in coasting and tobogganing," and who filled their Washington week ends with joy. He was "my childhood hero," said Anna, while "it was Mother's duty to counteract my tomboy tendencies and to teach me to sew and knit."[28] "I don't think Mother shared in the day-to-day fun in life at all," James agreed, "in things like skating, sledding, etc. She was very good about making arrangements, but she did not participate. We had more real fun with Mother when we were all much older when we went to the play with her, met people at her house, a few Sunday evenings."[29]

The burdens and perplexities of bringing up her own children made Eleanor appreciate more fully the heavy charge that had been placed on Grandma Hall when in 1892 she had taken in Eleanor and her two brothers. "My grandmother died," she wrote in her diary on August 14, 1919. "A gentle good woman with a great and simple faith. It is only of late years that I have realized what it meant for her to take Hall, Ellie and me into her home as she did. Pussie and Maude were wonderful about it too."

Not since the early days of their marriage when Franklin was a law clerk had Eleanor spent so much time with him, but time spent together can be abrasive as well as healing. He now often came home for lunch and tea, but good as his intentions were, he was still his old unpunctual self. He dallied at the office until an outraged telephone call from the "Missus" caused him to stuff papers in his briefcase, grab his hat and cane, and bolt for home. Even when she called for him at the office, she could not get him to leave on time. "Waited 35 minutes and returned to find Paul Hammond playing with the children waiting for us," she noted on one such occasion. Outwardly she smiled, inwardly she seethed.

They picnicked together in the country. They walked in the woods. Together with the Phillipses and the Millers they canoed up the old B & O Canal, lunched, and came back by way of the Potomac. The river ran fairly fast in spots. Pleasant but "not real excitement," Eleanor commented afterward.[30] Danger and roughness gave spice to life, and she did not like a slack and tepid existence. She tried to show Franklin that, but for him there were sanctuaries that belonged to men alone, into which he would not admit her.

If she did not hear from him she worried and when he was away she missed him, but when they were together he easily upset her, as was the case at the end of that 1919 summer. "I'm glad you enjoyed your holiday dear, & I wish we did not lead such a hectic life, a little prolonged quiet might bring us altogether & yet it might do just the opposite! I really don't know what I want or think about anything anymore!"[31] Yet when in October he went off to the Canadian woods with Livy and Lieutenant Commander Richard E. Byrd to hunt moose, she wrote him like a newlywed. "I hated to have you go off alone and shan't feel quite happy till you are safely home again," she wrote within hours after he left. When the postman brought his first letter she wrote in her diary, "No moose yet but sounds well, thank goodness. It was a joy to hear."[32]

She tried to be the kind of person he wished her to be. When he went off to a poker game, she used the time to make up the household-accounts book as he liked to have it done. "Now that I've done it, it doesn't take so long," she wrote Sara. "I hope Franklin will be pleased."[33] She took more time selecting her clothes. While they were in Paris she had ordered two dresses at Worth, and Franklin and Sara approved. The cape that Sara did not like she gave away to the "darling housemaid." She bought three hats ("$91—isn't it too awful...but I really took a long time to choose") from Miss Gandy, the mountain-climbing lady of whom she had been so jealous on her honeymoon.[34] In February, 1920, she splurged again, buying an evening dress and a gray satin afternoon dress at Miss Converse's. Franklin liked her in the evening dress, she noted a few weeks later with relief and pleasure.

The winter of 1920, a tonsillectomy was added to Franklin's usual ailments of sinuses and colds. "He looks rather poorly for him," Bertie Hamlin noted in her journal. Franklin asked Eleanor not to cancel their social engagements; Eleanor was getting out 2,000 invitations for Navy teas, he told Bertie. She got through the luncheons and the one big dinner they had scheduled, although it was "horrid" to do so without Franklin. Even with Franklin, dinner parties had again become ordeals. During one dinner that winter she went upstairs to tuck the children in and hear their prayers, and stayed away so long that Franklin became anxious. "I just can't stand to greet all those people," she said in tears. "I know they all think I am dull and unattractive. I just want to hide up here."[35]

Franklin was thirty-eight on January 30, and she had a party to celebrate the occasion: "all are coming as a character in a book, so it ought to be amusing."[36] The Lanes, Millers, Polks, Hallowells, McCauleys, Rodgers, and Alice and Nick Longworth were the guests. Their costumes were nowhere recorded, nor whether Eleanor found the evening bearable. On her own birthday the previous October she had noted, "I am 36. Margaret and Hall sent me a book, Mama and Tissie and Franklin wired" (Franklin was away making a speech in Rochester). It gave her pleasure to plan and organize gay birthday parties for others, but she always found reasons why hers should not be celebrated, especially when her feelings had been deeply hurt. Why should anyone wish to celebrate her birthday? She was not averse to making Franklin feel a little guilty.

Some of the gayest parties the winter of 1919–20 were given by Mrs. Marshall Field, whose liveliness, despite her age, evoked Washington's admiration. "We stayed at Mrs. Field's last night till 12:30 p.m. ending with a Virginia reel! On Sunday night too!" Eleanor reported.[37]

But other evenings turned out less happily. There was one disastrous revel at the Chevy Chase Club, of which there are two accounts. One is Eleanor's told years later when she could bear to speak of it; the other told by Alice Longworth with her usual "detached malevolence."[38] The women had, as usual, swarmed about Franklin, and he had been very gay while Eleanor felt more and more miserable. Finally she decided she would not be missed if she departed. He should stay and enjoy himself, she whispered to Franklin, but she was going home. She didn't, "as a rule," let him stay behind at a dance, said Mrs. Longworth. "She was rather firm about that; but this time she let him stay at the country club, and he came in with the Warren Robbinses. And it was they, of course, who hastened to tell me the next morning all about what had happened."

Eleanor had forgotten her latchkey and, unable to get in, had settled down on the doormat, propping herself against the wall, feeling sorry for herself and cross with Franklin. When he finally did turn up, close to dawn, Eleanor rose in the vestibule "like a wraith," said Alice, to confront him. The rest of the story we have from Alice.

"But darling, what's happened? What are you doing here?"

"Oh, I forgot my key."

"But couldn't you have gone to the Adolph Millers'? You could have spent the night there, or you could have gone to Mitchell Palmer's house, where there's a guard."

"Oh, no, I've always been told never to bother people if you can possibly avoid it." Here, Alice, in telling the story, interpolated, "So noble, so noble."

"You must have been hideously uncomfortable," Franklin went on.

"Well, it wasn't *very* uncomfortable."

She was quite sure, Eleanor commented later, that she had made Franklin "feel guilty by the mere fact of having waited" in the vestibule. They were not, she said in a massive understatement, the best years of her life.

Her immense physical vitality seemed to drain away, one of the few times in all her years that she registered such a complaint. "I was dead," she wrote on April 19, attributing her exhaustion to dinner guests who stayed "till 11.30."[39] The next day she noted again "I was a dead dog," having dined with Aunt Kassie at eight. And the evening after that she went to the Army and Navy League Ball. "I stood and received till 11 p.m. and went home 11:30 dead again." This would have been a normal reaction for most women, but Eleanor was always able to tap hidden springs of energy and her exhaustion was not normal. In May when she was at Hyde Park, she and Sara had a quiet dinner "but I might as well not have eaten it for I promptly parted with it all!"[40] She insisted it was "just weariness," but the weariness was only another manifestation of the conflict within her between a nature seeking to find its true vocation and the life of conformity that the effort to please her husband and mother-in-law had shaped.

While she sought to rebuild her relationship with Franklin, she began to turn against Sara. In July, 1919, when she had left Hyde Park and taken her younger children to Fairhaven, she confessed to her husband, "I feel as though someone had taken a ton of bricks off me and I suppose she feels just the same."[41] But Sara evidently was not aware of Eleanor's inner stress. "A letter from Mama this morning," Franklin wrote her. "It will amuse you as she says everything is going very smoothly."[42] At the end of September they all returned to Hyde Park. "Mama and I have had a bad time," she noted on October 3, "I should be ashamed of myself and I'm not. She is too good and generous and her judgment is better than mine but I can *learn* more easily."[43] (The italicized word is almost undecipherable, but "learn" seems to fit the context best.)

On a Sunday two days after this rebellious entry, Eleanor wrote, "Went to Church but could not go to Communion."[44] The words were austere and their implication stark, for she was the most faithful of churchgoers, the most sincere of communicants, for whom prayer was not a matter of rote but a daily influence in her life. Religion was of the utmost seriousness to her and prayer a kind of continuing exchange with God, a way of cleansing the heart and steadying the will. To say that she could not take Communion meant that she could not say that she "truly and earnestly" repented of her sins and that she was in a state of "love and charity" with those around her, as the Episcopalian Communion service required. She was temporarily cut off from divine grace, a condition that she must have found insupportable.

That week end she lost her temper with her mother-in-law one of the rare times in her life she did so. Her letter of October 6 begging Sara's forgiveness disclosed how deeply alienation and despair had taken command of her feelings. "I know, Mummy dear, I made you feel most unhappy the other day and I am so sorry I lost my temper and said such fool things for of course as you know I love Franklin and the children very dearly and I am deeply devoted to you. I have however, allowed myself to be annoyed by little things which of course one should never do and I had no right to hurt you as I know I did and am truly sorry and hope you will forgive me."

Although she was remorseful, her rebellion against Sara and the way of life Sara represented was only beginning, and it spread to Cousin Susie. When Eleanor went to New York to have dinner with the Parishes, "we had in some ways a very stormy evening."[45] She was finding Cousin Susie's self-indulgence and her unfriendly attitude toward people outside of her little circle difficult to bear. Eleanor "fairly jumped with joy," she wrote, when she and Franklin did not have to spend a summer week end with Cousin Susie, "though I'm sorry of course she isn't well."[46]

By the time she and Franklin left Washington her estrangement from Sara's and Cousin Susie's outlook was very deep. In early December, 1920, she spent an evening in New York talking with Sara and her two sisters, Dora and Kassie, and wrote Franklin afterward: "They all in their serene assurance and absolute judgments on people and affairs going on in the world, make me want to squirm and turn bolshevik." She was beginning to follow the "remorseless logic" of her love for others. Her desire to serve, which deference to her mother-in-law and Franklin had confined to the family circle, was breaking free. Humiliation and despair did not quench her ardent nature. Tenderness flowed into new channels. She clipped a poem, "Psyche," by Virginia Moore, out of the newspaper and wrote on it "1918," meaning that it conveyed her own slow climb out of the depths. It, too, like the Spring-Rice sonnet about the Saint-Gaudens statue, was filed among her bedside papers.

The soul that has believed
And is deceived
Thinks nothing for a while.
All thoughts are vile.

And then because the sun
Is mute persuasion,
And hope in Spring and Fall
Most natural,

The soul grows calm and mild,
A little child,
Finding the pull of breath
Better than death, . . .

The soul that had believed
And was deceived
Ends by believing more
Than ever before.

But her soul, which ended by "believing more," was moving toward wider, more general sympathies. Speaking of her wartime experience, Eleanor later wrote that from then on she saw herself and others more realistically. "No one is entirely bad or entirely good," and she no longer was sure of what was right and what was wrong; out of it all she emerged "a more tolerant person, far less sure of my own beliefs and methods of action, but I think more determined to try for certain ultimate objectives."[47]

III

---◇---

THE
EMERGENCE
OF
ELEANOR
ROOSEVELT

24. A CAMPAIGN AND FRIENDSHIP WITH LOUIS HOWE

"SHALL WE HAVE TO FIGHT EACH OTHER THIS FALL?" ALICE Wadsworth, the wife of the incumbent Republican senator, asked Eleanor. "I'd hate to have either of our good men beaten—so let's go after different jobs!"[1]

It was 1920, a presidential election year and the end of the Wilson years. The "club" dispersed. Lane resigned to take a job with Edward L. Doheny's oil company at $50,000 a year; it was strange employment for a man who had been one of the most progressive members of Wilson's cabinet, but he was already suffering with the illness that in a few months would kill him. Phillips was posted as U.S. minister to The Hague. Franklin spent much of his time out of Washington touring New York State to prepare the way to run either for governor or senator in the 1920 elections.

When Franklin left for San Francisco to attend the Democratic national convention, Eleanor did not know which office he would finally seek, but in either case he would need, if not the sponsorship, at least the neutrality of Tammany at the state convention. She was, therefore, surprised to read in the papers that he had helped wrest the state standard from a Tammany stalwart when the New York delegation refused to join in the demonstration in Wilson's honor. "You and Tammany don't seem to agree very well. Mama is very proud of your removing the State standard from them! I have a feeling you enjoyed it but won't they be very much against you in the State Convention?"[2]

Her letters to him sounded as if she, too, wanted to be in San Francisco. Two of his old Poughkeepsie supporters, John Mack and Thomas Lynch, were with him. "I can't help thinking what fun you will all have together." Politics interested her more than she sometimes acknowledged. She would like to have heard William Jennings Bryan's speech about the Democratic platform, she said, and then added a terse comment on the platform itself that might well apply to most such documents—"too much self praise and recrimination, too long but better than the Republican on the whole."[3]

She wished she could meet Franklin in Washington after the convention was over and hear all about it, she wrote, but on July 4 she transported her brood to Campobello. She did not dream that her husband might end up being the vice-presidential candidate, and since McAdoo, Cox, Palmer, and Smith seemed to be in a stalemate over who the candidate would be, Eleanor's major anxiety was that Franklin's arrival at Campobello would be delayed. "Please, please don't let your staying an extra day make any difference in coming up to us!"[4] She still did not know what had happened when she wrote him, "I suppose you started tonight for the East. I heard tonight in Eastport Cox was nominated but am in the dark as to the rest. I wonder if you are really satisfied."[5] Then the telegrams began to arrive. "It would have done your heart good to have seen the spontaneous and enthusiastic tribute paid when Franklin was nominated for Vice President today," Daniels wired her; "Franklin was nominated by acclamation," Lynch informed her. "This certainly is a world of surprises," she wrote Sara that evening. "I really think F. had a better chance of winning for the Senatorship but the Democrats may win, one cannot tell and at least it should be a good fight."[6]

So little was known about Eleanor that a long profile of Franklin Roosevelt in the Democratic *New York World* stated in the last sentence of the last paragraph, "Mrs. Roosevelt 'goes in' but little for society, finding her occupation in the management of her home and the welfare of her one daughter and her three sons." A Washington society reporter gave a somewhat different picture in the *New York Times*: "Mrs. Roosevelt is one of those women who, while she is absolutely at ease in the frilliest of social frills—she was born to them—yet finds them unimportant in her scheme of life."[7] After describing the Roosevelt family, the reporter continued, "She has her own circle of warm friends. She is—well, as one of her friends put it, she is too much of a Roosevelt to be anybody's prize beauty, but she's pure gold. . . . Few women are so generally esteemed by their acquaintance as Mrs. Roosevelt. . . . She was up to her eyes in war work . . . [but] she is essentially a home woman. She seems to particularly dislike the official limelight. . . . Just how she would endure the Vice-Presidential status . . . remains to be seen." "Papers are demanding your picture," Howe wired her from Washington. "Is there one at the house here that I can have copied?" "Are no pictures of me," she replied. As a result, the *Daily News* that Sunday published a picture of some other woman that it had cropped from a photograph of the Roosevelts at a baseball game, thinking it was the candidate's wife.

The *World* sent a correspondent from Eastport to Campobello to interview Eleanor. He came away with a brief, rather stilted statement that could hardly have satisfied his editor. "I am very much pleased and happy to know of Mr. Roosevelt's nomination," she said, "but I realize that it will take up much of his time during the coming campaign, and he may not have much time to enjoy a rest here. While he may not have looked for the honor, I am proud of his nomination and hope he will be elected."[8] An *Evening Post* reporter who went to Hyde Park, on the other hand, found a great dowager, quite at ease, overawed neither by press nor by the honors accorded to her son. "There is a stark and undeniable atmosphere of noncompromise about this house and its lady," the reporter commented, and found everywhere and in everything about Springwood—in the commodious and sturdily built mansion, the stone walls, the spreading trees—"a stamp of ancient solid things, of good beginnings which have persisted well."[9] Sara declined to talk about Franklin except for his connection with Hyde Park, the one place on earth, she said, that he loved best. In such surroundings, the perceptive reporter remarked, "there is no necessity ever to speak of what is one's belief; it is so certain and so sure."

Hyde Park did not want to be left out of the homecoming ceremonies that were being planned in Poughkeepsie, Sara advised her son. A rousing village welcome was being prepared, with their neighbor, Mr. Newbold, as chairman. "If and when you are elected, you will belong to the nation, now you are 'our boy' of Hyde Park and Dutchess." Motherly hopes were soaring: "My regards and best wishes to our future President."[10]

But Democratic national prospects were not good, as Eleanor had indicated in her letter to Sara. The country sensed that since Wilson's illness the government had been rudderless, and this was held against the Democrats. The people were tired of the heroic mode. There was a revolt against high taxes. The country was ready, as the Republican nominee Senator Harding phrased it, for a "return to normalcy." But for Roosevelt no political campaign was a lost cause. When Cox's representative in San Francisco had awakened Charles Murphy to tell him that Roosevelt was Cox's choice for vice president, the Tammany leader said, "He is not well known in the country." To campaign was an opportunity for Franklin to project himself onto the national stage and to conduct himself in such a way that no matter what happened in 1920, the party would turn to him in 1924.

Eleanor's hopes for Franklin's early arrival at Campobello dimmed as he conferred with local leaders on his way East and stopped off at Columbus to meet with Cox, a meeting at which the two men announced they wanted the election to be a plebiscite on the League of Nations. Eleanor finally went to Hyde Park instead. "In order to share the day with her husband, Mrs. Roosevelt traveled all night and all day from Eastport, Maine," the *New York Times* reported. She arrived too late for the "homecoming" at Springwood, where village neighbors with a band at their head met Franklin at the gate and escorted him to the house, but she did catch up with him for the ceremonies in Poughkeepsie.[11]

Sara wrote her son after the homecoming ceremony, "I will say nothing of my feelings on Tuesday last and in fact always for you know. I know you and I will never forget Tuesday the 13th of July, 1920! I kept wishing for your Father but I believe he knew and was with us...." Happy mother, unhappy wife. Eleanor could not identify with Franklin's triumphs in that instinctive and impulsive way. "Whatever Franklin achieves must be largely due to you," she had written Sara.[12] That was conviction, not courtesy.

Their closest friends saw it differently. Eleanor is "your real 'running mate,'" Aunt Kassie wrote. Isabella was thrilled because if Franklin was elected, Eleanor would also be in a position to do much to benefit the country, and she marveled at the steady progress Eleanor had made. The thought of Eleanor as the wife of the vice president caused Pauline Emmet to glow: "How splendid you will be dearest Eleanor (we must win!) graceful and gracious and charming!"

Eleanor was happy for Franklin, happy that he had attained something he wanted, but her feeling was also one of detachment and objectivity, as if she were looking at someone else's life from the outside. There were married couples who could say, as Beatrice Webb did of her marriage, "apart we each of us live only half a life, together we each of us have a double life." Eleanor had wanted that sort of relationship with Franklin, but the Lucy Mercer affair had killed her feeling that she really shared in his life or that she had abilities of her own. This was his career, not hers, his potentialities that were being realized, while hers continued to be circumscribed by family and friends.

She was ready for something more—how much so is suggested in an interview she gave at Hyde Park during the homecoming ceremonies.

Mrs. Roosevelt, the reporter wrote, "is first of all a domestic woman, but she has one outside interest, she admitted on Wednesday to a reporter of the (Poughkeepsie) *Eagle News*, in the only interview she granted. That is politics."

"Yes, I am interested in politics, intensely so, but in that I think I am no different from the majority of women, only that, of course, I have followed my husband's career with an interest that is intense because it is personal. But I have never," and she emphasized her words, "campaigned for him. I haven't been active in politics in any way, and so you see there isn't much of a story to be found in me.

"My politics? Oh yes, I am a Democrat, but," and here she paused, "I was brought up a staunch Republican,—and turned Democrat. I believe that the best interests of the country are in the hands of the Democratic Party, for I believe they are the most progressive. The Republicans are,—well, they are more conservative, you know, and we can't be too conservative and accomplish things.

"I am particularly interested in the League of Nations issue and I am firmly in favor of it, though I think we should adopt it with the reservation that Congress shall vote on whether or not we shall enter a war. But the League of Nations is, I believe, the only way that we can prevent war. We fought for it, and we should adopt it. If we don't adopt, it will be useless. The U.S. must be part of the alliance."[13]

These were the careful comments of a woman who was thinking for herself. The reporter was charmed by this "womanly" woman, as he described her. "Her hair is blond and fluffy, and her eyes of a deep shade of blue, make her look far younger than one would have imagined the mother of half-grown children to be. She is constantly smiling,—not the set, vapid smile of one who assents pleasantly rather than discuss a problem, but rather the smile that portrays a personality intensely interested in the questions under discussion and with a personal viewpoint on each of them." The reporter was interested that "as Mrs. Roosevelt sat and chatted...the Democratic nominee for Vice President frequently entered the library to ask her advice on questions that had come up...."

Back in Campobello Eleanor followed Franklin's progress through the papers. He and Cox were going to see the president, he wrote her, but he still planned to get to Campobello: "I can hardly wait, I miss you so much. It is very strange not to have you with me in all these doings."[14] "I like all your interviews," she replied, "and am dying to hear about your talk with the President. Oh! how I wish I could be in two places at once!"[15]

Franklin made the journey to Campobello on the destroyer *Hatfield*, piloting the vessel through the treacherous Lubec Narrows himself. While he was on the Island, he told the press, he intended to do some shooting, take cliff walks, begin work on another toy sailboat for the children, and teach James how to handle the *Vireo*, the boat that he had brought up, lashed to the deck of the *Hatfield*, to replace the *Half Moon*.[16] At the end of the week he, Eleanor, and Anna left for Washington, after which they would go to Dayton to attend the ceremony at which Governor Cox would be officially notified of his nomination. In Washington Eleanor arranged to give up their house—another indication of how little they expected to win—and Franklin said his good-by to the Navy by means of a formal letter of resignation to the president and an affectionate longhand note to Daniels. "You have taught me so wisely and kept my feet on the ground when I was about to skyrocket—and in all there has never been a real dispute or antagonism or distrust." In his diary, Daniels wrote, "He left in afternoon, but before leaving wrote me a letter most friendly and almost loving which makes me glad I had never acted upon my impulse when he seemed to take sides with my critics."[17]

While Eleanor and Anna went to Dayton to Franklin, Sara returned to Hyde Park with James and Elliott to prepare for Franklin's notification. Young Henry Morgenthau, Jr., managed the ceremonies at Springwood. Sara later grumbled to her children about what the crowds of politicians had done to her immaculate lawns,[18] but in her diary she wrote, "Very fine and impressive. About 500 came in the house. About 8,000 in all outside." Party notables, including Daniels, McAdoo, and Governor Smith were on Sara's porch, which one reporter called a "wonderful front porch—a long, broad stone veranda" that, he implied, put into the shadow the front porch from which Harding had said arrogantly he would conduct his campaign. The reporters wrote approvingly of the vine-covered stucco house and the old, wide-spreading trees, and described James and Elliott and their cousin Cyril Martineau as youngsters whose yellow hair stood on end like bristles, while Anna's tow hair fell down her back nearly to her waist. Eleanor Roosevelt wore a plain blue and white dress without ornaments, the press reported, and listened to her husband intently, perched on the balustrade that ran around the veranda with her feet resting on the edge of a camp stool.

When Franklin went West for his first campaign trip, Sara, Eleanor, and the three children returned to Campobello. "Keep some kind of diary *please*," he wrote her from St. Paul, "as I know I will miss some of the things that happen!"[19] That was his last letter. From then on if the family heard from him at all it was by telegram. "Splendid receptions Minnesota, South and North Dakota," he telegraphed on August 16. "So sorry miss Franklin's birthday give him my special love. All well. Telegraph Wednesday noon care Station Master Northern Pacific Railroad, Spokane, Washington."

Franklin's campaign office was still after her for photographs. "Bachrach in Washington has a good one with F. Jr. when a baby," she replied to Charles McCarthy on August 25, but those taken of her alone were rather poor. "I take such bad photographs." She went on to talk about the campaign:

> I am glad you feel Franklin's chances are good for I would be sorry to have him beaten after so much work & I really think & hope "Cox & Roosevelt" can do better for the country the next four, very hard years than "Harding & Coolidge." Personally, I had wanted Franklin out of government service for a few years at least, so in spite of the honor I really feel rather unselfish when I wish for his success!
>
> Would it be possible for you to send me some copies of Franklin's acceptance & some campaign buttons both Cox & Roosevelt? Several people are asking & writing for them & I would be most grateful if you can let me have them.

"Dearest, dear Honey," she wrote him on August 27, "I am positively hungry for news of you and it seems a long time since your last telegram and they are meagre enough." Her letter was full of family and political news. "So far the Republican papers having nothing very bad against you have simply been trying to treat you like an amiable, young boy, belittlement is the worst they can do." The Republican side of the family was lining up for Harding, a later letter reported. "Did you see that Alice is to go on the stump for Harding and that Auntie Corinne is to speak for him in Portland, Maine, on September 8th, starting his campaign there. Ted also speaks in Maine." Mrs. Selmes, Isabella's mother, had been at Henderson House when Franklin was nominated and reported that everyone there was "so nice" about

Franklin. But Franklin's success in the West worried the Republican high command. "Do you know," said the engineer on the Roosevelt train, "that lad's got a 'million vote smile'—and mine's going to be one of them." Theodore Roosevelt, Jr., was dispatched by the Republicans to trail Franklin. "He is a maverick," young Theodore said in Sheridan, Wyoming. "He does not have the brand of our family." This personal attack galled Franklin, and it was the beginning of bad feeling between the Oyster Bay and Hyde Park clans. Franklin thrust back shrewdly, although not personally, by recalling that "in 1912 Senator Harding called Theodore Roosevelt, first a Benedict Arnold and then an Aaron Burr. This is one thing, at least some members of the Roosevelt family will not forget."

Eleanor was restless at Campobello. When Franklin agreed to go to Brooklyn on Labor Day, she wrote to Sara a little irascibly, "Of course it is hard to refuse but I do think he should have cut Monday out and come here directly, however, there is no use in saying anything."[20] A reminder to Franklin to write to Aunt Dora revealed her own feelings: "I hate to add these personal things when you are under such a strain and wish I could do them but I can't and they are the kind of things which do mean so much to other people who don't happen to have all the interesting things you have to fill their minds."[21] He was in the privileged position; he had interesting things to do, and she was no longer content to sit on an island off the northeast coast of Maine while he had all the fun.

On September 20 Louis Howe wrote her that the staff was struggling with the Roosevelt pictures and packing as well as they could, and then he added, "I do not think Franklin has told you, but I am resigning for a month in order to avoid the civil service rules and going off with Franklin on the next western trip." And Franklin had not told Louis that he had also asked Eleanor to join the campaign train.

How this came about is not clear. She had written her husband at the beginning of September, "I would love to go down but as I know you must go on campaigning I would just be in the way." If she thought of herself as a burden, her friends saw her as a political asset. When Grace C. Root sent congratulations on Franklin's nomination, she added, "and not at all the least to you whose comprehension of things political might well be envied by the suffrage sisters!" Alice Wadsworth, relieved that "so far as *our* men are concerned the victory of one does not necessitate the defeat of the other," took it for granted that "both of us will probably be busy with *politics*—thanks to this dratted Suffrage!"

The 1920 election was the first national election in which women voted. "The woman's hour was striking," Mrs. Catt proclaimed at the victory convention of the National American Woman Suffrage Association. A candidate's wife could have an important effect upon his fortunes, and Franklin wanted Eleanor at his side. Before joining him, however, she took James to Groton, the first of four trips to deliver a son to the rector's Spartan disciplines. James was only twelve and it was difficult to leave him at boarding school, but it was family tradition, so she unpacked his trunk, arranged his cubicle, and finally said good-by to the Peabodys and to James. She would go through the same melancholy experience with each of the boys, increasingly dubious that separating youngsters from parents at so early an age was good for either; but it was Franklin's wish and she yielded, just as she did a few days later when James came down with a digestive upset and Franklin, on the basis of a reassuring message from the rector, urged her to stay with the train and let Sara go to Groton instead. It was the first time she had not been with an ill child and it was hard not to hasten back to her son's bedside, but as she wrote Sara, "I am going gaily on."

"This is the most killing thing for the candidate I ever knew," was her first report to Sara from the *Westboro*, as their campaign car was called.[22] There were good crowds, she wrote from Charleston, and she was particularly pleased to find that "Franklin has certainly made strides in public speaking and gets enough praise everywhere to turn anyone's head."[23] Days aboard a campaign train were more hectic than any she had ever experienced. "F. made 2 speeches & drove 26 miles over awful roads before we ever got any breakfast!" she reported from Kentucky. "There have been two town speeches since then and at least one platform speech every 15 minutes all day! We had coffee & sandwiches for lunch & a very hurried supper & now he still has to get off at Bowling Green at 10:10 for a speech in a hall! I never will be able to do without at least four large cups of black coffee again *every day!*"[24] She was relieved to learn from Sara that James' ailment had been diagnosed as colitis. "I don't know when I'll be back though I really don't see that I'm of the least use on this trip."

This was not Franklin's view, according to a few lines he added to the same letter. "I am still alive, tho' it has been about the most strenuous week of the campaign. It has been a great comfort to have Eleanor. Some day when this is all over I will regain my normal mode of life—& then I won't be horrid to you as I was last Sunday—& I will really try to do the many little things that do count! It is too bad about James."

Eleanor was able to leave the train in Terre Haute, Indiana, have a bath at the hotel, and write Sara.

We had a splendid meeting at Bowling Green last night, in the open at 10:30 p.m. must have been over a 1,000 people there. Franklin's voice is all right again & I should say he came through yesterday finely & it certainly was a big day, he must have talked to and tried to shake hands with at least 30,000 people, the newspapermen think. We arrived in this town about 12, a big crowd waiting came to shake hands & when Governor Cox's train came in we all went to speak to him & he had to say a few words & shake all the hands he could. He looks well but his voice is much worse than F's. F. went with him to Indianapolis, also Mr. Howe, Mr. McIntyre (whom I like very much) & Mr. Prenosil (the A.P. man). They return at 8:48 & we get on the train & go on to St. Louis.

Of course Franklin's looks bring all sorts of admiring comments & then we get asked if he's "Teddy" frequently. I almost hope he does not get elected for so many people are coming to see us in Washington & I shan't remember their names or faces.[25]

In St. Louis the station crowds appeared to her to be "rather apathetic," but she thought that was due to the "German descent" of so many of the city's inhabitants. In any case, Franklin had an "appreciative audience" in the armory, and afterward he had his hair cut "at 11 p.m. the only chance he had & then it was done on the car surrounded by an admiring audience of newspapermen!" She wanted Sara to send her "1 clean nightgown & shirt & 3 chemises & 3 drawers & any black stockings & handkerchiefs I may have. F. says he has enough." In a postscript about Franklin's impact on the crowds, she said his "head should be turned if it is ever going to be for there is much praise and enthusiasm for him personally almost everywhere."[26]

They went westward as far as Colorado and then returned East by another route. In Cincinnati mail and laundry caught up with them. Eleanor was still amazed at the pace and unhappy over her own uselessness. "I tell Franklin he will never settle down & give up the inevitable large cup of black coffee & cream with every meal again but I really think he will be so glad to rest he won't want to move for days. We enter N.Y. State the a.m. of the 21st & I shall go on to N.Y. as my only use has been so far that people are curious to see his wife but that won't be so in the East. . . ."[27] That Sunday in Cincinnati she was taken to church, "as they thought it wise to announce in the paper where *we* would go but only *I* went." Franklin's voice was again showing strain, she reported, and little wonder: "It is becoming almost impossible to stop F. now when he begins to speak, 10 minutes is always 20, 30 is always 45 & the evening speeches are now about 2 hours! The men all get out & wave at him in front & when nothing succeeds I yank his coat tails! Everyone is getting tired but on the whole the car is still pretty good natured! They tell us Gov. Cox's is all on edge."[28]

When the train reached Buffalo, Franklin went to speak in Jamestown, while Eleanor, with Louis Howe, decided to visit Niagara Falls, which she had never seen. This was a sign of their budding friendship. It had taken Eleanor a long time to appreciate Louis. At times she had resented his influence with her husband and had been swift to find fault with him. When Franklin went to Europe in 1918, she had complained that "the only item *every* paper gives is that Mr. Howe is running your office during your absence so he saw that was widespread news and how the naval officers must hate it!" But Howe was a sensitive, perceptive man who refused to be deterred by her coolness; he knew the blow she had been dealt by the Lucy Mercer business. She was the only woman on the *Westboro*, and he saw that many things bewildered or irritated her. At the end of the day Franklin would be tense and high-strung, and the men would gather at the end of the car to review the day's events, play a little poker, and hoist a few bourbons. Roosevelt "did not take life seriously enough," Steve Early, who was Roosevelt's advance man, later recalled. "He was just a playboy preferring poker to speech conferences."[29] Eleanor disliked the playboy in her husband; she felt he should save his strength and go to bed, and that a candidate for vice president should set an example.

She expressed her discontent obliquely; for example, she worried because she thought the car's porter was not able to get enough sleep because his berth was close to where the men played cards. She was timid with the newspapermen and wanted to be of more use than simply sitting with a rapt look listening to her husband make the same speech over and over again.

Louis sensed all this: her loneliness, her great sadness, her lack of self-confidence, her need of appreciation. He was aware also of her abilities—her good judgment, remarkable vitality, and organizational gifts. He saw the way people responded to her warmth and courtesy.

He began to tell her, and she desperately needed to hear such words, that she had a real contribution to make to her husband's campaign. He brought drafts of speeches to discuss with her. He explained the ways of newspapermen and encouraged her to meet them as friends. By the end of the trip she was on good enough terms with the press to be amused rather than upset when, from the rear of a hall, some of the reporters made funny faces at her to try to break the look of total absorption she adopted for her husband's speeches. They teased her when the ladies crowded around the candidate, and she took it good-naturedly. She was grateful to Louis for that. Together they discussed the issues of the campaign and the politics of the towns through which they traveled. Eleanor discovered that Louis had a wide range of knowledge, a nice sense of humor, a feeling for poetry and the countryside. Louis knew when to be silent and when to speak up. By the end of the trip they had become fast friends. His daughter Mary was at Vassar. "Will you ask Mary Howe to come up on Sunday?" Eleanor wrote ahead to Sara.

On the Monday before the election Franklin wound up his campaign with the traditional appearance in Poughkeepsie. The central issue, he said at the end of the campaign as he had at the beginning, is "whether the U.S. is to finish the war or to quit cold, whether we are to join the other forty odd nations in the great working League of Nations that will serve to end war for all time or whether we will turn our back on them. . . ." But he was a realist. Harding was a 10 to 1 favorite in the Wall Street betting. At 10:45 on Election Day morning, he and Eleanor and Sara arrived at the polling place in Hyde Park. It was raining but the village people were there and gave him a cheer. He was vote number 207 and Eleanor's was number 208, her first vote. Sara also voted, as did Rosy's wife Betty. But the hope that the millions of newly enfranchised women voters would cast a peace vote by voting for Cox, as Mrs. Catt had appealed to them to do, was quickly dashed. The special wire that brought the results into Springwood, where Franklin held open house for friends and neighbors, showed early in the evening that a Republican avalanche was in the making. "We all feel very badly over the result of the elections," Eleanor wrote Franklin a few days later.

Franklin took it philosophically, as did the inner group around him. They all were sure another chance would come. He hoped, wrote Renah Camalier, his secretary on the *Westboro*, "that when the clan meets again four years hence, it will have sense enough to see that there is but one man to put at the head of the ticket, that man, of course, being none other than my 'old boss.'" The Roosevelt organization dispersed except for Miss Marguerite LeHand. Young, pretty, highly competent, with a dry sense of humor, she had worked for Charles McCarthy in the Roosevelt offices at Democratic headquarters, and Franklin asked her to work for him permanently. She told him she would let him know "as soon as I have talked with my people. You were very nice to ask me." A month later she wrote him, "If you would still like to have me, I will be in New York on January third."

Louis was uncertain what he should do when a Republican secretary of the Navy took over—whether to go on Franklin's payroll or accept an outside business connection. Eleanor now became his staunch advocate, as he was hers. All the Howes spent Thanksgiving at Hyde Park with the Roosevelts, and afterward, Franklin left with Louis for Washington to join Hall for a hunting trip in Louisiana. "I have enjoyed Mrs. Howe," Eleanor wrote him. "I don't think she would bore you and she's a plucky little thing. They left at 9.03 cat and all, to take the midnight [train] and Mary went back to Vassar." The next day she added to the same letter, "I had a line from Louis also this morning telling me of your trip and safe departure from Washington."[30]

On Christmas Franklin sent the men who had been with him on the *Westboro* cuff links engraved with his initials and theirs, the beginning of the famous Cuff Links Club. The men in turn remembered Mrs. Roosevelt. "I wish you would send me a dollar and your visiting card," Louis Howe wrote Tom Lynch. "The boys have decided to send Mrs. Roosevelt a little pin for Christmas as a souvenir of the campaign and this is your assessment." "The very pretty pin you sent Mrs. Roosevelt," Lynch wrote Howe after the holidays, "was shown to me last week and will say you have very good taste, the gift was appreciated very much."

Eleanor had frequently suffered from her husband's uncommunicativeness, and she now had an ally in Louis, who gave her the feeling she craved of a closer identification with her husband's work. And Louis, who was never sure he knew all that was going on with the boss and even less sure of his influence, now had reinforcement in "holding Franklin down."

Long ago he had set his hand to making a king; now he began to make a queen.[31]

25. BAPTISM IN POLITICS

BY THE TIME THE FAMILY MOVED BACK TO NEW YORK ELEANOR
had a plan: she intended to help Franklin in whatever way he asked
and permitted, but she would also have work of her own to do.

"All men who make successes of their work," she counseled a lonely
woman years later,

> go through exactly the same kind of thing which you describe
> and their wives, in one way or another have to adjust themselves.
> If it is possible to enter into his work in some way, that is the ideal
> solution. If not, they must develop something of their own and if
> possible make it such a success, that they will have something to
> interest their husbands.[1]

Franklin charted a strenuous schedule for himself. He joined a law
firm which became Emmett, Marvin and Roosevelt. He became vice
president at $25,000 a year in charge of the New York offices of Van
Lear Black's Fidelity and Deposit Company of Maryland, the third
largest surety bonding house in the country. He was a Harvard over-
seer. He agreed to head the Navy Club and the Greater New York Boy
Scout Council. He also had ideas for some books he wanted to write.
It was too much of a program, Eleanor protested. "Of course I know
your remarkable faculty for getting through work when you get right
down to it," but if he was to carry through on his commitments, he
would have to cut out most formal parties, she said hopefully.[2]

Her own program was more modest. She enrolled in a business
school to learn typing and shorthand. She found a housewife to teach
her to cook. She began active work in the League of Women Voters.
Unable to move back into 49 East Sixty-fifth Street because the Lamont lease still had six months to run, she and her family camped in
Sara's house, but Eleanor quickly made it clear she did not intend to
return to the old pattern of always being available for a meal, a drive,

or pouring tea for Sara's friends and charities—in short, of subordinating her own interests to Sara's. She no longer felt the old obligation to write Sara about everything, nor did she share confidences with her or come to her with problems. She brushed aside Sara's view that a woman in her social position should confine her activity to serving on philanthropic boards. She did not want to be a name on a letterhead, an ornamental woman, without a job of her own to do. She wanted to be fully involved—with work, with people.[3]

A comment on Franklin K. Lane's death illuminated her frame of mind as well as the respect in which her wartime friends held her. Lane had checked into the Mayo Hospital in Rochester, Minnesota, and one of his last letters before undergoing the operation from which he did not recover was to Eleanor.

> Just because I like you very much, and being a very old man dare to say so, I am sending this line—which has no excuse in its news, philosophy or advice;—has no excuse in fact except what might be called affection, but of course this being way past the Victorian era no one admits to affections. I will not belittle my own feeling by saying that I have a wife who thinks you the best Eastern product— and probably she'd move to strike out the word Eastern. At any rate I think I should tell you that I am to be operated on tomorrow by Dr. Will Mayo and am glad of it. We shall see what we shall see. ... I'd love to see you and the gay cavalier—but let us hope it won't be long till we meet! Au revoir.

"It is a loss to the country," Eleanor wrote in her diary when she learned of Lane's death, "and I do not feel that we who are privileged to be his friends can gauge our loss but we must try in his memory to make the world a little better place to live in for the mankind which he loved so well."[4]

Among the organizations she turned to in the hope of being able to help improve the world was the League of Women Voters, the successor to the National Woman Suffrage Association. Its leaders had emerged from the long suffrage struggle as militant advocates of better working conditions for women, children's rights, reform of the political process, and peace. Mrs. Frank Vanderlip, the chairman of the New York State league, invited Eleanor to join the board and keep track of the league's legislative program. Eleanor hesitated, doubtful that she was equipped to handle such an assignment. She could have the help of a lawyer, Elizabeth F. Read, Mrs. Vanderlip said, to go through the Albany calendar and *Congressional Record* with her and indicate the bills of interest to the league.

Eleanor decided to accept, and one morning each week she went to Elizabeth Read's law office to review the documents and to select the bills she wanted to brief herself on more fully. She became acquainted with Esther Everett Lape, who had been active with Elizabeth Read in the suffrage movement, and shared a small apartment with her on East Eleventh Street. Esther, an energetic member of the league's state board who had taught at Swarthmore and Barnard and was an effective publicist, combined a driving political activism with tact and sensitivity; Elizabeth—calmer, more scholarly, more practical—stayed in the background. Both were highly qualified professional women. They were co-editors of the *City-State-Nation*, a weekly legislative review issued by the league, and although they were volunteers, they did an expert job. Franklin had stolen his wife's copy of the review, he wrote Esther Lape, and "I wish that the subscription list...might contain as many names of men as of women."[5]

Esther and Elizabeth's careful, documented workmanship shaped Eleanor's standards in her approach to public issues and helped her to do serious, sustained work. They were liberal in outlook but it was a pragmatic liberalism with which Eleanor sympathized. At meetings of the state board Esther was impressed with the way Eleanor "wanted always to know exactly what she could do before the next monthly meeting."[6] Her serenity had a stabilizing effect upon the board; she had a way of calmly rising above intramural disputes over personalities and jurisdictions to keep the board's attention focused on the league's larger purposes. "The rest of us," recalled Esther, "were inclined to do a good deal of theorizing. She would look puzzled and ask why we didn't do whatever we had in mind and get it out of the way. As you may imagine, she was given many jobs to do." Within a year the most tangled problems of reorganization were turned over to her to unsnarl.[7] Esther and Elizabeth were impressed with their new friend's attitude and performance, with her insistence upon doing her own work, with the strength and clarity that lay beneath the shyness. The esteem was mutual. Eleanor came to depend greatly upon their counsel and soon she was often spending evenings with them. They were cultivated, sensitive women with a strong sense of privacy, enormously useful citizens who had found in domestic arrangements that did not include men a happy adjustment. Their tender relationship was not unique in the suffrage movement, especially among women of great professional competence. They and several of their counterparts would in the next few years play a big part in what Eleanor herself called "the intensive education of Eleanor Roosevelt."

At the end of January, 1921, Eleanor attended the state convention of the League of Women Voters in Albany as a delegate from Dutchess County. It was a lively introduction to the league's activities. The Republican machine still smarted from the league's campaign against Senator Wadsworth, who had opposed the suffrage amendment even after New York voters had passed it. Regulars in both parties thought it was time that the women, heady with success, were tamed. The newly installed Republican governor, Nathan L. Miller, enraged the convention with a denunciation of the league as a menace to American institutions because of its social-welfare program and lobbying activities.

"I want to tell you why Governor Miller has suspicion of you," cried Mrs. Carrie Chapman Catt, the white-haired leader of the suffrage struggle and its most eloquent spokesman. "The League of Women Voters constitutes the remains of that army which for 50 years in the State of New York fought the battle for the enfranchisement of the sex." The women now intended to bring to the new struggle for welfare legislation the hard-hitting tactics they had learned in the suffrage battles.

The male politicians were very critical, but Miller's frontal attack soon proved to have been a blunder. Although Republican women outnumbered the Democrats by 5 to 1 at the convention, the league, led by Mrs. Vanderlip, a Republican, protested the governor's speech and reaffirmed the right of women "to work as a group outside the political party for political measures." The governor beat a quick retreat: he had been misunderstood, he said. The politicians realized that more subtle methods would have to be used to keep women in their place.[8]

Eleanor had long followed politics as an observer, but this was her apprenticeship in political activity on her own. Her role at the convention was limited to explaining to the delegates the work of her legislative committee: all bills introduced into the legislature would be reviewed, and the good and bad features of the key measures circulated to the league's membership. The next few months showed that there was more to the committee's activities than that.

The league decided to sponsor a bill requiring the political parties to give equal representation to men and women at all levels, and it was Eleanor's job to get the bill drafted and to obtain bipartisan sponsorship for it.[9] When the politicians in the legislature moved to weaken the direct primary law by excluding the governorship and other state-wide offices from its stipulations, the board asked Eleanor and Esther to formulate the league's opposition to the measure.[10] Eleanor led a state-board discussion of proposals to reorganize the state government which ended with the board's reaffirmation of its support of a longer term for governor, an executive budget, a shorter ballot, and departmental consolidation, reforms that in time would all be adopted. She had interested FDR in the work, enough so that the league minutes of March 1 read "on motion duly made and seconded, it was voted that a vote of thanks be sent Mr. Roosevelt for his help in the Legislative work." He was not making Governor Miller's mistake.

Franklin enjoyed coaching his wife in political tactics. The re-election of Narcissa Vanderlip as state chairman of the league was contested on the grounds that there had been electioneering in the vicinity of the polls. A committee was set up to investigate. Esther and Eleanor were both supporters of Mrs. Vanderlip and quite enraged over the investigation. At dinner at Sixty-fifth Street they told Franklin about the situation. "Eleanor, you be there early and sit up front," he advised. "Just as soon as the report is read, you get up and move that it be tabled. That motion is not debatable."

"It worked," recalled Eleanor gleefully. "You should have seen their jaws drop." Eleanor made a striking figure, thin and very tall. She had on a rose-colored suit, and a long fur, that went around her neck and down. It gave her a special pleasure to do what Franklin had told her to do.

In April, 1921, Eleanor was in Cleveland as a Dutchess County delegate to the league's second national convention. "I've had a very interesting day and heard some really good women speakers," she wrote her husband.

Mrs. Catt is clear, cold reason, Mrs. Larue Brown is amusing, apt, graceful, a Mrs. Cunningham from Texas is emotional and idealistic, but she made nearly everyone cry! I listened to Child Welfare all the morning and Direct Primaries all the afternoon, lunched with Margaret Norrie, drove out at five with Mrs. Wyllis Mitchell and called on Mrs. (Newton) Baker, dined and heard some speeches on Child Welfare and attended a N.Y. delegates' meeting and am about to go to bed, quite weary! Meetings begin tomorrow at ten.[11]

Twenty years later Eleanor still recalled the speech of Minnie Fisher Cunningham, veteran of a hundred reform battles in Texas, who made her feel "that you had no right to be a slacker as a citizen, you had no right not to take an active part in what was happening to your country as a whole."[12] She was moved particularly by Mrs. Cunningham's plea "that she hoped the day would not come when her children would look at her and say: 'You knew certain conditions existed and you did nothing about those conditions.'"

Mrs. Catt may have been "clear, cold reason" on the subject of direct primaries and other measures to weaken boss control of political parties, but she was all flame and passion when she ripped into President Harding, who in his first address to Congress a day earlier had declared "this Republic will have no part" in the League of Nations. Mrs. Catt threw aside a prepared speech.

> You have heard politics all day. I can't help saying something I feel I must. The people in this room tonight could put an end to war. Everybody wants it and every one does nothing. . . . I am for a League of Nations, a Republican league or any kind the Republicans are in.

She summoned the women, most of whom were by now on their feet, to "consecrate" themselves

> to put war out of the world. . . . Men were born by instinct to slay. It seems to me God is giving a call to the women of the world to come forward, to stay the hand of men, to say: "No, you shall no longer kill your fellow men."[13]

There was dead silence, followed by wave after wave of applause. Not until Eleanor Roosevelt achieved her full powers would another woman have a comparable authority over female audiences; but Eleanor had many years of training, discipline, and speechmaking ahead before she achieved such mastery. Back from Cleveland, a diary entry for April 23 noted that "worked in a.m. at typewriting review of legislative work for winter." The next day, Sunday, she went back to her typewriter after church, finished her notes on legislation, "and wrote out speech for Tuesday" for the Dutchess County chapter of the League of Women Voters. Margaret Norrie, her Staatsburgh neighbor, made the main report on the Cleveland convention. "I added a few words," Eleanor noted. The next day she went to New York to have her hair done and again say "a few words on legislation" to a league luncheon at the Colony Club. Speaking in public was a torment; her cultivated voice—which in conversation was relaxed and warm—rose several octaves and became high-pitched, and frequent distracting giggles reflected her self-consciousness. She was, however, determined to do better.

Regardless of the difficulties she had making speeches she was doing her job, and at the May meeting of the Dutchess County league was nominated for chairman but withdrew in favor of Margaret Norrie.[14] Also at that meeting she became involved in public controversy for the first time—in defense of civil liberties. In an article in the *Delineator* Vice President Coolidge had alleged that women's colleges were filled with radicals, Vassar being one of his targets, and in particular Professor Winifred Smith, who worried the vice president because she had contrasted the "moderation and intelligence" of the Soviet representative in Washington with the "narrowness" of the congressmen who were demanding his deportation. Coolidge thought Professor Smith's reactions were dangerous. Eleanor introduced the club's resolution on the subject. The club knew Miss Smith as "a public-spirited and devoted citizen," her resolution read, and in times of "public excitement" the national interest was best served by "calm and critical judgment." The resolution ended with a protest against "all thoughtless aspersion on such public-spirited citizens."

The *Poughkeepsie Eagle News* headlined the censure of the vice president: "Mrs. F. D. Roosevelt Offers Resolution Taking to Task Husband's Victorious Rival." The local press was "indignant" over the resolution, Eleanor noted in her diary, and added, "Foolish of me ever to do anything of the kind."[15] The criticism bothered her less than the fact that she had involved her husband. It was a problem she would face often in later years—did she have a right to engage in controversy if her husband might be adversely affected?

The circles in which Eleanor moved were greatly concerned with equal rights for women, and so was Eleanor. But the harsh stridency of some feminists irritated her; she was not what Franklin and Louis sarcastically called a "she-male." She attended a Westchester County

Democratic dinner where Franklin spoke, as did Harriet May Mills, who had been president of the New York Women's Suffrage party and was now a leading Democrat. Eleanor admired Miss Mills but thought she overdid the women question.[16] Eleanor enjoyed masculine society and working with the men. From Cleveland she had written Franklin, "Much, much love dear and I prefer doing my politics with you."[17]

Even though she was developing her own interests, her first choice still was to enter into her husband's work. Now the summer began that was to leave him crippled, with his survival as a public man dependent on her resolution, her encouragement, her readiness to serve as his proxy in politics. He had always needed her, more than she was ever able to recognize or than he usually could bring himself to say. After the summer, there no longer was need for words.

26. THE TEMPERING—POLIO

FRANKLIN WAS IMPATIENT TO GET BACK TO CAMPOBELLO IN 1921. For the first time since he began to campaign for public office, he planned to spend most of the summer on his beloved island. He needed its peace and he looked forward to being with his family. Public office had a disciplining effect on him, and when he was out of office he was restless, reckless, irrepressible. "Found Franklin in bed after a wild 1904 dinner and party," Eleanor noted May 24. Harriet, the maid, "frightened" her with the announcement that Mr. Roosevelt was in bed, but then when she learned why, she was "very indignant with him!"[1] Just before they went to Campobello, young Sheffield Cowles was married to Margaret "Bobbie" Krech, and Franklin's "uproarious" behavior at the wedding festivities surprised the Oyster Bay contingent, who had always thought of him as a little lacking in earthiness. "It was the Roosevelt spirits," they said, a claim that irritated Sara, who was sure her son was a Delano.

Orders went to Captain Calder at Campobello to get the *Vireo* and the motor launch in readiness, also the tennis court. Louis Howe, who had left the Navy Department, was planning to come to Campobello with his wife and his son, Hartley, which would give Franklin and Louis plenty of time to blueprint Franklin's bid for the governorship in 1922.

Sara was not in her house. Although sixty-seven, she returned to her pre-war practice of a yearly voyage to Europe to see her sister Dora and other Delano relatives. In London the spirit of adventure overcame caution, and she and Muriel Martineau took a twin-engine aeroplane from London to Paris.

> It was five hours from London to Paris. I had been told four hours, but I would not have missed it and if I do it again I shall take an open plane as one sees more and it is more like flying. Poor Muriel

soon began to feel ill and had to lie on the floor all the way and had a horrid time.

"Don't do it again," her son hastily cabled her, and she agreed. "In thinking it over I believe you really mean it, so I shall try not to fly back." After settling his family at Campobello, Franklin had to rush to Washington to deal with a Republican effort to "smear" his and Daniels' record. The specific charge was that they had sanctioned the use of entrapment procedures at Newport Training Station in a drive against homosexuality there. Louis brought Eleanor a copy of the report signed by two Republican senators. She was anxious to hear what Franklin intended to do. "Of course," he wrote back, "as I expected I found all the cards stacked, only even worse than I thought."[2] The Republican majority reneged on a promise to give him an opportunity to be heard. A Roosevelt press release denounced the committee's methods, denied any knowledge of the entrapment procedures and certainly of any supervision of them, and protested Republican use of the Navy as a political football.

"It must be dreadfully disagreeable for you and I know it worries you though you wouldn't own it," she wrote back, "but it has always seemed to me that the chance of just such attacks as this was a risk one had to take with our form of government and if one felt clear oneself, the rest did not really matter."[3] When she saw the newspapers the next day she was indignant, "but one should not be ruffled by such things. Bless you dear and love always." She added a postscript: "I liked your answer. You will be starting a week from today."

The presence of the Howes and other guests, including the Bibescos, enlivened the summer for her while Franklin was away. It was a sign of her growing fondness for Louis that she relaxed her puritan scruples about liquor. "Mlle.," the governess, had fallen into the water while cleaning the *Vireo*, "and I've just had to give her a little gin in hot lemonade," Eleanor informed her husband, "as she has never warmed up since!"[4] This was quite a concession from Eleanor, who was a strict teetotaler and a supporter of the newly ratified Prohibition amendment. Sara's attitude was more relaxed. She wrote from Paris,

I rather enjoy being where one had red and white wine on the table, very little said on the subject and no drinking of spirits, and I feel, as I always have, that we should have made our fight against the *spirits* and the saloon, and encouraged the French habit of wine and water, but Americans really like their whiskey best now, just as the English do.[5]

For the visit of Elizabeth Bibesco, the daughter of Herbert Asquith, leader of the British Liberal party for over a quarter of a century, Eleanor even permitted a cocktail to be made. "I had to break the lock of your drawer to get at the whiskey!" she informed Franklin, who no doubt was slightly startled and amused. It turned out to be a "very bad cocktail" made by Jefferson Newbold, but Elizabeth "was sweet and I like her better than ever."[6]

Louis was an ideal guest. A do-it-yourself carpenter, he had acquired Roosevelt's passion for model boats and had begun working with Captain Calder to build a workbench for Franklin in the boathouse. He was also an irrepressible writer of doggerel and a water colorist, and his place cards were a continuous delight. He had been a mainstay in the Drama League Players in Washington both as director and actor and was always ready at Campobello to entertain the children and play with them. He was a "godsend" when it came to keeping track of the island workmen who came to repair the pump. "Mr. Howe has endless patience in batting the ball to Elliott and Hartley," Eleanor wrote Sara, "and he thinks Elliott will be good though I can see no signs as yet."[7] But sometimes Eleanor's energy and enterprise were too much even for the willing Louis. She read aloud to them in the evenings, "but Grace and sometimes Louis snore before I get far and Russell [James' tutor] goes to bed before I begin and Mlle. won't go to bed but props her eyelids up with her fingers!"[8]

On July 30 Eleanor wrote Sara that she had expected Franklin that day but instead he was coming on Van Lear Black's yacht, the *Sabalo*. She was glad, she said, because the heat was awful and a trip by train would further tax his vitality. "I thought he looked tired when he left," Miss LeHand advised her. Thus began the harsh events that Eleanor later called "trial by fire," that left her husband unable to walk.

The cruise of the *Sabalo* proved strenuous. The weather in the Bay of Fundy was foul and the visibility low; Franklin was obliged to take the wheel for hours. Dropping anchor in Welchpool Harbor, he plunged into entertaining his guests. They went fishing for cod and he baited the hooks; at one point he slipped overboard and "never felt anything so cold as that water." His pace was too much for his New

York visitors, who discovered that imperative business required their presence in New York.[9]

The tempo of the household slackened only slightly. Roosevelt took his babies sailing on the *Vireo*; he and Louis worked on model boats; he played tennis with the older children; after supper they all turned out for baseball. Some friends sailed in on a yawl "and they spent a late evening with us ending up with a midnight supper!"[10] Though Franklin complained of feeling dull and tired, the vigorous life continued. On August 10, when the family was out on the *Vireo*, they spotted a forest fire and went ashore to flail at the flames with pine boughs. After the fire was under control, they dog-trotted, eyes smarting and smoke besmudged, for a dip in the relatively warm waters of Lake Glen Severn, then jogged back. Perhaps because he could not shake his loginess, Franklin took a quick dip in the Bay's icy waters but did not get "the glow I expected." When they returned to the house he sat around in his wet bathing suit looking through the mail, too tired to dress, and at supper complained of chills and aches and soon went to bed.

The next morning he felt worse. As he got out of bed his left leg dragged; soon it refused to move at all, and by afternoon his right leg was also powerless. His temperature was 102. Though he managed a smile and a joke for Anna when she brought him his tray, Eleanor was worried and sent for the family physician, old Dr. Bennett in Lubec, who thought it was a cold. But by Friday, August 12, paralysis had set in from the chest down. Eleanor, apprehensive, had sent the rest of the household on a previously planned three-day camping trip. A letter to Franklin's half brother, James Roosevelt Roosevelt, described the inception of the crisis. Harried and apprehensive as she was, the letter was composed, clear, and poignant.

> Campobello
> August 14, 1921
> Sunday
>
> Dear Rosy,
>
> We have had a very anxious few days as on Wed. evening Franklin was taken ill. It seemed a chill but Thursday he had so much pain in his back and legs that I sent for the doctor, by Friday evening he lost his ability to walk or move his legs but though they felt numb he can still feel in them. Yesterday a.m. Dr. Bennett and I decided we wanted the best opinion we could get quickly so Louis Howe

(who, thank heavens, is here, for he has been the greatest help) went with Dr. Bennett to Lubec and they canvassed the nearby resorts and decided that the best available diagnostician was the famous old Dr. W. W. Keen of Philadelphia and he agreed to motor up and spend the night. He arrived about 7:30 and made a most careful, thorough examination and the same this morning and he thinks a clot of blood from a sudden congestion has settled in the lower spinal cord temporarily removing the power to move though not to feel. I have wired to New York for a masseuse as he said that was vital and the nursing I could do, and in the meantime Louis and I are rubbing him as well as we can. The doctor feels sure he will get well but it may take some months. I have only told Franklin he said he could surely go down the 15th of Sept. He did say to leave then but not before on account of heat and to go to New York but it may have to be done on a wheel chair. The doctor thinks absorption has already begun as he can move his toes on one foot a little more which is encouraging. He has told the Dr. here just what medicines to give and what treatment to follow and we should know in the next ten days or two weeks how things are going.

Do you think you can meet Mama when she lands? She has asked us to cable just before she sails and I have decided to say nothing. No letter can reach her now and it would simply mean worry all the way home and she will have enough once here but at least then she can do things. I will write her a letter to quarantine saying he is ill but leave explaining to you or if you can't meet her to Uncle Fred or whoever does meet her. I hope you will think I am doing right and have done all I could. Of course write me if you think of anything else. I do not want particulars to get into the papers so I am writing the family that he is ill from the effects of a chill and I hope will soon be better, but I shall write Uncle Fred what I have told you and Langdon Marvin as Franklin cannot be at the office to relieve him.

Affly always,
Eleanor

For two weeks, until a trained nurse could come up from New York, Eleanor slept on a couch in Franklin's room and took care of her husband day and night. All the tenderness, solicitude, and devotion that so often were dammed up by his jaunty flirtatiousness now poured forth as she bathed him, rubbed him, attended to his every need. Looking at his collapsed legs brought to mind Michelangelo's *Pietà*, that universal symbol of woman, the mother, grieving over the broken body of man, the son, the piece of sculpture that in her girl-hood, reminding her of the wasted body of her father, had moved her to tears. She took her cue from Franklin's courage. Her vitality was equal to his darkest moments. Sometimes with Louis, often unaided, she raised and moved her husband's large, heavy frame. Dr. William W. Keen, who was witness to her twenty-four-hour ministrations, was worried.[11]

> You have been a rare wife and have borne your heavy burden most bravely. You will surely break down if you too do not have imme-diate relief. Even then when the catheter has to be used your sleep must be broken at least once in the night.

In later years the old doctor never ceased to praise Eleanor's tireless consecration. "She is one of my heroines," he wrote Roosevelt in 1926; "don't fail to tell her so." He was equally impressed with Franklin's courage and cheerfulness; indeed, he confided to Eleanor, he had "rarely met two such brave, cheerful and delightful patients. You see I count you as one although you are not going to take my medicine!"[12]

Franklin's cheerfulness at the time was a fugitive affair, as Eleanor's next letter to Rosy hinted. His temperature had returned to normal, she wrote on the eighteenth, "and I think he's getting back his grip and a better mental attitude though he has of course times of great discouragement." She had not yet told Franklin that Dr. Keen had warned that his recuperation would take a long time. "I dread the time when I have to tell Franklin and it wrings my heart for it is all so much worse to a man than to a woman but the 3 doctors agree he will be eventually well if nothing unfavorable happens in the next ten days or so and at present all signs are favorable, so we should be very thankful."

Dr. Keen had brought another doctor into the consultations, but in the meantime Uncle Fred, on the basis of Louis Howe's description of the illness, had consulted doctors in New York who leaned toward a diagnosis of infantile paralysis. "On Uncle Fred's urgent advice," Eleanor wrote Rosy,

> which I feel I must follow on Mama's account, I have asked Dr. Keen to try to get Dr. Lovett here for a consultation to determine

if it is I.P. or not. Dr. Keen thinks *not* but the treatment at this stage differs in one particular and no matter what it costs I feel and I am sure Mama would feel we must leave no stone unturned to accomplish the best results.[13]

Dr. Keen tracked down Dr. Robert W. Lovett, a specialist in orthopedics, at Newport, and he went to Campobello immediately. Dr. Lovett promptly diagnosed infantile paralysis, but would not commit himself as to the future course of the illness. Eleanor, determined to know the worst, begged Louis to ask Lovett what the chances were of Franklin's recovering the use of his lower limbs, because she felt that the doctor would be more frank with someone who was not a member of the immediate family.

It was impossible to tell, Lovett replied, but whatever chance there was depended on the patient's attitude. "If his interest in resuming active life is great enough, if his will to recover is strong enough, there is undoubtedly a chance." Eleanor should be prepared "for mental depression and sometimes irritability."

When she heard the diagnosis of polio she felt a momentary sense of panic because of the children, in addition to her anxiety over Franklin.[14] She had thought of polio as a possibility, she wrote Dr. Peabody at Groton, and while "it seemed incredible" she had kept the children out of Franklin's room, but that did not mean they were safe.[15] Lovett assured her, however, that since the children were not already stricken they had probably not been infected. When the trained nurse at last arrived from New York, Lovett and Keen, impressed with Eleanor's skillful care of her husband, felt that she should continue to share the nursing responsibility.

She also acted as Franklin's secretary and scribe. She wrote Langdon Marvin not to come up because "you wouldn't be allowed to see me if you came." Franklin could not get to the Sulphur Spring meeting, she advised the Fidelity and Deposit home office, but in her letter to Dr. Peabody asking whether James should return to Groton in September in light of his father's illness, she added, "Franklin says to tell you he can still do lots of work on the committee he hopes!" Miss LeHand, meanwhile, not knowing that Franklin was ill, had asked for a raise in salary. Mr. Roosevelt could not jump her to forty dollars but might manage to get her thirty-five, Eleanor wrote.

The most difficult letter was to Sara, who was due to arrive August 31.

Campobello
August 27, 1921
Dearest Mama,   Saturday

Franklin has been quite ill and so can't go down to meet you on Tuesday to his great regret, but Uncle Fred and Aunt Kassie both write they will be there so it will not be a lonely homecoming. We are all so happy to have you home again dear, you don't know what it means to feel you near again.

The children are all very well and I wish you could have seen John's face shine when he heard us say you would be home again soon.

Aunt Jennie is here with Ellen and we are having such lovely weather, the island is really at its loveliest.

Franklin sends all his love and we are both so sorry he cannot meet you.

Ever devotedly
Eleanor

Louis went to New York. "Everything in connection with your affairs is in the best possible shape," he reported. "I took breakfast with 'Uncle Fred' before your mama arrived, and filled him full of cheery thoughts and fried eggs. That night, being so exhausted with his day's labors, he decided to take dinner with me and we went together to the movies."[16]

As soon as she arrived Sara went to Campobello. The façade of cheer she found there did not fool her, but if Eleanor and Franklin were able to put up a brave front so would she. She was heartsick, but noted that Eleanor was doing "a *great* deal" for Franklin and commented, "This again illustrates my point that the lightning usually strikes where you least expect it." She wrote her sister, Doe (Mrs. Paul R. Forbes):

It was a shock to hear bad news on my arrival at the dock, but I am thankful I did not hear before I sailed, as I came directly here, and being very well and strong I could copy the happy cheerful atti-tude of Eleanor and even of poor Franklin, who lies there unable to move his legs, which are often painful and have to be moved for him, as they have *no* power. He looks well and eats well and is very keen and full of interest in everything. He made me tell him all about our four days in the devastated region, and told me what he saw when there. Dr. Lovett, the greatest authority we have on infantile paralysis, pronounced it that and says he *will* get well. At best it will be slow.[17]

"He and Eleanor decided at once to be cheerful," she reported to her brother Fred,

and the atmosphere of the house is all happiness, so I have fallen in and follow their glorious example.... Dr. Bennett just came and said "This boy is going to get well all right." They went into his room and I hear them all laughing. Eleanor in the lead.

Franklin persuaded his mother to go to Louise Delano's wedding as there was little for her to do at Campobello. "I am glad you sent her off to the wedding. It will do her good," Rosy wrote from Hyde Park. "Poor Tom Lynch I told him today about you, and he burst out crying." Lynch was not the only one. "I simply cannot bear to have beautiful, active Franklin laid low even for a time," Mary Miller wrote when the news caught up with her. Everyone found it difficult to think of "such a vigorous, healthy person ill," but they admired the "magnificent spirit," as Adolph Miller put it, which Franklin and Eleanor were showing. Husband and wife did not yield to self-pity, and they discouraged weeping and wailing by those around them. In the letters that Eleanor wrote for him, Franklin set a tone of optimistic banter that he expected those close to him to follow. "After many consultations among the medical fraternity," his letter to Langdon Marvin said,

my case has been diagnosed by Dr. Lovett as one of poliomyelitis, otherwise infantile paralysis. Cheerful thing for one with my gray hairs to get. I am almost wholly out of commission as to my legs but the doctors say that there is no question that I will get their use back again though this means several months of treatment in New York.... The doctors say of course that I can keep up with everything and I expect to do this through Mr. Howe, my former assistant in Washington who will act as my go-between from 65th Street to 52 Wall and the F & D Company.[18]

Howe and Miss LeHand went along with his tone of cheerful badinage. "By the way, Mr. Howe took me up with him in a *taxi*," Miss LeHand wrote Roosevelt; "isn't that scandalous? I love scandal!...

I have moved my desk and typewriter into your office right beside the telephone. Do you object?" Eleanor was grateful. "Your letters have amused him and helped to keep him cheerful." "Dear Boss," Louis wrote,

> I loved the way Eleanor telegraphed to go into Tiffany's to buy a watch for Calder without mentioning whether it was to be a $1200 Jorgerson or a Waterbury Radiolite; also to have it inscribed without mentioning what to inscribe on it! Lord knows I have acted as your alter-ego in many weird commissions, but I must positively refuse to risk my judgment on neckties, watches or pajamas.[19]

The watch was purchased and given to Captain Calder by Eleanor when the private railroad car that Uncle Fred had obtained pulled out of Eastport with Franklin aboard. It was the captain who, with the aid of some island men, had carried Franklin down the hill to the Roosevelt wharf on a stretcher that he had improvised and placed him on a motorboat for the two-mile crossing to Eastport. There, Louis, who stage-managed the whole move, skillfully diverted the waiting crowd while the stretcher was placed on a luggage cart and pulled up to the train. Each jolt was agony for Franklin, but Calder and his men could not have been gentler as they passed him through a window into the waiting car. Eleanor was deeply grateful to the captain and promised to let him know how Franklin stood the trip as soon as they arrived in New York. Her thoughtfulness as well as Roosevelt's evoked the sea captain's admiration.

> I went over to see Dr. Bennett yesterday afternoon and learned from him just how Mr. Roosevelt is taking everything. Isn't it wonderful to think how bravely and hopefully he is facing it all? . . . Say to Mr. Roosevelt that I carried his message to the engine driver who was so careful on the way to Ayer's Junction and he was more than proud.[20]

Calder also thanked her for the watch,

> which I can accept from you and Mr. Roosevelt, as the spirit in which it is given is so different, also for the real good friendly note which accompanied the same. Who could dare be disloyal to a friend like you? I only hope that Anna can be just like you as she grows older.

In New York Franklin entered Presbyterian Hospital and his case was taken over by Dr. George Draper, Harvard friend and orthopedic specialist. Whether Franklin could recover the use of his leg muscles was wholly uncertain. "I told them very frankly that no one could tell them where they stood," Lovett advised Draper. The case was a mild one and Lovett thought that "complete recovery or partial recovery to any point was possible, that disability was not to be feared." But then he hedged; it could go either way, he admitted. It looked to him "as if some of the important muscles might be on the edge where they could be influenced either way—toward recovery, or turn into completely paralyzed muscles." The doctor's ambiguity heightened the strain on Eleanor. A little later Draper wrote Lovett that he was concerned about his patient's "very slow recovery both as regards the disappearance of *pain*, which is very generally present, and as to the recovery of even slight power to twitch the muscles." Draper shrank from the moment when they would have Franklin sit up and he would "be faced with the frightfully depressing knowledge that he cannot hold himself erect." He felt strongly that

> the psychological factor in his management is paramount. He has such courage, such ambition, and yet at the same time such an extraordinarily sensitive emotional mechanism that it will take all the skill which we can muster to lead him successfully to a recognition of what he really faces without crushing him.[21]

Eleanor understood the psychological factor better than anyone. Franklin came back to New York believing he would soon be well enough to leave the hospital on crutches and resume work. At Campobello, all of them—Franklin, Louis, herself—had taken it for granted that he would soon be able to work again. They were returning to New York rather than Hyde Park, she had written Rosy, not only because that was where he could best be treated, but so that he could carry on his "various business activities." His determination to remain active was supported by his wife and by Louis, who underwrote his loyalty and faith in his friend's recovery by giving up his personal and family life and moving into the Roosevelt home in order to handle Franklin's affairs.

But the charade of a busy man of affairs which all three played at Campobello was based on the assumption of a relatively speedy and complete recovery. What would happen when Franklin realized that it might take years to regain the use of his legs or the even more somber possibility of permanent disablement? Any suggestion of retirement would diminish his recuperative powers, Dr. Draper felt. Eleanor was sure that if her husband was to hold onto the will to recover, he had to cling to his faith that he would return to politics and business.

Franklin was discharged from Presbyterian Hospital on October 28, but his record read "not improving" and some of the most painful days were ahead. At home he set about his exercises, but he was still running a temperature and his muscles were still tender.

Now the most excruciating pain began. The tendons behind his right knee began to jackknife and lock, and his legs had to be placed in plaster casts into which *wedges* were driven deeper and deeper, to stretch the muscles. It was as if his legs were on the rack. Not since Eleanor had seen her father go to have his leg rebroken had she witnessed such pain. But Franklin had a toughness and resilience her father had lacked, and he bore it stoically. He and Eleanor had taught the children to face illness and injury without tears or complaint; pain was to be borne silently. He followed his own Spartan precepts. Those who called him "feather duster," the political opponents who derided him as "Mama's boy," simply failed to see the iron fortitude behind the smiles and cheer. And if there were moments, as there must have been, when he was tempted to cry out against his fate, to surrender to his infirmities, Eleanor was there to brace him against them.

Their biggest problem was Sara. In her view, public service was an affair of *noblesse oblige*, not civic duty, and the life of a public man, especially of a politician, was less attractive than the quiet, secluded existence of a country gentleman. She now adamantly preached its virtues to Franklin and Eleanor. She was, moreover, genuinely afraid for her son. She was fearful that the callers whom Eleanor encouraged to come to the house sapped his vitality, that keeping up with his interests tired him. And she was sure that her mother's heart knew better than Franklin or Eleanor or Louis or the doctors what would speed his recovery. (She was not the only Hudson River matriarch with such views. Her good friend Mrs. Robert Livingston had prevailed upon her son to abandon the law and withdraw to the vacuous life of a country squire when his eyesight began to bother him. In later years his contemporaries, viewing his squandered talents, would say that Franklin had had Eleanor and Louis to save him from his mother while Robert

Livingston had been unprotected.)[22] All through the winter a struggle between the two women went on, usually with politeness and courtesy but sometimes with acrimony.

As Franklin and Eleanor stood firm in the contest of wills, Louis became the target of Sara's resentment, but it was Eleanor who bore the brunt of the struggle. Sara could be ruthless. With her, family was all that counted, and she resented outsiders with whom her children had close relationships. When Louis moved into the house, rather than being grateful to him for thus "marrying himself irrevocably to his crippled friend's future," Sara doggedly fought the influence with Franklin and Eleanor of "that ugly, dirty little man," as she called him.[23] She found it difficult to be civil to him and, in disapproval, withdrew to Hyde Park.

Sara was not content simply to argue with Eleanor over Franklin's care; she also used the children, too young to understand what was going on, shaken by the sight of their splendid, spirited father prostrate, their house astir with strangers. Since they were also resentful of Louis, Sara played on their resentment, especially Anna's. She was fifteen years old and having a difficult time fitting in at Miss Chapin's, where she felt she was treated by students and teachers as an "outsider." "I hated it but Mother decided I had to like it because she hoped I would develop the same feeling for Miss Chapin that she had for Mlle. Souvestre. So it was a year of complete withdrawal on my part from Mother, and Granny was feeling very excluded too."[24]

Anna was supposed to have the large room with bath on the third floor, but Eleanor had turned it over to Louis, relegating Anna to a cubicle on the fourth floor. Eleanor was sharing a room with the youngest boys, sleeping on a cot, but Anna did not think of that: "I agreed completely with Granny that I was being discriminated against." Moreover, Anna was confused by her mother's switch in attitude toward Louis; Eleanor and Sara had always agreed about that "dirty little man," and now only Sara was being consistent.

> Granny, with a good insight into my adolescent nature, started telling me that it was inexcusable that I, the only daughter of the family, should have a tiny bedroom in the back of the house, while Louis enjoyed a large, sunny front bedroom with his own private bath.
>
> Granny's needling finally took root; at her instigation, I went to Mother one evening and demanded a switch in rooms. A sorely

tired and harassed mother was naturally anything but sympathetic; in fact, she was very stern with her recalcitrant daughter.[25]

Eleanor carried a tremendous load. Since she was relieving the trained nurse, household arrangements could be complex. If she wanted to go out, as she did to take Anna to *Tosca* (she could not "resist seeing Anna at her first opera"), she had to make special arrangements with the nurse. Franklin wanted visitors and she saw to it that they came, but she also had to make sure they did not stay too long and would see them herself if necessary. Franklin had his ups and downs, and the one person with whom he did not have to dissemble was his wife.

"I am sorrier for you than Franklin," Caroline Phillips wrote from The Hague, "and I know what an ideal wife you are." It was, Eleanor said, the "most trying winter" in her life. Once Anna came upon her mother unexpectedly and found her slumped down in a chair, the picture of total dejection. Only Louis knew how to cope with Eleanor's moods. She must not give up in despair, he counseled; she had a great future, and so did Franklin. He could usually make her come out of her shell, but Anna only came to appreciate this later. At the time she was angry and resentful and it upset her to see Louis sitting in a comfortable armchair with her mother at his feet: "I would be violently jealous."[26]

Sara encouraged Anna to believe that her mother cared more for Louis than for her and this brought Eleanor close to the breaking point. Once that winter her self-discipline failed and the outward serenity and composure with which she usually guided the household shattered. She was reading to Franklin Jr. and John when she was suddenly swept by uncontrollable sobbing. The boys quickly left the room and so did Elliott, who happened to come in, saw his mother in tears, and fled. Louis tried to calm her but could do nothing. Finally she locked herself in a bathroom in her mother-in-law's house, until she was able to regain control. It was the only time that she went to pieces in that way, she said.

Sara's interference, on top of the burdens, was almost too much for Eleanor. "That old lady [Sara] with all her charm and distinction and kindliness hides a primitive jealousy of her daughter-in-law which is sometimes startling in its crudity," Caroline Phillips wrote in 1936 after a long talk with Helen Robinson in which she learned of the way Sara had used Anna against Eleanor.[27]

In the late spring of 1922 Anna came down with the measles and on top of that the mumps.[28] She was sent to Hyde Park and when Franklin went to Boston to be fitted for braces Eleanor went to Hyde Park too. One day Anna was writing a letter to her cousin, Helen Robinson, and "had just finished a few lines to the effect 'that the thing I like most about being up here is that Louis Howe is not up here,' when Mother walked in." Anna tried to hide the letter, but Eleanor sternly insisted that she wanted to read it. "I burst into tears," said Anna, "and gave it to her. She read it sitting at the end of the sofa and then said very coldly to me she would have to see to it I had no further contact with Louis the next winter when school started."

Sara was to take Anna and Jimmy to Europe later that month and the conversation turned to that.

> Suddenly to my horror Mother burst into tears and out poured her unhappiness. She had always looked forward to taking Jimmy and me to Europe, but she did not have the money to do so. So Granny was.

Eleanor softened when she saw how upset Anna was and said "she would really try to make things easier for me with regard to Louis," Anna noted.

After this incident, mother and daughter began to open up to each other. Their rapprochement was strengthened as a result of a run-in between Anna and her father. One day Anna was on a ladder shifting some books in the library at Hyde Park while Franklin directed her from his wheelchair when an armful of books slipped and crashed to the floor. "I saw Father start, and an expression of pain passed swiftly over his face. My apologies were interrupted by his voice very sternly accusing me of being too careless for words and no help at all." Anna fled in tears and

> ran into Mother. To her I sobbed out my story and my grief.... Mother told me of the battle Father was waging against great odds; of the naturalness of his nervous reaction; how lucky we were to have him alive and to be able to help him get well; how much more patience and grit he had to have than we; until I felt very sheep-ish and even more ashamed—but in a different way, a more adult, understanding way. Back I went to the library where, of course, I not only found forgiveness but also a sincere and smilingly given invitation to resume my place on the library ladder.[29]

Whatever the strain, Eleanor did not yield to Sara. After it was all over, Dr. Draper told his sister, Alice Carter, that if it had not been for Eleanor and Mr. Howe, Franklin would have really become an invalid.[30] Eleanor refused to treat Franklin as an invalid and did not allow others to do so. The struggle with her mother-in-law was finally over. "She dominated me for years," Eleanor later said. Franklin's illness completed her emancipation "and made me stand on my own two feet in regard to my husband's life, my own life, and my children's training."[31] She and Franklin both emerged from the ordeal tempered, tested, and strengthened. If she had yielded to Sara, Eleanor later said, she would have become "a completely colorless echo of my husband and mother-in-law and torn between them. I might have stayed a weak character forever if I had not found that out."

27. HER HUSBAND'S STAND-IN

ELEANOR ROOSEVELT NOW BEGAN A PERIOD OF INTENSIVE PUBLIC activity. Chroniclers of the Roosevelt era have studied her emergence in the years after her husband was stricken from the point of view primarily of the help it was to him. She became his stand-in with the Democrats. She kept his name before the public. She brought people to see him—key party officials and public personalities and the less well known whose points of view she felt should interest him.

All this was true. Equally true, although rarely noted either by herself because of modesty or by others because they were more concerned with Franklin Roosevelt, was her effectiveness in the organizations in which she worked. Interested in neither titles nor honors, she moved swiftly into positions of leadership. She became known for the honesty and vigor of her opinions. She accepted responsibility because there was a job to be done, and with the same ardent good will took on both "donkey work" and assignments that produced headlines. Her lack of pride and vanity and her sincere dedication to the public good inspired confidence in her fairness and judgment. By the time Franklin returned to political office some of the foremost women of the time, who had long been leaders in the struggle for women's rights, saw in Eleanor a new leader to whom they could pass on the torch.

Even before polio disabled Franklin, Louis had been encouraging her to take up interests of her own and to go into politics. As it became clear that Franklin would not return to public activity for a long time, Louis added an irresistible argument: Eleanor had to become actively involved in Democratic politics in order to keep alive Franklin's interest in the party and the party's interest in him. Doubtful as she was of her ability, once Louis put it to her as a matter of duty, his suggestions became easier for her to accept. And beneath the implacable promptings of conscience, there now were also the stirrings of ambition—the desire to show that she could succeed in this man's world of politics—and, even deeper, a repressed but sweetly satisfactory awareness that the fate of the man who had hurt her so deeply now depended upon the success she made of her work for him.

So when Nancy Cook, assistant to Harriet May Mills, chairman of the women's division of the Democratic State Committee, called to ask her to preside at a money-raising luncheon, she suppressed an impulse to say "no." Sara was among the hundred women gathered at the luncheon tables, and although she had undoubtedly come to give her daughter-in-law moral support, the presence of this increasingly critical lady could only have added to Eleanor's terror of the occasion. "I trembled so," she later wrote, "that I did not know whether I could stand up, and I am quite sure my voice could not be heard."[1] Since a few thousand dollars were raised as a result of her plea for funds, somebody must have heard her, and her performance was strong enough that she was subsequently asked to serve as chairman of the Finance Committee for the women's division. She invited Miss Cook, whose brisk enterprise she liked, to spend a week end at Hyde Park. Nancy was a striking, crisp-haired, crisp-voiced young woman with eager eyes, whose resourcefulness as an organizer and talents as a designer and craftsman (she was skilled at jewelry, pottery, copper, and brass work as well as cabinet making) made it easy for the members of the women's division to accept her managerial propensities. Through Nancy, Eleanor soon met Marion Dickerman, a soft-spoken, tall ("as a Gothic church window," someone said) woman of high principles and mournful countenance. They hailed from upstate New York, where they had been active in the suffrage movement, and had gone overseas to serve as volunteers in a British hospital. They returned home as the New York suffrage leaders were casting about for someone to run against Thad Sweet, the upstate Republican Speaker of the Assembly, who had blocked the progressive measures sponsored by the women. Finding that Marion lived in his district and was a Republican, they persuaded her to run against him. Nancy became her campaign manager. Backed by the Democrats, Socialists, Prohibitionists, and the women's groups, Marion's candidacy frightened Sweet sufficiently, though the district was traditionally Republican, that his backers slashed the tires of the women's cars, denied them halls to meet in, pressured the local printers to refuse their work. Marion lost but doubled the vote against Sweet. Harriet Mills was impressed with Nancy's work and asked her to come to New York City to work with her. Marion came down too, to teach and to work for the Foreign Policy Association. They found an apartment in Greenwich

Village. Marion came with Nancy to Hyde Park.[2] That was the way the friendship began. During the next few years Nancy, Marion, and Eleanor were almost inseparable.

On Franklin's urging, Eleanor put in as much time in Dutchess County politics as she did at the offices of the State Committee. An upstate Democrat had to have a firm local footing, Franklin felt, if he was not to be at the mercy of the New York bosses. He also believed that Democratic weakness upstate was a result of the neglect and apathy of those same bosses toward upstate issues and that systematic hard work could diminish, if not overcome, Republican upstate majorities. Franklin was the strategist and Eleanor the chief of the troops at his command. She and John Mack's daughter set out to organize the women in the county. That meant more speaking, and Louis took her in hand and coached her. He came to her meetings, sat at the back of the hall, and afterward gave her his critique. He was hard on her nervous giggle: "Have something to say, say it, and then sit down," was his terse advice.

The 1922 State Democratic convention was to take place at the end of September. William Randolph Hearst had gubernatorial aspirations. Franklin backed Al Smith and undertook to mobilize upstate support for him and especially to ensure a Dutchess County delegation committed to the former governor. Henry Morgenthau, Jr., helped, as did Mack, Tom Lynch, and Eleanor, who was his most tireless worker. She presided over a Dutchess County luncheon at which Elinor Morgenthau offered an anti-Hearst resolution that was unanimously adopted. She met the press and fired away at the Republicans: "It is impossible to be both a Republican and a progressive under the leadership of Governor Miller in this State."[3] She gave a picnic at Hyde Park for the wives of forty upstate mayors. She and Franklin received the Odd Fellows and Rebeccas at Hyde Park. One evening that summer as dessert was being served, Eleanor rose and said she had to go to speak in the Village. "It's only beginning," Rosy laughingly warned his younger half brother. "Once they mount the soapbox, mark my words, they never get off."[4]

Sara, who was in Europe with Anna and James, seemed to be feeling more benevolent about Eleanor's activities. "Eleanor's work among the women, will, I trust, bear fruit," she wrote Franklin.[5] Despite her political chores Eleanor took a refresher course in driving, and three times a week chauffeured Franklin and the two youngest children to Vincent Astor's place in Rhinebeck to use his "swimming tank."

There were mishaps. "Your running into our gate post was all right," Sara comforted her, "so long as you were not hurt."[6]

On August 13 Franklin addressed an open letter to Smith calling on him to run again, as the choice of "the average citizen." Smith said he was available. A telegram from Louis in Syracuse to Franklin in Hyde Park described the outcome: "AL NOMINATED WITH GREAT ENTHUSIASM. MORGENTHAU AND YOUR MISSUS LED THE DUTCHESS COUNTY DELEGATION WITH THE BANNER THREE TIMES AROUND THE HALL . . ." "Everything went along first rate," Smith wrote Roosevelt after the convention. "I had quite a session with our lady politicians as Mrs. Roosevelt no doubt told you. I was delighted to see her taking an active part and I am really sorry that you could not be there but take care of yourself—there is another day coming."[7]

The "lady politicians" had demanded two places on the ticket, but when Smith pledged to appoint women to high places in his administration, they gave way.

During the campaign Eleanor worked mainly in Dutchess County and learned how party politics worked on the village level. What she saw was not pleasant, especially the purchase of votes, but rather than withdraw in well-bred disgust, she was spurred on to work harder. On Election Day she chauffeured voters to the polls in the family Buick. The Republican margin in the county for Miller, which had been 6,200 in 1920, was reduced to little over 1,000. "I think what has been done in the county is amazing," Mrs. Norrie wrote approvingly to Franklin, "and I believe, now the start is made, a great deal more can be done."[8] So did Franklin and Eleanor. He was having a "strenuous time" over Hudson River politics, Franklin wrote a few months later. "We are doing some fine organizing work—especially with the aid of the ladies."[9]

"What job is Smith going to give you?" Hall wrote her from the West Coast after Smith's landslide election,[10] but a job on the public payroll was not what Eleanor had in mind. She was in politics primarily to serve her husband's purposes and beyond that to advance a point of view that began to take shape in her mind as she took on increasing responsibilities in the party. It was crystallized in an article entitled "Why I Am a Democrat," which the Junior League *Bulletin* asked her to write and which was to be run with one by Mrs. John Pratt on "Why I Am a Republican."[11]

She first discussed political parties and why principles, not personalities, should govern one's party allegiance. She felt that the Democratic party gave higher priority to human needs than did the Republican party. "On the whole the Democratic Party seems to have been more concerned with the welfare and interests of the people at large, and less with the growth of big business interests." Her next point showed how far she had moved from the viewpoint of the group with whom she had been raised.

If you believe that a nation is really better off which achieves for a comparative few, those who are capable of attaining it, high culture, ease, opportunity, and that these few from their enlightenment should give what they consider best to those less favored, then you naturally belong to the Republican Party. But if you believe that people must struggle slowly to the light for themselves, then it seems to me that you are logically a Democrat.

This Jeffersonian trust in the people was even more strongly reflected in Eleanor's growing involvement with the Women's Trade Union League. Founded in 1903 by Jane Addams and others "to aid women workers in their efforts to organize...and to secure better conditions," the Women's Trade Union League was the most militant women's group, and many of its leaders were aligned with the socialist movement. Eleanor joined the league in 1922 after attending a luncheon at the invitation of Mrs. James Lees Laidlaw. Rose Schneiderman, a redheaded packet of social dynamite who directed the New York League, said she first met Eleanor at a tea given by Mrs. Willard Straight to interest her friends in purchasing a home for the league. Rose was captivated by Eleanor's "simplicity" and "her lovely eyes." Eleanor was interested in Rose, too, and invited her to Sunday night supper at Sixty-fifth Street. While Eleanor scrambled eggs in a chafing dish and the silver coffee urn burbled, Rose recalled, "We talked about the work I was doing. Mrs. Roosevelt asked many questions but she was particularly interested in why I thought women should join unions."[12]

Rose and her associate, Maud Swartz, who had received her trade-union training in the British labor movement and was full of amusing stories about the trials and tribulations of a labor organizer, represented a new kind of friendship for Eleanor. Esther and Elizabeth, Nan and Marion, came of old American stock and were cultivated, well-bred women. But Rose, who had emigrated from Russian Poland and whose accent was still marked by the Lower East Side, was a fiery soapboxer. Her speech after the Triangle fire in 1911, the *New York Times* reporter said, brought emotion "to a snapping point." It took some time before Eleanor ventured to ask Sara to invite Rose and Maud to Hyde Park, as Sara was almost feudal in outlook. "She judged people almost solely by their social position," Eleanor later wrote, but "only people who knew her well could tell when she was really being rude."[13] "Of course, I can understand the point of view to which Cousin Susie and Sally arrive (a la Ku Klux)," Hall commiserated with her,

> but could never contemplate its use as they see it their duty to inflict same. If I lived in New York we should either never meet or else they would "lay off" of personalities. My feeling of the entire tribe is that they lack sympathy (original Greek meaning). I am only disturbed lest my children be brought up in the atmosphere of protection and utter uselessness to society.[14]

Eleanor went to work for the Trade Union League with the energy and thoroughness that characterized all her undertakings. While Dorothy Straight raised the $20,000 to make a down payment on a five-story brownstone at 247 Lexington Avenue, Eleanor, assisted by Mrs. Thomas W. Lamont, agreed to head up a committee to raise funds to pay off the mortgage, which in the end amounted to $35,000. Evening classes for women workers were organized at the new headquarters, and Eleanor came one night a week to read to the girls—to teach and to be taught. Marion Dickerman taught a class in literature. In 1925 Eleanor invited Rose and Maud to Campobello, and when she had to leave briefly while they were there she left the two women in charge of Franklin Jr. and Johnny and two of their friends. She had "more faith" in Maud Swartz handling the boys, she wrote Franklin, than she did in their tutor.[15]

Eleanor explained to her sons what the two women were doing and asked if they would like to give a Christmas party for the children of WTUL members. The boys agreed, but Sara was horrified. The diseases the two boys might pick up. . . . But this argument no longer carried weight with Eleanor. When she shyly approached Rose with the proposal, Rose was delighted. The invitations went out from Franklin Jr. and Johnny; Nancy Cook dressed the Christmas tree; Eleanor purchased the gifts—clothing, roller skates, dolls—and a cornucopia of candy for each child. At the last moment her boys balked; they could not understand "giving" presents: Christmas was a time for "getting" presents. They were more reconciled to their role the following year when it was explained to them that they were, in fact, deputies of Santa Claus.[16] For the Roosevelt boys this was their first contact with children of the slums and with trade unions. For their mother, it was another manifestation of a radical equalitarianism.

A Christmas party for slum children might still be considered in the Lady Bountiful tradition, even if it was under trade-union auspices, if it had not been buttressed by Eleanor's systematic work on behalf of league objectives—the forty-eight hour week, minimum wages, the abolition of child labor, the right to organize. She had become an influential figure in the League of Women Voters, the Women's City Club, and especially in the Democratic party, and wherever she carried weight, she rallied support for league programs. "Always generous and understanding, she never refused me anything I asked her," Rose wrote; for her part, Rose taught Eleanor all that she knew about trade unionism.[17]

Through Eleanor, Rose and Maud also became Franklin's teachers and spent many hours with him. Frances Perkins later said that Franklin's whole attitude toward trade unions might have been different had he not seen the theory and history of the trade-union movement through the eyes of these women. A labor leader once said to Madam Perkins that "you'd almost think he had participated in some strike or organizing campaign the way he knew and felt about it," and she credited his comprehension and grasp to the hours he had spent with Rose and her associates.[18]

In her article for the Junior League *Bulletin* on why she was a Democrat Eleanor had listed as a final reason the party's approach to the prevention of another war. The Democrats, she felt, were "more conscious of our world responsibility and more anxious to see some steps taken toward international cooperation than were the Republicans." It was a mild statement of the case. The times were not hospitable to militant advocacy of the League of Nations; the mood of the country was indifference, the policy of the Harding administration isolationist. Franklin, who had become head of the Woodrow Wilson Foundation, muted his support of the League and sought instead to keep an interest in Wilsonian principles alive. Wilson's attitude toward Franklin softened, especially after polio made Franklin a fellow in suffering. They exchanged letters, and when Eleanor went to Washington she called on Mrs. Wilson.

When Wilson died in early February, 1924, Franklin was on his houseboat in Florida waters. "I wired Mrs. Wilson today for us both," Eleanor wrote Franklin; "a people had never more surely contributed to a man's breakdown."[19] The president "must have been glad to go." She was aghast at Lodge's fulsome tribute to the dead president in the Senate: "I must say if I had been Lodge I would not have made his speech in the Senate, would you?" She took Anna to the hastily organized memorial service in New York at Madison Square Garden, which "was really almost filled even in the top gallery. Mr. John Davis and several others made good speeches but Rabbi Wise made the most stirring one."[20] That gifted orator called on his listeners to "embalm in oblivion the names and deeds of those who, to punish your and my leader—the hope-bringer of mankind—struck him down and broke the heart of the world!"

Franklin thought Wilson's death might help revive bipartisan faith in Wilson's ideals, but to Eleanor it seemed that the country was "so seething in partisan politics just now, it would seem hard to lift any subject out of them."[21] She spoke from melancholy personal experience. A promising and substantial effort to move international cooperation back into the realm of practical politics was foundering in a flare-up of faction and cowardice.

The previous May, Edward W. Bok, the former editor and publisher of the *Ladies' Home Journal* and a talented publicist, had proposed a nationwide competition for "the best practicable plan by which the U.S. may cooperate with other nations to achieve and preserve the peace of the world." To stimulate interest in the contest he offered $100,000 as the prize, half to go to the winner on the selection of the plan and the other half to be given to him when the plan received serious consideration in the Senate. It was, as the *New York Times* said, one of the most "princely" prizes ever offered for a noncommercial idea. Bok asked Esther Lape to direct the project, and she agreed to do so if she could have Eleanor Roosevelt work with her as a member of the policy committee. Bok readily agreed, and to establish the nonpartisan character of the competition they also asked Mrs. Frank Vanderlip, a Republican, to join the initial group.

The competition was announced on July 2, 1923. It was the lead story in the *New York Times* and rated headlines in all the great metropolitan dailies. "Isn't the American Peace Award going fine?" an exultant Bok wrote Franklin a month later, "and surely a great deal of the credit is due to that wonderful wife of yours. I am wondering whether she and Esther Lape ever sleep!"[22] Eleanor and Esther had assembled an impressive policy committee and had persuaded the big national organizations to set up a cooperating council. "She has been very busy with the Bok Award," Franklin wrote Hall. "I think it is a fine thing for Bok to start and will undoubtedly do much to hasten our eventual participation in world reconstruction, though I doubt if we see any immediate results. What do you think of it?"[23] Hall was more skeptical of its producing results: "The voting public of this part of the world, at least," he wrote, "has fallen into a state of lethargy as regards cooperation with the European Powers." Esther asked Franklin for a statement on the award. He was cautious. "I handed out a serious protest against the title," Roosevelt wrote Bok, "on the ground that it might make people think that we could get permanent peace by the mere establishment of a formula."[24]

With a quarter of a million inquiries and plans pouring in by the thousands, Eleanor was more sanguine than her husband and brother. The purpose of the competition, she said in her speeches, was not only to focus public thinking upon the form of association Americans felt their country ought to have with the rest of the world, but to submit the winning plan to the supreme test of practicality—passage in the Senate. "Esther wants me to do rather a job at the Bok office the next few weeks," she wrote Franklin at the end of October (the deadline for entries was November 15, 1923). "I told her after Election I'd devote my major activities to her and let up a bit on the Democrats!" On the closing day of the contest 700 plans were received, bringing the total to 22,165. "Amazing indeed, is the interest that has been called forth from every part of the country, and from every walk of life," the *Times* commented. On January 7 the winning plan was released. Again it was the lead story in the *Times*, which also published the full text. Briefly stated, it called for U.S. entry into the World Court and conditional support for the League of Nations, in effect cooperation without membership.

Promptly the Senate isolationists raised the cry that it was "a pro-League proposal pure and simple." An inquiry was launched headed by Senators Reed and Moses, two leading "irreconcilables," designed to show that the competition was a sinister propaganda exercise, that it was a rigged contest, and that the committee of jurors had been packed. Women crowded the hearing room, with Alice Longworth in a privileged seat on a huge leather sofa in back of the committee. Bok was treated with kid gloves at the hearing but Reed's examination of Esther Lape was so severe that other senators chivalrously came to her aid. How was the policy committee chosen, Reed demanded. Mrs. Roosevelt was the first one invited to join, Esther replied, and then Mrs. Vanderlip; Mr. Bok had left the selection of the remainder to the three women. "Do you mean that you three ladies then selected the rest of the members of the Policy Committee?" Reed asked incredulously. He was not alone in his outrage at such female presumption. "THREE WOMEN ENGINEERED BOK PEACE PRIZE CONTEST," was the Republican *New York Herald*'s headline. "The great Bok peace prize contest," the head of the *Herald*'s Washington bureau wrote, "was managed by two matrons of social distinction and a highly educated and most efficient young unmarried woman." Front-page photographs of Eleanor, Esther, and Mrs. Vanderlip accompanied the story. Franklin's unofficial press representative in Washington, Marvin McIntyre, came up to Esther, Elizabeth, and Eleanor after the committee excused Esther. "I think we're a thousand percent!" he told them. Miss Lape was one of "the most marvellously acute witnesses" to appear on the Hill, the *Boston Transcript* correspondent wrote. "They never went on with the hearings," Esther said. "They used Wilson's illness as a pretext to adjourn them."[25] But the isolationist orators called the Bok Peace Award a "peace-at-any-price" enterprise and equated internationalism with treason.

When Eleanor and Esther went to Washington March 17 to try to persuade some senators merely to introduce the winning plan, they were treated with cordiality and friendliness, but they were turned down. "It is discouraging to see people on an errand like this," Eleanor wrote her husband. "They have so little courage! They agree that their private views are met but the party isn't for it!"[26]

For Eleanor it was an intense education in the substantive issues as well as the politics of internationalism. Together with Esther and Elizabeth she read all of the entries, twenty of which Esther published in a book called *Ways to Peace*. The contest also helped Franklin crystallize his thinking on international cooperation. He had little sympathy for the isolationists ("You have doubtless seen the grand hullabaloo in the Senate over the Bok. Peace Award," he wrote George Marvin. "What fools Reed, Moses, etc. are. Eleanor is just back from Washington, where she went to hold Esther Lape's hand"), but he also had a healthy respect for political realities.

My objection to the accepted plan is that it is not practicable, i.e. politically practicable. The dear judges must have known that in choosing that plan they would revive the League of Nations very largely along existing lines. My plan avoided this by providing for an International Conference to establish a brand new permanent International organization.[27]

Because of his wife's membership on the policy committee, Franklin had not submitted his plan, but he did show it to Esther and it shaped his own approach to international cooperation when he was president.* The fundamental commitment to internationalism was there, but as a politician he thought it prudent to avoid open battle. Perhaps he felt he was bearing sufficient witness to the internationalist cause through the activities of his wife; since the public identified her advocacy with his convictions, that added to his reputation as a statesman without increasing the risks to him as a politician. He lapsed into relative silence but Eleanor pressed on. Public opinion admittedly was apathetic, even hostile; all the more reason to go forward with the work of education and organization. In her engagement book she transcribed the lines

Never dreamed, though right were worsted
Wrong would triumph,
Held we fall to rise, are baffled to fight better.

The peace-award group evolved into the American Foundation, whose main purpose was to work with those who shaped national opinion to promote U.S. entry into the World Court. Esther was the member-in-charge, Elizabeth the foundation's legal scholar, Eleanor the activist. A succinct statement on the "next step" in international cooperation that Eleanor wrote in 1925, when the House of Representatives approved U.S. participation in the World Court's activities and for a brief moment it looked as if U.S. acceptance was certain, revealed that although she would not compromise on goals, she advocated being flexible on tactics; a strong sense of practicality tempered her utopianism. Her speech was prepared for a meeting of women's clubs, and Louis went over it and made a few changes, chiefly shortening some of her sentences. Entry into the World Court was a first step in America's acceptance of its international responsibilities, she

---

* It is Esther Lape's recollection that Franklin did submit his plan and that "his objection to the winning plan was simply that it was not his."

stated. She was concerned with the "attitude of mind" with which a next step should be approached:

> Many of us have fixed ideas of what we think our own country and the various other countries of the world should do, but if we rigidly adhere, each to our own point of view, we will progress not at all. We should talk together with open minds and grasp anything which is a step forward; not hold out for our particular, ultimate panacea. Keep it in our minds, of course, but remember that all big changes in human history have been arrived at slowly and through many compromises.

The speech also showed how strongly her approach to politics was grounded in religious conviction:

> The basis of world peace is the teaching which runs through almost all the great religions of the world, "Love thy neighbor as thyself." Christ, some of the other great Jewish teachers, Buddha, all preached it. Their followers forgot it. What is the trouble between capital and labor, what is the trouble in many of our communities, but rather a universal forgetting that this teaching is one of our first obligations. When we center on our own home, our own family, our own business, we are neglecting this fundamental obligation of every human being and until it is acknowledged and fulfilled we cannot have world peace.

Peace was "the question of the hour," and for the women "this should be a crusade":

> The abolition of war touches them more nearly than any other question. Now when many of the nations of the world are at peace and we still remember vividly the horrors of 1914–1918 and know fairly generally what the next war will mean, now is the time to act. Usually only the experts, technical people, busy with war plans know, but at the moment we all know that the next war will be a war in which people not armies will suffer, and our boasted, hard-earned civilization will do us no good. Cannot the women rise to this great opportunity and work now, and not have the double horror, if another war comes, of losing their loved ones, and knowing that they lifted no finger when they might have worked hard?[28]

28. THE 1924 CAMPAIGN

SHORTLY AFTER THE BOK PEACE AWARD CONTROVERSY QUIETED
down and Eleanor was again concentrating on politics, Josephus Daniels wrote Franklin that he was relieved to learn that

> I am not the only "squaw" man in the country.... I think the *World*
> showed good taste when it announced that you were taking the
> helm of the Smith campaign they published the picture of your
> wife. I have had that experience on similar occasions and have
> always wondered how the newspapermen knew so well who was
> at the head of the family.

Franklin replied in the same tone:

> You are right about the squaws! Like you I have fought for years to
> keep my name on the front page and to relegate the wife's to the
> advertising section. My new plan, however, seems admirable—
> hereafter for three years my name will not appear at all, but each
> fourth year (Presidential ones) I am to have all the limelight. Why
> don't you adopt this too? It will make it much easier to put that
> Democratic national ticket of Daniels and Roosevelt across in 1928
> or 1932.[1]

Was Franklin wholly jesting? In less than two years Eleanor had
moved into a position of state leadership. Newspapers called her for
statements and she was beginning to speak over the radio as well as on
the stump. Her voice was still high, sometimes shrill, but her speaking
style had improved and she gamely stuck by the rules Louis had laid
down. The traits of helpfulness, modesty, and energy that made her
universally admired within the family now inspired equal admiration
in the public arena.

Franklin esteemed his wife's abilities highly, but he never happily surrendered the limelight to anyone. "Eleanor has been leading an even more hectic life than usual," he wrote Rosy. "Bok Peace Award, investigation by the Senate, Democratic females, in Philadelphia, etc. etc.—I think when I go away she will be more quiet as she will have to stay home more!"[2]

Eleanor understood how difficult it was for Franklin not to be front and center, especially in politics. "You need not be proud of me, dear," she wrote him on February 6, 1924:

> I'm only being *active* till you can be again—it isn't such a great desire on my part to serve the world and I'll fall back into habit of sloth quite easily! Hurry up for as you know my ever present sense of the uselessness of all things will overwhelm me sooner or later!

She had a stoic, almost fatalist, sense of resignation, yet like Marcus Aurelius, whose *Meditations* she admired, she was strongly motivated by a sense of the efficacy of moral effort. If the two attitudes were contradictory, it is a contradiction philosophers have never been able to resolve.

Directed by Franklin, coached by Louis, with a group of highly able women as co-workers—Esther, Elizabeth, Nancy, Marion, Caroline O'Day (widow of a Standard Oil heir) Elinor Morgenthau, Rose and Maud, a group to which in 1924 was added Mary W. Dewson, the new civic secretary of the Women's City Club—she was becoming a major force in public life. Whenever Eleanor was mentioned, wrote Isabella, who was now Mrs. John Greenway, "I say 'there is probably the greatest woman of this generation!'" A great many people were beginning to feel that way about her.

She made her office in the women's division of the Democratic State Committee. Caroline O'Day, socially prominent and strongly antiwar, had succeeded Harriet May Mills as chairman and Eleanor was chairman of the Finance Committee. Their efforts to organize the women, especially in the rural counties where there was no men's organization, and obtain recognition from the men, involved hard, often tedious work. Eleanor's journeyings with Nancy Cook or Marion Dickerman were fragmentarily recorded in her engagement book: "Left Massena in the rain. . . . The man Nan wanted to see was away." "Ran out of gas" in Ithaca and "searched for Mrs. T. unsuccessfully." "A good supper at St. James, proprietor a Democrat." "Gloversville— lovely country—meeting about 20 women and stayed till 3." Although they had requested modest lodgings, in one hotel they were ushered into "palatial suite. . . . Think F.D.R. may have to send us money to get home on."

By the spring of 1924 all but five counties of the state we organized, and the men were impressed. "Organization is something to which they are always ready to take off their hats," Eleanor said, but she realized how much women still had to learn before they would belong to the game as completely as did the men. In an interview with Rose Feld of the *Times* she related what she told women as she went around the state. "They have the vote, they have the power, but they don't seem to know what to do with it." Their lack of progress stemmed from the hostility of the men, and Eleanor summed up the real masculine attitude toward women in politics:

> You are wonderful. I love and honor you. . . . Lead your own life, attend to your charities, cultivate yourself, travel when you wish, bring up the children, run your house, I'll give you all the freedom you wish and all the money I can but—leave me my business and politics.

Her message to women was: "Get into the game and stay in it. Throwing mud from the outside won't help. Building up from the inside will."

A woman needed to learn the machinery of politics; then she would know how "to checkmate as well as her masculine opponent. Or it may be that with time she will learn to make an ally of her opponent, which is even better politics."[3]

At the Democratic state convention in April, 1924, called to launch the Smith boom for the presidential nomination, Eleanor led the women in rebellion against male monopolization of power. The issue was the selection of the delegates-at-large; the prime antagonist was Charles F. Murphy, the Tammany boss. "I have wanted you home the last few days," she wrote Franklin on the eve of the Albany meeting,

> to advise me on the fight I'm putting up on two delegates and two alternates at large. Mr. Murphy and I disagree as to whether the men leaders shall name them or whether we shall, backed by the written endorsement of 49 Associate County Chairmen. I imagine it is just a question of which he dislikes most, giving me my way or having me give the papers a grand chance for a story by telling the whole story at the women's dinner Monday night and by insisting

on recognition on the floor of the convention and putting the names in nomination. There's one thing I'm thankful for I haven't a thing to lose and for the moment you haven't either.[4]

Murphy held firm and Eleanor raised the flag of rebellion at the women's dinner at the Hotel Ten Eyck.

"We have now had the vote for four years and some very ardent suffragists seem to feel that instead of gaining in power the women have lost," she challenged her audience. If women wanted to achieve the objectives for which they had fought in winning the right to vote, they must not limit themselves to casting a ballot. "They must gain for themselves a place of real equality and the respect of the men,"[5] and that meant working "with" the men, not "for" them.

Then she went on with great deliberation,

It is always disagreeable to take stands. It is always easier to compromise, always easier to let things go. To many women, and I am one of them, it is extraordinarily difficult to care about anything enough to cause disagreement or unpleasant feelings, but I have come to the conclusion that this must be done for a time until we can prove our strength and demand respect for our wishes. We cannot even be of real service in the coming campaign and speak as a united body of women unless we have the respect of the men and show that when we express a wish, we are willing to stand by it.

The next day she headed a committee that called on Governor Smith, and when he supported the women's demands, Murphy capitulated. "Upstate women at the Democratic convention won the principal points in their contention that the selection of women delegates and alternates-at-large should be made by them rather than by Charles F. Murphy and other men leaders," the *New York Times* reported. "We go into the campaign feeling that our party has recognized us as an independent part of the organization and are encouraged accordingly," Eleanor told the press. "No better evidence could be shown that it is to the Democratic Party that the women voters of this State must turn if they desire to take a real part in political affairs." Governor Smith, she added, had been "a powerful factor" in bringing about this "very satisfactory conclusion."

That afternoon she presented the resolution to the convention that the New York State delegates to the Democratic national convention should be pledged to the governor. The resolution was adopted with a shout, and the chairman appointed Eleanor and Miss Martha Byrne to go to the governor's office to escort him to the platform. "It was Mrs. Roosevelt," noted the *New York Times* editorial, "a highly intelligent and capable politician," who introduced the Smith resolution at the convention.[6] The *Times* considered that a mark in Smith's favor.

The fight at the state convention she won, but the next she lost. Cordell Hull, chairman of the Democratic National Committee, appointed her chairman of a subcommittee of Democratic women to canvass the women's organizations and formulate planks on social-welfare legislation to submit to the Platform Committee at the national convention. The subcommittee she assembled was a strong one—the veteran Texas reformer, Minnie Fisher Cunningham, Mrs. Dorothy Kirchwey Brown of Massachusetts, who headed the Child Welfare Committee of the League of Women Voters, Mrs. Norrie, Elinor Morgenthau, Maud Swartz, Gertrude Ely, liberal Democrat from Bryn Mawr, Charl Williams of Tennessee, who was credited with lobbying through that state's legislature the final vote needed for ratification of the suffrage amendment, and Mrs. Solon R. Jacobs, former Alabama member of the Democratic National Committee and influential in the League of Women Voters. The subcommittee held hearings and drafted strong pro-league and Prohibition enforcement planks, equal pay for women workers, and a federal department of education, but its major objective was to commit the party to a resolution calling on the states to ratify the child-labor amendment. When the male-dominated Resolutions Committee rejected this proposal, Eleanor's committee sat outside its doors until the early hours of the morning demanding that it reconsider. The Resolutions Committee refused, by a vote of 22 to 18.

The resolute fight Eleanor and her friends made for progressive planks distinguished her group from two other claimants to leadership among women. One was Miss Elizabeth Marbury, who had been Democratic national committeewoman from New York since the passage of the suffrage amendment, for which she had fought. Though a remarkable woman, Miss Marbury gave the men no trouble; her chief interest in politics in the twenties, except for her opposition to Prohibition, was social, and her salon was famous for its mingling of high figures from the world of politics, fashion, and art. Eleanor and her colleagues were on good terms with her, but simply bypassed her. On the other side there were the embattled females of the Woman's party, who were too masculine for Eleanor's taste. Moreover, she thought the Woman's party opposition to protective legislation for women on the basis of equal rights was downright reactionary.

Although Eleanor's group was defeated in the Resolutions Committee, forces were gathering that in time would give them what they sought in the field of social-welfare legislation, including the abolition of child labor. Franklin Roosevelt returned to the political wars to nominate Alfred E. Smith with a speech that Walter Lippmann said was "perfect in temper and manner and most eloquent in its effect" and lifted the convention for a moment above "faction and hatred."

The national convention over, Roosevelt returned to his exercises, happy to have a legitimate reason to stand aside from the doomed national campaign, but Eleanor was deeply involved, more in support of the re-election of Smith as governor than in the campaign of John W. Davis. Because the national party had evaded the issue of ratification of the child-labor amendment, she was the more determined that the state convention should not. She appeared before the Platform Committee carrying a mandate from thirty women's organizations to urge a child-labor plank, and it was approved. She also represented the Women's Trade Union League in a plea for planks on the eight-hour day and minimum-wage legislation and these, too, were included in the platform.

Her speech seconding the renomination of Smith was one of the state convention's high points. A day earlier the Republicans had nominated her cousin Theodore Roosevelt, Jr., to oppose Smith, the same cousin who had called Franklin "a maverick" Roosevelt in 1920. Salt had recently been rubbed into that wound by Nicholas Longworth. "Mama is wild over Nick L. having called you in a speech a 'denatured Roosevelt,'" Eleanor wrote Franklin. Nick "was just trying to be funny," she told Sara, but she, too, was angry.[7]

"Of course he [Smith] can win," Eleanor said in her seconding speech. "How can he help it when the Republican convention yesterday did everything to help him?" The delegates did not miss the thrust, and applauded appreciatively. In the spring she had feigned concern because Louis Howe had rejoiced that some of the oil from the Teapot Dome scandal had spattered Teddy.[8] "I told him I was ashamed of such vindictiveness but he's been waiting to get even he says a long time!" In the campaign Louis' "vindictiveness" went further, and now he was actively abetted by Eleanor. Louis persuaded Eleanor and her lady Democrats to follow Teddy around the state in a motorcade that

featured a huge teakettle spouting steam, and in her speeches Eleanor
referred to her cousin as "a personally nice young man whose public
service record shows him willing to do the bidding of his friends."
Eleanor later said the teakettle affair was a "rough stunt."[9] The Oyster Bay clan sizzled, Louis beamed, and we may assume that Franklin
shed few tears.

There is a glimpse of Eleanor on the stump in the upstate rural
areas, in her own words.

"I guess you're campaigning," the speaker, a bedraggled woman
who looked fifty but probably was thirty, stood beside our car....
We were on a narrow back road in a hilly country and we were
campaigning so we acknowledged it and asked her politics, meanwhile taking a look at the farm and buildings. Everything bespoke
a helpless struggle, the poor land, run down buildings, the general
look of dirt and untidiness so we were not surprised to hear "Oh, I
ain't got much time for politics but Mr. Williams the R.F.D. man
says I must vote for Coolidge because he ain't had a chance yet and
I've always been a Republican anyways."

"No," she went on, "he ain't done much as I can see for farmers,
leastways I never had a worse time...."[10]

Eleanor was one of the few New York Democrats who stumped
in the rural districts, and her talks with farmers' wives shaped her
approach to agricultural distress. Her theme was rural-urban interdependence, which placed her in disagreement with those who felt
that a conflict between city and countryside was inevitable. "I live
in both city and country and so realize that the best interests of both
are to be promoted by better understanding of each other's situation
and cooperation rather than conflict." Because city problems had
been so obvious "all of the best brains in the land have concentrated
on solving them" and things had improved, and rural backwardness
could also be overcome "if city and country people will consider
the rural problem as a joint problem vital to both and give their best
thought to solving one of the greatest problems confronting our
nation today."[11]

Coolidge swamped Davis, who drew only 24 per cent of the vote,
not much better than LaFollette's 16 per cent. But in New York,
despite the Republican landslide, Smith won re-election.

29. LIFE WITHOUT FATHER

By THE END OF THE 1924 ELECTION CAMPAIGN SHE HAD BECOME
one of the busiest women in New York public life, but her responsibilities as wife, mother, and daughter-in-law were in no way diminished.
A crippled husband needed more attention than ever before, both
during the months when he was in New York attending to business
and politics and the household revolved about him, and in the long
stretches when he was away from New York in search of recovery and
had to be kept in touch with every household detail and especially
with his growing children.

Franklin's determination to recover the use of his legs turned into a
hunt for warm waters and balmy skies. He had discovered in Vincent
Astor's heated swimming tank that his legs regained some of their
power in warm water. In early winter 1923 he rented a houseboat, the
Weona II, on which he drifted through the waters off Florida in search
of good fishing and sandy beaches, and this was to be his pattern for
four winters. In the summer he went to Marion, Massachusetts, to
work with Dr. William McDonald on the exercises that this outstanding neurologist had devised for polio victims.

While Franklin was away Eleanor remained in New York on Sixty-
fifth Street and had to be both father and mother to the children, who
in 1924 ranged in age from eight (John) to eighteen (Anna). Alone,
too, she had to bear the brunt of Sara's harassment and discontent.

She made it seem easy and effortless, but a few lines in a thinly
veiled autobiographical article that she wrote for *Vogue* in 1930 suggested how difficult those years were for her and her loneliness in
facing them.

> Her husband was a busy man, loving her and loving his children,
> but as she sat there she realized clearly that for years to come other
> interests must come first with him and the irony of ironies, she,

who just now was groping for help, must be the one to make these other claims seem all important because she knew so well that without them the man would never be satisfied, and would never feel completely fulfilled.[1]

Her major comfort was Louis. Except for week ends which he spent with his family in Fall River, he lived in the house. Eleanor had moved him up to the fourth floor, but he came to breakfast, was often at dinner, and was always ready to counsel her. There was little she did not talk over with him. The children continued to be resentful of Louis. "I had the room next to his," James recalled.

We shared the bathroom. I thought him some kind of buddhist monk who burned incense. I didn't realize until later it was some kind of a health thing. I kind of resented the fact that he lived in the house and only later realized his contribution to Mother and Father.[2]

Sara remained a source of anxiety. The more confidently Eleanor formulated her views on the rearing of children, the more firmly she resisted Sara's interference, but the older woman had her own ways of bending the children to her will. "Those were the years," Franklin Jr. recalled, "when Granny referred to us as 'my children. Your mother only bore . . . you.'"[3] She countermanded Franklin and Eleanor by permitting the children to have things their parents withheld as a form of discipline. If she felt neglected, she would threaten to leave the offenders out of her will. "She would sometimes say before all the children together—'. . . is nicer to me than the rest of you. I think I will leave my money to him.'"[4]

James and Elliott were at Groton, but Anna, Franklin Jr., and Johnny were at home, the boys at the Buckley School, Anna finishing at Miss Chapin's. Eleanor arranged for each of the children in turn to spend part of their holidays with their father. She was in touch with Franklin's many friends who wanted to visit him—the Ledyards, de Rhams, Tom Lynch, Livy Davis, the Morgenthaus, Sir Oswald and Lady Cynthia Mosley. Disabled though Franklin was, he was usually gay and full of high jinks, and people were more than ever drawn to him.

Eleanor could squeeze in only brief visits, but she was not at home on a boat. Franklin loved a relaxed atmosphere with much laughter, prankishness, and hours devoted to stamp albums and book catalogues, which did not suit Eleanor, who was content only when she was doing something useful. Fortunately, Miss LeHand (now known as Missy) could go down and stay. Warm, competent, and attractive, she was totally devoted to the Roosevelts. Sara disapproved of this arrangement almost as strongly as she did of Louis living in the Sixty-fifth Street house, but Eleanor was grateful to the young woman. She knew that lack of mobility made the daily routines of life cumbersome and difficult for Franklin, and Missy's presence freed him from housekeeping anxieties and enabled him to stay in touch with the political world through a vast political correspondence, while it eased Eleanor's sense of guilt because she was unable to do more for him.

She herself went down for the first time in 1923, and the log of the *Weona II*, written by Franklin, suggested she was not unhappy to depart.

> Eleanor, Louis Howe, Esther Lape went fishing along the viaduct and caught 20 "Jacks." They packed each other's belongings (sic) and none of their own. From 3 p.m. till 5 they paced the hurricane deck in store clothes waiting anxiously for the train bearing the relief crew—(all of which were 2 hours late).[5]

Although Eleanor may have had reservations about joining Franklin in the South, her arrival each year was eagerly awaited. "Could we commence the Sabbath in any better way than to proceed to the station to greet the heavenly Mrs. Roosevelt [who] was expected on the morning train from Miami," wrote Julian Goldman, department-store magnate and legal client of Franklin's. The *Weona II* had been replaced by the *Larooco*, a ramshackle houseboat that Franklin and John S. Lawrence, Boston banker and Harvard friend, had jointly purchased. Frances de Rham recorded on the same day, "Mrs. F.D.R. unpacked—candy, mail, etc. and the serious business of cruising began. Mrs. F.D.R. entertained us at lunch with stories about the children." Her final entry that day reported "E.R. sleeps on deck peacefully!" Mrs. Roosevelt, Goldman elaborated,

> vindicated my high opinion of her by seizing the Heavenly deck for her sleeping quarters. Mosquitoes, flies, etc. mean nothing to her so long as the Citronella holds out.... The afternoon was spent by FDR...in catching a Fish—with Mrs. FDR...knitting and reading....After the usual evening meal Mrs. FDR...joined Capt.

Charley in Evening Services which were concluded by all singing "Onward Christian Soldiers."

Further entries in the log noted that they played bridge "at which E.R. and J.G. are again winners!" They tied up at Key West and Eleanor and Missy went ashore for mail, tickets, and papers.

Find the Admiral occupying most of the front page of the papers again with project for rejuvenating Democratic Party. . . . J.G. and E.R. spend many hours in conversation—many subjects ranging from love and marriage to the price of clothes—Mr. Goldman perfectly happy![6]

In her diary Eleanor wrote, "Mr. G. is so good and so nice but loves to talk about himself." Goldman left and the Henry Morgenthau, Jrs., arrived "tired and hot hollering for a bath. All overboard and have delightful half hour in the water. FDR swimming *much* better." A few days later Louis appeared "only 4 hours late . . . *much* conversation. . . . 4 beds arranged on the deck after violent discussion as to where which snore would annoy the least!" Louis and Eleanor played piquet, the rest parcheesi. The women swam in the early morning, clinging to the float because of sharks. "Much festivity in the evening," the log for March 17 reported, "due to the fact that it is the 20th wedding anniversary of the FDR's. Speech, green table-cloth, place cards and refreshments! Moving speech by H.M. Jr. and a presentation to the Hon. FDR of a pair of *linnen* panties." The next day there was "heavy gloom at the departure of E.R. and Missy."

"Missy weeps because last A.M. on boat!" Eleanor noted. The exclamation point indicated her own feeling that getting back to terra firma was scarcely a reason for tears.

Though she was not enthusiastic about life on a houseboat, Eleanor felt it was helping her husband. When in 1925, discouraged by the costliness of the *Larooco* and the vagaries of wind and tide, he wrote that he might sell it and concentrate on Warm Springs, she replied,

I am sorry you ever thought of giving up the boat. I think you must have had a touch of that sadness which in spite of all its sunshine the Florida landscape always gives me! It is a bit dreary as a country but I liked the life better this time than ever before and tho' I'd like to find an ideal spot where you could swim daily still I do feel it is the best thing now to do. I think you gain more at Warm Springs but it won't be practical in winter for a long time if it ever is and Florida does you *general* good which is important. I thought watching you swim you used your legs more than last summer. Don't worry about being selfish, it is more important that you have all you need and wish than anything else and you always give the chicks more than they need and you know I always do just what I want![7]

Eleanor accompanied Franklin when he first visited Warm Springs in 1924 at the suggestion of George Foster Peabody. The New York banker and philanthropist had acquired the ownership of this run-down resort built around "a miracle of warm water" gushing from a massive fissured rock "that never varied in temperature or quantity."[8] At the end of his first stay, Franklin wrote, "I walk around in water 4' deep without brace or crutches almost as well as if I had nothing the matter with my legs."[9] Warm Springs "does my legs more good than anything else." He saw its possibilities as a therapeutic center and began to negotiate for its purchase.

The financial end worried Eleanor. "Don't let yourself in for too much money," she begged Franklin,

and don't make Mama put in much for if she lost it she'd never get over it! I think you ought to ask her down to stay for a week, she's dying to go and hurt at not being asked. I'll bring her if you want and Missy could move out while she stayed.[10]

Roosevelt purchased Warm Springs from Peabody in 1926 for $195,000, most of it money he had inherited from his father. Basil O'Connor, who in 1925 had become Franklin's law partner, did the legal work on the transaction. "Something tells me Peabody's doing all right," he commented.[11] Dr. LeRoy W. Hubbard, a New York orthopedic surgeon with considerable experience in polio therapy, was persuaded to supervise the medical end, and brought Helena T. Mahoney, a trained physiotherapist, with him as an assistant.

"I know you love creative work," a dubious Eleanor wrote May 4, 1926,

my only feeling is that Georgia is somewhat distant for you to keep in touch with what is really a big undertaking. One cannot, it seems to me, have *vital* interests in widely divided places but that

may be because I'm old and rather overwhelmed by what there is
to do in one place and it wearies me to think of even undertaking
to make new ties. Don't be discouraged by me; I have great confidence in your extraordinary interest and enthusiasm. It is just that
I couldn't do it.

Warm Springs prospered under Franklin's leadership and was
approved by the American Orthopaedic Association. "Sixty-one
patients is grand but I don't see where you put them," Eleanor
exclaimed a year later. In 1928 the Edsel Fords contributed $25,000
with which to enclose the pool in glass so that it could be used the
year round. Franklin built a cottage which became, next to Hyde
Park, the place that he loved best, and he stayed there for longer and
longer periods. "I can't bear to have you away," Eleanor wrote him at
Thanksgiving, 1927. "Next year if you don't come home, I shall go up
to Groton!" She was "not keen to get into Warm Springs life at all,"
she told him when Johnny, her youngest, was about to enter boarding
school, yet she would have to get involved, she felt, if she stayed "long
or often." The atmosphere of the rural South, with its poverty and the
degradation of Negro and poor whites, depressed her.

She felt, too, that Warm Springs was Missy's domain, and there
were times she resented this and was even jealous. On her way to join
Franklin in Florida in 1925 she had chatted on a train with a lady who
told her how she lived in New York in the winter and in Long Beach
during the summer and was now on her way to Cuba to "visit some
folks." No, her husband did not mind; he was busy with the Elks and
Masons at night and was at his office all day. "An unconscious tragedy
told," Eleanor commented in her diary. She had escaped that kind of
loneliness by developing interests that were her own but that also fitted
into Franklin's long-range political plans. Nevertheless, she, too, was
a lonely woman. "No form of love is to be despised," she wrote in her
diary on the same trip, quoting from *The Constant Nymph*, which she
was reading. Franklin did not offer the love for which she yearned, and
she had to build her life around the acceptance of that fact. Theirs was
now a carefully arranged relationship, but while behavior and action
could be managed, she had less control over her feelings. She still was
attracted by this man, still hoped and grieved that he could not show
her the tenderness and unselfish devotion for which her spirit thirsted.
So she was grateful to Missy and treated her almost as one of her children, and kept the pangs she suffered to herself.

Real maturity, she wrote at the end of her life in the little book *You Learn by Living*, was the ability to look at oneself honestly and acknowledge the fact that there is

> a limitation in me. Here is a case where, because of some lack of experience or some personal incapacity, I cannot meet a situation; I cannot meet the need of someone whom I dearly love.... Either you must learn to allow someone else to meet the need, without bitterness or envy, and accept it; or somehow you must make yourself learn to meet it.... There is another ingredient of the maturing process that is almost as painful as accepting your own limitation and the knowledge of what you are unable to give. That is learning to accept what other people are unable to give. You must learn not to demand the impossible or to be upset when you do not get it.

That was the code she had worked out for herself; but her heart sometimes mutinied against that which her mind accepted as harsh necessity.

There were other reasons why she did not wish to become involved in Warm Springs. She was reluctant to have to fit into a life and place that belonged wholly to Franklin. Hyde Park bore the imprint of Sara's personality; Warm Springs that of Franklin's. She was developing her own style of life and did not want to give it up. She was, moreover, more useful to Franklin in New York. None of this persuaded Sara, who was constantly after her to spend less time on public activity and more with her husband and children. "It is nice to have Eleanor back,"[12] she wrote her son, "but I feel badly to have you so long without her." But this rarely was an issue between husband and wife.

Since Franklin was unable to help his younger sons in outdoor activities, Eleanor set about overcoming her own disabilities. She learned to ice skate; she finally mastered swimming by taking lessons at the Y; and she even made an attempt at tennis. "I practiced serving for half an hour today and nearly had apoplexy!" In 1925 she, Nan, and Marion took Franklin Jr., Johnny, Hall's son Henry, and Dr. Draper's son George Jr. on a camping trip through the Adirondacks in the old seven-passenger Buick, then up to Quebec and to Campobello. If there were no public camping sites, Eleanor, the most persuasive member of the group, talked farmers into giving them permission to pitch tents in their fields. "Where are your husbands?" one farmer wanted to know. "Mine is not with me and the others don't have husbands," she replied. "I don't want women of that kind," the farmer said with finality.[13]

Their arrival in Campobello was described in a letter Franklin, who was at Marion, sent to Rosy.

All goes well. Eleanor and the rest of the caravan reached Campobello in safety, the only accidents being first, Franklin Jr. cutting his foot with the axe, instead of the tree; second, skidding off the road into the ditch and having to be pulled out; and third, upsetting a dray just as they approached Lubec and dumping the load of lumber and the small boy who was driving it—total cost of damages, $10.[14]

James and Elliott spent the summer of 1925 on the C. M. Ranch in Wyoming. Judging by a letter sixteen-year-old James sent Eleanor, Sara evidently had tried to enlist him in her campaign to keep Eleanor at home.[15] "I did think that you were trying to do a little too much travelling and that you would get too tired out," he wrote, "but I guess you're the best judge of what you can do."

She made regular trips to Groton for the special events open to parents and to consult with the rector and the masters on less auspicious occasions. "I wonder if the Rector can't be induced to have a better science department," she wrote after one such visit.[16] There was a steady flow of letters from James and Elliott to Eleanor, which she forwarded to Franklin, and to Franklin, which he forwarded to her. She often intervened for Elliott. She had wanted to send him to public school but was too unsure of herself to insist in the face of tradition and the resistance of Franklin and Sara. Elliott was having a hard time with his older brother and needed encouragement. Eleanor thought Franklin should invite him South, and Franklin did. James entered Harvard in 1926, but although Elliott's grades improved he did not want to follow family tradition. "I wonder if his desire to go to Princeton will be a disappointment to you," she wrote her husband. "I think not being with James is a good thing and of course if he has his choice he will feel the obligation to make good."[17] In the end Elliott refused to go to college at all and wouldn't speak to Eleanor for months when she insisted that he had to pass his entrance examinations whether or not he went on to college.

Eleanor had an easier time with James. He had resented his mother's new friends, especially Louis, but by the end of 1926 he was playing bridge with Louis and being tutored by Marion Dickerman. Eleanor did not want him to go to Harvard. Franklin talked vaguely about sending him to Wisconsin University, but it was clear he hoped James would choose Harvard. James did, as did all the boys except Elliott.

James' first reports from college were full of the papers he had to write, the books he had to read, and the freshman elections, in which he was chosen class secretary-treasurer. Some of the undergraduate rites did not appeal to Eleanor; election to the Hasty Pudding and Fly Clubs involved substantial initiation fees and heavy drinking. "Too bad James needs the money," she wrote her husband. "You never can get away from your gold diggers, can you? I can't say three nights drunk fills me with anything but disgust!"[18] She and Franklin were worried that James would be too interested in social life and having a good time, and their fears were borne out when he was placed on probation. He had to give up running for the student council and his work with the Phillips Brooks House, and wrote a contrite letter to his mother: "I have learned what we talked about and it is better to learn it now when I can make the changes." The letter impressed Eleanor. "He's taking it very well and tho' I'm sorry about it still I think it was the best thing [that] could have happened."[19]

At the end of his freshman year James went abroad to bicycle around England, he told his parents. Eleanor suspected the real reason was to see Lucy Archer-Shee, whom James thought he wanted to marry, "but of course she or he may have changed a number of times before he is earning $5,000 a year which is the minimum I told him he could marry on much to his dismay!"[20] The next year James wanted to go abroad again, this time with Sara, who would finance the trip. His parents thought he should work that summer, but were not arbitrary. Eleanor had long ago concluded that discipline and scolding were ineffectual if the inner motivation to act differently was lacking. "I've had long talks with James and Elliott and the net result is that I think perhaps we've been making a mistake," she wrote Franklin.

It all comes down to the old question of necessity. If they saw the need it would be logical but as it is it is tyranny. Mr. Rawle has told James that the work of the college years is in college and the holidays should be used to see things they may not for many years have another chance to see or do, and work in a job should be left to be undertaken at the close of college and then pursued unrelentingly. His inclination, and Elliott's also, runs along with this and so it seems an unreasonable request. James looked very badly and was plainly troubled about money when he arrived and I think we can push too far and therefore hope you will let him go abroad with Mama and return in August stipulating that on his return he stay at H.P. You could tell him that he must get rooted there if he ever hopes to go into politics. Mama will pay his way over and back and the $500 you would have paid to take him to Houston will cover his time over there. Mama says she will give him a Ford in the autumn and I think now he's proved steady you'd better let him have it. She'll help on his allowance too I know. . . . I will stay with the little boys this summer and economize in every way on the house and tutor and travelling so you ought to be able to make your political contributions and still get by.[21]

Eleanor's greatest problems were with Anna, who was having a most difficult time. Eleanor was experiencing the usual anxieties mothers have about pretty daughters who have become conscious of the world of young men. "I was so guarded that even at 18 I was not allowed to go to a movie without a chaperone," Anna later said. "And on that Mother went along 100 per cent with Granny." Anna did not wish to come out. "Granny said I had to—and Mother went along." Her grandmother picked out her clothes and Cousin Susie invited her to tennis week at Newport "along with a couple of suitable young men to squire me. And Mother went along."[22]

When Anna finished Miss Chapin's, Sara again took her abroad in the winter and spring of 1925, and Anna gave her some hard times on the trip. To Sara's horror, a distant cousin took the girl on a tour of the Rome slums. Then an English lord became interested in her, and in desperation Sara telegraphed London to have a former governess come down and take charge. When they returned, Anna confided to her mother that she would never again travel on the continent alone with Sara. "We've had lots of talks and she's a dear and I'm glad you'll have a chance to give her some good advice."[23] The advice was needed about what Anna should do now that she was finished at Miss Chapin's. Sara did not want her to go to college, and cautioned her on the dangers of becoming a grind because young men would be intimidated by her and she would end up an old maid. This fear was not high on Eleanor's list. Her letters to Franklin spoke of "the inevitable young man" that was always somewhere in the vicinity. Anna had a feeling for outdoor life and a talent with animals, and felt that the summer she had spent with the Greenways on their Arizona ranch camping out on the desert was the best of her life. Her parents talked her into taking what she called "a short-horn agricultural course" at Cornell. Eleanor consulted with Henry Morgenthau, who suggested she first attend the Geneva (New York) State Experimental Station for six weeks as "it would provide the practical background for her Cornell course." Anna did not want to go, and when Eleanor drove her to Geneva they didn't say a word to each other the entire time. "Just now I am more worried about Anna than anyone," she wrote Franklin afterward.[24]

Though Anna no longer sided with her grandmother against Eleanor, she did not take her mother's admonitions kindly. "She doesn't care to write me, I evidently was too severe and we have not had a line since," Eleanor noted. Anna accepted her father's good-humored advice with better grace. "I am so pleased at her letter to you," Eleanor commented. "She has evidently not resented what you wrote in the way she did my letter and I'd rather have it that way for then you can be sure she'll take your advice on anything important."[25] She should not worry so much, Franklin advised her; it was just a matter of being nineteen.

Anna and James were both at the age when going out meant making a night of it, and Eleanor caught catnaps waiting for them to come in. "Wednesday night it was 4 a.m. and today 6 a.m.," she noted wearily, adding, "I will say, however, that even my suspicious nature could not imagine that he'd had too much to drink!" She napped on the sofa in Anna's room until Anna came in, and it was after one particularly trying vigil that she told Anna about the Lucy Mercer affair. It was the "first really adult conversation I had with my mother," Anna later said.[26]

Sara needn't have feared that Anna would become an old maid. The Cornell course, short as it was, was abandoned abruptly when Anna became engaged to Curtis Dall, a stockbroker about ten years her senior, and she was married at twenty. "I got married when I did because I wanted to get out," she said, to escape the tension and conflict between her mother and grandmother.[27] Typical of the friction between the two older women was the row precipitated by Sara's wedding gift to Anna and Curtis.

On Thursday Anna told me Mama had offered to give them an apartment . . . as a wedding present but she was not to tell me as she thought I would dissuade them from taking it. . . . While it is a lovely thing for her to do I am so angry at her offering anything to a child of mine without speaking to me if she thought I would object and for telling her not to tell me that it is all I can do to be decent and I've really tried to be thoughtful since Aunt Annie died. Sometimes I think constant irritation is worse for one than real tragedy now and then. I've reached a state of such constant self-control that sometimes I'm afraid of what will happen if it ever breaks![28]

It was not only Sara's deviousness that angered Eleanor. She felt that the luxurious apartment, which Anna did not want, would commit the couple to an expensive style of life that was Sara's, not theirs, and that they would be able to maintain it only by continual subventions from Sara.

Sara wrote a bland letter of explanation to her son. "I am sorry I could not consult with you and Eleanor, but as it is my wedding present, I feel I should do it alone, also two other people had options on it."[29] Eleanor had first decided not to say anything to Sara, but she finally did. "Eleanor dear," an upset Sara wrote her afterward:

> I am very sorry that I hurt you *twice*, first by not letting Anna tell you before it was decided and then by saying I would not give it to them. I certainly am old enough not to make mistakes and I can only say how much I regret it. I did not think I *could* be nasty *or* mean, and I fear I had too good an opinion of myself. Also I love you dear too much to ever want to hurt you. I *was hasty* and of course I shall give them the apartment. I only wanted them to decide for *themselves* and surprise you and Franklin. No doubt he will also be angry with me. Well, I must just bear it.
>   Devotedly
>   Mama

Eleanor sent this letter on to Franklin, saying, "I answered quite politely and apologized for answering her questions frankly and commenting on her subsequent remarks and told her you never demeaned yourself by getting angry over little things so you see I've been thoroughly nasty but I'll try to behave again now for a time."[30]

Anna and Curtis moved into the apartment in the autumn of 1926. "I want to help her," Eleanor wrote her husband,

> but not be about and do the superintending for I'm too executive not to do it all and then she'd never feel it was her own. Then next

week I'll go and do some arranging with her when she knows what she wants. Mamma says I'm cruel to "leave the poor child alone"![31]

Eleanor sent Franklin a column by Angelo Patri, an educator, on the relationship that should exist between parents and children. "The enclosed meets my views and I think you'll like it too," she commented. "You are entitled to one life—your own," Patri urged. "Live it, start the children on their way and then plunge back into your own again." Eleanor elaborated her own views on the subject in an article, "Ethics of Parents," that she submitted to *Collier's* in 1927.[32] "Why not try letting our children go for a change?" she asked. The fact that parents and children lived in the same house does not mean "inner understanding" of the younger by the older generation. It was important to help young people "in the way they wished to be helped and not in the way we think they should be helped." With too many parents their attitude "comes down to this very often. 'Do as I wish and I will help you in every possible way, but otherwise, oh, no!'" That statement reflected her bitter experience with Sara, but when she went on to say, "How about abstaining from criticism or advice when it is not asked?" she was voicing a lesson that she herself had had to learn. "I have yet to see the time when the unpleasant truths we 'feel it our duty' to tell our children really helped a difficult situation, but of course it relieved our own minds."

Collier's did not publish the article. "I have made three or four attempts to rewrite the story," associate editor Walter Davenport wrote her. "Each effort injured rather than helped.... At any rate, none seemed to arouse the enthusiasm of Mr. Chenery [the editor]." Eleanor filed the manuscript and started work on a piece for the *North American Review* on "Why Democrats Favor Smith," which was published.

Her first grandchild was born in March, 1927. "Such a 36 hours as we have had!" Eleanor reported to Franklin. Anna had her child at her mother's house.

everything was prepared but we waited all day. It wasn't hard and the new way is marvelous but it was long and tedious for the child. However, after an active second night the young lady appeared at 5 A.M. The boys will tell you about her. She weighs 7½ pounds, her eyes are blue, so far her hair is black, her mouth large, her ears very flat. Anna is tired but sleeping a lot.... Mama is thrilled.[33]

Sara wrote her son she was

> sorry the young grandfather could not be here for the great event.
> Eleanor sat all last night with Anna and came to my room this
> morning perfectly dressed and her hair perfect as if she had just left
> the dinner table! I think she is a wonder!

Sara never reconciled herself to the new order of things—Eleanor's
living her own life, Franklin's mixing the search for recovery with
continued activity in business and politics, Franklin and Eleanor's
unwillingness to interfere in the lives of the children as she had in
theirs. "I wish you could read Mama's last letter to me," Eleanor wrote
Franklin in exasperation.

> She is afraid of everything in it! Afraid of your going over bad and
> unfrequented roads, afraid I'll let the children dive in shallow water
> and break their necks, afraid they'll get more cuts! She must suffer
> more than we dream is possible![34]

Franklin had less patience with his mother than Eleanor. "I have seen
a strong man struggle half his life for emancipation from the gentle
but narrowing control of his mother," Eleanor wrote in the "Ethics of Parents" article, "and achieve it in the end only through what
seemed heartlessness and entire lack of consideration." After a surge
of annoyance and anger, Franklin's good nature and jollity reasserted
themselves. He had his problems with Sara, but there was not the
tension between Franklin and his mother that there was between
Eleanor and Sara. Perhaps he sensed that the struggle was over him,
but in any case he tried to stay out of it. He would sympathize with
Eleanor, and then would add, "I have always told you that if you give
Mama an inch she will take an ell."[35] Eleanor's letters were full of her
difficulties with Sara: "Mama has done nothing but get in little side
slaps today." "Mama was awful last Sunday and made us feel each in
turn that we'd like to chew her up." Sara, like her son, would be horrid
one moment and surprised that all was not forgiven and forgotten the
next. She considered the two houses on Sixty-fifth Street "absolutely
comfortable and well planned and nice in every way" while Eleanor
was looking at cooperative apartments so that they might move after
John went to Groton.[36] Sara criticized Eleanor's clothes, posture, taste,

and activities one day, and the next praised her extravagantly. "Eleanor is a wonder, so busy, and so sweet and so amiable all the time."

That is what she really thought—but jealousy often warped her judgment and reactions. "Your library will have no chintz covers," Eleanor indignantly wrote Franklin,

> because Mama told me she could make it attractive in half an hour and everyone liked her house better than mine and we had all the things to make a nice room only it needed taste, so I told her to go ahead and do it. Later she said she never liked to interfere so she didn't think she would and I said nothing would be done so I think you'll probably return to have to do it yourself! If it weren't funny I would probably blow up but I shan't.[37]

A week later she was still stubborn. "It wouldn't cost much to put slip covers in the Library, but I'm just obstinate after Mama's remarks and it is either done by her or not at all!"[38]

Eleanor could be stubborn with Louis, too, and not only over the issue of Prohibition. "It has been so hot that the furnaces have been let out in the house and in consequence a cold wave has swept in from the West and taken unfair advantage of us," he wrote his chief in Warm Springs.

> I expect to spend the balance of the springtime sitting around 49 East 65th Street in my overcoat with a quilt over my shoulders, for I rashly suggested to your Missus that one hot day did not make a summer and in consequence, as you can easily guess, 20 below zero would not let her admit that she was wrong by having the furnaces started up again.[39]

30. A LIFE OF HER OWN

ELEANOR'S BEST DEFENSE AGAINST SARA WAS TO GET AWAY FROM her, and by June, 1927, when she was writing Franklin that she "simply couldn't stand" staying at Hyde Park with Sara, she had a place of escape when Franklin and the children were not there, a place that she could share with her friends without having to negotiate with Sara whether it was all right for them to come. Sara was perfectly polite, always cordial, but she resented Eleanor's new friends. Rosy, whose reactions were much like Sara's, wrote Franklin, "Hope your Parlour Socialists are not living too much on the fat of the land with you, against their principles!!"[1]

Eleanor knew how the family felt about her friends, and when Franklin began to talk about a swimming pool near the Big House at Hyde Park, she persuaded him to combine it with a cottage that she, Nan, and Marion wanted to build beside the Val-Kill brook. "My Missus and some of her female political friends want to build a shack on a stream in the back woods and want, instead of a beautiful marble bath, to have the stream dug out so as to form an old-fashioned swimming hole," Franklin wrote Elliot Brown,[2] a friend from his Navy days whom he asked to supervise the project.

"We used to go up to Hyde Park for weekends and take the boys," Marion recalled.

We were having a picnic and Eleanor said, "This is our last weekend because Granny is closing the house for the winter." Franklin said "You girls are very foolish. Why don't you build a cottage for yourselves?" So we got to playing with the idea. Franklin then said, "if you mark out the land you want, I will give you a life interest with the understanding that it reverts to my estate with your death." So we drew up a paper that Louis, Franklin, Nan, Eleanor and I signed.[3]

Franklin, who had forceful views on the architectural style that was appropriate to the Hudson, decided the cottage should be made of field-stone and he worked with Henry Toombs, the architect, on the plans. The bids the women received seemed exorbitant. Finally Franklin told them, "If you three women will go away, Henry and I will build the cottage." On New Year's Day, 1926, the three women had their first meal there sitting on nail kegs, a crate being used as a table. The fol-lowing spring Sara was writing her son that while she, Curt, and Anna were at the Big House, Eleanor and the little boys were at the cottage,

> but they came over here for some hours today and tomorrow they lunch here. We three are invited for supper tomorrow at the cottage and they all lunch here on Sunday. Eleanor is so happy over there that she looks well and plump, don't tell her so, it is very becoming, and I hope she will not grow thin.[4]

"The cottage is beginning to look sweet," Eleanor wrote her hus-band, on "Val-Kill Cottage" stationery.[5] Nan and Marion lived there, but she used it often.

> I was delighted after I took all to the train at five to go back and say goodbye (to Mama) and come over here for a quiet evening with Nan. I've written two editorials and three letters and we have had supper and the peace of it is divine, but we have to take the 10:05 down tomorrow.[6]

The children loved the Big House, as did their father, but Eleanor never felt at home there. Even when Sara was away her spirit and pres-ence were everywhere. "This house seems too queer without you," Eleanor wrote her, "and there is no doubt in my mind but houses reflect the central spirit and are just empty shells without them!"[7]

Nan's undertaking to build the furniture for the cottage evolved into a more ambitious plan to start a furniture factory nearby to pro-duce authentic copies of early American pieces. Both Franklin and Eleanor shared a long-time concern with a better rural-urban bal-ance, and with his encouragement Eleanor helped establish the shop "primarily...to carry out a theory...about establishing industries in agricultural counties to give men and boys a means of earning money in winter and something interesting to do." Nan went to the

Metropolitan Museum in New York, to the Chicago and Hartford museums, and later to Monticello, to copy designs. Skilled Norwegian and Italian cabinet makers were employed to train the local boys. But Nan was the moving spirit here, hanging over her bottles and jars in search of the stain she wanted with the "passion of a medieval alchemist," and every piece, after the stain was applied, was rubbed and polished until the wood had the texture of velvet. Eleanor put up most of the capital—out of her growing earnings from radio and writing, as well as some of the little money she had inherited.[8]

As a first project, the women built the furniture for Franklin's new cottage in Warm Springs. "The furniture from the Val-Kill shop is a great success," Franklin wrote. By the spring of 1927 they were ready for their first exhibition, which was held at the Roosevelt Sixty-fifth Street house. The price list ranged from $40 for "trestle-table, round" to $175 for a large maple chest of drawers. "The work is handwrought and beautifully finished in every detail and copied with exactness from genuine antiques," said the *New York Times*.[9] Eleanor and Nan persuaded Abraham & Straus to send up buyers,

> and though they say they only sell cheap furniture, they've ordered $610 worth and are making an exhibit of it....I'm going to try Sloane's...and perhaps ask Grover Whalen if the Wanamaker shop in Philadelphia might be interested.[10]

Their early brochures spoke of "Roosevelt Industries," and Eleanor tried to interest the local women in weaving and other handiwork. She recruited women for a weaving class from the Hyde Park League of Women Voters and joined the class herself, but she did not have Nan's flair for design and craftsmanship. Her contributions to Val-Kill were those of executive, merchandiser, and inspirer.

Val-Kill Industries did not fully satisfy her need to do things herself, to develop skills of her own, to be useful professionally. In touch now with many professional women, she was bitter over her own inadequacies. "If I had to go out and earn my own living, I doubt if I'd even make a very good cleaning woman," she said. "I have no talents, no experience, no training for anything."[11] So when Marion, who was teaching at and vice principal of Todhunter, a private school for girls in New York City, was offered a chance to buy the school, Eleanor said, "I have no more children at home. Why don't we buy it together?"[12] With the shining example of Marie Souvestre in the back of her mind, she had always found teaching appealing. Franklin approved of the plan to buy the school and of Eleanor's decision to teach in it.

Her first efforts as a teacher evidently were disappointing. "I can't say I am set up by the exams my children did," she wrote Franklin. "I only flunked one but the others were none too good."[13] Yet when Marion asked her to take on a heavier schedule the following year she agreed.

She taught courses in literature, drama, and American history. Her drama course began with Aeschylus and ended with Eugene O'Neill, and her class in nineteenth-century English and American literature was equally wide-ranging. Notes for this class included biographical data on the writers she dealt with as well as remarks on their style and characteristics. She found her Allenswood notebooks quite useful. She was the moralist in literature; at that time it constricted her taste. She, Esther, and Elizabeth gave one night a week to reading French literature. Esther, on a trip to Paris, sent her André Gide's *Les Faux Monnayeurs*. The homosexual theme shocked her. "I read the book as the story of a sensitive relationship sensitively told," Esther said. "She read it in terms of a forbidden subject. She couldn't bring herself even to consider homosexuality. Generally her reaction was not so final, but in this case it was."[14]

In her history class, she emphasized "the connection between things of the past and things of today." Her examinations were given in two parts, one designed to test a knowledge of dates and facts, the other to encourage the girls to think for themselves. "Give your reason for or against allowing women to actively participate in the control of government, politics and officials through the vote, as well as your reasons for or against women holding office in the government." "How are Negroes excluded from voting in the South?" "What is the object today of inheritance, income and similar taxes?" (Most of her students came from families of wealth and high social standing.)

She was educating herself as well as her pupils. There were such reminders and admonitions to herself in her classbook as "look up Vikings" or "trace the trade routes better," and the general injunction, "be more exact." She used the "project method" in her homework assignments. When the class reached the Declaration of Independence she asked the girls to

read any life [of a signer] you like. Get any pictures you can. Visit the museum and see if you can find anything in the museum belonging to them. Write about any present day descendants. Look up furniture of the Colonial period in the museum. Make book with pictures.

Later she gave a class in current events, called "Happenings," for the older girls. "I would like them to see the worst type of old-time tenement," she wrote Jane Hoey of the Welfare Council.[15] She took them to courts, police line-ups, markets, and settlement houses so that they might have a firsthand picture of how the city was run.

Her courses in modern history and current events made greater use of newspapers and magazines than they did of textbooks. A teacher should start from a young person's own present interest, she felt, and lead them into a wider and deeper understanding of the world into which they were going. "It is the teacher's function," she told Eunice Fuller Barnard, the education editor of the *New York Times*, "to manage this relating process, to seize all opportunities, however unpromising, to make all history and literature and the seemingly barren study of the machinery of government somehow akin to the things pupils are doing in their daily life."[16] She modeled herself on Mlle. Souvestre. The *Times* observed that

no slipshod phrases escaped her, and again and again a girl was asked to define her terms. Nor did sonorous phrases parroted from textbook or dictionary get by. "That's what the book says," Mrs. Roosevelt would smile serenely. "Now, how would you put it?"[17]

Todhunter was progressive in its use of the project method in teaching, but it was also traditional.

We still have frequent tests and mid-term and final examinations as well as reports and marks of the traditional school. For we believe that the girls will have to take certain hurdles in life, and that hurdles in school are an important preparation.[18]

The way the school day began was also traditional. Promptly at ten minutes of nine, the hundred uniformed girls, ranging from five to eighteen, marched into the assembly room

to a stirring march on the piano. . . . And Mrs. Roosevelt and Miss Dickerman, stately figures in tailored dark red gowns and low-heeled oxfords, like those the girls are required to wear, stand behind a long table in front to receive them. There is a hymn, a prayer and announcements, and a friendly talk about school plans in which the girls take part. Then comes another song of the girls' own choosing, which may be as popular as they please. The morning I was there they sang "Polly-wolly-doodle" with great relish. And they march out again to classes.[19]

"Teaching gave her some of the happiest moments in her life," said Marion. "She loved it. The girls worshipped her. She was a very inspiring person." When Franklin was elected governor of New York in 1928, she determinedly retained her ties with Todhunter, leaving Albany on Sunday night, teaching two and a half days and returning to the capital Wednesday afternoon.

Many, perhaps a majority, of Todhunter girls were drawn from Social Register families. Eleanor tried to broaden their horizons and widen their sympathies, but the very concept of a "private" school gave her difficulty. In Europe, she noted, obligatory military service brought together men from all social backgrounds thus for a time wiping out class distinctions. Public schools should do this in the United States, "but unfortunately many of our children are so closely confined amongst the little groups of people which form their immediate circle of family and friends, that they have very little opportunity to develop any knowledge or judgment of human beings as a whole."[20] To bring up young people in the belief

that their own particular lives are typical of the whole world is to bring up extraordinarily narrow people and every parent should demand of the school in which they place their children that if possible, there be a wide range of types in order that the child may be given an opportunity to develop its knowledge of the world and its own powers of choosing desirable companions.[21]

She was critical of mothers who did not inquire how well a school stood scholastically "but only whether the children that her daughter will meet will benefit her when she is ready to enter into that strange thing called 'society,'" a word which, she indicated, had lost its magic and meaning.

There was a time in New York City when the City was comparatively small and much was heard of "the four hundred." Perhaps there were really only four hundred people who could afford the gaieties and elegant leisure of the society of the day, which was represented by an old lady in a magnificent house, who gave remarkable parties to a few people, many of whom, while they may have belonged to the society of the four hundred, scarcely can have been said to have either ornamented or elevated its standing in the greater social organization we call civilization.

But today there was no such thing

in the larger cities at least, as any one group which may be called "society.". . . there is no such thing possible in this country as an aristocracy of society based on birth. We set up a material basis as the final criterion of social eligibility, certainly in our larger cities.[22]

During her Washington days when she had come to New York she had told Sara that the people she wanted to see were Ruth Ledyard, Pauline Emmet, Nathalie Swan, Helen Wilmerding, Caroline Trevor, Mary Morgan, Helen Robinson, and Cousin Susie. She was still fond of these people, but she saw much less of them. "I've had a long sobbing letter from Cousin Susie who says I've only been there twice all winter so I must make an effort to see more of her!" She still paid her dues to the Monday Evening Sewing Class and the Colony and Cosmopolitan Clubs, but she no longer took "society" seriously. The most satisfactory friends, she had now discovered, were those with whom she worked.

31. SMITH'S DEFEAT, ROOSEVELT'S VICTORY

POLITICS IN ONE FORM OR ANOTHER TOOK MORE AND MORE OF Eleanor's time as the 1928 presidential campaign neared. "Women should not be afraid to soil their hands" by getting into politics, she urged everywhere. "Those who are not make the best politicians."[1] Together with Caroline O'Day, Elinor Morgenthau, Nancy Cook, and Marion Dickerman, she infused energy and purpose into the work of the women's division of the Democratic State Committee.

There was a great deal of drudgery. She had raised $6,000 toward the women's budget, she wrote her husband. "I have $24,000 to raise, do suggest some people to do it."[2] Each year it was a new struggle. "I hate the money-raising job and I wish I could resign," she wrote Franklin.[3] But she never did, and when, that same year, they began to publish a monthly magazine, the *Democratic News*, she took on the job of advertising manager as well as editor. "I've visited 12 or 15 men, can't do more than four a day and only have four ads, so far," she lamented.[4] "I'm learning the advertising business," her next letter exulted.

I spent an hour with Mr. Franklin Simon, who gave me advice, an "ad," and several names. This p.m. I'm getting my rate card done with H. M. Jr.'s "ad" man, so you see this bulletin is going to be a real business proposition before we get thro' if hard work can do it.

She wrote the editorials, solicited contributions from prominent Democrats—including her husband—and kept in touch with a network of correspondents in every county. Behind the scenes Louis was her chief collaborator. He taught her the tricks of layout, headline writing, and composing a terse lead, occasionally doing the job himself. Louis was pleased with Eleanor's progress as a politician and advised Franklin that his "Missus" was "gaining in political wisdom every day."[5]

She often went to Albany to do battle with recalcitrant legislators on behalf of legislation for women and children. When the assembly held a hearing, the manufacturers' lobby brought shop girls to Albany who asserted they were perfectly content with a 50- and 54-hour week, that a 48-hour bill would eliminate jobs. "What we want most of all is protection from the non-working and professional uplifters," an employee of the BMT declared. Disregard the "sob stuff," Eleanor urged the assemblymen when she rose to speak. The "great majority of the working women of this State are really in favor of this bill and would like to see it become law. I can't understand how any woman would want to work 54 hours a week if she only has to work 48 and could receive the same rate of wages."[6] The battle for the 48-hour law went into the 1926 and 1927 legislatures where she again clashed with the lobbyists for industry.[7]

Throughout the twenties the drive for progressive social and labor legislation in New York was directed by the Joint Legislative Conference, which had been initiated by the Women's Trade Union League and included the Consumers League, the League of Women Voters, the Women's City Club, the industrial board of the YWCA, the American Association for Labor Legislation, the WCTU, and the New York Child Labor Committee. One of its most stalwart members was Mary W. "Molly" Dewson, civic secretary of the Women's City Club, a no-nonsense lady who combined tough-mindedness with vision. She had worked for twelve years as superintendent of parole for girls in Massachusetts, gone to France during the war with the American Red Cross, and after the war, as research secretary of the National Consumers League, had helped Felix Frankfurter prepare the economic briefs in the District of Columbia and California minimum-wage cases. She had first met Eleanor the autumn of 1924, when, according to Molly, the president of the Women's City Club had introduced her to "a tall, slender woman who was hastening out of the room. "This is our new Vice President, Mrs. Franklin D. Roosevelt,' she said. . . . In that fleeting second, I felt her human warmth, sincerity and genuine interest in other persons."[8] Molly lived in the same cooperative house on West Twelfth Street as Nan and Marion, and she, too, became a co-worker of Eleanor's.

The program of the Joint Legislative Conference, Molly wrote in her memoirs, included such long-standing progressive objectives as unemployment compensation, minimum-wage legislation, old-age pensions.[9] The work of the conference, she thought, had had a large educational effect upon Franklin Roosevelt through Eleanor, who had served as chairman of the conference one year and who, by 1926, was militantly walking the picket line with Rose Schneiderman and using her considerable political influence within the Democratic party on behalf of the advanced goals of the conference. She had developed into a hard-hitting campaigner whom the Democrats frequently asked to present the party's viewpoint in debates, as she demonstrated in the 1926 senatorial campaign when Justice Robert F. Wagner was the Democratic candidate against incumbent James Wadsworth. Eleanor would have preferred Owen D. Young to Wagner, but Wagner was better than Wadsworth, whom she smilingly shrugged off in a debate as "a country squire of the 17th century in politics . . . in the 20th century." Warming up to this theme, she added that he had a "Marie Antoinette type of mind."

In 1926 she was elected to the holy of holies of the suffrage movement—the Leslie Commission, the group of nine women who presided over the disbursement of the fund that Mrs. Frank Leslie, widow of the publisher of *Leslie's Weekly*, had left Mrs. Catt in 1914 with which to advance the cause of women's rights. "You have qualified," Mrs. Catt wrote Eleanor on her election as a director. "I should add that you were nominated and seconded by two 'black Republicans.'"[10]

There were other signs of Eleanor's growing effectiveness. Radio was coming into its own and she was often asked to present the woman's viewpoint. She had become a practiced lecturer. Pearl Buck, a graduate student at Cornell in the mid-twenties, was on the committee to meet and escort her the day she came to Ithaca to lecture to the Home Economics Department. "It was her energy that struck me most that day." Her clothes were nondescript—an ankle-length purple satin dress, a brown tweed coat, bright tan oxfords—but her disregard of style did not matter. She had "a disarming kind of shyness. She was full of self-confidence and was anxious to please." Her speech was "good," and then there was a luncheon "invented" by the Home Economics Department. "It seemed to be mostly raw cabbage. . . . It was an uneatable meal so far as I was concerned. Mrs. Roosevelt ate it with great gusto, however, and congratulated the head of the department on having achieved this meal. . . . I remember her gay, high-pitched voice commenting on everything." Miss Buck was on the receiving line before dinner. "She shook each hand vigorously. She was the soul of good humor and not a whit Then they proceeded to dinner "and when we saw her off on the train I was completely exhausted."[11]

It was Louis Howe who had almost literally pitched her into the lecture circuit. "When I expressed some idea he thought was good he would snarl, 'For goodness sake, why don't you put it on paper?' Or else in his gruff but sweet manner he would say, 'Get out and talk.'"[12] Magazines had begun to invite her to write for them, and paid her generous fees. One article—"What I Want Most Out of Life," which appeared in *Success Magazine* in May, 1927—was highly personal yet representative of the new perplexities confronting women: what should they do with their vote and their growing leisure? "I suppose if I were asked what is the best thing one can expect in life, I would say—the privilege of being useful," the article began. She was particularly concerned with the woman over forty, whose children were grown and away from home and who did not have to worry too much about contributing to the family budget. She regretted that more women were not interested in politics. "More than anything else, it [politics] may serve to guard against the emptiness and loneliness that enter some women's lives after their children are grown." Even while children are growing up mothers should become

> accustomed gradually and while they are still comparatively youthful, to having lives, interests and personalities of their own apart from their households. . . . Home comes first. But—in second and third and last place there is room for countless other concerns. . . . And so if anyone were to ask me what I want out of life I would say—the opportunity for doing something useful, for in no other way, I am convinced, can true happiness be obtained.

It was not, in essentials, too different from the analysis of how to achieve happiness that she had written for Mlle. Souvestre a quarter of a century earlier.

Redbook asked her to write on women and politics, and she did a piece entitled "Women Must Learn to Play the Game As Men Do."[13] She was elated when *McCall's* offered her $500 "and only 2,500 words. . . . I suppose James will tell me he 'wouldn't write for such a magazine' as he did about the *Redbook* but I am glad of the chance!"[14]

S. J. Woolf, who interviewed her for the *New York Times Magazine*, was thoroughly taken with her:

> Seated at a small desk . . . she posed for a drawing, spoke about women in politics, answered innumerable telephone calls, arranged

her son's departure from the city and directed household affairs; and all before 10 o'clock in the morning for at that time she had to leave to give a talk at the girls' school at which she teaches.[15]

"She is the strongest argument," Woolf concluded, "that could be presented against those who hold that by entering politics a woman is bound to lose her womanliness and her charm." Mlle. Souvestre would have liked that.

By 1927 Democratic women were strongly organized throughout the state. Whenever Governor Smith's legislative program bogged down, he called Caroline and Eleanor to Albany to ask them to help get his bills through, and women by the hundreds came to the state capital at their call. They worked in a more disciplined way than the men, whom Eleanor ventured to criticize for their "inability to comprehend the value of sustained organization. Men think they can organize the vote six weeks before election, but women generally believe in all-year-round active political work."[16] In 1926 the women had achieved one of their goals—election to the Democratic State Committee on an equal footing with the men. To the six hundred women who gathered to celebrate the victory, Eleanor hailed it as the "breaking down of the last barrier." But once inside the fortress, they found it empty. Eleanor bridled at the "cut and dried" way in which matters were handled at State Committee meetings.[17] The power lay elsewhere, and the men still held it alone.

Alfred E. Smith, who was the governor of New York during the years of Eleanor's emergence, considered her a valuable ally—partly as the representative of her husband and partly in her own right as a leader among women. Eleanor admired the governor. Reflecting her rebellion against Sara and Sara's values, the fact that Smith had worked his way up from Oliver Street on the Lower East Side and still spoke its language of the streets added to his appeal. Franklin made the keynote speech at the 1926 convention that renominated the governor, and Eleanor was a member of the platform committee and spokesman for the women. Franklin could not campaign actively, but Eleanor could and did. "The Governor does get what he wants, doesn't he?" she wrote after election day the following year when an amendment he had opposed was defeated.[18]

What Smith most wanted was the Democratic nomination for president in 1928, and Eleanor was prepared to support him, even though she did not admire him unqualifiedly. She brought Florence

Kelley, the veteran social reformer, in the hope of converting him to the child-labor amendment. He stormed at the frail, elderly woman, paced angrily up and down his office, and finally Mrs. Kelley left in despair. Eleanor knew the governor well enough to understand that his show of anger masked his defensiveness; after Mrs. Kelley left she said to him, "You know that you are opposed to this amendment because the Church is opposed," and Smith agreed.[19] Some felt Smith's Catholicism disqualified him, but Eleanor quoted her Uncle Ted as having said he hoped to see the day when a Catholic or a Jew would become president.[20]

In the *North American Review* she argued the case for Smith, saying that unlike Wilson, who was "the Idealist, with no knowledge of practical politics, and therefore without the ability to translate his dreams into facts," Smith combined idealism with a "practical knowledge of how to achieve political results."[21] The issue in the 1928 elections, she wrote in *Current History*, was the age-old conflict between Jeffersonians and Federalists.

> The Democrats today trust in the people, the plain, ordinary, everyday citizen, neither superlatively rich nor distressingly poor, not one of the "best minds" but the average mind. The Socialists believe in making the Government the people's master; the Republicans believe that the moneyed "aristocracy," the few great financial minds, should rule the Government; the Democrats believe that the whole people should govern.[22]

In promoting Smith's candidacy with the Southern Women's National Democratic Organization, she argued that Smith, "in greater degree than any other man in public life, [has] the faculty of taking a complex problem of government and simplifying it so that people can go to the polls and vote on the issue intelligently," which she considered one of the most important functions of a leader in a democracy.[23] The governor's stand on Prohibition distressed her, but compared to his other qualities "his personal attitude on Prohibition is of minor importance." Mrs. Jesse W. Nicholson of Texas, the head of the Women's Democratic Law Enforcement League, bitterly opposed Smith's candidacy because he was a wet. If the league, whose membership was largely southern, was so concerned with upholding the Constitution, Eleanor wrote Mrs. Nicholson, why was it not making as great an effort "to enforce the 14th and 15th amendments relating to the right of all citizens to vote?"[24] Bravo, wrote George Marvin, writer, diplomat, and former Groton master, who addressed Franklin as "Francisco." "Whenever she gets ready to run for anything, she can count on two humble but husky votes in this 'Section.'"[25]

She had difficulties over Prohibition in her own household. When in 1924 she accompanied Mrs. Norrie to a convention of women in Washington to press for strict enforcement of the Volstead Act, she apologized to Franklin: "I know you will probably feel with Louis it is politically wrong to come but I do believe in it." While she felt that the Eighteenth Amendment

> works imperfectly I don't want it repealed or modified, for with all its faults, its virtues make it good.... Prohibition makes it harder to get alcohol.... There is less drinking now among young people than there was among our fathers. It is the example of the parents that is so dangerous.[26]

Franklin, whose approach to Prohibition was firmly political and opportunist, teased her about her support of Smith despite his wetness. "Thanks for sending me that awful picture of my Missus," he wrote Stanley W. Prenosil, the AP man who had covered his 1920 campaign. "She is apparently looking at a fly on the ceiling with the hope of finding out how to be wet and dry at the same time."[27]

Although Smith's "Kitchen cabinet" included neither Franklin nor Eleanor, he counted on them to play a major part in his drive for nomination and election. "Mrs. Moskowitz practically told me yesterday that you were to nominate the Governor," Eleanor informed Franklin.

> You will have to work hard to keep up your standard of four years ago! Also I am to head up a Woman's Committee for preconvention activities and we are to have an office in the Biltmore with Mrs. Moskowitz, etc. It won't mean much work once it is started but there was an implication of future work which horrified me as I ought to let them know I have to be at home this summer and yet you can't refuse what you haven't been offered, can you?[28]

"Elinor and Henry Morgenthau are like children in their joy that she [Elinor] should be made a delegate-at-large," Eleanor wrote wonderingly, a few weeks before the Democratic national convention in

Houston. "I never realized any one could care so much and only hope nothing happens to change the minds of the mighty!"[29]

One of her purposes in going into politics had been to keep Franklin's name before the public, especially the politicians. She succeeded. Mrs. Roosevelt's activity with the Democratic women, the *New York Herald Tribune* wrote in 1927, "has caused a revival in Tammany circles of the talk that Governor Smith favors Franklin D. Roosevelt...as Democratic candidate for Senator next year." Wherever she went in Democratic circles, people asked about Franklin. "I told everyone at the State Committee meeting yesterday you were going to Houston without crutches!"[30]

Franklin's return to the political scene would mean her withdrawal—there never was any doubt in her mind about that. She was sure that was the way it should be and had to be. But was she wholly content with the prospect? She did not go with him to Houston, but Elliott and Louis did, and when Sara sailed for Europe with James she was left in charge of Hyde Park, a chore she hated. Her last letter to Franklin before he left Warm Springs for the convention reported that "it is horrid, rainy weather and I am quite unreasonably depressed, partly because I feel uncomfortable about servants. . . ."[31] She would go to the railroad station to say good-by to Marion, Elinor, and Henry when they boarded the train for Houston, she added, and if Franklin saw Mrs. Nicholson of Texas, "give her an extra polite dig for me!" She would listen on the radio "and expire if it doesn't work!" It was not the letter of a woman who was satisfied to be removed from the scene of the action. When Smith was nominated on the first ballot she sent him her personal congratulations and to Franklin wrote that she was meeting Marion at the station and rather hoped the governor would be on the train as the papers had indicated he might be.

She had worried whether Franklin's nominating speech in Houston would meet the high standard of the "Happy Warrior" one. It did, said the *New York Times* editorially: "It is seldom that a political speech attains this kind of eloquence...a model of its kind." At state headquarters, Eleanor reported, "everyone was talking of your speech and feel you did untold good to the Governor's cause." But there was also dissatisfaction among the women, who were unhappy because they had not been consulted

> by the men leaders as to what women from New York should be given this or that place. It would be so easy for the men to do. I

can't understand why they prefer to stir up this current of discontent! However it is none of my business. I'm doing just what Mrs. Moskowitz asks me to do and asking no questions, the most perfect little machine you ever saw and after the National Committee meets and they appoint permanent people I'm going to get out and retire.[32]

She was not allowed to do so. In July the Democratic National Committee drafted her and Mrs. Nellie Tayloe Ross of Wyoming, the first woman governor, to head up the women's work in the campaign, with Mrs. Ross touring the country and Eleanor directing the work at headquarters. "She does a thorough job of it," the *New York Evening Post* reported. She was at her desk at nine, except when she had a class at Todhunter, and stayed until the work was done, which was often after midnight.

> Always courteous, never showing the slightest sign of impatience, she sees nearly every person who wants to talk to her and there are hundreds of them. It is said that she also dictates a personal answer to every letter she receives—about 150 a day.[33]

Malvina Thompson, young, tart, shy, a blend of New England and the Bronx, who had worked for the Red Cross and the Democratic State Committee, became Eleanor's personal secretary, and the campaign sealed a relationship that lasted through "Tommy's" life. She was also assisted by young Grace Tully, who had received her training as Cardinal Hayes' secretary. Under Eleanor's supervision, committees were organized to appeal to independent voters, business and professional women, college women, working women, social workers, new voters. Congresswoman Mary T. Norton ran the Women's Speakers Bureau and witty Mrs. June Hamilton Rhodes, the publicity department.

"Every morning," Eleanor wrote in a post-election account of the women's organization in the campaign, she "called a meeting of the various executive secretaries and went over their work with them, each one listening to the problems and questions of the other, thus learning what was going on and thus avoiding duplication. All work done in the various bureaus was under [my] direct supervision."[34] She prodded the states in which the organization was unsatisfactory and ironed out the inevitable disputes. One trouble spot was the midwest region, whose headquarters were in St. Louis. She telephoned Molly Dewson at her summer house in Maine.

Harry Hawes says the women in the Midwestern Headquarters of the Democratic National Committee are fighting and I must come out, but I cannot possibly leave headquarters in New York. Will you go in my place? I know only two women whom it would be safe to send and you are one of them.[35]

Of this request Molly later wrote, "scattered all over this country are, I imagine, a great many persons who have never been able to say 'no' to the Roosevelts or even 'I will think it over and telephone you.' I am no exception." The choice was a wise one, for Senator Hawes begged Molly "to stay through the campaign." After that, no campaign would be run without Molly's help.

Sara, still in Europe with James, wrote Eleanor that "I long to hear that my Franklin was not used up by Houston."[36] When she and James reached Vittels in the Vosges she informed Franklin that she had been given a first-hand account of the convention by Bernard Baruch.

Mr. B. Baruch is here and he came to our table last evening when he finished dinner and said he had been at the Convention and heard your fine speech. He seems to think Smith has a good chance, chiefly because many Republicans are anxious not to have prohibition.... Mr. Baruch says Elliott was perfect, helping you and taking the sheets as they fell from your hand. How lovely to have had James four years ago and Elliott now.[37]

Baruch also reported to Sara that the Smith forces were trying to draft her son for governor, but Roosevelt was firmly determined to avoid a draft for the governorship. Eleanor was less certain that he should turn down the nomination if it were offered to him. Agnes (Mrs. Henry Goddard) Leach, who was New York State chairman of the League of Women Voters, recalled being at Hyde Park around the time of the Houston convention. In the middle of luncheon Franklin was informed that Belle Moskowitz wanted to talk to him on the telephone. He refused to take the call, but then he was told Smith was on the phone and so he had himself wheeled out for what proved to be a long talk. "What did Smith want?" Eleanor asked on his return. "The same old thing," he replied. "He wants me to be the candidate for Governor. It's ridiculous."

"I don't think you should say it's ridiculous so quickly," Eleanor cautioned him.[38]

When the delegates began to arrive for the state convention in Rochester at the end of September, Franklin was ensconced in Warm Springs and evidently expected to stay there, for he had instructed Eleanor to have the *Times* and the *World* sent there for three months. Always buoyant and hopeful, he thought that with a few more years of exercises at Warm Springs he would be able to walk without braces. Moreover, he and Louis did not believe that 1928 was a good year for the Democrats, and he deliberately put himself out of immediate reach of Smith and his friends. As a result, their pressure to have him run focused on Eleanor and to a lesser degree on Louis. "My conviction that you should not run is stronger than ever and Eleanor agrees with me in this," Louis wired him on September 25. Tammany leader George Olvaney, Louis informed Franklin the next day, "has been trying to reach Eleanor who is speaking in New Hampshire apparently to persuade her to persuade you," and Franklin should let them know whether his decision "not to run is still final." If Franklin would head the ticket, Colonel Herbert Lehman told Eleanor, Lehman "would gladly run as Lt. Governor" so that Franklin could feel he "could go away each winter and leave [a] competent person in charge."

"I have to go to Rochester but I wish I didn't have to go for everyone makes me so uncomfortable," she wrote her husband. "They feel so strongly about your running and even good explanations can be made to sound foolish. The Governor called me yesterday and I told him to call you."[39] Smith had telephoned her from Milwaukee, and she arrived at the Hotel Seneca in Rochester almost at the same time he did. Roosevelt had sent a telegram to the governor reaffirming his reasons for refusing to run—that Smith did not need him in order to win and that he needed two more years to get rid of his leg braces; he owed it to his family to follow through his curative program to the end. A haggard Smith closeted himself with Mrs. Roosevelt. He wanted to know Franklin's *real* objections to accepting the nomination—health? Warm Springs finances? Would the governorship endanger his chances of walking again? At two she emerged from the governor's suite. "Will Mr. Roosevelt run?" the reporters wanted to know. "I don't think it is possible," she answered. Was she willing for him to run? She told them what she had told the county leaders who were insisting that it had to be Roosevelt: "It is entirely up to him. I am not trying to influence him either way." The reporters admired her poise.

The county leaders went into session again, but the discussion always came back to Roosevelt. Franklin was refusing to take Smith's calls and Eleanor agreed to get her husband on the phone; the rest would be up to Smith. As soon as Franklin answered, Eleanor turned the receiver over to Smith and raced for the train in order to be back in New York in time for the opening of Todhunter. "All day long," the *New York Evening Post* commented on the day's activities, "Mrs. Roosevelt had been in conference with the leaders, quiet, unruffled, probably the calmest person in all the crowded hotel."[40]

When she heard that he had yielded to the party's entreaties she wired Franklin: "Regret that you had to accept but know that you felt it obligatory." The pressure on Roosevelt was described in a Lippmann editorial in the *World:* "The demand for Mr. Roosevelt came from every part of the State. It could not be quelled. It could not be denied. The office has sought the man."

Sara was surprised but accepted the decision in good spirit, considering her earlier opposition to her son's remaining in public life. "Eleanor telephoned me before I got my papers that you have to 'run' for the governorship," she wrote Franklin.

> Well, I am sorry, if you do not feel that you can do it without too much self-sacrifice, and yet if you run I do not want you to be defeated! . . . Now what follows is *really private*. In case of your election, I know your salary is smaller than the one you get now. I am prepared to make the difference up to you.

One member of the family had no doubts. Anna wired her father, "Go ahead and take it," to which he replied, "You ought to be spanked."

But what did Eleanor really think about her husband's candidacy? When the press caught up with her at Democratic headquarters, she said

> I am very happy and very proud, although I did not want him to do it, he felt that he had to. In the end you have to do what your friends want you to. There comes to every man, if he is wanted, the feeling that there is almost an obligation to return the confidence shown him.

The reporters questioned her persistently about a story that had appeared in that morning's *World* under the headline "Mrs. Roosevelt's 'Yes' Final Factor." Based on what "intimate friends" of Mrs. Roosevelt told its reporter, it asserted that she had been on the phone with her husband in the late afternoon, that he had told her he might not be able to refuse in the end, unless she was not satisfied to have him run. "Mrs. Roosevelt held the receiver in silence for several minutes," the story stated. "The decision was left to her. Then she assured Mr. Roosevelt that she was of the opinion that he might enter the campaign, and, if elected, accept the office without harmful effects."[41]

She would not deny that she had talked to him, but insisted, "I was very surprised at the nomination. I never did a thing to ask him to run." Had she had a hand in changing his mind, the reporters wanted to know. "My husband always makes his own decisions. We always discuss things together, and sometimes I take the opposite side for the fun of the thing, but he always makes his own decisions."[42]

She did not think it right, as she had told Smith and John J. Raskob, then chairman of the National Democratic Committee, to ask him to do anything he felt he should not do, but did she herself want him to run? Edward J. Flynn, the Bronx Democratic leader, at Smith's request, had been sounding out Roosevelt during the summer on his real reasons for resisting the nomination. Flynn felt that among other things Roosevelt was concerned about what would happen to Warm Springs and the considerable money—all his fortune, in fact—that he had put into it if he could no longer give it his full attention. Eleanor, who was always practical and hard-headed in money matters, would no doubt have wanted to be assured on this score, as she would have had to be persuaded in her own mind that her husband had gone as far as possible to recover the use of his legs. But in the end it seemed to Flynn "that she was anxious that he should run, and that she would be happy if he would consent to it."

Thirty years later when she saw *Sunrise at Campobello*, she noted that the play depicting Franklin's victory over polio could have been a play about almost any other victim of infantile paralysis. There was another drama, she went on, "which came later in my husband's life" when "he made his decision as to whether he would devote himself to his efforts toward recovery or accept his disabilities in order to play a more active role in the life he was leading." Perhaps that was a subject for another play, she added.[43] "I think the most wonderful thing Eleanor did was to encourage him to run in 1928 when most people thought he was not up to it," said Esther Lape.[44]

If she did influence his decision, she kept it well hidden. Her account of what happened in Rochester in *This I Remember* ended with the ambiguous remark, "I sometimes wonder whether I really wanted Franklin to run."[45]

Her husband's decision to run did not alter Eleanor's primary political responsibility, which was to the Smith campaign organization. She kept an eye on the state through Elinor Morgenthau, Caroline, and Nancy and even helped them with the campaign caravans they were sending out all over the state, but she had her hands full with national problems. Her mail reflected the unprecedented bigotry and snobbery elicited by Smith's candidacy. "Can you imagine Mr. and Mrs. Smith in the White House as the leading family of the nation?" one letter from a Republican woman "who had always admired you" asked. Eleanor defended Smith in the Junior League *Bulletin*, saying that his "human" sympathies were wider than Hoover's; men worked *"under"* Hoover but "with" Smith; Hoover stressed "material prosperity," Smith would be concerned with "the human side of government." The many letters demanding to know how she, a supporter of the Volstead Act, could support a man who, if elected, would nullify Prohibition, were relatively easy to answer. But the southern propaganda was irrational. If Smith were elected, the pope would be coming to the United States on a battleship, "AL SMITH THE NEGRO LOVER" leaflets throughout the South proclaimed. "I want to assure you," Eleanor wrote an Alabama Democrat,

> that Gov. Smith does not believe in intermarriage between white and colored people. He has a full understanding of conditions as they are in the South and would never try to do violence to the feelings of Southern people . . . the Democratic Party has always better understood and sympathized with Southern feelings and prejudices than has the Republican.

As Election Day approached, Smith's defeat seemed likely, but Eleanor was a good trooper and sought to counteract a mood of defeatism. "I bring you good tidings," she told 2,500 women Democrats. "All the women of the country have been passing before me at my desk at headquarters. . . . The tide has turned and Gov. Smith's most recent speech has made us all feel that we are going to roll up a better and better vote."[46] But the day before election the betting odds favored Hoover and also Roosevelt. She made the traditional end-of-the-campaign swing through the Hudson Valley with Franklin, who was wearing the battered felt hat in which he had campaigned in 1920. The campaign ended with "Mr. Ottinger and I coming through it with the most kindly of feelings," he said. What were her husband's chances of success, a reporter asked Eleanor. "I don't know the State situation. I haven't been active with the State. I feel sure the Governor is going to win, though."[47]

She spent Election Day working at the polls, and in the evening was hostess at a buffet supper for their friends at the Biltmore. At nine Smith came by. "Frank, let's go down and hear the verdict." For a brief moment it looked as if Smith were carrying New York and the South, but then the returns moved decisively the other way. At midnight Smith dictated a telegram of concession, buttoned up his topcoat, put on his brown derby, and walked out. With heavy heart, Eleanor went to the Biltmore. "I may be here all night," Franklin said. It was "as exciting as a horse race." By morning he appeared to have survived the Democratic debacle. Smith lost New York by 103,481 votes; Roosevelt carried it by 25,564.

Smith's defeat notwithstanding, Eleanor had made her mark. Elizabeth Marbury, Democratic national committeewoman from New York and considered the dean of women politicians, conferred the accolade. "They won't need people like me. They've got their Mrs. Roosevelt now."[48]

But Eleanor grieved for Smith. "If the rest of the ticket didn't get in, what does it matter?" she said to a reporter who asked her how she felt about her husband's victory. "No, I am not excited about my husband's election. I don't care. What difference can it make to me?"[49]

But of course it would make a great deal of difference. Even before Election Day she had written the Democratic state chairman, resigning from the Democratic State Committee: "It seems to me now that my husband is actually back in active politics, it is wise for me not to be identified with any of the party committees."[50] She could not withdraw from a Consumers League dinner, she wrote Franklin, who had returned to Warm Springs after the election, "because I promised long ago but it is my last appearance as a speaker on any subject bordering on politics!"[51]

32. RETURN TO ALBANY

A TRIUMPHANT ROOSEVELT DEPARTED FROM WARM SPRINGS AND left it to his wife to arrange the move into the executive mansion. She was a far different person from the anxious young woman who had accompanied the ebullient new senator to Albany eighteen years earlier. She accepted an invitation from Mrs. Smith to come to Albany, and with great dispatch decided on the changes that would have to be made to fit the comfortable, loose-jointed mansion, with its turrets, cupolas, and broad red-papered halls, to the needs of the gregarious Roosevelt family.

The first structural change she wanted represented an act of thoughtfulness: to join the ladies' cloakroom to the back hall so that it could be used as a servants' dining and sitting room because the pantry where the servants had been eating was "not really decent."[1] Governor Smith's zoo was to be dismantled, and the three monkeys, one elk, one deer, one fawn, and six dogs dispersed. Republican approval was obtained to remove the three greenhouses and install a swimming tank—a real saving, Franklin carefully pointed out to the press, since the annual upkeep of the greenhouses was $6,000 for flowers which could be obtained from commercial florists for $750.

For her husband's bedroom Eleanor chose the "grandest sunny" room in the mansion, a corner room of the second floor with two exposures and a palatial dressing room and bathroom. The library downstairs would be his study and workroom, and the room upstairs that Smith had used as his office at the mansion would, with chintz curtains and Val-Kill furniture, make a cozy family sitting room and serve as her workroom. She suggested that the only single bedroom in the mansion be given to Missy; "We can talk that over," she wrote Franklin.[2]

How did she visualize her life in Albany, she was asked at a news conference. She would make the executive mansion into a home for her husband, she said, take the social side of things off his shoulders, and see that the house was run smoothly. She would carry on with the furniture factory at Val-Kill ("sold everything," she reported to her husband after their exhibit that autumn)[3] and with the weaving enterprise that she had recently started at Hyde Park village. These activities, she felt, were helpful to her neighbors and satisfied her craftsman's instinct. She was even more determined to continue her three-day teaching schedule at Todhunter School—"I teach because I love it, I cannot give it up." And she would arrange her life so that she could be immediately available to her children.[4] John, her youngest, had just joined Franklin Jr. and Elliott at Groton, and James was at Harvard. She must be able, at a moment's notice, to dash up to Groton or Cambridge, as she did soon after Franklin's election when "F. Jr. checked into the infirmary with a belly-ache in the right side" and Johnny, "the poor lamb," was on crutches after having banged his knee on a door "in a rush for crackers after calisthenics." She also discovered on that trip that Elliott, in his eagerness to get on the football team, had never told the school about his old rupture, which was giving him trouble. James, whom she visited in Cambridge on the way home, disclosed that he had become secretly engaged to Betsy Cushing, "a nice child ...but I regret that he wishes to tie himself down so young...in any case we can do nothing about it."[5] "A lot of things can happen to four boys away at school," she told the press with motherly understatement.

Mistress of the mansion, mother, teacher—thus she envisaged her role in the weeks after election. But the women with whom she had worked expected more of her; they rejoiced in Roosevelt's victory as much because it brought Eleanor into the executive mansion as because it put him into the governor's chair. They were sure she would transform the position of First Lady into one of unique usefulness. "What a First Lady you will make," exulted Emily Newell Blair, the one-time suffrage leader and veteran Democratic politician. "How splendid it is to have one in that place with the political acumen and feeling for women that you have."[6]

Eleanor was eager to make a place for women in government, and under her tutelage her husband had come to a more genial and enlightened view of woman's quest for equality; but she knew that basically he still considered politics a man's business. Having freed himself from his mother's domination, he would become impatient and evasive if she pressed her point of view in ways that did not fit his purposes and defer to his moods. She would need self-control as well as feminine intuition and guile not to irritate him. They dealt differently with both people and problems. Her responses were structured by the logic of love; his by the logic of power and governance. Her imagination was active on behalf of others and flowered in deeds of kindness; he was concerned with using others to further his political career and purposes. She disregarded convention and sometimes was impatient with legality when it stood in the way of benevolence; he often yielded to expediency and the more comfortable course. When she disapproved, tension would arise between them. But she had an inner conviction that he shared her concern to make life better for others; that, too, was part of his political purpose, and she believed that with tact, humility, and a service of anonymity she could be of help to him and to the causes to which she now was so actively committed.

Even before the new governor assumed office, she was influential in shaping the character of his administration. Roosevelt was uncomfortably aware that Smith meant to remain the power in the state. Smith had always patronized Roosevelt, the Hudson River patrician, and treated him, Roosevelt later wrote, as a piece of "window dressing that had to be borne with because of a certain value in non–New York City areas." Robert Moses, with his gift for wounding invective, had summed up the attitude of some of Smith's circle toward Roosevelt with the gibe "He'll make a good campaigner but a lousy Governor." The governorship need not interfere with Roosevelt's polio therapy, Smith had accommodatingly assured him in September. Once he was sworn in, he could decamp for the winter to Warm Springs, leave Lehman in charge, and return for a few days before the legislature adjourned. The suggestion that he govern by proxy had amused Franklin in September; it irked him when it was renewed with even more insistence after his victory and Smith's defeat. Smith pressed him to retain the Smith cabinet intact, and particularly to keep Robert Moses as secretary of state and Belle Moskowitz as his speech writer and strategist. The situation worried Roosevelt and he discussed his anxieties with his wife and Louis. They supported him in his determination not to be a front man for Smith.

They were particularly uneasy about keeping Mrs. Henry Moskowitz. She had been a Bull Moose progressive and was a brilliant publicist, but she was so arrogant that even Eleanor, the most tractable and cooperative of colleagues, found it difficult to work with her. She was politically astute and totally committed to Smith—as dedicated, persevering, and suspicious in his behalf as Louis was in Roosevelt's. "By all signs I think Belle and Bob Moses mean to cling to you," she warned her husband, "and you will wake up to find R.M. Secretary of State and B.M. running Democratic publicity at the old stand unless you take a firm stand."[7] Her next slightly anti-Semitic remark underscored how strongly she felt. "Gosh! the race has nerves of iron and tentacles of steel!" Roosevelt was perfectly clear in his own mind that he did not want Belle as part of his political household, but he could not bring himself to tell Smith. Eleanor was aware of how difficult it could be for him to be the messenger of bad news and how he hated situations where his charm and persuasiveness were impotent, but she kept after him. "Don't let Mrs. M. get draped around you for she means to be," she prodded in a letter to Warm Springs. "It will always be one for you and two for Al."[8]

"I hope you will consider making Frances Perkins Labor Commissioner," she wrote him, starting another campaign. "She'd do well and you could fill her place as Chairman of the Industrial Commission by one of the men now on [the] Commission and put Nell Schwartz (now Bureau of Women in Industry) on the Commission so there would be one woman on it." Then, as if she sensed male feathers being ruffled, she hastily added, "These are suggestions which I'm passing on, not my opinions for I don't mean to butt in."[9] And knowing that men will often hear with pleasure from other women what they will not accept from their wives, she had made sure that she would not be the only woman to make this suggestion. She instigated an invitation to Warm Springs for Molly Dewson, a reformer who nevertheless understood the political game; men liked Molly's down-East saltiness. She had come to Eleanor to ask how she could cash in on her services in the campaign and interest the governor-elect in the legislative program of the New York Consumers League, of which she was president.[10] "Go to Warm Springs to see Franklin before others see him," Eleanor advised, and promptly made it possible.

Molly arrived in Warm Springs well briefed. In the course of talking to Roosevelt about minimum-wage legislation she shifted the discussion to the department responsible for the administration of labor standards. "Why don't you appoint Frances Perkins your Industrial Commissioner?" she interjected. Franklin gave Molly the impression that he was not surprised by her request and that he was thinking about it favorably.[11]

The final confrontation between Roosevelt and Smith came during a four-hour meeting soon after his return from Warm Springs. All during December the battle had been fought behind the scenes and through stories planted by both sides, mostly in the Democratic *World*. "While [Smith] will retire to private life, probably to banking," wrote Ernest K. Lindley, who had covered Smith for many years, "no one doubts that he will continue to be a very powerful, if not the dominating influence in the Democratic Party in this State." Roosevelt means "to administer the office in his own name and by his own right," wrote another correspondent for the *World* on the same day. "This means," the story continued, "there will be changes in the Smith Cabinet." Lieutenant Governor-elect Herbert Lehman—a protégé of Belle's—confirmed on his return from Warm Springs, where he had gone to discuss the legislative program, that Roosevelt intended to be much more active as governor than had generally been assumed at the time of his nomination. And Roosevelt, tanned, buoyant, and "fit as a fiddle," underscored Lehman's observation. "I am ready," he announced as he left Warm Springs, "to carry on the duties of Governor of New York and to remain constantly on the job during the entire legislative period."

Eleanor had alerted Franklin that Smith wanted to see him as soon as possible after his return, and three days after Roosevelt's arrival in New York the two men talked. Moses "rubs me the wrong way," Roosevelt told Smith flatly, and that finished the campaign to keep him on. He was less definite about Belle, and an added complication was Smith's disapproval of Roosevelt's plan to appoint Frances Perkins as labor commissioner.[12] He was proud of Miss Perkins, Smith said—it was he who had appointed her chairman of the Industrial Commission, and she had performed ably—but a cabinet post carried administrative responsibilities, and, he said, "men will take advice from a woman, but it is hard for them to take orders from a woman." Smith's attitude did not surprise Eleanor. She had caught a glimpse of it in the way he had talked about the visit paid him by Nellie Tayloe Ross when she was governor of Wyoming, when Smith had gloated over her inability to produce the kind of figures that he always had at his fingertips. He did not feel a woman should be governor of a state or head of a department.[13]

Roosevelt, nevertheless, appointed Miss Perkins and also, as Eleanor had suggested, put Nell Schwartz on the Industrial Commission.

To the end of her life Eleanor would deny that she had had any part in the naming of Miss Perkins, and yet she kept a watchful eye on developments just to make sure there would be no last-minute hitches. At Miss Perkins' request, she arranged for her to come to Hyde

Park to have a relaxed talk with the governor-elect and to make sure that their ideas agreed on how far her writ would run. It was a "very satisfactory talk," Miss Perkins informed Eleanor afterward, "under conditions which couldn't possibly have occurred otherwise."[14] She wanted Eleanor to know "how much the women of the State admire your prospective relationship to Government." But that relationship, Eleanor knew, and her closest collaborators soon perceived, depended on how well she buried her tracks and how persuasively she disavowed that she had any influence. Molly sensed the hazards in Eleanor's path; if she had not emphasized how much Mrs. Roosevelt had helped her, she later wrote, it was "because I thought she was in a delicate position, and the less I said about her in connection with my work, the better."[15] Defeated on Moses and Perkins, Smith still fought on for Belle, and he appealed to Perkins, who was on good terms with both men, to intercede with Roosevelt. She did, but Roosevelt turned her down. Belle was "very, very able" and had done "a great deal for Al," as she would for any man who was governor, he conceded. But, and Miss Perkins suddenly became aware how much the man leaning back in his armchair had grown in strength and maturity, "I've *got* to be Governor of the State of New York and I have got to be it MYSELF. . . . I'm awfully sorry if it hurts anybody particularly Al."[16]

The battle to be governor in his own right was won, but Frances Perkins, who saw it from the inside, believed that Roosevelt might well have drifted into accepting Mrs. Moskowitz if it hadn't been for Eleanor.[17]

On the afternoon of January 31 the Smiths were at the executive mansion to await arrival of the Roosevelt motorcade from Hyde Park. When it came into view preceded by motorcycle outriders, Smith went down the steps. "God bless you and keep you, Frank," Smith greeted him. "A thousand welcomes. We've got the home fires burning and you'll find this a fine place to live." As Smith came toward him, Roosevelt added, "I only wish Al were going to be right here for the next two years." Mrs. Smith kissed the governor-elect and Smith embraced Mrs. Roosevelt. Both sides were cordial and considerate, a more difficult script for Smith to follow, for these final days in Albany with their outpourings of affection and "Auld Lang Synes" were something of a wake, but he carried it off in splendid style.

That evening Irving Lehman, associate justice of the court of appeals and Herbert's brother, swore in the new governor and lieutenant governor. Leaning on James's arm Roosevelt took the oath of office on the Old Dutch Bible that had been in the Roosevelt family since before Isaac the Patriot's day. Theodore Roosevelt had been sworn in as governor thirty years before in the same room.

The executive mansion quickly took on the easy informality of the Roosevelt household. It was always full, its nine guest rooms usually occupied, and large groups sat down to every luncheon and dinner. Informal meals were taken on the sun porch; the big state receptions and dinners were held in the large dining room. They came off "with full dignity," wrote one newspaperman who was often a guest at the mansion, "but with less stuffiness than such occasions acquire in the hands of less skilled hostesses."[18] House guests mingled with political leaders. Roosevelt's closest aides, and Eleanor's, became members of the household. Every afternoon when she was in Albany Eleanor served "a good substantial tea with chocolate cake" in the family sitting room, and whoever was in the house was invited: family, secretaries, newspapermen, friends, state troopers, distinguished guests. The servants were swept up in the warmth and friendliness of the governor and his lady, for their outstanding trait was that they enjoyed people.

A movie theater was set up in the hall on the third floor. Books, magazines, and papers were everywhere. Dogs raced through the halls—Chief, a large police dog, and the first Falla, a black Scottish terrier named after Murray of Fallahill, a remote Scotch ancestor. There was naturalness, noise, laughter, and continuous commotion. It was a home, not an official residence. At the center was Eleanor, managing the household, making life comfortable for its members, making guests feel at home, and making it all seem easy.

There is a picture of the Roosevelt hospitality in the diaries of Caroline Phillips. She and William arrived on a Friday afternoon to visit their old friends. "A very efficient-looking English butler" showed them upstairs "to a comfortable sitting room where we found Eleanor presiding over a tea table as quiet and peaceful as though she had nothing at all to do." Caroline noted, a little wonderingly, all the household people who drifted in for tea. John A. Warner, Al Smith's son-in-law and the head of the state police, and his wife came for dinner. And afterward they watched a movie starring the Barrymore brothers. "All the servants, black and white, seventeen in all, sat behind the house party and enjoyed the show with us." The Phillips marveled at the way Franklin and Eleanor were handling their jobs, "entering into the lives of their friends and household with greatest sympathy and courtesy. . . . Eleanor never seems to worry."

The fixed points in Eleanor's schedule during the Albany years were the Sunday evening train to New York and the noon train back on Wednesdays so that she would be in time for her Wednesday "at homes" from 4:30 to 6:00 P.M. Each Sunday before she left she obtained from Franklin a complete list of the people who would stay in the house while she was away and wrote out precise instructions for Harry Whitehead, the mansion's major-domo—menus, seating order at table, assignment of rooms, cars to meet guests, issuance of invitations. She settled servant problems, considered proposals for the purchase of labor-saving equipment, and made decisions on the one hundred and one little matters that are involved in the management of a large household. When friends expressed admiration for the ease and dispatch with which she managed the governor's house, she dismissed the praise: "Everything is done for me. I simply give the orders."[19]

Missy offered to take over some of the responsibility when Eleanor was away, but Eleanor firmly declined. She was grateful to the young woman, because if Missy were not living in the mansion it would be difficult to continue teaching. Yet it made her unhappy that Missy served as hostess at the all-male dinners Franklin gave while she was in the city and that he accommodated himself so genially to her absences; she would have liked him to protest.

Often Eleanor took early Sunday supper with Franklin and their guests, but usually the pre-supper talk flowed on until there was only time for her to gulp down milk and crackers and dash for the train. As a belated birthday present Nan and Marion had given her "a new kind of brief case bag" whose chief virtue was supposed to be an almost infinite expandability, and it soon bulged with the letters and documents that poured in upon her as the governor's wife. On the train she penciled out the replies she would dictate to Miss Thompson in New York—at the women's division office that she continued to share with Nancy. She also marked students' papers and worked on her lesson plans for the coming week. She had classes at Todhunter from nine to one on Monday, nine to five on Tuesday, and nine to eleven on Wednesday, which left time for her many other activities, and her calendar was always packed tight from morning to night. "If Mrs. Roosevelt did not hit two birds with every one stone, she never could have carried out her schedule," remarked Molly, who had been told to come and pour out her woes while Eleanor was on her way to the dressmaker.[20]

She worked with Louis Howe, whom she kept informed of Franklin's activities. Louis had remained in New York City, since the right position could not be found for him in Albany. To be the governor's secretary did not seem fitting, and he could not have headed a department. He, therefore, continued as Roosevelt's political chief-of-staff. Since he liked to work behind the scenes, the city seemed a better place from which to handle Roosevelt's political mail, so he continued to live at 49 East Sixty-fifth Street and serve as assistant to the chairman of the National Crime Commission. A guest room was set aside for him at the mansion for week ends. It was not as satisfying as being able to control access to Franklin, as he had done for so many years, but he adapted to the governor's necessities, as did everyone else around Franklin. Moreover, there was always Eleanor. At times the two seemed like conspirators in their efforts to hold the governor to a course of action they favored.[21]

Eleanor's political activities underwent a period of experimental adaptation. She no longer made political speeches, resigned from the boards of civic organizations that lobbied for legislation in Albany, and for a while declined to attend any meetings that "savor[ed] of politics," as she told Henry Morgenthau, Jr., when he invited her to a conference of master farmers. She also refused invitations to local Democratic dinners in four upstate counties, "so you see I'm being most discreet," she assured her husband.[22] She would miss not having "direct political responsibility," she told a farewell luncheon of the Women's City Club, especially after having worked so long to make women feel their political obligations.[23]

But this withdrawal from political activity was more a matter of form than substance. She removed her name from the masthead of the *Democratic News*, but continued to edit it behind the scenes, wrote editorials anonymously, and assigned the articles to be written.

By May, Franklin had lifted the prohibition on attending political gatherings as long as she did not make political speeches. In fact, he wanted her to go: it took another burden off his shoulders. The meetings were often exhausting affairs. She attended a Democratic luncheon on Staten Island, which she described to Franklin: "Arrived at 12:30, stood and shook hands till 1:30, ate till 3:30; talked till 5:20; home here at 6:40 nearly dead! They nominated you for President & you are the finest Gov. ever & I have all the virtues & would gladly have dispensed with half could I have left at four!"[24] A week later she was going to a Democratic dinner in Cohoes, "so let me know if you want anything done."

Her feminine grace and sympathy did not interfere with her

hard-headed astuteness as a politician. When the Women's Democratic Club of Buffalo wanted to know whether a woman could be
elected to office, she answered, "I think there is more opportunity
now than ever before for women in politics if they will keep their
ideals high and go in with the purpose of being of service rather than
with the purpose of obtaining an office." Offices would come as a
matter of course when the service was rendered. "Why not try to run
one Buffalo woman this coming autumn in a district which has some
chance?" was her closing advice.[25]

She championed the representatives of the women's groups lobbying
for protective legislation for children and women workers. All through
the twenties they had arrived faithfully on the Monday Empire State
Express while the legislature was in session, had spent long hours
waiting in corridors and anterooms to see legislators, and then were
brushed off. Now they went to the executive mansion "for tea, or dinner or even to stay overnight."[26] Sometimes she lectured the women
on the realities of wheeling and dealing in the legislative halls. "My
dear girls," she told a League of Women Voters' delegation brought to
Albany by Mrs. Leach, "you don't know what you are talking about,"
and then proceeded to tell them what the men really thought. "Of
course, I have Franklin so they don't dare talk that way to me."[27]

Molly, who did not require lectures on lobbying, was also helped
by Eleanor on occasion. She came to Albany to lobby for a bill to
reduce the working hours of women in retail stores. A compromise
bill had passed and was ready for the governor's signature, but it was
strongly opposed by business, and the governor had arranged a public
hearing. Molly found the hearing room "packed with elegantly tailored, prosperous looking gentlemen, the merchants, and not a single
backer of the bill except...[for the] representative of the League of
Women Voters. Somehow the Women's Conference had not received
their notice of the hearing."

She was pouring out her disgust later to Eleanor over a cup of tea
when Franklin came rolling in in his wheel chair, looking, Molly
thought, as fresh and cheerful as if he were going off for a week end.
Immediately Eleanor said, "What are you going to do about the bill?"
with what Molly felt was a touch of anxiety in her voice.

"Sign it, of course," he debonairly answered, and held out his hand
for tea.[28]

The twenty-fifth anniversary of the Women's Trade Union League
took place in 1929. The Finance Committee headed by Mrs. Roosevelt

and Mrs. Lamont had raised most of the money to pay off the mortgage on the league headquarters. They were arranging to celebrate the event with a party at the clubhouse when a letter came from Mrs. James Roosevelt inviting them to have their party at Hyde Park. Eleanor urged the governor to appear. "Don't forget the Women's Trade Union League party on June 8 from 2-6 PM, you are the *pièce-de-résistance*," she reminded him.[29] A boat was chartered and shopgirls and trade-union leaders made the trip up the Hudson.

"Did your ears ring all evening on Saturday?" Rose Schneiderman wrote Roosevelt afterward. "You were the main topic of conversation all the way down the river. The girls were saying over and over again, 'was not the Governor great' 'what a kind face he has' and 'How democratic he is' etc. etc. . . . As for myself—well, I wish there were a million more like you and Eleanor."[30]

Sara issued the invitation, Mrs. Lamont turned over the check, Franklin starred. Eleanor stayed in the background, but she was the link with the Women's Trade Union League, and it was often Eleanor who was in the lead on labor issues, rather than Franklin, on occasion even joining a picket line.[31] In April she presided at a luncheon of the Women's Trade Union League where the discussion centered on the five-day week. Merwin K. Hart, the manufacturers' lobbyist, commented that Mrs. Roosevelt would not want to be told she could work only five days a week. Taken by surprise, she agreed, but then qualified her agreement. "Work is living for me. The point is whether we live in our work."[32] Repeating a single motion throughout the day in a factory was drudgery, not to be compared with doing work that one enjoyed. And when in October, 1930, the International Ladies Garment Workers Union struck against the fashionable Fifth Avenue dressmakers and David Dubinsky was arrested for disorderly conduct, Eleanor came to his aid and endorsed the ILGWU's efforts to organize the unorganized.

"The Legislature adjourned, thank the Lord," Eleanor wrote, as the first session came to an end.[33] Franklin left for Warm Springs, and she began preparations for a trip to Europe which Franklin had suggested she take with Franklin Jr., who was called "Brother," and Johnny, together with Nan and Marion. The prospect of showing her sons her favorite places in Europe was appealing, but it also worried her. She was not sure she could handle Brother, going on fifteen, and Johnny, thirteen, and their inevitable wrestling matches. "I'm getting colder and colder feet about going abroad," she confessed in May. "It seems such a fearful effort."[34] She also fretted about the costs. There were large doctors' bills that spring, between Johnny's knee and Brother's broken nose and Elliott's rupture and James's digestive troubles—"if Franklin gets thro' under $6,000 he will be doing well." There were other money worries: "James asked me to beg you to send his check as he says it is a necessity. I wonder if you have forgotten Louis too? He has said nothing but Mary, when they were leaving last night, asked him for money & he was so hesitant to give it I wondered if he was short!" Sara as usual came to the rescue. "I am glad Mama is giving you a present because now I hope we will be able to pay all our many demands!"[35]

It was also Sara who a month later almost undid the European trip during a family dinner at the Big House. Eleanor was reviewing their plans for the trip—they were taking over the Buick and Chevvy and she, Nan, and Marion would do the driving; perhaps they might even do some camping. Suddenly Sara reared up, disapprovingly—it would be undignified for the wife of the governor and two of his sons to motor in an old touring car and even worse for the governor's wife to drive herself. Here young Franklin, unaware of the gathering storm clouds, chimed in, "Mom will probably land us in the first ditch," and described how the day before she had driven them into a gatepost, ending, cheerfully if illogically, "But we'll be all right." Eleanor then turned to the head of the table where Sara always sat opposite Franklin, and said in a cold voice, "Very well. I will take your grandsons in a manner consistent with what you think their positions ought to be." With that she hurried out of the dining room and took refuge on the screened porch. Here Franklin intervened, and in a voice more stern than Franklin Jr. had ever heard him use before—"or after"—told him to go after his mother, apologize, and not to return without her. Young Franklin was appalled to find his mother in tears and horrified that he should have hurt her so—"and there was the Old Man chained to his chair by his legs or otherwise he would have gone himself after Mother," he commented in recalling the incident.[36]

But Franklin did not contradict Sara. She again had her way, and the incident cast a shadow over the entire trip. The Chevvy was left behind. Nan and Marion took the Buick but Eleanor rented handsome chauffeur-driven limousines everywhere they went, beginning with a Daimler in England, and made the boys sit in the back with her although they longed to be up front with the driver. Not until Belgium, where they had a driver who charmed them all and who placed a little bouquet of flowers in the car for Eleanor every morning, did she relent. "Brother paid for that remark very dearly," commented Marion Dickerman. "Eleanor could be very hard."[37]

Before going abroad, Eleanor and the boys accompanied Franklin on an early-summer trip through New York State that was to become an annual event. During his first bout with the legislature, the governor had suffered several rebuffs from the Republican-controlled body, a fate he knew would be repeated unless he could build greater support for his objectives in the upstate areas. The city-oriented Democrats had long given up the farm areas as irretrievably Republican, but Roosevelt's formula was to cultivate the rural areas, and six years of crisscrossing the state on behalf of the women's division had convinced Eleanor that Democratic policies and organization could find a foothold upstate if the leadership worked at it. Roosevelt planned a summer cruise along the state's inland waterways that would enable him to inspect hospitals, mental institutions, and prisons as well as carry his programs to the people, especially the farmers. To Henry Morgenthau, Jr., who had sampled rural opinion on the issues of the 1929 legislature, he wrote, "What hits me most is the very high percentage of ignorance."

Eleanor joined enthusiastically in the preparations for the trip. A farm woman had written her a bitter letter against the Department of Education and school consolidation, she informed Dr. Frank Graves, the commissioner of education, and she wanted someone in his office to line up the facts for her "as concisely as possible." She intended to talk to the woman when she was in the western part of the state. "I think it would be a very good thing to put in the Women's *Democratic News*," she added, "besides being a very necessary thing for my own education."[38] The tour had another purpose. In May when Franklin had gone to Warm Springs there had been a flood of stories that he was an exceedingly tired man, which disturbed Eleanor and Louis. "It looks like a deliberate campaign to show how much will now have to be done when you are away," she wrote Franklin. "Lehman would not do it & I think others are responsible";[39] she detected "Belle's hand" in the operation. The most effective antidote to innuendos about the governor's physical capability was to go out and meet the citizenry face to face. So on July 7 Franklin, accompanied by his wife and sons, took command of the "good ship *Inspector* which has a glass roof" and headed westward along the Barge Canal to Buffalo.

There were frequent debarkations to meet local officials and inspect state institutions. The protocol of these inspections called for a tour of the grounds by automobile with the superintendent as guide and Roosevelt as commentator, pointing out for the benefit of the press what he wanted the legislature to do. Debarred by his crippled legs from going through the buildings, the governor would excuse himself and say Mrs. Roosevelt would be happy to do so. This was a new responsibility for Eleanor. She had at times looked at state hospitals for crippled children and similar institutions, but it was one thing to visit as a guest and quite another to inspect on behalf of the governor, who carried the ultimate responsibility for the management of these institutions. Franklin was not easily satisfied; the usefulness of the information—on which he had to act—depended on the ability of his deputies to spot the telling detail, fix it in their minds, and report it back coherently. He had made hundreds of inspections when he was assistant secretary of the Navy, and he knew what to look for; he now proceeded to instruct his wife.

Her first reports produced explosions of dissatisfaction. Was there overcrowding? It had not seemed so to her. How had she reached that conclusion? Had she estimated the distance between beds? Had she looked behind doors and into closets to see whether cots had been folded up and stacked away out of sight?

He was equally severe in regard to the food that was being served. The first time, she simply reported what she had read on the menus. He advised her to look into the pots in the kitchen and to make sure that what she saw there corresponded with what was listed on the menus. She began to look for the telltale signs, the grimace, the slightly cynical smile that might suggest morale problems between patients and staff or between staff and superiors. And then there was the problem of remembering it all. Franklin had a "really prodigious memory," and Eleanor had to discipline herself to hold the things she saw in her mind until she had passed them on to him.[40]

Her education in the techniques of inspection was further advanced by Corporal Earl Miller, a state trooper assigned to the governor's detail who often accompanied Eleanor when she went out alone. They became friends and he was soon giving her hints on the techniques officials used to take in unwary visitors. The surest way to get a true picture, he suggested, was to arrive unannounced, which she began to do; unhappy officials often could not conceal their consternation.[41]

It was a hard school. Once Franklin asked her to look at some upstate tree plantings that were to serve as a shelter belt, and he was clearly disappointed by her inability afterward to answer his questions. "I put my best efforts after that into missing nothing and remembering everything."[42] Before the Albany years were finished, she "had become a fairly expert reporter on state institutions."[43]

Eleanor continued to have mixed feelings about dropping everything to take the boys to Europe while her husband stayed behind to do the world's battles; it was too reminiscent of her lonely summers at Campobello. "Like most things in life," she confessed, "I want to go and yet I don't want to leave."[44] But they sailed from Montreal on July 26 after Franklin gave them a farewell dinner at the Mount Royal Hotel. "Well we are off & I am going to try to give the boys a good time and while I don't expect you to write please send me frequent cables," she wrote Franklin. "One for instance on Monday after you have been to Dannemora!"[45] Her mind was on the state's business, not Baedeker. There had been an outbreak of riots at Dannemora and Auburn prisons caused by overcrowding, poor food, and the enactment of the Baumes Laws, which made life sentence mandatory for fourth offenders. "I think the Baumes law makes reward for good behavior impossible and takes incentive away," her second shipboard letter stated. "Do write me what you find and your conclusions. The surplus will vanish in prison repairs if this goes on."[46] But he did not write, preferring to cable and telephone. "Hope you have a good trip. What shall I do with your casket?" his first communication read. "No one could imagine what it meant," Eleanor informed him, "but then I remembered the lunch basket which we discovered we left behind our first day out. . . ."

The boys disembarked at Belfast, where they joined James, who was staying with his fiancée at a country house overlooking the River Boyne that the Cushing family had taken outside Dublin. After a trip through the Lake district—in two cars—Nan and Marion went on to visit friends in Scotland, while Eleanor took the boat back to Dublin, where she found her boys very much involved with horses. James had even spent all his money on a colt that a fast-talking Irishman said could be trained to win all the races. When James later wired his father for his return passage, saying he would repay him out of his winnings, Franklin replied, "So happy about horse, suggest both of you swim home."[47] From the boys' talk Eleanor picked up the news that Elliott had gambled on the canal trip and lost twenty-five dollars to Corporal Miller and forty-five dollars to another member of the governor's staff. "I had a talk with him about gambling but I did not realize it was for sums like that he had played."[48] She was quite worried about Elliott. It was the summer he was refusing to go on to college. Franklin should talk to him about the right use of money, she advised, but without telling him they knew about his gambling losses.

In Dublin she went to the horse show and the races with her children. At a lunch at the legation, she met the "very nice Governor General" of Ireland, and the children of the founder and president of Czechoslovakia, the young Masaryks, were there—"very nice as usual"—and also "a most unpleasant Maharaja who strangled his wife (one of them) & threw her body down a well & looks it." Gossip had it that it had been the wife's punishment "for having disagreed with her lord and master." For the rest of the tour, they kept away from the world of officials. A Labor government had just come to power in London, but Eleanor made no effort to get in touch with political people, even though Franklin had suggested she go and see Prime Minister Ramsay MacDonald. This was to be a sightseeing trip for her boys, she insisted, and though she saw some old school friends in London and Aunt Dora in Paris, nothing was allowed to interfere with an exhaustive inspection of historical and cultural sites. She tried to keep the boys so busy during the day that they would be too weary for roughhousing, but almost every night she had to separate "two very angry brothers." They loved shopping at Harrod's and Burberry's: "I assure you I am ruined but they are swank and happy," she wrote Franklin. But they were bored with cricket and seeing the sites, and Eleanor was weary "of my incubus of a motor car," and so all were glad to cross the Channel for a tour of the Low Countries and the Rhine down to Bingen. In Luxembourg Nan, Marion, and the two boys toasted Franklin in the local champagnes; Eleanor "joined in, in Evian water!" Outside of Reims they inspected the Poméry wine cellars, where Eleanor observed that "very young boys were working under very unhealthy conditions" and Brother happily did some tasting. "F Jr. has had a taste of everything and likes it but I won't let him have it as a rule!" she reported.

At her husband's specific request they toured the battlefields, the underground forts at Verdun, Château-Thierry, Belleau Woods, and placed flowers near Quentin Roosevelt's grave. The rows and rows of crosses made a profound impression on the boys. "The thing that surprised me most was how France or Germany could go on and continue to be a world power when it had lost so many men," John wrote to his father.

Eleanor was disappointed not to find a letter from Franklin in Paris. "I hate not knowing what you have done about Elliott, and a thousand other things," she wrote. Had young Nesbitt, the son of a Hyde Park woman with whom she had become friendly, gotten into Cornell, she wanted to know, and would Franklin advance him money if he needed it.

As they were leaving Paris for Cherbourg, Franklin's only letter finally arrived, with the information that he intended to leave for Warm Springs soon after she returned. "I am very glad to be going with you as it will give us a little while to catch up & talk things over," she replied contentedly. She was glad she had made the trip, she finally concluded, "& will enjoy it in retrospect when the anxiety & necessary difficulties with two healthy youngsters is past. They have been good but a certain amount of trouble is inevitable. I think next summer we will separate them for a while." But her trials with the boys were not over. On their way to Cherbourg they visited Chartres and spent a night at Madame Poulard's at Mont-Saint-Michel, but the boys were in such a quarrelsome mood that she left them behind when she went to climb the ramparts and look at the old abbey and church. On her return, there was a commotion in the streets, and as she approached Madame Poulard's she heard screams. Franklin Jr. had pushed Johnny out of the window and was holding him head down dangling by the heels.[49]

They returned September 15, Todhunter classes resumed on October 1 and as vice principal she was soon involved in the preparations for the reopening of the school. Being mother, mistress of the executive mansion, and the governor's stand-in were all parts of her job, but the activities that she considered her own were teaching, writing, lecturing, helping run the Val-Kill Furniture Factory. She had agreed to serve as a member of the committee selecting books for the Junior Literary Guild. "She tells you with pride that this is a paid job; not her only one, for her school pays her a salary, too," Ida Tarbell wrote.[50] *Vogue* asked Eleanor to do an article, and she was pleased that the editor thought it "splendid," she noted in her reply to him, but he had said nothing about payment. "The only reason that I feel I must do this on a business basis is that other magazines pay me and I do not feel that unless it is for a purely educational or charitable publication, that it is quite fair not to ask the usual compensation."[51] She could use the money, but more important to her was the professional recognition that payment signified.

Though the activities that gave her the greatest satisfaction were those that she did in her own right, the public's growing interest in her was a result of the way she used the executive mansion as a springboard for good works, revealing the First Lady had a heart awake to the problems of other people. There was a person at the center of government, the individual citizen discovered, who answered any plea for help and took up every complaint against a bureaucrat. Neither by design nor appointment, and with her husband's concurrence, she began to perform an office that later generations would call "ombudsman."

She entered into the lives of her petitioners and thought of them as human beings, not cases. There were heart-rending appeals from the families of patients in the mental hospitals, which she sent on for investigation to Dr. Parsons, the commissioner of mental hygiene. "I enclose his report," she wrote to the family of a Miss P., "which indicates that the patient has a mild mental disturbance to which, generally speaking, she makes a satisfactory adjustment, but from time to time she overboils in the manner indicated in the letter." And thanking Dr. Parsons, she wrote, "I hope she eventually may be settled, . . . poor thing, she does not sound very happy." She was swamped with letters from old people begging her help with pension problems. She had every one of these "pathetic letters" reviewed in the hope that somehow they might be entitled to some kind of help. She looked into all requests for pardons, and if clemency was impossible, as was usually the case, "I can sometimes relieve their sorrow a little."

One of her most touching and insistent correspondents was a mother with a son in jail. "When she found I could not help her free him she begged that I go see him which I did. Now she begs that I go weekly and read the Bible to him!" A woman of eighty, so poor she could not pay for a dog license, had applied for an exemption. She sent Eleanor the "unfeeling letter" the state supervisor of dog licenses had written her; could Mrs. Roosevelt use her influence with the governor to have the tax remitted? It was Mrs. Roosevelt who paid the tax. She was overwhelmed by the trust people had in her. "I am the farmer's wife, that wrote you two years ago," one letter began. "You remember, I laid out my case then. Will you now see that I get my pension." "The farmer's wife," commented Eleanor wonderingly, "when there are dozens of them daily!"

But no letter went unanswered. Sometimes she sent a petitioner to his local district leader for help, but she did not leave it there. "Will you be good enough to let me know just what help your District

Leader gave you," she added. If she could do nothing in Albany, she would appeal to one of the many friends she had made throughout the state to look into a case for her, to see whether help might not be available locally.

Sometimes she showed these letters to Louis and, after she got to know him, to Corporal Miller, but as often as not she disregarded their warning that she was being taken in. "You're nothing but a cop," she said to Corporal Miller.[52] The appeals for help became a flood after the stock-market crash, and the rise in joblessness taxed even her resourcefulness in finding something affirmative to say to her correspondents. She strongly advised people not to come to New York to look for work: "At the present time there are countless numbers of people out of employment here and I am not able to get positions for any one." But still she did not give up. Did he have a job for Mr. K., statistician and Yale graduate, she asked Tom Lynch, who was now president of the State Tax Commission. "He has cried in my office like a whipped child."

Often she showed letters to her husband. "How shall I answer or will you?" she would pencil on the plea.

She functioned in a highly unorthodox way that defied all proper administrative charts. If she had been less tactful, less sensitive, if she had not always been careful to stay within the limits set by Franklin and to check with him to be sure that her activities were consistent with what he wanted done, her acts of compassion and her desire to be helpful could have degenerated into a scandal of meddlesomeness.

Roosevelt encouraged his state officials in the belief that he and "the Missus" were a team. She understood, and she was loyal. When she disagreed with him she told him, but it was kept within the family. He was the captain of the ship. "I sat next to you in the Senate chamber when the twenty million dollar relief bill was passed," an irate upstate judge wrote her. "Officials in Albany told me you were the boss. . . ." She had not been in the senate chamber when the relief bill was passed, she replied, "so you were wrong in thinking you sat next to me. Also any officials who told you I was boss of anything, were equally wrong."[53] Some members of Roosevelt's administration undoubtedly grumbled to their wives when she made requests they considered inconvenient, but more often they were glad to oblige. Not only was she the governor's wife and a political power in her own right, but, most important of all, she was a useful champion when their own programs were in trouble—or when they wanted the governor's support for new ideas.

It was to Eleanor that Frances Perkins came with a plan to overhaul and modernize the moribund Public Employment Service and its neglected network of state employment offices. Eleanor immediately saw its political implications as well as economic uses. "It looks good to me for it would take in employment of middle-aged and physically handicapped, etc. and you'd get the jump on Hoover, but they won't move till you let me know what you think," Eleanor wrote Franklin; the letter reached him a few days before the collapse of the stock market.[54] Roosevelt, according to Perkins, "at once saw the point of developing a good modern well-supported State Public Employment Service."

Eleanor had gotten to know a vast number of women in the small towns and rural areas and was now systematically getting to know more of them. Together with Elinor Morgenthau and Nancy Cook she was a faithful participant in the Home Economics Weeks that were organized by Cornell's Bureau of Home Economics and which annually brought thousands of rural women to Ithaca. Eleanor admired Martha van Rensselaer, the moving spirit behind the bureau, for the way she had made the bureau into a down-to-earth, sensible service to upstate women.

The women's division was ready for the 1930 gubernatorial campaign. Eleanor brought Molly Dewson into the division, and with Nancy Cook and Caroline O'Day they mapped strategy, organized meetings, issued literature—all behind the scenes. Her editorials in the *Democratic News* rallied the workers in the precincts to speak for the whole ticket. Her final editorial criticized the one-issue campaign of Republican candidate Charles H. Tuttle, who had concentrated on Tammany and corruption: what about the other big state-wide questions—taxation, farm relief, labor legislation, control of utilities, unemployment and public works, power?

What does it mean to be a candidate's wife, an interviewer wanted to know as the campaign drew to a close. "It doesn't mean a thing!" Eleanor replied. "In this particular case, at any event, the candidate's wife will go on pursuing the even tenor of her ways. Politics does not excite me. It never did. I take things as they come. If my husband is reelected, I shall be pleased. And if he isn't—well the world is full of interesting things to do."[55] In the meantime, however, she made sure that not the smallest thing was left undone that might help get her husband elected.

Roosevelt's landslide victory exceeded all expectations. He was swept in with a margin of 725,000, and was the first Democrat ever to carry upstate New York—by 167,000, which included Hyde Park, to Eleanor a "greater satisfaction than anything else." "Mrs. Roosevelt was a very great factor in Franklin D. Roosevelt's reelection," noted Molly Dewson, who was not given to flattery.[56]

The victory celebrations at Hyde Park on election night were prolonged, and Eleanor, who had to get ready for class next day, penciled a good-night note to her husband. "Much love & a world of congratulations. It is a triumph in so many ways, dear & so well earned. Bless you & good luck these next two years.—E.R."

33. ROOSEVELT BIDS FOR THE PRESIDENCY

———————◇———————

IN A YEAR OF DEMOCRATIC SUCCESSES, ROOSEVELT'S WAS THE handsomest. Overnight he became front runner among the Democratic aspirants for the presidency. It gave Eleanor pleasure to see him move toward the prize that he wanted above all others. She better than anyone appreciated how much determination and self-mastery his victory represented. She was happy, too, in the joy that the triumph brought her gnarled little friend Louis Howe, who behind the scenes had masterminded the comeback. Both men were now within sight of the goal they had been pursuing almost from the time of their first encounter. But she herself was a "fatalist," and the larger the ambition, the greater her feeling of its insubstantiality. She obtained her sense of fulfillment in service to others; to search out some hidden or defeated aspiration in the heart of a human being and then, in ways of her own, "to help this aspiration assume reality" gave her the greatest, perhaps the only, real joy in life. She had helped Franklin surmount the apparent devastation of his hopes by poliomyelitis. Now that he was the leading candidate for president, "that prospect did not interest me particularly."[1]

Her hopes were centered on a wholly different concern—making their marriage once again a covenant of spirit and feeling and not an arrangement to benefit the children and Franklin's career. A wife's job, Eleanor told an interviewer who had been advised by a group of distinguished women that she was "the ideal type of modern wife," was to be partner, mother, homemaker—and in that order, she emphasized. At one time she had placed the mother's role first, "but today we understand that everything else depends upon the success of the wife and husband in their personal relationship."[2]

She wanted to be close to her husband, to share, to be treated as equal not as instrument. But he had been brought up in a society where the ideal marriage was one that joined masculine egotism to feminine self-devotion. He was, moreover, self-centered in the way men become when they learn that few can refuse them anything. She could say "no" to him, and that was a part of her problem—how to press her point of view without making him feel guilty. For when that happened he became elusive, and as he was a consummate actor if he wished to be, he could keep even Eleanor guessing as to his true feelings and purposes. This made her feel shut out and destroyed the sense of companionship that she craved. She never gave up the hope that he would change. Perhaps now, in a common effort to make life better for other people, they could find their way to a new kind of partnership and at last efface the hurt he had done her in the Lucy Mercer affair.

The day after Roosevelt's victory, Jim Farley, the breezy politician whom Louis had groomed and nudged into the Democratic state chairmanship, told the press, "I do not see how Mr. Roosevelt can escape becoming the next presidential nominee of his party, even if no one should raise a finger to bring it about." Roosevelt had not told Farley he had made up his mind to run, but the statement had been carefully drafted with Louis, who, Jim assumed, knew the Boss's mind. A few days later Ed Flynn, whose rather nominal duties as secretary of state sheltered his role as one of Roosevelt's closest political advisers, was let in on the decision. They decided that the friendly, outgoing Farley was the man to send out to the regular organizations to round up delegates as the representative of the Friends of Roosevelt, an organization that Louis would direct. It was not Franklin who told Eleanor that he had decided to make his bid for president in 1932, although, of course, she had long known that the presidency was his goal. It was from Louis that she learned of his decision and that Louis was already at work planning the final strategy.[3]

Even though Franklin had not asked her how she felt about his running for the presidency, she was prepared to put her full strength—which was considerable—into the battle for the nomination, and he knew he could count on her. New York politicians, Farley said, recognized that she was "a strong and influential public figure in her own right."[4] Women figured importantly in the campaign plans and Farley, a new convert to women's role in politics, stood a little in awe of the work of the women under Eleanor's leadership. He was also grateful to her. "It wouldn't matter what Mrs. Roosevelt asked me to do, I would do it," he later told Emma Guffey Miller, Democratic national committeewoman from Pennsylvania. "If it hadn't been for her I would never have gotten where I am for she gave me my first big chance."[5] But it was political realism about the effectiveness of the women's organization more than gratitude to Eleanor Roosevelt which swayed the men. Farley credited the women's division with Roosevelt's margin of victory in 1928, and the 1930 campaign became known as the "waffle-iron" campaign because of the effective appeal the women had addressed to the housewives.[6] According to Farley's calculation, in counties where Eleanor's women were at work the total party vote picked up 10 to 20 per cent. "We felt the same kind of a job could be done on a national scale," he said.[7] As the recognized leader of the Democratic women of the state, Eleanor was the logical person for this job, but as the wife of the man who was both governor and candidate, she could not work openly, so Molly Dewson agreed to serve as her deputy. Molly hit it off well with Howe and Farley, and the team was complete.

By the spring of 1931 Louis had opened up the Friends of Roosevelt offices, and his "letter writing mill" was going full tilt.[8] So was Molly's, for whose signature Eleanor prepared the letters, and who, said Howe, managed a campaign correspondence "quite as large" as Farley's, though she did not use the green ink that became his trademark. In July Farley, in his role as Exalted Ruler of the Elks, made a highly productive western tour. At Eleanor's suggestion, Molly followed in his tracks a few months later. Her voluminous reports to Eleanor were also read by the men and perhaps were written with that in mind, for they reflected her and Eleanor's concern that Franklin should discuss the issues and that the women should not be ignored. At the end of her trip Molly reported from Salt Lake City: "I certainly got into pleasant relations with the ladies. . . . They undoubtedly were glad to see me. After all they are on the political coach, only by the eyelids— yet Hoover won by the women's vote." The women she had talked with considered Roosevelt "O.K." and a "vote getter" but Newton D. Baker, Wilson's secretary of war and a leading internationalist, also was "well liked." They were eager to hear Roosevelt "discuss national and international issues."[9]

Eleanor's campaign tasks for her husband were not limited to the women's division; she also helped the writers who wanted to do biographies of Franklin. Earle Looker, who had Republican inclinations and was a friend of the Oyster Bay Roosevelts, wanted to write a book about the Democratic Roosevelt. Eleanor furnished him opportunities to observe Roosevelt at first hand, and provided him with information. Looker did a great service for Roosevelt when the inevitable whispering campaign began about the candidate's physical incapacity to handle the presidency: he proposed publicly to challenge Roosevelt to submit to an examination by a panel of eminent physicians to be selected by the head of the New York Academy of Medicine. Roosevelt agreed and had the examination. The reprints of the panel's wholly affirmative findings, published by Looker in *Liberty*, were mailed out broadcast by Louis. "If polio did not kill him, the Presidency won't" was Eleanor's unsentimental reply when she was asked whether Franklin was physically up to the presidency.[10]

She was equally helpful to Ernest K. Lindley, who had covered Roosevelt, first for the *World* and then for the *New York Herald Tribune*. An outstanding reporter, he made his *Franklin D. Roosevelt: A Career in Progressive Politics* a sympathetic but objective biography that is still a source book for Roosevelt's Albany years. Roosevelt, who feigned dismay at the "whole library" of life stories that were being written about him, was not very cooperative with Lindley, but Eleanor and Louis were.[11]

Eleanor also took on such delicate, time-consuming tasks as the cultivation of Elizabeth Marbury, the still powerful Democrat, who wrote suggesting that Roosevelt come to Maine. "The best I can do is to send Eleanor to see you about the 20th of July," he replied. An ailing Missy accompanied Eleanor on a week's trip that included a stay in Newport with Cousin Susie and a stopover in Portland with Maude and David Gray. Eleanor was more concerned with Missy's health than with Miss Marbury's loyalties; Missy "smoked less today," she reported to her husband, "and I thought seemed more ready to sleep tonight. She is eating fairly well." They arrived at Miss Marbury's in time for lunch "& Miss Marbury has talked politics ever since except for a brief time when Missy & I went in swimming! Molly Dewson is here too for the night & tomorrow there is a grand jamboree!"[12]

Although she declined either in speeches or interviews to discuss politics or her husband's chances for the nomination, she was nevertheless an effective representative of his candidacy in the course of her extensive travels. In Winston-Salem, North Carolina, she spoke to the Altrusa Club, a nationwide organization of professional women, at a time when new Tammany scandals were breaking almost daily in New York City. Roosevelt's association with Tammany was seized upon by his rivals in order to embarrass him, and the nation watched developments as an index of his political independence. Eleanor did not deal with the issue directly in Winston-Salem; her subject was general and high-minded—"The Individual's Responsibility to the Community." In the course of her speech, however, she talked naturally about Tammany and how she had been raised to think that Tammany men had "horns and a tail," but "when one's party is not what one feels it should be, it is better to get into the organization and purify it from within instead of standing without and criticizing." Critics were disarmed. The *Times* correspondent observed that "Mrs. Roosevelt made many friends for herself and Governor Roosevelt. It was remarked by many political-minded folk at the dinner that she was a splendid advance agent, if such she could be termed, for her husband."[13] In Atlanta she spoke before the League of Women Voters. She sounded the theme that it was up to the women to end war, the reporter for the *Atlanta Constitution* wrote admiringly, "alternately bringing laughter with stories of her own education in politics and holding her listeners tense with her eloquence, Mrs. Roosevelt exhibited a versatility and political background worthy of the traditions of the Roosevelt family." She herself admitted to Molly that the time spent in North Carolina had been "rather profitable," although "nine speeches in three days was a bit strenuous!"[14]

Within New York State she continued to serve as Franklin's proxy. "I do not often go to the big places," she told Ida Tarbell with her usual modesty, "but often to the little places where they have difficulty in securing speakers. I don't do it as well as I wish I did, but after all what they want is to see the Governor's wife."[15] The *New Yorker* saw it differently: "No woman has a better grasp of the intricacies of state business and she has a decided flair for putting things aptly."[16]

She did not like to travel in the big state car, preferring to use her own and drive herself. This made Franklin uneasy, and he insisted that Earl Miller, now promoted to sergeant, accompany her.[17] Miller, one of the handsomest troopers in the state, a former amateur welterweight champion, an excellent horseman who did trick riding at the state fair, and an instructor in judo and boxing at the State Police School, was something of a self-styled Lothario. He had been Al Smith's bodyguard for four years and when the Roosevelts came to Albany was kept on the mansion detail. The boys in the barracks did not envy him his assignment with "that old crab," but Eleanor, with her kindliness and insatiable curiosity about people, quickly made a conquest of him. Soon he was telling her the story of his life—his beginnings in Schenectady, his years as circus acrobat, his war years in the Navy, his unhappy first marriage. Solicitude for his troubles made it easier for her to accept his helpfulness and brusque gallantries, and his barracks-room language, his cynicism, and his roughneck qualities were a new and interesting experience. She got to know his family and invited his niece to stay at the mansion. Earl, who had had no home since he was twelve, transferred the affection he would have felt for his parents to "the Boss" and "the Lady." Eleanor encouraged his friendship, and he helped her overcome fears that still remained from her years of self-subordination. He urged her to take up riding again and took care of her horse. He helped her gain enough confidence in her driving that she told Louis—who often insisted on doing the driving and some-times "scared her pink"—that she would "never take him again unless I'm doing *all* the driving."[18]

While she could deal with the press, she hated to be photographed because she was convinced she was ugly. She and Louis had a game—who could find the ugliest photograph of himself. "Please don't let them take my picture," she would plead with Miller. "Try to smile," he encouraged her; "smile for just one picture." He even stood behind the photographers and made funny faces at her.[19] Miller was not the only one who, from her photographs, had expected to encounter a woman of formidable plainness. The *New Yorker* correspondent was surprised at how "unjustly" the camera dealt with Mrs. Roosevelt because it could not capture "her immaculate freshness of appearance, her graciousness, and the charm of a highly intelligent, forceful and directed personality." In time, coached by Miller and pushed by necessity, she became as relaxed with photographers as with newspapermen.

Her friendship with Earl was cemented by the assistance he gave her with her alcoholic Uncle Vallie and with Franklin's old Groton tutor and crony of Navy days, George Marvin, who had similar problems. Marvin, full of self-pity, turned up in Albany lamenting his wasted literary talents and asking for help. Franklin had no time for him, so Eleanor undertook the task of rehabilitation, getting him a job with Henry Morgenthau's Conservation Department. But the process was painful and marked by frequent backslidings. When word reached her that George was on a tear, Earl was sent into action.

And when Vallie's drinking sprees resulted in his hiring a taxi and roaring up to the executive mansion, she and Miller took him back to Tivoli. At one point Vallie began associating with a young neighbor who had been arrested for raping a ten-year-old girl and who man-aged to smuggle in liquor. When the young man induced Vallie to buy a car and to permit other members of his family to stay at Tivoli,

Eleanor decided the time had come to step in. She took Vallie to his room while Miller proceeded to read the riot act to the young man. He told him to leave and followed him to the county line, where he warned him that if he returned he ran the risk of arrest. Vallie was more difficult: Earl had to subdue him by force. "As I wrestled him down, the cords stood out in his head. 'Hey! you're quite a strong fellow.'" Vallie finally conceded.[20]

Earl became part of the mansion household. He had been eating out in the kitchen with the other troopers, but was asked to eat with the family. He gave Eleanor the appreciation that her husband and her four sons so often neglected to show her. He took her side rather than Franklin's. And to be squired around by this handsome state trooper who paid her small masculine attentions and treated her as a woman appealed to long dormant feminine qualities in her. She even liked his lapses into a roughness that Nancy and Marion considered rudeness.[21] She became as devoted to Earl as she was to Louis; she loved everyone who gave her strength to meet and surmount difficult trials and fears.

Those she loved she mothered, as she did almost everyone who served her and Franklin. Gus Gennerich, a New York policeman who was Roosevelt's personal bodyguard, was another member of the family entourage. He had little education and always remained the New York "cop," but he was engaging and affectionate and loyal. The Roosevelts considered him a friend, and Franklin always insisted that he be considered part of his personal party. Eleanor often visited Gus's old and ailing mother, and she stayed with Gus after his mother died until the funeral.[22]

No matter what she may have felt about Missy's closeness to Franklin, Eleanor's maternal tenderness enveloped her as well. Inevitably, a romance developed between Earl and Missy which ended when Earl and Ruth Bellinger, a second cousin of his first wife, decided to get married. "Glad Earl told Missy," Eleanor wrote Franklin. "I was sure she would rather know from him."[23] Earl and Ruth were married at Hyde Park, with Anna Dall as bridesmaid and Elliott the best man.

The marriage ended gossip, at least temporarily, concerning Eleanor's relationship to Earl. It was not surprising that the habits and friendships of both Franklin and Eleanor caused raised eyebrows and provided food for "inside stories" at many dinner tables. Eleanor's frequent trips with Earl as her only companion, Missy's presence in the mansion and her role as the governor's hostess in Eleanor's absence, the affectionate familiarity among all of them, the obvious delight they took in each other's company left even good friends puzzled and confused as to the true character of their relationships.

When Bill and Caroline Phillips visited the Roosevelts in Albany, the observant Caroline noted that Earl Miller came to tea, but she could not quite figure out what his function was; she gave him the title of "Major" and decided he was probably an aide. She also noted that there was "a secretary whom everyone called Missie [*sic*]," who was, she commented, "a very nice young woman."[24] Missy's status also intrigued the Henry Goddard Leaches, who were among the guests that week end. Franklin proposed that they all motor down to Hyde Park for luncheon, and Eleanor said to Agnes Leach, "You'll understand that Franklin will not drive with us. He has this new car and he wants to show it off to Missy." Agnes concluded that he was very fond of Missy, and mentioned it later to Elinor Morgenthau. "Oh no," Elinor protested. "He loves Missy. She's quite essential to him. He loves Missy but as to an affair—no."[25] At Hyde Park they were met by Nancy Cook, "Eleanor's great friend," Caroline wrote in her diary, "short, stocky Miss Cooke [*sic*], with her poppy-out blue eyes and short wiry grey hair... was as always warmly embraced by Eleanor. She is a most determined person who began by being a paid worker at some Democratic organization and then a sort of political secretary to Franklin and she now runs the Val-Kill furniture factory at Hyde Park, as well as the Roosevelt family!"

The Phillipses came away from the week end with their two old friends feeling that they were both "living on *top* of their arduous job in a magnificent way.... The only flaw I could find in Eleanor is her disdain for any interest in food!... our meals were very unattractive, I must say. She was laughing at her mother-in-law who wanted to discuss with her what dishes would be most delicious for a dinner party, 'as though,' said Eleanor, 'anyone now-a-days had time to spend twenty minutes planning what to eat!'"

Eleanor's determination not to waste time on food made her insensitive to her husband's wishes, and she insisted that he was as indifferent to food as she was. "I am sorry to tell you that my husband and I are very bad about food. I do not know of any particular dish which he likes unless it is wild duck and the only recipe for that from his point of view is that it should fly through the kitchen."[26] It was no secret to others, however, that Roosevelt did not like the "plain foods, plainly prepared" that were served at the mansion, but evidently there was little he could do about it except when Eleanor was away. "Goodness, the Governor has no preferences," she told S. J. Woolf of the *New York Times*. "If I should give him bacon and eggs three times a day he would be perfectly satisfied."[27] She could be stubborn and she was always on guard against the pleasure-loving side in her husband.

Eleanor wanted her husband to talk to her about everything— friendships, managing the children, homemaking, and of course, politics and public affairs. She wanted to be his confidante and counselor, to be privy to his hopes and to be turned to when he met disappointment. But the nearer they came to the nominating convention and the decisive battle, the more ambiguous he became about his basic convictions and the less time he had for anything except the political game. When she feared that his pursuit of the presidency was engulfing her hopes of a true partnership, when it seemed to her that politics instead of being an instrument for the ennoblement of humanity was turning into a naked pursuit of an office, which, if achieved, would transform her into a ceremonial marionette, when it became evident that the more insistently she pressed these matters with him, the less he took her into his confidence, she fell into black despair.

She was worried about her children and the fact that her husband rarely saw them. Anna was having problems with her marriage. Elliott, not yet twenty-one, was restlessly moving from one job to another and rushing into marriage; he seemed "terribly young to prefer monogamy," commented David Gray,[28] and David's reservations were mild compared to Eleanor's. The youngest boys were driving too fast and too recklessly. Her husband did not take the drastic measures she urged, either because of the pressure of public duties or disinclination to face disagreeable situations. The fact that Franklin was governor meant a sacrifice for the children, she said; they could not be "first" with their father. At times she understood and accepted this as the inevitable consequence of his career as a public man but at the other times she was resentful that they should be robbed of his time, his companionship, his guidance. The reflected limelight was particularly injurious—favors were done for them; they were offered jobs and opportunities. There were always strings attached but they were too young to see that. "It may be so small a thing as being invited to park their cars where others are not permitted to," Eleanor said, unburdening herself to a friendly reporter. "It is bad for children to be allowed to infringe the rules."[29] She found herself in the role of "perennial deflator . . . sometimes it seems to me that I am everlastingly saying 'no.'" Her sigh as she said this reflected the burden that was thrown upon her by her husband's unavailability as disciplinarian. And if she did try to get Franklin to accept the responsibility for disciplining one of the children, "the punishment simply was not administered."[30]

In December, 1931, she wrote an article entitled "Ten Rules for Success in Marriage."[31] Though most readers probably assumed it described her relationship to her husband, actually it depicted what she wished marriage to be and what it was not. The article even discussed the circumstances under which divorce was justifiable, a hazardous topic for a public figure and a radical departure from the traditions of her grandmother and mother-in-law, who belonged to the generation described by Edith Wharton as dreading scandal more than disease. When in 1922 Hall had taken her to a little New York restaurant to tell her that he intended to divorce Margaret, she had been concerned with what it would mean "to the family, all of whom believed that when you made your bed you had to lie in it." But now she observed succinctly, "It is far better for two people who cannot get along to sep- arate than to lead a quarrelsome life. If there are no children, I would say that divorce is justifiable when either husband or wife, or both find that life together has ceased to have any spiritual value."

Her formula for married happiness emphasized "unselfishness— thoughtfulness—consideration of others. In marriage selfishness shows itself in one way that is particularly common, through the desire of either husband or wife to be the dominating person in the household." Expect to disagree, she said, but "do not dominate. In this respect victory for one is failure for the partnership."

But Franklin always had to be in command. He was a showman, and his charm and magnetism were so overpowering that the house- hold naturally gravitated around him; everyone's interests were sub- ordinated to his. A woman in love with a man could accept this, but that kind of love had died with the Lucy Mercer affair, Eleanor told herself. She was not in love with him. Yet she was prepared to render him a labor of love by serving his work (a distinction that she drew in an article for King Features, the Hearst Syndicate, published in Febru- ary, 1933, on the role of a public man's wife) if he would be thoughtful, considerate, and treat her as a partner and confidante. Perhaps these longings for a full partnership were inherently unfillable given her emotional needs and insecurities, and Franklin, on his side, could not be tenderly confiding and open in the way she craved. As she explained to her son James years later, "His was an innate kind of reticence that may have been developed by the fact that he had an older father and a very strong-willed mother, who constantly tried to exercise control over him in the early years. Consequently, he may have fallen into the habit of keeping his own counsel, and it became part of his nature not to talk to anyone of intimate matters."[32]

Many years later she wrote to a young friend in the service:

There is one thing I've always wanted to say to you, when you do come home and get engulfed in work, will you stop long enough now and then even if T. is working with you to make her feel she is *first* in your life even more important than saving the world? Every woman wants to be first to someone sometimes in her life and the desire is the explanation for many strange things women do, if only men understood it!

Stubbornly she fought for a more tender, intimate relationship with her husband. Life away from him was difficult; life with him could be equally so. In the spring of 1931 Sara, who was in Paris, became ill with pneumonia. Franklin wanted Eleanor to go to France, but she felt that it would do his mother much more good if he went without her, so he took Elliott instead. A touching letter from Eleanor followed. "I think I looked so tired chiefly because I hated to see you go, though I knew it was the best thing for you to do & the sensible thing for me not to go. We are really very dependent on each other though we do see so little of each other. I feel as lost as I did when I went abroad & I will never do that again.... Goodnight, dear.... Dear love to you.... I miss you & hate to feel you so far away." Franklin's visit, she wrote eighteen years later in *This I Remember,* "gave his mother just what was needed to accelerate her recovery."[33]

There were acute differences over issues and the compromises he felt obliged to accept in order to win the nomination. During the twenties she had developed a set of strongly held views and she used every channel in advancing them with her husband. "What did he think?...What was his reaction?" she would anxiously ask Louis, if he was in Albany, before she went in to sit on Franklin's bed and say good night. Or if she were leaving Albany, she would say to Missy, "You work on him."

As the Depression deepened and joblessness spread, she pressed more urgently for action. She was "not excited about the Communists," she told the Southern Women's Democratic Organization, but she was concerned about "the great number of people in New York who cannot get work."[34] Before the Brooklyn Emergency Unemployment Committee, she spoke of the right to work "as fundamental and inherent in our civilization. Suddenly to find that no work is to be had turns people bitter." She understood that bitterness and pleaded for the "alleviation of distress...now."[35] She was unhappy that Franklin was as elusive on the issue of child-labor legislation as Al Smith had been. Molly, on behalf of the advocates of unemployment compensation, asked Eleanor to urge the governor to make it a major objective. Eleanor regarded her thoughtfully as they drove through the congested garment district, Molly recalled, and then said, "I will speak to Franklin about it. I do not know whether he will consider it wise to take on another measure."[36] It was she who brought to her husband's attention a hard-driving, militant social worker named Harry L. Hopkins, whom Roosevelt selected to head up the state's program of unemployment relief.[37]

Some of Roosevelt's closest advisers—Sam Rosenman, his counsel and speech writer, and Doc O'Connor, his law partner and a political counselor, thought Eleanor was dangerously idealistic. Not long after Rexford G. Tugwell was drafted as a member of the Brains Trust in the spring of 1932, he was stunned to hear O'Connor say to him and Ray Moley, Columbia University professor and the first to be recruited into the Brains Trust, that he hoped they knew one of their first jobs was "to get the pants off Eleanor and onto Frank." Sam agreed.[38] Eleanor's "well-meant probings" annoyed them, so much so that they tended to avoid the dinners at the mansion that preceded a work-out with the Brains Trust. Conversation at dinner, Tugwell noticed, tended to be controlled by Eleanor, who always had "some good cause to further" and who "was apt to chide her husband when he claimed more than he should have for his efforts during the past four years."[39] Although Eleanor's "pronouncements infuriated Doc and Sam," Tugwell took them less seriously. He felt that even if her views were not profound, "they went cautiously in the right direction."[40]

The sharpest disagreements between Eleanor and her husband were occasioned by his shifts on Prohibition and the League of Nations. She remained a teetotaler, an ardent advocate of Prohibition, and a supporter of the Women's Christian Temperance Union. She would not have liquor or wine at her table and it offended her to learn that cocktails were served at the mansion in her absence. It had been difficult for her to go along with Franklin when at the 1930 Governors' Conference he suggested a states' rights solution of the enforcement problem. She had had great hopes for the Volstead Act, yet "when I see the terrible things that have grown out of it, such as graft and bootlegging, one begins to wonder about it," and she was realistic enough to see that enforcement was not working. But when Franklin went beyond states' rights and called for repeal of the Eighteenth Amendment, Eleanor disagreed sharply. "She was," commented Sam Rosenman, "a rather inflexible person, rather high-minded and averse to compromise. She had very set ideas."[41]

Although Louis was disdainful of Sam and Doc and was usually allied with Eleanor, on the Prohibition issue he, too, considered her unrealistic.[42] Eleanor's ally in this case was Sara, who was also a Prohibitionist by conviction. "I don't want my son to be elected if he has to be elected on a 'wet' ticket," she told a group of Roosevelt's political associates. But Roosevelt and Howe approached the issue politically, and were quite reconciled to see the "great experiment" torpedoed.

The other source of tension between Eleanor and her husband in the spring of 1932 was his retreat from supporting the League of Nations and the World Court. After he became governor, Roosevelt, one of the country's most prominent Wilsonians, fell silent on the issue of adherence to the Court on the grounds that as a governor he should stick to state affairs and not get involved in foreign-policy issues. Eleanor, on the other hand, continued to work with Esther Lape for ratification of the World Court. Pleas for action over her signature were sent to all Democratic senators, and she asked the Democratic national committeewomen from their states to get after any senators who did not respond.[43] "You do stick to the Court through thick and thin," Mrs. Catt wrote her admiringly in March, 1930.

Until 1932 Roosevelt had managed to escape attack on the issue through a policy of public silence and private assurances to World Court partisans that he was still with them. Now William Randolph Hearst, launching a boom for Speaker of the House John Nance Garner of Texas, began to fulminate against internationalism and the Wilsonians, urging instead an "America First" policy. His first blast named Roosevelt, Newton Baker, Owen D. Young, even Al Smith, but the attack was soon limited to Roosevelt. In front-page editorials with big black type the Hearst papers quoted his pro–League of Nations statements in 1920. By the end of January Howe was advising Franklin that "You may have to make a public statement before we get through, if this gets any more violent." The struggle over whether to appease Hearst raged among Roosevelt's advisers. Rosenman thought

Eleanor was rigid on this issue, too, even more so than on Prohibition: "She had an awful lot of faith in the World Court as the only thing to rally around once the League of Nations was out of the question."[44] Roosevelt tried to avoid public repudiation of the League and the Court by sending Jim Farley to the editors of Hearst's *New York American* to reassure them about Roosevelt's views on internationalism. The assurances should be given "to the public, publicly, not to me privately," Hearst stated on the front page next day. Finally, Roosevelt capitulated, and in a speech to the New York State Grange said he did not favor American participation in the League of Nations. He was even ready to turn his back on the Court, but Hearst seemed satisfied and the Wilsonians were up in arms. Cordell Hull, who had been drawn to Roosevelt by his internationalism and was one of the most influential supporters of his candidacy, was deeply upset by Roosevelt's speech. Colonel House warned Howe, "What you said about the League has already strained their loyalty, and many of them have told me that if you take the same position on the World Court they cannot support you."

Agnes Leach was one of the angry Wilsonians who had occasion to see Roosevelt at the time. "I couldn't believe my eyes," she said to him. "That was a shabby statement. I just don't feel like having lunch with you today."

Franklin was taken aback. "I am sorry you are in that mood. One reason I wanted you here today is that Eleanor is very fond of you and you can make peace between us. She hasn't spoken to me for three days."[45]

When Eleanor heard about the incident she immediately phoned her friend: "Agnes, you are a sweet, darling girl. I hear you upset Franklin very much. I didn't know you had it in you." He was eager for Eleanor's approval, Mrs. Leach felt, and cared "a terrific lot about her opinion" even if he disregarded it.

Roosevelt's reversal on the League, his ambiguities on Prohibition, and his efforts to avoid a showdown with Tammany produced widespread doubt about the strength of his convictions. Heywood Broun called him "a corkscrew," Elmer Davis thought him the "weakest" of the candidates for the nomination, and Walter Lippmann described him as "an amiable man with many philanthropic impulses" who was "not the dangerous enemy of anything." (Eleanor saved that column.) Many years later, Eleanor's radio and television agent, Thomas L. Stix, who idolized her, confessed that he had voted for Norman Thomas in 1932. "So would I," she reassured him, "if I had not been married to Franklin."[46]

Political discontent merged with personal unhappiness, as is revealed briefly in a letter she sent Molly after having lunch with her: "Of course there is no other candidate who will do more what we want. I simply had a fit of rebellion against the male attitude. I've had one before but sober sense does come to my rescue & I feel better when I realize that I've thought primarily about myself."[47]

"Can't you see that loyalty to the ideals of Woodrow Wilson is just as strong in my heart as it is in yours," one of Roosevelt's letters to an irate Wilsonian began, and went on to explain that his ideals had not changed, only his methods of achieving them—"and for heaven's sake have a little faith." He might almost have been arguing with his wife.

"It was all unnecessary," wrote Mrs. Charles Hamlin to Josephus Daniels about Roosevelt's repudiation of the League. But was it? A moment came in the Democratic convention three months later at the end of the third ballot when the stop Roosevelt movement still kept him short of the two-thirds vote needed for nomination. Several states—Mississippi, Arkansas, and Alabama—were being held in the Roosevelt ranks with difficulty. If Roosevelt did not gain decisively on the fourth ballot, his ranks might break and disintegrate. After consulting with Howe, Farley went to work on Texas, which along with California had been voting for Garner. Hearst was one of the keys to the California-Texas alliance, and Roosevelt leaders telephoned him at San Simeon to urge him to support a switch. He agreed. Would he have done so if Roosevelt had not satisfied him on the issue of the League? There is no absolute answer to the "ifs" of history, but it seems a reasonable conjecture that if Roosevelt had not compromised on this issue he might not have won the nomination. And if he had not been president when the Hitler menace broke out, would another man have promoted the Wilsonian cause as faithfully and effectively as he did?

Franklin was the politician, she the agitator, Eleanor said in later years.[48] "Mrs. Roosevelt's hand is almost exactly complementary to the hand of her husband," an authority in palmistry wrote. "By this I mean she has just the sort of character that will supplement and aid the character of the Governor."[49] They made a splendid team, but that was not the way it seemed to her at the time. She was a deeply divided woman as the convention neared. She was happy for Franklin—and Louis—as the states fell in line ("So Tennessee is in!" she wrote him on May 21, as things went according to schedule; "Jim Farley grins more broadly with each State!"), but she saw her husband's entry into the White House as portending a kind of gilded captivity for her.

Friends were baffled by her calmness, almost detachment, as the convention began. She took several hours off on the opening day to drive through a thunderstorm to visit Margaret Doane Fayerweather, an old friend who was recuperating from a very serious operation. For an hour she sat at Margaret's bedside, her knitting needles busy. Not till she left was there a word of politics. Then Margaret, unable to contain herself asked, "What are your plans?"

"Well, we shall either be flying to Chicago—or staying quietly at home."

"We shall be praying that you will be flying to Chicago."

"The time when we shall need your prayers will be if Franklin is nominated and elected."[50]

When the long night of the nominations began she was with Franklin, who was in his shirtsleeves, silent, waiting. Sara was at the governor's mansion as were Elliott and John, Missy, Grace Tully, and Sam Rosenman. When the speechmaking ended and the balloting began it was 4:20 A.M., and Eleanor sent out pots of coffee to the newsmen, who had established a listening post in the garage. As roll call followed roll call, Franklin chain-smoked and Eleanor knitted a turtle-neck sweater for asthma-wracked Louis who was in Chicago. At 9:15 A.M., after the inconclusive third ballot, the convention recessed. Sara found the suspense too upsetting and left for Hyde Park, indignant that some of the "gentlemen" in the New York delegation had voted against her son. The others tried to get a little sleep. Eleanor was the first to come down and was preparing to have breakfast with Louis Howe's grandson when she encountered two Associated Press reporters on their way out after the all-night vigil. Would Miss Hickok and Mr. Fay join her, she asked them. The breakfast went pleasantly, but to the two reporters Eleanor seemed withdrawn, not at all involved in the drama of the tense hours between the third and the final ballots. Fay thought she was worried that her husband would not get the nomination. More perceptively, Lorena Hickok, a woman in her late thirties, observed, "That woman's unhappy about something."[51]

At dinner that night the telephone call came for which Roosevelt had been waiting. "F.D., you look just like the cat that swallowed the canary," said Missy. Later the news was on the radio: McAdoo announced that California had not come to Chicago to deadlock a convention but to elect a president and was switching to Roosevelt.

"Good old McAdoo," said Roosevelt, smiling contentedly. "The rest of the study was a bedlam," Grace Tully recalled. "Mrs. Roosevelt and Missy LeHand embraced each other. Both embraced me. John and Elliott tossed scratch paper in the air and shook hands as if they hadn't seen each other in years. Mrs. Roosevelt came down out of the clouds before the rest of us. 'I'm going to make some bacon and eggs,' she announced."[52]

Albany neighbors gathered on the front lawn to cheer. Roosevelt exchanged quips with the photographers and reporters who had come crowding in from the garage. The women reporters, including the owl-eyed Miss Hickok, found Mrs. Roosevelt scrambling eggs. "Mrs. Roosevelt, aren't you *thrilled* at the idea of being in the White House?" one of them "gushed." Mrs. Roosevelt's only reply, Miss Hickok noted, was a look so unsmiling that it stopped all further questions along that line. Lorena Hickok's intuition that here was a woman strangely unhappy as her husband moved toward the presidency became a bond between the two women, and before the campaign was over she was receiving Eleanor's confidence. "I'm a middle-aged woman," she said to Miss Hickok on her forty-eighth birthday. "It's good to be middle-aged. Things don't matter so much. You don't take it so hard when things happen to you that you don't like."[53]

34. "I NEVER WANTED TO BE A PRESIDENT'S WIFE"

THE MORNING AFTER THE NOMINATION ROOSEVELT FLEW TO Chicago as a way of serving notice on the country that a new energetic leadership was prepared to take command. Eleanor accompanied him, as did Elliott and John, Sam, Missy, Grace, and two bodyguards, Gus and Earl. Eleanor was the first to emerge from the plane. "A fine job, Mr. Farley. Congratulations!" she said, extending her hand to the beaming chairman. Struck by her poise and composure, Emma Bugbee of the *New York Herald Tribune* commented that she was "one of the calm people of the world."[1] Someone asked her whether her life would not "belong to the public after this," and she quickly replied, "It never has and never could."

It was a discerning question. There was in her a craving for experience, a fear of pomp and ceremony. She did not wish to be shielded from the world but to take part in it and change it. She wanted to live a life without artifice, to do things herself, to live the truth. She had an ascetic strain—she called it the Puritan in her—and inner drives that in other times and other places had led women to renounce worldly pleasures and take vows of poverty and service. She carried about with her a prayer by Henry Van Dyke entitled "The Footpath to Peace," to which she added the words "with oneself." Among the prayer's injunctions were "to think seldom of your enemies, often of your friends and every day of Christ"; she had circled the phrase about Christ. "Christ was born in a manger," she wrote a few months later, "and worked all his life and in that way we were taught that the highest and best things in life may be linked with material hardship and the simplest of living." As completely as she could, she wanted to live according to Christ's teachings.

She feared that all these things would become impossible once she was First Lady, that she would become a prisoner of protocol and tradition. Louis, an inveterate scribbler of verse, had addressed himself to her anxieties in early 1932.

We are the hooded brotherhood of fears.
Barring the pleasant path that lay ahead.
Who, grim and silent, all these futile years,
Have filled your timid soul with numbing dread. . . .

Fool! Had you dared to speed your pace
Our masking cowls aside to tear
And meet us bravely face to face
We would have vanished into air.

Louis' assurances that there would be plenty for her to do in the White House did not end her worries; the closer Franklin came to the nomination, the more certain she became that she did not want to be First Lady. Nancy and Marion had accompanied Louis to Chicago, and Nancy received a letter from Eleanor saying these things. When she showed it to Louis, he ripped it to shreds and told her not to breathe a word of it to anyone.[2] From her own personal standpoint, Eleanor later wrote, she did not want her husband to be president: "It was pure selfishness on my part, and I never mentioned my feelings on the subject to him."[3]

Her dread of what she called "captivity" in the White House did not prevent her from pitching into the campaign with her usual vigor. While some of the party's conservatives were opposed to a strong women's division, especially a "militant" one, a major appeal was nevertheless going to be directed to the distaff side of the electorate. Molly moved over from Friends of Roosevelt to direct the drive, again as Eleanor's deputy. There was an easy and understanding relationship between the two. "I hate people to be grateful to me," Eleanor wrote Molly in Maine, where she had been sent to rest before the campaign, "just as much as you apparently hate them to be grateful to you so you need not worry. I love working with you for just the reasons I imagine you like working with me and you need not ever worry that I will not speak perfectly truthfully to you or that you should hesitate to say whatever you have on your mind to me."[4]

While Molly rested in Maine, Eleanor organized and staffed the women's division. She presented the Democratic National Committee, which Farley had assembled in New York for a strategy session, with the plan developed by Molly for work in the states. There was to be a vice chairwoman in every state to head up the women's work and a committeewoman in every county, especially in the rural areas, with whom Molly could correspond directly and to whom headquarters could send literature and gasoline money. The men agreed, although they were reluctant to have any money come into their states that was not channeled through them. They also agreed that the women in charge of their states would draft their work plans and send them to Eleanor. For the wife of the presidential candidate to hold such responsibility and to wield such authority was unprecedented in American politics, but in Eleanor's case it seemed the natural thing to do.

Eleanor and her colleagues had learned their lessons well in 1930 and knew exactly what they wanted. They did *not* want, a chagrined Howe discovered, the twelve-page brochures the men, including himself, had drafted. The women marched into his office, he later reported, "their noses visibly turned toward Heaven," and announced loftily, "You surely don't expect us to send that to our women do you?" "Why not?" Howe inquired. "Well, I don't know about you men, but we women have no time to waste reading through stuff like that." Women, Howe learned, had an "appalling desire for figures"; they preferred leaflets which presented a single argument. Finally they were given their own printing budget and told to produce their own literature. The ladies' "Rainbow Fliers," as they came to be called, were printed by the millions and were so successful that the men made extensive use of them. "They were written solely by women. No man had a hand in them," Molly commented rather smugly.[5]

Eleanor turned over to Molly a list of the "safe states" and the "fighting states," where Louis figured the election would be won or lost. The women precinct leaders in the latter states were notified just how their districts had voted in 1928 and how many additional votes were needed for a Democratic victory in 1932. The most intensive campaigning was done by a corps of "grass trampers," women who went from door to door and whose indefatigable work Louis later credited with bringing out the women's vote; he "would rather have a half-dozen women field workers than a hundred men any day," he concluded. Moreover, they made the same amount of money go twice as far; in fact, they were sometimes too frugal, and in a campaign it was necessary to use money speedily.[6]

Farley's and Molly's offices were at the Biltmore Hotel, while Louis and Eleanor remained across the street at the old Friends of Roosevelt office. One of Eleanor's jobs was to keep the channels of communication open between Farley and the ever-suspicious Howe, and she could occasionally be seen hurrying across Madison Avenue with Louis in tow to straighten out a misunderstanding, smooth over a hurt feeling. After the Walker hearings ended with Tammany Mayor Jimmy Walker's sudden resignation, Franklin took off on his campaign train accompanied by James and his wife Betsy and Anna Dall. Roosevelt liked to have his children with him, and he was especially fond of Betsy, who was pert, vivacious, and enjoyed coquetting with her irresistible father-in-law. From time to time Eleanor flew out to join the campaign train, and she was in Chicago when the whole family attended a World Series game between the Cubs and the Yankees. She was not a model of attentiveness, Jimmy later claimed, having slept through most of the game, one in which Babe Ruth and Lou Gehrig each hit home runs.[7] But during that same stay in Chicago when Bobby Fitzmaurice, who handled transportation schedules, fell ill, it was Eleanor who took the "Commissioner of the Ramps," as Roosevelt had fondly dubbed him, to the hospital, just as, a few weeks later, when Missy's mother died, it was Eleanor who accompanied Missy to Potsdam, New York, for the funeral.

The Depression was reaching its nadir and the grim signs were everywhere—the lengthening bread lines, the Hoovervilles, the silent, sullen countryside in which smoldered the fires of rebellion, the horrifying use of troops and tear gas to rout the veterans from Washington. Eleanor shifted her emphasis from the alleviation of distress to the need for basic change. A financial system that was "man-made" was also "man-controlled," she told the Chatauqua ladies. "We must reorganize our economic structure so it may be possible for those willing to work to receive adequate compensation." Her ideas were not more advanced than her husband's, Tugwell noted, but she was willing to talk about them "when he was not yet ready for commitment."[8] She counseled the girls of the Junior League to prepare themselves for the big changes that were coming by learning to earn their own living and to pull their weight by making a contribution to the world. When one of her Todhunter girls remarked that "you can get anything you want in the world if you have enough money," she asked the entire class to bring in "a list of things you think the Depression has taught people who have money and also a list of what you think it has done to people who are unemployed and have nothing." She urged "a spirit of mutual helpfulness" in easing the hardships of the Depression but insisted that the country's leaders probe deeply into its causes with a view to fundamental reform.

It was considered unseemly for her to campaign for her husband, but it was decided she should take the stump for Herbert Lehman, who had been nominated for governor over Tammany's objections and faced a hard fight. While Roosevelt, in Pittsburgh, to the delight of the conservatives among his advisers, condemned Hoover for his "reckless and extravagant" spending policies and promised a 25 per cent reduction in federal payrolls, Eleanor, in Syracuse a week later, was not so sure economy was such "a very wonderful thing...it can do a great deal of harm." The Republicans had cut $21 million out of the state budget, but "practically all of that came out of the appropriation for the Department of Public Works...[which] means that thousands of young engineers, draftsmen and laborers were thrown out of work." Since the Republicans subsequently were obliged to appropriate not only what they had cut out of the budget, but more for public relief, she wanted to know which would have been better—"to pay that money out in salaries for labor on public works, or to pay it in unemployment relief?"[9]

Roosevelt's goal was to get elected, and his rhetoric was shaped by that; Eleanor—as she ladled out soup on the bread lines, gave lifts to tramps, and sent hungry men to her house with instructions that they should be fed—was increasingly preoccupied with the necessity not only for fundamental changes but for preparing the country to accept those changes. Otherwise, she felt, Franklin's task might prove to be an impossible one.

She poured out her anxieties to Lorena Hickok on a midnight drive from Poughkeepsie to New York. She had attended Franklin's final rally but insisted on driving back to town afterward so that she could meet her nine o'clock class in the morning. "Of course Franklin will do his best if he is elected. He is strong and resourceful. And he really cares about people," she said, according to Hickok. "The federal government will have to take steps. But will it be enough? *Can* it be enough? The responsibility he may have to take on is something I hate to think about."[10]

The next day she was back in Hyde Park to cast her ballot and then returned to New York to prepare the buffet supper that she and Franklin gave for family, friends, and newsmen before going to the Biltmore Hotel to await the returns. Whatever her misgivings about becoming First Lady, outwardly she was as gracious and composed as ever. At the Biltmore, Franklin withdrew to a small suite upstairs to receive the returns with Flynn, Farley, and a few intimates. Eleanor

stayed downstairs in the ballroom to greet the hundreds of party workers who had gathered to celebrate the victory that appeared to be in
the making.

Smilingly she moved from ballroom to State Committee and
National Committee quarters, but as the returns began to come in she
slipped off to give Elliott's wife a glimpse of the lights and crowds and
excitement on Broadway on an election eve and to bring Sara down to
headquarters. As the fateful hour arrived, Louis turned gloomy, and as
if to emphasize his behind-the-scenes role, secluded himself with his
wife and son in his deserted offices across the street, calling Roosevelt
and Farley on the telephone but refusing to acknowledge that the early
returns were as good as they seemed. When victory seemed certain,
Eleanor and Farley went over to get him. The "two people in the
United States," Roosevelt saluted Howe and Farley, "more than anybody else, who are responsible for this great victory."

The reporters assigned to stay with Eleanor were, as one of them
wrote, "incredulous" at her composure in the midst of the klieg lights
and the mounting hysteria of victory. Nothing seemed to penetrate
her "profound calm." She consented to a press conference. Was she
pleased at the outcome of the election?

"Of course I'm pleased—if it really is true. You're always pleased
to have someone you're very devoted to have what he wants." Then
she paused and went on gravely, "It's an extremely serious thing to
undertake, you know, the guidance of a nation at a time like this. It's
not something you just laugh off and say you're pleased about."

The reporters had been reading Hickok's stories with their hints of
Mrs. Roosevelt's reluctance to become First Lady. Did she anticipate
returning to Washington and its social functions? one asked. "I love
people. I love having people in my house. I don't think I know what
'functions' are," was her smiling response.

Would she miss New York? would she find life in Washington too
restricting? the reporters pressed on. "I'm very much a person of circumstance," she said, again avoiding a direct reply. "I've found that I
never miss anything after it's gone. The present is enough to deal with.
Life is always full, you know."

The next morning the invisible bands whose fetters she had feared
began to tighten. The police guard outside the Sixty-fifth Street house
had been doubled, there were Secret Service men about everywhere,
and the crowd of reporters outside was prepared to dog her footsteps

all day. She was up early, and only Louis and Anna's daughter Sisty, who attended Todhunter and whom she would take to school, joined her at breakfast. A reporter for an afternoon paper sent in a message begging her to come out so that they might have a story for the early editions, and she interrupted her breakfast to oblige. She told the press what she intended to do that day. She "refuses to allow the new honor that has come to her husband to interfere with the varied interests of her own life," the *Sun* reporter wrote.

But at Todhunter the fiction she had insisted on maintaining—that she was just like any other teacher—was ignored. The girls could no longer be restrained. They stood as she entered, and one of them presented her with an Egyptian scarab to bring her good luck. "We think it's grand to have the wife of the President for our teacher," the girl shyly said.

She was not the wife of the president yet, she laughingly insisted, "and anyway I don't want you to think of me that way." In what was meant to be a reassurance to herself and a plea to those who knew her, she added, "I'm just the same as I was yesterday."

To Lorena Hickok, whom she now called "Hick," who accompanied her to Albany the next day, she unburdened herself more fully than she ever had before. "If I wanted to be selfish, I could wish Franklin had not been elected." She gazed out of the window at the long-familiar and reassuring vistas of the Hudson and the Catskills and continued, according to Hick, "I never wanted it, even though some people have said that my ambition for myself drove him on. They've even said that I had some such idea in the back of my mind when I married him. I never wanted to be a President's wife, and I don't want it now." She looked at Hick. "You don't quite believe me, do you?" she asked.

She was glad for Franklin, she went on, "sincerely. I couldn't have wanted it to go the other way. After all, I'm a Democrat, too."

"Now I shall have to work out my own salvation." Life in Washington was going to be difficult, but there was not going to be any First Lady—"there is just going to be plain, ordinary Mrs. Roosevelt. And that's all." She would very likely be criticized, "but I can't help it."[11]

The criticism was not long in coming. She continued to do what she had done for ten years—to live her own life as teacher, publicist, and business executive. She accepted a commercially sponsored radio contract, wrote articles for the Hearst syndicate and for the North

American Newspaper Alliance, and edited a MacFadden magazine, *Babies—Just Babies*. Although most of the proceeds went to charity and good works, many people reproached her for "commercializing her position" as the wife of the president-elect. When she continued to speak her mind on controversial issues, part of the press said she was embarrassing her husband.

She had contracted with MacFadden to edit *Babies—Just Babies* with Franklin's approval and after much discussion in the family. It gave a job as her assistant to Anna who was estranged from her husband. There was widespread ridicule as well as disapproval of the venture; the *Harvard Lampoon* parodied the magazine with an issue entitled "Tutors, Just Tutors." She had absolute control over the magazine's contents, she said defensively. "The job with the magazine I shall keep," she told the press. Versatility and enterprise, the *Hartford Courant* said, were admirable in a woman generally, "but the fact remains that being the first lady of the land is a full-time job in itself and that the dignity of the President and of the country cannot but suffer when his name is used for commercial purposes." Other papers echoed the *Courant* and suggested that "as a matter of propriety and in keeping with the dignity of the exalted position her husband is about to hold she ought to abandon some of her present occupations."[12] The debate became more heated when during a nationwide broadcast sponsored by a cosmetics firm she remarked that the average girl today "faces the problem of learning, very young, how much she can drink of such things as whisky and gin and sticking to the proper quantity." She was not urging girls to learn how to drink, but she was underscoring Prohibition's failure to curb excessive drinking; the conditions brought about by Prohibition, she said, required more strength of character and discipline than had been required of girls in her own youth. But that point was ignored by the drys and the "shocked protests" poured in. She was criticized in verse as well as prose.

> *Dear Madam: Pray take this tae mean*
> *A kindly counsel fra a freen.*
> *That ye hae reached the White House door*
> *Is just because the folk were sore.*
> *Noo, though ye talk an' though ye write*
> *Fair words wi' brilliant sapience dight,*
> *Tis better far for ye, I ken,*
> *To curb the tongue an' eke the pen . . . M'Tavish*

She defied convention in other ways that offended society. She went to Washington to call on Mrs. Hoover and look over the White House. She had received a telegram from Mrs. Hoover's secretary asking where she would like to have the White House car pick her up and whether she would like her military aide to be in uniform or civilian attire. No car and no military aide, she had replied; she would go down on the midnight train, have breakfast at the Mayflower, and walk to the White House. But that was not the end of the affair. Soon after breakfast Franklin's cousin, Warren Delano Robbins, who was then chief of protocol in the State Department, turned up with his wife and an official limousine to take her to the White House. No, Eleanor told them; she intended to walk.

"But Eleanor, darling, you can't do that," Warren protested. "People will recognize you! You'll be mobbed!" They argued with her, but to no avail. She liked to walk, Miss Hickok would accompany her, and that was that.

Whatever Ike Hoover, the chief usher, may have thought about her disregard of protocol in arriving at the White House, he could not but admire the dispatch with which she let him know what she wanted. She "rattled it off as if she had known it her whole life. She had already decided on every last detail of the social plans for Inauguration Day; told me who the house guests would be and what rooms they would occupy, though this was five weeks in the future; gave the menus for the meals, both regular and special; told me what household effects she would bring; what servants should be provided for; what the family liked for meals and when they liked to have them; in fact, everything the Chief Usher could wish to know except what the weather might be on March fourth."[13]

She had her defenders as well as critics. The *Nashville Tennessean,* recalling the way "Princess Alice" had been the joy of the newspaper world in the Theodore Roosevelt era, said approvingly, "It begins to look as if Anna Eleanor Roosevelt is going to make Alice Roosevelt Longworth look like Alice-Sit-by-the-Fire."[14] And Heywood Broun did not see why she should conform to the traditional idea of a president's wife and limit her role to saying "Yes, dear, you're entirely right" to her husband. "I would hold it against her rather than in her favor if she quit certain causes with which she has been associated simply on account of the fortuitous circumstance that he happens to have been chosen as President."[15] He was "delighted to know that we are going to have a woman in the White House who feels that like Ibsen's Nora, she is before all else a human being and that she has a right to her own individual career regardless of the prominence of her husband."

Despite such defenders, Eleanor thought it best to retreat. She intended to do no more commercial radio work, she announced; her writings would be confined to subjects that did not touch politics or her husband's interests, she would give up teaching, and she would refrain from linking her name to anything that might be used in advertising promotion.[16] The press applauded. "The President's wife, indeed, during the term of her husband is in the position of a queen, as far as the public is concerned," wrote the *Baltimore Evening Sun*.[17]

The episode confirmed her worst apprehensions that she was going to be a prisoner in the White House "with nothing to do except stand in line and receive visitors and preside over official dinners."[18]

While she was in Washington to call on Mrs. Hoover, Mrs. Garner had come to call on her. A plain woman, she had for years served as her husband's secretary and cooked his lunch on an electric grill in his office. She, too, was worried over what she could properly continue to do now that her husband was vice president–elect. Anxiously, she asked, "Mrs. Roosevelt, do you think I can go on being Jack's secretary?"

"I most certainly do!" Eleanor replied with vehemence.

Mrs. Garner's question may have influenced her own thinking about what kind of useful role she could play in her husband's administration that would not provoke public criticism and that would enable her to be the counselor and confidante of her husband. As she listened to the men surrounding the president-elect, she began to feel that the gravest danger facing him as president was that he would never hear the truth, that everyone would say yes to him. "From my life in Washington I know how difficult it is to keep in contact with public opinion once a man gets there." She was getting an enormous amount of mail—pleas for help, cries of despair, threats of rebellion. Why couldn't she serve as her husband's "listening post" and see to it that he obtained a balanced picture of what the country was thinking and feeling?[19]

She mentioned the "listening post" theme in remarks before a farewell dinner the Women's Trade Union League gave her. Some critics, she said, had asked her what right she had to set herself up "as knowing what other people are going through, what they are suffering. I cannot understand fully, of course. Yet I think I understand more than the people who write me think I do.... Perhaps I have acquired more education than some of you [who] have educated me, realize....

"I truly believe that I understand what faces the great masses of people in the country today. I have no illusions that any one can change the world in a short time. Things cannot be completely changed in five minutes. Yet I do believe that even a few people, who want to understand, to help and to do the right thing for the great numbers of the people instead of for the few can help."[20]

That is what she hoped her husband would be able to do. That is what she hoped she would be able to help him to do.

Finally she approached Franklin, but she did so hesitatingly, tentatively, afraid she already knew what his answer would be. Perhaps he would like her to do a real job and take over some of his mail, she suggested. He looked at her "quizzically" and softly turned her down; Missy would consider it interference, he said. "I knew he was right and that it would not work, but it was a last effort to keep in close touch and to feel that I had a real job to do."[21]

Eleanor could not have been her husband's secretary. She was not a Mrs. Garner, content to subordinate herself totally to her husband. A forceful personality in her own right, every whit as strong-willed as her husband, and with a clearer sense of direction, she would have found it difficult to handle his mail and make it exclusively a reflection of his thinking and purposes.

Though she knew this was true, her husband's rebuff hurt. The day before the inauguration she asked Lorena Hickok to pick her up at the Mayflower, where the Roosevelt and Howe families were staying until they moved into the White House. She directed the cab driver to take them out to the cemetery in Rock Creek Park, where they left the cab and walked to the cluster of pines that enclosed the Saint-Gaudens memorial to the wife of Henry Adams. They sat down on the stone bench that faced "Grief," as the statue had come to be called. After they had both gazed at the hooded figure in hushed silence, Mrs. Roosevelt spoke, quietly, almost as if she were speaking to herself, about what the statue meant to her.

"In the old days when we lived here, I was much younger and not so very wise. Sometimes I'd be very unhappy and sorry for myself. When I was feeling that way, if I could manage, I'd come here alone, and sit and look at that woman. And I'd always come away somehow feeling better. And stronger. I've been here many, many times."[22]

The wound left by the Lucy Mercer affair was still open, still painful. She was a woman of sorrow who had surmounted her unhappiness and managed to carry on, stoical toward herself, understanding and tender toward others. She had turned her sorrow into a strengthening thing before, and would do so again. As First Lady she would not be able to live her own life, but she would be able to render a service of love to her stricken country.

35. MRS. ROOSEVELT CONQUERS WASHINGTON

INAUGURATION DAY DAWNED GRAY AND CHILL. WHEN ELEANOR slipped out before breakfast to walk her Scottish terrier, the streets around the Mayflower were almost deserted and, in the dull, windy morning, cheerless.

They seemed to mirror the mood of the country. The greatest productive machine in the history of mankind had slowed almost to a halt. With at least thirteen million unemployed, no one felt his job was safe. Banks everywhere were closing, and almost everyone feared for his savings. Eviction and foreclosure had sent an icy finger through the middle class on the farm and in the city. For the first time there was not merely hunger but fear of starvation. "World literally rocking beneath our feet," wrote Agnes Meyer, the wife of the head of the Federal Reserve Board, in her diary.[1] In New York two young Socialists had been arrested by the police in the middle of the night for pasting on the closed banks stickers that said "Closed! Socialism Will Keep Them Open." Their evangelistic message was proclaimed to unseeing eyes. While the secretary of war of the departing administration had concentrated troops around some of the nation's cities because of what "Reds and possible Communists" might do, it was fear and apathy that endangered the republic, not revolt.

The Roosevelts recognized that the nation's crisis was primarily one of the spirit. Fear was the worst thing that happened to the country as a result of the Depression, Eleanor had written in December, "fear of an uncertain future, fear of not being able to meet our problems. Fear of not being equipped to cope with life as we live it today." What people needed was to have something "outside of one's self and greater than one's self to depend on.... We need some of the old religious spirit which said 'I myself am weak but Thou art strong oh Lord!'"[2]

Franklin Roosevelt soberly expressed the same feeling on the way to Washington. Religion and a belief in God, he said to Farley, as he looked out at the stricken countryside, "will be the means of bringing us out of the depths of despair into which so many apparently have fallen."

Before going to the White House to pick up the outgoing president and his wife, the whole Roosevelt household and the new cabinet attended services at St. John's Episcopal Church. The old rector of Groton, although he had voted for Hoover, was there at Roosevelt's invitation to lead the congregation in prayer: "May Thy son Franklin, chosen to be our President, and all of his advisers, be enlightened and strengthened for Thy service and may he direct and rule according to Thy will." Eleanor's head bowed low. The stirring hymn of faith and resolve rang out: "Eternal Father, strong to save."

Two limousines, with Roosevelt in the first and Eleanor in the second, moved toward the White House. There they were joined by the Hoovers. The crowds along Pennsylvania Avenue cheered. Roosevelt waved and doffed his silk hat, but Hoover, his face set stonily forward, was unresponsive to either the crowds or Roosevelt's effort to make conversation. What would Mrs. Hoover miss most? Eleanor asked her companion as they rode in the car behind. Not being taken care of, was the reply, not having train reservations made for her, not having her wishes anticipated and attended to. Eleanor made a silent vow never to permit herself to become so dependent.[3]

The immense crowds in the Capitol plaza cheered, but the country waited. On the inaugural stand the cold wind blew, and Eleanor, in a velvet gown and coat of "Eleanor blue," which it had taken her less than thirty minutes to select, was not dressed warmly enough. But she was impervious to the cold, intent on the response of the listening throng to her husband's words. Roosevelt's buoyant voice carried a message of action. In later years when the country had recovered its faith in itself, the electric line "the only thing we have to fear is fear itself," addressed to the crisis in spirit and morale, would be the one by which the speech was recalled. But on that gray day the millions of Americans who listened on their radios were most stirred by the call to battle stations: "This Nation asks for action, and action now. Our greatest primary task is to put people to work." If necessary to meet the emergency, he was prepared to ask Congress for power "as great as the power that would be given to me if we were in fact invaded by a foreign foe."

Here the president received his greatest burst of applause. Eleanor found it "a little terrifying. You felt that they would do *anything*—if only someone would tell them *what* to do," she commented afterward at the White House. She had a feeling "of going it blindly. We are in a tremendous stream and none of us knows where we are going to land." But what was important was "our attitude toward whatever may happen. It must be willingness to accept and share with others whatever may come and to meet the future courageously, with a cheerful spirit."[4]

She and the president set an example. His "exuberant vitality... high spirits... tirelessness... gave a lift to the spirits of millions of average men, stimulated them to higher use of their own power, gave them a new zest for life," wrote Mark Sullivan of the opening days of the Roosevelt presidency.[5] And Bess Furman of the Associated Press, reporting on Mrs. Roosevelt's debut as mistress of the White House, ended an exultant story, "Washington had never seen the like—a social transformation had taken place with the New Deal."[6] Eleanor was spontaneous, sensible, and direct, and the result was a shattering of precedents. She would run the little wood-paneled elevator herself, she firmly told Chief Usher Ike Hoover. When, because of constant interruptions, Hick was unable to finish an interview with Eleanor in the sitting room, they retreated to the bathroom. In her eagerness to get settled, she pushed furniture around herself. The thousand guests who had been invited for tea turned into three thousand, and for the first time tea was served in the East Room as well as the State Dining Room; Mrs. Henrietta Nesbitt, the Hyde Park neighbor whom Eleanor had brought to Washington as housekeeper, sent out repeatedly for more sandwiches, more little cakes. The tea guests had scarcely departed when dinner guests began arriving—seventy-five Roosevelt relatives, including Alice Longworth, all of whom Eleanor greeted at the door instead of waiting until they were assembled to make a ceremonious descent.

The most radical break with precedent was her decision to hold press conferences, the first ever given by a First Lady, in the White House, on the record. The contrast with Mrs. Hoover could not have been more marked. That silvery-haired, kindly woman had shielded herself from public notice. The handful of women who were assigned to keep track of her, who were known as the "Green Room girls," were permitted to observe her only at a distance at official receptions, teas, tree plantings, charity bazaars, and public appearances with the president. The few occasions on which she appeared in the press in her own right were in connection with the Girl Scouts. Behind the screen of protocol, within the confines of the White House, there was a motherly human being whose warmth, had the nation been permitted to share it, would have done something to relieve the impression of severity the Hoovers created. But only in the final days of the campaign did the Hoover managers realize that it had been a mistake to keep Mrs. Hoover at arms' length from friendly reporters. On the Roosevelt campaign train, Mrs. Roosevelt was talking daily to Lorena Hickok of the Associated Press, and out of the blue Bess Furman, the redheaded AP correspondent traveling with the Hoover campaign special, was told she could interview Mrs. Hoover, the only interview she was granted in four years of covering the First Lady. The ground rules, Mrs. Hoover informed her, were that she should not be directly quoted; Miss Furman would have to write about the biographical details Mrs. Hoover would now furnish her as if she had obtained them from a library.[7]

Mrs. Hoover had conformed to a pattern of behavior established for First Ladies from the time of Martha Washington. It was not a model Eleanor Roosevelt could follow without stultifying herself, and it was not a model she thought appropriate in a democratic society where the channels of communication between the people in the White House and the people in the country should, she felt, be open, lively, and sympathetic. So when Hick suggested that she hold press conferences, Eleanor agreed, and Bess Furman, whom she consulted, approved enthusiastically—as did Franklin and Louis. On Monday, March 6, two days before her husband's first press conference, an astonished and somewhat disapproving Ike Hoover, or so Eleanor thought, accompanied her into the Red Room, where thirty-five women reporters had assembled. The conference had been restricted to women, she explained, in order to encourage the employment of newspaperwomen and to make it more comfortable to deal with subjects of interest primarily to women. To further emphasize that she was in no way encroaching upon Franklin's domain, she had stipulated that no political questions could be asked. She brought with her a large box of candied fruits which she passed around—to hide her nervousness, she later claimed. The first news conference did not produce much news, but the women were elated, although some of them, especially May Craig of the *Portland* (Maine) *Press Herald*, having fought hard to break down masculine professional barriers, were uncomfortable that men were excluded. However, the attitude of the men was "Why in the world would we want to come to Mrs. Roosevelt's conferences?" Byron Price, the manager of the AP, predicted that the institution would last less than six months.[8] However, a few weeks later, when a bill to legalize 3.2 beer went up to Congress, Roosevelt was asked at his news conference whether beer would be served at the White House if the bill were passed; that would have to be answered by his wife, he replied off the record. Eleanor was on her way to New York, so Ruby Black of the United Press raced out to catch her at the airport. Would she, a teetotaler, permit beer to be served at the White House? "You'll have to ask my husband," was Eleanor's guarded reply. Told that the president had referred the press to her, she burst into laughter. She would have a statement for them at her next news conference, she promised. By Monday, when the women reporters trooped in for their meeting with Eleanor, masculine scorn had turned to anguish, and some of the men begged the women to fill them in later.

Beer would be served at the White House to those who desire it, Eleanor's mimeographed announcement read. She herself did not drink anything with an alcoholic content, but she would not dream of imposing her convictions on others. She hoped, however, that the availability of beer might lead to greater temperance, and to a reduction in the bootlegger's trade.[9]

The scoffing ceased. Eleanor proved to be such a good news source that Emma Bugbee, who had been sent by the *New York Herald Tribune* to report on the First Lady's inauguration activities, was kept in Washington by her Republican employers for four months. "Well, if it's going to be like that," Emma's office said, after their reporter had lunched with Mrs. Roosevelt and had been taken through the living quarters of the president's family, something Mrs. Hoover had not done until the final months of her husband's regime, "you had better stay down."[10] Another Monday the press conference became a classroom in diets—patriotic, wholesome, and frugal; the women learned the recipe for Martha Washington's crab soup and for dishes that Andrew Jackson ate in the days "when the onion and herb were as important as the can opener."[11] Sheila Hibben, the culinary historian whom Eleanor had invited to the news conference, even ventured a theory of history about White House menus: "The more democratic our Presidents have been, the more attention they paid to their meals." The lecture on the wholesome, inexpensive dishes that other First Ladies had served their husbands led up to an announcement that with the help of Flora Rose of Cornell, Eleanor had served "a 7-cent luncheon" at the White House—hot stuffed eggs with tomato sauce, mashed potatoes, prune pudding, bread, and coffee. In London a woman read this menu and exclaimed to a friend that "if Mrs.

Roosevelt can get her kitchen staff to eat three-penny, ha-penny meals, she can do more than I can with mine!"

"Oh, I don't know what she gives the servants," the friend replied. "She gives them to the President—and he eats them like a lamb."

Malnutrition, Eleanor concluded, was not only a result of a lack of food, but often of a lack of knowledge of menus that cost little and had high nutritional value. She thought the White House should set an example in the use of simple and nourishing foods. "Perhaps because of the depression we may teach people how really to feed their children."

Bess Furman contrasted the news-conference styles of president and First Lady: "At the President's press conference, all the world's a stage; at Mrs. Roosevelt's, all the world's a school."[12]

Eleanor's ban on political subjects did not mean a ban on issues of consequence and controversy. She hit out at sweatshops. She urged women to patronize the merchants who provided decent working conditions. She called for the elimination of child labor and urged more money for teachers' salaries. When in April the foreign dignitaries came flocking to the White House to confer with the president on the forthcoming World Economic Conference, she startled her press conference with the passion of her anti-isolationist plea. "We ought to be able to realize what people are up against in Europe. We ought to be the ready-to-understand ones, and we haven't been.... We've got to find a basis for a more stabilized world.... We are in an ideal position to lead, if we will lead, because we have suffered less. Only a few years are left to work in. Everywhere over there is the dread of this war that may come." She spoke, wrote Emma Bugbee, with "an intensity her hearers had never seen in her before."[13]

With many of her press-conference regulars, what began as a professional relationship soon ripened into friendship. Before the inauguration, Ruby Black (Mrs. Herbert Little) had shown Eleanor a photograph of her fourteen-month-old daughter. Eleanor had said she would love to see the child, and Ruby had thought it was an expression of courtesy rather than of intent. A week after she was in the White House, however, Eleanor telephoned her—could she come the next day to visit Ruby? She did, driving her little blue roadster to Ruby's house and making friends with the child. Newswomen found themselves being given lifts in the White House car, receiving Easter lilies from the White House greenhouses, lunching at the White House table, being invited to Hyde Park. Eleanor's gestures of thoughtfulness were not matters of calculation, of "being nice to the press"; one natural act of friendliness led to another. But friendship did not encroach upon journalistic responsibility. The women asked the questions to which they or their editors felt the public was entitled to know the answers. When a reporter cautioned the First Lady that an answer might get her into trouble, her colleagues made their displeasure known; the First Lady could take care of herself, they felt. And she did.

"Sometimes I say things," she said to her press conference,

> which I thoroughly understand are likely to cause unfavorable comment in some quarters, and perhaps you newspaper women think I should keep them off the record. What you don't understand is that perhaps I am making these statements on purpose to arouse controversy and thereby get the topics talked about and so get people to thinking about them.[14]

Most of the correspondents were friendly—too friendly, some of the men grumbled. The women alerted her as to what was on the public's mind and the questions she should be prepared to answer, and sometimes she consulted a few of them about the answers she proposed to give. Even the most "hard-boiled" were willing to help. This was, after all, a male-dominated capital and the women should stand together. Sometimes Eleanor blundered. Mrs. Mary Harriman Rumsey was running into public-relations difficulties as head of the Consumers Division of the National Recovery Administration, and Eleanor talked to Bess Furman and Martha Strayer, of the *Washington News*, about taking on second jobs, for which they would be paid, to help out Mrs. Rumsey. No, they told her regretfully; they were for the NRA and the whole New Deal, but accepting money from the government in any way could mean the loss of their jobs.[15] Publicity and newspaper work were closely allied, but the line between them was sharply drawn, particularly in Washington. They were right and she was wrong, and she did not press the offer. Lorena Hickok, who suddenly realized that her close relationship with Mrs. Roosevelt was affecting her detachment as a journalist, resigned her job with the AP to work for Harry Hopkins in the new relief administration, but her intimacy with Mrs. Roosevelt was unique. Friendship was another matter. Most of the women reporters felt they could be friends with the mistress of the White House without losing their objectivity, and marveled that she wanted to be their friend. In a city where human relations were usually governed by a careful consideration of interests and motivations were usually suspect, Eleanor's warmth and good will were refreshing. "I always thought when people were given great power it did something to them," Martha Strayer wrote to Eleanor. "They lost the human touch if they ever had it. To have been able to see you at close hand, demonstrating the exact contrary, means truly a great deal to me."[16] A few weeks after the inauguration, the Gridiron Club, a male journalistic stronghold, gave its annual dinner, which was attended by the president and his cabinet but from which women were barred. Eleanor organized a Gridiron Widows buffet supper for newswomen, cabinet wives, and women in government. "God's gift to newspaper women," the feminine press fraternity murmured.

What enchanted the press captivated the public. As First Lady, Eleanor's approach to people great and small remained as it had always been: direct and unaffected, full of curiosity and a desire to learn—and to teach.

On her return from a trip down the Potomac on the *Sequoia* with Prime Minister James Ramsay MacDonald and his daughter Ishbel as guests, she and Ishbel went on board a fishing schooner from Gloucester, Massachusetts, filled with fishing captains who had come to the Capital to ask for help for this "oldest industry." She invited the skippers to visit the White House, and twenty-seven came, escorted by their congressman. Eleanor herself took them around, and after the tour of the public rooms invited them to go through the family quarters on the second floor. Down the wide hall the weather-beaten men trailed, peering into historic rooms as Eleanor opened the doors and told some of the history that had taken place in them. The men chortled when she hastily closed a door behind which she had spotted Anna sleeping, and concluded, as one skipper put it, "There ain't too many ladies in her position who would have done what she did."[17]

A few weeks later she entertained Sara and the members of the Monday Evening Sewing Class at luncheon. Helen Wilmerding, a friend from the days of the Roser classes, was in the group. "All the old tribe we grew up with in New York have turned towards you like sunflowers," she wrote Eleanor later. "At first they were naturally more anxious than other people as to how you would stand up against the difficulties of your position. You are one of them and they cared more. Now they are sunflowers I need say no more." Eleanor appreciated Helen's note "very much," she replied, "for I felt the old crowd might disapprove of many things which I did."[18]

The "old crowd" was also somewhat astonished by the growing elegance of her clothes. In the twenties it had been fashionable to deplore Eleanor's lack of interest in what she wore. It conformed with society's stereotype of a strong-willed woman of good works to see her in bulky tweeds and a hair net, and to whisper that without a corset her stomach showed. Eleanor had dressed acceptably in the governorship years, but now the top couturiers of the country, who naturally wanted her patronage, pressed their advice and most stylish models upon her. If she did not devote more time than in the past to the selection of clothes, she was more willing to be guided by friends like June Hamilton Rhodes, who had helped in the campaign and now worked as a fashion publicist for the elegant Fifth Avenue shops. "I got a lot of clothes for myself and Anna in one afternoon last week," Eleanor wrote Franklin three weeks before the inauguration. "It is better to have plenty and not buy any new ones for quite a while!"[19] But the dress shops argued that such restraint in shopping did not help business recovery, and she evidently agreed, for in May, Lilly Daché shipped her six blue velvet hats "of the June Hamilton Rhodes material" and asked her to return those that did not please her entirely. "Mrs. Roosevelt kept all of the hats as she likes them all very much and would like to have you send a bill for them," replied Malvina "Tommy" Thompson who had come to Washington as her secretary.

"Your dress, hat and coat were lovely," Helen Wilmerding commented after the "old crowd's" visit to the White House. "I wanted to snatch them off and put them on myself...." Gentle Helen had not been among those who had mocked her taste in clothes, but since so many of her contemporaries had considered Eleanor a little dowdy in her dress, Helen's letter must have given her considerable gratification.

"Everyone makes very low prices," Eleanor had remarked on the afternoon she devoted to getting her White House wardrobe. She did not spurn them. She used to comment with amusement on the Scotch streak in Franklin, but it was a characteristic she shared. However, in spite of the Fifth Avenue shops' low prices, she was quite prepared to switch to less fashionable and less obliging establishments if that was the only way to get fair conditions for labor. "I feel sure that you will understand," she wrote to Milgrim's, "that I will have to wait before coming to you again until you have some agreement with your people which is satisfactory to both sides." A distraught Mr. Milgrim telegraphed her within the week that the ILGWU's strike had been settled and that both sides were satisfied. "I was quite upset when I received your letter and am very anxious to explain the facts when you come in for your fitting which will be ready Thursday, October 12th."[20]

This pro-labor gesture was in September, but in March she had already yielded to her incorrigible reforming impulses and struck out into precisely the kind of activities she thought she would have to give up as First Lady. "Friends who have wondered how long it would be before Mrs. Roosevelt's instinct for civic and social reform would assert itself in Washington had the answer today, when the story of her inspection trip to Washington's alleys was told for the first time," wrote Emma Bugbee.[21] Mrs. Archibald Hopkins, eighty-one, a "cliff dweller" with a social conscience, asked her to tour Washington's alley slums with her. By focusing public attention on these disease- and crime-ridden back streets perhaps they might be able to persuade Congress to do something about them. Eleanor made the tour, driving in her roadster. She reported her grim findings to the press and even suggested that Congress should act. Mrs. Hopkins' committee had prepared a bill to reconstruct the alley slums, she pointed out, and while it was a rule with her that she did not comment on pending legislation, she would say, "Of course I am sympathetic with the general theory of better housing everywhere." She spoke to Franklin about what she had seen and about the bill, and he permitted her to indicate to Mrs. Hopkins that he would help at the right moment. She enlisted the aid of the president's uncle, Frederic A. Delano, head of the National Capital Park and Planning Commission. "I have talked with Franklin and Uncle Fred about the bill," she reported to Mrs. Hopkins. "Franklin thinks that at the special session it will be quite impossible to get through any local bills of any kind, but I feel quite certain that at the regular session it can and will be done. Uncle Fred talked to me the other night and he feels he has convinced Senator King [chairman of the Senate District Committee] that the bill should be pushed. If it should happen to slide through well and good, but if it does not get through do not feel discouraged, for I feel sure it will go through at the next session."[22] Discouraged? Mrs. Hopkins, who had first visited the White House in Abraham Lincoln's time, at last had an ally on the distaff side. She felt invincible.

District institutions, Eleanor believed, should serve as a model for the nation. Instead, voteless and at the mercy of an economy-minded Congress that was, in addition, singularly indifferent to the Negroes who would be the chief beneficiaries of improved services, the residents of the District had among the worst hospitals, nursing homes, and jails in the nation. Her interest in the District would be a continuing one.

The Hoover action that had most offended the country was the eviction of the "bonus army" veterans from Washington in 1932. That Mr. Hoover, a Quaker, could have authorized the use of military force to drive jobless veterans out of their squatters' shacks seemed to Eleanor a dreadful object lesson in what fear could make a well-intentioned man do. As a consequence, when the Veterans National Liaison Committee informed the White House that the veterans were returning to Washington and expected the new administration to house and feed them, she pressed her husband to treat them with consideration and see to it that there was no repetition of the previous summer's panic. Louis—whose official title was secretary to the president and who called himself "the dirty-job man"—took on the job of handling the new bonus army.[23] The Veterans Administration directed to house the men lodged them in Fort Hunt, an old army camp across the river, provided them with food, medical care, even dental service. A military band entertained them. Louis kept in daily touch with the leaders and received reports on the mood among the men, including the activity of the Communists. The veterans having presented their case by the middle of May, Louis told them that twelve hundred of them could be enrolled in the CCC and tried to persuade them to pass a resolution to go home. The men debated and dallied, and then Louis played his trump card: he brought Eleanor to visit the encampment. The men were pleased and heartened to see the First Lady among them and quickly took her over, proposing that she tour the camp. She went with the men through tents, barracks, and hospital, ending up at the mess hall, where she mingled with the men in the mess line and was persuaded to make a little speech. She reminisced about World War days and her work in the railroad yards when the "boys," perhaps some of those who were here, had come through Washington on their way overseas. She also spoke of her post-war tour of the battlefields where they had fought and concluded, "I never want to see another war. I would like to see fair consideration for everyone, and I shall always be grateful to those who served their country." She led the men in singing "There's a Long, Long Trail" and departed amid cheers. "Hoover sent the army. Roosevelt sent his wife," said one left-wing veteran, who was chagrined over the Communists' loss of influence. Soon afterward the bonus marchers passed a resolution to disperse. "It is such fine things as that which bring you the admiration of the

American people," wrote Josephus Daniels from Mexico City, where he was the U.S. ambassador.[24]

Eleanor and Louis had not allowed the Secret Service to accompany them to the encampment, and there was considerable relief when they returned safely to the White House. Eleanor's insistence on not being shadowed by police and Secret Service enhanced the country's image of her as a woman unafraid, seeking to be herself, but it was a sore issue with those responsible for the safety of the president and his family. After the attempt on Roosevelt's life in Miami on February 15, 1933, he wanted to ask the Secret Service to assign a man to protect her. "Don't you dare do such a thing," she warned him. "If any Secret Service man shows up in New York and starts following me around, I'll send him right straight back where he came from." But Colonel Starling, the head of the presidential detail, brought the matter up repeatedly with the president and Louis. He was particularly worried over her insistence on driving herself around unescorted. She was unbudgeable, they explained.

Local police found her as stubborn as the Secret Service. When she came to New York to visit the headquarters of the Women's Trade Union League, she found four policemen in front of the building.

"What are you doing here?" she asked.

"We're here to guard Mrs. Roosevelt."

"I don't want to be guarded; please go away."

"We can't do that, the captain placed us here," the head of the detail explained in some embarrassment. She went inside and called Louis, who phoned police headquarters. The captain came immediately. "Please take them all away. No one's going to hurt me," Eleanor said to him.

"I hope not," the captain said doubtfully, but complied. Americans were "wonderful," she said. "I simply can't imagine being afraid of going among them as I have always done, as I always shall."[25]

She refused to succumb to fear. By self-discipline she had conquered her childhood dread of animals, of water, and of physical pain, and she kept these fears at bay by simply defying them.

She was an inveterate air traveler, sometimes pressing air personnel to fly even when they thought the weather too hazardous. The fledgling airlines found her a stalwart advocate of air travel, quite willing to lend herself to their promotional efforts; the country was benignly responsive to her sense of adventure and her delight in sponsoring the new and promising enterprise. In order to impress the public, especially women, with the ease and safety of air travel, Amelia Earhart invited Eleanor to join her on a flight to Baltimore in evening dress. Hall Roosevelt went along, as did a few newspaperwomen and Miss Earhart's husband, George Palmer Putnam. How did she feel being piloted by a woman, she was asked. Absolutely safe, was her reply; "I'd give a lot to do it myself!" She seriously discussed learning to fly with Miss Earhart and went so far as to take a physical examination, which she passed. But Franklin thought it was foolish to spend time learning to fly when she would not be able to afford a plane and she came to the same conclusion.[26]

Not long after she was settled in the White House she made her first transcontinental flight, to Los Angeles to see Elliott. Such a journey still was an event, and it was even more so when undertaken by the First Lady. From Fort Worth to the Coast, C. R. Smith, the president of American Airways, accompanied her, as did Amon G. Carter, the publisher of the *Fort Worth Star-Telegram*. Both men admired her stamina and poise; "her rapid air tour," wrote Carter, "twice spanning the continent, was a physical feat calculated to take the 'bounce' out of a transport pilot." She came through it "smiling."[27] Will Rogers found her performance sufficiently impressive to write a letter about it to the *New York Times*. Yes, it was a real boost for aviation, he said, "but here is really what she takes the medal for: out at every stop, day or night, standing for photographs by the hour, being interviewed, talking over the radio, no sleep. And yet they say she never showed one sign of weariness or annoyance of any kind. No maid, no secretary—just the First Lady of the land on a paid ticket on a regular passenger flight."[28]

Not since Theodore Roosevelt's days had the White House pulsated with such high spirits and sheer animal vitality. Colonel Starling took the Hoovers to Union Station and on his return to the White House a few hours later found it "transformed during my absence into a gay place full of people who oozed confidence."

"You know how it was when Uncle Ted was there—how gay and homelike," Roosevelt had remarked at Cousin Susie's before the inauguration. "Well, that's how we mean to have it!"[29]

As the official residence of the president, tradition and law limited the extent to which 1600 Pennsylvania Avenue could reflect the tastes and habits of the family that occupied it, but within those limits the Roosevelt personalities soon placed their gregarious and buoyant stamp on the historic dwelling.

There were grandchildren all over the place. Anna was separated from her husband, and she and her two children Sisty (Anna Eleanor), six, and Buzz (Curtis), three, stayed at the White House. Betsy and Jimmy and their daughter Sarah often visited, James to do chores for his father, Betsy because she was a favorite of her father-in-law. Franklin Jr. and Johnny, lively teen-agers, were in and out. There were nurseries on the third floor and a sandbox and jungle gym on the south lawn. There were also Eleanor's dogs Meggie and Major, both of whom had to be exiled to Hyde Park before the end of the year, Major for having nipped Senator Hattie Caraway and Meggie after biting reporter Bess Furman on the lip.

Some staid officials found the Roosevelt exuberance a little unsettling. The housekeeper was instructed to keep the icebox full for midnight snacks, and White House guards to let the teen-agers in even if they turned up in the early hours of the morning. What kind of place is this, an indignant Johnny wanted to know, when a fellow can't get into his own house? Eleanor had her own run-in with a too literal interpretation of regulations when Colonel Ulysses S. Grant III, in charge of public buildings and grounds, informed her that she could not attach an old-fashioned swing to the limb of a White House tree because it might injure the bark. "Well, of course, I shall do whatever he tells me, but for the life of me I cannot get this point of view." Eventually the children got their swing.[30]

But she would not do anything that detracted from the mansion's dignity, because it was a house that belonged to the nation. "I think it is a beautiful house with lovely proportions, great dignity, and I do not think any one looking at it from the outside or living in it can fail to feel the spell of the past and the responsibility of living up to the fine things which have been done and lived in that house."[31] The family quarters on the second floor were spacious but not intimidating. There were four large two-room suites, one at each corner of the floor, the larger room twenty-six by thirty feet, the smaller fourteen by seventeen feet. On the southern side the two corner suites were separated by the Monroe Room, a sitting room which Mrs. Hoover had furnished with authentic reproductions of Monroe furniture, and the Oval Room. On the opposite side of the house, looking toward Pennsylvania Avenue, there were two smaller guest rooms. The whole floor was bisected by a regal hall, eighteen feet wide, and the ceilings were seventeen feet high.

When Eleanor returned from the inaugural, she found the high-ceilinged rooms and the long hall devoid of all personal belongings a little depressing, but with the help of Nancy Cook and a White House warehouse full of old furniture, the family rooms soon bore the Roosevelt imprint.

Franklin took the Oval Room as his study, covering the walls with his naval prints and his desk with the gadgets and curios that he had collected all his life. Flanking the fireplace were the flags of the United States and of the president, and over the door he hung a pastel painting of Eleanor of which he was very fond. A door next to his desk led into a small bedroom. Eleanor felt that the bed there was too cumbersome and large, and ordered one made at Val-Kill. There were two bedside tables, one usually covered with documents and memoranda, the other with pencils, pads, and a telephone. Eleanor often left letters on this table with sections underlined and a notation in the margin, "F—read."

Her own suite was next to Franklin's in the southwest corner of the floor. The larger room had been Lincoln's bedroom, but she slept in the dressing room and used the other as her sitting room and study. She liked to be surrounded by photographs, and her walls were soon adorned with the framed portraits of family, friends, and people she had known and admired. Her Val-Kill desk was by a window overlooking a handsome magnolia that had been planted by Andrew Jackson. The view from her desk, as from the president's bed, swept across the south lawns to the Washington monument. Louis occupied the southeast suite and Missy had a small apartment on the third floor that had been used by Mrs. Hoover's housekeeper.

The western end of the second-floor hall had been used as a conservatory by Mrs. Hoover, who had fitted it out with heavy bamboo furniture, a green fiber rug, palm trees, and large cages of birds to give it an outdoor, California-like air. Eleanor turned it into a family sitting room where she presided over the breakfast table in the morning and the tea urn in the afternoon. The small silver tea service had been a wedding gift from Alice and the silver statuette of Old Mother Hubbard—a dining-table bell—had belonged to her mother. It was always at her right hand, its head, to the delight of the children, nodding solemnly back and forth when she rang.

When Eleanor saw that the breakfast tray had been brought in to Franklin, she would go in soon afterward to say good morning and exchange a few words. She did not stay long because he liked to be left alone to eat his breakfast and glance through the papers. In times of crisis there were always officials waiting in the hall to see him before he was wheeled over to the executive offices. Normally the three who went in after he had finished his breakfast to discuss the day's schedule were Louis, press secretary Steve Early, and Marvin McIntyre, who was in charge of appointments. The executive offices were practically under the same roof, but Franklin was "just as much separated as though he went to a building farther away," according to Eleanor. His day was taken up with a succession of people and crises, and he had little time for private affairs. It was sometimes hard on the children, who were having problems. Anna had decided to divorce Curtis ("So the news of our family is out," Sara lamented). Elliott was settling in Texas—"nothing could pay me to go back East again"—and was also separating from his wife. "That is terrible about Elliott and Betty," Johnny wrote from Groton, wanting to know whether there was anything he or Franklin Jr. could do. He, too, was making important decisions. He intended to work that summer at camp as a counselor, and "I'm going to Princeton College." Franklin Jr., senior prefect at Groton and bound for Harvard, alone among the children seemed to be serene. "It must be very satisfying to feel you've been married twenty-eight years,—especially in these times," he wrote his parents on their wedding anniversary, adding, "But to get to the point, first of all please don't forget to bring my full dress, all my stiff shirts...."

"We laugh about it a great deal when I formally make an appointment for the children to see their father at given hours when something comes up which really must be discussed and decided but it is not as much a laughing matter as we make it out to be...."[32] Usually Eleanor did not see Franklin until he returned from the executive offices to get ready for dinner. They rarely dined alone, and while conversation flowed freely at the dinner table, it was inevitably of an impersonal sort. After dinner, officials often came in to work with the president, leaving Eleanor to entertain their guests and bid them good night. Then she would go to her desk to work on her mail. Before she went to bed—"and sometimes that is very late"—she took her dogs for a walk around the White House circle and drank in the beauty and stateliness of the White House, with its portico "lighted only by the lights from the windows, and yet shining out in its whiteness against the darkness." Sometimes during the first few months officials stayed until the early morning and Eleanor did not dare to go to bed for fear of missing something that might happen while she was asleep.[33] In any event, she did not go to bed before going in to say good night to her husband, sit on his bed, and chat for a while. It was often the only chance she had to talk with him about the things she really had on her mind.

However late she stayed up, her day usually began at 7:30 A.M. with exercise or a ride in Rock Creek Park. Her horse, Dot, which she had bought from Earl, was stabled at Fort Myers and brought over to the park in an army van. Missy was occasionally her companion on these rides, but more often it was Elinor Morgenthau, with whom she was closer than any other woman in official Washington. Eleanor, in her riding habit and with a velvet ribbon around her soft, light-brown hair, became a familiar figure along Washington's bridle paths. Once her horse reared, frightened by a newspaper that blew across her path, and she was thrown. "I slid off very gracefully right into the mud," she told the reporters, who inevitably heard of the mishap.[34]

After breakfast she went to her desk and saw in turn the head usher, the social secretary, and the housekeeper. Ike Hoover, who had come to the White House during the administration of Benjamin Harrison and who died soon after the Roosevelts arrived, was succeeded as chief usher by Raymond Muir, a tall, dignified lawyer from the Veterans Bureau—always polite, always unruffled. The usher's room, which was at the right of the entrance as guests came in, was the clearing house of the establishment. Muir kept track of everyone who came into the White House living quarters—family, guests, people who had appointments with anyone in the White House. He saw that guests were met by a White House car and escorted them to their rooms if Eleanor could not do so herself. Mrs. Edith Helm was Eleanor's social secretary, as she had been Mrs. Wilson's. Mrs. Helm was tall, distinguished, erect, and correct, and bore the unmistakable stamp of someone who had grown up in one of the services. The daughter of an admiral and the widow of an admiral, she knew Washington's customs and conventions. Every morning she and Eleanor went over her lists and invitations and table orders. And finally Eleanor talked with Mrs. Henrietta Nesbitt, the housekeeper, who did the buying, prepared the menus, and supervised the household staff. Ike Hoover had been concerned because Mrs. Nesbitt was not a professional house-keeper, but Eleanor preferred Mrs. Nesbitt to a professional manager because she was conscientious and something of a business woman, and she was grandmotherly and unpretentious. She would do Eleanor's bidding, not vice versa.[35]

By the time Eleanor was finished with Mrs. Nesbitt, Tommy (now Mrs. Frank J. Scheider) had gone through the mail and taken out all the personal letters, communications from government officials, and any other letters that looked as though they might require immediate attention—some fifty letters a day, only a small proportion of the mail that Eleanor received. "Letters and letters and letters," she said of the first weeks in Washington. "Wire baskets on my desk, suit cases of mail going home even on Sundays" with Tommy, "a sense of being snowed under by mail." That first year 300,000 pieces of mail came to the White House addressed to her, and she loved it.

The letters that were not kept for Eleanor's immediate attention were sent to the Correspondence Unit, where they were opened and classified. (It was unofficially called the social bureau, indicating the nature of the bulk of the First Lady's correspondence in previous administrations.) There were two divisions: one, under Mrs. Helm, handled the social correspondence; the other, under Ralph Magee, worked with Tommy on the remainder of the mail. Magee's unit used form letters dating back to the Cleveland administration, which did not seem adequate to Eleanor, so she rewrote some; but generally she tried as far as was humanly possible to see that a letter received personal attention either from Tommy or herself. Some letters Tommy answered directly, and to others she dictated replies for Eleanor's signature, but for the fifty or so letters which were of special interest, Eleanor made a note of the kind of answer she wanted Tommy to compose or, in cases involving personal friends or controversy, she dictated a reply herself. In addition, there were letters she answered in longhand—to Hick, Earl, Nancy and Marion, her children, and old friends. So when she was not on the telephone, receiving callers, or otherwise engaged, there was always the basket of correspondence to get through, even if it meant working through the night after the last dinner guest had departed or slipping away from the movie that was being shown in the hall outside the president's study. However she managed to do it, by morning there was always a basket of outgoing mail on Tommy's desk.

When she was not writing letters, she was writing articles. With Louis Howe acting as her agent, she contracted to do a monthly 750-word piece for the North American Newspaper Alliance at $500 an article. They asked her to write "as one woman to another, of your problems as the woman of the household."[36] She signed the contract after exercising her option to cancel her arrangement with MacFadden to edit *Babies—Just Babies*. Criticism did not faze her, but ridicule did. Even her friends spoofed her about *Babies—Just Babies*. At the annual party of the Women's Press Club one of the songs began:

We are new to the business of running the show,
We're babies, just babies, just babies.[37]

When in addition to the ridicule there were editorial differences with publisher MacFadden, she decided to withdraw, and the magazine ceased publication. That same month, May, Louis Howe negotiated a contract for her with *Woman's Home Companion* to do a monthly column, "I Want You to Write Me," for which she received $1,000 each month. In addition, Anna was paid $325 a month for handling the correspondence that came flooding into the magazine as a result of the column. A friendly congressman alerted Marvin McIntyre that there was Republican criticism in the House Appropriations Committee of the number of letters that Eleanor referred to the Women's Bureau of the Department of Labor to be answered for her. It was assumed that this mail was the result of the *Woman's Home Companion* columns, and when it was pointed out that the mail that came in to the magazine was answered there, the criticism was dropped.[38] But there were other complaints.

He did not mean to be impertinent, a member of the staff of the *Writer's Digest* wrote, but weren't these writing offers made to her because her name would attract attention? She did not think him "the least impertinent" for asking such questions, Eleanor replied. "I do not like to think that my name is entirely responsible for my receiving these offers, although I realize it must be a part of it, as I cannot very well divorce myself from my name. I always honestly try to do every job to the best of my ability."[39]

But if there were many critics, most of the country approved. Here was the wife of the president, wrote historian Mary R. Beard, who through a massive correspondence, articles, press conferences, and speeches was giving "inspiration to the married, solace to the lovelorn, assistance to the homemaker, menus to the cook, help to the educator, direction to the employer, caution to the warrior, and deeper awareness of its primordial force to the 'weaker sex.'" The country was accustomed to "the Great White Father in the White House" instructing his people "in right conduct," commented Mrs. Beard; now the "Great White Mother emerges as a personality in her own right and starts an independent course of instruction on her own account." Mrs. Beard, a long-time feminist, clearly thought the country as well as the women had gained by this step forward in feminine evolution.[40]

Were they having guests the next week end? Franklin asked Eleanor at the beginning of April. "Probably a house full," she replied. Perhaps she had better put off some of them, he suggested. Why? Were they having some guests he had not mentioned? "I think, perhaps a few Prime Ministers." In April Eleanor discovered that "there were certain social duties which were entirely mine and which must be performed even if the skies seemed about to fall."[41]

Formal entertainments such as that occasioned by the visits of Ramsay MacDonald, Edouard Herriot, and the host of other foreign dignitaries who arrived to discuss the preparations for the London Economic Conference had an obligatory, ceremonial character. If she was sad because children and friends had to be seated at remote ends of the table, she reminded herself that it was the "people's hospitality" that she was dispensing, not her own, and that men and women had to be treated according to rank and precedence. Even with American public officials, the respect for their office and the pleasure their status conferred upon them were high among the inducements that had brought them to Washington, and this had to be recognized. "It is really the position which is invited and not the person!" And it was not Eleanor Roosevelt, the person, she realized, whom officials were anxious to meet, but the "wife of the President."

That was equally true of the thousands who came to her afternoon teas and receptions. Conventions came in great numbers to Washington in April, and they had to be received. One group would come in at four and another at five. Sometimes it was much worse, as in the case of the Daughters of the American Revolution, when Eleanor shook the hands of 3,100 women in an hour and a half: "If you don't think that rather trying, you want to try it sometimes."[42] A visit to the White House was an exalted occasion to the women she received. They wanted it to be memorable, and the smartly turned-out junior military aides who attended the First Lady and the very dignified ushers who escorted the guests to the Red Room or the Green Room helped make it so. With the help of Mrs. Helm, who admonished Eleanor gently and insistently upon the importance of protocol, she finally came to realize that the handshaking and receiving were more important than she thought. "I was a symbol which tied the people who came by me in the long ever-recurring receiving lines to their government," she noted later.[43] Once she understood the significance of the receptions and teas, she no longer rebelled. "Four hundred will be quite easy to have for tea," she assured Ruth Morgan, who was organizing the conference on the Cause and Cure of War.[44]

Nor was she unappreciative of ceremony that was evocative of American history or symbolic of the responsibility and power of the presidential office. She quickly came to know the history of the White House—its rooms, its portraits, its china—and enjoyed telling guests about it. Her pulse quickened to the ceremony of piping the president aboard the yacht *Sequoia* for the trip down the Potomac with the MacDonalds, and when they came back it was she who told the press of the little ritual at Mount Vernon that was performed by all passing naval vessels: "the bell rings, the flag dips, the sailors man the rail; if there is a bugler aboard he sounds taps; everybody stands at attention in silence."[45]

Although entertainment, especially of foreign visitors, was rigidly prescribed by protocol, even here her personality quickly made itself felt. MacDonald was accompanied by his daughter Ishbel. "What a difference," Bess Furman wrote, from their previous visit to the Hoovers in 1929, when Ishbel had been "shielded" from the press by Mrs. Hoover. Eleanor held two press conferences in the White House for the prime minister's daughter, who was a political personality in her own right, and had her sit in on her own. With the press in tow they went everywhere together, including a visit, unprecedented for a First Lady, to a congressional hearing on the thirty-hour bill while Frances Perkins was testifying. A young Republican congressman named Everett Dirksen gallantly vacated his seat for the Democratic First Lady. MacDonald wrote from London that they had felt themselves "so much at home at the White House."

Most of the formal entertaining decreed by protocol and tradition was over by inauguration day, but in the autumn Eleanor would have to confront her first social season, and a "deep gloom" settled upon her as she went over the dates and lists for the state functions. "One thing is certain," she told Mrs. Helm, "I can't even have a headache between the middle of December and the beginning of Lent!" Tuesday and Thursday nights were set aside for the large formal parties that were dictated by custom. The dinner for the vice president was unusually the first, in December. She knew that the president's dinner was "a command," Mrs. Garner wrote from Uvalde, but they wanted to stay in Texas for Christmas and "you know how Mr. Garner feels about dinners—so why not forget that it is a custom to give a dinner for the Vice President?" She had talked it over with the president, Eleanor replied, "and he says there is no reason why the dinner for the Vice President could not be given just as well in January. . . . I do not think the order in which the dinners come matters at all."[46]

Her success as a hostess was due neither to stamina nor to adherence to protocol but to her constant thoughtfulness for her guests, the little human gestures that made them feel welcome and at home amid all the trappings of power and ceremony. When the Amyas Ameses, who lived next door to the James Roosevelts in Cambridge, arrived to spend Easter at the White House Eleanor was at a meeting. After saying good evening to the president the Ameses were taken to one of the guest rooms opposite his study, and as they were unpacking there was a knock on the door, and there was Eleanor bearing a bowl of fruit. Mrs. Ames was pregnant and occasionally nauseated; James had told his mother of this, so Eleanor asked if her guest would like to have a snack between meals, and if so, what? "Cocoa and rye twist," Mrs. Ames said hesitantly. Eleanor saw to it that there was always a thermos and a plate of bread on the bedside table. On Easter Sunday when the whole household went to the cathedral for the service, Mrs. Ames went along doubtfully. "You won't want to stay through the whole thing," Eleanor told her; "I've arranged for the car to come back early and you can slip out before the sermon." She inquired whether there was anyone the Ameses wanted to see in Washington, and when they mentioned the Francis Plimptons, she invited them for Easter dinner. "The White House had an aura of power and impressiveness about it, but they were themselves," Mrs. Ames later recalled. "They acted as if they had always been there. It was like visiting friends in a very large country house. One was put instantly at one's ease. She was the fantastically most thoughtful hostess I have ever met in my life."[47]

In 1913 when Eleanor, then twenty-eight years old, had arrived in the Nation's Capital as the wife of the assistant secretary of the Navy, the social lists had dictated whom she received and entertained. The day was now long past when society as such had any interest for her; social standing did not foreclose an invitation to the White House, and neither did it insure one. Miss Mary Patten came, as full of gossip as ever, and so did the shy, almost speechless parents of a young hitchhiker to whom Eleanor had given a lift in upstate New York and had undertaken to get into a CCC camp, wiring Tommy that if he should turn up at the White House he should not be sent away. She reproached her cousin Muriel Martineau for thinking "we are not going to be able to see everyone just as we have always done," and also Rose Schneiderman, who had been to Washington on union business and had not let her know: "Please always come to lunch or to see me. I always feel badly when I miss any of my friends."

To be a successful hostess she felt one really had to give oneself to one's guests. This was easier to do when the people who were closest to her, who represented the private realm in her life, were somewhere near. Their arrivals, departures, and birthdays were carefully recorded in the little diary she began to keep on March 4. "Said goodbye to Hick." "Said goodbye to Earl & Ruth." "Nan to stay." "Rock Creek Cemetery with Hick." "Marion and 10s come 7:30 Hick for night." "E.R., Marion & Nan start upstate & Campo." "Hall's birthday." "Anna & children arrive." "Sisty's Birthday Party." "L.H. birthday. ...Supper for L.H." After the inaugural ceremonies, Elizabeth said to Esther, "Eleanor cares about having her friends go through things with her." She did and invited them to one big dinner after another. She never let go of a friend.

The two events she added to the list of formal entertainments were the White House Gridiron Widows party and a garden party for women executives in the government, many of whom had never been to the White House. The Roosevelt receptions and parties were "so carefully avoided by the 'nice people,'" a Washington cave dweller was heard to say, that Eleanor "had to invite the people who worked for the government in order to have any attendance at all." When these Washingtonians read the social news from the White House and found the names of those present unidentifiable, they sat back, disapproved, enjoyed Alice Longworth's cruel take-off of her cousin, and thought nostalgically of the days when the Washington that counted agonized over whether Alice, as the wife of the Speaker, or Dolly Gann, as sister and hostess of Vice President Curtis, should have social precedence.

These were trying days for Alice Longworth. Until the arrival of Franklin and Eleanor she had been Washington's "Roosevelt." She was still one of the most entertaining people in Washington as well as one of the most malicious. She had always been the star, Eleanor the retiring one, but now it was Eleanor of whom everyone talked. Even her burlesque of Eleanor, which everyone implored her to do, lost some of its savor when at a White House party Eleanor invited her to perform it for her. "Alice has a talent for that sort of thing," she said amiably, shrugging off questioners who hoped perhaps to stoke up a feud. It did not add to Alice's pleasure in the arrival of the Franklin Roosevelts to hear Auntie Corinne say that Eleanor was more like Theodore "than any of his children." Only a few of the Oyster Bay Roosevelts had not campaigned for Hoover; Auntie Corinne had refused to serve as a Republican elector—"You must understand my own beloved niece

is the wife of the Democratic Candidate"—and Kermit Roosevelt
had turned up at the Biltmore election eve to congratulate Franklin.
But Alice Longworth had campaigned for the Republican ticket. Like
her seventy-year-old stepmother, who had come out of retirement to
introduce Hoover at a Madison Square Garden rally, she could not bear
the idea that the name Roosevelt should be associated in the public
mind and affection with someone other than Theodore. But after the
election, Eleanor set aside political differences and wrote Alice, inviting her to feel free to come to all the parties, even though she must
never feel any obligation to come.

By the end of Roosevelt's first hundred days, he had piloted the
greatest budget of remedial laws in American history through Congress, and Eleanor had demonstrated to herself and to an astonished
country that the White House, far from being a prison, was a springboard for greater usefulness. The opportunities that came to her were
not of her own making. As First Lady she automatically commanded
national attention, was showered with good will, and could get anything she wanted. As the wife of a president who was lifting the hearts
of the nation with the example of his forcefulness, courage, and energy,
she shared in the adulation that flowed from a reviving people toward
the White House. It was not a life and existence that she had shaped
or willed for herself; it was something that was happening to her by
virtue of her husband's election and success. The pattern was set by
him. The purposes she served were his. Her real self, she felt, was
buried deep within her.[48]

Yet there was more to it than that. For by the end of the hundred
days, she as much as her husband had come to personify the Roosevelt
era. She as much as he had captured the imagination of the country.
Far from being a prisoner of the White House and having to content
herself with riding, catching up on her reading, and answering mail,
as she had predicted to friends, she found herself so busy that she had
no time to have her hair washed and would gladly have seen "the days
so arranged that one never had to sleep."[49] Most of the women who
molded public opinion shared the view expressed by Fannie Hurst in
her broadcast from the Chicago World's Fair on the women who were
making history for their sex: never before had the White House had
"a woman so closely allied to the tremendous responsibilities of her
position as wife of the President...." Her mail, which at the end of
the hundred days was heavier than ever, showed that hope was returning to the country, that morale and self-confidence were bounding

upward. That represented the nation's response to Roosevelt's fulfillment of his pledge of "action, and action now," and it also expressed the nation's recognition that in Eleanor as well as in Franklin it had again found leadership.

Cissy Patterson, whose fast behavior had shocked Eleanor in her debutante days, interviewed her for the *Washington Herald*, of which she was the publisher. What was Eleanor's secret, she wanted to know—the whole country was astonished by her energy and her ability to move through "these cram-crowded days of hers with a sure, serene, and blithe spirit." They were old acquaintances, Cissy said, who had moved in the same social circles, and she knew what a transformation had taken place in Eleanor. She was not satisfied with Eleanor's first answer—that she was blessed with a robust constitution. Nor did her second reply ("When I have something to do—I just do it") seem very enlightening. How did she escape the "sick vanity" and "wounded ego" that drained the vitality of most people? "You are never angry, for instance?"

"Oh, no. I really don't get angry.... You see I try to understand people."

"But when you were young, were you free like this? So free—so free of yourself?"

"No. When I was young I was very self-conscious."

Then how had Eleanor achieved mastery over herself? Somewhere along the line there must have been a struggle.

"Little by little," Eleanor replied. "As life developed, I faced each problem as it came along. As my activities and work broadened and reached out, I never tried to shirk. I tried never to evade an issue. When I found I had something to do—I just did it. Really, I don't know—."

Cissy then ventured the opinion that Eleanor was "a complete extrovert, of course." Either Eleanor didn't care for the question or did not care "for Dr. Freud," Cissy thought, for she did not answer. "She just glanced up over her knitting needles, with those clever grey eyes of hers."

Cissy gave up her effort to get Eleanor to talk about her "night of the soul." However Eleanor had achieved her self-mastery, of one thing Cissy was certain: "Mrs. Roosevelt has solved the problem of living better than any woman I have ever known."[50]

IV

---◆---

THE
WHITE
HOUSE
YEARS

36. THE POLITICS OF CONSCIENCE

_____

AN ALERT PUBLISHER RUSHED INTO PRINT A 40,000-WORD compilation of articles and speeches that Eleanor Roosevelt managed to put together in the course of getting settled in the White House. The book, entitled *It's Up to the Women*, had as its unifying theme the reforming role that women must assume if the nation was to come through the crisis of the Depression successfully. It chattily interlaced workaday advice on menus household budgets, child rearing, and getting along with one's husband and children with apostolic appeals to women to lead in the movement for social justice, to join and support trade unions, to set up consumers' groups to police the NRA, and to enter politics.[1]

The new order of things, Eleanor exhorted, should reflect not only "the ability and brains of our men" but also "the understanding heart of women," because especially in times of crisis women had "more strength of a certain kind than men."[2] "Perhaps it is better described as a certain kind of vitality which gives them a reserve which at times of absolute necessity they can call upon."[3] Above all, she wanted women to take the leadership in the movement to abolish war, and hoped that the adventure of building a better world might take the place of the excitement and glamor of war. She did not expect much from the men when it came to manifesting a will to peace: "Only the women and youth of any country can initiate this change. They will have the men to help them later on in the fight, but they will meet some of the same unbelief and lethargy that they have come up against in the past."[4]

It's Up to the Women was a call to action. It also indicated that the First Lady had her own set of priorities—peace, the abolition of poverty, and a concern for youth, women's rights, and the rights of minorities generally. Mary Beard concluded her enthusiastic review of the First Lady's book with the surprised observation that "the implications of some of her economic statements reach to the borderlands of political, social and cultural change."[5]

Eleanor's role as mistress of the White House was thrust upon her by virtue of being the president's wife, yet she also actively sought to shape that role in accordance with the laws and purposes of her inner being. "I am not a philosopher," she said.[6] Indeed, she was acutely conscious of her lack of a college education, which left her, she felt, at a disadvantage in the analysis and judgment of competing intellectual claims. Nevertheless, she did have a philosophy of living shaped by her religious upbringing and fed by a seemingly inexhaustible spring of human sympathy that turned the Golden Rule into a vital and moving force in her approach to men and institutions. In a Washington crowded with rebels and reformers her rigorous effort to live by the Golden Rule moved her into the vanguard of those who wanted the New Deal to mean a new, better order.

Her speeches and writings called for the building of a new world, and though her language was that of the Gospel and the Declaration of Independence rather than the *Communist Manifesto*, her underlying message was revolutionary. People "must understand what it is in the past which held us back, what it is in ourselves, in human nature as a whole, which must be fought down if we are successfully to have a new deal." The nation's goal had to be the creation of "a new social order based on real religion" rooted in people leading the lives "they would live if they really wished to follow in Christ's footsteps."[7]

She had her own concept of utopia. She sketched it softly, in phrases disarmingly modest and simple, in an article she wrote shortly after becoming First Lady, "What I Hope to Leave Behind Me." She would like to live in a community where every individual had an income adequate to provide his family with the ordinary comforts and pleasures of life but no individual had an income so large that he did not have to think about his expenditures. Such a community, she felt, "would have the germs of a really new deal for the race." But it would not happen without a shift in thought and a reconstruction of values—less concern with creature comforts and more cooperation in everything that might help people "acquire a little more graciousness and freedom in life."[8] If that was the type of community the Technocrats, who were much in the headlines at that time, were aiming at, she could view it sympathetically.

Eleanor Roosevelt was fundamentally a moralist. She believed that the Depression was caused as much by defects of spirit and character as of institutions. The nation had gone through a ten-year "orgy" of speculation and quick profits, "of money bringing returns which required no real work." Selfishness and a preoccupation with material things had been the hallmarks of the decade. Selfishness, she felt, had been responsible for America's imposition of higher tariffs and had flawed Americans' relationship with each other—the financial East ignored the distress in the farmlands, and everywhere the rich paid little attention to the poor.[9]

In the frenzy to make money, Americans had lost some of the qualities that made life worthwhile, the ability to enjoy simple things—a landscape, "the breath of a crisp October day," "the play of the sun and shadow," "the view from a high hill"—and above all the joy that came from sharing: "As I grow older I realize that the only pleasure I have in anything is to share it with some one else. . . . I could not today start out with any zest to see the most marvelous sight in the world unless I were taking with me someone to whom I knew the journey would be a joy."[10]

If the Depression had taught men any one thing, Eleanor hoped it was the lesson of "interdependence"—that "one part of the country or group of countrymen cannot prosper while the others go down hill, and that one country cannot go on gaily when the rest of the world is suffering." Perhaps the Depression might reunite the country and give it the sense of community that comes from shared hardships. The Pilgrim Fathers, in the small settlements that they had wrested from an unyielding continent, knew that to survive "they must survive together. . . . In our complicated modern civilization, we are so separated from each other, that we forget our interdependence. The depression has brought it back to us. . . . If we can get back to the feeling that we are responsible for each other, these years of depression would have been worth while."[11]

She invoked the Sermon on the Mount in order to persuade people, especially "the old crowd" with which she had grown up, to accept changes that meant higher taxes and fewer luxuries. If the country did just the temporary and expedient things "we will find ourselves again just where we are today, still building a civilization on human suffering."[12] What distinguished such pleas for benevolence and altruism from sentimental exhortation was the psychological understanding behind them. The personal disasters she had surmounted had taught her that although moments of stress and danger could paralyze and destroy, they could also liberate and strengthen. She had turned her father's death into a constructive, sweetening influence in her life. And instead of crushing her, the Lucy Mercer crisis and her husband's paralysis had become occasions of personal transcendence and growth. In the face of great emotional excitement, wrote William James, "proprieties and their inhibitions snap like cobwebs" and men are given courage to say "Yes" to life's challenges.[13] That was how Eleanor had responded to personal disaster; that was how she now responded to the nation's ordeal. It was a time of hardship and distress, but it was also a time when men and women might be more disposed than usual to subordinate selfishness, faction, and private interest to the common cause. Such moments had to be seized before hardness and the old cautions returned and used in order to bring about a basic reconstruction of institutions.

The National Industrial Recovery Act represented the kind of basic reform the nation needed, and Eleanor hoped the NRA codes would be charters of "fair play" among the various elements in the industrial process. But since she was also a realist about the relationship of power to justice, she helped the unions in their drive to organize under Section 7A, and when the codes turned into agreements for administered prices and restricted production she did her utmost to get consumer representation on the code authorities and state recovery boards and to strengthen the consumers' division under Mary Harriman Rumsey. "I wish I could tell you or that *you knew* how much you have helped the whole range of consumer problems and policies," Mary Rumsey wrote her. Eleanor was equally clear-eyed about another great pillar of the New Deal reconstruction, the Agricultural Adjustment Act. It seemed senseless when people were starving and in rags to pay farmers to plow under cotton and slaughter piglets: "While it may be necessary to raise farm prices, I do think some way should be found to take things which are not needed and give them to people who, in any case, will not be able to buy them."[14]

With seeming naïveté, she asked the AAA administrator over the telephone, "Why do you dump all these pigs into the Mississippi, when there are thousands of people in the country starving?" Before the startled official could reply, she went on, "Why not give the meat away to them?" Her strong objections to the destruction of food in the midst of hunger led to a scheme that anticipated the food-stamp plan. "Surplus farm products are being fed to the hungry instead of being destroyed because she asked a government official a question," reported Ruby Black in *Editor and Publisher* at the beginning of 1934.[15] "Of course all the male officials are convinced they would have thought of it themselves," Ruth Finney later wrote in the Scripps-Howard newspapers, "but they had not done so up to the time she insisted it was the thing to do."

Eleanor's greatest hope for bold, innovative moves to bring idle men and idle resources together lay with the Civil Works Administration set up by the president in November, 1933, and charged with the task of putting four million unemployed to work. "I hope that Mr. Hopkins, in his new corporation, will do some of the things which need to be done. He is really a remarkable person and gradually things may work out."[16]

She approved and defended her husband's program, but there was a radical charge to her advocacy of the New Deal that was absent from his. By the end of 1933 there was some improvement in the economic situation and considerable recovery of confidence. There was "more hope in the air," Eleanor wrote her friend Florence Willert in England, "in spite of the fight we have on our hands over here just now."[17] The fight was being waged by an owning class, which, its nerve restored, was beginning to resist further changes.

Eleanor devoted the opening lecture of her civics course at the New York Junior League to the need for continuing deep-rooted reform. She sought to bring home to the three hundred debutantes and society matrons who crowded the small auditorium the hunger and the cold that Lorena Hickok was reporting from the Dakotas, the desperation in Appalachia. People "simply won't live that way," she warned. She begged her listeners to make the effort to put themselves into the minds and hearts of the wretched and deprived because if they did so they would not be able to complain about higher taxes and government interference.

She told the story of a man who had gone to jail for stealing food to feed his starving family. He had been a model prisoner and was released for good behavior, yet as he left he swore to the warden he would do the same thing again if necessary. "I wouldn't blame him," Eleanor commented, and as her audience stirred uneasily she added, "You would be a poor wishy-washy sort of person if you didn't take anything you could when your family was starving."[18] The protests flooded in; editorialists and correspondents were horrified that the First Lady should seem to be encouraging lawlessness and violence. "I certainly did not tell the story of the starving man's stealing to feed his family to promote or encourage lawlessness or dishonesty," she answered one such critic. "I was merely trying to bring home to my audience, which was made up of people who know little of the suffering of poverty, that people were being driven to desperate ends." Give a job to the man whose case she cited, and to others like him, she said, and they would be the "most loyal and law abiding citizens."[19]

"Nothing I said in my talk justifies starting a revolution by violence," she replied to another critic.

> I simply pointed out the historical fact...that revolutions do not start until great groups of people are suffering and convinced of the hopelessness of their cause getting a fair hearing. I have always made it a point that we are going through a revolution without violence and I hope it will continue to be so, but certain changes must come and we should be willing to have them come.[20]

She directed her appeal to women and young people particularly, because she thought they were less involved with the past than the men and, therefore, freer to consider new ideas and accept drastic change. At Mrs. Meloney's annual *New York Herald Tribune* Forum she called upon youth to become socially militant and to face the fact "that it has to change politics, it has to change business ethics, it has to change the theories of economics and above everything else, it has to change— well, its own weaknesses." Young people should not be afraid of new ideas and should stick with them "until they have decided whether there is anything in that new idea which is worth while or not."[21]

Her praise of a little book, *Prohibiting Poverty*, by Prestonia Mann Martin, the granddaughter of Horace Mann, showed her own readiness to examine the most visionary of blueprints in the search for solutions. The book was in its fourth printing when it came to her attention in the autumn of 1933. Many of its ideas echoed Edward Bellamy's *Looking Backward*. At the heart of Mrs. Martin's "National Livelihood Plan" was the concept—taken over from Bellamy—of a Young Workers Corps or industrial army into which all young people of both sexes would be conscripted from the ages of eighteen through twenty-five. This Young Workers Corps—or National Service Corps, as Mrs. Martin also called it—would produce the "seven cardinal necessities" for everyone—food, clothing, shelter, transportation, etc. His eight-year service to the nation finished, the young "Commoner" would become a "Capital," free "to engage in the pursuit of wealth, fame, power, leisure....He may continue to work or not, as he chooses. His basic livelihood is in any case secure." The National Livelihood Plan, summarized Mrs. Martin, "is a project whereby collectivism would be applied to the production of Necessaries while individualism would be reserved for the production and sale of Luxuries and Surpluses for profit."

It was utopian and simplistic and its implementation would have involved a fantastic degree of regimentation. "Where would I be if I listened to that?" Franklin commented dryly when Eleanor gave it to him to read. Utopias taken literally are easy to caricature, but they must be seen, and that is how Mrs. Roosevelt saw *Prohibiting Poverty*, after an impetuous endorsement that was without qualification—as a stimulant to thought and debate, not as a working blueprint. *Prohibiting Poverty* was a utopia that was drafted by a woman and, therefore, more likely to interest women, Eleanor felt. It dramatically advocated a national purpose that she favored as strongly as the Socialists did, that given America's technological progress, poverty could and should be abolished. She was especially enthusiastic about Mrs. Martin's proposal that the energies of the young, rich as well as poor, girl as well as boy, should be enlisted in the war against want and in the service of the nation.

At the time Eleanor was in almost daily conference with Harry Hopkins on work projects for the unemployed, especially for women and young people. "It may be possible to try out some of these ideas under the emergency relief," she wrote an admirer of *Prohibiting Poverty*. "I wish they could lead us to the point where every one would have security, as far as the basic necessities of life are concerned."[22] Izetta Jewel Miller, a Democratic stalwart who had been commissioner of Welfare in Schenectady, asked whether she (Mrs. Miller) could do anything to promote the plan. Eleanor replied:

> I am afraid that we are due for some criticism for our work here. In the first place, operation. There is a germ of something along that line in the C.C.C. and in the Federal Relief camps for unattached women and girls that are being started this summer. I always speak about the book because the more people read it the more they will try to think along the lines of development for the young people of this country.

Mrs. Martin asked if her announcement could state that "Mrs. Roosevelt says everyone should read *Prohibiting Poverty*." Yes, Eleanor replied, "if you will qualify it by saying that I am not sure at the present time that all of the plans could be put into operation immediately, but I think it has many things that we should be thinking about constantly."[23] She pushed the book's thesis as "an informing power of the mind," not as a dream to be realized in practice.[24]

Among the Bellamyites who were delighted to discover an ally in the White House was Upton Sinclair, whose own plan, End Poverty in California (EPIC), was then sweeping that state and preparing the way for his race for the governorship. At the heart of the EPIC approach was its insistence on state responsibility for bringing together idle men with idle factories and exchanging their products with those of state-encouraged agricultural colonies. Sinclair and his wife were old friends of Prestonia Mann Martin, and he wrote the First Lady to ask if she would permit them to call upon her.[25] "Our friends gather round eagerly to ask what you are like, and more especially, what you think," he wrote after he and Mrs. Sinclair had visited the White House. He sent her a copy of *End Poverty in California*. "I will probably not be governor," he added, "but at least I hope to get some new ideas at work in this state."[26]

He was soon writing Eleanor again. He had heard from a friend that she was going to announce publicly her interest in his plan to end poverty in California. She pulled back from his effort to embrace her. Her reply, which was prudently marked "Private—not for publication," stated, "Some of the things which you advocate I am heartily in favor of, others I do not think are entirely practicable, but then what is impracticable today is sometimes practicable tomorrow. I do not feel, however, that I am sufficiently in accord with your entire idea to make any public statement at present."[27]

She was the teacher, the moralist, the dreamer, but she was also highly practical. The president carried the responsibility. Her proddings and probings had to be carried on in a way that would not embarrass him politically. When Sinclair, having captured the Democratic primary, turned to Mrs. Roosevelt in his effort to obtain White House support in the election, Roosevelt instructed his wife, "(1) Say nothing and (2) Do Nothing"—and she loyally complied.

There was another sign of her intense practicality—the way she backed up her exhortations to women to take leadership in the fight against war and social injustice with hard-headed political organization. Many women held important positions in the Roosevelt administration, she noted in *It's Up to the Women*, and were, therefore, in a stronger position to shape policy than ever before. The book did not

say what insiders in Washington knew, that at the center of this growing New Deal political sisterhood was Eleanor Roosevelt.

"About the most important letter I ever wrote you!" Molly Dewson scribbled on the margin of a seven-page enclosure she sent Mrs.
Roosevelt a few weeks after the Roosevelts arrived in Washington.
The letter reported on Molly's talk with James Farley, the postmaster
general, about women's patronage. He would make no appointments
of women, Farley assured Molly, without consulting Eleanor, so Molly
felt safe about the lists she had left with him, which described the jobs
the Democratic women wanted in categories of descending urgency.
"Imperative recognition" covered the four appointments to the staff
of the Democratic National Committee, followed by the names of
fourteen women who warranted "Very Important Recognition"
and twenty-five for whom jobs were sought under the classification
of "Very Desirable Recognition." Postmasterships and comparable,
minor appointments were listed under the heading of "Worthy of
Lesser Recognition."

"I think they are '100 percent' friendly toward recognizing the
work of the Women and that they will probably do it," Molly's letter
continued. But she cautioned Eleanor that the men were lobbying for
jobs so insistently "that continuous pressure will have to be brought
on Mr. Farley on behalf of the women. I mean continuous in the
sense of pressure on behalf of one woman today and another woman
tomorrow."[28]

Mrs. Roosevelt and Molly Dewson were determined that wom-
en's voices should be heard at every level of the new administration,
and they worked as a team to bring this about, although as far as the
world knew Molly was the chief dispenser of the New Deal's feminine patronage. The relationship between Eleanor and Molly was
harmonious and sympathetic. They had a common conception of the
importance of building party organization and of using the influence
of women to achieve the objectives of the New Deal.

Eleanor persuaded Farley to make the women's division a full-time
functioning department of the Democratic National Committee, and
then she and the president prevailed upon Molly Dewson to come to
Washington to head the department. On January 15, 1934, despite her
ban on political subjects, Eleanor presented Molly at her press conference to describe the new setup of the women's Democratic organization. When Molly said that women Democrats had long hoped for such

an organization and were now about to achieve it "for many reasons," Ruby Black of the United Press, who knew Mrs. Roosevelt's decisive role behind the scenes, mischievously blurted out, "name three." Eleanor gave her a humorously reproving glance, and Molly, after a pause, said, "This Democratic party really believes in women, and the plan was presented to it properly."[29] Molly arrived in the Capital with the names of sixty women qualified on the basis of their work in the campaign and their past records to hold high government positions. By April, 1935, the Associated Press reported that there were more than fifty women in such positions,[30] and many of them made public pronouncements under Eleanor's auspices. Secretary of Labor Frances W. Perkins announced the establishment of camps for unemployed women at one of Eleanor's press conferences. It was in Eleanor's sitting room that Mrs. Mary Harriman Rumsey, the chairman of the NRA Consumer's Advisory Board, described her group's effort to combat rising prices through local consumer organization. And the plans of the Civil Works Administration to provide 100,000 jobs for women were first disclosed by the new director of the CWA's women's work, Mrs. Ellen S. Woodward, at a joint press conference with the First Lady.

"I do happen to know, from my close connections with the business and professional women, of the resentment felt against Hoover because he did not recognize women," Judge Florence E. Allen of the Ohio supreme court wrote Eleanor in expressing her pleasure in the new administration's appointment of women.[31] Such recognition did not come automatically—not even in the New Deal. Molly fought vigorously to enlarge the number of positions open to women. Sometimes she won her point on her own, but if not, she went to Eleanor, and Eleanor, if she ran into difficulty, turned to Louis or Franklin. Occasionally nothing worked. When Secretary of State Hull recommended the appointment of Lucile Foster McMillin to the place on the Civil Service Commission that traditionally had gone to a woman, Molly complained to Eleanor, "Don't you really think that Secretary Hull has enough recognition and power in his own job not to take away from the regular organization women the few jobs that have always been marked out for them?" Why didn't he appoint Mrs. McMillin to a diplomatic post? But then, she added apologetically, "Of course, I realize I may be asking more from you than is possible at this stage of woman's development."[32] Hull had his way and Mrs. McMillin was named Civil Service commissioner, but several years later he did name two women as American ministers—"the first time in our history that women had been named to head diplomatic missions," he would proudly write, adding with male condescension, "They both proved competent, and made excellent records."[33]

Harry Hopkins was much more receptive to the wishes of the women, especially Eleanor. He was as passionate a reformer as she and just as ready for bold experimentation. He cultivated her interest in the Civil Works Administration and encouraged her to take the lead in setting up the women's end of the CWA. "You may be sure that under the new Civil Works program women will not be over-looked," Eleanor assured a woman correspondent who was upset that the president's announcement of the CWA omitted specific mention of women. A program for unemployed women was hammered out at a White House conference called and keynoted by Eleanor and attended by the leading figures in the field of social welfare. By the end of 1933, 100,000 women had CWA jobs.

The irascible and aggressive Harold L. Ickes was touchier to deal with. When Eleanor went to him with a request, she was usually care-ful to preface it with the statement that the president had asked her to do so. This was the case when she urged that the post of assistant commissioner of education, "which is now held by a woman [should] be retained by a woman" and that under the plan to provide work for unemployed teachers, half the positions should be allotted to women. Ickes agreed on both points.[34]

While she sought through patronage to build up the women's divi-sion of the party, Eleanor insisted that appointments had to be on the basis of merit, not just party loyalty, particularly as she felt that "during the next few years, at least, every woman in public office will be watched far more carefully than a man holding a similar posi-tion."[35] Farley, under pressure from a female party worker for one of the top jobs in the administration, turned to Eleanor, who noted that "as head of the Children's Bureau, she [the woman in question] would be appalling. . . . I imagine she is entitled to something if it can be had and I also imagine that she needs the money badly, but I would not sacrifice a good job for her."

While pressing for the appointment of Democratic women, Eleanor would not agree to the removal of outstanding women who happened to be Republicans. The head of the Children's Bureau, Grace Abbott, a Republican, had been one of the three top-ranking women in Wash-ington under Hoover. Although she militantly championed children's rights, ambitious Democrats tried to use Miss Abbott's party affiliation as an excuse for Farley to force her out. Eleanor advised Farley to write the woman who was after Dr. Abbott's job "that no change is being made in the Children's Bureau and that Miss Abbott has the backing of most of the organized groups of women interested in child welfare."[36]

Although she wanted the Democrats to become the majority party, which it was not in 1932, Eleanor did not hesitate to urge women to be ready to reject the party and its candidates "when the need arises."

> This will not be disloyalty but will show that as members of a party they are loyal first to the fine things for which the party stands and when it rejects those things or forgets the legitimate objects for which parties exist, then as a party it cannot command the honest loyalty of its members.[37]

Basically what she hoped might result from the inclusion of women was a humanization of government services and programs.

At a dinner honoring the new secretary of labor, Eleanor stressed that the post had been given to Frances Perkins "not only because there was a demand on the part of the women that a woman should be given a place in the Cabinet, but because the particular place which she occupies could be better filled by her than by anyone else, man or woman, with whom the President was acquainted."[38] But beyond that, Miss Perkins exemplified the new type of public servant who was being brought to Washington by the New Deal.[39]

> When Frances Perkins says "I can't go away because under the new industrial bill [NIRA] we have a chance to achieve for the workers of this country better conditions for which I have worked all my life," she is not staying because she will gain anything materially for herself or her friends, but because she sees an opportunity for government to render a permanent service to the general happiness of the working man and woman and their families. This is what we mean as I see it by the "new deal."

If this attitude toward public service struck people as new, "the women are in part responsible for it."

Louis Howe, who shared Eleanor's view that women were in the forefront of the revolution in thinking that was back of the New Deal, believed that revolution would soon make it possible to elect a woman president. "If the women progress in their knowledge and ability to handle practical political and governmental questions with the same increasing speed as they have during the last ten years, within the next decade, not only the possibility but the advisability of electing a woman as President of the United States will become a seriously argued question," he wrote, adding that if politics continued to divide along humanitarian-conservative lines and the people decided they wanted a New Deal approach to such issues as education, recreation, and labor, "it is not without the bounds of possibility that a woman might not only be nominated but elected to that office on the grounds that they better understand such questions than the men."[40]

Louis was so persuaded that the country might in the not-too-distant future say "Let's try a woman" that one day he came into Eleanor's sitting room, propped himself cross-legged on a daybed, and said, "Eleanor, if you want to be President in 1940, tell me now so I can start getting things ready."[41]

One politician in the family was enough, was her reply to such proposals, seriously meant or not. She did not deceive herself about the real attitude of the country, and doubted that the election of a woman was as imminent as Louis thought. "I do not think it would be impossible to find a woman who could be President, but I hope that it doesn't happen in the near future. . . . I do not think we have yet reached the point where the majority of our people would feel satisfied to follow the leadership and trust the judgment of a woman as President." Some day it might come to pass "but I hope it will not be while we speak of a 'woman's vote.' I hope it only becomes a reality when she is elected as an individual, because of her capacity and the trust which a majority of the people have in her integrity and ability as a person."[42]

Women would have to learn that no amount of masculine chivalry was going to give them leadership if they could not actually "deliver the goods." They should leave their "womanly personalities" at home and "disabuse their male competitors of the old idea that women are only 'ladies in business.'" Women must stand or fall "on their own ability, on their own character as persons. Insincerity and sham, whether in men or in women, always fail in the end in public life."

It's Up to the Women, which came out in November, 1933, was her first book, and like most first authors she soon was inquiring of her publisher, Frederick A. Stokes, how well it was going. "The book is not running away but is selling very steadily," he replied. Eleanor wanted to be successful, and she cared about her influence. Women leaders were conscious that the New Deal meant that more women were involved in government, that more strongholds of masculine privilege were being infiltrated, and that Eleanor Roosevelt was at the hub of this movement. "For some time I have had a collection of statesmen hanging upon my wall," wrote Carrie Chapman Catt, "but under the new administration, I have been obliged to start a new collection and that is one of stateswomen. Now it is ready and you are the very center of it all."[43]

Fundamentally Eleanor was neither stateswoman, politician, nor feminist. She was a woman with a deep sense of spiritual mission. Like Saint Theresa, she not only "had a powerful intellect of the practical order" but was a woman of extravagant tenderness and piety. There was always some prayer in her purse to recall her to her Christian vocation. Christ's story was a drama that re-enacted itself repeatedly in her thoughts and feelings. Amid the worldliness, the pomp, and the power of Washington she managed to hold vivid and intimate communion with Christ with a child's innocence and simplicity. Christ's life in this world, she wrote in a Christmas message,

> lasted only a short thirty-three years. This life began in a manger surrounded by poverty and the only thing apparently which the Christ Child was given was an abundance of love. All his life was spent in want as far as material things were concerned. And, yet from that life there has sprung the Christian religion and what we know as Christian civilization....
>
> Christ died a horrible death, probably at the time it was looked upon as a death of shame. He was buried by those who loved him in a borrowed tomb for he had never acquired any property of his own and yet from that death of shame and that borrowed tomb, has come to us all the teaching which has made progress possible in the love of human beings, one for another.
>
> What a tolerant person Christ was! He rarely condemned any one. Only when the money changers desecrated his Temple did he allow himself to drive them out.
>
> To those who were weak, however, and to those who had aspirations or a desire to do better, he was the understanding and forgiving master.

Her greatest admiration, she wrote in *It's Up to the Women,* went to the women in all ages "whose hearts were somehow so touched by the misery of human beings that they wanted to give their lives in some way to alleviate it." Preaching and exhortation were of little value unless followed up by living example. "The reason that Christ was such a potent preacher and teacher was because He lived what He preached," and missionaries—social as well as religious—"who want to accomplish the double task not only of alleviating human suffering but of giving faith to the people with whom they come in contact, must show by their own way of living what are the fruits of their faith."[44] She did so every hour of every day. She had disciplined herself never to evade an issue or an appeal for help, and in every situation she asked not only what was to be done but what she herself must do.

Among the many letters she received when she entered the White House was one from a young woman, Bertha Brodsky, who, in wishing her and the president well, added apologetically that she found it difficult to write because her back was crooked and she had to walk "bent sideways." Eleanor immediately replied with words of encouragement, her whole being alive with pity and sympathy. She sent the letter to the doctor in charge at the Orthopedic Hospital in New York, asking whether a free bed could not be found for Bertha. It was, and when Eleanor came to New York she visited the young woman, who was almost entirely encased in a plaster cast, although her eyes and mouth showed "a determined cheerfulness." The girl came from a very poor Jewish family, her father eking out an existence with a small paper route, and before the visit ended it was as if Bertha had become one of Eleanor's children. She visited her faithfully and sent flowers regularly. There was a package at Christmas, and flowers were sent to Bertha's mother at Passover. When Bertha was released from the hospital, Eleanor called Pauline Newman of the Women's Trade Union League, who found a job for her. She also helped Bertha's brother find a job, and when Bertha acquired a serious boyfriend she brought him to Eleanor to have her look him over. Eleanor attended Bertha's wedding, counseled her in moments of early marital strain, and was godmother to her child. "Dear Messenger of God," Bertha addressed her.

Her relationship with Bertha was not untypical. She yearned for situations that imposed duties. She responded to every appeal for help, indeed, sought to anticipate them. To friends who felt that she ought to save her energies for more important things, Eleanor replied that "whatever comes your way is yours to handle." Sometimes she was duped, but that was a risk she was prepared to take, and she even refused to condemn those who were not wholly honest with her. "I do not attempt to judge others by my standards," she said,[45] and she refused to dwell on injury.

Speaking of the Saint Theresas of this world, William James wrote at the beginning of the century:

> The world is not yet with them, so they often seem in the midst of the world's affairs to be preposterous. Yet they are the impregnators of the world, vivifiers and animators of potentialities of goodness which but for them would lie forever dormant. It is not possible to be quite as mean as we naturally are, when they have passed before us. One fire kindles another; and without that over-trust in human worth which they show, the rest of us would lie in spiritual stagnancy.... If things are ever to move upward, some one must be ready to take the first step, and assume the risk of it.[46]

To many New Dealers Eleanor seemed innocent on the subject of economics, and to the Marxists she appeared to be a sentimentalist about the struggle for power, yet long after the ideologists of the New Freedom and the New Nationalism, the Technocrats and the Bellamy-ites, the Socialists and the Communists retired or were driven from the battlefield, she would still be striding toward some further frontier of the struggle to liberate mankind's potentialities.

37. MRS. ROOSEVELT'S "BABY"— ARTHURDALE

———————————————◇———

"IF YOU WANT TO SEE JUST HOW BAD THINGS ARE," CLARENCE Pickett, the executive secretary of the Quaker social-action organization the American Friends Service Committee, advised Lorena Hickok, "go down to the southwestern part of the state [Pennsylvania] and into West Virginia." Hickok had checked in with Pickett before setting out on her travels as confidential agent for Harry Hopkins to report to him and to Eleanor on poverty in the United States.[1]

Pickett did not exaggerate the distress in Appalachia. Hickok's vivid communications from the coal towns registered incredulity that Americans could sink to such levels of degradation and hopelessness. No coal was being mined. Some of the miners had not worked for eight years. Human beings shuffled around like ghosts, and a miasmic silence hung over grimy company houses that clung to mountainsides along polluted gullies.

The only circumstance of hope that Hickok found was the work of the Quakers and the Agricultural Extension Service of the state university. They had persuaded some of the miners to launch a program of self-help: subsistence gardens had been dug into the unyielding hillsides; a furniture-making cooperative was thriving; the women were sewing and making clothes out of materials sent by the Red Cross; and, added Hickok, all of it "has done marvels for their morale."[2]

Nothing galvanized Eleanor into action more quickly than afflicted human beings in whom some spark of aspiration and hope still glowed. She was coming down, she informed Hickok, to see what the Friends were doing and hear what they had to propose. Pickett sent her a map "which will help you find Crown Mine, 14 miles south of Morgantown," and on August 18 Eleanor arrived, driving alone. That day and the next the Quaker workers took a tall woman whom they did not identify, wearing a dark blue skirt, white blouse, and a white ribbon around her hair, to see the most hopeful families and the most defeated ones. She listened to the miners' wives and took their babies on her lap. She went into the hovels alongside of Scotts Run, one of the worst slums in the county, where mine tipples rusted and the gully that was used for cooking and washing water also ran with sewage. The men, black-listed because of strikes, had been so long out of work that not even the Quakers could stir them out of their "sit and spit" listlessness.

What point was there in hating "our poor Communists," the two Quaker workers in the area, Alice Davis and Nadia Danilevsky, said to Eleanor when Hickok expressed her loathing for the Communists.[3] Their organizers were having as difficult a time as the Quakers in getting the beaten-down miners to stand up for their rights. Eleanor listened carefully and took notes. These two women had done relief work in Russia after the Revolution, an experience that had disenchanted them with Communism; they knew what revolution had done to Russia and did not want it for the United States. That gave special authority to their plea for help from Washington.

Action followed swiftly upon Eleanor's return to Washington. The little girl with the bad eyes should be sent to a hospital at her expense, she wrote Alice Davis. The CCC boy did not have t.b., as his parents had feared, but leg ulcers, and was now recovered. At a White House dinner she had told the story of the little boy who had clung to a pet white rabbit which his sister said they were going to eat, and William Bullitt had promised to send her a check for $100 in the hopes that it could keep the bunny alive.[4]

But these small acts of kindness did not touch the basic question of policy—what should be done with the thousands of miners who would never find work again in the mines, who were, in effect, stranded communities? The Quakers and the Extension Service workers in Morgantown thought they would have to be resettled in an area where they could make a living or, at the very least, grow their own food and begin to recover their self-respect. To the president, to whom Eleanor reported her findings, this seemed to be exactly the sort of situation the new Subsistence Homestead Program was designed to meet. The program had been authorized by the National Recovery Act, an omnibus bill which included a revolving fund of $25 million to set up "subsistence homesteads" with a view to achieving a better rural-urban balance.[5]

Urbanization and rural decay were old preoccupations of both the Roosevelts. "The bigger the city, the less thought of man," Eleanor had heard Franklin tell the students of North Carolina A. & M. back in 1913. A Jeffersonian faith in the virtues of a yeomanry had been a sympathetic theme in their friendship with Franklin K. Lane, who at the end of the war had urged a federal program to help returning soldiers acquire subsistence farms near their places of work—a form of soldiers' settlements. Eleanor's sponsorship of the Val-Kill industries was based on the theory she shared with her husband that men and women would stay on the farm if interesting and remunerative winter work could be found for them. Like her husband, she thought rural life superior to urban. Cities were absorbing and stimulating because of "the variety of human existence" to be found in them, she had written in 1930, "but I would rather live where trees and flowers and space and quiet give me peace."[6] As governor, her husband had advocated the development of rural-industrial communities, and the creative surge of his first hundred days as president gave him his chance to push his back-to-the-land ideas.

"I really would like to get one more bill," Roosevelt wrote Senator George Norris, "which would allow us to spend $25 million this year to put 25,000 families on farms at an average cost of $1,000 per family. It can be done. Also we would get most of the money back in due time. Will you talk this over with some of our fellow dreamers on the Hill?"[7]

He got his $25 million but there had been no discussion of the provision either in committee or on the floor of Congress. Ickes, who was given the Subsistence Homestead appropriation to administer, did not know what was intended. The housing people had their eye on the money, but Roosevelt knew what he wanted. He saw it as the beginning of a program under which in time a million families might be resettled into planned communities. The government would buy the land, build the houses, acquire the livestock and farm machinery, bring in roads, water, and utilities. The homesteaders would have thirty years in which to pay.[8] It was her husband's idea, Eleanor said of Arthurdale, as the first new community came to be called; "It's a plan he has talked about ever since I can remember." When she told him what the Friends thought needed to be done for the stranded miners, he decided this was the place to launch the homestead program.[9]

"The President thought you would be interested in knowing what is being done in the State University at Fairmont, West Virginia," Eleanor wrote Ickes after her talk with Franklin. The Extension Service people were doing "splendid work" in preparing the miners to go back to the farms:

The President thought this might be a good place to start and that perhaps it would be a good idea to send some one down to get more detailed information than I have. The conditions there are appalling, but the spirit and morale are good, and the people are doing everything they can to help themselves—whole families are weaving, making simple furniture, etc.[10]

Howe already had spoken to him, Ickes informed Eleanor; he (Ickes) had immediately dispatched two men to Morgantown, "and we are expecting an early report. It all sounds very interesting indeed and if the conditions are favorable we hope to go ahead at once with a subsistence project there."[11]

At the president's request, Ickes appointed M. L. Wilson, farmer-philosopher and former professor of agricultural economics, to head the Subsistence Homestead Division. "I'm interested in this and Mrs. Roosevelt's tremendously interested in it, and I think M. L. Wilson is the best man to take it over," the president had said.[12]

Wilson had scarcely settled his family in Washington when he and his wife were invited to the White House. What does one wear to dinner with the president? he amiably inquired at Garfinckel's, Washington's leading department store. Nor did he know what he would do with his car if he arrived at the White House in it. So he and Mrs. Wilson drove to within a few blocks of the president's house, parked and took a taxi the remaining way. Once inside such anxieties vanished before the thoughtfulness of the Roosevelts as hosts. The talk, moreover, was heady, the company congenial. The other guests were Frances Perkins, the Henry Wallaces, General Hugh Johnson, Admiral Byrd, the Leonard Elmhirsts, Louis Howe, and Nancy Cook. Most of the talk was about West Virginia and the possibility of resettling the miners. But it was more than that. New vistas of human betterment cast their spell over the evening. The real bond between the Roosevelts and Wilson was the dream they shared that the resettlement program could show the way to a new type of civilization for America. Rural sage, president, First Lady, Louis Howe, and the Elmhirsts, who were engaged in their own experiment in rural revitalization on a 2,000-acre medieval manor in Devon, England, exchanged ideas and hopes on the reshaping of village communities in order to serve the growth of a new type of socially minded individual.[13]

Dorothy Elmhirst, like Eleanor, had belonged to New York society when it was Society. She was the youngest child of William C. Whitney, financier and secretary of the Navy in Cleveland's first cabinet. Like Eleanor she had attended a Roser class which had met in her father's Fifth Avenue mansion, and also like Eleanor she had broken free from her environment and upbringing to become a woman of broad sympathies and unorthodox ideas. She and her husband Willard Straight had founded the *New Republic*. After his death she had married Leonard Elmhirst and with him had purchased Dartington in Devonshire, where they were trying out some of his ideas on how to halt the drift away from the countryside. In order to raise the standard of living they had introduced light industries and built housing, and they had encouraged the development of arts and crafts as a part of rural life and everyday amenity. Leonard Elmhirst, a student of medieval history, embellished his description of Dartington with references to the manorial system, where there had been security, a sense of belonging and rootedness, and, to a considerable degree, self-sufficiency. Everyone was fascinated. The Dartington concept was not too far from Wilson's "community idea."

"The conversation was very jolly. You felt completely at home," said Wilson. As he bid Mrs. Roosevelt good night she said she would ask Clarence Pickett of the Quakers to come down immediately so that they could talk further. "That's when we got started with Mrs. Roosevelt," Wilson added, as if he were recalling the advent of a hurricane.[14]

A few days later Wilson was informed by E. K. Burlew, Ickes's assistant, that it was evident "the President and Mrs. Roosevelt were going to have a great deal of interest in this. I think they will want Clarence Pickett to be associated with you in charge of it." The "rip-snorting pragmatist and Iowa farm-boy," as Wilson described himself, spent an afternoon with social-gospeler Pickett, who had been raised on a farm in Kansas, and they became friends. They agreed that Pickett would handle the resettlement of stranded miners in Appalachia and Wilson would concentrate on stranded farmers.[15]

Both men would have liked time in which to think their plans through carefully but West Virginia was not far from violence and the Roosevelts felt that a speedy demonstration of the government's concern was essential. "The situation has been considerably complicated," Pickett wrote after Eleanor's visit to West Virginia, "by the excessive interest of the President and Mrs. Roosevelt and Colonel Howe.

They want to establish one colony very quickly and have worked out some plans already, part of which are good and part of which are questionable."[16]

Louis Howe was as interested in resettlement as the president and Eleanor. To him its most promising feature was the chance it afforded to encourage industrial decentralization. The program, "if success-ful," he said on WNBC, "will revolutionize manufacturing industry" within twenty years and might be the answer to urban congestion.[17] Howe seemed to Wilson "all skin and bones," a man who sensed that he was in a race with death, and for that reason, thought Wilson, in a hurry to launch these new programs. He badgered, cajoled, and ordered Wilson and Pickett into action in West Virginia. A local committee composed largely of university agricultural experts rec-ommended the purchase of the Arthur Farm, fifteen miles south-east of Morgantown, near Reedsville, as the site for the first project. Used as an experimental farm by the university, the 1200-acre estate could be acquired cheaply since it was about to revert to the state for unpaid taxes.

But how did one purchase a farm as the agent of the government? "There were endless rules," Pickett discovered, "about purchasing land, letting contracts, and the circumstances under which local people might or might not be employed."[18] Had the limitations been respected Pickett doubted the four settlements for the stranded miners would ever have been built. Howe set them an example in cutting through bureaucracy and red tape. The president, Mrs. Roosevelt, and he were all agreed that the Arthur estate should be purchased, Howe told Wil-son. He wanted it appraised and he wanted an architect to go down and draw up plans for a community house, and he wanted this done in "two days." He also wanted a topographical map—he wasn't sure what for, but the president said they should get one made immediately.

The Treasury Department, after a phone call from Howe, provided the architect. Interior sent down the appraisers, but the topographical map engendered a minor crisis. The Land Office, "full of old people," was "flabbergasted" by Wilson's request and referred him to the Army. Burlew, a long-time Interior official who knew everything about the department, finally dug up two civil engineers in the Reclamation Service. It would take them thirty days to make a map, they reported to Wilson from Reedsville. "Where did you get them?" an indig-nant Howe wanted to know. Wilson said Burlew had provided them. "Who the hell is this man Burlew?" Howe flung out at him. Wilson explained that he had been around Interior a long time and was very knowledgeable. "Rabbit," Howe said, turning to his secretary, "get me E. K. Burlew in the Interior Department." When Burlew came to the phone, Howe introduced himself and said coldly, "I don't care how they do it or what they do to it, I want that map in a week," and then hung up. Howe then asked Wilson if he was in a position to buy the farm after it was appraised. Did he have a disbursing officer? "No, we haven't got anything yet—just Clarence Pickett and I and about three or four stenographers."

"You'd better get somebody who can pay some money pretty quickly because we're going to buy that farm," Howe said, bringing the interview to an end.

"What kind of an unreasonable man is Howe?" Burlew complained to Wilson, careful, nonetheless, to fulfill Howe's order. With the assistance of personnel from the Coast and Geodetic Survey and an Army plane, the map was provided within two days. Howe's face lit up when Wilson brought it in. "You go back and buy that place right away."[19]

On October 13 Ickes announced the purchase of the Arthur estate and said that 200 families would be resettled on this first project. Bushrod Grimes, a native of the area and the Extension Service worker in charge of the subsistence garden program in the county, was appointed manager of Arthurdale. (The new settlement was also called Reedsville, the town to which it was closest.)

"Yesterday Mr. Grimes took a group of men out to work at Arthurdale," Alice Davis reported to Eleanor. "I can't tell you what a delight it is to us that this plan has gone through. We had been looking toward it for such a long time with no real hope of substantial support, that we can hardly believe it when it happens.... None of us can ever tell you how grateful we are for what you have done for the community."[20]

All Eleanor's executive ability, her doggedness, and her influence were now placed at the disposal of the fledgling project, for she firmly believed that what was done in a single community might show the way to a nation. She saw Arthurdale as a laboratory for all the new communities. She wanted it to have the most advanced educational system, a model public-health service, producer and consumer cooperatives, and a program of handicrafts and music that would preserve the folk culture of Appalachia. This was a job Franklin had given her to do. Arthurdale was her "baby" and she interested herself in every detail—the selection of the homesteaders, the choice of a principal for the school, the initiation of a children's clinic. She shopped for refrigerators and inspected plumbing fixtures. Pickett took her to see a self-help group, the Mountaineer Craftsmen's Cooperative Association, which produced attractive maple furniture, including the Godlove chair. That led to a decision to transfer the Association, which was operating out of a junk shop in Morgantown, to Arthurdale and to equip the new homesteads with its products.[21]

Eleanor hired some of the staff. "This is just a note," she informed M. L. Wilson, "to tell you that I have taken on Nancy Cook and Eric Gugler as the advisory experts on the housing end of the West Virginia project." She had promised them expenses "plus whatever they deem their duties worth not in excess of $30 a day, which I understand is the pay for experts."[22] Guests came to the White House, heard the story of Scotts Run, and departed as recruits in a New Deal crusade. "It is magnificent, the way you are directing this big undertaking," wrote Dorothy Elmhirst, whose fund had agreed to finance a small clinic and hospital. "My dear, I am going back to England so proud of my country at last."[23]

By November 7 the first contingent of 25 miners and their families had moved from the coal-camp shacks to Arthurdale, temporarily quartered in the old Arthur mansion. Nine days later another 11 families followed. They would help to put up the fifty prefabricated houses that Louis Howe had ordered. There was even talk that some homesteaders would be eating Thanksgiving dinner in their own houses.

Henry Goddard Leach wrote Eleanor asking if she would do an article for the *Forum* about the "model mining village." Arthurdale was not a mining village, she corrected Leach. "It is for miners transplanted to a farming district with an industry planted there to give them a cash crop."[24] The key to Arthurdale's economic soundness— whether the transplanted miners would be able to make a living and also pay the government back the $1.5 million it had advanced to the project—was the establishment of an industry. In October the Public Works Administration allocated $525,000 to the Post Office Department in order to erect a furniture factory in Arthurdale where items of post-office equipment would be produced. The proposal seemed to pinch a neuralgic nerve in the body politic, and by January Congress was resounding with protests from the defenders of free enterprise. The factory would "wipe out private industry," Representative Taber warned. "Just a proposition to further the socialistic programs already launched by the administration," agreed his Republican colleague, Representative Foss of Massachusetts. Republican ideological protests were given point by more down-to-earth anxieties voiced by Democrats. The proposal would work an injustice on unemployed furniture workers "in my state and in every state which has a furniture factory," objected a North Carolina congressman. Representative Ludlow of Indiana whose district was the home of the Keyless Lock Company which manufactured locks for post-office boxes, went to see Louis Howe. The Arthurdale factory would take away business from it and throw men out of work, he complained, and he was sure that when Mrs. Roosevelt learned that the furniture-factory plan would cause distress and unemployment in Indianapolis she would gladly consider some alternative proposal to create employment in West Virginia. Howe sought to reassure Ludlow by telling him that the items to be manufactured at Arthurdale would not be competitive with those on which the Keyless Lock Company was a bidder.

Howe thought he had pacified Ludlow, but a House rider on a Treasury appropriation bill, January 26, 1934, introduced by Ludlow, prohibited the expenditure of Post Office funds for equipment manufactured at Arthurdale. "Three hundred EPIC Clubs pledged to end poverty in California by putting unemployed at productive labor are prepared to go to bat with reactionaries on this issue," Upton Sinclair wired from California. Eleanor sought to restrain Sinclair, because support from the former Socialist would only confirm congressional fears that a factory in Reedsville was a plunge into Socialism. "The chance for a government factory is still possible," she informed him. "I think a great deal has been made of this prematurely."[25]

The project would not harm industry, Ickes told a news conference. "It will be used as a yardstick to determine if the government has been paying too much for post office equipment, and thereby may hang a tale and may be the reason why some are opposing it."[26] Despite administration assurances, the House at the end of February reaffirmed its prohibition, brushing aside an impassioned plea for the project by its newest member, Eleanor's old friend Isabella Greenway, now a congresswoman from Arizona. Blocked in the House, the administration turned to the Senate, where Kenneth McKellar, the chairman of the Committee on Post Offices, was sympathetic.[27]

As administration pressure continued, so did the attacks. Dr. William A. Wirt, the Gary, Indiana, school superintendent, was enlivening the Capital with his exposé of an alleged conspiracy by "brain trusters" to foster a revolution with Roosevelt cast in the role of an American Kerensky, and he cited the Reedsville project to prove his point. It was a "communistic" plot to subvert the economy of Morgantown, West Virginia, he charged, for in resettling the miners at Reedsville they would be lost to Morgantown's rent and tax rolls. None of them had paid any rent or taxes for years, Eleanor noted, nor could she understand how it was communistic "to give people a chance to earn their own livings and buy their houses." In the Senate, Thomas D. Schall, the blind senator from Minnesota, came to Dr. Wirt's defense. Not only was Mrs. Roosevelt spending $25 million of the taxpayers' money on this "West Virginia commune," but she was profiteering on her own furniture factory in Val-Kill, charging fivefold the average price for its wares because she was the wife of the president. She intended to answer him at her news conference, Eleanor notified the senator, but before she did she wanted to tell him what she intended to say and give him a chance to retract. Would he come to the White House? He made an appointment but did not appear. The Reedsville factory would produce post-office boxes, not furniture, she subsequently told the press. It would be a yardstick operation and cost only a fraction of the $25 million. As for the Val-Kill furniture factory, it had always shown a deficit, and not one of the four investors ever received a salary or even traveling expenses.[28]

Bernard M. Baruch, whom Eleanor had begun to interest in Arthurdale, was delighted with her "beautiful handling of Senator Schall,"[29] and she invited him to see Arthurdale for himself. On June 7, 1934, when the first homesteaders were formally installed in their newly built houses, he and Mrs. Ickes went along. The hardheaded Baruch was moved. "I can never get out of my mind the faces of those people I saw the day we went to Reedsville," he wrote six months later. Baruch carried great weight on the Hill, where a considerable number of senators and representatives were beneficiaries of his largesse, but even Baruch's sympathetic interest in Arthurdale did not change House sentiment about the factory. In mid-June the proposal to have the government finance a factory was finally killed. "We are now busy figuring out, as we decided that it was better to drop the effort of putting through a post-office factory for fear of having a great deal of 'hot-air' in Congress and another attack on Reedsville written into the record, what shall be the industry down there," Eleanor wrote Baruch.[30]

The defeat of the government factory was a major setback. The efforts to get an industry for Arthurdale were further hampered by the rulings of Comptroller General McCarl, who refused to allow government funds to be used to subsidize private industry on the projects. McCarl is "not only a Republican," fumed Ickes, "but... a reactionary Republican."[31] At Baruch's suggestion, Eleanor spoke with Gerard Swope of General Electric, who was a supporter of the resettlement idea. For a brief period a subsidiary of General Electric operated a vacuum-cleaner assembly plant in Arthurdale but closed it down for a lack of orders. Throughout the thirties Eleanor tried to get an industry for Arthurdale. Businessmen who wanted entrée to the White House would raise her hopes with big schemes and promises, and one even established a branch of a shirt factory, but at no time during the decade was more than a third of Arthurdale's labor force employed by private industry. As the prospect of employment faded, the problem of how the homesteaders were to pay for their homes and achieve a decent standard of living became less soluble. It produced a series of clashes between Eleanor and Ickes.

The prime question was: if the government were creating a new community in which a factory it would build and the farmlands it would purchase would set the levels of livelihood, what should those levels be? Eleanor thought that Arthurdale—indeed, the $25 million set aside for the whole resettlement division—should be used as seed money to show what could be done through social and economic planning to create a better life for people. If the objective was to place "as many people as possible in as cheap houses as possible, then I think the 25 millions had much better be turned over to the relief administration," she stated. This was also Pickett's view. "It was only secondarily a relief measure," he said; "primarily it was thought of as the beginning of a decentralization program for workers in industry. It was hoped it might find wide application. The picture was of millions of workers living in small homesteads with some two or three acres of land for gardening."[32] If this was utopianism, then even the Chamber of Commerce shared it, because after a visit to the new community its president, Henry I. Harriman, endorsed Arthurdale and the program of the resettlement division as "fundamental and far-reaching" in that it would show the way "to the necessary decentralization of industry" and "the relief of mass congestion in the cities."[33]

In deciding what industry should be brought to Arthurdale, Eleanor wrote Baruch, at a time when she and Wilson thought they would have some choice in the matter, the important thing was "that a family shall have a sufficient means of livelihood and the assurance of an ability to pay their expenses covering a standard which we hope to

establish as something to shoot at in all rural industrial communities."[34] That standard, she felt, should include indoor bathrooms, a
new type of rural school that would be the center of community life,
and an innovative rural health program. Shown four alternative budgets for the homesteads by Ickes, she chose the most costly. She and
Howe fought for refrigerators. Charles F. Pynchon, a Chicago building
contractor whom Ickes, distrustful of Wilson, named to manage the
Homestead Division in a businesslike way, omitted refrigerators from
the Arthurdale plans. Everyone owned an icebox, he assumed, and the
homesteaders could bring along their old ones. But few of the miners
had them, Pynchon was told, when a furious Howe upbraided him for
the omission: "I know Mrs. Roosevelt will be shocked because she has
been looking over and picking out refrigerators for some time." Howe
was in charge of the "Electrical Committee" reviewing Arthurdale's
electrical requirements, the same letter said, and did not understand
why he was never consulted. "I think I will have to request the firing
of the man in charge of electrical matters as the President is particularly anxious that the electrical part is done under my supervision and
in close contact with me."[35]

At times Ickes seemed to agree with Mrs. Roosevelt that resettlement should be a pioneering division within the government and that
Arthurdale should be *the* demonstration project. He had heralded the
purchase of the Arthur estate as the beginning of an experiment that
would show "the way to a new life for many others."[36] But he was a
suspicious administrator who liked to keep a tight control over every
reach of his domain, and Wilson's direct access to the White House
vexed him. His office planted a secretary on the unsuspecting Wilson who notified Burlew whenever Wilson was called to the White
House. Obsessed by the fear of graft, Ickes insisted that the homestead
communities be administered by Washington. Wilson, a Jeffersonian,
wanted them to be self-governing, the responsibility local. So did
Eleanor. "She was a great community person," Wilson observed, "and
she believed that since these units were small, since they were experimental, there must be a maximum amount of local interest and local
initiative in them." In the spring of 1934 Ickes overrode Wilson and
federalized the fifty projects that had been announced, whereupon
Wilson resigned and returned to Agriculture as assistant secretary.[37]

The first fifty projects were of three types—experimental farm
colonies, homestead-garden colonies located within commuting distance of some type of industrial employment, and four settlements for

stranded miners in Appalachia. Of these Arthurdale alone escaped the secretary's executive clutch.

"I am becoming worried about the Reedsville, West Virginia project," he wrote in his diary, December 2, 1933.

> I am afraid that we are due for some criticism for our work there. In the first place, we undertook it too hastily. Colonel Howe, in a rash moment, told the President that we would start work within three weeks. . . . The result has been that we have rushed ahead pell-mell. I am afraid that we are spending more money than we have a right to spend. Another thing that bothers me is that Colonel Howe, with I think the approval of Mrs. Roosevelt, wanted us to enter into a contract for some 60 or 75 knockdown houses. I understand that these houses are only about ten feet wide and I am afraid that they will look a good deal like a joke.

Howe's prefabs became an albatross around Arthurdale's neck. He had ordered the fifty Cape Cod houses at a cost of $1,000 apiece over the telephone. Eleanor had tried unsuccessfully to argue him out of doing so, and when she visited Arthurdale she went straight for the first of the prefabs which had been put up. Pickett reported to Wilson her great disappointment. "She said she should have stopped Louis Howe from ordering those houses. She was afraid they would turn out to be just exactly what they were when she saw them." Their size was less a problem than their flimsiness, designed as they were for Cape Cod summers, not Appalachia winters.[38]

"We had fifty families out there in freezing winter weather sleeping under tents," Howe later said defensively. "We had to find accommodations for them somehow."[39] The houses were a blunder whatever the excuse. The blunder was compounded when the foundations that had been prepared for them proved to be too large. As a consequence the homesteaders who had hoped to be in their houses by Thanksgiving did not move in until June 7, 1934.

At Eleanor's suggestion, Eric Gugler was asked to redesign and reconstruct the houses. The president liked Gugler, she told Wilson and Pickett. "Eric Gugler turned out to be a very excellent person," said Wilson afterward. "He did a marvellous thing, but he said from the start, 'When you change plans, it's going to cost a lot of money.'"[40]

Ickes resented Eleanor's involvement in Arthurdale and was exasperated by her refusal to subordinate human values to cost consciousness, a point on which she was stoutly supported by Wilson and Pickett.[41] The debate over the size and design of the homestead houses, and, more generally, the standard of living that should be aimed at in the new settlements was fundamental and prophetic of later controversies over what constituted poverty and the government's responsibility to end it. Eleanor's view was that everyone had a right to a decent standard of living.[42] Ickes feared that failure to keep the costs down might mean loss of "the popular support that is absolutely essential if we are to carry through the program at all."[43] On the issue of the Arthurdale houses, the president at first sided with his wife. Ickes went to the White House to look at the sketches Gugler had prepared for these houses, and recorded in his diary that they

> were very attractive indeed but the cost of the thing is shocking to me. The President said we could justify the cost, which will run in excess of $10,000 per family, by the fact that it is a model for other homestead projects. My reply to that was to ask what it was a model of, since obviously it wasn't a model of low-cost housing for people on the very lowest rung of the economic order. . . . I don't see how we can possibly defend ourselves on this project. It worries me more than anything else in my whole department. The theory was that we would be able to set up families on subsistence homesteads at a family cost from $2,000 to $3,000 and here we have already run above $10,000 per family. I am afraid we are going to come in for a lot of justifiable criticism.[44]

The criticism was not long in coming. An article in the anti-administration *Saturday Evening Post,* "The New Homesteaders," focused on Louis Howe's prefabs, how "the camp houses" had been "slowly tortured" into shape and buried "in a meringue of wings, bay windows, fireplaces, porches, terraces and pergolas." Eight wells had been drilled and abandoned when the architect changed his mind about the location of the houses. Each enameled sink was equipped with a "large size patented grease trap which cost $37.50," and which the author said was unnecessary. Arthurdale, he wrote, was an example of New Deal bungling and an object lesson in what happens in a planned economy.[45]

A newspaper friend sent a batch of clippings prompted by the article to Eleanor in Hyde Park. Rumors about the house had been around a long time, the reporter said; "should we have told you?" Eleanor should be prepared to "explain frankly" when she returned to Washington.[46] She had tried to get Howe and Ickes to make a statement that these houses "had not worked out," she replied, and "that they were being made liveable, and that they would not cost the people moving in any more, as the basis for rent was to be set on the earning power of the community and not on the cost of development. For the first homesteads many things will have to be tried out which could not be paid for by the homesteaders." The homesteads were a demonstration of community building

> to show what might happen if industry could be decentralized and associated with agriculture and at the same time they are to experiment to find out how much of comfort and pleasure can be put into the lives of people living in this type of community.... I think all this should have been said long ago but that again is not my business.... I am begging them now to be entirely honest and very explicit. I am afraid I would always be more frank than is considered advisable by many.[47]

She was sure to be asked about Arthurdale at her first news conference when she came back to Washington, she advised Ickes, and she was writing out her statement "so that I will be sure to say the things which you all want me to say."[48]

Arthurdale also drew the fire of the Communists. While conservatives complained that the government was subsidizing a life of middle-class affluence, the Communists attacked the homestead as a design "for permanent poverty." Harold Ware, the Communist party's agricultural expert, collaborated on an article for *Harper's* in which he not only made fun, in a heavy-handed way, of Howe's truckloads of ready-made summer houses, but laboriously uncovered fascist implications in the homestead movement. If the West Virginia projects were a pattern for anything, they were "a pattern for the decentralization of poverty" and the establishment of "a state of serfdom." Ware supported this last charge with a reference to the thirty years that the homesteaders had in which to pay for the houses.[49]

"Of course, the Reedsville project is just one big headache and has been from the beginning," Ickes grumbled in his diary. There was Howe's initial mistake. "And then Mrs. Roosevelt took the Reedsville project under her protecting wing with the result that we have been spending money down there like drunken sailors—money that we can never hope to get out of the project. This project has been attacked in a number of articles and magazines and newspapers, and we are distinctly on the defensive about it."[50]

Ickes thought the president was swinging around to his views on cost: "As the President remarked to me: 'My Missus, unlike most women, hasn't any sense about money at all.' He added with respect to Louis Howe that Louie didn't know anything about money, being as he is an old newspaperman, although he did pay tribute to Louis's political sagacity."[51] Two days after Ickes made this entry the voters overwhelmingly endorsed the New Deal in the 1934 congressional elections. Buoyed up by this unprecedented vote of confidence, Roosevelt was determined to push forward with his program, including a massive expansion of the subsistence homestead movement. He had also decided to take the program away from Ickes. The day after the president told Ickes he was considering turning over the Subsistence Homestead Division together with a rural-housing program to Harry Hopkins, Ickes wrote in his diary, "I won't be at all put out if I lose Subsistence Homesteads. It has been nothing but a headache from the beginning."[52] But he continued to grumble about Eleanor's role in the affair.

> I am very fond of Mrs. Roosevelt. She has a fine social sense and is utterly unselfish, but as the President has said to me on one or two occasions, she wants to build these homesteads on a scale that we can't afford because the people for whom they are intended cannot afford such houses. The President's idea is to build an adequate house and not even put in plumbing fixtures, leaving that sort of thing to be done later by the homesteader as he can afford them. He remarked yesterday that he had not yet dared say this to the people (undoubtedly meaning Mrs. Roosevelt) who wanted the houses built with all modern improvements.

Roosevelt may have considered his wife extravagant, although within the family she was noted for frugality, or he may have been easing the blow to Ickes at the expense of his wife, for the president shrank from hurting people's feelings and many men have directed resentment away from themselves with the protest that they could not do anything with their wives. Whatever Ickes's impressions of the president's views on plumbing, Roosevelt told Tugwell and Dr. Will Alexander, when they took over the Resettlement Administration, the successor agency to the Subsistence Homestead Division: "These people ought to have plumbing. There's no reason why these country people shouldn't have plumbing. So put in plumbing. Put in bathrooms." But try as the Resettlement people did to get plumbing "within an economic budget," they never managed it. "It was always something that they couldn't pay for," Alexander recalled. On one occasion Tugwell went over to the White House to inform "the Boss" that "if he has his plumbing, he's got to let us subsidize it." Tugwell was gone all morning. His aides, all agog and sure that great matters of state must have been under discussion, demanded to know what had kept him when he returned. He had explained to the Boss their difficulty with fitting bathrooms into a house that the homesteaders would be able to pay for "and he [Roosevelt] got to drawing privies." The presidential anteroom was crowded with ambassadors, bankers, politicians, and the president had spent the morning drawing privies, Tugwell reported. Privies it was in the end. Resettlement became the Farm Security Administration in 1937, and the new agency eliminated indoor plumbing from the houses built in the South.[53]

Most of the Arthurdale houses, however, had already been built, and all had bathrooms. The cost issue there was how much the government should charge the homesteaders for the houses and how much should be considered government subsidy. Mrs. Roosevelt asked Baruch to examine the figures and give her a businessman's judgment. "You have told me to treat this as if it were my own matter," Baruch agreed, "and I propose to follow out your request until you tell me not to."[54]

She was grateful to Baruch for his help, and their relationship in the course of their work for Arthurdale had blossomed into friendship. There was, no doubt, an element of calculation on both sides, but also there was genuine affection. Baruch, before Chicago, had been one of the leaders of the stop-Roosevelt drive and while he had sought to make up for his mistake by the generosity of his campaign contributions, it was Roosevelt's policy to give him the feeling he was an insider while in fact keeping him at arm's length. When Baruch came to Hyde Park after the Chicago convention it had been Eleanor who drove him around, and increasingly it was Eleanor and Louis through whom he maintained access to Roosevelt. Eleanor had known Baruch in a distant way when he had served Woodrow Wilson. At that time she had been cool toward him both because he was Jewish and because he was a Wall Street speculator, but she was a different woman now and had come to appreciate his acumen in business and public affairs. He was ready to give advice, and she welcomed it. She knew she tended to be too trusting, to be carried away by her hopes, too inclined to believe that will alone could defeat economic realities. "I want you to be hardboiled, for it is a kind of 'hardboiledness' which is helpful," she had entreated him in a letter of thanks for agreeing to underwrite most of the costs of the experimental school at Arthurdale.[55] The tall, spare figure had become a familiar presence in her sitting room.

After a little trouble in getting what he called the "rock bottom figures," Baruch concluded that of the $1,597,707 that had been budgeted for Arthurdale, $1,037,000 would have to be charge-off to the government. To ask the homesteaders to pay more than $3,000, he thought, would place unbearable burdens upon them.[56] A million-dollar charge-off to the government did not seem lavish to him. The excess of actual costs over estimates was "not much larger relatively than a great many business and engineering precedents in other pioneering. . . . You are to be congratulated on your implacable insistence on accurate figures revealing the truth." And Eleanor could quote him if she wished.[57] She herself assembled statistics on the millions private industry spent on research; if such outlays were justified to develop new ways of manufacturing, the government was justified in putting "a little money into experimenting in new methods of living," she wrote. (These figures were included in a defense of Arthurdale which she did not publish because Ickes's man Pynchon thought that further publicity would only add fuel to the controversy.)

Risks had to be taken; one could not wait around for perfect solutions. "We do not think for a moment that we are doing anything more than experimenting," she wrote Florence Willert. "We know a lot of things have got to be thought through, but also think it is better to do something than to sit by with folded hands."[58]

The contrasting reports that came to her at the end of 1934 from Arthurdale and nearby Jere vindicated government action on the basis of plans and concepts that everyone realized would have to be revised not once but often. The Communists were making considerable headway among the Jere miners, reported Alice Davis, the Quaker relief worker who had first shown her around Scotts Run and who was now county welfare commissioner, and it seemed to her "just a race against time—whether we can get them into decent living conditions and decent ways of thinking before they are led to violence." The local unemployed organized by the Communists had marched on the Welfare Board and threatened to throw Alice and her caseworker into the river. "Of course, we laughed and said we furnished everything for stringing ourselves up but the rope, and they'd have to get together and make that themselves—but their faces were all twisted with hate and if they had had a little smarter leadership and a little more practice they *would* have put us in the river." She might be working with the Communists herself, she added: "If you and Mr. Roosevelt had not come to lead the people, I think many of us might have been thinking differently."[59] Eleanor put that letter into Franklin's bedside basket.

A few weeks later a wholly different report from West Virginia went into the president's basket, and Eleanor also sent a copy of it to Justice Louis D. Brandeis, who at dinner at the White House had been fascinated by her account of the efforts of the resettled miners, so like those of the Palestine settlers, to make a new life for themselves. This report was from Elsie Clapp, the progressive educator whom Eleanor had brought in as principal of the school in Arthurdale. It was about Christmas in Reedsville.

> Such joy. I wish you could have seen it. The toys you gave reached every boy, girl, child, baby. And, best of all, out of their abundance, the homesteaders on their own initiative made up several Christmas boxes for some people near us who are very poor and miserable. . . . We cut our tree, brought it in and decked it. We gathered our Christmas greens from the woods. . . . Christmas Eve at seven-thirty we gathered in the Assembly Hall. Carols which the children acted out orally, the old Bible story, presented by everyone. . . . The whole Christmas drew the community together . . . I was needed only to help. It was theirs entirely.

Eleanor set great store by the school. It would be up to the school, she had told Elsie Clapp when she interviewed her for the job of principal, not only to educate the children but to reawaken hope in the homesteaders, show them how to live more satisfying lives, indeed, to breathe life into this new community. The assignment did not faze Miss Clapp, a protégé of John Dewey who had been applying progressive education principles to rural education at the Ballard Memorial School in Kentucky. But she would need to bring in teachers with special training and get the advice of the best educators in the country, she told Eleanor, who agreed to both conditions and said she would find the money to employ qualified teachers. Eleanor also helped to establish a National Advisory Committee that included John Dewey,

Lucy Sprague Mitchell, and Dean William Russell. Jessie Stanton, the director of the Bank Street Nursery School in New York, set up the nursery school in Arthurdale, the first in the entire area. "If I can teach these mothers," Miss Clapp told Eleanor, "that cold pancakes and coffee aren't good for babies, my two-year-olds will be much healthier." The curriculum was adapted to the special needs of the community, the learning experiences organized around life problems that the community faced. Under Elsie Clapp's leadership, the school became the center of almost every community activity. She fostered a regional cultural movement, and a summer music festival that she and the homesteaders inaugurated featured "Jig-Dancing," "Ballad Singing," "Mouth-Harping," a "Fiddlers' Contest," and a "Square Dancing Contest" in which Eleanor was a participant.[60]

An expensive experimental school did not seem a legitimate charge upon the government, so Eleanor raised most of the operating expenses from private sources. Baruch was the most generous, beginning his contributions with a check for $22,000, a response, he wrote, to Eleanor's "rare combination of intelligence and great heart."[61] In order to be able to contribute herself, Eleanor resumed commercially sponsored radio broadcasts, the proceeds of which went to the American Friends Service Committee to be earmarked for the purposes she indicated. In the autumn of 1934 she received $18,000 for six 15-minute broadcasts of which $6,000 went for the salary of Elsie Clapp, another $6,000 to establish the handicraft center at Arthurdale under the direction of Nancy Cook, and the remaining $6,000 for health work.[62]

At times she seemed to be almost a commuter between Washington and Reedsville. When she was asked whether it was not a burden to travel to Arthurdale so often, she cut the questioner short with the reply that she enjoyed the company of the homesteaders. She liked them. She knew the names of the children, kept track of their ailments and their achievements. She chatted with their mothers about canning recipes and joined in the Virginia reel with their fathers. She had a "folksy and homelike way with the homesteaders," Wilson recalled, "as though she had always lived in the community and had just come back from having gone for a couple of weeks."

She had tried repeatedly to get Ickes to visit the project while the homesteads were still under his jurisdiction and wrote him that Baruch had come away "tremendously impressed" after his first visit, so much so that he was going "to help us to make it into the kind of experiment which we would all like to see." She hoped that the secretary would plan to go down, "for I feel that after all the trouble and anxiety that this project has caused you, you will get a sense of satisfaction from meeting the people and seeing how well it is turning out."[63] Ickes had promised he would go with her in August, but the visit never took place.

Although Ickes professed relief over the transfer of the homesteads to Tugwell, the shift rankled him. He became harshly critical of Eleanor, whom at times he even suspected of being part of a cabal to oust him from the cabinet. At the state dinner for the cabinet given by the president and Mrs. Roosevelt at the end of 1934, little pleased him: the menu hardly constituted a "Lucullan" repast, he disliked the domestic wines Eleanor insisted upon serving, and "the champagne was undrinkable." By January, 1935, he had come to the conclusion that Mrs. Roosevelt did not do her husband any good with her active involvement in public affairs. He began to cultivate Missy.[64]

Eleanor Roosevelt did present a problem to a strong, self-centered administrator like Ickes. He was never quite certain whether she was acting on the president's behalf or on her own. Nor was the president beyond taking advantage of the ambiguity.

Rexford G. Tugwell, who inherited the Subsistence Homestead Division from Ickes when, in May, 1935, Roosevelt combined it with the rural rehabilitation program of Hopkins's FERA and the soil-reclamation activities of the AAA, was also baffled by his relationship as Resettlement administrator to the First Lady, even though they were on terms of genuine cordiality. In December, 1933, when Tugwell was assistant secretary of agriculture, she had, at his urging, visited the department's National Research Center near College Park, Maryland, where Tugwell thought the nearby submarginal land could be turned into a garden city. A man of superior intelligence, more detached about his ambitions than Ickes, Tugwell admired the First Lady's relationship to government. She had rallied to his support when the food and drug interests fell upon him because of his sponsorship of an effective food and drug bill. The conservative press dug up a poem he had written as an undergraduate and quoted the line "I shall roll up my sleeves—make America over!" to prove his subversive intent, which had only strengthened Eleanor's admiration for him. They had enjoyed each other's company when they found themselves on the same plane bound for Puerto Rico, an historic visit prolific in New Deal benefits for this hitherto neglected island dependency.[65] They were good enough friends so that when she invited him for dinner or to Hyde Park he brought along his assistant, Miss Grace Falke, whom he later married, and when he delivered a speech at Dartmouth on the New Deal, Eleanor felt able to admonish him on the foolhardiness of his title, "Wine, Women and the New Deal." "Your sense of humor has led you into a trap, I am afraid," she wrote, envisaging a deluge of WCTU protests.[66]

She wanted to be helpful to Tugwell in his role as Resettlement administrator, but she considered Arthurdale her special responsibility. She fought stubbornly for what she considered to be the interests of the homesteaders, for she knew that Tugwell was basically wary of the back-to-the-land concept of resettling the unemployed and of industrial decentralization. In fact, he would have been happier if Roosevelt had not placed the Subsistence Homestead Division, which already was under fierce attack, in the Resettlement Administration.

Tugwell considered resettlement realistic as a way of moving farmers off exhausted soil but not as a remedy for industrial unemployment or urban congestion. People go to employment, not employment to people, he had stated, as if it were an iron law of economics; and if industries could be persuaded to decentralize, the new communities which formed around them would become company towns. Nor did he believe urban growth could be halted. But Eleanor refused to accept as inevitable what she felt ought to be resisted, even if the man she was opposing was as brilliant as Tugwell. She was, Tugwell wrote in *The Democratic Roosevelt,* "naive about many things—after all, she had a very defective education."

So although they were confederates, they had reservations about each other. He consulted her on the staff for the Resettlement Administration; she was enthusiastic about his plans for a Special Skills Division to instruct and encourage the settlers in the arts and crafts. She sent him an article on Arthurdale she had written for *Liberty,* which she wanted him to review. "This is a very moving little story," he commented. No, he had no objections to publication, but even if he had, they might have been difficult to offer since her note also said, "Franklin has seen this." She also urged him to expedite decisions on Arthurdale's requests for school-construction materials, which had been sitting "for ages on a desk in Washington." "I hope you will be patient with us for a month or two," he entreated her.[67]

Like Eleanor, Tugwell believed that these new communities should set a pattern for a new America and that the managers of the homesteads, therefore, had social and educational responsibilities, not simply economic and engineering ones. He convened a conference at Buck Hills Falls to assess these responsibilities. How could these communities be vitalized, Tugwell asked the group, which included anthropologists and psychiatrists as well as rural planners and managers. "A community does not consist of houses, and it does not consist of houses and schools and roads and water systems and sewers either. There is something else to a community besides that. We are trying to find out what it is if we can, and, if we can bring it into being, to make it come alive."[68]

The homesteaders were long-time casualties of the Depression, said Eleanor, who followed Tugwell onto the platform. They were not going to recover all of a sudden; they had lost their initiative and had suffered certain physical changes which had affected their mental and spiritual ability to face the world: "It is not purely a housing problem. You cannot build houses and tell people to go and live in them. They must be taught to live. Therefore this is a resettlement problem."[69]

Tugwell's emphasis on the social aspects of community building pleased Eleanor, who hoped there would soon be another conference on the same theme and that it would be held at Reedsville, which was, after all, supposed to be the demonstration center. She thought Arthurdale had come to life as a community and that it had done so because of Elsie Clapp's remarkable work with the school and the nursery. Baruch agreed with her. Whatever the cost of the school, he said, "the money has been well spent because it has demonstrated what can be done especially in the way of salvaging and redeeming old and young people. What has been done there can be duplicated in other places."[70]

Arthurdale had achieved the sense of community for which Tugwell was groping, and Eleanor hoped that that spirit would not be a casualty of the reorganization. She liked the plan which Tugwell had told her about at Buck Hills to form community corporations which would lease the land and houses from the government and in turn give long-term leases to the individual homesteaders. Outright sale of the houses, Tugwell feared, might expose the colonists to speculators and make land-use planning and corporate commercial farming more difficult. But Eleanor foresaw difficulties at Arthurdale, where the homesteaders had been led to believe that ownership of their homes would be vested with them individually, not with the community, and that the costs would be based on what they could pay. "I am afraid I am complicating your life very much," she wrote Tugwell apologetically after Buck Hills, "and I do not mean to do that but I thought I ought to tell you that I had told Franklin about it as I think he will be discussing it with you."[71]

Her readiness to go over Tugwell's head to the president did complicate the administrator's life and, carried away by the First Lady's patronage, the homesteaders also bypassed Resettlement Administration channels, and were even condescending to the administrator. "There is one thing I want to suggest to you," Eleanor cautioned Elsie Clapp,

> namely, Mr. Tugwell has the complete responsibility and when we are with him, I think you should make it a point to make him feel that we recognize his responsibility and do not even suggest that I do anything except stand ready to help in an unofficial way on educational and health questions. If you can, try to make him realize that while you feel identified with the people, and that they do seem to be your own, that you also fully realize the main responsibility is his and that they are "his people" and not "my people."[72]

It was sensible advice, but her own willingness to defer to Tugwell's "complete responsibility" was less than wholehearted. Limited funds compelled the Resettlement Administration to reduce the wages of the homesteaders who were employed on community construction projects, and the cuts were devastating the homesteaders, a frantic Elsie Clapp told Eleanor. "I quite realize that what has been done is necessary," Eleanor in turn wrote Tugwell, "but I think it ought to have been done in each of the homesteads not by a mere notice, but by some one who really understood the reason and who could put it to the people." If there was to be a wage reduction, she went on, there would have to be a corresponding reduction in the payments made by the homesteaders on their homes. "I can imagine that your problems are so many that what may happen to the people in one homestead does not loom very large, but after all this is the first and the one most criticized and under the public eye. I hope you will not think me an interfering old hen."[73] Despite the disarming final sentence, she did not relax her pressure on Tugwell. The homesteaders sent her a petition, underscoring the injustice of wage reductions without corresponding reductions in what they had to pay. She sent it straight to the president, telling him, as she informed Elsie Clapp, that "my feeling was that in the effort to be efficient from the economic standpoint, I thought perhaps the division was forgetting the important human element, and that I hoped he would keep in mind the fact that I wanted him to go down and get a picture of the human side of himself."[74]

Eleanor felt a responsibility to the homesteaders, to whom the government had made commitments, many of them through her. Sympathetic as she was with Tugwell's efforts to rethink the government's homesteading policy, she felt a new approach must take those commitments into account. "The opportunity to interpret thinking that lies behind some of the projects has not been easy with the present administration," the normally patient Pickett complained to her.[75] Yet she was alive to Tugwell's problems. When Elsie, in her zeal for the homesteaders, charged into Washington to get action on an Arthurdale payroll which had been delayed because of Treasury funding problems, Eleanor rebuked her. "The fact that you visited the Treasury caused three people to telephone Mr. Tugwell to find out if you were speaking with authority for him. As you know this would annoy a man who feels that his Administration must begin to function." It would be wiser for Elsie to keep out of the administrative side, she suggested, and if problems did arise to go through regular channels or through her.[76] She urged both Pickett and Elsie to be patient. Tugwell was "tired," as were many of the men who since March 4, 1933, had been working to the limit of their energies. She sensed, moreover, that Tugwell was "quite overcome to find that the old administration had worked out none of the fundamental problems."

When Baruch went to Reedsville to try to sort out the problems there that urgently called for decision he went alone because Eleanor thought the settlers might say things to him they would be reluctant to say in front of her. Baruch's survey had a wider application than Arthurdale. While some of its problems were unique, the more basic difficulties were characteristic of many of the new communities. A decision had to be made soon, he informed Eleanor, about how Arthurdale was to be governed. Would it be local or would it continue to be run from Washington? In any event, he wrote, "there must be some method of getting quicker decisions than there is now." Those in charge at Arthurdale, when Baruch finally got them to speak frankly, complained sharply of "their inability to get decisions or to cut the red tape, even in getting materials." The size of the community had to be settled; there would soon be 125 houses—should the government still aim for 200 as originally planned? Not if the people in them could not get work, Baruch felt, and he was highly pessimistic on that point. All the problems stemmed from that fact. The homesteads, he advised, should be sold at a price low enough to give the homesteader the chance to own them eventually, but the carrying charges could not be twenty dollars a month; a figure of $100 a year would be more realistic, especially in Arthurdale, where the possibilities of self-support had been further diminished by the belated discovery that its soil was not suitable for commercial crops.

It would be impossible to carry out the plan for a rural-industrial community as originally envisaged, Baruch advised Eleanor, but she must not feel that the effort had been wholly a wasted one. Arthurdale had demonstrated that there could be "human rehabilitation" after long periods of unemployment. Elsie Clapp's school had been particularly helpful in that connection, but there, too, they had to ask themselves whether the heavy private subsidies should continue or whether it was not time to normalize the school's relationship to the county and state educational system. "If we will learn not to put people where they cannot earn enough to care for themselves, whatever the cost, it will be cheap," Baruch concluded.[77]

It would take the war to show that the government was able, when the will was there, to direct industry to move to where people were, but Eleanor, while she abandoned neither the effort to get an industry for Arthurdale nor a vision of rural-industrial communes that would provide an escape from both urbanism and rural decay, was intellectually too insecure to press her own philosophy in the face of the practical judgments of a Baruch or the theoretical convictions of a Tugwell: "I think it is fairly well proved," she wrote a few months before a defense manufacturer began to operate in Arthurdale, "that even if industry is going to decentralize at all, it has to locate first and then the community grows around it."

Tugwell's emphasis as Resettlement administrator was on land reform. His program sought "to take poor people off poor land and resettle them where good land, good organization and good advice might rehabilitate them." In addition he promoted the brilliant concept of the "greenbelt towns," garden communities built in wooded areas adjacent to industrial centers, with low-cost housing as their cores.

Eleanor supported both programs, as did the president, but the mood of the country and especially of Congress was becoming hostile to the whole idea of planned communities. Although Tugwell contemplated sixty "greenbelt" projects, only three were built because they were attacked so savagely. And in the 1936 campaign, when the Republicans made the Resettlement Administration an issue, Tugwell noted that "we had no defenders and were told to keep quiet ourselves."

The environment had become unfriendly to social planning and experimentation, and this reinforced the individualistic and competitive attitudes of the settlers within the communities whom Eleanor, Tugwell, and Dr. Alexander had hoped to imbue with the community idea. It was difficult to build new communities with old minds. For years the miners had felt themselves to be social and economic outcasts, and now their deepest wish was not to be something special but to be like other Americans. "I realized when we began," Eleanor told the Women's National Democratic Club,

> that there must be an educational program when you take people from an area where they had been living for some time under impossible conditions, but I had no conception what the problem was. I understand it a good deal better than I did three years ago.... When these people were moved, they had to learn to stand on their own feet and make their own decisions, and sometimes they didn't quite know what was expected of them...nobody understood why these people didn't take hold. There is always grave danger in anything that is experimental. One must not do too much for people, but one must help them to do for themselves.[78]

The homesteaders had been encouraged to start cooperatives at Arthurdale and other settlements, but this, too, called for education. "They wanted cows tied to their back fences," Eleanor later said. "They trusted nobody, not even themselves. They had an eye out all the time to see who was going to cheat them next."[79]

"We were doomed to failure from the start," Tugwell wrote fifteen years later. The human stock was sound, he felt, but "the environment was hostile to the development of character" and to the development of the commitment and self-discipline necessary to make the communities work.[80]

The one instrumentality that had helped to reshape attitudes was Elsie Clapp's school at Arthurdale. Yet even this heavily subsidized school, with its progressive methods, made the homesteaders uneasy; they wanted their children to be taught the three R's like the rest of the children in West Virginia. Moreover, Arthurdale's bleak economic prospects worked against the initiative and self-reliance that the progressive curriculum sought to instill. Men without jobs found it difficult to plan and to keep ambition alive. That was the point made by the educational foundations when Baruch asked them to help finance the school. Without industries, without jobs, they told him, the school could not succeed. "I want to say again that in this I heartily concur," Baruch wrote to Eleanor.[81]

She went along with Baruch's conclusion, although reluctantly. He had spoken with Elsie Clapp about taking her task force of teachers to another community where the economic prospects might be more conducive to the long-term support of a costly experiment in progressive education, and Eleanor hoped the group might return to Arthurdale if the economic situation there were to become more stable. But without Baruch's moral as well as financial support she did not feel she could insist on going on with the school. She met with Tugwell and his aides to inform them of Baruch's decision and her own concurrence, as well as Elsie Clapp's. She had expected Tugwell to welcome the news since he considered it time the homesteaders tied in with the West Virginia school system, but Tugwell was unhappy, she reported to Baruch, and "rather took my breath away" with the statement that "the morale at Arthurdale and conditions there were ninety per cent better than in any other homestead, entirely due to the school." Her five-page single-spaced report to Baruch on what she had done about the school situation asked for his approval: "I hope you will feel I have acted wisely and have done what you would have done, for I value your good opinion and cooperation more than I can tell you."[82] She let him out of his commitment, but she continued to subsidize some of the school salaries. In 1939 her contribution was $2,677.49.

Eleanor went to Arthurdale to tell the homesteaders the decision about the school and explain the importance of carrying on the work "on their own responsibility and to tie themselves in in every possible way with the State, the county and the general neighborhood." She was not withdrawing her support for Arthurdale, she sought to reassure them. "I stressed to them that I was not in any way lessening my interest and would be there as often as I had been in the past" to work with their own school people.[83]

She kept her word by continuing to go to Arthurdale at commencement time to hand out diplomas until her last year in the White House. She also continued to bring friends to Arthurdale and to enlist their help for special projects—such as a library—voted by the homesteaders. In May, 1938, the president yielded to her proddings and made his often deferred visit to Arthurdale, hailing it as an example of "the

Eleanor (right) with her father and two brothers, Elliott and Hall, taken about 1892.

After her parents' deaths, Eleanor lived with her grandmother, Mrs. Hall, at Tivoli overlooking the Hudson. Here she is shown with her Aunt Maude, youngest of the beautiful Hall sisters.

The headmistress of Allenswood, Mlle. Souvestre, was at home in the worlds of high politics and high culture, and under her tutelage Eleanor blossomed.

In 1903 Eleanor and Franklin became secretly engaged. Here they are sitting on the porch of Sara's house at Campobello during Eleanor's visit in the summer of 1904.

Eleanor with Franklin's mother, Sara Delano Roosevelt, a daunting and remarkable woman. About 1904.

Honeymoon photograph taken in the Italian Alps.

Eleanor and Franklin on the steps at Hyde Park. Their first child, Anna, was born in May 1906.

Anna, now a one-year-old, with her delighted parents. The dog's name was
Duffy. 1907.

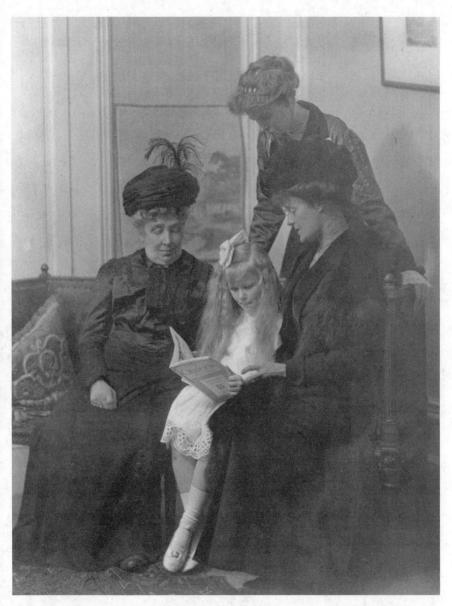

Four generations—Grandma Hall, Mrs. Stanley Mortimer (Aunt Tissie), Eleanor (standing), and Anna, who is looking at a copy of Theodore Roosevelt's magazine, the *Outlook*. About 1913.

Eleanor (right) loved to go on picnics. This is one at Campobello, August 1913.

Assistant Secretary of the Navy Roosevelt reviewing the Victory Fleet on its return from Europe, December 26, 1918. Eleanor is second from the left.

The notification ceremony at Hyde Park, August 9, 1920, after FDR had been nominated for vice president. At Eleanor's right are Secretary of the Navy Josephus Daniels, the McAdoos, Homer Cummings, and Governor and Mrs. Alfred E. Smith.

Family picture, 1920. Elliott sits just below his father. Franklin Jr. and John are in front with Chief, Anna's dog. Sitting on Eleanor's left is James, and in front of them, Anna.

Campaigning for Alfred E. Smith in 1924. A meeting at Eleanor's Sixty-fifth Street house in New York. Eleanor sits facing Louis Howe.

Nancy Cook, at Eleanor's right, and Marion Dickerman, at her left, became Eleanor's closest friends. Together they built a cottage and operated a furniture factory at Val-Kill. Marion ran Todhunter School where Eleanor was vice principal. Nancy Cook was director of the women's division of the New York State Democratic Committee, in which Eleanor became the key figure.

A Roosevelt family portrait on Hyde Park Terrace on September 15, 1931. (Left to right: Sara, FDR, Sistie, Anna, Buzzie. Back left to right: John, Betsy, James, Eleanor, Elliot, Curtis Dall, and Franklin Jr.)

The swimming pool at Val-Kill. From the left: FDR, Missy LeHand, and Eleanor.

New York City's ebullient Mayor Fiorello H. La Guardia, director of the Office of Civilian Defense, with Eleanor, after he had appointed her assistant director, calling her "America's No. 1 Volunteer."

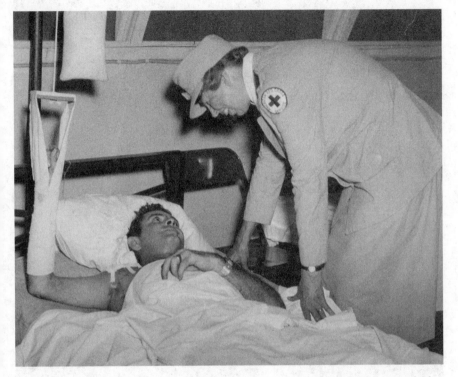

Journey to the South Pacific, 1943. "She went into every ward, stopped at every bed, spoke to every patient."

FDR, August 1944.

awakening of the social conscience of America." Businessmen who cultivated Eleanor in the hope of obtaining access to the president suddenly realized that she was cultivating *them* in the hopes of getting an industry for Reedsville. Arthurdale struggled along, but at the end of the thirties the weekly reports on unemployment showed that the majority of the homesteaders were still on the government work-relief payroll. The problem of an industry and full employment was finally solved in World War II; when the government began to offer defense manufacturers generous tax incentives and subsidies to expand their plants and facilities, Eleanor, backed by Baruch, pressed the men in charge of the defense program to keep the needs of the homestead communities in mind. Arthurdale's employment problem vanished when the Hoover Aircraft Corporation, attracted by its labor force and railroad facilities and with little risk to itself since the government was underwriting the expansion, leased several of the buildings the government had built in Arthurdale and began operations.[84]

Arthurdale was a chastening experience. It taught Eleanor that a president's wife who undertakes a specific job in the government faces double jeopardy: she is without real authority yet she is expected to perform miracles. When she does assert leadership it is resented and resisted. And if she does not, officials try to anticipate what she wants done. Tugwell was one of the most strong-minded and independent men in the Roosevelt administration, and yet he had been at a loss as to how to deal with the First Lady. "I had been told that he did not tell me his exact feelings because he felt everything I wanted must be carried out," Eleanor wrote Baruch.[85]

Eleanor's patronage of Arthurdale and the subsistence homesteads insured them plenty of publicity and attention, which had its good aspects, especially in helping the underprivileged feel that the government cared about them. Officials tried harder as a result of Eleanor's interest to make the experiment succeed. The public conscience was stirred. Eleanor's visit to the farm homestead project near Memphis was "a great encouragement to the families," Will Alexander, administrator of the Farm Security Agency, the successor to the Resettlement Administration, wrote her in late 1939, and then added: "Of course, our most discouraged and bewildered group are the families in the Migratory Labor Camps, about whom John Steinbeck wrote in *Grapes of Wrath*. It would mean a great deal to them if you could some time visit one of their Migratory Labor Camps."

But there were also adverse consequences to the publicity that

attended Eleanor's sponsorship and interest. A pilot program by defi-
nition must go through a period of trial and error, of mistakes and
failure. Eleanor's presence not only mobilized the administration's
friends but attracted its enemies, and critics pounced upon every mistake and magnified it to the limit. In this respect, Arthurdale might
have benefited from less publicity.

Then there was the effect of Eleanor's involvement on the homesteaders themselves. Her readiness to help and her belief in the experiment and in the homesteaders gave them courage and was an added
incentive to succeed. "I do not believe in discouraging people when
there is anything to encourage them about," she replied to a critic
who taxed her with closing her eyes to the problems in one of the
settlements; "I think there is a tremendous amount in the psychology
of hopefulness," she wrote Major Walker, one of the top officials of
the program, complaining that every time the regional staff people
visited the homesteads there was a slump in morale.[86] But the homesteaders, as she herself noted on other occasions, were not angels—far
from it—and her efforts to be helpful to them made them dependent
and too easy on themselves, so much so that on one occasion when
the school bus broke down they brought it to the White House garage
for repairs. Presidential aide "Pa" Watson stopped that.[87] That was
an extreme case, but too many homesteaders, Eleanor confessed in
1940, seemed to feel the salvation for all their problems was to turn to
the government, and she was disappointed by their unwillingness to
shoulder their share of responsibility.[88]

"How do you get these people to consent to such a program?" she
asked David E. Lilienthal, head of the Tennessee Valley Authority,
when he came to the White House to talk to her about the effect of
the TVA on people. Lilienthal, who considered her "a beautiful spirit"
but felt that she had a "social worker angle on a world that is tough and
bitter and hardly amenable to such tampering with systems," had long
hoped for a chance "to teach her some reality about economics." He
saw his opportunity when she gave a troubled account of the efforts
at Arthurdale and Crossville "and how she now saw that bringing in
factories from the outside wasn't the right way, even when it could be
done; that our way of making something happen out of the materials
at hand, and by knowing the particular problems intimately, was much
wiser." When Eleanor repeated her question about how the TVA got
people to change their way of doing things, Lilienthal told her of "grass
roots methods, and the technique of demonstration and learning by

doing and by example. And being close to the problem because we are a regional, not a Washington outfit."

"She is a very intelligent person," Lilienthal noted in his journal, "and she got it, and I think will pass it along to a member of the household who, God save the mark, can stand some education along the same line."[89]

But neither the conceptual mistakes of Eleanor Roosevelt and of M. L. Wilson nor the political vulnerability of Tugwell explain why this bold and imaginative attack on rural poverty and urban congestion was in the end liquidated by Congress. It was the firm commitment of the Farm Security Administration to the goal of ending rural poverty that alarmed the conservatives, because it threatened the traditional power structure in agriculture in general but particularly in the South, where many of the FSA benefits flowed to the Negro. And so when the war came, giving the New Deal's enemies the chance to kill off some of its most innovative programs under the pretext of cutting non-defense expenditures, the FSA was included. There were 99 communities at the time of its final liquidation; 10,938 homesteads had been built at a total cost of $108,095,328, or at a unit cost of $9,691, which included the cost of community facilities and management. Arthurdale, with a unit cost of $16,635, had been the most expensive.[90]

"These projects represent something new," President Roosevelt said in his Arthurdale address, "and because we in America had little or no experience along these lines, there were some failures—not a complete failure in the case of any given project, but partial failures due to bad guesses on economic subjects like new industries or lack of markets." But there were lessons to be learned from this "bold government venture," lessons that would save "a hundred times their cost in dollars."[91]

But the lessons were not learned. Instead of a planned approach to the related problems of the flight from the farms, urban congestion, and industrial decentralization, the outcome was left to the unchecked operation of social and economic forces that ultimately produced the crisis of the cities.

When Eleanor Roosevelt appraised the Arthurdale experience in the second volume of her autobiography, she acknowledged that money had been spent wastefully and that the financial returns to the government had not been satisfactory, but in extenuation she pointed to the human beings saved: "Oh, yes, the human values were most rewarding," she stoutly maintained.[92]

Her defensiveness was a tribute to the hold that the free-enterprise ethic had regained in the postwar era. "Sell it off—regardless" was the attitude of the National Housing Agency, which fell heir to Arthurdale.[93] The final cost to the government of liquidating Arthurdale's 165 houses, hillside inn, forge, weaving room, furniture-display room, and 57,250 square feet of factory space in 1946 was in the neighborhood of two million dollars. To Americans of the 70s, accustomed to the expenditure of billions on space and weapons research and hundreds of millions on health research, this will scarcely seem like heedless extravagance.

If experiments like Arthurdale were not justified, Eleanor wrote to a critic in 1934, then "we must go along the beaten path and be contented [sic] with the same type of living which has driven people out of rural districts in the past and into the cities where they have become equally unhappy under present industrial conditions."[94]

Unhappily, what in 1934 was a defense of a New Deal program turns out three decades later to have been accurate prediction.

38. PUBLICIST FOR
THE NEW DEAL—
COLUMNIST AND LECTURER

Had the census taker in 1932 asked Eleanor Roosevelt her job or profession, she would have said "teacher." But when she moved to the White House she had to give up professional teaching. Was there anything, she asked herself, that she could do professionally which would reflect her own knowledge and experience and not be entirely the result "of somebody else's work and position? . . . I turned naturally to speaking and writing."[1]

In 1934 she resumed the sponsored radio talks that she had given up when her husband had become president. People, especially women, were interested in her views. Speaking to them gave Eleanor a sense of fulfillment, and the largest audiences were those to be reached over the radio networks. Moreover, she wanted the money, chiefly for Arthurdale, and she decided to risk the criticism that she knew would come and see if she could ride it out. She would not touch the money from those talks herself, she explained to the press; her fees would be paid directly to the American Friends Service Committee to be disbursed at her direction. This announcement muted most of the criticism that had caused her to give up commercial radio in 1933, but not all of it. Her first sponsor was the Simmons Mattress Company, and the other mattress manufacturers, alarmed lest the nation flock to the Simmons product, protested to President Roosevelt that it did not seem fair for the First Lady to use her prestige to assist some single manufacturer. The president sent the protest to his wife. "Ask the President if he wishes to answer?" Eleanor queried. Howe advised against it. "I agree with Louis," wrote Steve Early, and a notification finally came back: "No ans. F.D.R."[2] A few weeks later, however, when a small manufacturer objected directly to her, she did defend herself by asking if she should not write for a single magazine because it would be unfair to its competitors, or buy from a favorite dress designer. "The principle involved in my broadcasting for a particular firm holds true in everything I do."[3] It was a debater's answer, and the criticism never wholly abated; but she was willing to accept it, and so, evidently, was Franklin. Her definitive reason was, "I could not help the various things in which I am interested if I did not earn the money which makes it possible."

Simmons paid her handsomely. "I think you are entirely right that no one is worth $500 a minute," she replied candidly to an irate citizen. "Certainly I never dreamed for a minute I was!" Her fees, it was noted, placed her in the same class as the highest-paid radio personalities of the time such as Ed Wynn.[4]

Her broadcasts were sufficiently popular to bring her another sponsor as soon as the Simmons series ended, this one the American typewriter industry, for whom she did six fifteen-minute talks on child education. These were subsequently issued as a pamphlet. Her 1935 sponsor was Selby Shoes who, for sixteen fifteen-minute talks, paid her $72,000, all of it sent directly to the AFSC. An article in *Radio Guide* praised her as a radio performer. Coached by studio technicians, who were enchanted with her because she was not a prima donna, she began to learn everything about radio delivery—timing, modulation, spacing—and by 1939 she was dubbed the "First Lady of Radio" by WNBC:

> Her microphone manners are exemplary.... She listens to suggestions from production men and cooperates in any plan to improve the reception of a broadcast. She arrives in time for rehearsals and accepts direction with no more ado than if she were an obscure personality.... She is not averse to a little showmanship here and there, but eschews tricks. Her voice is well-pitched and she speaks softly.... It is not an accident that Mrs. Roosevelt's radio voice is studied by students of speech.[5]

In 1936 Betty Lindley, the wife of Ernest Lindley and long a personal friend, became her radio agent and negotiated a contract with Pond's for thirteen talks at $3,000 apiece. Of this amount $200 was set aside for studio expenses, $300 went to Mrs. Lindley, and the remainder to the AFSC to cover the budget of the Arthurdale school; "after that it seems to me that the school should be taken over by the state."[6] She suffered a few mishaps as a radio performer. In her final broadcast for Pond's there were a "few terrible seconds" when a page disappeared from her script. If she had been following her own train of thought instead of a script as she was required to do, she could have handled it without a break, she said. As it was it took her "a second or two" to collect her thoughts.[7] What made her an outstanding radio performer was not so much her mastery of technique as her constant awareness of her unseen audience. She tried consciously to envision the women who were listening to her under conditions of the greatest diversity—on lonely ranches, in mountain cabins, in tenements—and to remember that they were weighing her words against their own experience. She made her listeners' interests and problems her own and tried out of her own experience to say meaningful things simply and concretely.

Her ability to identify with her listeners, to illustrate her thesis with homely stories, and to advance her point of view with such kindness and courtesy that even the most violent adversaries were stilled was even more evident in her lectures and speeches, where she was not bound by a script. Her custom, when she addressed live audiences, was to speak from a single page of notes. "Have something to say, say it and sit down," she advised students of public speaking, as Louis had advised her. "At first write out the beginning and the end of a speech. Use notes and think out a speech, but never write it down."[8] She did not like to speak if she did not have something affirmative to say. Often as the chairman introduced her she prayed for Divine guidance to say something that might be helpful to the people in front of her. Like Gandhi, Schweitzer, and other semi-religious figures with whom she later would be grouped, she was always the teacher. Everything she said was infused with moral purpose and affirmed the supremacy of love and truth.

Her speeches generally contained a challenge, but it was issued with such graciousness and modesty that few took offense. "Be conciliatory, never antagonistic, toward your audience," she advised, "or it may disagree with you, no matter what you say." Before the DAR convention she championed progressive methods in education, a campaign to eradicate illiteracy, and the "grand" adult-education work of the Relief Administration, and her tradition-bound audience listened attentively. She even poked gentle fun at a superpatriot's proposal to restrict the right to change laws to people of old stock (she and the president between them had only one ancestor who arrived later than colonial days, she noted, "so if anyone would have a right on that peculiar status, we would still qualify"), and ended with a plea for patriotism that "will mean living for the interests of everyone in our country and the world at large, rather than simply preparing to die for our country."[9] Novelist Dorothy Canfield Fisher wrote that she had "fairly bounded into the air with joy" because she had never dreamed that someone in authority could say right out what Eleanor had said to the DAR.[10]

A few weeks later she spoke extemporaneously at a federal prison for delinquent girls and women in Alderson, West Virginia. Her speech was Lincolnesque in its simplicity and feeling. She had been moved by the way the girls had sung the spirituals, she began, and then quoted the 121st Psalm: "I will lift up mine eyes unto the hills from whence cometh my help." That was the keynote of Alderson, she noted, set as it was in the mountains and run by a progressive penologist, Dr. Mary Harris, to help those who were there over the rough spots. That was also what government in general was now trying to do—"help the people it governs" over the rough spots. There was a new concept of social justice and government abroad in the land. "The fundamental change is just this, that instead of each person being out for himself for what he can get for himself . . . people must think . . . of the people around them" and ask of any action not only "what will be the effect . . . on me, but what will be the effect on those around me?" She then told of a recent visit to Puerto Rico and of a little rural school there that had been started by an obscure, humble individual but which was transforming the whole approach to rural education. "So when you get a chance to push something that is new and that helps the life of the people around you to be better, just remember what I have told you about Puerto Rico and help it along." Then she went into her own philosophy of life:

> It is a wonderful thing to keep your mind always full of something that is worth while doing. If you can get hold of something that you feel is going to help the people around you, you'll find that you're so busy trying to add one more thing to it that you won't have time to be sorry for yourself or to wonder what you're going to do with your spare time. . . . If I get sorry for myself, I'm no good to anybody else. It is just the best tonic I know, to get so interested in everybody that you want to see them happy always, and somehow or other you'll find that you haven't time for any of the things that filled your mind, that kept you from being a really useful person in the community that you were living in.[11]

It was a speech the girls understood, delivered with such earnestness and evident good will that even the most hardened yielded to its spell. "My prediction was correct," Dr. Harris wrote her afterward; "many of the girls have referred to it and quoted from it to me, and what I hear myself is only a small part of the comment it aroused."[12]

Her speeches held her listeners because they reflected her own efforts to think through to what was right and true. "You talk the language of the new America," wrote Frank P. Graham, the president of the University of North Carolina, after her talk at the university. A Negro woman, explaining her willingness to wait an hour and a quarter to get into one of Mrs. Roosevelt's lectures, put it more colloquially: "She's got a message. And gosh! she's given it to 'em hot!"[13]

By the end of 1935 Eleanor was in such demand as a speaker by forums and other groups accustomed to paying fees that she signed a contract with W. Colston Leigh to do two lecture tours a year under his management at a fee of $1,000 per lecture. The Leigh brochure advertised five subjects on which she was willing to speak:

RELATIONSHIP OF THE INDIVIDUAL TO THE COMMUNITY

PROBLEMS OF YOUTH

THE MAIL OF A PRESIDENT'S WIFE

PEACE

A TYPICAL DAY AT THE WHITE HOUSE

One thousand dollars was a large fee, larger than she would have commanded—at least at the outset—had she not been the president's wife, and since she did not feel obligated to turn over the whole of these fees to the American Friends Service Committee, some saw this as further proof that she commercialized and cheapened the First Ladyship. But she shrugged off such criticism, sensing perhaps that no one had done more to ennoble the First Lady's role; and if people came to her lectures because they were curious about the First Lady, they stayed and felt they had obtained their money's worth because of the personality with which they had come in contact.

Her first tour for Leigh began with an appearance at Grand Rapids, "and as usual I was very nervous until I found myself standing up and actually speaking." A confidential report to Leigh from his own correspondent in Grand Rapids was ecstatic. The audience of 1,700 to 1,800 "listened intently to every word." The observer noted that Eleanor was especially admired for the "dignified, authoritative manner" with which she handled all questions, including those meant to embarrass her. "Of course, everyone was amazed at all that she was able to do in a few hours that she was in the city....I am sure that she won over all of the Republicans who heard her that evening, and there were many."[14]

Eleanor liked Leigh because he was "hard-boiled" and sought to protect his lecturers from being overwhelmed by local hospitality, but Leigh's best efforts to shield her were unavailing. "All goes well but very hectically," she wrote Franklin. "It would be easy to be a lecturer or the wife of the President but both, Oh! my." She was to speak in Omaha on a Sunday evening to the Delphians, and would like to have a "quiet day," Tommy advised the local committee. A sympathetic reporter described that "quiet day." It began with Eleanor and Tommy's arrival by train at 7:00 A.M., when they were met by a half dozen Delphians and given flowers. En route to the hotel they were trailed by two detectives who kept themselves out of sight because Eleanor's distaste for bodyguards was by now well known. At 10:30, after they had bathed and breakfasted, Tommy let in the press for a half-hour's questioning. As they filed out, a delegation of WPA supervisors came in. "This time," the reporter noted, "Mrs. Roosevelt asked the questions." They were succeeded by representatives of the National Youth Administration, who invited her to inspect an exhibit of NYA handicrafts, which she did after lunch, donning low-heeled oxfords because she insisted on walking to the exhibit. An hour later, having changed to an afternoon dress, she met some forty Delphians at tea. Then came a group of women Democrats. After dinner in her suite alone with Tommy when she wrote her column, she looked in on a private party at the hotel, toured an exhibit in the hotel of bug extermination devices on display for the convention of the National Pest Control Association, and, thus "rested," wrote the reporter, "the First Lady left at 7:45 for the city auditorium to give the speech for which she had come to Omaha."[15]

In 1937, Leigh persuaded her to do the first three-week tour. A "bit too long," she confessed to Bess Furman afterward. "Two weeks is all I can do in one-night stands and keep feeling polite towards the people who meet you at seven a.m. with bouquets and flowers and expect you to wear a smile!" Sometimes the hotels were poor, she wrote her husband, and sometimes, as was the case with the Danville, Illinois, hotel from which she was writing, they were "delightful. When they like you we get much attention. When they don't we are completely neglected!" Yet exhausting as these tours were, when local sponsors wanted to make special arrangements for her, she objected. The lecture committee in Jackson, Mississippi, distressed to learn there would be no Pullman car from Meridian to Jackson, were arranging for a special car when Eleanor wired, "I do not mind riding in day coaches. Please do not put yourself or the railroad to extra expense."[16]

She might gently complain to her husband, to Bess, or to Tommy, but to those receiving her it was their comfort, their feelings that were always paramount with her. At Oak Park Junior College in Illinois she had been told that the subject of her speech would be "Peace" and was prepared to speak on that when she suddenly heard the chairman announce, "Mrs. Roosevelt will speak on 'A Citizen's Responsibility to the Community.'" She had no notes but went right ahead, saying "a little prayer that I would get through without them!" He was grateful, the embarrassed man wrote afterward, for her "courtesy in not changing the subject matter after I had announced it and the ability with which you handled the surprise subject."[17]

Women, of course, were interested in what she wore and how she carried herself. "I have seen five queens, and this queen is regal," remarked a cultivated Frenchman who watched her model a gown at a debutante cotillion. Dress designers chose her as "the best dressed woman in the United States" in 1934. "To have that title," she commented, especially in the light of her family's feeling that she never paid sufficient attention to her clothes, had been one of the "funniest" but also one of the "grandest" things that had happened to her. "I have come to the conclusion," she advised dress designer Lilly Loscher, "that a dress for this type of trip should be low cut but should have very thin sleeves coming over the shoulder which would not interfere with having a long-sleeved jacket to go with it. It should either be of lace or some crepe material which does not require a lining and which does not crush. If it is lace and has to have lining, the lining should be put into the dress because it is very annoying to have a lot of little snaps to keep straps together across the shoulders."[18]

She had a cultivated diction and pronounced her words with a singular clarity, although a few patriots objected to her preference for "*sh*edule" to "*sk*edule." Her platform voice was no longer a monotone but an instrument of shading and cadence, capable of a controlled intensity or easy relaxation. But it remained high-pitched until she was taken in hand by Mrs. Elizabeth von Hesse, a voice teacher: "Our Dear First Lady—may I speak frankly and to the point? I am a teacher of speech, particularly of tone production. . . . Mrs. Roosevelt, if I were permitted I would give you a simple set of exercises for the development of resonance and depth of tone that would give you richness of quality. You could project your voice without losing any of its beauty." The exercises were such that she could do them while dressing, even while riding. Eleanor was about to reply that she was "too busy" but changed her mind. What would they cost and what did Mrs. von Hesse think could be accomplished in two or three days "if I gave you an hour each day?" Not everything could be done in one week end, Mrs. von Hesse replied, but a set of exercises and speech habits could be established that would give her more effective use of her resonant chambers on which depended the richness of tone and would help her achieve "better diaphragm control."[19]

Mrs. von Hesse came down, charging $50 for the week end, and within a few months Eleanor was being congratulated on the improvement. Her voice did "carry better and more easily," Eleanor agreed, but she was playing truant from her exercises when she traveled: "I could probably exercise my head and my voice, but my body is out of the question because trains and hotel rooms do not lend themselves to space enough and there is a feeling the floor may not be clean which may have something to do with it."[20]

Because of her success with Eleanor Roosevelt, Mrs. von Hesse's professional reputation boomed, but when Mrs. von Hesse discussed with Colston Leigh lecturing under his management, Eleanor hastily wrote "I would not want to be used as Exhibit A, with a comparison of my defects and improvements," adding, however, that it was "quite all right for you to state in your publicity that I have had lessons from you."[21]

A "one-season-wonder" in the lecture field, Drew Pearson and Robert S. Allen wrote disparagingly in their newspaper column, "Washington Merry-Go-Round." As reporting, this was wildly inaccurate, since in November, 1938, when the column appeared, Eleanor had been lecturing for three years; as prophecy it was even worse since until nearly the end of her life she was one of Colston Leigh's most sought-after speakers. Evidently Pearson and Allen recognized their blunder because a few months later they wrote that "a check-up of Mrs. Roosevelt's lecture audiences shows that she has definitely made friends for her husband, despite large fees charged by her agent." The columnists particularly admired the way she subjected herself to a "grueling fire of questions" after her lecture, and her effective replies. In Akron, Ohio, she was asked, "Do you think your husband's illness has affected your husband's mentality?" Except for a slight firmness about her jaw, she betrayed no emotion as she read out the question, and replied: "I am glad that question was asked. The answer is Yes. Anyone who has gone through great suffering is bound to have a greater sympathy and understanding of the problems of mankind."[22] The audience rose and gave her an ovation.

Because she spoke from notes rather than from a text she had to think about what she was saying, and this kept her speeches "a little fresher," she thought, and prevented her from becoming bored.[23]

The naturalness, good sense, and spiritual energy, which made her a durable presence on the lecture circuit, also explained her success as a newspaper columnist. Two months after her arrival in Washington the United Feature Syndicate asked her to do a daily two-hundred-word article "on topics of general interest with particular emphasis on the home." Regretfully she had turned it down because of prior commitments to the North American Newspaper Alliance and to the *Woman's Home Companion*. In 1934 the latter publication, on its own initiative, increased her fee, but in 1935 it decided that "two years was about as long a time as we should continue a special feature of this type."

A few months later the United Feature Syndicate renewed its invitation to do a daily column, a diary of some four hundred to five hundred words in length. "When do I start?" was Eleanor's speedy reaction; her second question was, "What's my deadline?"[24] On December 31, 1935, she sent off her first piece of copy, carefully marking it PRESS RATES COLLECT.

No columnist had a more newsworthy setting or a more fascinating cast of characters upon whom to report. Her first column described the White House family quarters teeming with young people during the Christmas holidays. Her husband was in bed with a cold, she reported, "so I said a polite good night to everyone at seven-thirty, closed my door, lit my fire, and settled down to a nice long evening by myself." There had been sixteen that day for lunch, and one young guest had burst out, "Every meal is different in this house. Yesterday we talked about philosophies of government. Today we have talked about movies and punging." Eleanor did not explain, although a good reporter would have, that "punging" is a form of sleighing. The discussion about philosophies of government had been occasioned by

Franklin Jr. and John who, in discussing a sociology course at Harvard they were taking with Professors Zimmerman and Boldyraeff, had described the professors as being highly critical of the AAA, whereupon the president had suggested inviting the professors to dinner so they could confront Henry Wallace and Chester Davis. Eleanor's concluding comment revealed that she was not going to shun controversy: "There are so many things which you do not have to consider if you are developing and studying a thing in a classroom. . . . It is quite different to be faced with actual situations that have to be met in one way or another in a given period of time."[25]

It soon became evident that her appeal as a columnist was not based only on her relationship to the president. Readers were enchanted with the personality that disclosed itself in little flashes such as "I sallied forth and in two brief hours ordered all my Winter clothes" or how she had spent "half an hour having a whole new monetary system thrust upon me," or how, when speaking about the District Training School for Delinquent Girls, she had stated, "Never have I seen an institution called a 'school' which had so little claim to that name." She discoursed on plays and books, expressing her judgments crisply and unambiguously. "Crude in a way because the thoughts hit you like hammer blows," she said of Irwin Shaw's anti-war play *Bury the Dead*, "but it was a great performance." "One line from S. N. Behrman's play *End of Summer* will stick in my head for a long time—'At the end of every road you meet yourself.'" She had just finished Santayana's *The Last Puritan*: "There is altogether too much concentration on himself in Oliver's makeup. He was a fine character but missed, I think, the greatest fineness which is the ability to minimize your own importance even to yourself." John Golden was "funny" when he said there will never be any great women writers in the theater "because women do not know as much as men." The assumption of male superiority amused her "because as a rule women know not only what men know, but much that men will never know. For how many men really know the heart and soul of a woman?"[26]

She stayed away from politics but sometimes could not resist a gentle if oblique thrust. When the Supreme Court climaxed a series of rulings cutting down New Deal measures with its decision holding the AAA unconstitutional, she painted this picture of a relaxed reaction in the White House: she had gone down to the White House swimming pool for what she thought would be "a rather quiet and subdued swim at six o'clock. . . . My husband was already in the water, and before I reached the door, I dropped my wrapper, plunged into the water, and swimming about very quietly, I inquired hesitatingly how they were all feeling. To my complete surprise instead of either discouragement or even annoyance, I was told that everyone was feeling fine, and on that note we finished our swim." At dinner instead of the events of the day they discussed, violently, the Holy Roman Empire, the Dark Ages, and the Renaissance. At midnight she went in to say good night: "With the new day comes new strength and new thoughts."[27]

It was a picture of grace under pressure and at that moment of constitutional crisis her portrait of a steady-handed, non-vindictive president was worth more than a score of political pronouncements. As Anne O'Hare McCormick wrote two years later, after the tension-filled days of the Munich crisis, "No one should underestimate the reassuring effect on public opinion of the figure of the many-sided father of a family who slips in and out of the diary of the accomplished White House character who manages to sublimate the typical American woman in the person of the First Lady of the Land."[28]

Sometimes readers complained because Eleanor refused to be a pundit or to deal with serious matters all the time. "I am asked to write a diary and I cannot write on politics," she replied to one such critic; "I simply tell small human happenings which may interest or amuse the average reader.... Daily happenings are trivial, certainly, and not worth your time to read, but it may help some people to feel that lives they think must be important are after all filled with homely little things." To another faultfinder she wrote, "I learned a long time ago that too much crusading for any cause is almost as bad as too little. People get weary of too much preaching."[29]

She loved doing her column and longed to be accepted as part of the newspaper fraternity. She noted approvingly that at a Hyde Park picnic "before long we had to find a quiet spot where Mr. [Heywood] Broun could write his column." She wrote and filed her column under the most adverse circumstances; neither illness, travel, nor crowded calendars were permitted to interfere. She would arrive late in the day, she informed Flora Rose, the head of Cornell's Home Economics Department, and would ask if she could have a stenographer when she arrived "as I will have to do my daily column and get it off right away." When winter storms forced her to take a train rather than fly to Washington after visiting her daughter Anna in Seattle, her biggest worry was where would she file her column: "Yesterday all wires were down along the railroad for almost five hours and I thought I would never get my column filed in time. Today I'm taking no chances and am getting it off while we wait.... It is good for my typing anyway, as I have to do it myself, but I am a bit sorry for those who have to read it." On another occasion she dictated the column to Tommy, who was balancing her typewriter on her lap while Elliott drove them from Denton to Fort Worth, Texas.[30]

In September, 1936, she came down with the grippe and a fever so high that Franklin canceled some campaign speeches to hurry back to the White House to be with her. Who was doing Mrs. Roosevelt's column? he asked Tommy, and said he would be very glad to do it for her. "His offer was deeply appreciated," Eleanor reported to her readers. "We want to pass it on to you so that you will realize what you missed, but we refused courteously and rapidly knowing that if it once became the President's column we would lose our readers and that would be very sad."[31]

"Mrs. Roosevelt is a magnificent trouper and a real newspaper person to carry on under such circumstances," George Carlin, the manager of the United Feature Syndicate, said to Tommy.[32]

Eleanor's fellow-columnists enjoyed giving her advice, usually in their columns. "Of course Mrs. Eleanor Roosevelt is new at the column-and-diary profession or racket and one should not be too harsh," wrote Franklin P. Adams, whose "Conning Tower" in the *Herald Tribune* was devoted to a diary in the style of Samuel Pepys once a week. "In...yesterday's 'My Day,'...she tells of having tried to get, though not where, a Chuddar shawl for Colonel Howe, probably Louis McHenry Howe. She tried in three places, unnamed, and at the fourth, also unnamed, found that an effort would be made to get the shawl.... We are not her editor, but if we were we would say, 'Get names.'" The manager of the syndicate sent the column to her, saying "I agree with his comment heartily." She had not wanted to advertise the shops, she replied, or to use names without asking people's permission, but she would try to do better in the future. "I fear I have been trained to be too careful."[33]

Similar advice was offered by Damon Runyon a year and a half later. He wanted to know what she had for lunch, who were the interesting people to whom she referred, and what was interesting about them. She took the criticism in good spirit and tried to bear it in mind, but when she was hurried, which was often the case, her sentences were sometimes wordy, her verbs weak, her nouns abstract—so much so that the syndicate occasionally felt obliged to delete. Of one such paragraph, William Laas, the managing editor, complained that "the guests are not named, nor are the organizations they represent, and the question under discussion is not stated in so many words. These essential details are left rather mysterious."[34]

"I realize you are right," was her contrite reply.

She was not the only Roosevelt to begin a column in 1936. Alice Longworth had been recruited by a rival syndicate and was enlivening the Republican press with her political asperities. "I think Alice is having a grand time," Eleanor wrote their mutual friend Nan Wood Honeyman. "She certainly writes well. I wish I were as free as she, though I do not wish ever to be as bitter."[35]

The difference between the two was the basis of a skit, "Alice and Eleanor, or These Little Girls Make Big Money," which was put on at the stunt party of the Women's National Press Club in March, 1936. It showed a tall lady in riding clothes with a knitting bag at her side sitting at a desk next to a tea table. She poured tea, knitted, and picked away at her typewriter. The sign at her desk read, "Roosevelt, E." At another desk, labeled "Roosevelt, A.," sat a woman with a large handbag, a lot of cigarettes, and newspapers. She smoked, glanced at a paper, wrote fitfully, strode up and down. They finished their columns simultaneously and, crying "copy," left the stage. Then two distraught editors appeared. One, tearing his hair, read a tender, domestic little piece about a lovely tea hour around a roaring fire with Harry Hopkins reading fairy tales and Rex Tugwell piling logs on the Red Flames. That, screamed the hysterical editor, appeared in hundreds of newspapers under the name of Alice Roosevelt Longworth. The other editor, equally upset, found that under Eleanor Roosevelt's name there had appeared a column about the New Deal perishing of a potato diet and on the verge of being borsched to death.

The copy boy, the skit ended, was to blame, for "he had put Eleanor's syrup on Alice's desk and Alice's vinegar on Eleanor's desk."[36]

Whatever Eleanor's stylistic shortcomings, the column was popular. When editors left it out for a day readers protested. "I have a feeling," Bruce Bliven wrote in the *New Republic,* "that the New York sophisticates are all wrong and that the country as a whole likes the sort of person Mrs. Roosevelt has in her column demonstrated herself to be—friendly, unpretentious, possessed of inexhaustible vitality, a broad interest in all sorts of people and a human wish for their welfare." Her column was then appearing in 59 papers; a week later, right after the 1936 election, the *Pottsville* (Pennsylvania) *Republican* was added, a subscription that her syndicate considered "next only in importance to the President's carrying Pennsylvania." Though her circulation was smaller than some other columnists', it was respectable. In February, she appeared in 62 papers with a circulation of 4,034,552; Westbrook Pegler was in 110 papers with 5,907,389; Dorothy Thompson was in 140 papers with 7,500,000; Heywood Broun was in 42 papers with 2,829,487; and Raymond Clapper was in 49 papers with 3,653,000.[37]

When Eleanor first became a fellow-columnist, Westbrook Pegler approved of her; "about the only two things in the world that Pegler seems to like are 'Snow White and the Seven Dwarfs' and Eleanor Roosevelt," wrote Carlin.[38] Pegler's enthusiasm bubbled over in a column datelined San Francisco, March 17, 1938, in which he described her day there:

> It had been another routine day in the life of one who is stingily described as the "most remarkable" and "most energetic" woman of her time in this country, but who deserves more than that. I think we can take the wraps off and call her the greatest American woman, because there is no other who works as hard or knows the low-down truth about the people and the troubles in their hearts as well as she does.

Pegler went on to describe Eleanor's lecture on peace, a performance that he considered the more creditable "because she works in the straitjacket of diplomatic and political restraints. . . . Mrs. Roosevelt has been before us for five years now. We know her better than any other woman, and she knows the country better than any other individual, including her husband, and the profit is all on our side."

But not long after this column appeared Pegler soured on the New Deal, the Roosevelts, and the American Newspaper Guild, and he began to challenge Eleanor's credentials as a columnist. She was no more eligible for membership in the American Newspaper Guild, which she had promptly joined, he insisted, than he for membership in the DAR; she was "gainfully employed" as a journalist, as the guild constitution required of members, only because she was the wife of the president. The first step toward rehabilitating the guild would be to get rid of those who did not belong, starting with her. The president, with whom Mrs. Roosevelt discussed the column, advised her to ignore it. "Why get into a bad-smells contest?" he said.

She was not going to get into an argument with her "kindly fellow columnist," she wrote a few days later. She acknowledged that as the wife of the president she was in a different position than other columnists: "That has not always been the case and will not always be so in the future. In the meantime, I must worry along as best I can, facing situations that I find myself in, and doing the best I can with them as they are."[39]

In a private letter George Carlin, a good friend of Pegler's whom he also syndicated, protested Pegler's challenge to Mrs. Roosevelt's eligibility: "Big names come and big names go, but a big name goes nowhere unless, through the quality of the daily delivery, the author can hold a following." Recalling that in 1936, the year "My Day" had first appeared, Alice Longworth had also begun a column along the same lines, Carlin continued:

> If you will remember back, as long as I can remember, it had been the aim of newspapermen to get interviews with Princess Alice for twenty years without result. It had been thought that if she ever wrote, her stuff would make a great feature. The only trouble with the idea was that when it came to writing, she just couldn't write. Her stuff fell by its own weight and disappeared from the column field.
>
> *My Day* goes on and on, not because it is written by the wife of the President of the United States, but because it is an honest projection of one of the great personalities of our own time; a woman great in her own right, and, as a newspaper columnist, possibly the best trouper of them all, never known to miss a deadline.[40]

Much as she enjoyed doing her column, Eleanor's secret aspiration was to write a novel or a play—she had always been a fervent admirer of creative writers. "I have always been sorry that I did not have the courage to go to see you when you were living in Poughkeepsie," she wrote Dorothy Canfield Fisher, who, since she considered Eleanor Roosevelt the greatest woman in the country, was somewhat overwhelmed by this unaffected, almost hero-worshipful tribute.[41]

Eleanor did not think she had the technical knowledge to write a novel but she had long toyed with the thought of doing an autobiography. The preface and footnote material that she supplied for the volume of her father's letters she had edited had brought pleas from family and friends for more stories about her early years. Her conversation was filled with anecdotal material from those years, and on the

Florida Special on the way back from Puerto Rico in 1934 she had held a group of correspondents spellbound with reminiscences of her wedding day twenty-nine years earlier and how Uncle Ted had stolen the show from her and Franklin. She discussed the project of an autobiography with her literary agent, George Bye,* in the summer of 1936. He immediately saw its possibilities and begged her to begin, and by autumn, as she traveled with the president on the campaign train, sections were being dictated to Tommy.

Most authors would have considered writing an autobiography a full-time assignment in itself, but Eleanor did not slacken any of her other activities. She performed the election chores her husband assigned her, filed her column, did her lecture stint, discharged her official duties as White House hostess, and, of course, dealt with her voluminous mail. Some literary advice that she offered a farm woman from the Ozarks at that time shed light upon how she approached her own autobiography. Mrs. Alma W. Johnson of Rogers, Arkansas, had not sought literary guidance; like thousands of others she just wanted to pour out her troubles to the sympathetic soul in the White House. But Eleanor found in Mrs. Johnson's chatty twenty-page account of rural vicissitudes a sweetness of spirit so moving and readable that she sent it to Henry Goddard Leach, who published the "poignant document" in the *Forum*. The publishing world became interested, and Simon & Schuster thought there might be a book in her life story. But Mrs. Johnson did not quite know how to begin, so Eleanor dispatched a long letter of encouragement and advice:

> Block out your early youth, start with your very first memory, putting in as many incidents as possible which will show up your relationship to your parents, the effect of circumstances upon you, the things you learned and the way your character was formed by the circumstances of your life and the influence, conscious or unconscious, of your parents.
>
> If you do that and will send those chapters to me, I will correct grammatical errors and spelling and send them to Simon and Schuster.[42]

---

*Her first literary agent was Nannine Joseph. But since Nannine was also Franklin's agent Louis Howe placed Eleanor with George Bye, telling Nannine it was not right for her to be the agent for both the president and First Lady. Nannine became Eleanor's agent again in the late forties.

Although the lady in the Ozarks, even with Mrs. Roosevelt's help, was unable to produce a satisfactory draft chapter, Eleanor, adhering to the plan of work that she had outlined, and with her incredible ability to shut off the outside world and concentrate upon the task at hand, made steady progress with her own story. By late autumn an exhilarated George Bye was showing the first part of the book to Bruce and Beatrice Gould, who had recently taken over the *Ladies' Home Journal* and were on the lookout for features with which to reverse the magazine's declining fortunes. They promptly purchased the serial rights for $75,000 and urged Eleanor to push on. "An evening buried amongst old letters," she wrote. "Why does one keep old letters?" Some, unfortunately for future biographers, went into the fireplace that winter. The people at the *Ladies' Home Journal* were "all aglow" with what they had seen, Fannie Hurst reported; they were delighted with her "fine clean prose" and the "simplicity and forthrightness of the narrative."[43]

Although she was little more than halfway through, Eleanor was sufficiently satisfied with what she had written to attend a party that the Goulds gave to celebrate the appearance of the first installment. She was so excited at the prospect of being the guest of honor at a literary party that she first went to the wrong address. She finally arrived at the right place, breathless, wearing a large black hat whose sweeping lines reflected her exultation. Radiant and happy, she took her place in the receiving line along with the Goulds and other *Journal* authors, including Dorothy Thompson. "I have written as simple and as truthful a story as I could write," she told reporters at the party. "It was quite a job, but most exciting, all of it." She had such a good time at the party that she stayed "an unconscionable time." As she said her good-bys to the Goulds, she astonished them with the remark: "I can't tell you what it means to me to have this wonderful recognition for something I have done myself not on account of Franklin's position."[44]

The Goulds were not happy with the later chapters. While the early ones had been vividly evocative of a New York society that had vanished and of a childhood that had been unexpectedly painful and insecure, and were, the couple felt, "moving and veracious" and written with "startling honesty and courage," some of the chapters she was now bringing in were "superficial and thin." Suddenly her story had stopped being "the story of a human being and become almost a mere chronicle of events," Gould wrote her. "Now I don't think your life has become suddenly less interesting. But you have ceased suddenly to write about the most interesting aspects of it." He wanted her to tell "the inner story... because it is all women's story made more important because you are the person you are and occupy the position you occupy."[45]

She came to his office to work on revisions. They wanted the revealing phrase and telling detail. Could she give an exact description of her mother-in-law? Could she remember her husband's first words when he realized he had polio? Bruce Gould, a brusque man, burst out at one point, "But this chapter is simply a listing of places you went and people you met. It has nothing to say—in fact—it's terrible!" Mrs. Gould cast a reproving glance at her husband, but Eleanor took his criticism quietly. Insecure as a writer, she welcomed tough editing. She was herself a disciplined worker willing to do the best she could and would not waste time bewailing her failures and frustrations, but she offered a sympathetic shoulder to other writers on which to weep. "You do get yourself into a state of jitters," she consoled novelist-friend Martha Gellhorn, who was in the throes of a new book. "It is better to write it all down and then go back. Mr. Hemingway is right. I think you lose the flow of thought by too much rewriting. It will not be a lifeless story if you feel it, although it may need polishing."[46]

The Goulds rightly perceived that the later chapters dealing with her years in Washington and her own entry into politics after her husband was stricken with polio were not as well written as the early ones. But it was not, as they thought, that the chapters were "hastily written," but because there was so much she could not say. She could not let herself go as she had in speaking of her childhood. "Freedom is necessary for the development of the creative spirit," she had once said in explaining why women were not as creative in some of the arts as men. Women were obliged to defer to conventions to a far greater extent than men, and that blunted their creativity.

Franklin went over the manuscript carefully. He was a good editor, and in the earlier chapters his comments were chiefly stylistic, such as "the contrasts must be emphasized." In the final chapters, however, he was concerned with substance. He was displeased with her account of his efforts to get into a uniform during the war, which she had written from her own point of view, to explain why she had been unwilling to try to influence his decision either way. He made a large X through this section, commenting, "This is *at least* unfair to me." He wrote out his version of what had happened and she included it as he wrote it. He did not like some of the phrases she used describing the onset of his polio, such as "one night he was out of his head," and she deleted them. When she said that Elliott had never really liked Groton as James did, his comment was "too rough," even though it was an understatement, and when in writing about her brother Hall's divorce she quoted Mrs. Selmes as having said, "If you love a person, you can forgive the big things. Infidelity under certain circumstances need not ruin a relationship," he struck out the phrase about infidelity.[47]

Anna and John were also unhappy about the last chapters when she left the manuscript with them during a visit to Seattle. There was an undercurrent of "bitterness" in the later part of the work, and although it dealt with a most difficult time in her life, it did not show how she had mastered her bitterness and developed her present philosophy of life. They felt that her quarrel with Anna over the room that she had given to Louis Howe should be left out and hoped that she would modify expressions that made it appear "that you had little part in, and little interest in, your husband's career." She softened offending passages, rewrote others.[48]

As she reworked the last chapters, the Goulds began to purr. She had picked up the "dramatic thread" again, Bruce wrote encouragingly, but he pressed her to deepen her account of her husband's illness with additional material on how she felt upon seeing that her whole life would have to be revised. "What you have given of your philosophy of learning to adjust yourself to the difficult business of life is so sound, so illuminating, that you cannot blame us for wanting more."[49]

Nothing in *This Is My Story* as it finally was published was false but much was said circumspectly. The Lucy Mercer affair went unmentioned, and her struggle with her mother-in-law was muted; her "night-of-the-soul" could be glimpsed but dimly. And yet, in retrospect, considering that she was First Lady when the book was written, it was astonishingly frank, and this was the public's appraisal of the volume when it appeared.

There had been some criticism of the Goulds within the rabidly anti-Roosevelt Curtis publishing organization because they had accepted a Roosevelt book, but their editorial judgment was swiftly vindicated when the "smash success" of *This Is My Story* became a major factor in helping the *Ladies' Home Journal* overtake *McCall's* and the *Woman's Home Companion*. "Even more pleasing than this liking expressed in numbers was the exciting discovery that Eleanor Roosevelt's biography was read, in effect, by everyone—in government, parlors and slums."[50]

Following serialization, the autobiography was to be published in book form by Harper & Brothers. In advance of the book's appearance Eleanor had several sets of the *Ladies' Home Journal* containing the complete autobiography bound in limp leather and marked in gold letters for Franklin D. Roosevelt, Anna Roosevelt Boettiger, Malvina Thompson Scheider, and Earl R. Miller.* The copy she gave Franklin was accompanied by a jingle:

> *This may not look it but it is,*
> *A book which will some day appear*
> *It promises to be a whiz,*
> *So little less you'll get my dear!*

On her way through New York City in early November she went to Harper's to receive her copy of the book. "It looks much more important than I had ever imagined it would be, but I am still inexperienced enough to feel a real thrill and to be very proud when Mr. [Cass] Canfield said that they considered it a good piece of work and were glad to be the publishers."[51]

The book was widely acclaimed because the experiences she described in it were, she discovered, widely shared. The "harmless childish weaknesses of character" that she had written about in language that was "classic" in its "plain simplicity," said Dorothy Canfield Fisher, are universal. The painfully honest account of her struggle to overcome shyness and insecurity, wrote educator Alice V. Keliher, "will help young people in their adjustments to life more than anything else written." Women embraced the story as their own. "I saw so much in the story so far that every woman experiences," wrote one.

Old Bishop Atwood touched on another aspect of the book's appeal. Eleanor had been too harsh in judging her own character, the bishop thought, but had "succeeded in making a living picture of a social life now in the past." Karl Bickel, the former president of the United Press, thought it was one of "the greatest human documents he had

---

*Franklin, for Christmas, 1936, had distributed bound copies of the speech he had delivered at Chatauqua, New York, in August, 1936, "I Have Seen War, . . . I Hate War." Copy number 1 went to his wife; number 2 to his mother; the next five to children; number 8 to Missy; number 9 to Daisy Suckley, a Hudson River neighbor; number 10 to Grace Tully; number 11 to Marvin McIntyre; number 12 to Steve Early; number 13 to Doc McIntire; number 14 to Bill Bullitt; numbers 15 to 24 to the members of the cabinet beginning with Secretary of State Hull.

read in modern times," and Captain Joseph Patterson, the president of the *Daily News,* in a bold black scrawl let her know that "I think your book is splendid; and that it may become a classic." There was praise, sweet to her ears, from Alice Longworth, who at a party was heard to say "Have you read it? Did you realize Eleanor could *write* like that? It's perfect; it's marvellous; she can *write*...all at the highest pitch."[52]

As Alice Longworth acknowledged, Eleanor could write, but the basic appeal of *This Is My Story,* like the basic appeal she had as a lecturer and columnist, flowed from her personality. "You see I think you are a kind of genius," wrote Dorothy Canfield Fisher. "Out of your personality and position you have certainly created something of first-rate and unique value—not a book or statue or painting—an example."

39. WITHOUT LOUIS HOWE— THE 1936 CAMPAIGN

———————————◇———————————

THE 1936 CAMPAIGN WAS THE FIRST WITHOUT LOUIS HOWE. FOR Eleanor, whose life had been molded by this misshapen eccentric genius almost as much as by Mlle. Souvestre, his death left a void as impossible to fill as it was for Franklin, with whose rise to the presidency Louis' name would be forever linked.

Louis' final decline began in the autumn of 1934 when his breathing became more labored, his eyes more sunken, his thin frame more wasted. He found it an ordeal to walk to the office and began to stay in his paper-littered bedroom off the Lincoln room. It was directly across the hall from Eleanor's sitting room, and his pajama-clad figure, wracked with coughing, was often seen shuffling from one room to the other. In January, 1935, he took a turn for the worse, and the annual Cuff Links party of those who had been associated with Roosevelt's 1920 campaign was canceled. Franklin and Eleanor had no heart for a party without Louis, who had always been the impresario on such occasions, dreaming up stunts and writing scripts with Eleanor as a willing accomplice. In March, Eleanor warned his children, Mrs. Mary Baker and Hartley, that while there was no immediate danger, their father needed cheering up and letters would help. Ten days later, after a bronchial collapse, he drifted into unconsciousness. "He seems to cling to life in the most astonishing manner," Eleanor reported to Molly Dewson, "but I am afraid it is the end."[1]

But he rallied, opening his eyes two days later to ask for one of his Sweet Caporals. For another year, much of it spent under an oxygen tent, he battled for breath and life. When Louis' wife Grace could not be at the White House, Eleanor watched over him faithfully. She kept track of what he ate, insisted that he follow the doctor's orders, kept him informed on the comings and goings in the White House, and encouraged him in his hopes that he would manage the 1936 campaign as he had the others.

When the doctors recommended that he be moved to the Naval

Hospital it was Eleanor who took him there in the White House limousine and did not leave until she saw him settled. He went "peacefully," she reported to Grace, and only got into a "tizzy-whiz" because no telephone had been arranged.[2]

From his hospital bed he continued to plot strategy for the coming campaign by way of memos dictated to his secretary, Margaret Durand ("Rabbit"), and the telephone. When the inspiration seized him he insisted that "Hacky," the White House switchboard operator, put him through to Franklin immediately whether the president was at Hyde Park, Warm Springs, or in bed. The president finally requested that Louis' direct line to the White House be available only from 10:00 A.M. to 4:30 P.M., but he also asked his chief aides to treat Louis with respect and courtesy no matter what orders he issued by phone.[3]

The president visited Louis at the hospital and those were moments of cheer, for Roosevelt was a great jollier, but there were not as many visits as Louis wished. Not only were the pressures of the presidential office remorseless, but Roosevelt had a faculty for blotting from consciousness the people who were unable to keep up with him. It was Eleanor, who had taken so long to appreciate Louis, who was steadfast to the end. She came to see him every day she was in Washington, "but yesterday he was too busy," she wrote Grace Howe, for sometimes he played the same game with her he did with Farley—that "he was still a busy man of consequence." She brought friends like Baruch, who promised to be helpful to his son Hartley and also to underwrite the Good Neighbor League, an organization that Howe felt would be needed in the campaign to appeal to Republicans and Independents.

He was saving his strength for the campaign, Louis informed Rabbit, and when the time came he would leave the hospital and move his operations to the Biltmore Hotel in New York. All of his friends joined in the sad charade that Louis would be with them in the campaign.★ On the day Louis died Eleanor wrote Farley, "The President tells me that everything is to clear through both you and Louis and anything you are not entirely sure about is to come to him." That night, April 18, he slipped quietly away while asleep. Franklin was informed while he was at the Gridiron Dinner and Eleanor as she was giving her annual party for the Gridiron widows. The president ordered the

---

★Although Louis played along, he had moments of doubt. "But you will be there," protested John Keller, a young man who came to the hospital to read to him. "No," Louis disagreed softly. "I will not be there. Franklin is on his own now."[4]

White House flags to be half-masted, and the funeral services were held in the East Room. The choir of St. Thomas' Church, which Louis had joined when he first came to Washington with Franklin, sang the music he had always liked. The president and the First Lady accompanied the body to Fall River for the burial. "There is nothing to regret," Eleanor wrote in her column, "either for those who go, or for those who stay behind—only an inheritance of good accomplishment to be lived up to by those who carry a loving memory in their hearts."

There was one comforting thought, General Hugh Johnson wrote her: "In his impaired health he would have been very miserable as the campaign advances—and he not able to get into it vigorously." Eleanor agreed: "It was the happiest solution for Louis." She was grateful to Baruch: "You were wiser than the rest of us. You knew that it was medicine, food and drink to Louis to know that he was still in there fighting, doing something for Franklin."[5]

Even before Louis' death, she had felt that as a consequence of Louis' illness, Franklin was seeing a narrower range of people and his mail was being analyzed with insufficient sensitivity. "F.D.R.," she penciled on an aggrieved letter, "I think this letter answering is really vital. That was how L. H. built your popularity. I don't like R.C. but he's right about the way they feel. Couldn't one person take over this mail? E.R." He was "entirely right," she informed the writer, Russell Carney: "Louis Howe's not being on hand has meant that many people were not appreciated and had been forgotten." Molly Dewson complained that she was not able to get to see the president although the 1936 campaign was coming up and she had to get the women's division in readiness. Eleanor arranged for her and other women's division leaders to spend an evening with him. Afterward Molly commented, "I miss Louis Howe awfully."[6]

One of the jobs Louis had performed for Franklin was to keep track of the Roosevelt coalition, to evaluate by the statistical methods that were then available the inroads that were being made into the president's support from both left and right. The large followings attracted by the radical demagogues Huey Long, the Reverend Charles E. Coughlin, and Dr. Francis E. Townsend demonstrated that more rather than less action by government was necessary. Yet, on the other side, big business was outspokenly hostile to the New Deal, and men like the duPonts, Alfred Sloan, and John J. Raskob in alliance with conservative Democrats like Alfred E. Smith, Albert Ritchie, and John

Davis had established the American League to oppose Roosevelt and his New Deal reforms.

The progress of the demagogues frightened the New Dealers, who raised an anguished cry for more vigorous leadership by Roosevelt. In early 1935, they were asking what had happened to FDR. What should she say in reply? Eleanor asked Franklin, sending him several letters that reflected the liberals' complaint. Perhaps she also shared their restlessness, but in selecting these letters for his attention her primary purpose was to make sure that with Louis no longer analyzing the White House mail, Franklin was aware of the questions among significant groups of his supporters. She felt, more strongly than her husband perhaps, that the New Deal could not be considered complete, but she also believed that significant changes in national direction could not simply be declared. They had to be worked at long and patiently.

A young man who described himself as still in difficult circumstances said he was prepared "to starve a little . . . if I knew that the man in Washington who captured my imagination and admiration in 1933 was unchanged." "Would you like to answer or shall I?" Eleanor queried her husband, adding, "It is rather nice." Franklin asked her to write and presumably indicated the reply she might give. "Nothing has happened to F.D.R., but reforms don't come in two years."[7] An Iowa Republican who had voted Democratic in 1932 confessed that she was beginning to lose hope because the old order seemed unchanged. "I would write her," Roosevelt suggested, "that there is one thing to learn and that is not to believe everything she reads in the newspapers. Also tell her that the position of the Administration has not varied one iota and that it still has the same objectives."[8]

Molly Dewson was another who communicated to Eleanor her alarm over the president's failure to exert more vigorous leadership. Eleanor replied to Molly along lines suggested by Franklin:

These things go in cycles. We have been through it in Albany and we are going through it here. . . . He says to tell you that Congress is accomplishing a great deal in spite of the fact that there is very little publicity on what they have done. . . . The relief bill and the [social] security bill are bound to go slowly because they are a new type of legislation. If he tried to force them down the committee's throat and did not give them time to argue them out, he would have an even more difficult Congress to work with. . . .

Please say to everyone who tells you that the President is not giving leadership that he is seeing the men constantly, and that he is working with them, but this is a democracy after all, and if he once started insisting on having his own way immediately, we should shortly find ourselves with a dictatorship and I hardly think the country would like that any better than they do the delay.

The ups and downs in peoples' feelings, particularly on the liberal side, are an old, old story. The liberals always get discouraged when they do not see the measures they are interested in go through immediately. Considering the time we have had to work in the past for almost every slight improvement, I should think they might get over with it, but they never do.

Franklin says for Heaven's sake, all you Democratic leaders calm down and feel sure of ultimate success. It will do a lot in satisfying other people.[9]

Sometimes even Roosevelt became impatient and was tempted to twist arms and apply the whip to Congress, and it was Eleanor who urged patience and perseverance. She lunched with some friends of World War I days—Caroline Phillips, Mary Miller, Anne Lane. "She was as dear, as affectionate, as simple and spontaneous as she was at 17 when I first knew her 35 years ago," Caroline recorded in her diary. But she also looked "very tired" and was "worried about the harm Huey Long is doing." The president was ready "to take the whip to Congress and abandon his conciliatory attitude. Eleanor tries to prevent this, but has only a limited influence," Caroline noted.[10]

In mood and objective she was allied with the New Dealers, but she felt that education, not the "whip," was the way to move ahead. Congress must have time, she counseled an Iowa progressive who wondered whether the president had deserted the progressive group in Congress for big business: "If he went on the air and forced legislation through, there would be the cry of 'Dictator,' and no willing cooperation."[11] In Warm Springs at Thanksgiving time she urged her husband to adopt "the same method he had used in Albany of holding a school of his own members in Congress so that they can get a chance to talk out their own ideas and he can get his across to them."[12] But Roosevelt felt he did not have the time, he told Sam Rosenman, who agreed with Eleanor about a school for legislators, "and besides, there are so many of them that we could never get around to all."[13]

Eleanor had strong convictions, but she respected her opponents and believed, moreover, that in a democracy reforms had to be both gradual and subject to revision. The objectives set forth by people like Huey Long, she wrote a correspondent, were fine; the problem was to obtain them "without too much dislocation and too much hardship to everyone concerned."[14]

Nor did her strong disagreement with the American Liberty League alter her warm feeling for Al Smith, one of its chief architects. Louis had been "a hater" in politics, "the most intense hater I have ever known," she said; he never forgot and rarely forgave a politician who had crossed the president. But Eleanor, as columnist Arthur Krock noted, did not seem to take "her husband's political wars personally. She has seen a lot of feuds and reconciliations in politics." Krock's comment was prompted by the one-day sensation caused when it was disclosed that Eleanor had invited Al Smith to stay at the White House when he came to Washington to address the American Liberty League on January 25, 1936. Smith declined the invitation. Had not Mrs. Roosevelt understood, Krock wondered, that the invitation to Smith, when he was coming to Washington with the avowed purpose of blasting the president, would be considered suspect? People had to understand Eleanor Roosevelt's "simple and candid" nature, he was told by White House aides. She considered the White House her home. She was an extraordinarily direct person with a feeling of warmth for Smith, and had invited him without considering the political implications. The president had had nothing to do with it.[15]

One of the most bitterly fought measures in the 1935 Congress was the social security bill. There were differences among its advocates over a national versus a state approach, over the size and method of contribution, over whether it should be a new agency or lodged within the Labor Department. And there was the more basic opposition of the Republican party to the principle of social security, which conservative businessmen felt would lead to the "ultimate socialistic control of life and industry."

Eleanor's "old crowd" reflected the virulence of the conservative opposition. She invited the ladies of the exclusive Fortnightly Club to hold their March meeting at the White House and proposed that "social welfare" be the topic of discussion. Her cousin Helen Robinson, since the Club's Board of Governors did not dare write directly, was asked to convey to Eleanor their fears that they would not feel free while receiving her hospitality to criticize the administration and to disagree with pending legislation. It had not occurred to her that the social security bill was political, but if the board could think up another subject, she would have no objection: "Of course, I would have expected them to criticize administration measures where they touch on politics. I cannot see why everyone should be expected to think the same way about anything."[16]

Faced with strong opposition to the very principle of social security, Molly Dewson, although she had strong views on the specific features of the bill that were in contest, said she would take a bill "anyhow it's drafted." Eleanor felt similarly. She did not expect to get a complete "security program" in the next two years, she told her news conference, but hoped to see the program launched. Asked about the differences among the proponents of social security, she replied: "I have always been amused to note that those who want a great deal more, and those who want a great deal less done, find themselves, unconsciously to be sure, working together and preventing the accomplishment of a moderate middle-of-the-road program."[17]

"You've done more to influence thought in the past 21 months, than anyone except your husband," one of her newspaper regulars wrote her at the beginning of 1935.[18] Educate! Educate! Educate! That was her theme. It was part of the bond between herself and Molly Dewson. Molly sent her a leaflet advertising a Democratic rally in Michigan with speakers on the "New Work Relief Program" and on the CCC. "Dear Eleanor," Molly scrawled on it, "Aren't the men fun imitating the girls and becoming 'reporters' on special subjects instead of making general gas talks."[19]

She was "much more interested in possible far-away developments and [the] steady increase of women's influence, which, I feel, tends to ameliorate bad social conditions," she told Martha at an early stage in their friendship, "than I am in any immediate political developments." In a last interview that he gave to Bess Furman of the Associated Press, Louis Howe was equally sanguine about the long-range ameliorative effects that women could have on politics:

> If politics divides, as it may, very sharply along the lines of the humanitarian and there are ten years in which to see how this experiment of females in government is working...and if they make good, and if the great mass of the people conclude they want New Deal ideas in recreation, labor, schools, and want to support that line—and if in time there arises some woman who gets the confidence of the people as a whole, there might be the argument

advanced that the problems of the day are problems which have been neglected by man since George Washington, and men don't seem to understand what it's all about. The people may say: "Let's try a woman out." I don't think it's at all probable but there's nothing so clear now as the humanitarian issue.[20]

Eleanor had swiftly discouraged Louis when he had broached the idea that she might be the person the country might turn to—with a little prompting from him. But the idea was occurring to others. A Missouri congressman sent her a local column proposing that she be named the vice-presidential candidate in 1936 as a way of rescuing that post from oblivion; the congressman seconded the nomination. But, as Eleanor wrote Martha Gellhorn, she was interested in the mobilization of women's influence for basic reforms and sensed instinctively that she would be more effective as an educator if she were "in politics but not of it."*

Roosevelt's strategy for the 1936 election placed heavy stress on the campaign as an opportunity to educate and inform the electorate. He outlined his plans to the women at the dinner in mid-December, 1935, that Eleanor had arranged at Molly's request. It would be a New Deal, not a Democratic party, appeal, with a special effort made to reach the new groups which had a stake in the continuance of the Roosevelt policies—workers, farmers, Negroes, young people, women, independents. The opposition was formidable because of the wealth it commanded and because it had the support of 85 per cent of the press, and thus there had to be a major effort to counter its propaganda and get the truth into every home. The women's division had the most experience with a campaign based on truth-telling and falsehood-exposing. Roosevelt counted on the women's division, he told them, and wanted the party to make wide use of their educational techniques. Molly sent Farley a post-dinner synopsis of the session with the president with the admonition that "in carrying out his ideas, we rely on you." To insure doubly that Farley did not pigeonhole the decisions, Molly sent a copy to Eleanor.[21]

Under the plans outlined by Roosevelt the women were to be given more space at headquarters, their budget was to be increased, and they were to have the help of the men in obtaining government officials as speakers. His active campaign would begin with his address at the

---

*A distinction drawn by the sociologist Daniel Bell, discussing Eugene Victor Debs.

Jackson Day dinners, he told the women, and from that date on the ban on government officials making political speeches was off and the whole organization should be geared to countering Republican propaganda in the Republican-controlled press. He also said that he wanted a "Friends of Roosevelt" type of organization set up to appeal to those not functioning in the regular party organizations and an effort made to vitalize the Young Democrats through a national contest for the best speech on the New Deal.

Molly immediately drafted a letter that she asked Farley to send to the members of the cabinet. "Dear Henry, Frank, Harry, Harold, Frances, Arthur, etc." it read,

> The President has told the Women's Division of the National Democratic Committee to go ahead full steam in answering the avalanche of Republican propaganda after January 8th, when the Democratic campaign will open with the Jackson Day Dinners.
>
> He also said that after January 8th there is no ban against government officials speaking at political meetings. No one knows the record better.
>
> Will you please have prepared for the use of the Democratic National Committee a list of those in your department who are excellent, good and fair speakers upon whom we may call. . . .

During Howe's tenure the political chain of command had been clearcut: Roosevelt, Howe, Farley. That, at least, was how Molly Dewson saw it. "Mrs. Roosevelt told me in January that the 'high command' which I presumed meant the President, Mr. Farley and Mr. Howe had decided that the bulk of literature issued in the campaign should be the Rainbow Fliers. This statement was based on the reception given the fliers in the 1932 campaign."[22] With Louis gone the question of who was to carry out the commander-in-chief's directive became acute. Theoretically it was Jim Farley, national chairman, postmaster-general, and chief dispenser of patronage. He was loyal and effective, a professional politician who, however, did not particularly appreciate the New Deal as a movement of ideas and values or have much rapport with many New Dealers.

Farley was a technician, not a progressive crusader. During a national reconnaissance tour in late winter, 1936, Molly picked up reports on the West Coast that Farley was building a machine to make him president in 1940. "Just imagine JAF as President!!" she wrote incredulously to Eleanor; "for one thing he had better turn Methodist." Eleanor, who had a warm feeling about Jim, discounted the report: "Molly, I can't believe this is Jim's idea." She got along with the national chairman, but the exchange between the two women indicated their awareness of his limitations. Molly was under attack that spring by Emma Guffey Miller, the Democratic national committeewoman from Pennsylvania and sister of Senator Joseph Guffey, a highly influential Pennsylvania Democrat. Molly did not think Farley supported her in that contest with sufficient enthusiasm. "I go to your defense with loyalty and ardor practically every day," she wrote him. "The few times I have disagreed with you I have told you and no one else except Mrs. Roosevelt to whom I feel primarily responsible." Eleanor intervened on Molly's side. Farley retreated: "Regarding appointments," he wrote Eleanor, "please be assured that I will discuss them with you, and be governed by your wishes on anything I do relative to the activity of women."[23]

Like the president, Eleanor doubted that Farley and his headquarters staff, oriented as they were toward the traditional party organizations, were able to run a New Deal rather than a Democratic party campaign. Edward L. Roddan,* formerly the White House correspondent of the International News Service, was sent into headquarters to back up the redoubtable Charlie Michelson. Eleanor, like Franklin, communicated directly with Roddan although Michelson was supposed to be in charge of countering the attacks of the opposition. "Would you tell Mr. Michelson for me," Eleanor wrote Roddan, that she had heard that *Hell Bent for Election* by James P. Warburg, in which this young dissident Democrat charged that Roosevelt had carried out the Socialist rather than the Democratic party's program, was being "tremendously read and quoted, and perhaps should be answered." She had also heard that Marriner Eccles, the administration's leading defender of deficit spending, was very good at explaining "the whole monetary situation. Could he be induced to write an article...?" The pamphlet the committee had prepared, "Little Red Schoolhouse," was good for speakers and reference material, but the average person would have to be given "something a little easier to read. I have just given the President some campaign leaflets [the Rainbow Fliers] and

---

*One of "the three musketeers," as the three press-association correspondents assigned to the White House were dubbed. The other two were Frances L. Stephenson of the Associated Press and Frederick A. Storm of the United Press.

something of that kind is more useful for the average people in cities or rural districts."[24]

The communications to Roddan reflected White House dissatisfaction with the Farley-Michelson leadership. Roosevelt was almost abrupt in rebuking Farley after Farley's address to Michigan Democrats in which he predicted that "the governor of a typical prairie state" would be the Republican presidential nominee. "He, Too, Came from 'A Typical Prairie State'" the Republicans countered in a leaflet carrying a picture of Abraham Lincoln. "I thought we had decided any reference to Landon or any other Republican candidate was inadvisable," Roosevelt sternly wrote Farley. When an unrepentant Farley subsequently referred to Alfred M. Landon as the "synthetic" candidate, Roosevelt called in both Farley and Michelson and told them that no further statements should be issued without White House clearance. Roosevelt was in charge of the campaign, and to the extent that anyone was serving the role that Louis had in previous campaigns, Eleanor did in part, sitting in on budget meetings and through the women's division as well as through talks with Farley, trying to school him in her husband's concept of a New Deal campaign.

She accompanied her husband on the "nonpolitical" tour that he just happened to take at the same time the Republicans were meeting in Philadelphia. There were stops and speeches in Arkansas, Texas, Oklahoma, and Indiana. The nomination of Governor Landon was no surprise, Eleanor reported in one of her "nonpolitical" columns during the trip, but what platform would he run on? "For once the Republican Party seems to be made up of as many varying elements as the Democratic has often been!" But she was concerned about the Democratic platform: "We are on the move and things are better, but we have not yet arrived and we must not lull ourselves to sleep with a false sense of achievement."[25]

Two weeks later the Democrats convened in Philadelphia. Molly organized a breakfast for women delegates in order to deploy her forces. Eleanor thought it wiser not to come: "I would love to be at a breakfast in Philadelphia but am afraid I will only be able to come over for the day with Franklin. Otherwise, I might get myself into trouble!"[26] Although she was not at Philadelphia, her influence was felt. For the first time women were granted parity with the men on the platform committee, a measure of how far they had traveled since 1924 when Eleanor and her feminine colleagues had sat outside the locked door of the Resolutions Committee. "Women are more interested in the policies of the Democratic Party than in any question of power or patronage, and we are exceedingly grateful that the Convention has taken this tremendous step," a delighted Molly Dewson commented. Eleanor had conveyed the women's views on the Republican platform to Franklin, who was personally supervising the drafting of the Democratic document: "It might be useful in Democratic planks of interest to women." The women were jubilant over the Democratic document. "I have been telling you girls for years why I believed in the Democratic Party," Molly exulted to her cohorts, "but I could never tell you in such beautiful language." On every seat in the convention hall the women's division had placed a packet of Rainbow Fliers. There were 219 women delegates and alternates at Philadelphia compared to the 60 who had been at the Republican convention, and eight of the Roosevelt seconding speeches were made by women. Their large role at the convention symbolized the recognition they had achieved under Roosevelt. Much of the credit belonged to Molly Dewson, the best "she-politician" of his time, said Michelson, but Frances Perkins, after she had finished her formal speech at the women's breakfast, brought the audience to its feet in a spontaneous ovation when she added,

> I know that many women in this country when they go to vote in November for Franklin Roosevelt will be thinking with a choke in their throats of Eleanor Roosevelt. . . .
>
> She has gone out courageously, in the face of unfavorable criticism, not only to meet the people as a friend but to use that contact to make of herself a channel through which the needs and hopes and desires of people could be carried to places where solutions could be found to their problems.
>
> If ever there was a gallant and courageous and intelligent and wise woman, she is one.[27]

While this eulogy was being delivered in Philadelphia, Eleanor was at the Arthurdale commencement handing out diplomas. Two days later she accompanied the president to Philadelphia for his acceptance speech before the more than 100,000 people packed into Franklin Field. The Philadelphia Symphony had played, Lily Pons had sung, and John Nance Garner had formally accepted renomination as vice president. But it was a crowd that was waiting for Roosevelt. He arrived at the podium on the arm of his son James—after a "frightful five minutes" when in the crush his steel brace had buckled and, out of sight of the crowd, he had fallen. Composed, buoyant, and smiling, he came forward.

"We have conquered fear," his speech began, and he proceeded to recall the troubles of 1932–33 and what his administration had done to overcome them. Now there were "new difficulties, new problems" which must be solved. Freedom was "no half-and-half affair. If the average citizen is guaranteed equal opportunity in the polling place, he must have equal opportunity in the market place." This nation was poor, indeed, if it could not "afford to lift from every recess of American life the dread fear of the unemployed that they are not needed in the world." When he said "this generation of Americans has a rendezvous with destiny," the huge crowd "nearly went crazy," said Agnes Leach, one of the leaders of the women.

"The greatest political speech I have ever heard," commented Ickes. For ten minutes the crowd roared its approval, as Roosevelt, surrounded by his family, stood and waved. Eleanor's thoughts were less on the drama than on the expectations of the people as a consequence of her husband's speech: "A man must come to a moment like this with a tremendous sense of responsibility, but that must be very much augmented when he realizes by watching the crowd about him what his thoughts and words are going to mean to innumerable people throughout the nation."

To her schoolgirl friend Bennett (Mrs. Philip Vaughn) she wrote the same day: "For the good of the country I believe it is devoutly to be hoped that he will be reelected, but from a personal point of view I am quite overcome when I think of four years more of the life I have been leading!"[28]

Elated by the convention, several of the women—Molly, Agnes Leach, Caroline O'Day, Democratic national committeewoman Mrs. William H. Good, Frances Perkins, and Dorothy Schiff Backer, a recruit from the Republicans—turned up at Val-Kill the next day to rehash the convention and get their marching orders from Roosevelt. The president was in no hurry; he had his own clear picture of how he intended to pace his campaign: August in Washington with "nonpolitical" forays into the areas of flood and drought, no political speeches in September either, and four or five major political speeches in October. Two weeks after the convention he took off on a cruise with three of his sons; his destination was Campobello, where Eleanor would report to him on the situation at headquarters. "We are losing ground every day," Ickes fretted. "Meanwhile, the President smiles and sails and fishes and the rest of us worry and fume."[29]

While Franklin was cruising on the *Sewanna,* before going to Campobello his wife stopped in at headquarters to meet with Farley, who dealt with her as one professional to another, for she was a woman, he felt, who had a "real 'sense of politics'" and a "genuine gift for organization work."[30] She also had sessions with Molly Dewson, Stanley High, a former clergyman whose journalistic aptitude made him a fluent speech writer, and Michelson. Afterward she drafted several brisk memoranda. The basic one went to the president with copies to Farley, Michelson, High, Early, and Molly Dewson: "My feeling is that we have to get going and going quickly." She listed the questions she had brought up in her conferences at headquarters, to which she thought there ought to be answers in black and white that would reach "us" at Eastport by July 27 or 28 "when the President expects to be there." She urged that the publicity-steering committee be organized immediately, asked that minutes be kept of its meetings and that a copy be sent to the president, "and if the committee is willing, one to me as well." Some of the questions: Who was responsible for suggesting answers to charges, etc.? Who would actually do the radio work under the aegis of the publicity committee? Who was in charge of research? ("I gather if the President o.k.'s it, the aggressive campaign against Landon's record will begin before Landon's acceptance speech.") Who was collecting and organizing the Landon data? There were twelve questions in all, ending with the suggestion that Representative Sam Rayburn of Texas, who was to head the Speakers Bureau, should come in "at once to plan the policy and mechanics" and the additional suggestion that it would be well

to start some Negro speakers, like Mrs. [Mary McLeod] Bethune to speak at church meetings and that type of Negro organization. More and more my reports indicate that this is a close election and that we need very excellent organization. That is why I am trying to clarify in my own mind the functions at headquarters and have the President see a picture of the organization as clearly as possible in order that he may make any suggestions that he thinks necessary.

A supplementary letter to Farley expressed the hope "that when Ed Flynn gets back you will draw him into headquarters not only for consultation but for some definite responsibility. He is a pretty good executive organizer and Louis found him very valuable in the last campaign." Louis had trained her well.[31]

The memos she requested arrived at Campobello: two pages from Charlie Michelson; a "things are beginning to click" outline from Stanley High, who was heading up the Good Neighbor League; an explanation from Steve Early that he had been tied down at the White House and able, therefore, to spend only one day at headquarters; a letter from Rayburn's assistant saying he would reply when he arrived in New York (which turned out to be August 18); and a nine-page single-spaced letter from Farley. Yes, he would draw in Ed Flynn "full time." They were keeping minutes at headquarters and Eleanor and the president would receive copies. Leon Henderson, formerly chief economist of the NRA, was being brought in to head up research. Eddie Roddan was compiling the material on Landon. He (Farley) would cooperate in every way with the Labor party that Sidney Hillman was organizing in New York State and thought it would bring an added 150,000 voters to the national ticket. He reviewed the situation state by state and promised to send her all reports and letters that came in from the states. So far as Negro participation in the campaign was concerned, Will Alexander, Tugwell's deputy at the Resettlement Administration, was drafting the committee's plans. Farley did not think it wise to move too actively in August, he summed up, except to tool up the headquarters operation; but the president should, as he had planned, travel widely and inspect New Deal projects.

Though Farley was optimistic he was not yet ready to predict, as he did just before election, that Roosevelt would carry forty-six out of the forty-eight states. Far from it. In early August he forwarded to Eleanor a supporter's dream that Roosevelt "would win the election by a large majority, carrying 37 states... [including] Mr. Landon's home state," and his accompanying comment was that "we must get a few laughs out of the campaign." Uncertain about the outcome, Farley felt that the more militant New Dealers should be sidelined during the campaign, meaning especially Rex Tugwell and Harry Hopkins. Was it accidental that when the president's schooner pulled into Welchpool, Harry Hopkins was there, he and his wife having come as guests of Eleanor Roosevelt?

She herself was a controversial figure in the 1936 campaign, and some of the president's more skittish advisers, although not Farley, "felt that she ought to stay in the background."[32] Her support of Negro rights (see Chapter 44), her insistence on pursuing her own career, her outspoken views, often slightly in advance of those of her husband, and the widespread complaint that she had commercialized the First Lady's role caused some politicians to fear that the campaign might well turn into a referendum on whether the public preferred the old or new style of presidential wife. Alice Longworth hinted at this in an article she wrote on the ideal qualifications of a president's wife. She by no means disapproved of Eleanor's conduct as First Lady; in fact, as an activist herself with an insatiable interest in politics, she rather admired her cousin, but in her article she wondered whether people might not feel that "we didn't elect her, what is she horning in for?"[33]

The American Liberty League made Eleanor a primary target in its efforts to lure the Democratic South away from Roosevelt. Early in 1936 Raskob, duPont, and Sloan helped finance a gathering of southern Democrats in Macon, Georgia. Its purpose was to assault the New Deal root, branch, and leaf, and to launch a presidential boom for Georgia Governor Eugene Talmadge, idol of the wool-hat boys who referred to Roosevelt as "that cripple in the White House." As the "grass roots" Democrats filed into the hall for the meeting every seat had on it a copy of the *Georgia Woman's World,* featuring a two-column photograph which Vance Muse, the promoter of the meeting, described as "a picture of Mrs. Roosevelt going to some Nigger meeting, with two escorts, Niggers, on each arm." Harry Hopkins accused Sam Jones, a Washington public-relations man who worked for the Republicans, of having hatched the plans "to smear Mrs. Roosevelt in Georgia."[34]

Among the hate items circulated anonymously in the campaign was a bit of rhymed scurrility directed at both the Roosevelts:

You kiss the negroes
I'll kiss the Jews
We'll stay in the White House,
As long as we choose. . . .

Steve Early and Marvin McIntyre, both southerners and both among the president's more conservative advisers, were unhappy about Eleanor's racial views. Steve was furious, she knew, although he did not say anything to her, about her garden party for the girls from the reformatory in the District of Columbia. Eleanor had visited the District's Training School for Delinquent Girls early in May, 1936, and, "horrified" by the conditions she found there, she determined to draw the attention of Congress and the District commissioners to them. Consequently, she invited the head of the school to bring her girls, three-quarters of them Negro, to the White House. "They were treated exactly as any other guests are treated and taken to see exactly what any other guests are taken to see." She made one concession to local custom: the girls, Negro and white, remained in separate groups, segregated as they were at the school, and were served refreshments in separate tents. A few Negroes were offended that Eleanor, too, had deferred to the pattern of segregation, but the bulk of the Negro press realized that the important issue was not the segregation but that the First Lady had received as White House guests a group of girls most of whom were colored. The *Afro-American* noted that she did this in the wake of criticism "for appearing at colored gatherings and posing for photographs with colored people. . . . When she's right, the President's wife knows no such word as retreat." She knew that Steve had blown up to others, including the president, about this garden party; "Franklin, however, never said anything to me about it."[35]

She so worried some of the president's aides that there were reports she was considering curtailing some of her outside activities in view of the elections. To a friend who wrote expressing the hope that one such report was in error, she replied, "The piece in the paper had no basis—in fact I have neither talked to anyone or considered doing anything different from what I have always done."[36] Carrie Chapman Catt had been apprehensive that the campaign would increase the attacks on Mrs. Roosevelt. "The wife of a President or any other high official, suffered more from attacks upon him and his policies than did the man himself," she cautioned her friend, adding that she was sure "these were not altogether comfortable times for you." She was wasting her sympathy, Eleanor gently advised her: "I think I am more hardened to criticism than the President is, and it makes very little dent upon me, unless I think there is some real justification and something should be done."[37]

In March, the newspaperwomen had put on a skit at their annual party that underscored how drastically Eleanor Roosevelt had transformed the role of First Lady. A solemn-faced delegation appeared before a masked woman to inform her that her husband had been nominated for president and that she, as well as he, had to prove she was equal to the office. Then the delegation fired such questions at her as:

"How many speeches can you make in twenty-four hours?"

"Have you ever gone down in a coal mine?"

"Can you write a newspaper column with one hand and shake 500 hands with the other?"

"How's your radio voice?"

"How many places can you be at the same time?"

"Can you remodel a White House kitchen?"

"How many states of mind are bounded by Reedsville, West Va.?"

At this point the prospective First Lady fainted away.[38]

Ignoring the testimony of the newspaperwomen that the people liked their activist First Lady, the Republican strategists decided to make a campaign issue out of the proposition that Mrs. Landon would be different. Miss Nathalie Couch, a head of the Republican women's division, flew out to Topeka, Kansas, and after conferring with the Landons said she knew of no plans for Mrs. Landon's participation in the campaign. She expressed pointed admiration for the way Mrs. Landon was conducting herself, particularly her attempts to stay in the campaign background. "Mrs. Alf M. Landon does not intend to accompany her husband on any of his campaign trips and will devote the time from now until election to the care of her family," the *New York Times* began its account of one of the rare press conferences Mrs. Landon held. As the wife of the governor she had never held a press conference, Mrs. Landon noted, and intimated she would hold few in the future. "If Governor Landon is elected, Mrs. Landon will spend her time in the White House," Republican women orators proclaimed at their rallies.[39]

The homebody image the Republicans tried to create of Mrs. Landon caused great amusement among the Democratic women working in the campaign. "She did not dare open her lips. She was kept under very close control."

It was not Republican strategists alone who completely misread how women felt about the President's wife. A Democratic decision that although Eleanor could accompany the president on his campaign train she should stay out of sight did not survive the train's first stop. "Then it was discovered that the crowds wanted Mrs. Roosevelt. If she failed to appear on the platform they shouted for her until she did appear, and they cheered her just as heartily as her husband, sometimes more heartily. She smiled and waved but made no speeches. She never does when her husband is about."[40] Scripps-Howard columnist Thomas Stokes was struck by the way the faces of women "would blossom in smiles and up went their hands in salute" when they spotted Eleanor on the train, and wondered whether in the long run "the quiet pervasive influence of Mrs. Roosevelt" through women and the home "might not outweigh that of her husband."[41]

She celebrated her fifty-second birthday on the campaign train while it was crossing Nebraska and Wyoming. The Union Pacific Railroad provided a cake "large enough not only for our own party but for everyone on the train to share it." There was a telegram from the White House staff: "This is to assure a gracious lady who fills her days with good deeds on behalf of others that the home folk appreciate all of her kindness to them. All the workers in the Executive offices join me in wishing you joy and happiness on your birthday." It was signed by Steve Early.

She continued to do her column all through the campaign but it was carefully nonpartisan. The only marked deviation from this posture was a ladylike thrust at Cousin Alice, who was campaigning for Landon.★ She did not name her cousin but referred to Alice's attack on the president, headlined "His Mollycoddle Philosophy Is Called Typical of Roosevelt," in which Alice had contrasted Franklin Roosevelt's philosophy of security, dependency, and the so-called easy life with Theodore Roosevelt's credo of the strenuous life. It was Alice's view that her father had conquered his childhood disabilities and taught the nation the Spartan virtues of toughness and self-abnegation while Franklin Roosevelt, having learned to adapt to his illness, now was teaching the nation how to live with the Depression rather than to overcome it. "No man," wrote Eleanor, "who has brought himself back from what might have been an entire life of invalidism to physical, mental and spiritual strength and activity can ever be accused of preaching or exemplifying a mollycoddle philosophy. Most of my mollycoddles have had too much ease, too much dependency, too much luxury of every kind."[43]

By the time they returned from the western tour, it was becoming clear that a Roosevelt victory, perhaps even a landslide, was in the making. "The western trip was almost too successful," Roosevelt wrote Bill Bullitt. Eleanor had never seen crowds like those they were encountering in New England, she wrote as the campaign drew to an end. In Providence she was overcome by nostalgia for Louis Howe. She and Tommy went into the station restaurant for a cup of coffee

---

★Mrs. Longworth had seconded Landon's nomination, and as a columnist covering the Democratic convention wrote, "The talk is quite general that Mr. Roosevelt now is laying the groundwork for a third term" and asked the president to disavow such ambitions.[42]

and she thought of the many times she had been there with her friend and mentor: "I could see his little figure walking through that familiar station with the coat hanging from the sagging shoulders and the clothes looking much too big for him."

In the final days of the campaign the Republicans threw discretion to the winds. Landon, a man of moderate, often progressive, views and genial temperament, lost control of the campaign to the most reactionary and intransigent Republican politicians, and Molly Dewson deluged Eleanor with samples of Republican scare literature. The railroads were warning their men that if Roosevelt were re-elected the roads would be nationalized and thousands fired. Grocers were being advised their businesses would be destroyed by administration taxes and regulations. One national GOP bulletin directed all state headquarters in the final days of the campaign to stress that the administration was controlled by the Communists. Eleanor's old friend and ally in the labor wars, David Dubinsky of the ILGWU, had been nominated by the American Labor party as a Roosevelt elector; the Republican national chairman called Dubinsky—a Socialist and intransigent anti-Communist—a Communist, the American Labor party little better, and every day called upon Roosevelt to repudiate Dubinsky. Far from being daunted by these charges of Communism, Eleanor wrote Judge Dorothy Kenyon, who had explained that she was supporting the American Labor party as a party with "an enormous future," that "I, too, must admit that the American Labor Party tempts me!"[44]

The most reckless Republican tactic was the so-called pay-envelope campaign in which corporations inserted warnings in their employees' pay envelopes that some future Congress would divert the insurance funds of Social Security to other uses. An indignant Roosevelt ordered his speech-writing team to take the gloves off for the wind-up at Madison Square Garden; they gave him what he wanted and he added a few punch-lines himself. It was a speech designed to stir the audience to fighting pitch. It succeeded. There was a ringing enumeration of Roosevelt's commitments to the farmer, the consumer, the unemployed, the home owner, and the slum dweller, and after each pledge, almost like an incantation, "for all these things we have only just begun to fight." But the section that brought the vast crowd to its feet, that carried overtones of hubris, and was seized upon by the Republicans as confirmation of their charges that Roosevelt aimed to make himself dictator, was his harsh, almost exultant defiance of his enemies and detractors:

Never before in all our history have these forces been so united against one candidate as they stand today. They are unanimous in their hate for me—and I welcome their hatred.

I should like to have it said of my first administration that in it the forces of selfishness and of lust for power met their match. I should like to have it said of my second administration that in it these forces met their master.[45]

If Eleanor liked the speech, she did not say so in her column, which spoke only of the emotional quality of the audience's reaction. She had her own test of what a campaign speech should be. On the campaign train she had written, "And then when you listen to all of the President's speeches, you sharpen your critical faculties by asking yourself whether it is successfully informing the people of the nation." The Garden speech was a call to battle whereas she wanted campaigns to be schools in citizenship. Moreover, having gone through many campaigns in which the voters on both sides warned that victory for the other meant the doom of the republic, she no longer took such rhetoric seriously. "I wish," she wrote in mid-October, "I could convince myself that the defeat of either candidate would be so serious that it would make the victory for the side one believed in seem even more important. But the most I can feel is that we may have more difficult times if the opposition candidate is elected." And in another column that week end she wrote that her letters showed that the people wanted her husband's reelection "for very definite reasons, that they expect the next four years to bring some very definite achievements." She thought this was a good omen, for it showed that people were "really thinking and beginning to realize that their help is needed in order to accomplish any real forward steps."

How could she be so serene, people asked on the eve of the election. There was no point in making a fuss over the inevitable, was her reply: "What happens tomorrow is entirely out of our hands, the record of the past four years, the campaign that has been waged, all are over and whatever the decision may be one accepts it and builds as useful and pleasant a life as one can under whatever circumstances one has to live."[46]

The Roosevelts listened to the returns at Hyde Park. There was a buffet supper for family, friends, and close political associates, and by 6:00 P.M. everyone settled down to the business of listening to the returns. The president was in the dining room with his sons,

Missy, Sam, Tom Corcoran, leader of the new crop of bright young New Dealers, and McIntyre, with four telephones at hand. Corcoran improvised songs on his accordion; "Oh, Landon Is Dead," was one of them. Harry Hopkins moved in and out, as did Henry Morgenthau, Jr. Most of the guests were in the library being entertained by Mrs. James Roosevelt and Eleanor, who was wearing a flowing white chiffon gown with a huge red rose in her belt. She worried about the food, about the guests who had not yet arrived, about the grandchildren who were not yet asleep. She did not have the president's capacity for sitting back and savoring the moment, letting others worry about the details.

The results were not long in making themselves evident. "Very quickly the people who can compute percentages seemed to be confident that the verdict of the people was in favor of the President." Eleanor, as usual, was not so easily convinced, but when the leaders of the women's division, who had been listening to the returns at the Biltmore Hotel in New York City, telephoned that they were sure of the outcome and wanted to drive up to Hyde Park with Nancy Cook, she bade them come. "They were so much elated by the results of their labors and the success of Governor Lehman and the State ticket and of Mrs. O'Day that they did not leave until about two a.m.!" She finally induced Franklin and the children to go to bed around 3:00 A.M. after talking on the telephone with Elliott and his wife in Texas.[47] "You were right—so right," Roosevelt wrote Farley, who the day before election had predicted that he was "still definitely of the opinion that you will carry every state but two—Maine and Vermont."

Eleanor found the feeling of the country toward her husband as revealed in the election returns and the messages that flooded in upon her afterward "a little awe-inspiring. . . . You cannot help saying over and over again to yourself: 'What a responsibility for one man to carry!' Of course, no man could carry it unless the people carried it with him." Behind this last statement was a concept that later times would call "participatory democracy." That is what she had wanted the campaign to be. She thought the mandate her husband had received, overwhelming though it was, needed to be continually revitalized and renewed by an involved citizenry. The "fundamental" task, "for the leader of a democracy, is to bring to the people the realization that true democracy is the effort of the people individually to carry their share of the burden of government."[48]

To her husband she put it more concretely. He needed to build someone as his successor. The party organization had to be transformed, as the women's division had been, into an instrument of education and citizen involvement in public affairs.

"Do let me know," she wrote him just before he boarded the cruiser *Indianapolis* for a trip to Latin America, "if you've decided anything about Harry Hopkins, Ed Flynn, or Eddie Roddan. The people in certain positions seem to me very important these next few years."[49]

Then she struck a gayer note. "You should hear the messages that come to us from everywhere, by letter, by wire, by telephone! You could be a king or a dictator and they'd fight for you! Lucky you have no aspirations!"

40. WISE AS A SERPENT, GUILELESS AS A DOVE

$\diamond$

BY THE BEGINNING OF ROOSEVELT'S SECOND TERM, HIS WIFE had become a virtuoso in making her views known and her influence felt throughout the vast reaches of the federal government. Of her husband it would later be written that "there never was a prominent leader who was more determined about his objectives and never one who was more flexible about his means." Something similar might be said about his wife's adeptness in the uses of government, except that in her case the flexibility related to the ways by which a woman exercises influence in a milieu where power was in the hands of the men. She had learned from experience that if women wanted to be effective in politics and government they needed "the wisdom of the serpent and the guileless appearance of the dove!"[1]

Since she held no office and possessed no authority except that which derived from her husband, she left it to official Washington to guess what she did at his request and what she did on her own, what she did with his knowledge and what she did in order to place a situation before him and thus prod him and his aides into action. Officials received invitations to lunch with her at the White House, and when she steered the conversation into some field of interest to her, everyone wondered if the president had put her up to it, and usually she did not enlighten them. Sometimes she invoked the president, as in the case of a conference on leisure and recreation, when she wrote that "the President thinks it would be a very good thing if we could have a meeting on leisure time activities. He does not want to have it a White House Conference, but he felt if it could be called he could give it his blessing." What the recipients of the letter did not know was that because of her interest in the problem she had gone to the president and suggested the national conference in the first place. How could they know, when the president himself liked to keep his associates guessing as to his wife's authority since it often served his purposes to have her test a plan's acceptability before he embraced it fully.[2]

They assumed that if anyone knew where the president was heading, she did, and to a large extent they were right. How often, remarked Grace Tully, had she heard "Mrs. Roosevelt examining the Boss on what was going to be done about such and such a situation." But he did not disclose himself fully to anyone, and much that Eleanor wanted to know he did not tell her. Sometimes his reticence reflected a reluctance to discuss the seamier side of politics. (For example, Esther Lape was interested in a friend's candidacy to become ambassador to Russia, but Eleanor reported that she could not find out anything, for "these little political deals are not the things they tell the ladies readily as you know.") More often Franklin kept silent because he wanted to keep open as many options as possible. "I'm just not *ready* to talk about that yet, darling," he would say to her. On a lovely October day in 1937 in Hyde Park when the maples and oaks were in full autumnal glory the president talked with the press, and Eleanor in low-heeled shoes with a ribbon around her hair listened intently as the reporters tried to find out how he intended to "quarantine" an aggressor. She would have liked to have asked some questions, too, she wrote the next day. Of course, she could ask him in private, "but it always seems to me a little unfair to force anyone to talk shop when they might be thinking of something else."[3]

Yet when at her own press conference she was asked about the frequent coincidences between views expressed in her column and by the president, she replied with the conciseness for which the press admired her: "You don't just sit at meals and look at each other." During one insistent dinner-party cross-examination Anna cautioned her, "Mother, can't you see you are giving Father indigestion?" Some of Roosevelt's friends felt she harried him unduly. If there were matters she could not take up with him at dinner because of the presence of guests, she could bring them up when she went in to say good night or good morning—"if there's anything we want to talk about, we do." And on occasion she even hurried through the columned portico that led to the executive offices and slipped into his office to ask or tell him something, whispering in his ear if others were present. But she did not like to do that: "I always feel I am taking too much time and there are too many people waiting."[4]

She had other ways of finding out about Franklin's policies and plans. Often she passed on letters from troubled citizens to him asking how she should answer them, and occasionally these letters reflected her own uneasiness about some development. A Philadelphia woman asked her to use her influence "to defeat the awful increase in military preparedness." "FDR what is the answer?" she wrote across the top. "The answer to this type of letter is, I think, this," he replied, and summed up the argument against unilateral disarmament. "Write a letter along these lines," she in turn instructed Tommy.[5] A student at the University of Puerto Rico sent her a chapter of a book that dealt with democracy represented by the New Deal and asked, "Did I catch the real spirit of the New Deal?"

"FDR you are a better judge than I. Did she?" Eleanor inquired.

"I think this is pretty good," the president replied.

"Tell her an authority to whom I submitted her chapter thinks it 'pretty good,'" she instructed Tommy.[6]

"I was talking with a man the other day, and he said . . . ," she began a speech to a group of women. Impressed by the shrewd analysis that followed, one of her hearers asked, "Who was that man you talked to?"

"Franklin," said Mrs. Roosevelt.[7]

The officials in her husband's administration assumed she had his backing and knew she had a large public following, but the most important source of her influence was a personality that radiated goodness. "Charismatic authority," wrote Max Weber, represents leadership to which men submit "because of their belief in the extraordinary quality of a person." When the English novelist and pacifist Vera Brittain arrived at the White House for lunch she felt herself in the presence of a natural aristocrat; photographs of Eleanor had not prepared her for "the resolute, penetrating blue-grey eyes beneath their strongly marked brows" that caused her to forget every other feature of the First Lady's face and to hang on to every word she said.[8]

Eleanor refused to admit that she had any influence because of the power of her own personality, insisting that what she was able to accomplish had little to do with her as an individual. Rather, it had "a great deal to do with the circumstances in which I found myself."[9] She continually minimized her own importance. She advised a Texas woman whom she was encouraging to write and who decided an article about Eleanor Roosevelt was the way to break into the magazine market "not to tell only good things. . . . It will be more interesting if it is not too flattering. After all, you have only had the experience of helpful things whereas there are many people whom I have not been able to help and who probably feel that I could have done so if I had had the right understanding of their problem." When you know your own weaknesses, she said to a friend whose mother she had visited in her grocery shop, you know you are no better than other people, but because of your position you have a greater chance to do good. That is all. "You don't permit yourself false airs." She carried in her purse the prayer attributed to St. Francis in which the petitioner asks the Lord to grant "that I may not so much seek to be consoled as to console, to be understood as to understand, to be loved as to love . . ." We look at life as through a glass; the poet invests it with more poetry than it has in fact; the politicians see it as the struggle for power; Eleanor Roosevelt surrounded it with love. She profoundly influenced the thinking of some of her husband's aides, partly because she was the wife of the president but mostly by example. She insisted on being her natural self, and as Washington came to know her as a person rather than as a personage and began to sense her kindness, her genuine interest in people, her lack of egotism and boastfulness, it realized that here was no designing female Rasputin but a woman of mercy right out of First Corinthians. She ruled because she had learned to serve, and service became a form of control. She wanted people to feel that their government cared about them, and because she was in the White House she felt an added obligation to make people feel they knew her, had a right to tell her about themselves and to ask her for help.[10]

She showed compassion for all living things. "Can you suggest anything?" she asked Frances Perkins about a case that had come to her attention. "His legs are useless, his father is a drunkard, the home is very poor but he has put up a grand fight for an education." To Harry Hopkins at the Works Progress Administration, she wrote: "These poor gypsies seem to be having a difficult time. Is there any chance of their being put on a homestead in Florida or Arkansas, where they could be warm and where they might carry on their coppersmith work as well as farming? It seems to me the only solution for them." When Steve Vasilikos, the peanut vendor who stationed his cart near the White House, was driven away by the police, Eleanor wrote Steve Early from a sickbed at Hyde Park that he should take it up with the District authorities: "I would myself miss him on that corner. We had better let him stand at the White House gate." A protest against the manner in which Army mules were disposed of brought a memorandum to Steve Early: "Could the War Dept. either explain the reasons for doing so or make the whole situation clearer as I am quite sure they do not sell them without making sure they will have good homes."[11]

She transgressed against all the rules of tidy administration, though this, of course, was in the New Deal style. She asked help for suppliants whom officials often thought were malingerers and charlatans, and sometimes were. "Aside from the fact that I am disappointed in finding your story was made up entirely out of whole cloth," she wrote a woman in California, "I feel I must call your attention to the fact that when a letter is received which is as untrue as yours, it takes the time and energy of people here in Washington to follow it through which really should go toward trying to help someone who is really in difficulty."[12] She had not expected Governor Brann of Maine to help an applicant personally with a loan which she had referred to him, she wrote, slightly appalled, but since the governor and his aide had done so, Tommy informed them that "the money she [Mrs. Roosevelt] has is all pledged at the moment, but she does not want you and the Governor to suffer and she will take over the note and pay as she can."[13]

Officials often took her suggestions as commands when she had really meant them to use their own judgment, she said, but it was also true that she made her wishes known rather forcefully. Sometimes she was naïve and sometimes she asked for things that really meant a great deal of effort, yet only the most overweening in her husbands administration did not respond to the disinterested desire to be helpful that was back of her steady flow of communications to all the government departments. It might violate all the rules of political economy, but how was one to say no to a woman who felt the exhilaration of battling wind and snow on a wintry day and then immediately thought of what the foul weather meant to the poorly housed and poorly clothed?[14]

Her methods of getting the bureaucracy to respond varied with the degree of her outrage. Usually she sent a letter with a query— how should she answer? What was being done? Couldn't something be done? "Right in the mails she got a great many of these appeals," Will Alexander recalled. "She looked at the thing and decided whose business it was in the government to find out about it, and sent that letter with her own initials on it and wrote, 'Find out about this letter. You know what it's all about.' You'd better do it. She never forgot."[15] If she felt very strongly she invited the appropriate official to lunch and, since her right ear was slightly deaf, placed him on her left regardless of protocol. Or she asked him to tea. The day she received a delegation of sharecroppers in the Red Room she invited Henry Wallace and Dr. Alexander to be present. Sometimes she marched over to the offices of an agency in order to insure speedier action. On a letter she had from the National Federation of Federal Employees protesting the lack of housing for middle-income workers at a naval gun factory, she wrote,

Take to Mr. Hillman and Mr. Knudsen. Make appointment for me on Tuesday at 12 with Mr. Hillman and Mr. Knudsen together if possible. Call Mr. Hillman and ask if it can be so arranged and I will go to their office. I want to talk about housing. If Tuesday not possible would Thursday at 11:30 do?[16]

If an administrator's response to a letter seemed inadequate, she took it up with the president. She sent Acting Secretary of War Louis Johnson complaints she had received from residents of Maroc, California, that the Air Force's use of Maroc Dry Lake as a bombing range was endangering life and property; she did not like the Army's reply. "Give whole thing to F.D.R. and say I think answer of Mr. Johnson a bit lame!"

Experience and intuition taught her to which officials she was obliged to use the formidable words, "The President has asked me . . ." The readiness to do her bidding did not follow ideological lines. With Wallace and Ickes she usually invoked the president's authority. Wallace steered clear of her. On the way over to the White House, Wallace warned Will Alexander, whom he had just appointed administrator of the Farm Security Administration, "Now, Will, I want to give you some advice. You want to let that woman alone. She's a very dangerous person. You don't want to get mixed up with her." Wallace did not trust her judgment, Alexander thought. "I, of course, trusted Mrs. Roosevelt almost more than anybody I ever saw."[17] Ickes was as distrustful of her judgment as Wallace. With Hopkins and Jim Farley it was quite the opposite. Hopkins' aides were under standing instructions to give her whatever help she required, and Farley did her bidding even when he did not quite understand what she was after. Although Chester C. Davis, who succeeded George Peek as administrator of the AAA, was the leader of the "agrarians" as opposed to Rex Tugwell's "liberals" in the Department of Agriculture, he was a relaxed, kindly man, and Eleanor found him open-minded. When she came back from a trip to upper New York State where farmers had complained to her about the operations of the Federal Loan Bank, she got in touch with Davis about the matter. "Here is a concrete letter showing just what I mean," she followed up a few days after speaking to him about it. "Will you see that someone takes it up and looks into other conditions which I feel sure they will find throughout New York State?" No mention of the president.[18]

She lunched regularly with the wives of the cabinet and hoped her example might inspire some of them to join her in some of her undertakings. Few did. Young Jane Ickes, newly married to the secretary, wrote her in October, 1938, that because of a common devotion to progressive causes, Mrs. Roosevelt might be able to give her some advice on how to avoid Washington's pitfalls. Eleanor replied that she would be happy to do so.

> I think, however, that the person who can help you more than anyone else is Mrs. Morgenthau. She has succeeded in doing work which interests her in Washington, on things which are not controversial and which, therefore, do not jeopardize her husband's position. I think the general feeling is that our husbands have to do enough jeopardizing for themselves and therefore we should do as little as we possibly can along that line!
>
> It is a little easier for me.... Because of my years and old affiliations, I am apt to be blamed singly and not to put quite so much on my poor husband.[19]

She comforted herself with the thought that the country realized she had her own point of view with which Franklin might not agree. And he did have his ways of conveying to people that in her activities and opinions she was an independent personality. Once she entered his office while newsmen were jammed around his desk for a press conference. She wanted to bid her husband good-by as she prepared to leave in order to attend Cornell Week. The president looked out at the falling snow and told her to telephone if she got caught in a snowdrift.

"All right. I will telephone you from a snowdrift," Eleanor called over her shoulder as she left the room.

"And she would, too!" the president told the newsmen. This was more than husbandly admiration; it was testimony to his wife's independence.

Once she asked him whether her advocacy of the anti-lynching bill might hurt his efforts to get southern votes for his rearmament program. "You go right ahead and stand for whatever you feel is right," he said. She was not wholly persuaded that he had meant what he said and repeated her question. "Well, I have to stand on my own legs. Besides, I can always say I can't do a thing with you."[20]

Franklin never tried to discourage her, she wrote later, discussing some of the controversy she had created.[21] But it was more than that. He approved. Just because he had to ease up on his efforts to get New Deal legislation, he wanted her to press harder. It helped politically with the groups whose claims he had to postpone and, more important, it helped him resist the temptation of following the easiest course. That was her old role. One of the reasons he had married her was to keep him from sinning. "She had stronger convictions than he on the subjects of social welfare and social progress," observed Arthur Krock, who had occasionally been invited to small family dinners by Eleanor. "She was also a very determined woman—determined not only to make a career for herself so that she would not be just the President's wife, but also to make a career that would in her opinion put pressure on her husband to pursue the path of social and economic reform that he was embarked upon." She was not, she said in later years, "what you would call a 'yes-man' because that wasn't what he needed." Nor was it what the president particularly wanted, she added. "He might have been happier, if he had always been perfectly sure that I would have agreed. He wasn't. And it was probably good for him that he wasn't. But there must have been times when he would have liked it if he didn't have to argue things." She acted as a spur, she said, "because I had this horrible sense of obligation which was bred in me, I couldn't help it. It was nothing to be proud of, it was just something I couldn't help."

Rexford Tugwell recalled:

> No one who ever saw Eleanor Roosevelt sit down facing her husband and, holding his eyes firmly, say to him "Franklin, I think you should..." or, "Franklin, surely you will not..." will ever forget the experience.... And even after many years he obviously disliked to face that devastatingly simple honest look that Eleanor fixed him with when she was aware of an injustice amenable to Presidential action or a good deed that he could do.... It would be impossible to say how often and to what extent American governmental processes have been turned in new directions because of her determination that people should be hurt as little as possible and that as much should be done for them as could be managed; the whole, if it could be totalled, would be formidable.[22]

They were, in the White House years, consorts rather than bosom companions. Her relationship to him was less intimate than some wives had with their husbands after three decades of marriage but she was more influential. She had a point of view, a platform, a following, and he was a large and secure enough man to respect her for it.*

Cabinet officers often grumbled, some of them used her, but generally they complied with her requests. Some, like Henry Morgenthau, Jr., did so because there were times when they wanted her to find out what the president's mood was before they went in to see him, sometimes even to intercede with him.

On one occasion Morgenthau, sensing presidential displeasure with his views on tax policy, wrote in his diary that he had gone to Eleanor Roosevelt. "I told her that if she would be willing to accept the responsibility I would like to place myself in her hands as I felt that Franklin and I were drawing further and further apart. She said she was going to talk to the President." A few days later the president seemed to have softened toward Morgenthau's views and remarked at the cabinet meeting that "he and his wife had a discussion on economics in the country. . . . When he got through he gave me a searching look," Morgenthau wrote in his diary. When Morgenthau and Hopkins were trying to get the president to approve a $250,000 special outlay for milk for needy children in Chicago and were getting no response, Morgenthau went to Eleanor. "I'll ask Franklin about it tonight," she told him, "not as though you said anything, but as though I were troubled." Her intercession worked, commented Morgenthau.[23]

The bristly Ickes occasionally sought her patronage for one of his projects. When she was in Knoxville, for example, he wanted her to drive through the newly opened Great Smoky Mountains National Park. She did and expressed her pleasure in a column. He even tried to enlist her in his empire building. The wife of the naval governor of Samoa complained to her about the sanitary conditions on that island after thirty-seven years of United States' ownership. She sent the

---

* The *World-Telegram* in January, 1933, had spoken of a "connubial Presidency" after Eleanor, citing the danger of presidential isolation, said that her correspondence was an avenue

through which WE [*World-Telegram* capitals] can keep in touch with the public.

Not in the history of the American democracy and of the Presidency has a mistress of the White House spoken to the public in this extensive way, and so far as we know, not in the history of the democracies anywhere has the wife of a President, in alluding to the performance of the Presidential duties, used the first person plural "we" or "us." In the case of Mrs. Roosevelt she welcomes the public to write not in the capacity of a representative of the President but as one member of a sort of co-partnership of interest.

letter to Ickes because Roosevelt had placed the Division of Territories and Island Possessions in the Interior Department. But in doing so, Ickes informed Eleanor, the president had excluded Samoa and Guam. "Needless to say, I would be happy if in the process of governmental reorganization Samoa and Guam should be transferred to the Division of Territories and Island Possessions." Eleanor, however, did not take up the hint.[24]

She was glad to agree to requests to receive the staffs of federal agencies at the White House, but she deftly put such visits to her own use. The assistant to the public printer, Jo Coffin, brought the women who worked in her office to tea at the White House. "The nicest thing of all," she informed Eleanor afterward, "was the little conference when you gathered the girls around you on the lawn. You spoke of the urgent need of raising the standard of living of the colored people." The Children's Bureau brought its child-welfare field staff to Washington. "The opportunity for informal discussion of problems with Mrs. Roosevelt following the delightful tea was the highlight of the conference," Katherine Lenroot, chief of the bureau, wrote Tommy.[25]

Eleanor was careful in dealing with the members of Congress, fully aware of how jealous that body was of its status and how quick to resent what it considered pressure from the president or his wife. Occasionally a flare-up of moral indignation caused Eleanor to depart from her rule not to comment publicly on what Congress was doing, but she did so circumspectly, almost always asking Franklin's permission beforehand. If she sent a letter to a senator or representative, the note that accompanied it was studiedly neutral; it was simply for the gentleman's information to do with as he saw fit and generally elicited a courtly letter of thanks. But even in this area, when she was confronted with injustice she was not to be contained, especially if there was some bond of fellowship, either political or social, to make a direct appeal for help to a congressman appear to be the most natural course. That was the case in the matter of the sharecroppers.

Sherwood Eddy, clergyman, reformer, and publicist, came to her with an agitated account of the reign of terror in Arkansas instigated by the landlords to keep their sharecroppers out of the Southern Tenant Farmers Union. Many had been evicted, and Eddy wanted to resettle them on a cooperative farm he had purchased at Hill House, Mississippi. He asked Eleanor if these sharecroppers could be placed on relief until the first crop was brought in. "Is there any way in which you could be helpful, if you feel he should be helped?" she in turn asked Hopkins. "I want to be sure, of course, that you think something should be done, but I was horrified at the things he told me." It was Tugwell's job, Hopkins told her, and Tugwell, with whom she promptly communicated, said the Resettlement Administration would be prepared to take over the farm but they must then have the management of it. Eddy refused, and Eleanor informed Clarence Pickett, who had brought Eddy to her, that "under the circumstances I do not know what more could be expected" of the government.[26]

She did, however, write Senate Majority Leader Joseph Robinson, an old acquaintance. Eleanor had been on the delegation in 1928 that had gone to Arkansas for Robinson's notification ceremonies as vice-presidential candidate, and she wrote him without invoking the president's name. She was troubled about what the leaders of the sharecroppers and Eddy had told her, she said; "I am very anxious about it and know you must feel the same way"—would it be possible to send someone down on a mission of reconciliation? Robinson proved to be wholly on the side of the planters; there was no trouble between landlords and tenants except that which was instigated by "a group of agitators from time to time," he replied, going on to say that the landlords were willing to provide houses for the tenants who had been evicted "but they were prevented from doing so by the agitators." Eleanor pressed no further. She had made her views known and done all she could, and there was no point in alienating a mainstay of Franklin's working majority in the Senate. "The situation is a difficult and complex one," she wrote Robinson mollifyingly. "The whole system is apparently wrong and will take patience and a desire on all sides to straighten things out ultimately."

Yet her desire not to irritate Robinson did not hold her back a few months later when the Emergency Committee for Strikers' Relief telegraphed her that there was "a new reign of terror against 5,000 tenant farmers in Arkansas. Wholesale arrests of striking farm workers. Thirty-five Negro and white men held in small jail at Earle . . . workers charged with vagrancy. . . ." She requested Hopkins to have someone investigate and let her know if this was true. Their man in Arkansas had confirmed the arrests, Hopkins informed her a few days later, and the Department of Justice had a man down there to see whether there had been any infringement of federal law. Her next request was for Hopkins to arrange relief for the sharecroppers.[27]

Eleanor's efforts to improve the social-welfare institutions of the District of Columbia usually involved Congress and usually meant getting the president's explicit approval. Jail Lodge #114 of the American Federation of Government Employees called her attention to the "unsatisfactory working conditions" in the District jail. "Take up after I've been there," she noted on their letter, meaning that she should take it up in her column, and in the meantime she had Tommy send the substance of the letter to District Commissioner George Allen. Allen readily acknowledged that the complaint had merit, but it all went back to getting more money from Congress. "Would it be proper for me unofficially to draw attention of Committee to this condition?" Eleanor queried her husband. "Yes—sure—!" was the economic reply. A two-page letter detailing the conditions she had found in the District jail went to all members of the Appropriations Subcommittee concerned with the District's budget. "We did a good job for the National Training School for Girls," Senator Copeland replied; "Let's help the jail!" Senator Capper went further than his colleague: "I spent a couple of hours at the jail and became convinced that you had not overstated matters....I think it is wonderful that you are interested in a matter of this kind."[28]

The head of the League of Women Voters consulted Katherine Lenroot, the chief of the Children's Bureau, on how to persuade the Appropriations Committee to vote more money for improved children's services in the District. Miss Lenroot's advice was to ask Mrs. Roosevelt to convene a conference of citizens' groups and interested congressmen. Eleanor questioned whether such an approach might not stiffen congressional resistance, and the president, to whom she mentioned her doubts, agreed. "The President thinks the Congressional Committee might look upon it as an effort to coerce them," she wrote the league, but if they would get her a list of all the things the Social Service agencies wanted, she would ask the chairman "if he would get the Committee together and let me come up there and tell them that I realize I have more opportunity to see things firsthand than many of them," and they might like to know what she had learned. Congress did approve a budget for child welfare, but she was distressed, she wrote the chairmen of the House and Senate subcommittees a few weeks later, that no coordinator was named. "I know your deep interest in seeing that the children of the District are well cared for. This seems to me so vital that I am writing to you in the hope that you will immediately exert your influence to clear up that point." It was a moment when Roosevelt's influence with Congress was at its lowest point, and Eleanor's note ended, "I am sending this simply as a private citizen and I hope that you will not mention that I have sent it to you."[29]

Cautious as were her early approaches to Congress, by the end of the thirties they were increasingly unorthodox, occasionally even daring. In January, 1934, she told the Citizens Committee on Old-Age Security, "I could not possibly appear before a Congressional hearing on anything," but later she began to accept invitations to testify before congressional committees. She appeared before the Tolan Committee, which was investigating the problems of migratory workers, and was prepared to testify before a Senate subcommittee on discrimination against Negroes in defense industry. And in December, 1939, she created a sensation when she turned up uninvited at hearings of the House Un-American Activities Committee when it had subpoenaed her friends in the American Youth Congress.*[30]

Often she used a report on what she had seen on one of her endless journeys around the country as a peg with which to begin an exchange either with her husband or with the director of a government agency. "I can't say what happens to these reports," she was quoted as saying. "Some of them may never be read at all. Some of them I know have been. But I made them because I have been trained that way." She usually made notes on the things she thought might interest the president and local officials and the public generally took it for granted that what she saw went back to him. "No other President has had a trusted emissary going about the land talking to poor people, finding out what is good and what is bad about their condition, what is wrong and what is right in the treatment they receive," wrote Ruth Finney.[31]

Eleanor was as proficient as the president in the nonpolitical tour and inspection. Wherever she went she toured government projects, saw an endless stream of visitors, questioned reporters about local conditions—often as closely as they asked her about larger matters—and avoided public discussion of politics. Irrepressibly curious and a sympathetic questioner, she arrived in a community as her husband's inspector general, or so the local people thought, and came away its confidante.

"I would never presume to make recommendations," she insisted, speaking about the reports she submitted. But she defined "recommendations" in a Pickwickian sense, meaning they were not commands. "I forgot to tell you the other day how much impressed I was by the

*See Chapter 49, "FDR Administers a Spanking."

hospital for tubercular Indians at Shawnee, Oklahoma," she wrote Ickes in one of those missives she insisted were not recommendations. "I did feel, however, that the occupational therapy work might be made of more value if they could develop some of the arts in which some of the Indians must have skill and do a little better work than is being done at the present time." If less than a command, this was more than a suggestion. Ickes was in a benign mood; he thanked her for her letter: "It is gratifying that you found time during your busy trip to visit the Indian Sanitorium."[32]

Except for the homesteads, she was more deeply involved with the WPA than any other New Deal agency, and she did not hesitate to offer advice, often quite bluntly. She criticized the poor public-relations job the agency did, stating that some project officials seemed to avoid publicity "for fear of stirring up trouble. This is an age old attitude and never leads anywhere successfully." She admonished Aubrey Williams that the NYA representative in a discussion over which she had presided had been "rather dull.... Do you think a little coaching as to how to keep an audience on the *qui vive* would be advisable?" She returned from a visit to New York City and was immediately on the phone to Williams about the difficulties encountered there by the WPA-sponsored nursery school: "I think Dr. Andrus [the director of the nursery] is probably more interested in doing a good job than in government regulations. There ought to be a way by which both can be accomplished." Aubrey's follow-up report caused her to explode:

> The habit of having situations which arise investigated by the people about whom the complaint is made seems to me a most pernicious one and entirely futile. Exactly the same thing happened in the Illinois gravel pit situation. I do not see how you could expect a fair report from the people who are being accused of doing things which are not justifiable.

On the back of one of the letters in the series exchanged on this matter she wrote, "Give me these. Ask if he, Mrs. [Florence] Kerr & Harry [Hopkins] if he is in town would like to come & dine & talk NYA & WPA matters over. Will gladly have Mrs. Woodward also if they like." Her test of successful management was whether the job got done rather than whether a regulation was complied with. In Chicago she met at Hull House with the supervisors of Hilda Smith's Workers and Adult Education projects: "The main difficulty seems to be that Mr.

Maurer because of the set-up has to contact so many people every time he does anything that most of the time is spent running around to the people above him rather than supervising the teachers." Couldn't Aubrey "dynamite" the WPA official in charge?[33]

Often she worked through the women in her husband's administration. She and Molly Dewson kept a watchful eye over all appointments on the distaff side to make sure that women were not overlooked. The right of women to be considered on the basis of merit for all jobs was still far from established. She protested Hull's plan to send a woman to succeed Mrs. Owen in Denmark; she and Molly would "far rather" see him "send a man to Denmark and put a woman in some other place." In 1937 Molly accepted an appointment as one of the three members of the Social Security Board, and Mrs. Emma Guffey Miller, sister of Senator Guffey and Democratic national committeewoman from Pennsylvania, maneuvered to succeed her. Eleanor and Molly considered Mrs. Miller too close to the old-line organization, too traditional in her political methods. "Molly has had a conception of work for the Women's Division which I consider very valuable," Eleanor wrote Mrs. Miller, who had mounted a considerable campaign against Molly; "she has put education first and I think the women needed that more than anything else." Molly, backed by Eleanor, succeeded in having Jim Farley name Mrs. Dorothy McAllister of Michigan as director of the women's division. There was a weekly, sometimes daily, flow of memorandums from Mrs. McAllister asking for help, reporting on developments, building up regional meetings around her. Columnists spoke of the influence that Felix Frankfurter wielded in Washington through the many young lawyers, most of them graduates of Harvard Law School, whom he had spotted strategically throughout the New Deal. "Frankfurter's hot dogs," Hugh Johnson derisively named them. The women who looked to Eleanor for their marching orders and support were as numerous and perhaps more militant than Frankfurter's disciples.[34]

When women in the administration were attacked, as happened frequently, Eleanor defended them. There were periodic campaigns against Frances Perkins. "She has been quietly shoved in the wings," columnist Ray Tucker wrote in 1935, and her job was really being handled by the department's strong man, Edward McGrady. "FDR, this is being widely said. Is it part of the attack or has she not done well?" was Eleanor's query to her husband. "This is columnist's stuff and really silly," he assured her.[35]

Frances Perkins was one of the first targets of Representative Martin Dies, who accused her of malfeasance because she had not ordered the deportation of Harry Bridges, the radical leader of the Pacific Coast's longshoremen. When Dies threatened Miss Perkins with impeachment proceedings, her friend Ann (Mrs. Arthur Osgood) Choate sent an urgent call for assistance to Eleanor. She had talked with the president, Eleanor advised Mrs. Choate, who said he would appeal to the chairman of the House Judiciary Committee, Representative Hatton W. Sumners, on the basis of masculine chivalry to bring the matter to a vote—either to go ahead with impeachment proceedings or definitely turn them down. Then Eleanor offered some advice:

> I realize that Frances is under a strain and I wish she could take it more lightly because I think it is purely a political attack, and in public life women must accustom themselves to these things in the way that men have. She is alone and I wish that the women of this country, particularly in the organizations, could be induced to realize what the true story is on the whole Bridges question. Frances has it and, it seems to me, could give it to the heads of the different organizations if they would only request it. Then their backing could be made vocal. At present, many of the Federation of Women's Clubs members, who met down here, are down on Frances because they believe she is a Communist. When you get women started along those lines they are like sheep. They think Dies is doing a wonderful job and do not realize that he is doing something to make himself personally popular with the sole idea of being candidate for President, and Miss Perkins was the easiest victim.
>
> Frances does not know how to get on with newspaper people and neither has she a secretary who can do it. I did suggest that she try to get someone who would handle the press for her, but so far as I know she has never done it.[36]

Eleanor helped Frances, although she sensed a reserve in Frances's attitude toward her—perhaps it was Frances's fear that working too closely with Eleanor might make life more difficult for her in the man's world of the labor movement. The labor leaders had originally urged Roosevelt to appoint a man, and one of the stories current in Washington which, while not wholly accurate, was said to be in character so far as Eleanor was involved, described her as commiserating with her husband for the bad hour he must have put in with the labor leaders when he told them he had already made up his mind to appoint Miss Perkins. "Oh, that's all right," Roosevelt was said to have replied. "I'd rather have trouble with them for an hour than have trouble with you for the rest of my life." But it was Molly, not Eleanor, who had organized the campaign for Frances in 1933, and when in 1939 Roosevelt asked his wife to tell Miss Perkins, if she got the chance, not to oppose a reorganization measure that took the Employment Service out of the Labor Department, Eleanor passed the job on to Molly: "I think if you speak to her, it will have more weight than if I were to do it?"[37]

As at Albany, civic organizations prospered under Eleanor's patronage. She brought the White House closer to the civic-minded through their organizations, and by getting them a hearing from the president enabled him to hear viewpoints that otherwise might not have reached him. Organizations like the League of Women Voters, the National Association for the Advancement of Colored People, the National Public Housing Conference, the National Consumers League, the National Sharecroppers Fund, and the Conference on the Cause and Cure of War as well as the more radical groups such as the Workers Alliance and the American Youth Congress suddenly felt themselves on the inside of government, holding their sessions at the White House, being briefed by the First Lady on the president's plans and difficulties, and, because of her sponsorship, getting a hearing from press and public. "What on earth would I do without you in the White House?," Lucy Randolph Mason, a key CIO official in the South, exclaimed after an expression of interest by Eleanor had finally brought intervention by the Department of Justice in the case of a union organizer who had been badly beaten in Georgia.[38]

Eleanor's assistance to the housing groups when they convened in Washington in January, 1937, to press for passage of the Wagner Housing Act made up for what they considered the president's lack of enthusiasm for the bill in the previous session of Congress. Eleanor addressed the conference, invited its leaders to the White House to fill them in on the president's thinking, and relayed messages from them to the president and from the president to them.[39]

This time, with an assist from the president, the Wagner-Steagall bill was approved, and in September the United States Housing Authority was created. Nathan Straus was appointed administrator, and he promptly wrote Eleanor, hailing her as "one of the first 'housers' in the country" and expressing the hope that he could discuss his problems with her. "We are all very much pleased that, when it is organized, you will be able to have the new housing group at the White House for one meeting at which you will preside...." He regularly sent her the figures on the housing loans that he had approved and reports on the progress of the projects, and he even discussed the design of the apartments with her. To install closet doors, as she had suggested, would add approximately $225 to the cost of a dwelling unit, he advised her; every extra feature added to the costs and if he did not keep rehousing down to minimal standards he might endanger his hope to rehouse all slum dwellers. She did not protest, as she was more realistic now than she had been in 1934 about what Congress might be expected to sanction. "Surely closet doors are not worth $225 per house!" she agreed. "Come to lunch to talk it over."[40]

She mediated between Esther Lape's Committee of Physicians and the president in regard to improved medical services. Esther had moved the American Foundation, of which she was the member-in-charge, into the field of the organization of medical care. Organized medicine, particularly the American Medical Association, had successfully resisted the inclusion of compulsory health insurance in the social-security system when it was set up, and in order to keep the issue alive Roosevelt had appointed an Interdepartmental Committee to develop a program to strengthen the nation's health services. But this committee had gone about its studies in a leisurely manner and Roosevelt appeared to have forgotten about the group when Esther moved in. Together with a group of liberal doctors she had completed a massive survey of medical practitioners on whether and how medical care should be reorganized. The report, published in two large volumes, showed that the AMA's opposition to government involvement in the delivery of medical services and the maintenance of standards did not represent the views of the medical profession in general.

Esther wanted the president not simply to glance at the survey but really to digest it, she told Eleanor, even though she knew better than to expect the president to go through two fat volumes. Earlier Esther had mentioned some thoughts she had on government's relationship to business, and Eleanor told her to write them down and she would give them to Franklin. "Oh, he would not be interested," Esther protested. "Franklin is interested in any idea that can be written down on one page," Eleanor replied. Although the president had told Esther and Elizabeth when they had talked with him in July, 1936, that he would meet with their Physicians Committee "if they had agreed upon any clear point of view," Eleanor found him reluctant to do so when she brought up Esther's request for a meeting in February, 1937. She pried the reason out of him. "Somehow or other, Franklin had it in his mind that he would in some way have to line up with someone and he was not ready to do that." When Eleanor assured him that this would not be the case, she was able to arrange a date. She "infinitely" preferred one, Esther hastily notified her, when Eleanor could be present, even if it meant some delay. She sent along the names of her Physicians Committee.[41]

Franklin did not want to have dinner. "Lunch with me first," Eleanor had Tommy wire Esther. "Thursday April 8th. As much time as they want." In their talk with the president the doctors urged a partnership between government, medical schools, and hospitals in order to raise the standards of all medical care and to provide medical attention for the indigent. The first practical step was to establish a Planning Commission to formulate a national policy, they said, which led to the rediscovery of the Interdepartmental Committee under Josephine Roche, and the president asked Dr. McIntire to talk Esther's proposals over with the committee "and let me have a recommendation."

When the AMA learned what was going on at the White House it lifted the statement of principles Esther's committee had left with the president and endorsed them. Esther was not sure whether to be elated or alarmed, she wrote Eleanor; "Of course they tacked on some nullifying clauses designed to lodge everything with the AMA. This will never do. But it is revolutionary to have these principles put forth under those auspices." In any case it was more important than ever to go ahead with the Planning Commission.[42]

The president evidently thought so, too, for, Eleanor telegraphed Esther, "Franklin thinks it important to move at once. Will see you Monday or Tuesday a.m." In the end, Roosevelt decided not to appoint a new commission but to have Josephine Roche's committee bring in a report, which it did in February, 1938.

Guided by the Roche Report and urged on by Esther and her group, Roosevelt suggested to his Interdepartmental Committee that they convene a conference to secure the backing of medical science as well as public-health and citizens' groups for a program of action. Esther had reservations about the Roche Report, which she felt did not sufficiently reflect medical and administrative realities. But the president had one central concern: "Esther, my interest is in getting *some* kind of medical care to the submerged third that has now practically none."[43] The conference was held in July, 1938. Out of it emerged the Wagner

Health Act of 1939, but the AMA raised the cry of "socialized medicine" and the bill never came out of committee.

Esther refused to give up. Her group of doctors were "the genuine representatives of a powerful group of leading medical scientists opposed to the reactionary policy of the AMA," she wrote Eleanor begging her once more to arrange a meeting with the president. "Could you have the meeting here in September?" Eleanor queried her husband. By September war had broken out in Europe and Roosevelt had little time to think about health legislation, and in fact though there would have to be some health proposals ready for the 1940 session, he was hesitant about meeting with Esther's group. "Franklin says he does not want to get into any difficulty with the AMA just now when he has so much to contend with, and asks that this just be an off-the-record meeting." He saw them at the house rather than in the executive offices, and Eleanor served tea.[44]

Franklin was in retreat on domestic legislation in general. Although he adopted the reasoning of Esther's group, the "beginning" he suggested fell far short of their hopes. He asked Congress to authorize the construction of small hospitals in the needy areas of the country, "instead of waiting for a complete and perfected plan," such as the Wagner bill, "which would cost an awful lot of money."[45] This proposal, however, never emerged from committee either.

Roosevelt wanted medical care for the needy, but it is questionable whether he would ever have become as involved as he did without Esther's committee and Eleanor's mediation. Eleanor made a career of supplying the president with ideas of what might be done, placing him in touch with people and programs that otherwise might not have gained his attention.

Ickes did not approve of circumventing channels to reach the president, and called it getting in to see the president "through Mrs. R.'s back door." But this "back door" route to the president was open with Roosevelt's acquiescence. It enabled him to talk with people without the press knowing it and without the formality of giving them appointments. He recognized his wife's right to have as guests people who interested her as well as her friends, and if as a consequence Quaker pacifists, radicals, reformers, youth leaders, and "housers," who somehow neither he nor his secretaries ever managed to find time for, had a chance to talk with him, it was no disaster. He liked people and dominated the table talk no matter who the guests were, although he might comment to his staff the next morning that "Eleanor had a lot of 'do-gooders' for dinner and you know what that means." However, it was healthy for his staff to be aware that there were routes to his presence that they did not control. Eleanor did not abuse this prerogative. When she sensed that someone bored or irritated her husband, she had them to lunch or tea, and if she felt he might not want to see someone for political reasons, she made inquiries beforehand and guided herself accordingly. In any case, the list of dinner guests was always sent up to Missy, and if the guests did not interest him, Franklin pleaded work and dined in his oval study.[46]

As the thirties drew to a close, the jobless seemed to Eleanor to be a standing indictment of the American economy and an unredeemed claim on its conscience. She had grown close to Hopkins and the WPA because he and his top people were as ready as she to try unorthodox, even radical, methods to help the jobless. Franklin sensed political danger in the work projects started by the WPA for unemployed artists, musicians, writers, actors, and women, but Eleanor was all for them. There was "not the slightest doubt" in Aubrey Williams' mind "that had it not been for Harry Hopkins and Mrs. Roosevelt, for she was a powerful influence in support of width and variety in the work projects, the work program would have been much more limited in its variety and character."[47]

Eleanor wanted the well-off to visit the WPA projects because that would help them understand that "the unemployed are not a strange race. They are like we would be if we had not had a fortunate chance at life. . . . It is very hard for people who do not come face to face with suffering to realize how hard life can be." At Hyde Park Eleanor read aloud Martha Gellhorn's first story from *The Trouble I've Seen,* a series of WPA sketches, and some of her listeners wept. Then she was invited to the Colony Club to give a reading from the book. She trembled at the prospect, she said, but steeled herself to do it because it was important for the well-to-do to understand the situation of the unemployed.[48]

Because she felt the country had not as yet faced up in a fundamental way to the problem of the machine age, she was insistent that no plan, no point of view be rejected without someone giving it careful scrutiny. "There is a Mr. Albert Lytle Deane," she wrote Harry Hopkins, "who has submitted a plan to me. I, in turn, presented it to the President and he thinks it might be worthwhile to you to see Mr. Deane, and if, after talking to him, you think the plan has merit, the President will be glad to have you talk to him about it." Hopkins was a little annoyed: "Mr. Deane has discussed his plan with every official here in Washington at some time or other," he replied, and attached an analysis of the plan by Leon Henderson, who had found "very little of value" in it. Eleanor was not deterred. She wanted to be sure new ideas were not kept from the president. "This was sent me by a little man," Eleanor advised her son James, who was then acting as one of his father's secretaries, "and I just thought there might be something in it somewhere which would help you people who are working on the Supreme Court plan."[49]

A Tennessee farmer sent her a detailed proposal for establishing a silk industry in the United States. "He wants a silk industry. It was looked into but should we look further?" The president was sufficiently intrigued to send the proposal on to Wallace, inquiring, "Is there anything in this idea?" The labor costs were prohibitive, Wallace replied. "Did anyone go over this to find out if there is anything in it?" Eleanor asked her husband in regard to still another plan. "What can we say to Mrs. Roosevelt about this?" the president asked Lauchlin Currie, one of his administrative assistants. "A crank, and not worth bothering with," was Currie's summary judgment. But as long as someone looked into these matters Eleanor was satisfied. Usually they were wild goose chases, but one of the plans she passed on to Franklin was sent by Alexander Sachs, an economist with Lehman Brothers. In 1936 he had submitted a plan for agriculture, but in 1939 he came to the White House as the intermediary for Albert Einstein and other scientists who wanted to apprise the president about nuclear fission.[50]

In her search for a solution to the unemployment problem, Eleanor was as open to suggestions from the business community as from the labor movement and the left. It was through her★ that John Maynard Keynes' letter on the 1937 recession dealing with the impasse between the business world and the New Deal reached the president. Keynes wrote:

> I think the President is playing with fire if he does not now do something to encourage the business world, or at any rate refrain from frightening them further. If one is purporting to run a capitalist system, and not something quite different, there are concessions that have to be made. The worst of all conceivable systems is a capitalist one kept on purpose by authority in a state of panic and lack of confidence.[51]

★Leonard Elmhirst sent it to her, requesting that she pass it on to the president.

Baruch—also through Eleanor—was another who advised the president to ease up on the business community. He sent her the statement he had made before the Special Senate Committee on Unemployment in which he had warned that it was wrong to rush from a "regulate everything" position. She was not persuaded, Eleanor wrote Baruch later, but she was ready "to see us let business have some of the reforms which they think will solve their difficulties, not because I agree but because I think there is much in the psychological effect."[52] Her old friend Harry Hooker, now a Wall Street lawyer and counsel to Myron Taylor of U.S. Steel, was distressed to hear her say there was no solution known to her or to anyone else for full employment, and sent her a nine-page plan which called for repeal of the capital-gains tax, reduction in income taxes, and a ban on New Deal speeches attacking business. "Whether we like it or not, Capitalism is timid," Hooker summed up his recommendations.[53] Eleanor reported them to her husband, adding that she had also heard from a reputable economist that the way to bring about full employment was a large-scale housing program. She was for trying both. Fine, the president commented, but where was he going to get the money?

The First Lady was in advance of almost everyone in the administration in her emphasis on how much remained to be done despite New Deal achievements. At a Youth Congress dinner in February, 1939, a Republican speaker dismissed agencies such as the NYA and the CCC as ineffective and wasteful. "American youth does not want to be mollycoddled," the Republican official asserted; what it wanted was jobs. Eleanor was moved to make an impromptu answer. She agreed that WPA and NYA might not represent "fundamental" solutions; they were, she said quietly, stop-gap measures. But the NYA "gave people hope at a time when young people were desperate," and with the NYA and WPA we had "bought ourselves time to think." Although she believed in the measures enacted by the New Deal, she also noted that "they helped but they did not solve the fundamental problems. There is no use kidding ourselves. We have got to face this economic problem. And we have got to face it together. We have got to cooperate if we are going to solve it." Heywood Broun, who was in the audience, was so moved by her speech that he consulted his journalistic colleagues: "Am I just going into an impulsive handspring or is this one of the finest short speeches ever made in our times?"[54]

Because Eleanor was in advance not only of her husband but of almost all of his cabinet in urging that the "fundamentals" of the unemployment problem be confronted, she had to be careful not to give the opposition a chance to raise the cry of "petticoat government." Although the charge was completely inconsistent with the efforts to portray Roosevelt as a "dictator," that did not deter the administration's critics. When she was in Dallas in March, 1939, to lecture, Eleanor was presented by Governor W. Lee O'Daniel, a conservative Democrat. In his introductory remarks he said, "You've possibly heard of her husband. Any good things he may have done during his political career are due to her and any mistakes he may have made are due to his not taking up the matter with his wife." Was this southern courtliness or subtle Democratic aspersion? Eleanor promptly entered a gentle disclaimer: "A President's wife does not see her husband often enough to tell him what to do." Simeon Strunsky, who wrote the "Topics of the Times" column, enjoyed that. "Many a man who has had the privilege of talking with the President for five minutes in the course of a year or a whole administration has been known to go on ever after mysteriously assuming responsibility for most of the President's acts"; the First Lady was "too modest."[55]

But she knew the pitfalls of appearing to have any influence with Franklin. He had spent half a lifetime escaping the domination of his mother, and he resisted any kind of domination, especially a woman's. And Eleanor was a very strong-minded woman. "If the term 'weaker sex' is to be transferred from the female to the male of our society," commented Grace Tully, Missy's assistant, "much of the psychological groundwork must be credited to Mrs. Eleanor Roosevelt."[56] "Men have to be humored," Eleanor wrote in answer to Raymond Clapper's assertion that women were too emotional to be entrusted with large matters of policy. "I know that men have to believe that they are superior to women, and women from the time they are little girls have to learn self-discipline because they have to please the gentlemen. They have to manage some man all their lives." She loved the passage in Stephen Vincent Benét's "John Brown's Body" which described the lady of the plantation:

> She was often mistaken, not often blind,
> And she knew the whole duty of womankind,
> To take the burden and have the power
> And seem like the well-protected flower . . .[57]

Once, a student leader suggested the text of a message the president might send to a youth meeting; he noticed Tommy getting restive and finally she said tartly, "The President will write his own message." Later Tommy came to the young man and said apologetically she had not meant to hurt his feelings but if Mrs. Roosevelt were to go to the president and suggest what he ought to say "he will just get mad."[58] When Dr. D. E. Buckingham told the newspapers that Mrs. Roosevelt had secured him his job as District veterinarian, she wrote him sharply, "You must realize that I never actually ask for anyone's appointment. I simply stated your qualifications as I would have done for anyone who had done anything for us. You have placed me in a very embarrassing position, by having made it appear that I had used my influence." And she advised the president of the District Commissioners

> that in the future I will be very glad if my name is not used in con-
> nection with any recommendation which I make.
>
> I write these letters merely to give any information which I have
> when a man's name is up for consideration, and I would not, under
> any condition, want to influence your decision or have you do
> anything which was not in accordance with your best judgment.[59]

In a story about Ickes' appointment of Ruth Bryan Rohde to attend an Inter-American Travel Congress, the *New York Times* reported that Mrs. Roosevelt had suggested the appointment. She quickly wrote the secretary:

> I hope you do not think that I was the person who suggested Mrs.
> Rohde for any position. I simply wrote you because the President
> asked me to do so. There is such a concerted effort being made to
> make it appear that I dictate to F.D.R. that I don't want the people
> who should know the truth to have any misunderstanding about
> it. I wouldn't dream of doing more than passing along requests or
> suggestions that come to me.[60]

The issue of her influence with the president also arose in connection with her promptings of her husband during a press conference at Hyde Park. The president was accusing the anti-New Deal coalition in Congress of gambling with world peace and the economic well-being of the country, and in the informal atmosphere of Hyde Park

Eleanor spoke up to remind him of some vivid phrases that he had used at breakfast to illustrate his point. Mrs. Roosevelt "has come into the open as the guiding spirit and co-phrasemaker of her husband's program," Arthur Krock of the *Times* wrote afterward.[61]

"Did you notice that Mrs. Roosevelt during a press conference prompted the President?" John C. O'Laughlin, publisher of the *Army and Navy Journal,* excitedly wrote his friend Herbert Hoover.

Are they hereafter to cooperate rather than each to work one side of the street? Is the idea to advance Mrs. Roosevelt for something or other, even the Presidency? A fantastic notion, but in Washington suspicion follows any Roosevelt act. It may be, too, that the pair thought it advisable to show complete harmony in view. If so, the President will go much farther to the left during the remainder of his term, for you are aware of the extreme radicalism of the First Lady. . . . In any event, the incident is interesting and is welcome by the Republicans, who now feel they can attack Mrs. Roosevelt as a politician and thus avoid criticism for assailing a woman.[62]

"I should have learned by this time to keep quiet when I happen to sit in at the President's conferences," Eleanor told another member of the staff of the *Times,*

for every time I have ever opened my mouth at one I have got into trouble. But it seemed to be such a shame that the phrase he had used, telling us the same things at the breakfast table, couldn't be repeated for the correspondents, because it just wasn't as good a story without those graphic expressions. So I tried to help him out—and that's all to that.[63]

As much as possible she sought to minimize and conceal from public view her intercessions with the president. In December, 1939, Walter White of the NAACP sent her a report on an investigation of two lynchings in Mississippi, in the hope of publishing the report with her sponsorship. She sent it to the president. Back came a memo: "You should not accept a place as a member of the group but I suggest that you ask the Attorney General to look into this whole case to smell out any interstate activity or effect in the crime." Eleanor sent the report to Attorney General Murphy, saying that the president had suggested he look into it, and Murphy assigned Assistant Attorney General O. John

Rogge to the case. In writing to Walter White, however, she omitted any reference to the president. "I do not think it would be wise for me to give my name as a sponsor to the report you sent me, so I think this is one request I shall have to refuse. I am giving your letter to the Attorney General."

Louis Fischer, the writer and analyst of Soviet affairs, appealed to Eleanor to help get his wife and two sons out of the Soviet Union. At his request she agreed to speak to the president about it to find out if he would mention it to Soviet Ambassador Oumansky. The president had suggested that she invite Mrs. Oumansky for tea and talk to her about it, she reported to Fischer. The affair went well, and passports were issued to Fischer's family. When he later requested permission to describe the episode in a book he was writing and enclosed what he proposed to say, she wrote back:

> I hate to spoil anything you have written, but I would rather you left out my letter and any reference to the President. I do not want more than a mention of the fact that you came to see me and I said I would do what I could. I do not want it said that I interfered.[64]

She sought to hide her influence and effectiveness, and she held no office in government. Yet at the end of her husband's second term, Raymond Clapper included her among "The Ten Most Powerful People in Washington," saying that she was "a force on public opinion, on the President and on the government... a cabinet minister without portfolio... the most influential woman of our times." Grace Tully called her "a one-woman staff for the President," and Jesse Jones thought of her as "Assistant President." Without office she had developed an immense following throughout the country. It was never tested in a vote, but a poll on the subject published by Dr. Gallup at the beginning of 1939 showed that 67 per cent of those queried approved of the way she had conducted herself as First Lady, with women endorsing her activities by an even larger ratio than men.[65]

The philosopher Alfred North Whitehead, close to death in Cambridge, realized what she had accomplished during her husband's first two terms in office. Writing on behalf of Mrs. Whitehead and himself, he said, "We cannot exaggerate our appreciation of the wonderful work which you are doing in transforming the bleak social agencies of the past by the personal exercise of kindness, interest and directive knowledge." She was never able to forget, she told S. J. Woolf, "that this country or any other country is in the final analysis a collection of human beings striving to be happy, and it is the human element which is the most important consideration."[66]

Why does she bother him with such trivial matters, the president's aides sometimes complained and oftener thought. Life might have been more tranquil for Franklin if she had not done so, but the texture of the Roosevelt years would have been different, a human touch would have been missing, the people and their government would have been less intimately involved with each other.

41. CHANGES AT HYDE PARK

ELEANOR ROOSEVELT HAD MANAGED AS FIRST LADY TO REMAIN herself, to be a person, not a personage, and to have the human being thus disclosed accepted by the American public. But to remain human she had to keep official duties from stifling her personal life. Sometimes she felt she was leading a Jekyll and Hyde existence—one moment the public personality, the next the private human being.

In 1937 Forbes Morgan, who had been married to Aunt Pussie, died. Eleanor's ties with him dated back to the year of her debut when as one of Pussie's suitors he had danced with her. The funeral services were in Washington, and as usual in family crises much of the responsibility fell upon Eleanor. She comforted "Boy," Forbes's son, went with him to meet members of the family who converged upon Washington, and the next day accompanied him on the sad journey to Tivoli where Forbes was laid to rest in the Hall family vault. Yet all during the two days she also had to attend to such official duties as the annual breakfast of the Congressional Club, to which she had hurried after meeting her Aunt Maude at the train, for, she explained,

> these official duties, like the one yesterday and the one today, are scheduled so long in advance that it always seems to me unfair to break the engagement unless it is absolutely necessary.
>
> But in some ways it is a rather curious thing to have to divide one's life into personal and official compartments and temporarily put the personal side into its little hidden compartment to be taken out again when one's official duties are at an end.[1]

There were people who spoke to the passionate side of her nature, to whom she was bound by the memories of shared joys and sorrows— members of her family, a few co-workers, a few of the waifs for whom she felt a special responsibility. They represented the "personal side" of her life. She wrote of her Aunt Maude:

There are comparatively few people in the world whom you are always sure of finding equally interested, equally sympathetic, and equally entertaining as when you last met. When your ties go back into your childhood, however, and you have always found that a given person comes up to your expectations, you pick up the threads of relationship just where you dropped them when last you were together, and you feel a security of understanding which you do not feel with many people.[2]

The president was immersed in public affairs, and her children were grown and gone. She had, moreover, always felt she had shared both her husband and her children with another woman, Franklin's mother. She needed to have people who were close to her, who in a sense were hers, to whom she was the one and only, and upon whom she could lavish help, attention, tenderness. Without such friends, she feared she would dry up and die. When such friends were in trouble she expected them to turn to her, and she felt rebuffed if they did not. When they came to Washington she insisted they stay at the White House, and when she was in New York City or whatever part of the country in which they lived, she planned, long in advance, the things they would do together. It gave her pleasure to bring them gifts, to take them to a new restaurant, to go to the theater with them. She corresponded with them faithfully, often writing longhand letters in the early hours of the morning. Their birthdays were listed in a little black loose-leaf book, their Christmas gifts in another, and in the bulging little engagement book that she kept in her purse (the pages for which were Lorena Hickok's annual Christmas present to her), the birthdays, Christmas parties, and wedding anniversaries that she unfailingly celebrated with them were the first entries. "As you know, Mrs. Roosevelt is always a year ahead of all the rest of us in her engagements," Tommy wrote Hick. "She asked me to drop you a note to tell you that she would like to have the pages for next year when you have time to do them."[3]

Eleanor's cousin Corinne Alsop was staying with Alice Longworth, she informed Eleanor, but she would like to come and have dinner or tea with Eleanor when Alice was otherwise engaged: "I know that in casually saying I want to see you I am treating you as 'Eleanor' and not quite as the Mistress of the White House and I am always finding myself shy in so doing." "For Heaven's sake," Eleanor remonstrated, "why shouldn't you treat me as Eleanor! I never think of myself as mistress of the White House with casual people, much less with my family." Corinne, like Cousin Susie and Henry Parish and Harry Hooker and Isabella Greenway, reached back to her youth. There were the friends made during the years she entered public life—Esther Lape and Elizabeth Read, Nancy Cook and Marion Dickerman, and Elinor Morgenthau; those like Lorena Hickok and Earl Miller, who dated back to the days at Albany; and a few like Mayris Chaney, a dancer, who had been introduced to her by Earl in the Washington years. She went to great lengths to get together with these people.[4]

In the 1936 campaign reporters were mystified when a petite, shapely blonde appeared on the presidential train during Roosevelt's tour through the Midwest. Who was she? they wanted to know, and gawked even more when the lady who they decided was someone's *femme fatale* rode in presidential parades in the same car with Mrs. Roosevelt. Finally a woman reporter was delegated to ask Eleanor who she was since no one else in the official party seemed able to tell them. She was, Eleanor willingly replied, Mayris Chaney, or "Tiny" as she called her, a dancer and a friend. But why on the campaign train? "Well," explained Marquis Childs in his newspaper column, "they had promised themselves a holiday together and when Mrs. Roosevelt discovered she would not be on the West Coast that fall she wired for her friend, Mayris, to tour with the Presidential party. It was as simple as that."[5]

When Tiny came to New York she stayed at the little hideaway apartment that Eleanor and Tommy maintained on East Eleventh Street in the Village, in a little house owned by Esther and Elizabeth. So did Eleanor's brother Hall. So did Earl. Eleanor no longer used the house on Sixty-fifth Street. When she and Franklin moved to Washington they had thought of selling it, but only if that also was Sara's wish. They dropped the plan when Sara wrote her son,

> Yes, I should not care for being in New York and away from this house, which so exactly suits me and I have become fond of it. At the same time if we could get a good price, and if the money (half of the amount I get) would be a help to you, with your big family, I would willingly let it go and I should live in the country. Yet it would be a pity to sacrifice such fine property, for in time it will rise again in value.[6]

James and Betsy used the house briefly, as did Anna and her children after she divorced Curtis Dall, but Eleanor preferred her little apartment in the Village. "Dear Georgie," Tommy wrote the Negro maid, Miss Georgiana Turner, who worked for her and Eleanor in New York,

> Mrs. Roosevelt will be in on Monday just in time to go to the theatre. Will you leave for her some crackers and milk, so that she and Mrs. Morgenthau can just have a bite before they go to the theatre. Then will you leave some sandwiches and some iced Sanka and some fruit so that they can have something to eat when they return from the theatre. Mrs. Morgenthau will spend the night, so you will have a bed ready for her, as well as for Mrs. Roosevelt.[7]

If Eleanor considered any place home, it was Hyde Park. "I am always given the reputation of being constantly on the move," she said to a group of women who were meeting in Washington, and added, her voice becoming a little high-pitched as it still did when she repeated something that seemed to her quite absurd,

> in fact, one woman, I was told the other day, remarked that she did not see very much evidence that I ever stayed at home. As a matter of fact, I believe very strongly in deep roots in some piece of ground...some place that carried your memories and associations of many years. All of us need deep roots. We need to feel there is one place to which we can go back, where we shall always be able to work with people whom we know as our close friends and associates, where we feel that we have done something in the way of shaping a community, of counting in making the public opinion of that community.[8]

The Hudson Valley from Tivoli south to Hyde Park was that place for Eleanor, and Val-Kill particularly. For years the Stone Cottage, two miles east of the Big House—for which Franklin had given her, Nancy Cook, and Marion Dickerman lifetime use of the land (and where, as a measure of the intimacy of the three women, all the linen was marked EMN)—had been a refuge for her. There she found quietness when public life became too much, and devotion when, hurt by some new display of Franklin's casualness, she needed sensitive response and the feeling that she was really loved. Since the mid-twenties no one had been closer to Eleanor than Nan and Marion, especially Nan. But now her feelings began to change. She was constantly growing:

"There is something rather exciting about starting a new thing and one's ideas run riot!" she wrote in 1937 when she was fifty-three. "If the day ever comes when some one talks to me about something and it does not at once start a dozen trains of thought, I shall feel that the real springs of life are slowing up and that age is truly upon me!" She told the Todhunter graduating class, "Don't dry up by inaction but go out and do new things. Learn new things and see new things with your own eyes."[9]

She lived by this rule, her friends less so. There was a small sign that the relationship between her and her friends had changed when in late 1937 Marion asked Eleanor's help in planning the expansion of Todhunter. Like Val-Kill, Todhunter was an enterprise in which the three women were partners, even though Eleanor had given up teaching when she went to Washington, except for a current-events class. She still came, however, for opening-day ceremonies and commencement, and still gave an annual party for the staff and had each graduating class at the White House for a week end. Although the school was an excellent one, it was Eleanor's association with it that made it unique. Eleanor agreed to help Marion with her new plans, even though Franklin cautioned her, "You realize, of course, that if a campaign is undertaken, you will have to go to several dozen pep talk dinners and that the campaign is really based on your effective leadership." She did most of the things that Marion asked of her, but she refused to be quoted in the fundraising brochure as saying that she intended to make the school one of her chief interests after she left Washington; she hoped, in fact, that she would be able to go on with her column, her lectures, her radio work. "I am terribly sorry," she wrote the fund-raising firm, "but as I do not intend to make the school one of my chief interests, I feel it very much wiser to be absolutely honest. It will be one of my interests, but as I have no definite idea of what my other interests will be or where they will take me, I regret that I cannot change my statement." In the end, to Eleanor's relief, the expansion plans were abandoned because of the recession.[10]

But the shift in her interests might not have led to estrangement if Marion and Nancy had not reacted possessively. The break came when the three women decided to liquidate the Val-Kill Industries, which produced furniture, pewter, and woven materials. Eleanor wanted to take over the factory building, "The Shop" as it was called, and convert it into a house for herself and Tommy. According to Marion, they liquidated the factory because it had become too great a drain on Nancy: "The load that Nan carried nearly killed her," Marion was later quoted as saying. "I was carrying the school, but she carried the shop, the Democratic State Committee and was helping Eleanor with the homesteads."[11] Tommy's version was different: the furniture factory did not show a profit, and Eleanor was underwriting the losses; friends suggested that she get a business-minded person to manage the enterprise, and when Nancy objected they decided to dissolve the partnership.[12]

In return for clear title to the shop building, Eleanor proposed to relinquish her share in the Stone Cottage. It is not clear why Nan and Marion refused, except that they must have sensed that the new arrangements signified a change in Eleanor's feelings toward them and her withdrawal from a relationship that had been most significant in their lives. Franklin felt they had become too possessive; grateful as he was for the companionship they had given Eleanor—he had even agreed to their becoming members of the Cuff Links group—he was irritated, he told Agnes Leach, who was a good friend of all three women, by the way they went around saying "Eleanor this" and "Eleanor that," and he was outraged that after all Eleanor had done for them they should be making difficulties over the shop.[13]

That was the way matters stood when, in the summer of 1938, Marion went abroad. "While I was gone," she recalled three decades later, "something happened between Eleanor and Nancy. I don't know what. Nancy and Eleanor had a very tragic talk in which both said things they should not have said, but when I came back Nancy was crushed and Eleanor refused to see me. What took place I don't know."[14]

Eleanor did, however, spell out her version of what had happened in a letter to Marion on November 9, 1938, when she made a new attempt to gain clear title to the shop by turning over her share in the Todhunter School Fund to Nancy and Marion, and again, half a year later, when she finally insisted on withdrawing totally from Todhunter.

The talk I had with you last summer was a very preliminary one, but it was the result of a long period in which you may not have realized that you, Nan and I were having serious difficulties. After you left, I had a long and very illuminating talk with Nan which made me realize that you and Nan felt that you had spent your lives building me up. As I never at any time intended to put you in that position, and as I never had any personal ambitions, I was a little appalled to discover what was in Nan's mind, and of course must have been in yours. I know Nan well enough to know that you are a great influence and factor in her life.

In addition, on a number of occasions Nan has told me how extremely difficult my name made the school situation for you. You have told me that in spite of that, you wished me to continue my connection because we had begun together. However, in view of the fact that other factors have entered the situation which made me feel that we no longer had the same relationship that I thought we had in the past, there was no point in subjecting you to a situation which was detrimental. One real factor was that certain things came back to me through Franklin which made me realize many things which I had never realized before.

With a completely clear understanding, both financially and personally, I feel sure that we can have a very pleasant and agreeable relationship at Hyde Park. Any work I do in the future will of course be along entirely different lines which will not bring me into close contact with either of you in your work.

I shall always wish both you and Nan well in whatever you undertake, and I feel sure that we can all enjoy things at Hyde Park but not on the same basis that we have in the past.

I am looking forward very much to having you and Molly and the girls here on Friday. The arrangements which you suggested for Saturday have all been made, and the girls here invited for four o'clock.

She signed herself "affectionately." Marion replied that she had never used the expression "building up" nor even entertained the idea, and she knew nothing of what had come back to her from Franklin, with whom she had spoken for a few moments only after Eleanor had refused to talk with her for the second time. However, she accepted Eleanor's decision to sever her connection with the school and wished to consider a matter closed which had caused her much unhappiness and disillusionment. She, too, signed her letter "affectionately."

Eleanor's final transaction of giving up her share of the Todhunter School Fund, however, added to her disaffection from her friends. When Marion informed Franklin that she considered the fund a school trust and not the personal property of the three, Eleanor indignantly pointed out that they had all paid income taxes on their share of the fund which came out of the school profits; "If I were to die my executors would be obliged to get my share of that fund for my estate." If

Marion did not consider this a fair way of compensating Nancy for her share in the shop building, Eleanor was prepared to agree to a cash payment. "I have, however, as great a desire to feel during my life I am living in a building which I own as you have to feel that this fund which you have earned shall be used for purposes which you decide on. Therefore, I will only live in the shop building if there is a tangible settlement of the cash values according to Nancy's accounts." And when Harry Hooker told her that she did not have to file a gift-tax return in connection with the transfer of the fund to Marion and Nancy, Eleanor stubbornly insisted she "would rather pay the gift tax, as I want to have it registered that I gave up something which I had possessed. It is not a school fund. It belonged to the three of us jointly."[15]

Eleanor brought all the financial papers to Elizabeth Read, who did her income-tax returns. Elizabeth was horrified by the injustice of the settlement, but she was unable to get Eleanor to change her mind. "Elizabeth, what you say is true—but I can never forget that these two girls are afraid of the future and I am not."[16]

For Eleanor, the chapter of Nancy Cook and Marion Dickerman was closed. She continued to include them in the Cuff Links dinners at the White House and invited them to the big entertainments at Hyde Park when the president was there, and she sent them a turkey at Thanksgiving and small gifts at Christmas, but she brushed off every attempt to revive the old relationship. The real state of her feelings was indicated by Tommy, who in writing a well-meaning gentleman said, "I doubt if it would be of much help to you to consult Miss Cook about anything concerning Mrs. Roosevelt."[17]

Eleanor thought of herself as a countrywoman, and at times even imagined that if she had been born under other circumstances she might have made "a fairly adequate farmer's wife, having the necessary health and energy." Those she had, but other rural talents she lacked. She was all thumbs; try as she would she was never able to achieve the results with furniture stains, flower arrangements, and vegetables that Nancy managed effortlessly. Fortunately, there were always friends eager to serve her, and while communications between the two houses at Val-Kill, which were only 150 feet apart and connected by a flagstone walk, were, after 1938, restricted to the amenities, the costs of landscaping and the flower beds continued to be shared and for a time were under Nancy's supervision.

But Eleanor wanted the cottage to be her own and had made that clear even before the break. Otto Berge, who built the furniture, should bring it to the house, but "I don't want anything moved into its place until I am there to direct it."[18] There was a good deal of pine paneling in the new cottage and she had the woodwork rubbed down to look the way the furniture did, but she was the judge of when a satisfactory stain had been achieved. The pool was in front of the Stone Cottage; she invited the contractor who had built it to come to Val-Kill with his family for a picnic "and incidentally show some of the rest of us what has to be done about the pool so if anything happens to the man in charge, there would be more than one individual who understood the works." She supervised the spring planting around her cottage herself, and the excitement of returning to the country a few weeks later to find all her plants and bushes growing so fast she hardly recognized them had a special savor. "I love contrasts in flowers as I do in people, the pale columbine is a good foil for the sturdier zinnia," and no garden was complete for her without "some old fashioned yellow rose bushes, a bed of lilies of the valley in some shady spot and sweet peas and pansies to grow more abundant the more you pluck them."[19]

She was happy at Val-Kill; it was her house in a way none had ever been before—a rambling, two-story stucco structure with some twenty rooms of all sizes and shapes, each with its own books and pictures that Eleanor took pleasure in selecting herself. Since the house in time accumulated wings, there were unexpected step-ups and step-downs, alcoves and recesses everywhere, and guests, if they wanted it, could have complete privacy. Eleanor's bedroom overlooked the pond in which the sunrise and sunset were reflected. She slept on a sleeping porch surrounded by trees; in the morning there was the chirping of the birds to awaken her and at night a croaking chorus of frogs. On her bedside table was her father's copy of the New Testament with his interlineations, the one that had accompanied him all around the world and that he and Anna had read together in the days of their courtship.

Tommy, who had become much more than Eleanor's secretary, had her own apartment in the cottage. When they had started to work together in the twenties at the New York Democratic State Committee, there had been one immediate bond between them: Eleanor had been no more experienced in dictating letters than Tommy had been in taking shorthand, and as a result they had gotten along famously. "Now Mrs. Roosevelt can dictate enough letters in one hour to keep me busy for two days," Tommy told friends in 1936. Working for Eleanor Roosevelt was her life, and she wanted no other. She had begun as a shy, awkward girl from the Bronx, the daughter of a locomotive engineer, and now was a poised woman of the world. She had a strong, determined chin and could even say "no" to "Mrs. R.," as she called her, in order to protect her. Once when Eleanor started to dictate a letter to an official asking him to do something on behalf of a petitioner, Tommy let her hands fall to her side: "You can't do that," she told Eleanor. "Of course I can," was the reply, to which Tommy's rebuttal was: "Don't you know he'll be back and ask to be invited to the White House as a return favor?" The letter was not written. During her White House years Tommy refused to go out socially. "If I lost my job tomorrow, those people wouldn't give me house room," she used to say. "And anyway you're always expected to pay for such favors—in some way."

Eleanor reciprocated Tommy's loyalty. Copy number 3 of *This Is My Story* went to her, and when Tommy became ill in 1938 and was taken to the hospital, Eleanor canceled all her appointments to be at her bedside.

Tommy's apartment in the Val-Kill cottage had two bedrooms and a screened porch where, on genial summer days, breakfast and lunch were served. A living room served as Tommy's office and a kitchen served as a bar, usually presided over by Henry Osthagen, a gruff-voiced employee of the Treasury Department who had been gassed in the war and who became Tommy's companion after she and her husband separated. Guests at the cottage usually assembled in Tommy's office-living room for drinks before going to dinner, a ritual that Eleanor never allowed to become too protracted. It was a family joke that when mother announced dinner, there was no nonsense—"it was ready—now."

After dinner the guests went into the living room and sat around the fireplace. Conversation never flagged, with Eleanor, her fingers busy with some piece of knitting, setting the pace. She loved to read aloud, especially poetry, and often the much-used *Home Book of Verse* or Auntie Corinne's many books of poetry or, in the late thirties, "John Brown's Body" by Stephen Vincent Benét was brought out. She read well and without self-consciousness.

She managed an occasional week end at Val-Kill all through the winter but really lived there from Memorial Day until the end of September. The seasons in Dutchess County are very distinct, each with its own colors, shapes, and scents, and the changes and Eleanor's pleasure in them were faithfully chronicled in her letters and columns.

In winter she walked the snow-deep trails in high walking boots, a captive of the peacefulness of the winter landscape, and in summer she rode through the same woods on her horse Dot. Occasionally she saw a deer silhouetted against the trees and in July "an old friend," a blue heron, flying out of the marsh. In July, too, the purple loosestrife, which grew in marshy ground, enveloped Val-Kill in a violet haze. The marshes were also a breeding ground for large wood-flies, which sometimes kept her from riding until the wind blew them away.

She swam daily in the pool, and her effort to go off the diving board head first was a demonstration of sheer grit: she bent over the edge slowly, her fingers reaching toward her toes, at last tilting into the pool with a great splash. She never mastered it; she never gave up trying. She was always on the lookout for games and sports with which to amuse her guests and keep herself in trim. One season it was archery, another it was skiing ("I tried coming down one hill and to everyone's amusement landed in a heap at the bottom").[20] But it was only deck tennis that she could enjoy herself rather than through her friends' pleasure.

Her guest rooms were usually occupied, and rare was the day without its special excitement, whether it was the child star Shirley Temple and her parents, for whose visit Eleanor collected as many grandchildren as she could, or NYA administrators, who came to discuss their problems with her and whose presentation, when Franklin drove over and the officials crowded around his open car, she skillfully steered so that they put their best foot forward, for she wanted them to get more funds.[21]

Much as she loved the peacefulness of Val-Kill and a rainy day alone there before an open fire, she loved people more. Whoever interested her was invited to spend the day and told to bring his bathing suit. Eleanor would be at the Poughkeepsie station to meet him, a summery figure in a linen skirt and cotton blouse, white shoes and white stockings, a white ribbon around her hair.

One summer day she received a letter from Frank Harting, writing on behalf of himself and two friends with whom he shared an apartment. They were three young businessmen, he wrote, and were "rabid Eleanor Roosevelt fans"; she headed the list of people they would like to meet. "I was very much amused and somewhat flattered by your letter," she wrote back. "I like young people very much as I have so many around me all the time, and I should like to know you three." She invited them to spend a day at Hyde Park. "Tell Earl," she instructed Tommy, "if he feels he should protect me he can plan to spend that Sunday here!"[22]

She enjoyed masculine company, whether it was Earl Miller, still a health magazine's dream of virile manhood, the fussy but thoughtful Frank Harting, or the tall, saturnine Adrian Dornbush, head of the WPA's Technical Services Laboratory, who came to her cottage to paint. Auntie Bye, too, had always been surrounded by a coterie of male votaries whom the family had called "Joe-Bobs." Bob Ferguson had been one of them before he married Isabella, as had Joseph Alsop before he courted and married Corinne.

Eleanor still mothered Earl. She made a special Christmas for him, got him fight tickets through Jim Farley, and helped him finance the house he built near Albany. As chief inspector of prison guards in New York State, he was frequently in the vicinity of Val-Kill and kept an eye on it for "the Lady," as he called her; a guest room was always there for him. Divorced in 1934, he presented to Eleanor a succession of ladies upon whom she showered gifts and kindnesses until they faded away. In 1941 he remarried. Eleanor wrote him faithfully, letters full of warmth and affection. Some of her friends were puzzled by her attachment to this "cop," but if Franklin could make Missy a part of his household, she could do the same with Earl.

She encouraged his romances as, indeed, she did her best to help true love along whenever it showed up among her friends. She had liked John Boettiger, a newspaperman who had covered Franklin for the *Chicago Tribune,* and when Anna, separated from Curtis Dall, fell in love with him, Eleanor thought it was wonderful and shielded the courtship from prying eyes until Anna and John were ready to disclose it. Ever afterward Eleanor reminded her daughter that she had known John before Anna did. It gave her pleasure to lend her new cottage to Martha Gellhorn and Ernest Hemingway as a hideaway before they were married, and she did the same for the author of this book and Trude Pratt. Her gift of empathy enabled her to enjoy vicariously the love affairs of her friends: for her "there was no love/save borrowed love."[23]

It was approximately two miles from the Big House on the Hudson to Val-Kill over a winding dirt road that went through woods and fields that belonged to Franklin, as did the wooded paths and hills behind Eleanor's cottage, for Franklin was a canny accumulator of land and could not resist buying a farm if it came on the market and was in the vicinity of the Roosevelt acres, which now numbered about two thousand.

When Franklin was at Hyde Park Eleanor moved to the Big House, although she still worked at Val-Kill with Tommy. The Big House was dominated by Sara, who, though in her early eighties, kept a tight hold on the reins. At dinner Sara, as always, sat at one end of the table and Franklin at the other. She enjoyed the role of presiding dowager, and Eleanor was amused by Sara's calm assumption that it was to her and her son that the limelight belonged. When the Swedish crown princess visited Hyde Park, Eleanor was late because the royal party had come ahead of schedule, "but luckily," she reported, "my husband and my mother-in-law were the real hosts of the occasion so I managed to slip in unnoticed." Sara wanted to have the same precedence accorded her at the White House but Franklin said he could not overrule the protocol officers.[24]

There was a time when Sara's reproaches, complaints, and demands had upset Eleanor, but, as she wrote Maude, she was now so busy "I haven't time to worry about Mama and her feelings which is a help!"[25] She was considerate of her mother-in-law. It was still Eleanor who saw her off when she went abroad and was at quarantine to meet her on her return; but Eleanor lived her own life and when Franklin was not at the Big House she preferred her own cottage. For her part, Sara stayed aloof from Val-Kill, but Franklin did not. When he was at Hyde Park there was a steady flow of traffic between the Big House and the cottage. Eleanor had Franklin and his staff for steaks on her porch or, if he wanted to have a private luncheon at the Big House with some official, Eleanor had the rest of his household for a picnic, with James cooking the chops. On Labor Day the White House staff and newspaper people came for a picnic and baseball game. Usually, too, before the summer ended everyone journeyed to the Morgenthau farm at Fishkill for a "clambake," which, said Eleanor, Franklin enjoyed as much as any other early autumnal event in Dutchess County. She organized the newspapermen and women into a Virginia reel, with Franklin calling the numbers: "I feel very proud of my pupils," Eleanor noted in her column, "for I really started them . . . on the strenuous dance and they all seem to enjoy it and do it better each time I see them perform!" What the newspapermen thought is not recorded.[26]

Eleanor sometimes wondered how they would organize their lives after Sara died and the years in the White House were over. She thought the day of the very large estates was drawing to an end. "Here on the Hudson River it seems to face one every day," she wrote a former Hudson River neighbor; "I ride over the Rogers place and wonder what is going to happen to it, and now the Vanderbilt place is in the same condition. Ogden Mills has given his to the state, but the state, after all, can't be expected to take everybody's land along the River." Republican Howland Spencer, whose estate, Krum Elbow, on the west bank of the Hudson faced the Roosevelts', disposed of his as a form of revenge against Franklin. In 1936 he had announced he was leaving the United States to settle on his 7,000 acres in the Bahamas as a protest against New Deal taxes. What do you think of "your friend" now, Franklin twitted his mother. "Dearest Son, I was rather upset this morning about the horrid paper you sent about Howland Spencer, & your dictated note calling him *my* friend...." In 1938 Spencer declared that because of New Deal taxes he was unable to maintain Krum Elbow any longer and sold it to Father Divine, an eccentric self-appointed Negro preacher, for one of his "heavens." The country looked to Hyde Park. How would the president, with his strong streak of traditionalism and attachment for Hyde Park as it had been in his childhood, respond? It was Eleanor who commented through her column.

In Poughkeepsie I ran into some people who were much excited over the purchase by Father Divine of an estate across the river from my mother-in-law's home. I always feel sorry for anyone who has to sell a country place they have lived in for many years and enjoyed. One has so much more sentiment as a rule about one's country life. It must, however, be pleasant to feel that in the future this place will be "heaven" to some people, even if it cannot be to its former owner.[27]

Franklin wanted to keep Hyde Park not only the way it was in the thirties but the way it had been in his youth. The post offices that were built under his administration in Rhinebeck, Hyde Park, and Poughkeepsie were of gray fieldstone, an architectural style that he called "early Dutch colonial" and that he insisted was indigenous to the Hudson Valley. He persuaded Mrs. VanAlen, the niece of Frederick Vanderbilt, to offer the magnificent Vanderbilt estate, three miles north of the Roosevelts', to the federal government; he then got the Historic Monuments Division to accept and maintain it not only as an example of the millionaire style of life at the turn of the century but for its trees, some of which were several hundred years old and not to be found elsewhere on the North American continent. And when he arranged to have his papers housed at Hyde Park in a fieldstone library building and for the Big House to go to the federal government, he spoke nostalgically of the "small boy" who "half a century ago" took especial delight in climbing trees, digging in woodchuck holes and playing in creeks and fields that were not much different than they had been in the time of the Indians.

The Big House would always be his home but he, too, like Eleanor, wanted a place that would be built to his own specifications; he picked a hilltop behind Eleanor's cottage, where the sky seemed closer and over on the horizon the peaks of the Catskills could be glimpsed through the violet haze, to build "a little refuge to work in, where no one can come unless he invites them." Eleanor thought his plan to build a retreat on the Val-Kill side of his property "grand," and while he was cruising in Pacific waters on the U.S.S. *Houston* in the summer of 1938, her cables consisted chiefly of building progress reports: "Most of excavating for your house is finished"; "Walls of your house going up everything moving satisfactorilly."[28]

Although she was less a traditionalist than her husband and was more adaptable to change, Eleanor shared his feeling about Hyde Park and was actively involved in the affairs of the village and of the Hyde Park Improvement Association. Franklin declined her invitation to take part in its meetings at her cottage, but he did make suggestions on what could be done to improve the village at the annual meetings of the Roosevelt Home Club which took place on the grounds of his farmer, Moses Smith.[29]

Eleanor always hated to see the summer end—"the tang of fall makes me very sad because it brings the winter and all of its excitement very close." She was perfectly sure "that some day when I have no longer any obligation to do anything in this world, I am going to be very happy enjoying rural quiet and watching nature carry on its drama of life from the sidelines."[30]

42. LIFE WITH MOTHER AND FATHER

———————————————◇———————————————

THERE IS A PICTURE OF THE ROOSEVELT FAMILY ASSEMBLED AT Hyde Park in September of 1934 for Sara's eightieth birthday—a large clan, including several great-grandchildren, gathered around the matriarch. It was a much photographed family, chiefly because it was the family that currently occupied the White House, but also because its members made a handsome group together.

"As I looked at my two daughters-in-law," Eleanor wrote about her fifty-third birthday party at the White House, "I could not help thinking how lucky we are! All the boys seem to have chosen, not only people that one can enjoy looking at, but the better you know them the more you like them. Best of all apparently we can all have good times together and I think it is a good thing for a family to be able to look back at happy times." On that occasion she and her brother Hall located a pianist, and while he played they all danced; later everyone gathered around the piano and sang, including Franklin, who amused them by singing some old college songs. It was long after midnight before Jimmy and Betsy and the Morgenthaus were permitted to go home, and then only by grace of a plea from Eleanor, who felt that parties should end "when everybody is still apparently having a good time," which meant 1:30 A.M. at the latest. But the two Franklins stayed up. "When I went in to see my husband this morning, he looked at me disgustedly and said: 'It was three o'clock before I went to sleep!'"[1]

The four boys and Anna were built like their parents—tall, long-limbed, and long-armed, with strong bone structures, and they were brimful of energy. One summer when Franklin Jr. visited Eleanor's Aunt Tissie at her shooting in Scotland, she walked the moors all day and played poker with him most of the night and never seemed weary. Why had she never told them about the Hall side of the family, Franklin Jr. asked his mother on his return; how could they help bursting with vitality since they got it from both sides of the family—the Halls as well as the Roosevelts? The Delanos did not lack for vitality either, Eleanor reminded her son. The children had their parents' zest for life, and "love of adventure came to them naturally."[2]

Family reunions were rambunctious affairs, full of "tribal affection" and equally uproarious argument and high jinks. Ike Hoover had written of the way Theodore Roosevelt's exuberant children had taken over the White House so that it became "one general playground for them and their associates... roller skating and bicycle riding all over the house... giving the pony a ride in the elevator...." Eleanor and Franklin's children were older but equally high-spirited. Christopher Phillips recalled that at one Christmas party Franklin Jr. and John crept up behind the president's chair and tickled him. Roosevelt calmly reached his long arms behind him and pinioned them both. Muriel Martineau, over from London on a visit, thought the younger generation ill-mannered; the young girls staying at the White House were always late to dinner and kept the president waiting just because in New York it was fashionable to arrive a quarter to a half-hour late, and when the president came into the room many of the youngsters did not even get out of their chairs.[3]

But Franklin and Eleanor took youthful irreverence in their stride. Ickes described a dinner on the presidential train when they went to inspect the Grand Coulee dam site:

> It resolved itself into a debate between the members of the Roosevelt family, with all of them frequently talking at one and the same time. Mrs. Roosevelt precipitated the discussion by raising some social question and her three sons at once began to wave their arms in the air and take issue with her. She expressed belief in a strict limitation of income, whether earned or not, and the boys insisted that every man ought to have a right to earn as much as he could. The President joined in at intervals, but he wasn't President of the United States on that occasion—he was merely the father of three sons who had opinions of their own. They interrupted him when they felt like it and all talked at him at the same time. It was really most amusing. At one stage when they were all going on at once, I raised my voice and observed to the President that I now understood how he was able to manage Congress. Senator Wheeler followed my remark with the observation that Congress was never as bad

as that. That was about the sum and substance of outside contribution to the dinner talk that night, but it was all very interesting and very amusing.[4]

Eleanor and Franklin encouraged their children to have their own opinions and to express them without fear of embarrassing their parents. Yet Eleanor was slightly appalled when James, who was deeply involved in the politics of Massachusetts, a state with a large Catholic population, voiced his opposition to its ratification of the child-labor amendment. At the time newspaper publishers were insisting that the NRA Newspaper Code should permit employment of newsboys. "No civilization should be based on the labor of children," Eleanor said tersely. What about James' views, she was asked. She had written him in Boston asking for his reasons, she replied. "Of course, everybody is entitled to his own opinion," she added. "I am merely asking his. I would never dream of doing more. Jimmy must have reasons which seem sufficient to him. They wouldn't seem sufficient to me."[5]

She and the president were equally tolerant of Elliott in the late 1930s when, as a radio commentator over the Texas network of which he was an executive, he frequently voiced anti-New Deal views and as a politician allied himself with the anti-New Deal crowd which favored pledging the state's 48 votes to Garner in order to head off a third term. Elliott was a citizen of the United States and over twenty-one, and as such, Steve Early told the press, he was entitled to exercise his right of free speech. Although Eleanor and Franklin loyally defended Elliott's right to oppose his father's policies, a few months later Franklin, not without some satisfaction, filed in the family folder a news dispatch from Waco, Texas, reporting that supporters of a third term had drowned Elliott out with boos when he sought to introduce the keynoter, who favored pledging the state's delegation to Garner. And still later he filed another clipping, describing a thirty-minute ovation for the president that Elliott had precipitated at the Texas Democrats' state convention when he had defended New Deal spending and answered the charge of waste with the standard New Deal defense that hope had been kept alive.[6]

After his marriage to Anna, John Boettiger was offered and, with Franklin's encouragement and Eleanor's approval, accepted the publishership of the *Post-Intelligencer*, the Hearst paper in Seattle. "I shall miss them sadly but it does seem a grand opportunity and they will love it and so life is life, not always very pleasant," Eleanor wrote her husband, who was en route to Latin America on the U.S.S. *Indianapolis*. "I can hardly bear to have Anna & John go," she added a few days later, "but they are so happy that I wouldn't let them know for worlds but it is better than Europe for at least one can fly out if necessary."[7]

If Elliott and Ruth were associated with the anti–New Deal crowd in Texas, Anna and John were as staunch New Dealers as Eleanor herself, and this was an added bond between them. "Our voters reelected a complete New Deal delegation to Congress," John reported to his father-in-law in November, 1938. "So far as we are concerned in Washington [state], you can write your own ticket in 1940." The president did not comment on this last point when he replied to John; he was more concerned with his son-in-law's success as a publisher: "I am keen to hear all about the progress of the paper. Somebody told me that either you are in the black or about to get there. It goes to prove that a Hearst paper, minus Hearst's management, can be made to pay if it is run by a fellow like you." A few Seattle citizens were unhappy that, as a Hearst paper, the Boettigers published syndicated material critical of the president and First Lady; "they are not treating you and the President as they should as far as I can determine by the paper," one of them wrote Eleanor. "I assure you," she replied, "that they treat the President and myself with the highest respect and affection and the fact that they have one of Mr. Hearst's papers has nothing whatever to do with their attitude towards us personally."[8]

No sooner were Anna and John in their house in Seattle than Eleanor flew out, a "slow trip" because of low ceilings, to see them and to report to Franklin that their house was "lovely," that they were "making a real place for themselves," and that "Sis & Buzz are very well & happy. . . . Their teeth are being straightened so bars are rather in evidence."[9]

There were innumerable jokes, inside the family and out, about Eleanor's travels. "Dearest Babs," Franklin wrote her from the U.S.S. *Houston,* "The Lord only knows when this will catch up with my will o' the wisp wife, but at least I am proceeding according to schedule." Admiral Byrd set two places for supper at his South Pole hut just in case Mrs. Roosevelt should drop in; a child who heard the Robinson Crusoe story knew that the footprints in the sand were those of Mrs. Roosevelt; and the newswomen, in their 1936 stunt party, had Mrs. Roosevelt shooting to Mars in a rocket ship. The most famous story became a part of American presidential lore: the *New Yorker* cartoon in which two startled coal miners are looking up and saying, "Good gosh, here comes Mrs. Roosevelt." And when life did imitate art and Mrs. Roosevelt went down a coal mine in a miner's coveralls, Sara sent a barbed comment to her son, "I hope Eleanor is with you this morning.... I see she has emerged from the mine.... That is something to be thankful for." Sara never gave up trying. "So glad Eleanor is there with you dear," she wrote her son in Warm Springs, and sometimes she was even blunter: "I see Eleanor is back in Chicago, so perhaps you will have her at home tomorrow—I hope so."[10]

Yet much of Eleanor's traveling was done in order to keep in touch with the children. They were getting married (and divorced), settling down, having children, and setting up in business, and she was there to nurse them, to celebrate a birthday, to inspect a new grandchild, to counsel them, and to give them news of the rest of the family. She spent Christmas week, 1936, in Boston where Franklin Jr. was hospitalized for an operation on his sinuses, and stayed through New Year's Eve, sometimes in the company of, sometimes spelling, Ethel duPont, whom Franklin Jr. was to marry in June, 1937. Ten months later she was back in Boston to be with Johnny while he had four wisdom teeth removed, spending much of her time in the company of his fiancée, Anne Clark, a North Shore debutante. A few weeks later during Christmas of 1937 she canceled all engagements to fly out to be with Anna's family while Anna went into the hospital for an operation. And she made a special plane journey to Seattle to be with her daughter for the birth of her third child and to keep a promise to Buzz to be there for his ninth birthday, but she had to cancel the latter when the telephone rang at supper and she learned that Hall's son Danny had been killed in an airplane accident in Mexico. Dan Roosevelt had been a brilliant youngster, adventurous, with every promise of using the talents Hall had so tragically thrown away. "I am so deeply sorry for the boy's mother and my brother," Eleanor wrote an old friend, who had been one of the Morgan sisters of Staatsburgh. "Hall was so proud of Danny and was really very deeply affected. We can't put old heads on young shoulders and they seem always to confuse recklessness with courage." She left Seattle immediately to be with Hall and wrote him that "we must believe that there is a reason for all things in the universe, and turn to helping those, if we may, who are left behind, and will carry through life the scar of a great sorrow." She accompanied Hall to Dedham for the burial. "It meant a lot to us," Margaret Cutter, Hall's former wife, wrote her, "and I feel that you were the one person that kept Hall going. I was so terribly sad for him. Dan had been such a belated discovery and had proved such a perfect companion and was something for him to cling to."[11]

Eleanor was still the one the family turned to in moments of stress and tragedy. One wintry morning the telephone rang between 4:00 and 5:00 and she heard Franklin Jr.'s voice saying that he and Ethel had run into a car without lights parked on an icy road and were in the hospital. Would she come? When she reached the hospital, she discovered that Franklin Jr. had a concussion and did not remember having called her and could not imagine how she came to be there; "his action was probably subconscious," she recalled in *This I Remember,* "a reassertion of the childhood habit of turning to one's mother automatically when one is in trouble."[12]

She was "well conditioned to coping with family crises," she wrote. She could not afford to go to pieces because the president could not be worried more than was absolutely necessary.

The wedding of a Roosevelt to a duPont, the family which had heavily subsidized the American Liberty League, was one of the storybook romances of the thirties. The day before the wedding Eleanor walked into her husband's oval study, but seeing a group of gentlemen engaged in what seemed to be a very serious conversation, began to back away, when Franklin motioned to her. "The question under discussion is, what do I do tomorrow afternoon? I don't think I had better stand in the line." She was not very helpful, she said, but remembering the way the guests had abandoned her and Franklin at their wedding to cluster around their Uncle Theodore, she murmured, "It doesn't really matter what you do, as long as you don't steal the show." The wedding was beautiful—that is, "the church part of it," Eleanor reported to a newspaperman to whom she wrote frequently to encourage him in his effort to cure himself of alcoholism; "Ethel was a most beautiful bride. There were so many people at the house for the reception, the bridal party never sat down for five hours and they were utterly exhausted." Eleanor herself had to abandon the receiving line at the duPont home in Greenville, Delaware, to make a broadcast in Washington. "I don't know whether to be happy or sad," she told reporters as she left, "but simply say prayers that fundamentally their lives may so develop that they may be useful lives and therefore happy ones." That was her attitude, too, a year later when John married. "So our last child is leaving us," she wrote Caroline Phillips in Italy. "He seems so very young, but he is determined to get married and I do love Anne Clark very much." To Anne she gave the last string of pearls from the five-string choke collar that Sara had given her on her wedding day. Had she also given any "motherly advice" to Anne and Johnny, a relentless press wanted to know. "I am not good at giving advice," she replied. "I believe in letting them work out their own plans."[13]

She was not inclined either to give advice or to make predictions as to how a marriage might turn out. The younger the couple was, the greater the hopes and dreams that were vested in the marriage relationship, yet when the fires of infatuation cooled who could be sure that the partnership would not fall apart, especially if because of immaturity neither husband nor wife understood that any human relationship to prosper must be carefully tended? "It would be better if people did not marry too young," she felt, "and if they waited until they had more experience. Unfortunately, most people in this world have to learn by experience." She partly blamed herself for the early marriages of James, Elliott, and Anna. The Governor's Mansion had not been a home, and they did not feel that the Sixty-fifth Street house was theirs, nor even Hyde Park. That made them anxious to establish homes of their own and had added to their need to make money quickly.[14]

Elliott was the first to get a divorce. Anna was very close to him at the time, and at his bidding went to Chicago to talk things over with him. The family had heard rumors that he intended to get a divorce and marry Ruth Googins of Texas. "See if you can't keep him from rushing into it," Franklin asked his daughter. "He did not say he and Mother were opposed. He did not say 'don't do it' and when I called him from Chicago and told him Elliott was going to remarry right away, he was very annoyed, but his annoyance was at Elliott's doing it so quickly." Eleanor was more outspoken. She found it impossible to believe, she wrote her husband, that Elliott was considering remarriage, especially since he had no job. She flew to the West Coast to talk with him, but he was a restless young man, determined on his own course, and when he went ahead, despite his parents' pleas that he delay, they, of course, like most parents, loyally supported their headstrong child. Children should feel, Eleanor said, that they could always return to the home of their parents "with their joys or with their sorrows. We cannot live other people's lives and we cannot make their decisions for them." She had learned to accept "any change in her children's lives without making them feel guilty about it."[15]

She and Franklin had suffered so greatly from Sara's efforts to run their lives that they leaned over backward not to do the same with their children. They were unhappy when their children married too young and divorced too easily, but beyond being available to them for counsel and understanding when their private lives ran into difficulties, they resisted the impulse to interfere. Eleanor was more accessible than Franklin, for he, in addition to being tied down by his presidential duties, found it difficult to talk about intimate matters. Never once did either parent, although the children's divorces were a source of political embarrassment, advance political considerations as a reason for their not doing what they felt they had to do. The president said that "he thought a man in politics stood or fell by the results of his policies," Eleanor wrote; "that what their children did or did not do affected their lives, and that he did not consider that their lives should be tied to his political interests."[16]

Unlike Sara, Eleanor could not tell others what was right and what was wrong, since so often she was not sure herself. "Even if there were what the World calls sin," she replied to a woman who had written to criticize the Roosevelt children's divorces.

> I think we should remember that the Christian religion is patterned on the life of Christ, and that Christ showed in many of his actions that he believed one should judge not so much by what people had done but by the motives and a complete knowledge of the situation. Few people ever have that about other human beings. That knowledge is given only to the Lord.[17]

She found it difficult to condemn divorce if behind the decision to do so there had been careful consideration and a genuine effort to make the marriage work. She thought the real culprit in most divorces was incompatibility: "Incompatibility of temper sounds like a trivial cause for divorce and yet I am not sure that it is not the most frequent cause. It is responsible for quarrels over money, and it drives husbands and wives away from each other to other interests and other people and brings about the most serious acts for which divorce is usually granted." For that reason she thought people should be able to separate legally without moral stigma:

Naturally, the people who, like the Catholics, believe that marriage is consummated in Heaven, are not going to agree on this point, but I think people can be made far more unhappy if they find they have developed different standards and different likes and dislikes, than they sometimes are by really very serious things. It does not seem to me necessary to brand everyone who gets a divorce with something as serious as adultery or desertion, when frequently it is a case of different development and different opportunities for development.[18]

Eleanor rejoiced in the marriage of Anna and John because she felt they had not gone into their second marriage in any lightness of spirit. Both had profited by the sufferings and mistakes of their first marriages and now were drawn together by shared values and interests and by temperaments that were attuned to each other.

She no longer felt that a marriage should be preserved for the sake of the children. She deplored divorce, she wrote, "but never for a minute would I advocate that people who no longer love each other should live together because it does not bring the right atmosphere into a home." It was very sad when a couple was unable to make a success of marriage, "but I feel it is equally unwise for people to bring up children in homes where love no longer exists." Such views did not sit well with the church.

I am afraid I cannot claim to be a very good churchwoman. In fact, when I was tendered the *Churchman's* Award this year for promoting goodwill among certain groups, I carefully explained that while my husband was a good churchman, I was not particularly orthodox. I have a religion but it does not depend especially upon any creed or church.[19]

There was another reason why she hesitated to judge her children critically: being the children of public figures, especially of a president, they were at all times in the pitiless spotlight of publicity, so that every misstep or case of bad judgment became the subject of headlines, the slightest scrape was blown out of all proportions, the most improbable tale given the widest currency. "It seems so futile," she wrote a woman in Jamesport, Missouri, "to answer such foolish statements. ... However, I assure you that I have never seen any of my boys dance with a nude woman."[20]

"Incidentally, both our younger boys in college are having a very bad time as the sons of a man in public life," she wrote her Allenswood schoolmate, "Bennett." "It is not so easy . . . unless you never do anything or unless you have a Secret Service man with them all the time. Neither of these seems to go with the temperament of these two young things."[21]

The children resented the publicity. Franklin Jr. wanted to know why he should make headlines for actions which passed unnoticed when the Joneses or Smiths did them. His mother's reply that being the son of a president carried advantages as well as drawbacks, privileges as well as responsibilities never quite satisfied him. Franklin Jr., or "Brud" as he was called in the family, was a speed demon who held the unofficial Harvard-to-New-York record and was often stopped for speeding. "Will you speak seriously & firmly to F. Jr. & John about drinking & fast driving?" Eleanor begged her husband. "I really think it's important." Neither of the boys had any memory of their father having done so.[22]

"Father had great difficulty in talking about anything purely personal or private," Franklin Jr. recalled, "especially if it involved anything unpleasant. He left that to Mother." On one occasion, at Eleanor's insistence, Franklin finally agreed to speak sternly to "Brud" about his fast driving, but, Franklin Jr. recalled, his father "couldn't even bring himself to summon me to his little office on the porch of the Big House. It was Mother who had to say 'Your father wants to see you.'" When Franklin Jr. went in, his father hemmed and hawed and finally said, "'Your Mother tells me I must ask you to give me your license until you have learned your lesson.' He put it all on Mother. That was a basic trait with him. He couldn't fire anyone. I'm the same way. I hate an unpleasant showdown with anyone."[23]

Bad as the publicity was, it was equally injurious when officials excused offenses for which a Smith or a Jones would have been penalized. On one occasion when Franklin Jr. was picked up for speeding, instead of fining him the judge took him home for dinner.★ "Father was simply furious," Eleanor recalled. Her children, wrote Eleanor, were "five individualists who were given too many privileges on the one hand and too much criticism on the other."[24]

While Johnny was in Cannes in 1937 for the annual festival which

---

★ Franklin Jr. said his mother had sharpened the story to make her point. The judge fined him thirty dollars and *then* took him home for dinner.

ended in a "battle of flowers," he made international headlines when he was accused of having emptied a bottle of champagne in the mayor's plug hat. He denied the story, and William Bullitt, the U.S. ambassador to France, backed up his account. His parents believed the denial, and Eleanor was at the boat to meet him on his return:

> If it had been one of my other boys I would have felt the incident was more than probable, for they have great exuberance of spirit. It just happens that John is extremely quiet, and, even if he had been under the influence of champagne, I doubt if he would have reacted in this manner.[25]

But these episodes of publicity were minor compared to the steady attack on the older children on the grounds that they were trading on their father's position in order to make money and win favors for their associates. The children felt that the reverse was true—that government officials bent over backward when Roosevelts were involved in order to avoid the suspicion of favoritism. This was Elliott's complaint to his mother when she visited him in Texas. "He is dreadfully upset," Eleanor wrote her husband,

> that no decision is given on Ruth's station & says that it is hurting him in getting the management of stations he sells for everyone thinks the Com. [Federal Communications Commission] will give no decisions on stations if his name is connected with them. It does seem as tho' they had had ample time to make up their minds. Couldn't you or James say a word which w^ld hurry them? You know Elliott's disposition, he is beginning to think you are both agin' him.[26]

Despite this plea, according to James, who was at this time one of his father's principal secretaries, he and his father stayed out of it, and in time the FCC licensed the stations that Elliott sought in the name of his wife. Elliott was an able executive, but whether the FCC would have granted the licenses if his name had not been Roosevelt is a question to which no determinate answer is possible. But even if the commission had been influenced by the Roosevelt connection, was that so different from the advantages that all children reap who bear illustrious names?

James, particularly, had trouble over the nepotism issue. In late 1930, while he was still in law school, he teamed up with an insurance broker who offered him fifty dollars a week for part-time work. Although Louis Howe reported favorably on James' prospective employer and Eleanor wrote delightedly "James has got a job!," James said his father "was fit to be tied." Roosevelt cautioned James against allowing his name to be used to elicit political business and said that when he saw him he would explain "some of the reasons for the great willingness of some people to be awfully nice to you." James tried to avoid soliciting political business, but in his disarming memoir, *Affectionately, F.D.R.*, he acknowledged that the line sometimes was pretty close. "Possibly I should have been sufficiently mature and considerate enough of Father's position to have withdrawn from the insurance business entirely. But I was young, ambitious, spoiled—in the sense of having been conditioned to require a good deal of spending money—so I went right ahead in pursuit of what seemed to me the easiest solution."[27]

The issue arose in acute form when the president asked James to become one of his secretaries after Louis' death. Eleanor objected strongly and told Franklin he was being selfish. She also tried to talk to her son, telling him that she felt the appointment would draw down an unceasing political drumfire. "Why should I be deprived of my eldest son's help and of the pleasure of having him with me just because I am the President?" was Franklin's reply. Eleanor proved to be right and James was cartooned as "Crown Prince" and chivvied as "Assistant President." The attacks culminated in a *Saturday Evening Post* story by Alva Johnston entitled "Jimmy's Got It" in which it was insinuated that James' income from his insurance business and government connections ranged from $250,000 to $2 million a year. Eleanor was so angered by the Johnston piece that she wanted to answer it herself, but her husband dissuaded her. Instead, James submitted to questioning by Walter Davenport of *Colliers*, to whom he turned over his income-tax returns from 1933 to 1937. These showed that his income ranged from $21,714.31 in 1933 to $23,834.38 in 1937, reaching its highest point in 1941 with an income of $49,167.37.

"One of the worst things in the world," exclaimed the president to James' assistant, James H. Rowe, Jr., in a rare display of personal feeling, "is being the child of a President! It's a terrible life they lead!"[28]

Deeply devoted to his children yet preoccupied with public business, Franklin was less available to them than most fathers are to their offspring. He tried to make up for it by having at least one of them with him if it did not interfere with other things they ought to be doing, and one or two were always along when he traveled around the country on the presidential special or went for a cruise on a Navy vessel. "It was grand to have a couple of days wtih Anna and her family," Eleanor wrote Josephus Daniels in Mexico City, and then added poignantly, "and the President had one whole day in which he could be just a father and grandfather with no official duties."[29]

But she nevertheless felt that he should have devoted more attention to his children's problems. "Mother was very hard on Father for not doing so," Anna said.

> Mother could go tearing off to be with the boys in their crises. Father had to wait until the boys came to him and he was a very busy guy. He settled these things in his own way and it may not have been the perfect way. When I was sick Mother dashed out to spend Christmas with us in Seattle. I felt embarrassed. I felt Mother should have been at the White House. I had a husband and Mother should not have been with me.[30]

The attacks on James helped to break down his health, and by the middle of 1938 his stomach ulcers became so painful that, accompanied by Eleanor, he went out to the Mayo clinic in Rochester, Minnesota.

A decision was made to operate in September, and after six weeks of following the regimen prescribed by the doctors, James returned to Rochester, again accompanied by Eleanor. "The family as a whole seemed to feel that while he would probably be here only for a day still it would be a good idea for someone to go with him to make sure that he told us all the truth about what the doctors had to say!" Instead of allowing him to go home, the doctors reported that his illness was critical and recommended immediate major surgery. On September 11 Eleanor reported, "The President has arrived and shortly the operation for which the doctors have been preparing James will take place. I dislike operations!" She described the day of the operation in her next day's column:

> As I said before, I dislike operations! Like many other disagreeable things, however, they bring out the best that is in people. ... Jimmy's operation seemed to take a long time yesterday and when the young doctor who operated finally came to report to

my husband, he looked as though he had been through quite an ordeal....

I have discovered that there are a few advantages to being the President! Never before when I sat and waited for operations to be over, has anybody come and reported to me what was going on or what was the patient's condition. This time every now and then some one came to tell the President how far the work had progressed in that marvelous white operating room upstairs and I decided that this was on the whole one real advantage for which a President could be grateful![31]

The operation was successful, and no malignancy was found. Ten days later the doctors pronounced James out of danger and the president left—to face the Munich crisis. "I want to thank all of you," he said to the citizens of Rochester, "for what I can best describe as an understanding heart.... You have understood that I have come here not as President but as a father; and you have treated me accordingly." After a period of convalescence James resigned as secretary to the president, despite his father's protests, because he did not feel physically up to the White House job and because his marriage was breaking up. He took a job in Hollywood as assistant to Samuel Goldwyn at $25,000 a year, which created another storm: What did James Roosevelt have to offer Hollywood that made him worth $25,000 except his name? And Eleanor came under fire because she became a director of the insurance firm of Roosevelt & Sargent in order to protect Jimmy's interests.

This incident gave her a chance to say some of the things which Franklin had dissuaded her from writing a year earlier. Did the American people expect the children of their president to live lives of enforced idleness or to go out and earn their own livings, she asked. While the president's term in office is limited, she pointed out, it was long enough to ruin the lives of the younger members of his family if they were compelled to lead a completely restricted existence. As for her appointment to the board of Roosevelt & Sargent, she planned to attend meetings to cast her son's vote, not to sell insurance. Then she broadened the issue to defend her right to engage in private business. Did they expect the president's wife to sacrifice all her personal accomplishments and all the interests she had built up? If that were the case, some day a wife might refuse to go with her husband to the White House at such a sacrifice. When a man was elected to the presidency the voters did not give the rest of his family jobs, she emphasized.

The only concession she made to critics was an acknowledgment that there was an ethical obligation upon members of a White House family not to profit from special governmental favors in their business undertakings.*[32]

By and large, the public approved her statement. To Dr. Gallup's question, "Do you think the President's wife should engage in any business activity which interests her if she doesn't do it for profit?" 73 per cent of those polled replied "yes."[33] Whether the answer would have been the same about the children's business activities is more debatable. "They may be worth the high salaries they have been offered and accepted since their father became president of the United States," wrote the *Springfield News and Leader,*

> But we do not believe that William Randolph Hearst, whose place in national affairs is too well known to need recital, would have engaged Elliott Roosevelt, who knew nothing of radio, to become the head of the Hearst radio chain at a princely stipend had his father not been president, we do not believe Mr. Hearst would have engaged his son-in-law at a salary well in the five figures as a publisher almost the moment he married the president's daughter if it were not for his admittance into the Roosevelt family, we do not believe that Metro-Goldwyn-Mayer would have snatched up Jimmie Roosevelt at a Hollywood retainer if papa hadn't been sitting on the throne.[34]

So what? was the reply of the *Daily News.*

> That the President's power and influence don't do his children any harm is of course true. But how about, for instance, John D. Rockefeller Jr., Nelson Rockefeller, Junius Spencer Morgan, E. R. Stettinius Jr., Edsel Ford? Those men are all energetic, able and highly respected. But one potent reason why they are as far along in the world as they are today is that their fathers were or are wealthy men.
>
> It is taken for granted that a man who has made or inherited a wad of money in private business of some kind will help his children

---

* Her own income in 1938 totaled $61,128 of which $54,072 constituted remuneration for professional services—$1,000 from the Junior Literary Guild, approximately $17,000 from the United Feature Syndicate for her column, $23,000 from royalties and other writings, and $13,000 from lectures.

to get well started in the world. Nobody except a Red here or there objects to that.

But when a President of the United States merely LETS his children work at any trade at all, his political enemies caterwaul about nepotism and unfair advantages and undue influence. This, though the above-mentioned private fortunes are usually long-lived, while the Presidency up to now is only an eight-year job at the outside.[35]

"Dear Colonel Patterson," Eleanor wrote, "I deeply appreciate your writing as you did and am greatly heartened to have your support of my point of view."[36]

The attacks on the president and his wife for "exploiting" their connection with the White House were generally discounted as politics. "The long and the short of these attacks on the President's family is that they constitute dirty politics," the *Daily News* said, and added for itself that there were "far more substantial reasons for disagreeing with President Roosevelt, and far more decent sportsmanlike ways to fight him."

Years later James wrote that Father "should have been a lot tougher with all of us . . . he should have counselled us more instead of leaving us free to steer our own courses."[37] No doubt Eleanor thought so too, and her communications to Franklin were filled with such pleas as "tell him he *has* to live on his income . . . until he earns his own money." Yet she, too, leaned over backward not to interfere in her children's lives and rallied to their defense when they got into trouble.

Children who are raised in liberal, enlightened households often look back at their lives and the wasted opportunities and wish their parents had been tougher. They do not remember the many occasions when their parents were firm and their only reaction was defiance and obstinacy. Once when she returned to the White House Eleanor found Franklin Jr. there, home from Charlottesville, where he was enrolled in the University of Virginia law school. He had not decided whether to return that night or early in the morning. "In my most organizing spirit, I started to make his plans for him and he looked at me with the funniest expression and said: 'I don't like being orga-nized. I'm going to flip a coin!'" Eleanor was contrite. "It is good to be reminded every now and then of the bad habits which come with age. Grown persons do not like to have their minds made up for them. They like to arrive at a decision on their own volition. We mothers have a dreadful tendency to behave as though no one in the world could manage except ourselves."[38]

"No one ever lives up to the best in themselves all the time," Eleanor once wrote a friend, "and nearly all of us love people because of their weaknesses rather than because of their strengths." That was true of her attitude toward her friends. It was even truer of her feelings toward her children.:

> I don't know how other parents are, but I know that for myself, I can stand back and look at my children and what they do and think, once they are grown up, with a certain amount of objectiveness. On the other hand, I know quite well that there is a bond between us, and that right or wrong, that bond could never be broken. I am proud of them when I think they have acquitted themselves well, regardless of what the rest of the world may think, and even when I disagree and feel impelled to tell them so, I know that I understand them better than anyone else, perhaps. They are always my children, with the right to call upon me in case of need. The greatest contribution the older generation can give, I think, to the younger generation, is the feeling that there is someone to fall back upon, more especially when the hard times of life come upon them, and that is so even when we know that we have brought those hard times on ourselves.

"We could not ask that they give us peace and quiet," she wrote at the end of the White House years.[39]

43. THE DIVIDED WHITE HOUSE

THE DOMESTIC SIDE OF RUNNING THE WHITE HOUSE WAS LEFT to Eleanor. She issued the social invitations, planned the family reunions and parties, saw to it that none of their friends were overlooked. She was responsible for the housekeeping. The government paid for official entertainment, but the food the family and its personal guests consumed came out of the Roosevelt personal budget, so she kept two sets of accounts and five checkbooks. "The first of each month I am always rather breathless until I have balanced all my check books." Her biggest complication was the people who preferred to keep her checks as souvenirs rather than deposit them.[1]

The White House during the years of her mistress-ship was a place of warm hospitality, fun, and good-fellowship.

Although Eleanor was not witty, she liked fun and parties and had a sense of humor, especially about herself. She was too kind to take advantage of someone else's vulnerabilities for the purpose of a sally or a satire, but her laughter led the rest when her own foibles were lampooned.

The highlight of the Gridiron Widows parties were the skits in which she and Elinor Morgenthau acted and for which Elinor's versatile secretary provided the verses. In 1938 to the tune of "Gallagher and Shean" she and Elinor sang and danced:

MRS. R.: *Your welcome cheers me much—*
You know I still exist!
After my recent trip out west,
I found I'd not been missed!
One night I slipped away
Next morn, I'd gone halfway—
First stop, Seattle, to buy a rattle,
Then to Jimmie for a day.

MRS. M.:   *Oh, Mrs. Roosevelt! Oh, Mrs. Roosevelt!*
           Seems to me you have slighted Elliott and Ruth!

MRS. R.:   *No, we stood and talked like mad,*
           Twenty minutes all we had—
           Then I rushed to vote for Herbert, that's the truth!

MRS. M.:   *Oh, Mrs. R.! Oh, Mrs. R.!*
           People really think that you're a shooting star!

MRS. R.:   *Though Hyde Park was so remote,*
              Still the ticket got my vote!

MRS. M.:   *Positively, Mrs. Roosevelt—*

MRS. R.:   *Absolutely, Mrs. M.!*

The skits at the White House skirted controversy, but those put on by the newspaperwomen at the Women's National Press Club were highly political and often centered around the First Lady. In 1937 Eleanor was portrayed on a sit-down strike at the White House to obtain union hours for presidents' wives. The curtain rose, wrote Emma Bugbee, showing the White House portico draped with a huge sign on which was lettered,

THIS SHOP CLOSED. SIT DOWN STRIKE.

Eleanor's robust laugh rang through the room as a procession of pickets demanded "Union hours for First Ladies," "No more inaugural teas," "No more than 300 handshakes a day." Figures with banners representing the organizations accustomed to being sponsored by First Ladies—charities, battleships, peace movements, balls, musicales, thrift shops and hospital benefits, horse shows and amateur dramatics, high-school debates and baby contests—marched past the footlights expressing their dismay.

"Mrs. Roosevelt! Mrs. Roosevelt! We can't get our names in the papers any more," protested a delegation from the societies. There was no response from the sit-down striker. In marched a distressed group from the Society of Critics of Mrs. Roosevelt to implore her cooperation. Frances Perkins arrived to try to settle the strike, but retired moaning and defeated. Newsboys rushed across the stage, shouting, "Mrs. Roosevelt won't negotiate." But the show had to go on, so other skits were presented, with Mrs. Roosevelt still sitting down. The skit ended with the appearance of two strikebreakers at the White House, figures easily recognizable as representing Mrs. Herbert Hoover and Mrs. Alfred M. Landon. Eleanor ended the program with an off-the-record speech in which she "got even" with her friends of the Press Club, a speech that unfortunately was not recorded.[2]

If the laughter was at her expense, she was prepared to join in, and somehow it never seemed to detract from her graciousness and dignity. Yet to be the butt of ridicule was difficult for her. She had been a clumsy child whom her mother had made fun of as "Granny" and an awkward teen-ager who had been too tall and unfashionably dressed, so that her first impulse was to shrink from the limelight, especially from occasions where she might be burlesqued, but she presented a brave face to the world and encouraged others to do the same. She should not let her height worry her too much, she wrote a Philadelphia girl: "I have moments when I hate being tall. At other times I find it convenient, as, for instance in crowds.... After all, what we look like doesn't matter much to anyone except ourselves!" *Life* published a photograph of her asleep in an airplane with her mouth open. "She is fair game when caught by an enterprising photographer," a *Life* editor rationalized. "The picture gave me no concern, though some of my friends were rather appalled by it," Eleanor reassured the embarrassed photographer. "Nobody looks very nice when he goes to sleep with his mouth open, and this has served to remind me to carry a large heavy veil and swathe myself in it before I go to sleep on a plane again!"[3]

William Laas, who edited her column, explained why he had deleted the sentence, "I must not go to sleep on my good ear or the telephone will ring indefinitely and I will not hear it." The general public "can be very cruel," he wrote, "and it is seldom wise to leave one's self open to their gibes by revealing some personal idiosyncrasy." No one ever is as inwardly composed as they outwardly appear, Eleanor once wrote, "but it is a very good thing to cling to appearances."[4]

She was outwardly controlled, so much so that she had seemed to Cissy Patterson to be the most serene woman in Washington, yet there was an occasional reminder "of untamed Nature." An unknown writer felt it when she heard one of Eleanor's great bursts of laughter over the absurdity of some situation. Her hearty laughter reflected a natural exuberance but it was also a release from the resentment of a strong nature when it feels hemmed in by circumstances. With two such strong personalities as Franklin and Eleanor, it was a wonder the household was not torn apart between the president's realistic deference to what is and Eleanor's spirited impatience for what ought to be. It was held together not only by respect and mutual understanding and the interests that they shared in their children and their own careers, but by their ability to find a release from strain and tension in laughter and entertainment.

Louis, in addition to his other services to Franklin and Eleanor, had been a master of gaieties, and Eleanor, who had been his apprentice in this as in so many other things, carried on the tradition after he died. "I thought instead of making speeches at the dinner this year," her invitation to the 1938 Cuff Links dinner read, "it would be amusing if each person would come either in costume or with something to present to the President as a reminder of some special incident, and the President will be asked to guess what the incident is. . . . The ladies as usual will leave the gentlemen free after dinner for their usual enter-tainments." For Franklin's 1939 birthday party she asked everyone to come prepared "with a forecast of what may happen to the President in the coming year. It will be a general fortune-telling party."[5]

She enjoyed organizing the birthday parties for Franklin and mak-ing them gay occasions with Franklin the focus of all the to-do, and she did the same for close friends. For Elinor Morgenthau's birthday, she wrote Agnes Leach, "I am asking everyone to either write a poem or make a little speech to her on some event during the past year." But her own birthdays she preferred to have celebrated with as little fuss as possible. Franklin usually gathered the friends she really cared about for a birthday dinner, "but I was always glad when I ceased to be the center of attention."[6] She was unable to enjoy the limelight the way her husband—and her mother-in-law—did. At the president's birthday ball in New York City, Sara sat calmly amid a press of photographers in the glare of floodlamps enjoying "every bit of the commotion" that she caused, and when Helen Robinson left at 12:30 "she was still there, grand old war-horse that she is."[7]

At one of Franklin's birthday parties at the White House Eleanor contributed some verse which she read while wearing a chef's hat. It was a gentle apology to her husband because the menus at the White House were often not up to his gourmet standards.

Ducks, deer, salmon,
Turkey, pheasant, trout
Quail, moose and reindeer
All arriving by the ton

May be eaten with a pout
By the household, but the master
Never, never has enough.
On those who cook he's pretty rough
And when terrapin appears
Till he tastes it we're all ears
Fearing something's wrong again,
But without these delicacies
Life would lose full half its flavor
So to the senders in these races
For the Presidential favor
Go his thanks and our apology
Mistress, housekeeper, and cook we're the sorry trilogy!

Usually Eleanor could not admit that the White House menus were on the dull side and not what her husband wanted, yet it was a subject on which almost all guests and members of the family were agreed. Once Franklin stated his feelings in writing. The situation had improved, sizzled a memorandum to Eleanor, since he had protested being served chicken six times in one week; now he was getting sweetbreads—"about six times a week. I'm getting to the point where my stomach positively rebels and this does not help my relations with foreign powers. I bit two of them today."

One reason he wanted to be re-elected to a fourth term, he confided to Anna during the war years, and not wholly in jest, was "so I can fire Mrs. Nesbitt!" He was re-elected, James wrote, "but the housekeeper stayed on." James' account of his father's sufferings at the hands of Mrs. Nesbitt was one of the few points in James' book to which Eleanor took exception and asked her son to print her letter saying so. If the menus were not what the president wanted, it was her responsibility, since Mrs. Nesbitt submitted the menus to her; nor did Mrs. Nesbitt cook the food. "It was cooked by very competent cooks," and while Eleanor conceded that they had not known at first how to cook game and terrapin, the president had brought a man in once who did, and the cooks had learned from him.[8]

Partly, Franklin was a victim of the ascetic in Eleanor. She herself had little interest in food, she confessed, or, at heart, in other things that she considered time-wasting frippery. Once she distressed the nation's hairdressers with a columnar quip, "And now like all other women I must waste my time, at the hairdressers!" Why "waste"?

Ralph and Anna, the owners of a beauty shop, wanted to know. "We are as necessary as the milliner and dressmaker." "My dear *Ralph and Anna*," she hastily retreated, fearing she had dealt a blow to the nation's economy:

> The hairdresser is not wasting time; it is I who sit doing nothing while she works or while the drier works. The same is true of the time spent at the milliner's or dressmaker's, but we can't help wasting it and perhaps it is necessary for us all to do so now and then![9]

The puritan in her kept her from yielding to the frivolous and sensual as her husband could do on occasion. The Morgenthaus provided the champagne for one of her birthday parties; it had contributed to the gaiety of the occasion, her thank-you note said: "I think perhaps Franklin was more appreciative than I could have been, but I do know the champagne tasted very good."

It was not only that she punished herself by this form of self-denial but that she had to punish her husband. His very enjoyment of good food, high-living, and pleasure-loving company pushed her in the opposite direction. Such appetites were tied to the self-indulgent side of his nature from which she had suffered so greatly, as she had from her father's and her brother's, who was currently drinking himself to death.

When guests came to the White House for a family dinner one of the ushers showed them their places at the table on a seating chart; when all the guests had assembled in the Red Room, Eleanor came down, greeted them, and led them into the family dining room to join the president, who was already seated.

What went on at the executive-office side of the White House was controlled by Missy and the president's secretaries—Mac, Steve, Pa Watson, Jimmy—but in the family quarters her understanding with Franklin was that she gave the orders to the social secretary, the housekeeper, and the ushers. Even the invitations to the president's birthday dinners—the famous Cuff Links affairs—were left to her. "I am wondering," wrote Steve Early, "because I know how much pleasure the President gets out of Colonel Watson, whether you could care to include him among those invited to the birthday dinner. He is always loads of fun."[10]

The seating plan symbolized Eleanor's control of the social side of the White House, and she could mete out swift punishment to someone who tried to tamper with it. A Washington lobbyist whose ideas interested Eleanor and Franklin came for dinner, and when Mr. Crim, the usher, showed him the seating chart, the lobbyist expressed unhappiness that he was to sit some places removed from the president.

"My dear Mr. G...:" Mrs. Roosevelt wrote him later:

Mr. Crim tells me that you were extremely upset the other night because of the change I had made in the seating. However, you will remember I told you I would put you next to the President at dinner if I did not get you an appointment with him beforehand. Inasmuch as you had an appointment, I considered it was only fair that someone else should be given the opportunity to talk to the President at dinner.

Mr. Crim says you remarked that you were not here entirely for pleasure, but because you were doing things for the President. I realize quite well that you have taken a great deal of trouble and have done several things. However, I think in all probability the benefits have not been entirely one-sided.

In the future, I feel that it will be better for you to arrange your appointments with the President through Mr. McIntyre and keep them on a purely official basis.[11]

The gentleman felt himself undone. "To know you is a privilege and a joy and whether you are Mistress at the White House or living in a little one story frame house in Central Kansas, it would always be a grand human experience to travel out there and visit with you as often as possible," he wrote back hastily, giving his version of the incident. She appreciated his explanation, she replied, "and understand that your anxiety was caused by your desire to have a few minutes' talk with the President,"[12] but it was the end of their relationship.

His mistake was not only one of good manners; in undertaking to rearrange her seating order, he had also revealed that all his professions of loyalty to her were an expedient way of reaching the president. Franklin's charm was so overpowering, his instinct for predominance so strong, the power of his office so irresistible, that men and women who Eleanor thought were devoted to her and who shared her ideals often showed themselves more eager to have the president smile upon them when she introduced them into the White House circle than to stand with her for the principles they had previously voiced.

The White House was in a sense divided into two households—the president's and Eleanor's. She was much amused, Eleanor wrote in her column, to see a newspaper caption under a photograph of Missy, Grace Tully, and Betsy Roosevelt sailing for Europe describing Grace as her secretary. "I fear the lady must be much annoyed for she much prefers the gentlemen to the ladies and her affiliation with the White House staff is on the President's side."[13]

Both she and the president demanded a fierce and absolute loyalty from friends and associates. Harry Hopkins warned an attractive young woman for whom the president had shown a liking but who was a special friend of Eleanor's to be careful: Mrs. Roosevelt could freeze if she felt you were succumbing to the president's charm and abandoning her. He knew from personal experience, he added.[14]

Harry's introduction to the White House inner circle had been through Eleanor. It was she who had arranged occasions for the president to get to know him by having him and his wife Barbara, of whom Eleanor was very fond, visit Hyde Park and Campobello when the president was there. He was flattered by her constant calls. "Mrs. Roosevelt wants to see me about 'lots of things,' his diary for 1935 noted. The president, Louis, and Missy also were taken with Hopkins. Louis had found him "most congenial company," Aubrey Williams observed, and Missy was "a very devoted follower of his." During the 1936 campaign, Franklin gave Eleanor the impression that Harry might be his choice as Democratic candidate in 1940, and immediately after the election she began to press Franklin to act accordingly. Henry Morgenthau, Jr., and Harry were the only cabinet members she invited to the 1937 Cuff Links dinner and to her own birthday party. In 1938, she hinted at her advocacy of him as Franklin's successor, writing in her column that Hopkins "seems to work because he has an inner conviction that his job needs to be done and that he must do it. I think he would be that way about any job which he undertook." A few months later Roosevelt announced Hopkins' appointment as secretary of commerce, an appointment that was widely heralded as designed to transform the warmhearted social worker into a hard-headed business-statesman and thus pave the way for the presidential nomination.[15]

Another telling sign of Eleanor's fondness for Harry was her solicitude for him and his five-year-old daughter, Diana, after Barbara died in 1937:

This is just to remind you that we are counting on inviting you and Diana to stay with us over Christmas. Sara and Kate [James' children] feel that Santa Claus will be less apt to overlook them if they stay at the White House than if they stay at home, so they will be here Christmas Eve and Diana will have company.[16]

A memorandum Harry left for Diana underscored the closeness of their relationship:

> Just before Christmas in 1938 Mrs. Roosevelt came out to our house in Georgetown to see me. At that time I was feeling none too well. I had seen a great deal of Mrs. Roosevelt during the previous six months and the day she came out she told me she thought I seemed to be disturbed about something and wondered if it was a feeling that something might happen to me and that there was no proper provision for you. She told me that she had been thinking about it a good deal and wanted me to know that she would like for me to provide in my will that she, Mrs. Roosevelt, be made your guardian.[17]

Harry was greatly relieved at this offer and made out his will accordingly, and Eleanor took care of Diana until Harry's marriage to Louise Macy in July, 1942.

In 1939 Harry's health collapsed completely and he had to enter the Mayo clinic again; when he returned to Washington it was eight months before he could leave his Georgetown house. Eleanor and Missy kept him "in touch with Roosevelt's state of mind through frequent telephone calls and visits."[18]

She had seen Harry, Missy reported to Eleanor when she and the president came to Val-Kill for a Sunday lunch in January, 1940. He still seemed to feel he might run for president that year, Missy said, and someone should tell him that his health put it out of the question; perhaps four years later. Missy lamented that he was seeing too few people, and Eleanor agreed with her. Both women spoke affectionately of him.[19]

Missy was right about his health. On May 10, 1940, Hopkins went to dinner at the White House. "He was feeling miserable," wrote Sherwood, "and Roosevelt prevailed upon him to stay overnight. He remained, living in what had been Lincoln's study, for three and a half years."[20]

Mrs. Roosevelt would never admit it, Tommy said, but once he was in the White House Harry dropped her and transferred his complete loyalty to the president.[21]

Harry's companionship and help, even before he moved into the White House, filled much of the void that had been left in Franklin's life by Louis Howe's death, and Eleanor approved and encouraged it. But Louis had been her ally and confidant as well as Franklin's. She had inscribed Louis' copy of *It's Up to the Women:* "Dear Louis, Always my most helpful critic & best adviser." She hoped that Harry would play a similar role and, as Louis had done, hold the two sides of the White House together and instead of reinforcing the division there would help to heal it.

But Louis, as she noted, had helped to shape Franklin, had been his friend and counselor before he was surrounded by the aura of the presidency, while Harry, a younger man than the president, was shaped by him. On occasion Louis swore at the president and hung up the telephone on him. Harry had to tread warily. What Eleanor failed to acknowledge was that she, too, was a very different person from the insecure, inexperienced woman she had been in 1921 when Louis took her in hand. Louis said things to her that no one else could, and she had a greater respect for his political judgment than for any other man's except Franklin's. She, too, regarded herself as Harry's teacher, not his pupil, in politics. "In Harry Hopkins my husband found some of the companionship and loyalty Louis had given him," she wrote, "but not the political wisdom and careful analysis of each situation." She thought that Franklin might have avoided some of the mistakes of the 1938 purge if Louis had been around, and she wrote May Craig that "we wish with you that Harry Hopkins had not said a word about the primaries anywhere, but I haven't the faintest idea who urged him to." Mrs. Roosevelt still was "off of Harry," Ickes rejoiced in his diary after Roosevelt's election to a third term, and when she gets back from her lecture trip "she will put Harry in his place." Ickes lamented that the president was isolating himself "more and more" and that Harry, who played up to the president, was the only liberal seeing him.[22]

Harry, Eleanor wrote later, "frequently agreed with the president regardless of his own opinions, or tried to persuade him in indirect ways." When the president discussed a course of action with Harry, Sam Rosenman, or any of his own people and came to a conclusion, the discussion was closed. "That was not true with Eleanor. She stuck to it," said Rosenman. She had seen many people go in to talk with the president, prepared to tell him how much they disagreed with him: "They went in," Eleanor wrote, "but if I had a chance to see them as they came out, they usually looked at me blankly and behaved as though they never disagreed at all."[23]

"There were only two people who stood up to Franklin," Eleanor once said to Henry Morgenthau, Jr.; "you and Louis." Morgenthau demurred. "No, you are wrong. There were three people—Louis, myself and Eleanor Roosevelt." But Henry was as careful as Harry not to give Roosevelt the impression that he was in league with "the Missus." Henry's wife, Elinor, suffered keenly because she felt that the president kept her at arm's length. Once when she was sitting next to him at Sunday lunch she confronted him with her worry. "I want you to know that I am not a bearer of tales from your entourage to Mrs. Roosevelt's. I don't even report to my husband, nor does Henry tell me what goes on in your entourage."

"After that," Morgenthau commented, "things were all right between the two households."[24]

Even before Harry Hopkins moved into the White House, under Roosevelt's tutelage, the chief New Dealer had become much more political in his approach to issues. In the early New Deal years Harry repeatedly told his WPA staff that the political effects were not theirs to worry about; "we're here to implement a policy." But under Roosevelt's influence he changed. The day came when he said that the policy was right but he had to think about the political repercussions. After he moved into the White House he became occupied with the grand strategy of the war, and his angle of vision changed; he became impatient with those "goddam New Dealers" as, in a moment of irritability, he once described them to Robert E. Sherwood. Roosevelt, too, was prey to such moods. "I am sick and tired of having a lot of long-haired people around here who want a billion dollars for schools, a billion dollars for public health," he exploded to Henry Morgenthau in mid-July, 1939. "Here was Harry who was Mother's protégé to start with," said Anna, "and suddenly Harry became Father's protégé."[25]

Expecting an ally, Eleanor now often found in Harry an adversary and critic. And the vestigial puritan in her identified the shift in Harry's point of view with his taste for the elegant life and smart society—the parties on Long Island, the race tracks, the night clubs. It was a side of him she had not known and it offended her, although she said that Harry's top associate, Aubrey Williams, always remained the "idealist."[26]

Once not long after Hopkins moved into the White House, Eleanor's friends heard that she was ill with pleurisy, so ill that Tommy said, "It's the first time I've known her to turn her face to the wall." But when Eleanor came to New York to her little hideaway apartment on East Eleventh Street, she sent a message to Esther Lape that she wanted to talk with her. "I just want to tell you I haven't been ill at all. Something happened to me. I have gotten used to people who say they care for me but are only interested in getting to Franklin. But there was one person of whom I thought this was not true, that his affection was for me. I found this was not true and I couldn't take it."[27]

There was another reason why Harry's presence in the White House disturbed her. She feared that his fondness for high living encouraged the "playboy" in the president, a side of him that she disliked. When James once confessed to her that he was mystified by his father's pleasure in the companionship of a group of yachtsmen known as the "*Nourmahal* Gang," she agreed. She had never understood how he "could have gone on those cruises and relaxed with those people."[28]

But Franklin did enjoy "those people." "Father and Mother had a completely different way," said Anna:

> If Father became friendly with a princess or a secretary, he'd reach out and give a pat to her fanny and laugh like hell and was probably telling a funny story at the same time, whereas to Mother that was terrible.
>
> He loved to outrage Granny, to tease her. He could never do that with Mother. She was much too serious. Mother was inhibiting to him. She would never go along. That's why he turned elsewhere.[29]

This, too, was a dividing line in the White House—those persons like Missy and James' wife, Betsy, who played up to this side of the president's nature and the few who stood with Eleanor when she felt she had to be a hair shirt. It's not what the president wants, but what the president needs, she once said to a friend, but when Roosevelt turned on his charm there were few who did not succumb.[30] For a time, James and Betsy lived at the White House. Franklin was very fond of his daughter-in-law, who was gay and sophisticated in a way Eleanor could never be. Eleanor felt that Betsy was sometimes more concerned about pleasing her father-in-law than her husband. And when Betsy— without Franklin's saying so, perhaps even with his encouragement— began to encroach upon Eleanor's prerogatives as mistress of the White House, Eleanor put her foot down firmly.

"Mother was a very jealous person," said Anna.

She was jealous of Missy, of Betsy, of Louise, even of me. . . . They were all three women who had succeeded to some degree in usurping some of her responsibility as wife and First Lady. Mother came in late once, realized she had done nothing about the seating arrangements and asked for the chart and was told by the ushers Mrs. Hopkins had seated the table. She was furious.

Betsy never did anything for Father except always turn up for cocktails when he was alone. In those few minutes before the guests came in, there was always Betsy, chic and lovely, full of light quips. These were things Mother couldn't give him. She knew that, but she was a human being and never could quite accept it.[31]

"Tommy & I got back (by air) tonight," Eleanor wrote Maude Gray, "& I found Betsy here but leaving at once tonight. She does not kiss me but is very attractive to F.D.R. Aren't people funny?"[32]

Eleanor Roosevelt's most complex relationship was with Missy. There was affection and motherly solicitude—and also resentment. "Dearest ER," Missy wrote her in one of the early White House years. "Another Christmas, and thanks to your good example I am *not* exhausted by last minute wrapping. . . . I have had such a happy year—I hope you know how very much I appreciate being with you—not because of the White House—but because I'm *with you!*" Few letters to Franklin from his wife did not ask him to give her love to Missy, and when Missy's nieces were married, Eleanor attended the weddings and arranged for the gifts.

But Missy created problems, for the children as well as for Eleanor. While Anna was still in the East and spending a good deal of time in the White House, she admitted that she hated it when Missy was in a car with her father and had the preferred seat next to him. Franklin Jr., when asked by his mother whether he had ever resented Louis Howe, firmly said no, but he had resented Missy. Once he had said to Missy, "Are you always agreeable? Don't you ever get mad and flare up? Do you always smile?" She looked as if she were going to burst out crying, Franklin Jr. said.[33]

Anna was not wholly sure that "jealousy" was the right word to describe her mother's feelings toward Missy. Her presence in the White House made it possible for Eleanor to move around the country as much as she did. In 1938 Doris Fleeson wrote about Missy's role in the *Saturday Evening Post*. She described how Missy presided over the White House tea table when Mrs. Roosevelt was not there, how she wrote all the president's private letters, did the accounts, paid the bills, balanced his checkbooks, saw that the children got their allowances, kept track of his stamp, marine-print, and rare-book collections and ran the Little White House at Warm Springs "when Mrs. Roosevelt can't be there." Missy's service to the president was beyond price. "She was sweet and gentle," said Sam Rosenman, and continued:

> a very good hostess when Mrs. Roosevelt was away ... and far more intelligent than most people gave her credit for. I remember many occasions when letters passed over her desk that she did not think ought to go out. She would show them to me and Steve Early and if we agreed, she would put them in the desk and go back to him. ... When she had her stroke in 1941, I said, "A much greater loss to the country than the loss of a battleship."[34]

She wished, said Eleanor after reading Doris Fleeson's piece, that someone would write a similar article about Tommy, who made life possible for her.

But there was a murkier side to the relationship between Franklin and Eleanor in regard to Missy than the generous praise of Doris Fleeson's article disclosed, a side which Eleanor's great sense of dignity and pride caused her to keep well hidden, usually successfully.

Once a friend saw Eleanor go over and kiss Missy good night. "I thought to myself—how could she?" It required great strength and self-control for Eleanor to treat Missy with such warmth and friendliness. It was difficult for Missy, too. Fulton Oursler glimpsed that side of it. He ran the Macfadden publications, including *Liberty,* for which both Franklin and Eleanor had often written. Oursler's introduction to the Roosevelt household in the Albany days had been through Eleanor, but he found her too serious and high-minded. It was easier to relax with Missy, and by the mid-thirties the Ourslers were taking Missy to the races and she even considered summering near them on the Cape.

Oursler came down for dinner in May, 1935. It was a hot day. Since the president was off fishing and not expected back until dinner time, Missy invited Oursler up to the president's study for a drink. Then the president arrived and insisted on mixing the drinks. Mrs. Roosevelt was nowhere about, and in response to Oursler's inquiry the president remarked that he did not know where she was that night. Oursler was struck by the way he said it, and found it equally extraordinary that his only companion should be Missy. That evening Missy was hostess, "and she presided with a queenly dignity as a substitute for the apparently unmentionable First Lady of the Land," an evening, added Oursler, when it seemed to him that "everyone at the table wanted the President to have a good time." He was impressed with Missy's devotion. "She was young and attractive, and should have been off somewhere cool and gay on a happy weekend. Yet month after month and year after year she gave up date after date...here she sat with him knitting," keeping company with a very lonely man.[35]

Oursler again sensed the tangled relationship between Eleanor and Franklin and Missy during an overnight visit in January, 1938. It was the night of the reception for the judiciary, one of the season's more formal entertainments, and, as soon as they could, Missy and the Ourslers slipped away to have a drink upstairs. After a while Missy put in a call for the president. As she anticipated, he, too, had left the reception and was alone in his oval study. Why didn't they join him? he asked. They did and the president was in the middle of expressing his pleasure with Emil Ludwig's biography of him, which Oursler had commissioned for *Liberty,* when Eleanor, according to Oursler, came in "without any knocking." She declined an offer of beer but readily expressed herself on the Ludwig biography. It interested her because it gave a European point of view on the president, but it was inaccurate.* They moved into a discussion of public figures, and it became evident that Eleanor was partial to her Uncle Theodore. And while Franklin found this irritating, Oursler offered to publish an article by Eleanor on that theme. She would consider it, she said. Then she looked at the beer and asked, "Are my friends included in this?" and when Franklin said no, Eleanor left. The Ourslers, Missy, and the president then settled in for a long, relaxed talk. The president, in a genial mood, spoke freely about men and affairs of state that were then in the headlines, and the Ourslers found the talk exhilarating. After they bid good night to the president, Missy walked with them to their room. She, too, was exultant. "The President was never so

---

*She and Ludwig had not hit it off too well. "I understand you are the person responsible for your husband's interest in the underdog" had been Ludwig's opening remark, and she had quickly replied, "I am not." He had had a long talk with Mrs. Roosevelt, a skeptical Ludwig later told the Women's National Press Club, and found her "only too modest... she denies having influence."

frank before," she told them, and it was to her friends, Oursler noted in his journal, adding, "We feel we are part of a much darker quarrel which we can only guess about."[36]

Only rarely did Eleanor betray her feelings as she did in her thrust in front of the Ourslers about her Uncle Theodore. It was meant to gall, and Franklin's bristling response showed that it had reached home. Three days after that tension-filled episode, Oursler received a note from Eleanor, the "briefest" she had ever sent him: "I am sorry that I cannot write this article, but feel it would be in bad taste for me to do it."[37]

Eleanor's open expression of admiration for Theodore Roosevelt rankled Franklin because he was angry with most of the Oyster Bay kin, and Eleanor, too, regarded the Oyster Bay clan as the aggressors in the feud. "I am afraid Aunt Edith would not appreciate being mentioned in my column," she wrote a mutual friend who had asked her to praise Aunt Edith's "grit, hanging on despite a broken hip." "There is no love lost on that side of the family for this side of it." It was Alice who turned the knife. She infuriated Franklin at White House parties when she became the rallying center for anti-New Deal raillery and wisecracks. She was under no obligation to come to White House parties if she thought them a bore, Eleanor informed her—at Franklin's instigation, Alice thought. When James suggested to his father that Cousin Alice be appointed to a vacancy on a certain commission, "his reply, which I shall censor somewhat, was: 'I don't want anything to do with that woman!'"[38]

Eleanor, although she was more often the butt of Alice's barbs than Franklin, was more detached. She tried to keep politics from disrupting family ties, and when she was in Cincinnati for a lecture she lunched with Alice at the Longworth home. "It was strictly a family affair—we never allow politics to come between us," Alice later told the press. "I always enjoy my cousin," Eleanor wrote with an equability that must have annoyed her husband, "for while we may laugh at each other and quarrel with each other's ideas or beliefs, I rather imagine if real trouble came that we might be good allies. Fundamental Roosevelt characteristics gravitate towards each other in times of stress!" An irate Roosevelt loyalist tore this out and sent it to Eleanor along with a report of an Alice Longworth speech in which she accused Franklin of "buying his way to a third term with the W.P.A." On the margin of the clipping the gentleman had written, "so she's your dear, gravitating to you Roosevelts, cousin?"[39]

Since the death of Louis Howe, Eleanor had seen many people become White House familiars and then disappear. Each had imagined he was indispensable to the president; all were surprised at their dispensability. The president used those who suited his purposes. He made up his own mind and discarded people when they no longer fulfilled a purpose of his, she said. She could never conceive of his doing a reckless thing for a friend, except for Louis Howe. Perhaps all presidents have to be this way. Reserve is indispensable to the presidency. Yet this reserve also reflected the side of her husband that she hated. She had to have contact with people she loved; it was her way of refreshing her spirit. Franklin seemed to have no such bonds to people—not even to his children, Eleanor once said. She could never get accustomed to what she saw as his lack of real attachment to people. After Missy's stroke, Eleanor went in to Franklin on Christmas Eve to ask whether he had called her. He had not, he told her, and was not planning to do so. Eleanor could not understand that. Even Missy once confessed to Fulton Oursler that the president "was really incapable of a personal friendship with anyone."[40]

His father was a lonely man, James thought: "Of what was inside him, of what really drove him, Father talked with no one." Eleanor believed this was by choice. He never expressed regrets about the life of a public man or said that he wished things could have been different: "He lived his own life exactly as he wanted it."[41]

And while she was hurt by Missy's role and often annoyed by the procession of young women vying for the president's favor, she blamed him more than the women. And she was sorry for Missy, too, was a victim of this fascinating man's concentration upon himself and his objectives.

And at moments when his preoccupations hurt her, Eleanor told herself she did not love him, that she was simply rendering him a service of love, that she did not like to be First Lady and if it had been within her power would have lived quite differently. On her wedding anniversary in 1918 she had written Sara a letter full of thanks for the interesting and happy life Franklin had given her. In 1935 Sara mentioned this letter to her biographer, Rita Halle Kleeman, who asked Eleanor if she could see it. Eleanor was unable to find it, she said.[42] That was a measure of how differently she felt. Yet somewhere she still loved him; otherwise he would not have been able repeatedly to hurt her as he did. She loved him, for only a woman in love could have written as she did after one of his great electoral triumphs:

[undated]

The White House

Washington

Dearest Honey,

I haven't had a chance to say much to you but I want you to know
that I feel this should be a happy day because you have done much
for many people. Everyone has a happier feeling & you are doing a
grand job. Just go on thinking of others & not of yourself & I think
an undreamed of future may lie ahead for the masses of people not
only here but everywhere.

Much love

E.R.

She not only loved but respected him and believed in his leadership.
Franklin would sometimes say to his people in the White House, "My
Missus wants me to do this, and I can't." Fundamentally she accepted
his judgment of what was politically impossible because she knew that
he wanted the same things for the country that she did, and that when
he said he could not push a particular program it was not for lack of
caring but because Congress was opposed and the country unreceptive.
Sometimes in despair over public apathy she would say to him that she
wondered whether people were worth saving.

"Give people time, my dear," he would comfort her. "It takes time
to understand things. You are much too impatient and would never
make a good politician."

It was not a one-way relationship. She learned from him and
under his tutelage became one of the most accomplished politicians
of the time.

All during the White House years she would insist that whatever
praise she received for her activities as First Lady came to her because
she was the wife of the president. That was partly true humility, partly
superb tact, partly a canny woman's recognition that the public considered such deference to one's husband seemly. But it was also her
way of saying that she was doing all these things because of Franklin's
position and not because she wanted to do them. Yet after his death
she would go on with most of the public activities—the organizations,
the dinners, the benefits, the travels, the inspections—in which she
had engaged during the White House years. She would do so because
she wanted to, and she would do it better because of what she had
learned from him.

44. A GATHERING STORM

In 1932 when the National Association for the Advancement of Colored People sent questionnaires to Hoover and Roosevelt asking them to state their positions on various matters of urgent concern to Negroes, neither candidate replied personally, and if either party acknowledged the questionnaire, Walter White, the urbane but tenacious leader of the NAACP, did not consider the reply worthy of record.

He knew Eleanor Roosevelt only distantly at that time, but not long after the Roosevelts arrived in Washington word went around the Negro community that here was one person who considered them as human beings and whose sense of compassion and fairness embraced them. "I certainly believe that Mrs. Roosevelt likes colored people as her illustrious uncle did," a Harlem editor told a Negro social worker with Democratic connections, "but I don't know that her famous husband does. The mere fact that he has not made a single big appointment of any kind among colored people is my reason to believe thus." Eleanor underscored this part of the letter from Guilford N. Crawford, director of the Harlem Children's Fresh Air Fund, and sent it over to Franklin with "read" written next to it.[1]

Her efforts to bring the Negroes' plight to the attention of her husband and his cabinet colleagues—even some of the liberals among them—was a lonely enterprise. The Negro in the North, traditionally Republican, had voted for Hoover in 1932. The white South after its 1928 defection from Smith had rallied to the Roosevelt candidacy and was again solidly Democratic. Southern congressmen and senators controlled most of the committees in Congress which held the power of life or death over Roosevelt's legislative program. Even if Roosevelt were so minded, to support the legislative objectives of the Negro community meant to risk a break with his southern supporters. Nor was Roosevelt, when he first became president, driven by any commands of conscience to give such support. He had easily accommodated himself to the segregationist folkways of the South at Warm Springs, which did not admit Negroes.★ Two of his White House aides, Marvin H. McIntyre, his appointments secretary, and Stephen T. Early, his press secretary, were southerners. The president wanted to better the condition of the Negro, as of all disadvantaged groups, but he did not consider himself a second Emancipator. So Eleanor had to move warily if she was to have any influence with her husband or effectiveness in the country.

The race issue first confronted her in connection with the homesteads—whether Negroes should be admitted to Arthurdale. Negro families were among those she visited when she first went to Scotts Run. "Some of the Negroes think she is God," a local editor wrote the president afterward. She had consulted Clarence Pickett about the inclusion of Negroes in the project and he applied discreet pressure on the homesteaders to get them to do so, but they had voted it down. At Pickett's suggestion she invited a group of Negro leaders to the White House to discuss the matter. Walter White came, as did Mordecai Johnson of Howard, Robert Moton of Tuskegee, John Hope of Atlanta, and Charles Johnson of Fisk. It was, said Pickett, a memorable evening. Spurred on by Eleanor's quick and sympathetic comprehension, the Negro leaders turned the visit into a wide-ranging discussion of the general plight of their race. The talk went on until midnight, when the president was wheeled in and said a few friendly words. The whole occasion was unprecedented in Negro history. There were no decisions, but the consensus was that in the South desegregation, desirable as it was, should have a lower priority than Negro participation in the aid programs of the New Deal. As Dr. Will Alexander, a genial white southerner who was not at that meeting but who later became one of Eleanor's chief advisers on racial matters, put it:

> We had no racial doctrine, except that we were not to discriminate
> in the distribution of these benefits—the care of these people.... In
> the South we accepted the fact that Negroes usually lived in their
> own communities and so we provided projects for them—Negro
> projects. I frankly admit it. We accepted the pattern.[2]

★ "Mrs. Roosevelt?" an old-time resident of Warm Springs remarked to a *New York Times* reporter on the twenty-fifth anniversary of Roosevelt's death, "well, she was what you'd call a Negro lover, wasn't she?" (*New York Times,* April 13, 1970).

A few months later, when Eleanor addressed the Conference on Negro Education convoked by the Office of Education at the Department of the Interior, she pleaded for equal opportunity, not desegregation. By gently noting the facts, she criticized the states that spent less on the education of their Negro children than on that of their white children. In her view, "the one important thing is to see as far as possible that *every* child receives at least the best education that that child is able to assimilate." Illiteracy was the enemy of democracy, she went on, and "wherever the standard of education is low, the standard of living is low." She sent Harry Hopkins and Aubrey Williams a list of suggestions to insure full Negro participation in the emergency education program of the Federal Emergency Relief Administration. Williams, who was Harry's deputy, considered himself "a Southern rebel" and a fierce fighter for racial justice, was slightly piqued that Mrs. Roosevelt should think they needed prodding. He had an assistant send her his letter to state officials which declared that "equity demands that educational relief to Negroes be at least at the level of their percentage of the population in each state." It had already been signed before her memo was received, the accompanying note said.[3]

Eleanor knew that Harry Hopkins and Aubrey Williams were among the more courageous New Deal administrators on the race issue but she also knew the pressure they were under from the South to allocate funds in a way that would reinforce an economic structure based on Negro peonage. When Williams had gone to Mississippi during the Hoover administration to urge the establishment of minimal relief, the planters had opposed even the giving of seeds. "They did not want their 'niggers' planting gardens!" Despite Hopkins' benevolence and Williams' zeal, Walter White complained that their directives were being nullified at lower levels. Eleanor sent White's bill of particulars to Hopkins, adding, "I wonder if you will watch the colored situation quite closely and let me know from time to time how things are going for these people."[4]

An awakening Negro press wanted more. "The only way the Negro is going to get fair treatment," the Negro Press Association wrote Eleanor, "is for you to see to it that a strong, capable Negro woman is appointed to get things moving in the right direction for Negro relief." Were any important relief jobs being held by Negro women, Eleanor asked Hopkins. Did she have any suggestions, Hopkins responded. In 1927 she had met Mary McLeod Bethune, president of Bethune-Cookman College in Daytona, Florida, and they had worked together. Why not look into her qualifications?[5]

Eleanor was less successful with Frances Perkins. When the Negro Press Association urged the appointment of a Negro woman to the Women's Bureau, Eleanor asked Madam Perkins whether there was anything to the idea and if it would be possible to get one appointed. The secretary replied quite frankly that she was afraid to try it because of the prejudice against colored women. Frances Perkins "dreaded" dealing with the race problem in the South, Will Alexander said. He and Edwin Embree, the president of the Rosenwald Fund, were appalled to find that a Negro from Raleigh, North Carolina, whom Miss Perkins had employed to handle racial problems "was a white man's nigger if there ever was one."[6]

When the NAACP complained to Eleanor that some of the NRA codes being written for southern industries approved a wage differential for Negro workers, she contacted the head of the NRA, Donald Richberg, who sent her correspondence relating to the dispute. The issues were too complex for her to argue them on their merits; all she could do was submit Richberg's arguments to Walter White and forward his reply to them to Richberg, hoping that her interest would restrain officials from yielding too easily to southern demands for a wage differential based on race.

Opening another front, she inquired of Claude Swanson, secretary of the Navy and a former Virginia senator, whether it was true that Negroes were restricted to messmen jobs in the Navy? Yes, he informed her, but from 1923 to 1931 colored men had not been permitted to enlist at all.

> One of the chief reasons why the present restrictive policy exists is that in the event colored men be enlisted in a branch other than the messman branch, they would after training be subject to advancement to petty officers. In such a position they would be placed in charge of and have under them white men, all of which would result in a lack of team work, would create dissatisfaction, and would seriously handicap ship efficiency.

Eleanor decided there was nothing more she could do here and wrote the Negro editor who had complained about the policy: "These things come slowly and patience is required in all great changes."[7]

One of the most malign Depression phenomena was a resurgence of lynching; in 1933 there were twenty-eight, and twenty-four of the victims were Negroes. "I wanted to talk with you about what could be done to overcome the awful vogue for lynchings which seems to be spreading over the country," Jane Hoey, penologist and social worker, wrote Eleanor early in 1934. Had Miss Hoey noticed the meeting in Atlanta, Eleanor replied, "in which the women protested against that form of punishment? I think that the thing to do is to really try to bring to the South the feeling that the country as a whole has on the subject of lynchings."[8] But in addition to moral pressure she supported the NAACP drive for anti-lynching legislation, the NAACP's major legislative objective in Roosevelt's first administration. Walter White made few moves without keeping his new-found ally in the White House informed. The draft of the Costigan-Wagner bill and a brief by Charles H. Tuttle upholding its constitutionality awaited Eleanor on her return from Puerto Rico: "Welcome home!" White's covering letter said. She was his most reliable channel to the president, perhaps the only access he had, since he believed that McIntyre did not pass on his communications to Roosevelt. The Women's Missionary Council of the Methodist Episcopal Church South had unanimously endorsed the Costigan-Wagner anti-lynching bill, White wrote; would she pass on the news to the president? He also wanted her to know he had asked McIntyre to arrange for "a few minutes with the President." A week later White saw her at the White House, and she told him she had talked with Franklin and that he would sign the bill if it got to him, but it was his feeling that Congress might adjourn without passing many of the bills that were desirable, and he wanted an early adjournment. White sent her a tally showing 52 votes in favor of the bill and only 30 against it.

With backing from the president, the bill would pass, he felt. But two weeks after he had asked for an appointment with the president, McIntyre wired him, "Cannot arrange appointment requested at this time. President extremely busy on matters requiring immediate attention." Without presidential support, the bill stood no chance even of being debated. In desperation, White telephoned Eleanor. She wrote him about the outcome:

> The President talked to me rather at length about the lynching bill. As I do not think you will either like or agree with everything that he thinks, I would like an opportunity of telling you about it, and I would also like you to talk to the President if you feel you want to.[9]

An appointment was set up for May 7, 1934, a balmy spring Sunday. Eleanor was sitting with Sara on the south portico when White arrived at the White House, and since the president had not yet returned from an outing on the Potomac, White waited with the two women, and Eleanor used the time to brief him on some of the arguments that were being made against the bill. When the president came in he was full of good spirits and diversionary anecdotes, but finally Eleanor and White were able to get the conversation around to the anti-lynching bill. "But Joe Robinson tells me the bill is unconstitutional," Roosevelt remarked. White was ready for that one, and when this had happened several times, the president said sharply, "Somebody's been priming you. Was it my wife?" White smiled ambiguously. Franklin turned to Eleanor with the same query. She patted him affectionately and said she had to go upstairs to work on her mail.

Roosevelt then explained his difficulties with Congress. "I did not choose the tools with which I must work," he told White. "Southerners, by reason of seniority rule in Congress, are chairmen or occupy strategic places on most of the Senate and House committees. If I come out for the anti-lynching bill now, they will block every bill I ask Congress to pass to keep America from collapsing. I just can't take the risk."[10]

"I thoroughly enjoyed every minute of it and he was most generous in giving me so much time," White reported to Eleanor. "He doubtless has told you of his agreeing to a vote on the anti-lynching bill at this session of Congress but he told me frankly that he could not promise to withstand a long filibuster should one be attempted." High as White's hopes were as a result of his talk with Roosevelt and despite a favorable report by the Senate Judiciary Committee, the bill did not come up for debate on the floor because of the southern threat of a filibuster. White accompanied Senators Robert F. Wagner and Edward Costigan to the White House, and though he had come at their request, he had to wait outside while the senators conferred with Roosevelt. "Support growing but also threat of a filibuster," he informed Eleanor afterward. As the session drew to a close he again appealed to her to get some expression from the president that he favored a vote, but the endorsement she wrung from Franklin was circuitous and half-hearted: "If the sponsors of the bill will go at once to Senator Robinson and say that if, in a lull, the anti-lynching bill can be brought up for a vote, the President authorizes the sponsors to say that the President will be glad to see the bill pass and wishes it passed." When Wagner and Costigan communicated the president's message to the Senate majority leader, he did not even bother to reply, and the Senate adjourned without considering the bill. It was not on Roosevelt's "must" list and never would be.[11]

With the adjournment of Congress, Roosevelt put the bill out of his mind. Eleanor did not. When White came to visit her at Hyde Park during the summer, she took him in to say hello to the president.

In October, 1934, a particularly brutal lynching occurred. A Negro named Claude Neal was spirited out of a jail in Alabama, taken across the state line, and lynched in Marianna, Florida. The circumstances of this case were "peculiarly shocking," the Committee on Interracial Cooperation wired the White House. "Lynching advertised hours in advance, bringing together thousands of men, women and children eager to witness the spectacle. Lynching itself reported marked by unspeakable torture and mutilation. Local officers apparently indifferent throughout."

White wanted Eleanor to speak at a protest meeting at Carnegie Hall. "FDR I would like to do it," she appealed to him, "of course talking over the speech, but will do whatever you say." The answer came through Missy: "President says this is dynamite." Regretfully, Eleanor wrote White, "I do not feel it wise to speak on pending legislation but I will talk to the President and see what can be done in some other way on this." White sent her the NAACP report on its investigation of the Marianna lynching, and also relayed a newspaperman's report that the president was opposed to the Costigan-Wagner bill. Couldn't the Department of Justice act under the amended Lindbergh Kidnapping Law since Neal had been transported across the state line? "I talked with the President yesterday about your letter," Eleanor reported,

> and he said that he hoped very much to get the Costigan-Wagner bill passed in the coming season. The Marianna lynching was a horrible thing. I wish very much that the Department of Justice might come to a different point of view and I think possibly they will.[12]

Although White was heartsick over the gruesome details of the lynching at Marianna, Eleanor's description of the president's attitude lifted his spirits. But not for long. The president's State of the Union message to the new Congress, in which the Democratic majority was larger than before, made no reference to the Costigan-Wagner bill.

Deeply upset, White hastened to Eleanor. The president "wants me to say," she informed White later, "that he has talked to the leaders on the lynching question and that his sentence on crime in his address to Congress touched on that because lynching is a crime."[13]

Sentiment was running strongly against lynching, and to dramatize and deepen public feeling on the issue the NAACP arranged "An Art Commentary on Lynching." The exhibition included Reginald Marsh's "This Is Her First Lynching," a black-and-white drawing which showed a young white girl being held by her mother above the heads of a mob so the child could get a view of the lynching. There was also the famous print by the late George Bellows, "The Law Is Too Slow," showing a Negro being burned by a mob. A Thomas Benton oil portrayed a Negro being hanged from a telephone pole while lynchers replenished the fire beneath him. A "macabre exhibition," the *Times* headline said.

White wanted Eleanor to come, but the *Times* account made her uneasy that the publicity attending her visit might endanger the anti-lynching bill:

> The more I think about going to the exhibition, the more troubled I am, so this morning I went in to talk to my husband about it and asked him what they really planned to do about the bill because I was afraid that some bright newspaper reporter might write a story which would offend some of the southern members and thereby make it even more difficult to do anything about the bill.
>
> My husband said it was quite all right for me to go, but if some reporter took the occasion to describe some horrible picture, it would cause more southern opposition. They plan to bring the bill out quietly as soon as possible although two southern Senators have said they would filibuster for two weeks. He thinks, however, they can get it through.[14]

Roosevelt's hopes that the South would permit the bill to go to a vote after a *pro forma* filibuster were not realized. This time the president did support a vote making the measure the Senate's order of business after Costigan and Wagner, who were in charge of the bill, expressed in writing their readiness to have the motion temporarily laid aside for action on his "must" program, but he did not feel he could take action against the ensuing filibuster. White demanded that the president condemn the filibuster and publicly endorse the bill. He sent Eleanor an editorial from the *Des Moines Register* which savagely assailed the president's silence. Eleanor passed it on to Franklin with the comment—"Pretty bitter isn't it? I can't blame them though, it is human." On May 6 White, in protest, resigned as a member of the Virgin Islands Advisory Council, a post to which he had been appointed with Eleanor's backing.

"I am so sorry about the bill," Eleanor sought to console White. "Of course, all of us are going on fighting and the only thing we can do is to hope we have better luck next time."[15]

The president was angry with White and displeased with his wife. He did not say so directly, but a memorandum from Steve Early to Tommy no doubt reflected his views:

Personal and Confidential
MEMORANDUM FOR MRS. SCHEIDER
Dear Malvina: August 5, 1935.
I have been asked to send you a memorandum containing information for Mrs. Roosevelt concerning Walter White, Secretary, National Association for the Advancement of Colored People.

The memorandum is sent at this time because Walter White has been bombarding the President with telegrams and letters demanding passage of the Costigan-Wagner Anti-Lynching Bill before the adjournment of Congress: complaining about the War Department's policy regarding the assignment of negro reserve officers in C.C.C. camps, etc.

Walter White for some time has been writing and telegraphing the President. Frankly, some of his messages to the President have been decidedly insulting. For example, in a letter he wrote the President on May 6th when he resigned as a member of the Advisory Council for the Government of the Virgin Islands, after expressing great disappointment that the Pres. did not make a public pronouncement by means of a message to the Congress which would openly endorse the Anti-Lynching Bill, he said:

> "In justice to the cause I serve I cannot continue to remain even a small part of your official family."

His file of correspondence is voluminous.

I am advised by those familiar with White's actions at the Capitol that it was he who some time ago went into the restaurant within the Capitol Building and demanded that he be served, apparently deliberately creating a troublesome scene, compelling his eviction from the restaurant and giving rise to an issue, made much of in the press at the time. The belief in some quarters is that he did this for publicity purposes and to arouse negroes throughout the country through press accounts of his eviction from the Capitol and the refusal of Capitol authorities to permit him to eat in the restaurant there.

Mr. Forster advises that Walter White, before President Roosevelt came to the White House, because of his activities, has been one of the worst and most continuous of troublemakers.

Stephen Early

Eleanor, who was in Campobello, immediately wrote Early in defense of White:

I realize perfectly that he has an obsession on the lynching question and I do not doubt that he has been a great nuisance with his telegrams and letters, both now and in previous administrations. However, reading the papers in the last few weeks, does not give you the feeling that the filibuster on the lynching bill did any good to the situation and if I were colored, I think I should have about the same obsession that he has.

I do not think he means to be rude or insulting. It is the same complex which a great many people belonging to minority groups have, particularly martyrs. The type of thing which would make him get himself arrested in the Senate Restaurant is probably an inferiority complex which he tries to combat and which makes him far more aggressive than if he felt equality. It is worse with Walter White because he is almost white. If you ever talked to him, and knew him, I think you would feel as I do. He really is a very fine person with the sorrows of his people close to his heart.

E. R.[16]

She realized that her racial beliefs upset Early and McIntyre. "They were afraid," she later wrote, "that I would hurt my husband politically and socially. . . . There was no use in my trying to explain, because our basic values were very different, and since I was fond of them, I thought it better to preserve the amenities in our daily contacts."[17] By and large it was true that Roosevelt did not attempt to rein her in and that the activities she carried on in the field of welfare and race were with his knowledge and agreement. But there were times when her persistence annoyed him, and this, to judge by Early's memorandum, was one of them.

Early's hostility toward Negroes and Roosevelt's concern to protect his southern political flank were demonstrated again in September when Eleanor had Tommy submit a request from a Negro reporter to be allowed to attend her press conferences. She should not answer it, Early advised Tommy: "I have taken care of the Negro requests for the President's press conferences and if Mrs. Roosevelt opens hers it just makes the President more vulnerable. I think it is far the best thing to ignore the letter." Eleanor complied. Inside the White House she prodded, argued, and appealed to Franklin's better nature, but when he laid down the law, she generally let the matter rest there.[18]

Not always. If the purpose of the Early memorandum was to reduce White's access to the White House, she declined to understand it as such. But she was circumspect. She knew her activities were being exploited in the South by the extremists and demagogues. As early as August, 1934, Barry Bingham, whose father was president-publisher of the *Courier-Journal* in Louisville and Roosevelt's ambassador to Great Britain, wrote to McIntyre of one of the rumors that was afloat about the First Lady.

> The old propaganda story is being passed around in Louisville to the effect that Mrs. Roosevelt has made herself offensive to Southerners by a too great affection for Negroes. The tale is that she was visiting in South Carolina recently, and was scheduled to make a speech in one of the larger towns. She is said to have ridden to the auditorium, through the streets of the town, in an open car in which she sat next to a Negro woman, with whom she conversed sociably all the way.

Bingham thought the story was a fake, and it would give him "a good deal of satisfaction to know if I am right in saying that not only did such an incident not occur, but that Mrs. Roosevelt has not visited South Carolina in recent months." McIntyre passed the letter on to Eleanor. It was a hoax, she informed him; she had been to North, not South, Carolina in July, had made no speeches, and had driven into town in her own car accompanied only by Marion Dickerman and Nancy Cook and out the same way. "I am very much interested in the Negroes and in their betterment," her letter to Bingham said, but the tale that I was scheduled to speak somewhere and drove through the streets of a town with a negro woman beside me, happens to be untrue but I would, however, not have a single objection to doing so if I found myself in a position where it had to be done, but I probably would not do it in North Carolina.[19]

What had been a false rumor in 1934 took photographic form in 1935. Molly Dewson brought Eleanor a copy of the *Georgia Woman's World,* a racist sheet whose back page was given over to a photograph of Eleanor offering a flower to a tiny Negro child. The caption under the photograph quoted New York Representative Joseph A. Gavagan, House sponsor of the anti-lynching bill: "It has been increasingly evident that President Roosevelt, unlike his predecessor, as well as Mrs. Roosevelt, have drawn no color line at the White House."

"Who do you suppose is financing it?" Molly wanted to know. Eleanor thought it was Governor Talmadge. "I am afraid there is nothing much we can do," she noted. A later issue of the same paper had a two-column photograph of Eleanor being escorted to her car by a Negro in uniform. The photographs showing her in the company of Negroes, Eleanor calmly told her press conference, were taken with her permission, the last during a visit to Howard University, and the one with the Negro child at a slum-clearance project in Detroit. She did not object to their distribution. He was moved to tell her, Felix Frankfurter wrote from Cambridge, of the pride that he felt as a citizen

that the First Lady of the nation should deal with such a prickly problem in such a simple, straightforward, humane way as you did. I know it's the very law of your being so to act—and that makes it all the more a source of pride for the Nation. "They know not what they do," these racebaiters and exploiters of unreason. And you render deep service to the enduring values of civilization by serving the nation as a historic example of simple humanity and true human brotherhood in the highest places.[20]

Eleanor never wanted to offend anyone, even prejudiced whites, but she thought it more important to give Negroes the feeling that they were not alone. What did she want her to do, she wrote a woman who had protested her feeding a Negro girl at a Hyde Park picnic. "Surely you would not have refused to let her eat with the other representatives? . . . I believe it never hurts to be kind. Eating with someone does not mean you believe in intermarriage." She refused to be cowed by the bigots.[21]

What she did as a matter of heart and moral courage turned out to be astute politics, although that had not been her motivation. Republican hopes to split the South by exploiting the racial issue went unfulfilled. It again voted solidly Democratic despite efforts to portray the Roosevelts as "nigger lovers." And in the northern Negro precincts the same photographs that had been circulated in the South as anti-Roosevelt propaganda contributed to an historic shift in Negro voting allegiance from the party of Lincoln to the party of the Roosevelts.

But gratitude was matched by growing expectations. More perhaps than anyone else in the administration, Eleanor was cognizant of the explosive stuff that lay beneath the surface of Negro patience and bland affability.

New Dealers who had solutions for almost every social problem shied away from the color issue because they were themselves infected with prejudice. Henry Wallace was typical. Though he was the author of a splendidly forward-looking book, *Whose Constitution?*, the racial issue left him ill at ease. Will Alexander, whom Wallace had chosen to run the Farm Security Administration, found him "terribly afraid" of it—he "just wouldn't stand up to it," and "he was always afraid of Mrs. Roosevelt." Eleanor, on her side, felt that Wallace lacked sympathy and understanding of the problems of the American Negro, and she knew that he resented efforts to prod the Department of Agriculture to take a more positive approach to the Negro farmers' needs.[22]

Of all the members of the cabinet, Ickes, who had been president of the Chicago chapter of the NAACP, was the most stalwart on the Negro issue. In the early days of the New Deal, Will Alexander and Edwin Embree had persuaded the White House to agree that someone be appointed to see that Negroes were treated fairly. Ickes had named Clark Foreman, one of Dr. Alexander's aides whom Alexander described as a young man "of very great charm" but "very impetuous," as adviser to the secretary on the economic status of Negroes, his salary to be paid by the Rosenwald Fund. Foreman's assistant was Robert Weaver, the first Negro to obtain a Ph.D. in economics from Harvard. While Ickes was at times as distrustful of Eleanor's judgment as Wallace, on the racial issue they were allies. Unlike Early, Ickes did not resent it when Negroes like White militantly forced an issue such as eating in the Capitol restaurant. He "took the hides off people who turned away Negroes from the Interior restaurant," Alexander said. "You didn't dare take a Negro to lunch at Agriculture."[23]

Unless men like White had forced the issue, most of official Washington would have shut its eyes to discrimination hoping it would not rise up to confront them in a way that compelled a choice between conscience and expediency. They justified their noninvolvement by focusing on the substantial gains Negroes had made under the New Deal rather than on the injustice and degradation that still remained.

Eleanor refused to be insulated and shielded from a problem. The more perilous it was politically, the more twisted its roots in history, custom, and law, the more urgent that it be ferreted out, confronted, and dealt with. She received Negro sharecroppers in the White House and visited them in their tarpaper shacks in the cotton fields, and with kindly questions persuaded them to talk about themselves and their needs. After seeing Shaw's *Saint Joan,* she remarked on the remorse of the priest in the last scene,

> when with his own eyes he saw the suffering he had caused. "I did not know until I saw" is something which every human should recognize as being as true today as it was when people were tortured and burned at the stake. Only by seeing can we save ourselves the same kind of remorse that haunted the wicked, self-satisfied old priest.[24]

This was what the Negro wanted—that he be *seen* and recognized as an individual and accepted in the fullness of a humanity that he shared with the whites—and this was what the First Lady understood.

It represented for her an immense inner journey. "I quite understand the southern point of view," she replied to critics from that region, "because my grandmother was a Southerner from Georgia and her sister had a great deal to do with bringing us up when we were small children, therefore, I am familiar with the old plantation life."[25] Eleanor had absorbed the southern point of view along with her first lessons in reading from her Great-aunt Annie Gracie, who had held the children spellbound not only with her Br'er Rabbit stories but with her description of the personal slaves that she and Grandmother Roosevelt had been given on the Bulloch plantation, slaves who had slept at the foot of their beds and accompanied and served them wherever they went. Eleanor still called the Civil War the War between the States because "those who lose are apt to be more sensitive" than those who win, and while Walter White had sent her Dr. W.E.B. Du Bois' *Black Reconstruction,* praising it as a different way of looking at the Reconstruction period in American history, she was more influenced by *Gone with the Wind,* which she sat up several nights reading. The most interesting part for her was "the Reconstruction period. It is so easy to understand why the women of the South kept their bitterness toward their northern invaders." She still used terms like "pickaninny" and "darky"; a Tuskegee graduate reading the magazine installments of Eleanor's autobiography "couldn't believe [her] eyes" when she came across the "hated" and "humiliating" term "darky," and it was more hurtful because Mrs. Roosevelt, whom she considered "the paragon of American womanhood," had used it. A little bit on the defensive, Eleanor explained: "'Darky' was used by my Georgia great aunt as a term of affection and I have always considered it in that light. I am sorry if it hurt you. What do you prefer?"[26]

Eleanor admired Walter White, who with his blue eyes, fair skin, and blond hair could have escaped his Negro heritage had he chosen to do so. When White came to Hyde Park, she urged him to bring his wife and sister. She liked to talk things over with him—he clarified situations for her and helped her to see them more objectively. In his moments of deepest despair, White later wrote, when he was ready to give up on the white race, the thought of Mrs. Roosevelt was one of the few things that kept him from hating all white people.[27]

Mary McLeod Bethune was another Negro who became a friend as well as co-worker. "She's real black," a Negro policeman said, "she's black as a black shoe." Unlike Walter White, who was born into the Negro middle class, Mrs. Bethune was the fifteenth of seventeen children, some of whom had been sold in slavery, and she came from the rural South. Her mother was a matriarchal figure who sent her to be trained as a teaching missionary. Her heart's pride was Bethune-Cookman College, which she developed from a few adult classes and which was the center of her life until Aubrey Williams brought her to Washington to direct the NYA's Division of Negro Affairs. She had "the most marvelous gift of affecting feminine helplessness in order to attain her ends with masculine ruthlessness," a male colleague said admiringly. She was a great lady, but without Eleanor's support she could have accomplished little. Mrs. Bethune never came to see Eleanor without a long budget of requests—Negroes to be appointed, a conference to speak at, a Negro housing project to be financed, and, as a footnote, something that she wanted Mrs. Roosevelt to do for Bethune-Cookman College. She had to check into the hospital for two months, Mrs. Bethune informed Eleanor, first to lose thirty pounds, then to be operated on. "I realize how much the inactivity will irk you," Eleanor responded sympathetically, and she instructed the White House gardener to send flowers with her card once a week for two months to Mrs. Bethune at the Johns Hopkins Hospital. A personal experience with Mrs. Bethune taught her how deeply inbred racial feelings were among whites. She liked to kiss people whom she knew well when greeting them and when saying good-by, but it took some time and a conscious effort for Eleanor to give Mrs. Bethune a peck on the cheek, and it was not until she kissed Mrs. Bethune without thinking of it that she felt she had at last overcome the racial prejudice within herself.[28]

To Mary Bethune and Walter White, old fighters for their race who had learned to walk warily in the world of the white man, it was new and bracing to have someone else as close to the seat of power as the First Lady thinking of them, worrying about them as individuals. It made the world a friendlier place. But they were veterans who knew when to advance and when to retreat, how to swallow a humiliation with a smile and how to bide their time. A new, more rebellious generation was growing up to whom the dominant fact was not what the New Deal had done for the Negro but what the white race had done to the Negro.

"You do not remember me, but I was the girl who did not stand up when you passed through the Social Hall of Camp TERA during one of your visits in the winter of 1934—," wrote Pauli Murray, a WPA teacher, enclosing for Eleanor's attention an angry, defiant letter she had just sent the president: "I am a Negro, the most oppressed, most misunderstood and most neglected section of your population.... My grandfather, a Union Army soldier, gave his eye for the liberation of his race. As soon as the war was over, he went to North Carolina under the Freedmen's Bureau to establish schools and educate the newly freed Negroes." Although from that time on Miss Murray's entire family had been involved in educational work in North Carolina, she could not get into the University of North Carolina, which on its application asked for the "Race and Religion" of the applicant. The president had spoken the day before at Chapel Hill, hailing the university as a center of liberal thought and calling on Americans, especially the young people, to support a liberal philosophy based on democracy. "What does this mean for Negro-Americans?" Miss Murray demanded.

Does it mean that we, at last, may participate freely, and on the basis of equality, with our fellow citizens in working out the problems of this democracy? Does it mean that Negro students in the South will be allowed to sit down with white students and study a problem which is fundamental and mutual to both groups? Does it mean that University of North Carolina is ready to open its doors to Negro students . . . ? Or does it mean that everything you said has no meaning for us as Negroes, that we are again to be set aside and passed over for more important problems?

Prophetically, the letter closed, "Do you feel, as we do, that the ultimate test of democracy in the United States will be the way in which it solves its Negro problem?"

The letter stirred Eleanor deeply: "I have read the copy of the letter you sent me," she wrote Miss Murray.

and I understand perfectly, but great changes come slowly. I think they are coming, however, and sometimes it is better to fight hard with conciliatory methods. The South is changing, but don't push too hard. There is a great change in youth, for instance, and that is a hopeful sign.[29]

She was attracted to people, especially young people, who showed fight and indignation, and she encouraged Pauli Murray to write regularly and invited her to Hyde Park. When Miss Murray became secretary of National Sharecroppers Week, Eleanor spoke at the dinner. Eleanor also backed her in her decision to go to law school, and, as in the case of Mrs. Bethune, watched over her when she became ill.

Pauli Murray helped her understand the mood of Negro youth. So did Richard Wright. Because Wright was "a product of the WPA writers' enterprise," his publisher, Harper's, sent her *Uncle Tom's Children,* his first collection of stories. "It is beautifully written," Eleanor wrote the publisher, "and so vivid that I had a most unhappy time reading it." In all four stories a mob goes to work, and Wright showed with great graphic power that violence was the way civilization kept the Negro in his place. Wright thanked her for the help she had given him in bringing his book to public attention, adding, "I am at present engaged upon a long novel dealing with Negro juvenile delinquency, with Chicago's Southside as the background and locale." He was applying for a Guggenheim grant in order to finish it, and asked if he could use her name as reference. "Certainly," she replied. If the racial problem was to be dealt with it had to be understood, and Wright's vivid writing helped the white community to understand what it had done to the Negro people.[30]

"It is true," she wrote a woman in Philadelphia who complained that Negroes were ruining the neighborhood,

> that it may take years to educate the great mass of colored people to be good in desirable neighborhoods; but we are largely to blame. We brought them here as slaves and we have never given them equal chances for education, even after we emancipated them. They must be given the opportunity to become the kind of people that they should, and I often marvel that they are as good as they are in view of the treatment which they have received.... You are suffering from a difficult situation and it is always hard on the individuals who reap the results of generations of wrong doing.[31]

She refused to allow Negro "backwardness" to become a pretext for denying the Negro equality of treatment, but with Negro audiences she was equally firm in urging them not to permit white injustice to keep them from helping themselves and from putting forward their best efforts. Anyone in a minority group, she told Hampton Institute students,

> has to strive to do a better job, not just for himself as an individual, but because it is going to help the whole group that he belongs to and because it is going to have an effect on what all the others are going to be able to do. Every time we fail, every time we do not do our best, we don't just let ourselves down, we let down all the others that we might help if we did our best and if we did succeed.[32]

In February, 1936, Eleanor invited Marian Anderson, the Negro contralto, to sing at the White House. Thirty-three years later Miss Anderson, a woman of imposing majesty who had a voice that even in speech still enthralled her listeners, recalled the warmth and friendliness of the president and Mrs. Roosevelt that evening.[33] She might perform in the White House but in 1939 when Howard University approached the Daughters of the American Revolution to arrange for the use of Constitution Hall, the one auditorium in Washington large enough to hold the capacity audience that was expected to come out to hear Miss Anderson, the DAR refused and its president said that no Negro artist would be permitted to appear there.

People were aghast and Miss Anderson's fellow-musicians were outraged, but what turned a local episode of bigotry into a world-wide *cause célèbre* was Eleanor Roosevelt's decision to resign from the DAR. She did not reach it lightly. She was never sure resignations were effective. When Elinor Morgenthau had been excluded from the Colony Club because she was Jewish, Eleanor had quietly quit that group, but insisted she did so because she was no longer in New York City enough to make use of the club's facilities. An abrasive staged resignation over anti-Semitism, she felt, would have confirmed the ladies in their prejudice rather than softened hearts. But the DAR's ban on Negroes was a public matter from the very beginning; its openly proclaimed lily-white policy, if not challenged, was likely to set back the evolution of a more decent attitude in white America and further deepen the sense of estrangement of Negro America.

A few weeks earlier she had attended the founding meeting in Birmingham of the Southern Conference on Human Welfare, an organization which had the support of the CIO and southern New Dealers. There were a large number of Negro delegates, and the Birmingham city authorities insisted that the town's segregation ordinance be complied with or the conference would not be allowed to proceed. The delegates decided to go ahead with the meeting rather than disband, but Eleanor, coming in with Mrs. Bethune, refused to observe the segregation order. The police told her she was violating the law, so she had her chair placed in the center aisle, which the police had insisted must separate the white from the Negro delegates. Her action electrified black America. A National Conference of Negro Youth, the most restless, impatient group in the Negro community, had little affirmative to say about Washington's policies, but it enthusiastically passed a resolution thanking her for her moral courage in Birmingham.[34]

The DAR's defense of racism posed the same public challenge that Birmingham's enforcement of its segregation ordinance had. Eleanor talked with Walter White and others about whether she should resign, and finally she reached her decision. "I have been debating in my mind for some time a question which I have had to debate with myself once or twice before in my life," she wrote in her column:

The question is, if you belong to an organization and disapprove of an action which is typical of a policy, shall you resign or is it better to work for a changed point of view within the organization? In the past when I was able to work actively in any organization to which I belonged, I have usually stayed in until I had at least made a fight and been defeated. Even then I have as a rule accepted my defeat and decided either that I was wrong or that I was perhaps a little too far ahead of the thinking of the majority of that time. I have often found that the thing in which I was interested was done some years later. But, in this case I belong to an organization in which I can do no active work. They have taken an action which has been widely talked of in the press. To remain as a member implies approval of that action, and therefore I am resigning.[35]

Her resignation, said Walter White, "focused world-wide attention on the episode." It touched an awakening white conscience, and both conservative and middle-ground citizens approved. "I want you to know how proud I was of you the other day," Cousin Corinne Alsop, a staunch Republican and anti-New Dealer, wrote Eleanor from Avon; "you are the first lady of the land in your own right!" Dr. Peabody, the aging but still alert rector of Groton, found the action of the DAR "in line with the prejudice, I might say cruelty, with which we have dealt with the negro people. Your courage in taking this definite stand called for my admiration."[36]

There were dissenting voices, but a poll published March 19 by the American Institute of Public Opinion, Dr. George Gallup's organization, showed that 67 per cent of those polled approved of Mrs. Roosevelt's resignation, while 33 per cent opposed. In the blaze of public attention generated by Eleanor's act, Walter White and Marian Anderson's manager, Sol Hurok, came up with the idea of a free, open-air concert by Miss Anderson at the Lincoln Memorial. White went to Washington to speak to Oscar Chapman, the assistant secretary of the Interior, who, although Virginia-born, immediately rallied to the idea* and took it in to Ickes, who, "equally excited," hurried to the

---

*Chapman's version differs slightly from White's.[37] The Negro leader proposed that Miss Anderson sing in Lafayette Park, and when Chapman said the park did not lend itself to a concert, White asked, "What can you do?" Had he given any thought to the effect it might have "if we used Lincoln Memorial on Easter?"

"Oh, my God," White responded with fervor. "If we could have her sing at the feet of Lincoln!"

White House to catch the president before he left for Warm Springs to ask for his approval, which was given. A sponsoring committee was set up with Mrs. Caroline O'Day, the Georgia-born New York congresswoman-at-large, as chairman because White felt that Mrs. Roosevelt should not further expose herself "since reactionaries in the South were already pillorying her for her attitude on the Negro."

The concert took place on a Sunday afternoon. Ickes, who presided, estimated there were 75,000 people massed at the base of the memorial and extending up the Mall toward the Washington Monument, a majority of them Negro. The singer was almost overcome by the vastness of the crowd. Silencing the ovation with a slight wave of her hand, she began her recital. "America" was her opening number, and the liberty-breathing lines poured from her as if they were "a prayer." She ended with "Nobody Knows the Trouble I've Seen," a gentle lamentation that stirred its hushed audience to its roots. "I have never heard such a voice," Ickes wrote in his diary; "the whole setting was unique, majestic, and impressive."[38]

Eleanor thought it wise not to attend. "Thanks in large measure to you," Walter White reported to her, "the Marian Anderson concert on Sunday was one of the most thrilling experiences of our time. Only one thing marred it—that you couldn't be there. But I understand thoroughly the reason you could not come."[39] A new anxiety had arisen. Youthful members of the NAACP planned to picket the DAR during their annual conference in Washington, and Eleanor appealed to White to see if there were anything he could do to prevent it:

> In the first place Washington is a city where one could have serious trouble and I think it would not do any good to picket the D.A.R. It would only create bad feeling all the way around. At present the D.A.R. Society is condemned for the stand it took and if picketing is done it may result in the sympathy swinging to the other side.

Chapman said he would check into the legal position. He called in Felix S. Cohen, assistant to the solicitor, a brilliant lawyer. What would be the legal obstacles if the secretary should allow Marian Anderson to sing at the Lincoln Memorial?

"I haven't briefed it, but I would gamble my reputation that there is nothing that stands in your way except courage."

"That's all I want to know. I'm going to see the Secretary. Do a little briefing in case we run into trouble from the Park Service."

He had used almost identical language, White assured her, in urging that the plan be abandoned, and he had talked with board members of the NAACP and they agreed. The plan was abandoned.[40]

The Marian Anderson concert had important political consequences. Ickes dwelt on them in his diary, noting that up to the last, "no word was received from Garner, Farley, or Henry Wallace to the invitations sent to them to permit their names to be used as sponsors." But it was Garner, a leading conservative candidate to succeed Roosevelt, "who really got hurt," and when a furious Garner and his friends sought to spread the word that the vice president had never received a telegraph of invitation to be a sponsor, Roosevelt outlined to Ickes what he ought to tell Pearson and Allen "in order to nail down the story. . . . There was no doubt," wrote Ickes, that the president "enjoyed the tight hole in which the Vice President found himself. Here he is, a vigorous candidate for President, putting himself in a position of offending the Negro vote everywhere, although in several Northern states the Negro vote is likely to be the decisive vote in 1940."[41]

The politics of the racial issue interested Eleanor because she understood to what extent political considerations moved the men who held the power of decision in Washington. When Walter White invited the president to make a radio speech at the NAACP national conference to be held in June, 1940, a few weeks before the Democratic convention, Eleanor forwarded the invitation to the president, with the note, "It is a great chance to say some wise things to the Negro & to the rest of the nation!" The president declined the invitation, but Eleanor accepted the one extended to her.

Even as she counseled her young Negro friends to exercise patience, Eleanor sensed and sympathized with their bitterness and resentment. Addressing a meeting of the National Negro Congress to commemorate the signing of the Emancipation Proclamation, she called upon America to finish the job Lincoln had begun seventy-five years ago. She would not be silent, even in a campaign year, although some New Dealers were worried about a white backlash. When Will Alexander left the Farm Security Administration in June, 1940, to become vice president of the Rosenwald Fund, he went in to say good-by to his boss, Henry Wallace, who looked up and said, "Will, don't you think the New Deal is undertaking to do too much for the Negro?"[42]

Roosevelt, too, was restive under Negro pressure. A letter that was drafted for his signature on the occasion of the anniversary of Walter

White's twenty-five years of service to the Negro people was sent back with the memo, "Miss Tully brought this in. Says the President doesn't think too much of this organization—not to be too fulsome—tone it down a bit."[43]

The collapse of France in the spring of 1940 launched the country upon a vast preparedness effort and placed at the head of the Negro community's agenda the Negro's role in the defense effort. Between Wendell Willkie and Roosevelt, Negro leaders were going to drive as hard a bargain as they could with the administration in return for Negro support. Eleanor was the channel through which the Negroes maintained their pressure on the president, and because she was effective in gaining consideration of Negro demands, she was also instrumental in keeping the Negro vote Democratic.

Early in July Mrs. Bethune came to Eleanor with a bundle of papers citing chapter and verse on discrimination against Negroes in the armed forces, and the covering memorandum said there was "grave apprehension among Negroes lest the existing inadequate representation and training of colored persons in the armed forces may lead to the creation of labor battalions and other forms of discrimination against them in the event of war." Mrs. Bethune urged that the newly appointed secretary of war, Henry L. Stimson, name an outstanding Negro as his aide to insure fair treatment of Negroes in the armed services. A few days later Pa Watson called Mrs. Bethune, and, on the basis of a directive he had received from General Marshall's office, informed her that as part of the increase in the Regular Army there were to be several new Negro units.[44]

The Negro leadership bristled at this response. Walter White, accompanied by Aubrey Williams, hurried to Hyde Park to see Eleanor. They left with her a letter Thurgood Marshall had sent Stimson which listed the services that excluded Negroes and warned that when conscription was enacted, Negroes who were refused the right to serve in all branches would prefer to go to jail.

Eleanor turned this material over to the president, who asked his staff to remind him to take it with him to the cabinet meeting on August 16 and speak to the secretaries of war and Navy about the matter. Four days later Stimson wrote the president:

If selective service is approved, colored personnel will be inducted and trained in the Army of the United States in the ratio the available negro manpower bears the available white manpower. This personnel will be allotted to all arms and services except the Air Corps and the Signal Corps generally in proportion to the strength of those arms and services. With respect to aviation, there has been no development of colored personnel in this field. Therefore the War Department arranged with the Civil Aeronautics Administration to make a beginning by starting an aviation school at Glenview, Ill.[45]

Roosevelt sent a copy of Stimson's letter to his wife "for your information," and she sent it on to Walter White. But the Negro agenda was broader. James B. Nabrit, Jr., of Howard University wrote to Eleanor.[46] "As has usually been the case for the past seven years, whenever Negroes are unduly disturbed they have turned to you," he began, and asked that Negroes be included in every level of the selective-service machinery. "I think this should undoubtedly be done," Eleanor wrote in a follow-up memo to her husband, "and you should insist that in every locality where there is an appreciable percentage of Negroes, there should be one Negro at least on the draft board or on an advisory committee." Roosevelt's reply was not wholly responsive: "We have just put a Negro on Fred Osborn's Board," he informed her.[47] Meanwhile the requests of the Negro leadership for a cabinet-level meeting on integration in the armed services had not been granted. Eleanor sent her husband a pointed reminder:

I have just heard that no meeting was ever held between colored leaders like Walter White, Mr. Hill and Mr. Randolph, with the Secretary of War and Navy on the subject of how the colored people can participate in the services.

There is a growing feeling amongst the colored people, and they are creating a feeling among many white people. They feel they should be allowed to participate in any training that is going on, in the aviation, army, navy and have opportunities for service.

I would suggest that a conference be held with the attitude of the gentlemen: these are our difficulties, how do you suggest that we make a beginning to change the situation?

There is no use going into a conference unless they have the intention of doing something. This is going to be very bad politically, beside being [wrong] intrinsically, and I think you should ask that a meeting be held and if you can not be present yourself, you should ask them to give you a report and it might be well to have General Watson present.[48]

The conference took place on September 27. The president participated, as did Secretary of the Navy Frank Knox and Assistant Secretary of War Robert M. Patterson.

White's account of the conference, which he sent Eleanor a few days later when he thanked her for arranging it, reflected satisfaction that progress had been made with regard to the inclusion of Negroes in all branches of the Army and an increase in the number of Negro officers, although he regretted that nothing had been said about West Point, nor had any one "even thought of" nonsegregated units in the Army. Colonel Knox's rationalizations of why the Navy could do little were wholly unsatisfactory, he added, but the group was pleased with the president's sympathetic attitude, and it had left a memorandum with him embodying the Negro requests.[49]

In his diary Stimson gave an account of the meeting which White and his colleagues would have found extremely depressing.[50] Roosevelt had asked Stimson to come to the White House to answer what should be done

> to satisfy the Negro politicians who are trying to get the army committed to colored officers and various other things which they ought not to do and I sent Judge Patterson to this meeting because I really had so much else to do that I couldn't take it in. According to him it was a rather amusing affair—The President's gymnastics as to politics. I saw the same thing happen twenty-three years ago when Woodrow Wilson yielded to the same sort of demand and appointed colored officers to several of the Divisions that went over to France, and the poor fellows made perfect fools of themselves and one at least of the Divisions behaved very badly. The others were turned into labor battalions.

Although the president promised to get in touch with the Negro group again, several days passed and there was no word or action from the White House. And when it was finally issued, the White House statement boomeranged. The Negro leadership and press, instead of focusing on the allocation of Negroes to all branches of the armed services, interpreted it as a continuation of the traditional policy of segregation, and salt was added to the wound with the provision that, except for three already established Negro regiments, Negro units would be officered by whites. What particularly outraged the Negro leaders who had participated in the meeting with Roosevelt was a suggestion in the White House release that they had approved the policy of segregation. This not only was false but brought them under fire from their own groups. They demanded that Early issue a retraction. White appealed again to Eleanor, who talked with the president. Early finally wrote White expressing regret that the words he had used had embarrassed the Negro leaders.[51]

As the 1940 presidential campaign drew to an end and Willkie seemed to be gaining, the Democratic leaders grew touchy, particularly on the race issue. They were worried about the Negro vote and they were equally anxious not to do anything for the Negro that might further offend the white South. When Eleanor invited Mrs. Bethune's National Council of Negro Women to hold one of its convention sessions in the White House, Elinor Morgenthau received an anguished letter from, oddly enough, the Colored Division of the Democratic National Committee stating that "it would be well for Mrs. Roosevelt not to have contacts during these weeks before election, with colored groups in Washington which would be given widespread newspaper publicity.... It is neither politically necessary nor wise for a group of colored women to appear at the White House at this time." Eleanor addressed her reply to Oscar Ewing, Ed Flynn's deputy at Democratic headquarters, stating that the invitation was "a courtesy which had been extended to any number of women's groups and other groups, where the subject was one of interest to me or to the President. To withdraw that permission would seem to be a great discourtesy which would certainly not redound to anyone's credit."[52]

If the Colored Division was worried about offending the South, Harry Hopkins was more concerned with the Negro vote in the North, and he summoned Will Alexander to the White House to discuss Negro coolness toward Roosevelt. Ushers rushed him up to a bedroom where Hopkins sat astride a canopied bed cradling two telephones on which he was carrying on long-distance conversations. "Will, this fellow Willkie is about to beat the Boss, and we damn well better do something about it," Hopkins began, and then recited his worries over the Catholic vote now that George William Cardinal Mundelein was dead and his fear of the impact John L. Lewis's impending speech would have on the labor vote. Finally he came to the point: "The President has done more for the Negroes in this country than anybody ever did since Abraham Lincoln, and you can't get a word out of any of them. It looks as though they are all going to go against him.... If you can, tell me what to do."[53]

Alexander knew from Walter White, as did Eleanor and Franklin Jr., who had been reporting the same demands from Democratic headquarters in New York City, what Negroes wanted at this point. They wanted Colonel Benjamin O. Davis, who had been passed over on the promotion lists, made a brigadier general and they wanted Judge William Hastie appointed as civilian aide to Secretary Stimson. Alexander so advised Hopkins, and it was done. "Are you crazy appointing a nigger as General in the United States Army," one indignant telegram to the White House read.

But the agonizing over the Negro vote was not over. On a campaign trip to New York City with Roosevelt, Early, a quick-tempered southerner, kneed a Negro policeman assigned to guard the president when the officer refused to permit Early to cross a police line. The Republican press leaped happily upon the incident and blew it up to enormous proportions. Eleanor was besieged with phone calls about the need to repair the damage and the distressing effect it would have on the campaign. "It certainly was distressing," she commented, "but not only from the campaign angle." But she was loyal, and while she deplored his loss of temper, she assured Early's critics that "he would have behaved in exactly the same way, no matter who the person was. He has a hot temper."[54]

The Negro leaders knew that they had made significant gains and that their best hopes for the future lay in Roosevelt's reelection. "We must not let our indignation against the act of an individual rob us of cool judgment," White said in a statement to the Negro press. And on the Monday before election he sent Eleanor a note: "Please forgive me for imposing upon you so much. But I would be grateful if you would give the President the enclosed personal note of thanks for what he did in the matter of integration of Negroes in the armed forces of the United States." And to the president he wrote, "I want to send you this personal word of thanks for all you did to insure a square deal for Negroes in the defense of our country. We have worked night and day during recent weeks to take personally to the people the things you did and wrote. I am certain tomorrow will reveal that Negroes know the truth." He was right. An analysis of fifteen Negro wards in nine northern cities showed that Roosevelt had captured four in 1932, nine in 1936, and fourteen in 1940.[55]

Roosevelt was a friend of the Negro, said Roy Wilkins, assistant to Walter White, "only insofar as he refused to exclude the Negro from his general policies that applied to the whole country.... The personal touch and the personal fight against discrimination were Mrs. Roosevelt's. That attached to Roosevelt also—he couldn't hardly get away from it—and he reaped the political benefit from it."[56]

With Roosevelt's third term, Eleanor made a quantum jump in her thinking about the racial issue. Although at the beginning of the New Deal she had subordinated desegregation to equality of opportunity and benefits, her approach had now changed. "I have long felt," she wrote in 1941,

> that many of the things which we deplore, the prevalence of tuber-culosis, the mounting record of crime in certain sections of the country, are not due just to lack of education and to physical dif-ferences, but are due in great part to the basic fact of segregation which we have set up in this country and which warps and twists the lives not only of our Negro population, but sometimes of for-eign born or even of religious groups.[57]

At the top of Roosevelt's agenda at the beginning of his third term was aid to an embattled Britain. At the top of the black agenda was discrimination against Negroes in the armed services and the defense industries. Stimson was unhappy over Eleanor's support of the Negro campaign; he blamed a new drive for Negro officers on her, and in his diary scored "Mrs. Roosevelt's intrusive and impulsive folly," recall-ing that she had previously stirred up trouble many times on the race question.[58]

Walter White and Aubrey Williams complained to Eleanor about the failure of Sidney Hillman, head of the Labor Division of the Office of Production Management, to do more about the exclusion of Negroes from defense industries. Using a letter from the Washington Youth Council as a peg, Eleanor had a secretary write Hillman quot-ing the youth group to the effect that "discrimination against Negro youth in Washington has become more serious than ever with the restrictions that now exist against them in the defense program's activ-ities." Mrs. Roosevelt wanted to know whether such discrimination did in fact exist, the secretary wrote.[59] Of course, Eleanor already knew the answer; Aubrey Williams, for one, had told her. The NYA was training young workers for defense jobs, many of them Negroes, but no matter how good the Negroes were, Williams said, they were not being hired. Labor was as bad as management on this, he added. If Eleanor now wrote Hillman innocently asking for information in order to answer the Washington Youth Council, it was her way of moving into a situation where she knew she had no authority in her own right and where the president was not yet ready to act. It took Hillman eighteen days to reply, and his letter was filled with generalities. Eleanor was not impressed, but using his letter as an entering wedge, she invited the officials concerned with training, defense production, and the awarding of defense contracts to lunch at the White House. The guest list included Hillman, Weaver, Alexander, and Williams, but only the last knew who was coming, since he had advised Eleanor whom to invite.[60]

Alexander was Hillman's "Special Consultant," but he thought the labor leader "very timid about the race question." And while Hillman had named Bob Weaver chief of a Negro Employment and Training Branch, it was, said Alexander, a title "but that's all." Alexander and Weaver had begun to press Hillman to include a clause in defense contracts forbidding discrimination, but "Sidney wouldn't touch it. He was afraid of it. I think it was partly [his] being Jewish." That was in the background when they arrived at the White House for lunch on May 29. Eleanor finished eating quickly—"she never wasted much time on that," Alexander noted—and in her courteous and disarming way began to report what she had been hearing about employment of minority groups. What was the situation? she asked, turning to Hillman.

"Well, I'm sure Dr. Alexander and Dr. Weaver won't agree with me. We haven't agreed on it," Hillman began a little lamely. He should state his position, Eleanor said smilingly; then they could state theirs. According to Alexander, Hillman gave "a stumbling explanation." Progress was being made was his essential point. "Is that your impression, Dr. Will?" Eleanor asked. Alexander's report was considerably darker than Hillman's; little would be accomplished, he thought, unless a nondiscrimination clause was written into contracts with responsibility for compliance placed upon the contractors. He was supported by Bob Weaver, who, as leader of the "Black Cabinet," a resourceful group of young Negro intellectuals in New Deal agencies, knew the situation. His somber, disquieting bill of particulars confirmed Eleanor's own feeling that admonitory letters to defense contractors were not being effective and that the president was not aware of how bad the situation really was.[61]

The Negro community, meanwhile, had begun to act on its own. With the Office of Production Management refusing to budge, with a Senate resolution calling for an investigation of discrimination in defense industries stalled, and with the president unresponsive to requests for a meeting, A. Philip Randolph issued a call for a "March on Washington" on July 1 to protest the exclusion of Negroes from defense industries and their humiliation in the armed services.

This alarmed the president. Such a march could immensely complicate his situation on Capitol Hill and might even result in bloodshed. Steve Early asked Wayne Coy "to appeal to Mayor LaGuardia to exercise his persuasive powers to stop it." Eleanor was also enlisted. "I have talked over your letter with the President," she wrote Randolph,

> and I feel very strongly that your group is making a very grave mistake at the present time to allow this march to take place. I am afraid it will set back the progress which was being made, in the Army at least, towards better opportunities and less segregation.
>
> I feel that if any incident occurs as a result of this, it may engender so much bitterness that it will create in Congress even more solid opposition from certain groups than we have had in the past.[62]

But not even she could sway the Negro leadership. Wayne Coy advised Early that he thought the only way to head off the march was for the administration to support the Senate bill to establish a permanent investigating committee on the subject of discrimination. The president called in Aubrey Williams: "Go to New York," he ordered, "and try to talk Randolph and White out of this march.

"Get the missus and Fiorello and Anna [Rosenberg] and get it stopped," he added. When he heard of Williams' assignment, Pa Watson commented skeptically, "Hell, Williams will join them."[63]

The meeting took place in City Hall.

"You know where I stand," Eleanor said to Randolph and White. "But the attitude of the Washington police, most of them Southerners, and the general feeling of Washington itself are such that I fear that there may be trouble if the march occurs." When White explained that they had tried unsuccessfully all spring to see the president about

Negro grievances, she assured him she would get in touch with the president immediately, "because I think you are right."[64]

After the meeting Anna Rosenberg called Pa Watson to inform him LaGuardia's recommendation was that the president bring in Stimson, Knox, William S. Knudsen, and Hillman to meet with White and Randolph. "Fiorello thinks this will stop the march and nothing else will, except the President's presence and direction.... Anna, at the same time, said Mrs. Roosevelt was in full agreement with the Mayor as to the joint meeting."[65] That same day Roosevelt instructed Watson: "I will see Stimson, Knox, Knudsen, Hillman, White and Randolph on Friday next—or, if I do not go away and feel well enough, I will see them on Wednesday or Thursday." Aubrey Williams called Randolph and suggested that he halt preparations for the march "pending conference" with the president. The Negro leader refused, even though he praised Roosevelt for his "fine statement" that day requesting the OPM to reaffirm its policy of the full utilization of available and competent Negro workers in defense industry.[66]

The conference at the White House was held on June 18. Before it began the president saw Anna Rosenberg, who had become his link with LaGuardia and who briefed him on what the Negro leaders wanted which was essentially an order that would make nondiscrimination in defense industry not only a matter of policy but of mandate, with a Fair Employment Practices Committee set up to enforce it. The upshot of the June 18 conference was that the president asked the Negro group to meet with LaGuardia, Williams, and Mrs. Rosenberg to draft the kind of order they thought he should issue.[67]

The order was drafted and Eleanor, whom Aubrey Williams kept apprised of every move, left for Campobello. There was no electricity in the Campobello house and no phone, and Eleanor had to go a half-mile down the road to Mrs. Mitchell, the island's telegrapher, and sit on her steps until she could get a call through. She had just arrived on Campobello when she received a telegram from Aubrey Williams saying that he had to talk with her. When she called him he was out.[68] Finally when they did connect Williams told her that the draft of the order was sitting on the president's desk. White and Randolph feared it was being steadily whittled down. Williams had urged the president to sign, as had LaGuardia. Eleanor then talked with Franklin, who said these things took time. The draft had been sent over to the Budget Bureau; it had to go to the attorney general. On June 23 Randolph still planned the march and asked Eleanor (even though she opposed the march) to speak at the Lincoln Memorial rally which would climax the demonstration. Finally, according to Williams, spurred on by Eleanor, Anna Rosenberg bought a new hat, marched into the president's office, fished out the order, and cajoled him: "Sign it, Mr. President—sign it." There is a memo from Roosevelt to Rudolph Forster, the dignified executive clerk, "Fix up for me a sign & send to Attorney-General for language. Quick." Robert H. Jackson, the attorney general, returned it on June 25, and it was issued that day. He had been informed, Randolph telegraphed Eleanor at Campobello, that the order was on its way, and he was, therefore, postponing the march. She was glad, Eleanor replied: "I hope from this first step, we may go on to others."[69]

On July 19 the president named the commission, headed by Mark Ethridge of the *Louisville Courier-Journal,* a stalwart southern liberal. For a brief moment Walter White was content: "I have come to you on so many occasions with tales of woe," he wrote the First Lady,

> that I am certain there must be times when you dread the sight of me. That is why I am glad on this occasion to be able to report gratifying progress towards betterment of a condition in which improvement you played so major a part. I refer to the way in which the Fair Employment Practices Committee is going about its job. Mr. Ethridge has plunged in with his characteristic energy, forthrightness and courage.[70]

White's euphoria did not mislead Eleanor. After White had spoken to the International Student Service group at Campobello, she confided to a friend that she understood the black man's urgency. She sensed this "vast issue taking shape and every day coming closer to her." She had never seen such a seething restlessness among the Negro people. She could see it coming closer to her every day, she repeated, and all of us having to face up to it in unprecedented ways.[71]

45. THE YOUTH MOVEMENT

"I HAVE MOMENTS OF REAL TERROR," ELEANOR SAID IN MAY, 1934, "when I think we may be losing this generation. We have got to bring these young people into the active life of the community and make them feel that they are necessary."[1]

Harry Hopkins shared this sense of urgency. At a dinner at the White House Eleanor had noted gratefully his rejoinder to one of Franklin's advisers who had cautioned that a certain relief approach be "tried out very slowly." "Well, but I've got 10,000,000 unemployed to take care of," Harry objected. And one out of every four, perhaps one out of every three, of these unemployed, it was believed, were young people under twenty-five.[2]

In 1933 Eleanor had pressed Harry to develop "some kind of definite program" for this group, and in March, 1934, was after him again: "The youth of the country is still very much on my mind." One of Roosevelt's first actions during the "hundred days" had been the establishment of the Civilian Conservation Corps, but while Eleanor considered the reforestation camps a successful experiment, she was groping for a broader solution. She believed in the concept of universal youth service, of which the CCC might be the germ, but she did not like to see the camps administered by the Army. Of course, those who thought that the trouble with the young was that they lacked discipline and initiative—and this view was almost as prevalent in the thirties as in the sixties—considered the Army's involvement the best feature of the program. Compulsory training under the Army, one woman wrote Eleanor, would eliminate feminine neuroses and straighten out the "hitch-hikers...loafers...racketeers and that vast army of lazy men who really do not WANT to work." But Eleanor, who felt that the adult world, not youth, was to blame for the economic disaster that had befallen the nation, rejected this view, fearing that it was impossible "to give military training without having a trend toward using armies for military purposes."[3]

She saw universal youth service as a substitute for war, a way to satisfy "certain things for which youth craves—the chance for self-sacrifice for an ideal"—which war had furnished in the past.[4]

She was attracted to the plan Prestonia Mann Martin presented in *Prohibiting Poverty* because the Young Workers Corps suggested by Mrs. Martin provided a way in which to enlist the energies and enthusiasm of America's youth for national purposes that, unlike the labor youth battalions of Hitler and Mussolini, would be neither militaristic nor nationalistic. Henry Goddard Leach, publisher of the *Forum,* turned to Eleanor for a "precept" that would pull together the youth of America—student, CCC recruit, Girl Scout, "reds, pinks and white"—in the way the five-year plan kept Russian youth "whistling and active all day" and "racial purity" had German youth "marching through the streets . . . in a glow of high idealism."

The need for a creative formula was very much on her mind, Eleanor replied. Young people had to feel when they left school that they were of use somewhere: "I think we could start out and make them the producers of the necessities of life during the first two or three years and in return give them their living and a training of some kind which they can use later in earning a living." She would like to see them enlisted in a crusade for social justice, and, most important of all, shouldn't they themselves to be encouraged to formulate "what they think would be a fair deal all around as well as a new deal?"[5]

By May, 1934, her thinking had begun to crystallize. The problem of young people who were both out of school and out of work was not going to disappear, she feared, not even with economic recovery. She noted predictions that a hard core of five million unemployed would always remain, with the consequence that at least a million young people who left school each year would be jobless. "Now what are you going to say to our youth who are not wanted in industry? We have no plans for you! We offer you nothing, we simply restrict your activities. . . . I would like to see us institute a volunteer service to the country open to both boys and girls." She envisaged a two-year enlistment, with the volunteers, like the CCC boys, housed in camps and paid on the same basis, but put to work in the communities at public-service employment, in government jobs ("which would be better done if the personnel could be increased"), and in nonprofit-making organizations such as hospitals, settlement houses, schools and colleges, and libraries. The program would cost the country money, she conceded, but so did the idleness of young people in the form of vandalism and crime and increased expenditures on jails, asylums, and hospitals.

Here was the germ of the National Youth Administration. But Harry Hopkins and Aubrey Williams had to be sold on it, Franklin had to be persuaded, public opinion had to be educated, and young people had to be involved in shaping the program. In particular, she wanted young people to speak up. Although she declined an invitation to sponsor a magazine called *Modern Youth* because she thought it a little too flamboyant for the First Lady to endorse, she thought that there was "no question but what a forum is necessary" where young people could express themselves and clarify their thinking. One way to overcome the estrangement of young people from their elders and the society they had created, as she had suggested to Henry Leach, was to involve them in the search for a solution.

As honorary chairman of the Mobilization for Human Needs, the nation-wide community-chest drive that took place in the autumn, Eleanor was distressed to hear Newton D. Baker suggest at the Mobilization's 1934 conference that there were many places where young people today could earn a living if they had initiative and spirit. "I confess that my own imagination has been extremely lacking in the last few months!" she wrote him afterward. "If you have any convincing suggestions as to how to stimulate the imagination of young people and how to direct their energies, I shall be more than grateful. My mail is filled with pleas for help." Baker took refuge in a lawyer's argument: "I am afraid your question is unanswerable. The boys who have to be helped with suggestions are just the ones who have not the initiative to make a place for themselves even when the benches all seem full."[6]

She refused to indict the young: "a civilization which does not provide young people with a way to earn a living is pretty poor" was her view.[7] She attended a mobilization meeting whose sponsors wanted to educate the public as to the value of such organizations as the Boy Scouts, the Girl Scouts, the Campfire Girls, and the YMCA and YWCA, all of which were having trouble raising money during the Depression.

Twenty-five youthful representatives of these organizations were seated on a platform, and a selected audience of three hundred adults heard them discuss the problems they were facing and asked them questions. As Eleanor listened she became "more and more uncomfortable. It was perfectly evident that the young people hadn't really had a chance to argue things out. Their ideas were, many of them, very half-baked." It was equally evident to her that many of the older people who should have been sympathetic and understanding were quick to leap on the young people. "Well, I haven't any patience with you young people," one of them said. "You are afraid of life. Why of course you can get jobs if you want jobs."[8]

If they wanted to meet with her and go on with the discussion, she told the young people afterward, she would be happy to make available the Sixty-fifth Street house in New York for that purpose and also to help them contact some sympathetic adults who might be of use in thinking things through. They accepted. "We met once a month and I brought all kinds of people up from Washington." The group included representatives of the Boy Scouts and Campfire Girls, the Y's, a rabbinical student, and even a young Communist who truculently refused to accept her offer of tea. At the very first meeting members of the group challenged her about the discrepancy between the code of ethics they were taught in school, church, and home and their daily observation that grownups and the business world did not live by that code. "We want our young people to have these beautiful ideals," Eleanor commented as she recalled the exchange. "The only way for them to have them and keep them is for us to have lived by them but we haven't made a world in which it is very easy to live by them." The group had a little difficulty in deciding what it wanted to discuss, but by the second meeting it had adopted the suggestion of John Lang, the representative of the National Student Federation of America, that discussion should focus on "What the Federal Government Can Do to Establish a Youth Service Unit." This fitted in with Eleanor's thinking.[9]

All through 1934 the Office of Education had been holding conferences, preparing studies, and making reports on what the federal government might do, but with the cautiousness that was characteristic of entrenched federal bureaucrats, it moved at a snail's pace. "I am really concerned about our youth problems over here," Eleanor wrote Florence Willert in England early in 1934. "So many young people get to the age when they want to work and marry and cannot find any work to do. We are trying all sorts of things but I do not feel that we have gotten very far."[10]

The president was in no hurry to move beyond the CCC in having the government subsidize youth employment and training. When Eleanor handed him a report on youth joblessness to read during a trip down the Potomac he shrugged it off, handing it to his naval aide to read. The dismissive gesture may have reflected a burdened man's wish to be permitted to relax, but Fulton Oursler witnessed a heated exchange during a dinner at the White House which indicated that the president's impatience also reflected uncertainty over what the government's youth policies should be. The president, as he sometimes did when he was undecided as to what course to pursue, baited Eleanor. She hated to bring up business, she said to Franklin, but nowadays she had only "chance opportunities like these" to talk with him seriously.

"We are going to fix a regular time—in the morning," Franklin interrupted her with a smile at the Ourslers.

She had been talking with young people who represented the youth movement, Eleanor said, referring to the group that had been meeting at the Sixty-fifth Street house.

"What do they want?"

"They want jobs."

"They—and who else?" countered the president.

Eleanor reported what she sensed of the impatience of the young people with the older generation. He should listen to Charles Taussig on the subject, she suggested.

"Is he an American youth?" the president heckled her, knowing full well that Taussig was president of the American Molasses Company and a New Deal supporter. "He is *your* friend," Eleanor came back.

There was no young people's problem, Franklin said, starting another tack; there was only the problem of the whole people. "Another delegation could come to you, representing men over 40 who can't get jobs. . . . Such movements as a youth movement seem to be especially unnecessary." Well, what then would he do about jobs for them?

"They can join our CCC camps."

"The CCC is too militaristic."

This outraged Franklin. "It's the last thing in the world it really is."

"Well, after all, my dear, it is under the supervision of the Army."

"That does not make it militaristic."

The education in the CCC camps was not worthy of the name, Eleanor insisted, and the only job training the boys received was in forestry.

What can they be trained for? Franklin broke in—"brick layers?" Did she know how many unemployed bricklayers there were? "The CCC boys could be taught something useful," she insisted. Their teachers were terrible, and with all the unemployed teachers, the CCC could have its pick. Eleanor returned to her suggestion that he should meet with a group of young people. He balked. He would not do so unless they had something concrete to propose.

"They propose, as I told you, to have jobs!"

Eleanor shifted to the political argument. The young people would soon be voters; Hearst knew that, and he was cultivating the college editors. Franklin relaxed. "There is a great deal to what you say. Tell your friends I shall be glad to consider the matter." Her husband was "a practical politician," she later said.[11] If other arguments failed, he was always sensitive to the "purely political" argument.

"And will you see them?" she pressed home.

At this point, commented Oursler, "President Roosevelt winked at his wife."[12]

Public opinion was crystallizing. David I. Walsh, the chairman of the Senate Committee on Labor and Education, called upon Secretary Perkins to report on the extent of youth unemployment and what government should do about it. There were no accurate statistics, Madam Perkins informed the Senate, but estimates placed the number of out-of-school, out-of-work young people between the ages of eighteen and thirty at 3,300,000 to 3,363,000. The Labor Department recommended that some $85 million be allotted from relief funds to provide jobs for young people, that needy students be given stipends and that a few experimental camps be set up.[13]

This is what the president did a few months later when by executive order he established the National Youth Administration and allotted $50 million out of relief funds for the program. Hopkins and Williams had been reluctant to present the proposal to the president because a youth agency in the government might have had political repercussions. "We do not know that the country will accept it," they told Eleanor, and they did not even wish to ask the president and put him in the position of saying yes or no. She would present the proposition to him, she said, and find out how he really felt. She did so one evening when she went into his bedroom to say good night.

"Do you think it is right to do this?" Franklin asked her. It would be helpful to young people, she replied, but he should also be aware of Harry's and Aubrey's fears that it might boomerang politically and raise the cry that he was trying to regiment America's youth the way Germany was doing. "If it is the right thing to do for the young people," Eleanor recalled his saying, "then it should be done. I guess we can stand the criticism, and I doubt if our youth can be regimented in this way or in any other way."[14] That was another side of him. He was not only the politician.

NYA was close to Eleanor's heart. She defended it against the old-line agencies, especially the Office of Education, which wanted to take it over. "The teachers of the country have always felt that education should be administered through the Office of Education," a Richmond school official wrote her. The NYA was primarily a relief, not an educational, project, she replied, with incidental benefits to education. This was true, but her fundamental reason for keeping the new program out of the hands of the settled agencies was the need she felt for swift and venturesome action. Even Aubrey Williams, who headed up the NYA and was as hot-blooded a New Dealer as any in Washington, did not satisfy her sense of urgency. "Too late!" was her comment on a memorandum he sent her setting forth the need to concentrate on a training program for out-of-school young people instead of simply providing work jobs, as the initial NYA program did. As he chose his state directors, Williams sent the names to her, and he also sent over monthly reports on the status of youth work projects. These elicited such queries as "What has been done about the Juvenile Court at Jonesboro, Arkansas?" "Have projects now been approved for Virginia and New Jersey, as well as California?" "Was the Oregon library project accepted or not?" "How has the vocational guidance program developed?"[15]

A Tulsa school official complained about the multiplicity of forms the schools were required to fill out in connection with the NYA wages being paid to high-school students, and Eleanor asked Williams if they could be simplified. He agreed vehemently: "The only time I really get thoroughly discouraged is when the accountants, statisticians and procedure fellows get their way. We now have the matter ironed out so that instead of seven movements in the process of paying students, we now have only two." At the end of the first half-year of the NYA's operation, Williams published an article in *Progressive Education* entitled "Youth and the Government." He thought it was pretty good, and sent it to Eleanor. "I am glad the NYA is getting busy," was her restrained comment. When Ruby Black wrote Eleanor Roosevelt's biography in 1940, she told Tommy that she was calling the chapter on the NYA "Inspiration of the NYA" because "inspiration" had the double meaning of "causing something to exist and keeping it on its toes." And Mrs. Roosevelt should not be modest about her part in causing the NYA to come into existence, Ruby Black went on, "because both Harry Hopkins and Aubrey Williams without my even asking them, told me emphatically that Mrs. Roosevelt was responsible for the creation of the NYA."[16]

But the NYA and CCC together only partly met a problem whose dimensions were just beginning to be appreciated. Dr. Homer P. Rainey, the director of the prestigious American Youth Commission, a privately funded research group of educators, industrialists, and union leaders, estimated that the number of young people out of school and out of work was actually five and a half million, and he, too, as Eleanor had in 1934, stressed that it was not primarily a Depression phenomenon; even after recovery the nation could still be faced with the problem of idle young people.

Public-service employment, Eleanor began to feel, might have to be a permanent feature of the American system, a concept she hinted at in her support in 1936 for proposals to establish a Department of Education, Social Welfare, Health and the Arts. Such a department, she felt, should include a youth-service division that might embrace the NYA, CCC, and government-sponsored apprenticeship training programs. But she broached this idea very cautiously; in 1936 the Republicans were in full tilt against the NYA, using such battle cries as "it ignored the Office of Education," "its administrative costs were excessive," "it was bad for the morale of youth," and "relief should be returned to the localities."[17]

If the program was to be expanded rather than dismantled, the president had to be kept informed and indoctrinated. He was under unremitting pressure to reduce WPA expenditures. The school lobby remained hostile to the NYA and, at the National Education Association convention in 1936, publicly attacked the program. When Charles Taussig, whom the president had appointed chairman of the NYA Advisory Committee, showed Eleanor a sheaf of letters from high-school students expressing gratitude for the NYA jobs, she wrote on them, "Give me to show President. . . ." She invited the NYA Advisory Committee to hold its sessions at the White House and arranged to have the president sit in on part of them.

A plea from a group of girls who had been at the NYA's Camp Jane Addams at Bear Mountain Park in New York State underscored that more than the NYA was needed. They had regained health and an interest in life during their stay at the NYA camp, the girls said, but once back in New York City few of them had been able to find jobs.

"Now after four weeks of tramping through the streets more than one girl says there is nothing left except suicide or tramping on the roads." The girls had formed themselves into a unit of the Workers Alliance, a radical-led organization of the unemployed. What could Eleanor say to them? She sent a note to the regional director of the NYA, Mark McCloskey, "Will you see the girls and try to put them in touch with proper people?" But what could anyone tell them when there were no jobs?[18]

She repeatedly discussed with Aubrey Williams the problem of what to do with young people who were not absorbed by the business system. They considered the establishment of youth settlements—a kind of American kibbutz—with the government providing the land and the young people being put to work building houses for themselves, an idea that was being put into effect by the Resettlement Administration, but not as a youth project. She and Taussig tried to persuade some leading industrialists to turn over the development of new inventions to youth-staffed factories. When a young Texas couple wrote that because of Depression wages they were afraid to start a family, she asked her husband, "Couldn't the government extend a loan to such couples?"[19]

Her sense of the tentative and stop-gap qualities of the programs so far launched by the government to deal with an estranged younger generation quickened her own efforts to keep a channel of communication open with them. Some of the young people who had been meeting with her had become interested in the American Youth Congress, which had a reputation for radicalism. All the more reason, it seemed to her, that the adult world should try to stay in touch with the youth. For young people to want to rebel against a world of Depression, fascism, and war seemed to her a healthier way of relating to it than to drift along in a kind of mindless conformity.

"You have got to frame new objectives," she told the graduating class at the University of North Carolina. "You have got to decide what you want in this country. . . . I know that all of us would like to see a country in which there is no poverty, in which every one has a minimum income on which a decent standard of living can be sustained. How are we going to reach that objective . . . ? We have got to think out new ways for doing things." She had listened to economists, philosophers, and theorists "until sometimes I have a feeling that it would be a very good idea if some people would go out and try some new things and not be fettered always by a feeling that they must simply wait until somebody else has done something, until somebody

688 ELEANOR AND FRANKLIN

else can find out surely what thing is best to try. This will not get you into any trouble."[20]

She scorned the conformists. She noted that Brandeis as a young lawyer had been warned he was throwing away his career because the words "the public" appeared too frequently in his briefs and arguments. It had been her observation "through many long years that frequently the man who thinks he is throwing away his career because he believes in something and acts on his belief, in the end makes his career. Perhaps the most valuable lesson to youth in Justice Brandeis' 80th birthday is the way Justice Brandeis lived his life."[21] She preferred young people who were nonconformist, idealists, and willing to take risks on behalf of their ideals.

In the summer of 1934 an energetic, enterprising young woman named Viola Ilma sent her the program for an American Youth Congress to be held in cooperation with New York University. Miss Ilma wanted Eleanor to sponsor the congress, and while a wide range of youth and youth-serving agencies had said they would attend, Eleanor, a little unsure about Miss Ilma herself, was not prepared to be a sponsor. She did, however, send a letter which was read to the gathering in which she expressed an interest in the program "and hope that you will send me a report of the proceedings and any conclusions which you have come to."[22]

The congress was a tumultuous affair, and Viola and her friends, fearful of the radical youth groups, tried to keep a tight control of the proceedings. This played into the hands of the young Socialists and young Communists, who with the assistance of the Y's and the Jewish and Protestant youth groups, organized a coup in the name of democratic procedure and took over the leadership of the congress. Miss Ilma and her friends walked out. For a time there were two American Youth Congresses feuding bitterly with each other. A calumnious but effective article in the *New Masses* even suggested Nazi inspiration for Miss Ilma's initiative, noting that she had spent four months in Europe studying fascist youth movements, including a visit to Berlin, and that she had refused to disclose who had financed the congress. Several people sent the article to Eleanor, and Tommy wrote to ask how much truth there was in it. Her mother was Jewish, a distraught Miss Ilma replied, her staff was Jewish, and she herself was "an enthusiastic and confirmed democrat." She had refused to answer the *New Masses* demand that she disclose the sources of her money, but she was quite prepared to have the gentleman who had put up the money write Mrs. Roosevelt.[23]

Within Miss Ilma's congress, a group of young southerners organized another coup, and by April, 1935, Miss Ilma had repudiated the group. The left-wing American Youth Congress hastened to point this out to Eleanor when it protested her plan to attend a meeting of the more conservative group. She was prepared to attend the left wing's meeting, too: "If you can prove to me that you are a bona fide organization, representing a big group of young people, I shall be glad to come and listen to you under the same conditions." She acknowledged that she had not liked the southern group's slurs against those "who might happen to think along more radical lines, and I made the point very clearly that I believe every shade of thought should be represented in every Youth Congress and the young people should be given free expression."[24]

By January, 1936, the radical-leaning American Youth Congress was in complete possession of the field and it again invited her to address its National Council, which was to meet in Washington. This time she accepted. Other people were better qualified to address their meeting, she replied, "but I will gladly come to one of your sessions to answer any questions you may want to ask of me, to the best of my ability," and since there were some criticisms of the Youth Congress that she did not want to make publicly, a small group might want to come to tea at the White House, where she could talk more freely. Some of the president's advisers cautioned her not to go because the young people were so radical and would "ask unpleasant and critical questions," she disclosed later, but she answered them that

> We ought to be able to meet all young people and defend the things we believe in. It may not always turn out as we hope. We may find ourselves targets of criticism. I wonder if it does us much harm. The real thing that is harmful is the knowledge in our hearts that we are afraid to face any group of young people. Open discussion between the rising generation and the older generation is a really important thing.[25]

She arrived at Methodist Hall accompanied by Aubrey Williams. The young people came to the council meeting charged with hostility toward the government and all its representatives, including Eleanor

Roosevelt. The previous June when NYA officials had approached Waldo McNutt, chairman of the Youth Congress, for an endorsement of the newly established NYA, McNutt "laughed. The Congress laughed," a youth leader wrote. The NYA was derided as "a sop" and the Youth Congress drafted an American Youth Act which it itself conceded would cost $3.5 billion a year and which critics said would cost $20 billion. The questions at the National Council meeting were barbed. Young Communist vied with young Socialist in taxing Eleanor with the inadequacy of the NYA. "You don't have to tell me that the Youth Administration doesn't touch the whole problem. I know that," she replied. More was needed, she agreed, but she did not know the whole answer to the nation's economic and social problem—and neither did they. However, "it is wrong to be quite as divided as some of us are getting. I think it is good for some of us to get together sometimes." She understood youth's impatience. Changes did seem to "take forever," and "I used to be awfully impatient when I was your age," but a "free people eventually" found ways to put things right.[26]

The purpose of the Youth Congress session in Washington was to lobby for passage of the American Youth Act. At tea at the White House, Eleanor told the Youth Congress delegation, which included a Negro girl, that the Youth Act was unrealistic: it involved "too large" an expenditure. It also reflected "a keen distrust for administrators," an NYA analysis of the bill commented, but Eleanor was too tactful to put it that way. Its administrative features had not been "thought through," she said, and offered to put the group in touch with people who had drafting experience. Had she been disturbed by the questions that had been put to her at Methodist Hall? a member of the group asked hopefully. She laughed—the youngster reminded her of her own children when sometimes they had behaved scandalously and waited eagerly for her to respond with appropriate agitation. She had not been disturbed at all. Although the young representatives had tried to outdo each other in the militancy and truculence of their questions, which had covered the whole gamut of radical concern—unemployment, racial discrimination, suppression of liberties, militarization of youth—they had not bothered her at all.[27]

Mark McCloskey, the New York NYA official who, although a product of Hell's Kitchen, had his own problems with the young radicals, was struck by her patience and tact at Methodist Hall. He understood better, he wrote later, "how to work with some of our youth organizations, which at times, to say the least, are trying." She replied that "I have so much sympathy for those youngsters it is never hard to be patient. But I sometimes feel that the exact amount of honesty which they can stand is a question. I was really more honest with the few that came to see me later on."[28]

She would need a great deal of patience. Some of those who came to tea were filled with youthful swagger and the certainty that they in Marxism, not she in Christian ethics, had the key to history and human happiness.

"She's a good woman utterly lacking in knowledge of social forces and systems and why good men are helpless without organizations," one of the participants wrote to a friend.

> She thinks she can reform capitalists...by inviting them to the White House for dinner and a good talking-to. I'm convinced she's opposed to fascism, and that she as well as her husband would go much further if they felt they'd have support. But every time they take an even mildly progressive stand they antagonize some group or other within the Democratic Party which in their view it is important to hold together at all costs in order to insure re-election and other legislation which is not progressive. It was a pleasant tea. We stayed for two hours. We had little cream puffs and were waited upon by butlers. She was always sympathetic but helpless or sure that education alone would provide the solution.[29]

But not all the delegates to the National Council meeting were so condescending. "She stood the gaff wonderfully," one of them reported to the press. And even the Youth Congress *Bulletin* admitted to some admiration when it began its account, "For a solid half hour the First Lady stood up before a barrage of questions." Eleanor's success worried the Young Communist League, which sent her a stiff letter of rebuke for her "negative" attitude toward the American Youth Act. Her invitation to the young people to search for new answers since the old ones no longer served was "empty" rhetoric; since she refused to endorse the American Youth Act, "we are forced to conclude that you are not genuinely interested in helping the youth of America. What other conclusion can we reach?"[30]

She did not like to be misrepresented, especially when the purpose was so obviously to maintain young people in a state of belligerence and suspicion toward government and the older generation. She had not said the Youth Act would not meet the needs of youth, she replied.

"What I said was that the Youth Act is badly drawn and impractical, but it may serve as a basis for better legislation after it has been thoroughly discussed."

The extremist rhetoric of the Young Communist League did not surprise her, but that of the Youth Congress leaders did, as did their puzzling unresponsiveness to suggestions that would help them become more effective. At the end of the year she turned down an invitation to serve on the advisory board of the congress. She was too busy.

> Also, I am afraid that you have not done the things which would give me enough faith in you. I have heard you make statements which were not correct and after they had been explained and corrected, I have heard you make them again. While I am certainly in sympathy with the youth of today, I do not think anything will be accomplished unless every question and every problem is honestly and fairly dealt with.[31]

But then suddenly her pleas for greater realism began to have an effect, so it seemed to her. The Youth Act was revised—slightly, but revised—and the new version was sent to her by Abbott Simon, national legislative director, who asked to see her in connection with both the bill and a youth "pilgrimage" that was scheduled to descend upon Washington. "I spoke to the President," she advised him, "and if you are not afraid of the cold, he says he would be quite willing to come out on the south portico and say a few words to the group if they will gather at the back of the White House."[32]

Franklin had often teased Eleanor about the youth movement, but he, too, saw an unsolved problem in what to do about the hard core of jobless young people. He was preparing to recommend that the Civilian Conservation Corps be made a permanent government agency,* and while there was much good-natured rivalry and occasional friction between the two over the comparative virtues of the CCC and the NYA, when the latter proved to be more acceptable than the CCC, he became increasingly amenable to Eleanor's pleas that it, too, be envisaged as a permanent tool of government. At times he was even willing to admit that the educational program of the CCC left a great deal to be desired.[33]

---

*Although this recommendation was not adopted, the CCC was a highly popular activity and Congress did approve a three-year extension of the agency on June 24, 1937.

While two years earlier he had fled from meeting the youth leaders, now he was not only willing to have the legislative representative of the Youth Congress to dinner, but spent the evening advising him on the conduct of the pilgrimage sessions in Washington and the advisability, if the youth group wanted to get a hearing from Congress, of framing recommendations that were specific, concrete, and limited. "You indicated last evening," Simon wrote him, "how complex the solution of the problems facing young people must be and how interwoven with every other important phase of national planning, and I believe you will agree with me that these factors should also receive the necessary attention in formulating any definite policy." But Roosevelt's friendliness also heightened Youth Congress suspiciousness. They argued among themselves about whether the president was trying to set up a government-supervised youth movement. Although the Communist group in the congress, in line with its new Popular Front policy, was now intent on cooperation with the administration, the old dogmas still had an influence, and the young Communists were sensitive to the taunts of the young Socialists that cooperation between youth and the New Deal was "opportunistic," "reformist," and a "sell-out." Simon wrote, asking to see the president again: "I feel very strongly that before making the arrangements for the Conference absolute, that it would be of very great value to obtain more specifically the viewpoint of the President on a great many of the questions which our meeting will decide." The letter revived Eleanor's fears about the congress's sense of practicality. "Shall I ask for Sunday supper and give another chance?" she queried her husband. "The President says he is extremely sorry but he does not have a single free minute," she wrote Simon the next day. "I also regret that I cannot give you any more time as I have given you every opportunity I possibly can."[34]

Although the plan to have the president address the young people fell through, he did agree to receive a delegation of their leaders after the congress had paraded down Pennsylvania Avenue. This, too, was almost torpedoed by an act of youthful ebullience which some of its instigators labeled militancy, but which horrified the young Communists who were intent on working with Roosevelt. As the paraders reached the White House and the line slowly snaked around its rear, the shouts "Schools not battleships," "Pass the American Youth Act," and "Abolish the ROTC" became louder, the paraders more excited, and the District police more anxious. Orders were issued to the patrolmen on motorcycles to hurry the parade on to the finishing point. Sit-down strikes were very much in the air—Flint auto factories were occupied at that time by their workers—and the youthful paraders, spurred on by some of their leaders but not by the Communists, responded to police proddings by sitting down on the pavement and going limp. This threw the police into a frenzy, and they raced their motorcycles, exhausts wide open, in and out among the sit-downers. William Hinckley and Abbott Simon, the two youth leaders who had obtained the parade permits, were hauled off to jail. But then the White House intervened and told the police to take it easy. Marvin McIntyre received a group of youth leaders who had been scheduled to present American Youth Act petitions, and they demanded that Hinckley and Simon be freed. McIntyre told them to finish the parade and that the leaders would be released. Finally everything was straightened out, and calm returned. In the afternoon the president received a delegation of the congress, a meeting at which Eleanor and Aubrey Williams were also present. It was a friendly gathering. The president laughed off the "sit-down" incident. He had been arrested in Germany while on a bicycle tour, he recalled, suggesting that Germany had always been an overly bureaucratic state. He heard their story, the Youth Congress delegation reported, "on what the depression has done to millions of young people, admitted that we were on the right track in seeking federal aid for the nation's hard-hit young population, although he didn't agree with us on the sum the U.S Government could 'afford' for this purpose in 1937."

Baffled as the Roosevelts may have been by the dogmatism and occasional antics of the Youth Congress, the demonstration on the whole strengthened the administration's efforts to get congressional support for its youth program. "I know that your work has yielded some good results and will yield more," Aubrey Williams informed the Youth Congress later that day. "And I am in a pretty good position to know whether it yields anything or whether it doesn't." When William Hinckley, the chairman of the congress, asked the Roosevelts to send greetings to a "Model Congress" in Milwaukee over the July 4 week end, the president did so, and Eleanor wrote on the letter that she had received "I can only wish them wisdom and good luck."[35]

She felt her presence and help were having a calming effect upon the hotheads. She spoke to the opening session of the New York State Model Youth Legislature at City College in New York, the congress affiliate that was most heavily influenced by radical thinking. Her subject was peace, and she argued against the isolationism implicit in the Oxford Pledge, which thousands of young people had recited at campus peace meetings, vowing not to fight in any war the United States government might undertake. "We felt you had a difficult task on your hands," Mark McCloskey wrote afterward. The meeting had gone well, she thought.[36]

Hinckley, reflecting the viewpoint of the Youth Congress leadership, wrote that her speech had given "great help in counter-acting what I consider a very inappropriate tendency among some young people at the present time to hold that the Oxford Pledge is the answer of youth to the very complex problem of the organization of peace." But it was a pompous letter, and it was disingenuous—while public opinion, shocked by the advance of fascist aggression, was in flux, it is doubtful that the New York Youth Congress would have approved Roosevelt's call to "quarantine the aggressor" or voted down the Oxford Pledge and the Ludlow war-referendum amendment had there not been a change in Communist policy that reflected Moscow's search for allies against Hitler.* To Eleanor, a long-time battler for the Wilsonian principle of collective security, it appeared that "these young people are beginning to be a bit more stable and are a little bit better able to think things through."[37]

The president evidently agreed with this appraisal. Early in January, 1938, the officers of the World Youth Congress, which had been set up in Geneva, Switzerland, in August, 1936, and to which the American Youth Congress was affiliated, wrote asking Eleanor's help with the Second World Youth Congress, which was to take place at Vassar College in August, 1938. They wanted her to attend and to help them get financing. She asked her husband if she should accept and if Congress could be asked to make an appropriation toward its expenses as it had done for the meeting of the Rural Women of the World. "It is all right to accept this," the president told her, "but do not try for an appropriation because there are twenty or thirty international organizations that if we were consistent we would also have to help."[38]

Her sponsorship of the Second World Youth Congress displeased the Catholics, who were already irritated with her support of the Loyalists in Spain and her known advocacy of birth control. A priest sent her an editorial from *America,* the Jesuit weekly, called "Radicals at Vassar." It regretted her patronage of the congress and noted that the bishops through the National Catholic Welfare Conference

*See Chapter 49.

were discouraging attendance by young Catholics. It denounced the gathering as anti-Catholic, anti-religious, and pro-Communist. "I do not doubt that there are many Communists among them," she replied, "but they are not strong enough to rule the entire group. I have watched them and met with them over a period of four years and I have seen them grow into more sensible and reasonable young people. I think it is a great mistake to simply condemn them and do nothing about it."[39] To Eleanor, youth's radicalism was not a badge of untouchability but a plea for help and understanding. To James E. West, the adult executive of the Boy Scouts of America who wrote to explain his organization's avoidance of the Vassar sessions, she replied,

> I do not question the fact that because the conservative organi-
> zations have somewhat held back, it has left the predominating
> representation to the left-wing group but that is a fault on the part
> of the conservative organizations and no excuse from my point of
> view for not trying to keep in touch with these groups and helping
> them to be as sane as it is possible for youngsters to be.

The influence of the young Communists in the congress would be diminished to the extent that the congress took in "all groups of young people. I have always felt, however, that the attitude of staying away from a thing because you did not approve was not a helpful one and that it is better to try to fight anything which you felt harmful. This is better done from within than from without."[40]

How could the older generation be self-righteous and dogmatic? When younger people asked her what the generation in control had learned from the World War, she had to say honestly, "I don't know what we learned. I don't think we learned anything and I think we are going very much the same way that generations of people have gone before." She felt even more uncomfortable when these same young people then came back and said, "Well, you acknowledge that you don't know what you learned. You acknowledge that you don't like the world the way it is, but what are you doing about changing it?"[41]

The World Youth Congress assembled at Vassar College in August, 1938, two months before Munich. Rumors of Nazi mobilization swept the session and the worried Czech delegation cabled home for news. There were students from the battlefronts of Spain and China, and veterans of anti-colonial struggles in India and Indonesia and Cuba. The theme of the congress was affirmative—youth speaks out for peace—but the mood was militantly anti-fascist and anti-imperialist. The thirties, said the poet W. H. Auden, was "The Age of Anxiety," and of all those who shared in the torments and troubles of those years, Eleanor's heart was given most freely to the young. She could not stay away from the congress. She answered questions for an hour and a half and came back in the evening to participate in the entertainment. The eight hundred delegates from fifty-four countries seemed to her thoughtful and earnest, well-behaved and restrained. They did not seem to her the sinister characters some made them out to be, but "just like any other summer school students!" At the end of the congress she wrote:

> The more I see of this group made up of young people from many nations, the more important I realize it is that in every nation older people who can see the desirability of certain changes in our civilization should work with them. In this way their thought and action will not be one-sided and the impetuousness of youth should gain some benefit from the experience of age.[42]

The young seemed to her the messengers of the future, and, indeed, the world-mindedness of the Youth Congress, their consciousness of the existence of Asia and Latin America, even of Africa did foreshadow the collapse of empire of the postwar era. The themes of the Youth Congress and American Student Union pronouncements sounded in the thirties—equality of educational opportunity, federal aid to the arts, public provision of medical care for all, the creation of the city beautiful through slum clearance and housing, the conservation of natural resources, guaranteed jobs, civil liberties, and equal political rights—would form the platforms for which their children would be fighting decades later. "I welcome you here to Washington," Williams said after the sit-down demonstration; "I glory in the high, unequivocal grounds that you have taken.... I especially glory in the fact that you have taken such a fine and unequivocal stand with regard to no discrimination against race."[43]

Eleanor's subject at the *New York Herald Tribune* Forum a few weeks after the Vassar congress was "youth's contribution in keeping the mind of the nation young." She pleaded with her contemporaries, especially her husband, to keep themselves open to the influence of youth, to listen to the young people. The Youth Congress leadership was one more ally in the unceasing argument with Franklin over where to draw the line between what was needed and what was politically possible. Taussig invited Abbott Simon to attend a meeting of the NYA Advisory Committee. When the young man spoke at the session with the president, where others had been deferential he bluntly proposed that the NYA be extended to include 1,500,000 young people. The NYA had done valuable work, the president agreed, and should be continued, though he would not support increasing its responsibilities threefold. When the president's Advisory Committee on Education headed by Floyd Reeves warned of "a lost generation of young people" and proposed that the CCC be removed from War Department control and combined with the NYA to form a National Youth Service Administration, the American Youth Congress was prepared to sponsor legislation to that effect.[44]

Youth Congress officials spoke up where the NYA officials had to follow the president's lead, and Eleanor used them in her efforts to win the president over to doing more for young people. The NYA Advisory Committee met that fall (1938) at Val-Kill, and she invited Franklin to drive over to greet them. They clustered around his little Ford, and soon a "conference" was taking place under the trees in the bright October sunshine. May Craig, watching Eleanor, was greatly amused:

> She was really an advocate: she wants the Youth Administration to get funds and go forward. So she would say "Well you see Franklin" every now and then when she felt she could put in a helpful sidelight. She has been around to practically every state, seeing the Youth activities, so she could really steer the conference.
>
> The President hasn't been married to her for so long without knowing her methods—doesn't every husband? He knew she was trying to show him this Youth program because it is close to her heart. But he has an eye on the budget and knows how many other worthy projects need money.[45]

Part of Eleanor's problem with Franklin was his distrust of the Keynesian theories of priming the pump and compensatory spending. She sent him the keynote speech made at the convention of the American Student Union whose theme was "Keep Democracy Working by Keeping It Moving Forward." It was militantly New Deal in its outlook and enthusiastically pro-Roosevelt: "We must unite the campus for the objectives of the New Deal. We must unite the campus to play a decisive part in the 1940 election."

"This is an interesting letter and speech," the president commented in a memorandum:

> If you want to start a discussion among the young people some day, get them to discuss and answer the following question:
>
> The government deficit today is $3,000,000,000 a year. Such a deficit obviously cannot go on forever—expenditures $9,000,000,000, receipts from taxes $6,000,000,000.
>
> We could very easily and usefully spend another billion dollars a year on aids to and improvement of education.
>
> We could very easily and usefully spend another billion dollars a year in better health facilities throughout the country, and especially in the South and rural sections.
>
> We could very easily use another billion dollars a year in soil protection and flood prevention.
>
> We could very easily use another billion dollars a year in old age security and youth training.
>
> We could very easily use another billion dollars a year in slum clearance and better housing.
>
> That would mean a budget of $14,000,000,000 a year against tax receipts of $6,000,000,000.
>
> How can the $3,000,000,000 a year, present deficit, or the $8,000,000,000 a year, new deficit, if such projects are carried out, be financed?
>
> F. D. R.

Yet less than a month after this memo to his wife, which was dated January 16, 1939, and which reflected Roosevelt's unhappiness with deficit spending, he urged his son James, who had gone to work for Sam Goldwyn in Hollywood, to consider doing an educational film based on *An Economic Program for American Democracy*. Although this little book by seven economists from Harvard and Tufts embodied a Keynesian approach to full employment, the president considered it a "swell" expression of the economic philosophy of his administration. The seesawing in his mind reflected the pulling and shoving of the various factions and viewpoints in the administration.[46]

Eleanor helped her young friends in the Youth Congress—for friends she now began to consider them—to understand her husband's difficulties with Congress and that if they wanted change the place to work was with public opinion in the districts from which the congressmen hailed, but she never sought to silence the young people with the question "Where is the money going to come from?" And, in encouraging her husband to talk with the representatives of the youth organizations and to read their pronouncements, she was trying to educate him just as she herself was being educated. Her own ability to entertain new ideas was illustrated in an exchange with a reporter over Hitler's claim to have ended unemployment. Totalitarian countries did not class people who worked for the government as unemployed, she replied, whereas in this country persons on the rolls of the WPA, the CCC, the NYA were classified as unemployed even though they were doing useful work, beneficial to the public. In this respect, she thought there was something to be said for the approach of the totalitarian countries.[47]

In the congressional onslaught on relief and public works in the spring of 1939, the NYA was the only relief agency to have its funds increased to $100 million. "Many people have told me," Williams wrote her, "that we could have gotten the whole $123,000,000, if Mr. Rayburn had not made his motion but had allowed the thing to go ahead to a vote on the Collins Amendment." It was symptomatic of the change in the American Youth Congress that it no longer called for enactment of the American Youth Act, but had urged its constituent groups to write Congress and ask $250 million for the NYA. The president, moreover, had been converted to making the NYA a permanent agency. He separated it from the WPA and transferred it, along with the CCC and the Office of Education, to the newly established Federal Security Agency.[48]

Eleanor was still not satisfied that the CCC camps had the right kind of leadership and educational program. She learned of a report made by a group headed by Dr. Will Alexander that, in his words, "just took the lid off of the CCC camps." She did not think Franklin had seen it, she told Alexander; "they probably kept it from him." Or if he had seen it, "I don't think he got the implications of it." She asked Alexander to get a few of the educational advisers in the camps and bring them to dinner at the White House: "This is something Franklin's got to face."

Alexander located four college-trained men who he thought would make a good impression and gave them a little preliminary coaching. "You've got to look him right in the eye and tell him this. Mrs. Roosevelt wants you to, and when she wants you to do anything, it's perfectly safe. She's doing this, I'm not." The president sensed something was up and he began to filibuster, but Eleanor broke in; he should either talk to the young men or listen to them. Alexander thought his young men were "very convincing" and saw the president "begin to perspire." Before dinner was over Eleanor had one boy after another sit next to the president.[49]

In point of fact the battle was won, partly because Franklin had been persuaded that the camps should be under civilian administration and partly because with the outbreak of the war the Army was calling up reserve officers. "I am enclosing a copy of the memorandum which I am asking the President to sign tonight," Hopkins wrote Eleanor. "Alexander says this will do the business." The memorandum was addressed to Paul V. McNutt, the head of the Federal Security Agency, and suggested a special training agency to prepare new leadership for the CCC to replace the reserve officers being drained off by the armed forces.[50]

The danger of a jobless, alienated generation of young people was by no means over. "One third of the unemployed workers in the nation are young people fifteen to twenty-four years of age," the American Youth Commission reported as the war broke out. "The rate of unemployment is higher among youth between twenty and twenty-four than in any other age group and highest of all for young people between fifteen and twenty who are out of school and seeking work." But in the NYA and CCC and the Office of Education—if the latter could get more inspired leadership★—the tools were beginning to be available for a comprehensive attack on the problems of jobs and education for young people. They were not sufficient. When a Republican speaker at a Youth Congress dinner attacked the youth program of the government with the statement that "American youth does not want to be mollycoddled. . . . It sees no future in government agencies, in which it merely graduates from NYA to CCC and from CCC to WPA," Eleanor replied that she believed in the NYA, as she did in Social Security and other New Deal measures. "But never as fundamental answers, simply as something which has given us hope, which has given us perhaps a suggestion which might be followed by communities everywhere. . . . We have bought ourselves time in which to think, that is what we have done."[52]

★In July, 1939, Eleanor discussed with Aubrey Williams how to persuade the Carnegie Foundation, whose head admired Dr. John W. Studebaker, the commissioner of education, to finance an assignment for him outside of the government.[51]

It was a great satisfaction to her that the young people in the Youth Congress thought along lines so similar to her own. In July, 1939, the annual meeting of the congress, billed as a "Model Congress of Youth," seemed completely to vindicate her faith in the leadership of the group. The three thousand young people who attended the sessions were enthusiastic, informed, and united, it seemed, by a sense of shared goals and the feeling that everything was possible. They hit hard at the United States Congress, but Eleanor did not mind that, for this was the Congress that had killed the Federal Theatre Project and ruthlessly slashed the WPA and PWA appropriations. The demands of the young people were reasonable and concrete—a nationwide program of apprenticeship training, the extension to young workers of the provisions of the Wages and Hours Act, federal aid to education—and, in addition, to support an expanded NYA (the American Youth Act had been quietly shelved), the Youth Congress called for the establishment of a $500 million loan fund to help young people finish their schooling, establish homes, and get started in the world.

The high point of the pronouncements of the Youth Congress were the adoption of a creed and a resolution condemning all dictatorships, and Eleanor called the creed the finest thing she had seen come out of any organization. In affirmative terms it dedicated the congress to the service of the country and mankind, pledged itself to progress and social pioneering but only within the framework of the American system, vowed to keep America a nation where men and women could worship God in their own way, and ended with the Pledge of Allegiance to the Flag. And since this did not satisfy a disruptive group of delegates who were demanding that the congress exclude Communists, fascists, and Nazis, it went on record in opposition to "all forms of dictatorship, regardless of whether they be communist, fascists, nazi." The sessions in the burgundy-gilt decorated Manhattan Center ballroom, wrote *Time,* represented the "closest approach to a U.S. youth movement."[53]

"There are perfectly practical things that I want to say to you young people," Eleanor said in her remarks to the Youth Congress. "You will want to learn a little more parliamentary law. . . . It is all very well to have a great many very nice ideas but if you can't say them so that any child of five can understand them, you might just as well not have them. . . . The best English is always the simplest." She went on to urge them to get to know their own communities and to take on work that might not be as glamorous as marching in parades:

Organize first for knowledge, first with the object of making us know ourselves as a nation, for we have to do that before we can be of value to other nations of the world and then organize to accomplish the things that you decide to want. And remember, don't make decisions with the interest of youth alone before you. Make your decisions because they are good for the nation as a whole.

One of those present in the press box was H. L. Mencken. "I always like to listen to people who really believe in things," he commented.[54]

Eleanor took the creed and the resolution on dictatorship and sent them to the many people who were critical of the congress, including such good friends as Elinor Morgenthau, who had confessed that much as she wanted to help out anything Eleanor was interested in, "I myself have never been completely sold on the American Youth Congress."

"I for one am grateful for the courage of youth," Eleanor's covering letter read, and to the Catholic leaders who were outspokenly hostile to the congress, she wrote, "I do not see how anyone can say it is Godless."

46. FROM PACIFIST TO ANTI-FASCIST

✧

IN 1936, IRWIN SHAW, A YOUNG MAN JUST OUT OF BROOKLYN College, penned *Bury the Dead,* a dramatic broadside against war that was morally so shattering and sure in its sense of theater that it quickly moved from amateur performance to Broadway production. "What is there so dear that it is worth dying for?" Shaw argued. "Very few things...and never the things for which one nation fights another." The play's lines, as earlier noted, hit Eleanor like "hammer blows."[1]

Her own conviction about war's folly took shape in World War I, and was strengthened by her tour of Europe's battlefields and hospitals. She had returned a dedicated Wilsonian, resolved never again to sell a war bond, and when Carrie Chapman Catt, the suffrage battle won, summoned women to the struggle to prevent another war, she found an ardent recruit in Eleanor.

"How can we study history?" Eleanor cried out at the 1934 meeting of Mrs. Catt's organization, the National Conference on the Cause and Cure of War. "How can we live through the things that we have lived through and complacently go on allowing the same causes over and over again to put us through these same horrible experiences?... Anyone who thinks," she continued, "must think of the next war as they would of suicide." In New York a peace march going down Fifth Avenue carried placards proclaiming:

MRS. F.D.R. SAYS: "WAR IS SUICIDE!"

Out in Indianapolis, the headquarters of the American Legion, the women's auxiliary solemnly pronounced that "she is the number one pacifist in the country today."[2]

But though she preached the futility of war, Eleanor did not subscribe to the belief that it was never right to bear arms or to resist evil with violence. She had had too much experience with the clash of wills and the stubbornness of self-interest in American politics to ignore their reality on the international level. And if in her efforts to introduce some leaven of Christian forbearance and sacrifice into America's response to the world she leaned too heavily on the hope that trust and love might evoke an answering echo in nations as well as individuals, her husband was always there to remind her of harsher realities. As the aggressive designs of fascism unfolded in the thirties, Franklin Roosevelt went with his wife as far as he could to demonstrate America's will to peace—in response to his own convictions, it should be said, as well as to her pleas—but he also educated her and, through her, a large section of the peace movement, that in the absence of internationally agreed disarmament, a preparedness program also had a place in a strategy for peace.

"I am afraid that I am a very realistic pacifist," Eleanor wrote soon after the Roosevelts had entered the White House and protests came to her about her husband's proposals to build the Navy up to treaty limits. "We can only disarm with other nations; we cannot disarm alone." Was she correctly interpreting the president's policy, she asked Steve Early, sending him a copy of the letter that she was sending out in response to pacifist protests. Early forwarded her letter to the secretary of the Navy. It met his approval. Roosevelt's determination to build the U.S. Navy up to treaty strength reflected an anxiety about Japan. Germany, too, was arming, and, as Eleanor explained to pacifist leaders who felt the Western democracies were unresponsive to Hitler's demands for equality, it was "at present... very difficult to deal with Germany normally, because while she is demanding that other nations disarm, she herself is arming in every way she can under cover." But the real impetus for American rearmament, which in the first years of the Roosevelt administration was chiefly naval, came from the Pacific. Franklin, his wife later said, felt Japan had delusions of grandeur. "I remember his concern about Guam and the islands of the Pacific way back when he was Assistant Secretary of the Navy. I think his suspicions of Japan were based on his own outlook of what he felt made the Pacific safe for us. In all the war games, Japan was always considered the enemy in the Pacific."[3]

When the National Conference on the Cause and Cure of War came to Washington for its 1935 session, Eleanor had the leaders to dinner at the White House, and placed Mrs. Catt next to her husband. He promptly proceeded to explain to her, as he already had to Eleanor, why he felt that if peace was to be preserved America had to build a navy second to none and do it as fast as possible. "The President is a sincere friend of organized world peace," Mrs. Catt wrote afterward. "He would like to see the country in the League and the World Court, but what he really relied on to preserve peace is our Navy! And if I were in his shoes," the white-haired, grandmotherly woman declared with a show of spirit, "I would want the biggest navy in the world!"[4]

The chief concern of that White House dinner was to canvass the outlook for the World Court resolution which was moving toward a decisive vote in the Senate. In the absence of internationally agreed disarmament, Eleanor accepted her husband's arguments for a naval-building program, but her hopes for peace rested in international collaboration, and, since the League of Nations was still a taboo issue in American politics, in U.S. adherence to the World Court. At one of her first press conferences she had startled her listeners with the intensity of her plea that the United States had to find a basis on which to cooperate with the rest of the world if civilization was to be preserved, and it was largely the prodding of the women with Eleanor in the lead, that, once the Roosevelts had arrived in Washington, had moved court adherence back into the area of practical politics.[5]

Franklin had just about caught his breath after the difficult negotiations with Maxim Litvinov on recognition of the Soviet Union when Esther Lape was in pursuit of him through Eleanor about the World Court. She reminded Eleanor that in the spring of 1933 the president had indicated to the two of them that he intended to seek adherence to the court early in the 1934 session of Congress. "I know how many things seem more urgent in the domestic situation," Esther argued. "But the Court issue is critical also, and the ratification of the three Court treaties might, in our judgment, have a stabilizing influence on the international atmosphere out of proportion to what may seem to some the intrinsic importance of the issue." But Franklin, who was the greatest politician of his time, sent back word through Eleanor that "politically speaking and judging by the present time, it would be unwise to do anything about the World Court." The women were not convinced. They undertook to show the Senate that the court issue was not "cold."[6]

The peace lobby was effective. Even though Roosevelt told his Senate leaders he did not want action on the World Court at that session, the Senate Foreign Relations Committee was persuaded to hold a hearing on adherence. Would she attend, Esther asked Eleanor. "After all, the objective is simply a definite plank in 1932 Democratic Platform which we all support 100%." She was "terribly sorry," Eleanor replied the next day, "but Franklin thinks I had better not go to any hearings. I never go either to any of the code hearings or to any of the others at the Capitol. I hope to goodness that you have the votes to bring it out and that all will go well." She invited Esther to stay at the White House during the hearings, but Esther declined; it might be interpreted as committing the president "to a more aggressive line on court action than he wants to show at the moment." The hearings before the Senate Foreign Relations Committee were successful beyond Esther's hopes. The isolationists who thought they had buried adherence to the court along with the League of Nations were taken by surprise. Senators Hiram Johnson and William E. Borah acknowledged that the court supporters had marshaled enough strength to force a favorable report by the committee at that session of Congress.

But Franklin's political antennae still signaled danger. She had heard, Eleanor wrote, "what a very good hearing it was and [I] think it will do great good, but they are all convinced that the World Court shall not come up until after the next election as they feel that it would just give Mr. Hearst another thing to pin his attack on. So I am afraid there is not much chance." But Esther, remembering Roosevelt's previous vacillations on the issue, wondered if he would move in 1935. In October she transmitted to Eleanor a report of an evasive reply made by Senator David I. Walsh, the Massachusetts Democrat, when asked his position on the court: "I am a supporter of the President and when he recommends our joining it I shall vote in favor of doing so." In fact, Franklin's mind was made up, although he had not yet indicated so publicly. When the State Department had sent emissaries to Hyde Park in September to suggest that an adherence resolution be presented to the next session of Congress, they were pleasantly surprised that "Mr. Roosevelt readily agreed."[7]

The effort to win U.S. adherence came to a head in January, 1935. "We are banking everything on the Court getting through this week," Esther wired Eleanor on January 15, 1935. "We think only chance is to get it out of the way before legislative program gets complicated." The Senate Foreign Relations Committee reported the bill out on January 9, but Key Pittman, its chairman, refused to handle it on the floor because he was not in sympathy with the resolution and predicted a bitter fight. The bill was entrusted to Senate Majority Leader Joseph Robinson, who had polled the Democrats, as Senator Charles McNary had the Republicans, and estimated that the two-thirds majority for the resolution was easily there. The president evidently was dubious about the count for he asked for Esther's, and when she replied that even if one included the twelve doubtful votes in the opposition, there were not enough votes to defeat the resolution, Eleanor replied, "Please send me the names of any one on the doubtful list immediately."[8]

The Senate debate took place against a somber international background. Germany was rearming in disregard of treaties. Japan was preparing to push on from Manchuria into North China. Italy's campaign of threat and pressure against Ethiopia had begun. "At this period in international relationships," Roosevelt's message to the Senate read, "when every act is of moment to the future of world peace, the United States has an opportunity once more to throw its weight into the scales in favor of peace." But Senator Hiram Johnson, veteran of the battle against the League of Nations, looked at the same set of events and drew an opposite conclusion for American policy. The staccato sentences poured out: "All Europe sits over a volcano. No one knows when the explosion will come. But when the day comes Europe will drag us into the war as they did in 1917, and will hate us afterwards."[9]

Franklin had begun to work on the list of doubtful senators, Eleanor informed Esther, but the opposition also was mobilized. "Father Coughlin is down here now and I have been told that he got one Senator away from us. The President thinks he has a two-thirds vote but he wants to get his big appropriations bill through first. . . . He agrees with you about the record vote and wants it just as soon as the other bill is out of the way." As the record vote approached, isolationist pressure mounted. Every day, the Hearst press in front-page editorials called on its readers to write to their senators. The most deadly attack was leveled by Father Coughlin the Sunday before the vote. He denounced the court, which he said was favored by the "international plutocrats" who again would push the United States down the road to war, and entreated his vast listening audience to telegraph, today—"tomorrow may be too late"; a torrent of telegrams descended upon Capitol Hill.[10]

Esther and her friends frantically sought someone to go on the radio to try to offset the Hearst-Coughlin onslaught. Eleanor agreed to do so if they couldn't get someone more effective. "Sporting of you to do it," Esther wired after the speech, adding, "men are worms." Esther thought the president was not doing enough and that the Senate pro-court leadership was incompetent. Eleanor appealed to the women of her generation "who remember the World War and who desire to take any action they can to safeguard the youth of the future." In language simple and moving, she reviewed the arguments on behalf of this effort "to have questions settled by law and not by war.... We cannot escape being a part of the world. Therefore, let us make this gesture for peace, and remember there was no World Court in 1914 when the Great War began."

The telegrams from the women poured in, but in the Senate the speech boomeranged. It was the "only counterblow" to the Hearst campaign against the court, Arthur Krock commented in the *Times,* but it "has not had wholly favorable effect, to judge from the comment in the cloakrooms today." When the vote came adherence fell seven short of the required two thirds.[11]

A heartsick Esther went directly back to Philadelphia instead of going to the White House to say good-by. She hoped the president would resubmit the resolution promptly because "otherwise our whole international policy will be shortstopped."

Eleanor understood why, feeling as low as she did, Esther had not wished to spend the night at the White House.

It is discouraging that Mr. Hearst and Father Coughlin can influence the country in the way that they do but that is that.

Franklin says that he could not possibly resubmit the resolution.... Time may change the point of view of this country and the settling of American debts would make a tremendous difference. That is about all we can hope for.[12]

While some of the peace groups thought the president should have been more outspoken, Eleanor demurred.

In regard to the World Court vote—I doubt if any public word by the President would have helped matters much. He sent for every Democratic and Independent Senator and talked to him personally, besides sending his message. I am afraid that the pressure must come from the people themselves, and, until it does, we will never be become a member of the World Court.[13]

"I have been surprised all along that the President should make this such an issue as he has made it," Ickes commented in his diary. When he telephoned his friend Senator Hiram Johnson to congratulate him, Johnson told him that "a great many" senators "were bitter in their criticism of Mrs. Roosevelt for mixing up in this fight." Ickes did not understand how the president, able politician that he was, "allowed himself to become entangled as deeply as he was on this issue. He might have let the Senate pass on it without showing his own hand."[14]

Would the president have made the fight for the court if its adherents had not been able to focus their pressure on him through Esther and Eleanor? He was a convinced internationalist, searching for ways to indicate U.S. concern and interests in events in Europe and Asia. But would he have judged the political risks worth taking? In 1932 he had disappointed the Wilsonians when in pursuit of the presidential nomination he had capitulated to Hearst, renounced the League of Nations, and fallen silent about the court. Have faith in me, he had pleaded then. Perhaps the memory of a wife who on that occasion had refused to talk to him influenced him to make the court fight in 1935 despite adverse political signals. "When you disapprove of something you sit so straight your backbone has no bend," Franklin had once reproved her. And while the reproof had taught her a lesson and she had subsequently learned to treat political opportunism with tolerance and amused resignation, there still were occasions when she went cold and remote with anger, a prospect from which Franklin shrank. So if Roosevelt's involvement in the World Court was, as Ickes wrote, "a major political blunder," some of the responsibility was Eleanor's. But it was not really a blunder. He would make many efforts before war broke out to turn the country away from isolationism. All would fail, but the fight had to be made.

The Senate rebuffed international cooperation nine months before Mussolini's invasion of Ethiopia. It was a bad moment in which to weaken the authority, even if it was fragile and compromised, of the institutions that had been set up for the peaceful resolution of disputes. Yet even so committed an internationalist as Eleanor avoided advocacy of American support for the League of Nations. "I think I had better not speak for you," she wrote the League of Nations Association:

> I do hope to work for the World Court and I find that the feeling of Congress is so opposed to the League of Nations that those of us who are interested in trying to change the feeling on the World Court had better not be associated any more than is absolutely necessary with organizations for the League.[15]

The isolationist tide that ran against the League also engulfed the court. It was, as Franklin realized, a dead issue. The peace movement split, with many of the peace organizations turning from collaborative efforts to prevent the war that seemed to be coming to an attempt to insulate America from that war. The rationale for this shift was provided by the Nye Committee, which had been established to investigate the international traffic in munitions. Eleanor sympathized with the move to curb the "merchants of death," as the arms salesmen were characterized in the thirties. "Perhaps the first and most practical step that the nations of the world could take would be to buy out the munitions makers and make their business of war supplies a government business only," she said.*[16]

But the Nye Committee did not limit itself to the arms trade. It developed the thesis that the United States had been drawn into the Great War by bankers and munitions makers and that the threat to America's remaining at peace in the thirties arose not from the growing dangers in Europe and Asia but from the sale of munitions and loans to belligerents. The way to keep America out of another war, the Nye Committee argued, was to take the profits out of war through embargos on arms and limitations on loans, trade, and travel applied impartially against all belligerents. "In the Executive Branch it was evident that no one could withstand the isolationist cyclone," wrote Hull. Two months before the outbreak of the Italo-Ethiopian conflict, the Senate approved a mandatory arms embargo and denied the president any discretion in its application to aggressor and victim.[17]

There was some confusion in Eleanor's attitude toward the neutrality bill. The resolution was an "achievement" of the peace groups, she wrote John Haynes Holmes, a noted pacifist minister, "but the passage of that resolution does not prevent individual congressmen and senators from coming to the President to try to have a particular product of their district kept off any list which is considered 'munitions of war.'" That sounded as if she wanted even stronger legislation. Yet she also voiced the hope that when Congress reassembled women would impress upon their representatives that they did not want "any goods whatsoever sold to an aggressor nation which may even remotely contribute to continuance of war." But what if an aggressor's design could not be blocked without continuance, perhaps even expansion,

*The weakness of the "merchants of death" thesis has been shown since World War II when governments, including the United States, have become the chief purveyors of surplus arms and munitions.

of war? She had not faced the choice yet. Although some peace groups recoiled from League sanctions because they felt sanctions created a risk of enlarging the war, Eleanor favored economic sanctions against Italy because she thought they would stop the war and compel Italy to seek redress for its grievances through peaceful means.[18]

So she wrote her old German schoolfellow Carola von Schaeffer-Bernstein, who had criticized League sanctions against Italy as "against all laws of God and nature." The World War had ended the correspondence between Carola and Eleanor, but in April, 1933, when Roosevelt had come to power in the United States and Hitler in Germany, Carola again got in touch with "Dear Totty," explaining that she had not written in the intervening years because she had been ashamed of Germany's dishonorable role. But now with the overthrow of the Weimar Republic, Germany had been delivered from meanness and corruption and men with decent points of view had come to leadership. "Can you imagine what happiness it is for us to have our dear black-white-red flag again?"

Eleanor was astonished that Carola, a deeply religious woman, should have so high an opinion of the Nazi leaders, but, fond of Carola and curious as always to find out as much as she could about other countries and peoples, especially when they held views different from hers, she had replied and kept the correspondence going, limiting herself to chitchat about the family and her own busy life. But now she decided she had better let Carola know exactly how she felt about countries that resorted to war to satisfy what they considered to be their grievances. Carola had asked what right England had to think herself better than other nations and sit in judgment on them, and were not sanctions in fact another form of war?

"I do not know that it is England's fault any more than it is the fault of any other country," Eleanor replied a few weeks later,

> but it does seem to me perfectly ridiculous that intelligent human beings cannot sit around a table and satisfy their needs. Sanctions may be as bad as war, but if they would stop the war quickly, I would agree that it was advisable to use them. A brief period of war is better than a long period such as most wars bring us. Of course this country still feels very much detached from the rest of the world because of its size and distance, but that will not last forever. I would like to see some sane methods for settling these differences adopted.[19]

The issue of sanctions versus a mandatory arms embargo split the Conference on the Cause and Cure of War when it met in January, 1936. As the *Times* reported: "The problem of how this country should cooperate with other nations in collaborative efforts to maintain peace, and at the same time keep free from international commitments, proved a stumbling block in the adoption of a program for the coming year." This split in the peace movement was papered over by focusing on the aims on which there was agreement—disarmament, the need to unite the peace movement, and strengthening pacific alternatives to armed conflict.[20]

These were the purposes of the 1936 Emergency Peace Campaign, a movement initiated by the Quakers. Clarence Pickett, the head of the American Friends Service Committee, persuaded Eleanor to keynote the campaign with a nationwide broadcast. She liked Pickett, whom she considered an adviser without vanity or personal ambition, and she liked the way the Quakers validated their faith by good deeds rather than by theological disputation.

Other Americans, however, took a less favorable view of the Quakers, and especially of their pacifism. An Indiana Democrat protested to Jim Farley that Mrs. Roosevelt's association with the Quakers through the Emergency Peace Campaign embarrassed them politically, and in response Eleanor defended the Quakers: "They served as stretcher bearers in the war and were in the trenches with the wounded, and never back of the firing lines, and when the war was over they helped to rebuild what their conscience and religion would not allow them to destroy."[21]

On some points she did not agree with many of the organizations supporting the Emergency Peace Campaign, her letter continued. "I happen to believe that adequate armament for defense is necessary. Others may not; but I can join in any demonstration, at least, which has as its object the will for peace."

Felix Frankfurter was another who thought Eleanor's association with pacifists might prove an embarrassment in a presidential election year. He was especially concerned that George Lansbury, a venerated and saintly British pacifist who had just resigned his leadership of the British Labor party because he opposed the use of sanctions against Italy, was to participate in the Emergency Peace Campaign. Frankfurter asked Missy to pass on to the president a paragraph from "a wise English friend" who had learned that Eleanor was to speak on the same platform with Lansbury. This friend thought this a "dangerous enterprise. The Hearst press and others will pervert it, on the score of a pacifist Labor leader butting in to hamper the American movement of defense, etc."

Eleanor was furious. She spoke to the president and then wrote Frankfurter. "Many things will doubtless be said with which I do not agree" at the EPC meetings where she would be appearing together with Lansbury, she wrote,

> but I am responsible for my own opinions only and they have accepted these.
>
> What Mr. Hearst says or does not say seems to me to matter very little. Whatever he has to say has already been said, and so, though I appreciate your correspondent's concern, will you kindly tell him we will take our medicine and go on doing what things we want to do. The President will not be elected or defeated on anything I do.

Frankfurter swiftly replied disavowing any identification with the warning. He professed admiration for Eleanor's courage, praised Lansbury as "an old and deeply valued friend," and assured her that his correspondent was "a man of singularly fine and courageous character" who shared their contempt of Hearst. "And so," he concluded, "I am glad I passed on my correspondent's concern because it gave rise to these superb and forthright expressions of yours which were not new to me, but nevertheless give one courage and a new confidence every time they are expressed." On this effusive document Eleanor wrote a laconic "? thanks," which Tommy translated into "I understand perfectly your reasons for sending on the comments concerning Mr. Lansbury and I appreciate all the kind things you say."[22]

The Harvard professor should have known that Eleanor made few moves in the foreign-policy field without checking with Franklin and that in this area as in so many others, she was in effect a double agent—a spokesman inside the White House for the hopes of the peace movement, and her husband's deputy within the peace movement arguing for realism. It was not a role she could have played if Franklin had not been committed himself to peace and good neighborliness or if she herself had not tempered idealism with practicality.

Clarence Pickett drafted her speech for the Emergency Peace Campaign, but she turned it over to Franklin, and it was delivered as he corrected and amended it. Pickett's introduction was a recital in praise of what the U.S. government had done for peace, and even in these paragraphs the president made revisions that turned the speech into an exposition of his policy rather than of pacifist anxieties. Where Pickett had Eleanor saying, "I am glad to take part in the Emergency Peace Campaign which has as its great purpose—keeping the United States out of war," Franklin added, "while at the same time maintaining reasonable defense for the nation." To Pickett's sentence on disarmament, "We have pledged ourselves to build up our naval defenses only to treaty strength," Franklin added the warning phrase "as long as Treaties are operative," an addition which would be understood by the Japanese, who had just walked out of the London Naval Conference. Sentences that suggested the failure of the Versailles Treaty and the need for its revision were stricken out, since Hitler was moving toward the denunciation of the treaties that undershored European peace, but a Pickett sentence that urged America's active involvement in international efforts to redress the grievances of the have-not nations he allowed to remain: "We do not intend to be drawn into armed conflict," this sentence read, "but we certainly should be willing to use our resources and our unique position to bring about real results in conferences which deal with any questions remotely touching the peace of the world."[23]

Why should the president object to his wife's participation in the campaign when the keynote address reflected his policy? This was not guile. There was an area of common ground between the peace groups and the administration—the belief that the have-not nations had a case but not one that should be pressed by war and threat of war. Eleanor's relief that war did not follow as a result of Hitler's decision to send his troops into the Rhineland was symptomatic of a widespread view. Writing in 1950, Sumner Welles said that "determined action by France and Britain in the Rhineland crisis, would have changed the entire history of the past thirteen years." But the U.S. attitude, if Eleanor was any barometer, was as irresolute as the British and French:

> I am sure that everyone has been going around with a lighter heart today after reading that Hitler has agreed to join the League in the discussion about the present European situation. I have always felt that in a tense situation, if time could be given for everyone to discuss what was going on before they actually went to war, we might come to our senses. Most of us were taught as children to count thirty before we opened our mouths when we were angry and the same lesson should apply to nations. No one denies that

the Versailles Treaty was unjust in many ways and that revisions should be made. It is quite evident, however, that Germany has ignored the agreements under the Locarno pacts, but it seems more profitable to talk this over than to fight it out again to an unsatisfactory finish and to have another peace built on revenge and fears. France remembers previous invasions in this century, and no one can blame her for wanting to feel secure. There never was a time, however, when other nations were ready to see her point of view as they are today. But there is a tendency also to try to be fairer to all concerned, so let us pray that a spirit of fairness and friendliness to all will actuate the League's deliberations.[24]

The sense of the injustice and unfairness of Versailles weakened her response to Hitler's open violation of the Versailles Peace Treaty. Thomas Mann, at Hendrik Willem van Loon's suggestion, had been a dinner guest at the White House in mid-1935. The distinguished German exile did not believe compromise was possible with Hitler and felt that it was both too soon and too late for a sympathetic recognition of Germany's demands, but if he presented this point of view to the First Lady during his visit she was not yet prepared to accept it.[25]

Roosevelt, too, still hoped that disarmament coupled with economic appeasement of the have-not powers might be the way to halt the drift to war. A friend called Eleanor's attention to a statement by General Jan Christiaan Smuts that German proposals for a twenty-five-year nonaggression pact and disarmament offered a real opportunity to the United States to make its influence felt in the world. She brought the proposal to Franklin, who thought it worthy enough to suggest that she pass it on to Pickett, who "might be interested in talking to the various peace organizations about it."[26]

A few months later Roosevelt shared his thoughts about a "great design" for peace with *Times* columnist Arthur Krock when the latter was an overnight guest at Hyde Park. Roosevelt outlined a plan for a meeting of the heads of the great states. "Among the principals would be the Emperor of Japan, the Chancellor of the German Republic, the President of the French Republic, the King of Great Britain, and Stalin (if, which he doubted, he could get Stalin to sit down with Hitler). But, emphasized Roosevelt, the plenary committee would be a small one." Krock published the story on the understanding that Roosevelt would not deny it.[27]

Pickett was elated. "The President's Chatauqua speech* and now his hint at a conference of 'heads of nations' have stirred my imagination immensely as to possible steps toward peace. Despite a thousand diplomatic reasons against the conference idea it is, I am sure, the only adequately sound and dramatic step. Do encourage him to pursue it." In answering Pickett's letter, Eleanor informed him:

> Of course Arthur Krock was not authorized to tell that story. The President talked his idea over confidentially, and primarily as an idea, but never for publication at this time. However, he does think, in confidence, that only a small conference of the heads of nations, who really can speak for the nations, will ever take any real steps forward. I think if reelected, he will put through something of this kind if he can get the agreement of the other heads.[28]

But were the American people prepared to shoulder any commitment to keeping the peace, which such a conference implied? Educating the American public to the need to make such a commitment was Eleanor's major concern. She agreed to keynote the 1937 No-Foreign-War Crusade, successor to the Emergency Peace Campaign, because it gave her a chance to plead for U.S. support of international cooperation. For much the same reason Admiral Richard E. Byrd agreed to serve with her as chairman of the 1937 campaign. In June, 1936, when the admiral had lain near death at his advance base in Little America, separated for six months from his men, he had vowed to devote the remainder of his life to peace. The Quakers promptly invited him to head up the crusade. He had a "brain throb," Byrd wrote Eleanor on the eve of the crusade: the English-speaking nations led by the president should urge upon the world "a six months' moratorium on conflicting interests and consequent quarrels that appear to be leading inevitably to war."[29]

Admiral Byrd's proposal turned up in Eleanor's mail basket at the same time as an excited letter from Pickett did. He had just heard Sir George Paish, a British economist and foreign-affairs expert, who had "practical suggestions...as to what our country can do to turn

---

*Franklin D. Roosevelt, speech, "I Have Seen War...I Hate War," Aug. 14, 1936, in Franklin D. Roosevelt, *The Public Papers and Addresses,* ed. S. I. Rosenman, 13 vols. (New York, 1938–50), V, pp. 285–92.

the world back from chaos" including "a most important role which the President could play by dramatically appealing to all the nations." Eleanor thought this sufficiently germane to the president's own line of thinking to instruct Tommy, "Have typed copy of letter & send over by hand to Missy for FDR." Roosevelt saw Paish immediately, and he also encouraged Byrd, whose proposal for a moratorium on war had been made public in the meantime by Dr. Nicholas Murray Butler. Eleanor wrote to Byrd:

> Franklin says he thinks your plan is perfectly possible and, by the way, Sir George Paish has very much the same idea and was talking to him about it. Franklin says he wishes he could speak with you on April 6, but does not feel he should do it. He thinks it is grand for you to do it and he wishes that you might go abroad and see what influence you can exert in Italy, Germany, and Russia where our real difficulties lie today.
>
> Of course having your letter published did not upset Franklin at all. He likes to have other people try out ideas. You will have to convince him that there is any use in his calling a conference over the air. He does not think so. He insists that we are the most peace-loving people in the world and other countries are not.[30]

In the absence of encouragement from Europe's leaders, Roosevelt was reluctant to commit himself to a specific conference formula, but he wanted to keep the idea alive, and Admiral Byrd's speech for the No-Foreign-War Crusade in which he called for the establishment of an "efficient international organization" was broadcast from the White House after he had dined there.[31]

In July, Japan invaded North China, and by October Roosevelt's thoughts had shifted from economic appeasement to "quarantine." At Hyde Park the day after Roosevelt delivered his quarantine speech Eleanor listened with a curiosity equal to the newspapermen's as they pressed the president on what he had in mind by a "quarantine" and how such a policy could be reconciled with neutrality. "I can't tell you what the methods will be," Roosevelt put them off. "We are look-ing for some way to peace; and by no means is it necessary that that way be contrary to the exercise of neutrality." "They want to know so many things that I would like to know also," Eleanor commented afterward.[32]

One of the methods Roosevelt had discussed with Sumner Welles a few months before the quarantine speech was to embargo trade with Japan and to have the embargo enforced by an Anglo-American naval blockade. He abandoned the plan, Welles thought, because he had finally concluded "that public opinion would refuse to support any action that entailed even the remotest possibility of war."[33]

Peace-minded as Eleanor was, she was ready for such possibilities. Her whole thinking about war was being shaken to its foundations. The fascist pattern of military threat and racial incitement, the invasions, and the bombings of open cities and civilian populations in Spain and China altered her views about the use of force. On December 12, 1937, Japanese planes attacked and sank the U.S. gunboat *Panay* although it was marked with American flags clearly visible to the low-flying Japanese bombers. The United States demanded an apology and compensation. To pacifists who were dismayed by the firmness of the United States' reaction, Eleanor wrote:

> At the present time Japan is under the domination of a small military group. I do not think we have pushed her into her actions by anything we have done. Even the wife of the Japanese Ambassador nearly weeps whenever she talks about the Panay incident, and if you will go through the events of the past few weeks, you will notice that Japan has tried deliberately to find out how much England, France, and America would stand without going to war. I think her militarists have decided that we would not stand much more so we may be spared further exhibitions.

Then she added, and it was a measure of how drastically her thinking was changing:

> I have never believed that war settled anything satisfactorily, but I am not entirely sure that some times there are certain situations in the world such as we have in actuality when a country is worse off when it does not go to war for its principles than if it went to war.

The United States was a peace-loving nation, she replied to another objector, in no danger of becoming an aggressive one, but that did not ensure its safety: "You have but to look at China, the most peace-loving nation in the world, study its history, and you will see that unpreparedness and an unwillingness to fight have not succeeded in keeping people at peace."[34]

The fascist uprising in Spain, even more than the Japanese attack on China, drew Eleanor away from the peace movement into the ranks of the anti-fascists. "It gets clearer and clearer," Carola wrote her five months after the rebellion in Spain had begun, "that it is not a fight between the nations, but between two different points of view in the world: Bolshevism and Nationalism (in its good meaning)—Christ and anti-Christ." That was not the way Eleanor saw the struggle in Spain. Her young friend Martha Gellhorn had hastened to Madrid on whose outskirts Franco's armies had been stopped. Miss Gellhorn was vibrant, enthusiastic, and so beautiful that Ernest Hemingway, in Madrid to report the war, fell in love with her (a romance that Mrs. Roosevelt later was to encourage). After a few months in the beleaguered capital Martha rushed back to the United States to speak and agitate for the Loyalist cause. "We all listened to Martha Gellhorn while she told us of her experiences in Spain," Eleanor reported of the luncheon at the White House at which Martha spoke. "She seems to have come back with one deep conviction, the Spanish people are a glorious people, something is happening in Spain which may mean much to the rest of the world."[35]

Martha also had returned from Madrid to give what help she could to Joris Ivens, the Dutch film maker and Communist who had collaborated with Hemingway in the production of the film *The Spanish Earth*. She wanted Eleanor and, if possible, the president to see it, and Eleanor arranged to have it shown: "You are right in trying to make people realize that what is happening in Spain might happen anywhere. . . . The air raid on Valencia is terrible, but it is exactly what war seems to do to people. It makes them senseless and cruel and needlessly destructive."[36]

The film made a strong impression upon Eleanor and the president. Hemingway and Ivens were surprised when both Roosevelts wanted the film to be made stronger, because neither Franklin nor Eleanor had realized the degree to which land ownership was concentrated in the hands of the Church and the nobility and how much the peasants' hunger for land was at the root of the conflict. That should be brought out more explicitly, Eleanor suggested, for it was an experience so different from the American.[37]

Her help was solicited for an impartial Red Cross operation to feed the civilian population on both sides. "I talked to my husband," Eleanor wrote Anna Louise Strong, who was one of the many foreign Communists who had rushed from Moscow to Madrid:

He agrees with you that something should be done. However, the difficulty is that Franco will not give any guarantees and, therefore, there is no security that anything will be developed for any one. The other side, of course, will give it. Franco does not need food because he is in the country districts and, therefore, knows that his chances are greater if he keeps food away from the other side.[38]

With food ruled out, Miss Strong joined Clarence Pickett to establish a Joint Committee for Spanish Children to help children in fascist as well as Loyalist territory. Franco's troops were laying siege to the Basque stronghold in northern Spain, which though strongly Catholic was fervently Republican. The State Department, prodded by Eleanor, obtained a promise from Franco that children could be taken through the lines to safety zones.[39]

The friends of the Loyalists wanted to bring five hundred of the evacuated children to the United States, partly because it was a safe refuge, but also because of the propaganda value. Eleanor opposed this, feeling that it was fairer to the children and their parents to keep them as close to home as possible. When some of her friends began to accuse the State and Labor Departments of creating artificial obstacles, she showed annoyance: "Emotionally it is very easy to say that we should receive the children in this country, but it requires a little more than emotion to do the wise thing." It was difficult not to react emotionally in the face of Franco's indiscriminate bombing of Madrid and Bilbao, Martha said in defense of herself and others who supported the evacuation. She did not mean, Eleanor replied,

> that one should not feel emotionally about things that are happening in Spain. I should think, with your friends and your knowledge of what is going on, you would feel emotional. I simply meant that in our feelings towards the children we must not let our judgment be warped by our emotions...I think Allen Wardwell will be successful in raising the money and supplies for us to send both to Spain and to the neighboring countries.[40]

The money was raised and administered by the American Friends Service Committee

The Catholics were apprehensive over Eleanor's increasingly open expressions of sympathy for the Spanish Republic. Patrick Scanlan, managing editor of the diocesan paper the *Brooklyn Tablet*, noted that she was a sponsor of a fiesta the proceeds of which were to be used to purchase milk for the "distressed children" of Spain. "Might we ask, however, if the proceeds are to be used for needy children in Nationalist as well as Loyalist territory in the war...?" "Dear Sir," she replied with terse formality. "I make no distinction in children. Any needing help should be helped."[41]

American Catholics sided with General Franco as strongly as New Dealers did with Republican Spain. And guarded though Eleanor was in her expressions of sympathy with the Republican cause, they did not escape the watchful eyes of a Church hierarchy, which was becoming increasingly hostile to her on other scores. The Knights of Columbus criticized her views on divorce; the bishops did not like her patronage of the American Youth Congress; her sponsorship of an educational film *Birth of a Baby* was denounced by Catholic women's groups as an "offense" to Catholics; Church officials smarted when she protested Franco's aerial bombardment of Barcelona and wondered out loud why women everywhere did not rise up and refuse to bring children into this kind of world. He was outraged, wrote Gustave Regler, German novelist, Catholic, and commissar in the International Brigade, that the Catholics should be scandalized by the filming of a healthy baby in the process of birth and at the same time "not have one word for the dead children of Barcelona."[42]

A longhand letter came to Eleanor from Señora de los Rios, the wife of the Spanish ambassador. She spoke of the horrors of the bombardment of Barcelona, the deaths of hundreds of women and children. Could not the United States use its great authority to make an appeal in the name of democracy and humanity putting forward a formula for peace? Eleanor replied that she felt helpless: "I wish that I were not in the White House at the present time and could be free to make some statement."[43]

Catholic opposition to any move that might help the Loyalists immobilized the president. "When the audiences in my meetings started cheering Loyalist Spain," wrote Regler, "they often called and cheered the name Roosevelt at the same time as a soldier on the battlefield of freedom." But the president, fearful of isolationist sentiment, even more fearful of the loss of the Catholic vote which had been strongly New Deal, and intent on keeping his position aligned with Britain and France, supported the League's policy of nonintervention.

As German and Italian intervention became more blatant and

massive, friends of the Spanish Republic in the United States mounted an agitated campaign to lift the embargo on Spain. Within the White House Eleanor was its chief supporter. Journalist Louis Fischer, an authority on Soviet foreign policy, came to see her to argue the case for lifting the embargo. Eleanor wrote Fischer a few days later:

> I talked to the President and told him what you said. He agrees with you, but feels that it would be absolutely impossible to repeal the Neutrality Act, because the people of this country feel that it was designed to keep us out of war, and, on the whole, it is the best instrument to accomplish that end. He feels certain that we could not get the people to change this point of view without a period of education and perhaps from experiences which they have not yet had.[44]

Many thought the president had the authority without going to Congress to revoke the embargo on Spain, and the Lawyers Committee on American Relations with Spain prepared a brief to that effect. "FDR material you may like to see," Eleanor wrote on this. Witter Bynner, author and a Harvard classmate of Roosevelt's, pleaded the same case in a letter to Eleanor which she also passed on. "The only thing that can be said," Roosevelt advised her, "is that it seems *more* than doubtful that any action to lift the embargo can be taken legally." Bynner thought that "Frank," as he called him, while "sympathetically inclined towards the Loyalists," had been badly advised. Eleanor, too, was mistrustful of the State Department. "I rather gathered that the French assistance to the Spanish was not great," she agreed with Martha Gellhorn. "And I gather that even our own State Department has people who are not very anxious to do much for the Loyalists. Strange how easily our profits affect our feelings for democracy!"[45]

Max Lerner, sitting next to Eleanor at a refugee-aid dinner, warned her that he would have to attack the president sharply on the embargo issue. "Say what you think and feel," she replied unhesitatingly. "My husband would want you to. There are so many from the other side who are pushing him from their direction that we had better build our own fires to counteract their pressures."[46]

By the end of 1938 all of Loyalist Spain except Madrid had fallen. In one of its farewell gestures, the Republican government sent Eleanor a set of Goya etchings taken from the original. "It is a genuine emotion and not a formal state gesure to give these pictures to you," Martha assured her. The *Brooklyn Tablet* protested her acceptance of this gift. "In view of Franco's victory in Spain I think it would be highly improper for you to accept the Goya etchings stolen from the Spanish people," a Brooklyn reader of the *Tablet* wrote her. "Any sympathy you showed for the Loyalists in Spain was in very bad taste. As First Lady of the Land you should have assumed a neutral position."

"We are still recognizing the Loyalist Government," she replied defiantly:

> The Goya etchings are not "stolen" but done by a Spanish Loyalist and therefore the property of the Loyalist Government.
>
> I am not neutral in feeling, as I believe in Democracy and the right of a people to choose their own government without having it imposed on them by Hitler and Mussolini.

She refused to be intimidated, and sent the four books to the Corcoran Gallery to be placed on exhibition. "It is one of the five impressions done from old prints, and bound especially for me," her accompanying letter said. "I hope the people will enjoy seeing them."[47]

The war was lost. "At this very sad hour," Señora de los Rios wrote her from New York City, where her husband had accepted appointment to the Graduate Faculty in Exile, "I can only say that your kindness, courtesy and understanding have made much easier, circumstances which at times seemed beyond endurance."[48]

In Los Angeles a Catholic group threatened to boycott Eleanor's lecture unless she was introduced by someone other than Senator Robert W. Kenny, who, the Catholics said, was a sponsor of the Friends of the Abraham Lincoln Brigade, "a group who deliberately left this country to engage in a religious war in Spain." Eleanor rejected the demand. "As he [Franco] had the full support of the Italian and German fascist governments, it was natural that the democratic Loyalist Government had to turn for what help they could get to the communists. That did not, however, mean that they themselves were a communist government." As for the young Americans in the Abraham Lincoln Brigade, they had felt that democracy was threatened in Spain "and therefore I can not feel that any one supporting them is in any way anti-Catholic or pro-Communist."[49]

In the final days of the war, Leon Henderson, a militant New Dealer and Loyalist supporter, was at the White House when Eleanor brought up the subject of Franco's victory. "You and I, Mr. Henderson, will some day learn a lesson from this tragic error over Spain. We were morally right, but too weak." She turned toward the president as if he were not there. "We should have pushed *him* harder." The president did not defend his policy.[50]

47. A SPIRITUAL SHOCK

IT WAS IN SPAIN, WROTE ALBERT CAMUS, THAT MEN OF HIS GEN-eration "learned that one can be right and yet be beaten, that force can vanquish spirit, that there are times when courage is not its own recompense." After Spain came Munich to drive home the lesson that the force of dictators had to be met with force. Yet Eleanor Roosevelt was a reluctant convert.

Since the country had not been prepared to support sanctions, even against Japan, Roosevelt's follow-through on his quarantine speech was to recommend to Congress a vast rearmament program and to revert to the conference approach. In this he was abetted and advised by his newly named undersecretary of state, Sumner Welles.

Both the president and his wife found Welles more congenial than Cordell Hull. Eleanor's relationship with Hull was courteous and cool, as it was with the State Department generally. Hull kept her at arm's length. Letters that she sent to him were answered in State Department officialese. Once, when she was asked to take part in an international peace broadcast, she wrote on Tommy's memorandum, "I do approve but tell him the State Dept. wld have a fit if I said anything." She considered the department stuffy. When a vice-consul in Latin America asked in verse to be allowed to return home and was answered in verse by a State Department clerk, she commented, tongue in cheek: "Somehow or other I had not given credit to any one in the State Department for so much versatility and humor. It is nice to feel that what of necessity must be such a solemn branch of government may occasionally deal lightly with a situation."[1]

But it was not the department's stuffiness as much as its conservatism that bothered her. Harry Hopkins told her after his trip abroad in 1934 that American diplomats in Europe did not seem to know anything about the country they were in except what they were told by members of the upper crust, and they were not even interested in finding out from Hopkins what was going on in the United States. It

was only with the president's promotion of Welles to the undersecre-
taryship that Eleanor began to feel a genuinely sympathetic presence
in the department. "Sumner's mother and mine were great friends
and he went to school with my brother," she wrote. "Franklin never
knew him as well as I did but appointed him because of his abilities.
...I think Sumner was very much in sympathy with what Franklin
wanted to do."[2]

Welles proposed that the president call the Diplomatic Corps
together on Armistice Day and broach the conference idea as part of
a dramatic appeal for peace. The president was enthusiastic, but Hull
violently opposed such "pyrotechnics." Roosevelt gave up the Armistice Day appeal but wanted to go ahead with the conference. When
Welles saw Roosevelt he found him "harassed and irritated" by Hull's
relentless objections. Hull finally agreed on the condition that British
Prime Minister Chamberlain would be consulted first.[3]

It was about this time that Eleanor spoke to the annual Conference on the Cause and Cure of War, where she pushed the conference
idea: "If we are going to have peace in the world we will have to find
machinery to draw us together and make us function together and we
have got to find a way by which we can actually attack the problems
before they reach the point where people will want to go to war about
them....I don't think leadership lies along the path of isolation."[4]

Chamberlain's reply to the president's soundings, Welles wrote later,
was "a douche of cold water." The British leader protested that such a
conference would cut athwart British efforts to appease Germany and
Italy. Winston Churchill thought Chamberlain's rebuff of Roosevelt
represented "the loss of the last frail chance to save the world from
tyranny otherwise than by war." A few weeks after Chamberlain's
airy dismissal of the "proffered hand," Hitler moved against Austria.
Yet even if Chamberlain had accepted, how far could Roosevelt have
committed the United States? As Eleanor wrote at the time:

> Of course the trouble is that most people in this country think that
> we can stay out of wars in other parts of the world. Even if we stay
> out of it and save our own skins, we cannot escape the conditions
> which will undoubtedly exist in other parts of the world and which
> will react against us. That is something which I have preached from
> coast to coast on deaf ears I fear. We are all of us selfish—note Mr.
> Hoover's statement on his return from Europe—and if we can save
> our own skins, the rest of the world can go. The best thing we can

do is to realize nobody can save his own skin alone. We must all hang together.[5]

With Austria annexed Hitler began his moves against Czechoslovakia. In September the crisis came to a head. Chamberlain, believing Hitler could be appeased, flew to Berchtesgaden to confer with him. Although earlier in the year Eleanor had seemed to feel the time had come to stand up to the dictators, she recoiled from the prospect of war:

> I open the newspapers every day with a feeling of dread and I turn on the radio to listen to the last news broadcast at night, half afraid to hear that the catastrophe of war has again fallen on Europe. It seems to me that the Prime Minister of England did a fine thing when he went to visit the German Chancellor in a last effort to prevent bloodshed. It seems insanity to me to try to settle the difficult problems of today by the unsatisfactory method of going to war. If you kill half the youth of a continent, the problem will be no nearer a solution, but the human race will be that much the poorer.[6]

The British and French effort to resolve the crisis peacefully in effect reduced itself to an attempt to settle it at the expense of Czechoslovakia. The Czechs stood firm. Hitler threatened to march. "I thought as I looked at the pictures of the French Reservists leaving," Eleanor wrote, "how terrible it must be for those who remember 1914. How incredibly stupid it was for us to resort to force again!"[7]

Such pleas for peace played into the hands of the forces personified by Chamberlain who were prepared to sell Czechoslovakia down the river. It needs to be said, however, that responsible American leaders were in no position to urge Britain and France to stand up to Hitler when they knew the United States was not prepared to support the democracies if the result should be war. "The poor Zchecks! [sic]," Eleanor wrote her husband from Cousin Susie's, where "the quiet and calm" seemed "like another world.... I don't somehow like the role of England & France, do you? We can say nothing however for we wouldn't go to war for someone else."[8]

She read Thomas Mann's *The Coming Victory of Democracy.* The great humanist's quietly stated argument that force had to be met with force left her unsettled and confused. "I am sure that he feels as I do that the

World War and the attempts which we made at permanent settlements really left us with the seeds of the present complicated international situation," she wrote. Little had been done in the years since Versailles to correct its injustices. "Now, too late perhaps, we are conscious of this need when the world is faced again with the alternative of using force and building the same bitterness that we built up before, or else of allowing those nations which believe exclusively in force, to have everything their own way." Mann felt that "force must be met with force, but that is what we have been doing from generation to generation." She speculated on whether the world was witness again to another shift in the balance of power, or whether more was at stake. "It is very difficult for me to think this situation through. If we decide again that force must be met with force, then is it the moral right for any group of people who believe that certain ideas must triumph, to hold back from the conflict?"[9]

That was the critical question for her. If there was war, what was the United States? What was she prepared to do?

The British and the French had appealed to Roosevelt to use his influence to bring about a peaceful resolution of the crisis. An Allenswood classmate who moved in Court circles cabled from England:

DEAR ELEANOR ONE WORD FROM AMERICA WILL SAVE
EUROPE.
YOUR SCHOOLFELLOW MARGUERITE FEW ONCE BAXTER

Eleanor replied that she wished she knew "what the one word is which America could say to avert war. We are all deeply concerned but you seem to have a mad man in Europe who does not care how many people are killed." With the United States not prepared to intervene on the side of the democracies, Roosevelt could scarcely refuse to make the one move that was open to him. He cabled Hitler, Chamberlain, Daladier, and Beneš urging the parties "not to break off negotiations," stating that there was "no problem so difficult or so pressing for a solution" that it could not be settled by pacific methods.[10]

Beneš, Chamberlain, and Daladier promptly expressed their agreement with Roosevelt that the issue could be settled peacefully. But Hitler's reply, when it finally arrived, rehearsed Germany's case against Versailles and the League and ended on the chilling note that the responsibility rested "with the Czechoslovakian Government alone, to decide whether it wants peace or war." Roosevelt sent another appeal to Hitler. Eleanor was handed a copy, and she underlined the paragraph reading: "Present negotiation still stand open.... Should the need for supplementing them become evident, nothing stands in the way of widening their scope into a conference of all the nations directly interested in the present controversy." Next to the words "the nations directly interested," she wrote, "Are we?"

The question did not have to be answered because the next day Hitler invited Chamberlain, Daladier, and Mussolini to Munich. "In company with many people through out the world," Eleanor wrote that day,

> I breathe again this afternoon in the hope that this meeting in Munich may bring about peace instead of war. It may be harder to work out problems in a peaceful way, but it certainly seems to me worth the effort, for things which are imposed by force rarely are satisfactory.[11]

Her sense of relief was not unmixed:

> I can not help wondering, however, whether the patient in this case when he comes to and finds himself minus some arms and legs will not feel rather sad at having had them removed without being allowed a consultation.[12]

She was having great difficulty sorting out her ideas. The threat of war had lifted, but she disliked intensely the fact that the great powers had forced a small nation to submit, invoking a principle of self-determination they were unwilling to apply to themselves.

> Here the British, together with some others, have decided that the Sudeten Germans should have the deciding voice as to what country they wish to belong, and lo and behold, Palestine has a revolt. Perhaps they want to vote, and the Irish seem to have caught the fever and shall we be hearing from a few other peoples soon, I wonder? A complicated world, isn't it.

But in writing to her Allenswood classmate, Helen Gifford, she was less positive about the rights and wrongs of the Sudeten issue:

I feel with you that things are not definitely settled and I can well imagine that Mlle. Souvestre with her feelings about minorities might be very unhappy. However, I cannot help being glad that the countries involved did not send thousands of young people to be killed over this particular question. Czechoslovakia was set up in an arbitrary way and my whole feeling is that the question should have been discussed in a calm atmosphere and not at the point of a pistol.[13]

Another Allenswood classmate, "Bennett," wrote that she was relieved that war had been averted, but confessed that she was baffled by Carola, who had written enthusiastically about her son being in the German army.

and oh what a wonderful thought it was that he might give his life for his country. I may be unpatriotic, but I have not the slightest desire that my own sons should give their lives either for their own or anyone else's country if it can possibly be avoided! Indeed my chief feeling about Chamberlain's achievement is the deepest gratitude that they are not doing it now.

"Of course all you say about Carola is true," Eleanor replied,

and I cannot say that I want any of my children to go to war and be killed. Hitler has certainly managed to give the Germans a curious psychology, and how Carola can talk about being a Christian and not see the inconsistency of what they are doing is beyond my understanding. I think she realizes this, because I haven't heard from her in a long while, and we are becoming more and more articulate in this country as to our feeling.[14]

She was herself much clearer as to what she thought and less guarded in saying what she felt about neutrality revision and rearmament. A lecture trip in the midwest took her to Wisconsin. "The LaFollettes have been everywhere & are speaking against increased armament," she wrote the president, "but I had a good audience last night, people standing & no one took exception to my point of view."[15]

America's isolationism seemed to Eleanor to be nurturing a growing insensitivity to human suffering elsewhere, especially to the plight of the refugee. Her first effort to help refugees was undertaken at the request of the Grand Duchess Marie of Russia, who in 1934 had asked her to talk to the president about a bill to legalize the status of white Russian refugees who still had only temporary visas. Eleanor had spoken with the president, and the bill the Grand Duchess wanted— S. 2692—had been adopted by the Senate and signed by the president.[16]

But there were few such victories for the advocates of easing the immigration laws in order to provide a haven for Jewish and other anti-Nazi refugees from Hitler. All such moves foundered on the hard rock of a congressional resistance that was supported by American public opinion. "What has happened to us in this country?" Eleanor asked in her column at the beginning of 1939. "If we study our own history we find that we have always been ready to receive the unfortunates from other countries, and though this may seem a generous gesture on our part, we have profited a thousand fold by what they have brought us."

When she wrote this she was in the midst of a new effort to open America's doors a little wider. In early November the Nazis had horrified world opinion by *Kristallnacht* (night of the broken glass), when a wave of looting, arson, destruction, and cruelty had been let loose on Germany's hapless Jews in reprisal for the assassination of a German attaché in Paris by a young Polish Jew. Anti-Nazi and Jewish groups in the United States thought that perhaps in the light of events, which made it clear that the fate of Germany's Jews was sealed, U.S. public opinion might be willing to support legislation to ease the quotas for children.

At the end of December, Rabbi Stephen Wise's daughter, the brilliant and eloquent Justine Polier, who was a children's court judge in New York and active in the American Jewish Congress, conferred with Eleanor about a child-refugee bill which would provide for the admission of ten thousand children a year for two years in excess of the German quota. She would take it up with the president, Eleanor told Judge Polier. Franklin gave the bill the green light, and Eleanor outlined the strategy to Mrs. Polier:

> My huband says that you had better go to work at once and get two people of opposite parties in the House and Senate and have them jointly get agreement on the legislation which you want for bringing in the children.
>
> The State Department is only afraid of what Congress will say to them, and therefore if you remove that fear the State Department will make no objection.
>
> He advises that you choose your people rather carefully and, if possible, get all the Catholic support you can.[17]

The bill was introduced in early February, 1939, by Robert Wagner in the Senate and by Edith Nourse Rogers, a Massachusetts Republican, in the House. The supporting committee for the legislation included George William Cardinal Mundelein, Canon Anson Phelps Stokes, Herbert Hoover, Alfred Landon, and Frank Knox. Despite this impressive sponsoring group, the legislation immediately ran into objections from the American Legion, the DAR, and the American Coalition of Patriotic Societies, who contended that "charity begins at home."

"Are you willing I should talk to Sumner, and say we approve passage of Child Refugee Bill?" Eleanor cabled Franklin, who was on board the U.S.S. *Houston* in the Caribbean. "Mrs. Roosevelt's gentle persuasion did not work," wrote one critic of what he called Roosevelt's seeming indifference to the fate of the children. It was an unjust accusation, as Eleanor's letter to Judge Polier describing the president's attitude demonstrated. Eleanor had talked with James G. McDonald, the head of the president's Advisory Committee on Refugees, about what the president should do, she wrote Judge Polier,

and he told me he [McDonald] is in favor of the bill personally, but he has been told that pressing the President at the present time may mean that the people in Congress who have bills to cut the quota will present them immediately and that might precipitate a difficult situation which would result in cutting the quota by 90%, and that, of course, would be very serious. Therefore, the committee hestitates to recommend support of the bill when they do not know whether this will be the result or not.

I also talked with Sumner Welles. He says that personally he is in favor of the bill and feels as I do about it, but that it would not be advisable for the President to come out, because if the President did and was defeated it would be very bad. I told him I did not think it was any question of the President's actually coming out, though he was anxious to see the bill go through.

I cabled the President and he said I could come out and I could talk to Mr. Welles and say he would be pleased to have the bill go through but he did not want to say anything publicly at the present time.

Mr. Welles feels very strongly that pressing the bill at the present time might do exactly what Mr. McDonald says, because his desk is flooded with protests accusing the State Department at conniving in allowing a great many more Jewish people than the quota permits to enter the country under various pretenses.[18]

House and Senate immigration committees held hearings in April and May, and, as the State Department had feared, restrictionist groups led by the patriotic societies turned out en masse to denounce the legislation as "part of a drive to break down the whole quota system." At the beginning of June New York Representative Caroline O'Day asked the White House for an expression of the president's attitude. "File No Action," Roosevelt stoically scrawled on this query. A few weeks later Wagner withdrew his bill, which the Immigration Committee had modified so that the 20,000 children would come in—not in addition to but against the regular German quota.

"We used to be more sensitive to human need," Eleanor had remarked sadly to the Conference on the Cause and Cure of War at the beginning of the year. The defeat of the Child Refugee bill painfully underlined that judgment.[19]

An increase in anti-Semitism was another facet of the country's intensifying isolationism. "As to my husband's being a Jew," Eleanor replied to a woman who had passed this on as her friends' explanation of the Roosevelt administration's alleged partiality toward the Jews,

> there is one name, a great many generations back, which might have been a Jewish name and, as a joke, in my uncle Theodore Roosevelt's family it used to be said that some of the intelligence came from the ancestress. I feel, however, that if she was a Jew—and none of us know whether she was or not—the blood has been so much diluted that there is very little left in my husband's generation.[20]

Her own feeling about Jews, as about all ethnic, racial, and religious groups, had changed dramatically from her insecurity, dislike, and sense of strangeness with members of minority groups when she had been in Washington during the Wilson administration. Prejudice, she had come to understand, was worse for the person who felt it than for those against whom it was directed. "When a person holds deep prejudice, he gets to dislike the object of his prejudice. He uses it as an excuse for the fact that there is something unworthy in himself." And when you blame someone for your own undesirable qualities, "it becomes hard to be honest with yourself."[21] The Nazi persecution of the Jews reflected envy and insecurity: "It is the secret fear that the Jewish people are stronger or more able than those who still wielded superior physical power over them, which brings about oppression."[22]

People were good and bad, sensitive and calloused, greedy and generous—but not because they were Jews or Italians or Negroes or Anglo-Saxons.[23] And if a minority had certain disagreeable mannerisms or traits—the Jews, she felt, tended toward clannishness—that was because of what the dominant society had done to them. The gentile world had "pushed the Jewish race into Zionism and Palestine, and into their nationalistic attitude."[24] When a Jewish doctor inquired what Jews might do to stop "the ever-increasing tide of anti-Semitism," her answer essentially was assimilationist:

> I think it is important in this country that the Jews as Jews remain unaggressive and stress the fact that they are Americans first and above everything else; that they give help, together with the other citizens of this country, to the people who are being oppressed because of their race and religion; and, as far as possible, wipe out in their own consciousness any feeling of difference by joining in all that is being done by Americans.[25]

But basically she felt that the Jews were powerless and that their fate rested with the non-Jewish world.

> It depends almost entirely on the course of the Gentiles what the future holds. It can be cooperative, mutual assistance, gradual slow assimilation with justice and fair-mindedness towards all the racial groups living together in different countries, or it can be injustice, hatred and death. It looks to me as though the future of the Jews were tied up as it always has been with the future of all the races of the world. If they perish, we perish sooner or later.

Zionism and nationalism needed no apology, a Jewish editor protested; assimilation had not saved the Jews of Germany and Italy. "Mrs. Roosevelt read your editorial," Tommy wrote him, "and thinks you may well be right."[26]

An isolationist storm blew up at the end of January when, with a French observer on board, the latest model U.S. bomber crashed and it was disclosed that Roosevelt had authorized the sale of military planes to France. Eleanor defended the president's decision.

Do our sympathies lie with the other democracies or do they lie with the totalitarian states? Germany is geared to produce a thousand planes a month; France to produce one hundred planes a month. It seems quite evident why France would be interested in buying from us. It is also quite evident that Germany would naturally start a hue and cry that the U. S. was favoring France....

I want to see all the nations of the world reduce their armaments. Mr. Chamberlain has suggested it, but I have seen no acquiescence on the part of Mr. Hitler. Have you? Who is taking a belligerent attitude in the world today?[27]

The isolationist leaders thought it prudent not to reply to the First Lady, but the Nazi press did. The *Lokal Anzeiger* advised her to

leave politics alone.... One should ask her to keep her pen away from things of which she is ignorant. There are many other better fields of work for a militant writer; for instance, social questions concerning the 12,000,000 unemployed, lynching, child labor and public morals. It is not good for a nation if not only the husband but also the wife enters the political china shop.

Her press conference asked Eleanor what she thought of that. "I thought their whole attitude was that women didn't count," she replied. She was a "bad influence" on her husband, wrote *Popolo di Roma*, and "too many" of his decisions were swayed by her anti-totalitarian ideas.[28]

On March 17 Hitler moved again, occupying Prague and partitioning Czechoslovakia. Chamberlain, pushed by British public opinion and outraged by Hitler's failure to keep his word, pledged military assistance to Poland in the event of an attack by Hitler. Eleanor applauded:

The gentleman with the umbrella, finding that "appeasement" does not work where ethics do not exist, has gone the whole way in the opposite direction. It takes courage to do that, if you are in politics, and it cannot be done, except in a democracy. A dictator must always be "right." He can never be a human being, for his hold upon the people lies in the illusion that he is a superman.[29]

In a last-minute effort to stave off catastrophe, the president proposed to Hitler and Mussolini that in return for a specific pledge of nonaggression against thirty countries in Europe and the Near East, there would be an international conference in which the United States would participate to deal with access to markets, raw materials, territorial issues, and disarmament. "I am waiting anxiously, like everybody else, for the answer from the German and Italian heads of State to the plea for peace made by the President of the United States," Eleanor wrote.[30]

But Hitler and Mussolini, emboldened by the success of their tactics of terror and violence, were not disposed to negotiate, and turned down Roosevelt's plea with scorn and derision. Hitler called a special meeting of the Reichstag to do so, and at the same time denounced Germany's nonaggression treaty with Poland. Roosevelt had not really expected Hitler to respond otherwise, but he hoped this new demonstration of Hitler's hostility to collaboration would soften isolationist opposition to the more flexible neutrality for which he had been pressing Congress since January. But the isolationists drew the opposite conclusion. Every move Roosevelt made to prevent war in Europe confirmed them in their view that he was seeking a way to involve the United States in Europe's quarrels. An amendment of the neutrality laws to give him the power to use methods short of war which might have been a warning to the dictators that an attack upon Poland would range the United States on the side of the democracies remained stalled in committee.

The only positive indication that in a showdown precipitated by Hitler the democracies would stand together was the state visit to the United States in June of King George VI and Queen Elizabeth. "I need not assure you that it would give my wife and me the greatest pleasure to see you," Roosevelt had written the British monarch just as the Munich crisis was coming to a head, "and, frankly, I think it would be an excellent thing for Anglo-American relations if you would visit the United States." The visit was a great triumph; the United States embraced Their Majesties. Even Father Coughlin carefully referred to them as "lovely personalities" who, however, were being used "to nullify our basic foreign policy of no entanglements." Roosevelt was the impresario of the occasion. Every item of protocol, ceremony, and program underwent his scrutiny. Yet much of what made the visit distinctive bore his wife's unmistakable stamp.[31]

Not without some travail. "Oh dear, oh dear, so many people are worried that 'the dignity of our country will be imperiled' by inviting Royalty to a picnic, particularly a hot dog picnic," she wrote in her column two weeks before the royal couple arrived. In the forefront of the worriers was Sara, who forwarded a letter she had received begging her to rein in her daughter-in-law before she disgraced the country. On the back of the letter Sara had written a little message, "Only one of many such." "Poor darling," commented Eleanor; she did not know "that I have 'many such' right here in Washington."[32] Beneath Eleanor's boundless tact and perfect good taste was an irrepressible and occasionally impish democrat. Her critics should relax, she went on. What people remembered of a visit abroad were the differences, not the similarities with the way things were done at home, especially the customs that were a little queer and amusing: "We certainly don't want to make everything so perfectly English that there will be nothing for our guests to smilingly talk about afterwards." While she deleted this sentence from her column, she refused to be deterred by those who scoffed at what they considered her Yankee parochialism from showing the king and queen aspects of American life that were characteristic of the country and the Roosevelt reforms. And her husband supported her.

At the White House she presided over a lawn party where the king and queen met the heads of such agencies as the NYA, WPA, and Social Security that were distinctively New Deal. Dr. Will Alexander, the Farm Security administrator, was one of those whom she brought over to the king and queen to tell them what he was doing. He recorded later, "It was one of the most amazing performances and was an indication of where the hearts of President and Mrs. Roosevelt were."

The concert at the State Dinner also reflected Eleanor's special touch. There was Kate Smith, who was typically American, although Ickes grumbled that she was "a type one would expect to hear in a cheap music hall." Ickes did approve, however, of Marian Anderson, whose participation in this most select and glamorous social event of the Roosevelt years was the artistic high point of the evening as well as an unspoken rebuke to the snobbery and prejudice that had excluded her from the DAR auditorium. Another unorthodox performer in the concert for the royal couple was Alan Lomax, a gifted young collector and singer of folk songs, who seems, as a premature hippie, to have occasioned some shocked whispers since his locks were unshorn, his socks forgotten, and his political associations suspect.[33]

The semiofficial German News Bureau reported: "On Friday afternoon Mrs. Roosevelt has arranged a tea and a reception at which she hopes to bring the Left Radical members of the Federal

Government into conversations with the royal couple." The Italian propagandists took another line. "Mrs. Roosevelt did not kneel when introduced to Queen Elizabeth, despite the fact that this is court etiquette. This is the greatest scandal of the present era," noted *Popolo di Roma.*[34]

If Berlin and Rome were scandalized, the British ambassador was not wholly serene. He was unhappy that Eleanor presented her press-conference regulars to the king and queen, as Eleanor wrote Kathleen McLaughlin of the *New York Times:*

> I might have been able to do even more than that if one of your colleagues had not been fool enough to tell the British Ambassador that I was thinking of having a press conference when the Queen was there. I understand that the girls in Washington just about killed her![35]

She arranged for Harry Hopkins' six-year-old daughter Diana to meet the queen, whom she told beforehand that she thought Diana envisioned queens with crown and scepter. In that case, said the queen, it might be more satisfactory to the child if she saw her dressed for dinner. So that night Eleanor and Diana stood waiting in the hall for Their Majesties to come out of their rooms. When they did, Diana made her little curtsy to the queen who, Eleanor reported, lived up to a child's dream of how a queen should look, for "her spangled tulle dress with her lovely jewels and her tiara in her hair made her seem like someone out of a story book."[36]

From Washington the royal visitors went to Hyde Park with a stopover in New York to visit the World's Fair. At the Hyde Park picnic the menu included frankfurters and beer and the entertainment was equally distinctive, although some of the 165 guests found the Indian princess, Te Ata, boring and the voice of the young refugee singer, Charlotte Kraus, unexciting. "Not very good," recorded Helen Robinson of the entertainment, "but perhaps it was a novelty to the King and Queen—at any rate they were very polite about it, and the King was amusing himself by taking moving pictures." And throughout it all there was Eleanor "dashing about in a little brown gingham dress, seeing that the lunch was properly served and that everybody was comfortable, just as though it were only a family party." Afterward the president got into his little hand-operated Ford, with the queen beside him and the king in back, and drove away, "which looked very nice and informal."[37]

A dinner for the visiting royalty at the Big House was Sara's moment of glory. The king took her in, and the only toast of the evening was that of the president to the king's mother, a lovely tribute to two very awesome ladies. There were minor mishaps, and Eleanor could not resist the impulse to report them. An overloaded serving table crashed, and Eleanor's stepsister-in-law was heard saying to Sara, "I do hope that it wasn't *my* china that was broken." And later a tray of ice, water, and ginger ale hurtled to the floor when a butler slipped on his way to the library. "Why mention that?" the president asked when Eleanor checked her column with him. She thought people would like to know that accidents happen to housekeeping, even in the president's house. The president laughed and withdrew his objection. For the remainder of her life Sara would tell her children, "If *my* butler had been used instead of those White House people, none of these things would have happened."[38]

As the train carrying the king and queen pulled away from the Hyde Park station, the crowd of Roosevelt's Hyde Park neighbors which had gathered for the departure suddenly began to sing "Auld Lang Syne." It was a moving moment. "We all knew the King and Queen were returning home to face a war."

"Now for 'the visit,'" Eleanor reported to Maude Gray: "Everything went well.... Both [the king and queen] interested me & I think he feels things more than she does & knows more. She is perfect as a Queen, gracious, informed, saying the right thing & kind but a little self-consciously regal."[39] The king and queen had made a good impression, Ickes noted in his diary, "although I doubt whether there will be any relaxation of the wariness with respect to possible entanglements in foreign affairs."[40]

Public opinion was shifting away from isolationism, especially as signs multiplied that Hitler intended to force Poland to yield Danzig even at the risk of war with Britain and France, but the shift was not sufficiently pronounced to bring about amendment of the neutrality laws. By narrow majorities the House upheld the mandatory arms-embargo provisions of the legislation. "The vote last night was a stimulus to war," Roosevelt wrote Eleanor's old colleague and friend, Representative Caroline O'Day. But her vote with the majority was an indication of the sincerity and depth of conviction that gripped both sides in this historic controversy. Roosevelt turned to the Senate, but it postponed action until January, 1940, after Senator Borah disputed

Hull's warning that there might be war before then. His sources of information were better than the State Department's, Borah said.

The senators were eager to get away from the Washington heat, the president told Eleanor over the phone. She could not bring herself to believe there was nothing to be done to halt the looming conflict, but privately she was pessimistic:

> It would be marvelous if one could get all the nations around a table to discuss what they really need and put the money into something other than armaments. Unfortunately, however, my husband found when he sounded out the possibility of such a meeting that there was no cooperation forthcoming from the dictators. We pray daily that there will be no war although I must say our own Senators have made it more difficult to use one's influence to prevent a war.[41]

"I don't know what might happen now," she wrote Martha Gellhorn, "but it looks pretty hopeless to me and our hands, as far as prevention goes, are pretty well tied."[42]

On August 12 the president left Hyde Park for a few weeks of relaxation on the U.S.S. *Tuscaloosa*. "I think I shall spend most of the first few days sleeping," he told his wife. He was at Campobello on the fourteenth. "I look at the papers anxiously," Eleanor wrote him, "but hope you get the whole of your cruise, not just for your sake but for the sake of the poor people in Europe."

On August 21, Hitler secured himself against a two-front war by conclusion of the Nazi-Soviet Pact. "It would be a pact with the devil, if Britain signed an agreement with Russia," Carola had written "Bennett." The Englishwoman promptly wrote back, after revelation of the Hitler-Stalin pact, to ask whether "the devil had suddenly grown angel's wings in the sight of all good Germans!" Carola replied that "of course they were very much surprised but that everyone thought it wonderful!" Carola had been writing to her for months, Eleanor replied, "that only Christ's teachings could save us, and how one can reconcile Mr. Hitler with belief in Christ is more than I can tell."[43]

Within hours after the signing of the pact Hitler's demands for the return of Danzig had turned into a full-blown war crisis. The president broke off his cruise.

Again Roosevelt appealed for a peaceful resolution of the crisis—this time addressing himself to Hitler, the king of Italy, and the president of Poland. Carefully Eleanor commented that "blindly to ask for peace is no help in the present situation, for peace may be bought today at too high a cost in the future. It may be wise to buy it, but you must do so knowing what your objectives are for the future, and accepting the conditions which are a part of the price which is paid." Part of the price, she was suggesting, if war was to be averted, would be U.S. involvement in a settlement that would be fair as well as secure.[44]

"Negotiation, mediation or arbitration are just words," she wrote the next day, "but any one of them if put into practice now by people who really want to keep the peace might mean life instead of death to hundreds of thousands of young men." She asked Franklin over the telephone when he might be arriving at Hyde Park. Perhaps not for months, he told her, and his tone of voice implied that arrivals and departures were no longer of consequence, that in fact nothing relating to the plans of individuals counted any longer. Her heart sank, for it reminded her of 1914. "What a horrible situation it is," she wrote her husband that night.

"And still we wait from day to day hoping and praying for peace," she wrote on August 29. "I feel that every day that bombs do not actually burst and guns go off, we have gained an advantage." The thought of war desolated her. She looked again at Thomas Mann's tract on force having to be met with force, but the sentence that seemed most meaningful to her, so much so that she sent it on to Franklin, moved in the opposite direction. "War is nothing but a cowardly escape from the problems of peace," it read.

Then it came. "At five o'clock this morning our telephone rang," she reported from Hyde Park, "and it was my husband in Washington to tell me the sad news that Germany had invaded Poland and that her planes were bombing Polish cities. He told me that Hitler was about to address the Reichstag, so we turned on the radio and listened until six o'clock." She had just received a letter Carola had written August 19 begging Eleanor to try to see Germany's point of view and not to judge Germany too harshly. It was the same as in 1914, Carola felt, when the whole Western world had been arrayed against Germany, and just as in 1914 it would be said again that "it is only Germany's fault." But who could decide, since "meanings have always differed and will always differ about what is an offensive and what is a defensive war. . . . No nation is better than another and none is worse than another."[45]

There was no hatred for the German people in the United States, Eleanor replied, only an inability to understand how people of spirit can be terrified by one man and his storm troops to the point of countenancing the kind of horrors which seem to have come on in Germany not only where the Jews are concerned, but as in the case of the Catholics and some of the liberal German Protestants.

People judged Germany because of what they heard on the radio.

The radio makes a tremendous difference because one can actually hear these leaders make their speeches, and I listened, knowing enough German, to Mr. Hitler's speech to the Reichstag. He never mentioned that there was a God whom we are supposed to love, nor did he show the slightest sympathy for the people whom he had plunged into the war.

Her concluding paragraph showed that she was resigned at last to the Mann thesis that there could be no compromise with Hitler: "I hope that we are not facing another four years of struggle and I hope that our country will not have to go to war, but no country can exist free and unoppressed while a man like Hitler remains in power."[46]

Eleanor's old friend Harry Hooker saw her just after Britain and France had announced themselves at war with Germany. He reported to Anna Boettiger in Seattle that he felt Eleanor had "received a spiritual shock.... She has always worked so hard for peace and has had such faith in humanity."[47]

One question immediately met her everywhere: Could the United States keep out? "To that my answer always is the same and the only answer I can make, 'nobody knows. We hope so with all our hearts.'" But the next day, in a more downcast mood than ever, she wrote Maude Gray, "The attack on Poland by Russia has depressed F.D.R. He feels we are drawing nearer to that old decision 'Can we afford to let Germany win?' Stalin and Hitler are much alike, aren't they?"[48]

And to a conscientious objector who declared that "the man who goes to war for an ideal sacrifices his ideals in the process," she sadly replied: "I agree with you in theory but I would rather die than submit to rule by Hitler and Stalin, would not you?"[49]

48. MRS. ROOSEVELT AND THE COMMUNISTS

A CATHOLIC PRECEPT TEACHES MAN TO HATE THE SIN, NOT THE sinner. It was a rule Eleanor lived by and it is useful in an examination of her involvement with Communism and Communists in the thirties. Her attachment to democracy was too strong, her perception of realities too clear to permit her to be tempted by Soviet Communism; but her understanding of human weakness was so great and her sympathy for human beings in distress so all-encompassing that it was natural that Communists, too, would be embraced in the circle of her compassion.

Her views on Soviet Russia and Communism in the early White House years can be summed up quickly. She was convinced that Communism could gain a hearing in the United States only if this country's social system failed to provide Americans with jobs, security, and justice, but she also held the equally strong conviction that anti-Communism was exploited cynically by the privileged and powerful to prevent change. She felt a friendliness toward Soviet Russia as a nation and believed that the policy of nonrecognition should be ended in the interests of world peace and American trade. She was also interested in Soviet Communism as a social system based on planning and public ownership, but her interest was mixed with a repugnance for the Soviet regime's totalitarian aspects. Finally, she was convinced that America had to find its way toward a more just society on the basis of its own experience, tradition, values, and resources.

In 1933 she had seen the conditions that bred revolution when she was taken around the abandoned mines and desolate mining villages in West Virginia by Alice Davis, the county welfare commissioner. A remarkable woman, Miss Davis had worked with Quaker relief in Russia for eight years and had come out of that experience a confirmed anti-Bolshevik. She was grateful to the New Deal, she told Eleanor, because being a revolution itself, it helped to stave off the famine, suffering, and loss of freedom that she had seen after the Russian

Revolution. Once when friends whom Eleanor took to Arthurdale extolled the virtues of the Communist system on the basis of a brief visit to Russia, Miss Davis, although she was a Quaker, lost her temper and told them they knew nothing about Communism. "If you and Mr. Roosevelt had not come to lead the people," she wrote after that exchange, "I think many of us might have been thinking differently. But now it seems to me that every American must put all his strength into changes that will bulwark us against Communism."

In the spring of 1933 Louis Howe had taken Eleanor to the camp of the bonus veterans. The group that was most discomfited by her appearance there were the Communists, and the veteran who had exclaimed "Hoover sent troops, Roosevelt sent his wife" reflected the chagrin of the Communists who only began to make rapid headway among the bonus marchers after they had been routed from the capital by MacArthur's troops. The Communist party was minuscule in 1933; its membership was around 10,000, but many were dedicated revolutionaries, and it was a rapidly growing movement with a great attraction for intellectuals because of the contrast between what seemed to be a breakdown of capitalism and the purposefulness and rationality of Soviet Russia's Five-Year Plan. The Communists might have prospered had the new administration in 1933 taken the road of repression rather than relief and reform.[1]

That was evident from Lorena Hickok's letters and reports to Harry Hopkins from all over the nation. In mid-1933 her letters were full of the desperation of the unemployed and the hopes openly expressed by the Communists that the failure of government policies would lead to a general economic collapse. But a few months later, as relief funds began to reach the unemployed and hungry, Hickok was reporting from the Dakotas that the CWA was undermining the efforts of the Communists, who were "going about from farm to farm" trying to stoke the fires of revolt. And one of her final reports in March, 1936, recalled the headway that Communism had been making among middle-class Negroes until WPA and relief money saved many of them.[2]

Eleanor had a strong aversion to Communism, and an even stronger sense that the way to prevent it was to eliminate the conditions that bred revolutionary discontent. This was an old conviction of hers, first expressed in the 1912 campaign when she had written from the Democratic convention in Baltimore that "if we are not going to find remedies in Progressivism then I feel sure the next step will be socialism." She was not a Communist, she wrote a Michigan woman, but she had seen conditions "in this country where there were enough people being influenced by the communists, and I am afraid if I had been living under those conditions I might have been more easily influenced."[3]

Although the New Deal was clearly a democratic alternative to Communism, and Eleanor saw it as such, conservatives and reactionaries insisted on portraying it either as the forerunner of Communism or as its ally, and sometimes even as Communism itself. Dr. William A. Wirt, the Indiana school superintendent who testified before a congressional committee that Roosevelt was the Brain Trusters' "Kerensky," cited the Arthurdale project as one of the proofs of the administration's Communism. She did not understand how Dr. Wirt could consider it "communistic to give people a chance to earn their own livings and buy their own homes," Eleanor protested, but protests and explanations did not stop this line of attack. "They are putting on a little under-cover campaign of their own," reported Lorena Hickok in August, 1934, from the Rocky Mountain area.

> The Chamber of Commerce crowd... [doesn't] say much about the President. It's aimed mostly at Mrs. Roosevelt, Henry Wallace, Rex Tugwell, and what they rather vaguely describe as "the rest of the New Dealers." Mrs. Roosevelt especially is supposed to have strong Communistic sympathies and a tremendous and very bad influence on the President.

Eleanor's mail reflected this whispering campaign, and in answering one of these letters she wrote:

> I am at a loss to understand your remark "as to how far you and your friends intend to take him on the road to a government, such as they have in Russia, for instance." You do not seem to realize that it would be difficult for any one to influence the President against his own judgment, and you assume a desire on my part which is far from fact. I know of none of my friends or his friends who have any such idea.[4]

Some Americans were genuinely frightened. A Dorchester woman entreated Eleanor to have Emma Goldman deported, because, she said, the anarchist leader had instigated the assassination of McKinley and as long as she remained in the country President Roosevelt was in danger. "Emma Goldman is an old woman," Eleanor replied, "with absolutely no desire in her heart to do any harm to any one, or any opportunity to do so if she would want to."[5]

There was genuine fear of radicalism, but there was also the exploitation of such fears to preserve the status quo. Even the *Louisville Courier-Journal,* a newspaper sympathetic to the administration, editorialized against the Child Labor Amendment on the grounds that many of its sponsors were Communists. Frances Perkins begged Eleanor to write Robert W. Bingham, the publisher of the *Courier-Journal,* who was also Roosevelt's ambassador to the Court of St. James, and Eleanor did.

> I feel quite sure that you are not in sympathy with this editorial, but all the world has sent it to me and I wonder if you could say something, gently but firmly, to your editor about classing as communists those people who have worked for years for exactly what the administration has now done through its codes. Because of the codes, great numbers of states are rapidly ratifying this amendment, and this would put the administration, and the President himself, in the class of communists.

"Nothing could have been farther from the editor's mind than to associate the President, or his administration with Communism," a distressed Bingham replied. "Of course I should not tolerate any such thing for one moment. I am sure no reference has been made to this subject in the *Courier-Journal* beyond giving the history of some of the affiliations of some of the people who aided in founding the Children's Bureau." There was not the slightest objection to his paper stating its viewpoint, she assured him, except

> that it is unjust to classify the original supporters of the Child Labor Amendment as communists. Mrs. Kelly was a socialist but she worked all her life for many things which have since been adopted and are not considered socialistic today. Many people who knew her had great admiration for her and an editorial as bitter as was the one which was printed in your paper of course excites her friends.[6]

Many of the accusations referring to Eleanor's supposed Communist sympathies originated in *The Red Network,* compiled by Elizabeth Dilling and described by her as "A Who's Who and Handbook of Radicalism for Patriots." Just as the imaginative genealogist can find blue blood in anyone's lineage, so Mrs. Dilling, by diligent use of "guilt by association," managed to taint with subversion almost every liberal and New Dealer in the country. If one belonged to an organization to which Communists also belonged, or if the organization was praised by the *Daily Worker,* or if an organization or individual supported a cause which Communists also supported, that made one suspect; the possibilities of linkage were as inexhaustible as Mrs. Dilling's capacity for research. As Eleanor wrote a woman who inquired about Mrs. Dilling's charges:

The lady you speak of is probably quoting from a book written by Mrs. Dilling, called "The Red Net Work," in which I am accused of being a Red, as is everyone in this country who is working for better living conditions. She mentions Lillian Wald, who founded the Henry Street Settlement in New York, and who was a pioneer in establishing the splendid nursing service we have in this country. Mrs. Carrie Chapman Catt, who has worked to educate people on the causes and cures of war, and most of the men and women who have had any interest in the better treatment of their fellow human beings.

In her analysis of radical political trends, Mrs. Dilling labeled as "red" such figures as Gandhi, Einstein, and Frances Perkins. Of the great scientist she wrote: "Einstein, barred as a Communist from Germany, in January, 1934, was an overnight guest of the President at the White House." Among the 460 organizations that she described as "Radical-Pacifist controlled or infiltrated" were the Amalgamated Bank, the American Association for Old Age Security, the American Friends Service Committee, the Catholic Association for International Peace, the Federal Council of Churches, the League of Women Voters, the National Consumers League, the NAACP, and Union Theological Seminary. The itemization of suspect associations for Eleanor Roosevelt was substantial:

ROOSEVELT, MRS. FRANKLIN D.: Socialist sympathizer and associate; pacifist; Non-intervention Citz. Com. 1927; Nat. Wom. Tr. Un. Lg.; Nat. Cons. Lg.; co-worker with many radicals, some of whom have been appointed to Government positions by her husband; speaker, Nov. 24–25, 1933, Prog. Edu. Assn. meeting with radicals Norman Thomas, Reinhold Niebuhr, Harry A. Overstreet, etc. sent telegram expressing hope for success of World Peaceways; vice pres. N.Y. Lg. Women Voters; addressed pacifist Conference on Cause and Cure of War, introduced by Carrie Chapman Catt, who exulted that "for the first time in the history of our country we have a woman in the White House who is one of us"; she predicted unless we change our concept of patriotism "we most certainly will commit suicide"; she revealed that her recent declaration against toy soldiers for children had brought a "violent letter" from a man who dubbed her "preaching pacifism" as "inconsistent if your husband has to call the boys to the colors."[7]

Rather than intimidating liberals, the indiscriminate, often cynical efforts to brand as "Communist" all welfare legislation and organizations that were manifestly liberal had the opposite effect in the later thirties of causing liberals to shrug off charges of Communist control even when there was merit in the charges.

In the same letter in which she ridiculed Mrs. Dilling's *The Red Network,* Eleanor gave her assessment of Soviet Russia: "It happens that we in our country will never be content with the rather limited freedom that has come to the Russians, though to the Russians it may seem a great step in advance of what they have had before."

Eleanor had approved the president's decision to recognize the Soviet Union; she had, in fact, encouraged a change in policy. When, at the close of his fourth-term campaign in 1944, Roosevelt defended recognition of Soviet Russia in 1933 as "something that I am proud of," he added a "personal" note:

In 1933, a certain lady—who sits at this table in front of me—came back from a trip in which she had attended the opening of a schoolhouse. And she had gone to the history class—history and geography—children eight, nine or ten, and she told me that she had seen a map of the world with a great big white space upon it—no name—no information. And the teacher told her it was blank, with no name, because the school board wouldn't let her say anything about that big blank space. Oh, there were only a hundred and eighty or two hundred million people in it, which was called Soviet Russia.... For sixteen years before then, the American people and the Russian people had no practical means of communicating with each other. We re-established those means.[8]

Eleanor's interest in U.S. recognition of the Soviet Union was pragmatic, not ideological. A piquant glimpse of the attitude to the Bolshevik Revolution in the circles in which Eleanor and Franklin moved at the time it took place is afforded by Caroline Phillips' journals. In early 1918, at a meeting of "the Club" (the name that the Roosevelts and their closest friends in the Wilson administration gave their Sunday gatherings) at the Roosevelts', Caroline and the Adolph Millers performed a song and dance, and because the three of them had been arguing for a negotiated settlement of the war, Adolph sang extemporaneously, "For we are the gay Bolsheviki." A few months later, when Woodrow Wilson made the decision to intervene in Russia and to dispatch an expeditionary force, Eleanor's only comment was to lament that General William S. Graves and not Theodore Roosevelt's friend General Leonard Wood "goes in command to Siberia."[9]

But that was fifteen years earlier. By the time Roosevelt assumed the presidency enlightened U.S. opinion had long accepted the view that nonrecognition served neither the interests of the United States nor that of world peace. A committee that Esther Lape organized in 1932 to study the "Relations of Record" between the United States and the Soviet Union and to press the case for recognition reflected this shift in American opinion. Eleanor was a member of the committee, as were old Russia hands like Colonel Hugh Cooper, who had supervised the building of the Dnieperstroy Dam, and conservative Wall Street figures like Thomas W. Lamont and John W. Davis. "I think this group will be helpful," Eleanor advised her husband in July, 1933. Evidently he thought so, too, because he kept sending messages to Esther to speed up the report.

Roosevelt, however, was less interested in a scholarly report setting forth the "Relations of Record" between the two countries, Esther discovered, than in what the committee might do to lessen the feeling of American "church people" against recognition. Curious as to whose views Roosevelt listened to regarding U.S. policy toward Russia, Colonel Cooper one day asked the First Lady, "Mrs. Roosevelt, who is it now who really exercises influence with the President?" She exploded into laughter. "There never is one. Franklin plays one against the other. He is much too canny to be under the influence of any one individual."

If the report had little influence on the president, it was noted that when Soviet Foreign Commissar Maxim Litvinov arrived to carry on the recognition negotiations he had a copy of the committee's study in his hand, and after the complex talks ended in the exchange of ambassadors, Thomas Lamont wrote Esther that he thought Litvinov should raise an icon to her in Moscow.[10]

One subject touched on in the conversations between president and commissar related not to affairs of state but to the relations between husbands and wives with careers of their own. Mrs. Ivy Litvinov, the commissar's English-born wife, a highly cultivated woman, did not accompany her husband to the United States.

"Mrs. Roosevelt and I regret so much that your wife couldn't accompany you," the president said to Litvinov.

"Oh, well, you know. Very active woman, career of her own, constantly traveling, making speeches. Impossible to interrupt what she was doing. Came alone because she is individual in politics just as I am."

"I think I understand," Roosevelt commented.[11]

In 1936 the Soviet government sent a delegation of managers and technicians to study U.S. factories. Two women, Mme. Pauline Z. Molotov and Miss Ludmilla Shaposhnikova, were in the group, and Eleanor invited them to lunch at the White House along with Mrs. Hull, Mrs. Wallace, and Isabella Greenway. The Soviet women were the heads of Russia's soap and cosmetic industry and were studying American methods of manufacture and distribution. More than 50 per cent of the Russian women, even the farm women, were using the better grades of face soap and cosmetics, the Russian ladies boasted. Neither Mrs. Roosevelt nor Mrs. Greenway used cosmetics, and Isabella could not resist pointing this out to the representatives of the new Puritanism, quickly adding, however, "Of course, you must not judge the other women of this country by Mrs. Roosevelt or myself. I feel quite sure that if Mrs. Roosevelt began to do one eyebrow she would go out forgetting to do the other!"[12]

One source of information about Russia at this time was Sara Gertrude Millin, a South African writer whom Felix Frankfurter encouraged to write to Eleanor about her newly published life of General Jan Christiaan Smuts. She had been to Russia, Mrs. Millin's letter said, and it had turned out to be nothing

like I had imagined from the books I had read and the films I had seen. I had many-sided and extraordinary opportunities to see things—met Madame Litvinoff and her friends, newspapermen, foreign ministers, sincere communists, the simple people. I wish happiness only results for them, and I think that if Germany doesn't attack them they *may* emerge. But today—just this day—they are the most distressed people I have ever seen—worse off, in my mind, than the natives here.

There's only America for the hope of the world. Thank God for its President to maintain that hope.[13]

Another source of information on Russia during the thirties was Anna Louise Strong, indefatigable propagandist for Soviet Communism. Eleanor had her come to lunch at the White House when the president was there and evidently both Franklin and Eleanor enjoyed the conversation. How it went and the subjects covered may be surmised from the letter Miss Strong wrote to Eleanor a few days later. Evidently she had gone straight to the Soviet Embassy to discuss some of the questions the Roosevelts had brought up.

As for Stalin,—after leaving you I saw Troyanovsky, who is an old friend of my husband's. I asked him if he agreed with the picture of Stalin I gave you. He said: "I well remember Stalin from earliest days,—an unobtrusive youth sitting in conferences, saying little, listening much. Towards the end he would venture a mild suggestion and we began increasingly to see that we always took it. He summed up best the way to our joint purposes."

Stalin's authority, Miss Strong went on, arose from his ability to analyze events:

He has refused several chances to make himself the personal "god" of the people. . . . So the President asks whether people in these conferences don't feel that they "have to" agree with Stalin, the answer is both yes and no. Personal wire-pulling is not, I think, his characteristic, but the painstaking search for the adjustment of each bit of human material into a place where it can function, is. I have even been told by people in a position to know, that it was Stalin who tried to the last to "save Trotsky" against the rising ire of the Central Committee. I don't repeat this in America, not wishing to lose my reputation for sanity, but I can quite believe it myself.[14]

In addition to wanting to know how Stalin wielded power, Roosevelt pressed Miss Strong on how the Soviets raised money for their budget. Money did not seem to be an issue in the Soviet Union, she replied. The Soviet problem was time—"to get schools, factories, tractors—quickly rather than cheaply." She indicated that Roosevelt's problem was how "to get money from unwilling owners," but in the USSR the

> money problem becomes: which industries shall we run at a loss in order to establish them or to cut costs of basic necessities? Which shall we compel to pay for their plants out of three or four years income? On which shall we profiteer shamelessly in order to use the surplus for health, education and losses of needed industries?

Priorities were assigned.

Eleanor was politely skeptical. She did not understand how the Russian leaders managed to get diverse social groups—peasants, workers, managers, consumers—to act jointly if not by coercion. Moreover, she had the feeling that it was simpler to manage Russia's primitive economy than America's sophisticated and highly developed productive machine. "Their problem is simpler," Miss Strong replied, "because they have no fundamental clashes over ownership, but only clashes over which district or industry shall be developed first."

"But I see your tragedy," Miss Strong went on with the presumptuousness of someone who was sure that history was on her side. "The people trust you to use power for their benefit. And you want to do it. But you haven't power to use. Power resides in ownership of the means of production; the financiers have it, not you. But the people think you have it, and so, in spite of their great faith and your own sincerity, they will grow disillusioned." She was pessimistic about the future: "The financiers will force you steadily to the right and if you do not go, they will be ready, either through the ballot or by subsidizing veterans, to put in someone who will." Roosevelt would end up in the same plight as Ramsay MacDonald and the German Social-Democrats, she predicted. Having thus delivered herself of the party line on the future of the Roosevelts and the New Deal, she signed herself a little lugubriously, "with great admiration for you personally and utmost sympathy for the difficulties of your position."

Eleanor thanked her for her letter, adding, "However, we are much more hopeful than you are."[15]

Eleanor listened to Anna Louise Strong, and she also listened to the Quaker relief worker Alice Davis and her friends among the Russian *émigrés.* She and Lorena Hickok visited Miss Davis, who had moved to Dumbarton, Virginia, while Alexandra Tolstoy, a foe of Soviet Communism, was there. "Mrs. Roosevelt understands everything," Tolstoy's daughter said afterward. Miss Davis then added, "When you were here—I remember you questioned whether we would have to go through the same awful bloodshed that the countries abroad are having. I think that the reason we shan't have to is that you and the President do 'understand everything' or at least a very great deal about all sorts of people."[16]

Both the president and the First Lady had great confidence in themselves and in the redemptive power of American democracy, and were not afraid to talk with Communists. Eleanor felt that loyalty oaths were a reflection of fear, and any action motivated by fear seemed to her almost always to end up being unwise action. "Fear is not a constructive force," she told the *New York Herald Tribune* Forum in 1938. When the women cheered Representative Martin Dies, whose House Committee on Un-American Activities had just begun its probes of Communism, she wrote *Herald Tribune* publisher Helen Reid, "I was just grieved that a group of women so intelligent and outstanding could be carried away with and approve so spontaneously Mr. Dies." She was gravely concerned by

the constant battle going on between those who would have us fear the communists and those who would have us fear the fascists. You are thrown into the arms of one or the other in order to defeat the opposite trend of ideas. . . . You rarely see stressed anywhere the fact that it is difficult to win a negative battle. Why are we in this country not stressing a constructive campaign for democracy? We need not fear any isms if our democracy is achieving the ends for which it was established but we must fight for something.[17]

Occasionally she had held back from supporting a movement because it was too closely identified with the Communists, even though its professed purposes were worthy. By the late 1930s, however, she had become less concerned over being tagged a Communist because of Communist involvement in the organizations which she helped.

This was the period of the Popular Front when, because of the rise and advance of fascism, liberals and Communists joined together in defense of democracy and peace. Although conservative columnists portrayed this as a movement of liberals toward Communism, precisely the reverse was happening—the Communists were transforming themselves into militant New Dealers. Roosevelt, despite his stunning victory in the 1936 elections, found himself increasingly stalemated in Congress by a coalition of Republicans and southern Democrats, which kept buried in committee his bills to help the one third of a nation that was still impoverished.

Unable to muster support for his programs through the Democratic party organizations, Roosevelt began to look for allies in the unions and in the organizations that spoke for the ill-housed, ill-clothed, and ill-fed. The job fell to his wife; he wanted her to do it, and she wanted to do it. Inevitably it meant increased involvement with the left—with such organizations as the American Youth Congress, the League of Women Shoppers, and the National Negro Congress, as well as the NAACP, the trade unions (especially those affiliated with the CIO), the Southern Tenant Farmers Union, and the Southern Conference for Human Welfare.

Foreign developments also pushed Eleanor toward the left. To the more militant liberals, the enemies of the New Deal in the United States represented the same forces of appeasement that had brought fascism to power in Italy and Germany, were in rebellion against the Spanish republic, and were conniving with fascism in Britain and France.

The president felt similarly. "Over here there is the same element that exists in London," Roosevelt wrote U.S. Minister John Cudahy in Dublin. "Unfortunately, it is led by so many of your friends and mine. They would really like me to be a Neville Chamberlain—and if I would promise that, the market would go up and they would work positively and actively for the resumption of prosperity."[18] Countless committees sprang up, some organized by liberals, some by Communists—to aid Spanish democracy, for Chinese relief, to boycott German goods, to help Jews and intellectuals and other victims of fascism, committees to try to stop war by resisting fascism, not by appeasing it. Democrats of all hues, not only New Dealers, flocked into these groups. The presence of Communists was no deterrent, for during the years preceding the Nazi-Soviet Pact, Communists were considered among the staunchest foes of fascism, as was the Soviet Union, despite the terrible things that were happening inside its sealed frontiers.

The treason trials and purges in Moscow bewildered and horrified

Eleanor, as they did most New Dealers. Anna Louise Strong blandly defended the trials:

> You asked me what the reaction of the ordinary people in the USSR was to the trial. My husband has sent me some clippings from the newspapers of letters which poured in from the people. I am inclined to think that Stalin made a bad mistake in ever letting Trotsky out of the Soviet Union. The man is really incredibly dangerous, the more so because he has a very remarkable degree of magnetism which sweeps whole crowds of people off their feet. I know because I once gave him English lessons and I am still ashamed to remember how completely he could sway my convictions if he took the trouble.

Eleanor's reply was a noncommittal thank you. She was equally reticent in her comment on a letter from Marjorie Davis, the wife of Roosevelt's ambassador to Moscow, who had sent her a copy of the verbatim proceedings of the trials issued by the Soviet government with the comment, "At almost any place that you may open the book, there is much to impress the mind that a tremendous plot existed.... There seems to be such a predisposition on the part of the outside press to discount the facts of what the Government was up against, that I thought you would be interested in scanning this book."[19]

Dr. Jerome Davis, an old Russia hand who had been dismissed from Yale because of his activities with the American Federation of Teachers, thought he could find out the truth about the trials. He had been in charge of YMCA work in Russia during the war, had administered the prisoner-of-war camps in Turkestan, and had made several trips to Russia after the revolution. The new batch of trials, he wrote worriedly to Eleanor in March, 1938, would make any kind of understanding between the American people and the Soviet Union more difficult. "It will," Eleanor wrote next to this observation. Davis thought the United States should have an "unofficial observer" at the trials who could report directly to the president, and he volunteered for the assignment:

> I knew all these men from my work as he head of the YMCA during the World War. I have personally autographed pictures of Lenin and Stalin. I could go directly to Stalin and get the inside story of at least what he thinks is true.... I must say that all these trials make a bad impression on me as I know they must on the public at large.

"What would you think?" Eleanor queried her husband. The Russians would never consider it, he replied. She conveyed this message to Dr. Davis, adding, "I am afraid the world is not idealistic enough as yet."[20]

She listened to those who defended and apologized for the macabre proceedings in Moscow, and she also read the documents of the other side. Princess Alexandra Kropotkin lent her Vladimir V. Tchernavin's *I Speak for the Silent,* which she read, and Eleanor Levenson, the manager of the Rand School Book Store, a Menshevik stronghold, sent her the "Letter of an Old Bolshevik," which the school had just published.

"I wish that in some way we could get across to the people," Eleanor wrote her friend Mrs. William B. Meloney, organizer of the *New York Herald Tribune* Forums and editor of *This Week,* "that the thing we really fear and are horrified by in Russia is not the real communist theory which any peaceable people may decide to live under, but the same kind of dictatorship which takes toll of its people through force in the same way as does fascism." Theoretically Socialism and Communism could be achieved democratically; it was the departure from democracy, the corrupt reach for power of small groups and certain leaders "no matter what explanation they give, which brings about the horrors that we have watched in Russia and in other countries."[21]

The Communists in the Popular Front organizations insisted that to look at the Soviet Union and Stalin objectively, not to mention critically, was a disservice to the anti-fascist cause. Eleanor rejected this view and was pleased when the American Youth Congress resolution condemning dictatorships specifically mentioned the Communist as well as the fascist variety. On the other hand, she refused to allow the events in the Soviet Union and the Communist apologies for them to keep her away from organizations in which Communists were active.

The Workers Alliance held a "Right to Work" congress in Washington in June, 1939, to protest the congressional slashes in relief appropriations. Eleanor accepted honorary membership in the alliance even though she had been told it was a radical group. "There may be some things you believe in that I don't believe in," she said, "but I certainly am in sympathy with the meeting of any group of people who come together to consider their problems." Arthur Krock praised her, saying that she spoke "the enlightened truth, as she does so often, when she told the Workers Alliance that there are two ways in which to calculate the New Deal's public relief bill which posterity must pay or repudiate. She said in effect it was better for future national health to pass on a purely fiscal burden than one measured in terms of congenital, physical, moral and spiritual disease." But some columnists, like Frank R. Kent, preferred to ignore the issue of joblessness and concentrate on Communism: "It is almost incredible," Kent wrote, "that this Communist-saturated organization, whose object is to browbeat Congress and push the government to greater and greater expenditures for relief, should find its staunchest friends not only among the government officials who administer relief but in the White House itself."[22]

"I hope you will forgive me if I disagree with you in your feeling that I should not speak to the Workers' Alliance," she replied to the inevitable flood of critical letters:

> I believe that the people who turn to Communism do so because they feel that it might possibly answer some of their difficulties, and they are usually people who have difficulties.
>
> The Workers' Alliance is composed of WPA workers, many of them not even able to get on WPA. From long experience I have discovered that when people are unhappy, it is better to give them an opportunity to come into contact, even to ask questions, of someone whom they feel is responsible than to let them feel that they are shoved aside without any consideration. Going to speak to them doesn't foster Communism. They know exactly where I stand, but they also have a feeling that someone at least near to the seat of government is willing to listen to their troubles.[23]

Then the news came that Germany and the Soviet Union intended to sign a nonaggression pact. The pact was sealed on August 24; Hitler was free to launch his attack on Poland which he did on September 1.

"Some of the statements made in the last few days by various members of the Communist Party in this country seem rather odd," Eleanor wrote in a letter to Mrs. Strong dated August 28:

> I have always felt that, in theory, Communism was closer to Democracy than Nazism. In spite of the realization that Stalin was a dictator and that Russia was going through somewhat of the same kind of thing that all revolutions seems to have to go through, still one had the hope that in the future the theory of Communism would make a world in which Democracy and Communism might live together.
>
> This treaty does not seem to me to be in the interest of peace. It simply says to Hitler, "We will not attack you, so you are sure of having one less enemy. We need your machinery and you need our

raw materials, and we are quite willing for our mutual benefit, to have a trade agreement with you. As far as we are concerned, you can go ahead and take possession of any of the other countries that you choose without our help."

England and France will be in a much more difficult position. Of course, it seems quite possible that there may be in addition to this some secret agreement by which Russia will take her share of any particular country she is interested in controlling.

In a letter of September 5, Miss Strong was still enthusiastic about President Roosevelt, as she had not as yet realized the new orders from Moscow would mean a break with the Roosevelt administration. Her husband, she said—"supposedly a regular Bolshevik—goes wild with delighted excitement over the President's speeches, and declares that 'Just two countries, America and the Soviet Union, are the hope of the world.'" It was the first time, she went on, that she had ever heard him enthusiastic over anything "outside socialism and the USSR." It reminded her of Earl Browder's views that Roosevelt's actions, in Miss Strong's words,

> had caused a fundamental revision of the beliefs of the Communists; it had made them for the first time concede that real gains could be made for the working class under a "bourgeois democratic government," and that if the real democracy of the New Deal could be established, it should be possible to proceed from this, step by step, without violent overturn, to socialism.

Eleanor found this less impressive than Browder's readiness to accept Moscow's orders. That was as repugnant as Soviet policy itself: "The thing which is doing Russia the most harm in this country, no matter how much we all of us dislike the Dies Committee," she wrote, "is the fact that Earl Browder and various other American communists, are discovered not to have been acting as free agents but as directed ones."[24]

She was now perfectly clear in her own mind that cooperation with the Communists was impossible. In a few months she would reach the same conclusion about Popular Front organizations in which Communists not only were participants but, as it turned out, the controlling force.

49. FDR ADMINISTERS
A SPANKING

———————————◆————

A FEW WEEKS BEFORE THE NAZI-SOVIET PACT AND THE OUTBREAK
of war, Paul Kellogg, the editor of the *Survey,* and his wife Helen
Hall, the head of the Henry Street Settlement, congratulated Eleanor
Roosevelt on the "gallantry" she had displayed at the Model Congress
of Youth, "by that meaning your brave faith in them—for you were
certainly taking risks in view of the ugly and twisted attacks upon
them. You were in a sense putting yourself in their hands."[1]

The attacks on the Youth Congress, mixed as the motivations were,
had a basis in fact. For several years liberals and Communists had
worked together in a mottled array of Popular Front organizations
that were united on a program of support for Roosevelt, a strengthened New Deal, and collective security. The alliance had its critics
who contended that the real control in the Popular Front organizations rested with the Communists and that the latter, because of their
subservience to Moscow, were insincere adherents of the democratic
faith and untrustworthy partners in the democratic cause.

The test came after September, 1939. Before then, as the *New Republic* noted, the Communists had pursued the Popular Front policy so
ardently "that one can hardly tell them from New Deal Democrats."[2]
For a few grotesque weeks, after the signing of the Nazi-Soviet Pact,
the American Communists, while awaiting clarification from Moscow,
made a spectacle of themselves with their successive rationalizations
of the alliance. The new directives from Moscow arrived, and the
Communists dutifully about-faced. They characterized the war in
Europe as "imperialist," declared that the democracies were as guilty
as the fascist nations for its outbreak, accused Roosevelt of plotting
to push the United States into it, and called for all-out opposition to
Roosevelt's "war-hunger" program. Neither peace nor the immediate
interest of the masses, the Communists continued, could any longer
be promoted through "the Democratic Party or any faction of it." The
issue no longer was "a third term" but "a third party."

Eleanor read the statement with distaste and disbelief. She considered it tantamount to a declaration of loyalty to a foreign power. A group of veterans organizations challenged her on her support of the American Youth Congress. What basis did she have for her belief that its leadership was not Communist? The Youth Congress leaders should not be blamed, she replied, for the statements of Gil Green, the head of the Young Communist League, and Earl Browder, claiming credit for the growth and development of the Youth Congress. The Communist leaders, she said, seemed to owe their "first allegiance" to another country, and it would probably be to America's benefit "if we should allow these people to go to that country."[3]

As for her confidence that the Youth Congress leaders were not Communists, she reported that was based on hours of discussion with them, getting to know them as individuals. She had carefully examined their finances. She had attended their national and regional meetings, studied their minutes and resolutions. She had even sent for the FBI reports. Had groups such as the Legion, who criticized her support of the Youth Congress, been as painstaking and conscientious in their scrutiny?

Many of the witnesses before the Dies Committee cited the Youth Congress as an example of Communist deception and control, but the credibility of the Dies Committee and its witnesses was not very high at the White House. Established in 1938 with the encouragement of John Nance Garner and the votes of the southern bloc, in its first year the committee not only attacked Popular Front groups such as the Youth Congress without giving them an opportunity to reply but, using the technique of trial by headline, helped destroy the WPA's Federal Theatre and Writers' Projects. It contributed measurably to the defeat of Frank Murphy for re-election as governor of Michigan. It harassed Frances Perkins for her failure to deport Harry Bridges, the longshoremen's leader who was charged with being a Communist, and made itself a sounding board for attacks upon the CIO by old-line elements in the AFL. "The Dies Committee was from the outset on the track of the New Deal and all its works," wrote Walter Goodman in his objective study of the committee's history.

It was characteristic of the committee that, having obtained the lists of the Washington chapter of the American League for Peace and Democracy, a Communist-inspired anti-war organization, it made the lists public, including the names of 563 federal employees, a procedure that Roosevelt denounced as "sordid." By this "act of mass exposure, the Dies Committee obliterated all distinctions," Goodman observed.[4]

Although the White House shared the loathing of the committee and its methods that was felt by liberals and New Dealers, in late November, 1939, when an official of the Youth Congress telephoned Eleanor in New York City to say that the congress had received a telegram to appear at committee hearings the next day, she urged her young friends to be cooperative and not request a postponement. She was returning to Washington that night, she added, and would talk with them at the station before she left on the midnight train.

The young people, including the author of this book, who as head of the American Student Union had also been summoned to appear before the committee, were in a defiant mood when they met her at the train. They wanted to use their appearance to indict the committee, not to clear their organizations of the charges of Communism. Eleanor counseled otherwise. "Volunteer information," she urged, "try to cooperate with the Committee." The young people seemed like her children to her. "Don't assume a hostile attitude," she went on. Even if the committee was unfair, they should be restrained. She would try to get the president's permission to attend the hearings, she said, as she bade them good night.[5]

At 10:00 A.M. the youth group arrived in the caucus room. Neither Representative Dies nor J. B. Matthews, who had originally denounced the Youth Congress as a Communist front and was now the committee's chief interrogator, elected to be present. Representative Joe Starnes of Alabama, a fairer man with a sense of humor, was presiding, and he was in no hurry to call the youth group. Other witnesses were being questioned when without advance notice Eleanor, dressed in green, entered the caucus room alone at 11:15. A southern gentleman, Mr. Starnes stopped the questioning: "The chair takes note of the presence of the First Lady of the Land and invites her to come up here and sit with us." But Eleanor, who a few days earlier had said that she was willing to testify before the committee herself, declined the invitation to sit with the investigators. "Oh, no thank you," she replied smiling; "I just came to listen," and sat down with those to be investigated. The caucus room came alive. The press corps poured in and the moving-picture cameras were set up and focused, but the leisurely pace continued and it was not until four in the afternoon that the Youth Congress was called. Eleanor was still there, having—without premeditation, because she was a friendly woman and it seemed the natural thing to do—"scooped up" the young people, as one newspaper described it, and taken them to lunch at the White House. She now moved up to a press table to hear better.

The committee was on the defensive and Representative Starnes at his courtliest in dealing with the Youth Congress witnesses. He good-humoredly countenanced an appeal for funds that Youth Congress president Jack McMichael, who was tall, blond, a divinity student, and a southerner, managed to introduce in the midst of a discussion of Youth Congress finances. Starnes even permitted a congress resolution calling for the abolition of the Dies Committee to be read into the record; some of its statements were slanderous, Starnes noted, but the Youth Congress had a right to believe anything it wanted: "That is your right as American citizens."

"I can take six of you," Eleanor had said at lunchtime. Now she invited the same group to come to dinner and spend the night at the White House.

In addition to the six "guttersnipes," as someone dubbed them, there were at dinner that evening Melvyn Douglas, actor and militant New Dealer; his wife Helen Gahagan; Assistant Attorney General Norman Littell, who wanted to talk to Eleanor about how to pull the liberals together; his wife; Aubrey Williams, who was regarded with almost as much suspicion as the youth leaders by Mr. Dies; Colonel Francis C. Harrington, the head of the WPA; Eleanor; and the president, who was wheeled in after everyone had assembled in the family dining room.

The president, despite his preoccupation with Russia's two-day-old invasion of Finland, wanted to hear about the day's events on Capitol Hill. He punctuated his wife's and the young people's accounts with appreciative laughter. Perhaps he could be slipped into the next day's hearings under a sheet, he suggested roguishly. "You will be welcomed as a Ku Kluxer," observed Melvyn Douglas.[6]

"I have two real interests in this situation," Eleanor wrote in her column for the next day:

> One is that as far as is humanly possible, I give to young people whom I know and trust, the feeling that in any situation, particularly a difficult one, they may count on my assistance. My second interest is a desire to observe to what extent the government is not only striving to un-cover un-American activities, but is giving to youth the assurance that their government does not look upon

them with suspicion until they are proved guilty, and is anxious to help them in every way to build up the faith and trust in democracy which should be the heritage of every youngster in the United States.[7]

She did not lightly dismiss the warnings of some of her friends that she might be lending her prestige to a movement which could prove to be communistic. But she felt that the Youth Congress leadership could be trusted; perhaps even more strongly she felt that in dealing with human beings, trust and love were creative and must in time find an answering response. She had attended their weddings, had lent them money, had given them gifts, and she had helped them raise the Youth Congress budget, and found it inconceivable that young people would repay friendship with personal deception. But Aubrey Williams was worried. He did not share Eleanor's sense of trust and security in the Youth Congress leadership. After dinner, when the president had retired to his study and the youth leaders began a litany of praise for Eleanor's courage and steadfastness in accompanying them to Capitol Hill, Williams fixed the group with a piercing look and said, "Don't let her down; it will break her heart."

Eleanor's good friend Bernard Baruch was also worried for her. When he had heard the reports of the first day's session he telephoned from Hobcaw offering to come to Washington to supply her with a lawyer and to pay the expenses of the young people. She had not needed a lawyer, she wrote him after the hearings; "my mere presence created an atmosphere of great gentleness and even the young people needed no assistance." She did want Baruch to help with the Youth Congress budget, but when he saw her a few days later he had read the Youth Congress resolution attacking the Dies Committee and was quite upset by it. He felt the Youth Congress should have limited its criticism of the committee to its own specific grievances. She passed on Baruch's views to the leaders of the Youth Congress, but two days later decided she had leaned over too far in seeming to accept Baruch's appraisal of the work of the Dies Committee, and wrote him so:

I have been feeling ever since our talk that I ought to tell you that I agree with you getting Kuhn and Browder was a valuable contribution. However, on the whole, I think the Dies Committee is doing work which the Federal Bureau of Investigation could do a great deal better. What the Federal Bureau of Investigation discovers has to be proved in court and they have to have real evidence. They cannot just make statements about people and take any amount of time to prove them. . . .

I have a feeling that if we allow ourselves to be so conditioned that we cannot believe in people whom we see and meet and work with for fear that somewhere in the background there may be a sinister influence, we are never going to be able to do anything again. . . . Undoubtedly there are some people in any group that we would not approve of, but as long as the work done is creditable work, I think we must go ahead and help this group.[8]

The first real jolt to her confidence in the Youth Congress leadership came during the Washington "pilgrimage" in January, 1940. This project had been authorized, as a demonstration of youth's support of the president and the New Deal, in the halcyon summer days before the Nazi-Soviet Pact and the outbreak of the war. The emphasis was to be on civic education and persuasion, and it was called a "Citizenship Institute" in order to differentiate it from the militancy and sloganeering of earlier demonstrations.

Now the character of the institute was being transformed, but it was being done so subtly that it took a sophisticated observer to detect that it was not a spontaneous recoil at the outbreak of war but a result of Communist manipulation. The passion went out of the Youth Congress fight to revise the neutrality act to aid Britain and France; instead the emphasis was on keeping America out of war. There was a greater stress on liberties, with the implication that it was the administration's preoccupation with the war crisis that endangered them, as this same preoccupation endangered the continuation of the New Deal. However, such anxieties were not confined to the Communists. Ickes noted in his diary that he had brought up with the president the effort of "fat cats" to use the crisis to move back into positions of control in the government. "Don't think that I am not watching everything with an eagle eye," the president had sought to reassure him. It was the period of the "phony war" when the war aims of Chamberlain and Daladier were highly suspect and anti-involvement sentiment was running high in New Deal circles.[9]

At dinner with a few Youth Congress leaders the night before the institute opened, Eleanor told them how her son John, whom she had seen in Cambridge, had asked her to pass on to "Pa" his strong feeling that the United States ought to keep out of the war and not get involved on the side of either the Allies or Germany. John was worried about the way the president's policies gave the appearance that he was inching the country toward intervention. She had passed on John's message to the president, Eleanor said, her eyes twinkling as she added that she also noted that it came from his son, not from a Communist.[10]

Loyal to her Youth Congress friends, Eleanor, who rarely counted political risks, especially when she was dealing with young people, spared no effort to help the institute. She was beginning to be aware of "grass roots" efforts to change the policies of the congress, but she thought they reflected the way young people were feeling, not Communist manipulation.

She organized a committee of congressional wives, headed by Mrs. Garner and the wife of the Speaker, Mrs. Bankhead, to canvass official Washington for free lodgings for the overflow of youth delegates, and she sat at the telephone with George Allen, the district commissioner, seeking some 500 extra beds from hotels, a welfare institution, and Fort Myers, which set up cots for 150 boys. The Monday before the institute convened she had a congressional reception at the White House where the Youth Congress leaders pressed for action on the American Youth Act. She helped the Youth Congress obtain a government auditorium and administration speakers. She persuaded the president to speak to them from the rear portico of the White House.

He took a more objective view of his wife's young friends than she did. He was neither impressed by the logic of their growing isolationism nor persuaded that they were as innocent of Communist ties as they protested. Yet he, too, was not sure how the Communist problem should be handled in the organizations in which they were active. If there was a chance to save the organization he thought liberals should make the fight and not simply withdraw. That was the advice he had sent to Aubrey Williams in regard to the Workers Alliance, the organization of the unemployed. "FDR wld like to see Dave Lasser [the head of the Workers Alliance] change name & purge communists who put Russia first," Eleanor advised Williams.[11]

Eleanor also told the president of the split that had developed within the American Student Union and of the formation of a liberal caucus to oppose the Communists.* When the president saw Lasser later, he

---

* The author has dealt more fully with these events, including his disenchantment with the Communists, in *Eleanor Roosevelt, A Friend's Memoir* (New York, 1964). As he said in that book, nothing reported here about the position of the Youth Congress and Student Union

suggested that the Workers Alliance organize along similar lines and that a fight be made. Like his wife, he understood why, lacking jobs, unsure of their future, searching for a sense of brotherhood, young people and the unemployed responded sympathetically to radical doctrines. "The Communists are dangerous only as we ourselves fail," Eleanor wrote. It was a sentiment with which the president agreed, but he was also a realistic politician, and while he accepted this as a prescription for the long run, he had little patience for the point of view that he heard from his wife's young friends, a point of view that she at times seemed to share. In mid-January some Youth Congress leaders were present at a White House dinner when Eleanor asked the president whether she had been right to advise the Youth Congress leaders to revive and re-introduce the American Youth Act. Yes, he replied, provided the young people made clear in their proposals where he was to get the money. Young people felt, Eleanor retorted, that less money should go to armaments and more to social services. "All right," the president said, pushing back in his chair. "Let's accept the opinion of youth, but I want my protest recorded for history."

"Youth needs are a form of national defense," Abbott Simon of the Youth Congress volunteered. "Do we need all these battleships?" The president thought this was utopian nonsense and that the trouble was that the young people were plain ignorant about matters of naval strategy. Eleanor refused to let the argument rest there: Wasn't it the responsibility of leadership to give the country information so that they could decide such matters intelligently? Patiently Franklin outlined his picture of the possibilities. He was fearful of a Russo-German victory in Europe and seizure of the British fleet, followed by efforts to penetrate the Western hemisphere, first through trade and then through military and political arrangements. The United States had to be armed to prevent penetration of the continent and disruption of the hemispheric system, the president emphasized.

Wasn't it possible to combine both armaments and NYA? Of course, the country had to do both, he replied, but at the moment it was more urgent to arm than to increase the appropriation for NYA. Turning to Simon, he said, "You will have to wait a year. You can wait a year." "I want you to say all those things to the Youth Congress

---

leaders in 1939–40 should be construed as an indication of their viewpoint today. Most of the author's Youth Congress associates subsequently joined the ranks of the disenchanted, either energetically fighting the Communists or lapsing into political inactivity.

pilgrimage next month," Eleanor remarked to the president as he was being wheeled out.[12]

Soviet Russia's invasion of Finland proved to be another dividing line between Communists and non-Communists. At Hyde Park the week before the pilgrimage, the president drove over to Val-Kill with Missy for lunch. Eleanor asked him if he would deal with the fears of young people that the United States might get involved, especially if a government loan was made to Finland. He scoffed at such fears; neither Germany nor Russia would declare war on the United States because of such a loan. Nor was he willing to say, in response to a suggestion from a youth leader who was present, that however he felt about the issues it was healthy for young people to organize to keep America out of war. The United States had a stake in preventing a Russo-German victory, he replied. It was useful to keep Russia and Germany guessing as to whether the United States might not come in.

Presidential suspicions of the Youth Congress were strengthened when, a few days before its pilgrimage to Washington, a message came to press secretary Bill Hassett from a columnist stating that the youth group had been holding meetings in New York City at which it was voting on resolutions to censure the president because of his policies, including his desire to aid Finland. Did the president still plan to address the pilgrimage, the columnist asked. "Yes," Hassett replied, but Roosevelt took some precautionary measures, such as vetoing the request of the Congress to have its chairman speak from the portico. "You will notice the big 'NO' that the President put beside the paragraph, as to anybody else speaking,"[13]

Commissioner Studebaker of the Office of Education and Aubrey Williams were asked by Hassett to submit suggestions for the president's speech. Studebaker sent over seven pages of amiable generalities, none of which were used. The draft submitted by Williams had a little more fire to it but it flattered youth, and the president, bent on some plain talk, discarded that, too. The young people had begun to irritate him; his wife's leaning over backward to put the best face on their arguments irritated him even more. But he could not reproach her directly—there were, a Roosevelt assistant observed, "strange reticences" between the two.* What he could not say to her directly,

---

*A term used by Jonathan Daniels in a letter to the author, Jan. 9, 1970, when the latter wrote inquiring if Daniels knew whether a certain matter had been discussed between the two.

however, he could say in a speech to the Youth Congress and the country, and it was a speech he wrote himself.[14]

Saturday, the day of the pilgrimage, was a chill, rainy February day. The paint on the hundreds of placards ran and those that escaped disfigurement by the rain were blown about in the wind. But the blustery weather made the youthful marchers more defiant as they paraded up Constitution Avenue.

SCHOOLS NOT BATTLESHIPS

the front ranks shouted, reviving a slogan of the early thirties.

PASS THE AMERICAN YOUTH ACT

the answering cry came back. Occasionally the marchers broke into song:

> *No Major, no Major, we will not go,*
> *We'll wager, we'll wager, this ain't our show.*
> *Remember that we're not so green*
> *As the boys in seventeen.*

Their clothes sodden and their placards bedraggled but their spirits high, 4,466 marchers were clocked entering the White House gates. They had arrived an hour early and they stood, cold and miserable, awaiting the president, whose speech was scheduled to be broadcast at 12:30. McMichael led them in singing of *America* and *America, the Beautiful,* punctuated with the staccato chant:

PASS THE AMERICAN YOUTH ACT

When the president came out onto the portico, Eleanor, who in a rain cape had been circulating among the marchers with words of motherly cheer, went up to join him.

It was a stern speech with few pleasantries and no effort to play up to his youthful listeners, as the introductory paragraph made clear when the president told the group that it had a right to advocate change, although with a different form of government "this kind of a meeting on the White House lawn could not take place." The rain poured down and the statistics poured out—on how much better off the country was compared with 1932. Young people should not "seek or expect Utopia overnight," nor were young people the only ones in the country who had problems. Much still remained to be done, and his administration was ready to move "as fast as the people of the country as a whole will let us."

Up to this point his audience had been unenthusiastic but polite. Now the president swung into his "final word of warning": do not pass resolutions on subjects "which you have not thought through and on which you cannot possibly have complete knowledge." The New York Youth Council's condemnation of a loan to Finland as "an attempt" to force the United States into an imperialistic war was "unadulterated twaddle." A ripple of boos and hisses were quickly hushed; if the president heard them, he did not deign to notice. American sympathy was 98 per cent with the Finns, he continued, and it was "axiomatic" that America wanted to help with loans and gifts. It was silly and absurd to think that because of such loans the Soviet Union might declare war on the United States or that the United States was going to war with the Soviet Union. That brought him to the subject of the Soviet Union: whatever his earlier hopes from that experiment, it was today "a dictatorship as absolute as any other dictatorship in the world." The boos started again, and again they were suppressed.

Some of his audience were said to be Communists, the president continued, and they had a right to be so, provided they confined their advocacy of change "to the methods prescribed by the Constitution."[15]

It was a verbal spanking, one most of Washington sympathized with, taking Walter Lippmann's view that these young people were "shockingly ill-mannered, disrespectful, conceited, ungenerous, and spoiled."

When the Youth Congress returned to the Labor Department auditorium, most of its adherents, neither contrite nor shaken, were ready for a speaker who could give plausible and expressive shape to their resentment and hostility. CIO head John L. Lewis, a powerful orator and gifted phrasemaker and, like his youthful audience, resentful of Roosevelt who he felt had patronized him, was ready for them. With ten to twelve million unemployed, including four million young people, he began, "Americans cannot live on statistics." The audience exploded in glee. Ovation succeeded ovation as Lewis scored his points with a mocking commentary on Roosevelt's speech that did not omit Finland—the mineworkers had passed a resolution substantially like the one the president had labeled "twaddle"—and ending with a bid:

"as chairman of Labor's Nonpartisan League, I issue an invitation to the American Youth Congress to become affiliated, to come to a working arrangement with Labor's Nonpartisan League."

Bedlam ensued. The leaders of the Young Communist League did not conceal their satisfaction. The Youth Congress, despite its switch in policy, could still be a force. The rest of the day, the speeches of the delegates themselves, with a few minor exceptions, sounded the themes set forth by Joe Cadden, the secretary of the Youth Congress, and lent respectability by Lewis—"the government is letting us down," "all our social gains are threatened by the trend toward a war economy," the NYA was becoming an instrument for militarization of youth, and the CCC was being curtailed in order to force young people through economic pressure to join the Army.

Eleanor was present during Lewis's speech, sitting on the platform, knitting; her face was impassive, but inwardly she was shaken as she observed the group applauding positions which had some merit to them and reflected some real anxiety, some genuinely unmet need, but which, taken in the whole, were suspiciously close to the Communist line.

This was the atmosphere in which she brought the institute to a close on Sunday night with a question-and-answer period. For an hour she stood—tall, dignified, and unsmiling, in a black evening dress and wearing a corsage of orchids presented by the congress—dealing with the sheaf of questions given to her by Jack McMichael. "The nation probably has not seen in all of its history," wrote Dewey L. Fleming in the *Baltimore Sun,* "such a debate between a President's wife and a critical, not to say hostile, auditorium full of politically minded youths of all races and creeds."

Shouldn't the institute have passed a resolution condemning the Soviet invasion of Finland, was the first question. It was from Archibald Roosevelt, Jr., a grandson of Theodore Roosevelt who, with some other conservative critics, had been heckling the congress from the sidelines.

Eleanor had always been very careful not to impose her views on the congress. Her reply was double-edged: "No. I don't think you should go on record for anything you don't believe in—however, I think it is only fair to say that I do not think you fully understand some of the history underlying many situations in Europe, the Far East, and other places in the world."

There was a stir of dissent and an answering movement of approval.

She cut both short almost sternly: "I want you neither to clap nor hiss until I have finished and then you may do whichever you like." Aware that many in her audience wondered why so much solicitude was being shown for "poor little Finland" by people like Herbert Hoover who had shown none for other victims of aggression, she went on: "I agree with you that a stand should have been taken when Ethiopia was attacked. I agree with you in your sympathy for Spain. I agree with you in your sympathy for China and Czechoslovakia, but I also have sympathy for Finland."

In a remark that indicated she was aware of what was going on, one which the Youth Congress leaders decided to omit from the transcript of the "highlights" of her replies, she then said:

> I know the reasons advanced to justify the Russian invasion of Finland. Some of my Communist friends have told me. But in all fairness it ought to be said there is no excuse for a big nation attacking a little nation that has not attacked the big one.
>
> Therefore, our sympathy as a free people should be just as much with the Finnish people as it would be with any other small nation which is invaded.

A question on why the administration was cutting the budget for social legislation brought a blunt "I'll tell you why" response. That was what the people back in the localities wanted: "You will notice that even with the pared-down budget, Congress cut it further, which is an indication that you have not been busy forming public opinion in your communities, because Congress is responsive to you."

Her most moving statement came in response to a rhetorically worded question which said "we want jobs and education in America, not an M.A. in Flanders fields." The United States, Eleanor said, was "a very peace-loving nation. You are not the only ones who don't want war. I don't think there are many older people in this country who want war, and certainly none of us who know what war is like." She defended the president. The audience should not forget

> that we have four sons who are just the ages to go to war. Do you think that the President wants war? But nobody knows what they may face when the world is going through a cataclysm. I could agree with you right this minute that I don't want war, but I don't know what you might say under different conditions six months from now.

There was rebuke for Abbott Simon, who had criticized French treatment of the Spanish refugees. Was it fair to criticize France "when we do so little" and when, "mind you, there was a bill in Congress to bring in some children, all of whom were to be paid for, the money had been acquired, and which couldn't be passed because the people of this country wouldn't back it." The United States was in no position to "sit in too harsh judgment on other nations."

At the end of an hour, the audience ran out of questions. She thanked it for listening with patience and courtesy: "I am very, very fond of many of your leaders and I am sure I would like to know all of you personally," she said on leaving. She was given a standing ovation.[16]

The institute left her deeply troubled. The booing of the president had disconcerted her. Tommy was furious. When the Youth Congress leaders arrived at the White House for tea later that day she dressed them down. "How dare you insult the President of the United States?" she demanded. Later, the president sent for her, and when she marched into his study and stood before his desk, Roosevelt looked up at her and said quietly, "Thank you, Tommy." To his wife the president, perhaps because he sensed how bad she felt, spoke consolingly. "Our youngsters are unpredictable, aren't they?" Yet indignant as she was over the lack of respect for the presidential office, she regretted the president's speech. It had been too much like a lecture and was based on the assumption his audience had no brains.[17]

She had wanted the president to meet the young people and explain his point of view, to let them know his worries about the international situation and the political considerations that kept him from pushing harder for domestic legislation. Young people did not sense the mood in Congress. When Vice President Garner had told her that if Dave Lasser's Workers Alliance brought 100,000 unemployed to Washington they should be stopped by force, she had responded hotly that she would go down and join the demonstrators. The president was persuaded that if business did not provide people with jobs, government would have to get more heavily involved in business, but he also felt it would take another Depression to convince the country there was no other course. These were the considerations she had wanted the president to elaborate for the young people at the institute, but he felt they would not listen because they were under Communist influence.[18]

For a few months after the institute, Eleanor, on the assumption that the leaders of the Youth Congress were susceptible to reasoned argument, gave them every chance to show where they stood. She encouraged the large national organizations that remained in the Youth Congress to organize a liberal caucus inside the congress to fight the Communists, and found it enlightening that the officers of the congress were hostile to this caucus. She continued to help with the financing, but she also emphasized to the congress leadership that the "position of the American Youth Congress has got to be cleared up" on the Communist issue. At the request of the youth representatives who were fighting the Communists, she arranged an evening session at the White House with the president where, off the record, he might develop his thinking on many of the policies that worried young people. "He does not want it to be wholly Youth Congress, but to represent as many different groups as we can get together and whom we can trust not to go out and talk about it," she wrote one youth leader whom she asked to submit a list of young people who should be invited.[19]

The Nazis had overrun the Low Countries and were pressing their blitzkrieg into France when the president met with the group. For three hours he patiently answered every question put to him by the fifty young people seated on straight backed chairs in the State Dining Room. Though some of the questions implied that he had turned reactionary, he refused to be provoked. There were flashes of humor and occasionally the burden of his responsibilities touched his replies with sadness as he deftly sketched in the picture of a New Deal president conducting a two-front war—against Hitler and the dictators abroad and against the reactionaries at home.

The questions became repetitive. In one shape or another they reduced themselves to the plea that he should press harder for welfare legislation as a form of internal defense. And in one form or another his answer was that "merely shouting from the housetops—you cannot do it that way." And when he was wheeled out, his cigarette holder jauntily angled, Harry Hopkins and Eleanor took up the defense of the president against the implications in so many of the questions that he did not see the needs of the nation as well as the questioners did. "After all, anybody who has watched him in the last seven years knows he is a pretty good judge of public opinion and where it is," Hopkins noted, scarcely able to conceal his annoyance. Eleanor broke in: "A year and a half, two years ago, he said every single thing on defense that he said aloud today to individual members of Congress and gave the very same reasons ... and the reason that he can get them today is that circumstances hit the people of the United States in the head."[20]

It was extraordinary that in the midst of a grave international crisis the president of the United States was willing to devote an evening to the youth groups to explain and defend his policies. Why did he do so? Of course, he enjoyed the give and take of such a session, having for years handled the sharper, better informed questions of the White House press corps. He liked young people and had been comforted by the belief they were on his side, and it disturbed him that they should now be so distrustful and confused.[21] While he had questions about the Youth Congress leaders, he knew that there was widespread doubt, apprehension, and cynicism among young people who were in no way influenced by the Communists. His own sons were prepared to do their duty, but in varying degrees doubted that American involvement would have any happier outcome than it had in 1918. It grieved and worried him to see young people turn up in such large numbers at the isolationist rallies of America First. His speech calling for 50,000 planes brought a flood of telegrams, mostly favorable, but he found it striking that most of the 20 per cent who wrote in opposition were members of youth organizations or college students.

The Youth Congress leaders riding the isolationist bandwagon were not moved by the president's arguments. Eleanor had been struck by their failure to ask the president questions about his foreign policy and was subsequently outraged when at public meetings they proceeded to accuse him of wanting to send troops to Europe. At Eleanor's request Ed Flynn lent his home for a fund-raising meeting for the Youth Congress, but because they distrusted the Congress, people either did not come or refused to contribute. Unless the congress clarified its position by passing a resolution that specifically condemned aggression by Hitler and Stalin, Eleanor saw little prospect of its getting funds in the future. Again and again, before the annual meeting of the congress on July 4, she said to the leaders, "You have really got to prove at this convention that there is no outside domination."[22]

She refused to address or even to attend that meeting, despite the pleas of the congress officers. She arranged, however, to get reports from a number of observers, including Betty Lindley, her radio agent, and Thelma McKelvey, an official of the NYA. "We definitely felt that the minds of the delegates were made up before the speeches were given," they reported to her afterward. "We have absolutely no proof of who may or may not be communists, but there is sufficient evidence to indicate that they hold a strong place in the policy formation of the Congress."[23]

Eleanor still did not believe that the congress officials were Communists, but the resolutions and speeches at the Geneva meeting were along Communist lines and were exploited by Communist groups. She refused to go along with defeatist groups, and when she saw the Youth Congress leaders she advised them to read the section of *Mein Kampf* in which Hitler gave his methods of sowing dissension in the democracies.

To Dorothy Schiff Backer, a friendly newspaper publisher who before the Geneva congress had sent her an analysis made by Oliver Pilat of political alignments in the cabinet of the Youth Congress (David Dubinsky had sent her similar information), she had replied, "I do not feel that any one of them are permanently communists and I feel that I should cooperate in helping them solve the questions which really matter to them, because that is what will determine what they think and feel in the future." After the Geneva meeting, however, she no longer felt she could cooperate with the congress. "Whatever the reasons," she wrote congress leaders, "some of the resolutions you passed have a close affiliation with communist ideas and it does lay you open to being considered more or less organized and dominated by the communists." But she still continued to see its leaders privately. She was genuinely fond of them, and, moreover, profoundly believed in the redemptive power of trust and love.[24]

Until the Geneva conference, Eleanor had hoped that the non-Communist group in the congress might prevail. She hoped the congress might be salvaged because in a time of crisis she considered it essential that youth's voice be heard. But as she faced up to the implications of Geneva and as the Youth Congress settled into a "Yanks-are-not-coming" isolationism, which, except for its pro-Soviet bias, was as rancorous and absolute as that of America First, she shifted her support to the International Student Service, which, with her blessing, reshaped its program in order to assist young people who were looking for an alternative to the Youth Congress and American Student Union.

There were too many constructive things to be done to waste any more time on the American Youth Congress, she replied to questions about her relationship to it. "I don't think their present attitude is constructive and I don't have time if I do not think a movement is constructive, to work in it." She was now totally out of patience with the evasions of its leaders; they never spoke to her about Russia, she noted, but said only that they were followers of John L. Lewis. When the congress sent her its 1940 Armistice Day peace proclamation, she fired back a query: How did it reconcile opposition to aid to England on grounds that it would involve us in war while at the same time urging aid to China? "If conscription for one year is weakening and undemocratic here," she went on, "what do you think of Russia's conscript army [three years]?" In December the congress announced preparations for another Washington pilgrimage in February, 1941. They should expect no help from her, Eleanor wrote them:

> I have been thinking a great deal about my own position in all this lately, because while I believe in the complete sincerity of you, and while I respect the way in which you work for your convictions, and therefore feel no differently personally toward any of you than I ever have, still I find myself in complete disagreement with your political philosophy, and therefore with the leadership which you at present represent in the youth movement. I do not think that you represent the majority of youth, but I do think you have a right to try to further your ideas and to express your opinions and you should be heard in every gathering. However, when I do not agree with you, I also have an obligation not to help you and not to appear to agree with you.[25]

In June, 1941, the Nazis invaded the Soviet Union, and two months later the secretary of the Youth Congress wrote the president. "It has been some time since we have had the privilege of talking with you about our program and activities," the letter blandly started. The Youth Congress had several ideas on how to combat the "appeasement" forces at work in the United States and which were holding back the "strong anti-Hitler sentiment of our generation." They asked to see the president. Pa Watson attached a yellow slip to this letter on which his secretary typed, "Respectfully referred to Mrs. Roosevelt." Mrs. Roosevelt sent it back with a white slip, "My advice to you is simply to say that the President is too busy." The Youth Congress wanted her help, too, for an anti-Hitler youth conference in London. When she refused, they wrote back that she was "badly misinformed" about their views. They regretted their lack of an opportunity personally to tell her about their activities. "You seem to have forgotten," she replied, "conversations all of you had with me in the summer of 1940, and therefore do not realize the effect that your convention attitude of 1941, and the changed position you had taken since the invasion of Russia has had on me."[26]

She found it impossible to work with them, she wrote a friend. "I asked each one individually whether they had any connection with the Communists, and received what seemed to me their honest denial. I still believe in many of their objectives, but where there is deceit and lack of trust, I can not cooperate."[27]

Aubrey Williams had feared that Eleanor's experience with the Youth Congress might break her heart, but she was resilient and had a remarkable capacity to learn from disappointment and defeat. Her experience with Communist tactics in the youth movement, she later wrote, helped her to understand and cope with the Communist bloc in the UN.

Nor was she embittered toward the leaders of the Youth Congress, who were her friends, because of their failure to be candid and honest with her. Although she refused to work with them politically, she let them know that if they got into trouble personally she was always willing to help them as individuals.

She answered deception with understanding and injury with forgiveness, and at times put mercy above justice and legality.

50. THE THIRD TERM

"IF IT HAD NOT BEEN FOR MRS. ROOSEVELT," WROTE JAMES Farley of the 1940 Democratic convention which nominated Roosevelt for a third term, "it was doubtful that Wallace's nomination for Vice President would have carried." And if the convention had turned down Wallace, Roosevelt presumably would have issued the statement he had prepared declining the presidential nomination. That it was Eleanor who reconciled the mutinous delegates to her husband's choice of Wallace as a running mate represented high irony, for she was not a Wallace enthusiast and had not wanted Franklin to run because she did not see that Congress would be any readier to give him in a third term what it had refused him in the second, and now he would be carrying responsibility for decisions affecting not only the welfare but the lives of millions.[1]

But the irony of Eleanor making it possible for her husband to accept a nomination that she viewed with the utmost apprehension was not the only one of that convention: She performed this service after Franklin had kept her in the dark up to the very last moment about his decision to accept the nomination. This, of course, was the way he had behaved in 1930 when he had decided to make his first bid for the presidential nomination, but unlike 1930, in 1940 there was no Louis Howe to tell her what Franklin was up to and to argue away her fears. Harry Hopkins, who had moved into the White House on May 10 at Roosevelt's invitation, was in no position to risk the president's displeasure by sharing confidences with her.

Personally, she told her friends, she did not want to spend another four years in the White House. Sometimes she was humorous about what was required of the wife of a public man—especially when he was campaigning for office:

Always be on time. Never try to make any personal engagements. Do as little talking as humanly possible. Never be disturbed by anything. Always do what you're told to do as quickly as possible. Remember to lean back in a parade, so that people can see your husband. Don't get too fat to ride three on a seat. Get out of the way as quickly as you're not needed.

And when Bess Furman Armstrong went on from these rules to ask her to sum up thirty years as the wife of an officeholder, she said feelingly, "It's hell," a reply that staggered Bess. "Strong language comes startlingly from the lips of great ladies," she commented, "but surely there should be a special dispensation for her of whom it is said—'She always built him up, and she never let him down.'"[2]

In October, 1939, Eleanor took some time out of a busy day to allow a palmist to study her hands. It was not the first or the last time that she had her hands read, but this analysis of her character interested her particularly and she put it in the desk drawer where she kept the special items that heartened and inspired her, such as Spring-Rice's sonnet on the Saint-Gaudens memorial to Henry Adams's wife and some lines that Amelia Earhart had written on courage. The finger which showed leadership, the palmist wrote, "is much bolder in your left hand, which shows inherent potentialities, than it is in your right hand, which shows what actually happens. This leads me to believe that many times you've had to cramp your style."[3]

What was "man's chief end," asked an old friend of Franklin's who doubted that the president should run for a third term. Each one had to answer that question for himself, Eleanor replied, but perhaps it was "the full development of whatever we have in us." For herself that was impossible as long as Franklin was in the White House, or so she thought. Too many of the things she did as First Lady she had to do because of his position. In 1939, Tommy informed Emma Bugbee, "Mrs. Roosevelt had 4,729 for meals, 323 house guests, 9,211 tea guests, and she received 14,056, which means a total of 28,319. By 'received' I mean groups who are just received and not given food—D.A.R. etc."[4]

By dint of a remarkable vitality, of never consciously sitting down to relax, of being up for breakfast at 8:30 A.M. no matter how late she went to bed, Eleanor managed to combine these social duties with an amazingly varied and useful life. In April, 1940, United Feature Syndicate extended her contract to write "My Day" for another five years, which pleased her greatly, since it was renewed at a time when it appeared highly doubtful that Roosevelt would run again. She had delivered forty-five paid lectures in 1939 and was under contract for almost as many in 1940. In the spring she dashed off a little book on the religious basis of democracy—it was, she felt, the Golden Rule, "the fundamental thing which we must all have is the spiritual force which the life of Christ exemplifies." Magazines and publishers were prepared to buy whatever she wrote. In April she began a new radio series for WNBC. Her agents should find her a more suitable sponsor, advised Esther Lape, objecting to Sweetheart Soap; but Eleanor needed the money for her many charities and had long decided the benefits outweighed the criticism. She was commenting with "a noticeable increase of frankness and vigor" on politics and foreign affairs, a forthrightness that some interpreted as a sign that her husband did not contemplate another campaign.[5]

As the public speculated on whether or not Roosevelt would run for a third term, there were many proposals of jobs for Eleanor. Some wanted her to run for president or vice president. "If you will agree to let her serve your third term," William Allen White wrote the president, "I shall be for you against all comers. Every time she does anything she reminds me of T.R." A group of Bryn Mawr alumnae wanted her as president of their college, and the Denver chapter of the American Newspaper Guild proposed that she succeed the late Heywood Broun as president of the guild.[6]

There would be no lack of work for her after Franklin left the White House, of that she was sure, and it would be work of her own. At last she might be able to take on a job and see it through to a conclusion. But this was her personal preference, and because she felt it so strongly she kept silent about it, especially after the war began, believing that her husband should make his decision on the basis of the national interest.

★ ★ ★

AT THE END of an uncomfortable, cold, wet inauguration day in 1937, Eleanor wrote that her only consolation "was that there would never be for us another Inauguration, that this was really the last time here." What did she mean by that, the reporters immediately wanted to know. Did she exclude a third term? Third terms had "never been the custom of the country," she replied.[7]

Even before the 1937 inauguration she had begun to press her husband to groom a successor. She knew the temptation of power both for him and for the many officials in Washington who held it through him. As she went about the country, the politicians and officeholders thought they pleased her by their advocacy of a third term. When she spoke in July, 1937, to the Roosevelt Home Club, made up of the president's Hyde Park neighbors, she thought it time to oppose a third term publicly.

But this was her husband's decision to make, she felt, and when she realized, either because he told her or on the basis of her own political insight, that to close the door on a 1940 race would weaken his influence with Congress, she lapsed into public silence and became as adept as he at avoiding the traps the reporters set for her on the issue. Would her husband consider a third term in order to advance the New Deal, she was asked in Philadelphia. "You'll have to ask him that question." "But hasn't he told you?" "I haven't even asked him," she replied, cutting off that line of questions. What were her plans after 1940, she was asked in mid-1939. She had no idea where she would be after 1940, she replied. "If you have been married as long as I have to a man who has been in public office for a long time, you will learn never to think ahead and you will make up your mind to accept what comes along."[8]

In private she was less amenable about accepting whatever came along. When the Ickeses visited the Boettigers in Seattle the talk inevitably turned to a third term. Anna knew as little as they about her father's intentions, but she did know how her mother felt. Someone had suggested the possibility that the Roosevelt family might still be residing in the White House after 1940, Anna said. "Well, *I* don't intend to," her mother shot back. What was the use of being president, she wrote an old friend who asked about the possibility of Eleanor running for the presidency, "even if you wanted to be, if you cannot do the thing you ought to do?" Mrs. Meloney, whom Eleanor helped to secure administration speakers for the *Herald Tribune* Forum, always wanted the president. "FDR she wants you for a 3rd term and I thought this most unwise. You know I do *not* believe in it."[9]

Although at this time (1938) Roosevelt agreed with his wife and was encouraging the candidacy of Harry Hopkins by bringing Hopkins into the cabinet as secretary of commerce, he was not averse to getting some fun out of terrifying the conservatives with the possibility that he might be the candidate himself.

Helen Robinson, a Republican committeewoman from Herkimer and daughter of Franklin's half brother Rosy, dined at the White House a few days after the Munich crisis. "Franklin held forth as usual, and seemed in very good form," Helen reported in her diary.

The talk ran into a discussion of "third term" possibilities in the early history of this country, all pointing most definitely in my mind, from all that FDR said on the subject, to the fact that he has it very much in his mind to run again. This terrifies me beyond words. But I could only look pleasant and eat my dinner and keep a poker face.[10]

Helen may have misunderstood Roosevelt's historical references. His concern at the time was the selection of a successor who would carry on the New Deal. Andrew Jackson, he was telling Democratic leaders, including Garner and Farley, should have picked someone more in sympathy with his policies than Martin Van Buren if he wanted his policies continued. Franklin's foray into history was meant to be a warning to the party's conservatives.[11] Eleanor asked Franklin how she should reply to letters from friendly Democratic politicians who wanted to do the president's bidding, and his advice was reflected in her reply: "The thing for you to do is to work for delegates to the Convention who will only choose a liberal, New Deal candidate. Then, whoever is nominated, the ideas and policies will go on."[12]

But who was that candidate? It was evident by 1939 that the Hopkins' candidacy was stillborn. Perhaps if he had not been ill he might have been able to change that, but much of the time during the crucial pre-convention months he was either sick in bed or convalescing. There was no other New Dealer in sight to pick up the banner. The liberal cause looked desperate. Not only had the 1938 purge of conservative Democrats failed, but the Republicans had scored heavy gains. Congress was in a fractious mood, ready to vote down anything Roosevelt wanted just because he wanted it. In early 1939 a gloomy Ickes spoke of "the last-stand fight that the liberals are making under President Roosevelt's leadership," and Ickes and other New Dealers concluded that the president was the only liberal who could be nominated and elected.[13]

Eleanor disagreed, and had a long talk about it with Harry Hopkins during a luncheon with Hopkins and his daughter Diana in May. He described her attitude in a memorandum, dated May 28, 1939:

Mrs. Roosevelt was greatly disturbed about 1940. She is personally anxious not to have the President run again, but I gathered the distinct impression that she has no more information on that point than the rest of us. She feels the President has done his part entirely. That he has not the same zest for administrative detail that he had and is probably quite frankly bored. She thinks that the causes for which he fought are far greater than any individual person, but that if the New Deal is entirely dependent upon him, it indicates that it hasn't as strong a foundation as she believes it has with the great masses of people. Mrs. Roosevelt is convinced that a great majority of the voters are not only with the President, but with the things he stands for, and that every effort should be made to control the Democratic Convention in 1940, nominate a liberal candidate and elect him. She has great confidence in his ability to do this, if, and it seems to be a pretty big "if" in her mind, he is willing to take his coat off and go to work at it.[14]

It was a period in which Roosevelt kept his own counsel, his mind veiled from everyone. No one knew what he intended, neither his wife nor his children. In Texas Elliott campaigned for Garner. John Boettiger, to the delight of the New Dealers, lambasted Garner in an open letter and belabored Elliott, insisting that Roosevelt was the only Democrat who could carry the West. But Anna and John were as much in the dark as everyone else as to what the president wanted. Did he know what the president's reaction had been? John Boettiger wrote Ickes. The secretary was able to enlighten him: "Yesterday Pa Watson told me confidentially that the President had said to him and Steve Early, 'John put it over on Elliott, didn't he?'" But that reflected Roosevelt's attitude toward Garner, not toward a third term.[15]

Although Eleanor believed there was still time to build up a liberal successor to the president, she went along with the strategy of the advocates of a third term to enter Franklin's name in the primaries in order to head off Garner: "The Oregon primaries come early and Garner's name will most likely be put up. They will put your name up, but this does not require your consent."

She did not feel Franklin should run, and the outbreak of war did not change her view. The president had served his purpose in history, she told a young friend early in 1940, and youth should not cling to him for leadership. New leadership was needed for the next step ahead. Unless, she added, the international crisis made him indispensable.[16]

In Los Angeles for a lecture, her qualms about a third term came to the surface: "My own personal opinion—and not as the wife of a President—is that except in extraordinary circumstances we should stick to our traditions." The conditions were becoming extraordinary, a friend suggested, as Hitler had just invaded Denmark and Norway. Eleanor acknowledged that. "It is all horrible," she had written her husband from Denver,

> and goes deep in our theories of civilization, for if this is done then only force counts, our concepts that right and wrong had to be considered all go by the board and we return to the Middle Ages with inventions that make such concepts more dangerous to the human race.[17]

Despite the cataclysmic events in Europe, she had the impression after talking with the president on her return that he was considering a Hull-Farley ticket. She had asked him about Hull's social views, since she had always found the secretary "tight-lipped" on the subject. The president believed he was a liberal, yet she doubted that he was "strong enough to wage the fight that must be fought." As for Farley, while most of the New Dealers were in full cry against him, Eleanor liked him. He was straight, and when he made a promise he kept it. But he did not know half of what the New Deal was about. Many of the problems of government were too much for him, especially in the field of foreign policy. He often said to her, "Well, I don't understand it, but if you say it's o.k. Eleanor, that's enough for me." She drew the line at Garner; she could not stand him. If he were nominated, she would campaign against him, even though to go against the party would be heartbreaking. With Europe in flames, how could she resign herself to a ticket that was second best, she was asked. Wasn't it essential to have the strongest leader at the head of the ticket? For a moment she was silent. She did not like to contemplate the idea of the president's running again, she finally answered. It might result in the same stalemate between Congress and the executive that had rendered the president powerless in his second term.[18]

A few weeks later Hitler's mechanized armies and powerful air force struck westward, overrunning the Low Countries, knifing through the French at Sedan, and outflanking the Maginot Line:

> The last week has been pretty grim. FDR has expected it & so have I but the people are just waking up to the possibilities & everyone is worried. . . . FDR is getting more & more engrossed in the European problem but that is inevitable & one does feel a great futility in all human plans.[19]

The issue before the United States no longer seemed to be that of aiding the Allies but of American defense—perhaps even survival. If the Nazis came over she would give them a fight, Tommy impetuously exclaimed to her boss at the World's Fair; she would "kick, scream, pull their hair!" She and the president had spoken of the terrible world it would be if Hitler should achieve world conquest, Eleanor commented, and the president had said to her—one thing, anyway, they both would be dead. That was the mood in the White House early in June.[20]

During a trip East James asked his mother whether, as a Marine Corps reserve officer, he should get his business affairs in shape so that he could leave, and she reluctantly told him he had better. He was ready to go, James went on, but his heart was not in it; he did not see how anything would come out of America's entry into the war that would make it different from the last time. She had the same feeling, and, stirred by James's fatalism, mirroring as it did the mood of so many young people, she asked Franklin how people could avoid the sense of futility that came from fearing that the same old cycle would repeat itself—wars interrupted by short eras of peace. Why should young people feel that such a future was worth fighting for? "Don't you think that is a rather cowardly way to look at the future?" Franklin admonished her. He should give her one practical way to insure permanent peace, she pressed him. "Perhaps next time we shall have the sense to say there shall be no more armaments," he replied. The conversation ended, but he, too, was not sure. The next day he confessed to her that he had worried over the points she had raised until all hours of the morning. She felt terribly guilty.[21]

"The news is bad & F.D.R. edgy & not able to get away enough," Eleanor wrote Maude Gray in Dublin, where Maude's husband David had been posted as the U.S. minister.[22] The German army was on the outskirts of Paris. Mussolini about to enter the war. A desperate French premier was deluging Roosevelt with entreaties that the United States should declare war. Such men as Ickes, Archibald MacLeish, and Walter Millis, who had long preached the futility of war, were reluctantly admitting to themselves that they now favored a declaration of war. Roosevelt knew it was politically impossible, even though he had realized long before the others how inextricably involved U.S. interests were with those of the democracies. Eleanor, returning to the White House, found everyone "in the same tense mood they had been in when I left," she wrote the day Italy entered the war.[23] Roosevelt longed to strike a blow for freedom, yet he could not.

The third-term pressure on him became stronger. To the liberal plea that he had to run in order to preserve the gains of the New Deal was now added the much more powerful and irresistible argument that he could not walk away when the nation was in its most critical situation since it had gained its independence. Yet another part of him hesitated. At Hyde Park over the July 4 holiday, Franklin's cousin, Laura Delano, put the question to him while Eleanor sat nearby knitting. He cast his eyes despairingly toward the ceiling and exclaimed, "I am a tired and weary man." Part of him longed to return to the Hudson. He knew he would wield great influence from the sidelines. Perhaps the strongest check to his saying yes was his conservatism, his respect for established custom, his feeling for American history. As Eleanor later explained to Isabella, who had been one of her bridesmaids and whose support of Willkie after the Democratic convention grieved her, "Franklin felt more strongly about the traditional part of it than I did." Severely limited in what he could do to help Britain and France, uncertain as to what he should do about the third term, he became uncommunicative, even bad-tempered. "Those closest to him, including Missy," wrote Ickes after an exchange of confidences with Pa Watson and Doc McIntire, "do not know what is running in his mind as to important matters. Apparently he is taking absolutely nobody into his confidence."[24]

Although Eleanor did not learn from Franklin but from watching and listening to the others around him,* she concluded by the middle of June that he had been persuaded by the third-term advocates that with America in danger he could not refuse the nomination if it was offered to him. She could see, moreover, that if Franklin were to refuse now, it would be impossible to nominate anyone else acceptable to them and to the country.†[25]

She was still unhappy about his running again, but if he did she

---

*A month later, when Eleanor went to Chicago to address the convention, the ever-perceptive Emma Bugbee caught and noted the nuance in Eleanor's reply to the question whether she had known the president's decision in advance. She had not, she said, adding, "at least not from him."

†A *Fortune* survey released late in June showed that Roosevelt would be victorious but that there would be a GOP landslide with any other Democratic candidate.

wanted him to make his campaign a crusade for the fuller freedom that alone would give hope of an end to the old grim cycle. "Even though we arm," she wrote in her column, "still we must have more housing, better health services and jobs that insure a decent livelihood to every family."[26] Roosevelt agreed, but the draft that he sent out to Chicago said these things only weakly. When he told her firmly that he did not intend to go to the convention himself, nor should she go, she replied that in that case she would go to Hyde Park to her cottage. He did not ask her to stay. When a politician must move pragmatically and make compromises with city machines and southern senators that are difficult to square with his liberal principles, it is inconvenient to have a moralist around.

Val-Kill was at its most beautiful. At sunset, as the soft light filtered through the trees, the woods seemed to Eleanor to be filled with magic and mystery. Fat woodchucks and little white-tailed rabbits scuttled across the paths as she walked. The flowers beside the pool and house gleamed. On her sleeping porch she was lulled to sleep by the sound of frogs, and was awakened to the chirpings of a nest of baby robins. "This morning one of them is almost trying his wings. He almost flies out, but seems not to have the courage at the crucial moment. It reminds me of myself going off the diving board. I long to be able to communicate in some bird language that, if he just has self-confidence it will be all right." With the news from Europe unrelievedly grim, the simplicities of Val-Kill gave her some relief.[27]

She was at Val-Kill the week of the Democratic convention, work-ing with Tommy, swimming, riding, playing ring tennis, talking, and reading. Earl was in and out with a new girl whom he soon would marry. A young friend was present. She took her mother-in-law and Mrs. Betty Roosevelt to Norrie Point for dinner, had guests for lun-cheon, and in the evening listened to the convention proceedings over the radio, Tommy knitting a sweater, she monogramming linen. There were telephone calls from the White House and from Chicago, where Lorena Hickok, an employee of the Democratic National Committee and aware, therefore, of Farley's strong sense of alienation, kept her informed. Harry Hopkins, Eleanor remarked the day the convention opened, seemed to be making all the usual mistakes at Chicago; he did not seem to know how to make people happy. Frances Perkins called from Chicago to say that the situation there was "deadly"—couldn't something be done to lift the convention out of its squalid atmosphere of partisanship and factionalism? Frances wanted Eleanor to get the president to come out and speak, but Eleanor told her the president felt he had to stay close to Washington.

On Tuesday, the second day of the convention, Franklin called to tell her to listen to Senator Alben Barkley's keynote address, which contained a statement from him; he wanted to know what she thought of it. She had not known that Franklin was going to send a statement to the convention, although he had insisted upon it at a meeting with Flynn, Hopkins, Frank Walker, and James Byrnes the week before the convention opened. They had opposed his saying anything, but he wanted somehow to make it clear—to his conscience as much as to the delegates—that he was not seeking the nomination and that they were free to vote for any candidate. Perhaps that also accounted for his insistence to Eleanor that he had not told Harry Hopkins to set up a headquarters in Chicago, that Harry had just gone ahead and done so. "It was as if he did not want to make the choice," wrote Francis Biddle, "and preferred to have someone else make it for him." The statement read by Barkley said neither yes nor no, Eleanor pointed out to her friends. However, in failing to say no, it was in effect saying yes. She felt the statement should not have been made.[28]

By Wednesday the temper of the convention, which Frances Perkins had described as "deadly" on Monday, had turned ugly and rebellious as it became known that Roosevelt's choice of a running mate was Henry Wallace. Miss Perkins called again to tell Eleanor that she had to come to Chicago; the delegates needed the reassurance of her presence, and they would be comforted if she thought what they were doing was right. Eleanor demurred. She thought Frances was speaking nonsense, but if Franklin, with whom Frances had spoken, felt she ought to go, and Jim Farley invited her, she would fly out.

The president urged her to go, she told the little group at Val-Kill. But in *This I Remember* the president's quoted response sounded less enthusiastic: "It might be very nice for you to go, but I do not think it is in the least necessary." Chivalry? Or was it male unwillingness to acknowledge that he needed the help of a wife whom he had kept at a distance because she posed uncomfortable questions about how much control he might have even if he was re-elected, questions that the fractious mood of the delegates were proving to be quite pertinent. However, he did agree that she could be helpful to Jim and say things to him that he could not. So, ever the good soldier, she said she would call Jim, and if he wanted her to come out she would. She called Farley, who had felt so frozen out by Hopkins and Dave Niles, Hopkins's chief political adviser, that he was overcome with emotion by Eleanor's call and was unable to speak.

Why was she so reluctant to go to Chicago, she was asked by one of the small group at Val-Kill when she had settled down after dinner in her study to listen to the nominating speeches. She did not like the idea of speaking because the president could say things so much more effectively, she replied. If she said things he later said, she would be attacked for butting in. They would say that she made up the president's mind and he, understandably, would be annoyed.[29]

Franklin Roosevelt is "one part mush and three parts Eleanor," Doris Fleeson quoted Alice Longworth,* and the added quip that "Eleanor is a Trojan mare" did not sweeten the barb. A revealing exchange took place one evening in the president's study. Harry Hopkins asked who America's greatest women were. "Anne Hutchinson," Eleanor began. Harriet Beecher Stowe, someone followed up. "Mrs. Catt," Eleanor continued. "What was her husband's name?" the president asked, his derisive tone making it clear that he did not think much of marriages in which wives overshadowed husbands.[30]

She could never understand, Eleanor went on, why she was called upon to do things like going to Chicago. She was not important or influential. The function of women in politics was to ease things along, smooth them over; they were not main movers. She had tried to prevent the break between John L. Lewis and the president. "You and I, Mr. Jackson, are both working for the same kind of people," she had told Lewis's legislative aide Gardner Jackson with a candor that both charmed him and took his breath away. "They are both prima donnas. We've got to try to control the prima donna qualities in both of them." She had given up on Lewis when he had turned wholly

---

*Mrs. Longworth denied parentage:

Never, I never said that. I'm so glad you asked me about it. It wasn't true. They were both strong in different kinds of things. I think what happened is that I ran into a friend, Bill Hogg, and he said, "Have you heard what Jim Reed said about Franklin and Eleanor?" "Mush" is a bad, a silky word. There's no ring to "mush." How nice to have you ask me if I said that.

It was "maddening," she said, to have the story ascribed to her. (Author's interview with Mrs. Longworth.)

obstructionist, but she was still trying to prevent an irreparable break between the president and Farley.★[31]

She understood Farley's wanting to be president, she went on as the little group sat through the ritual of the nominating speeches, wanting it even more ardently because he was a Catholic and attributing his failure to get it to his religion. That was inevitable when one was part of a minority. She knew from her own experience how difficult it was to overcome the sense of insecurity and of being excluded, so she understood just how Jim felt. She was sad about Senator Carter Glass's uninspired speech nominating Farley, and when the radio carried the convention's singing of "When Irish Eyes Are Smiling," a tribute to Jim, she sang along in a low voice. But she also made the point that if he were to obtain the nomination, he would be obligated to the reactionaries and would be torn to pieces.

The nomination of Garner moved her to talk about his conservatism. He was a self-made man and in achieving success had become insensitive to the sufferings of others. He considered people in need of help failures and regarded all reform as a conspiracy to divest him of hard-won, personally achieved gains. The president, on the other hand, never having gone through bitter, personal struggle to achieve wealth and prominence, had no such feelings about his possessions and privileges. He was sensitive to suffering and privation and, once he understood, would go to the limit to change things; the problem was to get him to understand and to see a situation.

When Senator Lister Hill placed the president in nomination, she remarked that it looked like "a very rough campaign." The Democrats were highly vulnerable, she thought. If she were in the opposition she knew exactly what her campaign themes would be:

We haven't solved the unemployment problem.

We have broken a very great tradition.

It would be a very rough campaign, and she felt a great weariness in approaching it.

★When in the closing days of the campaign Lewis came out for Willkie, warning that if CIO members did not vote as he urged they would lose him as a leader, Eleanor wrote James Carey, a friend who was head of the United Electrical and Radio Workers Union and at that time close to Lewis: "That is a serious threat and a dangerous way to function in a democracy it seems to me. I cannot help wondering how Mr. Ford, Mr. Weir & Mr. Girdler welcome him as an ally" (Oct. 26, 1940).

The group at Val-Kill listening to the nominations did not break up until 3:00 A.M., but by 8:30 the next morning Eleanor had already been in for a swim and had jotted down some points she might use in her speech to the convention. She called Franklin to make sure she would not be saying things he intended to say, but his speech was not finished. He told her that Harry Hopkins had not been sent out by him, was not his personal representative, that he had no headquarters—that it was all a newspaper story. Earl and Tommy were skeptical.

With only an overnight bag and a briefcase bulging with mail and manuscripts, Eleanor left for New York in a small plane that C. R. Smith, the head of American Airlines and a good friend, had sent up for her. There was a quiet elegance about her silk coat and dress, both blue, and a small blue straw hat added a touch of chic. At LaGuardia she was joined by Franklin Jr., who had been sent by his father with whom he had been staying. Her mission, she told reporters at LaGuardia, was "to do whatever Jim Farley wants me to do as quickly as possible and then turn around and come right back."

Smith flew her to Chicago, where Farley met her at the airport. On the way to the hotel he filled her in on convention developments. There was a terrible situation caused by Wallace's nomination for vice president, he said; the delegates refused to accept Wallace. Although the president was insisting on Wallace, other candidates had to be nominated, and Farley said he was going to nominate Jesse Jones, who would tie in the party conservatives, and Elliott was going to second Jones. "The old man will have no one else but Wallace," Franklin Jr. interrupted.

Eleanor agreed to call the president and pass on Farley's views. He would not take Jones, Franklin told her. Suppose he—the president—died? What kind of a president would Jones make? "He doesn't speak our language." Barkley was loyal but lacked backbone; if he became president, the pressure groups would pull him apart. Byrnes was splendid but was a Catholic turned Episcopalian. Franklin had promised to support Wallace and would refuse the nomination if Wallace were not accepted. It was all right to name other candidates, he agreed in the end, if they were sure of the votes for Wallace. "*They* say they have the votes for Wallace," Farley responded, to which Eleanor said to herself, "Oh, my God."

At the convention hall she talked with Ed Flynn, who confirmed what Farley had said; he did not know whether they had enough votes for Wallace. Whatever the president had told her about not sending Hopkins out, Hopkins had set up the closest thing imaginable to a headquarters, Flynn commented, and he was summoning delegates and in general was functioning as the president's field commander. Flynn thought the move against Wallace was a move to compel the president to refuse the nomination. Eleanor considered that too Machiavellian, but at the White House an angry Roosevelt had prepared a statement declining the nomination in the event that Wallace was voted down.

She took a seat unobtrusively on the crowded platform and sent Franklin Jr. to look for Elliott. The convention did seem out of control, responding to Wallace's name with a roar of boos and catcalls. Mayors Frank Hague and Edward J. Kelly (from Jersey City and Chicago respectively) came up to speak to Eleanor, and she said to herself, "Oh Lord! I'll wager Pegler, Johnson and Clapper are all watching me." Elliott arrived and she cautioned him against supporting Jones in opposition to his father's wishes. The situation among the delegates was so "poisonous" that just before Barkley introduced Eleanor, Frances Perkins and Lorena Hickok panicked, although they had urged her to come to Chicago, and said it was terrible to put her on then. Eleanor calmed them. The audience was "like lambs," she later said.

MRS. ROOSEVELT STILLS
THE TUMULT OF 50,000

a headline read, and the United Press story began, "The hot and weary delegates caught her mood and gravity and fell silent."

A reporter had asked her upon her arrival whether she was happy about the president's nomination. "Happy!" she exclaimed, "I don't know how any one could be particularly happy about the nomination in the present state of the world. It is a tremendous responsibility to be nominated for the Presidency."

This was the theme of her speech. From the president's comments and from his choice of Wallace, who was a bad campaigner (even though the president was not going to leave the White House for the campaign), Eleanor concluded that he had chosen a running mate solely with the thought in mind that the man he chose might become president—almost "would" become president. The president obviously sensed "that the strain of a third term might be too much for any man." Whoever became president, she told her hushed audience, faced a heavier responsibility, perhaps, than any man has ever faced before in this country.... You cannot treat it as you would an ordinary nomination in an ordinary time.... So each and every one of you who give him this responsibility, in giving it to him assume for yourselves a very grave responsibility because you will make the campaign. You will have to rise above considerations which are narrow and partisan. This is a time when it is the United States we fight for.

In short, simple, eloquent sentences, she drove home the point, without mention of Wallace, that in asking the president to run again the delegates, too, assumed an obligation. "No man who is a candidate or who is President can carry this situation alone. This is only carried by a united people who love their country."

As she finished the hall was absolutely still. Petty rancors and rivalries had visibly subsided, and for the moment the convention was united. "She has done more to soothe the convention bruises than all the efforts of the astute Senators," the *Daily News* reported. "Thanks to her the roll call began in a fairly dignified atmosphere."[32]

A glowing Barkley thanked her, and the balloting for vice president began. It was very close. Many said that without her, Wallace would not have won. Along with the delegates, she listened to the president's acceptance speech, broadcast from the White House and piped into the convention hall. It explained why he had delayed issuing a statement of his attitude toward a third term until the opening of the convention. As commander-in-chief he was calling on men and women to serve their country; he had no right to decline such service himself. He stated, although in somewhat muted terms, that much remained to be done to meet domestic needs and drew once again the fundamental issue between dictatorship and democracy. Eleanor liked the speech but was unhappy over the bitter note he had sounded about the columnists. He had referred to them as "appeaser fifth columnists." She did not want the president even to be concerned with them.

As they left the platform, Frances Perkins observed ruefully that she was all for the democratic process, but a new party in birth was very painful. Eleanor replied that she was not so sure the new party was born yet. She spoke to Farley before she left and urged him to hold onto the chairmanship, even if he could not work actively. She thought he was weakening, and they agreed to spend a day together soon, planning the campaign.

Escorted by Franklin Jr., whose tie was awry and collar unbuttoned, they entered a car and, with an advance guard of police cars, sirens blowing, sped out to the airport. As the plane started to taxi down the runway, it was flagged back. Franklin was on the telephone to tell her she had done a very good job. Harry Hopkins was on another phone, also full of thanks. He brought up the mistakes he had made, and she was sure as he spoke that he must have been given to believe he was responsible for the convention. Her farewell words to Harry as she prepared to re-enter the plane were: "You young things don't know politics."

The letters poured in praising her performance at Chicago. It seemed to be "the determining influence in the final vote for Secretary Wallace," wrote Helen Reid, the publisher of the *New York Herald Tribune,* who had been present. Sam Rosenman, speaking for those who were with the president at the White House during the tense hours when he was determined to decline the nomination, said all of them had been "thrilled" by her talk at the convention: "It seemed to lift it above the petty political trading that was going and place it on a different level, far removed." One letter that especially pleased Eleanor was from the dean of American progressivism, Senator George Norris. He had listened to the Chicago proceedings with a growing apprehension, he wrote her, and just when it seemed

> as though the convention were going to "blow up" [and] the battle for righteousness was about to be lost, you came on the scene, and what you said in that short speech caused men of sense and honor to stop and think before they plunged.... You turned a rout into a victory. You were the Sheridan of that convention.... That victory was finally realized is due, in my opinion, more to you than any other one thing. That one act makes you heroic.[33]

The convention battle had been won, but Eleanor was not sure it meant victory for the purposes and programs that gave candidacies and politics their meaning. All through the summer months the issue that preoccupied her, as the Nazi war machine, supreme on the Continent, tried to bomb England into submission, was the question posed most sharply by Lord Halifax, once a leading spokesman of appeasement, in an address to the students of Oxford: "What is it that we fight for, and what prospect is there that we shall in the end secure the better world for which the fight is waged?"

Congress was debating conscription. The Army and Navy wanted a year's compulsory military service and nothing else. The Burke-Wadsworth bill reflected their recommendations. But Eleanor, who felt that the strengthening of democracy was an indispensable component of defense, favored a universal youth service that would be a force for democratization and national unity. She urged that military training be combined with other types of training. There was considerable talk in the press gallery, May Craig wrote from Washington, that she was "'bucking the old man' on the conscription bill," so Miss Craig was glad to see Eleanor's column making it clear she did not oppose the Burke-Wadsworth bill. "I am not bucking the President," Eleanor replied, "but would like to see a wider service." She did not want conscription to be exclusively administered by the Army, but felt that it should be geared in with the NYA and CCC. "National defense means more than military training," she told a news conference. "It means the building up of physique, of character and of a people conscious of what they owe to their country and what it means to them. ... It took more than a knowledge of the manual of arms to carry the British troops through the retreat from Dunkirk."

Why should the nation's young men alone be asked to serve in this supreme moment of danger? She favored total mobilization, a national muster in which everyone would be given a job to do, women as well as men, old as well as young, with burdens and sacrifices equally shared, a mobilization that would be at heart a commitment of spirit and of faith in the democratic future. When Dr. Harriet Elliott, the only woman on the National Defense Advisory Commission, went to Val-Kill to discuss what women might do in connection with the defense program, Eleanor was ready for her. The defense program should be used to serve the purpose of community revitalization, and women should be given training that would be useful in peace as well as in war. She suggested that they be taught how to prepare nutritious meals and that this be combined with a hot-school-lunch program; she urged training in the household arts, first aid, home nursing, and hygiene; and she recommended a physical-fitness and recreational program.[34]

But many of the president's advisers, as well as the president himself, feared that efforts to combine defense with reform might drive a crucial segment of business into the ranks of the isolationists and appeasers. Asked by an alert reporter to comment on Harriet Elliott's assertion that "defense is planes and guns" but also "building the health, the physical fitness, the social well-being of all our people.... Hungry people, undernourished people, ill people, do not make for strong defense," Roosevelt, instead of endorsing the plea, wisecracked that the issue of whether women should be admitted to the White House correspondents' dinner might also be considered a matter of national defense "but it is not immediate," no more so than whether his Christmas tree crop would be a success that year. He had to restrict defense assistance in the social field to needs that arose clearly from expansion of defense industry and facilities! "I draw the line. I have to." It was a sensible point, but still, as *Common Sense* noted, the wisecracks "came strangely from the head of the New Deal." When Eleanor questioned him about it, the president insisted he had not been referring to Miss Elliott or her report. "I've checked with others and it seems hard to understand how he could have missed the meaning of the question," Eleanor wrote to Selden Rodman. "I just can't feel that I've got to the bottom of it and yet I can't get the President now to think back."[35]

The contrasting fortunes of the conscription bill and a Treasury tax measure to take the profits out of war brought into sharp focus the compromises that Roosevelt was obliged to accept that summer. His tax message had asked for a steeply graduated excess-profits tax "so that a few do not gain from the sacrifices of the many." But Congress showed little enthusiasm for the Treasury bill, which was modeled on England's excess-profits legislation. "If you are going to try to go to war, or to prepare for war, in a capitalist country," Secretary of War Stimson wrote in his diary,

> you have got to let business make money out of the process or business won't work, and there are a great many people in Congress who think they can tax business out of all proportion and still have businessmen work diligently and quickly. That is not human nature.[36]

That was the point of view of the military men, who were primarily concerned with speed in production. On the other side, liberals like Eleanor Roosevelt and Henry Morgenthau, concerned with democratic morale, were indignant over the attitude of business. One week end at the beginning of August, Morgenthau went to Hyde Park to talk with the president about the tax bill, and afterward he visited Eleanor at Val-Kill to bewail the president's retreat. The Treasury's tax bill was out, Roosevelt had told him; the president would take the bill prepared by Congress, Morgenthau reported, which meant it would be drafted by the lawyers for the chambers of commerce. The manufacturers were on strike and were refusing to negotiate contracts until Congress enacted a tax bill that assured them their profits. "Only $900,000 in contracts have been negotiated and the President is scared."

"It's like the sit-down strike of capital against Léon Blum," broke in Elinor Morgenthau.

Couldn't something be done through the National Defense Advisory Commission, Eleanor asked. "You can't expect the businessmen on the Defense Council to go after fellow businessmen," Morgenthau replied. But disappointed as the secretary was, he cautioned Eleanor to let the president alone—"at least for 24 hours. He's in one of those moods."[37]

If she could not speak to the president directly, she had her column. People should not profit from the war financially while the nation's young men were being drafted, she wrote.[38] Each side in this debate had its own analysis of why France fell. While liberals spoke of the sit-down strike by French business against Léon Blum, conservatives like Eleanor's long-time friend and lawyer Harry Hooker were equally sure that the collapse of France had been due to the Blum reforms. Wendell Willkie had sounded this theme in his acceptance speech. The New Deal, like the Blum government, Willkie contended, was incapable of mobilizing industry's capacity to produce, and fomented division instead of unity. Eleanor gave a wholly opposite analysis of what had happened in France. Too many Frenchmen had cared more for their money than for France.

Unhappy as Eleanor was over Franklin's inability to give a stronger lead on those issues, Willkie offered no alternative, and the Republican party refused to follow his leadership on the Burke-Wadsworth bill, narrowly conceived as it was. Further, as if to underscore the unwillingness of the privileged to make any sacrifices, Willkie attacked the Russell-Overton amendment to the conscription bill, which would authorize the government to seize plants that refused to cooperate in the defense program. It would "sovietize" industry, Willkie charged: "It is said that if men are to be conscripted, wealth must be conscripted. If this statement is taken literally . . . I cannot understand what we are undertaking to defend." "Oh, yeah," Uncle David Gray wrote Eleanor from Dublin, Willkie "will send our boys to be massacred, but money is too sacred."[39]

But it was a losing battle. It took Congress all summer to complete action on conscription and taxes. Liberals predicted a "new crop" of war millionaires. "It was abandoning advanced New Deal ground with a vengeance," Ickes commented in his diary.[40]

It was worse than that. Earlier in the year, before France had fallen and he had consented to run again, Roosevelt had spoken of a revived NRA through which corporate enterprise would be subordinated to the public interest, and had talked to Ickes about regulatory and planning mechanisms modeled on the TVA. Now big business was setting the terms of its cooperation with the government, and the influence of the military had begun to grow. These were the dangers that Eleanor had foreseen for her husband if he ran for a third term, but as the campaign progressed and she saw the forces that lined up behind Wendell Willkie, she became increasingly reconciled to her husband's candidacy.[41]

"I think I'll have to do a little work at headquarters but no campaigning," she wrote shortly after the Chicago convention. "It is going to be a disagreeable fight! The convention was bad & Jim Farley's feelings & F.D.R.'s feelings made things no easier. They seem quiet now, however." Quiet they were, but the breach between the president and Farley was unbridgeable. Neither the president nor Eleanor was able to sway Farley from his determination to give up the national chairmanship. Roosevelt turned to Ed Flynn, who took on the job, reluctantly. "If I do anything political," Eleanor wrote Ruby Black, "I will surely let you know as I feel that the press would be entitled to know. However, I do not expect to do anything out in the open. Eddie Flynn is a very old friend of mine and I think, in some ways, we are even closer than I have ever been with Jim."

Flynn, she felt, understood the New Deal much better than Farley, and, indeed, the Bronx leader was keenly aware of Eleanor's strength and popularity with the New Deal segments of the Roosevelt coalition. He accepted her views on the organization of the women's work. She immediately implored Molly Dewson, who had written in July saying that she was "nearly reconciled to his running again," to leave her Maine refuge "to do some of the work with the men." Flynn asked Eleanor to serve as his link with Norris and LaGuardia, who were to head up an Independent Committee for Roosevelt and Wallace. But primarily Flynn wanted her nearby as an additional channel to the president. He knew how stubborn and remote Roosevelt could become, inaccessible even to his closest advisers.[42]

What was the strategy of the campaign, she was asked early in August. Before she could reply a friend observed, "The strategy eludes me except that the President is to continue being President and Mrs. Roosevelt First Lady." Flynn's advice to the president had been to confine himself to running the country and, as commander-in-chief, preparing for the dangers that beset it, and to leave partisan attacks to Flynn. There would be no campaign trips, Franklin informed Eleanor, but with the president silent, the pressure on her to campaign was stronger than in 1932 and 1936. She was sorry, she wrote a Roosevelt supporter,

> but I have never campaigned for my husband, and could not. The Democratic National Committee does not wish it either. The President must stand on his own record.
>
> If he is defeated we must believe it is for the best interest of the country.[43]

By the end of September she was no longer sure that the president's above-the-battle posture was right. She sent him a letter from a woman deploring the president's aloofness in the face of the GOP barrage of charges and claims. "FDR—I rather think she expresses the feelings of many," she wrote on the margin.

Flynn dispatched Franklin Jr., who was heading up youth work in the campaign, to plead with his father to make some political speeches. "What brings you to Washington?" Roosevelt teased his son as they dined alone in the oval study. "What is this 'urgent' business you had to see me about?" he went on as if he did not know.

"Everybody's worried at headquarters."

The president was amused. "Are they out ringing the doorbells?"

"Yeah, they're working their pants off."

"Good, good," the president beamed, "then they're not relying upon me."

Young Franklin protested: it was not enough; he had to get into it; Flynn had to know when he intended to start campaigning. "I'll let him know," the president said amiably.[44]

On October 11, Roosevelt went to Dayton, Ohio, but only to make a nonpolitical speech on hemispheric defense, and the short talks he made along the way were equally nonpolitical. Eleanor now felt that the president owed it to the public to discuss the issues that were being raised by Willkie: "I hope you will make a few more speeches. It seems to me pretty essential that you make them now as political speeches

& the people have a right to hear your say in opposition to Willkie between now & election day."[45]

The anti-Roosevelt underground campaign in 1940 was venomous, and Flynn accused the Republicans of conducting "the most vicious, most shameful campaign since the time of Lincoln." Much of the abuse centered on Eleanor and the Roosevelt family. Publicly she brushed it off as routine "mudslinging" but privately, as she confided in a long letter to Maude Gray reporting on her children, it caused offense and anguish:

> The campaign is as bad in personal bitterness as any I have ever been in. Scurrilous letters & publications pour in about Elliott, about the money we have all made & the way we have made it with innuendoes of all kinds so I'll be glad when it is all over. Of course from a personal standpoint I'd give anything to leave Washington & if Franklin is elected I sometimes wonder if the amount he can do will be worth the sacrifice that all of us have to make, but the choice is not ours to make.[46]

She feared what another four years of the presidential spotlight might do to her children. Franklin Jr., handsome, full of life, quick at jovial repartee with hecklers, was proving to be a great success as a campaigner; from all over the country politicians reported on how he captivated his audiences. His success pleased his mother, but his other traits worried her. In a stern letter reminiscent of the one Sara had written her son in 1906, Eleanor wrote her husband:

> Something has to be done to make F. jr. realize it is dishonest not to pay bills. I suggest you ask him to list *all* he owes. Pay it yourself & then take out of his allowance $100 a quarter. Tell him he *has* to live on his income, no going to "21" etc. until he earns his own money in toto & has no bills. Forbid Granny to give him anything except his Xmas & birthday presents beyond his allowance & that to be cut in proportion as his earnings make it possible.... Thank God for Anna & Johnnie who don't want to get rich quick & are willing to work & pay their way as they go.[47]

On October 23 the president went to Philadelphia for his first "political" speech. He was in fine form. The huge crowd loved it as he pulled out all the rhetorical stops in speaking of "the tears, the croc-odile tears" that the Republican leaders were now shedding for labor, youth, the unemployed, and the elderly after having opposed all the New Deal measures that he had introduced to help these groups: "In 1940, eight years later, what a different tune is played by them! It is a tune played against a sounding board of election day. It is a tune with overtones which whisper: 'Votes, votes, votes.'"

It was devastating, and the crowd roared in approval. Eleanor heard it in Barrytown, where she was visiting a Hudson neighbor, Alice Huntington. She listened to Willkie afterward. The contrast was ter-rific, she thought, and all to the president's advantage. She called Franklin and could sense that he, too, felt it had been a success. "Dar-ling," she interrupted his expressions of pleasure, "it's my call and it's costing me money and I have things to tell you."

Early in June, Esther Lape had expressed concern over a Republican whispering campaign that Roosevelt wanted to get the United States into the war, which she felt ought not to go unanswered. But the presi-dent refused to make statements that he feared would give aid and com-fort to the dictators. In October LaGuardia warned the White House that "the anti-third term propaganda would cease about the middle of October and a concerted drive [would] be made on anti-war."[48] LaGuar-dia was sufficiently worried to want Roosevelt to postpone the first call for draftees until after the election. The mayor's information was cor-rect. In the closing days of the campaign the GOP began to emphasize, to the exclusion of all else, the isolationist charge that Roosevelt was going to lead the country into war. Were there secret agreements to do so, Willkie demanded, and answered his own question with the predic-tion that on the basis of the president's past performance with pledges, the United States would be in the war by April. As Republican orators pounded away on this theme, there was something close to panic at Democratic headquarters. Although Roosevelt refused to postpone the drawing of the numbers under the Selective Service Act, in Boston he yielded to his political advisers and inserted an assurance to the "moth-ers and fathers [that] your boys are not going to be sent into any foreign wars.... The purpose of our defense is defense."

Quietly, the next day, in her column, Eleanor added her own foot-note to this pledge: "No one can honestly promise you today peace at home or abroad. All any human being can do is to promise that he will do his utmost to prevent this country being involved in war."[49]

Upon Flynn's urging, she consented in the final days of the campaign to appear at some Democratic rallies. The Republicans had sought to make her a campaign issue, distributing WE DON'T WANT ELEANOR EITHER buttons. These sometimes backfired. Gertrude Ely reported that she had gone to a Willkie Club meeting to present the Democratic position and started out by saying that she was one of the many women "who *did* want Eleanor, too," and to her utter amazement "this Administration-baiting group broke into sudden, spontaneous, enthusiastic applause."[50]

Throughout the campaign Eleanor had kept her column nonpolitical. George Carlin, the manager of the United Feature Syndicate, had advised her to do so because she had "become more and more loved by the Republicans as well as Democrats." Although nonpolitical, the column's spirit of grace and kindliness, its chatty reports on the doings of the president and his family, were more effective campaigning than any direct political utterance. That was the case, too, with her appearances at the huge receptions and rallies in and around New York City in the closing days of the campaign. A campaign worker wrote a friend:

> She came in smiling, very straight, giving the feeling of great strength and confidence, waving at old friends. She had that quality of noticing people in a crowd and letting them know it. All of us were made to feel our contribution had been of great importance. All of us felt enhanced. And when she spoke, every mother knew that she understood and shared their great anxiety about tomorrow—and so, they felt reassured that the President too would know and remember and protect them in every way.[51]

The Monday before election there was the traditional tour with the president through Dutchess County and his final appearance before his neighbors outside of the Nelson House in Poughkeepsie. Afterward Eleanor wrote:

> I remember what it was like the first time my husband ran for the State Senate....I think my feelings have always been much as they were the first time. I think I can say with honesty: "May what is best for the country happen today and may we all remember that whatever happens, this is just the beginning of some years of useful work!"[52]

To her Aunt Maude she wrote (and it was a measure of how her thinking had changed about her husband's candidacy): "Frankly I hate the next four years in Washington and dread what it may do to us all but there seemed nothing else for F. to do and once nominated for a number of reasons his defeat would have been undesirable."[53]

After luncheon at the Big House on Election Day, the president, Harry Hopkins, Pa Watson, and Doc McIntire settled down to a poker game to speed the afternoon along. Eleanor went to Val-Kill for a long walk with a friend, which took them through wooded paths drifted over with autumn leaves up to the hilltop house where in calmer days she and the president had entertained the British king and queen. She talked about the next four years. She hoped the president would now do all the things that he had wanted to do all along, that he knew had to be done but had not done because of political considerations. She was confident of victory, and she hoped that it would be clear-cut, a decisive mandate for liberal government. Repeatedly she spoke of the magnitude of the responsibility the president would assume with victory. The rapt expressions of trust and devotion on the faces of the people lining the streets as the president passed through had heightened her sense of the awfulness of the responsibility carried by the president in such perilous times. For herself, she had a real horror of four more years in the White House, with its lack of privacy, the ceremonial occasions, the things that had to be done in which she was not interested, and the people who would have to be entertained who meant little to her. She preferred to retire to Hyde Park, live with her friends, and be a useful citizen doing productive and helpful work, with a job of her own.[54]

As dusk descended everyone at the Big House except the president and his mother went to Val-Kill for a buffet supper of creamed chicken and rice, cake, ice cream, and coffee. Early returns from Connecticut were good, but talk was subdued as the forty-odd guests grouped themselves in different corners of Eleanor's dining and sitting rooms. Toward nine o'clock everyone returned to the Big House, where the president was already set up for business in the dining room. He was seated at the table with his jacket off and his necktie loosened. The tools of the evening were spread out before him—tally sheets, a large supply of sharpened pencils, and telephones that linked him with the White House and with Flynn at the Biltmore. In a little cubicle off the dining room, called the smoking room, AP, UP, and INS teletype machines clattered away. The group with the president changed from time to time except for Missy, Franklin Jr., and John. Harry Hopkins, to whom Roosevelt referred as "my house guest without portfolio," was often in and out, as were Judge John Mack, who had placed Roosevelt in nomination in 1932 and 1936, Uncle Fred Delano, and the members of a small group who gathered in a little study off the foyer: Pa Watson and Doc McIntire, Captain Daniel Callaghan (the president's naval aide), Judge Samuel Rosenman, Secretary Morgenthau, and Postmaster General Frank Walker.

The remainder of the party clustered around radios in the library. From time to time Missy or one of the boys came in from the dining room with "takes" from the tickers for Eleanor or written notes based on telephone talks with Ed Flynn and other political leaders around the country. Eleanor transmitted these tidbits calmly, as if nothing out of the ordinary were taking place. All evening, in an easy, effortless way, she made everyone feel at home and included, but she was detached about the returns, an observer rather than a participant in the mounting excitement. By eleven Flynn claimed victory, and scrambled eggs—an old Roosevelt custom—were being served. Some of the newspaperwomen came inside the house, and asked the president's mother how she felt. Beamingly she replied, "Am I proud of being a historic mother? Indeed I am." But there was no elation in Eleanor's reply to such questions: "This is too serious a time for the President to feel anything but a great sense of responsibility," she said.[55]

At midnight the traditional parade from the village arrived with red flares and a band playing "The Old Gray Mare." The floodlights of the movie cameramen went on and there was a great cheer as the president and his family went out and arranged themselves on the portico, with the president on the right, steadying himself on the arm of Franklin Jr., and Eleanor, in a flame-colored chiffon dress, tall and commanding, on the left. There was a sense of history having been made. Harry Hopkins was standing by himself at the rear of the portico. Suddenly he did a little pirouette of triumph and in a long, swinging arc brought his right fist down into the palm of his left hand. The words "we made it" could not have been spelled out more graphically or exultantly. After some banter with his neighbors, Roosevelt made a little speech, ending with the assurance that "you will find me in the future just the same Franklin Roosevelt you have known a great many years."

As the flares burned down and he called "Good night," there were shouts of "We want Eleanor," but smilingly she waved her hand and went into the house. A little later a delayed contingent of the Home

Club arrived, and Franklin Jr., came in saying, "Mother, they want you. There are 700 people still standing out there in the dark, asking for you. You'll have to go to them."

"I never do any talking when Father is around, you know that," she put him off. Then she added, "I hate to bother your father again, but if you think we should, I guess we will."

It was not until 2:30 in the morning that the president was satisfied that the results would not be upset. As he prepared to go to bed, he made the startling good-night observation, "We seem to have averted a *Putsch*, Joe." When his wife asked what he meant by that, he explained that he had received information that persons purporting to speak for Willkie and the German government had come to an agreement to compel Britain to make peace in return for which the United States would have unchallenged sovereignty in the Western hemisphere. "From all we hear," Eleanor later wrote Lady Florence Willert,

> we realize now that Mr. Willkie was backed by forces which were a greater menace than many of us were willing to believe. There was a fascist tendency for an appeasement policy toward Germany which terrifies many of us and makes us feel that the decision of the Willkie backers to keep up their organization is none too good for the country.[56]

Roosevelt's and his wife's feelings toward Willkie would change quickly. A few weeks after the election the president gave his defeated rival a cordial letter of introduction to Churchill, and Eleanor joined him on the dais at an NAACP dinner. But that was not the mood on election night at the Big House.

Perhaps she had been selfish, Eleanor said that night, and, wanting to get out of the White House, had tended to underestimate the importance of the president's re-election.

51. A JOB TO DO

A FEW WEEKS BEFORE THE THIRD-TERM INAUGURATION ELEANOR wrote: "So many people have been in and out of the house the last few days, and so many more will be these next few days that I ache at the thought. I'm always thankful for these hours from 1:00 to 3:00!" She was, of course, referring to the early morning.

It was a trying time. She was "immersed in lists and long talks with Mrs. Helm," who met her with a question every time she turned around. She was "so busy that I can only stay calm by being an automaton. At times like these I try to be a machine or I would burst into tears or run away."[1]

Some friends worried that another four years of an endless giving of herself to the thousands who passed through the White House, of an effort to make some affirmative response to every appeal for help must inevitably result in a self-protective numbing of the spirit. But tenderness and sympathy were self-regenerative, Eleanor felt. "I do not think I will ever become deadened," she replied to one such warning, "because I live in other people's lives. I must admit there are times when it weighs me down because I can't do some of the things I want."[2]

"Beware when God lets loose a person of conscience," Bonaro W. Overstreet would write of Eleanor's White House years. That conscience was more exigent than ever as she embarked upon her third term as mistress of the White House. "I looked at my children, at the President's mother, and then at the President himself," she wrote after the historic inaugural ceremony, "and wondered what each one was feeling down in his heart of hearts." She herself felt that "any citizen should be willing to give all that he has to give his country in work or sacrifice in times of crisis." She was writing about the president, but she felt the same way about herself. Although eight years in the White House repeatedly had revealed the pitfalls that lay in wait for a president's wife who tried to do a job, she longed to be of use.[3]

Just as the saints, even as they performed prodigies of resistance to temptation, worried endlessly whether they were pure enough to justify God's grace, so the question of her moral courage in the face of the pressures to conform was always on Eleanor's mind. She was deeply stirred by the hero of Lillian Hellman's *Watch on the Rhine,* a German anti-fascist who leaves family and comfort in the United States to go back to work in the German underground. How did one acquire that kind of courage, she wondered. What did it mean to say, as she did, that "we must do better than in 1918," if in yielding on such matters as the tax bill, health, housing, and minority rights the old cycle was being renewed? The time for courage was not later but now on issues relating to the way the war was being fought. What was required of her? Did she have a right to bother Franklin, who now carried the burdens not only of a nation but of a world? Yet if not she, who? And didn't she, too, carry a responsibility? The country had voted for him, but many had been reassured by her presence at his side.[4]

Hitherto her life had been disjointed. As First Lady she moved from one cause to another, patroness of all, involved fully in none. Her thoughts were equally fragmented. The war, which seemed to her to represent a mighty challenge to mankind to shape its future more decently, gave point and direction to her ideas and feelings, and since she did not permit herself to hold beliefs without accepting their consequences in action, she longed for a job of her own to do in the defense effort, one related to her basic conviction that the war had to be waged in ways that gave men and women the assurance not only of military victory but of a better world.

In the first months of the war she had offered to go to Europe for the Red Cross if Franklin thought it would be useful. He had been sympathetic, as he was thinking of a nationally coordinated refugee relief effort with Eleanor and ex-President Hoover at its head. But Hoover, driven by a bitterness against Roosevelt that verged on the neurotic, brushed aside his overtures. "Hoover turned us down," Eleanor informed Martha Gellhorn. "Said he would probably be busy organizing a political campaign next year and did not feel he could support the setting up of anything else, but that he would be willing to give his help and advice to the Red Cross. He refused to call on the President." In any event, the blitzkrieg moved faster than Eleanor's offer to go to Europe, and both Cordell Hull and Norman Davis, head of the American Red Cross, vetoed the journey after the Nazi breakthrough. They declined to take a chance on the president's wife being taken captive.[5]

With the continent occupied and England beset, in June, 1940, Eleanor undertook to act as the president's agent in establishing the U.S. Committee for the Care of European Children, which was to bring English and other European children to the United States for the duration of the war. When the provisional committee met in Eleanor's Greenwich Village apartment, its members were eager to have banker Winthrop Aldrich head the Finance Committee; but suddenly in his presence he was proposed as over-all chairman. Eleanor went into her bedroom and called the president for advice. He did not want a Republican stalwart in that position, he told her, so Eleanor composed herself, returned to the living room, and said in her most disarming manner: "It is kind of Mr. Aldrich to offer to be chairman, but is it not better from the point of view of geography to have someone from the Middle West?" At that, she turned to Marshall Field; she knew it was a bothersome responsibility, she said, but could he accept the chairmanship? Somewhat startled, the Chicago philanthropist and stalwart New Dealer did. Eleanor agreed to serve as honorary chairwoman.[6]

After the fall of France, she had in fact become, as one historian has written, "a kind of mother hen for all rescue agencies." Thousands of refugees, frantic at the prospect of being caught by Hitler's armies, were clamoring for visas to the United States. But the State Department, fearful that any liberalization of visa regulations would incur the wrath of Congress and the public, seemed, as Albert Einstein later informed Eleanor, to erect "a wall of bureaucratic measures" between the victims of fascist cruelty in Europe and safety in the United States. The department's visa operations were headed by Breckinridge Long, a narrow-minded conservative who was determined to hold refugee admissions down to a minimum.[7]

There was one sure way to bypass administrative bureaucracy in New Deal Washington—to appeal to the president through his wife. Eleanor was flooded with appeals to help obtain visas, and to each request she gave an affirmative response, often turning to Sumner Welles, who was sympathetic to the refugees. If Welles was unable to help, she went to Franklin, especially in the cases of the hundreds of intellectuals and political and trade-union leaders who were trapped in unoccupied France. Dr. Karl Frank and Joseph Buttinger, valiant leaders of the German underground, came to her apartment in New

York with lists of outstanding anti-fascists compiled by the Emergency Rescue Committee whom the committee was desperate to get out of Europe. She immediately called the president, who was a little impatient with her, irritated that it was not taken for granted that he was already doing all that was possible. It was a long call during which he kept bringing up the difficulties, while she pointed out the possibilities. Congress won't let them in; quotas were filled; we have tried to get Cuba and other Latin American countries to let them in but so far without success; our consuls can't locate people; Franco Spain won't admit even American refugees. Nevertheless, she took the lists and said she would see they were sent to U.S. consular offices in Europe.[8]

She sent them to the State Department with the plea:

> I hope, if it is safe and possible to do so, it can be put into the hands of our people in Europe with the request that they do everything they can to protect these refugees. I do not know what Congress will be willing to do, but they might be allowed to come here and sent to a camp while we are waiting for legislation.

Congress was unbudgeable, so the State Department, through administrative order, established an emergency visa procedure that would grant visitors' visas to the most endangered. How encouraging it was to have friendly support in the State Department, Karl Frank wrote Eleanor. "I know it is due to your interest. You will certainly know that many hundreds of people have been granted visitors visas. ... The biggest difficulty now, as you might know, is the problem of exit permits from France." But the joy of the refugee community as reflected in Karl Frank's letter was premature. "Is there no way of getting our Consul in Marseilles to help in getting a few more of these poor people out?" Eleanor wrote Welles on September 6, 1940, enclosing a letter from Frank. Although the State Department was authorizing visitors' visas, the local consuls were dilatory in issuing them.[9]

"FDR, a good case in point," Eleanor communicated to her husband in what had become a running argument between them. "They have been able to come for a long time but the consul won't grant visas." Clearly annoyed, the president retorted, "I do not think this is a good case in point at all." He went on to explain that the State Department's recommendation was on its way and that she should be patient. It took the pouch ten days to reach the consulate in question.[10]

Nevertheless, it was a fact that of the 576 names that the president's

Advisory Committee on Refugees had submitted to the State Department in August and early September, only about 40 visas had been issued by late September. At the end of November Eleanor was prodding Franklin again, on the basis of information supplied to her by Joseph Buttinger: "FDR—Can't something be done? ER" To Welles she was more emphatic: "I have had word from the Emergency Rescue Committee that the State Dept. promises to cable visas to Europe, but delays them. Is there anything that you could do to hasten this process so that the Committee will have assurance that the visas are cabled as soon as possible?" Her next message to Welles suggested that she had talked with the president: "I would like to have a report as to why so many of these people who actually have visas are finding so much difficulty. One fact is that they cannot get visas to go through Spain. Is there any way in which we could expedite them through Mr. Hayes?"[11]

Two decades later Mrs. Lion Feuchtwanger, the widow of the novelist, was writing an account of their escape from southern France. The American vice-consul in France had told Feuchtwanger, his wife wrote Eleanor, "that you were instrumental in his visa at a moment of ultimate danger." Was it she or the president who had been their good angel and enabled them to escape over the Pyrenees? "It was really my husband," Eleanor wrote back. "I could have done nothing except when he asked me to do it and I had his backing."[12]

Helping the rescue agencies was important work, but it still was not a job of her own. Nelson Rockefeller wanted her to go on a good-will mission to Latin America, but she turned him down. "So many things of interest have come up," she informed her husband; "I feel it quite impossible for me to go to South America." There is no date on this letter, but on January 9, 1941, she informed Rockefeller, "I have decided it would not be wise for me to go to South America now so I am giving up the idea."[13]

Her hopes of usefulness were pointed in another direction—to use the war emergency to build a unity of spirit, a readiness to share and sacrifice in the interests of a strengthened democracy. She demurred when James W. Gerard congratulated her as the president's "most effective campaigner." He gave her credit for something she had not done, she said, but she was willing to accept credit on another score: "I do, of course, believe sincerely that we must continue with the progressive social legislation as part of national defense and if, in supporting that, I have campaigned I am very glad."[14]

Civilian defense seemed to her the instrument for her purposes. Her friend Lady Stella Reading, head of the Women's Voluntary Services for Civil Defense, was doing a remarkable job in England both in the utilization of women and in the transformation of home defense into a force for social justice. Eleanor followed Lady Reading's work carefully, and after the election persuaded Franklin to request Mrs. Florence Kerr, who was in charge of WPA Community Service Projects, to prepare plans to make use of volunteer "women power" in America's defense effort. She became deeply involved in the elaboration of these blueprints, which, when they emerged, were entitled "American Social Defense Organization."

Many of the top women in Roosevelt's administration felt that only Eleanor could supply the leadership for such an organization, and Roosevelt himself evidently agreed for he advised his wife to refuse the chairmanship of a more limited group "because you belong logically with the larger nationwide group that Mrs. Kerr is about to make plans for."[15]

Franklin was aware of his wife's desire to be helpful in the defense program and even more keenly aware of her growing sense of apprehension that the New Deal was being abandoned. Perhaps in encouraging her to help with civilian defense he was not wholly innocent of the desire to shift her reforming impulses away from himself. At luncheon at Hyde Park just before the inauguration, there had been a tense moment over the issue of housing. The 1940 Lanham Defense Housing Act had specifically forbidden the use of the funds it authorized "to provide subsidized housing for persons of low income." The provision was aimed at Nathan Straus, a dedicated advocate of public housing, and at the United States Housing Agency which he headed. Eleanor wanted the president to see Straus, who feared that unless he or someone sympathetic to public housing administered the defense housing program it would be used to undermine the USHA. But Roosevelt, aware of Straus's unpopularity with Congress, refused to see him, and at the Hyde Park luncheon informed his wife that he was appointing Charles F. Palmer to the defense housing post. Would Palmer be sensitive to the need for low-cost housing, for schools, and other social services in defense areas, Eleanor wanted to know. Somewhat impatiently the president said he would, but Eleanor persisted. She had been told that he was partial to the real-estate people. Clearly annoyed, the president said, all right, he would appoint someone to watch for those things. Eleanor stuck to her guns: "Would he have any authority?" The president's mother, sensing her son's growing irritation, had signaled to the butler to wheel the president's chair to the table. Now she got behind his chair and helped wheel him away from a discussion which she saw did not please him.★[16]

Eleanor usually deferred to the president in matters of political strategy, yet these days she was haunted by the fear that the system of privilege and inequality within and among nations that had led to two world wars would inevitably breed more wars, despite a military victory, if the old division between haves and have-nots survived. When Harry Hopkins came back from the exploratory mission to England on which the president sent him early in January, 1941, she plied him with questions about how Lady Reading's organization was breaking down class distinctions and about Winston Churchill's war aims. Everyone was convinced there was no turning back, Harry assured her; they felt that Hitler must be defeated whatever the cost in privileges. Dozing on the couch of the president's oval study, Harry suddenly opened one eye and said to the president, "You know, Winston is much more left than you."[17]

Although Eleanor relished telling that story, she did not really believe that the president's commitment to liberalism had weakened. But she saw the pressures on him to abandon New Deal ground, and because she sensed the anxiety among Negroes, young people, and working men and women that their interests were being forgotten, she felt a compulsion to speak out more vigorously than ever on the whole range of home-front issues. She felt that the failure of many men to meet Army physical standards made a comprehensive national health program more rather than less urgent, and she said so. Her biggest disappointment with Harry Hopkins was his failure, now that he had become Franklin's closest adviser, to speak up for such a program: "Harry Hopkins could not be bothered." She fought for the farm tenant and for the young; "FDR insisted tonight neither farm security nor NYA was being curtailed." At the request of the Department of Agriculture, she alerted the president to moves in Congress to get rid of the school-lunch and food-stamp programs as "non-essential." She actively backed the fight for repeal of the poll tax, arguing that "we cannot be a democracy and deny the vote to any individual," especially

---

★Eleanor subsequently enjoyed a good working relationship with Palmer as housing coordinator. "Do help the USHA," she urged him. "Mr. Straus has done such a good job, but he does not understand getting on with Congress."

when many of the disenfranchised were being called to the armed forces. In public and private she pushed against the barriers that kept Negroes out of the defense industries and confined them to service jobs in the armed forces. She advocated rent controls and wage and price ceilings. If the vital energies of democracy were to be tapped, she said, democracy, like Communism and Nazism, must "give hope of a new order."[18]

While Roosevelt sometimes wearied of his wife's pressure, he, too, acknowledged, when the moment of irritation passed, that the conservatives were out to scuttle the New Deal and he, too, thought of civilian defense as "a social defense organization," as he would make clear in his Executive Order establishing the Office of Civilian Defense. Where was "that home defense thing," he was asked at a press conference early in March. "That's one of the most difficult things to put together in administrative form that I have yet had," he confessed, "because it covers so many different things in life."[19]

One of the major hurdles to issuing the order was to get agreement among the government agencies. Ickes was briefly involved in the planning of the home-defense setup. Too many women were being consulted, he huffily remarked, and Mrs. Kerr's plan was "cockeyed." He rallied to the side of Federal Security administrator Paul V. McNutt, who felt that Mrs. Kerr was trespassing on a proposal for an Office of Defense, Health, and Welfare Services, which he had drafted—also, it turned out, at the suggestion of the president. "It seems that Mrs. Roosevelt is mixed up in this," Ickes noted pessimistically, "and I told McNutt that he was likely to run into difficulties."[20]

In May the president issued his Executive Order. He had come down squarely on the side of the ladies, and the duties he assigned to the OCD were broad in scope. In addition to civilian protection, volunteer participation, and morale responsibilities, the new organization was given the job of securing the cooperation of the federal agencies in meeting the needs of communities resulting from the defense program. In effect, he deputized it to serve as home-front watchdog.[21]

The president appointed Fiorello LaGuardia to head up the organization. The ebullient little mayor had been pressing for a war assignment and Roosevelt had wanted to appoint him secretary of war, but Judge Rosenman, alerted by Justice Frankfurter, had talked the president out of that, describing LaGuardia as "a mad genius." A later suggestion that LaGuardia be appointed as the president's deputy with the defense-production group had also met with opposition. According to Ickes, it was felt that "LaGuardia would not work with the team but would run all over the field with the ball." When Ickes heard that LaGuardia had been named head of civilian defense, including morale, a field in which Ickes himself had ambitions, he wrote angrily that Fiorello "is not God" and could not handle home defense, campaign for re-election, and operate as chairman of the U.S.-Canadian Joint Defense Board. In this respect he had a point.[22]

The women wanted Eleanor to be in charge of volunteer work, and Roosevelt asked them to get in touch with LaGuardia, who saw the advantages to having the president's wife as his associate. It meant not only prestige and publicity, but unique leverage in establishing the new organization within the federal bureaucracy. He wanted her to join him, but she hesitated. Long experience had taught her that her presence incited jealousy as much as it elicited helpfulness, that officials in other agencies publicly acquiesced to her requests and privately grumbled because what they felt obliged to do for the wife of the president they would have refused to the assistant director of OCD. As for the publicity she would bring the fledgling, perhaps it was better for it to stay out of the limelight until a pattern of efficiency and usefulness had been established.[23]

She functioned most effectively when her leadership was exercised indirectly through someone like Molly Dewson. In June, Eleanor turned down the chairmanship of the women's division of civilian defense. She would only embarrass the president, she told friends; everything she said and did would be construed as officially coming from him and she did not want to add to his troubles.

She was more than willing, however, to help LaGuardia behind the scenes. Her interest was in the community-participation program, but the mayor's first thought in regard to women volunteers was to deck them out in attractive uniforms. He had set up a committee of New York's best fashion people, he informed Eleanor. "After you have seen the costumes and the insignia, do please let me have the benefit of your criticism." A stylish uniform, the mayor felt, would encourage women to volunteer, but Eleanor was not enthusiastic. It was "very unwise," she remonstrated, to release publicity on the uniforms "until we announce what work the women are going to do." Nor was she interested in elegance. She favored the "simplest kind of work uniform, one that was cheap and practical." The uniform that caught her eye at the New York display was a wrap-around apron of washable blue-gray cotton, a sort of cover-all, priced at under three dollars.[24]

Apart from uniforms for women volunteers, La Guardia was almost exclusively concerned with civilian protection—air-raid warning systems, practice blackouts, and especially fire precautions. Harry Hopkins was not surprised; it was an extension of the mayor's well-known fondness for dashing to three-alarm fires in New York City. "LaGuardia was in the President's hair," Baruch informed Ickes not long after the mayor took over the OCD job. "He is a poor executive and he won't work with anyone. He is too spectacular to keep his feet on the ground." The White House begged Anna Rosenberg, a hard-headed liberal who knew how to get along with the men, even the labor movement's rough diamonds, to stick close to the mayor and, above all, to keep him away from the president.[25]

Florence Kerr was in despair over the mayor's lack of interest in the volunteer-participation aspect of civilian defense. He not only was uninterested; he refused to let her do anything. "I was not allowed to do one single constructive thing. I did neither good work nor bad work—I did no work," she wrote later. The mayor's indifference became a form of pressure on Eleanor to become more actively involved in the program, and perhaps that was his intention. To get the mayor to move she offered him the use of the White House for the initial meeting of the Volunteer Participation Committee and asked the president to say a few words to the group: "I feel that you will have to make it clear that civilian participation is important. Otherwise the Mayor will not do much with his volunteers." The president did what she asked. "The Mayor's work is really in two parts," he told the forty-five members of the Civilian Participation Committee.

> The first is what I call quasi-military—a thing like preparing sand-bags . . . air raid alarms, and so forth and so on . . . but beyond that is your work, which is at least equally important—more important. . . .
> We know the fact that women in London—mothers of families—are just as important in the defense of Britain as men on a destroyer. They are all part of this defense. And I think we have a long ways to go in this country.[26]

The mayor did not construe the president's remarks as criticism of his leadership. He thanked Eleanor for her "splendid cooperation. I think it was you who made the meeting. I believe that it was most profitable and that we are going to get considerable help from all of the members for the *entire* program." Despite these fine words, the volunteer plans of OCD lagged. Eleanor said so at a press conference at end of August. As she explained to LaGuardia the next day,

> I was asked by one of the women reporters if I was completely sat-
> isfied with the work done by women volunteers in civilian defense,
> and I said I was not, and went on to explain that we are not fully
> launched on a real program, that there was still much to do.... I
> know that you feel as I do, that we have a big job ahead of us and
> are only just getting started.

With LaGuardia's approval she convened a meeting at the White House to discuss a civilian-defense program for young people, and at the meeting she criticized OCD's failure to enlist youth. When LaGuardia spoke to her about it afterward they made an oddly con-trasting pair—the mayor gesturing emphatically with his index finger as if to compensate for his shortness, the First Lady unruffled, benign, motherly, as if to minimize her tallness. "There are 135,000,000 peo-ple in this country," he said to her. "The criticism of 134,999,999 wouldn't touch me. Yours did." He was going to tell the president that he intended to draft America's Number 1 volunteer. "I'm wor-ried about the civilian defense job," she wrote that night, "because I don't want to do it but if the Mayor asks me I'll have to try. Just at the moment I feel very low."[27]

The two people who persuaded her to accept the civilian-defense post were Anna Rosenberg and Harry Hopkins. "Anna Rosenberg told me that only I could make the Mayor let anything be done on the civilian participation and she thought I wanted to do it." The pres-ident, Eleanor said, "was completely neutral, though he told me he thought it would help Mayor LaGuardia." Mrs. Rosenberg received a different impression of Roosevelt's attitude. "He wanted his wife to do it. He was glad to channel her energies into one area so that she would leave him alone in other areas. He knew that she felt frustrated because many of the liberal programs had to be put aside."[28]

"I spoke to the Mayor last night," she informed Anna Rosen-berg, "and he said I could ask for anything I wanted." Anna should send her—and here she enumerated the charts, job analyses, and field reports she wished to see. She planned to be in the office on Septem-ber 29 "at 9 a.m."[29] She had told the mayor she did not care how he straightened out the situation with the woman then in charge of vol-unteer participation.

I could say that I was working with her, but she must understand that my word goes and that we are together, going to plan to achieve two things:

    1) The participation of every individual throughout the country in a volunteer job who is able to do so.

    2) Make the volunteer jobs useful to the communities.

Before going into the office she planned to meet with OCD officials in the field during a trip to Seattle, but the trip had to be canceled. On September 7 the president's mother died. "Mama had a very wonderful end," Eleanor wrote Maude Gray.

> She had been somewhat of an invalid all summer but was home from Campo for a week, enjoyed Franklin's day at home tho' she had a slight temperature. About Sat. midnight a clot in the lung caused a circulatory collapse & she became unconscious & remained so till her breathing stopped at noon last Sunday. I think Franklin will forget all the irritations & remember only pleasant things which is just as well. The endless details, clothes to go through, check books, paper. I began on Sat.

Eleanor was "of course attending to everything," Helen Robinson reported in her diary.[30]

Eleanor wrote a tribute to her mother-in-law in her column: Sara was "a very vital person" whose "strongest trait was loyalty to her family.... She was not just sweetness and light, for there was a streak of jealousy and possessiveness in her where her own were concerned." The word "'grande dame' was truly applicable to her." Franklin could push unpleasant memories out of his mind, she wrote a friend, but not she:

> What ironical things happen in life & how foolish it all seems. I looked at my mother-in-law's face after she was dead & understood so many things I'd never seen before. It is dreadful to have lived so close to someone for 36 years & feel no deep affection or sense of loss. It is hard on Franklin however.[31]

She hoped Franklin would now be ready to make changes in the Big House so that it would be more livable and more theirs than Sara's. He did not say yes or no to her, but when Anna and John came East at his request, he told them that he wanted the house kept as it was. When Eleanor heard this from Anna, she said that she was unable to live in a museum: she would live in her cottage at Val-Kill and go to the Big House only when the president was there. The insistency with which she made it clear, even to strangers, that this had been her mother-in-law's house, not hers, betrayed how deeply she had been hurt: "My mother-in-law owned the house and ran it herself up until she died a year ago, and it is exactly as she left it. It never was my home in the sense that I had anything to do with the furnishing or running of it."[32]

September was one of the most difficult months in her life. No sooner had she begun to go through Sara's clothes and papers than she was summoned to Washington, where her brother Hall was in Walter Reed Hospital. He had had a few good years in the thirties as assistant to Frank Murphy when the latter was mayor of Detroit. But after the death of his son Danny he had disintegrated and had settled in Hyde Park where he was experimenting with prefabricated rural housing built on the president's land. "His liver is gone as they told him it would," she wrote Maude Gray. For the next ten days she lived at the hospital, sleeping in her clothes, keeping vigil with Hall's companion of his final years, the faithful Zena Raset.

> My idea of hell, if I believed in it, would be to sit or stand & watch someone breathing hard, struggling for words when a gleam of consciousness returns & thinking "this was once the little boy I played with & scolded, he could have been so much & this is what he is." It is a bitter thing & in spite of everything I've loved Hall, perhaps somewhat remissedly of late, but he is part of me. I do have a quieting effect on him & so I stood by his bed & held his hand & stroked his forehead & Zena stood by me for hours. She won't give up hope of his recovery & keeps asking me if I don't think he's strong enough to pull through till I could weep.

"It has been a hard two weeks," she wrote after Hall's death, "& from last Sunday until yesterday morning more harrowing than I could tell you, till the end which was quite peaceful. I wish all youngsters who drink & abuse their health could see the results of great strength with the liver gone." In her column she recalled a small boy with golden curls whom their young aunts called "cherub" which made her jealous. From the time he was eighteen, "the only way that anyone could hold him was to let him go.... He loved life, he could enjoy things more than almost anyone I have ever known." He had generosity, warmth of heart, courage amounting to recklessness, a brilliant mind, "and a capacity for work which, in his younger days, made him able to perform prodigious tasks, both physically and mentally." After a service in the East Room she accompanied the body to Tivoli for burial in the Hall family vault in St. Paul's churchyard.[33]

Two days later she reported for work at the OCD offices in Dupont Circle. The situation was not promising. "I had a talk with Corrington Gill today who has just come in to the Mayor's outfit & we agree that there is none [organization] & that we must have some." The Sunday before she went to work she had awakened at three in the morning and, finding herself wide awake, calm and rested, spent the next three hours mentally organizing the OCD work. At six she made some notes, which she gave to Tommy at breakfast to type out.[34]

The notes began with a section on "over-all objectives," enumerated the "goals of Department heads" to be achieved "by November 1," and then went on to a section that stated "our first job [is] to organize headquarters office." Each person was asked to "begin" by writing out for her the duties they had, salary agreements made, their staff in Washington and in the field.

Elinor Morgenthau, who had volunteered to come in to the office with her, "will confer when I am not available. All letters involving policy or any new procedure to be submitted to me *before* going out and not to be sent until approved. A copy of all letters on business matters to be sent at end of each working day to my secretary."

She wanted a detailed report on how work in the field was carried on and checked. A policy would have to be established on "our responsibility to the rest of organization and to the Mayor." This was followed by precise instructions on the handling of press and publicity. She enumerated the people who were to be put through on the phone, and added, "only listen in when I request it." All mail was to be opened but brought to her at first "until we can establish system." She set times for staff meetings. No visitors were to be put through except when they were on the appointment list or at the request of Mrs. Betty Lindley or Miss Dorothy Overlock.

She showed her plan to Baruch, who "approved my setup as far as charts went but I don't think he realizes what Defense Councils are going to be like to deal with!" The lack of organization, the absence of clearly defined tasks for the volunteers, the jealousies of the established departments, not to mention state and local defense councils, were even greater than she had anticipated:—"things are devious & I wonder if I have knowledge & courage to go on successfully."[35]

"We have an amazing reservoir of volunteers ready and willing," she wrote Lady Reading. "The difficulty has been in organizing the Washington office so it would be able to react down into the local communities and into our rural areas." The president had understated it in March when he had complained that working out the administrative setup for the OCD was one of the most difficult jobs he had ever faced.[36]

To develop a program involved painstaking negotiations with established government departments which were determined not to allow the upstart defense agencies to usurp responsibilities they felt were theirs. Speaking to a National Nutritional Conference in June, Eleanor had noted that deficiencies in diet were at the root of one third of the rejections from Selective Service on physical grounds. But when, in early November, the head of the Physical Fitness Division of the OCD proposed to print and distribute a nutrition chart, the Department of Agriculture and the Federal Security Agency refused to approve the chart. Her only interest, Mrs. Roosevelt wrote Paul V. McNutt, was to reach "the greatest number of people with information which is simple and fundamental about the things they should eat." She was quite willing to have Mr. Kelly transferred to Mr. McNutt's department if that would expedite matters. "I have no feeling whatsoever if you think it would work better to have him actually in your Department." She saw similar problems arising with other departments and some method of cooperation and coordination had to be reached. Not even the Red Cross "cooperated wholeheartedly," she confided to Belle (Mrs. Kermit) Roosevelt. "The Red Cross was supposed to train 20,000 women in six weeks. They trained—rather inadequately— some 3,000 in seven weeks."[37]

She inherited other organizational problems. The Army and the Navy often were not on speaking terms with each other, and both were impatient and scornful of requests from the OCD for cooperation. Every voluntary organization wanted to get into the civilian-defense setup, "which was fine, but also they wanted to run their own show in the way they thought it should be run." LaGuardia's part of the OCD staff in Washington was made up of mayors; James M. Landis, dean of the Harvard Law School, counted fifteen of them. They were talkers, not workers, and Landis "fired them all in one night," after he succeeded LaGuardia. As his deputy in charge of civilian protection, the mayor brought in General Lorenzo D. Gasser, a retired Army deputy chief-of-staff who was "extremely military-minded. He came into a conference—everybody stood up!"[38]

Eleanor realized that the job of the Volunteer Participation Division in Washington was not so much to recruit volunteers as to find significant activities for the volunteers who were locally recruited, and she staffed her office with strong program specialists who shared her vision of a better America. She asked Paul Kellogg, the distinguished editor of the nation's leading social-work magazine, to spend two days a week in Washington advising her. She persuaded Judge Justine Polier to give up her month's vacation to work up a family and child-welfare program with the interested government bureaus. As head of operations she appointed Hugh Jackson, who had done a brilliant job reorganizing New York City's Welfare Department. She made Jonathan Daniels, a gifted writer and recognized authority on regionalism, an executive aide, and brought in Mary Dublin, who as research director of the National Consumer's League and director of the Tolan Committee's hearings on migratory labor was familiar with the problems associated with the dislocation and movement of population. Together with Elinor Morgenthau, Betty Lindley, and Molly Flynn (an expert on welfare coordination), these persons constituted a program-planning committee.

Through her discussions with this group Eleanor began to develop a clear working conception of the scope and focus of her side of the OCD. Instead of civilian participation she now spoke of community mobilization. She wanted to make it, as Kellogg put it, "a yeasty force for interagency action at the federal level, and for effective community organization throughout the country." A conference in her office to discuss the wartime needs of children produced interagency agreement, no mean achievement, on a program of federal support for day care and additional grants to the States for maternal, child-health, and child-welfare services, which the president subsequently accepted as part of his social-security program. She was, said Kellogg, an "inspiring" force. Leila Pinchot, a volunteer in the Washington office, spoke of the impact of her "passionate integrity" in dealing with community representatives.[39]

Her appearance in a community created a sense of excitement and gave it the feeling that it was important in the defense program. If the organization still did not have the sweep and vitality of Lady Reading's in England, that was to be expected when no bombs were falling, cities were not being gutted, children were not being made homeless, and few took the threat of attack, not to mention invasion, seriously. Then came Pearl Harbor.

All afternoon on Saturday, December 6, Eleanor worked on OCD business in her sitting room with Judge Polier and Paul Kellogg. As they prepared to leave she took them in to say good night to the president. "Well, Justine," he greeted them, "this son of man has just sent his final message to the Son of God." He had played his last card for peace in the Pacific, he went on to explain to the startled trio, in a personal message to the Japanese emperor.[40]

The next day, Sunday, December 7, there was a large luncheon at the White House which Eleanor expected Franklin would attend since his cousin Ellen Adams and her children were among the guests. At the last moment, however, he sent word that he had decided to stay in his study and lunch with Harry. The first intimation of the attack on Pearl Harbor reached the president at 1:40 P.M. Eleanor heard the stunning news when she went upstairs after the luncheon "and found everyone telephoning." The president was busy all afternoon with Hull, the chiefs of staff, with calls to Churchill and others. But before she went over to the radio studio to do her weekly broadcast she went to talk with him. She found him "more serene than he had appeared in a long time," and sensed that it was "steadying to know finally the die was cast." This was the note she sounded in her broadcast:

> For months now the knowledge that something of this kind might happen has been hanging over our heads and yet it seemed impossible to believe, impossible to drop the everyday things of life and feel that there was only one thing which was important, and that was preparation to meet an enemy, no matter where he struck.
>
> That is all over now and there is no more uncertainty. We know what we have to face and we know that we are ready to face it.[41]

Fearful that the West Coast might soon be attacked—there were reports of Japanese submarines surfacing off San Francisco—Eleanor and Mayor LaGuardia quickly decided to fly out.* She spent the next morning at the OCD office, dashed back to the White House

---

*Landis, who doubled as head of the Harvard Law School and the New England OCD, tried to reach LaGuardia and finally did so at nine or ten in the evening. After he informed the mayor of the standby measures he had instituted, including an alert to all his wardens

to accompany the president to the Capitol to hear him ask Congress to declare a state of war in existence between the United States and Japan since December 7, a date that he predicted would "live in infamy." This was the second time Eleanor had heard a president ask Congress for a declaration of war. She remembered her anxieties in 1917 for her husband and her brother and "now I had four sons of military age."[43]

Overnight, Washington was a changed city. Soldiers with bayonets patrolled bridges, railroad junctions, the White House. Uniforms were everywhere in evidence. James and Elliott were in theirs when Eleanor saw them in the Whit House just before leaving for the West Coast, and her heart ached when James told her he wanted active duty with the Marines, even though his father thought he would be more valuable in the Capitol. He did not want to hold a desk job, he told his mother, and asked her to support him. She was sure the president would let him do his duty as he saw it, and within days she and the president were to say good-by to him.[44]

She, too, had her duty to do. At the airport she and LaGuardia said they were going to the coast to strengthen civilian-defense organization and morale. No one really knew what had happened at Pearl Harbor, the president had told her, except that no ships had escaped damage, the fleet was crippled, and the West Coast lay exposed to enemy raids. The trip did not begin auspiciously for the mayor. The plane hit an air pocket as he was being served dinner and a glass of milk spattered him, and he retired to his berth soon afterward. Eleanor was at work in her little compartment when the pilot brought her a flash from the Associated Press asking her to inform the mayor that San Francisco was being bombed. She paled and went to speak to LaGuardia. There was nothing to do but go on and fly directly to San Francisco instead of Los Angeles, he said. She liked that response. At Nashville she called Washington to verify the news and learned that the Army had failed to notify the mayor of San Francisco that it was merely holding a practice blackout. Everyone on the plane was

---

and auxiliary policemen, LaGuardia commented: "Very fine, but I think you want to get them to march. Can you get a big parade going in Boston tomorrow?"

"Mayor, my men don't march. They don't know how to march."

"You ought to get them to march."

"... They know marching isn't going to do anything here. They know exactly what their tasks are...."[42]

relieved, but no one that night believed it impossible or even improbable that San Francisco might be bombed.[45]

As they toured up and down the coast, they found that practically nothing had been done about civilian defense in most cities. "They all had beautiful plans on paper," but San Diego was the only city which had a plan in operation. Eleanor went to one meeting "where the Mayor, the Sheriff & the head of the Fire Dept. sounded off on what a lot they had done & would do when the Federal Government gave them the money. I hope I showed them that getting the money was a remote possibility & doing was different from saying!" The mayor of Los Angeles had "to practically be beaten over the head to make him acknowledge that there is any danger." But elsewhere she found people in a state of jitters. "One thing among others I've learned, if we have trouble anywhere that is where I must go because it does seem to calm people down."[46]

Pearl Harbor brought an immense spurt in civilian-defense activity. Defense councils multiplied, there were demands for plans to meet the remotest eventuality, and volunteers swamped federal and regional OCD offices. The organization was being vitalized, but Eleanor returned from the coast persuaded that LaGuardia had to be supplanted. She spoke immediately with Harold Smith, director of the budget, and Wayne Coy of the Office of Emergency Management, whom the president had asked to keep an eye on OCD, and they had reached the same conclusion. "Your committee on Civilian Defense is despondent and despairing of the activities of the organization," they had written the president just before Eleanor's return, and they had to have "a very frank discussion" with him about it. After hearing them, the president asked for a memorandum that he could use as a basis for telling LaGuardia that he wanted to relieve him of all administrative duties, having him continue perhaps as chairman of an OCD board. Eleanor, in the meantime, spoke with Dean Landis about taking over the administrative leadership.

A few days later Roosevelt saw LaGuardia. Smith told the president before the meeting that LaGuardia could not handle the job on a part-time basis, nor could he get and hold good people because of his "careless habit of firing people without much concern." LaGuardia sensed what was up as soon as he entered the president's office, and he did not make Roosevelt's task any easier. When the president said LaGuardia could not handle both the mayoralty and the directorship of the OCD and should get an assistant to take over the administrative work at the OCD, the mayor replied that he had been "unfairly criticized" in the press. Some people disliked him and the rest disliked Mrs. Roosevelt. Instead of being divested of administrative responsibilities, LaGuardia proposed that civilian protection be separated from civilian participation. The president was "fairly firm," commented Smith.[47]

At dinner on New Year's Day when Eleanor expressed misgivings about giving too much power to Wendell Willkie, whom the president thought he might put in charge of industrial mobilization, Harry Hopkins suggested that Willkie be placed in charge of civilian defense. Eleanor threw up her hands in mock horror—she preferred the mayor, she insisted, even though she was doing her best to have him promoted up and out of the organization. The day after the White House dinner, the president saw LaGuardia again and told him he wanted Landis appointed as executive officer. The mayor yielded. He would see Landis and if he accepted, the appointment could be announced the following week.[48]

It was none too soon. The day before Steve Early announced the Landis appointment, the House of Representatives voted to turn civilian-defense funds over to the War Department, which did not want them, and an amendment to supersede LaGuardia by a newly created assistant secretary of war failed by only one vote. In part these votes reflected a lack of confidence in LaGuardia's ability to handle both the civilian-defense job and the New York mayoralty, but basically the movement was fired by anti-New Deal feelings and forces. "Many people still feel that advantage is being taken of the emergency to further socialize America," said Representative Cox. The Democrats who supported the move against LaGuardia, said Republican Representative Creal, were joining hands "with the men who only a few days ago attempted to strangle every defense effort and everything else."[49]

The Landis appointment did not silence the critics. "Dean Landis is very 'pink,'" said Representative Ford, adding, "you would have a hard time getting somebody 'pinker,' but, nevertheless, we might have had Madam Perkins, with whose record you are all familiar." But interest in Landis suddenly subsided when a group of congressmen, abetted by the Hearst press, scented more exciting game in some of the people who had been appointed by Eleanor. They went after the author of this book whom the Hearst press disclosed to be a member of the Advisory Committee of the Youth Division of the OCD. Then Melvyn Douglas, the distinguished actor who was serving as head of an arts division, was savaged as another radical whom Eleanor had appointed, although she had had nothing to do with his selection. Some members of the advisory group assisting Eleanor in coordinating volunteer services were shown to have been members of organizations on Representative Dies' blacklist. That kept the story and the speechmaking alive. When it was learned that Mrs. Betty Lindley, Eleanor's chief of staff at $5,600, was also Eleanor's friend and had been her radio agent, that, too, stoked congressional indignation—as if every good executive does not staff his or her office with people in whom they have confidence and whose capabilities they have tested. But what had been a field day turned into a saturnalia with the discovery that Mayris Chaney, a dancer and close friend of Eleanor's, was employed as an assistant in the physical-fitness program at $4,600. "Twice as much as Captain Colin Kelly got," shouted Representative Faddis, "and he gave his life that this nation might continue." Congress and the press resounded with denunciations of "fan dancers" in the civilian-defense program. Representative Hoffman launched a "Bundles for Eleanor" campaign to help place "unfortunate idle rich people" in civilian-defense jobs. "It is not hard to get volunteers to take work at these figures," Representative Ford mocked. In vain did Eleanor insist that the valid criticism was that her division had moved "too slowly in getting able people to develop a necessary war program." With regard to salaries, they had tried to build "a nation-wide program with a staff that included only seventeen people in the Washington office who received over $2,600 a year; only four received $5,600 or more." The total paid staff numbered less than seventy-five.[50]

Such pallid statistics were overwhelmed by the hue and cry over Mayris Chaney. If she was worth $4,600, asked Representative Bennett, why not employ fan dancer Sally Rand, who should easily be worth $25,000?

In 1941, despite eight years of the New Deal, society still moved in the afterglow of an ethic of work and individualism which made "do-gooders" and "social workers" objects of derision and ridicule. Eleanor lent herself to caricature. Since the OCD was preaching physical fitness to the country, she felt it should set an example. So, during lunch hours and in the later afternoon there were calisthenics and square dancing on the roof of the OCD headquarters. It was done "with all the good heart in the world," said Landis, "but people weren't feeling that way"—and the press was tipped off. The government decreed nylon was not to be used for stockings, and when Eleanor appeared at headquarters the next day in dowdy cotton stockings every woman at OCD felt obliged to follow her example although many of them, having no wish to be classed as a bluestocking, hated it.[51]

And finally, to cap the charges of inefficiency, Communism, and do-goodism, there was, underlying the hostility of the southerners, the racial issue. A city like Atlanta did not want to let Negroes into its civilian-defense setup and the South generally resisted civilian-defense integration. "Now, Mrs. Roosevelt tackled that in her usual manner," Landis later recalled, "and naturally there were outcries against that, and a lot of people rallied to that banner."[52]

The Republicans were gleeful. John Callan O'Laughlin, editor of the *Army-Navy Journal* and one of Herbert Hoover's regular informants in the Capital, was pleased over Eleanor's growing difficulties in her OCD activities, partly because of skepticism of those activities and partly because of her sponsorship of "communists."[53]

"They burnt Mayris Chaney at the stake in Congress last week," wrote liberal columnist Samuel Grafton. "And one metropolitan newspaper ran four signed columns and three editorials attacking her within the space of two days." While Mrs. Roosevelt had "unwisely" given a job to Miss Chaney in civilian defense, Grafton went on, that was not the reason Congress was hot on her trail. "They've needed you, girl. For down below, the thing is still smoldering, the hatred of the last eight years, of the galling march of social change, so intimately connected with the name of Roosevelt."[54]

It was a time of cumulative military setbacks, almost disaster, but it was in vain that House leaders urged a sense of proportion and decency upon their colleagues. "What kind of statesmanship can condone the taking of a large part of two days' debate ranting about the employment of two individuals—not in the bill—and making no reference at all to vital items in the bill providing for the safety of millions along our eastern and western seaboards and making provision for the money necessary to carry on the war?" asked Representative Cannon, the chairman of the Appropriations Committee, but most of his colleagues were not disposed to listen. The OCD had become "a haven for so-called liberals," replied Representative Shafer, "who have long campaigned for America's participation in the war but who are now apparently seeking every means of avoiding the front-line trenches and doing any fighting." Even the level-headed and usually restrained Raymond Clapper joined in the hue and cry, summoning Westbrook Pegler to "come down here and do one of his justly celebrated scalping jobs on the Office of Civilian Defense. I mean on Mrs. Roosevelt, too, because half the trouble could be got rid of if the President would haul her out of the place." In a final thrust at Eleanor the House voted to ban the use of OCD funds for teaching "physical fitness by dancing" or for "promoting street or theatrical shows."[55]

Eleanor's recommendation of Mayris Chaney for a post with OCD had been unwise, a response of the heart rather than the head. Her unwillingness to turn her back on friends and associates whom unscrupulous critics stigmatized as "communists" made her vulnerable to attack. The exercise of power has its laws. The name of the codifier of those laws has entered the dictionaries as a synonym for political expediency, craft, and deceit. Those who place friendship, loyalty, and righteousness above power, wrote Machiavelli, are better off as private citizens.

Eleanor's love of people, when it came to her friends, expressed itself in a "loyalty...that is boundless—and even reckless, on occasion," said her old friend Henry Morgenthau, Jr.

"To know me is a terrible thing," Eleanor quietly remarked.[56] But even if she had not known or been fond of Mayris Chaney and the others under attack, she would have stood by them. Rare was the administrator or politician who was willing to employ someone whose background and record did not conform to conventional standards of success and propriety. But for Eleanor, to blow on the spark that encouraged another human being—defeated, flawed, despondent—to try to transcend his limitations gave life its savor. And an unconditional integrity made it predictable that she would not apply to others a "loyalty" test that she felt she herself would not pass if she were not First Lady.

The attacks on her confirmed her deepest forebodings about taking an official post in her husband's administration. She had come to OCD to help the program, and here she was, lessening its effectiveness. Her mail was heavy with letters about the Chaney-Douglas appointments, seven out of every eight critical, over half "more or less abusive" and, added Tommy, "still coming in." Eleanor had never had such an unfavorable press. The columnists who defended her were the exceptions, and one of them was Walter Winchell, who at the height of the hue and cry, concluded a weekly broadcast, "I remain your New York correspondent, Walter Winchell, who wishes the House of Representatives would again read the Bill they voted for on December eight.... It was a Declaration of War on the Axis—not Mrs. Roosevelt! Goodnight."

"I am not in the least disturbed by this latest attack," she wrote Kellogg. "It is purely political and made by the same people who have fought NYA, CCC, WPA, Farm Security, etc." Yet even before this final flareup she had concluded she must resign. The Interdepartmental Committee in OCD had to be under his chairmanship, she wrote Dean Landis. "You must preside over it, and you must have contacts with the other departments. I am afraid that being the President's wife would make it pretty awkward for a good many people if I were to do the job."[57]

It was awkward even for Dean Landis. It was "a perfectly impossible situation to have as an assistant director the wife of the President of the United States." She tried to do the best she could, according to Landis:

> For example, she had an office just one floor away, and this was a constant problem. I would call her up and say, "I'd like to see you about a matter," and she'd say, "Oh, no, I'll come up and see you." She made it a point always to do that so that outwardly the line of command would be there.
>
> But, after all, she would have channels of communication with the President considerably closer than mine! It was a difficult situation. And then, if she would take a position, that would involve the President; whereas if just an ordinary assistant director took a position it didn't involve the President. It might involve me but it didn't involve the President.[58]

Eleanor was glad to stay on as the executive in charge of community planning "for the time being," she had written Landis shortly after he came into OCD, "at least until everything is running smoothly, then if we can find just the right person, we can put him in."[59]

Landis talked to Roosevelt, who, he said, understood the difficulties of having as his associate the president's wife. On February 10, at Cornell, where Eleanor had gone to address the Home and Farm Week exercises, she stated in response to reporters' questions that she expected to resign "very soon. I always intended to resign once we were organized, but not until the civilian participation side is thoroughly organized." In her speech she added, "I realize how unwise it is for a vulnerable person like myself to try a government job."[60]

A week later she formally resigned. "By remaining in the Office of Civilian Defense I would only make it possible for those who wish to attack me, because of my beliefs, to attack an agency which I consider can prove its usefulness so completely to the people that it should be free of attack, in order to render its maximum service." Dean Landis had assembled the staff in the departmental auditorium for the occasion, and in a statement of its own the staff asserted that the resignation brought "a deep sense of personal loss to us all."

LaGuardia, accustomed as he was to brickbats in public life, was astonished at the "abuse" heaped upon the First Lady. He found it difficult to understand, he said, and "perhaps the real reason—the real cause—happened a long, long time ago. It happened, perhaps thirty-seven years ago this coming St. Patrick's Day, when a young man by the name of Franklin D. Roosevelt married the right girl."[61]

After Franklin's death, Eleanor, in a characteristic refusal to acknowledge she had any importance in the New Deal years except as the wife of the president, ascribed the attack upon her at the OCD to her relationship to the president: "I offered a way to get at the President and in wartime it is not politically wise to attack the President." But this did her position an injustice. The abuse and criticism were directed as much at her for what she represented as at the president for the power he wielded. She recognized this in a broadcast two days after she resigned, when as "a private citizen" she spoke her mind and assailed the "small and very vocal group of unenlightened men" who are now "able to renew, under the guise of patriotism and economy, the age-old fight of the privileged few against the good of the many." She reaffirmed her belief that defense included "better nutrition, better housing, better day-by-day medical care, better education, better recreation for every age. Perhaps we must all stand up more and be counted in this fight, the virtuous Westbrook Peglers on the one side, the boondogglers, so-called, on the other."[62]

Landis proved to be as unsympathetic to the volunteer participation program as LaGuardia had been. "Poor Jonathan Daniels," Eleanor wrote of her successor, "he's up against an impossible situation I fear— Landis is proving like LaGuardia & I know what he is going through." The OCD had six million volunteers. Landis acknowledged that there were a great many people in the country who wanted to do something in the war effort, "and perhaps the best thing for them was to baby sit for women working in munitions plants." But he shared congressional suspiciousness of social workers and do-gooders, and after six months Daniels resigned, and the dream of the OCD as a "people's movement" ended.[63]

52. GI'S FRIEND, I: JOURNEY TO BRITAIN

---◆---

ELEANOR CARRIED A NEW, A "WARTIME" PRAYER IN HER PURSE:

> Dear Lord,
> Lest I continue
> My complacent way,
> Help me to remember,
> Somehow out there
> A man died for me today.
> As long as there be war,
> I then must
> Ask and answer
> Am I worth dying for?

She grieved for the young men who were going off to war, for she knew what the last war "did to people's souls," and she dreaded it for this generation. She was anxious for her sons. One morning during the OCD travail a friend spoke to her on the telephone and, sensing distress and despair in her voice, rushed over, imagining some new disaster at the OCD. She and the president had just bade good-by to their two eldest sons. James was off to the West Coast to train with the Marine Raiders Battalion being organized by Major Evans Carlson, and the much maligned Elliott was under orders to join a bomber squadron. Eleanor began to sob as she spoke of how difficult it had been to say good-by. She knew they had to go, but it was hard. Simply by the laws of chance, not all of her sons—all four were in uniform— would return. Then she regained control of herself and firmly sent her visitor away. As she wrote Maude a few months later when James' battalion had moved to Midway Island preparatory to its daring raid on Makin Island, "perhaps we have to learn that life was not meant to be lived in security but with adventurous courage."[1]

An American Legion commander, reading a slight into her plea to the home front to safeguard the interests of the GIs or face the probability of a dangerous veterans' lobby after the war, suggested she make her contribution to the war effort by "keeping quiet for the duration." Asked at her press conference if she had any such plans, she shook her head and said simply, "None along that line." To lapse into silence, not to fight with every resource that she commanded, not to do everything that she was permitted to do was to betray the generation in uniform to which she had given her heart.

She was confident, she wrote Gil Harrison, who resigned from the OCD to join the RAF soon after she resigned, that there would be the courage "to make the kind of world we want . . . if youth is allowed to have its say and I, for one, am all for giving youth all the power it can handle." It was the older people who scared her:

> The democratic process is a slow one, and day by day I am becoming convinced that the people who hold it back are the elderly statesmen like Byrd, McKellar and Glass, and I think I am going to become an advocate of a fifty-year limit for activity, even though it will put a terrible crimp in my own feelings, and I realize it can never be made universal because I do pin many of my hopes for the future on people, including my husband who would be wiped out by such a limitation. Perhaps we will have to prove, in some way, that people's mentality remains younger than their years. [June 23, 1942]

Her letter ended with a bit of motherly advice: "remember to take your training very carefully and never to neglect the smallest detail. Flying is safe only for those who remember that it requires eternal vigilance."

Soon after Eleanor quit the OCD she departed on a swing around the country to see her children. At Fort Worth she found herself the only civilian on a plane full of ferry pilots. After the first moments of an awed "It's Mrs. Roosevelt," they clustered about the First Lady, delighted to talk, even to tease her. "We got into long arguments, would we be able to prevent more wars? Was there a moral equivalent for war? What about Russia after the war? etc. etc. Those boys are certainly doing some talking & thinking," she wrote a friend. She spent all of a day in San Diego with "James' boss" Major Evans Carlson, commander of the Second Marine Raider Battalion.[2]

He believes in the Chinese cooperatives. Those *not* government controlled, he thinks the profit motive must be eliminated & he's teaching his men that they must make all people their friends, they are fighting the system that forced all people to war, but they must not hate the people! His men are farm boys, many Southerners, C.C.C. boys but he talks to them. James gives them a "news review" on Sundays & answers questions afterwards. He preaches race equality & has taught them a Chinese rallying cry meaning "we cooperate"—He does everything they are asked to do & so does every officer. The Marine Corps thinks it is horrifying but the men think he & they are the finest things on earth.

To her husband she wrote almost bitterly that she was

finding it harder & harder to talk to these groups of boys. We spend now to send them to die for a "way of life," & a few years ago the very men who spend so willingly to speed them on their way were afraid of taxes to make this same way of life give them a chance to earn a living.[3]

There was no diminution of interest in all the groups and causes that turned to her for help, but first claim upon her ombudsman talents now belonged to the GI. General George Marshall assigned one, and later, two members of his staff to insure that the complaints which she transmitted from GIs, their wives, and parents and which were distinctively "flagged," and numbered in the hundreds, were investigated and corrective action taken if necessary. Although she was, according to Marshall's biographer, "the special advocate of Negro troops," no plea for help went unacknowledged. A corporal sent her a poem that he hoped to have published. Eleanor sent it to her agent, George Bye—could he help? He did. She suggested to Navy Secretary Knox that overseas news broadcasts to the armed forces be made more human and personal with news from the home towns of the boys, as the British were doing in the Middle East; perhaps, if it could be managed, even messages from the boys' families. She agreed with Mrs. Meloney that the message prepared for the president's signature to the "next of kin" was too cold and formal, and cooperated with Archibald MacLeish in drafting a more warmhearted communication. When a soldier at Fort Lewis complained that officers at the post were taking all the best seats at the USO shows she contacted General Osborn, chief of the

War Department's Morale Branch, who agreed that such situations were "deplorable" and said he was trying to change officer attitudes. She persuaded the National Gallery to stay open on Sundays for the benefit of servicemen visiting Washington, D.C., on leave and helped to obtain funds in order to have the National Symphony Orchestra play for the GI visitors. She persuaded the Army surgeon general to meet with a committee of psychiatrists who felt their services were not being well utilized. A pregnant wife complained that it was difficult to have a baby on a private's twenty-one dollars a month. Eleanor spoke to Franklin, who agreed that even with the contemplated increase in GI pay, it still would not be very much and authorized her to ask the American Red Cross to help. Viola Ilma, whose Vocational Foundation helped young men coming out of jail to obtain jobs, requested the members of her board to write to foundation boys going into the service. Eleanor took her quota of names. "Miss Ilma tells me that you like to be called Tony, but as this is my first letter I feel a little bit shy about doing so," she wrote Private Anthony Castorino. Every soldier who wrote her received a reply—not a formal, polite communication, but a chatty, news-filled letter. She had great hopes for this younger generation: "all the young men who worked for me in the O.C.D. or whom I've known in the college groups are somewhere in camp & they write such interesting letters. This generation is much more serious than the 1918 army was in regard to the future."[4]

As she went in and out of Union Station she noted large groups of servicemen standing in line to get something to eat and drink, or stretched out on the hard benches to sleep. She got after the Red Cross and the USO to open a canteen and to find some place in the station to put up cots. Her old friend from the NYA, Mark McCloskey, now with Charles Taft's Office of Defense, Health and Welfare Services, looked over the station and suggested that a possible sleeping area was the president's reception room, where the State Department received distinguished visitors. The State Department resisted. "A war need is more important than an occasional diplomat," Eleanor told Sumner Welles. The department yielded. Thanks, Taft wrote her, "for putting the heat on the State Department so effectively. I had given up completely."[5]

And the most difficult duty of all:

I've just visited the children & also all hospitals on the coast. Lots of casualties now coming but the rate of killed is 4–1 which seems appalling to me but is modern warfare. We do wonderful things for the wounded & I was happy to see seven out of the 14 boys in James' Makin Island raid all apparently getting well.[6]

The illusion of leisure that she had after she left the OCD was quickly dispelled by an inrush of new obligations, and by July she was writing Lady Willert in Oxford, "Somehow I do not seem to have had any free time this summer"; yet she also lamented, "I do not seem to be doing anything useful." Helen Ferris of the Junior Literary Guild asked her to write something for the Guild's *Bulletin* about her war work. She complied, but reluctantly; she did not think it would appeal to the young.

I try to put as much as I can in War Bonds; to pay my debts; to do what I can for people who write about their friends and relatives in the Services, and to answer the many letters from soldiers themselves. I visit hospitals and see innumerable people from other countries in order to try to find out how they are meeting their problems and pass along the information here which could be useful in meeting some of our problems.

I have tried to help all the women in the Government who are charged with specific problems that touch on the war situation. And I have, of course, given what I could to various war charities.[7]

As she contemplated the list, it seemed to her "pretty nebulous." From time to time there had been stories in the press that she might visit England, and Lady Reading had strongly urged her to do so. The papers were talking of her going to England in a bomber, she said to Franklin after he had met Churchill at Argentia. "Are you and Harry cooking up something?" "Winston" had said to give her his regards, Franklin had replied; he had not said he wanted to see her. That was September, 1941. Now, perhaps because he sensed his wife's discontent, he began to encourage the project. "There is a very remote chance that sometime FDR may let me go to England this summer or autumn or winter if by doing so I can serve some good purpose both there and here," she informed Maude. The British and American people ought to know "a great deal more about each other," she wrote her Allenswood classmate Bennett. She would like to bring home to some of the women in the United States "what the average household in England is going through."[8]

There were problems, too, between American and British troops where she thought she might be helpful, problems arising from the better food served American troops, their higher pay, and the posting of Negro GIs to England, although the latter vexed white Americans more than it did Englishmen. She had heard from several people, she wrote Stimson, that young southerners in England "were very indignant to find that Negro soldiers were not looked upon with terror by the girls in England and Ireland and Scotland. I think we will have to do a little educating among our Southern white men and officers." When Stimson learned that Eleanor was going to Britain he asked Roosevelt confidentially to caution his wife not to raise the issue during her visit. Roosevelt, Stimson noted in his diary, was sympathetic "to our attitude" and said he would pass the word on to Mrs. Roosevelt.[9]

By mid-September the visit had been arranged. The invitation from Queen Elizabeth expressed her and the king's pleasure if Eleanor would care to pay a visit to England and see something of the women's war activities, and hoped she would stay a few days with them at Buckingham Palace.

HER MAJESTY, THE QUEEN:
I am deeply appreciative of your very kind invitation to visit you in England. I shall try to come somewhere around the middle of October. I shall be very happy if I might spend two nights with you and His Majesty, the King, and after that I think I should devote my entire time to seeing all that I can of the British women's war effort, and our own groups over there. It will be a great pleasure to see you again.
Eleanor Roosevelt.

"I think it will be of immense value your going over," Lord Halifax, the British ambassador, assured her, "and you will have no difficulty in getting the kind of direct impression of typical people in their homes of which you spoke yesterday." Her English schedule was placed in the highly competent hands of Lady Reading. Mrs. Oveta Culp Hobby, who was in charge of the women's auxiliary of the Army, was accompanying her to England. She was not part of the official party, which was to consist only of Tommy and Eleanor, but Eleanor wanted to tour the women's military establishments with Mrs. Hobby. She also asked Ambassador John Gilbert Winant to find her "a simple, inexpensive hotel" in which to stay after she left Buckingham Palace—"I am afraid Claridge's is too expensive." Franklin instructed her to see "the Duchess of Kent and my godson, and Queen Mary and Queen Wilhelmina." She should also see, if they called on her, "King Haakon, Crown Prince Olav, King George of Greece, King Peter of Yugoslavia, The President of Poland, Beneš of Czechoslovakia, Lord and Lady Mountbatten, Margaret and Tony Biddle."[10]

The trip began under condition of secrecy so that the time of her departure should not be known to the enemy. She and Tommy were driven in a Secret Service car to a back entrance at the airport. The curtains were drawn in the flying boat in which they made the journey, and they were permitted to open them only after the autumn-hued coast line of Cape Cod was receding in a reddish-brown haze. It was a smooth twenty-hour journey, but transatlantic travel was still a novelty with some element of danger, and the sense of coming closer to the war was heightened when all on board were sworn to secrecy after they had sighted a convoy with its escorting destroyers zigzagging about like skittering insects. They landed at Foynes. There were many Nazi agents in Dublin, and it was thought prudent to keep the First Lady's arrival secret. Though no one was supposed to know of her presence, as Eleanor came up the gangplank and embraced Maude Gray, an onlooker said, "Why there's Mrs. Roosevelt." The weather made it impossible to proceed to London, so they spent the night at Kilgobbin, Lord and Lady Adare's great landed estate in County Limerick. The family felt extremely poor, Eleanor learned that night, but in the diary of the trip, she had begun to keep, she observed that "it is one of those cases of comparative poverty."[11]

The next day she, Tommy, Colonel Hobby, and the colonel's aide flew to Bristol in a plane that the prime minister sent. Ambassador Winant was there to meet her and to accompany her in the prime minister's special train to London. Eleanor liked Winant very much and had always found him helpful. When Harry Hopkins had told her that in London she did not have to bother with Winant but should deal with Averell Harriman, who was in charge of the Lend Lease operations in the British capital, she became quite angry and during her whole stay in England would have nothing to do with Averell, whom she had known since he was a small boy. As the train approached the end of its two-hour journey, she asked Winant why they had not flown to London. The ambassador was not sure; he had only been told that the king and queen never met anyone at the airport.

The prime minister's special train, the knowledge that she was to be met by the king and queen and spend two nights at Buckingham Palace, the appearance, as the train drew to a halt in Paddington Station, of the station master, as formally dressed and dignified as a lord of the realm, suddenly roused the insecurity she had suffered when as a bride of Franklin's they had stayed at some of the great houses in England. Why, she asked herself, had she ever let herself in for this? But outwardly she was serene and poised, and from the moment "she jumped from the train to grip the Queen's hand to a final informal chat sitting on the edge of a chair in the American Service Club in Edinburgh, 21 days later," noted the *London Daily Mail* after her departure, she created the image "of a personality as symbolically American as the Statue of Liberty itself."[12] The king was in a powder-blue uniform of an air marshal, the queen in a coat of black velvet, and Eleanor in a long, back-flared coat with a blue-fox scarf and a feathered hat of red, green, and white. "I hope you left the President in good health," the king, who seemed less at ease than the two women, said. "Yes, he is in very good health and wished that he could have come himself." "We welcome you with all our hearts," the queen added. Eleanor then presented Tommy, Colonel Hobby, and the aide, and proceeded to say a few words to the rest of the group who were assembled on the red carpet to greet her—Lady Reading, Foreign Secretary Anthony Eden, Lieutenant General Dwight D. Eisenhower, and Admiral Harold R. Stark.

As the royal limousine, a big Daimler, drove out of the station, a loud cheer went up. An alert reporter noted that through the whole welcoming ceremony the First Lady was carrying a large book, *Abraham Lincoln and the Fifth Column*. At Buckingham Palace, which, like Paddington Station, had its quota of bomb scars, the king and queen showed her to her rooms, apologizing for the windows, which had been blown out and replaced either by wooden or isinglass panels. Eleanor had an enormous suite and a bedroom which Elliott, when he saw it, compared to the long corridor in the White House.

She had tea with the king and queen around a set table, "as I used to have in my childhood," and met Princesses Elizabeth and Margaret. She found Elizabeth to be "quite serious and a child with a great deal of character and personality. She asked me a number of questions about life in the United States and they were serious questions." Tommy, in the meantime, had had tea with the ladies-in-waiting in their sitting room. Afterward she and Tommy did a little work—diary, column, and correspondence—before dinner at 8:30. Although the guests included some of the highest dignitaries in the realm—Prime Minister and Mrs. Churchill, General Smuts, Winant, the Mountbattens, and Elliott, whose reconnaissance squadron was based seventy miles outside of London—dinner was a three-course wartime meal. Eleanor sat between the king and Churchill. "I found the P.M. not easy to talk to, which was my experience in Washington," she noted. She got along well with the king, as she did with the queen. They still seemed to her, as they had in Washington, to be a young and charming couple who were doing a remarkable job of setting their people an example of character and devotion to duty. After dinner the company saw Noel Coward's film *In Which We Serve* and then Eleanor had a long talk with Elliott, until about two in the morning, and was pleased to note that his hostility toward the English was changing to admiration. "It is very good for the young to learn that their rather harsh, snap judgments are not always correct."[13]

The next morning there was a press conference at the embassy. Eleanor was visibly startled by the turnout, "a very formidable group but it went well, I was told." At lunch the queen brought together the heads of the women's organizations. Colonel Hobby was there, and, noted Eleanor, she "curtsied to the King and Queen." Altogether there were fourteen women alone with the king, he "seemed to take it with great calm."

That afternoon she began her round of inspections, tours, speeches, and receptions. "Hustle, did you say?" a British reporter wrote later; "she walked me off my feet!" She walked "fifty miles through factories, clubs and hospitals," reporters estimated later when, "glassy-eyed and sagged at the knees," they returned from a seven-day tour of the Midlands, Ulster, and Scotland.[14]

That first afternoon she went with the king and queen to view the destruction. The "City" was gutted. St. Paul's gaped open to the skies, and the dean told her that he and other church officials slept in the crypt during the bad blitzes in order to put out the fires more quickly. They toured London's East End and the queen remarked that the only solace in the destruction was that new housing would replace the slums that had been leveled. Eleanor stood aghast before the Guildhall ruins, and as she spoke with the different types of civilian-defense personnel who were gathered there—decontamination squads, fire-fighters, policewomen, many of whom were decorated for bravery—it was again borne in on her how England's home front was literally part of the battlefront.

That evening was Labor's night at the Palace. Ernest Bevin, the bluff and well-muscled minister of labor, was a guest, as was Lord Woolton. "He's your only Socialist peer, Sir," Bevin remarked to the king. Conversation with the Labor men was easier than with Churchill. Bevin told her about "Bevin's boys"—the three hundred Indian workers whom he had brought to England to teach skills and trade unionism. Woolton interested her because as a young man he had gone into the slums to experience conditions there and then had gone into business to prove that one could provide decent wages and good working conditions and still make money.

On Sunday the king, queen, and princess saw her off at the door after breakfast, more like friends saying good-by than any formal leave-taking, and she moved into the apartment the Winants had made available to her. She then went to visit the Washington Club, the American Red Cross Club in Mayfair. It was crowded, and the soldiers and sailors "mobbed" her. "Hi, Eleanor," some called out, and soon she was involved in a question-and-answer session. There were complaints about the slowness of the mail and the lack of American-style food in the messes, and the Red Cross ladies were concerned about the lack of woolen socks; the boys wore "cotton ones and their feet were blistered." She took that up with General Eisenhower the next evening. He had had his supply people check, he wrote her later:

> I find that we have not only made all normal issues, but we have at the minute two and one-half million pairs of light woolen sox in warehouses. Naturally, I cannot guarantee that every individual soldier has his full allotment, since it is entirely possible that some have been lost and replacement not yet made. However, I have already started the various commanders on a check-up to see that no man needs to march without proper footgear.

She journeyed to Chequers, the prime minister's country house. "After lunch we saw Randolph Churchill's little boy, Winston, who is a sweet baby and exactly like the Prime Minister. They sat on the floor and played a game and the resemblance was ridiculous." At Chequers she finished a letter to the president that she had begun at Buckingham Palace:

Dearest Franklin,

The Prime Minister is pleased with the ham & honey.

Our stay at the Palace is over but I am to see them again before leaving.

Saw a lot of boys at the Red + Washington Club this a.m. The woman in the dispensary even said they came in with terrible blisters because their socks are too tight. All coming here should be issued *wool* socks. No heat is allowed till Nov. & most of them have colds. The boys are very upset over the mail situation, some have been here two months & not a line from home. Also their pay in many cases is very late—& they buy bonds & don't get them. Someone ought to get on top of this situation & while they are about it they might look into the question of how promptly the families are getting allotments.

The spirit seems good but of course I've only seen a few.

The spirit of the English people is something to bow down to. Bevin & Woolton? dined with us at the Palace last night.

We came to Chequers to-day. Gen. & Mrs. Portal are here & Sir Anthony Eden & his wife. Tell Harry Robert was here looking well. Elliott too came to lunch & he spends tomorrow night in London with me. Winant insists on giving me his flat & moving upstairs, which is hard on him but grand for us. To-morrow will be a long day, so good night.

Tommy bears up well & now finds staying with Kings quite ordinary!

Love

ER[15]

The next day, accompanied by Mrs. Churchill, she inspected units of the Auxiliary Territorial Airforce. Chalmers Roberts of the London Office of War Information reported to his chief, Wallace Carroll:

In a pouring rain she walked the length of the parade ground between two rows of girls who had been standing at attention for some time, water trickling down their necks. Mrs. Roosevelt could have driven past but she told the commanding officer, "I would much rather walk, if that's all right." It was.[16]

It was "stupid" of her, she commented in her diary, to have sent her raincoat and rubbers back to London with her big bag. She spoke to the girls, who were gathered together in one of the hangars. There were cheers for her and Mrs. Churchill. They had tea, and then proceeded to the Auxiliary Territorial Service induction and training center at Guildford. She was especially interested in the cooking classes:

> The women are trained for two weeks at cooking small meals which they are obliged to eat themselves, then two weeks in making things out of left-overs and two weeks cooking out of doors on stoves which they built themselves out of old used tin cans, rubble like broken brick or stone, all held together by mud.

At a third camp, she slogged through the mud, fascinated by the way the girls were being trained to make repairs on heavy trucks.

Although there was every sign that she was doing very well indeed as unofficial ambassadress, she was still worried. On Tuesday Mrs. Churchill again accompanied her on an inspection of clothing-distribution centers of the Women's Voluntary Services. Halfway through Mrs. Churchill sat down on a marble staircase—Mrs. Roosevelt's pace was too much for her, she said; she would wait there. From this strenuous tour Eleanor proceeded to a luncheon given in her honor by the London County Council. It was an occasion saturated with centuries-old ceremonials, attendants in red coats, and a toastmaster who in measured voice called for order before each speaker in time-hallowed phrases: "I pray you silence, My Lords, Your Worships, Ladies and Gentlemen, the Honorable Mr. Chairman. The health of the king was proposed and that of the president. Eden offered the toast to her, saying that she was welcomed "first, as the first lady of the United States; second, as the wife of a great President of a mighty nation; and, third, and above all, for herself."[17]

"The horrible moment came for me to respond," she wrote later. She thought of Elliott's change of attitude toward the British, and that gave her a theme. She predicted that as the months went by many of America's young people

> will know more about Great Britain than they have ever known before. The growing understanding between us will perhaps mean more in the future not only to us but to the world than we can know. . . .
>
> I look to your young people and to our young people to be the kind of people most of us would like to be and really achieve some

of the things we hoped to achieve—at the end of the war. And then
I hope we will win the peace.

It seemed to go pretty well, she thought. That was an underestima-
tion; that afternoon Admiral Stark sent her a note in his own hand:
"We were all proud of you today."[18]

After luncheon she went to Fighter Command, where the WAAFs
filled every job from cook and waitress to control of the planes in the
air. She went to dinner that night at the Winston Churchill's, escorted
by Henry Morgenthau, who was in London. She and the prime minister had, as she put it in her diary, "a slight difference of opinion"
over Loyalist Spain. She had had a few talks with Churchill when he
had flown to Washington immediately after Pearl Harbor and stayed
at the White House. "He's very human & I like him the' I don't want
him to control the peace!" she had written then.*[19]

The subject of Spain came up when Churchill asked Morgenthau
whether the United States was sending food to Spain in sufficient
quantities. The secretary said yes, but Eleanor impulsively exclaimed
that it was a little too late, that the Loyalists should have been helped.
Churchill said he had been for Franco until Germany and Italy came
to his aid. Why couldn't the existing government have been helped,
Eleanor asked, reviving an argument she had so often had with her
husband. Churchill gave a reason Franklin had never suggested: if
the Loyalists had won the two of them would have been the first to
lose their heads. That argument did not impress Eleanor—it was of
no importance whether she lost her head. "I don't want you to lose
your head and neither do I want to lose mine," Churchill growled.
Here Mrs. Churchill intervened: "I think perhaps Mrs. Roosevelt
is right." That did not help matters, and Churchill's annoyance was
obvious. "I have held certain beliefs for sixty years and I am not
going to change now," he replied, almost angrily. At this point Mrs.
Churchill got up and walked away from the table as a signal that
dinner was over.[20]

---

*Six months later (June 23, 1942) she wrote Gil Harrison: "Mr. Churchill is with us again,
and I have just been reading an article about him by [Harold] Laski, which pretty well
agrees with my own feeling. Intellectually, Mr. Churchill knows that the day of traditional
class leadership in England is over, but the old feeling ties him to the old way and down
at the bottom he is fighting for that with courage and the best qualities that the old order
produced, but still without the vision of the new order."

Eleanor wondered about Mrs. Churchill, whom she found attractive, remarkably young looking, and full of charm. "One feels that she has had to assume a role because of being in public life and that the role is now part of her, but one wonders what she is like underneath." The prime minister's wife worked hard on Russian and Chinese relief, but "is very careful not to voice any opinions publicly or to associate with any political organizations. This I felt was true of the wives of all the public officials whom I met." How different from herself. Dr. George Gallup was in the midst of taking a poll which showed that Eleanor Roosevelt "probably is the target of more adverse criticism and the object of more praise than any other woman in American history." For every two persons who thought the First Lady talked too much Gallup's interviewers found three who approved of her courage and ability to speak out. It was a rare respondent who was neutral about her.[21]

She attended a luncheon with women members of Parliament arranged by Lady Astor, and her feminist heart noted that "these women seem to suffer from the same difficulties that women suffer from in the U.S.A. when they hold public office." They invited her to be present in the House when they raised questions about the inequalities which British women endured in such matters as income tax and compensation for war injuries, but Eleanor was staying out of political controversy. She was a guest, and though the cause of women's equality was one she felt strongly about, it would not have been seemly for her to get involved in British controversies over this principle. She also regretfully declined several invitations she received from the many groups espousing the cause of Indian self-government, including a request for an interview sent by the head of the India League, V. K. Krishna Menon.

One ardent feminist who wanted to see her but did not quite qualify for Lady Astor's luncheon was George Bernard Shaw. "Bring the First Lady to tea when you come," he wrote Lady Astor on one of the postcards that was his epistolary trademark. "When she returns home the first question they will ask her is 'Have you seen Shaw?' If she has to say No, it will cost Franklyn [sic] at least half a dozen votes in the next presidential election." H. G. Wells was more modest: "I don't think Mrs. Franklin D. Roosevelt's visit to London should include me," he wrote Winant, "but I think I might have a few words in private with the young man her son."

Churchill, despite his political set-to with the First Lady, rejoiced in the good that her visit was doing. He cabled the president:

I thought you would like to know that Mrs. Roosevelt's visit here is a great success. She has been very happy about it herself. I hope that the friendly reception by all people here has been reported as enthusiastically at home as it has been in this country. If you have any suggestions I will be glad to follow them—Elliott and Mrs. Roosevelt are well.

In between inspections and official luncheons and dinners, the procession of royalty had begun. Eleanor had just succeeded in getting her coat and hat off when the king of Norway and Crown Prince Olaf arrived: "We had almost an hour's talk and I like the King very much." When they left the young king of Yugoslavia, Peter, appeared with an aide. His visit was heavier sledding. He stayed three quarters of an hour "and somehow or other we managed to converse for that length of time." Later that day the president of Poland and Prime Minister Sikorski came:

> The conversation centered about getting Polish prisoners out of Russia. They were grateful for what had been done and they felt that Mr. Willkie had put the President's suggestions before Mr. Stalin and this had been a help, but they still have people like their greatest surgeon and greatest philosopher in prison in Russia and do not know how to get the Russian government to liberate them.

The Polish delegation was followed by the Greek king, and he was followed by Belgian Premier Pierlot, "who talked primarily about feeding children and young people in Belgium and was very insistent that this should be done." Another day she had a long talk with President Beneš and Jan Masaryk.

Her most daunting encounter, except for the night she spent with Queen Mother Mary, was her call on Queen Wilhelmina. "She greeted me warmly and allowed me to kiss her," Eleanor noted, "which gave me a sense of intimacy I had never expected to have but have never since lost." She spent an hour with the queen, and they talked about the postwar world.

Her night at Badminton with Queen Mary came after a full day with American troops, attending religious services, visiting a hospital, inspecting camp arrangements, chatting with men and officers everywhere, and ending with a visit to the American Red Cross Club run by Mrs. Theodore Roosevelt, Jr., where she beat time with her foot as the men sang "Home on the Range," which she told them was her husband's favorite song. It was just before the mid-term congressional elections, and the reporters tried to stir up a little political controversy between the First Lady and the Oyster Bay Eleanor, whose husband, when asked in 1933 his relationship to the incoming president, had quipped, "Fifth cousin—about to be removed." But both Eleanors were on their guard.

At precisely 6:30 P.M. General John Lee delivered Eleanor and Tommy to Beaufort Castle. The queen mother met her at the door and took her to her sitting room. After an exchange of pleasantries, Queen Mary showed her her room, which was vast as a barn and cold but "very grand with Chinese Chippendale furniture. She showed where the bathroom and the w.c. were & they were cold as well."

Dinner was not "a hilarious meal," but she made "valiant efforts" at conversation. Afterward they went into the drawing room and stood for fifteen minutes. Then the queen asked her and the princess royal to her sitting room. Tommy was left behind, "and soon escaped and went to bed" in order to keep warm. The queen mother and Eleanor talked for an hour, "but I found it hard to forget enough and yet remember enough! Conversation must flow but you must not sit down or leave until you are given the high sign!" The president had particularly wanted her to call on the queen mother because she had been so nice to his mother, and when Eleanor left Queen Mary gave her a photograph to give to the president as a fellow-conservationist. It showed the queen mother, fully dressed in hat, gloves, and veil, sawing a dead limb off a tree with one of her aides at the other end of the saw. The president loved it.[22]

Eleanor's visits to American troops continued. She inspected a parachute battalion which was about to fly to North Africa. As she watched the battalion parade, inspected the men's kits, and saw a few men jump, she sensed "a tension but nothing was said." She dropped in on a bomber squadron and persuaded two husky pilots to haul her up into the cockpit of the Flying Fortress "Phyllis." "I found I'm very fat for a pilot's seat," she said afterward; "it wasn't made to accommodate an old lady well over 50." She inspected Elliott's photo reconnaissance unit, her chauffeur getting lost on the way and having to telephone the embassy for additional directions, explaining in code words that "Rover has lost her pup." She inspected a tank corps which "had to stand in the cold and wet while I was shown everything from a tank to a jeep & I felt sorry for them, but they weren't any wetter or colder than I was!" She saw her first Negro troops and liked it when their officer, white, insisted that his men were the best in the Army.

She was in and out of London and toured the provinces, escorted by Lady Reading and accompanied by Dorsey Fisher and Chalmers Roberts and a sizable contingent of correspondents. She visited Bristol, Birmingham, and Liverpool, where she spotted a Liberty ship and asked to be taken aboard so she might look it over. She visited the barracks of the Negro troops in Liverpool. The original group had gone to North Africa, and the newly arrived transport troops were delighted to see the First Lady. She knew how bitterly Negroes resented their assignment to noncombat, menial jobs, but she was in England to improve morale not to reform the Armed Forces.*

Before she flew to Ulster and the great naval base at Londonderry she made a radio broadcast. The burden of her speech was that there must not be any easy relaxation after the war if a real victory for mankind was to be won. The British people who had performed so valiantly might well be tired when war came to an end "but we cannot be too tired to win the peace if our civilization is to go on."

The speech had a larger listening audience, the head of the BBC informed Winant, "than any previous talk at that time, which is the peak listening period. The estimated figure was 51.4 per cent of the total adult civilian population of Great Britain—a very large number indeed."[24]

In Londonderry at the naval base "we were warm and I secured from the Navy Hospital some kleenex which was a godsend since I had a vile cold in my head." Captain Davis, in charge of the hospital, asked her to tell Admiral McIntire that all he asked was to be let alone. She thought he was doing a good job, even though he objected strongly to Navy nurses: "He said women had no place in the Services.... One gathers from his conversation that he does not like ladies." After dinner they visited a Red Cross Club which was having a dance. A slightly drunken soldier followed her around asking her to dance until a major, thinking she was annoyed ("though as a matter of fact I was amused"), steered him away.

The next day in Glasgow began at eight in the morning, and at midnight she still was going strong in the great Rolls plant, where

---

*When she went to see Stimson on her return, the secretary was pleased to find her "very temperate" on the Negro question. She felt the Negro troops were doing well and praised the general in command.[23]

she made a brief speech in the hope that she then could bid her hosts good night. But the gentleman who spoke after her went on and on

> until I thought we were never going home to bed. The newspaper women sat in the front row and looked about to die. (I thought they were exhausted by the full day, but I learned afterwards that they had stayed up practically all night playing poker with officers in Londonderry.)

The final day of the trip through the provinces was also the most grueling. They journeyed down the Clyde on a steamer. The men in the shipyards gathered along the rails of the ships on which they were working to give her a cheer, and Eleanor stood in the prow for almost two hours, waving continuously. "I was so cold that my hands became congealed and I wish I had remembered to wear my black panties." Even her fur coat felt like cotton. Then she made a little speech to the men in a yard which had just finished an aircraft carrier, at the end of which Sir Harry Lauder stepped up and led the crowd in singing "To the End of the Road." And later at the luncheon in her honor, he sang, "Will Ye No Come Back Again?" A drive to Edinburgh during which she argued with the awesome Lord Rosebery about Russia's future, a reception at the lord provost's, and at last the night train to London.

There were a few final engagements in London, including a luncheon with women who had been at Allenswood with her, and a visit with the king to look at an apartment which he thought might be suitable for the president when he visited England.

There had been much transatlantic discussion about how she should travel home. The southern route by commercial plane was finally ruled out because Churchill and Winant both feared the Germans might force the plane down. "I don't care how you send her home," Roosevelt terminated the discussion; "just send her."

Mrs. Churchill came to see her on the day of her departure. The prime minister was in Chequers, but he sent her a note in his own hand: "You certainly have left golden footprints behind you." She should convey to Franklin his gratitude for all he had done "for the common cause and of my joy at the blessings which have crowned our truly united efforts. The British and Americans have worked together like brothers. So must it be to the end." As Eleanor's plane departed, Chalmers Roberts reported to his chief: "Mrs. Roosevelt has done more to bring a real understanding of the spirit of the United States to the people of Britain than any other single American who has ever visited these islands."

Her flight home was on a plane filled with ferry pilots, whose "short snorter" dollar bills she signed, as they did hers, showing that she had made a transoceanic flight. Much of her time was spent in thinking of ways by which to convey to the American people what she had seen and learned.

The trip went swiftly, and when the plane taxied to a halt in Washington's airport, "we looked out," Eleanor wrote as a final entry in her diary,

and saw several Secret Service men and several cars and knew that FDR had taken time off to come to meet us.... I really think Franklin was glad to see me back and I gave a detailed account of such things as I could tell quickly and answered his questions. Later I think he even read this diary and to my surprise he had also read my columns.

53. A CONSCIOUSNESS
OF COLOR

———————————————————✦

A FEW DAYS AFTER PEARL HARBOR, ELEANOR RECEIVED A FORE-
boding letter from Pearl S. Buck, whom she had known since the
twenties and with whom she had recently been working on Negro
problems. The novelist, on the basis of her long experience in the
Orient, wished to alert Eleanor and, through her, the president that
more basic than the Chinese antagonism to Japan was the colored
races' antagonism toward the white. A "deep secret colored solidarity is growing in the world," Miss Buck advised her friend. The
five-page letter echoed Eleanor's own views. She, too, realized that
white supremacy had become an international issue, after Pearl Harbor perhaps the fundamental one in the war. "Unless we make the
country worth fighting for by Negroes," she replied to a critic of her
racial views, "we would have nothing to offer the world at the end
of the war."[1]

Although in the weeks after Pearl Harbor Roosevelt was a frantically beset man, Eleanor passed on Pearl Buck's letter with a plea that
he read it. His sympathetic appreciation of the problem surprised her.
He told her he would have to compel the British to give dominion
status to India, and that it was essential to enlarge Negro rights in the
United States.[2]

His reaction was the more pleasing to her because of the presence
in the White House of Churchill. With great intellectual force that
eloquent statesman was pressing the case for a postwar world order
based on Anglo-American ascendancy. He had closed his first speech
in Washington with an expression of resolve that stirred the English-
speaking world but disquieted the Asian: "The British and American
people will for their own safety and the good of all walk together side
by side in majesty, justice, and peace."

"The Prime Minister is a thoroughly delightful person," Eleanor
wrote an old Hudson River friend. "My only difference of opinion

with him is that I do not believe we should stress the control of the English-speaking people when peace comes. It seems to me that we should include all people who believe in democracy." At times the president seemed to share Churchill's view. During Mackenzie King's visit to Hyde Park just before Pearl Harbor there had been discussion at the dinner table of postwar organization and the president had spoken of keeping a monopoly of military power in the hands of England and the United States after the war. "What about Russia?" Eleanor had asked, but he had simply shrugged off the question.[3]

Two days after Churchill left Washington, Pearl Buck was after the president again, this time by means of a telegram from herself, Walter White of the NAACP, Edwin R. Embree of the Rosenwald Fund, and others, pleading that the conferences with Churchill be followed by a meeting or some dramatic joint action with Chiang Kai-shek, as "already enemies are using Churchill visit as evidence of Anglo-Saxon will to world dominance. The battles in the Pacific are already being made to appear a war between white and yellow races."[4]

Although the telegram was sent directly to the president, to insure that it received his attention a copy went to Eleanor. And she did jog him on it with the observation, "Not such a bad idea, only Chiang Kai-shek can't leave." In the next few weeks Miss Buck wrote frequently to Roosevelt, either through his wife or directly to him with copies to Eleanor. The gist of what she had to say was embodied later in that remarkably farsighted book, *American Unity and Asia*. "Tell Pearl Buck I read her letter of March 7th with real interest," the president instructed his wife; "I am keeping it in my files." In these times, Miss Buck wrote gratefully to Eleanor, the fact that she was in the White House meant all the more to the people "who love our country and humanity, too. It is a great deal to be able to count on someone as millions of us count on you." Eleanor was not simply a "passer-on," even if that was the way she chose to describe herself. Pearl Buck also served Eleanor's purposes; arguments that the president shrugged off when they came from his wife he could accept from someone else, especially from a Nobel prize winner whose understanding of Oriental psychology was indisputable.[5]

Roosevelt's ideas about postwar world organization were evolving. When in May, again at dinner, a pert-nosed Vassar undergraduate asked him his ideas on the subject, he replied that he was certain of one thing: the aggressor nations would have to be policed after the war to see that they did not rearm. "Who would do the policing?" the Vassar miss came back at him—and perhaps that is why Eleanor had seated the young lady next to the president. Roosevelt replied, "The United States, the British, the Russians and the Chinese," adding, "if we hang together." Eleanor glanced at a friend who had heard his earlier statement about a British-American monopoly and smiled.[6]

While Churchill dreamed of an Anglo-American condominium, influential circles in the United States, with the Luce publications in the lead, spoke of an "American century." That concept appealed to Eleanor even less than Churchill's. "I do not think this is an American century," she wrote Gil Harrison, who had resigned from the OCD to volunteer in the RAF. "I like Vice President Wallace's 'people's century' better." One could not combat the Hitler ideology of Aryan superiority in Europe and expect the yellow and black peoples of the world, including the American Negro, to continue to submit supinely to the same doctrine, she wrote a critic:

> What you do not seem to realize is that no one is "stirring up" the colored people in this country. The whole world is faced with the same situation, the domination of the white race is being challenged. We have ten percent of our population, in large majority, denied their rights as citizens. In other countries you have seen the results of white domination, Burma, Singapore, et cetera. You have seen the results of intelligent handling in the Philippines.

It was "heartbreaking," Walter White told a Madison Square Garden meeting, that the color line at home in the war program was being mirrored in a color-line approach to international strategy, "and the tragedy of the situation is that only a few intelligent and brave souls like Mrs. Roosevelt, Pearl Buck, and one or two others in the white world are wise enough to see the picture as it is."[7]

More and more, the duty she had always felt to diminish human suffering seemed to Eleanor to pose the question of whether the sense of human fellowship could transcend the color barrier. There was little that the Negro people demanded of their government that did not end up as an appeal to her, and it was she who had to confront the men in authority with obligations from which they wished to flee; and the guiltier they felt, the more irritated they were with her. A memorandum from Harry Hopkins vividly described one such episode:

THE WHITE HOUSE
WASHINGTON

Memorandum   July 1, 1942

Mrs. Roosevelt called me four or five times today about the
Waller case.

This is the case of a negro tenant farmer who had murdered his
landlord and been sentenced to death. He was to be executed the
next morning.

A lot of pressure was being brought to bear on Mrs. Roosevelt to
intervene with the Governor. She spoke and wrote to the Governor
some days ago and, indeed, the President wrote a very strong letter
to the Governor in effect requesting the Governor to send the man
to prison for life instead of killing him.

The Governor had given six different reprieves and the President
felt that he could not intervene again. He thought the Governor
was acting entirely within his constitutional rights and, in addition
to that, doubted very much if the merits of the case warranted the
Governor reaching any other decision.

Mrs. Roosevelt, however, would not take "No" for an answer
and the President finally got on the phone himself and told Mrs.
Roosevelt that under no circumstances would he intervene with
the Governor and urged very strongly that she say nothing about it.

This incident is typical of the things that have gone on in Washington between the President and Mrs. Roosevelt ever since 1932.
She is forever finding someone underprivileged and unbefriended
in whose behalf she takes up the cudgels. While she may often be
wrong, as I think she was in this case, I never cease to admire her
burning determination to see that justice is done, not only to individuals, but to underprivileged groups.

I think, too, in this particular instance Mrs. Roosevelt felt that I
was not pressing her case with the President adequately, because in
the course of the evening he was not available on the phone and I
had to act as a go-between. At any rate I felt that she would not be
satisfied until the President told her himself, which he reluctantly
but finally did.

H. L. H.[8]

She pushed the president and Hopkins to the point of exasperation
because she felt that Odell Waller, condemned by a jury of landlords
from which Negroes had been excluded, had become a symbol of racial

injustice. "Times without number Negro men have been lynched or gone to their death without due process of law. No one questions Waller's guilt, but they question the system which led to it." She failed to save the condemned sharecropper, but her efforts in that direction helped preserve the faith of Negro Americans in their government. Walter White, Channing Tobias, Anna Arnold Hedgman, and other Negro leaders came to Washington the night before the execution to hold a death vigil. "The group definitely felt that you had done everything possible and had been a sympathetic friend to all of them," a friend wrote Eleanor later.[9]

Yet a few weeks later when her hotheaded young friend Pauli Murray upbraided the president for his evasive attitude on the Negro question, which Miss Murray contrasted with Wendell Willkie's forthright support of Negro rights, Eleanor rebuked her sharply: "I wonder if it ever occurred to you that Mr. Willkie has no responsibility whatsoever. He can say whatever he likes and do whatever he likes" without having to take into consideration the southerners who controlled the important committees in Congress. Nor should Miss Murray reproach the president because he was not as outspoken as his wife: "Of course I can say just how I feel, but I cannot say it with much sense of security unless the President were willing for me to do so."[10]

Her husband's willingness to have her speak out seemed to her to indicate not only his bigness as a person, but his sympathy with what she was saying. If to more cynical eyes it seemed that with her help he was getting the best of both worlds—credit among Negroes for support of their aspirations without any commitment that might create difficulties with the southern wing of his party—it must be said in extenuation that a more forthright espousal of Negro rights might have made it impossible for him to govern. Certainly the attacks upon Eleanor for her racial views were more savage, systematic, and unrelenting than any she had ever encountered. The war had dangerously elevated racial tension, and one of the uglier manifestations was the Eleanor Roosevelt rumor factory. The whole South teemed with Eleanor stories. One group of such rumors had her registering at a hotel in a small southern town and then demanding accommodations—in one version for four Negro women, in another for four Negro men; another group of stories had her spurning a dinner prepared by "the nice white people" of Tuskegee to go off in the company of "a big black Negro" to a colored banquet; a third variant portrayed her as registering at a small southern hotel and then ordering the bellboy,

"Go out and get me twenty Negro ladies, for I must have them to dinner with me."[11]

The most persistent and widespread rumors related to the "Eleanor Clubs," which supposedly cropped up in every state below the Mason-Dixon line. The purpose of these alleged clubs of Negro women was to get Negroes out of domestic service and white women into the kitchen by 1943. The aims of the clubs were said to be more pay, more privileges, fewer hours, and no criticism of Eleanor Roosevelt. Despite the hundreds of reports of the existence of such clubs, neither the FBI nor scholarly investigators like Howard W. Odum were able to find one. The FBI was brought in because some thought enemy agents were disseminating these stories, but Professor Odum in his careful survey concluded that their origin lay in the difficulties white women were experiencing with "the servant problem" as Negro women left domestic service for war-created jobs at higher wages. "Here's a new one," Ruby Black reported to Eleanor. In Bridgeport, Connecticut, it was said that Negroes were being hired in the war plants upon presentation of a slip which was written, "Give this man a job. E.R." Eleanor sent this item to Will Alexander, who was the minorities specialist for the War Manpower Commission. There was a labor shortage in Bridgeport, he explained, and the rumors were being circulated to keep the Employment Service from referring Negro women to defense jobs. "It doesn't make a pretty picture."[12]

In the summer of 1943 tension finally exploded into riot and bloodshed. Detroit was swept by racial strife more serious than anything since the First World War. Thirty-five persons were killed, twenty-nine of whom were Negroes, and the president had to send in federal troops. The orgy of race violence was triggered by a fist fight in a Detroit park, but the racial bigots blamed Eleanor Roosevelt. In a letter she referred to this:

> I've seen lots of people, black and white, who are disturbed about the race riots. There seems so little one can do & all agreed I should not go to Detroit just now since anything that happened would be blamed on me. The editorials in some papers blamed the race riots on me & of course that brings floods of letters from the South![13]

To accuse Mrs. Roosevelt, wrote the *Louisville Courier-Journal*, was "an example of the lowest of all the methods used up to this point by people who disagree with the political philosophy of the New Deal."

The causes were to be found in mass migration, overcrowded industrial areas, and "a new birth of self respect among Negroes." But that was the voice of reason, and at this time even usually sensible men were swept from their moorings by the gathering racial storm. Someone who worked for the OWI told a friend of Eleanor's in all seriousness that Roosevelt could not be re-elected in 1944 because of his wife's attitude on racial issues. She had gone to Detroit, he insisted, despite all proofs to the contrary, and in talking to Negro workers on the assembly line had told them to send all complaints to her—she would fix them.[14]

The southern picture of Eleanor Roosevelt as a racial firebrand had little relation to reality. Ironically, she was criticized in the Negro community because she counseled patience and moderation. She commended to Walter White an article in the *Reader's Digest* by Warren Brown which criticized the Negro press for sensationalism and inverted racism:

> I have seen a very considerable number of Negro papers recently and I feel that a certain number of them are not very responsible. For that reason I was glad to see that a colored man had the maturity to criticize in as temperate a way as Mr. Brown has in pointing out the faults of the press.

Her approval of the article distressed him, White replied. Brown's piece was being used to claim "that the grievances of the Negroes are illusory," and it played into the hands of "the enemies of the Negro and of democracy." White's reaction to the Brown article surprised Eleanor: "It seemed to me temperate and fair and mature." When an interracial group, Common Ground, solicited her opinion, she renewed her plea for journalistic restraint. "At a time when feelings were so tense, I thought he [Mr. Brown] wisely criticized such people as the Reverend [Adam Clayton] Powell who add to the tenseness. I do not see the Negro press regularly but I am often sent clippings and the headlines and articles seem pretty extreme at times."[15]

She again affronted the Negro leadership when she wrote an article for the *Negro Digest* entitled "If I Were a Negro," in which she suggested, "I would not do too much demanding. . . . I would take every chance that came my way to prove my quality and ability and if recognition was slow I would continue to prove myself, knowing that in the end, good performance would be acknowledged." With respect to discrimination in the armed forces, which was the flash point of Negro resentment, she wrote, "I would accept every advance that was made in the Army and Navy, though I would not try to bring these about more quickly than they were offered."[16]

"Am I to be blamed for asking, and even insisting, that I be treated as a man and a full fledged citizen in the land of my birth?" a Negro pastor protested, deeply pained that so sincere a friend of the Negro people should write in a way that put the Negro on the defensive. She had not meant to discourage the Negroes from claiming their rights, she replied:

In that sentence, "I would not do too much demanding," perhaps I did not make it clear that I thought colored people were quite right in stating the things they wanted and to ask for them but that when it came to the work of really fighting for them, they would probably get further if the white people who believe as they do, were urged to do most of the fighting and demanding. If it is possible, in the South it should always be done by Southerners themselves because they take it so much better than they do from a Northerner.

Dr. Will Alexander, for instance, can do twice as much with a Southern audience as I can.

In the Army and Navy, I feel that things are moving. They seem to move slowly but the advance in the aggregate has been very great in this war over the last. The Negro is serving in many different ways which were not open to him in the last war. Of course, you are right, they should neither have to ask for nor demand equal opportunity and equal treatment as citizens but I am talking about things as they are and not about things as they should be or as we wish they were. You know quite well there is an Executive Order against discrimination. There would always be "good reasons" for doing things when individuals want to do them. This change has to come slowly from the human heart and it takes a long while to bring about great changes.[17]

In this era of "black power," Eleanor Roosevelt's admonitions to the Negro militants of the forties sound conservative and patronizing. Even at the time, they drew the criticism of the *Amsterdam News*. "She is putting herself in the same boat with other so-called liberals and 'friends of the Negro,'" said the *News*, and wondered "if Mrs.

Roosevelt's regrettable article about Negroes was just another attempt by the Administration to curry the favor and support of the Southerners," especially in view of the approaching elections. Many southern whites, too, thought she was motivated in her racial views by a concern for votes—but they thought she was bidding for the Negro vote. The extremists on both sides, one in desperate defense of caste privilege, the other in desperate rebellion against a denial of rights, were cut off from that sense of fellow feeling for all human beings that was the strongest motivating force in her personality. What Eleanor feared was a massacre; what she hoped for was that changes might come without bloodshed. Pauli Murray, enraged by the moral neutrality of the president's statement after Detroit that "every true American regrets" the recent outbreaks of violence, wrote a bitter poem titled "Mr. Roosevelt."

"I am sorry," Eleanor wrote after she had received the poem, "but I understand."[18]

She understood, and although she counseled restraint she knew that the Negro faced Zionward and she would march with him as far and as fast as she dared. In the wake of the Detroit riots she wrote:

I'm enclosing a column I am filing the day I leave here. It's the most I thought F. would be willing to have me say. He feels he must not irritate the southern leaders as he needs their votes for essential war bills. I am not sure that they could be much worse than they are. The rest of the country seems to me sadly in need of leadership on labor questions and race relations.[19]

Her consciousness of color was heightened by Mme. Chiang Kai-shek's visit to the White House early in 1943. The generalissimo's wife, one of the famous Soong sisters, arrived in the United States at the end of November to be treated at the Medical Center in New York for the aftereffects of an automobile accident. Roosevelt, busy with the preparations for Casablanca, encouraged his wife to call upon her the day after her arrival, and the two women quickly established a sympathetic and warm relationship. Eleanor found Mme. Chiang to be "a very sweet person" but sensed also in China's First Lady great strength of character. Mme. Chiang has a personality, Eleanor wrote, which has "impressed itself on her people and made her a real partner with her husband in the most difficult period in China." In the first flush of enthusiasm for the exquisite visitor from China, Eleanor ascribed to her qualities which were more a description of herself than of Mme. Chiang. To have achieved what she has "she must be tough-minded, certainly no sentimentalist and yet she must have an understanding and sympathy for suffering and weakness," and she must be moved by "some overwhelming purpose."[20] If the beautifully embroidered clothes, the silk sheets that Mme. Chiang brought with her to the hospital—and later to the White House—if the carefully arranged hair, the soft, silky skin that obviously required much grooming seemed a little inconsistent with the picture of selflessness that Eleanor drew, if the peremptory tones that China's First Lady was reported to use with those about her when Eleanor was not present, indicated a certain mandarin coldness toward the lower orders, Eleanor—although she listened to Tommy's warnings that Mme. Chiang was not a Saint Teresa in Chinese silk—refused to accept their implications, perhaps because she felt that Mme. Chiang, being a woman, must be an ally in the struggle for equality and justice.

She listened carefully to the tart, occasionally catty observations of close friends like Tommy, Trude Pratt, and Elinor Morgenthau. She herself rarely said anything belittling of another person. "Yes, dear," was her smiling comment on her friends' cynical chatter, leaving them to guess whether she was taken in by someone like Mme. Chiang or, in the interests of her own larger purposes, preferred to accent the positive.

The president returned to Washington from Casablanca on January 31. Chiang had not been invited because, the president told Eleanor, Stalin had said he could not meet with Chiang and hope to stay out of war with Japan, but then Stalin himself, in the midst of the battle of Stalingrad, had not been able to come. Their exclusion enraged the Chinese, as Eleanor learned from Mme. Chiang, whom she visited, with a friend, before returning to Washington. The president, to whom she had spoken on the phone, asked her to inform Mme. Chiang that he had obtained agreements from Churchill that would much improve the airplane situation in China. When Eleanor conveyed this information to Mme. Chiang, the tiny figure looked up at her appraisingly, clearly unmoved. Sensing immediately what the coolness implied, Eleanor asked if she had heard from the generalissimo about Casablanca. At first Mme. Chiang refused to say but then in a torrent that mingled ice and fire, China's anger and resentment poured out.

China considered herself a full member of the United Nations, Mme. Chiang began. Global strategy could only be made by all of the United Nations, or at least the four main ones, never by two only, and then imposed on the rest or simply communicated to them. That was not a democratic way of working together, and if nations did not cooperate as equals during the war, no good peace was possible. China subscribed to the Atlantic Charter and was fighting for the Four Freedoms, not for herself alone, but for all peoples. She and the generalissimo were telling the Chinese people that while they had had a raw deal in the past, in the future it was to be different, that they were to be an equal member of the family of nations. If that was not to be the case, why should China fight on?[21]

It was an outburst that Eleanor, sensitive to the global nature of the "white supremacy" issue, listened to with sympathy. Would the generalissimo be willing to meet the president at some spot close to China? That would make two, Mme. Chiang answered, and there are four of us. Russia might be worried about Japan, Eleanor pointed out. Mme. Chiang acknowledged that this was a difficulty, but it did not preclude a meeting of Great Britain, the United States, and China.

When Eleanor spoke with the president the next night at dinner, he insisted that the Casablanca discussions had centered on military problems alone, "and they were not China's except where they concerned getting military supplies to China"—mostly planes, and General H. H. Arnold was on the way to Chungking to discuss the airplane situation. But there were other obstacles to the treatment of China as one of the Big Four. Churchill resisted it, because a strong China might threaten Britain's imperial position in the Far East. Roosevelt anticipated less trouble between the United States, Russia, and China, he told his wife, "than between any of us and Great Britain."[22]

Several times during Eleanor's visits to the hospital, Mme. Chiang had urged her to come to China, and Eleanor brought the matter up with Harry Hopkins, who had asked to talk to her about the need to set up some UN postwar planning machinery in such fields as food and education. That was all well and good, she wrote, but what was needed at the moment was

> more confidence in Russia & China that as a people we want to understand them & their problems & work *with* them. I asked Harry if he thought my going there now during the war would help here & there. He said if I thought so I should make Franklin let me go but to wait until Mme. Chiang came. She will be here next Wednesday & she is now at the Big House in Hyde Park. I think she is going

to surprise Franklin a good deal but she will charm him. She won't lean like Martha of Norway though! She can't be fooled either, somehow it seems to me that she compels honesty.[23]

Her tartness about Princess Martha was less an expression of irritation with the president for his flirtatiousness—for there was always a Martha for relaxation, she explained to a friend—than it was exasperation over the weakness of the feminine sex. The princess said little, but coquetted like a young girl, making sheep's eyes at the president's sallies and giving her protector, whom she addressed at his request as "dear godfather," the adoration in which he luxuriated. What man doesn't?[24]

Mme. Chiang arrived in Washington on February 17, and for almost two weeks Princess Martha was eclipsed. The president and Mrs. Roosevelt met her at Union Station. "My husband has a wonderful way of making people feel that he has known them for a long time," she wrote in an article for *Colliers* which she decided not to submit. "He calls it his fatherly attitude and I think he used it that day." At dinner that night there were only the president and Eleanor, Harry Hopkins and his wife, the former Louise Macy whom he had married in July, 1942, and Helen Gahagan Douglas. Eleanor must have advised Mme. Chiang that the president liked ladies to constitute an admiring audience. "She is wise. She listened at dinner & in her half-hour later with F.D.R. she listened but she will talk & she has already asked F.D.R. if I can go back with her!"[25]

Talk Mme. Chiang did, and most effectively for China's cause. "Mme. Chiang & Franklin had a wonderful press conference this morning. She is very quick." Eleanor sat with the president and Mme. Chiang, with her left hand resting reassuringly on the right arm of Mme. Chiang's chair. Occasionally during the conference they exchanged quick understanding smiles. Mme. Chiang played to the president, Raymond Clapper observed, "as the big strong man who could work miracles." The previous day, Eleanor had accompanied her to Capitol Hill for her speeches to Senate and House. Her appearance, Eleanor wrote, "marked the recognition of a woman who, through her own personality and her own service, has achieved a place in the world, not merely as the wife of the Generalissimo Chiang Kai-shek, but as a representative of her people." It was a revealing observation. She was still unwilling to admit that the place she herself had achieved in American life was due to her own efforts and personality, but her admiration went to the women who did succeed on their own. As she watched the slim figure in a long black Oriental dress, slit at the sides, come down the aisle escorted by senators who towered over her, Eleanor "could not help a great feeling of pride in her as a woman but when she spoke it was no longer as a woman that one thought of her."

She would remember "for a long time," she added, "the applause which both sides of the House gave her when she made a plea that we look upon Japan as our major enemy." So effective was Mme. Chiang in her advocacy that for a time the Combined Chiefs of Staff feared she might unhinge the "Germany First" strategy of fighting the war. She sometimes held long discussions with the president that went on so late into the evening that Eleanor would have to rescue her and send her to bed, a salvage operation that sometimes ended with Eleanor wading into the discussion herself.[26]

Mme. Chiang had scarcely left the White House when Prince Olaf and Princess Martha arrived for tea, giving at least one other guest at that tea party the feeling that the handsome princess did not wish to allow even a day to elapse without moving to wipe out the impression Mme. Chiang had made on the president. She was outrageously flirtatious, this guest thought, adding, "Mrs. Roosevelt seems to grow in situations like that and become even more a queen."[27]

Some of Eleanor's friends did not share her view that Mme. Chiang was a slit-skirt version of Eleanor Roosevelt. Tommy thought China's First Lady snobbish and spoiled. Harry Hooker, though something of a society gallant himself, was amused to hear Mme. Chiang's niece, Miss Kung, underscore that she was the seventy-sixth generation directly descended from Confucius. He had not known, Harry later confided to Eleanor, that China had its Newport Set.[28]

Pearl Buck came to dine with Eleanor shortly after Mme. Chiang's stay at the White House. It was a small party and Miss Buck, who, having experienced the generalissimo's rule in Nanking, was evading a public appearance with Mme. Chiang, felt free to speak critically. She questioned Mme. Chiang's use of the word "democracy." China's First Lady was beautiful but also imperious and expensive, Miss Buck said, and the generalissimo was a great man, but uncouth and, of course, a warlord. China would not develop democratically, she cautioned, unless the United States gave it a strong lead in that direction. Eleanor indicated that she understood; it had been "very interesting to have Madame Chiang Kai-shek at the White House."

The novelist was upset that publisher Henry Luce and his group had had so much to do with the arrangements for Mme. Chiang's tour of the United States. Here, too, Eleanor was sympathetic. Although she appreciated Mme. Chiang's desire to have Republican support for China, she had been a little taken aback at her lack of interest in a proposal Eleanor had conveyed from Walter White that Mme. Chiang address a mass meeting under NAACP auspices. Even though Eleanor had indicated her readiness to join Mme. Chiang on the NAACP platform, the Chinese First Lady had decided that she would appear only "under the auspices of her Chinese and American friends." Nor was she willing even to see White.[29]

Princess Martha need not have worried that Mme. Chiang might displace her. Eleanor, with a smile that suggested that behind the innocence there was great sophistication, told Pearl Buck that one day she had informed the president he would have the pleasure of dining alone with Mme. Chiang that evening as she (Eleanor) had to be elsewhere, and he had replied firmly, "Indeed I shan't! I am going to bed early!"

"I don't think that Franklin likes women who think they are as good as he is," Eleanor added wickedly.[30]

Although the president had enjoyed Mme. Chiang's company, he had few illusions about the hardness behind those calculating eyes. John L. Lewis was threatening a coal strike during the time of Mme. Chiang's White House stay, and the president asked her one evening at dinner how China would deal with such a labor leader. Swiftly and expressively she drew her small ivory hand across her throat. The president looked at his wife and later teased her, "Well, how about your gentle and sweet character?" And in later years Eleanor herself would say softly, "Those delicate little petal-like fingers—you could see some poor wretch's neck being wrung," and at that point she would make a twisting motion of her own fingers, which were as expressive as Mme. Chiang's.[31]

When Eleanor had first broached the idea of visiting China to her husband he seemed quite eager to have her go, but she thought it would be a mistake to visit China and not also go to Russia. During his White House visit in May, 1942, Foreign Minister Vyacheslav Molotov had asked to see her, and they had talked about women in Russia. Eleanor had said she was greatly interested and would like to visit Russia and see for herself. Molotov said he would remember that, and during Eleanor's visit to England the Soviet ambassador Ivan Maisky had made the invitation specific. But the president was reluctant to have her go to Russia: "F.D.R. feels the moment for that hasn't come." Admiral Standley, the U.S. ambassador in Moscow, was threatening to resign if any more dignitaries were sent to him; Willkie's visit had been quite enough for the duration.[32]

A few weeks later the president ruled out the trip to China, too. "I think he hopes to meet Stalin & Chiang this spring or summer & wants to wait on that," she wrote a friend. Perhaps he also feared that his wife's visit to China might strengthen the pressures on him to give the Chinese front a higher priority in Allied war plans. Representative Walter Judd, a former missionary in the Far East and a strong advocate of such higher priorities, lunched at the White House and afterward urged Eleanor to visit China, "perhaps going with Madame Chiang when she returns." Eleanor's cousin, columnist Joseph Alsop, who was with General Claire L. Chennault as a volunteer, was warning of a Chinese collapse "if there is not some sort of immediate, fairly spectacular action to revive the spirit of the Chinese people and troops." Perhaps the president feared his wife would join this "China lobby."[33]

She accepted his decision uncomplainingly. He must, however, have sensed her disappointment, for a few days later he told her he would like her to go to New Zealand and Australia. "I'm glad of course," she wrote, "as I may see James & I'll see many of our soldiers but it won't be as interesting as China or Russia!" But that suggestion, too, was subject to the vagaries of politics as well as of war: "FDR told me tonight after the Congressional party that the gentlemen were clamoring to go to the front & he thought it might be impossible to send them & in that case I would also be barred. I told him anything he decided was all right with me. I wanted to be a help & not a bother." However, C. R. Smith, who was at Air Transport Command, was asked to begin to plan her itinerary. "It would mean stopping everywhere. . . . Incidentally Australian and New Zealand officials have both asked but Franklin is still doubtful because of Congressional desires to visit in large numbers every front."[34]

Mme. Chiang came back to Washington after a triumphal tour of the country and again urged the president to permit Eleanor to visit her in Chungking, but the president would only vouchsafe a vague "sometime in the future" reply. Yet the increasingly clamorous "third world" could not be ignored. She wrote a friend that, "Next week the Liberian President comes, & won't that be a funny dinner? I really wish it wasn't a stag party for I'd like to observe Senators Connally & Barkley & one or two others!" She accompanied the president to a meeting with the president of Mexico on the U.S.-Mexican border and then went on to visit Japanese-American relocation camps in Arizona. "I just asked F.D.R. if I could take on an American-Japanese family but he says the Secret Service wouldn't allow it."[35]

With the conquest of North Africa completed, Churchill arrived in the United States to plan the next blows against Fortress Europe. "Mr. Churchill arrived at seven last night and Franklin says it is going to be the toughest of all the conferences." Command decisions were at the forefront, but India and the priority to be given to the Chinese theater were also high on the agenda, with Generals Stilwell and Chennault present to argue the case for more aggressive operations in the China-Burma theater. When Anthony Eden had been in Washington in March to discuss postwar plans, Roosevelt and Hull had tried to soften British resistance to acceptance of China as one of the Big Four. But Eden was dubious about China's stability, and he "did not much like the idea of the Chinese running up and down the Pacific." Mme. Chiang was still in the country, in New York City, when Churchill arrived, and Roosevelt thought she should meet Churchill. He asked Eleanor to invite her back to Washington. But, as Eleanor wrote a friend, Mme. Chiang balked:

A curious little drama has been going on. The Chinese gentleman sent his lady advice she didn't like so when I phoned to ask if she'd come down & lunch with these two gentlemen now here she said "No" the one she had not met could come to her! He wouldn't go & I could see Franklin thought they might fight if left alone so the brother was sent for & wires buzzed & now I believe she is coming but it may be Friday or Monday![36]

The meeting did not take place, and Mme. Chiang in June returned to Chungking. "I still like Mme. very much & Franklin said today that she had a brilliant mind," Eleanor wrote. From Chungking Mme. Chiang sent Eleanor some Before the Rain and Orange Blossom tea "which you like so much, and also two pieces of silk for the President for shirts.... Please do not forget that you are coming to visit me as soon as the cool weather sets in." Eleanor was leaving the middle of August, she replied, but for a short visit to the Southwest Pacific: "I talked to the President about getting out to you and he said just what he always says about so many other things—that I must not interfere with war plans. However, he said he would try to arrange it as soon as it seems practical."[37]

In the end she was not allowed to go to China, and she was also advised to stay away from Detroit, the scene of the racial riots. It was dangerous to permit a woman who refused to suppress the promptings of her conscience and imagination to visit the areas where the most searching test of the Christian ethic was taking shape.

54. GI'S FRIEND, II: THE FIRST LADY AND THE ADMIRAL

◇

ELEANOR PREPARED FOR HER JOURNEY TO THE SOUTHWEST Pacific with considerable trepidation because there were many "Eleanor stories" circulating among GIs in the South Pacific. A sergeant in New Guinea, she was informed, had written that they had heard that "dear Mrs. Roosevelt thinks it would be nice to keep us malaria-ridden forgotten men overseas until six months after the war." Of course she had never made such a remark, and she suspected it was enemy propaganda playing on the homesickness of the boys in the Pacific; but if such stories were believed, GIs might not be pleased to see her.

> This trip will be attacked as a political gesture, & I am so uncertain whether or not I am doing the right thing that I will start with a heavy heart. Well, enough of my doubts. I'll go because other people think I should, & if I see you that will be a joy, & if I don't I'll try to do a good job on seeing the women's work & where I do see our soldiers I'll try to make them feel that Franklin really wants to know about them.[1]

The four-engined Army Liberator in which she flew to the South Pacific carried a ton of mail and some military personnel as well as its distinguished passenger. It was not heated, so she slept "in that much scorned red flannel lining to my Red Cross coat as it grew fairly cold." Norman Davis had been delighted with her offer to visit the South Pacific in the uniform of the Red Cross as its "Special Delegate," and the uniform solved a wardrobe problem that was compounded by the necessity of taking a typewriter and yet staying within the 44-pound baggage limitation. She had decided not to take Tommy—"we will go together to China!"—and had learned to type again in order to be able to do her daily column.[2]

In Honolulu she showered at General William O. Ryan's house, did her exercises "to get the kinks out," breakfasted in a green bower alive with brilliantly plumaged birds, and then was off to Christmas Island, a coral atoll that they reached at dusk. She was worried about snakes, associating their presence with tropical climates, and was relieved to learn from the commanding officer that there were none on the atolls. But when she stopped by her quarters before going to the movie that was a standard item on the daily schedules of these isolated Pacific outposts, she was horrified to find the floor crawling with large bugs. "I might have screamed if I had not been the only woman on the Island and I knew a feminine scream would attract a good deal of attention." She stamped hard instead, and the bugs quickly vanished through the cracks in the floor.

Soon after reveille the next day she was ready to go, with—at her request—two enlisted men as her escorts. She toured the hospital, visited military installations, took the names of the boys who wanted to have her write their home folks that she had seen them, and drove forty miles in a jeep to visit the island rest camp. Afterward she wrote her husband that older men did not stand up to the debilitating heat as well as the younger ones, and that if possible no one should be stationed in such a climate for more than two years. "I think the men here have been glad to have me come," she wrote Tommy. That was a relief to her, for she had feared that the officers and men might find her visit a bore and an imposition. She reminded them more "of some boy's mother back home, than the wife of the President of the United States—and we all loved it," the correspondent for the *Pacific Times* wrote.[3]

In the Cook Island group, her next stop, after she had made her rounds she wrote, that "there seems to be no trouble anywhere out here between Southern white and colored. They lie in beds in the same wards, go to the same movies and sit side by side and work side by side." But at Aitutaki, as she wrote Tommy, a different picture was given to her by the officer in command:

The Colonel, regular army, Mass. Republican, and snobby was not pleased to see me. I'm sure he would sleep with a Maori woman but he told me he does not believe in mixed marriages, and he would like some Army nurses because some of his younger officers want to marry some of the native girls. He has both white and colored troops and is much worried since he has some white Southerners and he is afraid some day a white boy will find his native girl that he went out with last night is off with a colored boy the next night and then there would be a shooting and a feud would start between

white and colored troops. He thinks we should have all colored or
all white on an island, but he owns that the colored have done very
good work so he just prays hell won't break loose.[4]

The colonel regarded her as a "do-gooder," and she was determined
to show him there was nothin effete about this particular reformer.
He drove her in his jeep to the island's radar station: "I have never
seen a steeper road but since I was sure he took me to see if I would be
afraid, I summoned all my experience with Hall and tried to behave
as tho' I usually drove over such roads!" In the Fijis she enjoyed a real
mattress for the first time since leaving the United States; an Army
cot, she wrote, "would not be my permanent choice for a bed." More
should be done for the men's recreation. Phonographs and needles—
and women—were needed. "Two commanding generals have now
spoken to me about the fact that seeing no white women had the effect
of making officers and men forget that certain kinds of intercourse
with the natives was not desirable, and when it is safe to let women
on duty come to these areas I think it will be a very good thing." The
absence of wine and beer was bad: "last night four men died from
drinking distilled shellac." She visited two hospitals in the Fijis, one
with 903 patients, the other with 843. "Malaria [is] more of an enemy
than combat though there were some serious wounds." The boys were
"plenty hardboiled," she wrote as the plane winged on to New Caledonia and Admiral William F. Halsey's headquarters in Noumea, "but
as far as I can tell my being here is giving them a kick."

She was anxious about her meeting with Admiral Halsey. Most of
the men in the hospitals in the Fijis were casualties from the great battles that had taken place in the Solomons. Her heart was set on going
to Guadalcanal, which for her was the symbol of the war in the South
Pacific and of all the hardships and suffering to which American boys
were being subjected. How could she look wounded men in the eye
in the future and say she had been in the South Pacific but had not
been to Guadalcanal? She felt as strongly about going there as Franklin had about going to the front in the First World War when he had
insisted on visiting a battery of 155s under fire, and even firing one of
its guns. But he had been unwilling to give her a firm "yes" and left
the decision up to Halsey.

The conqueror of the Japanese fleet in the South Pacific also classed
Eleanor Roosevelt as a "do-gooder" and "dreaded" her arrival. What
were her plans, he asked almost as soon as she had stepped from the

plane. "What do you think I should do?" she countered, hoping to get her way by subordinating herself to his wishes. But the admiral was wise to that feminine tactic.[5]

"Mrs. Roosevelt," he said, "I've been married for thirty-odd years, and if those years have taught me one lesson, it is never to try to make up a woman's mind for her." He suggested that she spend two days in Noumea, proceed to New Zealand and Australia, and then return to Noumea for two days on her way home. She agreed, and the admiral began to relax when she produced a letter from the president that said he had told his wife that he was "leaving the decision wholly up to the Area Commanders" as to where she should go. "She is especially anxious to see Guadalcanal and at this moment it looks like a pretty safe place to visit," the president concluded.

"Guadalcanal is no place for you, Ma'am!" Halsey brusquely responded.

"I'm perfectly willing to take my chances," she said. "I'll be entirely responsible for anything that happens to me."

"I'm not worried about the responsibility, and I'm not worried about the chances you'd take. I know you'd take them gladly. What worries me is the battle going on in New Georgia at this very minute. I need every fighter plane that I can put my hands on. If you fly to Guadalcanal, I'll have to provide a fighter escort for you, and I haven't got one to spare."

Eleanor looked so crestfallen that Halsey found himself adding, "However, I'll postpone my final decision until your return. The situation may have clarified by then." He thought this cheered her up, but she wrote to the president:

Ad. Halsey seems very nervous about me, the others I can see think I could safely go to Guadalcanal, he says on my return I may go to Espiritu Santo & he will then decide, conditions may be more favorable. I realize final responsibility is his but I feel more strongly than ever that I should go & I doubt if I ever go to another hospital at home if I don't for I know more clearly than ever what it means to the men.... I won't get near any dangerous spots in Australia either. In some ways I wish I had not gone on this trip. I think the trouble I give far outweighs the momentary interest it may give the boys to see me. I do think when I tell them I bring a message from you to them, they like it but anyone else could have done it as well & caused less commotion![6]

But she had a job to do, and early the next morning she started her round in New Caledonia. By the time she departed for New Zealand Admiral Halsey had become her most ardent partisan in the theater:

> Here is what she did in twelve hours: she inspected two Navy hospitals, took a boat to an officer's rest home and had lunch there, returned and inspected an Army hospital, reviewed the 2nd Marine Raider Battalion (her son Jimmy had been its executive officer), made a speech at a service club, attended a reception, and was guest of honor at a dinner given by General Harmon.

And, the admiral might have added, pecked away at her typewriter in the dead of night, doing a column. Halsey's report continued:

> When I say that she inspected those hospitals, I don't mean that she shook hands with the chief medical officer, glanced into a sun parlor, and left. I mean that she went into every ward, stopped at every bed, and spoke to every patient: What was his name? How did he feel? Was there anything he needed? Could she take a message home for him? I marveled at her hardihood, both physical and mental, she walked for miles, and she saw patients who were grievously and gruesomely wounded. But I marveled most at their expressions as she leaned over them. It was a sight I will never forget.[7]

Her itinerary in New Zealand was much the same as it had been on the atolls—hospitals, Red Cross clubs, and camps, in addition to official receptions and visits to war factories where girls who were filling explosives, running lathes, and turning out precision parts paused to give her a resounding cheer. "I did the important broadcast tonight so that is behind me. Tomorrow night we leave and go to receive a Maori welcome." The racial issue was never far away, and her response to it was impulsively honest. From the moment that she touched foreheads with her Maori guide in the Maori style of greeting, the tribesmen were enchanted by her simplicity and friendliness. They christened her "Kotuku," or the "White Heron of the One Flight," which according to Maori tradition is seen but once in a lifetime. But back in the southern United States the photographs of her "rubbing noses" with her Maori guide were advanced as further proof of the First Lady's "nigger-loving" propensities.

She received a radio message from the president that the reaction to her trip so far was favorable—"but he never reads the unfavorable people," she advised Tommy, "so I'm anxious to hear from you. I wonder if I ever will!" To be without news from home, to feel cut off from the people she loved was almost unbearable—"I feel a hundred years away as though I were moving in a different and totally unattached world"—and she asked Tommy to send messages to her special people. That night they flew to Canberra, and Major George Durno, a former newspaperman who had been assigned to her by Air Transport Command, sent Tommy a batch of unanswered letters and telegrams. "For your information," he added, "Mrs. R. literally took New Zealand by storm.... She did a magnificent job, saying the right thing at the right time and doing a hundred and one little things that endeared her to the people."[8]

A letter to Tommy written on the way to Australia sounded a more prosaic note:

> I drew a check today for two hundred dollars. Since I am counted royalty I have only spent money on tips but they are very high and the one hundred and sixty I left with will be spent by tonight. I dread Australia for thirteen days but they will come to an end. Even the British trips couldn't touch these schedules.

"My being 'social & polite' day is over," she wrote the president after a hectic round of official activities in the Australian capital. "Yesterday was busy & wearying—however, I like Mr. Curtin [Australian prime minister] very much & I hope you will ask him to come to the U.S. again." She thought the government people were "very happy" that she had come, but nevertheless she was discontented. Russia and China were still on her mind. "Last night both the Chinese & Russian representatives pressed me to know when I was going to visit their countries so hurry up with your meetings Sir!" As for Australia, "Truth to tell however, I very much doubt that these trips have any real value & they certainly put our high-ranking officials to much trouble & travail of spirit!" But Nelson T. Johnson, the U.S. minister in Canberra, felt quite differently, as he wrote to her later:

> The authorities expected the stiff formality which through the years has characterized the visits of members of the royal family. You gave to Canberra and Australia not only the thrill that comes from a visit of royalty but the intellectual thrill of realizing they were

meeting a very fine woman with a very warm personality of her own.... The success of your visit to Canberra was due very much to yourself and to the warm informality which you gave to the proceedings everywhere.[9]

"I have walked through miles of hospital wards," her diary read shortly after she began her tour of Australia. In Melbourne, she mounted a platform in the largest American hospital in Australia, facing tiers of wounded and hospitalized men. She brought them the president's greetings and went on to talk about the postwar world, saying that all veterans deserved what she had come to know they expected: "Jobs at a living wage and the knowledge that the rest of the world is getting things worthwhile so your children may live in a world at peace." She did not mind the strenuous hospital schedules, and when she learned that Franklin had cabled to Australian officials suggesting that "she should not do so much," she wrote Tommy to tell the president that "if I wasn't busy I'd go crazy or go home tomorrow."[10]

She wanted to go to New Guinea but, as she wrote sardonically to Doris Fleeson, "General MacArthur was too busy to bother with a lady." Her letter to Franklin was irate:

Word came last night from Gen. MacArthur that it would require too many high-ranking officers to escort me in Port Moresby & he cld not spare them at this time when a push is on. This is the kind of thing that seems to me silly. I'd rather have a Sergeant & I'd see & hear more but I must have a General & I'm so scared I can't speak & he wouldn't tell me anything anyway. Generals Eichelberger & Byers & Ad. Jones are dears but I'd much rather be unimpeded. The papers here complain that I see none of the plain people. Neither do I really see any of the plain soldiers. I have an MP escort everywhere that wld do you credit. I have all the pomp & restriction & none of the power! I'm coming home this time & go in a factory!

The weather is fine, the days full, & I feel fine & I'm not doing anything which couldn't better be done by Mr. Allen of the Red + who could go see their people nearer the battle front & should come out here now.

I grow fatter daily since we eat at every turn.
Much love
ER.[11]

General MacArthur would not be bothered with her, and the staff aide whom he detailed to escort her in Australia was anything but pleased when the assignment was first handed to him. However, like Admiral Halsey, the aide, Captain Robert M. White, came away a changed man. In an article he later wrote for the *Christian Advocate* he said:

> As far as I was concerned, Mrs. Roosevelt or anybody else could come and go, but what I didn't like was to leave my post to accompany them. I traveled 10,000 miles to find Japanese and do what I could do to end the war, not to travel around with brass hats.... But wherever Mrs. Roosevelt went she wanted to see the things a mother would see. She looked at kitchens and saw how food was prepared. When she chatted with the men she said things mothers say, little things men never think of and couldn't put into words if they did. Her voice was like a mother's, too. Mrs. Roosevelt went through hospital wards by the hundreds. In each she made a point of stopping by each bed, shaking hands, and saying some nice, motherlike thing. Maybe it sounds funny, but she left behind her many a tough battletorn GI blowing his nose and swearing at the cold he had recently picked up.[12]

She talked with the men in the military hospitals, carried her tin tray down the chow line in mess halls, and sat chatting with the enlisted men after meals. She rode with them in jeeps and was forever answering their questions. On the north coast of Australia the hospitals were filled with wounded from New Guinea, and outside Townsville she came upon troops in battle dress, heading for the front. She insisted on walking down the road, which was scarred with rocks, to tell each truckload good-by and wish the boys good luck. At one point her voice quavered, but she quickly recovered and continued on down the line.

Film actress Una Merkel was one of a group of entertainers who toured the Southwest Pacific shortly after Eleanor's trip, and she later told John Golden, the producer, what it was like to follow the First Lady. "How's Eleanor?" the boys often yelled, and Gary Cooper would reply, "Well, we saw her tracks in the sand at one of the islands where we stopped, but we couldn't tell which way they were headed." Miss Merkel also heard at one hospital that the First Lady had been brought to the bed of a young boy whose stomach had been pretty well shot to pieces and who was being kept alive with blood plasma and tubular feeding. Eleanor had leaned over and kissed the boy gently and lovingly, and with that, Miss Merkel was told, "the will to live revived somehow."[13]

As her tour of Australia ended, Eleanor was still furious over being protected by admirals, generals, and MPs who treated her

> like a frail flower and won't let me approach any danger. The boys last night all asked if I wasn't coming to New Guinea & I feel more strongly than ever about their restrictions.... I've never been so hedged around with protection in my life. It makes me want to do something reckless when I get home, like making munitions![14]

But the next day when she arrived in Noumea, the world turned brighter, for Admiral Halsey, the New Georgia campaign finished, consented to let her visit Guadalcanal. "I feel happy to-night for we are going to Guadalcanal.... I left Australia friendly & happy I think. For the rest I only hope it was a good job. I know I should have gone to New Guinea."

With the visit to Guadalcanal ahead of her, Eleanor's energy returned and she wore down her escort touring New Caledonia. "Listen, Hi," a member of a Medical Base Detachment on the island wrote an anti–New Deal Republican at home, "do you think it is a cinch to come over here, and especially a woman? It's dangerous and tiresome and it's a wonder a person her age could stand it." And if Eleanor's home-front critics complained that her trip cost too much and used some gasoline, "as far as our bunch is concerned we would all be willing to turn over our pay for the rest of the war to help compensate you fellows on the home front for any inconvenience you suffered by Mrs. Roosevelt's trip."[15]

At 8:00 A.M. the flight north began. Miss Colette Ryan of the Red Cross, a friend of Admiral Halsey's, accompanied her. They landed first at Efate, on which some of the biggest hospitals were located, and again she toured acres of hospital beds with something to say to each boy. In the afternoon they flew further north to Espiritu Santo, headquarters of the Navy Air Force; there they dined with the admiral, went to an outdoor movie where Eleanor made a little speech, and got to bed at 11:00 P.M. Two and a half hours later she was called for a 1:30 take-off.

Eleanor and Miss Ryan perched on two little seats over the bomb bay as the plane took off in the darkness. It became cold, and a "youngster" handed them blankets and later brought them cups of coffee.

Landing on Guadalcanal after the three-hour flight through the darkness was for Eleanor the most exciting moment of the trip. They breakfasted at the airfield with General Nathan Twining, the commanding officer of the Thirteenth Air Force, and then the Army came to get her. Trucks loaded with Seabees were arriving at the field as she drove off, and when she leaned out to wave her presence created a sensation. "Gosh, there's Eleanor," one boy shouted. The commanding officer was horrified that she should be treated with such levity, but she felt it was a great compliment: "They were evidently so pleased to see women there one had to laugh and go on waving." To some her presence was not such a surprise; it had been announced at the movies the night before that no man would be allowed to walk around the following day without shirt or shorts.

She toured the island, went through the hospitals, visited the cemetery, experienced an alert, and saw a Negro boy, Cecil Peterson, in whom she was interested. The following is an account of her visit written by the author, who was then stationed on Guadalcanal:

Mrs. Roosevelt has been here and gone—a very tired Mrs. Roosevelt, agonized by the men she had seen in the hospitals, fiercely determined because of them to be relentless in working for a peace that this time will last, a very loving and motherly Mrs. Roosevelt, and despite the heat, the weariness and the tragedy, a gracious and magnificent lady.

For me it was a grand day. . . . Early in the morning I learned she was here and having breakfast with General Twining about a hundred yards away. I dashed madly out to shave and just as I finished I received a telephone call from Colonel Higgins to report to General Howard at 12:30. It was hard waiting through the morning, but I had seven letters from you, and so I wrote you and the hours passed swiftly. I did get a glimpse of Mrs. Roosevelt being photographed with the General as I was going for the mail, but I thought it best not to bollix up the Army's program and drove rapidly away.

At 2:30 I drove down to headquarters and as I sat in Colonel Higgins' tent and heard her hearty laugh—you know how it rings out and dominates the whole table—the robust Roosevelt laugh—I fidgeted impatiently. Finally the lunch with the senior officers was over, and a note was slipped to Mrs. R. that I was here, and army protocol crashed as we embraced one another. The press was there but did not get any photographs. Mrs. R. then talked to the reporters, and then we went into the General's bedroom and talked for fifteen minutes before she had to go off to more hospitals.

General Howard gave me a note where to meet them at 3:30. Mrs. R. said she wanted to come back to our headquarters to visit the weather station and take a peek at our tents. I said the boys would greatly love that, except the tent part, if it was all right with General Twining, and he readily acceded.... So I dashed ahead to the Weather Station to tell them Mrs. R. was coming and then dashed to the Mobile Hospital where I was to meet her at 3:30. I had had no lunch, foolishly thinking I would be invited to lunch with the Lady, so I did in two tootsie rolls.

At 4:30 it turned out that Mrs. R. was to meet several Senators and Admiral Halsey who were arriving there. So the General told me to get into the station wagon, one of the snazziest I have ever seen, and we drove over to the rendezvous place. The poor General must have been baffled by the conversation between us which was of color schemes for the 11th Street house, furniture and a person named "Trude."

When we arrived at the rendezvous, I stayed in the car while Mrs. R. and the General went out to greet the gentlemen, and then to my horror Admiral Halsey who is a legendary figure in these parts flanked by the Commanding-General of these parts, came over with Mrs. Roosevelt to the station wagon. Now a Sergeant doesn't smugly remain seated when a four-star Admiral comes over, so I decided to hell with the press and the Senators and jumped out and stood at attention. And then Admiral Halsey put out his hand and Mrs. Roosevelt introduced us: "So this is the young man," he said, and inspected me critically as the photographers snapped their cameras. I hope the damn pictures were suppressed. I don't want to finish the Admiral. I can see the *Chicago-Tribune* with a caption—THIS IS WHY OUR CAMPAIGN IN THE SOUTH PACIFIC IS NOT MOVING FORWARD.

Then we dropped Mrs. Roosevelt and General Howard at another hospital and I was there alone with the Admiral. So I gulped and said nothing, knowing the man has great cares, anyway a Sergeant doesn't speak until spoken to. He asked me about my work as an "aerologist" (Navy term for weather man) and then said some amusing things about the Senators, who seem to have left him severely alone. Admiral Halsey is a jovial man but with a reputation for remarkable bluntness and directness so I guess the Senators decided it was best not to tangle with the old seadog.

Then I went back to get Mrs. Roosevelt in the Weather Station's car. We got rid of the MPs who were greatly relieved and I drove Mrs. R. down to our area. I introduced her to Van who had voted for Willkie in '40 but was now urging his friends to vote for FDR in '44, and she told a wonderfully amusing story which you undoubtedly have heard about the sad marine whose unit was to leave these parts, and who felt he couldn't leave until he had shot a Jap. So his officer advised him to stand up on the ridge and shout "To hell with Hirohito," and a Jap would certainly appear and then he could bag him. Next day the officer came on the Marine he still was depressed. "What happened?" asked the officer. "I did as you said, Sir, and a Jap did climb out of his foxhole, but he yelled 'To hell with Roosevelt' and how could I shoot a fellow Republican."

Then despite all my grimaces Mrs. R. came down to our tent, and she will report her impressions. By this time everyone in the area was clustering around. Lucky that no one thought to ask her for an autograph for I never would have been able to get her back to the General by 5:15. "How do these weather men rate?" asked Marines, GIs, swabbies.

So I drove her back disregarding the speed limit of 25 miles as I could afford to with Mrs. R. in the car. We drove by a river, and 50 Marines drove frenziedly into the shallow water when one of them spotted Mrs. R. Three sailors before they knew who was in the car signalled for a lift. They clambered in raucously, saw Mrs. R., gulped and were the silentest swabbies I have met in the service as Mrs. R. told them about things back home.

I came back again in the evening and we sat on a screened porch and talked until 11:30 but I have never seen her so weary. And today she had to be up at 4:15 and fly and then another round of hospitals. So though I hated to let her go, because for a little while I was back in the world of those I love, at 11:30 I left. You and Tommy must make her rest, really rest, when she returns, impatient though she may be to tell the American people about the boys here. Honestly, Trude, I have never seen her as tired as she was last night. She must have been going a terrific pace, because while she was going through hospitals here this afternoon, the officers who have been with her gratefully took time out to sleep.[16]

Having covered seventeen islands, New Zealand, and Australia, and, by George Durno's estimate, having seen about 400,000 men in camps and hospitals, she began her homeward journey. It was, she confessed to Doris Fleeson, "most exhausting emotionally as well as physically." But she left the South Pacific with "a sense of pride in the young people of this generation which I can never express and a sense of obligation which I feel I can never discharge."[17]

When Admiral Halsey said good-by to her he told her it was impossible for him to express his appreciation for what she had done for his men. "I was ashamed of my original surliness," he wrote later. "She alone had accomplished more good than any other person, or any group of civilians, who had passed through my area. In the nine months left to me as COMSOPAC, nothing caused me to modify this opinion." But his misgivings were warranted, since the Japanese bombed Guadalcanal the night before her arrival and the night after her departure.[18]

The long flight home gave her a chance to think through the recommendations she wished to make to officials in Washington, beginning, of course, with her husband. First she prepared a report for the Red Cross, which, with its covering letter, came to nine pages single-spaced. Most of her other notations related to postwar planning and were items that she intended to take up with the president. She was fearful that once the war was over the returning veterans would be forgotten in a general slackening of national spirit and relaxation of controls. Legislation providing for jobs and education for veterans should be passed now and made known to the men in the services. There were other memos: "I do not like General..." "Men not chief concern anywhere. Officers have too much men too little [Guadalcanal]." "French natives poorly cared for."

Had his wife told him about her trip, reporters asked Roosevelt shortly after Eleanor's return. Yes, he replied, she has been talking almost ever since she got back.

In press conference and radio broadcast she spoke of her admiration for the generation that she had seen in the South Pacific. She had been told that this generation was soft. "Golly, if that generation is soft I don't know what it is going to be when it gets tough." Often the mother in her spoke out: "If you had seen the gatherings at the post offices each time we unloaded a bag of mail and it was distributed, you would know what your letters mean."

She ended the radio broadcast in which she reported on her trip
with a plea for racial and religious tolerance:

> I wonder if I can transmit to you the feeling which I have so strongly.
> In a nation such as ours every man who fights for us is in some way,
> our man. His parents may be of any race or religion, but if that man
> dies, he dies side by side with all of his buddies, and if your heart
> is with any man, in some way it must be with all.[19]

55. THE 1944 CAMPAIGN

NOT LONG AFTER ELEANOR RETURNED FROM THE PACIFIC, Franklin told her that the meetings he had long sought with Stalin and Chiang Kai-shek were at last to take place.

She wanted to accompany him because the tide of battle was turning, and the moment had arrived for political decisions that would shape the destinies of men and nations for decades to come. She wanted to be there when those decisions were made, perhaps to be able to interpose her "but Franklin" when in moments of weariness or irritation he seemed to be yielding to expediency or when the pulls of a class with which she had broken more decisively than he began to assert themselves.

If she asked to go and did not wait for his invitation, she was emboldened to do so by the picture she nowadays always carried with her of the broken boys she had visited in the hospital wards: "If we don't make this a more decent world to live in I don't see how we can look these boys in the eyes. They are going to fight their handicaps all their lives & what for if the world is the same cruel, stupid place."[1]

At Harvard, Churchill had broached the idea of a common Anglo-American citizenship. That worried Eleanor, and when she mentioned her concern to Henry Wallace, the two agreed that Churchill was pushing for a U.S.-British alliance—"and we believed in a United Nations one. We thought Franklin did but it might not yet be the moment to shout about it when Eden, Hull & Stalin were meeting and the principals may meet in November or December. So I asked FDR & gathered he would like us all to keep quiet."[2]

She did what he asked, yet within the privacy of the family she continued to prod and press for a United Nations approach. She did not like the role of goad, especially when she realized that Franklin was beginning to show signs of wearing out, but she was driven by the sense that a moment of opportunity had arrived when history was open, a moment that must not be lost. Not even illness turned her aside.

In October the president came down with intestinal flu. The founding conference of the UN Relief and Rehabilitation Administration was scheduled to meet a few weeks later in Atlantic City, and former Governor Lehman and Frank Sayre, who were in charge of the preparatory work, still did not know what the United States was prepared to offer. Should Eleanor bother the president, who was just beginning to recover? She decided that Lehman and Sayre had to have a chance to talk to him and put it up to her husband:

> Tonight the Lehmans' & Sayres' come to dine & get a chance to tell F. some of their troubles. The Relief Com. meeting is the 9th & they feel that no one is fighting for them or telling the country about their needs. They should lay in stores of food, clothing, seeds, farm machinery & they fight here with local demands. Now 44 nations will have to agree to take their quotas. It looks like our first test on working together & we are not even sure what our own Congress & our own agencies will do.[3]

What the United States might be prepared to do to save the liberated peoples from starvation related to its ability to enlarge its food output without a price inflation. And that, in turn, depended on subsidy payments, which were the administration's chief weapon for keeping down the cost of living. But Congress, in rebellion against wartime controls, was hostile to subsidies. Eleanor had been urging her husband to press Congress on the issue, and a week before he opened the UNRRA Conference he sent a message to Congress proposing a comprehensive food program. It delighted her. She found in it, she told friends, much that she had long advocated but which she had thought he had never accepted.[4]

That was Franklin's way. He fought her. He baited her. He used her to develop a case with which he might be in eventual, though not practical, sympathy. He tried to escape from her. And then he turned around and accepted her point of view. While the politician in him, the gay cavalier, the Hudson River squire, and the now weary and harassed president was often impatient with her, sometimes even angry, the idealist in him recognized her indispensability and valued the presence within the household of a loving and principled opposition.

So she thought she might be of help in the conferences at the summit and asked to go. But he put his foot down and said no; no women would be there. Some journeys he wanted her to make and some he vetoed.[5] There were times he wanted her with him and others when he did not. He set the pattern. He was in command. He ordered matters to suit himself. In continuing to serve him she walked a lonely path.

He did not want his wife to accompany him to Cairo and Teheran, but he liked to have members of his family with him and arranged to have Elliott, Franklin Jr., and John Boettiger, all of whom were in the European theater of war, meet him. Eleanor questioned having Franklin Jr. leave his destroyer, the *Mayrant*, which had been badly damaged in the Palermo bombing. It was scheduled to return to the States for repairs, and Franklin Jr., who had behaved with great gallantry in that action, felt he should be with his men on the difficult return journey. "I tried to make Pa *ask* but not *order*," Eleanor wrote James, "but he said he needed him & that was that." All the way from Oran to Tunis Roosevelt tried to persuade his son that the *Mayrant* could do without him. He needed him, the president said. "You know, I *am* the Commander-in-Chief and I can *order* you to join me." At this his son grinned and said he hoped his father would not do that. Finally the president gave up:

> F. jr. met the travelers in Tunis & blandly F. wrote me it seemed wiser for F. jr. to return with his own ship! I'm glad F. jr. had the sense of responsibility & F. respected it. Of course, I should never get excited for things always turn out this way![6]

The two Franklins arrived back in the United States at about the same time. It was a happy Christmas. Anna, Franklin Jr., John, and their families, including seven grandchildren, gathered in Hyde Park. When the grandchildren became too obstreperous in the library while their grandfather was with the photographers, Eleanor distracted them with carol singing. "It was busy but I think everyone enjoyed it," she wrote, and before the holidays were over she had been told pretty much everything that had taken place at Cairo and Teheran. She knew from a letter from Mme. Chiang that the president had gotten on well with the generalissimo and that largely due to the president's statesmanship the conference had been "a great success." The president felt he had been equally successful at Teheran in mediating between Stalin and Churchill. With the artistry of a practiced storyteller, he described his first encounter with Stalin. He had scarcely been installed in his quarters, he said, when the door opened and there stood the marshal.

He had paused on the threshold for a moment, taking Roosevelt's measure while Roosevelt took his. Then Roosevelt grinned and Stalin reciprocated, and they shook hands firmly. The president felt that by the end of the conference he and Stalin were coming to understand and trust each other. Roosevelt and Churchill told Stalin the date and plans for the cross-channel invasion of Europe, and Stalin informed Roosevelt of Russia's intention to enter the war against Japan once Hitler was defeated. The breakup of the Reich had been discussed and tentatively agreed to, but the decisions that most interested Eleanor were those dealing with the plans for a postwar peacekeeping organization:

> He found in a box yesterday a plan which he wrote when he was flat on his back years ago & Mr. Bok offered an award for a "peace plan" & I was on the jury so he never sent it in.... It shows F. says that you may forget what you once produced but it remains in your subconscious mind. Today it is virtually, with changes, the same as has been agreed on by some important people as the basic machinery to be set up.[7]

As happy and relaxed as Roosevelt was at Hyde Park during Christmas week, he returned to Washington an ailing man. Diagnosed as flu the malady proved persistent and nagging, and after two weeks in Washington, the president was ready for another rest. "FDR left for a week in H.P.," Eleanor wrote her Aunt Maude, "& I know he will return made over." The stay at Hyde Park helped him, but the old zest seemed to be lacking: "FDR says he feels much better but I don't think he longs to get back & fight." That was something new. In the past the rout of an infection had been accompanied by a return of political combativeness. The previous winter he had left Hyde Park after a siege of flu "full of health" and, as he wrote Winston Churchill, feeling like "a fighting cock." Now he could not shake his weariness. From a physical point of view the time had come for him to lay down his burdens, but Eleanor, who had strongly opposed a third term, did not feel that way about the fourth. As she was to tell her old Albany friend Margaret Doane Fayerweather just before Roosevelt departed on his last trip to Warm Springs: "I think he faced the fact, five years ago, that if he had to go on in office to accomplish his work, it must shorten his life, and he made that choice. If he can accomplish what he set out to do, and then dies, it will have been worth it. I agree with him."[8]

She agreed with him—a striking statement, for it showed that as

critical as Eleanor often was of his compromises, she trusted his judgment and leadership. And leadership carried a responsibility which
must be discharged even at the price of life. In her eyes, as well as his
own, he, too, was a soldier in the service, and with almost five million
young Americans overseas, how could he not finish the job? "Halsey
has been here & Eisenhower," she wrote Maude in January, 1944, "&
today F. is reported to have said the war will last another 18 months
which means I fear that we stay here & you stay in Ireland."

In November, 1943, Franklin had cheered her by saying that he
intended to fight on the domestic situation:

> F. said he knew we were at a low point at home, he knew liberals
> were discouraged but it was better to have it so now than later. He
> had to deal with realities & get all that was needed for war purposes
> & immediate postwar needs by keeping conservatives with him.
> If he had to run, & he hoped he wouldn't have to, he'd put in a
> fighting Nat. chairman & make a liberal campaign & clean out a
> lot of people playing with the Republicans whom he couldn't do
> without till certain things were sewed up. He also remarked that
> internationally he had to deal with many prima donnas & at home
> they were almost as bad.[9]

But the conservative coalition was more completely in control than
ever when Congress reassembled in January, 1944. "Congress seems
to behave worse daily," Eleanor grieved, and while Roosevelt spoke
his mind freely on such issues as an economic bill of rights, soldier
vote legislation, and equitable taxes, in order to get any legislation
whatsoever he increasingly had to make use of conservative-minded
men. So the new national chairman, instead of being a fighting liberal, as Franklin had hoped he would be, was a man with whom the
bosses felt comfortable. "I had a talk with our new Nat. Democratic
Chairman, Mr. Robert Hannegan, Irish Catholic from St. Louis,"
she wrote. "Practical politician, but that may be necessary." That was
Hannegan's last visit in a long time. Despite repeated invitations to
come to see her, he stayed away. Eleanor may have frightened him,
especially with her stand on civil rights.[10]

More alarming to Eleanor than Hannegan's appointment was the
president's portrayal of himself as "Dr. Win-the-War." "The remedies
that old Dr. New Deal used were for internal trouble," he told a press
conference, "But at the present time, obviously the principal emphasis,

the overwhelming first emphasis should be on winning the war." Afterward, with victory, reform would be in order again, but "we don't want to confuse people by talking about it now." Eleanor was sufficiently disturbed by the president's statement to dissent publicly— something she rarely did—when she was asked about it at her press conference. She, for one, she replied, had not laid the New Deal "away in lavender." Of course, the New Deal "has become rather old, rather stable and permanent, too, in many ways." But if it were to be dropped as a goal, the country needed something more in its place than "win-the-war."

She did not doubt the president's purposes, but she felt it necessary to offset the steady drumbeat of conservative pressures that played on the White House. In February, Congress overrode Roosevelt's veto of the tax bill, which he said provided relief "not for the needy but the greedy." The president, Eleanor said,

> is more philosophical daily. He knows he will only be elected if they can't find anyone else & I really think he doesn't care except he means to say & do as he thinks right at home. He's also fighting the British now at every turn & perhaps he's getting a bit weary but he'll go on as long as the people want him.[11]

She had to be away in March on the third of her wartime trips. "I'm leaving Miami with Tommy on the 6th to go to our stations in the Caribbean. F. wants me to go & so apparently does the Army & Navy. There won't be overseas wounded on this trip but they think the men feel out of it & forgotten."

Just before she left she received the upsetting news that Ruth and Elliott were getting a divorce:

> It has been a hard day, Ruth wrote announcing that she had heard from Elliott & in ten days would send him papers to sign & file for her divorce. I had hoped they would wait till after the war & I am sick at heart & grieve for the children. I said goodbye to Johnny. When his ship leaves they go straight to the Pacific....You said I was strong, well, I feel remarkably weak tonight, my "tummy" has felt queer all day & I'd like a shoulder to weep on![12]

In the first few days of her Caribbean tour, she covered Puerto Rico, which she had not seen since 1934 (Rex Tugwell was now its governor), the Virgin Islands, and Jamaica. The routine was much the same as it had been in the South Pacific and England—hospitals, military installations, speeches, press interviews, state receptions. Her husband must have cautioned her to be nice to officers as well as enlisted men, for she assured him in her first letter that she was seeing *"officers & men,"* underlining the words. Their wedding anniversary was on the seventeenth: "I'm sorry I won't be home but will you get something you want & let me pay for it on my return? I have $50-earmarked & I'd like you to squander it."[13]

She teased the president about a communication that came to her in Curaçao. A local merchant presented her with a medallion, and the accompanying note said that in the early part of the century President Roosevelt, "then Lieutenant on an American warship, visited our Island and at his request we gave him a small goat as mascot on the ship."

"Show FDR," she wrote on this, "& ask what he has been holding out on me all these years?" The president replied in kind:

> I have an alibi. The only time I was ever in Curaçao in my life was in 1904 when I went through the West Indies on a Hamburg-American Line "yacht." I was accompanied by and thoroughly chaperoned by my maternal parent.
>
> I was never given a goat—neither did anyone get my goat!
> This looks to me like a German plot![14]

She got as far west as the Galapagos Islands and as far east as the tip of Brazil, visiting American bases at Belém, Natal, and Recife, and writing Sra. Vargas, wife of the president of Brazil, afterward, "It is such a great country with potentialities for development which seem limitless." The commanding officers said her visit had been "helpful with Brazilians and good for our men," she informed her husband, obviously pleased that she was doing a good job. In addition to Brazil, she covered bases in Venezuela, Colombia, Ecuador, Panama, Guatemala, and Cuba. Although her primary purpose in these countries was to visit American troops, the welcome she received from the local populace showed how far her reputation had spread. The press was struck by the "spontaneous ovations" accorded her, especially as her movements were rapid, her arrivals in most cases unheralded. Noteworthy, too, they thought, was the turnout of women everywhere, who clearly saw her not only as a symbol of democracy and good neighborliness but as a champion of the rights of women. Even Cor-dell Hull, usually not one of her enthusiasts—for he rightly regarded her as a partisan of Sumner Welles, whom he hated—wrote her that she had made "an important contribution" to hemispheric solidarity.[15]

She returned to Washington to find Franklin still miserable and Dr. McIntire sufficiently concerned, especially by Franklin's "racking cough," to insist on a complete medical checkup. "FDR is not well but more will be known by Monday & I think we can help keep him in good health but he'll have to be more careful. I think the constant tension must tell & tho' he has said nothing, I think he has been upset by Elliott & Ruth." She was to see the doctors after the tests, but she herself felt the causes of his illness were not simply physical: "The nervous tension as well as the long burden of responsibility has a share in the physical condition I am sure."[16]

The results of the tests, Dr. McIntire later wrote, showed "a mod-erate degree of arteriosclerosis, although no more than normal in a man of his age; some changes in the cardiographic tracing; cloudiness in his sinuses; and bronchial irritation."* The doctors said he had to quit smoking in order to get rid of the sinus and throat trouble, and they also prescribed a vacation. He decided to go to Hobcaw, Bernard Baruch's 23,000 acre plantation in South Carolina. Perhaps Eleanor would have been less than happy about this plan had she known that Lucy (Mercer) Rutherfurd wintered not too far away and would be a secret visitor to the plantation while Franklin was there.[17]

He stayed at Hobcaw almost a month. During the first week Eleanor had no word from him at all but she heard through the Secret Service that he was leading a most restful existence. At the end of the second week she flew down for the day with the Curtins of Australia.

---

* This presumably is what Dr. McIntire told Eleanor, and it may be that she did not appre-ciate the nature of his illness. A young heart specialist, Dr. Howard G. Bruenn, who was brought in to examine the president at this time—the end of March—diagnosed "hyper-tension, hypertensive heart disease, cardiac failure (left ventricular) and acute bronchitis"—conditions, he added, that "had been completely unsuspected up to this time."

"I'm sure Mother did not know he had congestive heart failure," Anna asserted, "and if they said he had hypertension it would have meant very little to her." Neither was Anna told about the congestive heart failure. In 1956 Eleanor was interviewed by Clayton Knowles of the *New York Times* on the subject of the president's health. She said that the president's doctors had told him less than three months before his campaign for a fourth term that he "could quite easily go on with the activities of the Presidency," and that despite recurrent rumors to the contrary, he had never had a heart attack.

F. looks well but said he still has no "pep." Dr. McIntire says they will do final tests when he gets home in Sunday & put him on a strict regimen. He ought soon to get well. I'm trying to get him to come to Hyde Park at the end of June & only return two or three days a month during the summer months.[18]

Part of her husband's problem, she thought, was that he suspected the doctors did not really know what was the matter with him, and that worried him. Yet Dr. McIntire assured her that he was "confident the doctors do know & he [Franklin] is getting better." After Roosevelt returned to Washington, McIntire brought in the specialists again for a final examination in May. They found that he had recovered from "the infection in his sinuses and chest," but recommended avoidance of overwork, "a rest period after luncheon and free evenings, certainly after nine o'clock, so that he could relax." Despite the doctors' reassuring report, Eleanor continued to be anxious, for Franklin tired very easily and still had indigestion so that no outsider was allowed to come to meals. And that was an additional anxiety, for she thought it was "bad for him to have so much of the same people tho' of course he does have a good many in the office." What she meant was that access to the president would now be almost wholly controlled by his secretaries and that her opportunity to introduce dissenters and liberals through the luncheon- and dinner-guest list would be considerably reduced. "Pa is enjoying not doing things which bore him," she wrote James, "and he's getting so much pleasure out of having Anna around that I think he's going to shirk any but the office hour things for some time but it isn't necessity—just preference!"[19]

She had a toughness about physical ailments, always minimizing her own, and she tended to take the same attitude toward her husband's. Franklin Jr. told her before he left for the Pacific that he believed "the old man" loved to play the delicate one in order to have her concerned and to have her around a lot.[20] While she thought Franklin Jr. was right that his father exaggerated his frailty, she also received the impression that Franklin needed her more:

I must really live in the Big House this year, but whenever I can I want to be at the cottage.... My heart is in the cottage. I'll never like the Big House but suddenly F. is more dependent, the children & grandchildren look upon this as home & the cottage is just mine, so I must try to keep this lived in & really pleasant. Never from choice would I live here however & never alone.[21]

She knew Hyde Park's restorative powers for Franklin, and while he was still at Hobcaw she had written urging that he spend more time at Hyde Park, putting it in terms of Anna and her children rather than his health:

Anna has arranged to bring the children East & we will have to open & run the Big House from about the middle of June on. Couldn't you arrange to go up & stay a month at a time & only come back for two or three days once a month? It would be heavenly for us all.

I want to buy some little upholstered chairs & some few little things to make the servants' rooms more livable. I won't spend much & I think there is enough in the House account to do it. May I? Also, if I made a diagram of Mama's room so everything could be put back in place could I arrange it as a sitting room with a day bed in case someone had to sleep there? It could be very livable I think but we might have to repaper or paint over in that room.[22]

What a pathetic request. It was over forty years since Franklin had first brought her to Hyde Park, and Sara had been dead three years, yet Eleanor still felt she had to ask his permission to rearrange the furniture in Sara's bedroom.

She had made it pleasant, she announced triumphantly, in time for the first big week end in June when the president came up, accompanied as he often was by Princess Martha and her entourage: "I can work in it & not feel her [Sara's] presence in the room but over here there is no getting away from the bigness of the house & the multitude of people." There were compensations. Anna's children—Sistie, Buzz, and Johnny—were there, as was Elliott's first child, Bill. "It is years since I've had to see children go to bed & I love it & am having a good time."[23]

Franklin was more dependent, but he was also more in need of an uncritical companionship that she could not give. The surest sign was the way he turned to his daughter, Anna Boettiger, whose husband was overseas with the Army's military-government branch. When Hearst officials used his absence to bring the *Post-Intelligencer*'s editorial policies into line with the chain's, Roosevelt suggested that Anna come back East, live at the White House, and help him. He was a lonely man—Missy was gone; the Hopkinses had moved to their own house in Georgetown, and, moreover, there was at this time some estrangement in his relationship with Harry; Eleanor was too independent, too strong, ethically too unrelenting to provide him with the kind of relaxed, unjudging company that he wanted. The one thing she was not able to bring him, wrote her son, James, "was that touch of triviality he needed to lighten his burden."[24]

Yes, Anna said, she would love to move into the White House and help him, "'but not until I have talked with mother.' She was very frank with me. It would be wonderful for her. She personally would love it but she did not want to go through with me what she had gone through with Louise Hopkins."[25] It was the old story. Eleanor did not want another woman, even her daughter, pre-empting her prerogatives as mistress of the White House. Just before her trip to the Caribbean, Eleanor had discovered that Missy, a helpless invalid since 1941 when she had suffered a stroke and now under constant care in Massachusetts, had been invited to stay at the White House during her absence. She canceled the visit. "I was away last week when Grace [Tully] and Franklin arranged for you to come down on the 7th of March," she wrote Missy. "I am terribly sorry that they did not realize that I want to be here when you come." She should come for a week in April: "I am very sorry that they did not consult me before making plans but it is hard to get everyone together and I have been away for a few days at a time." She instructed Tommy to "show Grace letter & my answer. FDR has seen & approved answer."[26]

Since Anna had no wish to make life more difficult for her mother, there seemed to be no problem, and so Anna, with Johnny Boettiger, her youngest child, moved into the White House in the spring of 1944. But whatever mother and daughter's intentions, the relationship was shaped by the president—his needs, his weariness, his desire to be shielded from the one person who knew him beyond all masquerade and stratagem. More and more he lunched and dined alone with "Sis." More and more frequently Eleanor was heard to say, "Anna is the only one who would know about that"; "I'll have to ask Anna"; "We'll have to get Anna to ask the President."

There were other ladies whose company he liked. Princess Martha continued to entertain him, as did two spinster cousins, Margaret "Daisy" Suckley and Laura "Polly" Delano. Laura Delano was full of spice, snobbery, and malice, but like Daisy she did not contradict the president. Eleanor might remonstrate quietly about de Gaulle, whom the president detested and ridiculed, but Laura would egg him on. He should be tough on "that unspeakable person."[27]

Someone else who came to dinner at the White House—when Eleanor was away—was Lucy Rutherfurd, she of the "Mona Lisa smile." Mrs. Rutherfurd was another good listener. There was, too, when she and Franklin saw each other, the magic of remembered love to cast its glow over their present encounters. There were always other people around—Anna, Daisy Suckley, Laura Delano, the Secret Service, White House secretaries like Pa Watson, Steve Early, and Bill Hassett. It was all aboveboard, except that Eleanor was not told. They said to themselves that they were protecting her and they wanted to do so, for she was a woman of commanding dignity and of an almost saintly selflessness, whom all admired and some even loved. Within the limits of their loyalty to Franklin they were eager to do everything possible to protect her from hurt and humiliation. Yet for a woman who was intransigent about knowing the truth and facing up to it, such a deception, if and when she learned of it, would prove to be almost the final indignity. Franklin knew that even if no one else did.

May, 1944, was dominated by the impending invasion of Europe: "I feel as though a sword were hanging over my head, dreading its fall and yet know it must fall to end the war. I pray that Germany will give up now that the Russians are approaching and our drive in Italy has begun. However, I have seen no encouraging signs."[28] A service at the tomb of the unknown soldier at Arlington was almost more than she could bear—"I dread the invasion so much that it is getting on my nerves a bit I guess." The OWI asked her to prepare a radio speech to be used after the invasion began. "It is addressed to the mothers of the U.S.A.," she wrote, "& I can't think of what I want to say. I only know I don't want to say any of the things they suggested!"

She heard the invasion news from Franklin on June 5 before she went to bed, and she slept very little that night. Although it could not be a happy day because of the inevitable suffering, loss, and destruction, the tension was eased. The president seemed to her to be his old self again: he "keeps us all a bit undecided by saying he doesn't know what he will do & that when he hears Hitler is ready to surrender he will go to England at once & then in the next breath that he may go to Honolulu & the Aleutians!" If he did go to London, he informed Eleanor a few weeks later, he wanted her to accompany him.

There was other news in June that indicated a turning point in the war. Rome fell to the Allied armies and Marshall Pietro Badoglio's government, which had been denounced by liberal opinion as fascist-tainted, was replaced with a cabinet headed by a prominent anti-fascist. "I'm beginning to think I ought to be more patient for in the end FDR does seem to get pretty much what we want."[29]

The State Department began to move faster on its postwar planning. Eleanor wanted women to be drawn in and presided over a conference at the White House on "How Women May Share in Post-War Policy Making." "I wish very much," she wrote Jonathan Daniels, now one of the president's secretaries, "that you and Judge Rosenman would divide the day and come in as observers." Daniels did attend, and one of the items he received was "a roster of qualified women." It was clear from the comments of the participants that Eleanor Roosevelt led the list, even though her name was not on it.[30]

She was deeply concerned with the issue of full employment after the war. She invited Walter Reuther, whom she described to Baruch as "a rather intelligent young labor leader," to come to Hyde Park to discuss with her his ideas about industrial reconversion. She passed on Reuther's suggestions to the president, who advised her that "Jimmy Byrnes should really look this over and have a talk with Reuther." She also transmitted to Baruch, whose own recommendations on "War and Postwar Adjustment Policies" were then languishing in Congress, Reuther's point-by-point questions and disagreements with Baruch's approach. "You will notice that he thinks you will have to be worked on," her accompanying note said. "I do not think you really need that, but I would love to have a chance to talk over these questions and suggestions with you sometimes."

"Perhaps I do need to be worked on," Baruch replied, "but he needs better to understand the report." At Eleanor's instigation a correspondence sprang up between Reuther and Baruch with Eleanor acting as mailman, believing that each could educate the other and, in the process of doing so, educate her and give her some voice in what was shaping up as the key domestic issue. "To speak to Baruch," a memo that Tommy typed out for her began: "In regard to the sale of war plants is Aluminum Company, for example, going to be allowed to expand its monopoly or is the government going to reconvert the plants so as to break their monopoly?"

Harry Hopkins, who, because of illness, had been away from Washington since January, shared Reuther's concern about full employment but did not like Baruch's recommendations. "After being away for six months and reading and thinking of the kind of world we would like to have," he wrote Eleanor, who was in Hyde Park, "I am appalled at what must be done in this country if we are to accomplish anything like full employment. I am persuaded that the Baruch Plan will not do as a pattern, largely because it completely ignores all the human aspects for whose benefit our great industrial system should be organized." Eleanor advised Hopkins to talk with Baruch, adding with some asperity, "He does have more influence at the present time than any of us. We do have to work with Congress, you know, and he has more influence than you or I or the CIO, or most people who feel as we do, that the human things and full employment are the most important thing before us." She believed that Baruch was ready "to go along on anything that will be helpful, if he is convinced that it is good."[31]

Eleanor also served as mailman between her husband and Earl Browder, the leader of the American Communists.* In this case it was a form of reluctant servitude. "I do not like American Communists," she wrote Josephine Truslow Adams—painter, descendant of John Adams, and inveterate fellow-traveler—"because they have caused a great deal of trouble here and did all they could to hamper us before Germany went into Russia. Now that it suits their purposes they cooperate." That was written in November, 1943.

It was through Miss Adams that Browder's messages were being sent to the president via Eleanor. Because of her impeccable genealogical credentials, the Communists had given her a stellar role in the campaign to release Browder from the Atlanta penitentiary where he had been serving a four-year sentence for traveling on a false passport. Miss Adams was a middle-aged lady in tennis shoes, a vivid personality with flashes of imaginative brilliance that sometimes shaded into hallucination. She had taught art at Swarthmore College in the thirties, had an encyclopedic knowledge of flowers, and did first-rate flower paintings, one of which Esther Lape, who knew her, had given to Eleanor. On the basis of this frail connection, Miss Adams had written Eleanor after Pearl Harbor pleading for the release of Browder in the interests of national unity. Paul Robeson, one of her letters stated, felt that Browder was the only man who could overcome Negro bitterness because of their exclusion from defense jobs. But Eleanor could not forget Communist behavior during the Nazi-Soviet Pact. "I have

---

* My account of this episode is based on Eleanor Roosevelt's correspondence with Josephine Truslow Adams and interviews with Earl Browder and Esther Lape, a friend of Miss Adams'.

your letter," she replied, "but I do not feel I should ask the President about Mr. Browder."

In May, 1942, the president did commute Browder's prison term on the ground that a four-year sentence was far in excess of what was usual in passport-fraud cases. "I am sure now that the whole left wing is working only for victory," Miss Adams wrote Eleanor.

Browder, after his release, wanted a discreet channel of communication with Roosevelt, and Miss Adams, who was known among her friends as something of a fabulist, sold herself to the Communist leader as a person who had access to the president, even though the only time she had entered the White House was in 1939 as a member of a Philadelphia delegation that presented a petition to one of the president's secretaries. But Eleanor Roosevelt had answered her letters, and out of such flimsy materials Miss Adams managed to weave a persuasive picture of an intimate relationship with the White House.

By the end of 1943 Miss Adams's letters increasingly quoted Browder. "Willkie flirts heavily with the left," Miss Adams reported Browder as saying, "but those I know made up their minds to keep certain promises we made on national unity in case of the ending of the Atlanta situation." A month later a penciled note from Miss Adams described how "E.B." had kept James Patton, president of the National Farmers Union, who was leaning toward Willkie, in line for Roosevelt. To be sure, Mrs. Roosevelt understood this was a message intended for the president, Miss Adams ended her letter. "It would be tragic I think if the President did not have this story." Evidently Eleanor did not grasp who "E.B." was, or did not wish to, and replied as she did to all communications about a 1944 candidacy: "I am sure the President is only concerned with winning the war and not about who is the candidate."

"The man who argued Patton into supporting the President is a prominent left-wing leader," Miss Adams wrote back, scarcely able to conceal her vexation with the First Lady's obtuseness. "It would be quite natural perhaps if you did not trust him.... The President would I am sure take into consideration at least what he said and what he did from the point of view of realistic and practical politics without the least being sold on him or his ideas."

By the beginning of January, 1944, it was clear to Eleanor that Miss Adams's letters were intended for the president. "Type," she instructed Tommy, "give FDR & say I know nothing about her reliability." Evidently Roosevelt was interested, for from that time on all the letters from Miss Adams were sent over to him. There was every reason for the president to be intrigued, since Browder was well informed on what was going on in left and labor circles and the information that he transmitted, along with reports on what the Communists were doing to build national unity behind the war effort, including their moves to cool the ghettos and to keep labor from striking, clearly served the country's purposes.

The Communist drive for unity and harmony on the home front stopped short, however, of those whom Browder called "Trotsky-ites" and who, in fact, included all liberal and labor leaders who were actively anti-Communist. His messages via Miss Adams were filled with warnings—against James Loeb of the Union for Democratic Action, against Roger Baldwin of the American Civil Liberties Union, against labor leaders like Reuther, Dubinsky, and Alex Rose. There was a long attack on James Carey, secretary of the CIO, who was denounced as "a Catholic ending in the same camp with the Trotsky-ites out of his bitter natural hate of the Communists." Eleanor rarely commented on the contents of the Adams letters, but Carey was a personal friend. She had given the letter to the president, Mrs. Roosevelt wrote Miss Adams, "but I know you are wrong about Mr. Carey."

"I am glad to be wrong about Mr. Carey," Miss Adams wrote molli-fyingly. "The thing that upset me was the Town Hall debate in which he disputed the section of the President's message referring to the labor draft." Eleanor saw no perfidy in Carey's opposition to a labor draft. "Any official of the C.I.O. must be against a Universal Draft because his constituency is," she replied, "but that does not mean he is opposed to the President." When Browder, through Miss Adams, attacked the *Nation*, the *New Republic*, the *New Leader*, and "the special Trotskyite section of *PM* headed by Wechsler" for being unduly critical of the president, Eleanor defended Wechsler and the liberal weeklies. "He has a good mind and is honest," and the publications that Browder has crit-icized "make more sense to me than your confusing Trotskyite talk."

The president found Browder's all-out support helpful, but he was content to let the correspondence be handled by his wife. It was Browder's impression that the president felt more kindly toward him than Mrs. Roosevelt, although it was Mrs. Roosevelt who wrote the attorney general and the commissioner of immigration in 1944 when a deportation order was issued against Browder's Russian-born wife Irene. "I think she did so because the President asked her to," said Browder. "She was not sympathetic either to me or to my wife." The president, as Browder had correctly surmised, was a realistic politician, and whatever served the purposes of his policy he was prepared to use. Mrs. Roosevelt, the moralist, found it more difficult.

Just as Baruch, Hopkins, and Reuther all felt it was important to have Eleanor on their side in the conflict that was taking shape over reconversion policies, so the more socially minded nuclear scientists were coming to her with their anxieties about the uses of atomic energy. She had first learned about this most closely guarded secret of war in July, 1943, from a young physicist working on the A-bomb project. "He was convincing & rather frightening & we must have peace in the future" was her reaction to her meeting with the young man in a letter that she wrote afterward in which she did not indicate what it was that had frightened her.[32]

Scientist Irving S. Lowen was employed at the Metallurgical Laboratory, the Chicago phase of the Manhattan Project, which had among its workers Enrico Fermi, Leo Szilard, and Eugene Wigner. The last two had persuaded Einstein to send the letter to Roosevelt that led to the launching of the atomic project, and it was under Fermi's leadership that the first chain reaction had been achieved. The MetLab scientists were among the most creative at work in the Manhattan district and were also the ones most concerned with the political and social implications of this new force that they were freeing for man to use. In 1943 their anxiety centered on the fear that the Nazis might develop the bomb first. A message had reached them from a German scientist named Fritz Houtermans. "Hurry up—we're on the track" was the substance of his warning to his colleagues. The MetLab scientists felt that the military men in charge of the project thought of it as a weapon for the next war and did not grasp the need for speed. They were equally sure that the Army's bringing in of the duPont Corporation for the construction of the reactors at Oak Ridge and Hanford meant a nine-month "learning period" delay. The costly preparations that duPont set about making seemed, the scientists felt, to betoken the corporation's interest in obtaining exclusive postwar control of this new energy source.

By the summer of 1943 they were sufficiently exercised over these matters (Arthur H. Compton, the director of MetLab, later wrote that he had had a "near rebellion" on his hands) to decide to go out of channels and try to reach the president directly—and Mrs. Roosevelt seemed the best way to do that. Lowen, an associate of Wigner's, thought he could get an introduction from an NYU colleague,

Professor Clyde Eagleton, and volunteered to go to her not as a representative of the worried scientists, but on his own.

Eleanor saw Lowen at her Washington Square apartment in late July and immediately called the president to urge him to see the scientist. The president proposed that he talk with Dr. Vannevar Bush and Dr. James Conant, director and deputy director, respectively, of the Office of Scientific Research and Development. "Dearest Franklin," Eleanor wrote afterward, typing out the letter herself:

> Mr. Irving S. Lowen, the man whom I telephoned about will be in Washington tomorrow.
>
> Mr. Lowen says that Dr. Bush and Dr. Conant would be of absolutely no use because they have been so close to the project that they have perhaps lost the sense of urgency which these younger men have.
>
> There is they believe, a chance that a very brilliant man who is working on this in Germany may have been able to develop it to the point of usefulness. The Germans are desperate and would use this if they have it ready. It is imperative they feel that we proceed quickly to perfecting it and these young scientists believe that they are already two years behind all that they might have accomplished if they had been allowed to progress.
>
> They want an investigation by an impartial outsider who can see the possibilities of what might happen, but who is not a scientist, a man of judicial temperament who will weigh the possibilities.
>
> Mr. Lowen thinks you might want to speak to some of the other men
>
> Professor H. C. Urey, Columbia
> Professor Wigner
> Professor Szilard
> Professor Fermi
> Professor Oppenheimer
> Dr. Gale Young
> Professor A. H. Compton...[33]

"I hope you see Lowen. He impresses me with his own anxiety," she added in longhand.

Roosevelt did see Lowen the next day and evidently the young man made an impression, for when the president talked about the bomb to James Byrnes that summer, he told Byrnes that he thought the Germans were ahead in the race to develop it. Roosevelt also instructed Lowen that if he wished to send him a personal message again, he should place it in a sealed envelope for the president's eyes only and send it to him via Grace Tully.

If the intention of this directive was to cut his wife out of the chain of communication (the president must have been annoyed at the breach in the project's secrecy that the scientists' going to Eleanor represented), it was ineffective. A few months later when Lowen asked to see the president again because nothing materially had changed and the Germans, in the view of some of the MetLab leading scientists, were "about to use the weapon we all fear," Roosevelt, about to leave for Casablanca, referred him to Conant. A desperate Lowen again went to Eleanor.

With the president in Casablanca she did not know to whom to turn. "The announcement from Germany yesterday of a secret force to be used to destroy in great & unprecedented ways," she wrote her husband, "has made one young scientist jittery again & he is calling me on the phone this morning but what can I do?" She decided she had to do something, and arranged for Lowen to see Early and Rosenman as well as Baruch.★[34]

"This fellow came into Steve's office, a little wild-eyed," Judge Rosenman recalled. "Is your room tapped?" was the scientist's first remark to Early. "If he had not been sent by Mrs. Roosevelt, Steve would have thrown him out then and there," said Rosenman. Then Lowen darted over to a closed door and threw it open to see if anyone was listening at the keyhole. Reassured that all was secure in the White House, he told them about the A-bomb project and the fears of the scientists that the project was moving slowly because of military red tape and duPont's interest in a postwar monopoly of atomic energy.

"Do you know anything about this?" Early asked Rosenman after the man had left.

"Not a thing."

"What should we do?"

"You and I," suggested Rosenman, "should get into a car and go to

---

★The announcement that had alarmed the scientists was an Associated Press dispatch from London, December 3, 1943, which read: "Again threatening retaliation for the air war upon Germany, the Berlin radio said today that the German High Command 'intends by one fell drastic stroke to end the unbridled mass murder,' and added that 'mankind is not far from the point where it can at will blow up half the globe.'"

see Bob Patterson." They did. Judge Patterson, the assistant secretary of war, confirmed that a bomb, thousands of times more powerful than dynamite, was being developed and expressed complete confidence in General Leslie R. Groves, who was in charge of the project. "The first thing to be done is to transfer this fellow," added Patterson.

Baruch saw Lowen the next day.

> The young man was in a highly nervous state. All I could get from him was that he was engaged in developing a secret process at the University of Chicago, and that he was convinced that his work was being obstructed. I could learn no more, but I had heard enough to know that the matter was not in my bailiwick. I asked Dr. Conant to see the troubled physicist.

There was no way around Conant, who, the Chicago group felt, constituted part of the problem. "I should like to take this opportunity to tell you," Conant reported to the president upon the latter's return from Casablanca,

> that in my opinion, based on intimate knowledge of this whole project, everything is going as well as humanly possible. I believe we are very fortunate in having in General Groves, the Director of the enterprise, a man of unusual capability and force. Criticisms like Mr. Lowen's are based on an incomplete view of the total picture on the one hand and on the other represent the inevitable emotional reactions of human beings involved in an enterprise of this sort.[35]

One consequence for Lowen was that he was transferred out of the project. "I seem to be pretty effectively stopped from doing any more fighting," he reported to Eleanor. If she wanted any more information, Lowen continued, Wigner, Szilard, and Fermi would be happy to come to Washington to supply it.[36]

In a memo to the president, Eleanor suggested that he might ask Dr. Conant to see Wigner, Szilard, and Fermi "to tell about their work which has such important implications for the future."

Roosevelt was getting a little impatient. "Dear Van," he wrote Dr. Bush, "This young man has bothered us twice before and I think Jim Conant has seen him twice. I fear, too, that he talks too much. Do you think we should refer the matter to Conant?" Five days later Bush reported back:

Conant had a long talk in Chicago with Fermi and Wigner, and tells me they are quite satisfied with the arrangements now in effect and do not share Lowen's views. I spent all day with Szilard yesterday. His criticism boils down to the feeling that his group have not been fully used. There has, of course, been a reluctance to introduce scientists of foreign origin to the full knowledge of a matter of potentially great military importance. There is also a matter of early patent applications which has its difficulties.

My conclusion is that there have been no more missteps and delays than ought to be anticipated on a matter of this novelty and complexity and that the organization is sound and in capable hands.[37]

Conant's report to the president was not wholly correct, according to Wigner: "By that time I felt it was too late for a change, but we certainly did not tell Conant we did not share Lowen's views." While reconciled to the arrangements with duPont, the MetLab men were more than ever concerned with long-range development and control of the atom. Eleanor saw Lowen again, three weeks after D day. "We now have the discovery, I'm told, which he feared Germany would have first but I gather no one wants to use it for its destructive power is so great that no one knows where it might stop." "Our fears were political," recalled Wigner. "They were fears about letting this destructive force loose upon the world."[38]

To the nuclear scientists, and to the country generally, Eleanor and Franklin were partners. In the 1944 presidential campaign those who viewed her as a "dangerous" woman counted this against Roosevelt, but to the New Deal wing of the Roosevelt coalition her presence at his side was a reassurance as to Roosevelt's purposes. The prospect of a fourth term gave Eleanor fewer problems than had the third: "I don't know what F. will decide but if he thinks he is needed I'm sure he'll make the fight & if he loses, I shant be as sorry as I would be if he didn't accept the responsibility when he felt he should."[39]

She listened to the Republican convention, which nominated a Dewey-Bricker ticket at the end of June:

All promises & no performance. We'll promise too in our convention & how little any of us really know what we can do after the war. All one should say is: "Build a character that can meet new conditions without fear, develop the power to think things thro' &

face facts & recognize the interdependence among men!" I wonder why we can't all be humble & less bombastic?[40]

May Craig, who stopped at Hyde Park en route home from the Republican convention, told Eleanor that the Republican campaign was to be keynoted to youth as against "a tired old man." "Fortunately, he looks pretty vigorous," was Eleanor's comment to May, as it was to a discouraged young friend who wrote her that the Democratic party had turned timid and respectable. The president had to compromise at the moment because winning the war was the most important thing, Eleanor replied. "When the war is over even an elderly gentleman like the President may do some surprising things."[41]

The president's health fluctuated wildly and deceptively. His wife could write about Franklin's postwar plans, yet Ed Flynn, who saw him after his return from Hobcaw, was so shocked by his appearance and by a querulousness and apathy that were wholly foreign to his old friend that he begged Eleanor to use her influence to keep him from running again. There is no evidence that she did; on the contrary, and especially after the Republicans had nominated Thomas E. Dewey, she found herself contemplating the possibility of her husband's defeat with apprehension for the country, even though from her "own point of view four more years in the White House is almost more than I can bear. I am very conscious of age & the short time I have in which to live as I like & I know that is such selfish thinking that one has no right even to let it be in one's mind."[42]

She had a profound trust in her husband's leadership, but it did not keep her from disagreeing with him. She did her utmost to keep him from dropping Wallace as his running mate even though she had to agree with him that Wallace was not a good politician. "I wrote a column on Wallace but Franklin says I must hold it till after the convention. I wish I were free!" She accompanied Franklin to the West Coast while the Democratic convention was in progress. "Wallace is fighting," she reported, sadly adding that his radio speech "was nice but not inspiring." She sought to console Wallace when he lost. "I had hoped that by some miracle you could win out, but it looks to me as though the bosses had functioned pretty smoothly. I am told that Senator Truman is a good man, and I hope so for the sake of the country." A week later she wrote more positively about Truman to Esther Lape: "I am much more satisfied with Senator Truman than I would have been with some of the others who were seriously considered."[43]

Publicly her role in the 1944 campaign was little different from what it had been in earlier ones: "I have been very busy making 'non-political' speeches about registering and voting!" But her behind-the-scenes participation was considerably reduced. Farley and Flynn had always consulted her, indeed, had sought to pull her into the campaign as deeply as she allowed, but Hannegan gave her a wide berth, avoiding her invitations before the Democratic convention to come in and talk to her. Not only was she a strong Wallace partisan, but she was a transmitter of messages that neither he nor the president wanted to receive, such as Walter White's warning that the Negro vote should not be taken for granted. White had telephoned Eleanor just before the convention to warn that the majority of Negroes would vote Republican unless a very strong civil-rights plank was adopted at the convention. She tried, unsuccessfully, to get the president to see White, but the Democratic leaders feared that a strong plank would mean a split with the southern democrats. So Hannegan kept away from Eleanor, and after the convention when he very much wanted to see her, there was always a reason why she could not fit him in. She was no political novice.[44]

Another reason that she was less involved in the 1944 campaign was Roosevelt's own aloofness from it. He was withdrawn and indifferent. "I don't think Pa would really mind defeat," Eleanor wrote James. "If elected he'll do his job well. I feel sure and I think he can be kept well to do it but he does get tired so I think if defeated he'll be content. ...I am only concerned because Dewey seems to me more and more to show no understanding of the job at home or abroad." Pa Watson remarked that the president "just doesn't seem to give a damn." As usual, when every other approach failed, the White House staff and the politicians turned to Eleanor to persuade her husband to come down "into the dusty political arena" and begin to swing.[45]

Eleanor felt that the president owed it to the country to campaign—it was "only through the actual sight and feel of the crowds that the man in public life really gets to know what the people who back him believe in." Moreover, he looked well to her after his return from Honolulu and the Aleutians, although he did look older: "Whatever he had last spring took a toll, but I guess he feels his experience and equipment will help him to do a better job than Mr. Dewey." She thought so, too, even though within the family she fought the conservative pressure on him, which, if yielded to, she feared might mean losing the peace. She and the president drove down to Fishkill to have tea with the Morgenthaus. The future of Germany came up, and Morgenthau chided the president for appointing Robert Murphy as political adviser to Eisenhower in Germany: "Why pick Robert Murphy for the job? In the minds of the people it connoted Darlan★ and everything that goes with it." Eleanor intervened to say that given the attitude of the pope it was a mistake to send a Catholic to Germany. The president came to the pope's defense, reported Morgenthau, "particularly in regard to this last speech the Pope made on private property. The President said the Pope had always been for private property and was against Communism." Morgenthau did not find the president's line of reasoning reassuring or convincing, but he was gratified to note Eleanor's attitude on the future of Germany: "She had been slightly pacifist before the war and I thought she might think we should go a little easy on the Germans, but she doesn't."[46] Eleanor accompanied the president to Quebec for his talks with Churchill on the future of Germany. "I hope for the sake of these negotiations & the future that F. is elected & continues vigorous in action till the major trends are established."[†47]

With Roosevelt silent, the polls in early September showed an alarming drop in his strength and a rise in Dewey's. The clamor that he campaign actively increased, and Eleanor quietly abetted the efforts of his associates to get him to do so. She seated a personable friend, Trude Pratt, who was working at Democratic headquarters, next to him at dinner at Hyde Park:

> I had a long talk with the Boss, sticking out my neck—trying to convince him to speak more often—and before crowds. . . . He said

---

★ The U.S. decision to recognize the authority in French North Africa of the Vichyite Admiral Jean Darlan when Allied troops landed there had provoked an uproar that only abated when Darlan was assassinated a few weeks after the invasion began.

† "As to your feelings about 'unconditional surrender,'" Eleanor wrote Helena Hirst in London (Sept. 28, 1943),

> I think that was my husband's phrase because he uses it very often. I think the feeling is that Germany needs to be made to feel that civilized people do not associate with people who accept brutality such as they have meted out to the Jews and other conquered peoples. One can not pin all the blame on Hitler. The people accepted him and though it was done through education, they will have to take the consequences I fear, until new generations have grown up. I am afraid I have very little sympathy for any people or any nationality whether German, Italian or Japanese, who accept tamely, actions of their governments and then think they are not to blame for them.

he did not want to speak—his voice was bad. I told him he had to—and his ills were imaginary—and if he did not really want to win he should not have run (after that I almost died)—but he said, I was right—and would I go on. Yes, I said, it's a tragedy that both Hannegan and Porter were green and that you have to do it all alone. Yes, he said, that was bad—what else? They could think only of the Democratic Party, I said, and had no courage. Yes, he said, *he* was interested in a new liberal party—and that's why he wanted to see Wendell (whose death may be very bad for us). What else? By that time I was no longer afraid of him, so we talked about the kind of thing that should be done.... [48]

The proddings were effective, or perhaps he enjoyed the proddings because they pushed him in the direction he had always planned to go. A week before he went to Hyde Park he surprised his news conference by announcing that he would make a political speech to the Teamsters Union on September 23. That speech proved to be a political classic:

These Republican leaders have not been content with attacks on me, on my wife, or on my sons. No, not content with that, they now include my little dog, Fala. Well, of course, I don't resent attacks, and my family doesn't resent attacks, but Fala *does* resent them.... He has not been the same dog since. [49]

He was still champ. He began to campaign as energetically as he had in 1940, and as he campaigned, wrote Robert Sherwood, he "improved visibly in strength and resilience," even regaining the use of his legs sufficiently to stand and speak from the rear of his campaign train. Sherwood did not know how Roosevelt had accomplished this, but he believed that "it was largely due to the determination of Mrs. Roosevelt who supported him in refusal to accept physical defeat as she had done when he was first stricken in 1921."[*][50]

The Monday before the election, Roosevelt made what he called "another sentimental journey" in an open car through the Hudson Valley. Eleanor did not go along. "They always stop at the same places," she explained, "and I think the one in Beacon is the very spot where

---

[*] There was "a complete disregard of the rest regimen" in October, Dr. Bruenn wrote. "He really enjoyed going to the 'hustings,' and despite this his blood pressure levels, if anything, were lower than before."

the President made his very first campaign speech when he entered politics as a young man, running in a 'hopeless' district for the State Senate." She caught up with Franklin at his last stop in Poughkeepsie, where he was introduced by Dean Mildred Thompson of Vassar, and then she dashed down to headquarters in New York City to thank the campaign workers on the president's behalf.

This election night at Hyde Park was the same as the others had been, yet somehow different: the neighbors came in and the president's intimates were there, as were Eleanor's; but all four sons were overseas, and Anna and her son Johnny were the only members of the immediate family who were present. There were other faces missing as well. When at 9:00 P.M. the dining room was cleared and "the real business," as Eleanor put it, of tabulating the votes began, she thought of Louis Howe, "who really enjoyed sitting in his shirt sleeves and calculating the percentages," of Missy, who always sat with the little group of men around the president, and of Sara, who could never understand Eleanor's detachment on such occasions.

At 11:40 the traditional torchlight parade from the village arrived, and this time Roosevelt permitted himself to be wheeled out to address them from the wheel chair, instead of putting on his heavy braces and standing up. It was too early to make any statement, he told his neighbors, "but it looks like I'll be coming up here from Washington again for another four years." The president was wheeled back into the house, and Eleanor beckoned the scores of shivering reporters and photographers to come in and warm themselves in front of the library's fires, which she ordered stoked up, and to share in the cheese, crackers, and coffee that were being served. The president returned to the dining room. The returns grew progressively better, and at 3:15 in the morning Dewey conceded.

"There was a great deal of excitement all through the evening among many people about us," Eleanor wrote afterward, "but I can't say that I felt half as much excited as I will feel the day that I hear the war is over."[51]

Although the president's popular margin was reduced in comparison to the 1940 returns, his victory was substantial and included a sizable increase in Democratic strength in Congress. To Eleanor, victory immediately posed the question: "What for?" When they returned to Washington she put that question to the president and Harry Hopkins in a talk she had with them about the next four years and which Hopkins recorded:

Mrs. Roosevelt urged the President very strongly to keep in the forefront of his mind the domestic situation because she felt there was a real danger of his losing American public opinion in his foreign policy if he failed to follow through on the domestic implications of his campaign promises. She particularly hoped the President would not go to Great Britain and France and receive great demonstrations abroad for the present, believing that that would not set too well with the American people.

She impressed on both of us that we must not be satisfied with merely making campaign pledges; the President being under moral obligation to see his domestic reforms through, particularly the organizing of our domestic life in such a way as to give everybody a job. She emphasized that this was an overwhelming task and she hoped neither the President nor I thought it was settled in any way by making speeches.[52]

Of this Hopkins note Sherwood wrote that Eleanor was known as the president's "eyes and ears" but that there were many others who reported to him. The unique function that she performed for her husband was "as the keeper of and constant spokesman for her husband's conscience."

Her allegedly radical influence upon the president had been an issue in the campaign, a "phony" one, she said. She had never had any real power or influence, she maintained. In any case, "these aren't the things people make decisions about. But, the election showed that the people on the whole believe even a woman has a right to do what she believes is the right thing." With the world "rocking on its foundations," she did not intend to play the part of "a Dresden doll."[53]

56. DEATH OF THE COMMANDER-IN-CHIEF

———————————————————◆

ELEANOR WAS "IN FOR IT" FOR ANOTHER FOUR YEARS, ESTHER Lape wrote her on Election Day, adding that Eleanor had an obligation to think of how she could use her power most effectively. "She's not the only one to tell me I have a responsibility but I feel inadequate," Eleanor wrote on Esther's letter.[1] Her sense of inadequacy did not keep her from expressing her views to Franklin more forcefully than ever.

At the time of the Democratic convention when Eleanor had protested the party's "pussyfooting" on all controversial issues, the president had put her off with the plea "wait till November." She was fearful then that in November there would be other "compelling reasons . . . for tactics which may be wise but which I feel are just appeasement."[2] That was what now happened. The reorganization of the State Department that followed Hull's resignation alarmed and outraged her. She expressed herself forcefully in a letter to her husband, who had left for Warm Springs. The letter is worth quoting in some detail for it shows how tough, relentless, and perhaps unfair, she could be:

> Dearest Franklin: December 4, 1944
> I realize very well that I do not know the reasons why certain things may be necessary nor whether you intend to do them or do not intend to do them.
>
> It does, however, make me rather nervous for you to say that you do not care what Jimmy Dunne thinks because he will do what you tell him to do and that for three years you have carried the State Department and you expect to go on doing it. I am quite sure that Jimmy Dunne is clever enough to tell you that he will do what you want and to allow his subordinates to accomplish things which will get by and which will pretty well come up in the long time results to what he actually wants to do.
>
> In addition, it seems to me pretty poor administration to have a man in whom you know you can not put any trust, to carry out

the things which you tell him to do. The reason I feel we can not trust Dunne is that we know he backed Franco and his regime in Spain. We know that now he is arguing Mr. Winant and the War Department in favor of using German industrialists to rehabilitate Germany because he belongs to the group which Will Clayton represents, plus others, who believe we must have business going in Germany for the sake of business here.

I sent you a memo on Yugoslavia, not because I want it sent to Mr. Stettinius because he has a duplicate, but just because I want you to read it while you have the time. This does not look as though Tito refused to send for things which would relieve his civilian population.

One of the young officers who worked for Gen. Donovan in Yugoslavia and who is now on leave, came to see me and said he had written a report which they promised to send you. He is afraid you have never seen it. In it he tells certain things which are gradually turning most of the people against us and toward Russia. He said that at first, Europeans everywhere thought America would help them but if we really want Russian influence to be paramount, we are going about it in the best possible way.

Neither you nor I can, of course, tell Bill Donovan that this young man told me these things, but you might ask whether there are any conflicting reports on the situation in Spain. The fine Catholic hand is visible in Europe and in our State Department.

With Dunne, Clayton and Acheson under Secretary Stettinius, I can hardly see that the set-up will be very much different from what it might have been under Dewey.

I hope the weather will be warmer and that you are getting some swimming and I am glad you are going to stay a little bit longer.

I suppose I should trust blindly when I can't know and be neither worried or scared and yet I am both and when Harry Hopkins tells me he is for Clayton, etc. I'm even more worried. I hate to irritate you and I won't speak of any of this again but I wouldn't feel honest if I didn't tell you now.

Much love,

E. R.

Two days later she was back at him again. The United States had protested Churchill's veto of Count Carlo Sforza, the distinguished Italian anti-fascist, as foreign minister in the new Italian cabinet:

I like the statement on Sforza and our attitude toward the other governments very much indeed, but, are we going to use any real pressure on Winston? I am afraid words will not have much effect.

All of the newspapers which were agin you and all of the people who were agin you in the election are now loudly praising the State Department set-up. It does make me nervous and perhaps it is all right if you can make them all behave like reformed characters so the rest of us who have been doubting Thomases will have to take our hats off to them.

While the president gave his wife the impression that he did not agree with her criticism of the new command group in the State Department, in Warm Springs some of his actions showed that her criticisms had struck home. He refused to approve a press release submitted to him by Secretary of State Stettinius announcing the appointment of six new assistant secretaries because the name of Archibald MacLeish was not included. William D. Hassett, his press secretary, quoted him as saying that "Archie was the only liberal in the bunch, which is top-heavy with Old Dealers."[3] Who rendered him a greater service of love—Eleanor with her criticism, or Laura and Daisy, who were at Warm Springs (as was Lucy Rutherfurd the first few days of his stay) and who were concerned only with making this overburdened man's life as pleasant as possible and introducing no jarring political note?

Eleanor wanted to see him on his return from Warm Springs, she warned him, "before you begin to look weary!"[4] But he was in no hurry to see her. She, haunted by the fear of a war fought in vain, pressed her husband more strongly than ever. He, with the responsibility for victory or defeat, not to mention ten million lives, his energy and patience quickly exhausted, put her off more abruptly than ever before, sometimes without even a softening jollification. Anna, caught in the middle, sympathized with her father:

> Although she knew the doctors had said he should have half an hour of relaxation, no business, just sitting around, maybe a drink, she would come in more and more frequently with an enormous bundle of letters which she wanted to discuss with him immediately and have a decision.[5]

On one occasion when Anna was mixing cocktails and her mother came in with her usual budget of questions and problems, "Father blew his top. He took the bundle of letters and pushed it over to me. 'Sis, you handle this.' And here I was striving to be neutral. What she wanted was o.k. but for him it was one more thing at the end of a tough day."

Yet more than anyone else Eleanor helped him conserve his physical energy and emotional vitality. Missy had died in August while the president was in the Pacific,* and it was Eleanor who had attended the funeral, as she did the Mass for Alfred E. Smith in October and the memorial service for Wendell Willkie a few days later. At the inaugural receptions, while the president saw only a few intimates in the Green Room—chiefly family and Princess Martha and her entourage—she stood for hours, until she was drawn and exhausted doing the ceremonial things, shaking hands with hundreds of her husband's supporters, visiting the National Democratic Club to shake more hands, then moving on to a gathering of the Democratic faithful at Oscar Ewing's and ending the evening at the Electors' Dinner. She was always ready to ease Franklin's burdens by taking them on herself, but problems had to be faced and decisions made, and she could not remain silent when it seemed to her, as in the case of the State Department appointments, that he was following "the line of least resistance."[6] With an invincible belief that will and spirit could transcend infirmity, she was reluctant to treat him as an invalid or to have him accept invalidism. Indelibly engraved in her memory was the precedent to be avoided, if humanly possible, of Mrs. Woodrow Wilson standing between a nation calling for leadership and her invalid husband.

He had rallied so often before, but this time it seemed to be different:

For the first time I was beginning to realize that he could no longer bear to have a real discussion such as he always had. This was impressed on me one night when we were discussing with Harry

---

*A statement issued at the White House in Roosevelt's name said:

Memories of more than a score of years of devoted service enhance the sense of personal loss which Miss LeHand's passing brings. Faithful and painstaking, with a charm of manner in speech, by tact and kindness of heart, she was utterly selfless in her devotion to duty. Hers was a quiet efficiency, which made her a real genius at getting things done.

How much Roosevelt valued Missy was shown by his will when it was filed for probate after his death. It provided that Missy's medical expenses should be taken care of out of the income from his estate up to 50 per cent, the remainder going to Eleanor.

Hooker the question of compulsory military service for all young men as a peacetime measure. Harry Hooker had long believed in this and had worked for it. I disliked the idea thoroughly and argued against it heatedly, probably because I felt Harry was so much in favor of it that Franklin seemed to be getting only one side of the picture. In the end, I evidently made Franklin feel I was really arguing against him and I suddenly realized he was upset. I stopped at once, but afterwards Harry Hooker took me to task and said I must not do that to Franklin again. I knew only too well that in discussing the issue I had forgotten that Franklin was no longer the calm and imperturbable person who, in the past, had always goaded me to vehement arguments when questions of policy came up. It was just another indication of the change which we were all so unwilling to acknowledge.[7]

Two days after the inauguration the president left for the Yalta Conference. Eleanor had asked to go along, but as in the case of the Cairo and Teheran conferences he had turned her down:

Franklin felt that if I went it would only add to the difficulties as everyone would feel they had to pay attention to me, but since Sarah Churchill was going, Franklin thought Anna would be a help and a comfort and I am sure she will be. I am very proud of her, she has grown into such an extremely capable person and a fine person as well as a lovely one.[8]

So Eleanor wrote to Lady Willert two weeks after the travelers left, but what she said of her pride and pleasure in Anna's having accompanied her father only partially disclosed her feelings. She was worried about Franklin's condition, his irritability, his impatience, his tendency to follow the path of least resistance. "FDR and Anna go tomorrow night and I'm not really happy about this trip but one can't live in fear, can one?"

Just before his departure Roosevelt sent to Congress his nomination of Wallace to succeed Jesse Jones as secretary of commerce and head of the Reconstruction Finance Corporation. The battle that broke out in Congress seemed to Eleanor symptomatic of the "bigger" fight: "Are we to be Liberal or Conservative?" Roosevelt's letter dismissing Jones did not help Wallace because it made it appear that the only reason he was asking Jones to take another job in his administration was to repay Wallace for a political loyalty in 1944 that entitled him to whatever job he wanted—except secretary of state. "The Jones-Wallace fight is on," Eleanor reported to her husband in Yalta:

> Of course Jones has behaved horribly & your letter when published was hard on Wallace. I know you wrote it hoping to make Jones feel better but I guess he's the kind of dog you should have ousted the day after election & given him the reasons. He would not have published that letter!... People like Oscar Ewing are telling newspaper men that "Henry is a nice fellow, but he shouldn't have R.F.C." So to-morrow I'm going to call Mr. Hannegan & ask what he and the Com. are doing to back Wallace.[9]

It was time to stop being blackmailed by the conservatives, she wrote a soldier correspondent stationed in China: "Either we are going to give in to our diehard Southern Congressmen or we are going to be the liberal party."[10]

She tried to get more help from her husband for Wallace: "Your message came through to Barkley but we wish you had added a little word for Wallace. We assume you take it for granted we know you believe Wallace will help you to do the job, but a little reassurance would be helpful!" But Roosevelt was unresponsive. As cabled messages came in about the Wallace situation from Sam Rosenman as well as from Eleanor, Roosevelt handed them on to James Byrnes, who was with him, with "little indication of personal interest."[11]

Eleanor sensed that: "I wish I knew what you really thought & really wanted. I've explained your letter to Jones & wondered if I was doing some wishful thinking & Mary Norton asked me the other day if you really wanted Wallace."

This was written on February 13. The few messages he sent her from Yalta were, although affectionate, either silent or equivocal on the subject of Wallace. "Dearest Babs," he wrote her the day he left the Crimea:

> We have wound up the conference—successfully I think and this is just a line to tell you that we are off for the Suez Canal and then home but I doubt if we get back till the 28th. I am a bit exhausted but really all right.

I do hope all goes well. It has been grand hearing from you and I expect another pouch tomorrow.

Ever so much love.

Devotedly

F[12]

On February 11 the results of the Yalta Conference were announced in a joint statement by Roosevelt, Churchill, and Stalin. "We seem to be almost united as a country in approval of the results of the Conference," Eleanor reported to her husband, happy to be able to send him good tidings for a change:

I think you must be very well satisfied & your diplomatic abilities must have been colossal! Jonathan is happy. John is happy. All the world looks smiling! I think having the first U.N. meeting in San Francisco is a stroke of genius. At last will Marshal Stalin leave his own country, or won't you three have to be on hand?[13]

The travelers returned, and Eleanor was grateful that the president seemed ruddy and rested and stoical about the death of Pa Watson, which had occurred at sea:

He says he felt well all the time & he feels evidently that all went well. He liked Stalin better & felt they got on better than before. He says his one complete failure was with Ibn Saud on Palestine but says F. "he is 75 & has been wounded 9 times, it will be easier to deal with the son who comes to power." I believe there are 49 sons! He does not seem upset over DeGaulle. We do go out to open the San Francisco Conference.[14]

She liked his report to Congress on Yalta partly because he was conciliatory and resisted the temptation to strike back at his critics. But a few weeks later when the news about the agreement to give Soviet Russia three votes in the UN General Assembly was leaked, she began to have misgivings:

The secret agreement at Yalta sounds to me very improbable but I do know F. remarked Molotoff was interpreting certain things differently from the way they had been understood. Of course I don't know what happened & can't ask over the telephone but I just don't think FDR would be stupid enough to make secret agreements![15]

U.S. differences with Russia over what had been agreed to at Yalta, she later learned, related to the more vital matters of Poland and the liberated areas generally and not to Russia's three UN votes, to which the president had acquiesced. It is doubtful that Eleanor's presence at Yalta would have changed the course of events there. In later years she said that Franklin got as good an agreement from the Russians as was possible given the presence of the Red Army in Eastern Europe and the desire of U.S. military leaders to insure Russian's entry into the war against Japan once Hitler was defeated.[*][16]

The president's willingness to address Congress sitting down, because of the weight of his steel braces, had meant to her that he was accepting "a certain degree of invalidism." All through March he had been impatient to get away to Warm Springs, and she was pleased when he decided to do so, taking Laura Delano and Margaret Suckley with him. "I know they would not bother him as I should have by discussing questions of state; he would be allowed to get a real rest and yet would have companionship—and that was what I felt he most needed."[17]

Margaret Fayerweather was at the White House when he arrived from Hyde Park on his way to Warm Springs. The president seemed to her "terribly thin and worn and gray," and it was painful to her to watch the way his hands shook. She asked Eleanor about it. "She says a loss of muscular control is noticeable," Mrs. Fayerweather noted in

---

*David Lilienthal recorded in his diary in 1953 a discussion about Yalta at J. J. Singh's where Eleanor was a guest, as were Lin Yutang, Anne O'Hare McCormick, Louis Fischer, and Walter White. "When Franklin came back from Yalta," Eleanor began, and, noted Lilienthal, the whole chattering table immediately grew quiet,

I told him how disappointed I was, and rather shocked, that Esthonia, Lithuania, and Latvia had been left with the Soviet Union, upon Stalin's insistence, instead of being given their independence and freedom.

Franklin said—now mind you I don't say he was right or wrong, but this shows the reasoning he had in his mind—Franklin said (and I can still see his face as he said it) he had thought about this for a long time. He asked me: "How many people in the United States do you think would be willing to go to war to free Esthonia, Latvia, and Lithuania?" I said I didn't suppose there would be very many. "Well," he said, "if I had insisted on their being freed I would have had to consider what I would do to back up that decision, which might require war. And I concluded that the American people did not care enough about the freedom of those countries to go to war about it."

her diary. "He no longer *wants* to drive his own car at Hyde Park—lets her drive, which he never did before, and lets her mix cocktails if Colonel Boettiger is not present." And yet, added Eleanor, she had to smile when people spoke of how tired Franklin must be:

> I am all ready to hand over to others now in all that I do and go home to live in retirement; but Franklin said to me last Sunday, "You know, Eleanor, I've seen so much now of the Near East and Ibn Saud and all of them, when we get through here, I believe I'd like to go and live there. I feel quite an expert, I believe I could help to straighten out the Near East." "Can't you think of something harder to do?" I asked. "Well, yes," he answered quite seriously. "It's going to be awfully hard to straighten out Asia, what with India and China and Thailand and Indo-China. I'd like to get into that." Does *that* sound tired to you, Margaret? *I'm* all ready to sit back. *He's* still looking forward to more work.[18]

Her letter to Maude was gloomier:

> FDR with whom I talked to-day seems settled in Warm Springs & the rest will do him good. He should gain weight but he hates his food. I say a prayer daily that he may be able to carry on till we have peace & our feet are set in the right direction.... Elliott cables that he hopes the end will come soon in Germany. The boys in the Pacific are not so optimistic. All three are there now & I suppose in this battle. I can't help worrying about them all, they've been in so long, will their luck hold.[19]

With the president in Warm Springs and less accessible than ever, the calls on Eleanor for help were greater than ever. Mrs. Gladys Tillett, assistant chairman of the Democratic National Committee, wanted her to ask Stettinius to appoint women as advisers to the U.S. delegation to the San Francisco Conference; she did. Charl Williams of the National Education Association was worried about a bill that might permit federal aid to church-related schools; off went a memo to the president: "It seems to me unwise to strengthen the sectarian and private schools." James Carey, who had attended the founding conference of the World Federation of Trade Unions in London, sent her his report; "Frances dear," Eleanor wrote the secretary of labor, "what do you think of these recommendations?" She asked

Ugo Carusi, the commissioner of immigration, why unused quotas could not be added to current quotas to ease the barriers against refugees, a thought-provoking question, even though the commissioner felt legislation would be needed. The sharecroppers in southeastern Missouri, whom she had helped before, were now threatened with eviction from their FSA homes; Eleanor asked presidential assistant James Barnes to see what he could do on the Hill to stop it. She conferred with Senator J. W. Fulbright and Assistant Secretary of State MacLeish about the proposed International Education and Cultural Organization. She attended Mary Bethune's meeting of the National Council of Negro Women and left with a new batch of assignments. She went after General Frank J. Hines for his stale and unimaginative management of the Veterans Administration, using an article in *Harper's*—"The Veterans' Runaround" by Charles Bolte, head of the fledgling American Veterans Committee—to instigate a discussion that involved Byrnes, Baruch, and her husband. She transmitted to General George C. Marshall and other military leaders her weekly accumulation of complaints and appeals from GIs, their mothers, and their wives. She saw Algernon Black of the Ethical Culture Society, who wanted to go overseas to work with Negro troops, and gave him a letter to the undersecretary of war. A young Nigerian prince told her of a plan to obtain scholarships for Nigerian boys and girls, and she promised to help him set up his committee. Rabbi Isaac H. Steinberg came to see her about a proposal to settle Jewish refugees in Australia; she sent it on to the president. There was a request from nuclear physicist Leo Szilard to see her. He had composed a memorandum on how to avoid a nuclear-arms race with Russia. "I was not certain that this memorandum would reach the president if I sent it 'through channels.'. . . I intended to transmit my memorandum through her—in a sealed envelope—to the President." He was informed Mrs. Roosevelt would see him on April 12.

She had told Margaret Fayerweather that she was quite willing to hand over all that she was doing to someone else, but that reflected her yearning to step out of the public spotlight, not a readiness for a career of idleness. This was made clear in a reaction she expressed after a long day of seeing petitioners: "I was wondering yesterday when I leave the White House what my value will be in any of these things & what people will still be around!"[20]

That was April 6. Soon she would discover that the tasks she discharged as ombudsman were self-imposed, rooted in her sense of duty and her need to be of service, not in her position as the wife of the president. The week end of April 8 she and Tommy went to Hyde Park to unpack cases and barrels of china and glass. "We ache from our unwonted exercise," she wrote her husband, "but we've had fun too! In May I'll finish the job." She had seen Franklin Jr.'s wife, Ethel: "I think she'd be very pleased if you asked her to come & bring Joe [Franklin III] to San Francisco." She did not feel sleepy, her letter went on, so she had written "James, Elliott, & Frankie, Elinor Morgenthau [who had had a heart attack in Florida], Rommie & Sisty" She asked to be remembered to Margaret Suckley and Laura Delano. "I'm so glad you are gaining, you sounded cheerful for the first time last night & I hope you'll weigh 170 pounds when you return. Devotedly, E.R." That was the last letter between them.

On the morning of April 12 Eleanor had her regular press conference. She was asked about San Francisco, and some of the questions seemed to assume that the power of decision lay in the hands of the United States alone. "We will have to get over the habit of saying what we as a single nation will do," Eleanor said, once again using her news conference as a school for the country. "When we say 'we' on international questions in the future, we will mean all the people who have an interest in the question. A United Nations organization is for the very purpose of making it possible that all the world's opinion will have a clearing place." Her luncheon guest that day was Nila Magidoff, a lecturer for Russian War Relief, whose excited cross-breeding of Slavic phrases with English was such a delight to listen to that Eleanor persuaded Anna to forsake her little Johnny at the Navy Hospital to come to lunch to meet her. Afterward she saw Malcolm Ross of the Fair Employment Practices Commission.

At three o'clock Charles Taussig, an adviser to the U.S. delegation to San Francisco, was ushered into her sitting room. He wanted her help in ascertaining the President's wishes on trusteeships. She would call the President, she said, and try to find out. At this point Tommy signaled her urgently to take the phone. It was Laura Delano calling from Warm Springs to say the President had fainted and had been carried to his bed. Eleanor asked a few questions guardedly, in order not to alarm Taussig, hung up, and, ending the interview immediately, spoke with Dr. McIntire. He was in touch with Warm Springs, he said, and although he gave her the impression that he was not alarmed, he suggested that they fly down to Warm Springs later in the day. She should not cancel her next engagement, the annual benefit for the

Thrift Shop at the Sulgrave Club, he advised her, since to do so and then depart for Warm Springs would inevitably set the rumors flying. So she drove to the Sulgrave Club and made her little speech. The entertainment had just begun when she was called to the telephone. "Steve Early, very much upset, asked me to come home at once. I did not even ask why. I knew in my heart that something dreadful had happened." But the amenities had to be preserved, so she went back to the party, made her apologies, and left. "I got into the car and sat with clenched hands all the way to the White House. In my heart of hearts I knew what had happened, but one does not actually formulate these terrible thoughts until they are spoken."[21]

"When she came back," Early later was to tell the press, "Admiral McIntire and I went to her sitting room and told her the President had slipped away. She was silent for a minute and her first words were: 'I am more sorry for the people of this country and of the world than I am for ourselves.'" Although later Eleanor could not remember that she had made this statement and doubted that she had, it was characteristic of the selflessness and self-command with which she responded to the news of her husband's death. "A lesser human being would have been prostrated by the sudden and calamitous tidings," the *Times* wrote, "but Mrs. Roosevelt at once entered upon her responsibilities." Her first thought was of others and what had to be done. She sent for Vice President Harry Truman. Her cable to her sons—

HE DID HIS JOB TO THE END AS HE WOULD WANT
YOU TO DO

—became the order of the day for a stricken people and their government. She asked Steve Early to hold up the announcement of the president's death for fifteen minutes so that Henry Morgenthau could have a doctor break the news to his wife because she did not want her ailing friend to hear the news over the radio. She arranged to fly down to Warm Springs with Early and McIntire.[22]

The vice president, who did not know why he had been summoned to the White House so urgently, soon arrived and was ushered into Eleanor's sitting room. Anna and John Boettiger were with her, as was Early. Eleanor came forward and placed her arm gently on the vice president's shoulder.

"Harry," she said quietly, "the President is dead."

For a moment a stunned Truman could not bring himself to speak.

Finally, finding his voice, he asked, "Is there anything I can do for you?" He would never forget, he later wrote, her "deeply understanding" reply.

"Is there anything *we* can do for *you?*" she asked. "For you are the one in trouble now."

As the arrangements went forward to swear in the vice president, he asked Eleanor whether there was anything she needed to have done. She told him she would like to go to Warm Springs at once and asked if it would be proper for her to make use of a government plane. He agreed immediately, and minutes after the new president was sworn in, she left for Warm Springs. As she walked, tall and erect, to the White House limousine, a group of newspaperwomen were standing beneath the portico. "A trouper to the last," one of them whispered.

She was completely composed when she arrived at Warm Springs just before midnight. She swiftly embraced Laura Delano and Margaret Suckley and kissed Grace Tully, who murmured how deeply sorry she was for Eleanor and the children. "Tully, dear," she replied, "I am so very sorry for all of you." She sat down on the sofa and asked Laura and Margaret to tell her exactly what had happened. She listened quietly, exchanged a few words, and then went into the bedroom where her husband lay. She closed the door and remained inside for about five minutes. "When she came out her eyes were dry again, her face grave but composed," Grace Tully wrote.[23]

She then heard from Laura that Lucy Rutherfurd had been there when the president had died. She had come on April 9 from Aiken, bringing with her Mme. Shoumatoff to do a portrait of the president. Mrs. Rutherfurd, she also learned from Laura, had been to dinner at the White House, when Eleanor was away. Anna had been present as hostess, and Laura and Daisy had been there too.[24]

How did she respond to that bitter discovery? Was it another dark night of the soul for her? She gave no outward sign of anger or hurt, and she did not mention Mrs. Rutherfurd's presence at Warm Springs when she came to write her account of the White House years in *This I Remember*. And yet the concluding paragraphs of her book unmistakably refer to it. She was accounting for the "almost impersonal feeling" that she had during the days after Franklin's death; she could not think of it as a personal sorrow: "It was the sorrow of all those to whom the man who now lay dead, and who happened to be my husband, had been a symbol of strength and fortitude." Partly it was a protective device. From the time the war began she had been schooling herself to the thought that some or all of her sons might be killed and that her husband might die.

But that did not wholly explain her feelings, she went on:

> Perhaps it was much further back I had had to face certain dif-
> ficulties until I decided to accept the fact that a man must be what
> he is, life must be lived as it is, circumstances force your children
> away from you, and you cannot live at all if you do not learn to
> adapt yourself to your life as it happens to be.
>
> All human beings have failings, all human beings have needs
> and temptations and stresses. Men and women who live together
> through long years get to know one another's failings; but they also
> come to know what is worthy of respect and admiration in those
> they live with and in themselves. If at the end one can say: "This
> man used to the limit the powers that God granted him; he was
> worthy of love and respect and of the sacrifices of many people,
> made in order that he might achieve what he deemed to be his task,"
> then that life has been lived well and there are no regrets.
>
> He might have been happier with a wife who was completely
> uncritical. That I was never able to be, and he had to find it in some
> other people. Nevertheless, I think I sometimes acted as a spur, even
> though the spurring was not always wanted or welcome. I was one
> of those who served his purposes.[25]

As the funeral train moved north to Washington, she remained alone for most of the long, sad journey. Even after darkness fell,

> I lay in my berth all night with the window shade up, looking out
> at the countryside he had loved and watching the faces of the people
> at stations, and even at the crossroads, who came to pay their last
> tribute all through the night.
>
> The only recollection I clearly have is thinking about "The
> Lonesome train," the musical poem about Lincoln's death. ["A lone-
> some train on a lonesome track / Seven coaches painted black /
> A slow train, a quiet train / Carrying Lincoln home again..."]
> I had always liked it so well—and now this was so much like it.[26]

In Washington the funeral cortege with the black-draped caisson drawn by six white horses moved in slow, solemn processional
toward the White House. When it arrived under the portico, a squad

of service men lifted the coffin from the caisson and carried it up the steps into the White House. Immediately behind it walked Eleanor, alone, leading her children. And at the funeral service in the East Room, reporters noted that she was wearing one piece of jewelry on her widow's weeds as she walked down the center aisle followed by her children. It was the small golden pin shaped like a fleur de lys that her husband had given her as a wedding gift.

Was she still in love with him? She told friends that she had not been, not since her discovery of the Lucy Mercer affair, but that she had given her husband a service of love because of her respect for his leadership and faith in his goals. "That is what she told me," Esther Lape said. "That was her story. Maybe she even half believed it. But I didn't. I don't think she ever stopped loving someone she loved."[27]

And then Esther, unaware that her old friend had once responded to Franklin's proposal of marriage with the same lines from Elizabeth Barrett Browning, recited from memory:

> Unless you can think when the song is done
>   No other is left in the rhythm;
> Unless you can feel when left by one,
>   That all men else go with him;
> Unless you can know when upraised by his breath,
>   That your beauty itself wants proving;
> Unless you can swear, "For life, for death!"
>   Oh, fear to call it loving!

Bibliographical Note

I HAVE INDICATED AT THE APPROPRIATE PLACES in the following footnotes the manuscript collections which I consulted in the writing of this book. There are at the Franklin D. Roosevelt Library, in addition to the Franklin D. Roosevelt and Eleanor Roosevelt papers, an important group of family letters and materials, sometimes referred to as the Halsted Collection because it was Anna Roosevelt Halsted who saw to it that they were deposited at the library for safekeeping. The family retains control over access to these papers. The diaries of Helen Roosevelt Robinson are in the private possession of her daughters. The diaries of Caroline Drayton Phillips, to which references are made in this book, were supplied to me by her son Christopher.

The transcripts of the interviews conducted by the Oral History Project at Columbia University were an invaluable source, as was the *New York Times'* collection of clippings on Eleanor Roosevelt, which I was able to consult through the kindness of John B. Oakes. A. H. Raskin and Thomas Lask helped me to identify some lines of poetry that turned up in Eleanor Roosevelt's papers. Herman Kahn of the Yale University Library helped me to verify quotations from the diary of Henry L. Stimson, and the George Gallup organization in Princeton, New Jersey, permitted me to consult their files on public attitudes toward Mrs. Roosevelt.

The following persons gave me their recollections and evaluations of Mrs. Roosevelt: Mrs. Amyas Ames, Dr. Viola W. Bernard, James and Dorothy Bourne, Earl Browder, Emma Bugbee, Mrs. Gladys Brooks, Mrs. Edward Carter, Benjamin V. Cohen, Mrs. Corinne Robinson Cole, Maureen Corr, Mr. and Mrs. W. Sheffield Cowles, Mrs. Margaret Cutter, Howland S. Davis, the Baroness Emily de la Grange, Laura Delano, Marion Dickerman, Leonard K. Elmhirst, James Farley, David Gray, David Gurewitsch, Anna Roosevelt Halsted, Mrs. Susan Hammond, Duncan Harris, James Hendrick, Mrs. Rhoda Hinckley, Mrs. Anna Rosenberg Hoffman, Mr. and Mrs. Hartley Howe, Nannine Joseph, Esther Everett Lape, David Lilienthal, Mrs. Margaret Dix Lawrence, Mrs. Agnes Leach, Mrs. Edith Lehman, the Reverend James Elliott Lindsley, Mrs. Alice Longworth, Isidore Lubin, Earl R. Miller, Raymond Moley, Mrs. Gerald Morgan, Pauline Newman, Christopher Phillips, Justine Wise Polier, Mrs. Belle Roosevelt, Elliott Roosevelt, Franklin D. Roosevelt, Jr., James Roosevelt, John Roosevelt, Samuel I. Rosenman, Mr. and Mrs. Durward Sandifer, Mrs. Dorothy Schiff, Thomas L. Stix, Dr. Belinda Straight, Daisy Suckley, Aileen Tone, Eugene Wigner, Mrs. Helen Wilmerding.

References

1. HER FATHER

Young Elliott Roosevelt's letters to his family are in the Halsted Collection, Franklin D. Roosevelt Library (FDRL). Many of them were published by Eleanor Roosevelt, ed., *Hunting Big Game in the Eighties* (New York, 1933), where also will be found on pp. viii and 181 the quotations describing young Eleanor's feeling for her father. Additional family material—the papers of Anna Roosevelt Cowles, especially her "Story of the Roosevelt Family," Houghton Library, Harvard University; the papers and letters of Theodore Roosevelt at the Widener Library, Harvard University, called the Theodore Roosevelt Memorial Association Collection; Theodore Roosevelt, Diaries, Library of Congress: and a few letters relating to Elliott and the first Theodore Roosevelt at the Theodore Roosevelt Association, New York City. An engaging account of President Theodore Roosevelt's youthful years with vivid glimpses of Elliott is contained in Corinne Roosevelt Robinson, *My Brother Theodore Roosevelt* (New York, 1921). Her friend Frances Theodora Parsons' memoir of the Theodore Roosevelts, *Perchance Some Day* (privately printed, New York, 1951), was also helpful in the writing of this chapter. Writers of Teddy Roosevelt's youth and family background are indebted to Carleton Putnam's unfinished *Theodore Roosevelt: A Biography* (New York, 1958). William Sheffield Cowles, Jr., is my authority for the size of Cornelius Van Schaack Roosevelt's estate, and Putnam, p. 337, for the amount of the legacies the first Theodore left his four children. On the evolution of the Oyster Bay Roosevelts from hardware merchants to investment bankers, see William T. Cobb, *The Strenuous Life: The Oyster Bay Roosevelts in Business and Finance* (New York, 1946). I also made use of Allen Churchill, *The Roosevelts: American Aristocrats* (New York, 1965). Colonel M. L. Crimmins has written an account of "Elliott Roosevelt's Visit to Texas in 1876–1877," *Southwestern Historical Quarterly,* Vol. 48, Oct., 1944. on "Mittie" Roosevelt's position in New York society, see Mrs. Burton Harrison, *Recollections Grave and Gay* (New York, 1911), p. 278.

2. HER MOTHER

Material on the Hall family, including Anna Hall's letters and notebooks, Halsted Collection, FDRL. For the position of the Livingstons of Clermont in American history and New York society, see George Dangerfield, *Chancellor Robert R. Livingston of New York* (New York, 1960), and Staughton Lynd, *Class Conflict, Slavery and the United States Constitution* (New York, 1967), Pt. I. For Eleanor Roosevelt's recollections of her great-grandmother Elizabeth Livingston Ludlow, see her *This Is My Story* (New York, 1937), hereafter referred to as *TIMS,* and Joseph P. Lash, *Eleanor Roosevelt, A Friend's Memoir* (New York, 1964). For the impression Anna Hall Roosevelt made on her contemporaries, see a memoir written by "Three Friends," *In Loving Memory of Anna Hall Roosevelt* (privately printed, New York, 1892); also, "Representative Society Ladies—VIII. Mrs. Elliott Roosevelt," *Leslie's Weekly,* Oct. 12, 1889.

3. THE WORLD INTO WHICH ELEANOR WAS BORN

1. For descriptions of New York society in the 1880s and 1890s: Mrs. Winthrop Chanler, *Roman Spring* (Boston, 1934); Edith Wharton, *A Backward Glance* (New York, 1936); *The Age of Innocence* (New York, 1920), and *The House of Mirth* (New York, 1905); Ward McAllister, *Society As I Found It* (New York, 1890); Mrs. John King van Rensselaer, *The Social Ladder* (New York, 1925); Florence J. Harriman, *From Pinafore to Politics* (New York, 1923); and *Town Topics.* On Browning's reaction to Anna Hall Roosevelt, see the letter from Anna

Hall Roosevelt to Bamie Roosevelt, Aug. 5, 1887; letter from Theodore Roosevelt to Henry Cabot Lodge, Sept. 5, 1887.

2. John Sargeant Wise, *Recollections of Thirteen Presidents* (New York, 1906), pp. 241–43.

3. See New York newspapers of Oct. 11, 1884: *Times, Tribune, Herald, World, Sun, Evening Post.*

4. E. Roosevelt, ed. *Hunting Big Game in the Eighties,* cited (Ch.1), pp. 36–37.

5. *Ibid.*

6. E. Roosevelt, *TIMS,* cited (Ch. 2), p. 7; *New York Herald,* May 23, 1887.

7. Letter from Joe Murphy to Eleanor Roosevelt, May 6, 1937.

8. E. Roosevelt, *TIMS,* pp. 17–18.

4. THE CRACK-UP

1. Eleanor Roosevelt, draft of article. "Conquer Fear and You Will Enjoy Living," *Look,* May 23, 1939.

2. Cowles, "Story of the Roosevelt Family," cited (Ch. 1).

3. *New York Tribune, New York World, New York Sun,* Aug. 18, 1891, and the *New York Times,* Dec. 4, 1891, and Jan. 19, 1892.

5. HER MOTHER'S DEATH

1. Recollections of Elliott Roosevelt in Abingdon appeared in the Washington County, Va., newspaper, March 4, 1933; also, "When a Roosevelt Found Health in Virginia Hills," *Richmond* (Virginia) *Times-Dispatch,* May 24, 1935.

2. "Three Friends," *In Loving Memory of Anna Hall Roosevelt,* cited (Ch. 2).

3. Letter from Eleanor Roosevelt to Katherine Ellsworth, Nov. 20, 1929.

4. E. Roosevelt, *TIMS, cited* (Ch. 2), pp. 19–21.

5. *Ibid.*

6. "HE LIVED IN MY DREAMS"

1. Eleanor Roosevelt, "Ethics of Parents" (unpub. article, 1927). Italics are author's.

2. Eleanor Roosevelt, If You Ask Me," *McCall's,* Jan., 1950.

3. E. Roosevelt, ed., *Hunting Big Game in the Eighties,* cited (Ch. 2), p. 181.

7. THE OUTSIDER

1. Two compositions written at a considerably later date were sketched out in the "Commonplace Book" that Eleanor's Aunt Pussie turned over to her. They spoke directly of her father.

She had waited so long, so long. One night she awoke. Someone was whispering in her ear. Suddenly the room seemed to be filled by millions of shadowy forms who whispered to her, "He has broken his word. He has broken his word." She could stand it no longer & she cried out in the dark "Oh my father come" & a voice answered "I am here" & he stood beside her & his cool hand lay on her hot head. She clasped it in both hers & sighed contentedly. "Oh I knew you must come" but he answered, I have kept my word I have come back but I must go away again, & the child cried out Oh! Take me with you I have waited so long & it has been so hard I cannot stay alone. He bent down & kissed her & she fell asleep. The next morning the people who had never understood came in & looked pityingly at her lying cold & dead & they said "poor child to die so young (how sad) & a few tears were shed & then she like all those who have ceased to move in this earthly sphere sank into oblivion.

A child stood at a window watching a man walking down the street, the little face was white & set & the big tears stood in the brown eyes but the mouth smiled till the man was out of sight & the sob which was choking her did not break out till he was gone & she could see no more. Her father [was] the only person in the world she loved, others called her hard & cold but to him she was everything lavishing on him all the quiet love which the others could not understand. And now he had gone she did not know for how long but he had said "what ever happens little girl some day I will come back" & she had smiled. He never knew what the smile cost. His letters came often telling of the life he was leading, his hopes & fears & sometimes there would come a letter without any news, filled only with love for her & these were the letters she loved & kissed before she went to bed. But a time came when there were no more letters & a grown up person told the child that her Father was dead, but the child did not cry. Dead people did not come back & her father had promised to come & he never broke his word. At first she could not bear to hear him spoken of as dead but at last she grew accustomed to it, they were making a mistake but what was the difference? The years went by & she still believed but doubts came sometime now....

2. Interviews with Mrs. Lucius Wilmerding (Helen Cutting) and Mrs. Charles W. Lawrance (Margaret Dix). Additional information about the Roser classes supplied by Mrs. Francis (Corinne Robinson) Cole, Mrs. Paul (Susan Sedgwick) Hammond, and the Baroness Emily (Sloane) de la Grange.

3. Interview with Corinne Cole.

4. Interview with Margaret Lawrance.

5. The Reverend Elliott Lindsley, rector of St. Paul's Church, Tivoli-on-the-Hudson, helped me reconstruct the settings and arrangements at Oak Terrace and made available to me Hall family documents and photographs that came into his possession as well as shared with me his knowledge of the various families that lived along the Woods Road.

6. E. Roosevelt, "Ethics of Parents," cited (Ch. 6).

7. Eleanor Roosevelt, Introduction, *John Martin's Book: Tell Me a Story* (Jacket Library Edition, 1932).

8. Lillian Rixey, *Bamie: Theodore Roosevelt's Remarkable Sister* (New York, 1963), pp. 112–14.

9. Interview with Alice Longworth; Eleanor Roosevelt, *You Learn by Living* (New York, 1960), p. 28.

10. Hermann Hagedorn, *The Roosevelt Family of Sagamore Hill* (New York, 1905), pp. 27, 32, 40.

11. Interview with Corinne Cole.

8. THE SPARK IS STRUCK

1. Letter from Marie Souvestre to Mrs. Hall, Feb. 18, 1901.

2. Leon Edel brought Henry James's letters to my attention, and I am also indebted to him for defining the sense in which James used the term "middle class."

3. Interview with Helen Gifford, *London Daily Mail,* Oct. 21, 1942.

4. *Ibid.*

5. Interview with Corinne Cole.

6. Letters from Carola von Schaeffer-Bernstein to Joseph P. Lash, March 19, 1968, and April 24, 1968.

7. Letter from Dorothy Strachey-Bussy to Eleanor Roosevelt, Sept. 26, 1942.

8. Draft of an article written by Eleanor Roosevelt in the late forties.

9 Beatrice Webb's appraisal of Marie Souvestre, in *My Apprenticeship* (London, 1926) and *Our Partnership* (London, 1948).

10. Eleanor Roosevelt, "My Day," syndicated column, Feb. 21, 1946.

11. *Ibid.*

12. Michael Holroyd, *Lytton Strachey: The Unknown Years* (New York, 1967).

13. Richard Harrity and Ralph G. Martin, *Eleanor Roosevelt: Her Life in Pictures* (New York, 1958), p. 18.

14. Eleanor Roosevelt, "What Religion Means to Me," *Forum,* Dec., 1932.

15. E. Roosevelt, *TIMS,* cited (Ch. 2), p. 8.

16. Letter from Marie Souvestre to Mrs. Hall, Jan. 24, 1902.

17. Interview with Helen Gifford, *London Daily Mail,* Oct. 21, 1942.

9. YOUNG IN A YOUNG COUNTRY IN A YOUNG TIME

1. Harold U. Faulkner, *The Quest for Social Justice, 1898–1914* (New York, 1931), p. 105.

2. Margaret Dix, "Rosemary for Remembrance," privately printed.

3. Ralph Barton Perry, *The Thought and Character of William James* (Boston, 1935), II, pp. 312–14.

4. Quoted in Charles and Mary Beard, *The Rise of American Civilization* (New York, 1942), II, p. 405.

5. Junior League *Handbook,* published by the Association of Junior Leagues of America.

6. Chanler, *Roman Spring,* cited (Ch. 3), p. 117; *New York Herald,* Jan. 12, 1903.

7. Letter from Marie Souvestre to Eleanor Roosevelt, July 7, 1902.

8. Interview with Duncan Harris.

9. Interview with Helen Wilmerding.

10. *Town Topics,* Dec. 18, 1902.

11. Interview with Laura Delano.

12. Interview with Corinne Cole.

13. Rixey, *Bamie: Theodore Roosevelt's Remarkable Sister,* cited (Ch. 7), p. 35.

14. Chanler, p. 228.

15. Rixey, p. 230.

16. Mark Sullivan, *Our Times: The United States 1900–1925,* 6 vols. (New York, 1926), II, p. 28.

17. Eleanor Roosevelt, "Lady Bountiful Rolls Up Her Sleeves," *Reader's Digest,* March, 1938.

18. M. and C. Beard, II, pp. 421–22.

19. Annual reports of the College Settlement, later known as the Rivington Street Settlement, 1903–5.

20. Interview with Margaret Cutter.

21. Letter from Eleanor Roosevelt to Franklin D. Roosevelt, Jan. 20, 1904.

22. *Ibid.,* Jan. 26, 1904.

23. *Ibid.,* Feb. 9, 1904.

24. E. Roosevelt, *You Learn by Living,* cited (Ch. 7), pp. 103–4.

10. "FOR LIFE, FOR DEATH"

Franklin D. Roosevelt's letters, unless otherwise noted, will be found in Franklin D. Roosevelt, *F.D.R.: His Personal Letters,* ed. Elliott Roosevelt, 4 vols. (New York, 1947, 1948, 1950), hereafter referred to as *Letters.*

1. Harrity and Martin, *Eleanor Roosevelt: Her Life in Pictures,* cited (Ch. 8), p. 17.

2. Franklin D. Roosevelt, Diaries, in FDRL.

3. Sara D. Roosevelt, Journals, in Halsted Collection, FDRL.

4. Interview with Corinne Cole.

5. Interview with Alice Longworth.

6. Interview with Laura Delano.

7. Maxine Cheshire, column, *Washington Post,* Feb. 19, 1967.

8. Interview with Mrs. Paul Hammond.

9. Associated Press, Oct. 11, 1934.

10. Thomas Lask, of the *New York Times Book Review,* tracked down this line to its source.

11. Harrity and Martin, p. 19; A. Churchill, *The Roosevelts: American Aristocrats,* cited (Ch. 1), p. 226.

12. Interview with David Gurewitsch.

13. The poem is Elizabeth Barrett Browning's "A Woman's Shortcomings."

14. E. Roosevelt, *TIMS,* cited (Ch. 2), p. 111.

15. S. D. Roosevelt, Journals, Dec. 1, 1903.

16. Eleanor Roosevelt, "I Remember Hyde Park: A Final Reminiscence," published posthumously, *McCall's,* Feb., 1963.

17. Letter from Eleanor Roosevelt to Franklin D. Roosevelt, Dec. 6, 1903.

18. E. Roosevelt, *TIMS,* p. 111.

11. MOTHER AND SON

1. Interview with Corinne Cole.

2. Interview with Helen Wilmerding.

3. Frank Freidel, *The Apprenticeship,* vol. I of *Franklin D. Roosevelt,* 3 vols. (Boston, 1952), p. 13.

4. Rita Halle Kleeman, *Gracious Lady* (New York, 1935), pp. 82–83.

5. Joseph Alsop and Robert Kintner, "Roosevelt Family Album," *Life,* Sept. 9, 1940.

6. Eleanor Roosevelt, in conversation with Arnold Michaelis, on the recording "A Recorded Portrait" (1958).
7. Kleeman, p. 177; E. Roosevelt, "I Remember Hyde Park," cited (Ch. 10).
8. Kleeman, p. 170.
9. Sara D. Roosevelt, *My Boy Franklin* (New York, 1933), p. 13.
10. H. N. MacCracken, *Blithe Dutchess* (New York, 1958), p. 90.
11. S. D. Roosevelt, *My Boy Franklin,* p. 4.
12. Frank D. Ashburn, *Peabody of Groton* (New York, 1944), p. 43.
13. For this description of Peabody and Groton I have leaned heavily on Ashburn and on George Biddle, *An American Artist's Story* (New York, 1939).
14. Franklin D. Roosevelt, "The Roosevelt Family before the Revolution," in FDRL.
15. Interview with Sheffield Cowles, Jr.; also Cowles, Oral History Project, Columbia University, hereafter referred to as OHP.

12. JOURNEY'S END
1. E. Roosevelt, *TIMS,* cited (Ch. 2), p. 110.
2. Interview with Alice Longworth.
3. See Freidel, *The Apprenticeship,* cited (Ch. 11), p. 27, on Roosevelt's desire to go to Annapolis; see *Ibid.,* p. 48, on Roosevelt's desire to enlist during the Spanish-American War.
4. Clara and Hardy Steeholm, *The House at Hyde Park* (New York, 1950), p. 113.
5. Kleeman, *Gracious Lady,* cited (Ch. 11), p. 240.

13. EPITHALAMION
1. Interview with Corinne Cole.
2. *Ibid.*
3. Franklin D. Roosevelt, *The Public Papers and Addresses of Franklin D. Roosevelt,* ed. Samuel I. Rosenman, 13 vols. (New York, 1938–50), 1938, p. 38, hereafter referred to as *Public Papers.*
4. E. Roosevelt, *TIMS,* cited (Ch. 2), p. 123.
5. Halsted Group, "Engagement Presents and Wedding Presents," listed in Eleanor Roosevelt's own hand.
6. Interview with Margaret Lawrance.
7. *New York Times* and the *New York Herald,* March 17 and 18, 1905.

14. HONEYMOON
1. A. Steinberg, *Mrs. R.: The Life of Eleanor Roosevelt* (New York, 1958), p. 54; C. and H. Steeholm, *The House at Hyde Park,* cited (Ch. 12), pp. 114–15.
2. E. Roosevelt, "My Day," cited (Ch. 8), Nov. 13, 1939.
3. Interview with Franklin D. Roosevelt, Jr.
4. Interview with Anna Roosevelt Halsted.
5. The honeymoon letters of Eleanor and Franklin D. Roosevelt to Sara D. Roosevelt, in F. D. Roosevelt, *Letters,* cited (Ch. 10), II, pp. 2–85.
6. Interviews with Maureen Corr and David Gurewitsch.
7. Franklin D. Roosevelt, speech, in FDRL.

15. SETTLING DOWN
1. E. Roosevelt, *TIMS,* cited (Ch. 2), p. 138.
2. *Ibid.,* p. 139.
3. *Ibid.,* pp. 142–46.
4. *Ibid.,* p. 162.
5. Interview with Corinne Cole.
6. E. Roosevelt, *TIMS,* p. 162.
7. Kleeman, *Gracious Lady,* cited (Ch. 11), p. 246.
8. E. Roosevelt, "I Remember Hyde Park," cited (Ch. 10).
9. Interview with Laura Delano.
10. Interview with David Gray.
11. Stefan Lorant, *F.D.R.: A Pictorial Biography* (New York, 1950), p. 43.
12. *Boston Globe,* July 26, 1942.

16. THE WIFE OF A PUBLIC OFFICIAL

1. Helen Robinson, Diaries, in the possession of her daughters.
2. Grenville Clark, in the *Harvard Alumni Bulletin,* April 28, 1945.
3. Kleeman, *Gracious Lady,* cited (Ch. 11), p. 252.
4. Earle Looker, *This Man Roosevelt* (New York, 1932), p. 48.
5. Franklin D. Roosevelt, General Correspondence, in FDRL.
6. S. J. Woolf, "A Woman Speaks Her Political Mind," *New York Times Magazine,* April 8, 1928.
7. For Beatrice Webb's attitude toward suffrage, see her *My Apprenticeship,* cited (Ch. 8), p. 354; for her rejection of Joseph Chamberlain, see Kitty Muggeridge and Ruth Adam, *Beatrice Webb: A Life, 1858–1943* (New York, 1968), pp. 92–93.
8. Kleeman, p. 253.
9. E. Roosevelt, *TIMS,* cited (Ch. 2), p. 167.
10. Franklin D. Roosevelt, Diaries, in FDRL.
11. Langdon P. Marvin, OHP.
12. *Poughkeepsie Daily Eagle,* May 30, 1911.
13. *Knickerbocker News,* July 7, 1920.
14. Letter from Eleanor Roosevelt to Maude Waterbury, July 5, 1912.
15. E. Roosevelt, *TIMS,* pp. 192, 193, and Eleanor Roosevelt, *This I Remember* (New York, 1949), pp. 65, 66, hereafter referred to as *TIR.*
16. Interview with Margaret Cutter.

17. THE ROOSEVELTS GO TO WASHINGTON

1. Josephus Daniels, *The Wilson Era* (North Carolina, 1944), pp. 124–27.
2. E. Roosevelt, *TIMS,* cited (Ch. 2), p. 195.
3. *Raleigh* (North Carolina) *News and Observer,* May 27, 1913.
4. Letter from Eleanor Roosevelt to Maude Waterbury, May 27, 1913.
5. Edith B. Helm, *Captains and Kings* (New York, 1954), p. 37.
6. For Eleanor Roosevelt's account of climbing up the mast, see her *TIMS,* p. 207; for an officer's account of the same incident, see Yates Stirling, *Sea Duty* (New York, 1939), pp. 142, 143.
7. E. Roosevelt, *TIMS,* p. 205.
8. Daniels, p. 55.
9. *New York Evening Post,* March 19, 1913.
10. Letter from Eleanor Roosevelt to Maude Waterbury, May 13, 1913.
11. Interview with Aileen Tone.
12. E. Roosevelt, *TIMS,* p. 237.
13. Cecil Spring-Rice, *The Letters and Friendships of Sir Cecil Spring-Rice,* 2 vols. (Boston, 1929), I, p. 53, hereafter referred to as *Letters.*
14. Helm, p. 47.
15. Eleanor Roosevelt, in conversation with Trude Lash, March 28, 1944.
16. William Phillips, *Ventures in Diplomacy* (privately printed, 1952), pp. 68, 69.
17. Letter from Eleanor Roosevelt to Franklin D. Roosevelt, July 10, 1913.
18. Letter from Isabella Ferguson to Eleanor Roosevelt, 1914.
19. E. Roosevelt, *TIMS,* p. 206.

18. BRINGING UP HER CHILDREN

1. E. Roosevelt, "Ethics of Parents," cited (Ch. 6).
2. E. Roosevelt, *TIR,* cited (Ch. 16), Ch. II.
3. Parsons, *Perchance Some Day,* cited (Ch. 1), p. 249.
4. Eleanor Roosevelt, "My Children," draft of an article written in 1934 or 1935.
5. James Roosevelt and Sidney Shalett, *Affectionately, F.D.R.* (New York, 1959), p. 38.
6. E. Roosevelt, "My children," *op. cit.*
7. J. Roosevelt and Shalett, p. 83.
8. *Ibid.,* p. 48.
9. E. Roosevelt, "I Remember Hyde Park," cited (Ch. 10).
10. E. Roosevelt, "My Children," *op. cit.*
11. J. Roosevelt and Shalett, pp. 39–42.

12. Interview with Anna Roosevelt Halsted.
13. Phillips, *Ventures in Diplomacy*, cited (Ch. 17), p. 69.

19. THE APPROACH OF WAR
1. Phillips, *Ventures in Diplomacy*, cited (Ch. 17), pp. 68–69.
2. *Ibid.*, p. 70.
3. Letter from Eleanor Roosevelt to Franklin D. Roosevelt, July 10, 1913.
4. Caroline Phillips, Journals, Aug. 10, 1914.
5. Letter from Eleanor Roosevelt to Franklin D. Roosevelt, Aug. 7, 1914.
6. Caroline Phillips, Journals, Aug. 10, 1914.
7. Letter from Eleanor Roosevelt to Franklin D. Roosevelt, June 10, 1915.
8. E. Roosevelt, *TIMS*, cited (Ch. 2), p. 232.
9. Letter from Eleanor Roosevelt to Franklin D. Roosevelt, Aug. 22, 1915.
10. Daniels, *The Wilson Era*, cited (Ch. 17), p. 124.
11. E. Roosevelt, *TIMS*, p. 241.
12. Freidel, *The Apprenticeship*, cited (Ch. 11), p. 267.
13. Letter from Eleanor Roosevelt to Sara D. Roosevelt, Jan. 23, 1917.
14. Spring-Rice, *Letters*, cited (Ch. 17), II, p. 374.
15. Franklin K. Lane, *The Letters of Franklin K. Lane* (Boston, 1922), pp. 239–40.
16. E. Roosevelt, *TIMS*, p. 245.

20. PRIVATE INTO PUBLIC PERSON
1. Letter from Eleanor Roosevelt to Sara D. Roosevelt, March 6, 1918.
2. F. J. Harriman, *From Pinafore to Politics*, cited (Ch. 3), p. 222.
3. Letter from Eleanor Roosevelt to Sara D. Roosevelt, May 10, 1917.
4. Freidel, *The Apprenticeship*, cited (Ch. 11), p. 315.
5. Interview with Franklin D. Roosevelt, Jr.
6. E. Roosevelt, *TIMS*, cited (Ch. 2), p. 250.
7. *Ibid.*, p. 251.
8. Letter from Eleanor Roosevelt to Sara D. Roosevelt, March 14, 1918.
9. *New York Times*, July 16, 1917.
10. Letter from Eleanor Roosevelt to Franklin D. Roosevelt, July 20, 1917.
11. Helm, *Captains and Kings*, cited (Ch. 17), p. 53.
12. Letter from Eleanor Roosevelt to Sara D. Roosevelt, Jan. 22, 1918.
13. *Ibid.*, May 12, 1918.
14. *Ibid.*, Jan. 14, 1918.
15. *Ibid.*, Oct., 1918.
16. E. Roosevelt, *TIMS*, p. 262.
17. Letter from Eleanor Roosevelt to Sara D. Roosevelt, Nov. 11, 1918.
18. E. Roosevelt, *TIMS*, p. 252.
19. Letter from Eleanor Roosevelt to Sara D. Roosevelt, March 31, 1919.
20. *Ibid.*, May 7, 1920.
21. Archibald MacLeish, *The Eleanor Roosevelt Story* (Boston, 1965), Intro.

21. TRIAL BY FIRE
1. Letter from Eleanor Roosevelt to Joseph P. Lash, Oct. 25, 1943.
2. This chapter is based on the author's conversations with Eleanor Roosevelt as well as on interviews with Anna Roosevelt Halsted, Corinne Cole, Alice Longworth, Aileen Tone, Margaret Cutter, Marion Dickerman, and David Gurewitsch. In addition, Jonathan Daniel's *The End of Innocence* (Philadelphia, 1954) and *Washington Quadrille: The Dance beside the Documents* (New York, 1968) were very helpful.
3. Letter from Sara D. Roosevelt to Eleanor Roosevelt, March 24, 1915.
4. Arthur Schlesinger, Jr., "F.D.R.'s 'Secret Romance,'" *Ladies' Home Journal*, Nov., 1968.
5. Letter from Walter Camp to Franklin D. Roosevelt, July 25, 1917.
6. Arthur C. Murray, *At Close Quarters* (London, 1946), p. 85.
7. Phillips, *Ventures in Diplomacy*, cited (Ch. 17), p. 68.
8. Letter from Adm. Cowles to Franklin D. Roosevelt, Aug. 18, 1917.

9. Letter from Eleanor Roosevelt to Sara D. Roosevelt, April 24, 1918.

10. Letter from Eleanor Roosevelt to Franklin D. Roosevelt, July 24, 1918.

11. Letter from Eleanor Roosevelt to Sara D. Roosevelt, July 18, 1918.

12. Letters from Eleanor Roosevelt to Franklin D. Roosevelt: July 19, 1917—"I hope you continue to lunch and dine out"; Oct. 29, 1917—"I hope you enjoy Mrs. Marshall Field tonight"; June 18, 1918—"I'm so glad you dined with Alice and I hope you go out somewhere on Sunday."

13. Letter from Franklin D. Roosevelt to Eleanor Roosevelt, "Thursday" (1916).

14. Letter from Eleanor Roosevelt to Franklin D. Roosevelt, Aug. 17, 1916.

15. Letter from Franklin D. Roosevelt to Eleanor Roosevelt, July 16, 1917.

16. *Ibid.,* July 23, 1917.

17. Letter from Eleanor Roosevelt to Franklin D. Roosevelt, July 27, 1917.

18. Letter from Franklin D. Roosevelt to Eleanor Roosevelt, July 26, 1917.

19. Letter from Eleanor Roosevelt to Franklin D. Roosevelt, July 28, 1917.

20. *Ibid.,* Aug. 15, 1917.

21. Letter from Lucy Mercer to Eleanor Roosevelt, Sept. 2, 1917; letter from Eleanor Roosevelt to Franklin D. Roosevelt, Sept. 8, 1917.

22. Letter from Franklin D. Roosevelt to Eleanor Roosevelt, Sept. 9, 1917.

23. Letter from Eleanor Roosevelt to Sara D. Roosevelt, March 18, 1918.

24. Interview with Alice Longworth.

25. Henry Brandon, "A Talk with an 83-Year-Old Enfant-Terrible," *New York Times Magazine,* Aug. 6, 1967.

26. Eleanor Roosevelt, in conversation with the author.

27. Daniels, *Washington Quadrille,* p. 145.

28. Brandon, *op. cit.*

22. RECONCILIATION AND A TRIP ABROAD

1. Letter from Eleanor Roosevelt to Sara D. Roosevelt, Nov. 19, 1918.

2. Letter from Eleanor and Franklin D. Roosevelt to Sara D. Roosevelt, Nov. 25, 1918.

3. Letter from Eleanor Roosevelt to Sara D. Roosevelt, Nov. 19, 1918.

4. *Ibid.,* Oct. 23, 1918.

5. *Ibid.,* Nov. 19, 1918.

6. *Ibid.*

7. *Ibid.,* Dec. 2, 1918.

8. *Ibid.,* Dec. 16, 1918.

9. *Ibid.*

10. *Ibid.,* Nov. 26, 1918.

11. Caroline Phillips, Diaries, Dec. 5, 1918.

12. Letter from Eleanor Roosevelt to Sara D. Roosevelt, Nov. 11, 1918; E. Roosevelt, *TIMS,* cited (Ch. 2), p. 290.

13. For this account of Eleanor Roosevelt's trip abroad, I have made use of her diary, her letters to Sara D. Roosevelt, and the diary of Livingston Davis, in FDRL.

14. Helm, *Captains and Kings,* cited (Ch. 17), p. 135.

15. Interview with Sheffield Cowles, Jr.

16. Letter from Eleanor Roosevelt to Sara D. Roosevelt, March 4, 1919.

17. *Ibid.,* Oct. 10, 1919.

18. Alice R. Longworth, *Crowded Hours* (New York, 1933), p. 292.

19. Letter from Eleanor Roosevelt to Sara D. Roosevelt, Feb. 16, 1920.

20. *Ibid.,* Feb. 27, 1920.

21. Letters from Eleanor Roosevelt to Franklin D. Roosevelt, Oct. 22 and 23, 1919.

22. Letter from Eleanor Roosevelt to Sara D. Roosevelt, Oct. 28, 1919; E. Roosevelt, *TIMS,* p. 304.

23. THE REBELLION BEGINS

1. Eleanor Roosevelt, Diary, Oct. 5, 1919.

2. "The Wisdom of Eleanor Roosevelt," *McCall's,* p. 111.

3. Mrs. Roosevelt spoke to the author about the meaning of the Saint-Gaudens statue to her

when she took him on New Year's Day, 1941, to Rock Creek Cemetery to see it; see also Lorena Hickok, *Reluctant First Lady* (New York, 1962), pp. 91–92.

4. Letter from Eleanor Roosevelt to Trude Lash, June, 1941.

5. Livingston Davis, Diary, cited (Ch. 22), Feb. 9, 1919.

6. Letter from Eleanor Roosevelt to Trude Lash, June, 1941.

7. Letter from Eleanor Roosevelt to Pauline Emmet, Jan. 11, 1939.

8. Letter from Eleanor Roosevelt to Sara D. Roosevelt, Jan. 21, 1917.

9. *Ibid.*, March 24, 1919.

10. *Ibid.*, March 4, 1919.

11. *Ibid.*, March 13, 1919.

12. *Ibid.*, summer, 1919.

13. *Ibid.*, March 24, 1919.

14. Letter from Eleanor Roosevelt to Franklin D. Roosevelt, July 22, 1919.

15. Letter from Franklin D. Roosevelt to Eleanor Roosevelt, July 23, 1919.

16. Letter from Eleanor Roosevelt to Franklin D. Roosevelt, July 24, 1919.

17. Letter from Franklin D. Roosevelt to Eleanor Roosevelt, July 25, 1919.

18. Letter from Eleanor Roosevelt to Sara D. Roosevelt, June 3, 1919.

19. *Ibid.*, May 11, 1919.

20. *Ibid.*, May 13, 1919.

21. *Ibid.*, Nov. 25, 1918.

22. *Ibid.*, June 2, 1918.

23. *Ibid.*, Aug. 18, 1919.

24. *Ibid.*, Nov. 8, 1918.

25. Interview with Mrs Van Wyck Brooks.

26. Interview with Margaret Cutter.

27. Interview with Corinne Cole.

28. Interview with Anna Roosevelt Halsted.

29. Interview with James Roosevelt.

30. Letter from Eleanor Roosevelt to Sara D. Roosevelt, Sept. 8, 1919.

31. Letter from Eleanor Roosevelt to Franklin D. Roosevelt, Sept. 28, 1919.

32. Eleanor Roosevelt, Diary, Oct. 29, 1919.

33. Letter from Eleanor Roosevelt to Sara D. Roosevelt, May 4, 1919.

34. *Ibid.*, Oct. 20, 1919.

35. Arthur Schlesinger, Jr., *The Crisis of the Old Order: 1919–1933*, vol. I of *The Age of Roosevelt*, 3 vols. (Boston, 1957), p. 369.

36. Letter from Eleanor Roosevelt to Sara D. Roosevelt, Jan. 30, 1920.

37. *Ibid.*, spring, 1919.

38. For Eleanor Roosevelt's account of this incident, see *You Learn by Living*, cited (Ch. 7), pp. 80–81; interview with Alice Longworth, in Jean Vanden Heuvel, "The Sharpest Wit in Washington," *Saturday Evening Post,* Dec. 4, 1965.

39. Eleanor Roosevelt, Diary, April 19, 1919.

40. Letter from Eleanor Roosevelt to Franklin D. Roosevelt, "May," 1919.

41. *Ibid.*, July 23, 1919.

42. Letter from Franklin D. Roosevelt to Eleanor Roosevelt, July 23, 1919.

43. Eleanor Roosevelt, Diary, Oct. 3, 1919.

44. *Ibid.*, Oct. 5, 1919.

45. *Ibid.*

46. Letter from Eleanor Roosevelt to Franklin D. Roosevelt, Aug. 19, 1919.

47. E. Roosevelt, *TIMS,* cited (Ch. 2), pp. 259–60.

24. A CAMPAIGN AND FRIENDSHIP WITH LOUIS HOWE

1. Letter from Alice Wadsworth to Eleanor Roosevelt, June 25, 1920.

2. Letter from Eleanor Roosevelt to Franklin D. Roosevelt, July 3, 1920.

3. *Ibid.*

4. *Ibid.*, July 5, 1920.

5. *Ibid.*, July 7, 1920.

6. Letter from Eleanor Roosevelt to Sara D. Roosevelt, July 7, 1920.

7. *New York World,* July 7, 1920; *New York Times,* July 10, 1920.

8. *New York World,* July 8, 1920.

9. *New York Evening Post,* July 8, 1920.

10. Letter from Sara D. Roosevelt to Franklin D. Roosevelt, July 8, 1920.

11. *New York Time,* July 13, 1920.

12. Letter from Eleanor Roosevelt to Sara D. Roosevelt, July 7, 1920.

13. *Poughkeepsie Eagle News,* July 16, 1920.

14. Letter from Franklin D. Roosevelt to Eleanor Roosevelt, July 17, 1920.

15. Letter from Eleanor Roosevelt to Franklin D. Roosevelt, July 19, 1920.

16. *Bangor Daily News,* July 25, 1920.

17. Frank Freidel, *The Ordeal,* vol II of *Franklin D. Roosevelt,* 3 vols. (Boston, 1954), p. 76.

18. Kleeman, *Gracious Lady,* cited (Ch. 11), p. 262.

19. Letter from Franklin D. Roosevelt to Eleanor Roosevelt, Aug. 15, 1920.

20. Letter from Eleanor Roosevelt to Sara D. Roosevelt, "Thursday evening" (1920).

21. Letter from Eleanor Roosevelt to Franklin D. Roosevelt, Aug. 27, 1920.

22. Letter from Eleanor Roosevelt to Sara D. Roosevelt, Sept. 29, 1920.

23. *Ibid.,* Sept. 30, 1920.

24. *Ibid.,* Oct. 2, 1920.

25. *Ibid.,* Oct. 3, 1920.

26. *Ibid.,* Oct. 5, 1920.

27. *Ibid.,* Oct. 17, 1920.

28. *Ibid.,* Oct. 19, 1920.

29. Harold Ickes, *The Secret Diary of Harold Ickes* (New York, 1953), I, p. 699, hereafter referred to as *Secret Diary.*

30. Letter from Eleanor Roosevelt to Franklin D. Roosevelt, Nov. 29, 1920.

31. Corinne Cole's observation, during an interview.

25. BAPTISM IN POLITICS

1. Letter from Eleanor Roosevelt to Mrs. McFadden, Sept. 16, 1930.

2. Letter from Eleanor Roosevelt to Franklin D. Roosevelt, Dec. 3, 1920.

3. E. Roosevelt, *TIMS,* cited (Ch. 2), pp. 325–26.

4. Eleanor Roosevelt, Diary, May 18, 1921.

5. Letter from Franklin D. Roosevelt to Esther Lape, Dec. 13, 1921.

6. Interview with Esther Lape.

7. League of Women Voters Minute Books for 1921, 1922, and 1923, inspected at Barnard College and the offices of the league.

8. *New York Times,* Jan. 27, 28, and 29, 1921.

9. League of Women Voters Minute Books, Feb. 8, 1921.

10. *Ibid.,* April 19, 1921.

11. Letter from Eleanor Roosevelt to Franklin D. Roosevelt, April 11, 1921.

12. Eleanor Roosevelt, speech at the League of Women Voters Biennial Convention, May 1, 1940.

13. *New York Times,* April 13, 1921.

14. *Poughkeepsie Eagle News,* May 24, 1921.

15. Eleanor Roosevelt, Diary, May 24, 1921.

16. *Ibid.,* May 18, 1921.

17. Letter from Eleanor Roosevelt to Franklin D. Roosevelt, April 11, 1921.

26. THE TEMPERING—POLIO

1. Eleanor Roosevelt, Diary, May 24, 1921.

2. Letter from Franklin D. Roosevelt to Eleanor Roosevelt, July 21, 1921.

3. Letter from Eleanor Roosevelt to Franklin D. Roosevelt, July 22, 1921.

4. *Ibid.,* July 18, 1921.

5. Letter from Sara D. Roosevelt to Eleanor Roosevelt, July 20, 1921.

6. Letter from Eleanor Roosevelt to Franklin D. Roosevelt, July 20, 1921.

7. Letter from Eleanor Roosevelt to Sara D. Roosevelt, July 25, 1921.

8. Letter from Eleanor Roosevelt to Franklin D. Roosevelt, July 25, 1921.

9. Letter from Grace Howe to Mary Howe, Aug. 7, 1921; quoted in Alfred B. Rollins, *Roosevelt and Howe* (New York, 1962), p. 179.

10. Letter from Eleanor Roosevelt to Sara D. Roosevelt, Aug. 4, 1921.

11. Letter from Dr. William W. Keen to Eleanor Roosevelt, Aug. 26, 1921.

12. *Ibid.*, Aug. 30, 1921.

13. Letter from Eleanor Roosevelt to James Roosevelt Roosevelt, Aug. 23, 1921.

14. E. Roosevelt, *TIMS,* cited (Ch. 2), p. 332.

15. Letter from Eleanor Roosevelt to Endicott Peabody, Aug. 28, 1921. The origin al of this letter is in the Houghton Library, Cambridge, Mass.

16. Letter from Louis Howe to Franklin D. Roosevelt, Sept. 1, 1921.

17. Letter from Sara D. Roosevelt to Dora Forbes, Sept. 3, 1921.

18. Letter from Franklin D. Roosevelt to Langdon Marvin, Sept. 3, 1921.

19. Letter from Louis Howe to Franklin D. Roosevelt, Sept. 1 1921.

20. Letter from Capt. Calder to Eleanor Roosevelt, Sept. 18, 1921.

21. Dr. George Draper and Dr. Robert W. Lovett, quoted in John Gunther, *Roosevelt in Retrospect* (New York, 1950), pp. 225–26.

22. Interview with Howland Davis.

23. Rollins, p. 185.

24. Interview with Anna Roosevelt Halsted.

25. Anna R. Halsted, "My Life with FDR," the *Woman,* July, 1949.

26. Interview with Anna Roosevelt Halsted.

27. Caroline Phillips, Journals, Jan. 13, 1936.

28. Interview with Anna Roosevelt Halsted.

29. Halsted, *op. cit.*

30. Interview with Alice Carter.

31. Harrity and Martin, *Eleanor Roosevelt: Her Life in Pictures,* cited (Ch. 8), p. 89.

27. HER HUSBAND'S STAND-IN

1. "The Wisdom of Eleanor Roosevelt," cited (Ch. 23), p. 106.

2. Interview with Marion Dickerman.

3. *New York Times,* Aug. 6, 1922.

4. Interview with Mrs. Gerald (Mary Newbold) Morgan.

5. Letter from Sara D. Roosevelt to Franklin D. Roosevelt, Aug. 27, 1922.

6. Letter from Sara D. Roosevelt to Eleanor Roosevelt, July 13, 1922.

7. Letter from Alfred Smith to Franklin D. Roosevelt, Oct. 9, 1922.

8. Letter from Margaret Norrie to Franklin D. Roosevelt, Nov., 1922.

9. Letter from Franklin D. Roosevelt to Abram I. Elkus, Aug. 20, 1923.

10. Letter from Hall Roosevelt to Eleanor Roosevelt, Nov. 9, 1922.

11. Eleanor Roosevelt, "Why I Am a Democrat," Junior League *Bulletin,* Nov., 1923.

12. Rose Schneiderman, *All for One* (New York, 1967), p. 50.

13. E. Roosevelt, "I Remember Hyde Park," cited (Ch. 10).

14. Letter from Hall Roosevelt to Eleanor Roosevelt, Dec., 1922.

15. Letter from Eleanor Roosevelt to Franklin D. Roosevelt, July 25, 1925.

16. Interviews with Franklin D. Roosevelt, Jr., and John Roosevelt.

17. Schneiderman, p. 8.

18. Frances Perkins, *The Roosevelt I Knew* (New York, 1946), pp, 32, 33

19. Letter from Eleanor Roosevelt to Franklin D. Roosevelt, Feb. 3, 1924.

20. *Ibid.,* Feb. 6 and 10, 1924.

21. *Ibid.,* Feb. 6, 1924.

22. Letter from Edward M. Bok to Franklin D. Roosevelt, Aug. 3, 1923.

23. Letter from Franklin D. Roosevelt to Hall Roosevelt, July 10, 1923, and Hall Roosevelt's reply, July 17, 1923.

24. Letter from Franklin D. Roosevelt to Edward M. Bok, Aug. 14, 1923.

25. Interview with Esther Lape.

26. Letter from Eleanor Roosevelt to Franklin D. Roosevelt, March 27, 1924.

27. Letter from Franklin D. Roosevelt to George Marvin, Jan. 29, 1924.

28. Eleanor Roosevelt, speeches and articles, 1925.

28. THE 1924 CAMPAIGN

1. Letter from Josephus Daniels to Franklin D. Roosevelt, May 8, 1924, and Roosevelt's reply, May 26, 1924.
2. Letter from Franklin D. Roosevelt to James Roosevelt Roosevelt, Jan. 23, 1924.
3. *New York Times,* April 20, 1924.
4. Letter from Eleanor Roosevelt to Franklin D. Roosevelt, April 9, 1924.
5. *New York Times,* April 14, 1924.
6. *Ibid.,* May 2, 1924.
7. Letter from Eleanor Roosevelt to Franklin D. Roosevelt, March 1, 1924.
8. *Ibid.*
9. E. Roosevelt, *TIR,* cited (Ch. 16), p. 32.
10. Eleanor Roosevelt, article written in 1924 and submitted to *Town Tidings* in 1928.
11. *Ibid.*

29. LIFE WITHOUT FATHER

1. Eleanor Roosevelt, typed article, dated Dec. 23, 1930, submitted to *Vogue* but not accepted.
2. Interview with James Roosevelt.
3. Interview with Franklin D. Roosevelt, Jr.
4. Bruce and Beatrice Gould, *An American Story: Memoirs and Reflections of Bruce and Beatrice Gould* (New York, 1968), p. 283.
5. Franklin D. Roosevelt, Log of the *Weona II,* Feb. 25, 1923.
6. Julian Goldman, Log of the *Larooco,* March 8, 11, 13, 15, 16, 17, and 18, 1925.
7. Letter to Franklin D. Roosevelt from Eleanor Roosevelt, March 26, 1925.
8. Turnley Walker, *Roosevelt and the Warm Springs Story* (New York, 1953), p. 10.
9. Letter from Franklin D. Roosevelt to Abram I. Elkus, Oct. 24, 1924.
10. Letter from Eleanor Roosevelt to Franklin D. Roosevelt, April 6, 1926.
11. Walker, p. 120.
12. Letter from Sara D. Roosevelt to Franklin D. Roosevelt, March 1, 1927.
13. Interview with Marion Dickerman.
14. Letter from Franklin D. Roosevelt to James Roosevelt Roosevelt, July 22, 1925.
15. Letter from Eleanor Roosevelt to Franklin D. Roosevelt, July 1, 1925.
16. *Ibid.,* March 14, 1928.
17. *Ibid.,* March 21, 1927.
18. *Ibid.,* Oct. 25, 1927.
19. *Ibid.,* April 26, 1928.
20. *Ibid.,* April 10, 1927.
21. *Ibid.,* undated (1928).
22. Interview with Anna Roosevelt Halsted.
23. Letter from Eleanor Roosevelt to Franklin D. Roosevelt, April 22, 1925.
24. *Ibid.,* July 13, 1925.
25. *Ibid.,* July 25, 1925.
26. Interview with Anna Roosevelt Halsted.
27. *Ibid.*
28. Letter from Eleanor Roosevelt to Franklin D. Roosevelt, March 28, 1926.
29. Letter from Sara D. Roosevelt to Franklin D. Roosevelt, March 31, 1926.
30. Letter from Eleanor Roosevelt to Franklin D. Roosevelt, March 31, 1926.
31. *Ibid.,* Oct. 27, 1926.
32. *Colliers* rejected it.
33. Letter from Eleanor Roosevelt to Franklin D. Roosevelt, March 25, 1927.
34. *Ibid.,* Aug. 4, 1925.
35. Interview with Anna Roosevelt Halsted.
36. Letter from Eleanor Roosevelt to Franklin D. Roosevelt, March 19, 1926.
37. *Ibid.,* Nov. 7, 1927.
38. *Ibid.,* Nov. 13, 1927.
39. Letter from Louis Howe to Franklin D. Roosevelt, April 22, 1927.

30. A LIFE OF HER OWN

1. Letter from James Roosevelt Roosevelt to Franklin D. Roosevelt, Feb. 17, 1926.
2. Letter from Franklin D. Roosevelt to Elliot Brown, Aug. 5, 1924.
3. Interview with Marion Dickerman.
4. Letter from Sara D. Roosevelt to Franklin D. Roosevelt, April 2, 1926.
5. Letter from Eleanor Roosevelt to Franklin D. Roosevelt, April 12, 1926.
6. *Ibid.,* Oct. 17, 1926.
7. Letter from Eleanor Roosevelt to Sara D. Roosevelt, Oct. 11, 1926.
8. Letter from Malvina Thompson Scheider to F. E. Compton, Sept. 16, 1933; E. Roosevelt, *TIR,* cited (Ch. 16), pp. 32–34; Mrs. Daniel O'Day, "The Art of Creating Heirlooms," *Motordom,* March, 1929.
9. *New York Times,* May 17, 1927.
10. Letter from Eleanor Roosevelt to Franklin D. Roosevelt, April 22, 1928.
11. Eleanor Roosevelt and Lorena Hickok, *Ladies of Courage* (New York, 1954), p. 262.
12. Interview with Marion Dickerman.
13. Letter from Eleanor Roosevelt to Franklin D. Roosevelt, Feb. 2, 1928.
14. Interview with Esther Lape.
15. Letter from Eleanor Roosevelt to Jane Hoey, April 9, 1930.
16. Eunice Fuller Barnard, article, *New York Times,* Dec. 4, 1932.
17. *Ibid.*
18. *Ibid.*
19. *Ibid.*
20. Eleanor Roosevelt, "What Do We Want As an Education for Our Girls?," *Woman's Journal,* Oct., 1930.
21. *Ibid.*
22. *Ibid.*

31. SMITH'S DEFEAT, ROOSEVELT'S VICTORY

1. *New York Times,* Jan. 25, 1927.
2. Letter from Eleanor Roosevelt to Franklin D. Roosevelt, Feb. 5, 1924.
3. *Ibid.,* April 6, 1925.
4. *Ibid.,* April 25, 1925.
5. Letter from Louis Howe to Franklin D. Roosevelt, March 21, 1927.
6. *New York Times,* Feb. 25, 1925.
7. *Ibid.,* March 22, 1926; the *World,* Jan. 23, 1927.
8. Dewson papers, especially unpublished memoir, *An Aid to the End,* in FDRL.
9. *Ibid.*
10. Letter from Carrie Chapman Catt to Eleanor Roosevelt, July 7, 1926.
11. Theodore F. Harris, *Pearl S. Buck* (New York, 1969), pp. 298, 290.
12. S. J. Woolf, "Energy: Mrs. Roosevelt Tells How She Conserves It," *New York Times Magazine,* May 28, 1939.
13. Eleanor Roosevelt, "Women Must Learn to Play the Game As Men Do," *Redbook,* March, 1928.
14. Letter from Eleanor Roosevelt to Franklin D. Roosevelt, April 14, 1928.
15. Woolf, "A Woman Speaks Her Political Mind," cited (Ch. 16).
16. *New York Times,* Sept. 27, 1926.
17. *Ibid.,* Jan. 25, 1927.
18. Letter from Eleanor Roosevelt to Franklin D. Roosevelt, Nov., 1927.
19. Eleanor Roosevelt, in conversation with author, Aug. 4, 1940, recorded in his diaries, hereafter referred to as Lash Diaries.
20. *New York Times,* Jan. 25, 1928.
21. Eleanor Roosevelt, "Why Democrats Favor Smith," *North American Review,* Nov., 1927.
22. Eleanor Roosevelt, "Jeffersonian Principles the Issue in 1928," *Current History,* June, 1928.
23. *New York Times,* May 31, 1928.
24. Letter from Eleanor Roosevelt to Mrs. Jesse W. Nicholson, Jan. 28, 1928.
25. Letter from George Marvin to Franklin D. Roosevelt, Feb. 2, 1928.

26. Letter from Eleanor Roosevelt to Franklin D. Roosevelt, April 1, 1928.
27. Letter from Franklin D. Roosevelt to Stanley W. Prenosil, Aug. 23, 1928.
28. Letter from Eleanor Roosevelt to Franklin D. Roosevelt, April 26, 1928.
29. *Ibid.,* April 27, 1928.
30. *Ibid.,* April 18, 1928.
31. *Ibid.,* June 22, 1928.
32. *Ibid.,* July 4, 1928.
33. *New York Evening Post,* Oct. 2, 1928.
34. Written for the *Bulletin* of the Women's National Democratic Club.
35. Dewson papers.
36. Letter from Sara D. Roosevelt to Eleanor Roosevelt, July 3, 1928.
37. Letters from Sara D. Roosevelt to Franklin D. Roosevelt, July 26, 1928, and Aug. 4, 1928.
38. Interview with Agnes Leach.
39. Letter from Eleanor Roosevelt to Franklin D. Roosevelt, Sept. 30, 1928.
40. *New York Evening Post,* Oct. 2, 1928.
41. *World,* Oct. 2, 1928.
42. *New York Herald Tribune,* Oct. 3, 1928.
43. E. Roosevelt, "My Day," cited (Ch. 8), Feb. 3, 1958; Emma Bugbee, in the *New York Herald Tribune,* Jan. 31, 1958.
44. Interview with Esther Lape.
45. E. Roosevelt, *TIR,* cited (Ch. 16), p. 46.
46. *New York Times,* Oct. 28, 1928.
47. *New York Evening Post,* Nov. 8, 1928.
48. *Ibid.,* Nov. 7, 1928.
49. *Ibid.,* Nov. 8, 1928.
50. Letter from Eleanor Roosevelt to William Bray, Oct. 30, 1928.
51. Letter from Eleanor Roosevelt to Franklin D. Roosevelt, Nov. 13, 1928.

32. RETURN TO ALBANY
1. Letters from Eleanor Roosevelt to Franklin D. Roosevelt, Dec. 1 and 2, 1928.
2. *Ibid.*
3. *Ibid.,* Dec. 6, 1928.
4. *New York Times,* Nov. 11, 1928.
5. Letters from Eleanor Roosevelt to Franklin D. Roosevelt, Nov. 11 and 24, 1928, and Dec. 6, 1928.
6. Letter from Emily Newell Blair to Eleanor Roosevelt, Dec. 19, 1928.
7. Letter from Eleanor Roosevelt to Franklin D. Roosevelt, Nov. 13, 1928.
8. *Ibid.,* Nov. 19, 1928.
9. *Ibid.,* Nov. 22, 1928.
10. Dewson, *An Aid to the End,* cited (Ch. 31).
11. *Ibid.*
12. Franklin D. Roosevelt, letter "Written for the Record," April 6, 1938.
13. E. Roosevelt, *TIR,* cited (Ch. 16), p. 42.
14. Letter from Frances Perkins to Eleanor Roosevelt, Dec. 17, 1928.
15. Letter from Molly Dewson to Lorena Hickok, 1953 (in Dewson papers, cited, Ch. 31).
16. Perkins, *The Roosevelt I Knew,* cited (Ch. 27), pp. 52, 53.
17. Frank Freidel, *The Triumph,* vol. III of *Franklin D. Roosevelt,* 3 vols. (Boston, 1956), p. 17 (based on an interview with Miss Perkins).
18. Ernest K. Lindley, *Franklin D. Roosevelt* (New York, 1931), pp. 338–40.
19. Ida M. Tarbell, in the *Delineator,* Oct., 1931.
20. Dewson, *An Aid to the End.*
21. Interview with Anna Roosevelt Halsted; Rollins, *Roosevelt and Howe,* cited (Ch. 26), p. 254; Rexford G. Tugwell, *The Brains Trust* (New York, 1969), p. 55; interview with Earl Miller.
22. Letter from Eleanor Roosevelt to Franklin D. Roosevelt, Nov. 19, 1928.
23. Eleanor Roosevelt, speech to the Women's City Club, Jan. 9, 1929, reported in the Women's City Club *Quarterly,* March, 1929.

24. Letter from Eleanor Roosevelt to Franklin D. Roosevelt, May 1, 1929.
25. Letter from Eleanor Roosevelt to Mrs. Pfohl, June 17, 1929.
26. Dewson, *An Aid to the End.*
27. Interview with Agnes Leach.
28. Dewson, *An Aid to the End.*
29. Letter from Eleanor Roosevelt to Franklin D. Roosevelt, May 15, 1929.
30. Letter from Rose Schneiderman to Franklin D. Roosevelt, June 12, 1929.
31. *New York Times,* Dec. 3, 1926.
32. *Ibid.,* April 9, 1929.
33. Letter from Eleanor Roosevelt to Sara D. Roosevelt, March 30, 1929.
34. Letter from Eleanor Roosevelt to Franklin D. Roosevelt, May 19, 1929.
35. *Ibid.*
36. Interviews with Franklin D. Roosevelt, Jr., John Roosevelt, and Marion Dickerman.
37. Interview with Marion Dickerman.
38. Letter from Eleanor Roosevelt to Dr. Frank Graves, June 12, 1929.
39. Letter from Eleanor Roosevelt to Franklin D. Roosevelt, April 24, 1929.
40. E. Roosevelt, *TIR,* pp. 55, 56.
41. Interview with Earl Miller.
42. Steinberg, *Mrs. R.: The Life of Eleanor Roosevelt,* cited (Ch. 14), p. 162.
43. E. Roosevelt, *TIR,* p. 56.
44. Letter from Eleanor Roosevelt to Franklin D. Roosevelt, July 27, 1929.
45. *Ibid.*
46. *Ibid.,* July 28, 1929.
47. J. Roosevelt and Shalett, *Affectionately, F.D.R.,* cited (Ch. 18), p. 211.
48. Letter from Eleanor Roosevelt to Franklin D. Roosevelt, Aug. 1, 1929.
49. *Ibid.,* Aug. 5, 7, 11, 14, 15, 19, 22, 25, 30, and 31, 1929, and Sept. 3, 1929.
50. Tarbell, in the *Delineator.*
51. Letter from Eleanor Roosevelt to the managing editor of *Vogue,* March 12, 1930.
52. Interview with Earl Miller.
53. Letter from Henry Neil to Eleanor Roosevelt, Sept. 15, 1931, and Eleanor Roosevelt's reply, Sept. 28, 1931.
54. Letter from Eleanor Roosevelt to Franklin D. Roosevelt, Oct. 2, 1929.
55. *Evening World,* Oct. 2, 1930.
56. Dewson, *An Aid to the End.*

33. ROOSEVELT BIDS FOR THE PRESIDENCY

1. E. Roosevelt, *TIR,* cited (Ch. 16), p. 61.
2. *Good Housekeeping,* Aug., 1930.
3. E. Roosevelt, *TIR,* p. 65.
4. James A. Farley, *Behind the Ballots* (New York, 1938), p. 353.
5. Letter from Emma Guffey Miller to Eleanor Roosevelt, Sept. 13, 1947.
6. Samuel I. Rosenman, *Working with Roosevelt* (New York, 1952), pp. 42, 43.
7. Farley, p. 83.
8. Edward J. Flynn, *You're the Boss* (New York, 1947), p. 83.
9. Letter from Molly Dewson to Eleanor Roosevelt, Dec. 9, 1931.
10. Looker, *This Man Roosevelt,* cited (Ch. 16), p. 140.
11. Letter from Ernest K. Lindley to Joseph P. Lash when the latter was assisting Elliott Roosevelt in editing vols. III and IV of his father's letters.
12. Letters from Eleanor Roosevelt to Franklin D. Roosevelt, July 22 and 24, 1931.
13. *New York Times,* Nov. 20, 1931.
14. Dewson papers, cited (Ch. 31).
15. Ida M. Tarbell, in the *Delineator,* cited (Ch. 32).
16. Helene Huntington Smith, "Profile," *New Yorker,* April 5, 1930.
17. Interview with Earl Miller.
18. Letter from Eleanor Roosevelt to Louis Howe, May 17, 1932.
19. Interview with Earl Miller.
20. *Ibid.;* letter from Eleanor Roosevelt to Maude Gray, July 12, 1930.

21. Interview with Marion Dickerman.
22. Flynn, p. 216.
23. Letter from Eleanor Roosevelt to Franklin D. Roosevelt, May 18, 1932.
24. Caroline Phillips, Journals, April 1, 1932.
25. Interview with Agnes Leach.
26. Letter from Eleanor Roosevelt to the *Ladies' Home Journal,* Sept. 29, 1929.
27. S. J. Woolf, in the *New York Times,* Oct. 11, 1932.
28. Letter from David Gray to Eleanor Roosevelt, Jan. 24, 1932.
29. Lorena Hickok, Associated Press dispatch in the *Knickerbocker Press,* Albany, Sept. 6, 1932.
30. J. Roosevelt and Shalett, *Affectionately, F.D.R.,* cited (Ch. 18), p. 236.
31. Eleanor Roosevelt, "Ten Rules for Success in Marriage," *Pictorial Review,* Dec., 1931.
32. Letter from Eleanor Roosevelt to Joseph P. Lash, Jan. 19, 1943.
33. E. Roosevelt, *TIR,* p. 64.
34. *New York Times,* March 4, 1930.
35. *Ibid.,* Jan. 20, 1931.
36. Dewson papers.
37. Gertrude Macy, in conversation with the author.
38. Tugwell, *The Brains Trust,* cited (Ch. 32), p. 57.
39. *Ibid.*
40. *Ibid.*
41. Interview with Samuel I. Rosenman.
42. Interview with Hartley Howe.
43. Eleanor Roosevelt–Esther Lape correspondence, 1929–31.
44. Interview with Samuel I. Rosenman.
45. Interview with Agnes Leach.
46. Interview with Thomas L. Stix.
47. Letter from Eleanor Roosevelt to Molly Dewson, March 11, 1932.
48. Eleanor Roosevelt, in conversation with the author.
49. Alice B. Jennings, in the *Atlanta Journal,* Dec., 1930.
50. *Syracuse Herald,* Oct. 1, 1932.
51. Hickok, *Reluctant First Lady,* cited (Ch. 23), pp. 32, 33.
52. Grace Tully, *F.D.R. My Boss* (New York, 1949), pp. 51, 53.
53. Hickok, p. 44.

34. "I NEVER WANTED TO BE A PRESIDENT'S WIFE"

1. Emma Bugbee, in the *New York Herald Tribune,* July 2, 1932.
2. Interview with Marion Dickerman.
3. E. Roosevelt, *TIR,* cited (Ch. 16), p. 68.
4. Letter from Eleanor Roosevelt to Molly Dewson, Aug. 4, 1932.
5. Molly Dewson, North American Newspaper Alliance, Jan. 2, 1933.
6. Louis Howe, in the *Boston Globe,* Dec. 25, 1932; Dewson papers, cited (Ch. 31).
7. Interview with James Roosevelt.
8. Tugwell, *The Brains Trust,* cited (Ch. 32), p. 86.
9. *New York Herald Tribune,* Oct. 28, 1932.
10. Hickok, *Reluctant First Lady,* cited (Ch. 23), Ch. I.
11. *Ibid.*
12. *Springfield Union,* Dec. 22, 1932.
13. "Ike" H. Hoover, *Forty-two Years in the White House* (New York, 1934), p. 226.
14. *Nashville Tennessean,* Feb. 15, 1933.
15. Heywood Broun, in the *New York World-Telegram,* Feb., 1933.
16. *New York Evening Post,* Feb. 4, 1933.
17. *Baltimore Evening Sun,* Feb., 1933.
18. Perkins, *The Roosevelt I Knew,* cited (Ch. 27), p. 69.
19. *New York Times,* Jan. 22, 1933.
20. *Ibid.,* Feb. 15, 1933.
21. E. Roosevelt, *TIR,* p. 76.
22. Hickok, p. 92.

35. MRS. ROOSEVELT CONQUERS WASHINGTON

1. Quoted in William E. Leuchtenburg, *Franklin D. Roosevelt and the New Deal, 1932–1940* (New York, 1963), p. 39.
2. Eleanor Roosevelt, "What Religion Means to Me," the *Forum,* Dec., 1932.
3. E. Roosevelt, *TIR,* cited (Ch. 16), p. 78.
4. Hickok, *Reluctant First Lady,* cited (Ch. 23), pp. 104, 105.
5. Sullivan, *Our Times,* cited (Ch. 9), II, p. 399.
6. Bess Furman, *Washington By-Line* (New York, 1949), p. 151.
7. *Ibid.,* pp. 133, 134; see also pp. 46–61.
8. *Ibid.,* p. 153; May Craig, in the *Portland Press Herald,* April 27, 1933.
9. *New York Times,* April 4, 1933.
10. Interview with Emma Bugbee.
11. *Washington Star,* March 30, 1933.
12. Furman, p. 194.
13. *New York Herald Tribune,* April 25, 1933.
14. Interview with Emma Bugbee.
15. Letter from Martha Strayer to Eleanor Roosevelt, undated.
16. *Ibid.*
17. *New York Times,* April 24, 1933; the *New York Herald Tribune,* April 24, 1933.
18. Letter from Helen Wilmerding to Eleanor Roosevelt, June 14, 1933, and Eleanor Roosevelt's reply, June 23, 1933.
19. Letter from Eleanor Roosevelt to Franklin D. Roosevelt, Feb. 15, 1933.
20. Letter from Eleanor Roosevelt to Herman Milgrim, Sept. 28, 1933, and Milgrim's reply, Oct. 9, 1933.
21. *New York Herald Tribune,* March 20, 1933.
22. Letter from Eleanor Roosevelt to Mrs. Archibald Hopkins, May 19, 1933.
23. Rollins, *Roosevelt and Howe,* cited (Ch. 26), pp. 291, 386–88.
24. Letter from Josephus Daniels to Eleanor Roosevelt, May 26, 1933.
25. *New York Times,* March 16, 1933.
26. Letter from Amelia Earhart to Eleanor Roosevelt, Nov. 20, 1933; letter from Eleanor Roosevelt to Amelia Earhart, Dec. 4, 1933.
27. Letter from Amon G. Carter to Eleanor Roosevelt, June 25, 1933, enclosing an editorial from the *Fort Worth Star-Telegram,* "All American Woman."
28. Will Rogers, letter to the *New York Times,* June 7, 1933.
29. Parsons, *Perchance Some Day,* cited (Ch. 1), p. 340.
30. *New York Herald Tribune,* April 24, 1933.
31. Eleanor Roosevelt, article for the North American Newspaper Alliance, April 1, 1933; Hickok, p. 105.
32. Eleanor Roosevelt, article for the North American Newspaper Alliance, April 28, 1933.
33. *New York Times,* March 14, 1933.
34. *Ibid.,* April 13, 1933.
35. Eleanor Roosevelt, radio broadcast, March 15, 1935.
36. Letter from Merritt Bond to Eleanor Roosevelt, April 8, 1933.
37. *New York Times,* March 20, 1933.
38. Letter from Marvin McIntyre to Eleanor Roosevelt, Dec. 26, 1933.
39. Letter from Eleanor Roosevelt to Aron Mathieu, May 9, 1933.
40. Mary Beard, review of Eleanor Roosevelt's *It's Up to the Women* (New York, 1933; hereafter referred to as IUTTW), in the *New York Herald Tribune Books,* Nov. 14, 1933.
41. Eleanor Roosevelt, radio broadcast, 1934.
42. Eleanor Roosevelt, speech, Massena, New York, May 5, 1933.
43. Eleanor Roosevelt, radio broadcast, 1934.
44. Letter from Eleanor Roosevelt to Ruth Morgan, Dec. 4, 1933.
45. Furman, p. 167.
46. Letter from Mrs. John Nance Garner to Eleanor Roosevelt, Sept. 8, 1933, and Eleanor Roosevelt's reply, Oct. 7, 1933.
47. Interview with Mrs. Amyas Ames.
48. E. Roosevelt, *TIR,* pp. 350–51.

49. Letter from Eleanor Roosevelt to Mrs. F. Hirst, Nov. 7, 1933.
50. *Washington* (D.C.) *Herald,* April 5, 1933.

36. THE POLITICS OF CONSCIENCE

1. E. Roosevelt, *IUTTW,* cited (Ch. 35).
2. *Ibid.,* p. 204.
3. *Ibid.,* p. 174.
4. *Ibid.,* pp. 246, 247.
5. Mary Beard, in the *New York Herald Tribune Books,* cited (Ch. 35).
6. E. Roosevelt, *IUTTW,* p. 260.
7. Eleanor Roosevelt, speech, Baltimore, Oct. 13, 1933, and speech to the Affiliated Schools for Workers, Oct. 24, 1933.
8. Eleanor Roosevelt, "What I Hope to Leave behind Me," *Pictorial Review,* April, 1933.
9. Eleanor Roosevelt, undated speech drafted in late 1932 or early 1933.
10. E. Roosevelt, "What I Hope to Leave behind Me," *op. cit.*
11. Eleanor Roosevelt, in the *Democratic News,* Dec., 1932.
12. E. Roosevelt, speech, Baltimore, Oct. 13, 1933.
13. William James, *The Varieties of Religious Experience* (New York, Modern Library, 1902), p. 257.
14. Letter from Eleanor Roosevelt to Eliza Keates Young, Oct. 17, 1933. On Eleanor Roosevelt's help to consumer groups, see also her letter to Elinor Herrick, Aug. 30, 1933; letter from Eleanor Roosevelt to Hugh Johnson, Jan. 17, 1934; letter from Mary Rumsey to Eleanor Roosevelt, Oct. 30, 1934; letter from Eleanor Roosevelt to Louis Howe, Dec. 13, 1933. On her role in starting the food-stamp plan, see Pearson and Allen, "Washington Merry-Go-Round-of-the-Air." Nov. 26, 1935; Emma Bugbee, in the *New York Herald Tribune,* March 1, 1936; Kathleen McLaughlin, in the *New York Times,* July 5, 1936.
15. Ruby Black, in *Editor and Publisher,* Feb. 10, 1934.
16. Letter from Eleanor Roosevelt to Eliza Keates Young, Oct. 17, 1933.
17. Letter from Eleanor Roosevelt to Lady Florence Willert, Dec. 4, 1933.
18. *New York Times,* Nov. 9, 1933; International News Service, Nov. 10, 1933.
19. Letter from Eleanor Roosevelt to David Gaines, Nov. 15, 1933.
20. Letter from Eleanor Roosevelt to Mrs. Alderman, Dec. 5, 1933.
21. *New York Times,* Oct. 13, 1933.
22. Letter from Eleanor Roosevelt to Mr. Roberts, Oct. 31, 1933.
23. Letter from Eleanor Roosevelt to Izetta Jewel Miller, May 18, 1934; letter from Eleanor Roosevelt to Mrs. Martin, Oct. 9, 1934.
24. A distinction drawn by Northrup Frye in "Varieties of Literary Utopias," *Utopias and Utopian Thought,* ed. Frank E. Manuel (Boston, 1967), p. 31.
25. Letter from Upton Sinclair to Eleanor Roosevelt, Oct. 21, 1933.
26. *Ibid.,* Oct. 31, 1933.
27. Letter from Eleanor Roosevelt to Upton Sinclair, Jan. 26, 1934.
28. Letter from Molly Dewson to Eleanor Roosevelt, April 27, 1933.
29. Ruby Black, in *Editor and Publisher,* Feb. 10, 1934.
30. Furman, *Washington By-Line,* cited (Ch. 35), p. 230.
31. Letter from Judge Florence E. Allen to Eleanor Roosevelt, May 1, 1933.
32. Letter from Molly Dewson to Eleanor Roosevelt, April 29, 1933.
33. Cordell Hull, *Memoirs,* 2 vols. (New York, 1948), p. 183.
34. Letter from Eleanor Roosevelt to Harold L. Ickes, Dec. 13, 1933, and Ickes' reply, Dec. 18, 1933.
35. E. Roosevelt, *IUTTW,* p. 213.
36. Letter from Eleanor Roosevelt to James Farley, undated.
37. E. Roosevelt, *IUTTW,* p. 199.
38. Eleanor Roosevelt, speech, March 24, 1933.
39. E. Roosevelt, *IUTTW,* p. 200.
40. Louis Howe, draft of an article, "Women's Ways in Politics," *Woman's Home Companion,* July, 1935.
41. Malvina Thompson Scheider, in conversation with the author.

42. Eleanor Roosevelt, radio broadcast, Sept. 5, 1934.
43. Letter from Carrie Chapman Catt to Eleanor Roosevelt, Aug. 15, 1933.
44. E. Roosevelt, *IUTTW,* pp. 204 and 178 respectively.
45. S. J. Woolf, in the *New York Times,* May 24, 1939.
46. James, pp. 349–50.

37. MRS. ROOSEVELT'S "BABY"—ARTHURDALE

1. Hickok, *Reluctant First Lady,* cited (Ch. 23), p. 136.
2. Lorena Hickok, reports to Harry Hopkins, in FDRL.
3. Letter from Alice Davis to Eleanor Roosevelt, Aug., 1933.
4. Letters from Eleanor Roosevelt to Alice Davis, Aug. 24, 1933, and Nov. 7, 1933.
5. Title II, Sect. 208, National Industrial Recovery Act.
6. *New York Times,* Jan. 23, 1930.
7. Letter from Franklin D. Roosevelt to George Norris, April 17, 1933.
8. Arthur Schlesinger, Jr., *The Coming of the New Deal,* vol. II of *The Age of Roosevelt,* 3 vols. (Boston, 1959), p. 365, and M. L. Wilson, Memoir, OHP.
9. *New York Times,* Nov. 3, 1933.
10. Letter from Eleanor Roosevelt to Harold L. Ickes, undated, but probably Aug. 23, 1933.
11. Letter from Harold L. Ickes to Eleanor Roosevelt, Aug. 25, 1933.
12. Wilson, OHP.
13. *Ibid.;* letter from Leonard Elmhirst to Joseph P. Lash, Nov. 18, 1968.
14. Wilson, OHP; Paul R. Conkin, *Tomorrow a New World* (Ithaca, N.Y., 1959), p. 102.
15. Wilson, OHP.
16. Letter from Clarence Pickett to Elizabeth Marsh, Aug. 24, 1933, cited by Holly Cowan, "Arthurdale," master's thesis submitted to Columbia University History Dept., 1968.
17. Louis Howe, WNBC broadcast, Aug. 20, 1933.
18. Clarence Pickett, *For More Than Bread* (New York, 1953), p. 44.
19. Wilson, OHP.
20. Letter from Alice Davis to Eleanor Roosevelt, Oct. 14, 1933.
21. Pickett, p. 46.
22. Letter from Eleanor Roosevelt to M. L. Wilson, Nov. 17, 1933.
23. Letter from Dorothy Elmhirst to Eleanor Roosevelt, Sept. 20, 1933.
24. Letter from Eleanor Roosevelt to Henry Goddard Leach, Nov. 20, 1933.
25. Letter from Upton Sinclair to Eleanor Roosevelt, Jan. 31, 1934, and Eleanor Roosevelt's reply, Feb. 6, 1934.
26. *New York Times,* Feb. 21, 1934.
27. Roosevelt File, Jan. 20, 1934; letter from Silliman Evans to Kenneth Mckellar, Feb. 17, 1934.
28. Eleanor Roosevelt, statement to the press, April 24, 1934.
29. Letter from Bernard Baruch to Eleanor Roosevelt, May 2, 1934.
30. Letter from Eleanor Roosevelt to Bernard Baruch, June 13, 1934.
31. *Ickes, Secret Diary,* cited (Ch. 24), I, p. 335; Conkin, p. 206.
32. Eleanor Roosevelt, speech, undated, Group XXXVI, Roosevelt papers; Pickett, p. 44.
33. *New York Times,* July 29, 1934.
34. Letter from Eleanor Roosevelt to Bernard Baruch, June 13, 1934.
35. Letter from Louis Howe to Charles F. Pynchon, July 24, 1934, and Pynchon's reply, July 26, 1934.
36. *New York Times,* Oct. 13, 1933.
37. Wilson, OHP.
38. *Ibid.*
39. Associated Press, Jan. 23, 1935.
40. Wilson, OHP.
41. Conkin, p. 121.
42. *St. Louis Post-Dispatch,* Nov. 14, 1934.
43. Ickes, I, p. 162.
44. *Ibid.,* p. 152.

45. Wesley Stout, "The New Homesteaders," *Saturday Evening Post,* Aug. 4, 1934.
46. Letter from Martha Strayer to Eleanor Roosevelt, Aug. 20, 1934.
47. Letter from Eleanor Roosevelt to Martha Strayer, Aug. 27, 1934.
48. Letter from Eleanor Roosevelt to Harold L. Ickes, Sept. 8, 1934.
49. Harold M. Ware and Webster Powell, "Planning for Permanent Poverty," *Harper's,* April, 1935.
50. Ickes, I, p. 207.
51. *Ibid.,* pp. 218–19.
52. *Ibid.,* p. 227.
53. Will Alexander, OHP; Conkin, p. 171.
54. Letter from Bernard Baruch to Eleanor Roosevelt, Dec. 4, 1934.
55. Letter from Eleanor Roosevelt to Bernard Baruch, July 14, 1934.
56. Letter from Bernard Baruch to Eleanor Roosevelt, Dec. 6, 1934.
57. *Ibid.,* Jan. 28, 1935.
58. Letter from Eleanor Roosevelt to Lady Florence Willert, April 28, 1934.
59. Letter from Alice Davis to Eleanor Roosevelt, Oct. 15, 1934.
60. Elsie Clapp, *Community Schools in Action* (New York, 1939) and *The Use of Resources in Education* (New York, 1952); E. Roosevelt, "My Day," cited (Ch. 8), Aug. 2, 1937.
61. Letter from Bernard Baruch to Eleanor Roosevelt, April 20, 1935.
62. Letter from Clarence Pickett to Eleanor Roosevelt, Sept. 21, 1934.
63. Letter from Eleanor Roosevelt to Harold L. Ickes, June 13, 1934.
64. Ickes, I, pp. 248–60; *ibid.,* p. 285.
65. This episode is described by Tugwell, OHP memoir.
66. Letter from Eleanor Roosevelt to Rexford Tugwell, May 3, 1934.
67. *Ibid.,* June 3, 1935, and Tugwell's reply, June 3, 1935.
68. Rexford G. Tugwell, Minutes of the conference at Buck Hills Falls.
69. Associated Press, July 2, 1935.
70. Letter from Bernard Baruch to Eleanor Roosevelt, Oct. 24, 1935.
71. Letter from Eleanor Roosevelt to Rexford Tugwell, July 8, 1935.
72. Letter from Eleanor Roosevelt to Elsie Clapp, July 8, 1935.
73. Letter from Eleanor Roosevelt to Rexford Tugwell, Aug. 3, 1935.
74. Letter from Eleanor Roosevelt to Elsie Clapp, Aug. 9, 1935.
75. Letter from Clarence Pickett to Eleanor Roosevelt, Aug. 26, 1935.
76. Letter from Eleanor Roosevelt to Elsie Clapp, Aug. 23, 1935.
77. Letter from Bernard Baruch to Eleanor Roosevelt, Oct. 24, 1935, Jan. 27, 1936, and April 6, 1936.
78. Eleanor Roosevelt, speech to the Women's National Democratic Club, Jan. 24, 1936; Schlesinger, Jr., *The Coming of the New Deal,* pp. 371–72.
79. Steinberg, *Mrs. R.: The Life of Eleanor Roosevelt,* cited (Ch. 14), p. 210.
80. Rexford G. Tugwell, Foreword to E. C. Banfield, *Government Project* (Glencoe, Ill., 1951), p. 12.
81. "Diary of a Homesteader's Wife," *Liberty,* Jan. 2, 1937; letter from Bernard Baruch to Eleanor Roosevelt, June 22, 1936.
82. Letter from Eleanor Roosevelt to Bernard Baruch, July 12, 1936.
83. *Ibid.*
84. Letter from Raymond Kenny to Eleanor Roosevelt, June 8, 1940; letter from Eleanor Roosevelt to Maj. Dillon, June 15, 1940; letter from James Rowe to Eleanor Roosevelt, July 31, 1940.
85. Letter from Eleanor Roosevelt to Bernard Baruch, July 12, 1936.
86. Letter from Eleanor Roosevelt to Mrs. Marshall, May 25, 1938; letter from Eleanor Roosevelt to Maj. Walker, July 5, 1938.
87. Letter from Pa Watson to Malvina Thompson Scheider, March 26, 1935.
88. Lash Diaries, May 27, 1940.
89. David E. Lilienthal, *The Journals of David E. Lilienthal* (New York, 1964), I, p. 236.
90. Conkin, p. 167.
91. F. D. Roosevelt, *Public Papers,* cited (Ch. 13), 1938, p. 356.
92. E. Roosevelt, *TIR,* cited (Ch. 16), p. 133.

93. "Eden Liquidated," *Business Week,* July 27, 1946.
94. Letter from Eleanor Roosevelt to C. D. Beebe, Sept. 5, 1934.

38. PUBLICIST FOR THE NEW DEAL—COLUMNIST AND LECTURER

1. Eleanor Roosevelt, speeches and articles, 1934.
2. President's Personal File 2, Sept. and Oct., 1934.
3. Letter from Eleanor Roosevelt to L. Denison, Nov. 2, 1934.
4. *New York Times,* May 21 and 14, 1934, respectively.
5. *Radio Guide,* Nov., 1935; "First Lady of the Land Is First Lady of Radio," NBC Feature Service, 1939.
6. Letter from Eleanor Roosevelt to Clarence Pickett, March 4, 1937.
7. E. Roosevelt, "My Day," cited (Ch. 8), July 15, 1937.
8. Letter from Eleanor Roosevelt to Granville B. Jacobs, Aug. 13, 1937.
9. Eleanor Roosevelt, DAR speech, April 21, 1934.
10. Letter from Dorothy Canfield Fisher to Eleanor Roosevelt, April 23, 1934.
11. Eleanor Roosevelt, Alderson speech, May 28, 1934.
12. Letter from Mary Harris to Eleanor Roosevelt, May 31, 1934.
13. Letter from Frank P. Graham to Eleanor Roosevelt, June 17, 1935; Negro woman, quoted in *St. Louis Globe Democrat,* Nov. 5, 1939.
14. E. Roosevelt, "My Day," March 10, 1936; report to W. Colston Leigh in Eleanor Roosevelt file, March 14, 1936.
15. Virginia James, article in Omaha morning newspaper, undated.
16. Letter from Eleanor Roosevelt to Bess Furman, March 29, 1937; letter from Eleanor Roosevelt to Franklin D. Roosevelt, Nov. 10, 1937; Associated Press, March 22, 1937.
17. E. Roosevelt, "My Day," Nov. 10, 1936, and letter from T. P. Carpenter to Eleanor Roosevelt, Nov. 19, 1936.
18. The Frenchman's remark quoted by June Rhodes to Eleanor Roosevelt, Nov. 4, 1935; Eleanor Roosevelt chosen as best-dressed woman, Dec. 28, 1934; letter from Eleanor Roosevelt to Lily Loscher, Sept. 16, 1939.
19. Letter from Elizabeth von Hesse to Eleanor Roosevelt, Aug., 1937; letter from Eleanor Roosevelt to Elizabeth von Hesse, Feb. 1, 1938, and Elizabeth von Hesse's reply, Feb. 4, 1938.
20. Letter from Eleanor Roosevelt to Elizabeth von Hesse, Oct. 25, 1938.
21. Letter from Elizabeth von Hesse to Eleanor Roosevelt, Nov. 18, 1939; letter from Eleanor Roosevelt to Elizabeth von Hesse, April 10, 1939.
22. Letter from Leon Pearson to Eleanor Roosevelt, Dec. 3, 1938, and Eleanor Roosevelt's reply, Dec. 13, 1938.
23. Associated Press, Sept. 27, 1938.
24. Margaret Marshall, "Columnists on Parade," *Nation,* Feb. 26, 1938.
25. E. Roosevelt, "My Day," Dec. 31, 1935.
26. *Ibid.,* April 30, 1936, May 7, 20, and 10, 1936, July 27, 1936, and March 5, 1937.
27. *Ibid.,* Jan. 7, 1936.
28. Anne O'Hare McCormick, in the *New York Times,* Oct. 16, 1938.
29. Letter from Eleanor Roosevelt to Mrs. Frank, June 15, 1939, and to Mrs. Auer, Feb. 3, 1937.
30. E. Roosevelt, "My Day," Aug. 31, 1936; letter from Eleanor Roosevelt to Flora Rose, Feb. 13, 1937; E. Roosevelt, "My Day," Dec. 19, 1937, and March 10, 1937.
31. E. Roosevelt, "My Day," Sept. 21, 1936.
32. Letter from George Carlin to Malvina Thompson Scheider, Sept. 17, 1936.
33. Letter from Monte Bourjaily to Eleanor Roosevelt, Jan. 16, 1936, and Eleanor Roosevelt's reply, Jan. 17, 1936.
34. Damon Runyon, syndicated column, Nov. 1, 1937; letter from William Laas to Eleanor Roosevelt, March 23, 1940.
35. Letter from Eleanor Roosevelt to Nan Wood Honeyman, Jan. 22, 1936.
36. Women's National Press Club skit, in the *New York Times,* March 3, 1936.
37. Bruce Bliven, in the *New Republic,* Nov. 4, 1936; letter from United Features Syndicate to Eleanor Roosevelt, Nov. 16, 1936; Marshall, *op. cit.*

38. Letter from George Carlin to Eleanor Roosevelt, April 2, 1938.

39. Pegler, syndicated column attacking Eleanor Roosevelt, Aug. 6, 1940; for Franklin D. Roosevelt's comment, Lash Diaries, Aug. 5, 1940; Eleanor Roosevelt's reply to Pegler in "My Day," Aug. 9, 1940.

40. Letter from George Carlin to Eleanor Roosevelt, Aug. 7, 1940.

41. Letter from Eleanor Roosevelt to Dorothy Canfield Fisher, April 23, 1934.

42. Alma W. Johnson, "Farm Woman Battles the Depression," *Forum,* July, 1936; letter from Eleanor Roosevelt to Alma W. Johnson, Sept. 28, 1936.

43. E. Roosevelt, "My Day," Jan. 5, 1937; letter from Fannie Hurst to Eleanor Roosevelt, Feb. 13, 1937.

44. The Goulds, *An American Story,* cited (Ch. 29), p. 188; *New York Times,* Feb. 25, 1937; E. Roosevelt, "My Day," Feb. 26, 1937.

45. The Goulds, p. 272.

46. Letter from Eleanor Roosevelt to Martha Gellhorn, Jan. 16, 1937.

47. E. Roosevelt, *TIMS* MS., in FDRL.

48. Letter from Anna and John Boettiger to Eleanor Roosevelt, undated.

49. Letter from Bruce Gould to Eleanor Roosevelt, May 7, 1937.

50. The Goulds, p. 198.

51. E. Roosevelt, "My Day," Nov. 3, 1937.

52. Lady Florence Willert reported Alice Longworth's reaction to Eleanor Roosevelt in a letter, March 30, 1937.

39. WITHOUT LOUIS HOWE—THE 1936 CAMPAIGN

1. Letter from Eleanor Roosevelt to Mary Howe Baker, March 11, 1935; letter from Eleanor Roosevelt to Molly Dewson, March 22, 1935.

2. Letter from Eleanor Roosevelt to Grace Howe, Aug. 23, 1935.

3. Lela Stiles, *The Man behind Roosevelt* (Cleveland, 1954), pp. 289–94.

4. John Keller and Joseph Bouldt, "Franklin's on His Own Now," *Saturday Evening Post,* Oct. 12, 1940.

5. E. Roosevelt, "My Day," cited (Ch. 8), April 20, 1936; letter from Eleanor Roosevelt to Bernard Baruch, quoted in Stiles, p. 294.

6. Letter from Eleanor Roosevelt to Russell Carney, Nov. 1, 1935; letter from Molly Dewson to Eleanor Roosevelt, Nov. 5, 1935, and Dec. 19, 1935.

7. Letter from Eleanor Roosevelt to Charles E. Kizer, May 20, 1935.

8. Letter from Franklin D. Roosevelt to Eleanor Roosevelt, March 18, 1935.

9. Letter from Eleanor Roosevelt to Molly Dewson, March 9, 1935.

10. Caroline Phillips, Diaries, Feb. 12, 1935.

11. Letter from Eleanor Roosevelt to R. Gifford, March 20, 1935.

12. Letter from Eleanor Roosevelt to June Rhodes, Nov. 22, 1935.

13. Rosenman, *Working with Roosevelt,* cited (Ch. 33), p. 54.

14. Letter from Eleanor Roosevelt to Mrs. W. N. Prince, Feb. 13, 1935.

15. *New York Times,* Dec. 29 and 31, 1935; letter from Eleanor Roosevelt to Alfred Smith, Dec. 18, 1935; letter from Alfred Smith to Eleanor Roosevelt, Dec. 26, 1935; letter from Eleanor Roosevelt to Alfred Smith, Dec. 31, 1935.

16. Letter from Helen Robinson to Eleanor Roosevelt, March 7, 1935, and Eleanor Roosevelt's reply, March 12, 1935.

17. Eleanor Roosevelt, radio broadcast, March 17, 1935, and news conference, Feb. 17, 1935; letter from Molly Dewson to Eleanor Roosevelt, March 13, 1935.

18. Letter from Martha Strayer to Eleanor Roosevelt, Jan., 1935.

19. Letter from Molly Dewson to Eleanor Roosevelt, mid–1935.

20. Letter from Eleanor Roosevelt to Martha Gellhorn, June 26, 1936; Louis Howe, in an interview, in Furman, *Washington By-Line,* cited (Ch. 35), pp. 234–35.

21. Letter from Molly Dewson to Jim Farley, Dec. 21, 1935.

22. Letter from Molly Dewson to Charles Michelson, July 17, 1936.

23. Letter from Molly Dewson to Jim Farley, April, 1936; letter from Jim Farley to Eleanor Roosevelt, May 9, 1936.

24. Letter from Eleanor Roosevelt to Edward L. Roddan, April 18, 1936.

25. Eleanor Roosevelt, *My Days* (New York, 1938), p. 44 (a selection of Mrs. Roosevelt's columns).

26. Letter from Eleanor Roosevelt to Molly Dewson, May 22, 1936.

27. *New York Times,* June 24 and 25, 1936; *New York Herald Tribune,* June 26, 1936.

28. E. Roosevelt, "My Day," June 28, 1936; letter from Eleanor Roosevelt to Mrs. Philip Vaughn ("Bennett"), June 27, 1936.

29. Ickes, *Secret Diary,* cited (Ch. 24), I, p. 639; Franklin Roosevelt outlined his campaign in a letter to John Nance Garner, July 19, 1936.

30. Farley, *Behind the Ballots,* cited (Ch. 33), p. 354.

31. Letter from Eleanor Roosevelt to Franklin D. Roosevelt, July 16, 1936; letter from Eleanor Roosevelt to Jim Farley, July 16, 1936.

32. Ruth Finney, series of articles on Eleanor Roosevelt, in Scripps-Howard papers, May 26–31, 1937.

33. Alice Longworth, "The Ideal Qualifications of a President's Wife," *Ladies' Home Journal,* Feb., 1936.

34. *New York Times,* Nov. 8, 1936.

35. *Afro-American,* May 23, 1936; the attitudes of Steve Early and Marvin McIntyre in E. Roosevelt, *TIR,* cited (Ch. 16), p. 164.

36. Letter from Eleanor Roosevelt to Mrs. C. Whitney, Oct. 25, 1935.

37. Letter from Eleanor Roosevelt to Carrie Chapman Catt, April 18, 1936.

38. Emma Bugbee, in the *New York Herald Tribune,* March 3, 1936.

39. *New York Times,* July 12 and 22, 1936, and Aug. 21, 1936.

40. Finney, *op. cit.*

41. Thomas L. Stokes, *Chip Off My Shoulder* (Princeton, 1940), pp. 453 and 363 respectively.

42. *New York Herald Tribune,* June 24, 1936.

43. E. Roosevelt, *My Days,* pp. 79–80; interview with Alice Longworth

44. Letter from Eleanor Roosevelt to Dorothy Kenyon, Nov. 9, 1936.

45. Rosenman, pp. 134–35; F. D. Roosevelt, *Public Papers,* cited (Ch. 13), 1936, pp. 566–73.

46. E. Roosevelt, "My Day," Nov. 1, 1936; E. Roosevelt, *My Days,* pp. 82–84; "My Day," Nov. 2, 1936.

47. E. Roosevelt, "My Day," Nov. 4, 1936.

48. *Ibid.,* Nov. 15, 1936, and E. Roosevelt, *My Days,* p. 90.

49. Letter from Eleanor Roosevelt to Franklin D. Roosevelt, from Kansas City, Nov. 14, 1936.

40. WISE AS A SERPENT, GUILELESS AS A DOVE

1. Rexford G. Tugwell, *The Democratic Roosevelt* (New York, 1957), p. 332; E. Roosevelt, *My Days,* cited (Ch. 39), p. 129.

2. Letter from Eleanor Roosevelt to Josephine Roche, March 6, 1939; letter from Eleanor Roosevelt to Sanford Bates, Feb. 17, 1939.

3. Tully, *F.D.R. My Boss,* cited (Ch. 33), p. 110; letter from Eleanor Roosevelt to Esther Lape, Sept. 21, 1936; E. Roosevelt, "My Day," Oct. 6, 1937.

4. Geoffrey Hellman, "Mrs. Roosevelt," *Life,* Feb. 5, 1940; Tully, p. 110; *New York Times,* Nov. 17, 1936.

5. Letter from Ira Chandler to Eleanor Roosevelt, Feb. 16, 1936; letter from Franklin D. Roosevelt to Eleanor Roosevelt, Feb. 24, 1936.

6. Letter from Ana Maria O'Neil to Eleanor Roosevelt, May 13, 1938, enclosing unpublished book, *The Intangible Frontier,* which had just won a $1,000 prize offered by Northwestern University.

7. Helene Huntington Smith, in *McCall's,* July, 1935.

8. Max Weber, *From Max Weber: Essays in Sociology,* eds. H. H. Gerth and C. Wright Mills (New York, 1946), p. 295; Vera Brittain, *Thrice a Stranger* (New York, 1938), pp. 386–87.

9. Eleanor Roosevelt, speech on receiving the *Churchman* Award, Nov. 29, 1939.

10. Letter from Eleanor Roosevelt to Mrs. Walker, May 17, 1939; Lash Diaries, May 10, 1940; Eleanor Roosevelt, *Churchman* Award speech.

11. Letter from Eleanor Roosevelt to Frances Perkins, Sept. 14, 1939; letter from Eleanor Roosevelt to Harry Hopkins, May 3, 1937; letters from Eleanor Roosevelt to Steve Early, Sept. 23, 1936, and Aug. 27, 1937.

12. Letter from Eleanor Roosevelt, May 4, 1935.

13. Letter from Eleanor Roosevelt to Helen Hanson, May 19, 1939; letter from Malvina Thompson Scheider to Helen Hanson, Aug. 13, 1939.

14. E. Roosevelt, *TIR*, cited (Ch. 16), p. 6; E. Roosevelt, *My Days*, p. 13.

15. Alexander, OHP.

16. *Ibid.*

17. *Ibid.*

18. Letter from Eleanor Roosevelt to Chester Davis, Aug. 31, 1936.

19. Letter from Eleanor Roosevelt to Jane Ickes, Oct. 10, 1938.

20. Snowdrift episode, Associated Press, Feb. 16, 1937; Eleanor Roosevelt, in conversation with author.

21. E. Roosevelt, *TIR*, p. 164.

22. Arthur Krock, *Memoirs: Sixty Years on the Firing Line* (New York, 1968), p. 149; Michaelis, "A Recorded Portrait," cited (Ch. 11); Tugwell, in *Roosevelt Day Dinner Journal* of Americans for Democratic Action, Jan. 31, 1963.

23. John Morton Blum, *Years of Urgency* (New York, 1964), pp. 27–28, 436.

24. Letter from Harold Ickes to Eleanor Roosevelt, July 19, 1937.

25. Letter from Jo Coffin to Eleanor Roosevelt, May, 1936; letter from Katherine Lenroot to Malvina Thompson Scheider, April 7, 1938.

26. Letter from Eleanor Roosevelt to Harry Hopkins, April 9, 1936; letter from Eleanor Roosevelt to Clarence Pickett, April 21, 1936.

27. Letter from Joseph Robinson to Eleanor Roosevelt, April 20, 1936; and Eleanor Roosevelt's reply, April 21, 1936; Emergency Committee telegram to Eleanor Roosevelt, May 21, 1936; letter from Harry Hopkins to Eleanor Roosevelt, June 4, 1936.

28. Letter from Sen. Capper to Eleanor Roosevelt, Feb. 12, 1937.

29. Letter from Mrs. Ottenburg to Eleanor Roosevelt, Feb. 1, 1939, and Eleanor Roosevelt's reply, Feb. 2, 1939; letter from Eleanor Roosevelt to Rep. Ross Collins and Sen. James O'Mahoney, May 19, 1938.

30. Letter from Eleanor Roosevelt to the Citizens Committee on Old Age Security, Jan. 2, 1934; she appeared before the Tolan Committee Dec. 11, 1940.

31. Kathleen McLaughlin, in the *New York Times*, Jan. 21, 1940; Finney, series of articles, cited (Ch. 39).

32. Letter from Eleanor Roosevelt to Harold Ickes, April 18, 1937; letter from Harold Ickes to Eleanor Roosevelt, April 23, 1937.

33. Letter from Eleanor Roosevelt to Col. Harrington, April 15, 1939; letters from Eleanor Roosevelt to Aubrey Williams, March 7, 1936, Oct. 13, 1938, Dec. 12, 1938, and Oct. 21, 1938.

34. Letter from Eleanor Roosevelt to Franklin D. Roosevelt, Aug. 27, 1937; letter from Eleanor Roosevelt to Emma Guffey Miller, July 15, 1937.

35. Letter from Eleanor Roosevelt to Franklin D. Roosevelt, Nov. 18, 1935, and Franklin Roosevelt's reply, Nov. 22, 1935.

36. Letter from Eleanor Roosevelt to Ann Choate, Feb. 2, 1939.

37. H. H. Smith, "The First Lady," *McCall's*, Sept. 1935; letter from Eleanor Roosevelt to Molly Dewson, April 30, 1938.

38. Letter from Malvina Thompson Scheider to Frank Murphy, Jan. 13, 1940; letter from Lucy Mason to Eleanor Roosevelt, Jan. 23, 1940.

39. Letter from Eleanor Roosevelt to Mary Simkhovitch, Jan. 26, 1937, letter from Helen Alfred to Eleanor Roosevelt, Jan. 27, 1937.

40. Letters from Nathan Straus to Eleanor Roosevelt, Dec. 23, 1937, April 26, 1938, and May 23, 1938.

41. Letter from Eleanor Roosevelt to Esther Lape, Feb. 11, 1937, and Esther Lape's reply, March 10, 1937.

42. Letter from Esther Lape to Eleanor Roosevelt, June 8, 1937.

43. Telegram from Eleanor Roosevelt to Esther Lape, June 10, 1937, letter from Esther Lape to Joseph P. Lash, March 26, 1964.

44. Letter from Esther Lape to Eleanor Roosevelt, Aug. 10, 1939; letter from Eleanor Roosevelt to Esther Lape, Dec. 6, 1939.

45. Franklin D. Roosevelt, press conference, Dec. 22, 1939; F. D. Roosevelt, *Public Papers,* cited (Ch. 13), 1939, p. 598.

46. Ickes, *Secret Diary,* cited (Ch. 24), III, p. 396; Tully, p. 78.

47. Aubrey Williams, *A Southern Rebel,* unfinished autobiography, in Williams papers, in FDRL.

48. Eleanor Roosevelt, speech to the Washington Conference of WPA Directors of Women's and Professional Projects.

49. Letter from Eleanor Roosevelt to Harry Hopkins, Jan. 29, 1937, and Hopkins' reply, Feb. 15, 1937; letter from Eleanor Roosevelt to James Roosevelt, June 16, 1937.

50. Letter from Robert Cohn to Eleanor Roosevelt, Aug. 10, 1939; letter from Franklin D. Roosevelt to Henry Wallace, Aug. 24, 1939; letter from Eleanor Roosevelt to Franklin D. Roosevelt, Oct. 19, 1939; letter from Alexander Sachs to Eleanor Roosevelt, Jan., 1936.

51. Letter from Leonard Elmhirst to Eleanor Roosevelt, Dec. 11, 1937.

52. Bernard Baruch, statement to the Special Senate Committee on Unemployment, Feb. 28, 1938; letter from Eleanor Roosevelt to Bernard Baruch, March 15, 1939.

53. Letter from Harry Hooker to Eleanor Roosevelt, April 14, 1939.

54. *New York Herald Tribune* and the *New York Times,* Feb. 22, 1939. Heywood Broun, "It Seems to Me," *New York World-Telegram,* Feb. 24, 1939.

55. *New York Times,* March 13, 1939.

56. Tully, p. 105.

57. Eleanor Roosevelt, "Men Have to Be Humored," *Woman's Day,* Aug., 1940.

58. Lash Diaries, June 28, 1941.

59. Letter from Eleanor Roosevelt to Dr. D. E. Buckingham, Nov. 22, 1935; letter from Eleanor Roosevelt to Melvin Hazen, Nov. 29, 1935.

60. Letter from Eleanor Roosevelt to Harold Ickes, April 4, 1939.

61. *New York Times,* Aug. 9, 1939.

62. Letter from John C. O'Laughlin to Herbert Hoover, Aug. 10, 1939, O'Laughlin MS., Library of Congress.

63. Kathleen McLaughlin, article in the *New York Times,* Jan. 20, 1940.

64. Letter from Eleanor Roosevelt to Louis Fischer, Dec. 6, 1939.

65. Raymond Clapper, "The Ten Most Powerful People in Washington," *Look,* Jan. 28, 1941; Tully, p. 107; Jesse Jones, *Fifty Billion Dollars* (New York, 1951), p. 264; Gallup Poll files in Princeton, N.J.

66. Letter from Alfred North Whitehead to Eleanor Roosevelt, April, 1942; S. J. Woolf, in the *New York Times,* May 24, 1939.

41. CHANGES AT HYDE PARK

1. E. Roosevelt, "My Day," cited (Ch. 8), April 22, 1937.

2. *Ibid.,* June 19, 1939.

3. Letter from Malvina Thompson Scheider to Lorena Hickok, May 20, 1938.

4. Letter from Corinne Alsop to Eleanor Roosevelt, Jan. 10, 1936, and Eleanor Roosevelt's reply, Jan. 15, 1936.

5. Marquis W. Childs, *I Write from Washington* (New York, 1942), p. 117.

6. Letter from Sara D. Roosevelt to Franklin D. Roosevelt, Nov. 29, 1932.

7. Letter from Malvina Thompson Scheider to Georgiana Turner, May 20, 1939.

8. Eleanor Roosevelt, speech to the Conference on the Cause and Cure of War, Jan. 21, 1936.

9. E. Roosevelt, "My Day," April 7, 1937; *New York Times,* June 4, 1938.

10. Letter from Franklin D. Roosevelt to Eleanor Roosevelt, Dec. 17, 1937; letter from Eleanor Roosevelt to Caleb Coffin, March 3, 1938; letter from Eleanor Roosevelt to Harry Hooker, April 28, 1938.

11. Interview with Marion Dickerman.

12. Malvina Thompson Scheider to author, Lash Diaries, Aug. 9, 1940.

13. Interview with Agnes Leach.

14. Interview with Marion Dickerman.

15. Letter from Eleanor Roosevelt to Marion Dickerman, Nov. 9, 1938; letter from Eleanor Roosevelt to Harry Hooker, Feb. 4, 1939.

16. Interview with Esther Lape.

17. Letter from Malvina Thompson Scheider to Max Abelman, June 16, 1939.

18. Letter from Eleanor Roosevelt to Nancy Cook, May 26, 1937.

19. Letter from Eleanor Roosevelt to Matthew Hasbrouck, May 18, 1937; Eleanor Roosevelt, speeches and articles, in FDRL.

20. E. Roosevelt, "My Day," Jan. 15, 1939.

21. May Craig, in the *Portland Press Herald,* Nov. 3, 1937.

22. Letter from Eleanor Roosevelt to Frank Harting, July 16, 1937.

23. Edwin A. Robinson, "Aunt Imogen."

24. E. Roosevelt, "My Day," July 4, 1938; interview with Helen Wilmerding.

25. Letter from Eleanor Roosevelt to Maude Gray, Sept. 6, 1935.

26. E. Roosevelt, "My Day," Sept. 12, 1937.

27. Letter from Eleanor Roosevelt to Aileen Webb, Sept. 1, 1938; letter from Sara D. Roosevelt to Franklin D. Roosevelt, Feb. 17, 1936; E. Roosevelt, "My Day," July 31, 1938.

28. Letter from Eleanor Roosevelt to Leo Casey, July 3, 1938; letter from Eleanor Roosevelt to Franklin D. Roosevelt, July 30, 1938.

29. See Franklin D. Roosevelt, speech, "Informal, Extemporaneous Remarks before the Roosevelt Home Club," Aug. 27, 1938, in F. D Roosevelt, *Public Papers,* cited (Ch. 13), 1938, pp. 502–5.

30. Letter from Eleanor Roosevelt to Esther Lape, Aug. 28, 1938; E. Roosevelt, "My Day," July 20, 1939.

42. LIFE WITH MOTHER AND FATHER

1. E. Roosevelt, "My Day," cited (Ch. 8), Oct. 12, 1937; for her remark about when parties should end, see the *New York Herald Tribune,* May 27, 1938.

2. E. Roosevelt, *TIR,* cited (Ch. 16), p. 11.

3. Hoover, *Forty-two Years in the White House,* cited in (Ch. 34), pp. 28–29; interview with Christopher Phillips; Caroline Phillips, Diaries, Jan. 1, 1935.

4. Ickes, *Secret Diary,* cited (Ch. 24), I, p. 184.

5. *New York Times,* Feb. 20, 1934.

6. Clippings of Elliott's activities in Texas, dated May 28, 1940, and Sept. 11, 1940.

7. Letters from Eleanor Roosevelet to Franklin D. Roosevelt, Nov. 22 and 30, 1936.

8. Letter from Eleanor Roosevelt to an insurance man in Seattle, March 30, 1938.

9. Letter from Eleanor Roosevelt to Franklin D. Roosevelt, May 2, 1937.

10. Letter from Franklin D. Roosevelt to Eleanor Roosevelt, July 5, 1934; *New York Herald Tribune,* March 1, 1936; Sara D. Roosevelt's reaction quoted in J. Roosevelt and Shalett, *Affectionately, F.D.R.,* cited (Ch. 18), p. 273; letter from Sara D. Roosevelt to Franklin D. Roosevelt, March 15, 1940.

11. Letter from Eleanor Roosevelt to Mrs. Lewis Thompson, April 25, 1939; E. Roosevelt, "My Day," April 19, 1939; letter from Margaret Cutter to Eleanor Roosevelt, May 21, 1939.

12. E. Roosevelt, *TIR,* p. 176.

13. E. Roosevelt, "My Day," June 29, 1937; Eleanor Roosevelt to newspaperman, July 7, 1937; *New York Times,* June 30, 1937; letter from Eleanor Roosevelt to Caroline Phillips, May 21, 1938; *New York Times,* June 18, 1938.

14. Letter from Eleanor Roosevelt to Mrs. Douglas, Jan. 26, 1940; E. Roosevelt, *TIR,* p. 18; interview with Anna Roosevelt Halsted.

15. Interview with Anna Roosevelt Halsted; letter from Eleanor Roosevelt to Franklin D. Roosevelt, July, 1933; letter from Eleanor Roosevelt to Mrs. Douglas, Jan. 26, 1940.

16. E. Roosevelt, *TIR,* p. 165.

17. Letter from Eleanor Roosevelt to Mrs. Douglas, Jan. 26, 1940.

18. Letter from Eleanor Roosevelt to Beatrice Gould, Jan. 7, 1938.

19. Letter from Eleanor Roosevelt to Mrs. Douglas, Jan. 26, 1940.

20. Letter from Eleanor Roosevelt, Aug. 22, 1938.

21. Letter from Eleanor Roosevelt to Mrs. Philip Vaughn ("Bennett"), Nov. 11, 1935.

22. Letter from Eleanor Roosevelt to Franklin D. Roosevelt, Sept. 2, 1933.

23. Interview with Franklin D. Roosevelt, Jr.

24. E. Roosevelt, *TIR,* p. 10.

25. Letter from Eleanor Roosevelt to Miss Toynton, Jan. 7, 1939.

26. Letter from Eleanor Roosevelt to Franklin D. Roosevelt, March 8, 1937.
27. J. Roosevelt and Shalett, p. 218.
28. *Ibid.*, pp. 291, 269, 264.
29. Letter from Eleanor Roosevelt to Josephus Daniels, Oct. 5, 1937.
30. Interview with Anna Roosevelt Halsted.
31. E. Roosevelt, "My Day," Sept. 6, 8, 11, and 12, 1938.
32. *Washington Times,* Dec. 19, 1938.
33. *New York Times,* Jan. 6, 1939.
34. *Springfield News and Leader,* Dec. 18, 1938.
35. *New York Daily News,* Dec. 21, 1938.
36. Letter from Eleanor Roosevelt to Col. Patterson, Dec. 27, 1938.
37. J. Roosevelt and Shalett, p. 37.
38. E. Roosevelt, "My Day," April 6, 1938.
39. *Ibid.,* Nov. 8, 1938; E. Roosevelt, *TIR,* p. 11.

43. THE DIVIDED WHITE HOUSE
1. Eleanor Roosevelt, radio broadcast, July 6, 1937.
2. Emma Bugbee, in the *New York Herald Tribune,* March 2, 1937.
3. Letter from Eleanor Roosevelt to Helen Weiss, Jan. 20, 1938; letter from Eleanor Roosevelt to Mrs. Jane Barrett, Nov. 23, 1938.
4. Letter from William Laas to Eleanor Roosevelt, March 23, 1938; Eleanor Roosevelt, in the *Democratic Digest,* 1937.
5. Letter from Eleanor Roosevelt to Marion Dickerman, Jan. 13, 1938; letter from Eleanor Roosevelt to Harry Hopkins, Jan. 10, 1939.
6. Letter from Eleanor Roosevelt to Agnes Leach, Jan. 27, 1937; E. Roosevelt, *TIR,* cited (Ch. 16), p. 155.
7. Helen Robinson, Diaries, cited (Ch. 16), Jan. 31, 1938.
8. J. Roosevelt and Shalett, *Affectionately, F.D.R.,* cited (Ch. 18), p. 237; letter from Eleanor Roosevelt to James Roosevelt, July 30, 1959.
9. Letter from Eleanor Roosevelt to Ralph and Anna (owners of a beauty parlor), Oct. 28, 1938.
10. Letter from Steve Early to Eleanor Roosevelt, Jan. 25, 1937.
11. Letter from Eleanor Roosevelt to Mr. G——, May 7, 1936.
12. *Ibid.,* May 16, 1936.
13. E. Roosevelt, "My Day," cited (Ch. 8), Sept. 5, 1937.
14. Lash Diaries, Jan. 31, 1942.
15. Williams, *A Southern Rebel,* cited (Ch. 40) p. 94; E. Roosevelt, "My Day," Aug. 22, 1938.
16. Letter from Eleanor Roosevelt to Harry Hopkins, Dec. 9, 1937.
17. Harry Hopkins, memorandum, Jan. 19, 1945.
18. Robert E. Sherwood, *Roosevelt and Hopkins: An Intimate History New York, 1948), p. 171.*
19. Lash Diaries, Feb. 5, 1940.
20. Sherwood, p. 173.
21. Talk with Malvina Thompson Scheider at Campobello, June 28, 1941.
22. E. Roosevelt, *TIR,* p. 168; letter from Eleanor Roosevelt to May Craig, June 10, 1938; Ickes, *Secret Diary,* cited (Ch. 24), III, p. 371.
23. Interview with Samuel I. Rosenman; E. Roosevelt, *TIR,* pp. 4–8, 167–68.
24. Henry Morgenthau, Jr., in conversation with the author, May 30, 1963.
25. Information provided by Mrs. Winslow Carlton, who worked for Harry Hopkins; Blum, *Years of Urgency,* cited (Ch. 40), pp. 41–42; Sherwood, p. 285; interview with Anna Roosevelt Halsted.
26. E. Roosevelt, *TIR,* p. 173.
27. Interviews with Esther Lape and Trude Lash.
28. J. Roosevelt and Shalett, p. 277.
29. Interview with Anna Roosevelt Halsted.
30. Lash Diaries, Aug. 5, 1940.
31. Interview with Anna Roosevelt Halsted.
32. Letter from Eleanor Roosevelt to Maude Gray, June 9, 1940.

33. Interview with Anna Roosevelt Halsted; statement by Franklin D. Roosevelt, Jr., as recorded in Lash Diaries, June 4, 1941.

34. Interview with Samuel I. Rosenman.

35. Fulton Oursler, *Behold the Dreamer* (New York, 1964), pp. 424–25.

36. *Ibid.,* p. 435; Furman, *Washington By-Line,* cited (Ch. 35), pp. 271–72.

37. Letter from Eleanor Roosevelt to Fulton Oursler, Jan. 14, 1938.

38. Letter from Eleanor Roosevelt to "Doc" Cropley, Oct. 14, 1937; interview with Alice Longworth; J. Roosevelt and Shalett, p. 294.

39. Associated Press, Nov. 14, 1938; E. Roosevelt, "My Day," Nov. 14, 1938.

40. Lash Diaries, March 20, 1941, and Jan. 1, 1942; Oursler, pp. 424–25.

41. J. Roosevelt and Shalett, pp. 315, 319.

42. Letter from Eleanor Roosevelt to Rita Halle Kleeman, May 29, 1935.

44. A GATHERING STORM

1. Letter from Guildford N. Crawford to Eleanor Roosevelt, May 9, 1933.

2. Letter from C. E. Smith to Eleanor Roosevelt, Oct. 31, 1933; Clarence Pickett, quoted by Holly Cowan, "Arthurdale," cited (Ch. 37); Pickett, *For More than Bread,* cited (Ch. 37), p. 49; Alexander, OHP.

3. Letter from C.F. Klinefelter (of FERA) to Malvina Thompson Scheider, Nov. 6, 1934; letter from Aubrey Williams to state relief administrators and chief state school officers, Nov. 2, 1934.

4. Williams, *A Southern Rebel,* cited (Ch. 40); letter from Eleanor Roosevelt to Harry Hopkins, Nov. 2, 1934.

5. Letter from Eleanor Roosevelt to Harry Hopkins, Oct. 10, 1934; Rackham Holt, *Mary McLeod Bethune* (New York, 1964), p. 35.

6. Letter from M.J. Chisum to Eleanor Roosevelt, Jan. 29, 1934, and Eleanor Roosevelt's reply, Feb. 24, 1934; Alexander, OHP.

7. Letter from Claude Swanson to Eleanor Roosevelt, Dec. 6, 1935; letter from Eleanor Roosevelt to C.A. Franklin, Dec. 10, 1935.

8. Letter from Eleanor Roosevelt to Jane Hoey, Jan. 17, 1934.

9. Letter from Eleanor Roosevelt to Walter White, May 2, 1934.

10. Walter White, *A Man Called White: The Autobiography of Walter White* (New York, 1948), pp. 179–80.

11. Letter from Walter White to Eleanor Roosevelt, May 7, 1934; *ibid.,* May 29, 1934; letter from Walter White to Edward Costigan, June 8, 1934; letter from Edward Costigan to Sen. Robinson, June 11, 1934.

12. Letter from Walter White to Eleanor Roosevelt, Nov. 8, 1934; *ibid.,* Nov. 20, 1934; letter from Eleanor Roosevelt to Walter White, Nov. 23, 1934.

13. Letter from Eleanor Roosevelt to Walter White, Jan. 23, 1935.

14. *New York Times,* Feb. 12, 1935; letter from Eleanor Roosevelt to Walter White, Feb., 1935.

15. Letter from Eleanor Roosevelt to Walter White, May 8, 1935.

16. Letter from Eleanor Roosevelt to Steve Early, Aug. 8, 1935.

17. E. Roosevelt, *TIR,* cited (Ch. 16), p. 164.

18. Letter from Steve Early to Malvina Thompson Scheider, Sept. 11, 1935.

19. Letter from Barry Bingham to Marvin McIntyre, Aug. 29, 1934; letter from Eleanor Roosevelt to Barry Bingham, Sept. 4, 1934.

20. Letter from Eleanor Roosevelt to Molly Dewson, Dec. 30, 1935; letter from Felix Frankfurter to Eleanor Roosevelt, April 30, 1936.

21. Letter from Eleanor Roosevelt to Miss Conrad, Sept. 7, 1938.

22. Alexander, OHP; Sidney Baldwin, *Poverty and Politics: The Rise and Decline of the Farm Security Administration* (North Carolina, 1968), p. 332.

23. Alexander, OHP.

24. E. Roosevelt, "My Day," cited (Ch. 8), May 13, 1936.

25. Letter from Eleanor Roosevelt to John Flyner, Dec. 17, 1935.

26. Letter from Eleanor Roosevelt to Lucy Stewart, Feb. 21, 1939; on Eleanor Roosevelt's reaction to *Gone with the Wind,* see "My Day," Aug. 20, 1936; Eleanor Roosevelt's exchange with Esther Cary on the use of the word "darky," April 13, 1937.

27. Poppy Cannon, *A Gentle Knight* (New York, 1956), p. 9.

28. Samuel S. Battle OHP; letter from Mary McLeod Bethune to Eleanor Roosevelt, April 16, 1940; interview with Anna Roosevelt Halsted.

29. Letter from Eleanor Roosevelt to Pauli Murray, Dec. 19, 1938.

30. Letter from Harper's to Eleanor Roosevelt, Feb. 10, 1938, and Eleanor Roosevelt's reply, March 4, 1938; letter from Richard Wright to Eleanor Roosevelt, Aug. 22, 1938, and Eleanor Roosevelt's reply, Aug. 29, 1938.

31. Letter from Eleanor Roosevelt to Mrs. Lydia Wischan, March 1, 1938.

32. *New York Times,* April 22, 1938.

33 Marian Anderson, speech at the Memorial Day exercises in the Hyde Park rose garden, May 30, 1939.

34. Clark Foreman, "A Decade Hope," *Phylon,* Vol. XII, No. 2, 1951; Proceedings of the NYA National conference of Negro Youth, Jan. 12, 1939.

35. E. Roosevelt, "My Day," Feb. 28, 1939.

36. White, p. 182; letter from Corinne Alsop to Eleanor Roosevelt, Feb. 27, 1939.

37. Interview with Oscar Chapman; White, p. 182.

38. Ickes, *Secret Diary,* cited (Ch. 24), II, p. 615.

39. Letter from Walter White to Eleanor Roosevelt, April 12, 1939.

40. Letter from Eleanor Roosevelt to Walter White, April 12, 1939; letters from Walter White to Eleanor Roosevelt, April 14 and 17, 1939.

41. Ickes, II pp. 615–16.

42. Alexander, OHP, p. 332.

43. Memorandum, no date (probably 1942), President's Personal File 2.

44. Mary McLeod Bethune's memorandum, July 12, 1940; directive from the war Dept. to Gen. Watson, July 15, 1940.

45. Letter from Henry Stimson to Franklin. Roosevelt, Aug. 20, 1940.

46. Letter from James Nabrit, Jr., to Eleanor Roosevelt, Sept. 17, 1940.

47. Letter from Franklin D. Roosevelt to Eleanor Roosevelt, Sept. 24, 1940.

48. Letter from Eleanor Roosevelt to Franklin D. Roosevelt, undated.

49. Letter from Walter White to Eleanor Roosevelt, Oct. 3, 1940.

50. Henry Stimson, Diary, Sept 27, 1940, Yale University Library.

51. White, p. 187; letter from Eleanor Roosevelt to Viola Ilma, Oct. 26, 1940.

52. Letter from Crystal Bird Fauset to Elinor Morgenthau, Oct. 15, 1940; letter from Eleanor Roosevelt to Oscar Ewing, Oct. 25, 1940.

53. Alexander, OHP.

54. Letter from Eleanor Roosevelt to Mrs. Wender, Nov. 13, 1940.

55. Leuchtenburg, *Franklin D. Roosevelt and the New Deal,* cited (Ch. 35), p. 322; *Crisis,* XLVII, 1940.

56. Roy Wilkins, OHP.

57. Eleanor Roosevelt, unpublished foreword to Pearl S. Buck's letter to the *New York Times,* Nov. 15, 1941, which was to be published as a pamphlet, a project that was dropped after Pearl Harbor.

58. Stimson, Diary, Jan. 24, 1941.

59. Letter from Eleanor Roosevelt's secretary to Sidney Hillman, May 5, 1941.

60. Letter from Aubrey Williams to Eleanor Roosevelt, May 29, 1941; letter from Sidney Hillman to Eleanor Roosevelt, May 23, 1941; White House luncheon on May 29, 1941.

61. The luncheon is described by Alexander, OHP.

62. Letter from Eleanor Roosevelt to A. Philip Randolph, June 10, 1941.

63. Letter from Wayne Coy to Steve Early, June 21, 1931; letter from Aubrey Williams to Joseph P. Lash, March 1, 1964.

64. White, p. 190.

65. Letter from Gen. Watson to Franklin D. Roosevelt, June 14, 1941.

66. Letter from A. Philip Randolph to Franklin D. Roosevelt, June 16, 1941.

67. Interview with Anna Rosenberg (Mrs. Paul Hoffman).

68. Telegrams from Aubrey Williams to Eleanor Roosevelt, June 20 and 24, 1941.

69. Letter from Aubrey Williams to Joseph P. Lash, March 1, 1964; telegram from Aubrey Williams to Eleanor Roosevelt, June 25, 1941; Lash Diaries, June 23 and 26, 1941; Franklin

D. Roosevelt, memorandum to Rudolph Forster, in Official File; telegram from A. Philip Randolph to Eleanor Roosevelt, June 24, 1941, and Eleanor Roosevelt's reply, June 26, 1941.

70. Letter from Walter White to Eleanor Roosevelt, Sept. 22, 1941.

71. Lash Diaries, Aug. 1, 1941.

45. THE YOUTH MOVEMENT

1. *New York Times,* May 7, 1934.

2. *Ibid.*

3. Letters from Eleanor Roosevelt to Harry Hopkins, March 24, 1934, and Oct. 5, 1934; letter from Eleanor Roosevelt to Mrs. Bostwick, Nov. 7, 1933.

4. *New York Times,* Nov. 25, 1933.

5. Letter from Henry Goddard Leach to Eleanor Roosevelt, Jan. 10, 1934, and Eleanor Roosevelt's reply, Jan. 22, 1934.

6. *Woman's Home Companion,* May, 1934; letter from Eleanor Roosevelt to Newton D. Baker, Oct. 4, 1934, and Baker's reply, Oct. 8, 1934.

7. Letter from Eleanor Roosevelt, Dec. 3, 1934.

8. Eleanor Roosevelt described this experience in a speech to the Altrusa Club, El Paso, Texas, March 11, 1938.

9. Interview with Rabbi Arnold Lasker, one of the participants; Minutes of the Youth Today Meeting, Nov. 22, 1934; E. Roosevelt, speech, Altrusa Club.

10. Letter from Eleanor Roosevelt to Lady Florence Willert, Jan. 16, 1935.

11. In questions and answers submitted by Harper's when she was writing *TIR.*

12. Oursler, *Behold the Dreamer,* cited (Ch. 43), pp. 393–400; Smith, "The First Lady," cited (Ch. 40).

13. Frances Perkins, report to the Senate, April 5, 1935.

14. E. Roosevelt, *TIR,* cited (Ch. 16), pp. 162–63.

15. Letter from Eleanor Roosevelt to Cornelia S. Adair, Oct. 23, 1935; Eleanor Roosevelt's "too late" comments on the Williams letter, Aug. 20, 1935; letters from Aubrey Williams to Eleanor Roosevelt, Nov. 22 and 23, 1935; letter from Eleanor Roosevelt to Aubrey Williams, Nov. 30, 1935.

16. Letter from Aubrey Williams to Eleanor Roosevelt, Nov. 20, 1935; Aubrey Williams, "Youth and the Government," *Progressive Education,* Dec., 1935; Ruby Black, *Eleanor Roosevelt* (New York, 1940); letter from Ruby Black to Malvina Thompson Scheider, July 5, 1940.

17. Letter from Eleanor Roosevelt to Homer Rainey, March 24, 1936; letter from Eleanor Roosevelt to John Lang, March 21, 1936; Eleanor Roosevelt, radio broadcast, March 18, 1936; Republican criticism of the NYA made by Mrs. Eugene Meyer in radio debate, Feb. 27, 1936.

18. Letter from Camp Jane Addams' girls to Eleanor Roosevelt, June 25, 1936.

19. Letter from Aubrey Williams to Eleanor Roosevelt, Oct. 14, 1936; letter from Charles Taussig to Eleanor Roosevelt, June, 1940; letter from Mrs. Carroll to Eleanor Roosevelt, Aug. 13, 1936.

20. Eleanor Roosevelt, speech at the University of North Carolina, June 1, 1935.

21. E. Roosevelt, "My Day," cited (Ch. 8), Dec. 6, 1936.

22. Letter from Viola Ilma to Eleanor Roosevelt, June 15, 1934, and Eleanor Roosevelt's reply, Aug. 15, 1934.

23. Letter from Viola Ilma to Eleanor Roosevelt, Dec. 7, 1934.

24. Letter from Eleanor Roosevelt to Waldo McNutt, April 23, 1935.

25. Letters from Eleanor Roosevelt to William Hinckley, Jan. 16 and 21, 1936; Associated Press, Feb. 9, 1936.

26. Summary of the Proceedings of the National Council of the American Youth Congress, Jan., 1936; William Hinckley, in *Progressive Education,* Dec., 1935.

27. Summary of the Proceedings of the National Council of the American Youth Congress, *op. cit.;* for the NYA's analysis of the American Youth Act, see the memorandum from Dorothy I. Cline, undated.

28. Letter from Mark McCloskey to Eleanor Roosevelt, Feb. 4, 1936, and Eleanor Roosevelt's reply, Feb. 11, 1936.

29. Letter from Joseph P. Lash to a friend, Jan. 29, 1936.

30. Letter from John Little, New York chairman of the Young Communist League, to Eleanor Roosevelt, May 4, 1936, and Eleanor Roosevelt's reply, May 9, 1936.

31. Letter from Eleanor Roosevelt to William Hinckley, Nov. 30, 1936.

32. Letter from Abbott Simon to Eleanor Roosevelt, Jan. 7, 1937; letter from Eleanor Roosevelt to Abbott Simon, Jan. 14, 1937.

33. See letters from Eleanor Roosevelt to Robert Fechner, director of the CCC, Dec. 11, 1935; from Robert Fechner to the War Dept., Dec. 12, 1935; from Robert Fechner to Eleanor Roosevelt, Dec. 12, 1935.

34. Letters from Abbott Simon to Franklin D. Roosevelt, Feb. 11 and 12, 1937; letter from Eleanor Roosevelt to Abbott Simon, Feb. 13, 1937; Minutes of the National Executive Committee, American Student Union, March 20 and 21, 1937.

35. Letter from the American Youth Congress to affiliates, March 8, 1937; letter from Aubrey Williams to William Hinckley, Feb. 22, 1937.

36. Letter from Mark McCloskey to Eleanor Roosevelt, Feb. 11, 1938, and Eleanor Roosevelt's reply, Feb. 15, 1938.

37. Letter from Eleanor Roosevelt to Mark McCloskey, Feb. 15, 1938.

38. Letter from Eleanor Roosevelt to Franklin D. Roosevelt, Jan. 7, 1938.

39. *America,* Aug. 6, 1938; letter from Eleanor Roosevelt to Father Murphy, Aug. 16, 1938.

40. Letter from Eleanor Roosevelt to James West, Aug. 13, 1938.

41. E. Roosevelt, speech, Altrusa Club.

42. E. Roosevelt, "My Day," Aug. 16, 17, and 21, 1938.

43. Letter from Aubrey Williams to William Hinckley, Feb. 22, 1937.

44. Eleanor Roosevelt, speech to the *New York Herald Tribune* Forum, *New York Times,* Oct. 25, 1938; Abbott Simon, report to the American Youth Congress, Feb. 17, 1938; Minutes of the American Youth Congress Resident Board, May 2, 1938.

45. May Craig, syndicated columns, Oct., 1938.

46. Joseph P. Lash, speech "Students in the Service of Democracy," Dec. 27, 1938; memorandum from Franklin D. Roosevelt, Jan. 17, 1939; letter from James Roosevelt to Franklin D. Roosevelt, Feb. 2, 1939, and Franklin Roosevelt's telegram in reply, undated.

47. Associated Press, Jan. 31, 1939.

48. Letter from Aubrey Williams to Eleanor Roosevelt, June 21, 1939; Minutes of the American Youth Congress Resident Board, May 18, 1939; F. D. Roosevelt, *Public Papers,* cited (Ch. 13), 1939, p. 332.

49. Alexander, OHP.

50. Letter from Harry Hopkins to Eleanor Roosevelt, Sept. 18, 1940.

51. Letter from Aubrey Williams to Eleanor Roosevelt, Aug. 1, 1939.

52. "A Program of Action," issued by the American Youth Commission, Oct., 1939; Eleanor Roosevelt, speech to the American Youth Congress, Feb. 21, 1939.

53. "Proceedings of the Model Congress of Youth, July 1–5, 1939," American Youth Congress; *Time,* July 17, 1939.

54. *Ibid.*

46. FROM PACIFIST TO ANTI-FASCIST

1. Irwin Shaw, in the *New York Times,* May 3, 1936; E. Roosevelt, "My Day," cited (Ch. 38), May 20, 1936.

2. Eleanor Roosevelt, speech, Jan. 24, 1934; *New York Times,* May 19, 1934, and Jan. 3, 1935.

3. Letter from Eleanor Roosevelt to Lewis Chamberlain, Feb. 19, 1934; letter from Steve Early to Claude Swanson, May 23, 1934, and Swanson's reply, May 26, 1934; letter from Eleanor Roosevelt to Jeannette Rankin, Oct. 23, 1933; Franklin D. Roosevelt's attitude toward Japan based on Eleanor Roosevelt's reply to a question submitted by Lorena Hickok in connection with the writing of *TIR.*

4. Mary Gray Peck, *Carrie Chapman Catt* (New York, 1944), p. 351.

5. *New York Herald Tribune,* April 24, 1933.

6. Letter from Esther Lape to Eleanor Roosevelt, Dec. 10, 1933; letter from Franklin D. Roosevelt to Eleanor Roosevelt, Dec. 19, 1933; letter from Esther Lape to Eleanor Roosevelt, mid-Jan., 1934.

7. Letter from Esther Lape to Eleanor Roosevelt, March 18, 1934, and Eleanor Roosevelt's

reply, March 19, 1934; letter from Esther Lape to Eleanor Roosevelt, March 19, 1934; *New York Times,* March 23, 1934; letter from Eleanor Roosevelt to Esther Lape, April 12, 1934; letter from Esther Lape to Eleanor Roosevelt, Oct. 9, 1934; Hull, *Memoirs,* cited (Ch. 36), p. 388.

8. Wire from Esther Lape to Eleanor Roosevelt, Jan. 15, 1935.

9. F. D. Roosevelt, *Public Papers,* cited (Ch. 13), 1934, pp. 40–41; *New York Times,* Jan. 16, 1935.

10. Letter from Eleanor Roosevelt to Esther Lape, Jan. 24, 1935.

11. Eleanor Roosevelt, speech on WNBC, Jan. 27, 1935.

12. Letter from Eleanor Roosevelt to Esther Lape, Feb. 1, 1935.

13. Letter from Eleanor Roosevelt to Mrs. Kendall Emerson, Feb. 12, 1935.

14. Ickes, *Secret Diary,* cited (Ch. 24), I, pp. 284–85.

15. Letter from Eleanor Roosevelt to the League of Nations Association, Feb. 20, 1935.

16. Eleanor Roosevelt, speech in Chicago, *New York Times,* Nov. 1, 1935; on the defects of the "merchants of death" thesis, see George Thayer, *The International Trade in Armaments* (New York, 1969).

17. Hull, pp. 398–400.

18. Letter from Eleanor Roosevelt to John Haynes Holmes, Oct. 23, 1935.

19. Letter from Carola von Schaeffer-Bernstein to Eleanor Roosevelt, Jan. 3, 1936, and Eleanor Roosevelt's reply, Jan. 28, 1936.

20. *New York Times,* Jan. 24, 1936.

21. Letter from Eleanor Roosevelt to Miss Schillinger (with a copy to Farley), April 22, 1936.

22. Letter from Felix Frankfurter to Missy LeHand, April 14, 1936; letter from Eleanor Roosevelt to Felix Frankfurter, April 18, 1936; letter from Felix Frankfurter to Eleanor Roosevelt, April 21, 1936, and Eleanor Roosevelt's reply, April 30, 1936.

23. Clarence Pickett's draft of Eleanor Roosevelt's speech for the Emergency Peace Campaign with Franklin D. Roosevelt's corrections, Eleanor Roosevelt file.

24. Sumner Welles, *Seven Decisions That Shaped History* (New York, 1950), p. 4; E. Roosevelt, *My Days,* cited (Ch. 39), pp. 28–29.

25. Letter from Hendrik Willem Van Loon to Eleanor Roosevelt, June 23, 1935; letter from Eleanor Roosevelt to the Thomas Manns, June 22, 1935.

26. Letter from George F. Peabody to Eleanor Roosevelt, April 2, 1936; letter from Eleanor Roosevelt to Clarence Pickett, April 2, 1936.

27. *New York Times,* Aug. 28, 1936; Krock, *Memoirs,* cited (Ch. 40), p. 183.

28. Letter from Clarence Pickett to Eleanor Roosevelt, Aug. 28, 1936, and Eleanor Roosevelt's reply, Aug. 31, 1936.

29. Letter from Adm. Richard Byrd to Eleanor Roosevelt, Jan. 27, 1937.

30. Letter from Eleanor Roosevelt to Adm. Richard Byrd, Jan. 27, 1937.

31. *New York Times,* April 7, 1937.

32. See F. D. Roosevelt, *Public Papers,* 1937, pp. 406–11, for "quarantine" speech delivered Oct. 5, 1937, and *ibid.,* pp. 422–25, for the press conference held the next day at Hyde Park; E. Roosevelt, "My Day," Oct. 6, 1937.

33. Welles, pp. 71–73.

34. Letter from Eleanor Roosevelt to Miss Baker, Jan. 2, 1938; letter from Eleanor Roosevelt to Mrs. Graham, Feb. 2, 1938.

35. Letter from Carola von Schaeffer-Bernstein to Eleanor Roosevelt Dec. 13, 1936; E. Roosevelt, "My Day," May 27, 1937.

36. E. Roosevelt, "My Day," June 1, 1937.

37. *Ibid.,* July 9, 1937; letter from Martha Gellhorn to Eleanor Roosevelt, July 18, 1937.

38. Letter from Eleanor Roosevelt to Anna Louise Strong, May 18, 1937.

39. Letter from Eleanor Roosevelt to Martha Gellhorn, June 14, 1937.

40. *Ibid.,* June 24, 1937.

41. Letter from Patrick Scanlan to Eleanor Roosevelt, Aug. 10, 1937, and Eleanor Roosevelt's reply, Aug. 10, 1937.

42. *New York Times,* April 30, 1938, and May 2, 1938; *New York Herald Tribune,* April 18, 1938; E. Roosevelt, *My Days,* p. 238.

43. Letter from Sra. de los Rios to Eleanor Roosevelt, April 2, 1938.

44. Letter from Eleanor Roosevelt to Louis Fischer, Feb. 25, 1938.

45. Letter from Franklin D. Roosevelt to Eleanor Roosevelt, Dec. 8, 1938; letter from Eleanor Roosevelt to Martha Gellhorn, June 29, 1938.

46. Max Lerner, in the *New York Post,* Nov. 9, 1962.

47. Letter from Catherine Delehanty to Eleanor Roosevelt, Jan. 30, 1939, and Eleanor Roosevelt's reply, Feb. 7, 1939; letter from Eleanor Roosevelt to C. P. Minnigerode of the Corcoran Gallery, Feb. 19, 1939.

48. Letter from Sra. de los Rios to Eleanor Roosevelt, March 31, 1939.

49. Letter from Annie T. Ganey to Eleanor Roosevelt, March 18, 1939, and Eleanor Roosevelt's reply, March 24, 1939.

50. Gunther, *Roosevelt in Retrospect,* cited (Ch. 26), p. 191.

47. A SPIRITUAL SHOCK

1. Eleanor Roosevelt's answer to Malvina Thompson Scheider's memorandum, Nov. 23, 1935; E. Roosevelt, "My Day," cited (Ch. 8), Sept. 9, 1936.

2. Lash Diaries, April 20, 1940; E. Roosevelt, notes in preparation for the writing of *TIR.*

3. Welles, *Seven Decisions That Shaped History,* cited (Ch. 46), pp. 22–23.

4. Eleanor Roosevelt, speech to the Conference on the Cause and Cure of War, Jan. 19, 1938.

5. Sumner Welles, *The Time for Decision* (New York, 1944), pp. 66–67; Winston Churchill, *The Gathering Storm* (Boston, 1948), pp. 254, 255; letter from Eleanor Roosevelt to Martha Gellhorn, April 5, 1938.

6. E. Roosevelt, "My Day," Sept. 16, 1938.

7. *Ibid.,* Sept. 20, 1938.

8. Letter from Eleanor Roosevelt to Franklin D. Roosevelt, Sept. 21, 1938.

9. Thomas Mann, *The Coming Victory of Democracy* (New York, 1938); E. Roosevelt, "My Day," Sept. 23, 1938.

10. Letter from Eleanor Roosevelt to Marguerite Few, Sept. 28, 1938.

11. E. Roosevelt, "My Day," Sept. 28, 1938.

12. *Ibid.,* Sept. 30, 1938.

13. *Ibid.,* Oct. 7, 1938; letter from Eleanor Roosevelt to Helen Gifford, Oct. 14, 1938.

14. Letter from Mrs. Philip Vaughn ("Bennett") to Eleanor Roosevelt, Dec. 14, 1938, and Eleanor Roosevelt's reply, Jan. 4, 1939.

15. Letter from Eleanor Roosevelt to Franklin D. Roosevelt, Oct. 21, 1938.

16. Letter from the Grand Duchess Marie to Eleanor Roosevelt, April, 1934; letter from Eleanor Roosevelt to the Grand Duchess Marie, July 2, 1934.

17. Letter from Eleanor Roosevelt to Judge Justine Polier, Jan. 4, 1939.

18. Letter from Eleanor Roosevelt to Franklin D. Roosevelt, Feb. 22, 1939; letter from Eleanor Roosevelt to Judge Justine Polier, Feb. 28, 1939.

19. Franklin D. Roosevelt, memorandum, June 2, 1939; E. Roosevelt, speech to the Conference on the Cause and Cure of War.

20. Letter from Eleanor Roosevelt to Mrs. Clark, Aug. 22, 1938.

21. Weldon Wallace, carbon copy of a story written for the *Baltimore Sun,* based on an interview with Eleanor Roosevelt which took place in 1954 on the subject of racial prejudice.

22. Eleanor Roosevelt, "The Future of the Jews," *Liberty,* Nov. 25, 1938, written in reply to an article on the same subject by H. G. Wells.

23. Letter from Eleanor Roosevelt to Mrs. Paxton, Feb. 15, 1937.

24. E. Roosevelt, "The Future of the Jews."

25. Letter from Eleanor Roosevelt to Dr. Hyman, Nov. 19, 1938.

26. Letter from S. Margoshes to Eleanor Roosevelt, Dec. 24, 1938; letter from Malvina Thompson Scheider to S. Margoshes, Jan. 3, 1939.

27. E. Roosevelt, "My Day," Feb. 2, 1939.

28. *New York Times,* Feb. 5 and 8, 1939, and March 1, 1939.

29. E. Roosevelt, "My Day," April 3, 1939.

30. *Ibid.,* April 17, 1939.

31. F. D. Roosevelt, *Letters,* cited (Ch. 10), IV, pp. 867–68; the Rev. Charles E. Coughlin's comment, in the *New York Times,* June 12, 1939.

32. E. Roosevelt, "My Day," May 28, 1939.

33. Alexander, OHP; Ickes, *Secret Diary,* cited (Ch. 24), II, pp. 642–50.

34. *New York Times,* June 10 and 14, 1939.

35. Letter from Eleanor Roosevelt to Kathleen McLaughlin, June 29, 1939.

36. Harry Hopkins, Papers, in FDRL.

37. Helen Robinson, Diaries, cited (Ch. 16), June 11, 1939.

38. E. Roosevelt, "I Remember Hyde Park," cited (Ch. 10).

39. Letter from Eleanor Roosevelt to Maude Gray, June 13, 1939.

40. Ickes, II, pp. 642–50.

41. E. Roosevelt, "My Day," July 20, 1939.

42. Letter from Eleanor Roosevelt to Mrs. Helen Hirst, July 25, 1939; letter from Eleanor Roosevelt to Martha Gellhorn, Aug. 8, 1939.

43. Letter from Mrs. Philip Vaughn ("Bennett") to Eleanor Roosevelt, Nov. 26, 1939, and Eleanor Roosevelt's reply, Dec. 15, 1939.

44. E. Roosevelt, "My Day," Aug. 24, 1939.

45. *Ibid.,* Sept. 1, 1939; letter from Carola von Schaeffer-Bernstein to Eleanor Roosevelt, Aug. 19, 1939.

46. Letter from Eleanor Roosevelt to Carola von Schaeffer-Bernstein, Sept. 6, 1939.

47. Letter from Harry Hooker to Anna Roosevelt Boettiger, Sept. 11, 1939.

48. *New York Times,* Sept. 16, 1939; letter from Eleanor Roosevelt to Maude Gray, Sept. 17, 1939.

49. Letter from Eleanor Roosevelt to Mrs. Barmore, Oct. 3, 1939.

48. MRS. ROOSEVELT AND THE COMMUNISTS

1. Letters from Alice Davis to Eleanor Roosevelt, Dec. 24, 1933, and Oct. 15, 1934; E. Roosevelt, "My Day," cited (Ch. 8), Dec. 4, 1936.

2. Lorena Hickok, reports to Harry Hopkins, in FDRL.

3. Letter from Eleanor Roosevelt to Miss Holden, Nov. 7, 1934.

4. Letter from Lorena Hickok to Aubrey Williams, Aug., 1934; letter from Eleanor Roosevelt to Mrs. Goodspeed, Oct. 4, 1934.

5. Letter from Eleanor Roosevelt to Mrs. Deane, June 7, 1934.

6. Letter from Eleanor Roosevelt to Robert W. Bingham, Jan. 8, 1934, and Bingham's reply, Jan. 14, 1934; letter from Eleanor Roosevelt to Robert W. Bingham, Jan. 27, 1934.

7. Elizabeth Dilling, *The Red Network* (published by the author, Milwaukee, 1934), p. 317; letter from Eleanor Roosevelt to Mrs. Trautman, July 1, 1936.

8. Franklin D. Roosevelt, address to the Foreign Policy Association, Oct. 21, 1944, in F. D. Roosevelt, *Public Papers,* cited (Ch. 13), 1944, pp. 342–54.

9. Caroline Phillips, Journals, Feb. 13, 1918; letters from Eleanor Roosevelt to Franklin D. Roosevelt, July 20, 1918, and Aug. 8, 1918.

10. Letter from Esther Lape to Joseph P. Lash, Oct. 12, 1970; interview with Esther Lape.

11. Krock, *Memoirs,* cited (Ch. 40), pp. 149–50.

12. E. Roosevelt, "My Day," Feb. 20, 1936.

13. Letter from Sarah Millin to Eleanor Roosevelt, Nov. 17, 1936.

14. Letter from Anna Louise Strong to Eleanor Roosevelt, Jan. 29, 1935.

15. Letter from Eleanor Roosevelt to Anna Louise Strong, Feb. 13, 1935.

16. Letter from Alice Davis to Eleanor Roosevelt, Dec. 11, 1936.

17. Eleanor Roosevelt, speech at the Women's Faculty Club, Harvard University, Dec. 5, 1935; letter from Eleanor Roosevelt to Helen Reid, Nov. 8, 1938; E. Roosevelt, "My Day," Sept. 26, 1938.

18. Letter from Franklin D. Roosevelt to John Cudahy, April 16, 1938, may be found in F. D. Roosevelt, *Letters,* cited (Ch. 10), IV, p. 776.

19. Letter from Anna Louise Strong to Eleanor Roosevelt, Feb 13, 1937, and Eleanor Roosevelt's reply, Feb. 24, 1937; letter from Mrs. Joseph Davies to Eleanor Roosevelt, April 12, 1938, and Eleanor Roosevelt's reply, April 27, 1938.

20. Letters from Jerome Davis to Eleanor Roosevelt, March 1 and 26, 1938, and Eleanor Roosevelt's reply, April 15, 1938.

21. Letter from Eleanor Roosevelt to Mrs. William B. Meloney, Nov. 28, 1938.

22. Arthur Krock, in the *New York Times,* June 8 and 9, 1939; Frank Kent, in the *Baltimore Sun,* June 5, 1939.

23. Letter from Eleanor Roosevelt to Mrs. Bernstein, June 21, 1939.
24. Letter from Eleanor Roosevelt to Anna Louise Strong, Oct. 25, 1939.

49. FDR ADMINISTERS A SPANKING
1. Letter from Paul Kellogg to Eleanor Roosevelt, July 5, 1939.
2. The *New Republic,* quoted in Walter Goodman, *The Committee* (New York, 1968), p. 74.
3. *New York Times,* Nov. 22, 1939.
4. Goodman, p. 74.
5. Lash Diaries, Nov. 29, 1939.
6. *Ibid.*
7. E. Roosevelt, "My Day," cited (Ch. 8), Dec. 1, 1939.
8. Letter from Eleanor Roosevelt to Bernard Baruch, Dec. 2, 1939; *ibid.,* Dec. 12, 1939.
9. Ickes, *Secret Diary,* cited (Ch. 24), II, p. 721.
10. Lash Diaries, Jan. 16, 1940, and Feb. 9, 1940.
11. Eleanor Roosevelt's marginal note on Aubrey Williams' letter to her, Nov. 11, 1939.
12. Lash Diaries, Feb. 5, 1940.
13. Letter from Harlan Miller to William Hassett, in the President's Secretary's File; E. M. Watson to William Hassett, Feb. 7, 1940.
14. Letter from John W. Studebaker to William Hassett, Feb. 5, 1940, and letter from Aubrey Williams to William Hassett, Feb. 5, 1940. Both Hassett and Judge Samuel I. Rosenman, whom the author consulted when he was writing *Eleanor Roosevelt, A Friend's Memoir* (cited, Ch. 2), said they thought the president had written this speech himself.
15. Franklin D. Roosevelt, speech to the American Youth Congress, Feb. 10, 1940, in F. D. Roosevelt, *Public Papers,* cited (Ch. 13), 1940, pp. 87–94.
16. "This Is Youth Speaking: Record of the National Citizenship Institute, Feb. 9–12, 1940," American Youth Congress; Dewey L. Fleming, in the *Baltimore Sun,* Feb. 11 and 12, 1940.
17. Lorena Hickok recalled the episode of Tommy's lacing into the Youth Congress leaders in a letter to Nannine Joseph, Feb. 5, 1954; E. Roosevelt, *TIR,* cited (Ch. 16), p. 201; Lash Diaries, March 6 and 29, 1940.
18. Lash Diaries, Feb. 19, 1940, and May 9, 1940.
19. Letter from Eleanor Roosevelt to Joseph P. Lash, March 8, 1940.
20. Transcript 649 A, contained in Roosevelt press conferences, in FDRL, June 5, 1940.
21. In 1936, Roosevelt told David Lilienthal of his hopes that the thoughtfulness of youth and women about economic issues would ensure the growth and consolidation of liberalism. See Lilienthal, *The Journals of David E. Lilienthal,* cited (Ch. 37), I, p. 64.
22. Letter from Eleanor Roosevelt to Joseph Cadden, May 12, 1940.
23. Betty Lindley and Thelma McKelvey, report, in Eleanor Roosevelt files, 1940.
24. Letters from Eleanor Roosevelt to Mrs. Dorothy Backer, May 12 and 14, 1940; letter from Eleanor Roosevelt to the Youth Congress leaders, undated.
25. Letter from Eleanor Roosevelt to the Youth Congress leaders, Dec. 16, 1940.
26. *Ibid.,* Sept. 17, 1941.
27. Letter from Eleanor Roosevelt to Polly Raymond, Oct. 22, 1941.

50. THE THIRD TERM
1. James A. Farley, *Jim Farley's Story* (New York, 1948), p. 302.
2. Bess Furman Armstrong, "Public Man's Wife," the *New York Times Magazine,* May 14, 1939.
3. Letter from Anne Shriber to Eleanor Roosevelt, Oct. 24, 1939.
4. Letter from Eleanor Roosevelt to Lionberger Davis, Sept. 13, 1940; letter from Malvina Thompson Scheider to Emma Bugbee, Jan. 10, 1940.
5. Eleanor Roosevelt, *The Moral Basis of Democracy* (New York, 1940), p. 69; Emma Bugbee, in the *New York Herald Tribune,* Jan. 21, 1940.
6. Letter from William Allen White to Franklin D. Roosevelt, Dec. 22, 1939; *New York Times,* Dec. 20, 1939.
7. E. Roosevelt, *My Days,* cited (Ch. 39), p. 108; newspaper clippings: *New York Times, New York Herald Tribune, New York Post, New York Sun, New York World Telegram,* and the *New York Daily News,* Jan. 21, 1937.
8. *New York Times,* Jan. 15, 1938, and Nov. 6, 1939.

9. Ickes, *Secret Diary,* cited (Ch. 24), II, p. 456; letter from Eleanor Roosevelt to Lady Florence Willert, Jan. 12, 1938; letter from Eleanor Roosevelt to Franklin D. Roosevelt, Aug. 12, 1938.

10. Helen Robinson, Diaries, cited (Ch. 16), Oct. 8, 1938.

11. Farley, p. 164; F. D. Roosevelt, *Public Papers,* cited (Ch. 13), 1939, p. 64.

12. Letter from Franklin D. Roosevelt to Eleanor Roosevelt, May 13, 1939; letter from Eleanor Roosevelt to George Taylor, May 29, 1939.

13. Ickes, II, p. 589.

14. Sherwood, *Roosevelt and Hopkins,* cited (Ch. 43), p. 117.

15. Ickes, II, p. 606.

16. Memorandum from Eleanor Roosevelt to Franklin D. Roosevelt, undated; Lash Diaries, Feb. 4, 1940.

17. Letter from Eleanor Roosevelt to Franklin D. Roosevelt, April 11, 1940.

18. Lash Diaries, April 20, 1940.

19. Letter from Eleanor Roosevelt to Maude Gray, May 17, 1940.

20. Lash Diaries, June 3, 1940.

21. *Ibid.,* Eleanor Roosevelt, speech to the Junior Chamber of Commerce, Jan. 2, 1941, in which she described this conversation with the president; United Press, Jan. 2, 1941.

22. Letter from Eleanor Roosevelt to Maude Gray, June 9, 1940.

23. E. Roosevelt, "My Day," cited (Ch. 8), June 10, 1940.

24. Letter from Eleanor Roosevelt to Isabella (Mrs. Harry) King, Aug. 22, 1940; Ickes, III, p. 207.

25. E. Roosevelt, *TIR,* cited (Ch. 16), pp. 212–14; Emma Bugbee, in the *New York Herald Tribune,* July 19, 1940; *Fortune* survey, reported in the *New York World Telegram,* June 24, 1940.

26. E. Roosevelt, "My Day," June 27, 1940.

27. *Ibid.,* July 17, 1940.

28. The author was at Val-Kill the week of the convention and recorded his observations in his diary, July 15–19, 1940; Francis Biddle, *In Brief Authority* (New York, 1962), p. 140.

29. Farley, pp. 283, 299; E. Roosevelt and Hickok, *Ladies of Courage,* cited (Ch. 30), pp. 281–84; E. Roosevelt, *TIR,* p. 215; E. Roosevelt, "My Day," July 19 and 20, 1940; Lash Diaries, July 15–19, 1940.

30. *New York Daily News,* June 24, 1940; interview with Alice Longworth; the incident in the president's oval study is recorded in Lash Diaries, Feb. 5, 1941.

31. Gardner Jackson, OHP.

32. *New York Daily News,* July 19, 1940.

33. Letter from Helen Reid to Eleanor Roosevelt, July 19, 1940; letter from George Norris to Eleanor Roosevelt, July 19, 1940.

34. Letter from May Craig to Eleanor Roosevelt, Aug. 6, 1940, and Eleanor Roosevelt's reply, Aug. 8, 1940; Eleanor Roosevelt, press conference, *New York Times,* June 3, 1940; copy of memorandum from Eleanor Roosevelt on mobilization of the entire country sent to Harry Hooker, undated; letter from Eleanor Roosevelt to Nan Honeyman, July 18, 1940; E. Roosevelt, "My Day," Aug. 5, 7, and 28, 1940; Eleanor Roosevelt, speech to the *New York Herald Tribune* Forum, Oct. 22, 1940.

35. Franklin D. Roosevelt, press-conference transcript, Sept. 24, 1940; letter from Selden Rodman to Eleanor Roosevelt, Sept. 26, 1940; letter from Eleanor Roosevelt to Franklin D. Roosevelt, Oct. 8, 1940; letter from Eleanor Roosevelt to Selden Rodman, Oct. 28, 1940.

36. Henry L. Stimson, *On Active Service* (New York, 1947), p. 353.

37. Lash Diaries, Aug. 4, 1940.

38. E. Roosevelt, "My Day," Aug. 5, 1940.

39. Letter from David Gray to Eleanor Roosevelt, Aug. 29, 1940.

40. Ickes, III, p. 295.

41. Lash Diaries, Feb. 4, 1940.

42. Letter from Eleanor Roosevelt to Maude Gray, Aug. 9, 1940; letter from Eleanor Roosevelt to Ruby Black, Aug. 6, 1940; letter from Molly Dewson to Eleanor Roosevelt, July 13, 1940, and Eleanor Roosevelt's reply, Aug. 8, 1940; letter from Eleanor Roosevelt to Fiorello LaGuardia, Aug. 24, 1940.

43. Lash Diaries, Aug. 14, 1940; letter from Eleanor Roosevelt to Leon Gilson, Oct. 8, 1940.

44. Interview with Franklin D. Roosevelt, Jr.

45. Letter from Eleanor Roosevelt to Franklin D. Roosevelt, Oct. 11, 1940.

46. Letter from Eleanor Roosevelt to Maude Gray, Oct. 17, 1940.

47. Reaction to Franklin D. Roosevelt, Jr.'s campaigning in President's Personal File 5; letter from Eleanor Roosevelt to Franklin D. Roosevelt, Oct. 17, 1940.

48. Letter from E. M. Watson to Franklin D. Roosevelt, Oct. 1, 1940.

49. F. D. Roosevelt, *Public Papers,* 1940, p. 517; E. Roosevelt, "My Day," Oct. 31, 1940.

50. Letter from Katherine Littell to Malvina Thompson Scheider, Oct. 29, 1940.

51. Recollection of Trude Lash.

52. E. Roosevelt, "My Day," Nov. 5, 1940.

53. Letter from Eleanor Roosevelt to Maude Gray, Nov. 3, 1940.

54. Lash Diaries, Nov. 5, 1940.

55. Accounts of election night at Hyde Park in New York newspapers, Nov. 6, 1940; Lash Diaries, Nov. 5 and 6, 1940.

56. Lash Diaries, Nov. 5 and 6, 1940; letter from Eleanor Roosevelt to Lady Florence Willert, Nov. 16, 1940.

51. A JOB TO DO

1. Letter from Eleanor Roosevelt to Joseph P. Lash, Jan. 14, 1941.

2. Letter from Esther Lape to Eleanor Roosevelt, Dec. 15, 1940, and Eleanor Roosevelt's reply, Dec. 19, 1940.

3. Bonaro W. Overstreet, in the *National Parent Teacher,* May 1950; E. Roosevelt, "My Day," cited (Ch. 8), Jan. 21, 1941.

4. Eleanor Roosevelt's reaction to Lillian Hellman's *Watch on the Rhine* in Lash Diaries, April 20, 1941.

5. Letter from Eleanor Roosevelt to Martha Gellhorn, Sept. 27, 1939; Lash Diaries, May 29, 1940.

6. Lash Diaries, June 15, 1940.

7. Henry L. Feingold, *The Politics of Rescue: the Roosevelt Administration and the Holocaust, 1938–1944* (New Brunswick, N.J., 1970), p. 160; on the State Dept.'s visa policy after the fall of France, see Feingold, Ch. VI; Arthur D. Morse, *While Six Million Died* (New York, 1967), pp. 294–304; David S. Wyman, *Paper Walls: America and the Refugee Crisis, 1938–1941* (Mass., 1968), pp. 138–50; letter from Albert Einstein to Eleanor Roosevelt, July 26, 1941.

8. Lash Diaries, June 24, 1940; letter from Eleanor Roosevelt to A. A. Berle, June 25, 1940.

9. Letter from Karl Frank to Eleanor Roosevelt, Aug. 15, 1940.

10. Memorandum from Franklin D. Roosevelt to Eleanor Roosevelt, Oct. 2, 1940. The exchange was occasioned by Mrs. Roosevelt's efforts to help Dr. Edith Vogel of Keuka College to get her mother and sister out of Prague.

11. Letter from Eleanor Roosevelt to Franklin D. Roosevelt, Nov. 27, 1940; letters from Eleanor Roosevelt to Summer Welles, Dec. 11 and 30, 1940.

12. Letter from Mrs. Lion Feuchtwanger to Eleanor Roosevelt, May 17, 1960.

13. Nelson Rockefeller replied, Jan. 14, 1941, saying that he hoped her decision was "not final as I know nothing would be more helpful at this time than your visit to South America."

14. Letter from James Gerard to Eleanor Roosevelt, Nov. 6, 1940, and Eleanor Roosevelt's reply, Nov. 9, 1940.

15. Letter from Lady Stella Reading to Eleanor Roosevelt, Dec. 1, 1939, and Eleanor Roosevelt's reply, Dec. 28, 1939; letter from Eleanor Roosevelt to Mrs. Schoonmaker, Dec. 29, 1939; letter from Florence Kerr to Eleanor Roosevelt, Dec. 4, 1940; letter from Ellen Woodward to Eleanor Roosevelt, Jan. 2, 1941; letter from Harriet Elliott to Eleanor Roosevelt, Jan. 2, 1941; memorandum from Franklin D. Roosevelt to Eleanor Roosevelt, Jan. 5, 1941.

16. Lash Diaries, Jan. 16, 1941.

17. *Ibid.,* Feb. 27, 1941.

18. See E. Roosevelt, *TIR,* cited (Ch. 16), p. 239, for Hopkins' attitude toward the health program; letter from Eleanor Roosevelt to Aubrey Williams on the NYA and Farm Security, Jan. 12, 1942; on the food-stamp program, see the letter from Henry B. Sell to Malvina Thompson, Nov. 8, 1942; *New York Times,* Oct. 30, 1941; *New York Herald Tribune,* Feb. 1, 1941.

19. F. D. Roosevelt, *Public Papers,* cited (Ch. 13), 1941, p. 44; see also pp. 162–66.

20. Ickes, *Secret Diary,* cited (Ch. 24), III, pp. 406–8.

21. F. D. Roosevelt, *Public Papers,* 1941, pp. 162–66.

22. Interview with Samuel I. Rosenman; Ickes, III, pp. 398, 518.

23. Letter from Florence Kerr to Franklin D. Roosevelt, May 22, 1941; letter from Harriet Elliott to Franklin D. Roosevelt, May 22, 1941.

24. Letter from Fiorello LaGuardia to Eleanor Roosevelt, June 5, 1941, and Eleanor Roosevelt's reply, June 10, 1941; *New York Herald Tribune,* June 18, 1941.

25. Ickes, III, p. 572; interview with Anna Rosenberg Hoffman.

26. On Florence Kerr's troubles with Mayor LaGuardia, see her letter to Eleanor Roosevelt, Feb. 16, 1942; letter from Eleanor Roosevelt to Franklin D. Roosevelt, July 22, 1941; Franklin D. Roosevelt, remarks to the Civilian Participation Committee, July 24, 1941, in F. D. Roosevelt, *Public Papers,* 1941, pp. 277–81.

27. For Eleanor Roosevelt's criticism of volunteer-participation plans, see the *New York Times,* Aug. 28, 1941; letter from Eleanor Roosevelt to Fiorello LaGuardia, Aug. 29, 1941; on the White House meeting on civil defense, see the letter from Eleanor Roosevelt to Jane Seaver, Aug. 31, 1941; Minutes of the White House meeting on civil defense, Sept. 3, 1941; Lash Diaries, Sept. 6, 1941; letter from Eleanor Roosevelt to Joseph P. Lash, Sept. 3, 1941.

28. On Anna Rosenberg's and Harry Hopkins' persuading her to take the OCD job, see the letter from Eleanor Roosevelt to Florence Kerr, Feb. 18, 1942; E. Roosevelt, *TIR,* p. 240; interview with Anna Rosenberg.

29. Letter from Eleanor Roosevelt to Anna Rosenberg, Sept. 6, 1941.

30. Letter from Eleanor Roosevelt to Maude Gray, Sept. 14, 1941; Helen Robinson, Diaries, cited (Ch. 16), Sept. 7, 1941.

31. E. Roosevelt, "My Day," Sept. 7, 1941; letter from Eleanor Roosevelt to Joseph P. Lash, Sept. 9, 1941.

32. Lash Diaries, Oct. 23, 1941; letter from Eleanor Roosevelt to Miss Rank, Aug. 31, 1942.

33. Letter from Eleanor Roosevelt to Joseph P. Lash, Sept. 14, 1941; letter from Eleanor Roosevelt to Maude Gray, Sept. 26, 1941; E. Roosevelt, "My Day," Sept. 26, 1941.

34. Letter from Eleanor Roosevelt to Joseph P. Lash, Sept. 16, 1941.

35. *Ibid.,* Oct. 2, 1941.

36. Letter from Eleanor Roosevelt to Lady Stella Reading, Oct. 4, 1941.

37. Letter from Eleanor Roosevelt to Paul V. McNutt, Nov. 9, 1941; letter from Eleanor Roosevelt to M. L. Wilson, Nov. 6, 1941; letter from Eleanor Roosevelt to Belle Roosevelt, Nov. 5, 1941.

38. James Landis, OHP.

39. Interview with Justine Polier; letter from Paul Kellogg to Francis Biddle, Jan. 13, 1942; letter from Leila Pinchot to Eleanor Roosevelt, Feb. 20, 1942; letters from Kathrine Lenroot to Eleanor Roosevelt, Aug. 27, 1942, and Dec. 3, 1942; letter from Katherine Lenroot to Frances Perkins, Dec. 23, 1942.

40. Interview with Justine Polier; letter from Paul Kellog to Eleanor Roosevelt, July 28, 1942.

41. E. Roosevelt, *TIR,* p. 233; Eleanor Roosevelt, radio broadcast, Dec. 7, 1941.

42. Landis, OHP.

43. E. Roosevelt, *TIR,* p. 234.

44. Lash Diaries, Dec. 8, 1941.

45. *Ibid.,* Dec. 8 and 9, 1941.

46. Letter from Eleanor Roosevelt to Alice Huntington, Dec. 16, 1941; letters from Eleanor Roosevelt to Joseph P. Lash, Dec. 11 and 13, 1941.

47. Letter from Wayne Coy to Franklin D. Roosevelt, Dec. 13, 1941; letter from Eleanor Roosevelt to James Landis, Dec. 16, 1941; Harold Smith, Diary, in FDRL.

48. Last Diaries, Jan. 1, 1942; Smith, Diary, Jan. 2, 1942.

49. *Congressional Record,* Jan. 8, 1942.

50. *Ibid.,* Jan. 12, 1942, and Feb. 6, 1942; Eleanor Roosevelt, press conference, Feb. 10, 1942, and Eleanor Roosevelt's staff chart, Feb. 18, 1942.

51. Landis, OHP.

52. *Ibid.*

53. Letter from John C. O'Laughlin to Herbert Hoover, Feb. 7, 1942.

54. Samuel Grafton, in the *New York Post,* Feb. 11, 1942.
55. *Congressional Record,* Feb. 9, 1942.
56. *New York Times,* Feb. 13, 1942.
57. Letter from Eleanor Roosevelt to Paul Kellogg, Feb. 10, 1942; letter from Eleanor Roosevelt to James Landis, Jan. 30, 1942.
58. Landis, OHP.
59. Letter from Eleanor Roosevelt to James Landis, Jan. 30, 1942.
60. Landis, OHP; *New York Times,* Feb. 12, 1942.
61. Fiorello LaGuardia, WNYC broadcast, Feb. 15, 1942.
62. E. Roosevelt, TIR, p. 250; Eleanor Roosevelt, radio broadcast, Feb. 22, 1942.
63. Letter from Eleanor Roosevelt to Joseph P. Lash, July 26, 1942; Landis, OHP.

52. GI'S FRIEND, I: JOURNEY TO BRITAIN
1. Letter from Eleanor Roosevelt to Joseph P. Lash, Feb. 5, 1942; Lash Diaries, Dec. 26, 1941; letter from Eleanor Roosevelt to Maude Gray, June 7, 1942.
2. For remarks of the American Legion official, see the *New York Times,* April 6, 1942, and for Eleanor Roosevelt's reply, see *ibid.,* April 18, 1942; letter from Eleanor Roosevelt to Joseph P. Lash, March 20, 1942.
3. Letter from Eleanor Roosevelt to Franklin D. Roosevelt, March 23, 1942.
4. Forrest C. Pogue, *George C. Marshall: Ordeal and Hope* (New York, 1965), pp. 115–16; letter from George Bye to Eleanor Roosevelt, March 19, 1942; letter from Eleanor Roosevelt to Frank Knox, March 11, 1942; letter from Eleanor Roosevelt to Archibald MacLeish, March 15, 1942; letter from Gen. Frederick H. Osborn to Eleanor Roosevelt, Sept. 18, 1942; letter from Eleanor Roosevelt to Maj. Gen. Magee, July 21, 1942, and Magee's reply, July 25, 1942; letter from Eleanor Roosevelt to Anthony Castorino, May 28, 1942; letter from Eleanor Roosevelt to Maude Gray, May 9, 1942.
5. Letter from Eleanor Roosevelt to Summer Welles, March 9, 1942; letter from Charles Taft to Eleanor Roosevelt, March 24, 1942.
6. Letter from Eleanor Roosevelt to Maude Gray, Oct. 6, 1942.
7. Letter from Eleanor Roosevelt to Lady Florence Willert, July 9, 1942; letter from Eleanor Roosevelt to Helen Ferris, Oct. 19, 1942.
8. Letter from Eleanor Roosevelt to Lady Stella Reading, Oct. 4, 1941; letter from Eleanor Roosevelt to Maude Gray, July 31, 1942; letter from Eleanor Roosevelt to Mrs. Philip Vaughn ("Bennett"), Aug. 11, 1942.
9. Letter from Eleanor Roosevelt to Henry Stimson, Sept. 22, 1942; Stimsom, Diary, cited (Ch. 44), Oct. 2, 1942.
10. Letter from Lord Halifax to Eleanor Roosevelt, Sept. 17, 1942; letter from Eleanor Roosevelt to Gilbert Winant, Sept. 22, 1942; memorandum from Franklin D. Roosevelt to Eleanor Roosevelt, Oct. 16, 1942.
11. The account of the trip, unless otherwise noted, is drawn from Eleanor Roosevelt, "Diary of Trip to Gt. Britain—Oct. 21 to Nov. 17, 1942," unpublished.
12. *London Daily Mail,* Nov. 18, 1942.
13. Eleanor Roosevelt, Diary; Eleanor Roosevelt, press-conference transcript, Nov. 19, 1942; E. Roosevelt, TIR, cited (Ch. 16), p. 264.
14. *London Daily Mail,* Nov. 18, 1942.
15. Letter from Eleanor Roosevelt to Franklin D. Roosevelt, Oct. 25, 1942.
16. Chalmers Roberts, "Mrs. Roosevelt's Visit to Britain," confidential memorandum to Wallace Carroll written at the end of Mrs. Roosevelt's trip.
17. *London Times,* Oct. 27, 1942.
18. Handwritten note from Adm. Harold R. Stark to Eleanor Roosevelt, Oct. 27, 1942.
19. Letter from Eleanor Roosevelt to Joseph P. Lash, Jan. 4, 1942.
20. E. Roosevelt, Diary; E. Roosevelt, TIR, p. 275.
21. Gallup poll, reported in the *New York Times,* Dec. 9, 1942.
22. E. Roosevelt, Diary; E. Roosevelt, TIR, p. 251; letter from Eleanor Roosevelt to Joseph P. Lash, Nov. 1, 1942.
23. Stimson, Diary, Nov. 20, 1942.
24. Letter from Sir Cecil Graves to Gilbert Winant, Dec. 2, 1942.

53. A CONSCIOUSNESS OF COLOR

1. Letter from Pearl Buck to Eleanor Roosevelt, Dec. 18, 1941; letter from Eleanor Roosevelt to R. J. Divine, Jan. 29, 1942.

2. Lash Diaries, Dec. 26, 1941.

3. Letter from Eleanor Roosevelt to Alice Huntington, Jan. 3, 1942; letter from Joseph P. Lash to Trude Pratt, May 31, 1942.

4. Telegram from Pearl Buck *et al.* to Franklin D. Roosevelt, Jan. 16, 1942.

5. Memorandum from Franklin D. Roosevelt to Eleanor Roosevelt, March 11, 1942; Eleanor Roosevelt, review of Pearl Buck, *American Unity and Asia* (New York, 1942), in the *New Republic,* Aug. 3, 1942; letter from Pearl Buck to Eleanor Roosevelt, July 29, 1942.

6. Jane Plimpton was the Vassar student leader; the dinner exchange was reported by the author to Trude Pratt, May 31, 1942.

7. Letter from Eleanor Roosevelt to Gil Harrison, June 23, 1942; letter from Eleanor Roosevelt to Mrs. M. Clark, Sept. 18, 1942; Walter White, speech at Madison Square Garden, June 16, 1942.

8. Robert Hopkins made a copy of his father's memorandum available to Anna Roosevelt Halsted.

9. Eleanor Roosevelt's comment on the Odell Waller case is quoted here from her letter to A. M. Kroeger, Aug. 20, 1942; Mrs. Oswald B. Lord, with the OCD in New York, described the attitude of the Negro leaders in her letter to Eleanor Roosevelt, July 8, 1942.

10. Letter from Pauli Murray to Eleanor Roosevelt, July 23, 1942, and Eleanor Roosevelt's reply, Aug. 3, 1942.

11. Letter from Malvina Thompson to Steve Early, July 30, 1943; Howard W. Odum, report, "On Trying to Analyze Southern Racial Tensions...," 1943.

12. Odum, *op. cit.;* letter from Eleanor Roosevelt to Mrs. Dowling, Dec. 31, 1942; letter from Ruby Black to Eleanor Roosevelt, Oct. 6, 1943; letter from Will Alexander to Eleanor Roosevelt, Oct. 16, 1943.

13. Letter from Eleanor Roosevelt to Joseph P. Lash, July 1, 1943.

14. *Louisville Courier-Journal,* July 2, 1943; letter from Trude Pratt to Joseph P. Lash, June 29, 1943.

15. Warren Brown, "Negro Looks at Negro Press," *Reader's Digest,* Jan., 1943; letter from Eleanor Roosevelt to Walter White, Jan. 4, 1943, and White's reply, Jan. 11, 1943.

16. Eleanor Roosevelt, "If I Were a Negro," *Negro Digest,* Oct., 1943.

17. Letter from the Rev. Nelson to Eleanor Roosevelt, Oct. 30, 1943, and Eleanor Roosevelt's reply, Nov. 11, 1943.

18. *Amsterdam News,* Nov. 6, 1943; letter from Eleanor Roosevelt to George Hawkins, Oct. 23, 1943; letter from Eleanor Roosevelt to Pauli Murray, July 26, 1943.

19. Letter from Eleanor Roosevelt to Joseph P. Lash, July 11, 1943.

20. Eleanor Roosevelt, unpublished article on Mme. Chiang Kai-shek.

21. Letter from Trude Pratt, who accompanied Mrs. Roosevelt, to Joseph P. Lash, Feb. 1, 1943.

22. Letters from Eleanor Roosevelt to Joseph P. Lash, Feb. 1 and 12, 1943.

23. *Ibid.*

24. Letter from Trude Pratt to Joseph P. Lash, May 30, 1943.

25. Letter from Eleanor Roosevelt to Joseph P. Lash, Feb. 17, 1943.

26. Raymond Clapper, in the *New York World-Telegram,* Feb. 20, 1943; E. Roosevelt, "My Day," cited (Ch. 8), Feb. 18, 1943; letter from Eleanor Roosevelt to Joseph P. Lash, Feb. 19, 1943.

27. Letter from Trude Pratt to Joseph P. Lash, March 3, 1943.

28. E. Roosevelt, *TIR,* cited (Ch. 16), p. 285.

29. Harris, *Pearl S. Buck,* cited (Ch. 31), p. 292; letter from Eleanor Roosevelt to Walter White, Feb. 16, 1943.

30. Harris, pp. 292–93.

31. E. Roosevelt, *TIR,* p. 284; interview with Maureen Corr.

32. Letter from Eleanor Roosevelt to Joseph P. Lash, Feb. 28, 1943; letter from Trude Pratt to Joseph P. Lash Feb. 24, 1943.

33. Letter from Eleanor Roosevelt to Joseph P. Lash, March 12, 1943; letter from Walter

Judd to Eleanor Roosevelt, March 22, 1943; Joseph Alsop, quoted in Sherwood, *Roosevelt and Hopkins,* cited (Ch. 43), p. 731.

34. Letters from Eleanor Roosevelt to Joseph P. Lash, March 17, 1943, April 10, 1943, and May 22, 1943.

35. *Ibid.,* May 21, 1943, and April 22, 1943.

36. Sherwood, p. 716; letter from Eleanor Roosevelt to Joseph P. Lash, May 18, 1943.

37. Letter from Mme. Chiang Kai-shek to Eleanor Roosevelt, July 8, 1943, and Eleanor Roosevelt's reply, July 26, 1943.

54. GI'S FRIEND, II: THE FIRST LADY AND THE ADMIRAL

1. Letter from Eleanor Roosevelt to Mrs. Fife, Aug. 5, 1943; letter from Eleanor Roosevelt to Joseph P. Lash, July 25, 1943.

2. My account of Mrs. Roosevelt's trip to the South Pacific, unless otherwise noted, is drawn from her diary.

3. Letter from Eleanor Roosevelt to Franklin D. Roosevelt, Aug. 20, 1943; *Pacific Times,* Aug. 29, 1943.

4. Letters from Eleanor Roosevelt to Malvina Thompson, Aug. 19, 22, 23, and 25, 1943.

5. William F. Halsey and J. Bryan, *Admiral Halsey's Story* (New York, 1946), p. 166.

6. Letter from Eleanor Roosevelt to Franklin D. Roosevelt, Aug. 26, 1943.

7. Halsey, p. 167.

8. Letter from Eleanor Roosevelt to Malvina Thompson, Sept. 3, 1943; letter from George Durno to Malvina Thompson, undated.

9. Letter from Eleanor Roosevelt to Franklin D. Roosevelt, Sept. 5, 1943; letter from Nelson T. Johnson to Eleanor Roosevelt, Sept. 7, 1943.

10. *New York Times,* Sept. 6, 1943; letter from Eleanor Roosevelt to Malvina Thompson, Sept. 7, 1943.

11. Letter from Eleanor Roosevelt to Doris Fleeson, Oct. 4, 1943; letter from Eleanor Roosevelt to Franklin D. Roosevelt, Sept. 6, 1943.

12. Robert M. White, "A Mother at the Front," the *Christian Advocate,* Dec. 30, 1943.

13. *New York Times,* Sept. 12, 1943; letter from Una Merkel to John Golden, April 17, 1944.

14. Letter from Eleanor Roosevelt to Malvina Thompson, Sept. 13, 1943.

15. Russell Smith in Martins Ferry, *Daily Times Leader,* Nov. 12, 1943.

16. Letter from Joseph P. Lash to Trude Pratt, Sept. 19, 1943.

17. Letter from Eleanor Roosevelt to Louis Weiss, Sept. 30, 1943; letter from Eleanor Roosevelt to Doris Fleeson, Oct. 4, 1943.

18. Halsey, pp. 167–68.

19. Eleanor Roosevelt, press conferences; in Honolulu, Sept. 21, 1943, in San Francisco, Sept. 23, 1943, and in Washington, D.C., Sept. 27, 1943; Eleanor Roosevelt, radio broadcast for war bonds, Sept. 27, 1943.

55. THE 1944 CAMPAIGN

1. Letter from Eleanor Roosevelt to Joseph P. Lash, Aug. 26, 1944.

2. *Ibid.,* Oct. 15, 1943.

3. *Ibid.,* Oct. 28, 1943.

4. F. D. Roosevelt, *Public Papers,* cited (Ch. 13), 1943, pp. 466–97; letter from Trude Pratt to Joseph P. Lash, Nov. 2, 1943.

5. Letter from Eleanor Roosevelt to Mme. Chiang Kai-shek, Jan. 3, 1944.

6. Letter from Eleanor Roosevelt to James Roosevelt, in J. Roosevelt and Shalett, *Affectionately, F.D.R.,* cited (Ch. 18), p. 345; letter from Eleanor Roosevelt to Joseph P. Lash, Dec. 5, 1943.

7. Letters from Eleanor Roosevelt to Maude Gray, Dec. 2, 1943, and Jan. 2, 1944; letter from Trude Pratt to Joseph P. Lash, Dec. 19, 1943; letter from Eleanor Roosevelt to Joseph P. Lash, Jan. 3, 1944; F. D. Roosevelt, *Letters,* cited (Ch. 10), IV, p. 1488.

8. Letter from Eleanor Roosevelt to Maude Gray, Jan. 22, 1944; letter from Eleanor Roosevelt to Joseph P. Lash, Jan. 27, 1944; letter from Franklin D. Roosevelt to Winston Churchill, March 17, 1943; F. D. Roosevelt, *Letters,* IV, p. 1413; Margaret Fayerweather, "My Diary in the White House," unpublished MS., in FDRL.

9. Letter from Eleanor Roosevelt to Joseph P. Lash, Nov. 11, 1943.

10. *Ibid.*, Feb. 1, 1944.

11. Franklin D. Roosevelt, press conference, Dec. 28, 1943, reprinted in F. D. Roosevelt, *Public Papers,* 1943, pp. 569–75; Eleanor Roosevelt, press conference, reported in the *New York Times,* Jan. 3, 1944; F. D. Roosevelt, *Public Papers,* 1944, pp. 80–82; letter from Eleanor Roosevelt to Joseph P. Lash, Feb. 24, 1944.

12. Letter from Eleanor Roosevelt to Maude Gray, Feb. 12, 1944; letter from Eleanor Roosevelt to Joseph P. Lash, March 2, 1944.

13. Letter from Eleanor Roosevelt to Franklin D. Roosevelt, March 13, 1944.

14. Letter from C. L. Maduro to Eleanor Roosevelt, March 20, 1944; letter from Franklin D. Roosevelt to Eleanor Roosevelt, April 5, 1944.

15. Letter from Eleanor Roosevelt to Mme. Vargas, March 15, 1944; letter from Eleanor Roosevelt to Franklin D. Roosevelt, March 17, 1944; "Analysis of Press Comment Prepared in the Office of Nelson Rockefeller, Coordinator of Inter-American Affairs," 1944; letter from Cordell Hull to Eleanor Roosevelt, April 3, 1944.

16. Ross T. McIntire, *White House Physician* (New York, 1946), p. 143; letters from Eleanor Roosevelt to Joseph P. Lash, March 30, 1944, and April 2, 1944.

17. McIntire, p. 184; Howard G. Bruenn, "Clinical Nature of Illness and Death of President Franklin D. Roosevelt," *Annals of Internal Medicine,* vol. 72, April, 1970.

18. Letter from Eleanor Roosevelt to Maude Gray, May 1, 1944.

19. Letter from Eleanor Roosevelt to Joseph P. Lash, April 25, 1944; McIntire, p. 187; letter from Eleanor Roosevelt to Joseph P. Lash, May 15, 1944; letter from Eleanor Roosevelt to James Roosevelt, May 29, 1944.

20. Letter from Trude Pratt to Joseph P. Lash, May 25, 1944.

21. Letter from Eleanor Roosevelt to Joseph P. Lash, May 19, 1944.

22. Letter from Eleanor Roosevelt to Franklin D. Roosevelt, April 21, 1944.

23. Letter from Eleanor Roosevelt to Joseph P. Lash, June 16, 1944; letter from Eleanor Roosevelt to Maude Gray, July 4, 1944.

24. Interview with Anna Roosevelt Halsted; J. Roosevelt and Shalett, p. 317.

25. Interview with Anna Roosevelt Halsted.

26. Letter from Eleanor Roosevelt to Missy LeHand, Feb. 18, 1944.

27. Letter from Trude Pratt to Joseph P. Lash, July 3, 1944.

28. Letter from Eleanor Roosevelt to Doris Fleeson, May 15, 1944; letter from Eleanor Roosevelt to Joseph P. Lash, April 9, 1944, and May 15, 1944.

29. Letter from Eleanor Roosevelt to Joseph P. Lash, June 6 and 11, 1944, and July 18, 1944.

30. Letter from Eleanor Roosevelt to Jonathan Daniels, June 12, 1944.

31. Memorandum from Franklin D. Roosevelt to Eleanor Roosevelt, July 16, 1944; letters from Eleanor Roosevelt to Bernard Baruch, Feb. 22, 1944, and July 4 and 23, 1944; memorandum from Eleanor Roosevelt to Bernard Baruch, undated; letters from Bernard Baruch to Eleanor Roosevelt, July 11 and 28, 1944; letters from Eleanor Roosevelt to Walter Reuther, July 13, 1944, and Aug. 7, 1944; letters from Walter Reuther to Eleanor Roosevelt, July 11, 1944, and Aug. 28, 1944; letter from Harry Hopkins to Eleanor Roosevelt, Aug. 9, 1944, and Eleanor Roosevelt's reply, Aug. 12, 1944.

32. Letter from Eleanor Roosevelt to Joseph P. Lash, July 27, 1943.

33. Letter from Prof. Clyde Eagleton to Eleanor Roosevelt, July 20, 1943; letter from Eleanor Roosevelt to Franklin D. Roosevelt, July 27, 1943.

34. Letter from Eleanor Roosevelt to Franklin D. Roosevelt, Dec. 5, 1943; interview with Samuel I. Rosenman.

35. Bernard M. Baruch, *The Public Years* (New York, 1960), p. 359; letter from James Conant to Franklin D. Roosevelt, Dec. 30, 1943.

36. Letter from Irving S. Lowen to Eleanor Roosevelt, Feb. 15, 1944.

37. Letter from Eleanor Roosevelt to Franklin D. Roosevelt, Feb. 25, 1944; letter from Franklin D. Roosevelt to Vannevar Bush, March 2, 1944; letter from Vannevar Bush to Franklin D. Roosevelt, March 7, 1944.

38. Interview with Eugene Wigner; letter from Eleanor Roosevelt to Joseph P. Lash, June 25, 1944.

39. Letter from Eleanor Roosevelt to Joseph P. Lash, April 30, 1944.

40. *Ibid.,* June 27, 1944.

41. *Ibid.,* July 2, 1944; letter from Eleanor Roosevelt to Betty Hight, July 4, 1944.

42. Flynn, *You're the Boss,* cited (Ch. 33), p. 179; letter from Eleanor Roosevelt to Joseph P. Lash, July 16, 1944.

43. Letter from Eleanor Roosevelt to Joseph P. Lash, July 14, 1944; letter from Eleanor Roosevelt to Mrs. Philip Vaughn ("Bennett"), April 22, 1944.

44. Letter from Eleanor Roosevelt to Alice Huntington, Oct. 23, 1944; letters from Trude Pratt to Joseph P. Lash, July 5 and 7, 1944.

45. Sherwood, *Roosevelt and Hopkins,* cited (Ch. 42), p. 820; letter from Eleanor Roosevelt to James Roosevelt, in J. Roosevelt and Shalett, p. 353.

46. E. Roosevelt, "My Day," cited (Ch. 8), Nov. 4, 1944; letter from Eleanor Roosevelt to Joseph P. Lash, Aug. 23, 1944; John M. Blum, *Roosevelt and Morgenthau* (New York, 1970), pp. 580–81.

47. Letter from Eleanor Roosevelt to Joseph P. Lash, Sept. 11, 1944.

48. Letter from Trude Pratt to Joseph P. Lash, Sept. 8, 1944.

49. F. D. Roosevelt, *Public Papers,* 1944, p. 290.

50. Sherwood, p. 824; Bruenn, *op. cit.*

51. E. Roosevelt, "My Day," Nov. 8, 1944.

52. As quoted in Sherwood, p. 831.

53. Associated Press, Nov. 10, 1944; Eleanor Roosevelt, "How to Take Criticism," *Ladies' Home Journal,* Nov., 1944.

56. DEATH OF THE COMMANDER-IN-CHIEF

1. Letter from Esther Lape to Eleanor Roosevelt, Nov. 8, 1944.

2. Letter from Eleanor Roosevelt to Maude Gray, July 4, 1944.

3. William D. Hassett, *Off the Record with F.D.R., 1942–1945* (Rutgers, 1958), p. 304.

4. Letter from Eleanor Roosevelt to Franklin D. Roosevelt, Dec. 12, 1944.

5. Interview with Anna Roosevelt Halsted.

6. Letter from Eleanor Roosevelt to Joseph P. Lash, Jan. 10, 1945.

7. E. Roosevelt, *TIR,* cited (Ch. 16), p. 343.

8. Letter from Eleanor Roosevelt to Lady Florence Willert, Feb. 8, 1945; letter from Eleanor Roosevelt to Joseph P. Lash, Jan. 21, 1945.

9. Letter from Eleanor Roosevelt to Franklin D. Roosevelt, Feb. 20, 1945; letter from Franklin D. Roosevelt to Jesse Jones, in F. D. Roosevelt, *Letters,* cited (Ch. 10), IV, pp. 1566–67; letter from Eleanor Roosevelt to Franklin D. Roosevelt, Jan. 26, 1945.

10. Letter from Eleanor Roosevelt to Lt. George Wells, Feb. 22, 1945.

11. James F. Byrnes, *All in One Lifetime* (New York, 1958), p. 256.

12. Letter from Franklin D. Roosevelt to Eleanor Roosevelt, Feb. 12, 1945.

13. Letter from Eleanor Roosevelt to Franklin D. Roosevelt, Feb. 13, 1945.

14. Letter from Eleanor Roosevelt to Joseph P. Lash, Feb. 28, 1945.

15. *Ibid.,* April 2, 1945.

16. Lilienthal, *The Journals of David E. Lilienthal,* cited (Ch. 37), III, pp. 363, 364.

17. E. Roosevelt, *TIR,* p. 343.

18. Fayerweather, "My Diary in the White House," cited (Ch. 55) March 28, 1945.

19. Letter from Eleanor Roosevelt to Maude Gray, April 1, 1945.

20. Letter from Eleanor Roosevelt to Joseph P. Lash, April 6, 1945.

21. E. Roosevelt, *TIR,* pp. 343–44.

22. Bernard Asbell, *When F.D.R. Died* (New York, 1961), p. 53; *New York Times,* April 13, 1945; Henry Morgenthau, "A Tribute to Eleanor Roosevelt."

23. Tully, *F.D.R. My Boss,* cited (Ch. 33), pp. 365–66.

24. Interview with Anna Roosevelt Halsted.

25. E. Roosevelt, *TIR,* pp. 348–49.

26. Asbell, p. 161.

27. Interview with Esther Lape.

Index